Alan Rogers

Europe

Quality camping & caravanning sites

INSPECTED CAMPSITES & SELECTED

Compiled by: Alan Rogers Guides Ltd

Designed by: Paul Effenberg, Vine Design Ltd

Maps created by Customised Mapping (01769 560101)
contain background data provided by GisDATA Ltd

Published by: Alan Rogers Guides Ltd,
Spelmonden Old Oast, Goudhurst, Kent TN17 1HE
www.alanrogers.com Tel: 01580 214000

British Library Cataloguing-in-Publication Data:
A catalogue record for this book is available from the
British Library.

ISBN: 0-9545271-3-5

Printed in Great Britain by J H Haynes & Co Ltd

CONTENTS

the Alan Rogers approach

IT IS NEARLY 40 YEARS SINCE ALAN ROGERS PUBLISHED THE FIRST CAMPSITE GUIDE THAT BORE HIS NAME. SINCE THEN THE RANGE HAS EXPANDED TO SIX TITLES WITH GUIDES TO ITALY AND SPAIN & PORTUGAL ADDED IN 2004, AND A NEW GUIDE TO CENTRAL EUROPE AND CROATIA FOR THIS YEAR. WHAT'S MORE, ALAN ROGERS GUIDES HAVE BECOME ESTABLISHED IN HOLLAND TOO: ALL SIX TITLES ARE ALSO AVAILABLE IN THE NETHERLANDS, STOCKED BY WELL OVER 90% OF ALL DUTCH BOOKSHOPS.

There are many thousands of campsites in Europe of varying quality: this guide contains impartially written reports on no less than 815 of the very finest, in no less than 25 countries. Each one is individually inspected and selected. This guide does not include sites in Britain and Ireland, for which we publish a separate guide, and it contains only a limited selection of sites in France, Italy, Spain & Portugal and the Central Europe countries as we also publish separate guides for these destinations. All the usual maps and indexes are included, designed to help you find the choice of site that's right for you. We hope you enjoy happy and safe travels – and some pleasurable 'armchair touring' in the meantime!

INDEPENDENT AND HONEST

Whilst the content and scope of the Alan Rogers guides have expanded considerably since the early editions, our selection of campsites still employs exactly the same philosophy and criteria as defined by Alan Rogers in 1968.

'warts and all'

Firstly, and most importantly, our selection is based entirely on our own rigorous and independent inspection and selection process. Campsites cannot buy their way into our guides – indeed the extensive Site Report which is written by us, not by the site owner, is provided free of charge so we are free to say what we think and to provide an honest, 'warts and all' description. This is written in plain English and without the use of confusing icons or symbols.

"...the campsites included in this book have been chosen entirely on merit, and no payment of any sort is made by them for their inclusion."

Alan Rogers, 1968

A question of quality

The criteria we use when inspecting and selecting sites are numerous, but the most important by far is the question of good quality. People want different things from their choice of campsite so we try to include a range of campsite 'styles' to cater for a wide variety of preferences: from those seeking a small peaceful campsite in the heart of the countryside, to visitors looking for an 'all singing, all dancing' site in a popular seaside resort. Those with more specific interests, such as sporting facilities, cultural events or historical attractions, are also catered for.

The size of the site, whether it's part of a campsite chain or privately owned, makes no difference in terms of it being required to meet our exacting standards in respect of its quality and it being 'fit for purpose'. In other words, irrespective of the size of the site, or the number of facilities it offers, the essentials (the welcome, the pitches, the sanitary facilities, the cleanliness and the general maintenance) must all be of a high standard.

Expert opinions

We rely on our dedicated team of Site Assessors, all of whom are experienced campers, caravanners or motorcaravanners, to visit and recommend sites. Each year they travel some 100,000 miles around Europe inspecting new campsites and re-inspecting the older ones. Our thanks are due to them for their enthusiastic efforts, their diligence and integrity and their commitment to the philosophy of the Alan Rogers Guides.

We also appreciate the feedback we receive from many of our readers and we always make a point of following up complaints, suggestions or recommendations for possible new sites. Of course we get a few grumbles too – but it really is a few, and those we do receive usually arrive at the end of the high season and relate mainly to overcrowding or to poor maintenance during the peak school holiday period.

Please bear in mind that although we are interested to hear about any complaints we have no contractual relationship with the campsites featured in our guides and are therefore not in a position to intervene in any dispute between a reader and a campsite. If you have a complaint about a campsite featured in our guides the first step should be to take the matter up with the site owner or manager whilst on the campsite.

Widely regarded as the 'Bible' by site owners and readers alike, there is no better guide when it comes to forming an independent view of a campsite's quality. When you need to be confident in your choice of campsite, you need the Alan Rogers Guide.

- ✔ Sites only included on merit
- ✔ Sites cannot pay to be included
- ✔ Independently inspected, rigorously assessed
- ✔ Impartial reviews
- ✔ 36 years of expertise

Written in plain English, our guides are exceptionally easy to use, although a few words of explanation may be helpful. This guide is divided firstly by country, subsequently (in the case of larger countries) by region. For a particular area the town index at the back provides more direct access.

Indexes

Our three indexes allow you to find sites by country, site number and name, by country and site name (alphabetically) or by the town or village where the site is situated.

Campsite Maps

The maps of each country are designed to show the country in relation to others and will help you to identify the approximate position of each campsite.

The Site Reports – *Example of an entry*

Site no **Site name**

Postal Address (including region)

A description of the site in which we try to give an idea of its general features – its size, its situation, its strengths and its weaknesses. This column should provide a picture of the site itself with reference to the facilities that are provided and if they impact on its appearance or character. We include details on pitch numbers, electricity (with amperage), hardstandings etc. in this section as pitch design, planning and terracing affects the site's overall appearance. Similarly we continue to include reference to pitches used for caravan holiday homes, chalets, and the like. Importantly at the end of this column we indicate if there are any restrictions, e.g. no tents, naturist sites.

Facilities

Lists more specific information on the site's facilities, as well as certain off site attractions and activities.

At a glance

Welcome & Ambience	✓✓✓✓	Location	✓✓✓✓✓
Quality of Pitches	✓✓✓✓✓	Range of Facilities	✓✓✓✓

Our inspectors grade each site out of five, giving a unique indication of certain key criteria that may be important when making your decision.

Directions

Separated from the main text in order that they may be read and assimilated more easily by a navigator en-route. Bear in mind that road improvement schemes can result in some road numbers being altered. Websites like **www.mappy.com** and others give detailed route plans.

Charges 2005

Reservations

including contact details

Open

Site opening dates.

Facilities

Toilet blocks: We assume that toilet blocks will be equipped with at least some British style WCs, washbasins with hot and cold water and hot showers with dividers or curtains, and will have all necessary shelves, hooks, plugs and mirrors. We also assume that there will be an identified chemical toilet disposal point, and that the campsite will provide water and waste water points and bin areas. If not, we comment. We continue to mention certain features that some readers find important: washbasins in cubicles, facilities for babies, facilities for those with disabilities and motorcaravan service points. Readers with disabilities are advised to contact the site of their choice to ensure that facilities are appropriate to their needs.

Shop: Basic or fully supplied, and opening dates.

Bars, restaurants, takeaway facilities and entertainment: We try hard to supply opening and closing dates (if other than the campsite opening dates) and to identify if there are discos or other noisy entertainment.

Children's play areas: Fenced and with safety surface (e.g. sand, bark or pea-gravel).

Swimming pools: If particularly special, we cover in detail in the first column but reference is always included in the second column. Opening dates, charges and levels of supervision are provided where we have been notified.

Leisure facilities: For example, playing fields, bicycle hire, organised activities and entertainment.

Dogs: If dogs are not accepted or restrictions apply, we state it here. Check the quick reference list at the end of the guide.

Off site: This briefly covers leisure facilities, tourist attractions, restaurants etc nearby. Geographical tourist information is more likely to be in the first column.

At a glance: All Alan Rogers sites have been inspected and selected – they must meet stringent quality criteria. A campsite may have all the boxes ticked when it comes to listing facilities but if it's not inherently a 'good site' then it will not be in the guide.

These 'at a glance' ratings are a unique indication of certain key criteria that may be important when making your decision. Quite deliberately they are subjective and, modesty aside, are based on our inspectors' own expert opinions at the time of their inspection.

Charges: These are the latest provided by the sites. In those few cases where 2004 or 2005 prices are not given, we try to give a general guide.

Telephone numbers: The numbers given assume you are actually IN the country concerned. If you are phoning from the UK remember that the first '0' is usually disregarded and replaced by the appropriate country code – this system is currently undergoing changes. For the latest details you should refer to an up-to-date telephone directory.

Opening dates: Are those advised to us during the early autumn of the previous year – sites can, and sometimes do, alter these dates before the start of the following season, often for good reasons. If you intend to visit shortly after a published opening date, or shortly before the closing date, it is wise to check that it will actually be open at the time required. Similarly some sites operate a restricted service during the low season, only opening some of their facilities (e.g. swimming pools) during the main season; where we know about this, and have the relevant dates, we indicate it – again if you are at all doubtful it is wise to check.

Reservations: Necessary for high season (roughly mid-July to mid-August) in popular holiday areas (ie beach resorts). You can reserve via our own Alan Rogers Travel Service or through tour operators. Or be wholly independent and contact the campsite(s) of your choice direct, using the contact details shown in the site reports.

Points to bear in mind

Some site owners are rather laid back when it comes to opening and closing dates. They may not be fully ready by their opening date – grass and hedges may not all be cut or perhaps only limited sanitary facilities open. At the end of the season they also tend to close down some facilities and generally wind down prior to the closing date. Bear this in mind if you are travelling early or late in the season – it is worth phoning ahead.

The Camping Cheque low season touring system goes some way to addressing this in that participating campsites are encouraged to have all facilities open and running by the opening date and to remain fully operational until the closing date.

Whether you're an 'old hand' in terms of camping and caravanning or are contemplating your first trip, a regular reader of our Guides or a new 'convert', we wish you well in your travels and hope we have been able to help in some way. We are, of course, also out and about ourselves, visiting sites, talking to owners and readers, and generally checking on standards and new developments.

The Alan Rogers Team

service
and value

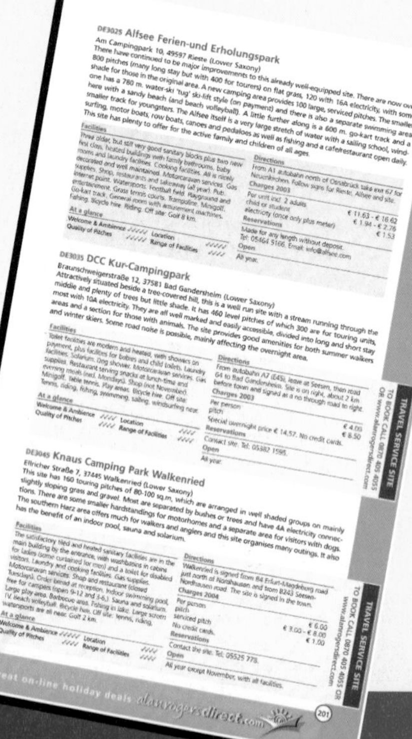

DE3025 **Alfsee Ferien-und Erholungspark**

Am Campingpark 10, 49597 Rieste (Lower Saxony)

There have continued to be major improvements to this already well-equipped site. There are now over 800 pitches (many long stay but with 400 for tourers) on flat grass, 120 with 16A electricity, with some shade for those in the original area. A new camping area provides 100 large, serviced pitches. The smaller one has a 780 m. water-ski 'tug' ski-lift style (on payment) and there is also a separate swimming area here with a sandy beach (and beach volleyball). A little further along is a 600 m. go-kart track and a smaller track for youngsters. The Alfsee itself is a very large stretch of water with a sailing school, windsurfing, motor boats, row boats, canoes and pedaloes as well as fishing and a cafe/restaurant open daily. This site has plenty to offer for the active family and children of all ages.

Facilities

Three older, but still very good sanitary blocks plus two new first class, heated buildings with family bathrooms, baby rooms and laundry facilities. Cooking facilities. All is nicely decorated and well maintained. Motorcaravan services. Gas supplies. Shop, restaurants and takeaway (all year). Pub. Internet point. Watersports. Football field. Playground and entertainment. Grass tennis courts. Trampoline. Minigolf. Go-kart track. General room with amusement machines. Fishing. Bicycle hire. Riding. Off site: Golf 8 km.

At a glance

Welcome & Ambience ✓✓✓✓✓ Location ✓✓✓✓✓
Quality of Pitches ✓✓✓✓✓ Range of Facilities ✓✓✓✓

Directions

From A1 autobahn north of Osnabrück take exit 67 for Neuenkirchen. Follow signs for Rieste, Alfsee and site.

Charges 2003

Per unit incl. 2 adults € 11.63 - € 16.62
child or student € 1.94 - € 2.76
electricity (once only plus meter) € 1.53

Reservations

Made for any length without deposit. Tel: 05464 5166. Email: info@alfsee.com

Open

All year.

DE3035 **DCC Kur-Campingpark**

Braunschweigerstraße 12, 37581 Bad Gandersheim (Lower Saxony)

Attractively situated beside a tree-covered hill, this is a well run site with a stream running through the middle and plenty of trees but little shade. It has 460 level pitches of which 300 are for touring units, most with 10A electricity. They are all well marked and easily accessible, divided into long and short stay areas and a section for those with animals. The site provides good amenities for both summer walkers and winter skiers. Some road noise is possible, mainly affecting the overnight area.

Facilities

Toilet facilities are modern and heated, with showers on payment, plus facilities for babies and child toilets. Laundry facilities. Solarium. Dog shower. Motorcaravan services. Gas supplies. Restaurant serving snacks at lunch-time and evening meals (not Mondays). Shop (not November). Minigolf. Table tennis. Play areas. Bicycle hire. Off site: Tennis, riding, fishing, swimming, sailing, windsurfing near.

At a glance

Welcome & Ambience ✓✓✓✓ Location ✓✓✓✓
Quality of Pitches ✓✓✓✓ Range of Facilities ✓✓✓✓

Directions

From autobahn A7 (E45), leave at Seesen, then road 64 to Bad Gandersheim. Site is on right, about 2 km. before town and signed at a no through road to right.

Charges 2003

Per person € 4.00
pitch € 8.50
Special overnight price € 14.57. No credit cards.

Reservations

Contact site. Tel: 05382 1595.

Open

All year.

TRAVEL SERVICE SITE
TO BOOK CALL 0870 405 4055 OR www.alanrogersdirect.com

DE3045 **Knaus Camping Park Walkenried**

Ellricher Straße 7, 37445 Walkenried (Lower Saxony)

This site has 160 touring pitches of 80-100 sq.m. which are arranged in well shaded groups on mainly slightly sloping grass and gravel. Most are separated by bushes or trees and have 4A electricity connections. There are some smaller hardstandings for motorhomes and a separate area for visitors with dogs. The southern Harz area offers much for walkers and anglers and this site organises many outings. It also has the benefit of an indoor pool, sauna and solarium.

Facilities

The satisfactory tiled and heated sanitary facilities are in the main building by the entrance, with washbasins in cabins for ladies (some curtained for men) and a toilet for disabled visitors. Laundry and cooking facilities. Gas supplies. Motorcaravan services. Shop and restaurant (closed Tuesdays). Order bread at reception. Indoor swimming pool, free for campers (open 9-12 and 3-6.). Sauna and solarium. Large play area. Barbecue area. Fishing in lake. Large screen TV. Beach volleyball. Bicycle hire. Off site: Tennis, riding, watersports are all near. Golf 2 km.

At a glance

Welcome & Ambience ✓✓✓✓✓ Location ✓✓✓✓
Quality of Pitches ✓✓✓✓ Range of Facilities ✓✓✓✓

Directions

Walkenried is signed from B4 Erfurt-Magdeburg road just north of Nordhausen and from B243 Seesen-Nordhausen road. The site is signed in the town.

Charges 2004

Per person € 6.00
pitch € 3.00 - € 8.00
serviced pitch € 1.00
No credit cards.

Reservations

Contact the site. Tel: 05525 778.

Open

All year except November, with all facilities.

TRAVEL SERVICE SITE
TO BOOK CALL 0870 405 4055 OR www.alanrogersdirect.com

Germany

Great on-line holiday deals alanrogersdirect.com

201

The Alan Rogers Travel Service was set up to provide a low cost booking service for readers. We can tailor-make a holiday to suit your requirements, giving you maximum choice and flexibility: exactly what we have been offering for some 5 years now.

Alternatively you can opt for one of our new Value+ holidays, pocketing a 20% saving off base price in return for accepting various restrictions (see opposite).

And because we organise so many holidays we can offer outstanding Ferry Deals too!

Unbeatable Ferry Deals

WE ARE ALWAYS NEGOTIATING NEW OFFERS ON CHANNEL CROSSINGS. MAKE SURE YOU ASK US ABOUT OUR FAMOUS DEALS!

- ✓ **CARAVANS GO FREE**
- ✓ **TRAILERS GO FREE**
- ✓ **MOTORHOMES PRICED AS CARS**

SEE PAGES 15-16

At the Alan Rogers Travel Service we're always keen to find the best deals and keenest prices. There are always great savings on offer, and we're constantly negotiating new ferry rates and money-saving offers, so just call us on

0870 405 4055

and ask about the latest deals.

or visit

www.alanrogersdirect.com

THE AIMS OF THE TRAVEL SERVICE ARE SIMPLE.

- To provide convenience - when booking a campsite yourself can be anything but convenient.
- To provide peace of mind - when you need it most.
- To provide a friendly, knowledgeable, efficient service - when this can be hard to find.
- To provide a low cost means of organising your holiday – when prices can be so complicated.

HOW IT WORKS

1 Choose your campsite(s)

2 Choose your dates

3 Choose your ferry crossing

Then just call us for an instant quote

0870 405 4055

or visit
www.alanrogersdirect.com

LET US BOOK YOUR PITCH AND FERRY FOR YOU

For full details see our FREE 2005 brochure

0870 405 4055

Ask about our incredible Ferry Deals:

- ✓ Caravans GO FREE
- ✓ Motorhomes Priced as Cars

NEW Value+ Holidays SAVE 20%

We can book many campsites for you, with complete flexibility: any dates, any duration, any arrival/departure day, any ferry and so on.

But some readers do not necessarily need such choice and would prefer 'off the shelf' convenience and even lower prices. So for 2005 we are introducing our new **Value+** holidays where, in return for meeting certain conditions, we can reduce your base price by a massive 20%.

We can offer **Value+** holidays at over 50 campsites within our 2005 programme. To qualify for huge savings please understand that your holiday must be...

- \+ Ferry-inclusive
- \+ Single site only – no overnight campsite stops
- \+ Minimum of 7 nights
- \+ Either 7, 14 or 21 nights duration
- \+ Booked at least 30 days in advance of travel
- \+ Subject to availability on each site

See our new 2005 brochure for details
or call us today for a no-obligation quote.

0870 405 4055

PRICING YOUR HOLIDAY

WE ACT AS AGENTS FOR ALL THE CAMPSITES AND FERRY OPERATORS FEATURED IN THE TRAVEL SERVICE. AS SUCH, WE CAN BOOK ALL YOUR TRAVEL ARRANGEMENTS WITH THE MINIMUM OF FUSS AND AT THE BEST POSSIBLE PRICES. THE BASE PRICES BELOW INCLUDE 14 NIGHTS PITCH FEES AND RETURN FERRY CROSSING.

	Base Price 2 adults + car 14 nights		Extra adult		Child	Extra/fewer nights	
First night on site	Tailormade	**Value+**	Tailormade	**Value+**	(0-13)	Tailormade	**Value+**
Before 17 May	**£318**	£254.40	**£25**	£20	FREE	**£12**	£9.60
17/5 - 17/6	**£338**	£270.40	**£25**	£20	FREE	**£12**	£9.60
18/6 - 1/7	**£369**	£295.20	**£25**	£20	FREE	**£12**	£9.60
2/7 - 12/8	**£439**	£351.20	**£25**	£20	FREE	**£12**	£9.60
13/8 - 22/8	**£399**	£319.20	**£25**	£20	FREE	**£12**	£9.60
From 23/8	**£338**	£270.40	**£25**	£20	FREE	**£12**	£9.60

The base price of your holiday includes 14 nights pitch fees and a mid-week return ferry crossing from Dover to Calais with P&O Ferries for a car and 5 passengers (outward sailing times must be between 14:01 and 06:59. Inward sailing times must be between 20:01 and 14:59). Additional supplements are payable for caravans, trailers and motorhomes at many times and for cars at weekends and times outside those given above. There will also usually be a campsite supplement payable (see opposite). Call us on **0870 405 4055** for details and a quote.

If your holiday is longer or shorter than 14 nights, simply add or subtract the extra/fewer night rate. Tailor-made holidays must be for a minimum of 3 nights, with ferry (many sites have a minimum stay requirement). For holidays longer than 21 nights please call for a quotation. You may stay on as many sites as you wish, subject to individual site requirements, with a one-off £10 multi-site fee. Value+ holidays are subject to various restrictions. Please see page 9 for details.

LOW £100 DEPOSIT

A special low deposit of just £100 secures your holiday

(full payment is required at the time of booking for travel within 10 weeks)

14 nights pitch fees + ferry for car and passengers	from **£324** DOVER - CALAIS
14 nights pitch fees + ferry for motorhome and passengers	from **£346** PORTSMOUTH - LE HAVRE
14 nights pitch fees + ferry for car and caravan and passengers	from **£324** DOVER - CALAIS

Sample Value+ holiday at Camping Jarny Ocean, Vendée in May.

Motorhomes **Priced** as Cars

Caravans and Trailers **GO FREE**

Site Supplements

All sites operate their own independent pricing structure, and in order to reflect the differences in cost from one site to another, a nightly 'site supplement' needs to be added to the Base Prices indicated above.

All supplements are given in our 2005 brochure. Additional supplements can often apply for electricity, water and drainage or special pitches.

The simplest next step is to request a brochure or just call us for an immediate price quotation for your chosen site and all the available options, as well as any other important information, such as any minimum stay requirements.

CALL US NOW **0870 405 4055** FOR AN INSTANT QUOTE
OR VISIT **www.alanrogersdirect.com**

Leave The Hassle To Us

- **All site fees paid in advance – you won't need to take extra currency with you.**
- **Your pitch is reserved for you – travel with peace of mind.**
- **No endless overseas phone calls or correspondence with foreign site owners.**
- **No need to pay foreign currency deposits and booking fees.**
- **Take advantage of our expert advice and experience of camping in Europe.**

Already Booked Your Ferry?

We're confident that our ferry inclusive booking service offers unbeatable value. However, if you have already booked your ferry then we can still make a pitch-only reservation for you. Your booking must be for a minimum of 10 nights, and since our prices are based on our ferry inclusive service, you needto be aware that a non-ferry booking will always result in somewhat higher prices than if you were to book direct with the site.

You still benefit from:

- **Hassle-free booking with no booking fees and foreign currency deposits.**
- **Comprehensive Travel Pack.**
- **Peace of mind: site fees paid in advance, with your pitch reserved for you.**

FULL DETAILS IN OUR 64 PAGE 2005 COLOUR BROCHURE CALL

0870 405 4055

book on-line and save money

www.alanrogersdirect.com is a website designed to give you everything you need to know when it comes to booking your Alan Rogers inspected and selected campsite, and your low cost ferry.

Our glossy brochure gives you all the info you need but it is only printed once a year. And our friendly, expert reservations team is always happy to help on **0870 405 4055** – but they do go home sometimes!

Visit www.alanrogersdirect.com and you'll find constantly updated information, latest ferry deals, special offers from campsites and much more. And you can visit it at any time of day or night!

alanrogersdirect.com

book on-line and save

Campsite Information

- ✓ Details of all Travel Service campsites - **instantly**
- ✓ Find latest special offers on campsites - **instantly**
- ✓ Check campsite availability - **instantly**

Ferry Information

- ✓ Check ferry availability - **instantly**
- ✓ Find latest ferry deals - **instantly**
- ✓ Book your ferry online - **instantly**
- ✓ Save money - **instantly**

BOOK YOUR CAMPSITE AND FERRY - INSTANTLY

Perfect Match

Find the campsite that's right for you

With so many sites to choose from it can be difficult to find a short-list. With the unique Alan Rogers Perfect Match system you can quickly find a campsite that meets your requirements. This powerful and searchable database of top campsites, all Alan Rogers inspected and selected, means you can quickly find an ideal site, book it on-line and relax in the knowledge that your holiday is safely reserved.

INSPECTED CAMPSITES & SELECTED

have you visited www.alanrogers.com yet?

Thousands have already, researching their holiday and catching up with the latest news and special offers.

Launched in January 2004 it has fast become the first-stop for countless caravanners, motorhome owners and campers all wanting reliable, impartial and detailed information for their next trip.

It features a fully searchable database of the best campsites in the UK & Ireland, and the rest of Europe: over 2,000 campsites in 26 countries. All are Alan Rogers inspected and selected, allowing you to find the site that's perfect for you, with the reassurance of knowing we've been there first.

And now it has been re-launched for the 2005 season, with more than ever before.

Crossing the Channel

One of the great advantages of booking with the Alan Rogers Travel Service is the tremendous value we offer. Our money-saving Ferry Deals have become legendary: see below. As agents for all the cross-Channel operators we can book all your travel arrangements with the minimum of fuss and at the best possible rates.

Just call us for an instant quote

0870 405 4055

or visit

www.alanrogersdirect.com

Book on-line AND SAVE

Short Sea Routes

Hop across the Channel in the shortest possible time and you can be on your way. We offer all main routes at great prices (when you book a pitch + ferry 'package' through us). And why not take advantage of our Ferry Deals? Caravans and trailers can go **FREE** on Dover – Calais with P&O Ferries.

Dover - Calais

hoverspeed

Dover – Calais
Newhaven - Dieppe

Folkestone – Calais

Harwich – Hook of Holland

Short Sea Routes SPECIAL OFFERS

Caravans **Go FREE** - Trailers **Go FREE** - Motorhomes **Priced as Cars**

Dover – Calais

Caravans **Go FREE***

Available all year between 1 May 2005 – 31 Oct 2005 excluding high season weekends.

Motorhomes **Priced as Cars***

Available between 1 May 2005 – 31 Oct 2005 on midweek, low season sailings and apply at all times of the day.

High season is 26-28 May and 15/7-31/8 outward and 4-5 June and 23/7-4/9 inward. Weekends are Fri/Sat outward, Sat/Sun inward.

* Applies to certain sailings only. Over-length supplements may apply. Please ask for details.

Folkestone – Calais/Coquelles

FREE Caravans between midnight and 06:00.
Low caravan supplements on off peak crossings.

Don't delay – this offer is strictly subject to availability and will be first come, first served.

Just call us for an instant quote **0870 405 4055**

or visit **www.alanrogersdirect.com** BOOK ON-LINE AND SAVE

Longer Routes

Sometimes it pays to take a longer crossing: a more leisurely journey perhaps. Or a chance to enjoy dinner on board ship, followed by a night in a comfortable cabin, awaking refreshed and ready for the onward drive. Either way there are still savings to be had with our super Ferry Deals (when you book a pitch and ferry 'package' through us).

Portsmouth – St Malo/
Caen/Cherbourg
Plymouth – Roscoff/Santander
Poole – Cherbourg
Portsmouth – Le Havre

Portsmouth – Bilbao
Hull – Rotterdam/Zeebrugge

Poole – St Malo
Weymouth – St Malo

1st time abroad?

PREPARATIONS FOR THAT FIRST TRIP CAN BE DAUNTING. BUT DON'T WORRY - WE'RE WITH YOU ALL THE WAY.

Longer Routes **SPECIAL OFFERS**

Motorhomes Priced as Cars - Caravans FROM JUST £13 each way

Portsmouth – Le Havre**

Motorhomes **Priced as Cars*** on 'special sailings' from Portsmouth in low season (midweek AND weekend). Le Havre is now just £4 each way supplement over Dover-Calais on lead-in sailings for cars. Caravan supplement starts at just £13 each way on Portsmouth - Le Havre.

Many supplements for high season have reduced – **call us for an instant quote.**

Condorferries Poole/Weymouth – St Malo

Motorhomes **Priced as Cars** on all crossings direct to St Malo and via the Channel Islands. Travel must be on a Tuesday or Wednesday (either direction). Offer excludes high season (27/5-29/5 and 15/7-24/8 out, 3/6-5/6 and 22/7-4/9 in).

* Applies to certain sailings only. Over-length supplements may apply. Please ask for details.
** At the time going to press Portsmouth – Le Havre crossings are operated by P&O Ferries. This route may, in time, be operated by Brittany Ferries, subject to the outcome of negotiations.

Don't delay – this offer is strictly subject to availability and will be first come, first served.

Just call us for an instant quote **0870 405 4055**
or visit **www.alanrogersdirect.com** BOOK ON-LINE AND SAVE

The tiny independent principality of Andorra is situated high in the Pyrenees between France and Spain. With a diverse landscape of mountains, valleys, forests, lakes and hot springs, it is probably best known for skiing and duty-free shopping.

Andorra

Shopping and skiing aside, Andorra has plenty to offer the visitor in terms of leisure activities. One of the most unspoilt areas of the country is the hamlet of Llorts. Set amidst fields of tobacco overlooked by mountains, it's a great place for hiking. The enormous spa complex in Caldea offers the perfect place to relax. Fed by natural thermal springs, it houses lots of pools, hot tubs and saunas. Village festivals are a popular event with many Andorran towns and hamlets celebrating their heritage with music, dancing, wine and feasts. Most fall in the high season.

Administratively Andorra is divided up into seven parishes: Canillo, Encamp, Ordino, La Massana, Andorra la Vella, Sant Julià de Lòria and Escaldes-Engordany. The Principality of Andorra can be accessed by road from France through Pas de la Casa and the Envalira Pass and from Spain via Sant Julià de Lòria. The nearest main cities are Barcelona (185 km) and Lleida (151 km) on the Spanish side and Toulouse (187 km) and Perpignan (169 km) on the French side.

Population

66,334

Capital

Andorra la Vella

Climate

The climate is temperate, with cold winters with a lot of snow and warm summers. The country's mountain peaks often remain snowcapped until July

Language

The official language is Catalan, with French and Spanish widely spoken

Currency

The Euro

Telephone

The country code is 00 376

Banks

Mon-Fri 09.00-13.00 and 15.00-17.00, Sat 09.00-12.00

Shops

Mon-Sat 09.00-20.00, Sun 09.00-19.00

Public Holidays

New Year's Day; Epiphany; Constitution Day, Mar 14; Holy Thursday to Easter Monday; Labour Day; Ascension; Whit Sunday; Whit Monday; St John's Day Jun 24; Assumption; National Day Sep 8; All Saints' Day Nov 1; St Charles' Day; Nov 4; Immaculate Conception; Dec 8; Christmas Dec 24-26; New Year's Eve

Motoring

There are no motorways in Andorra. Main roads are prefixed 'N' and side roads 'V'. Certain mountain passes may prove difficult in winter and heavy snow-falls could cause road closures. Expect traffic queues in the summer, with a high volume of motorists coming to and from France

Tourist Office

Embassy of the Principality of Andorra
63 Westover Road, London SW18 2RF
Tel/Fax: 020 8874 4806
Personal visits by appointment only

IF YOU FANCY A TRIP ACROSS THE BORDERS, TOULOUSE IN FRANCE IS ONLY 187 KM, EASILY ACCESSIBLE BY CAR OR TRAIN, AND FREQUENT BUSES RUN TO THE SPANISH TOWN OF LA SEU D'URGELL, ONLY 9 KM. AWAY.

AN7143 Camping Xixerella

Ctra de Pals, Erts, La Massana

Andorra is a country of narrow valleys and pine and birch forested mountains. Xixerella is attractively situated in just such a valley below towering mountains and beside a river. The site is made up of several sections, accessed by tarmac or gravel roads. There are some terraced pitches, although generally they are not marked out which results in very informal patterns of pitching. They are on grass, mainly with a small degree of slope. Electricity (3/6A) is available for most of the 220 places. Barbecues and picnic area with bridge access to walks in the woods. Pleasant bar and restaurant with pool-side terrace. The site can be very busy from mid-July to mid-August, but otherwise it is usually quite peaceful. Do not forget to explore Andorra for that duty free shopping.

Facilities

The satisfactory main sanitary building is fully equipped, including British style WCs (no paper) and some children's toilets, some washbasins in cabins, showers with curtains. Laundry and dishwashing facilities under cover. Further modern facilities in novel round building by the pool, including toilets, a laundry, baby bath and dishwashing sinks. Small shop, bar and restaurant (closed May and Oct). Swimming pool and paddling pool (open mid-June - mid-Sept). Sauna planned. Play area. Minigolf. Volleyball. Basketball. Table football. Electronic games. Disco in season. Torch useful. Off site: Volleyball and basketball pitch close by. Riding 3 km. Skiing possible at Arinsal (5 km) or Pal (6 km).

At a glance

Welcome & Ambience	✓✓✓✓	Location	✓✓✓✓✓
Quality of Pitches	✓✓✓✓	Range of Facilities	✓✓✓✓✓

Directions

Site is 8 km. from Andorra la Vella on the road to Pal (this road can only be accessed on the north side of town), via La Massana.

Charges 2004

Per person	€ 4,20
child	€ 3,80
caravan or tent	€ 4,20
car	€ 4,20
motorcaravan	€ 8,40
electricity (3A)	€ 3,95

Reservations

Contact site. Tel: 836 613.
E-mail: c-xixerella@campingxixerella.com

Open

All year.

AN7145 Camping Valira

Avda Salou, s/n, Andorra la Vella

This is a small and unusual site in the town of Andorra La Vella, with a steep curving entrance which can become congested at peak times. You pass the pleasant restaurant and bar and the heated indoor pool as you enter the site. Maximum use has been made of space here and it is worth looking at the picture of the site in reception as it was in 1969. The 160 medium sized pitches are mostly level on terraces with some shading. One of the family will guide you to your place which can be an interesting experience if the site is busy. All pitches have electricity and there are water points around the site. As this is a town site there is some ambient noise but the site is ideal for duty free shopping. There is a free 'birds eye' view of any event in the sports stadium.

Facilities

The facilities are modern and spotless, with provision for disabled campers, plus separate room with toddler's toilet and good baby room. Two washing machines and dryer. The two blocks can be heated in winter. Bar/restaurant with good menu at realistic prices. Well stocked small shop (town shops less than 1 km). Small heated indoor pool. Paddling pool. Play area. Barrier closed 11 pm - 7 am. Off site: Town shops less than 1 km.

Open

All year.

At a glance

Welcome & Ambience	✓✓✓✓	Location	✓✓✓✓
Quality of Pitches	✓✓✓✓	Range of Facilities	✓✓✓✓

Directions

Site is on the south side of Andorra La Vella, on left travelling south behind sports stadium. It is well signed off the N145. Watch signs carefully – an error with a diversion round town will cost you dear at rush hour.

Charges 2004

Per person	€ 4,50
child (1-10 yrs)	€ 4,00
caravan or tent	€ 4,50
car	€ 4,50
motorcycle	€ 4,00
motorcaravan	€ 9,00

Reservations

Not usually necessary. Tel: 722 384.
E-mail: campvalira@andorra.ad

Austria is primarily known for two contrasting attractions, the capital Vienna with its fading Imperial glories, and the variety of its Alpine hinterland. It is an ideal place to visit year round, whether you want to admire the spectacular scenery and participate in winter sports activities or visit the historical sites and cultural attractions.

Perhaps the best know area and the most easily accessible part of the country is the Tirol in the west. A charming region with picturesque valleys to explore, you'll be able to enjoy folk-lore entertainment year round. Situated in the centre is the Lake District and Salzburg. With its ancient castles, curative spas and salt mines to visit, Salzburg also has plenty of music, art and drama festivals to enjoy. Vienna too offers plenty of cultural pursuits with its museums, opera and famous choirs. The neighbouring provinces of Lower Austria, Burgenland and Styria, land of vineyards, mountains and farmland, are off the tourist routes, but provide good walking territory. Further south, in the Carinthia region, lakes and mountains dominate the landscape. The beautiful scenery and rural way of life offers a quieter retreat. There are a few large towns to explore, lots of pleasant villages and good, often uncrowded roads.

Population

8.1 million

Capital

Vienna

Climate

Temperate, with moderately hot summers, cold winters and snow in the mountains

Language

German

Currency

The Euro

Telephone

The country code is 0043

Banks

Mon, Tues, Wed & Fri 08.00-12.30 and 13.30-15.00. Thurs 08.00-12.30 and 13.30-17.30

Public Holidays

New Year; Epiphany; Easter Mon; Labour Day; Ascension; Whit Mon; Corpus Christi; Assumption 15 Aug; National Day 26 Oct; All Saints 1 Nov; Immaculate Conception 8 Dec; Christmas 25, 26 Dec

Shops

Mon-Fri 08.00-18.30, some close 12.00-14.00; Sat 08.00-17.00

Motoring

Visitors using Austrian motorways and 'A' roads must display a Motorway Vignette on their vehicle as they enter Austria. Failure to have one will mean a heavy, on-the-spot fine. Vignettes are obtained at all major border crossings into Austria and at larger petrol stations. From 1 January 2004, all vehicles above 3.5 tonnes maximum permitted laden weight using the Austrian network of motorways and expressways are required to attach a small device called the 'GO-Box' to their windscreen. The Go-Box uses the high frequency range to communicate with the around 400 fixed-installation toll points covering Austria, making it possible to effect an automatic toll deduction without slowing the flow of traffic. The on-board devices can be obtained for a one-off handling fee of Euro 5.00 at about 220 sales centres in Austria and in neighbouring countries or via the Internet. For further information visit the website at http://www.vignette.at

Tourist Office

Austrian National Tourist Office (ANTO)
PO Box 2363, London W1A 2QB
Tel: 020 7629 0461
Fax: 020 7499 6038
Email: info@anto.co.uk
Internet: www.austria-tourism.co.uk

tip

WELL-KNOWN LOCAL DELICACIES ARE *WIENER SCHNITZEL*, A VEAL ESCALOPE, AND THE FAMOUS DESSERT, THE *STRUDEL*, A BAKED DOUGH FILLED WITH FRUITS AND A SPRINKLING OF RAISINS AND CINNAMON.

AU0010 Alpencamping Nenzing

Garfrenga 1, A-6710 Nenzing (Vorarlberg)

Although best known for its ski-ing resorts, the forests and mountains of the Vorarlberg province make it equally suitable for a peaceful summer visit. Alpencamping Nenzing, is some 690 m. above sea level, set in a natural bowl surrounded by trees with some views across the pleasant countryside. You wind your way up from the main road or motorway, following a narrow road (you leave by a different, equally narrow route). On the left is a large building with the reception and restaurant and in front an old farm cart loaded with brightly coloured flowers. Some of the 166 level, but small, tourist pitches are in a flat area with others on neat terraces beyond. All have electricity (12-16A) and 100 also have water, drainage, sewage, TV, gas and phone connections. As a member of the Top Camping Austria association, the site has a 'Topi' club providing a range of activities, sport and competitions for children and daily activities for adults that includes a variety of guided walks for different ages, the Bernina Glacier Express, sports and music. Being open all year, the site can be a base from which to ski in winter.

Facilities

Two cramped, but heated, sanitary blocks - one under the reception building and another in the centre of the site (these are stretched in high season). Baby room. Facilities for disabled visitors. Motorcaravan service point. Small shop. Bar. Restaurant. Heated swimming pool (20 x 8 m). Play areas. Topi Club. Practice climbing wall. Sauna, solarium, massage. Off site: Bicycle hire, riding and fishing near.

Open

All year except Easter - 30 April.

At a glance

Welcome & Ambience	✓✓✓	Location	✓✓✓✓
Quality of Pitches	✓✓✓	Range of Facilities	✓✓✓✓

Directions

From A14 Feldkirch - Bludenz motorway take exit for Nenzing on B190 road and then follow the small 'Camping' signs with site logo - a butterfly.

Charges 2004

Per unit incl. 2 persons	€ 15,00 - € 26,20
incl. 2 children	€ 22,20 - € 31,80
electricity	€ 0,65
full services	€ 1,50

No credit cards.

Reservations

Only accepted for 8/7-16/8 (and necessary). Tel: 05525 62491. E-mail: office@alpencamping.at

AU0232 Terrassencamping Sonnenberg

Hinteroferst 12, A-6714 Nüziders bei Bludenz (Vorarlberg)

A friendly welcome awaits you at this well equipped site on the western end of Austria, at the junction of five alpine valleys. The views are captivating and ever-changing, ideal for keen photographers. The site is mostly terraced with pitches for longer stay units having gravel hardstandings at one side of the site, while shorter stay units have an area closer to the entrance. There are 130 good sized pitches, all with electricity (13A), 15 have a drain, and 24 are fully serviced. Traditional Tirolean musical evenings are a feature of this site. Herr Dünser senior takes parties of campers on guided walking tours, highly recommended, but do make sure that you are properly equipped, and reasonably fit. Good English is spoken.

Facilities

A superb new two storey building contains high quality facilities. On the lower floor you will find WCs, spacious hot showers, and washbasins (some in cubicles), and a baby room. The upper floor has a drying room, laundry, and a dishwashing room. TV and cinema room. Secure storage room for campers' bicycles, a ski and boot room, and seven studio apartments. Playground. Table tennis. Motorcaravan service point. Gas stocked. Baker calls daily in July/August. Only one dog per unit is allowed. Off site: Village 500 m. Fishing 3 km. Riding and bicycle hire 4 km. Golf 8 km.

At a glance

Welcome & Ambience	✓✓✓✓✓	Location	✓✓✓✓✓
Quality of Pitches	✓✓✓✓	Range of Facilities	✓✓✓✓✓

Directions

Nüziders is about 25 km. southeast of Feldkirch. From A14 exit 57 (Bludenz) turn north on road 190 and left at roundabout into village following camping signs.

Charges 2005

Per person	€ 5,00 - € 5,20
pitch incl. electricity	€ 8,90 - € 12,40

No credit cards.

Reservations

Advised for peak season. Tel: 05552 64035. E-mail: sonnencamp@aon.at

Open

30 April - 3 October.

AU0150 Camping Riffler

Bruggenfeldstraße 2, A-6500 Landeck (Tirol)

This small, pretty site is almost in the centre of the small town of Landeck and, being on the main through route from the Vorarlberg to the Tirol, would serve as a good overnight stop. Square in shape, it has just 50 pitches on either side of access roads on level grass, with the main road on one side and the fast flowing River Sanna on the other edge. Trees and flowers adorn the site giving good shade and all pitches have electricity (10A). Activities in the area include walking, mountain biking, paragliding, kite flying, rafting, canoeing and climbing.

Facilities

The small toilet block has been rebuilt to a good standard. Washing machine and dryer. Basic motorcaravan services. Restaurant (closed Oct). Shop. Small general room. Play area. Table tennis. Fishing. Off site: Supermarket just outside the gate, other shops 100 m. Restaurants about 300 m. Bicycle hire and swimming pool 500 m.

Open

All year except May.

At a glance

Welcome & Ambience	✓✓✓✓✓	Location	✓✓✓✓✓
Quality of Pitches	✓✓✓✓	Range of Facilities	✓✓✓✓

Directions

Site is at the western end of Landeck on the main no. 316 road.

Charges 2004

Per person	€ 4,40
child (5-14 yrs)	€ 3,70
pitch	€ 4,50 - € 8,30
car	€ 2,30
electricity	€ 2,30

Winter prices slightly more. No credit cards.

Reservations

Write to site. Tel: 05442 64898. E-mail: riffler@aon.at

AU0155 Aktiv-Camping Prutz

A-6522 Prutz (Tirol)

Aktiv-Camping is a long site which lies beside and is fenced off from the River Inn. Most of the 131 individual level pitches are for touring and range in size from 70 to 90 sq.m. They all have 6A electrical connections and in the larger area fit together sideways and back to back, so at times, it can give the appearance of being quite crowded. There is a separate overnight area for motorcaravans. This is an attractive area with many activities in both summer and winter for all age groups and you may well consider using this site not just as an overnight stop, but also for a longer stay.

Facilities

The sanitary facilities are of a high standard, with some private cabins, good facilities for the disabled, washing machine, dog shower, small mini-market, takeaway, rest room, children's play room, dry ski room, skating rink Children's entertainment. Guided walks, skiing (free shuttle service). Off site: Indoor pool at Feichten, Pilgrim's Church at Kaltenbrunn. Kaunertaler Glacier.

Open

All year.

At a glance

Welcome & Ambience	✓✓✓	Location	✓✓✓
Quality of Pitches	✓✓	Range of Facilities	✓✓✓

Directions

Travelling west from Innsbruck on the E60/A12 for about 65km. turn south onto the B180 signed Bregenz/Arlberg/Innsbruck/Fernpass. for approx. 11km. to Prutz. Site is signed from the B180 over the bridge.

Charges 2005

Per person	€ 6,70 - € 7,80
child (10-15 yrs)	€ 3,50
pitch incl. electricity	€ 7,00 - € 11,00

Reservations

Contact site. Tel: 05472 2648.
E-mail: info@aktiv-camping.at

AU0035 Camp Alpin Seefeld

Leutascherstrasse 810, A-6100 Seefeld (Tirol)

Alpin Seefeld is a pleasant, modern campsite with very good facilities in an attractive setting some 1,200 metres high. With excellent views of the surrounding mountains and forests there are 140 large, individual pitches mainly on flat grass (plus a few hardstandings), all with gas, TV, electricity (16A) and waste water, with 10 water points around, but no shade. Some pitches at the back and edge of the site are terraced. This is a good base for both summer and winter activity, whether you wish to take a gentle stroll or participate in something more demanding, including skiing direct from the site.

Facilities

Excellent heated sanitary facilities include nine private bathrooms for hire, some private cabins. Washing machines and dryer. Sauna, Turkish bath and solarium. Shop. Bar, snack bar and takeaway. Fishing. Play area. Bicycle hire. Off site: Sports centre with heated indoor and outdoor pools and restaurant are close. The popular Tirolean village of Seefeld 1 km. Golf 1.5 km.

Open

All year.

At a glance

Welcome & Ambience	✓✓✓✓	Location	✓✓✓✓✓
Quality of Pitches	✓✓✓✓	Range of Facilities	✓✓✓✓

Directions

Seefeld is about 17 km. northwest of Innsbruck. The site is about 2 km. from Seefeld on the road signed to Leutasch. It is well signed as you approach the town.

Charges 2004

Per person	€ 3,50 - € 9,50
over 65 yrs	€ 3,00 - € 8,00
child (3-14 yrs)	€ 2,00 - € 7,50
pitch	€ 4,00 - € 12,50

Reservations

Contact site. Tel: 05212 4848.
E-mail: info@camp-alpin.at

AU0227 Comfort Camp Grän

Engetalstr. 13, A-6673 Grän (Tirol)

In a village location in the Tannheimer Tal, with panoramic mountain scenery, Comfort Camp Grän is a family run site with excellent heated sanitary facilities and a stylish modern indoor swimming pool complex. It makes a good base for exploring this border region of Austria and Germany. The site has 210 pitches of 80-100 sq.m. (170 for tourists) all with 16A electric hook-ups, on fairly level grass, over gravel terrain with some shallow terraces. The main services are grouped at the entrance and include a hotel, restaurant, bar and a mini market. A 'wanderbus' service to various locations and walking trails runs from the village from end of May until early October.

Facilities

At the rear of the reception building, the main sanitary unit is very impressive with superb facilities, spacious, light and airy. There are controllable hot showers, washbasins in cubicles, a childrens section in the ladies, a baby room and many family bathrooms for rent. First aid room. No dedicated facilities for disabled people. The second smaller unit at one end of the site is equally good. Indoor pool complex (access with key card) with relaxation areas, sauna and steam room. Solarium. Mini-market. Restaurant and bar. Small playground plus indoor playroom for under 12s. Teenagers' room with playstation, babyfoot, table tennis. Off site: Haldensee (lake) 3 km. German Border 10 km.

At a glance

Welcome & Ambience	✓✓✓✓	Location	✓✓✓✓
Quality of Pitches	✓✓✓✓	Range of Facilities	✓✓✓✓✓

Directions

Grän is close to the German border, to the southwest of Füssen. From Germany on A7, turn off at exit 137, and go south on road 310 to Oberjoch, then road 308 (road 199 in Austria) east to Grän. At eastern end of village turn north (Pfronten) to site (1.5 km).

Charges guide

Per person	€ 6,50 - € 7,20
child (2-14 yrs)	€ 4,60 - € 6,70
pitch	€ 4,00 - € 8,20
electricity	€ 0,65

Reservations

Advised for peak season. Tel: 05675 6570. E-mail: comfortcamp@aon.at

Open

23 May - 2 November; 15 December - 18 April.

AU0040 Ferienanlage Tiroler Zugspitze

Obermoos 1, A-6632 Ehrwald (Tirol)

Although Ehrwald is in Austria, it is from the entrance of Zugspitzcamping that the cable car runs to the summit of Germany's highest mountain. Standing at 1,200 feet above sea level at the foot of the mountain, the 200 pitches (120 for tourists), mainly of grass over stones, are on flat terraces with fine panoramic views in parts. All have electricity connections (16A). The modern reception building at the entrance also houses a fine restaurant with a terrace which is open to those using the cable car, as well as those staying on the site. A further large modern building, heated in cool weather, has an indoor pool and fitness centre. This excellent mountain site, with its superb facilities, provides a good base from which to explore this interesting part of Austria and Bavaria by car or on foot.

Facilities

Two excellent sanitary blocks provide some washbasins in cabins and 20 private bathrooms for rent. Separate children's sanitary unit. Baby room. Unit for disabled people. Washing machines, dryers and dishwashers. Drying rooms. Motorcaravan service point. Shop. Bar. Restaurant. Indoor pool with sauna, whirlpool and fitness centre with solarium and massage room. Outdoor pool and children's pool with slide. Table tennis. Bicycle hire. Play area. Organised activities in season. Off site: Hotel, souvenir shop and cable car station 100 m. Sports in Ehrwald 5 km.

At a glance

Welcome & Ambience	✓✓✓✓	Location	✓✓✓✓✓
Quality of Pitches	✓✓✓✓	Range of Facilities	✓✓✓✓✓

Directions

Follow signs in Ehrwald to Tiroler Zugspitzbahn and then signs to camp.

Charges guide

Per person	€ 10,00 - € 12,00
child (4-15 yrs)	€ 7,50 - € 8,50
pitch	€ 6,00 - € 8,00
electricity per kw.	€ 0,80

Reservations

Write to site with deposit (€ 73). Tel: 05673 2309. E-mail: ferienanlage@zugspitze.com

Open

All year.

AU0060 Ferienparadies Natterer See

Natterer See 1, A-6161 Natters (Tirol)

Above Innsbruck, seven kilometres southwest of the town, this excellent site is in a quiet and isolated location around two small lakes. One of these is for bathing with a long 67 m. slide (free to campers, on payment to day visitors), while boats such as inflatables can be put on either lake. There are many fine mountain views and a wide variety of scenic excursions. For the more active, signed walks start from the site. There are 210 individual pitches (180 for tourists) of varying size. Some are quite small, either on flat ground by the lake or on higher, level terraces where views can be obscured by trees in the summer and some access roads are narrow. All pitches have electricity (6A), with 50 also having water and drain. Many are reinforced by gravel (possibly tricky for tents). For winter camping the site offers ski and drying rooms and a free ski-bus service. A toboggan run and langlauf have been developed on the site, with ice skating, ice hockey and curling on the lake. Occasional services are held in the small chapel. The excellent restaurant with bar and large terrace overlooking the lake has a good menu. Three 'theme pavillions' overlooking the water provide special dinners (4-8 persons). Very good English is spoken. This family-run campsite must rate as one of the best in Austria and can therefore become very busy. It was awarded Camping Cheques' Campsite of the Year 2001. Used by a tour operator (20 pitches).

Facilities

Two large sanitary blocks have under-floor heating, some washbasins in cabins, plus excellent facilities for babies, children and disabled people. Laundry facilities. Motorcaravan services. Fridge boxes for hire. Bar/restaurant (20/3-2/10). Pizzeria and takeaway. Good mini market (20/3-2/10). Playgrounds. Children's activity programme with Indian 'topi' tents. Child minding (day nursery) in high season. Sports field. Archery, basketball, beach volleyball and water polo. Table tennis. Youth room with games, pool and billiards. TV room with Sky. Internet point. Mountain bike hire. 'Aquapark' with water trampoline, bumper boats, slide and other attractions (1/5-30/9). Surf-bikes and wind-glider. Canoes and mini sailboats for rent. During main season (mid May-mid Oct) extensive daily entertainment programme for children and adults offers different sports, competitions, amusement and excursions. No dogs are accepted in high season (2/7-27/8). Off site: Tennis, minigolf nearby.

Open

All year except 1 November - 14 December.

At a glance

Welcome & Ambience	✓✓✓✓✓	Location	✓✓✓✓✓
Quality of Pitches	✓✓✓✓✓	Range of Facilities	✓✓✓✓✓

Directions

From Inntal autobahn (A12) take Brenner autobahn (A13) as far as Innsbruck-sud/Natters exit (no. 3) without payment. Turn left by garage onto the B182 to Natters. Turn first right and immediately right again and follow signs to site 4 km. Note: Care is needed when negotiating site entrance and there is a separate entrance for large units or vehicles over 3 m. high - ask reception.

Charges 2005

Per person	€ 5,70 - € 7,60
child (under 14 yrs)	€ 4,40 - € 5,20
pitch	€ 7,80 - € 10,00
with water and drainage	€ 9,30 - € 12,50
dog (excl 2/07-27/08)	€ 3,00 - € 3,70
electricity (6A)	€ 3,20 - € 3,50

Special weekly, winter, summer or Christmas packages.

Reservations

Made for min. 7 days with deposit (€ 37). Tel: 0512 546732. E-mail: info@natterersee.com

AU0220 Ötztal Arena Camp Krismer

Dorf 387, A-6441 Umhausen (Tirol)

This is a delightful site with lovely views, in the beautiful Ötz valley, on the edge of the village of Umhausen. Situated on a gentle slope in an open valley, it has an air of peace and tranquillity and makes an excellent base for mountain walking, particularly in spring and autumn, or skiing in winter. The 98 pitches, some on individual terraces, are all marked and numbered and have electricity (12/16A); charges relate to the area available, long leads may be necessary. The reception building houses an attractive bar/restaurant, a TV room and the sanitary facilities. The enthusiastic family owners speak good English and are very helpful and welcoming. Just above the site is an archaeological open air park depicting the life and times of 'Ötzi the Ice Man' whose remains were found in the mountains beyond the park. The walk up to the Stuibenfall is highly recommended but is quite strenuous – allow at least one hour.

Facilities

With under-floor heating, open washbasins, hairdressing room and showers on payment, the toilet facilities are of good quality. A small toilet/wash block at the far end of the site has been refurbished for summer use. Baby room. Dishwashing. Washing machine and dryer, iron from reception, drying room. Basic motorcaravan services. Bar/restaurant (May-Sept, Dec-April). No shop but bread can be ordered at reception. TV room with satellite. Ski room. Fishing. Bicycle hire. Table tennis. Off site: Swimming pool and tennis 100m. Shops in village 200 m. Play area 300 m. Para-gliding, mountain walks, Stuiben waterfall and 'Ötzi Dorf' nearby.

At a glance

Welcome & Ambience	✓✓✓✓✓	Location	✓✓✓✓✓
Quality of Pitches	✓✓✓✓	Range of Facilities	✓✓✓✓

Directions

Take Ötztal Valley exit 123 from Imst - Innsbruck A12 motorway, and Umhausen is 13 km. towards Solden on the B186; site is well signed to south of village.

Charges 2004

Per person	€ 5,60
child (2-13 yrs)	€ 4,10
pitch	€ 2,40 - € 8,00
electricity (plus 0.75 per kw)	€ 2,54

Reservations

Write with deposit (€ 37). Tel: 05255 5390. E-mail: info@oetztal-camping.at

Open

All year.

AU0225 Romantik Camping Schloß Fernsteinsee

Am Fernpaß Tirol, A-6465 Nassereith (Tirol)

This is a secluded, attractive site in a sheltered location in the protected area of the Fernstein Lakes and part of the Schloss Fernsteinsee estate. There are 120 pitches, all for tourists, in two separate areas and 80 have electric hook-ups (4A). The pitches are on level grass in the area in front of the reception and services building, on four shallow terraces, divided by low rails or shrubs, with good shade and gravel access roads. The second area, which is further from the services, is more open, served by a central tarmac road and pitching is less formal. The reception building houses a good quality heated sanitary unit, a sauna and solarium, a small bar and terrace, and shop for basics. The upmarket Hotel Schloss Fernsteinsee is a 500 m. walk from the site and provides a restaurant and bar, and close to the hotel is small chapel. Tennis courts, an indoor swimming pool, horse riding, rafting and boating, diving, fishing and cycling are all available nearby. A little English is spoken.

Facilities

Modern heated facilities with a generous supply of controllable hot showers, all washbasins in cubicles, a suite for disabled people, and a baby changing facility. Dishwashing and laundry rooms. Table tennis, Boules courts, small playground, games room. Drinks machine. Communal barbecue facility. Sauna and solarium. Fishing and boating on the lake. Off site: The Hotel Schloss Fernsteinsee with bar and restaurant 500 m. Nassereith village, shops and indoor swimming pool 1.5 km. The Fern Pass and alpine road.

Open

15 April - 26 October.

At a glance

Welcome & Ambience	✓✓✓✓	Location	✓✓✓✓
Quality of Pitches	✓✓✓✓	Range of Facilities	✓✓✓✓

Directions

Nassereith is about 15 km. north of Imst, just south of the Fern Pass. From Imst take road 189 north for 13 km., then left on road 179 and continue past Nassereith, taking a tarmac entry road about 500 m. before the river bridge (well signed). From north, pass hotel entrance, cross bridge, first entrance is off car-park, but second entry after 500m. is better quality.

Charges guide

Per person	€ 4,70
child (3-14 yrs)	€ 2,80
pitch	€ 2,50 - € 6,90
electricity	€ 2,10

Reservations

Contact site. Tel: 05265 5210.
E-mail: hotel@schloss-fernsteinsee.at

AU0170 Camping Innsbruck-Kranebitten

Kranebitter Allee 214, A-6020 Innsbruck (Tirol)

With good facilities, this site is in a pleasant situation just outside Innsbruck. The 120 pitches are numbered, but not marked out, on mostly sloping grass, with good shade cover. With three separate terraces for caravans and motorcaravans, all pitches have electricity (6A, long leads are on loan for some). By the side of the site, with access to it, is a large open field with a good playground and plenty of space for ball games. Being so near to the attractive town of Innsbruck, the site makes an excellent base from which to visit the ancient city and also to explore the many attractions nearby. The 'Innsbruck-Card', available from the site, gives various discounts for attractions in the city, plus free travel on public transport (park-and-ride from the site, even if you don't stay overnight). A private taxi also runs a shuttle service to and from the city for 5. Some road and aircraft noise may be heard. Good English is spoken.

Facilities

The large, toilet block, although showing signs of age, is heated, clean and acceptable, with some washbasins in cabins. Washing machines and dryers. Motorcaravan services. Bar/ restaurant with terrace (open all year, but open times may vary). Internet point. Shop for basic supplies. Playground with large play field adjoining. Games for children and barbecues in summer. Free mountain hiking and cycling tours in summer, free ski bus in winter. Bicycle hire. Off site: Swimming pool 2 km.

Open

All year.

At a glance

Welcome & Ambience	✓✓✓✓	Location	✓✓✓✓
Quality of Pitches	✓✓✓	Range of Facilities	✓✓✓✓

Directions

From A12 Innsbruck - Arlberg motorway, take Innsbruck-Kranebitten exit 83 from where site is well signed, directly on B171 (Telfs-Innsbruck non-toll road).

Charges 2005

Per person	€ 5,00 - € 5,35
child (4-14 yrs)	€ 3,50
caravan	€ 3,00
car	€ 3,00
motorcaravan	€ 5,00 - € 6,00
electricity	€ 3,00

Less 10% for stays over 10 days.
Special offers for sporting groups.

Reservations

Contact site. Tel: 05122 84180.
E-mail: campinnsbruck@hotmail.com

AU0080 Schloß-Camping

A-6111 Volders (Tirol)

The Inn valley is not only central to the Tirol, but is a very beautiful and popular part of Austria. Volders, some 15 kilometres from Innsbruck, is one of the little villages on the banks of the Inn river and is perhaps best known for the 17th century Baroque Servite Church and monastery. Conveniently situated here is the very pleasant Schloss-Camping, dominated by the castle from which it gets its name that towers at the back of the site with mountains beyond. The 160 numbered grass pitches are on level or slightly sloping ground. Electricity connections throughout (16A). The well laid out camping area is in two areas, divided by a fence and is closely mown, making this a most attractive site and the English speaking Baron who owns and runs it gives a most friendly welcome. There are rooms to let in the castle. This is an excellent base from which to explore the region and visit Innsbruck, Salzburg, the Royal Castles at Schwangau, the Bavarian Alps and northern Italy over the Brenner Pass for day trips.

Facilities

The small, sanitary block of old design is near the entrance and has some washbasins in cabins. Washing machine and covered dishwasing area. Motorcaravan service point. Bar/restaurant. Snack bar with terrace. Shop for basics (all May - end Sept). Fenced and heated swimming pool (mid May-mid Sept). Minigolf. Playground. Games and entertainment for children in high season.
Off site: Supermarket 400 m. Bicycle hire 500 m. Golf and riding 7 km.

Open

15 April - 15 October.

At a glance

Welcome & Ambience	✓✓✓✓	Location	✓✓✓✓
Quality of Pitches	✓✓✓✓	Range of Facilities	✓✓✓✓

Directions

From A12 motorway, travelling east, leave at exit 68 for Hall, going westwards, take exit 61 for Wattens and follow the B171 and signs for Volders where site is signed.

Charges guide

Per person	€ 5,70
child (3-14 yrs)	€ 3,30
caravan or tent	€ 3,30
car	€ 3,30
m/cycle	€ 1,00
motorcaravan	€ 6,60

No credit cards. Reductions for stays of 3 nights or more in low season.

Reservations

Made for any length of stay with deposit and small fee. Tel: 05224 52333. E-mail: campingvolders@utanet.at

AU0250 AlpencampingMark

Bundesstraße 12, Maholmhof, A-6114 Weer bei Schwaz (Tirol)

This pleasant Tirol site is run by a family who provide not only a neat, friendly site and a warm welcome, but also a variety of outdoor activities. Formerly a farm, they now breed horses, giving a free ride each day to youngsters and organise treks. Herr Mark junior (a certified alpine ski guide and ski instructor) runs courses for individuals or groups in climbing (there are practice climbing walls on site), rafting, mountain bike riding, trekking, hiking, etc. Guided alpine tours can be arranged and there are pleasant walks up the lower slopes of the mountains directly from the site. Set in the Inn valley, between mountain ranges, the site has 96 flat, grass pitches (71 for touring units) on either side of gravel roads, with electricity connections (6/10A). Trees provide shade in some areas. This site could be used for a night stop when passing through from Innsbruck to Salzburg, but is even better for a longer stay for adventurous youngsters or for a holiday in the Tirol area. The Mark family would very much welcome visits by rallies in the Spring season and are happy to arrange programmes of entertainment and excursions. Good English is spoken.

Facilities

Good quality, modern, heated sanitary facilities are provided in the old farm buildings. Freezer. Washing machines and dryer. Motorcaravan services. Small, cheerful bar/restaurant and shop (1/6-1/9). Small heated pool (15/5-15/9). An attractive wooden chalet houses reception and the activities are administered from here. Activity programme with instruction. Bicycle hire. Riding (free for children). Glacier tours. Table tennis. Large play area with good equipment. A further barn is for use by children in wet weather.
Off site: Imtal Valley, good for mountain biking.

Open

1 April - 31 October.

At a glance

Welcome & Ambience	✓✓✓✓	Location	✓✓✓✓
Quality of Pitches	✓✓✓✓✓	Range of Facilities	✓✓✓✓

Directions

Site is 200 m. east of the village of Weer on Wattens - Schwaz road no. B171 which runs parallel to the A12, just 10 km east of Innsbruck. (If using A12 take exit 61 from west or 53 from east).

Charges 2005

Per person	€ 4,30 - € 5,50
child (under 14 yrs)	€ 3,00 - € 3,50
pitch	€ 4,50 - € 6,00
electricity	€ 2,50
dog	€ 3,00

Reservations

Necessary for July/August and made without deposit. Tel: 05224 68146. E-mail: alpcamp.mark@aon.at

AU0070 Camping Hofer

Gerlosstrasse 33, A-6280 Zell-am-Ziller (Tirol)

Zell am Ziller is in the heart of the Zillertal valley at the junction of the B169 and B165 Gerlos Pass road and nestles round the unusual 18th century church noted for its paintings. Camping Hofer, owned by the same family for over 50 years, is on the edge of the village just five minutes walk from the centre on a quiet side road. The 100 pitches, all with electricity (6/10A),(long long leads may be needed) are grass on gravel. A few trees decorate the site and offer some shade. A pleasant development provides a bar/restaurant and terrace, games and TV room, a small heated pool which can be covered and a sun deck. Once a week in summer the owner takes those who wish to rise at 4 am. to a nearby mountain to watch the sun rise. A little road train gives a free service round the village. The pleasant owner, who speaks good English, does his best to provide a friendly, family atmosphere

Facilities

Good quality, heated sanitary provision is on the ground floor of the apartment building and has some washbasins in cabins. Baby room. Washing machines, dryers and irons. Gas supplies. Motorcaravan services. Restaurant with bar (closed 1/11-10/12 and 30/4-31/5), offers special theme weeks with international dishes; Greek, Italian, Mexican etc. Shop opposite. Swimming pool (1/4-31/10). Bicycle hire. Organised entertainment and activities in high season. Guided walks, cycle tours, barbecues, biking, skiing. Ski room. Youth room. Off site: Town and supermarket within walking distance. Gerlos pass high alpine road.

Open

All year.

At a glance

Welcome & Ambience	✓✓✓✓✓	Location	✓✓✓✓✓
Quality of Pitches	✓✓✓✓	Range of Facilities	✓✓✓✓

Directions

Site is well signed from the main B169 road at Zell am Ziller. Site is at southern end of town close to the junction of the B169 and B165.

Charges 2004

Per person	€ 4,50 - € 7,50
child (under 14)	€ 3,00 - € 5,00
pitch	€ 5,50 - € 9,50
electricity	€ 2,50
dog	€ 2,00

Special low season and winter packages.
No credit cards (debit cards accepted).

Reservations

Necessary for July/Aug and Christmas; made for any length with deposit. Tel: 05282 2248.
E-mail: office@campinghofer.at

AU0100 Camping Seeblick Toni Brantlhof

Reintalersee 46, Moosen, A-6233 Kramsach (Tirol)

Austria has some of the finest sites in Europe and Seeblick Toni-Brantlhof is one of the best. In a quiet, rural situation on the edge of the small Reintalersee lake, it is well worth considering for holidays in the Tirol with so many varied excursion possibilities nearby. Kramsach, a pleasant, busy tourist resort is some three kilometres from the site. The mountains which surround the site give scenic views and the campsite has a neat and tidy appearance. The 243 level pitches (215 for tourists) are in regular rows off hard access roads and are of good size with grass and hardstanding. All pitches have electricity (10A), 100 are fully serviced including cable TV and phone connections. The large, well appointed restaurant has a roof-top terrace where one can enjoy a meal, drink or snack and admire the lovely scenery. A path leads to the lake for swimming, boating and a sunbathing meadow. With a good solarium, sauna, whirlpool and fitness centre, this site provides for an excellent summer holiday and, with ski areas near, an excellent winter holiday also. This is a family run with good English spoken and there is a friendly welcome.

Facilities

Two heated sanitary blocks of quite outstanding quality include some washbasins in cabins. The main block has been extended to include en-suite toilet/basin/shower rooms (free), the second one, on the opposite side of the camping area, also has individual bathrooms to let. Both blocks are heated in cool weather. Facilities for disabled visitors. Baby room. Washing machines and dryers. Drying rooms. Freezer. Motorcaravan services. Restaurant (all year). Bar. Snack kiosk. Well stocked mini-market. Fitness centre. Playground. Tepi club, kindergarten and organised activities for children in high season. Youth room. Fishing. Bicycle hire. Riding. Internet point (July/Aug. only).

Open

All year.

At a glance

Welcome & Ambience	✓✓✓✓✓	Location	✓✓✓✓✓
Quality of Pitches	✓✓✓✓	Range of Facilities	✓✓✓✓✓

Directions

Take exit 32 for Kramsach from A12 autobahn and turn right at roundabout, then immediately left following signs 'Zu den Seen' in village. After 3 km. turn right at camp sign. Note: there are two sites side by side at the lake – ignore the first and continue through to Seeblick Toni.

Charges 2005

Per person	€ 5,50 - € 8,00
child (under 14 yrs)	€ 4,50 - € 5,50
pitch	€ 7,10 - € 10,20
electricity	€ 3,20
dog	€ 4,20 - € 5,10

Reservations

Essential for July/Aug. and the skiing season and made for min. 1 week with deposit.
Tel: 05337 63544. E-mail: camping@seeblick.co.at

AU0102 Seen Camping Stadlerhof

A-6233 Kramsach (Tirol)

This child-friendly family run site is in a beautiful location near the Krummsee. It has a small restaurant and bar, excellent sanitary facilities, heated outdoor pool complex with cafe and Wellness Centre, and a comprehensive children's playground that will keep them amused for an entire holiday. There are 130 sensibly sized pitches (99 for tourists) all with electric hook-ups (10A). Many are individual and divided by hedges and shrubs, and some mature trees offer shade in parts. Some multi-serviced pitches are available. The Wellness Centre provides pampering and luxury for the adults with sauna, solarium, steam room, aromatherapy, massage rooms, skin therapy treatments, fitness centre, plus a relaxation area and an FKK naturist terrace. The children meanwhile, have an enticing array of play equipment including climbing frames, tubes, fort, bridge, conventional swings and slides, a skateboard ramp, table tennis and a games room with machines. The site also has its own small lake, a panorama walk and a dog walk. Reasonable English is spoken. A Quickstop facility with grassy pitches and electric hook-up for overnighting is also offered.

Facilities

Spacious sanitary facilities include controllable hot showers, some washbasins in cubicles, and 5 family bathrooms for rent. Laundry and dishwashing facilities. No dedicated facilities for disabled people. Small restaurant and bar. Basic provisions available. A magnificent new building contains the 'Wellness Centre', an outdoor heated stainless steel swimming pool (12.5m. x 6m and open in winter) with spa pool and childrens pool, and a cafe. Comprehensive playground. Drying room, ski room. Off site: Kramsach is within walking distance. Reintalersee 3 km.

Open

All year.

At a glance

Welcome & Ambience	✓✓✓✓	Location	✓✓✓✓✓
Quality of Pitches	✓✓✓✓	Range of Facilities	✓✓✓✓✓

Directions

Kramsach is approximately mid-way between Innsbruck and Kufstein. From A12 exit 32 turn right at roundabout and immediately left following signs for 'Zu den Seen' in village. Site is just outside village on left hand side, after a right hand bend.

Charges 2004

Per person	€ 4,60 - € 5,80
child (under 14 yrs)	€ 2,95 - € 3,80
electricity	€ 2,50
dog	€ 3,00 - € 3,50

No credit cards.

Reservations

Advised for peak season. Tel: 05337 63371.
E-mail: camping@tirol.com & info@camping-stadler

AU0065 Camping Seehof

A-6233 Kramsach (Tirol)

Camping Seehof, an excellent site in every respect, is situated in a marvellous, sunny and peaceful location on the eastern shores of the Reintalersee lake. Add to this that it is very much a family run site and you have almost perfection itself. It separates into two areas, a small area next to the lake, with a good sunbathing area, and a bigger one nearer the large excellent sanitary block. All the large pitches are served by good access roads and have electricity and TV point and many have waste water drainage. Water points are conveniently located around the site. Seehof provides an ideal starting point for walking, cycling or riding (with a riding stable nearby), and in the winter for cross-country skiing, ice-skating and curling. A free shuttle bus operates from the site during the skiing season.

Facilities

Excellent sanitary facilities include four bathrooms, which are free for campers' use, and a further six to rent for private use. The second suite of showers, under reception, should be completely refurbished before 2005. Baby room. Facilities for disabled visitors. Medical room; including bed. Dog shower. Washing machine and dryer. Ski room. Motorcaravan service point. Small shop for basics. Restaurant. Playground and children's playroom. Internet access. Bicycle rental. Fishing. Off site: Kramsach and not too far away Kristallwelten and the Swarovski Factory.

At a glance

Welcome & Ambience	✓✓✓✓✓	Location	✓✓✓✓✓
Quality of Pitches	✓✓✓✓✓	Range of Facilities	✓✓✓✓✓

Directions

From the A12 take exit 32 into Kramsach. At roundabout turn right and immediately turn left. At T-junction turn right and at next T-junction turn left. Site is about 2.8 km. along this road and you turn right towards it. Reception is next to the restaurant.

Charges 2004

Per pitch with electricity	€ 8,00 - € 10,00
adult	€ 4,20 - € 5,70
child (2-14yrs)	€ 3,00 - € 4,00

Reservations

Advised for July/Aug. Tel: 05337 63541.
E-mail: info@camping-seehof.com

Open

All year.

AU0140 Euro Camping Wilder Kaiser

A-6345 Kössen (Tirol)

The village of Kössen lies to the south of the A8 Munich - Salzburg autobahn and east of the A93/A12 motorway near Kufstein. It is therefore well situated for overnight stops but even more for longer stays. Wilder Kaiser is located at the foot of the Unterberg with views of the Kaisergebirge (the Emperor's mountains) and surrounded by forests. Being about two kilometres south of the village, it is a quiet location, away from main roads. The well constructed main building at the entrance houses reception, a restaurant with terrace, well stocked mini market and the sanitary facilities overlooking the small, fenced heated swimming pool and children's pool. About 125 of the 190 pitches (grass over gravel) are available for tourists, plus an area for tents. Around 100 are of a good size, with electricity (10A), water, drainage, TV and gas points, they are arranged on either side of paved roads. A little shade from specimen trees and all have views. English spoken.

Facilities

The heated, central sanitary block is of good quality with spacious showers, some washbasins in cubicles and a baby room. Washing machines and dryers. Motorcaravan services. Shop. Large restaurant/bar (closed Nov). Snack bar (high season). Club room with TV. Heated swimming pool (May - Oct). Youth room. Sauna and solarium. Tennis. Table tennis. Large imaginative adventure playground. In high season, special staff run a Topi club and other activities for adults and children, with the weekly programme displayed on notice boards.

Open

All year.

At a glance

Welcome & Ambience	✓✓✓✓	Location	✓✓✓✓
Quality of Pitches	✓✓✓	Range of Facilities	✓✓✓✓

Directions

From A8 autobahn (München - Salzburg), take Grabenstatt exit 109 and go south on B307/B176 to Kössen where site is signed. From A93 (Rosenheim - Kufstein) autobahn take Oberaudorf exit and go east on B172 to Walchsee and Kössen.

Charges guide

Per person	€ 5,50 - € 6,50
child (under 14)	€ 3,00 - € 5,00
pitch with electricity and TV	€ 6,00 - € 8,00
pitch with all services	€ 7,00 - € 9,00
electricity	€ 3,00
dog	€ 3,00 - € 4,00

Reductions for long off-season stays.

Reservations

Made with deposit and fee for exact dates in high season; no minimum stay except at Christmas (3 weeks). Tel: 05375 6444.
E-mail: info@eurocamp-koessen.com

AU0110 Tirol Camp

Lindau 20, A-6391 Fieberbrunn (Tirol)

This is one of many Tirol campsites that cater equally for summer and winter (here seemingly more for winter, when reservation is essential and prices 50% higher). Tirol Camp is in a quiet and attractive mountain situation and has 280 pitches all on wide flat terraces, set on a gentle slope (193 for touring units). Marked out mainly by the electricity boxes or low hedges, they are said to be 80-100 sq.m. and all have electricity (6A), gas, water/drainage, TV and telephone connections. A small, heated outdoor swimming pool with a paddling pool is open in summer. A new 'Wellness Centre' (free to campers) with indoor/outdoor pool complex sauna, steam room, solarium, aromatherapy massage etc was opened in 2004. For winter stays, the site is very close to a ski lift centre and a 'langlauf' piste. Good English spoken.

Facilities

The original refurbished toilet block in the main building is excellent with some washbasins in cabins and some private bathrooms on payment. A splendid, modern heated block at the top end of the site has spacious showers and all washbasins in cabins. Facilities for the disabled. Washing machines, dryers and drying room. Motorcaravan services. Self-service shop and snacks. Restaurant (closed Oct, Nov and May). Separate general room. Internet point. Sauna. Tennis. Outdoor swimming pool (12 x 8 m; 1/6-30/9). Indoor pool and Wellness Centre (all year). Lake fishing. Riding. Bicycle hire. Outdoor chess. Playground and children's zoo. Entertainment and activity programmes for adults and children (July/Aug).

At a glance

Welcome & Ambience	✓✓✓✓	Location	✓✓✓✓✓
Quality of Pitches	✓✓✓✓	Range of Facilities	✓✓✓✓✓

Directions

Site is on the east side of Fieberbrunn, which is on the B164 St Johann-Saalfelden road. Turn south off the B164, 2 km. east of Fieberbrunn and follow camp signs up the hill to the site.

Charges guide

Per person	€ 6,00 - € 10,00
child (4-15 yrs)	free - € 5,00
pitch	€ 5,00 - € 25,00
electricity (per kw/h on meter)	€ 0,70
dog	€ 5,00

Winter charges higher. Special weekly package deals with half-board offered in summer. Reductions for over 60s.

Reservations

Any length (with deposit in winter only).
Tel: 05354 56666. E-mail: office@tirol-camp.at

Open

All year.

AU0180 Sport-Camp Woferlgut

Kroessenbach 40, A-5671 Bruck (Salzburg)

The village of Bruck lies at the junction of the B311 and the Grossglocknerstrasse in the Hohe Tauern National Park, with Salzburg to the north and Innsbruck to the northwest. Sport Camp Woferlgut, a family run site, is one of the best in Austria. Although surrounded by mountains, the site is quite flat with pleasant views. The 350 level, grass pitches are marked out by shrubs (300 for touring units) and each has electricity (16A), water, drainage, cable TV socket and gas point. The fitness centre has a fully equipped gym, whilst the other building contains a sauna and cold dip, Turkish bath, solarium (all free) massage on payment and a bar. In summer there is a free activity programme, evenings with live music, club for children, weekly barbecues and guided cycle and mountain tours. The site's own lake is used for swimming and fishing, surrounded by a landscaped sunbathing area. In winter a cross-country skiing trail and toboggan run lead from the site and a free bus service is provided to nearby skiing facilities. A high grass bank separates the site and the road. The management is pleased to advise on local attractions and tours, making this a splendid base for a family holiday. Good English is spoken. Used by tour operators (45 pitches).

Facilities

Three modern sanitary blocks - the newest in a class of its own - have excellent facilities, providing private cabins, under-floor heating and music. Washing machines and dryers. Facilities for disabled visitors. Family bathrooms for rent. Motorcaravan services. Cooking and dishwashing facilities. Well stocked shop, bar, restaurant and takeaway (20/12-20/4 and 13/5-1/11). Small, heated outdoor pool and children's pool (13/5-30/9). Fitness centre. Two playgrounds, indoor play room and children's cinema. General room. Tennis. Volleyball. Football area. Bicycle hire. Hobby room with billiards, table tennis and TV. Fishing. Watersports and lake swimming. Hiking and skiing (all year) nearby. Collection of small animals with pony rides for young children. Off site: ATM 500 m. Skiing 2.5 km. Golf 3 km. Boat launching and sailing 3.5 km.

At a glance

Welcome & Ambience	✓✓✓✓	Location	✓✓✓✓
Quality of Pitches	✓✓✓✓	Range of Facilities	✓✓✓✓✓

Directions

Site is southwest of Bruck. From road B311, Bruck by-pass, take southern exit (Grossglockner) and site is signed from the junction of B311 and B107 roads (small signs).

Charges 2005

Per person	€ 4,70 - € 6,10
child (under 10)	€ 3,90 - € 5,10
caravan and car	€ 9,10 - € 11,80
motorcaravan	€ 7,50 - € 11,80
electricity (plus meter)	€ 2,10
dog	€ 3,10 - € 4,20

Special offers for low season, longer stays.

Reservations

Contact site. Tel: 06545 73030.
E-mail: info@sportcamp.at

Open

All year.

AU0265 Park Grubhof

A-5092 St Martin bei Lofer (Salzburg)

Park Grubhof is a well organised spacious site in a scenic riverside location, once the pleasure park of the adjacent Schloss (now a hotel). The 200 pitches all with electric hook-ups (10A, long leads may be required), have been carefully divided into separate areas for different types of camper - dog owners, couples, young people, families and groups. There are wooded areas with plenty of shade, other more open areas, and some very attractive log cabins which have been rescued from the old logging camps. This site is particularly good for tenters. A major feature is a large alpine flower meadow, which is left unmown except for a couple of pathways. To one side of the site is a restaurant, well stocked shop, and a small games room with table tennis. The main activities are based around the River Saalach, where you will find open barbecue areas, weekly trials and demonstration of canoeing and white water rafting, fishing and swimming (when the river level reduces). Free children's entertainment is organised in main season. The long flat valley is ideal for easy cycling with many marked routes and there are good walking trails from the site. Good English is spoken. Parents of small children should be aware that the site is adjacent to a fast flowing river which is unfenced.

Facilities

Two sanitary units - the most recently built unit by the riverside, and the original larger, but more dated unit nearer reception, give a good provision of all facilities including some washbasins in cubicles, laundry and dishwashing sinks. A suite for disabled campers is in the older unit. Motorcaravan service point. Shop, restaurant and bar. Playground. Games room. Watersports. Off site: Lofer 1 km. Gorges and caves 5-7 km. Salzburg 40 minutes drive. Many marked walking and cycling trails.

Open

1 May - 30 September.

At a glance

Welcome & Ambience	✓✓✓✓	Location	✓✓✓✓✓
Quality of Pitches	✓✓✓✓	Range of Facilities	✓✓✓✓

Directions

St Martin bei Lofer lies about 40 km. east of Kufstein. From A12 exit 17 (south of Kufstein) take road B178 east to St. Johann in Tyrol, then continue on the B178 north west to Lofer, and finally south on B311. Just past Schloss Grubhof at the northern edge of St. Martin, turn left (site signed) and follow lane to site.

Charges 2004

Per person	€ 5,20
child (under 15 yrs)	€ 3,20
pitch	€ 2,20 - € 5,40
electricity	€ 2,00
dog	€ 1,20

Reservations

Contact site. Tel: 06588 8237.
E-mail: park-grubhof@salzburg.co.at

AU0160 Seecamp Zell am See

Thumersbacherstraße 34, A-5700 Zell-am-See (Salzburg)

Zellersee, delightfully situated in the south of Salzburg province and near the start of the Grossglockner-strasse, is ideally placed for enjoying the splendid southern Austria countryside. Seecamp is right by the water about 3 km. from the town of Zell and with fine views to the south end of the lake. One is immediately struck by the order and neat appearance of the site, with 176 good level, mainly grass-on-gravel pitches of average size, all with electricity (10/16A). About half have water, drainage and TV connections. Units can be close together in peak season. A large, modern building in the centre, houses the amenities. The lake is accessible for watersports, including both surfing and sailing schools. All in all, this is a splendid site for a relaxing or active holiday. Good English spoken.

Facilities

Excellent, heated sanitary facilities include facilities for disabled visitors and a baby room. Washing machines, dryers and irons. Motorcaravan services (access difficult for larger units). Restaurant (closed for 2 weeks after Easter and Oct-Nov). Shop (June-Aug. and Dec-mid Jan). Beach volleyball. Play area. Playroom with playstations. Fishing. Bicycle hire. Topi Club and summer entertainment for children. Activity programme for adults with rafting, canoeing, mountain biking, water ski-ing and hiking. Winter ski packages and free ski bus. Glacier ski-ing possible in summer. Off site: Free entry to nearby lake beach, swimming pools and ice skating. Nearby Schloss Prielau and the pretty villages along the eastern side of lake.

Open

All year.

At a glance

Welcome & Ambience	✓✓✓✓	Location	✓✓✓✓✓
Quality of Pitches	✓✓✓✓	Range of Facilities	✓✓✓✓

Directions

Approaching from the north on the B311 take the Thumersbach exit just before tunnel entrance (2 km. north of Zell-am-See town). After 500 m. turn left and site entrance is 750 m. on the right. Note: This road has a 3.5 ton weight restriction but it is the only access to site.

Charges 2004

Per person	€ 7,40
child (5-15 yrs)	€ 4,00
simple pitch	€ 8,30
comfort pitch	€ 10,70
tent pitch	€ 4,00
car	€ 2,50

Gas on meter; local tax (over 15 yrs) € 0.90. Less 20% in low season. Special winter package prices.

Reservations

Made for min. 7 days - contact site for form.
Tel: 06542 72115. E-mail: zell@seecamp.at

AU0185 Campingplatz Seewiese

Tristachersee 2, A-9900 Lienz (Tirol)

High above the village of Tristach and 5 km. from Lienz, this is a perfect location for a good campsite. When we arrived the owner said, "This is a green paradise at the gateway to the Dolomites" – it did not take us many minutes to agree totally with his assessment. The 110 pitches all have 6A electricity and the 11 pitches for motorcaravans near reception each have electricity, water and internet access. Caravans are sited on a gently sloping field which has level areas although pitches are unmarked and unnumbered. At the bottom of this field is a small lake which can be used for swimming and a volley-ball pitch. There are many opportunities for sporting activities including kayaking, rafting, mountain biking, climbing and paragliding. The more sedate may be happy with walking or golf that can also be found nearby.

Facilities

Toilet facilities are clean, heated and modern with free showers. Washing machine and dryer. Motorcaravan service point. Excellent restaurant/bar. Small play area. Internet access. Swimming in adjoining lake. Off site: Lienz 5 km.

Open

5 May - 30 September.

At a glance

Welcome & Ambience	✓✓✓✓	Location	✓✓✓✓✓
Quality of Pitches	✓✓✓✓	Range of Facilities	✓✓✓✓

Directions

In Lienz initially follow signs for Spittal and at traffic lights turn right towards Tristach. Go under the railway and over a small bridge then turn left, still towards Tristach. Go through village of Tristach and after about 1.5 km. turn right up to the site, which is at the top of a 1:10 climb.

Charges 2004

Per unit incl. 2 persons	€ 20,50
incl. electricity	€ 22,50
extra person	€ 5,70
child (5-14 yrs)	€ 3,80
dog	€ 2,20

Reservations

Advised in high season. Tel: 04852 69767. E-mail: seewiese@osttirol.com

AU0262 Oberwötzlhof Camp

Erlfeld 37, A-5441 Abtenau (Salzburg)

High up in the Lammertal Valley is this small farm site with amazing views of the surrounding mountains. Part of a working farm, it has a total of 70 pitches, of which 30 are for long stay units, leaving 40 places for tourers. All are serviced with electricity hook-ups (10A), water and drainage. Amateur astronomers will appreciate the lack of site lighting, but campers may find a torch useful. The small fenced swimming pool (10 x 5 m.) is unheated, and has paved surrounds. The restaurant is only open during the winter, but breakfasts, drinks and ices are available during the summer season. Despite the slightly dated facilities, we think that the friendly atmosphere and stunning location amply compensate for any shortcomings. Places to visit should include Postalm, real alpine meadow country with some excellent walking (brochure from reception). There are many opportunities for rafting, hydrospeeding, canyoning, paragliding and mountain biking in the area. No English is spoken.

Facilities

The current sanitary unit is a little dated and could be stretched if the site was full, but it does provide some washbasins in cubicles, laundry and dishwashing facilities, drying room, and solarium, however there are no special facilities for babies or disabled campers. A new unit is under construction but it could be some time before it is finished (the shell was complete at the time of our visit, but needed internal fitting and decorating). Restaurant open in winter only. Swimming pool. Internet terminal. Off site: Abtenau is 2.5 km. (about 25 minutes walk we were told). Skiing 2.5 km. Riding 8 km. Hallstättersee and salt mines 30 km.

Open

All year.

At a glance

Welcome & Ambience	✓✓✓✓✓	Location	✓✓✓✓✓
Quality of Pitches	✓✓✓✓	Range of Facilities	✓✓✓✓

Directions

Abtenau lies to the south east of Salzburg. From A10 exit 28 (Golling), take B162 east for 14 kms., and site is signed to the left about 2.5 km before Abtenau.

Charges 2005

Per person	€ 5,50
child (under 15 yrs)	€ 3,50
pitch	€ 5,00 - € 5,50
motorcaravan	€ 8,00 - € 10,00
electricity	€ 3,20

No credit cards.

Reservations

Contact site. Tel: 06243 2698. E-mail: oberwoetzlhof@sbg.at

AU0240 Camping Appesbach

Au 99, A-5360 St Wolfgang (Upper Austria)

St Wolfgang, a pretty little village on the lake of the same name which was made famous by the operetta 'White Horse Inn', is ringed round by hills in a delightful situation. The location of Appesbach, on the banks of the lake with a good frontage, is one of its main assets. The lake is used for all types of sailing and wind-surfing and bathing is possible if it's not too cool. The site has 170 pitches, with 100 for tourists with some in regular rows and the rest on open meadows that could become full in high season. Pitches near the lakeside have higher charges. All have electricity (10A). Also on site is a good restaurant and takeaway. The welcoming owners, Maria and Christian Peter both speak good English.

Facilities

The two toilet blocks have been combined into one, extended and refurbished to a good standard. Drive over Motorcaravan service point, with adjacent chemical disposal facility, sink and water. Good shop. Bar (1/5-31/8). Restaurant with TV (Easter-30/9). Snack bar with terrace (Easter-30/9). Small playground. Table tennis, billards, darts. Off site: Tennis nearby. Village 1 km. Many excursions possible including Salzburg 50 km.

Open

Easter - 31 October.

At a glance

Welcome & Ambience	✓✓✓✓	Location	✓✓✓✓
Quality of Pitches	✓✓✓✓	Range of Facilities	✓✓✓✓

Directions

From B158 Salzburg-Bad Ischl road, turn towards St Wolfgang just east of Strobl and site is on the left 1 km. before St Wolfgang.

Charges 2004

Per person	€ 4,10 - € 5,60
child (3-15 yrs)	€ 2,55 - € 3,55
pitch	€ 4,00 - € 11,00
electricity	€ 2,50
dog	€ 2,00

10% discount for CCI card holders.

Reservations

Made for min. 1 week with deposit. Tel: 06138 2206. E-mail: camping@appesbach.at

AU0212 Panoramacamping Stadtblick

Rauchenbichl, Rauchenbichler Straße 21, A-5020 Salzburg (Salzburg)

With a panoramic view over the city of Salzburg this site is well named, and you can be sure of a warm welcome from the multi-lingual owner, Herr Wörndl. The site has 70 pitches all with electric hook-ups (4A) and water points, on grass over gravel terraces, plus 10 grassy tent pitches. They are reasonably sized for a city site location, and the view and the good value restaurant amply compensate for any shortcomings. This is an ideal site for a short stay to see all the sights of the city, with a bus stop within walking distance, and local tour buses pick up from the site. The site also sells the Salzburg Card.

Facilities

The single toilet unit is in the older style, but is neat, clean and well maintained. Some washbasins in cabins, controllable hot showers with limited changing space, but there are no facilities for babies or the disabled. Laundry. Two dishwashing sinks. Motorcaravan service point. Shop. Restaurant (May-Sept). TV, lounge, and babyfoot. Play area. Off site: Golf 3 km. or 10 km. Bicycle hire 3 km.

Open

20 March - 5 November; 28 December - 6 January.

At a glance

Welcome & Ambience	✓✓✓✓✓	Location	✓✓✓✓✓
Quality of Pitches	✓✓✓✓	Range of Facilities	✓✓✓✓✓

Directions

From A1 exit 288 (Salzburg Nord) turn south towards city. Approaching first set of lights you need to be in right hand lane, turn right on a minor road (site signed). Continue to top of hill, and follow site signs.

Charges guide

Per person	€ 5,90
child (2-15 yrs)	€ 2,90
pitch	€ 3,70 - € 6,20
pet	€ 1,45

Reservations

Advised for peak season. Tel: 06624 50652. E-mail: info@panorama-camping.at

AU0280 Camping Stumpfer

A-3392 Schönbühel (Lower Austria)

This small, well appointed site with just 60 pitches is directly on the River Danube, near the small town of Schönbühel, and could make a convenient night stop being near the Salzburg - Vienna autobahn. The 50 unmarked pitches for touring units, all with electricity (16A), are on flat grass and the site is lit at night. There is shade in most parts and a landing stage for boat trips on the Danube. The main building also houses a Gasthof, with a bar/restaurant of the same name. This is very much a family run site.

Facilities

Part of the main building, the toilet block is of good quality with hot water on payment. Facilities for disabled visitors include ramps by the side of steps up to the block. Washing machine and dryer. Motorcaravan services. Small shop for basics. Playground. Fishing. Off site: Swimming pool, bicycle hire or riding within 5 km.

Open

1 April - 31 October.

At a glance

Welcome & Ambience	✓✓✓✓	Location	✓✓✓✓
Quality of Pitches	✓✓✓	Range of Facilities	✓✓✓✓

Directions

From Salzburg - Vienna autobahn take Melk exit and go towards Melk Nord. Just before bridge turn right (Schönbühel, St Polten), at T-junction turn right and continue down hill. Turn right just before filling station (Schönbühel).Site is 3 km. next to Gasthof.

Charges 2004

Per person	€ 4,40
pitch incl. electricity	€ 4,70 - € 7,70

Reservations

Write to site. Tel: 02752 8510. E-mail: office@stumpfer.com

AU0345 Seecamping Gruber

Dorfstraße 63, A-4865 Nußdorf am Attersee (Upper Austria)

The Attersee is the largest of a group of lakes just to the east of Salzburg in the attractive Salzkammergut area. Seecamping Gruber is a small crowded site halfway up the western side of the lake. There are 150 individual pitches, with an increasing number of seasonal units taking the larger pitches, there still are some 60 pitches for tourers, all with 16A electricity, 16 with water and waste water as well and many with shade. Pitches tend to be small to medium size and the access roads are narrow making entrance and egress difficult and this is not help by the seasonal pitches erecting fences etc to utilise every last inch of their pitches. Sadly only from the 25 metre swimming pool and the shallow children's play pool (both heated and with sunbathing areas) are there views across the lake to the hills beyond.

Facilities

Modern sanitary facilities offer some private cabins, washing machine and dryer, good unit for the disabled and baby room. Restaurant and takeaway. Shop. Play area. Swimming and paddling pools. Sauna, solarium and gym. Fishing. Off site: Windsurfing, sailing, both with courses available. Mountain bikes, diving and balloon rides nearby.

Open

15 April - 15 October.

At a glance

Welcome & Ambience	✓✓✓✓	Location	✓✓✓✓
Quality of Pitches	✓✓✓	Range of Facilities	✓✓✓✓

Directions

From the A1/E55/E60 between Salzburg and Linz, take exit 243 to Attersee and then south on the B151 to Nußdorf. Site is on the southern edge of the village.

Charges 2004

Per unit incl 2 persons and electricity	€ 27,00
dog	€ 3,00

Reservations

Recommended for July/Aug. Tel: 07666 80450. E-mail: gruber@camping.co.at

AU0340 Camping am See

Winkl 77, A-4831 Obertraun (Upper Austria)

It is unusual to locate a campsite so deep in the heart of spectacular mountain scenery, yet with such easy access. Directly on the shores of Halstattersee, near to Obertraun and the Dachstein mountain range, this 2.5 hectare, flat site, with 160 pitches is an excellent, peaceful holiday base. Owners cum professional artists, Carola and Lorenzo, both speak English and their talents are reflected around the central amenity building. The grass site is basically divided into two, with tents in a more shady area, whilst caravans and motorcaravans are more in the open. There are no specific pitches although the owners, within reason, control where you place your unit. At the time of our visit there were only 36 electricity hook-ups. Hallstatt is an UNESCO listed alpine village with the oldest salt mines in the world – a major attraction. This region is ideal for peace and quiet, walking for all abilities, fishing, biking, climbing and much more.

Facilities

Completely refurbished, fully equipped and modern, the toilet block includes a small baby room. Washing machine. New, open barn style area for dishwashing and a similar area with purpose built barbecues, seating and tables. Bar and limited restaurant with hot meals and fine wines available to order. Basic daily provisions kept such as bread and milk. Small playground. Off site: Activities nearby include walking for all ages and abilities, bird watching, fishing, mountain biking, rock climbing, scuba diving and much more. For naturists, 100 m. from the site there is a delightful popular area designated as an FKK strand (naturist beach).

At a glance

Welcome & Ambience	✓✓✓✓	Location	✓✓✓✓✓
Quality of Pitches	✓✓✓✓	Range of Facilities	✓✓✓✓

Directions

Due south from Bad Ischl on road B145, take road B166 to Hallstatt. After single carriageway tunnel, site is 4 km. on left on entering village of Winkl. Road is a little narrow in places so care is needed.

Charges guide

Per unit incl. 2 persons	€ 20,10
small tent incl. 2 persons	€ 4,50
electricity	€ 3,00

No credit cards.

Reservations

Necessary for high season. Tel: 06131 265. E-mail: camping.am.see@chello.at

Open

1 May - 30 September.

AU0302 Aktiv Camping Neue Donau

Am Kaisermühlendamm 119, A-1220 Wien-Ost (Vienna)

This is the sister site of Camping Wien-Sud and, whilst closer to Vienna, it is not in such a pleasant location. Near to two busy motorways there is inevitably some background traffic noise. However it is perhaps easier to find and has similar facilities and standards. With 320 level touring pitches with electricity and a further 12 with water and drainage also, the site has a large and changing population. The site is close to the 'Donauinsel', a popular recreation area. The Neue Donau (New Danube), a 20 km. long artificial side arm of the Danube provides swimming, sports and play areas, while the Danube bicycle trail runs past the site. This is a good location for visiting old Vienna and the Danube.

Facilities

Modern toilet facilities are clean, and well maintained with free showers. Facilities for disabled visitors. Washing machines and dryers. Motorcaravan service point. Campers' kitchen with cooking, fridges, freezers and TV. Shop. Small restaurant. Play area. Volleyball. Internet access. Barbecue areas. Off site: Vienna 5 km.

Open

Easter - end September.

At a glance

Welcome & Ambience	✓✓✓✓	Location	✓✓✓✓
Quality of Pitches	✓✓✓	Range of Facilities	✓✓✓✓

Directions

Site is close to the A23 and A22. From A23 heading east turn off at first exit after crossing the Donau (signed Lobau). At first traffic lights, near Shell station, turn left and after 200 m. turn right into site.

Charges 2004

Per person	€ 5,50 - € 6,50
child (4-15 yrs)	€ 3,50 - € 4,00
pitch	€ 7,00 - € 8,00
serviced pitch	€ 9,00 - € 10,00
electricity	€ 3,40 - € 4,00

Reservations

Advised in July and August. Tel: 01 202 4010.
E-mail: camping.neuedonau@verkehrsbuero.at

AU0304 Camping Wien-Sud

Breitenfursterstr. 269, A-1230 Wien-Atzgersdorf (Vienna)

This site, which is in a former Palace park and was closed for some years, reopened in 2003 with new facilities and new management. It is now probably the best site in the greater Vienna area, with good public transport links to the city centre and a friendly and welcoming atmosphere. With 170 touring pitches (all with electricity (12/16A) and 32 with water and drainage), the site provides a good base for city sightseeing. Right next door is a Merkur supermarket which is well worth a visit for storing up whichever way you are heading. With lots of mature trees and some shade you will find this a peaceful and quiet site. Walking and cycling are popular in the Vienna woods nearby and the Jubliäumswarte offers a wonderful view of the city.

Facilities

Excellent modern toilet facilities are clean and well maintained with free showers. Facilities for disabled visitors. Washing machine and dryer. Some cooking facilities. Motorcaravan service point. Small restaurant. Small play area. Off site: Vienna 6 km.

Open

1 May - 30 September.

At a glance

Welcome & Ambience	✓✓✓✓✓	Location	✓✓✓✓
Quality of Pitches	✓✓✓✓	Range of Facilities	✓✓✓✓

Directions

From the A2 turn onto the A21 towrds Linz (if you're heading north the slip is just past IKEA). Turn off the A21 at first exit, Brunn am Gebirge, and head north. Site is well signed but keep going on this road to site on the right in Atzgersdorf.

Charges 2004

Per person	€ 5,50 - € 6,50
child (4-16 yrs)	€ 3,50 - € 4,00
pitch	€ 7,00 - € 8,00
serviced pitch	€ 9,00 - € 10,00
electricity	€ 3,50 - € 4,00

Reservations

Advised for July/Aug. especially for serviced pitches.
Tel: 01 867 3649.
E-mail: camping.sued@verkehrsbuero.at

AU0306 Camping Wien West

Hüttelbergstrasse 80, A-1140 Wien (Vienna)

Our Austrian agent has recommended this modern site located to the west of Vienna and we plan to conduct a full inspection in 2005. Camping Wien West can be found at the edge of the Wienerwald, but just 8km from the city centre, with good public transport links. Pitches are generally flat and of a good size, all with electrical connections. Sanitary facilities are of a good standard and include special facilities for disabled customers. Numerous cycling and walking trails lead though the Vienna woods, passing close to the site. Chalets for rent.

Facilities

Small shop, restaurant, motor home service point, kitchen facility, games room, children's playground. Off site: Vienna centre 8km, Schönbrunn palace, cycle and walking trails, swimming pool, tennis.

Open

All year (except February).

Directions

The site is best accessed from the A1 Salzburg - Vienna motorway. Upon arrival in Vienna, drive over the Bräuhausbrücke (bridge). Proceed on the Bergmillergasse until you reach Hüttelbergstrasse after the first traffic lights.

Charges 2005

Pitch (inc. electricity 6 amps)	€ 4,00 - 9,00
adult	€ 5,50 - 6,70
child (4 - 15 years)	€ 3,50 - 4,00
electricity	€ 3,00 - 4,00

Reservations

Contact site. Tel: 01 9142314.
Email: camping.west@verkehrsbuero.at

AU0300 Camping Rodaun

Breitenfurter Straße 487, An der Au 2, A-123 Wien-Südwest-Rodaun (Vienna)

This good little site is within the Vienna city boundary and is a pleasant base for visiting this old, interesting and world famous city. Just 9 km. from the centre, there is an excellent public transport system for viewing the sights as car parking is almost impossible in the city. Situated in a southern suburb, it has space for about 40 units on flat grass pitches or on concrete bases and an additional area for about 20 tents. With little shade, the pitches are not numbered or marked, either in the centre or outside the circular tarmac road running round the camping area, with electricity provided (6A).

Facilities

The toilet block has some washbasins in cabins and hot showers for which a token is needed, buy them at reception. Laundry service provided by Frau Deihs. Off site: Supermarket and restaurant within 250 m. Swimming pool 2 km.

Open

1 April - 5 November.

At a glance

Welcome & Ambience	✓✓✓	Location	✓✓✓✓
Quality of Pitches	✓✓✓	Range of Facilities	✓✓✓

Directions

Take Pressbaum exit from Westautobahn or Vosendorf exit from Sudautobahn and follow signs. It is worth writing for a brochure which gives a good sketch map showing how to find the site.

Charges 2004

Per person	€ 5,50
child (3-13 yrs)	€ 3,30
pitch incl. car	€ 5,46 - € 6,10
electricty	€ 0,70
dog	€ 1,50

Reservations

Are advised; write to site. Tel: 01 8884 154.

AU0290 Donaupark Camping Tulln

Hafenstraße, A-3430 Tulln (Lower Austria)

The ancient town of Tulln (the 'city of roses') lies on the southern bank of the River Danube, about 20 miles northwest of Vienna. The city can be reached by train in about 30 minutes and one can sail on the river through the Wachau vineyards, orchards and charming villages viewing the ruined castles and church belfries. Tulln was founded by the Romans and was the capital until replaced, first by Klosterneuburg and then Vienna. There are interesting old buildings in the town and music concerts are held on the river promenade. Donaupark Camping, owned and run by the Austrian Motor Club (OAMTC), is imaginatively laid out village-style with unmarked grass pitches grouped around six circular gravel areas. Further pitches are to the side of the hard road which links the circles and these include some with grill facilities for tents; 100 of the 120 tourist pitches have electricity (3/6A) and cable TV sockets. Tall trees surrounding the site offer shade in parts. Tucked neatly away at the back of the site near two of the three toilet blocks, are 120 long stay caravans. Activities are organised in high season with guided tours around Tulln on foot, by bike and on the river by canoe. This is a quiet location some 100 m. from the Danube, excellent for families. The manager speaks good English and is pleased to advise on tourist matters.

Facilities

Three identical, modern, octagonal sanitary blocks can be heated. One is at reception (next to the touring area), the other two are at the far end of the site. Facilities for disabled visitors. Washing machines and dryers. Cooking rings. Gas supplies. Bar and restaurant with terrace which keeps open quite late.(1/5-15/9). Shop (15/5-15/9). Play areas, space for ball games and Topi club (July/Aug). Tennis. Volleyball. Bicycle and canoe hire. Excursion programme. Off site: Lake swimming in adjacent park. Entry free for campers. Fishing 500 m. Bus service into Vienna 9/7-24/8. Half-hourly train service to Vienna. Steamer excursions available.

At a glance

Welcome & Ambience	✓✓✓✓	Location	✓✓✓✓
Quality of Pitches	✓✓✓✓	Range of Facilities	✓✓✓

Directions

From Vienna follow south bank of the Danube on B14; from the west, leave the A1 autobahn at either St Christophen or Altenbach exits and go north on B19 to Tulln. Site is on the east side of Tulln and well signed.

Charges 2004

Per person	€ 6,00
child (5-14 yrs)	€ 3,00
pitch	€ 7,50 - € 11,00
electricity	€ 1,80
small tent with car or motorcycle	€ 4,50

Reservations

Write to site. Tel: 02272 65200.
E-mail: camptulln@oeamtc.at

Open

Easter - 15 October.

AU0502 Camping Im Thermenland

Bairisch Kölldorf 240, A-8344 Bairisch Kölldorf (Steiermark)

Near to both the Slovakian and Hungarian borders and set in the rolling countryside of southeast Austria, this is a real hidden gem. Not shown on many maps, but well worth the trip, if you want a good quiet site with modern amenities and excellent standards then come right here. There are 100 pitches of which 70 are for touring and all have electricity, water and drainage. The site is near to numerous spas and thermal baths and close to Styrassic Park, a must for younger campers.

Facilities

Excellent toilet facilities are clean, well maintained and include free showers. Facilities for disabled visitors. Washing machine and dryer. Dog shower. Restaurant (all year). Unheated outdoor, but covered, swimming pool (May - Sept). Small play area. Off site: Styrassic Park 4 km. Fishing 100 m. Golf 3 km.

Open

All year.

At a glance

Welcome & Ambience	✓✓✓✓	Location	✓✓✓✓
Quality of Pitches	✓✓✓✓	Range of Facilities	✓✓✓✓

Directions

Leave A2 at exit 157 and head towards Feldbach on the 68. Continue on the 66 to Bad Gleichenberg, go straight over first roundabout and turn left at second. After 2.8 km. just past fire station, turn left by chapel and immediately right towards the site (600 m).

Charges 2004

Per person	€ 6,15
pitch	€ 3,99 - € 7,25
electricity	€ 0,50

Reservations

Made with deposit. Tel: 03159-3941.
E-mail: gemeinde@bairisch-koelldorf.at

AU0330 Camping Central

Martinhofstraße 3, A-8054 Graz (Steiermark)

Although not as well known as Vienna, Salzburg and Innsbruck, Graz in the southern province of Styria is Austria's second largest city. Camping Central's name is misleading as it is situated in the southwest of the town in the Strassgang district, 6 km. from the centre. The 136 level tourist pitches are either in regular rows either side of tarmac roads under a cover of tall trees or on an open meadow where they are not marked out. All have electricity (6A). Adjoining the site is the town sports stadium which includes a huge open air swimming pool. At 110 x 100 m. it is reputed to be the largest pool in Europe. Except when there are activities at the stadium, Camping Central is a quiet place which makes a good night stop when travelling from Klagenfurt to Vienna or a base from which to explore the region.

Facilities

The new, well built toilet block is of good quality and the other two blocks have been refurbished. Each can be heated in cool weather. Facilities for disabled visitors. Washing machines and dryer. Swimming pool (May - Sept, small charge). Small restaurant at the pool. Tennis, table tennis, playground, jogging track and minigolf. Limited animation during high season. Off site: Two other restaurants within 300 m. Good shop about 400 m.

Open

1 April - 31 October.

At a glance

Welcome & Ambience	✓✓✓✓	Location	✓✓✓✓
Quality of Pitches	✓✓✓✓	Range of Facilities	✓✓✓✓✓

Directions

From the west take the exit 'Graz-west', from Salzburg exit 'Graz-sud' follow signs to Central and Strassgang and turn right just past traffic lights for site (signed).

Charges 2004

Per unit incl. 2 persons	€ 25,50
extra person	€ 7,75
child (4-15 yrs)	€ 5,00
tent (1 person)	€ 13,75

No credit cards.

Reservations

Not necessary, but choice of pitch limited.
Tel: 06763 785 102. E-mail: freizeit@netway.at

AU0505 Camping Leibnitz

Rudolf Hans Bartsch-Gasse 33, A-8430 Leibnitz (Steiermark)

Near to the Slovakian border, close to the small town of Leibnitz, this site is set in the rolling wine-growing countryside of southeast Austria. A small site with only 52 pitches, it is set in a lovely park area and close to an excellent swimming pool complex which is available for campers' use (with access arrangements for disabled visitors). Minigolf, tennis, volleyball and a multitude of local cycle paths are nearby. All the pitches are of a good size, level and with 16A electricity connections, and some have shade. The town has shops and restaurants with weekly events held at the Jazz Club.

Facilities

Excellent toilet facilities are clean and well maintained. Showers cost € 0.50. Facilities for disabled visitors. Washing machine. Small restaurant but many more within walking distance. Small play area. Off site: Leibnitz 500 m. Leisure centre with two heated outdoor swimming pools 100 m.

Open

1 May - 15 September.

At a glance

Welcome & Ambience	✓✓✓✓✓	Location	✓✓✓✓✓
Quality of Pitches	✓✓✓✓	Range of Facilities	✓✓✓✓

Directions

From A9 take Leibnitz exit, go straight over two roundabouts (through outlet centre), over lights and after 300 m. turn left (site signed). Over roundabout into Leibnitz, turn right and site is about 500 m.

Charges 2004

Per person	€ 4,00
pitch incl. car	€ 4,70 - € 5,80
electricity	€ 1,80

Reservations

Advised in July and August. Tel: 03452 82463.
E-mail: leibnitz@camping-steiermark.at

AU0520 Camping am Badesee

A-8822 Mühlen (Steiermark)

Set in an beautiful open alpine valley alongside a lake in the southern part of the Steiermark region, this family run site will provide you with a warm welcome, and a relaxing holiday. The 60 good sized pitches are well spaced on open grassy terraces, and with only 10 long stay units, there should be around 50 for tourists. All have electricity (6A). From reception you can order shopping - bread, milk and eggs and basic requirements. The small cafe/snack bar with a terrace which overlooks the lake, serves regional dishes and drinks. Once a week in season the site organises a barbecue, pasta or goulash evening, and activities for all the family. There is a small traditional playground, a brightly painted caravan and a pets corner. The lake is used for swimming, fishing, canoes and non-powered craft.

Facilities

A modern heated sanitary unit provides spacious hot showers, some washbasins in cubicles, with child size showers and basins. Hairdressing and shaving areas. Dishwashing sinks outside under cover. Laundry room also has a baby bath and changing facility. No dedicated facilities for disabled persons. Communal barbecue. Playground. Pets corner. Basketball net. Trampoline. Table tennis. Babyfoot. Lake for swimming, fishing and boating. Bicycle hire. Off site: Two restaurants and services in Mühlen (15 minutes walk). Riding 1 km. Neumarkt (6 km.) has more comprehensive shopping facilities. Golf 14 km.

At a glance

Welcome & Ambience	✓✓✓✓✓	Location	✓✓✓✓✓
Quality of Pitches	✓✓✓✓	Range of Facilities	✓✓✓✓

Directions

Mühlen is southwest of Judenburg. From the west on A10, take exit 104 (St. Michael im Lungau) and head east on road 96 through Murau to Scheiffling. Turn right (south) on B317 to Neumarkt, and towards the end of village turn left on B92 to Mühlen. Site is 5.8 km on right hand side.

Charges guide

Per unit with 2 persons and electricity	€ 17,40

Reservations

Advisable for peak season. Tel: 03586 2418. E-mail: office@camping-am-badesee.at

Open

1 May - 30 September.

AU0490 Camping Terrassen Maltatal

Malta 6, A-9854 Maltatal (Carinthia)

Just six kilometres from the autobahn and 15 from Millstättersee, this site is good for an overnight stop but its pleasant situation and the good-sized swimming pool on site encourage many to stay longer. The pool is over 300 sq.m. with a grassy lying out area and is open to all (free for campers). There are 200 grassy pitches on narrow terraces (70-100 sq.m.) and mostly in rows on either side of narrow access roads. Numbered and marked, some separated with low hedges, all have electricity (6/10A) and 20 have water and drainage connections, (the electric boxes are often inconveniently located on the next terrace). The 'Kärnten-card' is available from the site which gives free travel on public transport and free entry to various attractions. Note: Local church bells ring at 6 am. every morning.

Facilities

Two toilet blocks, one with under-floor heating, have about half the washbasins in cabins and six family washcabins. Good facilities for babies and children. Washing machines, dryers and irons. Motorcaravan services. Only basic provisions kept. Restaurant (all season). Swimming pool (20/5-15/9). Sauna. Playground. Bicycle hire. Riding. Entertainment programme, many walks and excursions. Off site: Village 500 m. Fishing or golf 6 km.

Open

12 April - 31 October.

At a glance

Welcome & Ambience	✓✓✓✓	Location	✓✓✓✓
Quality of Pitches	✓✓✓	Range of Facilities	✓✓✓✓

Directions

Site is 6 km. up a mountain valley from an exit at the southern end of the A10 Salzburg - Carinthia autobahn. Take autobahn exit 129 for Gmund and Maltatal and proceed up Maltatal 6 km. to site.

Charges guide

Per person	€ 5,20 - € 6,60
child (3-14 yrs)	€ 3,40 - € 4,10
pitch with electricity	€ 6,60 - € 8,90
plus water and waste water	€ 8,90 - € 10,50
dog	€ 2,20 - € 2,60

Reservations

Made with deposit. Tel: 04733 234. E-mail: info@maltacamp.at

AU0440 Schluga Camping

Obervellach 15, A-9620 Hermagor-Presseggersee (Carinthia)

Schluga Camping is under the same ownership as Schluga Seecamping, some 4 km. from that site in a flat valley with views of the mountains. The 223 tourist pitches are of varying size, 84 with water and TV connections. Electricity connections are available throughout (10A). Mainly on grass covered gravel on either side of tarmac access roads, they are divided by shrubs and hedges. A weekly sheet details events at both Schluga sites and nearby. The site is open all year, to include the winter sports season.

Facilities

Four sanitary blocks are heated in cold weather. Most washbasins in cabins. Family washrooms for rent. Baby rooms and suite for disabled people. Washing machines and dryers. Drying rooms and ski rooms. Motorcaravan services. Well stocked shop (1/5-30/9). Bar/restaurant (closed Nov). Heated pool (12 x 7 m; 1/5-30/9). Playground. Internet point. Badminton. Off site: Tennis nearby.

At a glance

Welcome & Ambience	✓✓✓✓	Location	✓✓✓✓
Quality of Pitches	✓✓✓✓	Range of Facilities	✓✓✓✓✓

Directions

Site is on the B111 Villach-Hermagor road just east of Hermagor town.

Charges 2005

Per person	€ 5,00 - € 7,70
pitch	€ 6,60 - € 8,60

Reservations

Contact site. Tel: 04282 2051.
E-mail: camping@schluga.com

Open

All year.

AU0425 Seecamping Berghof

Ossiachersee Süduferstraße 241, A-9523 Villach-Hlg. Gestade (Carinthia)

This surely must be the ultimate camping experience, a perfect location, excellent facilities, great pitches and a welcome to match. The Ertl family and their staff manage this 500 pitch site to perfection. Use of the natural topography means that you actually think you are in a small site wherever you camp. With lovely lake views from almost every spot this is a great site to stop for a short or long stay. There are 120 pitches with water, electricity and drainage and many pitches have access to the internet. Eighteen family cabins with WC, washbasin and shower are available to rent in the various toilet blocks. The large Ossiacher See provides numerous opportunities for water sports. There are caravans, mobile homes and small rooms for rent. Listed as one of Austria's top 10 and recognised as of one the leading campsites in Europe, this is a site not to miss!

Facilities

Five modern toilet blocks spread around the site, provide the usual facilities including special provision for young children and babies in two blocks. Facilities for disabled people. Large, central building housing well stocked supermarket and helpful reception. Pleasant restaurant with terrace, takeaway meals and games room for older children. Good play area and daily club for 4-11 year olds all season. Table tennis. Games room. Bicycle hire. Watersports; including boat hire and windsurfing school. Volleyball. Minigolf. Lake swimming. Off site: Fishing. Villach 5 km.

At a glance

Welcome & Ambience	✓✓✓✓✓	Location	✓✓✓✓✓
Quality of Pitches	✓✓✓✓✓	Range of Facilities	✓✓✓✓✓

Directions

From A10 exit 178(travelling south, just after tunnel). Head towards Ossiacher See and after 1 km. turn right towards Ossiacher See Sud. At lights turn left. Site is 3.5 km. on left in hamlet of Heiligengestade.

Charges 2004

Per person	€ 5,20 - € 7,60
pitch	€ 27,00 - € 50,50

Reservations

Necessary in high season for large pitches.
Tel: 04242 41133. E-mail: office@camping-ertl.at

Open

1 April - 20 October.

AU0400 Camping Arneitz

Seeuferlandesstraße 53, A-9583 Faak am See (Carinthia)

Directly on Faakersee, Camping Arneitz is one of the best sites in this area, central for the attractions of the region, watersports and walking. Family run, Arneitz led the way with good quality and comprehensive facilities. The 400 level, marked pitches are mainly of gravel, off hard roads, with electricity available. Some have good shade from mature trees. Grass pitches are available for tents. There is a delightfully appointed restaurant at the entrance where there is entertainment in high season. Day trips can be made to Venice and other parts of northern Italy, and the surrounding countryside.

Facilities

Splendid family washroom with family cubicles around the walls and in the centre, washbasins at child height in a circle with a working carousel in the middle. Extra, small block nearer the lake. Washing machines, spin dryer, irons. Motorcaravan services. Supermarket. Self-service restaurant, bar and terrace. General room with TV. Small cinema for children's films. Beauty salon. Sauna/solarium. Minigolf. Playground. Fishing. Riding. Bicycle hire.

At a glance

Welcome & Ambience	✓✓✓✓	Location	✓✓✓✓
Quality of Pitches	✓✓✓✓	Range of Facilities	✓✓✓✓

Directions

From A11 take exit 3 and head towards Egg, turn left at T-junction. Go through Egg to site.

Charges 2004

Per person	€ 6,80 - € 7,50
pitch incl. electricity	€ 10,00 - € 13,00

Reservations

Only made for outside the main season.
Tel: 04242 26898. E-mail: camping@arneitz.at

Open

28 April - 30 September.

AU0410 Strandcamping Turnersee

A-9123 St Primus (Carinthia)

The southern Austrian province of Kärnten is a gentle rural area of mountains, valleys and lakes. Strandcamping lies between Villach and Graz, just south of the A2 Villach - Vienna motorway, giving the opportunity to visit Croatia and northern Italy. The neat, tidy site is situated in a valley with views of the surrounding mountains. The 300 marked and numbered pitches for touring units vary in size, on level grass terraces. Although there are many trees, not all parts have shade. All pitches have electricity (6A) and 50 also have water, drainage, TV and phone connections. There are 110 static caravans. At the lakeside is a large well-mown grass area for sunbathing, with a wooden decking area right next to the water with steps down for swimming in the lake. It is very much a site for families where children are catered for rather than just tolerated and has a pleasant atmosphere. Membership of the Top Camping Austria association provides a Topi Club with games and entertainment for children. There is also a daily programme for adults.

Facilities

Four modern sanitary blocks spread around the site, providing the usual facilities including special provision for young children and babies in the largest block. Facilities for disabled people. Large, central building housing well stocked shop, pleasant restaurant with terrace (10/5-14/9), takeaway (7/6-23/8) and play room for small children. Good play areas for children and small zoo with goats and rabbits. Topi club and organised activities for adults and children. Table tennis, games room, bicycle hire, watersports and volleyball. Internet access. Off site: Fishing and golf 1.5 km. Riding 3 km. Boat launching 5 km.

Open

3 April - 3 October.

At a glance

Welcome & Ambience	✓✓✓✓	Location	✓✓✓✓
Quality of Pitches	✓✓✓✓	Range of Facilities	✓✓✓✓✓

Directions

Leave A2 motorway at exit 296 signed Grafenstien. Go onto road 70 for a few kilometres and turn right for site via Tainach and St Kanzian. Site is on left before St Primus.

Charges 2004

Per person	€ 4,50 - € 7,50
child (4-14 yrs)	€ 3,00 - € 5,10
pitch	€ 6,00 - € 10,00
incl. services	€ 8,00 - € 12,50
dog	€ 1,50 - € 3,00

Special deals for families.

Reservations

Necessary for high season. Tel: 04239 2350. E-mail: info@breznik.at

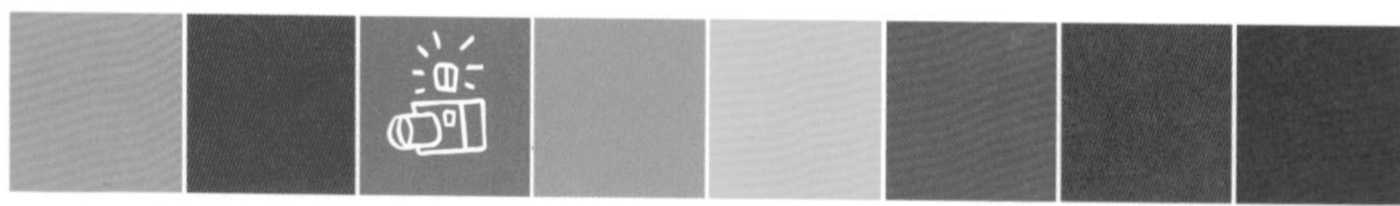

AU0415 Camping Rosental Roz

Gotschuchen 34, A-9173 St Margareten im Rosental (Carinthia)

In the picturesque Drau valley, southeast of Flagenfurt, Rosental Roz has magnificent views along the valley and of the cliffs that form the northern boundary. The site is also close to the Slovakian and Italian borders. With 430 pitches (all for touring) and 4 mobile homes to rent around a small swimming lake, the site is good for short or long stays. All pitches have 6A electricity and 50 pitches have water and drainage. An active children's club provides lots to occupy the youngsters and guided walks for adults are organised from the campsite. There are separate areas for dogs and a special area for dogs to romp around, plus dog shower.

Facilities

Toilet facilities are clean and modern with free showers, 10 family washrooms and a large shower facility for young children. Washing machine and dryer. Restaurant/bar (1/5-30/9). Shop (1/6-15/9). Children's club (1/6-30/8). Playgrounds and large games area. Off site: Fishing 1 km. Riding 2 km. Many walks.

Open

Easter - 15 October.

At a glance

Welcome & Ambience	✓✓✓✓	Location	✓✓✓✓
Quality of Pitches	✓✓✓✓	Range of Facilities	✓✓✓✓

Directions

Site is southeast of Klagenfurt. From the 91 road turn onto the 85 towards Feriach. Before getting to St Margareten in the centre of the small hamlet of Gotschuchen turn left towards site. It is about 1.5 km. but well signed (watch the overhanging gutters especially when passing another vehicle).

Charges 2004

Per person	€ 6,80
child (1-18 yrs)	€ 4,80 - € 5,80
pitch	€ 7,90 - € 10,10
dog	€ 2,90

Reservations

Necessary in July/Aug; contact site. Tel: 04226 81000. E-mail: camping.rosental@roz.at

AU0480 Komfort-Campingpark Burgstaller

Seefeldstraße 16, A-9873 Döbriach (Carinthia)

This part of Austria deserves to be better known as it is a most attractive region and has some excellent camp sites. Burgstaller is the largest of these and makes a good base from which to explore Carinthia, northeast Italy and Slovenia. The site entrance is directly opposite the park leading to the bathing lido, to which campers have free access. There is also a heated swimming pool. The 600 pitches (560 for tourists) are on flat, well drained grass, backing onto hedges and marked out, on either side of access roads. These vary in size (65-120 sq.m.), all with electricity, water and drainage and there are special pitches for motorcaravans. 130 pitches also have sewer and satellite TV connections. Much activity is organised here, including games and competitions for children in summer with a winter programme of skiing, curling and skating. At Christmas, trees are gathered from the forest and there are special Easter and autumn events. This is an excellent family site for winter and summer camping with a very friendly atmosphere, particularly in the restaurant in the evenings. Good English spoken.

Facilities

Two very good quality sanitary blocks, the larger part of the central complex. It has some washbasins in cabins, facilities for children and disabled visitors, dishwashers and underfloor heating for cool weather. Some private sanitary rooms are for rent. Motorcaravan services. Good restaurant with terrace (May-Oct). Shop (May-Sept). Bowling alley. Disco (July/Aug). TV room. Sauna and solarium. Secluded roof terrace used for nude sunbathing. Two play areas (one for under 6s, the other for 6-12 yrs). Beach volleyball. Basketball. Bathing and boating in lake. Special entrance rate for lake attractions. Fishing. Bicycle hire. Mountain bike area. Riding. Comprehensive entertainment programmes. Covered stage and outdoor arena provide for church services (Protestant and Catholic, in German) and folk and modern music concerts. Off site: Mountain walks, climbing and farm visits all in local area.

At a glance

Welcome & Ambience	✓✓✓✓✓	Location	✓✓✓✓✓
Quality of Pitches	✓✓✓✓	Range of Facilities	✓✓✓✓✓

Directions

Site is well signed from around Döbriach.

Charges 2004

Per person	€ 5,00 - € 7,85
child (4-14 yrs)	€ 3,50 - € 5,90
pitch	€ 4,50 - € 11,00
dog	€ 2,00 - € 2,60

Discounts for retired people. No credit cards.

Reservations

Write to site. Tel: 04246 7774.
E-mail: service@qualitycamp.com

Open

All year.

We are grateful to the Audiovisual Library of the European Commisssion and to the individual National Tourist Boards for providing photographs and material for this guide.

May 2004 saw the accession of ten new countries into the European Union, eight of which are in Central Europe.

With the overall quality improvements of campsites in these countries, we have decided that the time is right for a new Alan Rogers guide dedicated to this 'New Europe',

The following countries are included in this new guide: Slovenia, Hungary, Slovakia, Czech Republic, Poland, Lithuania, Latvia and Estonia . We have also included Croatia, which whilst outside the EU, we feel enhances our new guide (see map on page 51).

This guide to the whole of Europe includes just a selection of the campsites in each of these countries.

The largest and most southerly of the Baltic states. The landscape is made up of wonderful rolling hills, gentle plains, flowing rivers and lakes. Most of the Baltic shoreline is separated from the open sea by a long narrow strip of sand dunes called the Curonian Spit.

For centuries, amber has been washed up onto the golden sands of the coastline and has historically become known as 'Lithuania's gold'. The unique sand spit here, created by wind and water is an impressive formation stretching from the southwest to Klaipeda and enclosing the vast Curonian Lagoon. Old villages are said to be buried beneath but today there are several fishermen's settlements in their place. The capital Vilnius is often known as 'Baltic Jerusalem' which becomes quite apparent when you see the many churches, towers and medieval courtyards.

Kaunas is the second largest city with buildings that combine together in a mix of arts and architecture of different eras. Klaipeda, the country's main seaport, is well worth a visit. It is a modern city of quays and warehouses and a restored fortress, Kopgalis, is now a marine museum, aquarium and dolphinarium.

Throughout the regions, there are five national parks which have been established for the protection and study of the natural, cultural and historical heritage of the country. This is the place to be for a breath of fresh air and the chance to embark on activities such as walking, cycling, horse riding and fishing.

Population

3.4 million

Capital

Vilnius

Climate

Maritime/continental. Snow is on the ground for about three months of the year; summers are warm

Language

Lithuanian. Russian, Polish and German are widely spoken as is English in the major cities

Currency

The Litas (Lt)

Telephone

The country code is 00 370

Banks

Mon-Fri 08.00-13.00 and 14.00-17.00

Shops

Mon-Fri 09.00-12.00 and 14.00-18.00. Some stay open at midday. Sat 09.00-midday

Public Holidays

New Year's Day; Lithuanian Statehood Restoration Day 16 Feb; Lithuanian Independence Restoration Day 11 March; Easter (Catholic) Sun, Mon; International Labour Day 1 May; Mother's Day - first Sun of May; Feast of St John 24 June; State Day 6 July; Assumption of the Blessed Virgin 15 Aug; All Saints Day 1 Nov; Christmas 25, 26 Dec

Motoring

From the beginning of September through to March, dipped headlights are required at all times. Ensure your car is well equipped during the winter months as weather conditions can be severe. It is recommended that you use guarded car parks in larger towns, especially if leaving your car somewhere overnight.

Tourist Office

No active tourist office in the UK

Embassy of the Republic of Lithuania
84 Gloucester Place
London W1U 6AO
Tel: 020 7486 6401
Fax: 020 7486 6403
Internet: www.tourism.lt

LITHUANIAN PEOPLE ARE REGARDED AS OUTGOING AND YOU ARE SURE TO MAKE MANY FRIENDS DURING YOUR VISIT HERE.

LI2060 Camping Viktorija

Vilkaviskio Sav., 4270 Vistytis (Lithuania)

Vistytis is just inside Lithuania, near the border at the point where Poland, Russia (Kaliningrad region) and Lithuania meet. In fact most of the adjoining lake is in Russia. At the present time this is probably one the best campsites in the Baltic States, where standards are generally lower than seen in western Europe and more akin to Russia where there exists what might best be described as pre-war sanitation. Not surprisingly the site gets busy in high season especially at weekends. There are 40 touring pitches, all with electricity, and further open areas for tents beside the lake. English is spoken in reception.

Facilities

A small sanitary block has toilets which are poor. However the new building houses 6 bathrooms, each with new, clean and modern facilities (WC, washbasin and shower). Chemical disposal point. Bar and restaurant at hotel. Boat and bicycle hire. Old huts for rent. Dogs not accepted.

Open

1 May - 1 October.

At a glance

Welcome & Ambience	✓✓✓✓✓	Location	✓✓✓✓✓
Quality of Pitches	✓✓✓	Range of Facilities	✓✓✓✓✓

Directions

From Kalvarija on A5 (E67) take road west towards Vistytis. After about 35 km. on entering the village turn left heading south down the side of lake Vistytis. Site is on right after about 5 km.

Charges 2004

Per person	LTL 4,00
pitch incl. electricity	LTL 40,00

Reservations

Not needed. Tel: 83 42 4 75 21.
E-mail: viktorija@viktorija.lt

LI2030 Kempingas Slenyje

Slenio g. 1, 4050 Trakai (Lithuania)

This excellent site in a National Park beside Lake Galve is situated north of Trakai and about 35 km. from Vilnius. There are 50 touring pitches, all with 16A electricity and views across the lake to Trakai Castle which was Lithuania's former capital. Vilnius has much to offer the visitor, from the old town – don't miss Pilies Gatve (translated as 'the gates of dawn') – to the modern, new city centre. Most of the symbols of Soviet occupation have now been destroyed and a modern vibrant city is being constructed. The geographical centre of Europe is only 25 km. north of the capital and is also worth visiting.

Facilities

Small sanitary block has toilets and hot showers which are good and clean. Chemical disposal point. Bar, restaurant and café in adjoining complex. English spoken in reception. Hot air balloon and steamboat rides. Off site: Vilnius and Trakai.

Open

All year.

Reservations

Not needed Tel: 370 528 538 80.
E-mail: kempingasslenyje@one.lt

At a glance

Welcome & Ambience	✓✓✓✓	Location	✓✓✓✓✓
Quality of Pitches	✓✓✓✓	Range of Facilities	✓✓✓✓✓

Directions

From Vilnius, take Kaunas road. After 25 km. near Rykantai, turn right towards Trakai. After 7 km. turn right for 'Kempingas slényje - 0.5 km'. Once down the hill, take the narrow asphalt road which takes you round the shore of the lake to site. Coming from Kaunas, as soon as you pass Vievis turn right at sign 'Trakai - 17 km'. After 13 km., turn left towards Uztrakis at sign 'Slenis - 2 km'. Then follow the signs.

Charges 2004

Per person	LTL 16,00
pitch	LTL 5,00 - 13,00
car	LTL 6,00
electricity	LTL 9,00

LI2010 Apple Island

Lake Grabuostas, Zalvariai, Moletai

Camping Apple Island is a new site which is attractively located on an island on Lake Grabuostas, around 60 kilometres north of Vilnius. This region is predominantly made up of forests, lakes and rolling hills. In all, there are more than 300 lakes, including the largest in Lithuania, Lake Asveja. A little bridge leads to Camping Apple Island, and the site offers some attractive tent pitches (no electricity). Additionally, there are 24 pitches with electricity, water and drainage, all of which are level and of a good size. Leisure facilities here include tennis and minigolf, and there is an attractive lakeside beach with barbecue facilities. The central building houses a café/bar with a terrace, and games room on the first floor.

Facilities

The sanitary block is modern and generally well maintained. Shower tokens are sold at reception (1 lt. each). Café - bar, Mini golf. Fishing. Tennis. Sauna. Rowing boat hire. Lakeside beach. Off site: Moletai (nearest large town with some interesting museums and monuments).

Open

All year.

At a glance

Welcome & Ambience	✓✓✓	Location	✓✓✓
Quality of Pitches	✓✓✓	Range of Facilities	✓✓✓

Directions

From A14 (Vilnius – Utena) road, follow signs to Luokesa (before reaching Moletai). Follow signs to Ambraziskiai and pass through Zalvariai village. Site is signed on left (across the bridge onto the island).

Charges 2004

Per pitch incl. 2 persons	LTL 35,00
with electricity, water and drainage	LTL 65,00

Reservations

Contact site. Tel: 383 50073.
E-mail: strenko@strenko.lt

This is the central of the three Baltic countries, sitting on the Eastern coast between Estonia and Lithuania. It is a land of forests, plains, lakes, river valleys and white sandy beaches.

The capital city of Riga is situated on both banks of the River Daugava, separating it into two parts. In this historic centre you will find a wealth of theatres, opera houses, concert halls, restaurants and art galleries representing cultural life.

The region of Kurzeme is well known for its many fishing villages, nestled among pines, forests and large ice-free ports. The furthest point north is the Kolka Horn, a stretch separating the Baltic Sea from the Riga Gulf. If it's windy you may see waves from the Gulf meeting waves from the open sea. Another water spectacle, near Kuldiga, is the Ventas Rumba, one of the widest waterfalls in Europe.

Vidzeme is the Northern region and houses the Gauja National Park. Along the stretch of the River Gauja you will come across a combination of medieval castles, legendary caves and a wonderful hilly landscape. Sigulda, the 'Switzerland of Latvia' is where you will find Latvia's downhill skiing centre and bobsled track.

The east is the 'land of blue lakes', several hundred in fact, making this region a fisherman's paradise. Particularly beautiful is Lake Ezezers which has more bays and islands than any other in Latvia.

Population

2.3 million

Capital

Riga

Climate

A temperate climate but with considerable temperature variations. Summers are warm and winters can be very cold with snow

Language

Latvian. Russian, English and German are also widely spoken

Currency

The Lat (LVL)

Telephone

The country code is 00 371

Banks

Most banking hours are 9.00-17.00 Mon-Fri, some are open on Saturdays from 9.00-13.00

Shops

Mon-Fri 09.00-12.00 and 14.00-18.00. Some stay open at midday. Sat 09.00-midday

Public Holidays

New Year's Day; Easter Good Friday, Sun, Mon; Labour Day 1 May; Mother's Day - first Sun of May; Midsummer's Eve; Ligo Day 23 June; Jani Day 24 June; Proclamation of the Republic of Latvia 18 Nov; Christmas 25, 26 Dec; New Year's Eve 31 Dec

Motoring

Traffic is relatively light in Latvia (except in the capital) and main roads are well maintained, Some rural roads may be unsurfaced. Dipped headlights are required at all times. If involved in an accident do not attempt to remove your vehicle until the police give permission. Motorway speed limits are low (90-100 kph).

Tourist Office

Latvian Tourism Information Centre
72 Queensborough Terrace
London WH 3SH
Tel: 020 7229 8271
Email: london@latviatourism.lv
Internet: www.latviatourism.lv

tip

LATVIA OFFERS OVER 12,000 RIVERS AND 3,000 LAKES PROVIDING A FANTASTIC OPPORTUNITY FOR BOATING, WALKING AND GENERALLY ENJOYING THE OUTDOORS.

LA1020 Camping Meleku Licis

4032 Dzeni

This site is typical of many of the 'Old Russian' standard sites in the Baltic States – an excellent location, great pitches and disgusting sanitary provision. So, unless you are prepared to use your own facilities, give this site a miss. Having said that, it is right next to the Baltic coast with a great sandy beach, it is quiet and has a pleasant restaurant and bar. There are 75 touring pitches, 20 with electricity. Located about 20 kilometres south of the Estonian border, it is south of the small town of Salacgriva in the Limbazu Region.

Facilities

The small sanitary block has toilets which were filthy and cold showers. So if you come here be prepared to use your own facilities. Chemical disposal point. English spoken in reception. Small restaurant and bar. Off site: Baltic coast.

Open

1 May - 30 September.

At a glance

Welcome & Ambience	✓✓	Location	✓✓✓✓
Quality of Pitches	✓✓✓✓	Range of Facilities	✓✓

Directions

This Dzeni did not appear on our map of the Baltic States, however it is 72 km. north of Riga on the Tallinn highway near Salacgriva. It is well signed.

Charges 2004

Per unit incl. 2 persons and electricity	€ 7,70

Reservations

Not needed. Tel: 371 928 4555.
E-mail: aktivs@apollo.lv

LA1040 Riga City Camping

Kipsalas iela 8, 1048 Riga (Latvia)

The old town of Riga is certainly well worth a visit and this new site provides the opportunity. Based on a small island in the Daugava River in a mixed urban area, this small site provides 40 touring pitches; 16 with electricity connections. Much of the old town has been rebuilt since the war and the informative and disturbing Museum of Occupation near the Town Hall is worth visiting as is the Art-Nouveau architecture of Riga's residential area. The market, which occupies the former Zeppelin hangers, should also be seen. Latvia's answer to fast food is also an essential part of your visit – 'pelmeni' (which are meat dumplings fried, boiled or swimming in soup) and pancakes are cheap, filling and tasty and are served throughout the town.

Facilities

Two small sanitary blocks in 'portacabin' style units have toilets and hot showers which are clean and useable. The adjoining building provides a bar and snacks. Chemical disposal point. Bicycle hire. English is spoken in reception. Off site: Shopping centre within 800 m. Riga 20 minutes walk away.

Open

1 June - 30 September.

At a glance

Welcome & Ambience	✓✓✓	Location	✓✓✓✓
Quality of Pitches	✓✓✓	Range of Facilities	✓✓✓

Directions

Kipsalas is a small island in the Daugava River in central Riga. From the old town cross the new suspension bridge and at the end of the bridge go down the slip road, turn right after 300 m. (large campsite sign) and the site is 800 m. on the left.

Charges 2004

Per person	LVL 1,00
pitch	LVL 5,00 - 8,00
electricity	LVL 3,00

Reservations

Not needed. Tel: 706 5000. E-mail: camping@bt1.lv

LA1060 Camping Nemo

Atbalss 1, 2008 Jurmala

Jurmala is the favourite seaside resort of the Latvian people, and also many Russians, and the name literally means 'seaside'. Nemo is, in fact, a small water theme park where many of the visitors camp on the flat, grassed areas inside the park. Technically the site has 40 touring pitches, all with electricity, but more than three times that number were camping there when we visited so you should expect little space. There are also many basic wooden huts to rent which sleep four people. During late July and August the park is crowded and the sanitary facilities inadequate and dirty. Riga is about 40 minutes drive to the east and it is possible to use public transport.

Facilities

2 small sanitary blocks have toilets and cold communal showers with no screens; with the site so crowded they are over used and dirty. Chemical disposal point. Restaurant and bar. Disco till the early hours every Friday and Saturday. Small water theme park, but no swimming pool. English spoken in reception. Off site: Riga and the Baltic coast.

Open

1 May - 1 October.

At a glance

Welcome & Ambience	✓✓	Location	✓✓✓✓
Quality of Pitches	✓✓	Range of Facilities	✓✓

Directions

Nemo is in the Vaivari area of Jurmala. Approach Jurmala from Riga on the A10, you have a choice - pay LTL 2 (you need change) for a 48 hour toll pass (Nemo 14 km.) or turn right (Nemo 22 km). On the toll road go straight on through Jurmala. Nemo is signed and turn right into site after 14 km.

Charges 2004

Per person	LTL 1,00
caravan or motorcaravan	LTL 8,00 - 9,00
tent	LTL 1,00

Reservations

Not taken. Tel: 77 32 349. E-mail: nemo@nemo.lv

A small country in Northeast Europe bordering the Baltic Sea and sitting just below Finland. Now relieved from its communist rule, Estonia offers the chance to discover a new and refreshingly genuine experience. A country with a history-filled past, surrounded by beautiful castles, old cities, manor houses, forests, beaches and islands, to one with a progressive future.

Northern Estonia is the Baltic Sea coast region lined by dramatic cliffs across the Gulf of Finland. Along this 200 km long stretch from Tallinn to Narva, medieval castles, restored manor estates and beautiful waterfalls can be seen. Narva Castle is an impressive hallmark of the region. A nature lovers' paradise can be found at Lahemaa National Park, one of Estonia's most popular nature reserves complete with jagged coasts, vast forests, wetlands and numerous hiking trails.

The two largest islands off the coast are Saaremaa and Hiiumaa, both inviting retreats. The smaller islands include Muhu, Kihnu and Ruhnu and, along with their laid-back, and friendly atmosphere are typical examples of the Estonian landscape dotted with windmills, thatched cottages and sleepy fishing villages.

Tartu is Estonia's second city and is a good starting point for exploring Southern Estonia. Any visit here should include Polva and Voru, home of the Estonian Setus. Witness a step back in time, villages with wooden huts and small farms where these ancient peoples retain their own unique language and culture and are famous for their colourful folk dress and distinctive style of singing.

Population

1.4 million

Capital

Tallinn

Climate

A temperate climate with warm summers and fairly severe winters

Language

Estonian

Currency

Estonian kroon (EEK)

Telephone

The country code is 00 372

Banks

Mon-Fri 9.00-16.00

Shops

Shopping hours vary widely. In larger towns and cities many shops are open fom 09.00 to 19.00, with reduced hours at weekends.

Public Holidays

New year's Day; Independence Day 24 Feb; Good Friday; May Day; Whitsun; Victory Day 23 June; Midsummer's Day 24 June; Re-Independence Day 20 Aug; Christmas 25,26 Dec

Motoring

Dipped headlights are compulsory at all times and winter tyres must be fitted Oct-April. You are required to carry wheel chocks in your vehicle. Do not drink before driving. When parking in many towns, you must buy and display a ticket (available from local shops etc.)

Tourist Office

No active tourist office in the UK

Embassy of the Republic of Estonia
16 Hyde Park Gate
London SW7 5DG
Tel: 020 7589 3428
Fax: 020 7589 3430
Internet: www.visitestonia.com

tip

TO THE SOUTH YOU WILL DISCOVER PINE FORESTS AND ROLLING HILLS AND TOTALLY UNSPOILED NATURE - PERFECT FOR FISHING OR HORSE RIDING.

ET0030 Camping Kalev

Kloostrimetsa tee 56A, 11913 Tallinn

No trip to Estonia would be complete without a visit to Tallinn and in particular, the Old Town. Whilst Camping Kalev may not be the most picturesque or the best equipped campsite it is ideally situated for visiting Estonia's capital. Located directly under the 314 m. television tower and next to the botanical gardens, it is easy to find. The site has 18 pitches, with electricity, although more than double that number of campers were there when we visited in August. Tallinn just a 15-minute bus ride away.

Facilities

Small sanitary block has toilets which are clean and serviceable but the hot showers are in need of refurbishment and are tatty (but they work). Chemical disposal point. English spoken in reception. Off site: Tallinn.

Open

1 May - 30 September.

At a glance

Welcome & Ambience	✓✓✓	Location	✓✓✓✓
Quality of Pitches	✓✓	Range of Facilities	✓✓

Directions

Site is northeast of Tallin, directly under the Soviet built TV Tower, which is over 300 m. high and can be seen for miles. Coming from the east turn off route 1 before Tallinn and just head towards the tower.

Charges 2004

Per caravan or motorcaravan	EEK 300,00
tent and car	EEK 240,00

Reservations

Not possible. Tel: 372 623 9191.
E-mail: motorlubikalev@hot.ee

ET0040 Camping Eesti Karavan

45501 Võsu

This Eesti Caravan Club site is simply a large level grassed field screened by trees next to the Baltic Coast. There are 120 touring pitches, most with electricity connections available. In the village of Võsu there are shops, bar and a bank with automat. The restored manor house and park at Palmse are well worth a visit if only to see the 'Rolls Royce' used by Khrushchev that broke down during a state visit to Estonia, during the Soviet occupation, and was too expensive to repair so it was left behind. The parks around the manor and the café, in the old bathhouse, are particularly worthy of a visit. There is also a former Soviet Coast Guards barracks at Kasmu, which is now a maritime museum.

Facilities

Small sanitary block has toilets and showers, which are basic but clean. Chemical toilet disposal point. English spoken in reception. Off site: The Lahemaa National park, Palmse Manor and the Baltic coast.

Open

1 May - 30 September.

At a glance

Welcome & Ambience	✓✓✓	Location	✓✓✓✓
Quality of Pitches	✓✓✓	Range of Facilities	✓✓✓

Directions

The village of Võsu is north of Palmse and off the route 1 the Narva - Tallinn highway. As you approach Võsu you can turn left towards Kasmu in which case you turn right at the next crossroads and the site is about 400 m. on the left. If you go on through the village and bear left near the beach site is on right.

Charges 2004

Per unit incl. electricity	EEK 100,00

Reservations

Not needed. Tel: 03 24 46 65.

ET0050 Toila Spa Kamping

Ranna 12, 41702 Toila

Coming to this site after three weeks in Russia and having crossed the border into Estonia at Narva only 30 minutes earlier, we thought it must be a mirage – a clean, level, green field right beside the coast, fenced and secure with clean toilets, hot showers and water! Having quickly settled in, we realised it was not a mirage and set about enjoying all this quiet site has to offer. There are 25 touring pitches all with electricity. Toila, along a former trade route of the Vikings, is famous for its gardens. Here stood the majestic Oru Castle, built by the famous St Petersburg businessman Yelisseyev in the 19th century. Having been used as the Estonian President's summer residence between the wars it was subsequently destroyed. Now the village is home to parts of the parkland that has been reconstructed and the views of the Baltic Glint are quite spectacular. Here the Glint forms part of the Saka-Ontika-Toila landscape reserve. Although the site is next to the coast there are some 120 steps down to the beach.

Facilities

Small sanitary block has toilets and hot showers, which are immaculate. Adjoining hotel provides a bar, restaurant and indoor swimming pool, complete with sauna. In addition the spa complex offers a variety of treatments that are all available to campers. Chemical toilet disposal point. English spoken in reception. Internet access in the hotel. Cottage accommodation. Off site: Toila and the Baltic coast.

Open

1 May - 15 October.

At a glance

Welcome & Ambience	✓✓✓	Location	✓✓✓✓
Quality of Pitches	✓✓✓	Range of Facilities	✓✓✓✓

Directions

The village of Toila is 12 km. northeast of Johvi which is on route 1, the Narva - Tallinn highway. Turn north towards Toila and just as you enter the village a sign indicates a left turn towards the Toila Sanatoorium (Spa Hotel). Having turned left, drive about 800 m. and just before the hotel car park turn right, then left and left again. Site is ahead on the right.

Charges 2004

Per caravan incl. electricity	EEK 110,00

Reservations

Not needed. Tel: 372 332 5328.
E-mail: info@toilasanetoorium.ee

The Baltic States

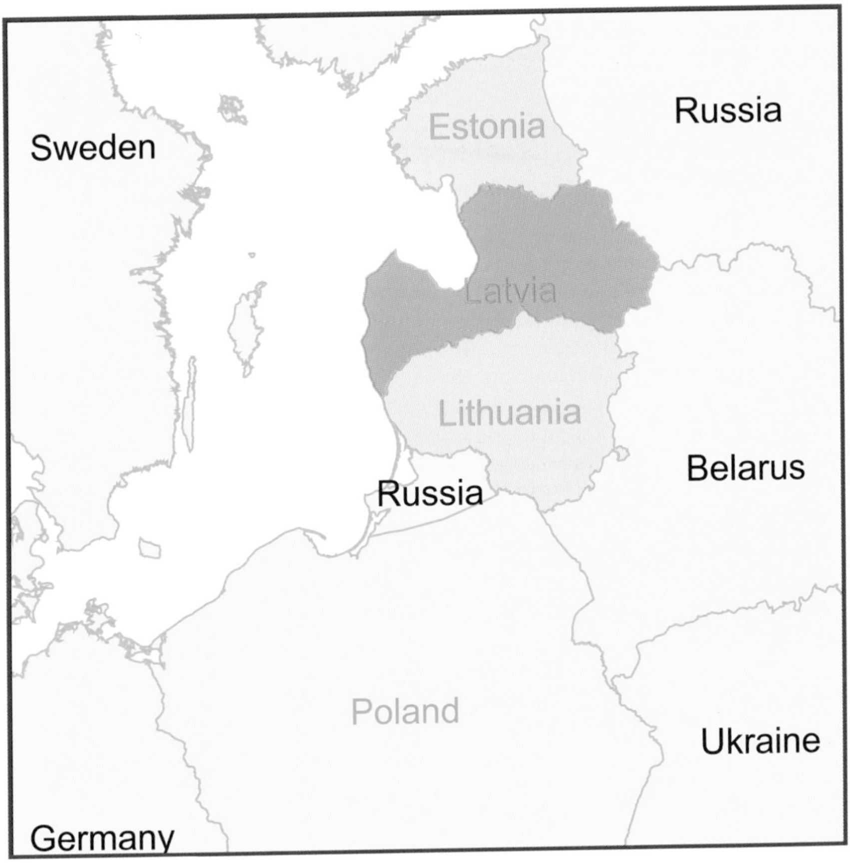
Sweden
Estonia
Russia
Latvia
Lithuania
Russia
Belarus
Poland
Ukraine
Germany

Whilst there is a good selection of campsites in the three Baltic states, many fall well short of standards which are the norm in western Europe. Sites, whilst in attractive locations, suffer from poor (and sometimes very poor) sanitary facilities. Showers will be poor, often with cold water only, toilets are usually Turkish. Indeed many sites are reminiscent of standards we may have tolerated in the 1950's. Changes are happening but it is certainly going to take some years for things to change to any substantial extent. Motorcaravan draindown points are very rare, so you may need to resort to other methods. Inevitably, sites of most recent construction offer the best standards. Our recommendations, we feel, are all to a good and reliable standard.

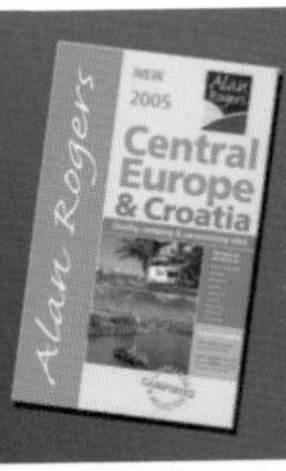
Alan Rogers
NEW
2005
Central
Europe
& Croatia

Alan Rogers

This is a just a sample of the campsites we have inspected and selected in Central Europe & Croatia. For more campsites and further information, please see the Alan Rogers Central Europe & Croatia guide.

Belgium

A small country divided into three regions, Flanders in the north, Wallonia in the south and Brussels the capital. Belgium is rich in scenic countryside, culture and history, notably the great forest of Ardennes, the historic cities of Bruges and Ghent and the northern coastline with its sandy beaches.

Brussels is at the very heart of Europe and doubles as the capital of the European Union. A multi-cultural and multi-lingual city full of remarkable monuments, interesting museums and highly acclaimed restaurants. In the French speaking region of Wallonia lies the mountainous Ardennes, an area famous for its forests, lakes, streams and grottoes, making it a popular holiday destination, especially for those who like nature and walking. The safe, sandy beaches on the northern coast run for forty miles. Here lies Ostend, a popular seaside resort with an eight kilo-metre long beach and a promenade coupled with a bustling harbour and shops. Bruges is Europe's best preserved medieval city and is certainly one of the most attractive, whether you want to relax on a boat trip along the canals, explore the narrow streets or visit one of the many churches and art museums.

Population

10.2 million

Capital

Brussels

Climate

Temperate climate similar to Britain

Language

There are three official languages. French is spoken in the south, Flemish in the north, and German is the predominant language in the eastern provinces

Currency

The Euro

Telephone

The country code is 00 32

Banks

Mon-Fri 09.00-15.30. Some banks open Sat 09.00-12.00

Shops

Mon-Sat 09.00-17.30/18.00 hrs - later on Thurs/Fri; closed Sundays

Public Holidays

New Year; Easter Mon; Labour Day; Ascension; Whit Monday; Flemish National Day 21 July; Assumption 15 Aug; All Saints 1 Nov; Armistice Day 11 Nov; Christmas Day

Motoring

For cars with a caravan or trailer, motorways are toll free except for the Liefenshoek Tunnel in Antwerp. Maximum permitted overall length of vehicle/trailer or caravan combination is 18 m. Blue Zone parking areas exist in Brussels, Ostend, Bruges, Liège, Antwerp and Gent. Parking discs can be obtained from police stations, garages, some shops and the Royal Automobile Club Belgique

Tourist Office

Belgian Tourist Office Brussels & Wallonia,
217 Marsh Wall, London E14 9FJ
Tel: 0906 3020 245 Fax: 020 7531 0393
Email: info@belgiumtheplaceto.be.
Internet: www.belgiumtheplaceto.be

Tourism Flanders-Brussels,
31 Pepper Street, London E14 9RW
Tel: 020 7867 0311 Fax: 020 7458 0045
Email: office@visitflanders.co.uk

IF CHOCOLATE IS YOUR WEAKNESS, HEAD TO ONE OF BELGIUM'S 2,130 CHOCOLATE SHOPS AND TRY A FAMOUS BELGIUM PRALINE: A DELICATELY SCULPTED CHOCOLATE SHELL CONCEALING A RICH CENTRE – DELICIOUS!

BE0555 Recreatipark Klein Strand

Varsenareweg 29, B-8490 Jabbeke (West Flanders)

A interesting site in a convenient location, only 10 km. from Bruges, this site has its own lake and sandy beach. It is in two distinct areas divided by an access road. The static and residential units are closest to the lake, and this area also has most of the amenities. These include the main reception building, two restaurants (French, Chinese), takeaways, bar, mini-market, and most of the sports facilities. There is a water-ski school (charged for) at the lake which also has a swimming area with waterslide (lifeguard), and boat and kayak rental. A comprehensive programme of activities and entertainment is provided in July/August. Indeed, this is a family holiday site with plenty of activities for all members of the family. The touring site is a short walk away with The Dolphin Cafe and touring reception (both July/August only), a large fenced play area for younger children, with a children's pool. For older children there is an adventure playground island surrounded by a moat. Overall there are 650 pitches, of which 123 are for tourists. All are on grass, a good number quite large with hedges, and all have 10A electricity. Despite the active nature of the site and the proximity of the motorway this is a surprisingly relaxing place.

Facilities

A single modern, heated, toilet block in the touring area includes good sized showers (tokens € 0.75 for 3 minutes) and vanity style open washbasins. Facilities for disabled campers. Dishwashing (€ 0.50). Laundry. Motorcaravan service point. Besides the amenities already mentioned, also on site are indoor and outdoor tennis courts, a climbing wall, fishing lake, bicycle hire, and boules courts. Barrier card deposit € 25. Off site: Golf 10 km. Riding 5 km.

Open

All year.

At a glance

Welcome & Ambience	✓✓✓✓	Location	✓✓✓✓
Quality of Pitches	✓✓✓✓	Range of Facilities	✓✓✓✓

Directions

Jabbeke is 10 km. southwest of Bruges. From Ostend or Dunkirk on A10 take exit 6 (Jabbeke) and turn right on N367. In 500 m. turn right by filling station (Constant Permekelaan). At end of street turn left, then first right for 1 km. to site entrance on left.

Charges 2004

Per person	€ 4,00
child	€ 1,50
pitch and car	€ 9,00
electricity	€ 1,50

Reservations

Advisable for peak season. Contact site.
Tel: 050 811 440. E-mail: info@kleinstrand.be

BE0520 Camping de Blekker

Jachtwakersstraat 12, B-8670 Koksijde aan Zee (West Flanders)

This family-owned site, adjacent to a 186-hectare nature reserve on the Belgium coast, is divided into two sections: Blekker and Blekkerdal. De Blekker has 178 pitches of which 75 are allocated for tourists. The pitches are grassy with some dividing hedges and trees, and all have 10A electricity connections. Visitors should drive to the Blekker reception but will be given a choice of where to park. Local attractions include the Koksijde annual Flower Market and Floral Pageant, National Fishery Museum and horseback shrimp fishing in Oostduinkerke or Clown City in De Panne.

Facilities

Each section has a single modern sanitary unit including washbasins in cubicles, dishwashing and laundry sinks, washing machine and dryer, facilities for babies and a suite for disabled persons (other than for washbasins, hot water is on payment throughout). Laundry. Dogs are not accepted. English is spoken. Off site: Shop in nearest village 300 m. Restaurant and bars 400 m. - 3 km.

Open

15 February - 15 November.

At a glance

Welcome & Ambience	✓✓✓✓✓	Location	✓✓✓✓
Quality of Pitches	✓✓✓✓	Range of Facilities	✓✓✓✓

Directions

From A16 (E40) exit 1A, take N8 towards Koksijde. At roundabout take N396 towards Koksijde Dorp and then turn towards Koksijde-aan-zee. Follow small yellow camp signs. Site entrance road is on the right.

Charges 2004

Per unit incl. 4 persons	€ 19,00 - € 27,00
extra child (under 12 yrs)	€ 4,00

Special rates for holiday weekends.

Reservations

Advised for high season and peak weekends; contact site. Tel: 058 51 16 33.
E-mail: camping.deblekker@belgacom.net

BE0560 Camping De Lombarde

Elisabethlaan 4, B-8434 Lombardsijde (West Flanders)

De Lombarde is a spacious holiday site, between Lombardsijde and the coast. It has a pleasant atmosphere and modern buildings. The 360 pitches are set out in level, grassy bays surrounded by shrubs, all with electricity (16A, long leads may be needed). Vehicles are parked in separate car parks. There are many seasonal units and holiday homes, leaving 180 tourist pitches. There is a range of activities (listed below) and an entertainment programme in season. This is a popular holiday area and the site becomes full at peak times. A pleasant stroll takes you into Lombardsijde or you can catch the tram to the beach.

Facilities

Three modern heated, clean sanitary units are of an acceptable standard, with some washbasins in cubicles. Facilities for disabled people. Large laundry. Motorcaravan services. Shop (1/4-30/9). Restaurant/bar and takeaway (July/Aug. plus weekends 21/3-11/11). Tennis. Table tennis. Basketball. Boules. Fishing lake. TV lounge. Animation programme. Playground. Torch useful. Off site: Sea 400 m. Riding and golf 500 m. Bicycle hire 1 km.

Open

All year.

At a glance

Welcome & Ambience	✓✓✓✓	Location	✓✓✓✓✓
Quality of Pitches	✓✓✓✓	Range of Facilities	✓✓✓✓

Directions

Coming from Westende, follow the tram-lines. From traffic lights in Lombarsijde, turn left following tram-lines into Zeelaan. Continue following tram-lines until crossroads and tram stop, turn left into Elisabethlaan. Site is on right after 200 m.

Charges guide

Per unit incl. electricity	€ 13,00 - € 24,00
small pitch incl. 2 persons	€ 2,60 - € 3,10
dog (1 per pitch)	free

Reservations

Write or fax for details. Tel: 058 23 68 39. E-mail: info@delombarde.be

BE0578 Camping Ter Duinen

Wenduinesteenweg 143, B-8421 De Haan (West Flanders)

Ter Duinen is a large, seaside holiday site with 120 touring pitches and over 700 privately owned static holiday caravans. Pitches are laid out in straight lines each side of tarmac roads and the site has three immaculate toilet blocks. Other than a bar, a playing field and a little shop, the site has little else to offer, but it is only a 400 metre walk to the sea and next door to the site is a large sports complex with a sub-tropical pool and several sporting facilities. Best places to visit for a day trip are Oostende with the Atlantic Wall from WW II, Knokke (which holds many summer festivals) and Brugge.

Facilities

Three modern toilet blocks have good fittings, washbasins in cubicles (cold water only) and showers (€ 1.20). Baby bath. Facilities for disabled visitors. Two launderettes. Motorcaravan service point. Shop (closed Wed). Snack bar. Off site: Sea with sandy beach 400 m. Bicycle hire 400 m. Riding 1 km. Golf 3 km. Boat launching 6 km.

Open

1 March - 15 October.

At a glance

Welcome & Ambience	✓✓✓✓	Location	✓✓✓✓✓
Quality of Pitches	✓✓✓	Range of Facilities	✓✓

Directions

On E40 in either direction take exit for De Haan/Jabbeke. In De Haan drive through centre and turn right in front of the station (don't cross the tram-lines). Follow the Wenduinsesteenweg to the site on the right.

Charges guide

Per unit incl. 2 persons, electricity	€ 14,50 - € 18,00
extra person	€ 2,25
child (under 10 yrs)	€ 1,50

Reservations

Necessary for high season. Tel: 050 41 35 93.

BE0580 Camping Memling

Veltemweg 109, B-8310 Brugge (West Flanders)

This traditional site, ideal for visiting Brugge, is located behind a bistro in a quiet suburb. The 100 unmarked pitches (60 for touring units) are on slightly undulating grass, with gravel roads and trees and hedges providing some shade. Electricity (6A) is available to 40 pitches. There is a separate area for tents. Bars, restaurants, local shops and supermarkets are within walking distance. Brugge itself has a network of cycleways and for those on foot a bus runs into the centre from nearby. It may be best for visitors with large units to telephone in advance to ensure an adequate pitch.

Facilities

Heated toilet facilities are clean and tidy, including some washbasins in cubicles. Facilities for babies and disabled visitors. Dishwashing sinks (H&C). Laundry with washing machine and dryer. Freezer for campers' use. Tiny playground. Bicycle hire. Off site: Municipal swimming pool and park nearby. Supermarket 250 m, hypermarket 1 km.

Open

All year.

At a glance

Welcome & Ambience	✓✓✓✓✓	Location	✓✓✓✓
Quality of Pitches	✓✓✓	Range of Facilities	✓✓✓

Directions

From R30 Brugge ring road take exit 6 on N9 towards Maldegem. At Sint-Kruis turn right at traffic lights (site signed, close to supermarket).

Charges 2005

Per person	€ 4,00
child (under 15 yrs)	€ 3,00
pitch and car	€ 4,00 - € 7,50

Reservations

Write or fax for details. Tel: 050 35 58 45. E-mail: info@camping-memling.be

BE0610 Camping Blaarmeersen

Zuiderlaan 12, B-9000 Gent (East Flanders)

Blaarneersen is a comfortable, well managed municipal site in the west of the city. It adjoins a sports complex and a fair-sized lake which provide facilities for a variety of watersports, tennis, squash, minigolf, football, athletics track, dry ski slope, roller skating and a playground. The 208 individual, flat, grassy touring pitches are separated by tall hedges and mostly arranged in circular groups; with electricity to 178. There are 26 hardstandings for motorcaravans, plus a separate area for tents with barbecue facility. Some noise is possible as the the city ring road is close. In Gent, tour the markets, free of charge, with the Town Crier (May-Sept, Sunday 10.30). Central Gent is three kilometres - the bus stop is 150 m. and buses run every 20 minutes to the city centre. There are also good networks of paths and cycle routes around the city.

Facilities

Four sanitary units of a decent standard vary in size. Most of the 36 free hot showers are in one block. Showers and toilets for disabled people. Laundry. Motorcaravan services. Shop, café/bar (both daily March - Oct). Takeaway. Sports facilities. Playground. Fishing on site in winter, otherwise 500 m. Lake swimming. Off site: Bicycle hire 5 km. Riding and golf 10 km.

Open

1 March - 15 October.

At a glance

Welcome & Ambience	✓✓✓✓	Location	✓✓✓✓
Quality of Pitches	✓✓✓✓✓	Range of Facilities	✓✓✓✓✓

Directions

From E40 take exit 13 (Gent-West) and follow dual carriageway for 5 km. Cross second bridge and look for Blaarmeersen sign, turning sharp right and following signs to leisure complex. In city avoid overpasses - most signs are on the lower levels.

Charges 2004

Per unit incl. 2 persons	€ 10,75 - € 14,25
extra person	€ 3,25 - € 4,00
child (5-12 yrs)	€ 1,50 - € 2,00
electricity (10A)	€ 1,25

Reservations

Most advisable in main season; made for any period (no deposit) and kept until 5 pm.
Tel: +32 9 266 81 60.
E-mail: camping.blaarmeersen@gent.be

BE0570 Camping Jeugdstadion

Leopold III Laan 16, B-8900 Ieper (West Flanders)

Camping Jeugdstadion is a small developing municipal close to the historic old town. At present there are only 21 caravan pitches, 12 on hardstandings and all with electricity (16A), plus a separate area for 15 tents. The barrier key also operates the lock for the toilet block. At the end of Leopold III Laan is the Menin Gate built in 1927, which bears the names of British and Commonwealth soldiers who lost their lives between 1914-1918. The last post is sounded beneath the gate at 8 pm. every evening in their honour. The interactive museum entitled 'The Flanders Experience' in the Cloth Hall is a moving experience. The Commonwealth War Graves Commission is a little further away in Elverdingestraat. In mid August each year there is a festival for young people in the town, when the campsite is usually fully booked.

Facilities

The modern, heated but fairly basic toilet block has cold water to washbasins and three sinks for dishwashing outside. Bicycle hire. Minigolf. Boules. Barrier key deposit € 24.79 or £20. Off site: The adjacent sports complex has courts for volleyball, petanque and squash, whilst indoor and outdoor swimming pools are only 500 m. away, and there is a very large comprehensive playground. Minigolf. During school holidays these facilities are extensively used by local children and can therefore be fairly busy and lively.

Open

16 March - 31 October.

At a glance

Welcome & Ambience	✓✓✓	Location	✓✓✓✓✓
Quality of Pitches	✓✓✓	Range of Facilities	✓✓✓✓

Directions

Site is southeast of the city centre. From N336 (Lille) at roundabout by the Lille Gate, turn left on Picanolaan and take first right into Leopold III laan. Jeugdstadion entrance is on the right. Use roadside parking spaces and book in at 'Kantine' (08.00-19.00 hrs) on left inside gates. The vehicle access is at the rear of the site, signed from Steverlyncklaan (2nd left off Picanolaan), but reception will give you a map and a barrier key. Alternatively go straight to the vehicle gate and walk through the site to book in (easier for large units). Signposting around the city is difficult to follow.

Charges guide

Per person	€ 3,00
child (6-12 yrs)	€ 1,50
caravan pitch incl. electricity	€ 4,50
tent	€ 1,50
dog	€ 1,00

Reservations

Write to site for details. Tel: 057 21 72 82.
E-mail: info@jeugdstadion.be

BE0600 Camping Groeneveld

Groeneveldreef, Bachte-Maria-Leerne, B-9800 Deinze (East Flanders)

Quiet and clean is how Rene Kuys describes his campsite. Groeneveld is a traditional site in a small village within easy reach of Gent. It has a friendly atmosphere and is also open over a long season. Although this site has 108 pitches, there are a fair number of seasonal units, leaving around 50 large tourist pitches with electricity (8A). Hedges and borders divide the grassy area, access roads are gravel and there is an area for tents. Family entertainment and activities organised in high season include themed, musical evenings, barbecues, petanque matches, etc. The village of Bachte-Maria-Leerne has a butcher, general store, café and bar, chemist, two restaurants, baker, plus a newsagent and tabac. The site has produced a location map of these for guests. The city of Gent is just 15 kilometres north of the site and five kilometres to the south is the pleasant town of Deinze.

Facilities

Two clean sanitary units of differing age and design provide British style WCs, washbasins and free hot showers. Motorcaravan services. Bar/café (July/Aug. and weekends) with a good range of snacks, and a comprehensive range of speciality and local beers. Small coarse fishing lake. Floodlit petanque court. Adventure style play area. TV room.
Off site: Shops and restaurants nearby. Golf 3 km. Swimming pool 5 km. Kayaking 5 km.

Open

26 March - 12 November.

At a glance

Welcome & Ambience	✓✓✓✓✓	Location	✓✓✓✓
Quality of Pitches	✓✓✓✓✓	Range of Facilities	✓✓✓✓

Directions

From A10 (E40) exit 13, turn south on N466. After 3 km. continue straight on at roundabout and site is on left on entering village (opposite a large factory). Note: yellow signs are very small.

Charges guide

Per unit incl. electricity	€ 13,60 - € 17,40
hikers (2 persons and tent)	€ 2,50 - € 3,00
dog	free

No credit cards.

Reservations

Write to site. Tel: 093 80 10 14.
E-mail: info@campinggroeneveld.be

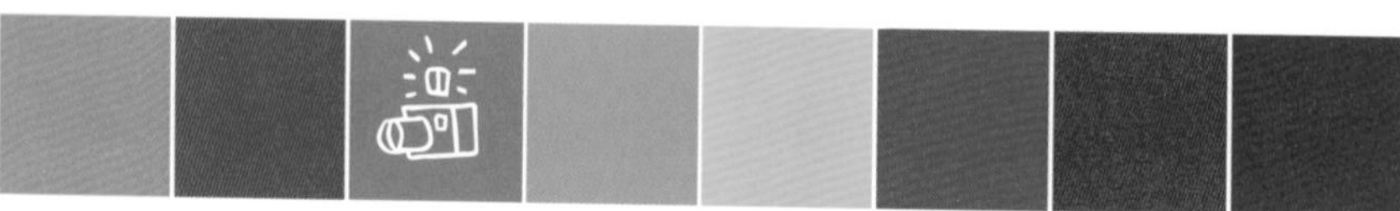

BE0590 Camping De Gavers

Onkerzelestraat 280, B-9500 Geraardsbergen (East Flanders)

Domein de Gavers is a modern, well organised holiday site in a peaceful location. It is adjacent to a large sports complex, located about five kilometres outside Geraardsbergen. It can be a busy site in season. There is good security and a card operated barrier. Most of the 448 grassy, level pitches are taken by seasonal units but about 80 are left for tourists. Pitches are arranged on either side of surfaced access roads with some hedges and few trees to provide shade in parts, with electricity (5/10A) available to most. The site offers an extensive range of sporting activities (see below) and a full entertainment programme over a long season.

Facilities

Six modern, heated and well equipped sanitary buildings provide hot showers on payment (€ 0.50). Modern rooms for disabled people and babies. Launderette. Motorcaravan services. Shop (July/Aug). Cafeteria, restaurant, bars and takeaway (daily April - Sept, otherwise weekends). Excellent playground. Tennis. Volleyball. Basketball. Mini-football. Boules. 'Midget' golf. Fishing. Canoes, windsurfers, pedaloes, yachts and row boats for hire. Bicycle hire. Tourist train. Swimming pool should be ready for 2003. Swimming and beach area. Climbing. Off site: Outdoor pool, bars and restaurants within 1.5 km.

Open

All year.

At a glance

Welcome & Ambience	✓✓✓✓	Location	✓✓✓✓
Quality of Pitches	✓✓✓✓	Range of Facilities	✓✓✓✓✓

Directions

From E429/A8 exit 26 towards Edingen, take N255 and N495 to Geraardsbergen. Down a steep hill, then left at camp sign towards Onkerzele, through village and turn north to site. From E40/A10, exit at junction 17 on to N42, turn left on to N495 and follow instructions as above.

Charges guide

Per caravan or motorcaravan incl. electricity	€ 9,00 - € 18,00
tent incl. 2 persons	€ 9,00
dog	free

Discounts of 5-30% for longer stays.

Reservations

Write or fax for details. Tel: 054 41 63 24.
E-mail: gavers@oost-vlaanderen.be

BE0620 Camping Roosendael

Schriekenstraat 27A, B-9290 Berlare-Overmere (East Flanders)

This new site with many mobile homes is of top quality and is located in a very special area. Less than 250 m. away is Donkmeer, the site of Belgium's finest group of lakes, offering all types of watersports including fishing, with attractive bars and cafés at which to sit and watch the world go by. The site is on the outskirts of the busy village of Berlare-Overmere which has a shop. It is a neat, well laid out site with 80 piches in total (30 for touring units) connected by paved roads. All the pitches are fully serviced with electricity (10A), cable, water and waste water (hence the small toilet block). They are level and quite large with some shade near hedges or trees. The warden is extremely helpful with lots of local knowledge and he will provide visitors with maps for walking and cycling.

Facilities

The small, yet superb, toilet block has spacious shower rooms (€ 0.25 per minute) and good en-suite facilities for disabled visitors. All was very clean and tidy. Washing machines and dryers. Family room. Small play area for under fives. Play field. Boules. Barbecues are not permitted.
Off site: Watersports at lake 500 m.

Open

All year.

At a glance

Welcome & Ambience	✓✓✓✓✓	Location	✓✓✓✓✓
Quality of Pitches	✓✓✓✓✓	Range of Facilities	✓✓✓✓

Directions

From E17 Gent - Antwerp take exit 11 for Overmere. Take E445 signed Zele and after 6 km. turn right for Donkmeer (turn is on right just past supermarket and garage). Go through village past the lakes. At a right hand bend you will see the Café De-Kalvaar on the left - turn left and site is at end of Kapellebergstraat.

Charges guide

Per unit all inclusive € 16,00

Reservations

Made with deposit (€ 14.30). Tel: 093 67 87 42.

BE0630 Camping Grimbergen

Veldkantsraat 64, B-1850 Grimbergen (Brabant)

A popular little municipal site with a friendly atmosphere, Camping Grimbergen has 90 pitches on fairly level grass, of which around 50 have electricity (10A). The municipal sports facilities are adjacent and the site is well placed for visiting Brussels. The bus station is by the traffic lights at the junction of N202 and N211 and buses run into the city centre every 15 minutes. In Grimbergen itself visit Norbertine Abbey, St Servaas church, and the Sunday morning market. Also worth a visit are the nearby towns of Lier and Mechelen, and the botanical gardens at Meise. The site is not really suitable for large units.

Facilities

Older style sanitary facilities are acceptable, but not luxurious, and cleaning can be variable at times. They can be heated in colder months. Three dishwashing sinks under cover. Separate facilities for disabled people. Motorcaravan services. Adventure playground. Off site: Fishing 800 m.

Open

1 April - 31 October.

At a glance

Welcome & Ambience	✓✓✓✓	Location	✓✓✓
Quality of Pitches	✓✓✓	Range of Facilities	✓✓✓

Directions

From Brussels ring road take exit 7 (N202) to Grimbergen for about 2.5 km, turn right at traffic lights on N211 towards Vilvoorde (site signed), then left at second lights to site on right in approx. 500 m.

Charges 2005

Per person	€ 4,00
child (under 12 yrs)	€ 1,00
pitch incl. car	€ 3,00
electricity	€ 2,00

No credit cards.

Reservations

Contact site. Tel: 0479 76 03 78.
E-mail: camping.grimbergen@pandora.be

BE0640 Camping Druivenland

Nijvelsebaan 80, B-3090 Overijse (Brabant)

This small, peaceful site is within easy reach of Brussels and also close to 25,000 hectares of woodland where you can enjoy some of the best Belgian countryside by foot or by cycle. Neat and mature, the site is well looked after and family run. It has a large open touring field or further pitches available in the sheltered area of the static park. The pitches are slightly sloping but almost all have views over the countryside – in total there are 150 pitches, with 80 for touring units and 80 electricity connections (8A). This is a very pleasant relaxing site at which to stay and tour this part of Belgium.

Facilities

Fully equipped toilet block with some washbasins in cabins and toilets for children. Well laid out provision for disabled visitors (shower room and toilet/washroom). Dishwashing sinks (€ 1). Laundry sinks, washing machine and dryer. Limited shop with some fresh food. Table tennis. Boules.

Open

1 April - 30 September.

At a glance

Welcome & Ambience	✓✓✓✓✓	Location	✓✓✓✓
Quality of Pitches	✓✓✓✓	Range of Facilities	✓✓✓

Directions

From E411 Brussels - Namur road take exit 3 to Overijse (not exit 2). After 1 km turn right signed Tombeek, Waver and Terlanen. Site is 1 km. on right (it is quite a long walk from the barrier to reception).

Charges guide

Per unit incl. 2 persons and electricity	€ 14,50 - € 17,00
extra person	€ 1,25

Reservations

Contact site. Tel: 02 687.93.68.
E-mail: camping.druivenland@pandora.be

BE0750 Camping de Molen

Thonetlaan, B-2050 Antwerp (Antwerp)

This is a convenient municipal site located on the bank of the River Schelde opposite the city centre. It is possible to walk into the heart of this ancient and interesting city (the tunnel is approx. two kilometres from the campsite, and is about 500 m. long), although cycling may be a better option. The site is fairly level with tarmac roads, and has 77 pitches (20 seasonal units, leaving 55 for tourists), most with access to 10A electricity hook-ups. You will need the adapter cable (deposit payable) as the electric hook-ups are not like any you have seen before, and some long leads may be necessary. Antwerp's ancient city centre and the diamond district are well worth a visit.

Facilities

Basic toilet facilities, clean when visited, could be hard pressed at times, especially when everyone returns from a hard day's sightseeing. Basic facilities for disabled persons. Dishwashing and laundry sinks under cover. Overall the facilities are quite acceptable given the very modest campsite fees. Double axle caravans are not admitted.
Off site: Shops, hot food, bar and outdoor pool near.

Open

April - September.

At a glance

Welcome & Ambience	✓✓✓✓	Location	✓✓✓✓✓
Quality of Pitches	✓✓✓✓	Range of Facilities	✓✓

Directions

From the north follow ringroad around Antwerp through the Kennedy tunnel and keep right to 'Linkeroever'. Turn right at Esso petrol station, then left at first traffic lights. Turn left at St Annastrandens tunnel on the 'Thonetlaan'. Site is on right after 2 km.

Charges 2004

Per person	€ 2,50
child (3-11 yrs)	€ 1,00
pitch	€ 1,25
car	€ 1,00
electricity	€ 1,25

Reservations

Not possible. Tel: 03 219 8179.
E-mail: harry.bastin@cs.antwerpen.be

BE0655 Camping De Lilse Bergen

Strandweg 6, Gierle, B-2275 Lille (Antwerp)

This attractive, quietly located holiday site has 503 shady pitches, of which 241 all with electricity (10A) are for touring units. Set on sandy soil among pine trees and rhododendrons and arranged around a large lake, the site has a Mediterranean feel. It is well fenced, with a night guard and comprehensive, well labelled, fire fighting equipment. Cars are parked away from units. The site is really child-friendly with each access road labelled with a different animal symbol to enable children to find their own unit easily. The lake has marked swimming and diving areas (adult), a sandy beach, an area for watersports, plus a separate childrens pool complex (depth 60 cm.) with a most imaginative playground. There are lifeguards and the water meets 'Blue Flag' standards. A new building by the lake houses changing rooms, extra toilets and showers and a baby room. There are picnic areas and lakeside or woodland walks. An entertainment programme is organised in high season.

Facilities

Four of the six main toilet blocks have been fully refitted to a good standard and can be heated. Some washbasins in cubicles and good hot showers (on payment). Well equipped baby rooms. Facilities for disabled campers. Laundry and dishwashing rooms. Barrier 'keys' can be charged up with credit units for operating showers, washing machine etc. First aid post. Recycling centre. Drive-over motorcaravan service point. Restaurant (all year, weekends only in winter), takeaway and well stocked shop (Easter - 31/9; weekends only outside July/Aug). Fishing. Tennis. Table tennis. Minigolf. Boules. Multicourt. Volleyball. Climbing wall. Playground, trampolines and skateboard ramp. Pedaloes, windsurfers, lifejackets & bicycles for hire. Childrens electric cars and pedal Kart tracks (charged for).
Off site: Golf 1 km. Riding 1 km.

At a glance

Welcome & Ambience	✓✓✓✓	Location	✓✓✓✓
Quality of Pitches	✓✓✓	Range of Facilities	✓✓✓✓

Directions

From E34 Antwerp-Eindhoven take exit 22, turn towards Beerse, and almost immediately turn second left by car park (avoiding motorway slip road), and follow forest road to site entrance.

Charges 2004

Per unit incl. electricity (10A)	€ 11,00 - € 21,00
dog	€ 3,00

Reservations

Contact site. Tel: 014 55 79 01.
E-mail: info@lilsebergen.be

Open

All year.

BE0660 Camping Baalse Hei

Roodhuisstraat 10, B-2300 Turnhout (Antwerp)

The 'Campine' is an area covering three-quarters of the Province of Antwerp, noted for its nature reserves, pine forests, meadows and streams and is ideal for walking and cycling, while Turnhout itself is an interesting old town. Baalse Hei is a long-established friendly site with 454 pitches. A separate touring area of 61 large pitches (all with 16A electricity and TV connections and shared water point) on a large grass field has been thoughtfully developed with young trees and bushes planted. Cars are parked away from the pitches. Large motorhomes can be accommodated although it is advisable to telephone in advance. It is 100 m. from the edge of the field to the modern, heated, sanitary building. There is a small lake for swimming with a beach, a boating lake and a large fishing lake (on payment). Entertainment and activities are organised July/Aug. Walk in the woods and you will undoubtedly come across some of the many red squirrels or take the pleasant 1.5 km. riverside walk to the next village. Arrival after 4 pm. departure by 10 am.

Facilities

The toilet block provides hot showers on payment (€ 0.50), some washbasins in cabins and facilities for disabled visitors. Dishwashing facilities (hot water € 0.12), Launderette. Motorcaravan services. Café/restaurant (daily 1/6-30/9, w/ends only other times, closed 16/11-25/1). Breakfast served in high season. Shop (all year). Club/TV room. Lake swimming. Fishing. Two tennis courts. Table tennis. Boules. Volleyball. Basketball. Football. Adventure play area. Bicycle hire. Off site: Riding or golf 1.5 km.

Open

16 January - 15 December

At a glance

Welcome & Ambience	✓✓✓✓✓	Location	✓✓✓✓
Quality of Pitches	✓✓✓✓✓	Range of Facilities	✓✓✓✓✓

Directions

Site is northeast of Turnhout off the N119. Approaching from Antwerp on E34/A12 go onto Turnhout ring road to the end (not a complete ring) and turn right. There is a small site sign to right in 1.5 km. then country lane.

Charges 2005

Per unit all inclusive	€ 15,00 - € 19,00
2 cyclists and tent	€ 10,00 - € 13,00
electricity	€ 1,00
dog	€ 1,25

No credit cards.

Reservations

Contact site. Tel: 014 44 84 70.
E-mail: info@baalsehei.be

BE0800 Camping Zilverstrand

Kiezelweg 17, B-2400 Mol (Antwerp)

Zilverstrand offers something for everyone: a holiday environment for all age groups, with nothing lacking for the discerning holidaymaker. The main attraction is a 'subtropical' pool complex with a central swirl-pool, two shallow pools for toddlers, long water flume, jacuzzi and sunbeds (cheaper to campers). There is provision for wheelchair users. An ultra-modern tavern, restaurant and snack bar overlook the lake with its beach. Another two lakes cater for fishermen. There are two sand-based play areas for small children and one among the trees with adventure equipment for older children. Furthermore there is an extensive entertainment programme in July and August. Camping facilities are equally as good. Of the 100 touring pitches, all with fresh water tap, waste water disposal and electricity connection, 13 are set aside for motorcaravans. These pitches are huge and each have a tarmac area suitable for the drive wheels during inclement weather.

Facilities

A single modern sanitary block includes an excellent children's room (bath in the shape of a car, 3 raised showers, child-size toilets, baby changing station), and 2 family suites suitable for visitors with disabilities. Further toilet facilities in the pool complex. Restaurant, bar, tavern and takeaway. Supermarket. Play areas including a new play area for 5-12 year olds. Boules, volleyball, football. Lakes for fishing. Lake with beach area and slide.
Off site: Bicycle hire and golf 0.5 km. Riding 5 km. Supermarket 7 km. Abbey and zoo 7 km. Walking and cycling routes (maps from reception).

At a glance

Welcome & Ambience	✓✓✓✓✓	Location	✓✓✓✓✓
Quality of Pitches	✓✓✓✓	Range of Facilities	✓✓✓✓✓

Directions

From Antwerp, take E313 and exit at junction 23. Take N71 to Mol (towards Lommel), turn left onto N712 signed Kielzelweg and Zilverstrand is on the left.

Charges 2004

Per person	€ 3,00
child (under 11 yrs)	€ 1,00
pitch	€ 12,50 - € 18,00
dog	€ 1,25

Reservations

Min. 7 nights (Sat. - Sat.) in July/Aug.
Tel: 014 81 00 98.
E-mail: zilverstrand.bvba@pandora.be

Open

1 March - 1 November.

BE0780 Family Camping Wilhelm Tell

Hoeverweg 87, B-3660 Opglabbeek (Limburg)

The Limburg region is a relaxing area with much to do, including shopping or touring the historic towns with a very enjoyable choice of food and drink! Wilhelm Tell is a family run site that caters particularly well for children with its indoor and outdoor pools and lots of entertainment on offer throughout the season. The entertainment team are very active. There is a total of 128 pitches with 70 available for touring units, some separated, others on open fields. There are 60 electricity connections (10A) and, for winter use, 20 hardstandings. The super bar/restaurant has access for wheelchair users. M. Lode Nulmans has a very special attitude towards his customers and tries to ensure they leave satisfied and want to return. For example, in his restaurant he says 'it serves until you are full'.

Facilities

Toilet facilities are adequate. Extra facilities around the pool supplement at busy times. Baby room in reception area. Two excellent modern en-suite units for disabled visitors. Two dishwashing and two laundry sinks. Washing machine and dryer. Motorcaravan service point. Fridge hire. Bar/restaurant and snack bar (times vary acc. to season). Swimming pools (well supervised), the outdoor pool with slide and wave machine. Play area. Table tennis.

Open

All year.

At a glance

Welcome & Ambience	✓✓✓✓	Location	✓✓✓✓
Quality of Pitches	✓✓✓✓	Range of Facilities	✓✓✓✓

Directions

From E314 take exit 32 'Maaseik' and follow 730 road towards As. From As follow signs to Opglabbeek. In Opglabbeek take first right (Weg van Niel) and then first left (Kasterstraat) to site.

Charges 2004

Per person	€ 6,00
child	€ 3,00
pitch	€ 13,00
electricity per k/w	€ 0,25
dog	€ 4,00

Less 30% in low season.

Reservations

Necessary for high season. Tel: 089 85 44 44. E-mail: receptie@wilhelmtell.com

BE0740 Camping L'Eau Rouge

Cheneux 25, B-4970 Stavelot (Liège)

A popular, lively and attractively situated site, L'Eau Rouge is in a sheltered valley close to Spa and the Grand Prix circuit. There are 140 grassy pitches of 110 sq.m. on sloping ground either side of a central road (speed bumps) - 70 are taken by permanent units and 70 for tourists. The main building houses the busy reception, shop, café, bar and the main sanitary facilities. There are plenty of sporting activities in the area including skiing and luge in winter. The site is close to the motor race circuit at Spa Francorchamps and is within walking distance for the fit. The site's Dutch owners are not only embarking on a five year programme upgrading the infrastructure, but also have other ideas in the pipeline.

Facilities

There is a main block but a smaller unit serves the touring area. It includes good numbers of British WCs, mostly open washbasins, but rather fewer hot showers (free) - which could be stretched at times. Additional facilities should be available in the near future. Dishwashing and laundry sinks. Shop. Baker calls daily at 9.30 am. in season. Café. Bar. Football. Boules. Table tennis. Archery (free lessons in high season). Barbecues. Playground. Entertainment in season. Off site: Bicycle hire 6 km. Riding 10 km. Spa Francorchamps motor racing circuit.

At a glance

Welcome & Ambience	✓✓✓✓	Location	✓✓✓✓
Quality of Pitches	✓✓✓✓	Range of Facilities	✓✓✓

Directions

From E42 take exit 11 (Malmedy) in the direction of Stavelot. Site is signed.

Charges 2004

Per person	€ 2,25
child (4-12 yrs)	€ 2,00
pitch	€ 10,00
electricity (10A)	€ 2,00

Reservations

Write to site. Tel: 080 86 30 75. E-mail: info@camping-leaurouge.be

Open

All year.

BE0735 Camping Petite Suisse

Al Bounire 27, 6960 Dochamps

A member of the same group as Parc de la Clusure (BE0670) this site has been recommended to us and we plan to conduct a full inspection in 2005. Attractively located within the Ardennes, the site is an ideal base for walking and cycling holidays. Pitches are terraced and grassy, mostly of a good size and all with electrical connections. Many have panoramic views and some also have satellite TV connections. The site organises a varied activity programme, including archery and walking trips. Mobile homes and chalets for rent.

Facilities

Heated toilet block. Restaurant, bar and takeaway meals. Shop. Swimming pool, paddling pool and water slide. Tennis. Archery. Children's playground and club. Entertainment programme in high season. Off site: La Roche en Ardennes 10 km. Baraque de Fraiture (ski resort) 10 km. Golf 20 km.

Open

All year.

Directions

From La Roche take the N89 to Samrée. Here, take the N541 towrds Dochamps and the site can be found on the left after 600 m.

Charges 2004

Per unit incl. 2 persons and electricity (6A)	€ 17,50 - € 22,00
extra person	€ 4,00 - € 4,50
child (under 4 years)	free

Reservations

Advised for high season; contact site.
Tel: 084 444 030. E-mail : info@petitesuisse.be

BE0730 Camping Moulin de Malempré

1 Malempre, B-6960 Manhay (Luxembourg)

This pleasant countryside site, very close to the E25, is well worth a visit and the Dutch owners will make you very welcome. The reception building houses the office and a small shop, above which is an attractive bar and restaurant with open fireplace. The 140 marked tourist pitches are separated by small shrubs and gravel roads on sloping terrain. All have electricity (10A), 40 have water and drainage as well and the site is well lit. The star of this site is the main sanitary unit, an ultra modern, two storey Scandinavian style building; this is complemented by a unisex unit. There is a little traffic noise from the nearby E25 (not too intrusive). English is spoken.

Facilities

Modern toilet facilities include some washbasins in cubicles and family bathrooms on payment. The unisex unit can be heated and has a family shower room. Unit for disabled people with automatic taps, hoists and rails. Baby room. Dishwashing sinks and laundry. Motorcaravan services. Shop for basic provisions only (1/7-15/9). Baker calls daily 08.30 - 09.15. Restaurant (1/7-15/9 and weekends). Bar (1/7-15/9 and weekends). Heated swimming pool and children's pools (one with mushroom fountain (15/5-15/9). TV. Table tennis. Pool table. Boules. Playground and trampoline. Off site: Bicycle hire 3 km. Riding 6 km. Fishing 10 km. Places to visit include the Hotton Grottoes, one of the prettiest Belgian caves (open daily Apr-Oct).

At a glance

Welcome & Ambience	✓✓✓✓✓	Location	✓✓✓✓
Quality of Pitches	✓✓✓✓	Range of Facilities	✓✓✓✓

Directions

From E25/A26 (Liege-Bastogne) exit 49, turn towards Lierneux on N822, follow signs to Malempré and site.

Charges 2005

Per unit incl. 2 persons	€ 17,00
extra adult	€ 4,00
child (3-11 yrs)	€ 2,75
electricity	€ 2,50
dog	€ 2,50

Less 20% in low season.

Reservations

Made with deposit of half the total fees - contact site.
Tel: 086 45 55 04.
E-mail: camping.malempre@cybernet.be

Open

22 March - 31 October.

BE0670 Camping Parc La Clusure

Chemin de la Clusure 30, B-6927 Bure-Tellin (Luxembourg)

Set in a river valley in the lovely wooded uplands of the Ardennes, known as the L'Homme Valley touring area, La Clusure has 425 large marked, grassy pitches (350 for touring units). All have access to electricity (16A), cable TV and water taps and are mostly in avenues off a central, tarmac road. It's a busy site that could feel crowded during the high season. There is a very pleasant, well lit riverside walk (the river is shallow in summer and popular for children to play in), a heated swimming pool and children's pool with pool-side bar/terrace. The site is used by a tour operator (number of pitches varies). The nearby main Brussels - Luxembourg railway line is due to be re-routed. The famous Grottes of Han are nearby, also Le Club at Marche-en-Famenne - a centre for karting, quad biking, jet-ski, paintball and bowling. Those preferring quieter entertainment might enjoy the Topiary Park at Durbuy.

Facilities

Four sanitary units (one heated in winter) include some washbasins in cubicles facilities for babies and family bathrooms. Dishwashing and laundry facilities may be stretched at times. Motorcaravan services. Well stocked shop, bar, restaurant, snack bar and takeaway (all 25/3-2/11). Bicycle hire. Tennis. Badminton. Volleyball. Swimming pools (29/4-11/9). New playgrounds. Organised activity programme includes courses in canoeing, mountain biking and climbing (July/Aug). Fishing (licence essential). Barrier card deposit (€ 20). Off site: Riding 7 km. Golf 25 km.

At a glance

Welcome & Ambience	✓✓✓✓	Location	✓✓✓✓
Quality of Pitches	✓✓✓✓	Range of Facilities	✓✓✓✓✓

Directions

Site is signed north off the N803 Rochefort - St Hubert road at Bure, 8 km. southeast of Rochefort with a narrow, steepish, winding descent to site.

Charges 2005

Per pitch incl. 2 persons	€ 22,00
extra person	€ 4,50
electricity (16A)	€ 3,00

Reservations

Advisable for Easter, Whitsun and for July - mid-Aug. Made with deposit and fee (€ 17.50). Tel: 084 360 050. E-mail: info@parclaclusure.be

Open

All year.

BE0720 Camping Tonny

Tonny 35, B-6680 Amberloup (Luxembourg)

With a friendly atmosphere, this family campsite is in pleasant valley by the River Ourthe. It is an attractive small site with 75 grassy touring pitches, with wooden chalet buildings giving a Tyrolean feel. The pitches (80-100 sq.m.) are separated by small shrubs and fir trees and electricity (4/6A) is available. Cars are parked away from the units and there is a separate meadow for tents. Surrounded by natural woodland, Camping Tonny is an ideal base for outdoor activites. The main chalet has a café/bar and open fireplace, with a nice shady terrace for relaxing outside and is open all year (according to demand). Nearby St Hubert has a Basilica, the St Michel Furnace Industrial Museum and a wildlife park, with wild boar, deer and other native species - all worth a visit.

Facilities

Two fully equipped sanitary units (both heated in cool weather) include dishwashing and laundry sinks (all hot water is on payment). Baby changing area and laundry. Freezer for campers use. Small shop. Cafe/bar. TV lounge and library. Sports field. Boules. Games room. Playgrounds. Skittle alley. Bicycle hire. Fishing. Canoeing. Cross country skiing.

Open

15 February - 15 November.

At a glance

Welcome & Ambience	✓✓✓✓✓	Location	✓✓✓✓
Quality of Pitches	✓✓✓✓	Range of Facilities	✓✓✓✓

Directions

From N4 take exit for Libramont (N826), then to Amberloup (4 km.) where site is signed.

Charges guide

Per person	€ 3,50
pitch	€ 8,00
electricity (4A)	€ 1,60
dog	€ 2,00

Off season discounts for over 55s and longer stays.

Reservations

Essential for high season; contact site. Tel: 061 68 82 85. E-mail: camping.tonny@belgacom.net

BE0770 Camping Le Vieux Moulin

Petite Strument 62, B-6980 La Roche-en-Ardenne (Luxembourg)

Located in one of the most beautiful valleys in the heart of the Ardennes, Le Vieux Moulin has 187 pitches and, although there are 127 long stay units at the far end of the site, the 60 tourist pitches do have their own space. Some are separated by hedges, others for tents and smaller units are more open, all are on grass, and there are 50 electric hook-ups (6A). The 19th century water mill has been owned and operated by the owner's family for many years, but has now been converted into a small hotel and a fascinating mill museum (visits with an audio guide in English). La Roche is a pretty little town in an unspoiled area, a very scenic region of rolling tree-clad hills and small deep valleys, with rocks for climbing, castles to explore and rivers to fish.

Facilities

A newly constructed, centrally located toilet block is between the tourist and long stay areas. It can be heated in cool weather and provides washbasins in cubicles and controllable hot showers on payment. Dishwashing and laundry sinks with washing machine. No facilities for disabled persons. A further older unit is at the end of the mill building. Restaurant and bar with hotel (8 rooms). Mill museum. Off site: Town facilities 800 m.

At a glance

Welcome & Ambience	✓✓✓✓✓	Location	✓✓✓✓✓
Quality of Pitches	✓✓✓✓	Range of Facilities	✓✓✓

Directions

From town centre take N89 south towards St Hubert, turning right towards Hives where site is signed. Site is 800 m. from the town centre.

Charges guide

Per person	€ 2,50
child (under 5 yrs)	free
pitch	€ 7,50

Reservations

Advisable for high season, contact site.
Tel: 084 411 380. E-mail: strument@skynet.be

Open

1 April - 11 November.

BE0725 Camping Le Val de L'Aisne

Rue du T.T.A., 6997 Blier-Erezee (Luxembourg)

This site has been recommended by a reader and we hope to conduct a full inspection in 2005. Camping Le Val de l'Aisne is a lakeside site at the heart of the Ardennes and forms part of a leisure complex which also includes a restaurant and a number of gites. The pitches are large and grassy, many with attractive views over the lake towards the Chateau de Blier. All the pitches are equipped with 10 amp electricity, some also with water and drainage. A range of activities are available here, notably mountain biking, hiking, fishing tournaments, pot-holing and various watersports. Mobile homes and gites for rent.

Facilities

Facilities: Lakeside beach, canoes, pedaloes, tennis, restaurant, café, adventure park, cycle hire, fishing, children's playground, children's club, entertainment /activity programme in high season. Off site: Riding, cycle and walking trails in the Ardennes woods.

Open

All year.

Reservations

Contact site. Recommended for high season.
Tel: 086 47 00 67. E-mail: info@levaldelaisne.be

Directions

Take the E411 from Brussles towards Namur-Arlon. Leave at exit 18 (Courrière), then follow the N4 to Marche-en-Famenne. Continue to Hotton, crossing the bridge over the Ourthe, and then following signs to Soy et Erezée. Follow this road for around 9km until you reach a roundabout. Here, follow signs to La Roche and you will find the site on your left after 900m.

Charges 2005

Pitch (inc. 2 persons)	€ 18,00
extra adult	€ 3,00
child (under 3 years)	free
electricity (10A)	€ 3,00

Reductions in low season.

BE0530 Camping du Waux-Hall

Avenue Saint-Pierre 17, B-7000 Mons (Hainault)

Waux-Hall is a useful and convenient site for a longer look at historic Mons and the surrounding area. It is a well laid out municipal site, close to the town centre and E42 motorway. The 75 pitches, most with electricity (10A), are arranged on either side of an oval road, on grass and divided by beds of small shrubs; the landscape maintenance is excellent. A large public park with refreshment bar, tennis, a children's playground and lake is adjacent, with direct access from the site when the gate is unlocked. Places to visit include the house of Van Gogh, the Fine Arts Museum, Decorative Arts Museum and the Collegiate church.

Facilities

A single, heated toilet block is of older style, basic but clean, with most washbasins in cubicles for ladies. Washing machine and dryer. Dishwashing and laundry sinks under cover. Soft drinks machine, ice cream. Bicycle hire. Tennis. Playground. Off site: Public park adjacent. Town centre shops and restaurants within easy walking distance. Fishing 300 m. Riding 2 km. Golf 4 km.

Open

All year.

At a glance

Welcome & Ambience	✓✓✓✓	Location	✓✓✓✓
Quality of Pitches	✓✓✓✓✓	Range of Facilities	✓✓✓✓

Directions

From Mons inner ring road, follow signs for Charleroi, La Louviere, Binche, Beaumont. When turning off ring road, keep to right hand lane, turning for site is immediately first right. (signed Waux-Hall and camping).

Charges 2004

Per person	€ 3,35
child	€ 2,15
pitch incl. 2 nights electricity	€ 5,25 - € 6,15
car	€ 0,90
electricity more than 2 nights (10A) per k/w	€ 0,15

No credit cards.

Reservations

Write or phone for details. Tel: 065 33 79 23. E-mail: ot1@ville.mons.be

BE0710 Camping Colline de Rabais

Rue de Bonlieu, B-6760 Virton (Luxembourg)

Colline de Rabais is a large site with an unusual lay-out. This consists of a circular road with smaller roads leading to circular pads with wedge shaped pitches. In a hill top setting, the site is surrounded by forest. A large sports complex is a walk away at the bottom of the hill offering tennis, fishing and much more. The forest is open to walkers and cyclists alike - you can go for ages without seeing another person. The present Dutch owners took over in 1997 and are slowly revamping the site. Various activities are organised throughout the season. There are around 250 pitches for touring units, all with 16A electricity (some long leads needed), plus 43 mobile homes and bungalows for rent and 22 tour operator tents. Site lighting is poor - a torch is recommended.

Facilities

Three toilet blocks including one which has been modernised with shower/washbasin cubicles and an en-suite room for disabled people. Cleaning and maintenance can be variable and not all blocks are open in low season. Laundry sinks, washing machines and dryers. Motorcaravan service point. Bar/restaurant and shop (opening times vary). Small outdoor swimming pool with wood decking for sunbathing. Bicycle hire. Off site: Fishing 1 km. Riding 3 km.

Open

All year.

At a glance

Welcome & Ambience	✓✓✓	Location	✓✓✓✓
Quality of Pitches	✓✓✓	Range of Facilities	✓✓✓

Directions

From E25/E411 take exit 29 towards Etalle and Virton. Follow signs for Vallée de Rabais. Turn right at sports complex. At crossroads (with phone box) turn right and uphill to site at end of road.

Charges 2004

Per unit incl. 2 persons	€ 19,50
extra person (over 3 yrs)	€ 4,50
electricity	€ 3,00
dog	€ 5,00

Reservations

Necessary for high season. Tel: 063 57 11 95. E-mail: info@campingvalleederabais.be

BE0680 Camping Sud S.p.r.l.

Voie de la Liberté 75, B-6717 Attert (Luxembourg)

This is a pleasant family run site which would make a good base for a short stay and is also well sited for use as an overnight halt. The 86 touring pitches are on level grass with 6A electricity hook-ups and are arranged around an oval loop access road. There are 11 drive-through pitches especially for one-nighters, plus four hardstandings for motorcaravans and a tent area. The far end of the site is close to the N4 and may suffer from some road noise. On-site facilities include a small restaurant/bar with takeaway facility and a shop for basics. An outdoor swimming pool (12 x 6 m) has a separate paddling pool and there is an open sports field at the far end of the site.

Facilities

A single building provides modern sanitary facilities including some washbasins in cubicles and baby areas. Showers are free in low season but are limited to one per person per day in July/August by use of a charge 'key' system. Extra showers can be purchased if required. No facilities for disabled campers. Laundry and dishwashing sinks under cover. Small bar/restaurant and takeaway (1/4 - 25/10) TV in bar. Swimming pool (May-Sept). Small playground. Children's entertainment (4-12 yrs) three afternoons per week during July/August. Off site: Attert village has two churches and a museum and the Liberation Route passes the site. Internet cafe and Roman Museum in Arlon 8 km. Local nature parks. Riding 5 km. Golf 8 km. Supermarket 5 km.

At a glance

Welcome & Ambience	✓✓✓✓	Location	✓✓✓
Quality of Pitches	✓✓✓✓	Range of Facilities	✓✓✓✓

Directions

Attert is about 8 km. north of Arlon. From N4 take Attert exit, continue east for about 1 km. to Attert village, site entrance is immediately on your left as you join the main street.

Charges 2004

Per person	€ 4,00
child (2-11 yrs)	€ 2,25
pitch	€ 8,00
electricity	€ 2,25
dog	€ 1,50

No credit cards.

Reservations

Made with deposit of 40% of total fees and booking fee of € 11.50. Tel: 063 223715. E-mail: campingsud@hotmail.com

Open

1 April - 25 October.

Once a Yugoslavian province, Croatia has thrown off old communist attitudes and blossomed into a lively and friendly place to visit. A country steeped in history, it boasts some of the finest Roman ruins in Europe and you'll find plenty of traditional coastal towns, clusters of tiny islands and mediaeval villages to explore.

The heart-shaped peninsula of Istria, located in the north, is among the most developed tourist regions in Croatia. Here you can visit the preserved Roman amphitheatre in Pula, the beautiful town of Rovinj with its cobbled streets and wooded hills, and the resort of Umag, well-known for its recreational activities, most notably tennis. Islands are studded all around the coast, making it ideal for sailing and diving enthusiasts. Istria also has the highest concentration of campsites.

Further south, in the province of Dalmatia, Split is the largest city on the Adriatic coast and home to the impressive Diolectian's Palace. From here the islands of Brac, Hvar, Vis and Korcula, renowned for their lively fishing villages and pristine beaches, are easily accessible by ferry. The old walled city of Dubrovnik is 150 km south. At over 2 km. long and 25 m. high, with 16 towers, a walk along the city walls affords spectacular views.

Population

4.7 million

Capital

Zagreb

Climate

Predominantly warm and hot in summer with temperatures of up to 40°C

Language

Croat

Currency

Kuna

Telephone

The country code is 00 385

Banks

Mon-Fri 08.00 - 19.00

Shops

Mainly Mon-Sat 08.00-20.00, although some close on Monday and Sundays

Public Holidays

New Year's day; Epiphany 6 Jan; Good Friday; Easter Monday; Labour Day 1 May; Statehood Day 30 May; Day of Anti-Fascist Victory 22 June; Thanksgiving Day 5 Aug; Assumption 15 Aug; All Saints 1 Nov; Christmas 25, 26 Dec

Motoring

Croatia is proceeding with a vast road improvement programme. There are still some roads which leave a lot to be desired but things have improved dramatically. Roads along the coast can become heavily congested in summer and queues are possible at border crossings. Tolls: some motorways, bridges and tunnels. Cars towing a caravan or trailer must carry two warning triangles. It is illegal to overtake military convoys.

Tourist Office

Croatian National Tourist Office
2 The Lanchesters
162-164 Fulham Palace Road
London W6 9ER
Tel: 0208 563 7979
Fax: 0208 563 2616
Email: info@cnto.freeserve.co.uk
Internet: www.croatia.hr

WITH ITS WARM SEAS, CRYSTAL-CLEAR WATERS AND OVER ONE THOUSAND ISLANDS TO EXPLORE, CROATIA IS AN IDEAL PLACE TO TRY SCUBA DIVING. DIVING CENTRES CAN BE FOUND AT THE LARGER RESORTS.

CR6712 Camping Stella Maris

Savudrijska cesta bb, 52470 Umag (Istria)

This extremely large, sprawling site of 4.5 hectares is split by the Umag – Savudrija road. The camping site is to the east and reception and the amazing Sol Stella Maris leisure complex where the Croatian open tennis tournament is held (amongst other competitions) is to the west. Located some 2 kilometres from the centre of Umag, the site comprises some 400 pitches of which 130 are seasonal and 20 are for tour operators. They are arranged in rows on gently sloping ground, some are shaded. Campers select their pitches and a considerable amount of walking can be involved in organising connection of electricity (10A). The site's real strength is its attachment to the leisure complex, with numerous facilities available to campers. There are two swimming pools (one sea water) and a very pretty pebble beach area where sun loungers may be hired for €1 per day. There is a huge entertainment area and the choice of seven restaurants and bars including a cocktail bar and buffet bar with great sea views at night. Boats may be launched or hired at the marina and bikes hired for some challenging tours of the area.

Facilities

Three sanitary blocks are clean but dated. Half the washbasins and all the showers have hot water. Facilities for disabled visitors in the northern block only (key from reception). Dishwashing and laundry sinks, some with hot water. Apart from the toilet blocks there is no supply of fresh water or waste water disposal facility on site. Supermarket (07.00-22.00 hrs opposite reception). Huge range of restaurants, bars and snack bars. International Tennis centre. Water sports. Fishing (permit required from Umag). Animation programme for children. Off site: 'Land train' every 15 minutes into Umag and a local bus service to towns further along the coast. Excursions organised. Golf 25 km. Riding 1 km.

Open

Easter - 15 October.

At a glance

Welcome & Ambience	✓✓✓✓	Location	✓✓✓✓✓
Quality of Pitches	✓✓✓	Range of Facilities	✓✓✓✓✓

Directions

Site is 2.5 km. north of Umag. On entering Umag look for signs on the main coast road to all campsites and follow the Stella Maris signs.

Charges 2004

Per person	€ 3,00 - € 4,70
child (5-11 yrs)	€ 1,70 - € 2,60
pitch	€ 3,80 - € 6,10
electricity	€ 2,20
dog	€ 2,00 - € 2,90

For stays less than 3 nights in high season add 10%.

Reservations

Contact site or Istraturist reservations service:
tel: 052 719 100, fax: 052 719 999.
Site tel: 052 710 900.
E-mail: camp.stella.maris@istraturist.hr

CR6715 Camping Park Ladin Gaj

Karigador bb,, 52466 Novigrad (Istria)

This extremely large site is very well planned in that just 50% of the 127 hectares is used for the pitches, thus leading to lots of open space around the pitch site and an uncluttered beach area. It is the largest of the Istraturist group of sites. The very long curved beach is of rock and shingle with grassy sunbathing areas. There are many watersports on offer which more than compensates for the lack of a pool (although there are plans for a toddlers' paddling pool). There are 1,440 pitches of varying sizes, all with electricity (10A), for tourers and 350 seasonal pitches. Shade is sparse. Two of the restaurant/bars offer excellent views over the sea and are most attractive for a romantic dinner. The site is very popular with the Dutch and a friendly and happy atmosphere is prevalent even in the busiest times. Some noise is transmitted from the road alongside the site and there is a late night disco which may disturb some campers. The ancient towns of Umag and Novigrad are close and served by buses for those who wish to explore their fascinating past. The supporting entertainment and other events including sports facilities, combined with good value for money make this a great choice for your camping holiday.

Facilities

There are 10 toilet blocks which include 2 bathrooms with deep tubs. Two blocks have children's WCs but there are currently no facilities for disabled campers. The site has plans to update these facilities. Dishwashing and laundry sinks. Fresh water and waste water points only at toilet blocks. Drive over motorcaravan service point. Range of shops and supermarket. Bar, snack bar and restaurant (musical entertainment some evenings) all open early morning to midnight (one until the small hours). Tennis. Fishing (permit from Umag). Football, minigolf, table tennis. Watersports. Off site: Riding near. Bus service to Umag and Novigrad.

Open

20 April - 1 October.

At a glance

Welcome & Ambience	✓✓✓✓✓	Location	✓✓✓✓
Quality of Pitches	✓✓✓✓	Range of Facilities	✓✓✓✓

Directions

Site is located on the Umag - Novigrad road approx. 6 km. south of Umag. Look for large signs.

Charges 2004

Per person	€ 1,90 - € 4,50
child (5-11 yrs)	€ 1,20 - € 2,40
pitch acc. to season and type	€ 5,30 - € 10,10
electricity	€ 2,20
dog	€ 2,00 - € 2,80

For stays less than 3 nights in high season add 10%.

Reservations

Contact site or Istraturist reservations service:
tel: 052 719 100, fax: 052 719 999, or site,
Site tel: 052 725 040.
E-mail: camp.ladin.gaj@istraturist.hr

CR6722 Autokamp Zelena Laguna

52440 Porec (Istria)

A busy medium sized site (by Croatian standards), Zelena Laguna (green lagoon) is very popular with families and boat owners. Part of the Plava Laguna Leisure group that has three other campsites and seven hotels in the vicinity. It is long established and is improved and modernised each year as finances permit. Within the last 10 years, amongst other things, a new pool has been built. The 1,100 pitches (540 for touring units) are a mixture of level, moderately sloping and terraced ground and range in size from 40-120 sq.m. Slopes will be encountered on the site with a quite steep hill leading to the highest point allowing impressive views over the sea. Access to the pitches is by hard surfaced roads and shingle tracks which generally allow adequate space to manoeuvre. There are plenty of electrical hook-ups (10A; some German plugs in most). 42 super pitches are very popular and in other areas there is around one water point to every four pitches. Like all others in the area, Zelena Laguna can get very crowded in late June, July and August and as it can get very hot in high summer (40 degrees Celcius), the pitches nearest the sea and therefore the sea breezes, are recommended (book ahead). The sea runs along two sides of the site and has a mostly rocky beach with blue flag status into which paved sunbathing areas have been inserted. At one end of the beach is an impressive marina where visitors may park their yachts. Approximately 25% of the beach area is reserved for naturists. There are cold open air showers on the beach and toilets are a short walk away. There are many attractions to amuse you here or ample opportunity to just chill out as it is quite peaceful.

Facilities

The sanitary blocks are good but being improved for 2005. About half the washbasins have hot water and there are free hot controllable showers in all blocks. Toilets are mostly British style and there are facilities for disabled campers. Supermarket and mini-market. Several restaurants and snack bars (from 1/5). Swimming pool. Sub-aqua diving (with instruction). Tennis (instruction available). Five-a-side football. Bicycle hire. Boat hire (motor and sailing). Boat launching. Beach volleyball. Riding. Aerobics. Animation programme for the family. Off site: Small market and parade of shops selling beach wares, souvenirs etc. immediately outside site. Regular bus service and also a small 'land train' known as the 'Bumble Zug' from the adjacent hotel complex into the centre of Porec (alternatively it is 15 minutes drive but parking tends to be somewhat chaotic) but for the adventurous a water taxi to Porec harbour. Nearest large supermarkets are in Porec (4 km). Fishing 5 km (permit required). Riding 300 m.

At a glance

Welcome & Ambience	✓✓✓✓	Location	✓✓✓✓
Quality of Pitches	✓✓✓✓	Range of Facilities	✓✓✓✓

Directions

Site is between the coast road and the sea with turning approx. 2 km. from Porec towards Vrsar. It is very well signed and is part of a large multiple hotel complex.

Charges 2004

Per person	€ 3,60 - € 6,50
child (5-12 yrs)	free - € 4,50
pitch	€ 5,40 - € 12,50
electricity	€ 2,20 - € 2,80
dog	€ 2,90 - € 5,20

Reservations

Only made for certain pitches, with fee. Contact Plava Laguna Group, Rade Koncara 12, 52440 Porec. Tel: 052 410 101. Fax: 052 410 601. E-mail: mail@plavalaguna.hr

Open

1 April - 30 September.

CR6720 Naturist Centre Ulika

Cervar, 52440 Porec (Istria)

One of the many naturist campsites in Croatia, Ulika is run by the same concern as Zelena Laguna (CR6722) and Bijela Uvala (CR6724) and offers similar facilities. The site is well located, occupying a small peninsula of some 15 hectares. This means that there is only a short walk to the sea from anywhere on the site. The ground is mostly gently sloping with a covering of rough grass and there are 388 pitches with electricity connections. One side of the site is shaded with mature trees but the other side is almost devoid of shade and could become very hot. There are many activities on site (see below) and an excellent swimming pool. The reception office opens 24 hours for help and information. Single men are not accepted. All in all, this is a pleasant, uncomplicated site which is well situated, well managed and peaceful. The site won a Blue Flag award for the cleanliness of its beaches.

Facilities

Six toilet blocks provide mostly British style WCs, washbasins (half with hot water) and showers (around a third with controllable hot water). Each block has facilities for disabled visitors. Dishwashing and laundry sinks (half with hot water). Laundry. Supermarket (seven days per week). Restaurant, pizzeria and snacks. Bicycle hire. Swimming pool. Fishing. Tennis. Table tennis. Minigolf. Water sports - water skiing, windsurfing, etc. Volleyball. Boating - marina on site Off site: Riding nearby. Porec the nearest town is 6 km. – a must to visit – a regular local bus service runs from site reception.

At a glance

Welcome & Ambience	✓✓✓✓	Location	✓✓✓✓
Quality of Pitches	✓✓✓	Range of Facilities	✓✓✓✓✓

Directions

Site is approx. 3 km. off the main Novigrad - Porec road, signed in village of Cevar.

Charges 2005

Per person	€ 2,40 - € 4,70
child (5-12 yrs)	free - € 3,27
pitch	€ 3,58 - € 6,80
pitch incl. 10A electricity	€ 4,45 - € 9,20
dog	€ 2,10 - € 3,32

Reservations

Only made for certain pitches, with € 25,56 fee. Tel: 052 436 325. E-mail: mail@plavalaguna.hr

Open

April - October.

CR6724 Camping Bijela Uvala

Bijela Uvala, Zelena Laguna, 52440 Porec (Istria)

Bijela Uvala is a large friendly campsite with an extensive range of facilities and direct sea access which makes the site very popular in high season. The topography of the site is undulating and the gravelled or grassy pitches are divided into zones which vary considerably. As the coastline winds along the site, the rocky and intermittently paved sea access is increased with boat launching facilities, beach volleyball and eateries dispersed along it. The 2000 pitches, 1476 for touring, are compact and due to the terrain some have excellent sea views and breezes, however as usual these are the most sought after so book early. They range from 60-120 sq.m. and all have electricity , 400 also have water connections. Some are formal with hedging, some are terraced and most have good shade from established trees or wooded areas. There is also very informal areas where pitches are not demarcated and generally on uneven ground. The smaller of the two pools is in a complex adjacent to the sea along with a large animation area where the active animation program can be seen and a family style restaurant. There are many sporting facilities and fair ground style amusements (at extra cost). The adjoining campsite Zelenga Laguna is owned by the same organisation and access to its beach (including naturist section) and facilities is via a gate between sites or along the beach. A large sports complex is also within walking distance. This site is very similar to Camping Zelegna Laguna with fewer permanent pitches.

Facilities

Eight sanitary blocks are clean and well equipped with mainly British style WCs. Free hot showers but no hot water for dishwashing or laundry. Washing machines. Facilities for disabled visitors. Motorcaravan service point. Gas. Fridge boxes. Two restaurants, three fast food cafes, two bars and a bakery. Large well equipped supermarket and a mini market. Two swimming pool complexes, one with a medium size pool and the other a larger lagoon style with fountains.T ennis. Beach volleyball. Playground. Amusements. TV room. Animation centre with active children's club. Minigolf. Table tennis. Football. Boat launching and harbour. Off site: Zelenga Laguna campsite facilities. Sports complex 100 m. Naturist beach 25 m.

At a glance

Welcome & Ambience	✓✓✓✓	Location	✓✓✓✓
Quality of Pitches	✓✓✓✓	Range of Facilities	✓✓✓✓

Directions

The site adjoins Zelena Laguna. From the main Porec to Vrsar coast road turn off towards coast and the town of Zelena Laguna approximately 4 km. south of Porec and follow campsite signs.

Charges 2004

Per person	€ 3,60 - € 6,50
child (5-12 yrs)	free - € 4,50
pitch	€ 5,40 - € 11,20
electricity	€ 2,20 - € 2,80
dog	€ 2,90 - € 5,20

Reservations

Made with € 25.56 fee. Contact the Plava Laguna Group. Tel: 052 410 551.
E-mail: mail@plavalaguna.hr

Open

Easter - end October.

CR6716 Lanternacamp

Lanterna, 52440 Porec (Istria)

This is one of the largest sites in Croatia with an amazing selection of activities and high standards. Reception is buzzing in high season as around 10,000 guests are on site. Set in 90 hectares with over 3 kilometres of beach, there are 3,000 pitches of which 2,600 are for touring units. Facilities at Lanterna are impressive with the whole operation running smoothly for the campers. The land is sloping in parts and terraced in others. There is a large pool and pretty bay with rocky beaches. Some of the marked and numbered pitches are shaded and they are arranged to take advantage of the topography. Pitches are 60-120 sq.m with some superb locations right on the the sea, although these tend to be taken first so it is advisable to book ahead. Some of the better pitches are in a reserved booking area. Terracing has improved the view in many areas. Electrical connections are 8A. Many activities and quality entertainment for all are available both on and off site – you are spoilt for choice here including a vast choice of places to eat. Prices tend to be higher than other sites in the area but you get value for money with the supporting facilities.

Facilities

The fourteen sanitary blocks are clean and good quality, with some private bathrooms, baby care areas, some Turkish style WCs, hot showers with some blocks providing facilities for disabled people. Three supermarkets sell most everyday requirements. Four restaurants, bars and snack bars and fast food outlets. Adult's pool and two children's swimming pools. Sand-pit and play areas, with animation for all in high season. Tennis. Table tennis. Bicycle hire. Watersports. Boats for rent. Minigolf. Riding. Dogs are restricted to a certain area. Off site: Nearest large supermarket in Novigrad, 9 km. An hourly bus service runs from the reception area. Fishing. Riding 500 m.

Open

1 April - 15 October.

At a glance

Welcome & Ambience	✓✓✓✓	Location	✓✓✓✓
Quality of Pitches	✓✓✓✓	Range of Facilities	✓✓✓✓✓

Directions

The turn to Laternacamp is well signed off the Novigrad to Porec road approximately 8 km. south of Novigrad. Continue for about 2 km. down the turn off road towards the coast and the campsite is difficult to miss on the right hand side.

Charges 2004

Per person	€ 4,05 - € 6,20
child	€ 2,90 - € 4,35
pitch incl. electricity	€ 7,00 - € 11,45
dog	€ 3,25 - € 4,45

Prices for pitches by the sea are higher.

Reservations

Not normally necessary, but will be made with € 30.68 fee (non returnable). Contact the Riviera Group: tel: 052 434 900 or 408 000; fax: 052 451 440 or 451 331. Site tel: 052 404 500. E-mail: lanternacamp@riviera.hr

CR6728 Camping Turist Vrsar

52450 Vrsar (Istria)

Part of the Riviera group, this site is very close to the fishing port of Vrsar, and there is direct access from the site. The views of the many small islands from the site are stunning and it is very relaxing to sit on the beaches and enjoy the Croatian sunshine with a beer in your hand. The site is very proud of its Blue Beach status, a safe rock pool has been made for children and a splash pool is at the base of the large flume in the beach area. This is a 30 hectare site with 833 pitches of which 593 are available to tourists. Marked and numbered, the pitches vary in size with about 90 sq.m. being the average. The ground is undulating with sandy soil, grass and some terracing. There is ample shade from mature pines and oak trees,16A electricity and 60 pitches with water and electricity. The site has no pool but a long beach area with attractive coves provide easy access for sea bathing from rock surfaces. A public area is in the centre of the beach areas but fenced off. The restaurant is excellent, with a lovely view and there is a snack bar and beach bar. The direct access to the old town of Vrsar is very popular as it gives easy access to its huge range of cafés, bars and restaurants.

Facilities

Three old and four new toilet blocks provide a mixture of British and Turkish style WCs, and washbasins and showers, not all with hot water. Some have facilities for disabled campers, private cabins and baby rooms. Dishwashing and laundry sinks, some with hot water. Restaurant/bars. Beach bars. Chemical disposal. Laundry. Supermarket (1/5-15/9). Bar/restaurant (1/5-15/9). Sports centre. Cinema. Bicycle hire. Only gas barbecues are permitted. Dogs allowed in some areas. Fishing. Off site: Golf 7 km. Riding 3 km. Excursions. Shops in Vrsar, although the nearest serious shopping centre is at Porec. Riding 3 km.

Open

22 March - 15 October.

At a glance

Welcome & Ambience	✓✓✓✓	Location	✓✓✓✓✓
Quality of Pitches	✓✓✓✓	Range of Facilities	✓✓✓✓✓

Directions

Site is on the main Porec (7 km) - Vrsar (1 km) road, well signed.

Charges 2004

Per person	€ 3,60 - € 5,65
two children free, 3rd child	€ 2,60 - € 4,55
pitch incl. 10A electricity	€ 6,20 - € 10,30
dog	€ 3,25 - € 4,45

Highest prices are for pitches by the sea.

Reservations

Contact the Riviera Group, address as site. Tel: 052 441 330. Fax: 052/441 010 or 451 440. E-mail: turist@riviera.hr

CR6725 Camping Porto Sole

Porto Sole, 52450 Vrsar (Istria)

Located near to the pretty town of Vrsar and its charming marina, Porto Sole is a large campsite with 800 pitches. The pitches vary, some are in the open with semi shade and are fairly flat, others are under a heavy canopy of pines on undulating land. There is some terracing near the small number of water frontage pitches. The site could be described as almost a clover leaf shape with one area for rental accommodation and natural woods, another for sporting facilities and the other two for pitches. There is a large water frontage and two tiny bays provide delightful sheltered rocky swimming areas. In peak season the site is buzzing with activity and the hub of the site is the pools, disco and shopping arcade area where there is also a pub and both formal and informal eating areas. The food available is varied but simple with a tiny terrace restaurant by the water.

Facilities

Five older style toilet blocks with British and Turkish style WCs were clean and well maintained. The low numbers of showers (common to most Croatian sites) result in long queues. Facilities for disabled visitors. Washing machines, dishwashing and laundry (cold water). Large well stocked supermarket. Small shopping mall. Pub. Pizzeria. Formal and informal restaurants. Swimming pools. Play area (alongside beach). Boules. Tennis. Table tennis. Minigolf. Massage studio. Disco. Animation in season. Scuba diving courses. Boat launching. Off site: Marina 1 km. Historic town of Vrsar 2 km.

At a glance

Welcome & Ambience	✓✓✓✓	Location	✓✓✓✓
Quality of Pitches	✓✓✓✓	Range of Facilities	✓✓✓✓

Directions

Follow signs towards Vrsar and take turn towards Koversada, then follow campsite signs.

Charges 2004

Per person	€ 4,40 - € 5,80
child (5-12 yrs)	free - € 3,80
pitch	€ 6,20 - € 11,60
dog	€ 3,50 - € 5,00

Reservations

Contact site. Tel: 052 441 198.
E-mail: petalon-portosole@anita.hr

Open

1 April - 1 October.

CR6730 Camping Amarin

Monsena bb, 52210 Rovinj (Istria)

Situated four kilometres from the centre of the lovely old port town of Rovinj this site has much to offer. The complex is part of Adria Resorts. It has 12.6 hectares of land and is adjacent to the Monsena bungalow complex, campers can take advantage of the facilities afforded by both areas. There are 670 pitches for touring units on various types of ground and between 80-120 sq.m. Most are separated by foliage, 10A electricity is available. A rocky beach backed by a grassy sunbathing area is very popular, but the site has its own superb, supervised round pool with corkscrew slide plus a splash pool for children. Boat owners have a mooring area and launching ramp, and a breakwater is popular with sunbathers. The port of Rovinj contains many delights, particularly if you are able to contend with the hundreds of steps which lead to the church above the town from where the views are well worth the climb.

Facilities

Thirteen toilet blocks have a mixture of British style and Turkish toilets. Half the washbasins have hot water. Some showers have hot water, the rest have cold and are outside. Some blocks have one private cabin on the female side and a unit for disabled visitors (shower, toilet and washbasin). Plenty of dishwashing and laundry sinks all with hot water. Fridge boxes for hire. Washing machines. Security boxes. Drive over motorcaravan service point (key for hose from reception). Waste bins are emptied daily using an electric powered silent vehicle. Supermarket Small market selling beach wares, and fresh fruit and vegetables. Two restaurants, taverna, pizzeria and terrace grill. Swimming pool. Flume and splash pool. Watersports. Bicycle hire. Fishing (subject to permit). Daily animation for children and adults. Barbecues are not accepted. Hairdresser. Massage. Dogs accepted. Off site: Hourly minibus service to Rovinj. Excursions from site including day trips to Venice. Riding nearby.

At a glance

Welcome & Ambience	✓✓✓✓	Location	✓✓✓✓
Quality of Pitches	✓✓✓	Range of Facilities	✓✓✓✓

Directions

Follow signs towards Rovinj and if approaching from the north turn off approximately 2kms before the town towards Monsena and Valalta. Then follow signs to Monsena and the campsite. From Rovinj continue through town towards Vrsar for 2kms and then turn off as above.

Charges 2004

Per person	€ 3,40 - € 5,40
child (5-11 yrs)	€ 1,70 - € 2,70
pitch incl. electricity	€ 5,40 - € 8,30
dog	€ 3,00

For stays less than 3 nights in high season add 10%.

Reservations

Contact site or Istraturist reservations service:
tel: 052/5280 0376, fax: 052/5281 3497.
Site tel: 052 802 000. E-mail: monsena@jadran.tdr.hr

Open

1 May - 30 September.

CR6727 Camping Valkanela

Valkanela, 52450 Vrsar (Istria)

Camping Valkanela is located in a beautiful green bay, right on the Adriatic Sea, between the villages of Vrsar and Funtana. It offers 875 pitches, all for tourers and 400 with 10A electricity. Pitches near the beach are numbered, have shade from mature trees and are slightly sloping towards the sea. Those towards the back of the site are on open fields without much shade and are not marked or numbered. Most numbered pitches have water points close by, but the back pitches have to go to the toilet blocks for water. Access roads are gravel. For those who like activity, Valkanela has four gravel tennis courts, beach volleyball and opportunities for diving, waterskiing and boat rental. There is a little marina for mooring small boats and a long rock and pebble private beach, with some grass lawns for sunbathing. It is a short stroll to the surrounding villages with their bars, restaurants and shops. There may be some noise nuisance from the disco outside the entrance.

Facilities

Fifteen toilet blocks of varying styles and ages provide toilets, open style washbasins and controllable hot showers. Child size toilets, basins and showers. Bathroom (free). Facilities for disabled visitors. Laundry with sinks and washing machines. Dishwashing under cover. Two supermarkets. Souvenir shops and newspaper kiosk. Bars and restaurants with dance floor and stage. Patisserie. Tennis. Minigolf. Fishing. Bicycle hire. Games room. Marina with boat launching. Boat and pedalo hire. Disco outside entrance. Daily animation programme for children up to 12 yrs. Excursions organised. Off site: Riding 2 km.

At a glance

Welcome & Ambience	✓✓✓✓	Location	✓✓✓✓✓
Quality of Pitches	✓✓✓	Range of Facilities	✓✓✓✓✓

Directions

Follow campsite signs from Vrsar.

Charges guide

Per person	€ 3,50 - € 5,10
child	free - € 3,60
pitch incl. electricity	€ 5,00 - € 10,30
dog	€ 2,70 - € 4,00

Reservations

Write to site in English. Tel: 052 445 216. E-mail: valkanela@anita.hr

Open

7 April - 30 September.

CR6733 Camping Vestar

52210 Rovinj (Istria)

Camping Vestar, just five kilometres from the historic harbour town of Rovinj, is one of the rare sites in Croatia with a partly sandy beach. Right behind the beach is a large area, attractively landscaped with young trees and shrubs, with grass for sunbathing. The site has 750 large pitches, of which 600 are for tourers, all with 16A electricity (the rest being taken by seasonal units and 14 pitches for tour operators). It is largely wooded with good shade and from the bottom row of pitches there are views of the sea. Pitching is on two separate fields, one for free camping, the other with numbered pitches. The pitches at the beach are in a half circle around the shallow bay, making it safe for children to swim. Vestar has a small marina and a jetty for mooring small boats and excursions to the islands are arranged. There is a miniclub and live music with dancing at one of the three bar/restaurants in the evenings. The restaurants all have open air terraces, one covered with vines to protect you from the hot sun.

Facilities

Four old, one modern and one refurbished toilet block with mainly Turkish style toilets and some British style, open washbasins and controllable hot showers. Child size basins. Family bathroom. Facilities for disabled people. Laundry service. Fridge box hire. Dishwashing (cold water only) under cover. Shop. Three bar/restaurants. Playground. Tennis. Volleyball. Fishing. Boat and pedalo hire. Miniclub (5-11 yrs). Excursions. Off site: Riding 2 km. Rovinj 5 km.

Open

1 May - 1 October.

At a glance

Welcome & Ambience	✓✓✓✓	Location	✓✓✓✓✓
Quality of Pitches	✓✓✓✓	Range of Facilities	✓✓✓✓

Directions

Follow site signs from Rovinj.

Charges guide

Per person	€ 3,00 - € 5,60
child	€ 1,50 - € 2,80
pitch incl. electricity	€ 4,00 - € 8,50
dog	€ 3,00

Reservations

Write to site in English. Tel: 052 829150. E-mail: vestar@jadran.tdr.hr

CR6729 Naturist Camping Koversada

Koversada, 52450 Vrsar (Istria)

According to history, the first naturist on Koversada was the famous adventurer Casanova. Today Koversada is an enclosed holiday park for naturists with bungalows, 1,700 pitches (700 for tourers, all with 6/8A electricity), a shopping centre and its own island. The main attraction of this site is the Koversada island, connected to the mainland by a small bridge. It is only suitable for tents, but has a restaurant and two toilet blocks. Between the island and the mainland is an enclosed, shallow section of water for swimming and, the other side of the bridge, an area for mooring small boats. The pitches are of average size on grass and gravel gound and slightly sloping. Pitches on the mainland are numbered and partly terraced under mature pine and olive trees. Pitching on the island is haphazard, but there is also shade from mature trees. The bottom row of pitches on the mainland have views over the island and the sea. The site is surrounded by a long beach, part sand, part paved.

Facilities

Seventeen toilet blocks provide British and Turkish style toilets, washbasins and controllable hot showers. Child size toilets and basins. Family bathroom (free). Facilities for disabled visitors. Dishwashing under cover. Laundry service. Supermarket. Kiosks with newspapers and tobacco. Several bars and restaurants. Playing field. Tennis. Minigolf. Fishing. Boats, surf boards, canoes and kayaks for hire. Paragliding. 'Tweety club' for children. Live music. Sports tournaments. Off site: Riding 2 km.

Open

15 April - 30 September.

At a glance

Welcome & Ambience	✓✓✓✓✓	Location	✓✓✓✓✓
Quality of Pitches	✓✓✓✓	Range of Facilities	✓✓✓✓✓

Directions

Site is just south from Vrsar. From Vrsar, follow site signs.

Charges 2004

Per person	€ 4,50 - € 6,00
child (5-11 yrs)	free - € 3,30
child (12-18 yrs)	€ 3,10 - € 4,30
pitch	€ 6,10 - € 14,20
dog	€ 3,20 - € 4,50

Reservations

Write to site in English. Tel: 052 441 222.
E-mail: koversada-camp@anita.hr

CR6731 Naturist Camping Valalta

Cesta Valalta-Lim bb., 52210 Rovinj (Istria)

When we visited in August there were 6,000 naturist campers here but there was still a pleasant open atmosphere. The passage through reception is efficient and pleasant and this feeling is maintained around the well organised site. A friendly, family atmosphere is to be found here and whilst there are no restrictions on entry, cautious monitoring within the site ensures the well being of all the naturist guests. An outer and inner reception adds to the security. All pitches are the same price with electricity (16A), although they vary in size and surroundings. The variations include shade, views, sand, grass, sea frontage, level ground or terracing. It is not possible to reserve a particular pitch and campers do move pitches at will. The impressive pool is in lagoon style with water features and cascades. Unusually for Croatia, the beach has soft sand (with some help from imported sand). All manner of sports are available. The high standards here and throughout the site ensure that customers return regularly throughout its 35 years of operation. We were impressed by this well ordered and smart naturist site.

Facilities

Twenty high quality new or refurbished sanitary blocks of which four are smaller units of plastic 'pod' construction. Hot showers (coin operated). Facilities for disabled campers. Washing machines. Supermarket. Four restaurants. Pizzeria. Two bars. Large lagoon style pool complex. Doctor. Beauty saloon. Running track. Minigolf. Tennis. Football. Bocce. Sailing. Play area. Bicycle hire. Beach. Beach volleyball. Boat launching. Diving club. Windsurfing. Internet. Animation all season. Animals are not allowed. Off site: Gas close by. Riding 7 km.

Open

24 April - 2 October.

At a glance

Welcome & Ambience	✓✓✓✓✓	Location	✓✓✓✓✓
Quality of Pitches	✓✓✓✓	Range of Facilities	✓✓✓✓✓

Directions

Site is located on the coast 8 km. north of Rovinj. If approaching from the north turn inland (follow signs to Rovinj) to drive around the Limski Kanal. Then follow signs towards Valalta about 2 km. east of Rovinji. Site is at the end of the road and is well signed.

Charges 2004

Per unit	€ 6,50 - € 11,60
person	€ 4,10 - € 6,65
child (3-14 yrs)	€ 2,00 - € 3,70

Reservations

Contact site. Tel: 052 804 800.
E-mail: valalta@valalta.hr

CR6736 Camping Valdaliso

Monsena bb, 52210 Rovinj (Istria)

Unusually Valdaliso Camping has its affiliated hotel in the centre of the site. The advantage for campers is that they can use the hotel and, as breakfast is served there but not in the restaurant, it may appeal to some. The fine Barabiga restaurant within the hotel offers superb Istrian and fish cuisine and the pool is also within the hotel. You are close to the beautiful old town of Rovinj and parts of this site enjoy views of the town. A water taxi makes exploring Rovinj very easy, compared with the impossible parking for private cars. A bus service is also provided but this involves considerable walking. The pitches are mostly flat with shade from pine trees and the site is divided into three sections all with 16A electricity. The choice of formal numbered pitches, informal camping or proximity to the sea impacts on the prices. We are told that 2005 will see some 'super' pitches installed. The kilometre plus of beach has crystal clear water and a pebble beach. The animation programme is extremely professional and there is a lot to do at Valdaliso, which is aimed primarily at families. The variety of activities here and the bonus of the use of the hotel make this a great choice for campers

Facilities

Two large clean sanitary blocks have hot showers (coin operated), The northeastern block has facilities for disabled campers. Hotel facilities. Shop. Pizzeria. Restaurant. Table tennis. Volleyball. Basketball. Tennis. Fitness centre. Games room. Billiards. Children's games. Bicycle hire. Summer painting courses. Exchange. Water taxi. Bus service. Boat rental. Watersports. Boat launching. Beach volleyball. Fishing. Diving school. Internet in both receptions. Animals are not accepted. Off site: Town 1 km. Excursions.

At a glance

Welcome & Ambience	✓✓✓✓	Location	✓✓✓
Quality of Pitches	✓✓✓	Range of Facilities	✓✓✓✓

Directions

Follow signs to Rovinj on the main coast road then turn north 2 km. west of Rovinj and follow signs towards Monsena and campsite signs.

Charges 2004

Per person	€ 3,30 - € 5,50
child (7-12 yrs)	€ 2,00 - € 3,30
pitch	€ 5,00 - € 13,50

Reservations

Contact site. Tel: 052 815 025.
E-mail: info@rovinjturist.hr

Open

23 March - 15 October.

CR6765 Camping Kovacine

Cres, 51557 Cres (Dalmatia)

Camp Kovacine is located on a peninsula on the beautiful Dalmatian island Cres, just 2 km. from the town of Cres. Kovacine has 417 numbered, mostly level pitches, of which 382 are for tourers (300 with electricity). On sloping ground with shade provided by mature olive and pine trees, pitching is on the large, open spaces between the trees. Some places have views of the Valun lagoon. Kovacine is partly an FKK (naturist) site, which is quite common in Croatia, and has a pleasant atmosphere. Here one can enjoy Croatian camping with local live music on a stage close to the pebble beach, where there is also a restaurant and bar. The beach, part concrete, part pebbles, has a jetty for mooring boats and fishing. It is close to the historic town of Cres, which offers a rich history in fishing, shipyards and traditional houses.

Facilities

Five modern, comfortable toilet blocks (two refurbished) offer British and Turkish style toilets, open plan washbasins (some cabins for ladies) and hot showers. Bathroom for hire. Facilities for disabled people (although access is difficult). Washing machine. Fridge box hire. Motorcaravan services. Supermarket. Bar, restaurant and pizzeria. Playground. Children's club. Evening shows with live music. Boat launching. Fishing. Diving centre. Motor boat hire.

At a glance

Welcome & Ambience	✓✓✓✓	Location	✓✓✓✓✓
Quality of Pitches	✓✓✓✓	Range of Facilities	✓✓✓✓

Directions

From Rijeka take road 2 south towards Labin. Take ferry at Brestova. Continue to Cres and follow signs.

Charges guide

Per person	€ 3,90 - € 7,50
child	€ 1,90 - € 2,90

Reservations

Write to site in English. Tel: 051 571 161.
E-mail: camp.kovacine@ri.htnet.hr

Open

15 April - 15 October.

CR6768 Camping Slatina

Martinscica, 51556 Otok Cres (Dalmatia)

Camping Slatina lies about halfway along the island of Cres, beside the fishing port of Martinscica on a bay of the Adriatic Sea. It has 370 pitches for tourers, some with 10A electricity, off very steep, tarmac access roads, sloping down to the sea. The pitches are large and level on a gravel base and enjoy plenty of shade from mature laurel trees, although hardly any have views. Whilst there is plenty of privacy, the site does have an enclosed feeling. Some pitches in the lower areas have water, electricity and drainage. Like so many sites in Croatia, Slatina has a private diving centre, which will take you to the remote island Lastovo. Lastovo is surrounded by reefs and little islands and the crystal clear waters of the Adriatic make it perfect for diving. Martinscica owes its name to the medieval church of the Holy Martin and has a Glagolite monastery, standing next to the 17th century castle, built by the Patrician Sforza. Both are well worth a visit.

Facilities

Five refurbished and one old, 'portacabin' style toilet block provide toilets, open style washbasins and controllable hot showers. Facilities for disabled visitors. Laundry with sinks and washing machine. Fridge box hire. Dishwashing under cover. Dog shower. Car wash. Shop. Bar, restaurant, grill restaurant, pizzeria and fish restaurant. Playground. Minigolf. Fishing. Bicycle hire. Diving centre. Boat launching. Beach volleyball. Pedalo, canoe and boat hire. Excursions to the 'Blue Cave'. Off site: Martinscica with bars, restaurants and shops 2 km.

Open

Easter - 31 October.

At a glance

Welcome & Ambience	✓✓✓✓	Location	✓✓✓✓✓
Quality of Pitches	✓✓✓✓	Range of Facilities	✓✓✓✓

Directions

From Rijeka take no. 2 road south towards Labin and take ferry to Cres at Brestova. From Cres go south towards Martinscica and follow site signs.

Charges 2005

Per person	€ 4,09 - € 6,65
child	€ 2,05 - € 3,07
pitch	€ 3,40 - € 4,00
dog	€ 1,02 - € 1,53

Reservations

Write to site in English. Tel: 051 574 127.
E-mail: slatina@ri.htnet.hr

CR6782 Camping Zaton

PO Box 363, Siroka ulica bb, 23232 Zadar (Dalmatia)

The Zaton Holiday Village is a newly built, family holiday park, close to the historic town of Nin and just a few kilometres from the bustling seaside resort of Zadar. This park itself is more like a town and has every amenity one can think of for a well spent holiday on the Dalmatian south coast. The village is divided into two areas separated by the shopping centre and a large parking area, one for campers close to the sea, the other for a complex with holiday bungalows. Zaton has 1,400 mostly level pitches for tourers, of which about 900 have electricity, water and waste water, the rest having electricity only. All numbered pitches have shade from mature trees and some have views over the extensive, pebble beach and the sea. Access is off hard access roads and some of the pitches at the far end are on terraces. Zaton caters for everybody's needs on site with numerous bars, restaurants, shops and two swimming pools. Excursions are organised to the Krka waterfalls, the Zrmanja Canyon and the Kornati, Paklenica and Plitvice National Parks.

Facilities

Five modern and one refurbished toilet blocks have British and Turkish style toilets, washbasins (some in cabins) and controllable hot showers. Child size basins. Facilities for disabled visitors. Campers kitchen with gas hobs. Dishwashing. Motorcaravan service point. Dog shower. Car wash. Shopping centre. Restaurants and kiosks. Enormous playground with giant slides, trampolines and bump cushions (charged). Mini-car track. Riding. Trim track. Scuba diving. Professional animation team (high season). Teen club. Games hall. Internet point. Live shows on stage by the beach. Off site: Historic towns of Zadar and Nin.

Open

1 May - 30 September.

At a glance

Welcome & Ambience	✓✓✓✓	Location	✓✓✓✓✓
Quality of Pitches	✓✓✓✓	Range of Facilities	✓✓✓✓✓

Directions

From Rijeka take no. 2 road south and leave at exit for Zadar. Drive north towards Nin and site is signed a few kilometres before Nin.

Charges guide

Per person	€ 3,40 - € 6,00
child	€ 2,30 - € 4,60
pitch incl. electricity	€ 6,00 - € 16,00
dog	€ 2,80 - € 5,20

Reservations

Write to site in English. Tel: 023 280 280.
E-mail: camping@zaton.hr

CR6755 Camping Pila

Obala 94, Punat, 51521 Krk (Dalmatia)

Autocamping Pila is right beside the bustling seaside resort of Punat on the biggest Croatian island Krk, which is connected to the main land by a bridge. Krk is the first island on your way from Europe to the Mediterranean and the Romans called it the 'Golden Island'. Autocamp Pila is just 100 m. from the Adriatic and has 600 pitches for tourers, all with 16A electricity on grass and gravel. Some are slightly sloping. Some 250 of the pitches are marked and numbered, most with shade from mature trees, the remainder are unmarked on a separate field. It can get very busy in high season and pitching can become cramped. Krk lies in the Kvarner Cove of the Adriatic sea and Punat is in the southern, greener part of the island. It is an easy 200 metres walk from the site to the centre of the resort where there are many bars, restaurants and souvenir shops. An evening walk along the promenade to enjoy the deep blue, crystal clear waters of the Adriatic and the view on the little island Kosljun (to where a day trip can be booked) is certainly recommended.

Facilities

Four modern, comfortable toilet blocks with toilets, basins and showers. Child size showers and basins. Baby room with bath and changing mat. Facilities for disabled visitors. Campers kitchen with cooking rings. Dishwashing (inside). Motorcaravan service point. Supermarket, bar with terrace and restaurant (all season). Snack bar. Small playground on gravel. Minigolf. Aerobics and aquarobics. Video games. Daily evening programme for children. Internet. Lessons in the Croatian language. Pebble beach. Off site: Punat with shops, bars, restaurants. Pedalo and boat hire 200 m.

At a glance

Welcome & Ambience	✓✓✓✓	Location	✓✓✓✓✓
Quality of Pitches	✓✓✓	Range of Facilities	✓✓✓✓

Directions

On Krk follow no. 29 road and take exit for Punat. In Punat follow good site signs.

Charges 2005

Per person	€ 3,50 - € 4,95
child	€ 1,60 - € 3,40
pitch incl. electricity	€ 8,50 - € 10,90
dog	€ 1,60 - € 2,40

Reservations

Write to site in English. Tel: 051 854 020. E-mail: pila@ri.htnet.hr

Open

1 May - 30 September.

CR6830 Kamp Paklenica

Dr. Franje Tudmania 14, 23244 Paklenica (Dalmatia)

This is a relatively small site next to the Alan Hotel in Plaklenica. It has 250 pitches, all for tourers and 150 with 16A electricity, on level, grass and gravel ground (firm tent pegs needed) under mature trees that provide useful shade. The front pitches have beautiful views of the blue waters of the Adriatic. Paklenica is only 100 m. from the entrance of the Paklenica National Park and excursions to the Park and to the Zrmanja Canyon can be booked on the site. Paklenica has its own beach, paved with rock plates, that gives access to a sheltered lagoon for swimming and boating. On site are a pizzeria and good value restaurant with a large, open-air terrace and a supermarket is only a 200 m. walk. The Alan Hotel provides a children's club, an outdoor swimming pool, games room with billiards and a fully equipped fitness centre (all free of charge for camp guests). Some entertainment is organised with live musical nights (quality variable) and games (you could win a five day free stay).

Facilities

Two good toilet blocks provide British and Turkish style toilets, open washbasins and controllable, hot showers (free). Child size toilet, shower and basin. Excellent facilities for disabled visitors. Dishwashing. Fridge box hire. Motorcaravan service point. Bar/restaurant and pizzeria. Oval shaped pool (150 sq.m) with paddling pool. New playground (on gravel). Tennis. Minigolf. Fishing. Bicycle hire. Beach volleyball. Jet ski, boat and scooter hire. Children's club. Live music night with entertainment. Games room with billiards and arcade machines. Communal barbecue area. Off site: Supermarket 200 m.

At a glance

Welcome & Ambience	✓✓✓✓	Location	✓✓✓✓
Quality of Pitches	✓✓✓	Range of Facilities	✓✓✓✓

Directions

From Rijeka, take no. 8 coast road south along the Dalmatian coast towards Starigrad-Paklenica. In town, ignore signs for N.P. Paklenica but continue for another 200 m. and turn right at sign for 'Hotel Alan'. Turn right to site.

Charges 2004

Per person	HRK 20,50 - 45,00
child (3-12 yrs)	HRK 11,50 - 26,50
pitch incl. car	HRK 37,50 - 64,00

Reservations

Necessary for high season; contact site. Tel: 23 36 92 36. E-mail: alan@zadar.net

Open

Easter - 15 October.

CR6850 Camp Seget

Hrvatskih zrtava 121, 21218 Seget Donji (Dalmatia)

Seget is a pleasant, quiet site with only 120 pitches, just 2 km from the interesting old harbour town of Trogir. It is an ideal base for exploring this part of the Dalmatian Coast, or for visiting Trogir and Split. The site is set up on both sides of a tarmac access lane that runs down to the Adriatic Sea. Pitches to the left are off three separate, gravel lanes. They are fairly level and from most there are views of the seac. Pitches to the right are slightly sloping and mostly used for tents. Of reasonable size (50-80 sq.m) the pitches are on grass and gravel firm tent pegs may be needed), mostly in the shade of mature fig and palm trees. All have access to 16A electricity (long leads may be necessary). To the front of the site a paved promenade gives access to the pebble beach. Via the promenade it is an easy five minute stroll to the first restaurants (we can recommend 'Frankie's'), where you can enjoy good quality meals.

Facilities

One good and one 'portacabin' style toilet block with British style toilets, open style washbasins and controllable, hot showers (free). Campers' kitchen. Fridge box hire. Dishwashing. Shop. Beach. Fishing. Boat rental. Barbecues permitted only on communal area. Off site: Golf, riding and bicycle hire 1 km. Boat launching 500 m.

Open

15 April - 31 October.

At a glance

Welcome & Ambience	✓✓✓✓	Location	✓✓✓✓
Quality of Pitches	✓✓✓	Range of Facilities	✓✓

Directions

Follow no. 8 coastal road south towards Split and in Trogir follow site signs. Site is signed on the right. It is a sharp right and a descending bend off the main road.

Charges 2004

Per person	HRK 19,00 - 24,00
child (5-12 yrs)	HRK 13,00 - 16,00
pitch incl. car	HRK 31,00 - 60,00
electricity	HRK 15,00
dog	HRK 7,50

No credit cards.

Reservations

Necessary for high season; contact site.
Tel: 21 88 03 94. E-mail: kamp@kamp-seget.hr

CR6890 Autocamp Solitudo

Iva Dulcica 39, 20000 Dubrovnik (Dalmatia)

Auto-camp Solitude belongs to the Babin Kuk hotel chain and is located on the north side of Dubrovnik. Its location is close to perfect, just a few kilometres from the historic old town of Dubrovnik and on the beach which makes it an ideal base for both sightseeing and relaxing. There are 238 pitches, all for tourers and all with 12A electricity, arranged on four large fields that are opened according to demand. The back field to the right is mainly used for tents and pitches here are small. The back field to the left has pitches of up to 120 sq.m. and takes many motorcaravans. From some pitches on this field there are beautiful views of the mountains and of the impressive Dr. Franco Tudmani Bridge. All pitches are numbered and level (some on terraces) and most are shaded by a variety of mature trees. The ground is hard and stony (firm tent pegs needed). There are few amenities on the site (except for two excellent toilet blocks), but the hotel complex 1 km. down the road provides bars, restaurants, tennis courts, sports fields and a shopping centre.

Facilities

Good and attractively decorated, modern toilet blocks have British style toilets, open washbasins and controllable, hot showers. Good facilities for disabled visitors. Laundry with washing machines, iron and ironing board. Dishwashing. Motorcaravan service point. Shop. Snack bar. Tennis. Minigolf. Fishing. Bicycle hire. Beach with pedalo, beach chair, kayak and jet ski hire. Excursions organised to Elefati Islands. Off site: Outdoor pool 500 m. Bar, disco and restaurant 500 m.

Open

1 April - 15 October.

At a glance

Welcome & Ambience	✓✓✓✓	Location	✓✓✓✓✓
Quality of Pitches	✓✓✓	Range of Facilities	✓✓✓✓✓

Directions

From Split follow no. 8 road south towards Dubrovnik. Site is very well signed (starting 110 km. before reaching Dubrovnik) throughout the city.

Charges 2004

Per person	€ 3,40 - € 5,40
child (5-12 yrs)	€ 1,65 - € 2,65
pitch	€ 7,00 - € 10,20
with electricity	€ 8,75 - € 11,95
dog	€ 2,65 - € 4,00

Reservations

Contact site. Tel: 0201 44 86 861.
E-mail: maro.konjerod@babinkuk.com

The Czech Republic is a land full of fascinating castles, romantic lakes and valleys, picturesque medieval squares and famous spas. It is divided into two main regions, Bohemia to the west and Moravia in the east.

Although small, the Czech Republic is crammed with attractive places to explore. Indeed, since the new country first appeared on the map in 1993, Prague has become one the most popular cities to visit in Europe. Steeped in history with museums, architectural sights, art galleries, and theatres, it is an enchanting place. The beautiful region of Bohemia, known for its Giant Mountains, is popular for skiing, hiking and other sports. The town of Karlovy Vary, world famous for its regenerative waters, is Bohemia's oldest Spa town, with 12 hot springs containing elements that are said to treat digestive and metabolic ailments. It also has many picturesque streets to meander through and peaceful riverside walks. Moravia is quieter, the most favoured area is Brno and from here it is easy to explore historical towns such as Olomouc and Kromeriz. North of Brno is the Moravian Karst, with around 400 caves created by the underground Punkya River. Some caves are open to the public, and boat trips are available along the river and out of the caves.

Population

10.3 million

Capital

Prague

Climate

Temperate, continental climate with four distinct seasons. Warm in summer with cold, snowy winters

Language

The official language is Czech

Currency

The Koruna

Telephone

The country code is 00420

Banks

Mon-Fri 0830-1630

Shops

Mon-Fri 08.00-18.00, some close at lunchtime. Sat 09.00 until midday

Public Holidays

New Year; Easter Mon; May Day; National Day 8 May; Saints Day 5 July; Festival Day 6 July; Independence Day 28 Oct; Christmas 24-26 Dec

Motoring

There is a good and well signposted road network throughout the Republic and, although stretches of cobbles still exist, surfaces are generally good. An annual road tax is levied on all vehicles using Czech motorways and express roads, and a disc can be purchased at border crossings, post offices and filling stations. Do not drink any alcohol before driving. Dipped headlights are compulsory throughout the winter months. Always give way to trams and buses.

Tourist Office

Czech Tourist Authority
95 Great Portland Street, London W1N 5RA
Tel. 020 7291 9925
Fax. 020 7436 8300
Email: ctainfo@czechcentre.org.uk
Internet: www.visitczech.cz

TRY THE LOCALLY PRODUCED BEER AND WINE. PILSEN, IS THE HOME OF PILS, AND BREWERY TOURS ARE AVAILABLE.

Czech Republic

CZ4640 Autocamping Areal Jadran

Jezerni 84/12, 35101 Frantiskovy Lazne (Zapadocesky)

Autocamping Jadran is on the outskirts of the spa town Frantiskovy Lázné and is the perfect base to visit the many restored spa baths with healing waters. Besides visiting the spa baths you can tour the beautiful West Bohemian countryside. Marie Novotny with her husband Jiri, owner of the site, welcomed us very warmly and is really looking forward to meeting you. She told us that the site has been open for eight years and that she loves to welcome British and Dutch campers. There are 150 pitches for tourers, all with 16A electricity, and the site has its own lake for cooling down in the hot summer months. The pitches are partly shaded and some are of at least 120 sq.m. Adjacent to the site is Hotel Jadran which serves fine meals for very reasonable prices and has a pleasant bar.

Facilities

The heated toilet blocks (two older, one refurbshed) are simple, but are clean and tidy. They include toilets, washbasins with hot and cold water, controllable showers, a launderette with 2 washing machines and sinks with free hot water (not covered). Restaurant (1/4-31/10). No shop but fresh bread available every morning in the restaurant. Giant chess, draughts and other games. Russian bowling. Volleyball. Fishing. Riding. Bicycle hire. Inflatables allowed in the lake. Off site: Riding 400 m. Fishing 6 km.

Open

All year.

At a glance

Welcome & Ambience	✓✓✓✓✓	Location	✓✓✓✓
Quality of Pitches	✓✓✓✓	Range of Facilities	✓✓✓

Directions

Take the no. 6 road from Karlovy Vary to Frantiskovy Lázné and from there the signs to Hotel Jadran. Site is behind the hotel.

Charges guide

Per person	€ 2,60
child (3-12 yrs)	€ 1,60
tent or caravan	€ 3,10
motorcaravan	€ 4,10
pet	€ 1,00
electricity	€ 2,80

Less 10% for stays over 7 days or repeat visits.

Reservations

Possible but probably not necessary.
Tel: 354 542 412. E-mail: atc.jadran@centrum.cz

CZ4650 Autocamping Luxor

Plzenska, 353 01 Velká Hled (Zapadocesky)

An orderly site, near the German border, Luxor is adequate as a stopover for a couple of days. Like some other sites in the Czech Republic, it has now come under the management of a local hotel. It is in a quiet location by a small lake on the edge of the village of Velká Hled'sebe, four kilometres from Marianbad. The 100 pitches (60 for touring units) are in the open on one side of the entrance road (cars stand on a tarmac park opposite the caravans) or in a clearing under tall trees away from the road. All pitches have access to electricity (10A) but connection in the clearings section may require long leads. Forty bungalows occupy one side of the site. There is little to do here but it is a good location for visiting the spa town of Marianbad.

Facilities

Toilet buildings are old and should be refurbished, but the provision is more than adequate. Cleaning could be better. No chemical disposal point. Restaurant with self-service terrace (1/5-30/9). Rest room with TV, kitchen and dining area. Small playground. Fishing. Bicycle hire. Off site: Very good motel restaurant and shops 500 m. in village. Riding 5 km. Golf 8 km.

Open

1 May - 30 September.

At a glance

Welcome & Ambience	✓✓✓✓	Location	✓✓✓✓
Quality of Pitches	✓✓✓	Range of Facilities	✓✓✓

Directions

Site is directly by the Stribo-Cheb road no. 21, 500 m. south of Velká Hled'sebe.

Charges guide

Per unit incl. 2 persons and electricity	CZK 380
extra person	CZK 53
child (0-9 yrs)	free

No credit cards.

Reservations

For information write to Interhotel Cristal Palace, 353 44 Mariánské Lánzé or phone 0165/2056-7. Fax: 0165/2058. Tel: 165 623 504. E-mail: autocamping.luxor@seznam.cz

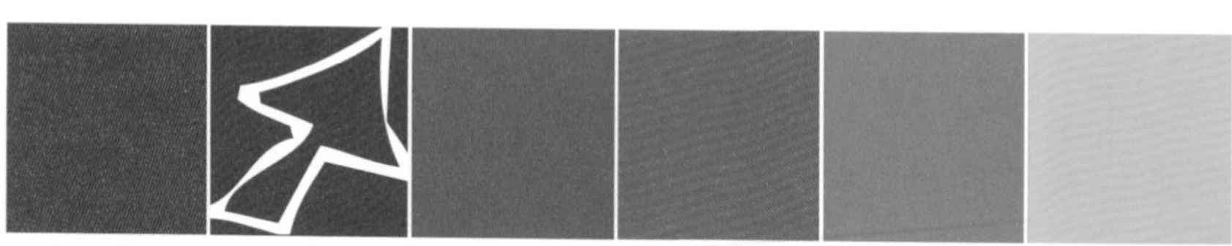

CZ4750 Camping Bilá Hora

Ul.28.rijna 49, 301 62 Plzen (Zapadocesky)

Even non-drinkers probably know that Pilsen is famous for its beer (Pils) and as the home of the Skoda car factory. Traffic in the town centre is heavy so, if you wish to visit the city where beer has been brewed since 1295, find a campsite and use the bus. Visits to the brewery may be arranged. Camping Bilá Hora is a suitable site and is situated amidst trees in the suburb of Bilá Hora, about three kilometres from the city centre on the edge of town. The 50 pitches are on a gentle slope in a clearing, but level concrete tracks have been made for caravans and motorcaravans, with electricity available at 30 pitches. It is a pleasant, quiet site with its own restaurant. Bungalows are quite separate from the camping area.

Facilities

A new sanitary block (British style WCs, bath and laundry) is in the camping area, plus another with the bungalows - they are good by Czech standards. Washing machine and iron. Motorcaravan services. Kitchen. Restaurant. Kiosk with small terrace (all year). Bicycle hire. Playground. Table tennis. Volleyball. Off site: Shops 200 m. Fishing 500 m. Swimming and tennis near. Bus stop at site entrance.

Open

15 April - 30 September.

At a glance

Welcome & Ambience	✓✓✓	Location	✓✓✓✓
Quality of Pitches	✓✓✓✓	Range of Facilities	✓✓✓✓

Directions

Site is to the north of the town on the Plzen(Pilsen) - Zruc no. 231 road where it is signed.

Charges guide

Per person	CZK 50
child (10-15 yrs)	CZK 20
caravan or tent	CZK 70
car	CZK 70
motorcycle	CZK 20
motorcaravan	CZK 140

Reservations

Not necessary. Tel: 377 562 225.

CZ4780 Autocamping Konopiste

256 01 Benesov u Prahy (Stredocesky)

Benesov's chief claim to fame is the Konopiste Palace, the last home of Archduke Franz Ferdinand whose assassination in Sarajevo sparked off the First World War in 1914. Autocamp Konopiste is part of a motel complex, with excellent facilities situated in a very quiet, tranquil location south of Prague. On a hillside, rows of terraces separated by hedges provide 65 grassy pitches of average size, 50 with electricity (10A). One of the best Czech campsites, it has many different varieties of trees and much to offer those who stay there. A fitness centre and heated swimming pool are shared with motel guests. The whole complex has a well tended, cared for air. Near the motel, is the Stodola restaurant, open each evening from 6 pm. until 1 am. this attractive replica of an old Czech barn is well worth a visit. With local specialities served by girls in local costume in a candlelit atmosphere and accompanied by a small, live music quartet, it is an evening to remember (booking essential).

Facilities

The good quality sanitary block is central to the caravan pitches. Washing machine and irons. Kitchen. Site's own bar/buffet (high season) with simple meals and basic food items. Motel bar and two restaurant (all year). Swimming pool (1/6-31/8). Tennis. Minigolf. Volleyball. Table tennis. Bicycle hire. Badminton. Fitness centre. Children's playground. Club room with TV. Chateau and park. Off site: Shop 200 m. Fishing 1.5 km. Riding 5 km. Prague 48 km. (public transport available).

Open

1 May - 30 September.

At a glance

Welcome & Ambience	✓✓✓	Location	✓✓✓✓
Quality of Pitches	✓✓✓✓	Range of Facilities	✓✓✓✓

Directions

Site is signed near the village of Benesov at Hotel Konopiste (no connection) and Motel Konopiste on main Prague - Ceske Budejovic road no. 3/E55.

Charges 2004

Per person	CZK 70 - 90
child (6-15 yrs)	CZK 40 - 60
caravan	CZK 170 - 290
large tent	CZK 150 - 250
small tent	CZK 70 - 100
car	CZK 80 - 100

Electricity included.

Reservations

Contact site. Tel: 317 722 732.
E-mail: hotel@hotelkonopiste.cz

CZ4830 Camping Horjany

Horejany 3 Tochovice, 26272 Breznice (Stredocesky)

Arthur and Jelly de Baan started Horjany about six years ago on old farm premises. The location of the site alone is worth a stay for a couple of days to enjoy, especially from the pitches at the back of the site under the trees, the wide views over the woods and the farming fields. Camping Horjany is truly a 'back to nature' campsite - not all of the 50 pitches (40 with 3A electricity) are marked out and the grass between the pitches is not well cut. However, this doesn't cause any inconvenience because the site roads are cut well and if you need extra space on your pitch (adding up to 200 sq.m!) Arthur just mows an extra piece for you. The site breathes friendliness and cosiness and many campers come here every year. If you want to enjoy the true Czech country life on an authentic Czech farm, this is the place to go. A real piece of art is the perfectly designed bar in the old pigsty. With a warm and comfortable atmosphere, there are a few pleasant sofas to rest in after a long day's walking or cycling and a nice new bar where you can enjoy a beer or a glass of wine. You can even bring your own musical instruments and join in with the site's band. It is a pity this site is only open for eight weeks a year – it is a perfect place to relax, to enjoy and to make new friends.

Facilities

The single toilet block in a converted stable provides toilets, washbasins (open style and in cabins) with hot and cold water, controllable showers, child size washbasins, baby bath, sinks for washing up, a dryer, freezer and sinks (inside) with free hot water. No shop but bread to order. Swimming pool (12 x 6 m). Swings for children. Tennis. Live music. Disco. Soccer competitions against locals. Russian bowling. Library. Board games. Torches are necessary.
Off site: Riding 2.5 km.

Open

July and August only.

At a glance

Welcome & Ambience	✓✓✓✓✓	Location	✓✓✓✓✓
Quality of Pitches	✓✓✓✓	Range of Facilities	✓✓✓

Directions

Follow road no. 20 Plzen - Pisek road and turn onto no. 19 road towards Rozmital and Breznice. Go left over the bridge in Breznice towards Tochovice and turn right in Tochovice to Horejany. Go through the village towards Tusovicky and you pass the site (not signed). Follow the A4 from Prague to Pribram and from there towards Strakonice. Turn right towards Kletice, Tusovice and Tusovicky which leads to Horejany and the site.

Charges guide

Per unit incl. 2 persons	€ 10,00
extra person (max 6 per pitch)	€ 2,00
electricity	€ 2,00
dog	€ 1,50

Reservations

Necessary as it is a short season - contact the Dutch owners on 0031 182 530635. Tel: 737 353 785.
E-mail: sophiartgouda.BV@12move.nl

CZ4840 Camping Oase Praha

Zlatniky 47, 25241 Dolni Brezany (Prague)

Camping Oase Praha is a quiet site, yet it is only five kilometres from Prague, with easy access. You can take the bus (from outside the site) or drive to the underground stop (10 minutes). The site has 85 pitches, all around 90 sq.m, with 10A electricity and 16 with water and drainage, on level, well kept fields. The site is very well kept and has just everything one may expect, including a new Western style toilet block, a well maintained swimming pool and separate paddling pool, a restaurant and a bar. Children can amuse themselves with trampolines, the new playground or volleyball and basketball. The main attraction here is, of course, the Czech capital. However, this site will provide a relaxing environment to return to and another advantage is that Mr Hess, the owner, speaks English.

Facilities

An outstanding, new toilet block includes washbasins (open style and in cabins) with hot and cold water, spacious, controllable showers and child size toilets. Facilities for disabled visitors. Laundry with washing machines and dryer. Campers kitchen with hob, fridge and freezer. Motorcaravan services. Restaurant and bar. No shop but basic groceries are available in reception. Swimming pool (9 x 15 m) and separate paddling pool with slide (both 1/5-31/8). New adventure style playgrounds. Trampolines. Table tennis. Volleyball. Basketball. Minigolf. Internet point. TV and video. Board games. Bicycle hire. Closed circuit security cameras. Off site: Fishing 2 km. Riding 3 km. Golf 10 km. Boat launching 15 km.

Open

15 April - 15 September.

At a glance

Welcome & Ambience	✓✓✓✓	Location	✓✓✓✓
Quality of Pitches	✓✓✓✓	Range of Facilities	✓✓✓✓

Directions

Go southeast from Prague on the D1 towards Brno and take exit 11 to Jesenice via road 101. From Jesenice follow the camp signs to the site in Zlatniky.

Charges 2004

Per person	CZK 90
child (under 12 yrs)	CZK 60
pitch incl. electricity	CZK 400
dog	CZK 60

Less 20% discount 15/4-31/5 and 1/9-30/9. Less 3% discount for payment in cash.

Reservations

Made before 1/5; min. 1 week (Sat. - Sat).
Tel: 241 932 044. E-mail: post@campoase.cz

CZ4590 Holiday Park Lisci Farma

Dolni Branna 350, 54302 Vrchlabi (Vychodocesky)

This is truly a site that could be in Western Europe considering its amenities, pitches and welcome. However, Eurocamp Lisci Farma is a fully Czech-owned site and has a pleasant Czech atmosphere. The 242 pitches are fairly flat, although the terrain is slightly sloping, and some pitches have shade. The pitches on the new area at the entrance are terraced. The site is well equipped for the whole family to enjoy with its adventurous playground with trampolines for children, archery, beach volleyball, Russian bowling and outdoor bowling court for older youngsters. A beautiful sandy, lakeside beach is 800 metres from the entrance. More active visitors can go paragliding or rock climbing with experienced guides. This site is very suitable for relaxing or exploring the culture of the area. Excursions to Prague are organised and, if all the sporting possibilities are not enough, the children can take part in the activities of the entertainment team, while you are walking or cycling or enjoying live music at the Fox Saloon.

Facilities

One old, but refurbished sanitary block and one modern block include spacious, controllable showers (on payment), child size toilets, baby room, facilities for disabled visitors, and a launderette. Motorcaravan service. Bar/snack bar with pool table. Games room. Swimming pool (6 x 12 m). Adventure style playground on grass. Trampolines. Tennis courts. Minigolf. Archery. Russian bowling. Bowling court. Beach volleyball. Paragliding. Rock climbing. Bicycle hire. Excursions to Prague. Off site: Fishing and beach 800 m. Riding 2 km. Golf 5 km.

At a glance

Welcome & Ambience	✓✓✓✓	Location	✓✓✓✓✓
Quality of Pitches	✓✓✓✓	Range of Facilities	✓✓✓✓✓

Directions

Follow road no. 14 from Liberec to Vrchlabi and Dolni Branna. Site is signed in Vrchlabi in the direction of Prague.

Charges guide

Per person	CZK 90,00
child (4-14 yrs)	CZK 70,00
pitch incl. 6A electricity	CZK 360,00
dog	CZK 70,00

Reservations

Contact site. Tel: 499 421 473.
E-mail: hotelcamp@liscifarma.cz

Open

All year.

CZ4690 Camping Slunce

471 07 Zandov (Severocesky)

Away from larger towns, near the border with the old East Germany, this is pleasant rural country with a wealth of Gothic and Renaissance castles. Zandov has nothing of particular interest but Camping Slunce is a popular campsite with local Czech people. There is room for about 50 touring units with 35 electrical connections (12A) on the level, circular camping area which has a hard road running round. Outside this circle are wooden bungalows and tall trees. The general building at the entrance houses all the facilities including the reception office.

Facilities

The satisfactory toilet block is good by Czech standards. Kitchen with electric rings, gas cooker and fridges. Restaurant (all year) under separate management has live music in high season. Kiosk for basics (May - Sept). Tennis. Swimming pool. Volleyball. Mountain bike hire. Playground. Large, room for games and TV. Barbecues not permitted. Dogs are not accepted. Off site: Fishing 1 km. Riding 2 km.

Open

2 May - 30 September.

At a glance

Welcome & Ambience	✓✓✓✓	Location	✓✓✓✓
Quality of Pitches	✓✓✓	Range of Facilities	✓✓✓✓

Directions

Zandov is 20 km. from Decin and 12 km. from Ceske Lipa (Ceské Lipy) on the minor road between these two towns. Signed in the centre of Zandov village.

Charges guide

Per person	CZK 97
child	CZK 61
caravan or tent	CZK 97
car	CZK 97
motorcycle	CZK 55
motorcaravan	CZK 189

Reservations

Not made. Tel: 487 861116.

CZ4860 Autocamping Orlice

PO Box 16, 517 41 Kostelec n Orlice (Vychodocesky)

Kostelec does have an ancient castle, although not a lot else to commend it, but is a good centre from which to explore the interesting town of Hradec Kralove, East Bohemia, the Orlicke Hory and other high districts near the Polish border. Autocamping Orlice, situated on the edge of town near the swimming pool, has a river running by and is in a quiet location (except when children play in the weir!) and a pleasant appearance. Surrounded by tall trees, the grass pitches are of generous size although not marked or numbered, on each side of a concrete grid road which runs the length of this rectangular site. There is room for 80 units, half having electric points (16A) and with shade in parts. The friendly manageress speaks good English and will be pleased to advise on local attractions. There is a hotel alongside the camp but advice is to seek a better restaurant in town for meals. A good site for those seeking rest and quiet and not needing organised activities, there is a friendly welcome.

Facilities

The central sanitary block includes hot water in washbasins, sinks and good showers - it is of a good standard for the Czech Republic. Unlike most Czech sites, showers have dividers, space for dressing, a door that locks, and even a chair! Limited food supplies are available in a bar/lounge during July/Aug. Café/bar (15/5-30/9). Off site: Town swimming pool near (15/6-31/8; new pool planned for 2003). Tennis 100 m. Fishing 500 m. Riding 5 km.

Open

15 May - 30 September.

At a glance

Welcome & Ambience	✓✓✓✓	Location	✓✓✓✓
Quality of Pitches	✓✓✓	Range of Facilities	✓✓✓

Directions

Site is signed from the centre of town.

Charges guide

Per person	CZK 42 - 46
child (6-14 yrs)	CZK 20 - 24
caravan	CZK 70 - 78
tent	CZK 58 - 68
car	CZK 58 - 68
motorcycle	CZK 30 - 40

Reservations

Write to site. Tel: 494 322 768. E-mail: orlice@wo.cz

CZ4820 Caravan Camp Valek

Chrustenice 155, 26712 Lodenice (Stredocesky)

Only 2.5 kilometres from the E50 motorway, this well maintained, family owned site creates a peaceful, friendly base enjoyed by families. Surrounded by delightful countryside, it is possible to visit Prague even though it is about 28 km. from the city centre. It is best to use public transport and at Zlicin, a ten minute drive from the site there is a 'park and ride' with guarded car parks costing 20p per day (no height restriction, arrive before 09.00). This is also the start of the 'B' metro line transporting one rapidly to Mustek, the heart of the city and the main sights (return fare 50p! - tickets can be bought in advance from reception). On leaving the car park to return, there is a large shopping centre including a Tesco superstore! The medium sized, gently sloping grass site is divided in two by a row of well-established trees (some shade) and the toilet block. Most pitches are relatively flat, in the open and not specifically marked. However this does not appear to cause overcrowding and generally there is plenty of space. Electricity (10A) is available. Some places have pleasant views of the sunbathing area in front of the pool with a pine-forested hillock as a backdrop. The 20 x 60 metre pool is fed by a river and better classified as a lake with rough concrete sides, access steps and a water chute. Very small dinghies, air beds and large rubber rings can be used in the 'lake' allowing children to really enjoy themselves.

Facilities

The single clean toilet block has limited numbers of toilets and showers, but during our visit in high season coped well. Small shop with fresh rolls daily, plus milk, sweets and ice cream. Tastefully decorated waiter service restaurant with terrace has an extensive menu with customers praising, quality, quantity and price of the meals. Natural swimming pool (20 x 60 m) with constantly changing water checked regularly by the authorities to ensure its purity. Extensive games room with arcade machines and internet. Live musical nights on Saturday. Tennis. Off site: Prague 28 km. Plzen 69 km.

Open

1 May - 30 September.

At a glance

Welcome & Ambience	✓✓✓✓	Location	✓✓✓✓
Quality of Pitches	✓✓✓✓	Range of Facilities	✓✓✓✓

Directions

From E50 (D5) motorway take exit 10 for Lodenice. Follow camping signs and or Chrustenice. Site is 300 m. on right on leaving Chrustenice.

Charges 2004

Per adult	CZK 95
child (6-14 yrs)	CZK 45
caravan	CZK 115
tent	CZK 65 - 115
car	CZK 95
motorcycle	CZK 75

Less 10% 1-31 May and 1-30 September.

Reservations

Contact site. Tel: 311 672 147.
E-mail: info@campvalek.cz

CZ4880 Camping Roznov

Horni Paseky 940, 756 61 Roznov pod Radhostem (Severomoravsky)

Roznov pod Radhostem is halfway up the Roznovska Becva valley amidst the Beskydy hills which extend from North Moravia into Poland in the extreme east of the Republic. It is a busy tourist centre which attracts visitors to the Wallachian open-air museum and those who enjoy hill walking. There are 300 pitches (200 for touring units), some of which are rather small, although there are some new landscaped pitches of 90-100 sq.m. Arranged on flat grass and set amidst a variety of fruit and other trees, there are 120 electrical connections (16A) and shade in some parts. Although right by a main road with some traffic noise, the site is surrounded by trees and hills and was reasonably quiet during our visit.

Facilities

The good quality central toilet block has hot water in basins and sinks. New, well equipped toilet block with washbasins and WCs en-suite for ladies. Washing machine. Very basic food items fromshop and restaurant, not always open. Swimming pool (25 m. and heated July/Aug). Tennis. Off site: Restaurant or snack-bar night club at the modern hotel 300 m. Fishing and golf 1 km. Riding 4 km.

At a glance

Welcome & Ambience	✓✓✓✓✓	Location	✓✓✓✓
Quality of Pitches	✓✓✓✓	Range of Facilities	✓✓✓✓

Directions

Site is at eastern end of Roznov on the main 18/E442 Zilina-Olomouc road opposite sports stadium.

Charges guide

Per person	CZK 99
pitch incl. car	CZK 100 - CZK 170

Reservations

Write to site. Tel: 571 648 001. E-mail: info@camproznov.cz

Open

All year.

CZ4785 Camp Drusus

Trebonice 4, 15500 Praha (Prague)

Camp Drusus is a friendly, family site on the western edge of Prague. It provides a good base from which to explore this beautiful city with the metro station only 15 minutes walk away. The site has 65 level pitches (all for tourers), 50 with 10A electricity and varying in size (60-90 sq.m). Access off a circular, grass and gravel road. There is no shop here but basics can be ordered at reception and one of the biggest shopping areas in Prague is only 2 km away. You could enjoy a real Czech breakfast in the restaurant which also opens for dinner and serves as a bar. This is a pleasant, well kept and quiet site with good connections to the Czech capital.

Facilities

Portacabin style toilet facilities that look basic but are clean, contain British style toilets, open washbasins and free, controllable hot showers. Laundry. Kitchen. Dishwashing. Motorcaravan service point. No shop, but basis to order at reception. Bar/restaurant. Small fitness centre. Playground. Games room with billiards. Off site: Shops 2 km. Metro station for Prague 15 minutes. Golf 12 km. Riding 10 km.

Open

15 April - 15 October.

At a glance

Welcome & Ambience	✓✓✓✓	Location	✓✓✓✓
Quality of Pitches	✓✓✓	Range of Facilities	✓✓✓

Directions

On E50/E48 take exit 19 for Reporyje. In the centre turn left on K Trebonicum to site on the right.

Charges 2004

Per person	CZK 70 - 90
child (5-14 yrs)	CZK 40
pitch incl. car	CZK 140 - 200
electricity	CZK 80
dog	free

Reservations

Necessary for high season. Tel: 235 514 391. E-mail: drusus@drusus.com

CZ4870 Autocamping Morava

Bezrucova, 789 85 Mohelnice (Severomoravsky)

This is an interesting area of contrasts - heavy industry, fertile plains and soaring mountains. Mohelnice is a small industrial town but the campsite is in a peaceful setting surrounded by trees on the northern edge. The amenities on offer, particularly for children, may tempt one to stay longer. The site is roughly in two halves with the camping area on a flat, open meadow with a hard access road. The 100 touring pitches are not numbered or marked so siting could be a little haphazard. There are 80 electricity connections (10A). There is little shade but the perimeter trees should screen out road noise. The other part of the site is given over to a two storey motel and bungalows with a good quality restaurant between the two sections. Good English is spoken at reception and it is a very pleasant, well organised site.

Facilities

The toilet block is satisfactory. Electric cooking rings. Restaurant (May - Oct). Kiosk/snack bar. Small shop (May - Oct). Live music (high season). Swimming pool (May - Oct). Tennis. Minigolf. Bicycle hire. Road track - driving and cycling learning area. Playground. TV room.

Open

15 May - 15 October (motel all year).

At a glance

Welcome & Ambience	✓✓✓✓	Location	✓✓✓✓
Quality of Pitches	✓✓✓	Range of Facilities	✓✓✓✓

Directions

Site is signed on the western edge of town on the Olomouc - Hradec Kralove road no. 35/E442.

Charges guide

Per person	CZK 40
pitch	CZK 60 - 90
electricity	CZK 40

No credit cards.
Less 10% for 5 days or more, paid on arrival.

Reservations

Write to site. Tel: 583 430 129.

CZ4770 Camping Dlouhá Louka

Stromovka 8, 370 01 Ceské Budejovice (Jihocesky)

The medieval city of Céske Budejovice is the home of Budweiser beer and is also an industrial centre. It lies on the River Vltava with mountains and pleasant scenery nearby. Dlouhá Louka is a motel and camping complex 2 km. south of the town on the Céske Budejovice - Cesky Krumlov road. The camping part is a flat, rectangular meadow surrounded by trees which give some shade around the edges. There are some marked, hedged pitches and hardstanding, but many of the grass pitches are not marked or numbered so pitching can be rather haphazard. This is a useful night stop between Prague and Linz or for longer stays if this region is of interest.

Facilities

The single sanitary block, with British style WCs, is at one end making a fair walk for some. Washing machine and irons. Kitchen with electric rings. Very pleasant bar and restaurant (all year). Small kiosk for basic supplies (1/7-3/8). Tennis. Volleyball. Table tennis. Playground. Off site: Shops 200 m. Bicycle hire 2 km. Fishing and golf 10 km.

Open

All year.

At a glance

Welcome & Ambience	✓✓✓✓	Location	✓✓✓✓
Quality of Pitches	✓✓✓	Range of Facilities	✓✓✓

Directions

From town follow signs for Ceske Krumlov. After leaving ring road, turn right at Motel sign. Take this small road and turn right 60 m. before Camp Stromovky. Camp site name cannot be seen from the entrance - only the word Motel.

Charges guide

Per person	CZK 70
pitch	CZK 120 - 140

No credit cards.

Reservations

Write to site. Tel: 387 203 601.

CZ4710 Camping Chvalsiny

Chvalsiny 321, 38208 Chvalsiny (Jihocesky)

Camping Chvalsiny is Dutch owned and has been developed from an old farm. Pitches are more or less flat, the grass is well cut, there is a newly built sanitary block. The 200 pitches are of average size but look larger because of the open nature of the terrain which also means there is little shade. Chvalsiny is a family site and children are kept occupied with painting and stories, soccer and rafting competitions. The location in the middle of the Blanky Les nature reserve, part of the vast Sumava forest, provides excellent opportunities for walking, cycling and fishing but it also has a rich culture and heritage.

Facilities

Modern, clean and well kept toilet facilities include washbasins in cabins and controllable showers (coin-operated). Laundry. Kiosk (1/6-15/9) with daily necessities. Snack bar (1/6-15/9). Play attic. Lake swimming. Climbing equipment and swings. Crafts, games, table tennis. Bicycle hire. Torches useful. Off site: Village restaurants close.

Open

1 May - 15 September.

At a glance

Welcome & Ambience	✓✓✓✓	Location	✓✓✓✓✓
Quality of Pitches	✓✓✓✓	Range of Facilities	✓✓✓✓

Directions

Take exit 114 at Passau in Germany towards Freyung. Continue to Philipsreut and take no. 4 road towards Vimperk. Turn right on road 39 to Horni Plana and Cesky Krumlov. Turn left 4 km. before Cesky Krumlov on no. 166 to Chvalsiny and follow camp signs.

Charges 2004

Per person	CZK 90,00
child (under 12 yrs)	CZK 50,00
pitch with electricity	CZK 300,00

No credit cards.

Reservations

Possible via 0528 221137. Tel: 380 739123.
E-mail: info@campingchvalsiny.nl

CZ4720 Camping Frymburk

Frymburk 184, 38279 Frymburk (Jihocesky)

Camping Frymburk is beautifully located on the Lipno lake in southern Bohemia and is ideal for the active camper. From this site, activities could include walking, cycling, swimming, sailing or rowing and afterwards you could relax in the small bar and restaurant. The site has 170 level pitches on terraces (all with electricity). From the lower terraces on the edge of the lake there are lovely views over the water to the woods on the opposite side. A ferry crosses the lake from Frymburk and the site has a small beach.

Facilities

Four toilet blocks, two old, one modern and one refurbished, with toilets, washbasins (open style and in cabins) with cold water only, pre-set showers on payment (with curtain) and an en-suite bathroom with toilet, basin and shower. Launderette. Bar. Playground. Canoe, bicycle, pedaloes, rowing boat and surfboard hire. Kidstown. Rafting. Bus trips to Prague. Torches useful. Off site: Shops and restaurants in the village 900 m. from reception.

Open

15 April - 1 October.

At a glance

Welcome & Ambience	✓✓✓✓	Location	✓✓✓✓✓
Quality of Pitches	✓✓✓	Range of Facilities	✓✓✓✓

Directions

Take exit 114 at Passau in Germany (near the Austrian border) towards Freyung in the Czech Republic. Continue on this road till Philipsreut and from there follow the no. 4 road towards Vimperk. Turn right a few kilometres after the border towards Volary on no. 141 road. From Volary follow the no. 163 road to Horni Plana, Cerna and Frymburk. Site is on the 163 road, right after the village.

Charges 2004

Per pitch incl. electricity	CZK 380,00

No credit cards. Less 20% 15/4-15/6 and 1/9-1/10.

Reservations

Contact site. Tel: 380 735 284.

CZ4815 Triocamp Praha

Ustecka Ul, 18400 Praha (Prague)

This site on the northern edge of Prague is a great place to stay for a few days to visit the city. It has 70 pitches (all for tourers) with 6/15A electricity. Most are in the shade of mature trees, which can be very welcoming after hard day sightseeing. The ground is slightly sloping but most pitches are level and access is off one circular, tarmac road, with cabins and pitches on both sides. There is one hardstanding for a motorcaravan. Triocamp has a bar and a restaurant with a comprehensive menu and covered terrace attractively decorated with a variety of flowers. Toilet facilities are in good order and comfortable. Bus tickets can be purchased at the site reception, including tickets for bus tours through the city or for a boat excursion on the Moldau River.

Facilities

Modern, comfortable toilet facilities provide British style toilets, open washbasins and free, pre-set hot showers. Facilities for disabled people. Laundry with washing machine. Dishwashing. Shop. Attractive bar/restaurant. Play area. Volleyball. Off site: Prague is a few kilometres by public transport.

Open

All year.

At a glance

Welcome & Ambience	✓✓✓✓	Location	✓✓✓✓
Quality of Pitches	✓✓✓✓	Range of Facilities	✓✓✓✓

Directions

On E55 in either direction, take exit 1 towards Zdiby and continue straight ahead on 608 road. Site is on right after about 3 km.

Charges 2004

Per person	CZK 120 - 140
child (5-15 yrs)	CZK 70 - 80
pitch incl. car	CZK 170 - 300
electricity	CZK 70
dog	free - CZK 70

Reservations

Contact site in writing. Tel: 283 850 795.
E-mail: triocamp.praha@telecom.cz

CZ4896 Camping Country

Hluboke Masuvky 257, 67152 Hluboke Masuvky (Jihormoravsky)

Camping Country is a well cared for and attractively landscaped site, close to the historical town of Znojmo. It is a rural location close to a National Park and close to the Austrian border which would make it ideal either as a stopover on your way south and for a longer stay to enjoy the new cycling routes which have been set out in the National Park. Camping Country has 60 pitches (all for tourers), 30 with 6A electricity, on two fields - one behind the main house taking 6 or 8 units, the other one larger with a gravel access road. The fields are connected by two wooden bridges (one is only fenced on one side). Varieties of low hedges and firs partly separate the pitches. To the front of the site is a paddock with two horses and facilities for minigolf, volleyball, basketball and tennis. In the garden of the main house is a paddling pool. Colourful flowers and trees give the site a pleasant atmosphere. We feel that Camping Country is certainly one of the better Czech sites.

Facilities

Modern and comfortable toilet facilities provide British style toilets, open washbasins (cold water only) and free, controllable hot showers. Campers' kitchen. Dishwashing. Bar/restaurant with one meal served daily. Play area. Tennis. Volleyball. Basketball. Minigolf. Riding. Some live music nights in high season. Tours to Vienna, Brno and wine cellars organised. Torch useful. Off site: Fishing, boat launching and beach 10 km.

Open

1 May - September.

At a glance

Welcome & Ambience	✓✓✓✓	Location	✓✓✓✓
Quality of Pitches	✓✓✓✓	Range of Facilities	✓✓✓✓

Directions

Coming from the northwest on the E59 road exit to the east at Kasarna onto the 408 road and continue north on the 361 road towards Hluboké Masuvky. Site is well signed.

Charges 2004

Per person	CZK 90
child (3-12 yrs)	CZK 45
pitch incl. car	CZK 90 - 145
electricity	CZK 60
pet	CZK 35

Reservations

Contact site. Tel: 515 255 249.
E-mail: camping-country@cbox.cz

Alan Rogers

This is a just a sample of the campsites we have inspected and selected in Central Europe & Croatia. For more campsites and further information, please see the Alan Rogers Central Europe & Croatia guide.

Denmark offers a diverse landscape all within a relatively short distance. The countryside is green and varied with flat plains, rolling hills, fertile farmland, many lakes and fjords, wild moors and long beaches, interrupted by pretty villages and towns.

Denmark is the easiest of the Scandinavian countries to visit, both in terms of cost and distance. There are many small islands but the main land masses that make up the country are the islands of Zealand and Funen and the peninsula of Jutland, which extends northwards from the German border. Zealand is the most visited region, its main draw being the capital, Copenhagen. This vibrant city has a beautiful old centre, an array of museums and art galleries plus a boisterous night life. Funen is the smaller of the two main islands and known as the Garden of Denmark, with its neat green fields and fruit and vegetable plots. Sandy beaches and quaint villages can be found here. Jutland has the most varied landscape ranging from heather-clad moors, dense forests to plunging gorges. It's also home to one of the most popular attractions in Denmark, Legoland, and the oldest town in Scandinavia, Ribe.

Population

5.3 million

Capital

Copenhagen

Climate

Generally mild although changeable throughout the year

Language

Danish, but English is widely spoken

Currency

Danish Krone

Telephone

Mon-Wed & Fri 09.30-16.00, Thurs to 18.00. Closed Sat. In the provinces opening hours vary

Banks

The dialling code for Denmark is 00 45

Shops

Hours may vary in the main cities. Regular openings are Mon-Thu 09.00-17.30, Fri 09.00- 19.00/20.00, and Sat 09.00-13.00/14.00

Public Holidays

New Year's Day; Maundy Thursday; Good Friday; Easter Monday; Ascension; Constitution Day 5 Jun; Whit Mon; Christmas 24- 26 Dec; New Year's Eve

Motoring

Driving is much easier than at home as roads are much quieter. Driving is on the right. Do not drink and drive. Dipped headlights are compulsory at all times. Strong measures are taken against unauthorised parking on beaches, with on the spot fines

Tourist Office

The Danish Tourist Board
55 Sloane Street, London SW1X 9SY
Tel: 020 7259 5959.
Fax: 020 7259 5955
Email: dtb.london@dt.dk
Internet: www.visitdenmark.com

EATING OUT IN DENMARK CAN BE EXPENSIVE, TRY STICKING TO *DAGENS RET* – THE DAY'S SPECIALITY WHICH IS USUALLY GOOD VALUE.

DK2010 Hvidbjerg Strand Camping

Hvidbjerg Strandvej 27, DK-6857 Blavand (Ribe)

A family owned, 'TopCamp' holiday site, Hvidbjerg Strand is on the west coast near Blåvands Huk, 43 km. from Esbjerg. It is a high quality, seaside site with a wide range of amenities and facilities. Most of the 570 pitches have electricity (6/10A) and the 130 'comfort' pitches also have water, drain and satellite TV. Many are individual and divided by hedges, in rows on flat sandy grass, with areas also divided by small trees and hedges. On-site leisure facilities include an impressive, tropical style indoor pool complex with stalactite caves and 70 m. water chute, 'the black hole' with sounds and lights plus water slides, spa baths, Turkish bath and a sauna. The latest indoor suite of supervised play rooms is designed for all ages with Lego, computers, video games, TV, etc. The most recent sanitary facilities are also impressive, thatched in the traditional style and one with a central, glass covered atrium. A Blue Flag beach and windsurfing school are adjacent to the site and the town offers a full activity programme during the main season (mid June - mid Aug).

Facilities

Four superb toilet units, two just renovated to very high standards, include washbasins (many in cubicles), roomy showers, spa baths, suites for disabled visitors, family bathrooms, kitchens and laundry facilities. The most recent units include a children's bathrooms decorated with dinosaur or Disney characters, racing car baby baths, low height WCs, basins and showers, plus many high quality family bathrooms, suites for disabled visitors and two new kitchens with hobs, microwave ovens and cosy dining areas. Some family bathrooms for rent. Motorcaravan services. Supermarket. Café/restaurant. TV rooms. Pool complex, solarium and sauna. Play areas. Supervised play rooms (09.00-16.00 daily). Barbecue areas. Minigolf, football, squash and badminton. Riding. Fishing. Dog showers. ATM machine. Off site: Legoland 70 km.

At a glance

Welcome & Ambience	✓✓✓✓	Location	✓✓✓✓
Quality of Pitches	✓✓✓✓✓	Range of Facilities	✓✓✓✓✓

Directions

From Varde take roads 181/431 to Blåvand. Site is signed left on entering the town (mind speed bump on town boundary).

Charges 2004

Per person	€ 9,52
child (0-11 yrs)	€ 7,03
pitch	€ 2,07 - € 12,41
serviced pitch	€ 3,45
electricity (6/10A)	€ 3,59 - € 4,14
dog	€ 3,17

Reservations

Made without deposit. Tel: 75 27 90 40.
E-mail: info@hvidbjerg.dk

Open

16 March - 26 October.

DK2140 Jesperhus Feriecenter and Camping

Legindvej 30, DK-7900 Nykobing Mors (Viborg)

Jesperhus is an extensive, well organised and busy site with many leisure activities, adjacent to Blomsterpark. It is a 'TopCamp' site with 662 numbered pitches, mostly in rows with some terracing, divided by shrubs and trees and with shade in parts. Many pitches are taken by seasonal, tour operator or rental units, so advance booking is advised for peak periods. Electricity (6A) is available on all pitches and water points are in all areas. The indoor and outdoor pool complex (daily charge) has three pools, diving boards, water slides with the 'Black Hole', spa pools, saunas and a solarium. Although it may appear to be just part of Jutland, Mors is an island in its own right surrounded by the lovely Limfjord. It is joined to the mainland by a fine 2,000 m. bridge at the end of which are signs to Blomsterpark (Northern Europe's largest flower park which also houses a Bird Zoo, Butterfly World, Terrarium and Aquarium) and the camp site – both under the same ownership. The flower park, situated well to the north of Denmark, is an incredible sight from early spring to late autumn, attracting some 4,000 visitors a day to enjoy over half a million flowering plants and magnificent landscaped gardens. With all the activities at this site an entire holiday could be spent here regardless of weather, but Jesperhus is also an excellent centre for touring a lovely area of Denmark.

Facilities

Four first rate sanitary units are cleaned three times daily. Facilities include washbasins in cubicles or with divider/curtain, family and whirlpool bathrooms (on payment), suites for babies and disabled people. Free sauna. Superb kitchens with full cookers and hoods, microwaves, dishwashing sinks and a fully equipped laundry. Supermarket (1/4-1/11) with gas. Restaurant. Bar. Café, takeaway. Pool complex with solarium. Activities include a 10 lane bowling centre, 'space laser' game, attractive minigolf, volleyball, tennis, go-carts and other outdoor sports. An indoor hall includes badminton, table tennis, and children's 'play-world'. Playgrounds. Pets corner. Golf. Fishing pond. Practice golf (3 holes). Off site: Riding 2 km. Bicycle hire 6 km. Beach 2 km.

At a glance

Welcome & Ambience	✓✓✓✓✓	Location	✓✓✓✓
Quality of Pitches	✓✓✓✓	Range of Facilities	✓✓✓✓✓

Directions

From south or north, take road no. 26 to Salling Sund bridge, site is signed Jesperhus, just north of the bridge.

Charges 2004

Per person	DKK 68,00
child (1-11 yrs)	DKK 49,00
pitch	free - DKK 50,00
electricity	DKK 30,00
dog	DKK 10,00

Reservations

Advised for holiday periods - write for details.
Tel: 96 70 14 00. E-mail: jesperhus@jesperhus.dk

Open

All year.

DK2020 Mogeltonder Camping

Sonderstregsvej 2, Mogeltonder, DK-6270 Tonder (Sønderjylland)

This site is only five minutes walk from one of Denmark's oldest villages and ten minutes drive from Tønder with its well preserved old buildings and magnificent pedestrian shopping street. From here you can visit the Schackenborg Castle Gardens (with guided tours) – the castle is owned by the Danish royal family and was built in 1283. A quiet family site, Møgeltønder has 285 large, level, numbered pitches on grass, most with electricity (10A), divided up by new plantings of shrubs and small hedges. Only 35 pitches are occupied by long stay units, the remainder solely for tourists, and there are 15 cabins. The site also has an excellent outdoor heated swimming pool and children's pool and a good playground.

Facilities

Two superb, modern, heated sanitary units include roomy showers (on payment), washbasins with either divider/curtain or in private cubicles, plus excellent bathrooms for families and disabled visitors. Baby room. Two kitchens with hobs and dishwashing sinks (all free). Laundry with sink, two washing machines and dryer. Motorcaravan services. Shop for essentials only (bread ordered daily). Swimming pool (10 x 5 m.) and paddling pool. Minigolf. Playground. TV and games rooms. Internet access. Off site: Golf and bicycle hire 10 km.

At a glance

Welcome & Ambience	✓✓✓	Location	✓✓✓✓
Quality of Pitches	✓✓✓✓	Range of Facilities	✓✓✓

Directions

Turn left off no. 419 Tønder - Højer road, 4 km. from Tønder. Drive through Møgeltønder village (on cobbles) and past the church where site is signed.

Charges 2004

Per person	DKK 54,00
child (0-12 yrs)	DKK 27,00
electricity	DKK 20,00

Reservations

Not normally necessary. Tel: 74 73 84 60. E-mail: moegeltoender.camping@post.tele.dk

Open

All year.

DK2000 Nordsø Camping

Tingodden 3, Årgab, DK-6960 Hvide Sande (Ringkøbing)

Located beside the North Sea, behind the sand dunes and next to a fjord, Nordsø not only has beach access but also provides a splendid indoor pool complex. There are 300 regularly laide out, level pitches, quite close together, most of which have 16A electricity with 80 fully serviced and 43 cabins. The site has a wide range of activites for children with a restaurant for evening use and a pizzeria for day time. The site is situated on the West Coast Path, a 40 km. long cycle path for children and adults.

Facilities

Two fully equipped toilet blocks one heated. Family bathrooms (charged). Facilities for the disabled visitors. Laundry. Restaurant, bar, pizzeria and takaway. Supermarket. Kitchen. Outdoor and indoor pool complex (Dkr. 10-20). Sauna, solarium and spa bath. Tennis, table tennis, minigolf. TV and games room. Play areas. Fishing.

Open

11 April - 14 September.

At a glance

Welcome & Ambience	✓✓✓	Location	✓✓✓✓
Quality of Pitches	✓✓✓	Range of Facilities	✓✓✓✓

Directions

From E20 take exit 73, Korskroen. Take main road 11 to Varde then 181 towards Nymindegab and Hvide Sande. Site is 6 km. south of Hvide Sande.

Charges 2004

Per person	€ 8,78
child (0-11 yrs)	€ 5,68
pitch	free - € 6,76
electricity (10A)	€ 3,78

Reservations

Contact site. Tel: 96 59 17 22. E-mail: info@nordsoe-camping.dk

DK2015 Ådalens Camping

Gudenåvej 20, DK 6710 Esbjerg V-Sædding (Ribe)

Owned and run by Britta and Peter Andersen, this superb site is in the northeast of Esbjerg and is a great starting point from which to tour the city with its harbour, museums and sea water aquarium. It is also convenient for those arriving on the ferry from Harwich (16 hours). From the attractive, tree lined drive, gravel lanes lead to large fields with well-mown grass and good services. Ådalens has 193 pitches for touring visitors and 30 seasonal places. The pitches are split into groups of 5 or 10 by mature trees that provide some shade. There are 16 concrete hardstandings for large caravans or motorcaravans, 4 of which are fully serviced. Ådalens is close to the beach but also has an attractive outdoor pool with slide and paddling pool. Everything is in pristine order, with amenities that will ensure a pleasant stay.

Facilities

Two modern toilet blocks with free hot showers. Special children's section in bright colours and family shower rooms. Excellent facilities for disabled visitors. Baby room. Laundry. Kitchen. Motorcaravan services. Basics from reception (bread to order). Outdoor pool (15 x 10 m). Playground with cable track. Animal farm. Giant chess. Minigolf. Internet access. TV room with library. Off site: Fishing, golf, bicycle hire 5 km. City centre 5 km.

At a glance

Welcome & Ambience	✓✓✓✓	Location	✓✓✓✓✓
Quality of Pitches	✓✓✓✓✓	Range of Facilities	✓✓✓✓

Directions

From Esbjerg, take the 447 road northeast and continue along the coast. Turn right at sign for site.

Charges 2004

Per person	€ 8,00
child (1-11 yrs)	€ 4,80
pitch	€ 3,40
electricity (10A)	€ 3,50

Reservations

Contact site. Tel: 75 15 88 22. E-mail: info@adal.dk

Open

All year.

DK2165 Skiveren Camping

Niels Skiverenrej 5-7, DK-9982 Skiveren/Aalbæk (Nordjylland)

This friendly seaside site, a member of the Danish 'TopCamp' organisation, is set up in 'maritime style' with the pitches separated by low wooden poles connected by a sailor's rope. Skiveren Camping has 670 pitches (595 for tourers), almost all with 6/10A electricity. The level pitches are of a good size (up to 120 sq.m), some having a picnic table and all are separated from the main tarmac access road by the low wooden fences. Toilet facilities look immaculate and the main block has a new attractive, light-blue children's section in maritime style again, with a lighthouse and a boat. The site has its own fitness centre with an outdoor pool, sauna, steam bath and solarium. However, this whole area is also great for a seaside holiday on the Ålbæk Bugt beaches. Other possibilities are walking and cycling on the surrounding moors or a visit to the interesting old harbour town of Skagen.

Facilities

Three immaculate toilet blocks with the usual facilities, free family showers and private facilities with shower, toilet and basin for rent. Facilities for disabled visitors. Laundry. Kitchen. Motorcaravan services. Supermarket. Café for meals, drinks and takeaway meals. Outdoor pool (15 x 8 m) with whirlpool and sauna. Playground. Football field. Tennis. Games room with wide-screen TV and air hockey. Beach volleyball. Bicycle hire. Children's club. Live music and dancing. Off site: Fishing 14 km. Golf 7 km. Riding 10 km.

Open

Easter - 30 September.

At a glance

Welcome & Ambience	✓✓✓✓	Location	✓✓✓✓
Quality of Pitches	✓✓✓✓	Range of Facilities	✓✓✓✓

Directions

From the no. 40 road going north from Ålbæk, turn left at sign for 'Skiveren'. Follow this road all the way to the end.

Charges 2004

Per person	DKK 50,00 - 68,00
child (1-11 yrs)	DKK 32,00 - 44,00
pitch	DKK 20,00 - 50,00
with water and drainage	DKK 45,00 - 65,00
electricity (6/10A)	DKK 25,00 - 30,00

Credit cards 4% surcharge.

Reservations

Contact site. Tel: 98 93 22 00.
E-mail: info@skiveren.dk

DK2180 Nordstrand Camping

Apholmenvej 40, DK-9900 Frederikshaven (Nordjylland)

An excellent site, Nordstrand is 2 km. from Frederikshaven and the ferries to Sweden and Norway. It is another 'TopCamp' site and provides all the comforts one could possibly need with all the attractions of the nearby beach, town and port. The 430 large pitches are attractively arranged in small enclosures of 9-13 units surrounded by hedges and trees; 250 pitches have electricity (10A) and drainage, a further 20 have water and there are 16 on hardstandings. There are 64 seasonal units, plus 23 site owned cabins. The roads are paved and the site is well lit. The beach is a level, paved 200 m. walk. There is much to see in this area of Denmark and this site would make a very comfortable holiday base.

Facilities

Centrally located, modern, large toilet blocks provide spacious showers (on payment) and washbasins in cubicles, together with some family bathrooms, rooms for disabled people and babies. Laundry with free ironing. All are spotlessly clean. Good kitchens at each block provide mini-ovens, microwaves, hobs (free) and dishwashing sinks with free hot water. Motorcaravan services. Supermarket (all season). Cafè (15/6-15/8). Pizza service. Indoor swimming pool. Sauna. Solarium. 'Short' golf course, minigolf, tennis, table tennis, billiards and chess. Bicycle hire. Play areas. Internet access (free). Off site: Frederikshavn with shops, etc.

At a glance

Welcome & Ambience	✓✓✓✓	Location	✓✓✓✓
Quality of Pitches	✓✓✓✓	Range of Facilities	✓✓✓✓

Directions

Turn off no. 40 road 2 km. north of Frederikshavn at roundabout north of railway bridge. Site is signed.

Charges 2004

Per person	DKK 52,00 - 65,00
child (0-11 yrs)	DKK 35,00 - 45,00
pitch	DKK 30,00 - 40,00
electricity	DKK 26,00

Reservations

Essential for high season and made with deposit (DKK 400). Tel: 98 42 93 50.
E-mail: nordstrand-camping@post10.tele.dk

Open

1 April - 20 October.

DK2150 Solyst Camping

Logstorvej 2, DK-9240 Nibe (Nordjylland)

You will always be near to the water in Denmark, either open sea or, as here, alongside the more sheltered waters of a fjord - Limfjord. Sølyst is a family run site providing 200 numbered pitches, most with electricity (6A), on gently sloping grass arranged in fairly narrow rows separated by hedges (150 for touring units). There are facilities for watersports and swimming in the fjord, the site also has a small heated swimming pool (8 x 16 m), waterslide and splash pool with a children's pool all with paved sunbathing area, and paddle boats can be rented. A little train provides rides for children. Good paths have been provided for superb, easy walks in either direction, and indeed right into the nearby town of Nibe. This is a delightful example of an old Danish town with picturesque cottages and handsome 15th century church. Its harbour, once prosperous from local herring boats, is now more concerned with pleasure craft.

Facilities

A central sanitary unit includes washbasins in cubicles, four family bathrooms, a baby room and facilities for disabled visitors. Very good kitchen with hobs, microwave, oven, dishwashing sinks and small dining area. Fully equipped laundry. A second unit provides extra facilities including two more family bathrooms. Hot water (except in washbasins) is charged for. Motorcaravan services. Mini-market. Snack bar and takeaway (open main season). Swimming pool. Solarium. Play area. Minigolf. Boules. TV room. Games room with amusement machines. Fishing. Bicycle hire. Boat launching. Beach. Off site: Riding 1 km. Town of Nibe 1 km. Golf 4 km.

At a glance

Welcome & Ambience	✓✓✓✓	Location	✓✓✓✓✓
Quality of Pitches	✓✓✓✓	Range of Facilities	✓✓✓✓

Directions

Site is clearly signed from the no. 187 road west of Nibe town, with a wide entrance.

Charges 2004

Per person	DKK 55,00 - 63,00
child (under 12 yrs)	DKK 29,00 - 33,00
pitch	DKK 25,00

Reservations

Advised for peak periods - write for details.
Tel: 98 35 10 62. E-mail: soelyst@dk-camp.dk

Open

All year.

DK2170 Klim Strand Camping

Havvejen 167, Klim Strand, DK-9690 Fjerritslev (Nordjylland)

A large coastal, family holiday site, Klim Strand is a paradise for children. It is a privately owned 'TopCamp' site with a full complement of quality facilities, including its own fire engine and trained staff. The site has 560 numbered touring pitches, all with electricity (10A), laid out in rows, many divided by trees and hedges and shade in parts. Some 220 of these are fully serviced with electricity, water, drain and 18 channel TV hook-up. On site activities include an outdoor water-slide complex, a newly renovated indoor pool complex, tennis courts, pony riding (all free), numerous play areas, an adventure playground with aerial cable ride, roller skating area and ramp. Recent additions include a kayak school and a large bouncy castle for toddlers. Live music and dancing are organised twice a week in high season. Suggested excursions include trips to offshore islands, visits to local potteries, a brewery museum and bird watching on the Bygholm Vejle.

Facilities

Two large, central toilet blocks, recently renovated to high standards, are heated. Spacious showers and some washbasins in cubicles. Separate children's room with child size/height WCs, basins and half height shower cubicles. Baby rooms. Bathrooms for families (some charged) and disabled visitors. Sauna, solariums, whirlpool bath, hairdressing rooms, fitness room. Dog bathroom. Two smaller units are by reception and beach. Laundry. Well equipped kitchens and barbecue areas with dishwashing sinks, microwaves, gas hobs, and two TV lounges. Motorcaravan services. Supermarket. Pizzeria. Restaurant and bar. Internet cafe. TV rental. Pool complex. Play areas. Crèche. Bicycle hire. Off site: Golf 10 km. Boat launching 25 km.

At a glance

Welcome & Ambience	✓✓✓✓	Location	✓✓✓✓✓
Quality of Pitches	✓✓✓✓	Range of Facilities	✓✓✓✓

Directions

Turn off Thisted-Fjerritslev no. 11 road to Klim from where site is signed.

Charges 2004

Per person	€ 8,28 - € 9,38
child (1-11 yrs)	€ 5,52 - € 6,34
pitch	€ 8,28 - € 12,41
electricity	€ 3,86
dog	€ 2,48 - € 2,76

Reservations

Essential for mid June - end August.
Tel: 98 22 53 40. E-mail: ksc@klim-strand.dk

Open

1 April - 20 October.

DK2130 Hobro Camping Gattenborg

Skivevej 35, DK-9500 Hobro (Nordjylland)

This neat and very well tended municipal site is imaginatively landscaped and has 130 pitches on terraces arranged around a bowl shaped central activity area. Most pitches (100 for touring units) have electricity (10A) and there are many trees and shrubs. Footpaths connect the various terraces and activity areas. There are 30 seasonal units and 10 cabins. The reception building with a small shop and tourist information, has a covered picnic terrace behind, and houses a large TV lounge. The small, heated, outdoor swimming pool with water-slide is free to campers and open in high season, weather permitting. Extra unusual facilities include billiards, giant chess, and a woodland moon-buggy track. The site is 500 m. walk from the town, close to the Viking Castle of Fyrkat and the lovely old town of Mariager.

Facilities

The main heated sanitary building towards the rear of the site includes washbasins in cubicles and hot showers (on payment). Two family bathrooms. Facilities for disabled people. Baby room. New kitchen with hobs, dishwashing sinks and free herbs. Small laundry with washing machine and dryer. Tiny unit in the centre of the site has two unisex WCs and basins (cold water only) and a small kitchen. Additional WC and basins at reception. Motorcaravan services. Shop (order bread before 9 pm). Swimming pool (high season). Play areas. Table tennis. Basketball. Football. Minigolf. TV lounge with board games and library. Off site: Bicycle hire near. Town 500 m. Fishing 7 km. Beach 1 km. Golf 25 km.

At a glance

Welcome & Ambience	✓✓✓✓✓	Location	✓✓✓✓
Quality of Pitches	✓✓✓✓	Range of Facilities	✓✓✓

Directions

From E45 exit 35, take road 579 towards Hobro Centrum. Site is well signed to the right, just after railway bridge.

Charges 2004

Per person	DKK 53,00 - 62,00
child (2-11 yrs)	DKK 28,00 - 32,00
electricity	DKK 22,00

Reservations

Contact site. Tel: 98 52 32 88. E-mail: hobro@dk-camp.dk

Open

4 April - 26 September.

DK2100 Blushoj Camping

Elsegårdevej 55, DK-8400 Ebeltoft (Århus)

This is a traditional type of site where the owners are making a conscious effort to keep mainly to touring units – there are only six seasonal units and four rental cabins. The site has 200 pitches on levelled grassy terraces surrounded by mature hedging and shrubs. Some have glorious views of the Kattegat and others overlook peaceful rural countryside. Most pitches have electricity (10A), but long leads may be required. There is a heated and fenced swimming pool (14 x 7 m) with a water-slide and terrace and the beach below the site provides opportunities for swimming, windsurfing and sea fishing. The owners also arrange traditional entertainment - folk dancing, local choirs, and accordion music some weekends in high season. This is a fine location for a relaxed family holiday, with numerous excursion possibilities including the fine old town of Ebeltoft (4 km), with its shops and restaurants, and the world's largest wooden sailing ship, the Frigate Jylland, now fully restored and open to the public.

Facilities

One toilet unit includes washbasins with dividers and showers with divider and seat (on payment). The other unit has a kitchen with electric hobs, dishwashing sinks, dining/TV room, laundry and baby facilities. A heated extension provides six very smart family bathrooms, and additional WCs and washbasins. Motorcaravan service point. Well stocked shop. Swimming pool (20/5-20/8). Minigolf. Play area. Games room. Beach. Fishing. Off site: Riding, bicycle hire, boat launching and golf 5 km.

Open

1 April - 15 September.

At a glance

Welcome & Ambience	✓✓✓✓✓	Location	✓✓✓✓✓
Quality of Pitches	✓✓✓✓	Range of Facilities	✓✓✓✓

Directions

From road 21 northwest of Ebeltoft turn off at junction where several sites are signed. Follow signs through the outskirts of Ebeltoft turning southeast to Elsegårde village. Turn left for Blushøj and follow camp signs.

Charges 2004

Per person	DKK 60,00 - 68,00
child	DKK 31,00 - 35,00
electricity	DKK 22,00

No credit cards.

Reservations

Contact site. Tel: 86 34 12 38.

DK2060 Askehøj Camping

Askehøjvej 18, Laven, DK-8600 Silkeborg (Århus)

Askehøj Camping is a small family site on sloping ground near Silkeborg. This is the Danish Lake District in the centre of the country's most beautiful natural area. The 250 pitches here are in rows on small rectangular fields, each taking 6-10 units. Although the ground slopes, most pitches are level and the rows are separated by walls and high bushes. Askehøj takes 190 touring units, all with 6/10A electricity. The site is surrounded by mature trees. There is a swimming pool (free) with a small slide and a separate paddling pool. According to the owner, most people come here to enjoy walking, cycling and fishing (there is a lake nearby) or to visit Silkeborg or Århus. Try a tour on the lake on Denmark's oldest steamboat or visit the Himmelbjerget viewing point, from where there are beautiful views of the lake, the woods and the surrounding countryside.

Facilities

One traditional style toilet block provides basic, but clean facilities with free showers and a special section for children. En-suite facilities for disabled people. Laundry with washing machines, dryers and spin dryer. Campers' kitchen. Shop (bread to order). Takeaway. Swimming pool (15 x 8 m) with slide and paddling pool. Playground. Football field. Minigolf. Boules. Entertainment programme for children three times a week in high season. Extensive games room with arcade machines, air hockey and table football. Off site: Fishing 2 km. Boat launching 3 km. Golf 5 km. Beach 8 km.

At a glance

Welcome & Ambience	✓✓✓✓	Location	✓✓✓✓
Quality of Pitches	✓✓✓✓	Range of Facilities	✓✓✓✓

Directions

From Silkeborg follow the 15 road southeast towards Århus. Turn right towards Svejbæk at the sign and continue towards Laven. Follow the camp signs.

Charges 2004

Per person	DKK 55,00
child (1-12 yrs)	DKK 33,00
pitch	DKK 15,00 - 30,00
electricity	DKK 23,00

Min. price per pitch DKK 107 (mid-season) – DKK 122 (high season). No credit cards.

Reservations

Contact site. Tel: 86 84 12 82.
E-mail: askhoj@dk-camp.dk

Open

11 April - 19 September.

DK2070 Fornæs Camping

Stensmarkvej 36, DK-8500 Grenå (Århus)

In the grounds of a former farm, Fornæs Camping is about 5 km from Grenå. From reception a wide, gravel access road descends through a large grassy field to the sea. Pitches to the left are mostly level, to the right slightly sloping with some terracing and views of the Kattegat. The rows of pitches are divided into separate areas by colourful bushes and each row is marked by a concrete tub containing a young tree and colourful flowers. Fornæs has 320 pitches of which 240 are for tourers, the others being used for seasonal visitors. All touring pitches have 10A electricity. At the foot of the site is a pebble beach with a large grass area behind it for play and sunbathing. There is also an attractive outdoor pool with two slides, a paddling pool, sauna, solarium and whirlpool near the entrance. Here also a comprehensive room serves as a restaurant, takeaway and bar, and in a former barn there is a games room. Fornæs provides a good base from which to explore this part of Denmark or for taking the ferry to Hjelm island or to Sweden.

Facilities

Two modern toilet blocks have British style toilets, washbasins in cabins and controllable hot showers (Dkr 2). Child-size toilets. Family shower rooms. Baby room. Facilities for disabled people. Fully equipped laundry. Campers' kitchen. Motorcaravan service point. Shop. Café/grill with bar and takeaway (evenings). Swimming pool (80 sq.m) with paddling pool. Sauna and solarium. Play area. Minigolf. Volleyball. Basketball. Boules. Fishing. Watersports. Off site: Golf and riding 5 km.

At a glance

Welcome & Ambience	✓✓✓✓	Location	✓✓✓✓
Quality of Pitches	✓✓✓✓	Range of Facilities	✓✓✓✓

Directions

From Århus follow the 15 road towards Grenå and then the 16 road towards town centre. Turn north and follow signs for Fornæs and the site.

Charges 2004

Per person	DKK 60,00 - 68,00
child (1-12 yrs)	DKK 32,00 - 36,00
electricity (10A)	DKK 25,00

Credit cards 5% surcharge.

Reservations

Call or e-mail the site. Tel: 86 33 23 30.
E-mail: fornaes@1031.inord.dk

Open

Easter - 28 September.

DK2080 Holmens Camping

Klostervej 148, DK-8680 Ry (Århus)

Holmens Camping lies between Silkeborg and Skanderborg in a very beautiful part of Denmark. The site is close to the waters of the Gudensø and Rye Møllesø lakes which are used for boating and canoeing. Walking and cycling are also popular activities. Both Skanderborg and Silkeborg are worth a visit and in Ry you can attend the Skt. Hans party which takes place at midsummer. Holmens has 225 grass touring pitches, partly terraced and divided by young trees and shrubs. The site itself is surrounded by mature trees. Almost all the pitches have 6A electricity and vary in size between 70 – 100 sq.m. A small tent field is close to the lake, mainly used by those who travel by canoe. The lake is suitable for swimming but the site also has an attractive pool complex consisting of two circular pools linked by a bridge and a paddling pool with water canon. There are plenty of opportunities for activities including boat hire on the lake and for fishing (the site has its own fishing pond).

Facilities

One traditional and one modern toilet block have British style toilets, washbasins (open and in cabins) and controllable hot showers (on payment). En-suite facilities with toilet, basin, shower. Baby room. Excellent facilities for disabled visitors. Laundry. Campers' kitchen. Small shop for basics. Open-air pool with jet stream and paddling pool with water canon (free for campers). Pool bar. Extensive games room. Playground. Football field. Tennis. Minigolf. Fishing. Bicycle hire. Boat rental. Off site: Golf 14 km. Riding 2 km. Beach 2 km.

At a glance

Welcome & Ambience	✓✓✓✓	Location	✓✓✓✓✓
Quality of Pitches	✓✓✓✓	Range of Facilities	✓✓✓✓

Directions

Going north on E45, take exit 52 at Skanderborg turning west on 445 road towards Ry. In Ry follow the camp signs.

Charges 2004

Per person	€ 8,29 - € 9,57
child (3-11 yrs)	€ 4,57 - € 5,14
pitch	€ 2,14
electricity (6A)	€ 3,30 - € 4,86

Reservations

Contact site. Tel: 86 89 17 62.
E-mail: info@holmens-camping.dk

Open

27 March - 26 September.

DK2044 Hampen Sø Camping

Hovedgaden 31, DK-7362 Hampen (Vejle)

If you are heading up towards Denmark to cross to Norway or Sweden, then this site in a natural setting close to lakes and moors could be a useful stop-over. There are 230 pitches in total, with 80 seasonal units plus 34 cabins, but there will always be space for touring units. The pitches are arranged in large grassy bays taking around 15 units, and there are 10A electric hook-ups (some long leads may be needed). The nearby Hampen See lake is a pleasant walk through the forest and is said to be one of the cleanest lakes for swimming in Denmark. Many people stay here to visit Legoland, the Lion Park and Silkeborg, in addition to walking and cycling in this pleasant area. English is spoken.

Facilities

Two toilet blocks, one at the upper end, the other near the entrance, one basic, the other with newer facilities. En-suite facilities for disabled people. Laundry. Good supermarket and restaurant open all year and to the general public. Takeaway. Kitchen. Games and TV rooms. Small outdoor pool. Covered minigolf. Playground. Trampolines. Table tennis. Free bicycles. Race track for mini cars. Internet access. Off site: Riding 500 m. Fishing 3 km. Golf 18 km.

Open

All year.

At a glance

Welcome & Ambience	✓✓✓✓	Location	✓✓✓✓
Quality of Pitches	✓✓✓✓	Range of Facilities	✓✓✓✓

Directions

Site lies on road no. 176, approx. 500 m. southwest of its junction with road no.13 between Vejle and Viborg (around 50 km. south of Viborg). Look for Spar mini-market and camping signs.

Charges 2004

Per person	€ 8,11
child (0-11 yrs)	€ 4,05
electricity	€ 3,38
dog	€ 0,68

Reservations

Contact site. Tel: 75 77 52 55.
E-mail: info@hampen-soe-camping.dk

Denmark

DK2050 Terrassen Camping

Himmelbjergvej 9 A, Laven, DK-8600 Silkeborg (Århus)

Terrassen Camping is a family run site arranged on terraces, overlooking Lake Julso and the countryside. There are 260 pitches with good views, most with electricity (6/10A) and three new hardstanding pitches for motorcaravans. A small area for tents (without electricity) is at the top of the site where torches may be required. There are also 29 seasonal units, and some site owned cabins. The solar heated swimming pool (8 x 16 m, open June-end August) has a paved terrace and is well fenced. This is a comfortable base from which to explore this area of Denmark where a warm welcome and good English will greet you. Take a trip on Lake Julso on Hjejen, the world's oldest paddle steamer.

Facilities

The main modern sanitary unit is heated and includes many washbasins in cubicles, controllable showers (on payment), family bathrooms, children's bathroom, baby room, and facilities for disabled visitors. Kitchen with hobs, ovens and dishwashing sinks. An older re-furbished unit contains another kitchen, plus 4 more shower cubicles with external access - despite their outward appearance they are newly re-tiled and immaculate. Motorcaravan services. Well stocked shop. Swimming pool (15/5-31/8). Games/TV rooms. Adventure playground, trampolines, bouncing cushion, toddlers indoor play room and pets corner. Basketball, volleyball and boules courts. Covered barbecue area. Canoe hire. Off site: Restaurant just outside the site. Fishing 200 m. Golf and bicycle hire 5 km. Boat launching 5 km.

At a glance

Welcome & Ambience	✓✓✓✓✓	Location	✓✓✓✓✓
Quality of Pitches	✓✓✓✓	Range of Facilities	✓✓✓✓

Directions

From the harbour in the centre of Silkeborg follow signs and minor road towards Sejs (5 km.) and Ry (20 km). Site lies on the northern side of the road at village of Laven (13 km.). Note: Height restriction of 3 m. on railway bridge over this road.

Charges 2004

Per person	DKK 62,00
child (1-11 yrs)	DKK 38,00
pitch	free - DKK 40,00
electricity	DKK 26,00
dog	DKK 10,00

Reservations

Essential for high season; contact site. Tel: 86 84 13 01. E-mail: info@terrassen.dk

Open

18 March - 18 September.

DK2040 Riis Camping & Fritidscenter

Osterhovedveg 43, DK-7323 Give (Vejle)

Riis is a good quality touring site ideal for visiting Legoland (18 km) and Lion Park (3 km). It is a friendly, family run 'TopCamp' site with 280 large touring pitches on sheltered, gently sloping, well tended lawns surrounded by trees and shrubs. Electricity (6A) is available to 220 pitches, and there are 51 site owned cabins. The outdoor heated pool and water-slide complex and the adjacent small bar that serves beer, ice cream, soft drinks and snacks are only open in main season. There is also a small, well stocked shop next to reception for necessities. More comprehensive shopping and restaurants are in nearby Give. This is a top class site suitable for long or short stays in this very attractive part of Denmark.

Facilities

Two excellent sanitary units include washbasins with divider/curtain and controllable showers (on payment). Suites for babies and disabled visitors, family bathrooms (one with whirlpool bath, on payment) and solarium. Two excellent kitchens with hobs, ovens, and dishwashing sinks (on payment). Large dining room/sitting room with TV, plus a covered barbecue grill area. Laundry. Motorcaravan services. Shop. Pool complex (charged in July). Cafe/bar. Table tennis. Minigolf. Outdoor bowling alley. Train ride for children. Comprehensive playground. Animal farm. TV lounge. Bicycle hire. Off site: Fishing and golf 4 km. Beach 23 km.

Open

30 April - 5 September.

At a glance

Welcome & Ambience	✓✓✓✓✓	Location	✓✓✓✓
Quality of Pitches	✓✓✓✓	Range of Facilities	✓✓✓✓

Directions

Turn onto Osterhovedvej southeast of Give town centre (near Shell Garage) at sign to Riis and site. After 4 km. turn left into tarmac drive which runs through the forest to the site. Alternatively, turn off the 442 Brande-Jelling road at Riis village north of Givskud.

Charges 2004

Per person	DKK 64,00
child (0-11 yrs)	DKK 44,00
pitch	free - DKK 40,00
comfort pitch plus	DKK 30,00
electricity	DKK 25,00
dog	DKK 10,00

Reservations

Site can become full in July/Aug. Reservations are advisable. Tel: 75 73 14 33. E-mail: info@riis-camping.dk

DK2048 Faarup Sø Camping

Fårupvej 58, DK-7300 Jelling (Vejle)

This site was originally set up on the old farm woodlands of Jelling Skov where local farmers each had their own plot. Owned since January 2004 by the Dutch/Danish Albring family, this is a rural location on the Fårup Lake. This family site is ideal for those who want to enjoy a relaxed holiday on the lakeside beaches or walking or cycling through the surrounding countryside. Some of Denmark's best-known attractions such as Legoland and the Lion Park are nearby. Fårup Sø Camping has 240 pitches, mostly on terraces (from top to bottom the site has a height difference of 53 metres). The terraces provide beautiful views of the countryside and the Fårup lake. There are 180 pitches for touring units, most with 10A electricity, and some tent pitches without electricity. Next to the top toilet block is an open-air barbecue area with a terrace and good views. A neighbour rents out water bikes and takes high season excursions onto the lake with a real Viking Ship which campers can join. The last weekend of May the site celebrates the Jelling Musical Festival when it is advisable to book in advance.

Facilities

One modern and one older toilet block have British style toilets, open style washbasins and controllable hot showers (card operated). Family shower rooms. Baby room. Facilities for disabled visitors. Laundry. Campers' kitchen. Motorcaravan services. Shop (bread to order). Outdoor swimming pool (15 x 5 m). Playground. Football field. Minigolf.. Basketball. Volleyball. Games room. Pony riding. Lake with fishing (charged), watersports and Viking ship. Off site: Golf and riding 2 km. Boat launching 10 km. Legoland 20 km. Lion Park 8 km.

At a glance

Welcome & Ambience	✓✓✓✓	Location	✓✓✓✓
Quality of Pitches	✓✓✓✓	Range of Facilities	✓✓✓

Directions

From Vejle take the 442 road northwest towards Jelling. In Jelling turn south towards Fårup Sø and the site.

Charges 2004

Per person	DKK 59,00
child	DKK 32,00
pitch	DKK 25,00
electricity	DKK 25,00

Reservations

Contact site. Tel: 75 87 13 44.
E-mail: faarup-soe@dk-camp.dk

Open

4 April - 5 September.

DK2036 Gammelmark Strand Camping

Gammelmark 16, DK-6310 Broager (Sønderjylland)

This site combines Danish hospitality with historical interest. In 1864 war was waged between the Danes and the Germans over the Flensburger Förde and this site organises excursions to the war museum in Dybbøl Banke where you can learn all about this devastating period in Danish history. Especially interesting for children, in summer a guide will take them out for a day to show them how tough it was to drag the canons uphill. Gammelmark is also close to a Royal Palace, now owned by Prince Frederick and Mary. When they are not at home it is possible to visit the Royal Gardens. The Siegers, a Danish/Dutch couple, have owned this site since 2001. Gammelmark has 240 level, grasss pitches (180 for tourers), all with 10A electricity. From the top terraces there are some great views of the Flensburger Förde. This site is useful as a stop over on your way to north, but also for the active camper. There are several marked walking routes and opportunities for diving and fishing.

Facilities

Modern, heated facilities with British style toilets, washbasins (open and in cabins) and controllable hot showers (Dkr 2). Child size toilets and basins. Baby room. En-suite facilities for disabled visitors. Laundry with sink, 2 washing machines, dryer and ironing board. Dishwashing. Motorcaravan services. Shop. Playground. Animal farm. Football field. Fishing. Riding. Sailing. Diving. Beach. Daily activity programme in high season. Musical nights. TV room. Torch useful. English is spoken. Off site: Bar, restaurant and takeaway 2 km. Bicycle hire 6 km. Golf 10 km.

At a glance

Welcome & Ambience	✓✓✓✓	Location	✓✓✓✓
Quality of Pitches	✓✓✓✓	Range of Facilities	✓✓✓

Directions

From Flensburg take no. 7 road north and at exit 75 turn east towards Sønderborg. Take exit Dynt and follow site signs.

Charges 2004

Per person	DKK 60,00
child (1-11 yrs)	DKK 30,00
pitch	DKK 15,00 - 30,00
electricity	DKK 27,00
dog	DKK 8,00

Reservations

Call or e-mail the site. Tel: 74 44 17 42.
E-mail: info@gammelmark.dk

Open

1 April - 30 September.

DK2032 Augustenhof Camping

Augustenhofveg 30, DK-6430 Nordborg/Als (Sønderjylland)

People looking for real peace and quiet are well off on this remote site on the Lillebælt waters. As we learned from one of the guests, because of the remote location of the site, there's not much traffic around. Augustenhof has been developed on the land of a former farm giving feeling of space, mainly because of the marvellous views of the sea from most pitches. The site borders the beach, which lies about 5 m. lower – this part of the site is not fenced. The climb down to the beach is via a stairway. This site is an ideal starting point for long beach walks, cycling tours, surfing and sailing. Augustenhof has 190 large, grassy pitches with 115 for touring units. Most have 6/13A electricity and in rows off gravel roads separated at the rear by low hedges. Because the site is relatively high, in good weather it is possible to see Jutland and Funen. There is very little shade, but a firm sea breeze will normally cool things down in summer.

Facilities

Two traditional toilet blocks with British style toilets, washbasins (open style and in cabins) and controllable hot showers (Dkr. 2). Child size toilets, showers and basins. Comfortable family rooms with toilet, basin and shower. Baby room. En-suite facilities for disabled visitors. Laundry with sinks, washing machine and dryer. Campers' kitchen. Dishwashing (free hot water). Motorcaravan services. Shop (daily in season). Playground. TV room. Minigolf. Fishing. Bicycle hire. Watersports and boat launching. Beach. Torch useful. English is spoken. Off site: Golf 5 km.

Open

All year.

At a glance

Welcome & Ambience	✓✓✓✓	Location	✓✓✓✓
Quality of Pitches	✓✓✓✓	Range of Facilities	✓✓✓

Directions

From Sønderborg continue on 8 road to Augustenborg, then follow 405 road to Nordborg. In Nordborg turn right at the sign 'Nordborg Skole' and camp signs. Follow signs to site.

Charges 2004

Per person	DKK 57,00
child (0-12 yrs)	DKK 30,00
electricity	DKK 22,00
dog	DKK 8,00

Reservations

Taken but normally not necessary.
Tel: 95 74 95 03 04.
E-mail: augustenhof@dk-camp.dk

DK2034 Stensager Camping

Oluf Ravnsvej 16, Binderup Strand, DK-6091 Bjert (Sønderjylland)

For children the main attraction of this site is sure to be the giant, 48 metres long, brand new water slide – at the time of our visit it was just one week old. It ends in a separate pool, from which one can slip into the main fun pool and next to that is a paddling pool with a slide for toddlers. Stensager has large pitches on well kept, grassy fields. Pitches are separated at the rear by high bushes and around the site are many different sorts of trees. The site is on sloping ground, but the 270 pitches (145 for tourers) are level and all have 6/10A electricity. Although Stensager is only a couple of hundred metres from the sea, none of the pitches has views. According to Mrs Gustafson, the owner, most campers come here to relax, lie on the beach and to visit the historic town of Kolding with its Castle, once belonging to the Danish royal family. This is also a good site for those who like fishing, walking and cycling.

Facilities

Two modern blocks provide British style toilets, washbasins in cabins and controllable hot showers. Child size toilets, basins and showers. Family shower rooms. Baby room with bath. En-suite facilities for disabled people. Laundry with sink, 3 washing machines and dryer. Dishwashing. Motorcaravan services. Shop (daily in season). Swimming pool with giant slide, paddling pool and sauna. Playground. Football field. Minigolf. Watersports and boat launching. Beach. Beach volleyball. Basketball. Daily entertainment programme for children in high season. TV room. English is spoken. Off site: Fishing 8 km. Golf 12 km.

Open

1 April - 15 September.

At a glance

Welcome & Ambience	✓✓✓✓	Location	✓✓✓✓
Quality of Pitches	✓✓✓✓	Range of Facilities	✓✓✓✓

Directions

Follow E45 north towards Kolding and take exit 66 towards Christiansfeld and follow 170 road north. At Taps exit towards Åsturp, Sjølund and Grønninghoved and follow to Binderup, Bjert and Bjert Strand.

Charges 2004

Per person	DKK 60,00
child	DKK 31,00
electricity	DKK 23,00

Less 15-25% in low season.
Credit cards accepted with a 4% surcharge.

Reservations

Call, write or e-mail the site. Tel: 75 57 22 31.
E-mail: stensager@dk-camp.dk

DK2022 Vikær Diernæs Strand Camping

Dundelum 29, Diernæs, DK-6100 Djerindes (Sønderjylland)

The warm and humorous welcome at Vikær Diernæs will start your holiday off in the right way. This family site in Southern Jutland lies in beautiful surroundings, right on the Diernæs Bugt beaches – ideal for both active campers and relaxation seekers. For the active there are several routes for walking and cycling and, of course, sea fishing trips are possible. In the area are a newly developed swamp nature reserve, Schackenborg Castle and the battlefields of Dybbøl Banke. The attractively laid out site has 330 grass pitches (210 for touring units), all with 10/16A electricity and separated by low, partly newly planted, hedges. Access is off long, gravel access lanes. The upper part of the site provides newly developed fully serviced pitches with electricity, water, sewage, TV aerial point and internet. From these, and from the front pitches on the lower fields, there are marvellous views over the Diernæs Bugt. The site is next to a 'Blue Flag' beach providing safe swimming. In high season the site organises excursions to the Dybbøl heritage centre.

Facilities

Two modern toilet blocks with British style toilets, washbasins in cabins and controllable hot showers. Family shower rooms. Baby room with bath and changing mat. En-suite facilities for disabled visitors. Laundry with sink, 2 washing machines and dryer. Campers' kitchen. Dishwashing. Motorcaravan services. Shop (Thursday – Sunday 7.30 – 21.00). Playground. Football field. Minigolf. Fishing. Archery. Watersports and boat launching. Petanque. Play house for children with Lego and Play Station. Daily activities for children in high season.
TV room. Billiards. Torch useful. English is spoken.
Off site: Golf 30 mins. Riding 2 km.

At a glance

Welcome & Ambience	✓✓✓✓	Location	✓✓✓✓
Quality of Pitches	✓✓✓	Range of Facilities	✓✓✓

Directions

From German/Danish border follow E45 north. Take exit 69 and follow to Hoptrup. From Hoptrup follow to Diernæs and Diernæs Strand.

Charges 2004

Per person	DKK 62,00
child (under 12 yrs)	DKK 35,00
pitch	DKK 12,00 - 55,00
electricity	DKK 26,00
dog	DKK 10,00

Reservations

Call, write or e-mail site. Tel: 74 57 54 64.
E-mail: info@vikaercamp.dk

Open

11 April - 28 September.

DK2030 Sandersvig Camping

Espagervej 15-17, DK-6100 Haderslev (Sønderjylland)

An attractively laid out, family run site, Sandersvig offers the very best of modern facilities in a peaceful and beautiful countryside location, 300 metres from the beach. The 470 very large grassy pitches (270 for tourers) are divided by hedges, shrubs and small trees into small enclosures, many housing only four units, most with electricity (10A). The site is well lit, very quiet at night and there are water taps close to most pitches. The playground boasts Denmark's largest bouncing cushion! Opposite the site, on the road to the beach, the site owners have planted new woodland. Sandersvig makes a very comfortable base for excursions. Visit nearby historic Kolding with its castle, museums and shops, the beautiful old town of Christiansfeld or the restored windmill at Sillerup. The drive to the island of Fyn takes less than an hour, with miles of country lanes around the site for cycling and walking.

Facilities

Three heated sanitary blocks offer some washbasins in cubicles and roomy showers (on payment). Suites for disabled visitors, six family bathrooms and baby rooms. Excellent kitchens with ovens, electric hobs, dishwashing sinks. Very good laundry. Fish cleaning area. Motorcaravan services. Well stocked supermarket and fast food service, with dining room adjacent (Easter-15/9). Takeaway (15/6-15/8). Outdoor heated swimming pool (15/5-1/9). Solarium. Playground. New football field. Games room with pool table, 'air hockey' and arcade machines. TV lounge. Two hard tennis courts. Boat launching. Off site: Riding 4 km. Bicycle hire 6 km. Fishing 7 km. Golf 16 km.

At a glance

Welcome & Ambience	✓✓✓	Location	✓✓✓✓
Quality of Pitches	✓✓✓✓	Range of Facilities	✓✓✓✓

Directions

Leave E45 at exit 66 and turn towards Christianfeld. Turn right at roundabout onto 170 and follow signs for Fjelstrup and Knud village, turning right 1 km. east of the village from where site is signed.

Charges 2004

Per person	DKK 54,00
child (0-11 yrs)	DKK 30,00
pitch	DKK 10,00 - 25,00
electricity (10A)	DKK 23,00
dog	free

Reservations

Essential for high season (25/6-7/8). Tel: 74 56 62 25.
E-mail: sandersvig@dk-camp.dk

Open

27 March - 15 September.

DK2046 Trelde Næs Supercamp

Trelde Næsvej 297, Trelde, DK-7000 Fredericia (Vejle)

Trelde Næs Supercamp is one of the larger Danish sites with 500 level and numbered pitches. The 400 touring pitches all have 10A electricity and there are 37 fully serviced pitches with electricity, water, waste water and internet. Seasonal units take up the remaining 100 pitches. Pitching is off tarmac access roads on well-kept, grassy fields with some shade from bushes at the rear. The toilet buildings are older in style but the fittings are good. At the front of the site is a heated, open air, fun pool with large slide, bubble bath, water curtain and play island. This is connected to a room with a sauna, Turkish baths and massage chairs, with play stations for children. Trelde Næs is right next to the beach, but also close to the nature reserve of Trelde Næs which has been part of the Royal estates since the 14th century. The historic town of Fredericia is close. Here we recommend you take the tour of the Walls, built by King Christian IV, and visit Den Historiske Miniby, a miniature model park of Fredericia.

Facilities

Four traditional but refurbished toilet blocks have British style toilets, washbasins in cabins and controllable hot showers (card operated). Child size toilets and basins. Family shower room. Baby room. Laundry with sinks, 3 washing machines and dryer. Dishwashing. Fun pool (10 x 20 m.) with island, large slide, Turkish bath, solarium and sauna. Shop. Takeaway. Several playgrounds. Football field. Minigolf. Fishing. Watersports. Full entertainment programme in high season for children. TV room. English is spoken. Off site: Boat launching 1 km. Golf 6 km. Bicycle hire 6 km.

At a glance

Welcome & Ambience	✓✓✓✓	Location	✓✓✓✓✓
Quality of Pitches	✓✓✓✓	Range of Facilities	✓✓✓✓

Directions

From Fredericia follow road no. 28 north and take Trelde exit. Follow signs for Trelde and Trelde Næs.

Charges 2004

Per person	DKK 66,00
child (0-11 yrs)	DKK 40,00
pitch	DKK 0,00 - 50,00
with services	DKK 30,00 - 70,00
electricity	DKK 25,00

Reservations

Necessary for high season. Call, write or e-mail the site. Tel: 75 95 71 83. E-mail: info@supercamp.dk

Open

All year.

DK2200 Bojden Strandcamping

Bojden Landevej 12, Bojden, DK-5600 Fåborg (Fyn)

Located in one of the most beautiful corners of southwest Fyn, this is a well equipped site separated from the beach only by a hedge. Many pitches have sea views as the site slopes gently down from the road. The 314 pitches (200 for touring units) all have electricity and include 32 fully serviced pitches (water, drainage and TV aerial point). A swimming pool (13 x 9 m) and paddling pool with a sun terrace are open during suitable weather. Everyone will enjoy the beach (Blue Flag) for swimming, boating and watersports. The water is too shallow for shore fishing but boat trips can be arranged. Bøjden is a delightful site for an entire holiday, while remaining a very good centre for excursions.

Facilities

The superb quality, heated toilet block is centrally located and includes washbasins in cubicles, controllable showers, family bathrooms (some with whirlpools and double showers), a baby room and excellent facilities for disabled people. Well appointed kitchen. Washing machine and dryer. Motorcaravan services. Supermarket. Takeaway. Swimming pool (20/5-20/8). Solarium. Play areas. TV and games rooms. Barbecue area. Bicycle and boat hire. Fishing. Riding. Minigolf. Off site: Beach adjacent. Restaurant and bar 100 m. Golf 12 km.

At a glance

Welcome & Ambience	✓✓✓✓	Location	✓✓✓✓✓
Quality of Pitches	✓✓✓✓	Range of Facilities	✓✓✓✓

Directions

From Faaborg follow road no. 8 to Bøjden and site is on right 500 m. before ferry terminal (from Fynshav).

Charges 2004

Per person	DKK 59,00
child (under 12 yrs)	DKK 35,00
pitch (18/6-15/8)	DKK 30,00 - 60,00
electricity	DKK 26,00

Reservations

Advised for high season. Tel: 62 60 12 84. E-mail: bojden@dk-camp.dk

Open

1 April - 15 September.

DK2220 Helnæs Camping

Strandbakken 21, Helnæs, DK-5631 Ebberup (Fyn)

Helnæs Camping is on the remote Helnæs peninsula to the southeast of Fyn (Funen in English), connected to the mainland by a small road. The site is adjacent to a nature reserve making it ideal for walkers, cyclists and bird spotters, or for those who enjoy sea fishing (we were told this is a great location for sea trout). The road to the site takes you through a breathtaking environment with colourful flowerbeds on the Bobakkerne Wall to the north and large outer marches in the south. Helnæs Camping has 160 pitches, some terraced, on grassy fields sloping down towards to the sea. From almost all the pitches there are beautiful views of Helnæs Bugt and the site is only 300 m. from the beach. Low rock walls and different types of newly planted trees and low shrubs separate pitches. All have 6A electricity. The owner since 2002, Mr. Kristensen, has built a new playground, which is fenced with a low rock wall and a new minigolf course.

Facilities

Two toilet blocks, one partly refurbished, one new, with British style toilets, basins in cabins and controllable showers (Dkr. 2). Baby room (heated). Laundry with 2 washing machines, 2 dryers and spin dryer. Dishwashing. Campers' kitchen. Shop. Takeaway. New adventure type playground. Football field. Minigolf. Bicycle hire. Canoe hire. Watersports. In high season small circus for children. TV lounge. Covered barbecue area. English is spoken. Off site: Sea fishing.

At a glance

Welcome & Ambience	✓✓✓✓✓	Location	✓✓✓✓✓
Quality of Pitches	✓✓✓✓	Range of Facilities	✓✓✓

Directions

From Nørre Åby follow 313 road south to Ebberup. In Ebberup turn south to Helnæs and signs to Strand.

Charges 2004

Per person	DKK 56,00
child	DKK 28,00
electricity	DKK 22,00

No credit cards.

Reservations

Call, write or e-mail the site. Tel: 64 77 13 39. E-mail: info@helnaes-camping.dk

Open

1 April - 17 October.

DK2210 Bøsøre Strand Ferie Park

Bøsørevej 16, DK-5874 Hesselager (Fyn)

A themed holiday site on the eastern coast of Fyn, the tales of Hans Christian Andersen are evident in the design of the heated indoor pool complex and the main outdoor children's playground at this site. The former has two pools on different levels, two hot tubs and a sauna and features characters from the stories, the latter has a fairytale castle with moat as its centrepiece. There are 300 pitches in total, and with only 25 seasonal units there should always be room for tourists out of main season. All have 6A electricity, there are 124 multi-serviced pitches and 20 hardstandings. In common with several other sites in Denmark, Bøsøre operates a debit card system. Upon payment of a minimum Dkr. 100.00, the card will allow use of the facilities (showers, washing machine etc).

Facilities

Sanitary facilities are housed in one main central block and a smaller unit close to reception. Family bathrooms, special children's section, baby rooms, facilities for disabled people. They could be stretched in high season. Motorcaravan services. Shop. Restaurant. Pizzeria. Take-away in peak season. Kitchen (water charged). Solarium. Indoor pool complex. Playground. Animal farm. Internet. Bicycle hire.

Open

Easter - 17 October.

At a glance

Welcome & Ambience	✓✓✓✓	Location	✓✓✓✓
Quality of Pitches	✓✓✓✓	Range of Facilities	✓✓✓✓

Directions

The site lies on the coast midway between Nyborg and Svendborg. From road 163 north of Hesselager, take turn towards coast signed Bøsøre Strand.

Charges 2004

Per person	DKK 62,00
child (0-11 yrs)	DKK 41,00
pitch	free - DKK 50,00
serviced pitch	DKK 25,00
electricity	DKK 28,00

Reservations

Contact site - advised for high season. Tel: 62 25 11 45. E-mail: info@bosore.dk

DK2205 Løgismosestrand Camping

Løgismoseskov 7, DK-5683 Hårby (Fyn)

A countryside site with its own beach and pool, Løgismosestrand is surrounded by picturesque villages and the owners are a friendly young couple. The 220 pitches here are arranged in rows and groups divided by hedges and small trees which provide a little shade. All the 140 pitches for touring units have 6-10A electricity points. A barbecue area has gas grills and there are swimming (8 x 14 m.) and paddling pools (small charge). Recent additions include a café and pizzeria, plus a new football pitch.

Facilities

Heated toilet units, kept very clean, include washbasins in cubicles, roomy showers (on payment), baby room, bathrooms for families and disabled people. Good laundry with washing machine and dryer. Excellent fully fitted kitchen with gas hobs, microwave (cooking facilities charged). Motorcaravan services. Shop. Café with pizzeria. Takeaway (high season). Swimming pool (1/6-1/9). Minigolf. Table tennis. Bicycle and boat hire. Pony riding. Adventure playground. Play field. Off site: Riding 2 km. Golf 12 km.

Open

27 March - 18 September.

At a glance

Welcome & Ambience	✓✓✓✓	Location	✓✓✓✓
Quality of Pitches	✓✓✓✓	Range of Facilities	✓✓✓✓

Directions

Southwest of Hårby via Sarup and Nellemose to Løgismose Skov, site is well signed. Lanes are narrow, large units should take care.

Charges 2004

Per person	DKK 59,00
child (under 12 yrs)	DKK 35,00
pitch	DKK 10,00 - 40,00
electricity	DKK 26,00
dog	DKK 5,00

Credit cards accepted with 5% surcharge.

Reservations

Essential for high season - write for details. Tel: 64 77 12 50. E-mail: info@logismose.dk

DK2215 DCU Camping Odense

Odensevej 102, DK-5260 Odense (Fyn)

Although within the confines of the city, this site is hidden away amongst mature trees and is therefore fairly quiet and is an ideal base from which to explore the fairy-tale city of Odense. The 225 pitches, of which 200 have electricity (10A), are on level grass with small hedges and shrubs dividing the area into bays. There are a number of seasonal units on site together with 14 cabins. A good network of cycle paths lead into the city. The Odense Adventure Pass (available at the site) allows unrestricted free travel on public transport within the city limits, free admission to the swimming baths and a free daily newspaper, with varying discounts on other attractions.

Facilities

Large sanitary unit provides up to the minute facilities including washbasins in cubicles, family bathrooms, baby room and excellent suite for disabled visitors. Well equipped kitchen with gas hobs, extractor hoods and dishwashing sinks. Washing machines and dryer. Motorcaravan services. Shop. Small swimming pool. Games marquee. Table tennis. TV room. Large playground with bouncing cushion. Ball games field. Minigolf. Free bicycles. Off site: Cycle track through the zoo to city centre. Hans Christian Andersen's house. Bicycle hire 700 m. Golf 4 km. Fishing 10 km.

At a glance

Welcome & Ambience	✓✓✓✓	Location	✓✓✓✓
Quality of Pitches	✓✓✓	Range of Facilities	✓✓✓✓

Directions

From E20 exit 50, turn towards Odense Centrum, site entrance is 3 km. on left immediately beside the Texaco Garage.

Charges 2004

Per person	DKK 64,00
child (0-11 yrs)	DKK 32,00
pitch	DKK 20,00

Reservations

Contact site. Tel: 66 11 47 02. E-mail: odense@dcu.dk

Open

22 March - 20 October.

DK2235 Sakskobing Gron Camping

Saxes Allé 15, DK-4990 Sakskobing (Lolland)

This small, traditional style site provides a useful stop-over on the route from Germany to Sweden within easy reach of the Puttgarden - Rødby ferry. There are 125 level grassy pitches, most with electricity and, although there are a fair number of seasonal units, one can usually find space. The pool at the nearby sports centre is said to be the most modern in Europe. The site has a well stocked shop, although the attractive town centre is semi-pedestrianised and has a good range of shops and a supermarket. The town is noted for its unusual 'smiling' water tower, which you pass on the way to the site.

Facilities

Two sanitary units provide basic, older style facilities, including push-button hot showers (Dkr. 2 token), some curtained washbasin cubicles and a baby room, plus cooking, dishwashing and laundry facilities. Motorcaravan services. Shop. Play area. Off site: Town 500 m.

Open

1 April - 27 October.

At a glance

Welcome & Ambience	✓✓	Location	✓✓✓
Quality of Pitches	✓✓✓✓	Range of Facilities	✓✓✓

Directions

From E47, exit 46, turn towards town on road 9. Turn right at crossroads towards town centre (site is signed), cross railway and then turn right again, and site entrance is 250 m. on left.

Charges guide

Per person	DKK 55,00
electricity	DKK 20,00

Reservations

Advised for last week June to end of July. Tel: 54 70 47 57.

DK2250 Hillerød Camping

Blytækkervej 18, DK-3400 Hillerod (Sjælland)

The northern-most corner of Sjælland is packed with interest, based not only on fascinating parts of Denmark's history but also its attractive scenery. Centrally situated, Hillerød is a hub of main roads from all directions, with this neat campsite clearly signed. It has a park-like setting in a residential area with five acres of well kept grass and some attractive trees. There are 92 pitches, of which 50 have electricity (10A) and these are marked. The site amenities are all centrally located in modern, well maintained buildings which are kept very clean. The centre of Hillerød, like so many Danish towns, has been pedestrianised making shopping or outdoor refreshment a pleasure. Visit Frederiksborg Slot, a fine Renaissance Castle and home of the Museum of Danish national history. Hillerød, however is a fine base for visiting Copenhagen and only 25 km. from the ferries at Helsingør and the crossing to Sweden.

Facilities

The bright, airy toilet block is older in style and includes washbasins with partitions and curtain. Facilities for babies can be used by disabled people. Campers' kitchen adjoins the club room and includes free new electric hot plates and coffee making machine. Dishwashing sinks. Laundry room (free iron). Motorcaravan services. Small shop with basic supplies. Good comfortable club room with TV and children's corner. Playground. Free bicycles, some with buggy for small children. Off site: Tennis courts and indoor swimming pool 1 km. Riding 2 km. Golf 3 km. Excellent new electric train service every 10 minutes (20 mins. walk) to Copenhagen. The site sells the Copenhagen card.

At a glance

Welcome & Ambience	✓✓✓✓	Location	✓✓✓✓
Quality of Pitches	✓✓✓	Range of Facilities	✓✓✓

Directions

Follow road no. 6 bypassing road to south until sign for Hillerod S. Turn towards town at sign for 'Centrum' on Roskildvej road no. 233 and site is signed to the right.

Charges 2004

Per person	DKK 60,00
child (2-11 yrs)	DKK 30,00
electricity	DKK 30,00
dog	free

Reservations

Not made. Tel: 48 26 48 54.
E-mail: hillcamp@post8.tele.dk

Open

Easter - 30 September.

DK2255 Topcamp Feddet

Feddet 12, DK-4640 Fakse (Sjælland)

This interesting spacious site with ecological principles is located on the Baltic coast. It has a fine, white, sandy beach (Blue Flag) which runs the full length of one side, with the Præstø fjord on the opposite side of the peninsula. There are 862 pitches, generally on sandy grass, with mature pine trees giving adequate shade. All have 10/13A electricity and 20 are fully serviced (water, electricity, drainage and sewage). There are 676 pitches for touring units. Two, recently constructed sanitary buildings have been specially designed to have natural ventilation, with ventilators controlled by sensors for heat, humidity and smell. The shaped blades on the roof increase ventilation on windy days. All this saves power and provides a comfortable climate inside. Heating is by a wood chip furnace (backed up by an oil seed rape furnace), is CO_2 neutral and replaces 40,000 litres of heating oil annually. The buildings are clad with larch panels from sustainable local trees, and are insulated with flax mats. Rainwater is used for toilet flushing, but showers and basins are supplied from the normal mains, and urinals are water free. Water saving taps have an automatic turn off, and lighting is by low wattage bulbs with PIR switching. Recycling is very important here, with separate bins for glass, metal, paper, cardboard and batteries. The site has a Danish Green Key award for its environmental standards.

Facilities

Both sanitary buildings are impressive, equipped to very high standard and include family bathrooms (with twin showers), complete small children and baby suites. Facilities for disabled people. Laundry. Kitchens with ovens, hobs and rental fridges, dining room and a TV lounge. Each block has a chemical disposal facility complete with handbasin, soap, and paper towel. Excellent drive-over motorcaravan service point. Well stocked licensed shop. Licensed bistro and takaway (1/5-20/10 but weekends only outside peak season). Minigolf, games room and table tennis. Indoor toddlers' playroom and several playgrounds for all ages, trampolines and bouncing cushion. Event camp for children. Pet zoo. Bungee jump. Internet access. Gym, massage, reflexology and sunbeds. Watersports. Fishing. Off site: Many other activities with guides or instructors, including Land Rover safaris, abseiling, Icelandic pony riding, educational courses, ocean kayaking, and seal watching in Fakse Bay. Indoor pool complex nearby. Amusement park.

At a glance

Welcome & Ambience	✓✓✓✓✓	Location	✓✓✓✓
Quality of Pitches	✓✓✓✓	Range of Facilities	✓✓✓✓

Directions

From south on E47/55 take exit 38 towards Præsto. Turn north on 209 road towardds Fakse and from Vindbyholt follow site signs. From the north on E47/55 take exit 37 east towards Fakse. Just before Fakse turn south on 209 road and from Vindbyholt, site signs.

Charges 2004

Per person	DKK 66,00
child (0-11 yrs)	DKK 45,00
pitch	DKK 25,00 - 47,00
electricity	DKK 30,00
dog	DKK 15,00

Reservations

Advised for high season; contact site.
Tel: 56 72 52 06. E-mail: info@feddetcamping.dk

Open

1 April - 19 October.

Denmark

DK2260 DCU Nærum Camping

Ravnbakken, DK-2850 Nærum (Sjælland)

Obviously everyone arriving in Sjælland will want to visit 'wonderful, wonderful Copenhagen', but like all capital cities, it draws crowds during the holiday season and traffic to match. This friendly, sheltered site is near enough to be convenient but distant enough to afford peace and quiet (apart from the noise of nearby traffic) and a chance of relaxing after sightseeing. Nærum, one of the Danish Camping Union sites, is only 15 km. from the city centre and very near a suburban railway that takes you there. The long narrow site covers a large area alongside the ancient royal hunting forests, adjacent to the small railway line and the main road. Power lines do cross the site but there is lots of grassy open space. The 275 touring pitches are in two areas - in wooded glades taking about six units each (mostly used by tents) or on more open meadows where electrical connections (6/10A) are available. Nærum is a useful site to know for Copenhagen, but is also very near to the interesting friendly shopping complex of Rødøvre and the amusement park at Bakken. Note: Should you wish to drive into the city, there is a useful car park on the quayside. It is within easy walking distance of the centre and is located where the Kalvebød Brygge meets the Langebrø bridge (suitable for motorcaravans and caravans).

Facilities

Two modern toilet blocks, one in the meadow area has been refurbished and includes partitioned washbasins. Good block at reception can be heated and also provides a laundry, dishwashing and a campers' kitchen. Good facilities for babies and disabled people. Four family bathrooms (free). Motorcaravan service point. Reception and shop for basics (closed 12.00-14.00 and 22.00-07.00). Café/restaurant near. Club room and TV. Barbecue. Play field and adventure playground. Off site: Full range of sporting facilities within easy reach of the site and café/restaurant within a few hundred metres. Train service to Copenhagen (400 m. on foot, change at Jaegersborg).

At a glance

Welcome & Ambience	✓✓	Location	✓✓✓✓
Quality of Pitches	✓✓✓	Range of Facilities	✓✓✓

Directions

From E55/E47, take Nærum exit (no. 14), 15 km. north of Copenhagen. Turn right at first set of traffic lights (site signed), right on road 19 at second lights, cross bridge and turn left, following signs to site.

Charges 2004

Per person	DKK 62,00
child (0-11 yrs)	DKK 31,00
pitch	DKK 20,00
electricity	DKK 25,00

Reservations

Write for details. Tel: 45 80 19 57. E-mail: info@dcu.dk

Open

19 March - 25 September.

DK2265 Camping Charlottenlund Fort

Strandvejen 144B, DK-2920 Charlottenlund (Sjælland)

On the northern outskirts of Copenhagen, this unique site is within the walls of an old fort which still retains its main armament of twelve 29 cm. howitzers (disabled, of course). The fort was constructed during 1886-1887 and was an integral link in the Copenhagen fortifications until 1932. The site is only six kilometres from the centre of Copenhagen, with a regular bus service (every 20 minutes) from just outside the site. Alternatively you could use the excellent cycle network to visit the city. There are 63 pitches, mostly on grass, all with 10A electric hook-ups. The obvious limitation on the space available means that pitches are relatively close together, but many are quite deep. The site is very popular and is usually full every night, so we suggest that you either make a reservation or arrive well before mid-day.

Facilities

Sanitary facilities located in the old armoury are rather basic, but clean, well maintained and heated. Showers on payment, but kitchen facilities include gas hobs and a dining area. Laundry. Motorcaravan service point. Small kiosk in front of site. Bicycle hire. Beach. Off site: Small restaurant (separate management) is adjacent, with good sea views to Sweden and the spectacular Oresund Bridge. Riding 1.5 km. Golf 2 km.

Open

15 May - 14 September.

At a glance

Welcome & Ambience	✓✓✓✓	Location	✓✓✓✓
Quality of Pitches	✓✓	Range of Facilities	✓✓

Directions

Leave E47/E55 at junction 17, and turn southeast on Jægersborgvej. After a short distance turn left (east) on Jægersborg Allé, following signs for Charlottenlund (5 km) and follow all the way to the end. Finally turn right (south) on to Strandvejen, and site entrance is on left after 500 m.

Charges 2004

Per person	DKK 70
child (3-12 yrs)	DKK 27
electricity	DKK 25

Reservations

Essential for high season; contact site. Tel: 39 62 36 88. E-mail: camping-fort@mail.dk

Situated in the far north, Finland is a long and mainly flat county, dominated by huge dense forests and glorious lakes. The unspoilt wilderness of this country makes it a perfect place for relaxing in natural, peaceful surroundings.

There is a considerable difference in the landscape between north and south, with the gently rolling, rural landscape of the south giving way to the hills and vast forests of the north and treeless fells and peat-lands of Lapland, where reindeer and moose run free. Forests of spruce, pine and birch cover three quarters of the country's surface and are inhabited by hares, elks and occasional wolves and bears.

The other outstanding feature of Finland is its thousands of post-glacial lakes and islands. The main Lake District is centred on the beautiful Lake Saimaa in the south east, where you can swim, sail and fish. In the south, the capital Helsinki retains a small town feel, with open air cafes, green parks, waterways and a busy market square surrounded by 19th century architecture and museums. The flat western coastal regions include Turku and the Åland islands, ideal for sailing and fishing.

Population

5.2 million

Capital

Helsinki

Climate

Temperate climate, but with considerable variations. Summer is warm, winter is very cold

Language

Finnish

Currency

The Euro

Telephone

The country code is 00 358

Banks

Mon-Fri 09.15- 16.15 (regional variations may occur)

Shops

Mon-Fri 09.00-17.00/18.00. Sat 09.00-14.00/15.00, department stores usually remain open to 18.00. Supermarkets usually open to 20.00 Mon-Fri

Public Holidays

New Year; Epiphany; Good Friday; Easter Mon; May Day; Ascension; Midsummer's Day; All Saints Day; Independence Day 6 Dec; Christmas 25, 26 Dec

Motoring

Main roads are excellent and relatively uncrowded outside city limits. Traffic drives on the right. Horn blowing is frowned upon. There are many road signs warning motorist of the danger of elk dashing out on the road. If you are unfortunate enough to hit one, it must be reported to police. Do not drink and drive, penalties are severe if any alcohol is detected

Tourist Office

Finnish Tourist Board
PO Box 33213
London W6 8KX
Tel: 020 8600 5680
Fax: 020 8600 5681
Email: finlandinfo.lon@mek.fi
Internet: www. finland-tourism.com

TAKE A CRUISE ALONG THE LAKES. DAILY TOURS AND LONGER CRUISES OPERATE IN THE SUMMER. POPULAR ROUTES ARE BETWEEN HAMEENLINNA AND TAMPERE, TAMPERE AND VIRRAT AND ALONG THE SAIMAA LAKES.

FI2990 Camping Tenorinne

99950 Karigasniemi (Lapland)

This is probably the most northerly campsite in Finland and makes an excellent stop over en-route to North Cape. By the time you arrive here, you will have been driving inside the Arctic Circle for three or four days! This is a small site with space for about 30 units, on three levels with a small access road sloping down to the river. Electricity points (16A) are available throughout the site but the pitches are unmarked. This area is still largely unpopulated, scattered with only small Sami communities and herds of reindeer. Karigasniemi is a slightly larger town as it is a border post with Norway and is close to both the Kevo Nature reserve and the Lemmenjoki National Park. Finland has 19 nature reserves covering an area of 1,520 square kilometres; Kevo takes up almost half of that area. The campsite is on the banks of the Tenojoki River and is an excellent base for walking and bird watching. A little further north you will find Nuvvus-Ailigas, the holy fell of the ancient sami, which rises to a height of 400 m. above the level of the Teno river. Karigasniemi is at the junction of the 970 with route 92 and is a good base to absorb all that Finnish Lapland has to offer.

Facilities

Sanitary block includes showers, toilets and sauna. Launderette. Kitchen. Reception includes small shop and TV.

Open

1 June - 15 September.

At a glance

Welcome & Ambience	✓✓✓✓	Location	✓✓✓✓
Quality of Pitches	✓✓✓	Range of Facilities	✓✓✓

Directions

If you are travelling south on the 970 the campsite is on the right just as you enter the town. If you are travelling west on the 92, turn right immediately before the Norwegian customs point, the site is a short way on the left past the petrol station. The site entrance is quite steep.

Charges 2005

Per tent or caravan	€ 15,00 - € 17,00
electricity	€ 3,00

Reservations

Not needed. Tel: 016 676113.
E-mail: tarmo_lehtosalo@hotmail.com

FI2995 Ukonjarvi Camping

Pl 118, 99801 Ivalo (Lapland)

Ukonjarvi Camping lies on the banks of Lake Inari, situated in a forested area alongside a nature reserve. It is a quiet, peaceful site, ideal for rest and relaxation. All 50 pitches have electricity and are surrounded by pine and beech trees. Cottages are available to rent. A bar and restaurant are located at reception; a range of local dishes are produced including reindeer casserole. There is also a barbecue hut, located in the centre of the site, if you prefer to cook your own food. A climb up to the nearby view point offers spectacular views over the lake – you can even see over to Russia, which is just a few kilometres away. The lake also provides plenty of opportunities for boating and fishing.

Facilities

Sanitary block includes toilets and showers. Lakeside sauna (extra cost). Barbecue hut with logs. Small beach. Fishing and boating on lake. Off site: Local attractions in the area include the Tankavaaran kansainvalinen Kulamuseo, a gold mining experience where you can try your had at gold panning – keeping what you find! The Northern Lapland Centre and the Sami Museum, displaying cultural and natural history exhibitions.

At a glance

Welcome & Ambience	✓✓✓✓	Location	✓✓✓✓✓
Quality of Pitches	✓✓✓	Range of Facilities	✓✓✓

Directions

Ukonjarvi Camping is 11 km. north of Ivalo on Route 4. Look for signs to Lake Inari viewpoint; site is approximately 1 km. down the narrow road on the road.

Charges 2004

Per unit incl 2 persons and electricity	€ 16,00

Reservations

Not essential. Tel: 016 667501.
E-mail: nuttu@ukolo.fi

Open

June - September.

FI2985 Camping Sodankylä Nilimella

Kemijärventie 1361, 99600 Sodankylä (Lapland)

Camping Sodankyla Nillimella is a small, quiet site situated alongside the Kemijarvi River, just one kilometre from the centre of Sodankyla. The site is split into two areas by a small, relatively quiet, public road. The good sized pitches are situated behind the reception and all are clearly marked with hedges and have 10A electricity. The reception area also serves drinks and snacks. Sodankyla town itself, at the junction of routes 4 and 5, is home to a small Sami community and is an important trading post, so you will find a variety of shops including a small supermarket. The town is also home to the Geophysical Observatory, which constantly surveys the earth's magnetic field and measures earthquakes using seismic recordings. The Sodankyla Light Infantry Brigade, (the Finnish version of the SAS) which specialises in survival in cold climates is also based near here. This whole area is ideal for walking and bird watching; there are plenty of way marked paths to choose from. You can try the 4 km Luosto Game trail or the 15 km Kaares Fell hiking trail, which will take you right into the wilderness. There are many easier walks in the Urho Kekkonen National Park, which is close by, some 10 km. north of Vuoso.

Facilities

Two good sanitary blocks with toilets, hot showers and saunas. Off site: Shops and supermarket in Sodankyla town.

Open

1 June - 31 August.

At a glance

Welcome & Ambience	✓✓✓✓	Location	✓✓✓
Quality of Pitches	✓✓✓	Range of Facilities	✓✓✓

Directions

If travelling north on Route 4 turn right onto Route 5. The site is on the left just after you cross the river, it well signed and easy to find.

Charges 2004

Per unit incl. 2 persons and electricity	€ 16,00

Reservations

Recommended for July. Tel: 016 612181.
E-mail: matkailu.neuvonta@sodankyla.inet.fi

FI2980 Ounaskoski Camping

Jäämerentie 1, 96 500 Rovaniemi (Lapland)

Ounaskoski Camping is situated almost exactly on the Arctic Circle, 66 degrees north and just five miles south of the Santa Claus Post office and village, on the banks of the Kemijoke River. The site has 88 marked, but ill defined pitches, (63 with electricity), plus a further a small area for tents. One problem that arises is the Finnish four metre rule, so if you're not the first one there some pitches may be unusable. The site has a small sandy beach alongside the river but don't try swimming in it. Rovaniemi attracts almost 65,000 UK visitors each year, almost all in the weeks leading up to Christmas, who fly direct to the local airport and pay Santa Claus a visit. The town has much to offer with a good selection of shops and some restaurants. Reindeer Chop Suey at the Chinese restaurant was well worth trying! Not to be missed is the Artikum Museum where you will learn much of how people in the North live with nature and on her terms. Slightly further a field you can visit Vaattunkikon-gas and enjoy one of the many walks, which are suitable for everyone, from the one kilometre walk to the most challenging 9 kilometre path. Alternatively sit back and enjoy the summer sun on the riverbank. Note: It is important to note the check out time of 15.00 hours!

Facilities

There are two sanitary buildings each providing toilets, showers and a laundry. One also houses a kitchen and sauna. Café. Shop. Many organised coach trips on offer. Off site: Ranua Zoo. The Kemijoki, Finland's largest river, offers numerous opportunities for sightseeing by boat.

Open

End of May - late August.

At a glance

Welcome & Ambience	✓✓✓✓	Location	✓✓✓✓
Quality of Pitches	✓✓✓	Range of Facilities	✓✓✓

Directions

Ounaskoski Camping is on the banks of the Kemijoki River in the middle of Rovaniemi. From the 4/E75 go via the centre across the river and turn right. The site is between the Jatkankynttilasilta Bridge and the Rautatiesilta Bridge.

Charges 2005

Per unit incl 2 adults and children under 16 yrs	€ 20,00
extra adult	€ 8,00
electricity (16A)	€ 4,00

Reservations

Essential in July and August when the site gets really busy. Tel: 016 345 304.

Finland

FI2970 Nallikari Camping

PL 55, 90 015 Oulun Kaupunki (Oulu)

This is probably one of the best sites in Scandanavia, set in a recreational wooded area alongside a sandy beach on the banks of the Baltic Sea, with the added bonus of the adjacent Eden Spa complex. Nallikari provides 200 pitches with electricity (some also have water supply and drainage), plus an additional 79 cottages to rent, 28 of which are suitable for winter occupation. Oulu is a modern town about 100 miles south of the Arctic Circle that enjoys long, sunny and dry summer days. The Baltic however is frozen for many weeks in the winter and then the sun barely rises for two months. In early June though the skies were blue and the days very long and warm with the sun setting at about 23.30 and rising at 01.30! Nallikari, to the west of Oulu, is three kilometres away, along purpose built cycle paths and the town seems to have much on offer. Nordic walking, with or without roller blades, seems to be a recreational pastime for Finns of all ages! You might even be tempted to buy a pair of these long brightly coloured walking sticks yourself! Oulu hosts events such as the Meri Oulu Festival in July and the Oulu Music Video Festival and forms the backdrop to the mind boggling, mime guitar playing world championships.

Facilities

The modern shower/WC block also provides male and female saunas, kitchen and launderette facilities. Playground. Near reception is a cafeteria and BBQ area. Off site: The adjacent Eden centre provides excellent modern spa facilities where you can enjoy a day under the glass-roofed pool with its jacuzzis, saunas, Turkish Baths and an Irish Bath.

Open

All year.

At a glance

Welcome & Ambience	✓✓✓✓	Location	✓✓✓✓
Quality of Pitches	✓✓✓✓	Range of Facilities	✓✓✓✓

Directions

Leave Route 4 E75 at the junction with route 20 and head west down Kiertotie. The site is well signed, Nallikari Eden, but just continue straight on, just after the traffic lights you cross a bridge take the second on the right. Continue to the Eden Complex and turn right and the site is ahead where the road turns right.

Charges 2004

Per caravan or motorcaravan incl. 1 person	€ 18,00 - € 20,00
tent and car	€ 17,00 - € 18,00
tent	€ 15,00 - € 17,00
electricity	€ 3,50

Reservations

Recommended during the summer.
Tel: 08 5586 1350. E-mail: nallikari.camping@ouka.fi

FI2960 Koljonvirta Camping

Ylemmäisentie 6, 74120 Iisalmi (Kuopio)

Korljonvirta Camping is a large but quiet site located about five kilometres from the centre of Iisalmi. There are 120 marked grass pitches, all with electricity (16A). The site adjoins a lake and has a small beach and facilities for boating and fishing. Iisalmi town itself is on the northern edge of the Finnish Lake District and provides a good variety of shops, including some factory outlets, and an interesting variety of events during June, July and August. These vary from the world famous Wife-Carrying World Championships to the Lapinlahti Cattle Calling Competition and the International Midnight Marathon. Alternatively you can visit one of the town's museums or the St Eliah Church. Close to the campsite is a well-known battlefield from the Swedish-Russian war (1808-1809) when Finland was still part of Sweden. Numerous re-enactments take place over dinner where you can meet Colonel Sandels, Prince Dolgoruki and fight side by side with Soldier Bang. The site has cottages available to rent.

Facilities

The sanitary blocks provide showers, toilets and a sauna in one block. Launderette. Shop. Snack bar. Motorcaravan service point. Lake and small beach with facilities for boating and fishing. The site exhibits large wooden sculptures of animals.

Open

May - September.

At a glance

Welcome & Ambience	✓✓✓✓	Location	✓✓✓✓
Quality of Pitches	✓✓✓	Range of Facilities	✓✓✓

Directions

From road 5 turn east onto the 88 (towards Oulu) just north of Iisalmi. Go straight over the roundabout and the site is about 1 km. on the left.

Charges 2004

Per unit	€ 15,00
electricity	€ 4,00

Reservations

Probably not needed but worth checking in July and August. Tel: 017 825252. E-mail: tuulatimo@surfen.fi

FI2922 Camping Taipale

Leiritie, 78250 Varkaus (Kuopio)

Camping Taipale is situated right in the middle of an area of a thousand lakes, along the banks of Lake Haukivesi, which stretches to Savonlinna. Being at latitude of 61 degrees, daylight at Camping Taipale lasts for almost twenty four hours during the months of June and July. Built in 1988 this is a modern site, with 52 pitches, (all with electricity) in two lightly wooded areas, with a further grassy area for 90 tents and 16 log cabins to rent. To the south of the site there is a fine sandy beach and a small island with its own fishing dock for campers use. Slightly further a field is Savonlinna which is the hub of the Lake Saimaa waterways traffic. The town is famous for its medieval castle Ovalinlinna, which is transformed each year for the world famous opera festival. To the north of the site is Kuopio, where Lake Kallavesi encircles the town centre. From the Puijo tower you can admire one of the most spectacular panoramas of Finnish lakes and forest while having lunch in the towers revolving restaurant.

Facilities

Two sanitary blocks with good clean toilets and showers. The central block also provides a laundry with washing machines, driers, ironing facilities and good kitchen facilities. Two lakeside saunas (charged: € 12.50 per hour for a family or € 6.70 per person per hour). Motorcaravan service point. Off site: An old canal and museum is less than 1km from the site. The steamship 'Paul Wahl' has cruises on the lake from the local marina. Varkaus 3 km. away is the home to the museum of mechanical music. Very popular cruises are available from Kuipio and an annual dance festival in June.

Open

Mid-May - August.

At a glance

Welcome & Ambience	✓✓✓✓	Location	✓✓✓✓
Quality of Pitches	✓✓✓✓	Range of Facilities	✓✓✓

Directions

Leave the main road 5 at Varkhaus and proceed into and through the town. The site is well signposted and is about 9 km. from the route 5 junction. Turn at the traffic lights towards Taipale and then bear left; the site is on the right about 1 km. further along this quite road.

Charges 2005

Per unit incl 2 persons	€ 16,50
incl. 1 person	€ 10,00
electricity	€ 3,50

Reservations

Essential for July, accepted by email.
Tel: 017 552 6644.
E-mail: tuija.jalkanen@campingtaipale.inet.fi

FI2850 Rastila Camping

Karavaanikatu 4, 00980 Helsinki (Uusimaa)

No trip to Finland would be complete without a few days stay in Helsinki, the capital since 1812. This all year round site has exceptional transport links with the metro; only five minutes walk from the campsite gates. It provides 150 pitches, all with electrical hook-ups, plus an additional small field for tent campers. Recent improvements include shrub planting between the tarmac pitches and new-grassed sections for all pitches. All visitors will want to spend time in the Capital and a 24 hour bus, tram and metro pass costs a little over €4 and can be bought from the metro station. Once on the metro you're in the city centre within 20 minutes on this regular fast train service. Essential visits will include Senate Square, in the heart of the city, and Suomenlinna a marine fortress built on six islands in the 1700s. This garrison town is one of the most popular sights in Finland and is the world's largest maritime fortress. Helsinki, on the other hand, is one of Europe's smallest capitals and walking around the centre and port is a popular pastime as is visiting the market square alongside the ferry port. The city also has a wide variety of art galleries and museums, many of which are free with the Helsinki card.

Facilities

Three heated, clean and well maintained sanitary buildings provide showers, toilets and kitchens. Full kitchen available for campers use. Motorcaravan service point. TV and games room. Snack bar/licensed restaurant near the small beach. Off site: Tallin the capital of Estonia is only 90 minutes away from Helsinki by fast jetline ferry.

Open

All year.

At a glance

Welcome & Ambience	✓✓✓✓	Location	✓✓✓✓
Quality of Pitches	✓✓✓✓	Range of Facilities	✓✓✓✓

Directions

Well signed from the 170 or Ring I. From the 170 you turn at the Itakeskus shopping complex towards Vuosaari. After crossing the bridge go up the slip to Rastila. At the top of the slip road turn left and the site is directly ahead.

Charges 2005

Per pitch incl. 1 person	€ 8,00 - € 13,00
electricity	€ 4,00 - € 7,00

Discounts for weekly or monthly bookings.

Reservations

Not needed. Tel: 09 321 6551.
E-mail: rastilacamping@hel.fi

From the hot sunny climate of the Mediterranean to the more northerly and cooler regions of Normandy and Brittany, with the Chateaux of the Loire and the lush valleys of the Dordogne, France offers holidaymakers a huge choice of destinations to suit all tastes.

The largest country in Western Europe, France boasts every type of landscape imaginable ranging from the wooded valleys of the Dordogne to the volcanic uplands of the Massif Central, the rocky coast of Brittany to the lavender covered hills of Provence and snow-capped peaks of the Alps. Each region is different and this is reflected in the local customs, cuisine, architecture and dialect. Many rural villages hold festivals to celebrate the local saints and you can also find museums devoted to the rural arts and crafts of the regions.

France has a rich architectural heritage with a huge variety of Gothic cathedrals, châteaux, Roman remains, fortresses and Romanesque churches to visit. Given the varied landscape and climate there is also great scope for outdoor pursuits with plenty of hiking and cycling opportunities across the country, and rock-climbing and skiing in the mountains. And of course a trip to France wouldn't be complete without sampling the local food and wine.

Population

60.2 million

Capital

Paris

Climate

France has a temperate climate but this varies considerably from region to region

Language

French

Currency

The Euro

Telephone

The country code is 00 33

Banks

Mon-Fri 09.00-1200 and 14.00-16.00

Shops

Mon-Sat 0900-1830. Some are closed between 1200-1430. Food shops are open 0700-1830/1930. Some food shops (particularly bakers) are open Sunday mornings. Many shops close Mondays

Public Holidays

New Year; Easter Mon; Labour Day; VE Day 8 May; Ascension; Whit Mon; Bastille Day 14 July; Assumption 15 Aug; All Saints 1 Nov; Armistice Day 11 Nov; Christmas Day

Motoring

France has a comprehensive road system from motorways (Autoroutes), Routes Nationales (N roads), Routes Départmentales (D roads) down to purely local C class roads. Tolls are payable on the autoroute network which is extensive but expensive, and also on certain bridges

Tourist Office

The French Government Tourist Office (FGTO)
178 Piccadilly
London W1V 0AL
Tel: 0906 8244 123
Fax: 0207 493 6594
Email: info.uk@franceguide.com
Internet: www.franceguide.com

EAT, DRINK AND BE MERRY! VISIT THE VINEYARDS OF FRANCE, SAMPLING THE LOCAL WINES, OR JOIN ONE OF THE REGIONAL COOKERY CLASSES HELD FOR VISITORS.

FR29130 Camping des Abers

Dunes de Ste. Marguerite, 29870 Landéda (Brittany)

This delightful twelve acre site is beautifully situated almost at the tip of the Sainte Marguerite peninsula on the north-western shores of Brittany in a wide bay formed between the mouths (abers) of two rivers, L'Aber Wrac'h and L'Aber Benoit. With soft, white sandy beaches and rocky outcrops and islands at high tide, the setting is ideal for those with younger children and this quiet, rural area provides a wonderful, tranquil escape from the busier areas of France, even in high season. Camping des Abers is set just back from the beach, the lower pitches sheltered from the wind by high hedges or with panoramic views of the bay from the higher places. There are 180 pitches arranged in distinct areas, partly shaded and sheltered by mature hedges, trees and flowering shrubs, all planted and carefully tended over 30 years by the Le Cuff family. Landscaping and terracing where appropriate on the different levels avoids any regimentation or crowding. Easily accessed by good internal roads, electricity is available to all (long leads may be needed). Speaking several languages, the family who own and run this site with 'TLC' will make you very welcome.

Facilities

Three toilet blocks (one part of the reception building and all recently refurbished) are very clean, providing washbasins in cubicles and roomy showers (token from reception €0.80). Good facilities for disabled visitors and babies have been added at the reception block. Dishwashing sinks. Fully equipped laundry. Motorcaravan service point. Mini-market stocks essentials (1/6-15/9). Simple takeaway dishes (1/7-31/8). Pizzeria and restaurant next door. Table tennis. Good play area (on sand). Games room. Live music, Breton dancing and Breton cooking classes, and guided walks arranged. Splendid beach reached direct from the site with good bathing (best at high tide), fishing, windsurfing and other watersports. Torch useful. Gates locked 22.30-07.00 hrs. Off site: Miles of superb coastal walks. Tennis and riding close. The nearby town of L'Aber Wrac'h, a well known yachting centre, has many memorable restaurants.

At a glance

Welcome & Ambience	✓✓✓✓✓	Location	✓✓✓✓✓
Quality of Pitches	✓✓✓✓	Range of Facilities	✓✓✓✓

Directions

From Roscoff (D10, then D13), cross river bridge (L'Aber Wrac'h) to Lannilis. Go through town taking road to Landéda and from there signs for Dunes de Ste Marguerite, 'camping' and des Abers.

Charges 2005

Per person	€ 3,30
child (1-7 yrs)	€ 1,80
pitch	€ 5,50
car	€ 1,50
electricity	€ 2,40
dog	€ 1,60

10% reduction outside 15 June - 31 August.
Camping Cheques accepted.

Reservations

Write to site. Tel: 02 98 04 93 35.
E-mail: camping-des-abers@wanadoo.fr

Open

1 May - 30 September.

France

TRAVEL SERVICE SITE

TO BOOK CALL 0870 405 4055 OR www.alanrogersdirect.com

FR29010 Castel Camping Le Ty-Nadan

Route d'Arzano, 29310 Locunolé (Brittany)

Ty Nadan is a well organised site set amongst wooded countryside along the bank of the River Elle. The 183 pitches for touring units are grassy, many with shade and 152 with 10A electricity. An exciting and varied programme of activities is offered throughout the season – canoeing, rock climbing, mountain biking, aqua-gym, riding or walking – all supervised by qualified staff. A full programme of entertainment for all ages is provided in high season including concerts, Breton evenings with pig roasts, dancing, etc. (be warned, you will be actively encouraged to join in!) The pool complex with its slides and paddling pool is very popular and now has an attractive viewing platform. Super recent additions include a large indoor pool complex and an indoor games area with a climbing wall. Several tour operators use the site (90 pitches). This is a wonderful site for families with children of all ages.

Facilities

Two older, split-level toilet blocks are of fair quality and unusual design, including washbasins in cabins and baby rooms. An impressively equipped block opened in 2002 provides easier access for disabled people. Dishwashing facilities in two attractive gazebo style units. Washing machines and dryers. Good sized restaurant, takeaway, bar and well stocked shop (all open all season). Crêperie (July/Aug). Heated outdoor pool (17 x 8 m) with water slides and paddling pool. New indoor pool. Small beach on the river (unfenced). Tennis courts, table tennis, pool tables, archery and trampolines. Indoor badminton and rock climbing facility. Exciting adventure play park and new 'Minikids' park for 5-8 yrs. Riding. Bicycle hire. Boat hire. Fishing. Canoe and sea kayaking expeditions. High season entertainment. Paintball. Off site: Beaches 20 minutes by car. Golf 12 km.

At a glance

Welcome & Ambience	✓✓✓✓✓	Location	✓✓✓
Quality of Pitches	✓✓✓✓✓	Range of Facilities	✓✓✓✓✓

Directions

Make for Arzano which is northeast of Quimperlé on the Pontivy road and turn off D22 just west of village at camp sign. Site is approx. 3 km.

Charges 2004

Per person	€ 7,10
child (under 7 yrs)	€ 4,50
pitch	€ 16,00
electricity (10A)	€ 5,70
dog	€ 4,80

Camping Cheques accepted.
Less 15-20% outside July/Aug.

Reservations

Made for exact dates with deposit (€ 50) and fee (€ 25). Tel: 02 98 71 75 47.
E-mail: TY-NADAN@wanadoo.fr

Open

15 May - 15 September.

FR29050 Castel Camping L'Orangerie de Lanniron

Château de Lanniron, 29336 Quimper (Brittany)

L'Orangerie is a beautiful and peaceful, family site in 10 acres of a XVIIth century, 42 acre country estate on the banks of the Odet river. It is just to the south of Quimper and about 15 km. from the sea and beaches at Bénodet. The family's five year programme to restore the park, the original canal, fountains, ornamental 'Bassin de Neptune' (where visitors may now fish), the boathouse and the gardens and avenues is now complete. The original outbuildings have been attractively converted around a walled courtyard. The site has 200 grassy pitches, 146 for touring units. Of three types (varying in size and services), they are on fairly flat ground laid out in rows alongside access roads with shrubs and bushes providing pleasant pitches. All have electricity and 88 have all three services. The restaurant in the beautiful XVIIth century Orangerie, and the Gardens are both open to the public and in Spring the rhododendrons and azaleas are magnificent, with lovely walks within the grounds. Used by tour operators (34 pitches). All facilities are available when the site is open.

Facilities

The main heated block in the courtyard has been totally refurbished and is excellent. A second modern block serves the newer pitches at the top of the site and includes facilities for disabled people and babies. Washing machines and dryers. Motorcaravan service point. Shop (15/5-9/9). Gas supplies. Bar, snacks and takeaway, plus restaurant (open daily from 25/5-5/9, reasonably priced with children's menu). Heated swimming pool (144 sq.m.) with paddling pool. New pool planned. Small play area. Tennis. Minigolf, attractively set among mature trees. Table tennis. Fishing. Archery. Bicycle hire. General reading, games and billiards rooms. TV/video room (cable and satellite). Karaoke. Animation provided including outdoor activities with large room for indoor activities. Off site: Two hypermarkets 1 km. Historic town of Quimper under 3 km. Beach 15 km.

At a glance

Welcome & Ambience	✓✓✓✓✓	Location	✓✓✓✓
Quality of Pitches	✓✓✓✓	Range of Facilities	✓✓✓✓

Directions

From Quimper follow 'Quimper Sud' signs, then 'Toutes Directions' and general camping signs, finally signs for Lanniron.

Charges 2004

Per adult	€ 6,00
child (2-7 yrs)	€ 4,00
pitch (100 sq.m.)	€ 14,00
with electricity (10A)	€ 18,00
special pitch (120/150 sq.m.)	
with water and electricity	€ 21,00
animal	€ 3,50

Less 15% outside July/Aug.
Camping Cheques accepted.

Reservations

Made with deposit (€ 70) and fee (€ 20).
Tel: 02 98 90 62 02. E-mail: camping@lanniron.com

Open

15 May - 15 September.

France

TRAVEL SERVICE SITE

TO BOOK CALL 0870 405 4055 OR www.alanrogersdirect.com

FR29080 Camping Le Panoramic

Route de la Plage-Penker, 29560 Telgruc-sur-Mer (Brittany)

This medium sized, traditional style site is situated on quite a steep, ten acre hillside, with fine views along the coast. It is well tended and personally run by M. Jacq and his family who all speak good English. The site is in two parts, divided by a fairly quiet road leading to a good beach. The main upper site is where most of the facilities are situated, with the swimming pool, terrace and a playground located with the lower pitches across the road. Some up-and-down walking is therefore necessary, but this is a small price to pay for such pleasant and comfortable surroundings. The 200 pitches are arranged on flat, shady terraces, mostly in small groups with hedges and flowering shrubs and 20 pitches have services for motorcaravans. A good area for lovely coastal footpaths. A 'Sites et Paysages' member.

TRAVEL SERVICE SITE

TO BOOK CALL 0870 405 4055 OR www.alanrogersdirect.com

Facilities

The main site has two well kept toilet blocks with another very good block opened for main season across the road. All three blocks include British and Turkish style WCs, washbasins in cubicles, facilities for disabled people, baby baths, dishwashing, plus washing machines and dryers. Motorcaravan services. Small shop (1/7-31/8). Bar/restaurant with good value takeaway (1/7-31/8). Barbecue area. Heated swimming pool, paddling pool and jacuzzi (all 15/5-7/9). Playground. Games and TV rooms. Children's club in season. Sports ground with tennis courts, volleyball. Bicycle hire. Off site: Fishing 700 m. Good sandy beach 700 m. downhill by road, bit less on foot. Riding 6 km. Golf 14 km. Sailing school nearby.

At a glance

Welcome & Ambience	✓✓✓✓✓	Location	✓✓✓✓
Quality of Pitches	✓✓✓	Range of Facilities	✓✓✓✓

Directions

Site is just south of Telgruc-sur-Mer. On D887 pass through Ste Marie du Ménez Horn. In 11 km. turn left on D208 signed Telgruc-sur-Mer. Continue straight on through the town and site is on right within 1 km.

Charges 2005

Per person	€ 5,00
child (under 7 yrs)	€ 3,00
pitch	€ 12,00
electricity (6-10A)	€ 3,10 - € 4,50
water and drainage connection	€ 2,50
dog	€ 1,60

Less 20% outside July/Aug.

Reservations

Made for any period; contact site.
Tel: 02 98 27 78 41.
E-mail: info@camping-panoramic.com

Open

1 June - 15 September.

FR29030 Camping du Letty

29950 Bénodet (Brittany)

Built around their former farm, the Guyader family have ensured that this excellent and attractive site, with direct beach access, has plenty to offer for all the family. The site on the outskirts of the popular resort of Bénodet spreads over 22 acres with 493 pitches, all for touring units. Groups of eight to ten pitches are set in cul-de-sacs with mature hedging and trees to divide each cul-de-sac. Markers indicate the limits of each pitch which are slightly smaller than average (none more than about 80 sq.m), although they do not feel too small since they are not hedged or fenced. Most pitches have electricity, water and drainage. At the attractive floral entrance, former farm buildings provide a host of facilities including an extensively equipped fitness room. There is also a modern, purpose built nightclub and bar providing high quality live entertainment most evenings (situated well away from most pitches to avoid disturbance). Although there is no swimming pool here, the site has direct access to a small sandy beach, and has provided a floating pontoon with a diving platform and water slides into the sea (safe bathing depends on the tides).

Facilities

Six well placed toilet blocks are of good quality and include mixed style WCs, washbasins in large cabins and controllable hot showers (charged). One block includes a separate laundry and dog washing enclosures. Four well equipped baby rooms. Separate facility for disabled visitors. Launderette. Hairdressing room. Motorcaravan service points. Well stocked mini-market. Extensive snack bar and takeaway (22/6-30/8). Bar with games room and night club. Library/reading room. Games lounge with billiard and card tables and entertainment room with satellite TV. Fitness centre (no charge). Saunas, jacuzzis and solarium (all on payment). Table tennis. Two tennis and two squash courts (charged). Boules, volleyball, basketball and archery. Well equipped play area. In July/Aug. entertainment and activities organised for the whole family.

At a glance

Welcome & Ambience	✓✓✓✓	Location	✓✓✓✓✓
Quality of Pitches	✓✓✓	Range of Facilities	✓✓✓✓

Directions

From N165 take D70 Concarneau exit. At first roundabout take D44 to Fouesnant. Turn right at T-junction. After about 2 km. turn left to Fouesnant (still D44). Continue through La Forêt Fouesnant and Fouesnant, picking up signs for Bénodet. Shortly before Benodet at roundabout turn left (signed Le Letty). Turn right at next mini roundabout and site is 500 m. on left.

Charges 2004

Per adult	€ 5,00
child (under 7 yrs)	€ 2,50
pitch	€ 7,00
car or motorcaravan	€ 1,70
m/cycle	€ 1,20
electricity (1, 2, 5 or 10A)	€ 1,50 - € 4,00

Reservations

Not made. Tel: 02 98 57 04 69.
E-mail: reception@campingduletty.com

Open

15 June - 6 September.

FR29180 Camping Les Embruns

Rue du Philosophe Alain, Le Pouldu, 29360 Clohars-Carnoët (Brittany)

This site is unusual in that it is located in the heart of a village, yet is only 250 metres from a sandy cove. It is also close to beautiful countryside and the Carnoët Forest. The entrance with its card operated barrier and wonderful floral displays, is the first indication that this is a well tended and well organised site, and the owners have won numerous regional and national awards for its superb presentation. The 180 pitches (100 occupied by mobile homes) are separated by trees, shrubs and bushes, and most have electricity, water and drainage. There is a covered, heated swimming pool, a circular paddling pool and a water play pool. It is only a short walk to the village centre with all its attractions and services.

Facilities

Two modern sanitary blocks, recently completely renewed, include mainly British style toilets, some washbasins in cubicles, baby baths and good facilities for disabled visitors. New family bathrooms. Dishwashing and laundry sinks under cover. Washing, drying and ironing facilities. Motorcaravan service point. Small shop (3/4-15/9). Bar and terrace (1/7-31/8) overlooking a covered, heated swimming pool (3/4-15/9) and paddling pool. Takeaway (20/6-5/9). Large games hall with pinball machines and table tennis. Play area. Football field, volleyball and minigolf. Communal barbecue area. Daily activities for children and adults organised in July/Aug. Off site: Nearby sea and river fishing and watersports. Bicycle hire 50 m. Riding 2 km. Good cycling in the surrounding countryside. Beach 250 m.

At a glance

Welcome & Ambience	✓✓✓✓	Location	✓✓✓✓
Quality of Pitches	✓✓✓✓	Range of Facilities	✓✓✓✓✓

Directions

From N165 take either 'Kervidanou, Quimperlé Ouest' exit or 'Kergostiou, Quimperlé Centre, Clohars Carnoët' exit and follow D16 to Clohars Carnoët. Then D24 for Le Pouldu and site signs in village.

Charges 2004

Per unit incl. 2 persons	€ 9,90 - € 21,50
fully serviced pitch	€ 13,90 - € 25,50
extra person	€ 3,70 - € 4,90
child (under 7 yrs)	€ 2,40 - € 3,00
electricity on ordinary pitch	€ 3,00
animal	free - € 1,00

Less in low seasons.
Use of motorcaravan services € 1.83.

Reservations

Advised for high season. Tel: 02 98 39 91 07.
E-mail: camping-les-embruns@wanadoo.fr

Open

9 April - 17 September.

FR29060 Camping Caravaning Le Pil-Koad

Route de Douarnenez, Poullan-sur-Mer, 29100 Douarnenez (Brittany)

Pil Koad is an attractive, family run site just back from the sea near Douarnenez in Finistère. It has 190 pitches on fairly flat ground, marked out by separating hedges and of quite good quality, though varying in size and shape. With 100 pitches used for touring units, the site also has a number of mobile homes and chalets. Nearly all pitches have electrical connections and the original trees provide shade in some areas. A large, modern room, named the 'Woodpecker Bar', is used for entertainment with discos and cabaret organised in July and August. A small shop selling basics is part of the same complex. The gates are closed 10.30 - 07.00 hrs. The village is 500 m. with a choice of restaurants and the town of Douarnez is 6 km. A variety of beaches is within easy reach (the nearest sandy beach is 5 km), and this coast offers some wonderful scenery and is ideal for walking.

Facilities

Two main toilet blocks in modern style include mainly British style WCs and washbasins mostly in cabins. Laundry facilities. Motorcaravan service point. Gas supplies. Small shop for basics (15/6-11/9). Takeaway (25/6-4/9). Heated swimming pool and paddling pool (no bermuda-style shorts). Tennis court. Table tennis. Minigolf. Volleyball. Fishing. Bicycle hire. Playground. Weekly outings and clubs for children (30/6-30/8) with charge included in tariff.
Off site: Restaurants in village 500 m. Riding 4 km. Nearest sandy beach 5 km. Douarnenez 6 km.

Open

15 May - 28 September.

At a glance

Welcome & Ambience	✓✓✓✓	Location	✓✓✓✓
Quality of Pitches	✓✓✓✓✓	Range of Facilities	✓✓✓✓

Directions

Site is 500 m. east from the centre of Poullan on D7 road towards Douarnenez. From Douarnenez take circular bypass route towards Audierne; if you see road for Poullan sign at roundabout, take it, otherwise there is camping sign at turning to Poullan from the D765 road.

Charges 2004

Per person	€ 3,00 - € 4,50
child (under 7 yrs)	€ 1,50 - € 3,00
pitch	€ 6,20 - € 13,00
electricity (10A)	€ 3,50
dog	€ 2,00 - € 3,00

Camping Cheques accepted.

Reservations

Made for min. 1 week with 25% deposit and fee (€ 19). Tel: 02 98 74 26 39.
E-mail: info@pil-koad.com

FR29190 Camping Les Prés Verts

Kernous-Plage, 29900 Concarneau (Brittany)

What sets this family site apart from the many others in this region are its more unusual features - its stylish pool complex with Romanesque style columns and statue, and its plants and flower tubs. The 150 pitches are mostly arranged on long, open, grassy areas either side of main access roads. Specimen trees, shrubs or hedges divide the site into smaller areas. There are a few individual pitches and an area towards the rear of the site where the pitches have sea views. Concarneau is just 2.5 km. and there are many marked coastal walks to enjoy in the area, plus watersports or boat and fishing trips available nearby. A 'Sites et Paysages' member.

Facilities

Two toilet blocks provide unisex WCs, but separate washing facilities for ladies and men. Pre-set hot showers and washbasins in cabins for ladies, both closed 9 pm - 8 am. Some child-size toilets. Dishwashing and laundry sinks, washing machine and dryer. Pizza service twice weekly. Swimming pool (1/6-31/8; around 18 x 11 m.) and paddling pool. Playground (0-5 yrs only). Minigolf. Off site: Path to sandy/rocky beach (300 m.) and coastal path. Riding 1 km. Supermarket 2 km. Bicycle hire 3 km. Golf 5 km.

Open

1 May - 22 September.

At a glance

Welcome & Ambience	✓✓✓	Location	✓✓✓✓✓
Quality of Pitches	✓✓✓✓	Range of Facilities	✓✓✓

Directions

Turn off C7 road, 2.5 km. north of Concarneau, where site is signed. Take third left after Hotel de l'Océan.

Charges 2004

Per unit incl. 2 adults	€ 16,48 - € 20,60
extra adult	€ 4,76 - € 5,95
child (2-7 yrs)	€ 3,12 - € 3,90
dog	€ 1,16 - € 1,45
electricity (2-6A)	€ 2,90 - € 4,43

Reservations

Contact site. Tel: 02 98 97 09 74.
E-mail: info@pres-verts.com

FR29140 Haven Camping Domaine de Kerlann

Land Rosted, 29930 Pont-Aven (Brittany)

Haven Europe have, with careful and imaginative planning, ensured that their mobile homes here blend naturally into the environment. The remaining 20% of around 110 touring pitches (some 80 sq.m, some 120 sq.m, all with electricity) have been left in a more natural situation on rough grass with a small stream flowing through and with some mature trees providing shade. Land drainage is poor due to the park being on low lying ground. The 'piece de resistance' is the amazing pool complex comprising three outdoor pools with separate toboggan, attractively landscaped with sunbathing terraces, and an indoor tropical style complex complete with jacuzzi and its own toboggan. Much holiday camp style entertainment (with a French flavour) takes place on the bar terrace with its stage overlooking the complex.

Facilities

The main large toilet block on the centre of the mobile home area includes washbasins in cubicles, outside dishwashing and laundry sinks. Good laundry. A second block in the touring section opens in high season. Mini supermarket. French style restaurant, snack restaurant, takeaway and bar. Impressive pool complex including indoor and outdoor pools with lifeguards. Well equipped play areas. All weather multi-sports court, tennis courts, minigolf. Video games room, pool tables and satellite TV in the bar. Three children's clubs for different age groups. Gas barbecues are not permitted. Off site: Pont-Aven with its Gauguin connection, art galleries and museums is well worth visiting. Small ports and villages nearby. Beach 5 km.

At a glance

Welcome & Ambience	✓✓✓	Location	✓✓✓
Quality of Pitches	✓✓	Range of Facilities	✓✓✓✓

Directions

From Tregunc - Pont-Aven road, turn south towards Névez and site is on right.

Charges 2004

Per pitch incl. up to 2 persons with electricity	€ 13,00 - € 34,00
extra person	€ 3,00 - € 6,00
extra vehicle	€ 1,00 - € 4,00

Reservations

Accepted at any time for min. 4 days; no booking fee. Contact site or Haven Europe in the UK on 0870 242 7777 for information or reservation. Tel: 02 98 06 01 77. E-mail: kerlann@haven.fr

Open

18 March - 30 October.

FR35000 Camping Le Vieux Chêne

Baguer-Pican, 35120 Dol-de-Bretagne (Brittany)

This attractive, family owned site is situated between Saint Malo and Mont Saint Michel. Developed in the grounds of a country farmhouse dating from 1638, its young and enthusiastic new owner has created a really pleasant, traditional atmosphere. It offers 200 good sized pitches, most with electricity, water tap and light, in spacious rural surroundings on gently sloping grass. They are separated by bushes and flowers, with mature trees for shade. A very attractive tenting area (no electricity) is in the orchard. There are three lakes in the grounds and centrally located leisure facilities include an attractive pool complex. Some entertainment is provided in high season. Used by a Dutch tour operator (10 pitches).

TRAVEL SERVICE SITE

TO BOOK CALL 0870 405 4055 OR www.alanrogersdirect.com

Facilities

Three very good, unisex toilet blocks include washbasins in cabins, a baby room and facilities for disabled people. All recently been refurbished and can be heated. Small laundry with washing machine, dryer and iron. Motorcaravan services. Shop. Takeaway. Café with terrace overlooking the pools (all season). Medium sized, heated swimming pool, paddling pool, slides, etc. (17/5-14/9; lifeguard July/Aug). TV room (satellite) and games room. Tennis court, minigolf, giant chess. Play area. Riding in July/Aug. Fishing is possible in two of the three lakes. Off site: Supermarket in Dol 3 km. Golf 12 km. Beach 20 km.

At a glance

Welcome & Ambience	✓✓✓✓✓	Location	✓✓✓✓
Quality of Pitches	✓✓✓✓	Range of Facilities	✓✓✓✓✓

Directions

Site is by the D576 Dol-de-Bretagne - Pontorson road, just east of Baguer-Pican. It can be reached from the new N176 taking exit for Dol-Est and Baguer-Pican.

Charges 2004

Per person	€ 5,00
child (under 10 yrs)	€ 3,00
pitch	€ 5,50 - € 14,00
electricity (5A)	€ 4,00

Reservations

Made with deposit (€ 30) and fee (€ 15).
Tel: 02 99 48 09 55. E-mail: vieux.chene@wanadoo.fr

Open

1 April - 1 October.

FR35040 Camping Le P'tit Bois

35430 St Jouan des Guerets (Brittany)

On the outskirts of Saint Malo, this neat, family oriented site is very popular with British visitors, being ideal for one night stops or for longer stays in this interesting area. Le P'tit Bois is a busy site providing 274 large level pitches (around 140 for touring units) which are divided into groups by mature hedges and trees, separated by shrubs and flowers and with access from tarmac roads. Nearly all have electrical hook-ups and over half have water taps. Behind reception, an attractive, sheltered terrace around the pools provides a focus during the day along with the bar and snack bar. There are site-owned mobile homes and chalets which means that facilities are open over a long season (if only for limited hours).

TRAVEL SERVICE SITE

TO BOOK CALL 0870 405 4055 OR www.alanrogersdirect.com

Facilities

Two fully equipped toilet blocks, one in the newer area across the lane, include washbasins in cabins, baby baths and laundry facilities. Simple facilities for disabled people. Motorcaravan service point. Small shop (from 15/5). Bar where entertainment and discos are organised (July-Aug). Snack bar with takeaway, small bar, TV room (large screen for sports events) and games rooms. Swimming pool with paddling pool and two slides (from 15/5). Indoor pool with jacuzzi and turkish bath. Playground and multi-sports court. Tennis court, minigolf, table tennis, and outdoor chess. Charcoal barbecues are not permitted. Off site: Beach 1.5 km. Fishing 1.5 km, bicycle hire or riding 5 km, golf 7 km.

At a glance

Welcome & Ambience	✓✓✓✓	Location	✓✓✓✓
Quality of Pitches	✓✓✓✓✓	Range of Facilities	✓✓✓✓✓

Directions

St Jouan is west off the St Malo - Rennes road (N137) just outside St Malo. Site is signed from the N137 (exit St Jouan or Quelmer).

Charges 2005

Per person	€ 6,00 - € 8,00
child (under 7 yrs)	€ 3,00 - € 5,00
pitch and car	€ 10,00 - € 20,00
electricity (6A)	€ 4,00

Reservations

Made on receipt of 25% of total cost, plus fee (€ 30) in July and August. Tel: 02 99 21 14 30.
E-mail: camping.ptitbois@wanadoo.fr

Open

16 April - 10 September.

FR44090 Camping Château du Deffay

B.P. 18 Le Deffay, Ste Reine de Bretagne, 44160 Pontchâteau (Brittany)

A family managed site, Château de Deffay is a refreshing departure from the usual formula in that it is not over organised or supervised and has no tour operator units. The landscape is natural right down to the molehills, and the site blends well with the rural environment of the estate, lake and farmland which surround it. For these reasons it is enjoyed by many. However, with the temptation of free pedaloes and the fairly deep, unfenced lake, parents should ensure that children are supervised. The 142 good sized, fairly level pitches have pleasant views and are either on open grass, on shallow terraces divided by hedges, or informally arranged in a central, slightly sloping wooded area. Most have electricity. The facilities are located within the old courtyard area of the smaller château (that dates from before 1400). The larger château (built 1880) and another lake stand away from this area providing pleasant walking. The reception has been built separately to contain the camping area. Alpine type chalets overlook the lake and fit well with the environment.

Facilities

The main toilet block, housed in a converted barn, is well equipped including washbasins in cabins, provision for disabled people and a baby bathroom. Washing machines, and dryer. Maintenance can be variable and, with the boiler located at one end of the block, hot water can take time to reach the other in low season. Extra facilities are in the courtyard area where the well stocked shop, bar, small restaurant with takeaway and solar heated swimming pool and paddling pool are located (all 15/5-15/9). Play area. TV in the bar, separate room for table tennis. English language animation in season including children's mini club. Torches useful. Off site: Golf and riding 5 km. Close to the Brière Regional Park, the Guérande Peninsula, and La Baule with its magnificent beach (20 km).

At a glance

Welcome & Ambience	✓✓✓✓✓	Location	✓✓✓✓
Quality of Pitches	✓✓✓✓	Range of Facilities	✓✓✓✓

Directions

Site is signed from D33 Pontchâteau - Herbignac road near Ste Reine. Also signed from the D773 and N165.

Charges 2004

Per person	€ 2,80 - € 4,55
child (2-12 yrs)	€ 1,95 - € 3,00
pitch	€ 6,75 - € 10,25
with electricity (6A)	€ 10,40 - € 13,90
with 3 services	€ 11,90 - € 15,65

Camping Cheques accepted.

Reservations

Accepted with deposit (€ 10 per day) and fee (€ 16). Tel: 02 40 88 00 57.
E-mail: info@camping-le-deffay.com

Open

7 May - 17 September.

FR44030 Camping Le Pré du Château de Careil

33 rue du Château, Careil, 44350 Guérande (Brittany)

This small site has a quiet atmosphere and is popular with couples, retired people and those with young children (it is not really recommended for families with older children or teenagers). In the grounds of the Château de Careil, a building dating from the 14th century which may be visited, this small site, shaded by mature trees, contains just 50 good sized pitches. All are equipped with electricity and water, some also have drainage. There is a small swimming pool.

Facilities

Toilet facilities in the main building include four unisex shower and washbasin rooms. Facilities for disabled people. Baby room. Washing machine. In season (15/6-5/9) bread can be ordered. Small swimming pool (open 15/6-5/9). Playground. TV room. Table tennis. Off site: Supermarket near. Bicycle hire 2 km. Beach 2.5 km. Riding 5 km.

Open

22 May - 12 September.

At a glance

Welcome & Ambience ✓✓✓✓✓ Location ✓✓✓✓
Quality of Pitches ✓✓✓✓ Range of Facilities ✓✓✓

Directions

Take D92 from Guérande to La Baule and turn east to Careil before the town. From D99 Guérande - St Nazaire road, turn onto D92, following signs to 'Intermarche' and Château de Careil. Entrance gate is fairly narrow and located between two bends.

Charges 2004

Per unit incl. 2 persons, electricity	€ 18,00 - € 22,00
electricity (10A)	€ 1,60

Reservations

Possible with deposit (€ 21.34) and booking fee. Tel: 02 40 60 22 99. E-mail: chateau.careil@free.fr

FR44100 Sunêlia Le Patisseau

29 rue du Patisseau, 44210 Pornic (Brittany)

Le Patisseau is situated in the countryside just a short drive from the fishing village of Pornic. It is a relaxed site with a large number of mobile homes and chalets, which is popular with young families and teenagers. Touring pitches, all with 6A electricity, are divided between the attractive 'forest' area with plenty of shade from mature trees and the more open 'prairie' area. Several barbecues are provided helping to create a sociable atmosphere. A railway runs along the bottom half of the site with trains two or three times a day, but they do finish at 22.30 hrs and the noise is minimal. The spacious restaurant and bar overlook the indoor pool. Outside two waterslides are cleverly concealed amongst the trees. This is a lively site and the Morice family work very hard to maintain a friendly atmosphere.

Facilities

There are three sanitary blocks, one of which is being rebuilt for 2005. They include washbasins in private cabins, child-size toilets, baby baths, laundry rooms and dishwashing facilities. Maintenance can be variable. Shop (main season). Bar and restaurant (3/4-12/9). Takeaway (1/7-31/8). Indoor heated pool with sauna, jacuzzi and spa (all season). Outdoor pools with slides (1/5-12/9). Play area. Volleyball and table tennis. Bicycle hire. Off site: Fishing 1.5 km. Beach 2.5 km. Riding 4 km. Golf 5 km.

Open

3 April - 12 September.

At a glance

Welcome & Ambience ✓✓✓✓✓ Location ✓✓✓✓
Quality of Pitches ✓✓✓ Range of Facilities ✓✓✓✓

Directions

Site signed at roundabout junction of D751 (Pornic - Nantes) road. From town centre take Rue du General de Gaulle then Rue de Nantes, crossing the D751. At the next roundabout turn left and follow the signs.

Charges 2004

Per unit incl. 2 persons	€ 19,00 - € 29,00
incl. electricity (6A)	€ 23,00 - € 33,00
extra person	€ 5,00 - € 7,00
child (1-7 yrs)	€ 3,00 - € 5,00

Camping Cheques accepted.

Reservations

Made with deposit (€ 50) and fee (€ 30); contact site by letter, phone or fax. Tel: 02 40 82 10 39. E-mail: contact@lepatisseau.com

FR44150 Camping La Tabardière

44770 La Plaine-sur-Mer (Brittany)

Owned and managed by the Barre family, this campsite lies next to the family farm. Pleasant, peaceful and immaculate, this site will suit those who want to enjoy the local coast and towns but return to an 'oasis' for relaxation. It still, however, provides activities and fun for those with energy remaining. The pitches are mostly terraced either side of a narrow valley and care needs to be taken in manoeuvring caravans – although the effort is well worth it. Most pitches have access to electricity. The site is probably not suitable for wheelchair users. Whilst this is a rural site, its amenities are excellent with pools and a water slide and a challenging 18 hole minigolf. The beautiful beaches are 3 km.

Facilities

Two good, clean toilet blocks are well equipped. Laundry facilities. Motorcaravan service point. Bar. Shop. Snacks and takeaway. Good sized swimming pool (supervised). Play area. Minigolf. Table tennis. Volleyball. Basketball. Half size tennis. Boules. Off site: Beach 3 km. Golf, riding 5 km.

Open

1 April - 30 September.

At a glance

Welcome & Ambience ✓✓✓✓✓ Location ✓✓✓✓
Quality of Pitches ✓✓✓✓ Range of Facilities ✓✓✓✓✓

Directions

Site is well signed, situated inland off the D13 Pornic - La Plaine sur Mer road.

Charges 2004

Per unit incl. 2 persons	€ 12,00 - € 19,00
child (2-10 yrs)	€ 2,50 - € 3,50
electricity (3/6A)	€ 2,70 - € 3,60

Reservations

Made with deposit (€ 60) and fee (€ 16). Tel: 02 40 21 58 83. E-mail: info@camping-la-tabardiere.com

FR44190 Camping Le Fief

57, chemin du Fief, 44250 St Brévin-les-Pins (Brittany)

This site has been recommended by our agent and we plan to inspect it during 2005 with a view to future inclusion in this guide. Le Fief is a lively family site with an excellent swimming pool area (a new pool complex is planned for 2005). A lively entertainment programme is organised here throughout the high season. Mobile homes for rent.

Facilities

Modern toilet blocks. Shop. New restaurant planned for 2005. Takeaway. Swimming pool complex with cascades, fountains and a 'lazy river'. Covered pool. Play area. Table tennis. Games room. Off site: Beach 400 m. Water sports. Fishing. Planète Sauvage safari park.

Open

26 March - 15 October.

Directions

From the St Nazaire bridge, take the St Brevin - L'Ocean exit from the D213. Continue over the first roundabout and bear right at the second, to join the Chemin du Fief. The site can be found on the right and is well signed.

Charges 2004

Per pitch incl. 2 persons	€ 12,00 - € 28,00
extra person	€ 3,50 - € 6,50
child (0-7 yrs)	€ 1,75 - € 3,25
electricity	€ 4,00

Reservations

Contact site. Tel: 02 40 27 23 86.
E-mail: camping@lefief.com

France

FR44180 Camping de la Boutinardière

Rue de la Plage de la Boutinar, 44210 Pornic (Brittany)

This campsite has it all - two kilometres from the beautiful harbour town of Pornic and 200 metres from the sea, together with the very best of amenities and facilities (unusually all open and functioning 1 May - 22 Sept). This is truly a holiday site to suit all the family whatever their age. The site has 250 individual good sized pitches, 100-120 sq.m. in size, many bordered by three metre high, well maintained hedges for shade and privacy. All pitches have electricity available. This is a family owned site and English is spoken by the helpful, obliging reception staff. Beside reception is the site shop which is excellent in size, range and quantity of goods for the holidaymaker. Across the road is a new complex of indoor and outdoor swimming pools, paddling pool and a twin toboggan water slide. Facing the water complex, the bar, restaurant and terraces are also new and serve excellent food, be it a snack or in the restaurant or perhaps a takeaway. On site there are also sports and entertainment areas. This site is difficult to better in the South Brittany, Loire Atlantic area.

Facilities

Toilet facilities are in three good blocks, one large and centrally situated and two supporting blocks. Whilst the blocks are of traditional build the quality, maintenance and cleanliness are amongst the best. Washbasins are in cabins, dishwashing is under cover. Laundry room with sinks, washing machines and dryers. Excellent shop (15/6-15/9). New complex of bar, restaurant, terraces (1/4-22/9). Three heated swimming pools, one indoor, a paddling pool and water slides (15/5-22/9). Games room. Sports and activity area. Playground. Minigolf. Table tennis. Off site: Sandy cove 200 m. Golf, riding, sea fishing, restaurants, cafes, fishing harbour, boat trips, sailing and windsurfing, all within 5 km. of site.

At a glance

Welcome & Ambience	✓✓✓✓	Location	✓✓✓✓
Quality of Pitches	✓✓✓✓✓	Range of Facilities	✓✓✓✓✓

Directions

From north or south on D213, take Nantes D751 exit. At roundabout (with McDonalds) take D13 signed Bemarie-eb-Retz. After 4 km. site is signed to right. Note: do NOT exit from D213 at Pomic Ouest or Centre.

Charges 2004

extra person	€ 3,00 - € 6,00
child (2-10 yrs)	€ 2,00 - € 4,50
electricity (3-10A)	€ 3,50 - € 5,00
animal	€ 2,00 - € 3,50

Reservations

Made with deposit (€ 62) and fee (€ 23).
Tel: 02 40 82 05 68. E-mail: info@laboutinardiere.com

Open

1 April - 30 September.

FR56120 Camping Les Iles

La Pointe du Bile, 56760 Pénestin-sur-Mer (Brittany)

You will receive a warm and friendly welcome at this family run campsite where the owner, Madame Communal, encourages everyone to make the most of this beautiful region. The 107 pitches are mostly of a reasonable size (although larger caravans and American motorhomes are advised to book) and all have electricity. All services are fully open 14/5-16/9, with a limited service at other times. There is direct access from the site to cliff-top walks and local beaches (you can even walk to small off-shore islands at low tide). Used by one tour operator (26 pitches).

Facilities

The large central toilet block has mostly British style WCs and washbasins in cabins (with hairdryers for ladies). Dishwashing and laundry sinks. Facilities for disabled people and two baby baths. Motorcaravan service point across the road at 'Parc des Iles', the mobile home section of the site. Shop. New bar and restaurant with takeaway overlooking new pool complex (14/5-16/9). Modern multi-sports pitch for football, basketball and volleyball. Tennis court across the road. Bicycle hire. Riding. Full range of activities and entertainment for adults and children in July/Aug. Off site: Windsurfing 500 m. Sailing school 3 km.

Open

1 April - 4 October.

At a glance

Welcome & Ambience	✓✓✓✓	Location	✓✓✓✓✓
Quality of Pitches	✓✓✓✓✓	Range of Facilities	✓✓✓✓✓

Directions

From Pénestin take D201 south, taking a right fork to Pointe du Bile after 2 km. Turn right at crossroads just before beach and site is on left. Take care on arrival - the barrier is fairly close to the entrance, but there is some parking along the road outside.

Charges 2004

Per unit incl. 2 adults	€ 19,50 - € 31,50
extra person (over 10 yrs)	€ 3,20 - € 5,00
child (2-10 yrs)	€ 1,60 - € 2,50
pet	€ 1,80 - € 2,30
electricity (6A)	€ 2,80

Reservations

Made with deposit (€ 100) and fee (€ 20).
Tel: 02 99 90 30 24.
E-mail: contact@camping-des-iles.fr

TRAVEL SERVICE SITE

TO BOOK CALL 0870 405 4055 OR www.alanrogersdirect.com

FR56020 Camping de la Plage

Plage de Kervilaine, 56470 La Trinité-sur-Mer (Brittany)

The area of Carnac/La Trinité is popular with holiday makers and the two La Trinité sites of La Plage and La Baie have the great advantage of direct access to a good sandy beach. Both sites are owned by the same family, and each is very well maintained, both having a small (12 m.) heated pool with a slide. The grassy pitches, which have electricity and water (70% with drainage also), are separated by hedges and shrubs and at La Plage there are attractive flower beds. Situated on a low cliff, the terrace with its views across the bay is a very popular place for a meal or a drink. Reception areas are welcoming and friendly with tourist information on display. Both sites have a number of tour operator pitches.

Facilities

Toilet blocks have washbasins in cubicles and facilities for disabled people and small children. Washing machines and dryers. Well stocked shop with bakery. Bar, restaurant, crêperie, takeaway. Swimming pools with new water slides, etc. Good play areas including ball pool. Tennis, basketball, minigolf, table tennis. Large TV screen. Lively entertainment programme in high season for all ages and some evening entertainment in nearby disco. Bicycle hire. Beach. Guided tours on foot or bicycle. Internet access. Small communal barbecue areas (only gas ones permitted on pitches). Not suitable for American motorhomes or twin axle caravans. Off site: The village of La Trinité is 20 minutes walk along the cliff path and 10 minutes (approx) by car. Carnac is a 10-15 minutes drive in the opposite direction.

At a glance

Welcome & Ambience	✓✓✓✓	Location	✓✓✓✓✓
Quality of Pitches	✓✓✓✓	Range of Facilities	✓✓✓✓

Directions

Site is signed in different places from the D186 coast road running from La Trinité to Carnac-Plage.

Charges 2004

Per unit incl. 2 persons	€ 16,40 - € 31,10
extra adult	€ 4,00
child (2-18 yrs)	€ 2,80 - € 3,00
electricity (6/10A)	€ 2,00 - € 3,70
dog	free - € 1,20

Reservations

Contact site; when booking it is important to state size of unit in order that appropriate size pitch can be allocated. Tel: 02 97 55 73 28. E-mail: camping@camping-plage.com

Open

7 May - 17 September.

FR50080 Camping Haliotis

Chemin des Soupirs, 50170 Pontorson (Normandy)

The Duchesne family have achieved a remarkable transformation of this former municpal site. Situated on the edge of the little town of Pontorson and next to the river Couesnon, Camping Haliotis is within walking, cycling and canoeing distance of Le Mont Saint-Michel. The site has 110 pitches, including 95 for tourers, and there are plans to extend the site. Most pitches have electricity. A new swimming pool with a jacuzzi has been built, and the large, comfortable reception area developed to incorporate a bar and restaurant.

Facilities

Very clean, renovated and well-equipped wash block. Bar and restaurant. No shop or takeaway on site, facilities available in nearby town. Swimming pool with jacuzzi, separate paddling pool. Good fenced play area. Large games room. Free tennis court. Free fishing in the River Couesnon. Off site: Local services in Pontorson within walking distance. Bicycle hire 1 km. Riding 5 km. Golf 18 km. Beach 30 km.

Open

25 March - 15 November.

At a glance

Welcome & Ambience	✓✓✓✓✓	Location	✓✓✓✓
Quality of Pitches	✓✓✓✓	Range of Facilities	✓✓✓✓

Directions

Site is 300 m. from the town centre, west of D976, alongside the river, and is well signed from the town.

Charges 2005

Per adult	€ 4,20 - € 5,00
child (under 7 yrs)	€ 1,95 - € 2,50
caravan or tent, and car	€ 4,00 - € 4,50
motorcaravan	€ 4,00 - € 4,50
electricity	€ 2,50 - € 3,00

Camping Cheques accepted. No credit cards.

Reservations

Contact site. Tel: 02 33 68 11 59. E-mail: info@camping-haliotis-mont-saint-michel.com

FR76130 Camping de la Forêt

Rue Mainberthe, 76480 Jumieges (Normandy)

This is a pretty family site with a friendly laid back atmosphere. It is located just ten kilometres from the A13 Paris – Caen autoroute, and is best accessed by ferry across the River Seine. The great abbey at Jumieges was founded in 654 by St Philibert, rebuilt by the Normans and consecrated in the presence of William the Conqueror – well worth a visit! The site was formerly a municipal and has recently been taken on by the Joret family. The 90 grassy pitches (76 for tourers) are attractively located in woodland. Virtually all pitches are reasonably shaded and most have electrical connections. A good range of shops, cafes, restaurants etc. can be foung in Jumieges, just 600 m. away.

Facilities

Two toilet blocks, both of modern construction and maintained to a good standard with British toilets and pre-set showers. Washing and drying machines. Shop. Small swimming pool (heated 1/6-30/8). Playground. Chalets and mobile homes to let.

Open

2 April - 30 October

At a glance

Welcome & Ambience	✓✓✓✓	Location	✓✓✓
Quality of Pitches	✓✓✓✓	Range of Facilities	✓✓

Directions

Jumieges is around 10 km. north of the A13 Paris – Caen autoroute (Bourg-Achard exit). Take D313 towards Caudebec-en-Caux. Then, either take the ferry across the Seine (with toll) from Heurtauville to Jumieges, or continue over the Pont de Brotonne and double back on D982 to Jumieges. Site is clearly signed in the village.

Charges 2005

Pitch incl. 2 persons	€ 14,20 - € 15,00
extra person (over 4 yrs)	€ 3,40 - € 3,80
electricity	€ 2,50

Camping Cheques accepted.
Reduced charges in low season.

Reservations

Conatct site. Tel: 02 35 37 93 43.
E-mail: info@campinglaforet.com

FR02060 Camping Municipal Guignicourt

14 Bis Rue Godins, 02190 Guignicourt (Northern France)

This very pleasant little municipal site has 100 pitches, 50 for long stay units and 50 for tourists. These two sections are separated by the main facilities on a higher terrace. Pitches are generally large and level, although you might need an extra long electricity lead for some, but there are few dividing hedges. Pitches along the river bank have most shade, with a few specimen trees providing a little shade to some of the more open pitches. The town is quite attractive and is worthy of an evening stroll. At the junction of the N44 and D925, 7 km. west of the town, is the Chemin des Dames, Monument des Chars d'Assaut - a memorial to the WW1 tank campaign at Berry-au-Bac, with two remarkably well preserved tanks. Further to the west is the Caverne du Dragon, a former stone quarry which sheltered troops during the 1914-18 conflict, which is now a museum depicting everyday life on the front line. You may notice a low level hum from the nearby Generale Sucrière factory, a major industry of the town, but you may also hear the site's nightingales.

Facilities

The modern sanitary unit has British and Turkish style toilets, washbasins (cold only except for the one in a cubicle), push-button hot showers, dishwashing and laundry sinks. Bar (1/4-30/9). Playground. Tennis and boules courts. Fishing. Off site: The town has all services including a supermarket and bank. Golf 3km. Beach 15 km.

Open

1 April - 30 September.

At a glance

Welcome & Ambience	✓✓✓✓	Location	✓✓✓✓
Quality of Pitches	✓✓✓✓	Range of Facilities	✓✓✓

Directions

Guignicourt is about 20 km. north of Reims, just east of the A26, junction 14. The site is well signed from D925 in the village.

Charges 2004

Per adult	€ 2,00
child (2-10 yrs)	€ 1,20
pitch incl. electricity (6/10A)	€ 7,80 - € 15,60
animal	€ 1,00

Reservations

Contact site. Tel: 03 23 79 74 58.
E-mail: camping.guignicourt@free.fr

FR02030 Caravaning La Croix du Vieux Pont

02290 Berny-Riviere (Northern France)

Attractively located on the banks of the River Aisne, La Croix du Vieux Pont is a very smart, modern site offering a high standard of facilities. Many pitches are occupied by mobile homes and tour operator tents, but there are 52 pleasant touring pitches, some on the banks of the Aisne. The 34 hectare site is maintained to a high standard with some excellent amenities, notably four heated swimming pools, one indoors with a waterslide and jacuzzi. There are two tennis courts, an amusement arcade and volleyball court. At the heart of the site is a well-stocked fishing lake which is also used for pedaloes and canoes.

Facilities

The six toilet blocks are modern and kept very clean, with washbasins in cabins and free hot showers. Washing and drying machines. Facilities for disabled visitors. Large supermarket. Bar, takeaway and good value restaurant (most amenities 1/4-30/9). Swimming pool complex (covered pool 1/4-30/10, outdoor 1/5-30/9). Play area. Fishing. Bicycle hire. Coach trips organised on a regular basis to Paris, Parc Asterix and Disneyland. Appartments to let. Dogs are not accepted. Off site: Riding 100 m. Golf 30 km.

Open

1 January - 31 December.

At a glance

Welcome & Ambience	✓✓✓✓	Location	✓✓✓✓
Quality of Pitches	✓✓✓✓✓	Range of Facilities	✓✓✓✓✓

Directions

From Compiegne take N31 towards Soissons. At Vic-sur-Aisne turn right, towards Berny-Riviere and site is on right after 400 m.

Charges 2005

Oer unit incl. 2 persons and electricity	€ 19,00 - € 21,50
incl. 4 persons	€ 27,00 - € 29,50

Camping Cheques accepted.

Reservations

Essential for high season and made with deposit (€ 40). Tel: 03 23 55 50 02.
E-mail: info@la-croix-du-vieux-pont.com

FR60010 Camping Campix

B.P. 37, 60340 St Leu-d'Esserent (Northern France)

Opened in 1991, this informal site has been unusually developed in a former sandstone quarry on the outskirts of the small town. The quarry walls provide very different boundaries to most of the site, giving it a sheltered, peaceful environment. Trees have grown to soften the slopes. Not a neat, manicured site, the 160 pitches are arranged in small groups on the different levels with stone and gravel access roads (some fairly steep and possibly muddy in poor weather). Electricity (6A) is available to approximately 140 pitches. Torches are advised. There are very many secluded corners mostly for smaller units and tents and plenty of space for children to explore (parents must supervise - some areas, although fenced, could be dangerous). A footpath leads from the site to the town where there are shops, restaurants and an outdoor pool (in season). This site is best suited to those not needing sophisticated on-site facilities, or for visiting local places of interest and the friendly, English speaking owner will advise. These include Chantilly, the Asterix Park and the Mer de Sable, a Western theme amusements park, both 20 km. Disneyland is 70 km. It is also possible to visit Paris by train (information at reception).

Facilities

At the entrance to the site a large building houses reception and two clean, heated sanitary units - one for tourers, the other usually reserved for groups. Two suites for disabled people double as baby rooms. Laundry facilities with washing machine and dryer. At quieter times only one unit is opened but facilities may be congested at peak times. Motorcaravan service facilities. Bread and milk delivered daily. Basic snack bar operates from mobile unit (July/Aug). Off site: Fishing 1 or 5 km, riding or golf 5 km.

Open

7 March - 30 November.

At a glance

Welcome & Ambience	✓✓✓	Location	✓✓✓
Quality of Pitches	✓✓✓	Range of Facilities	✓✓✓

Directions

St Leu-d'Esserent is 11 km. west of Senlis, 5 km. northwest of Chantilly. From the north on the A1 autoroute take the Senlis exit, from Paris the Chantilly exit. Site is north of the town off the D12 towards Cramoisy, and is signed in the village.

Charges 2005

Per unit	€ 3,50 - € 5,00
person	€ 3,00 - € 5,00
child (under 9 yrs)	€ 2,00 - € 3,00
small tent	€ 2,50 - € 4,00
electricity	€ 2,50 - € 3,50
dog	€ 1,00 - € 2,00

Reservations

Advisable for July/Aug. Tel: 03 44 56 08 48.
E-mail: campixfr@aol.com

FR62060 Caravaning L'Orée du Bois

Chemin Blanc, 62180 Rang-du-Fliers (Northern France)

This fairly peaceful but extensive campsite is in a natural woodland setting, and only 3 km. from a large sandy beach. From reception you pass through a corner of the mobile home (privately owned) section, then through an area of natural, preserved woodland which separates the touring area. This has 80 individual, touring pitches, all with shade and electric hook-ups. On sandy grass which can be slightly undulating, most are separated by hedges and bushes, but the emphasis is on 'nature'. Also on the touring site are 67 wooden camping lodges. A separate clearing in the woodland is reserved for tents, and useful for cyclists or backpackers is 'Camp Sherpa' comprising eight 2-berth wooden tents. A modern sanitary unit is central in the touring area, with a second smaller unit in the mobile homes area, useful when walking between your pitch and the bar/brasserie with takeaway, tennis courts, pétanque etc. Berck Plage is only 3 km. and has a magnificent sandy beach and promenade, with extensive free parking areas, with many bays for disabled motorists. Indeed the site and the area are well suited to disabled visitors of all ages.

Facilities

Modern facilities with open and cubicle washbasins, controllable hot showers, a laundry with washing machines and dryer, and good facilities for disabled persons (with low level dishwashing and laundry sinks), small children and babies. Note: water for the toilets is obtained from a borehole, and has a slight brownish colour. Basic motorcaravan service point by reception, with a full service area located close to the nearby Intermarché. Bar/brasserie (30/3-20/10). Animation and dancing in July/Aug. Multi-court tennis. Several playgrounds. The woodland area conceals a football field, volleyball, a fitness trail, a course for quads and all terrain bikes, and a fishing lake.
Off site: Small supermarket adjacent, large Intermarché complex 700 m. Sports centre at Berck-Plage. Also close by is Le Parc de Bagatelle, the largest amusement park in northern France. Beach 3 km. Cycle hire 2km, horse riding 1.5km, boat launching 3km, golf 8km. Market in Berck-Plage Tues/Wed/Thurs/Sat/Sun, and in Rang du Fliers Thursday.

At a glance

Welcome & Ambience	✓✓✓✓	Location	✓✓✓✓
Quality of Pitches	✓✓✓	Range of Facilities	✓✓✓✓

Directions

Rang du Fliers is just east of Berck Plage and about 15 km. south of Le Touquet. From Berck Plage take D917 east to roundabout by Intermarché supermarket, turn left (north) at next roundabout (site signed), site entrance is 500 m. on left. From A16 exit 25, follow D917 towards Berck Plage. After four roundabouts, a railway crossing, and two more roundabouts, turn right at the seventh roundabout (site signed), site entrance is 500 m. on left.

Charges 2004

extra person	€ 3,00 - € 5,50
child (3-7 yrs)	€ 2,00 - € 3,50
animal	€ 2,00

Discounts for stays of 14 days.
Barrier card deposit €50.

Reservations

Essential for July/Aug, and advisable at other times. Made with deposit of 25% of total fees.
Tel: 03 21 84 28 51. E-mail: oree.du.bois@wanadoo.fr

Open

30 March - 20 October.

FR80060 Camping Le Val de Trie

Bouillancourt-sous-Miannay, 80870 Moyenneville (Northern France)

Le Val de Trie is a natural countryside site in a woodland location, near a small village. It is maturing into a well managed site with modern facilities. The 100 numbered, grassy pitches are of a good size, divided by hedges and shrubs with mature trees providing good shade in most areas, and all have electricity and water. Access roads are gravel (the site is possibly not suitable for the largest motorcaravans). There are good walks around the area and a notice board keeps campers up to date with local market, shopping and activity news. The site has a friendly, relaxed atmosphere and English is spoken. Very much off the beaten track, it can be very quiet in April, June, September and October. If you visit at these times and there is no-one on site, just choose a pitch or call at the farm to book in. There are a few Dutch tour operator tents (5).

Facilities

The two sanitary buildings are well maintained and cleaned, and include washbasins in cubicles, units for disabled people, babies and children, plus laundry and dishwashing facilities (and a microwave to warm babies food). Washing machine and dryer. Basic motorcaravan services. Extended shop (from 1/5) provides basic necessities, farm produce and wine, bread can be ordered each evening and butcher visits twice weekly in season. Plans include an extended bar, and snack-bar (with takeaway), with the addition of a TV room (15/5-15/9). There is a terrace and (in high season) a children's club. Pleasant, heated small swimming pool (6 x 12 m. open 1/5-31/8), fenced with large paddling pool and jacuzzi. Table tennis, boules and volleyball. Fishing lake (free). Bicycle hire. Children's play areas and small animal enclosure. Off site: Riding 2 km. Golf 10 km. Beach 12 km.

At a glance

Welcome & Ambience	✓✓✓✓✓	Location	✓✓✓✓✓
Quality of Pitches	✓✓✓✓	Range of Facilities	✓✓✓✓

Directions

From exit 2 on A28 near Abbeville take D925 to Miannay and turn left on D86 to Bouillancourt sous Miannay: site is signed in village

Charges 2005

Per unit incl. 2 persons	€ 12,00 - € 17,60
with electricity	€ 15,00 - € 21,00
extra person	€ 2,90 - € 4,40
child (under 7 yrs)	€ 1,90 - € 2,80
dog	€ 0,80 - € 1,30

Camping Cheques accepted.

Reservations

Made with dates, plus deposit (€ 31; no fee for AR readers). Tel: 03 22 31 48 88.
E-mail: raphael@camping-levaldetrie.fr

Open

1 April - 1 November.

FR80040 Camping Le Royon

1271 route de Quend, 80120 Fort-Mahon-Plage (Northern France)

This busy family run site, some two kilometres from the sea, has 300 pitches of which 100 are used for touring units. Of either 95 or 120 sq.m, the marked and numbered pitches are divided by hedges and arranged either side of access roads. Electricity (6A) and water points are available to all. The site is well lit, fenced and guarded at night (€ 30 deposit for barrier card). Entertainment is organised for adults and children in July/Aug. The site is close to the Baie de l'Authie which is an area noted for migrating birds.

Facilities

Four toilet blocks provide mostly unisex facilities with British or Turkish style WCs and some washbasins in cubicles. Units for disabled people. Baby baths. Dishwashing and laundry sinks under cover. Small shop (July/Aug). Mobile takeaway calls each evening in July/Aug. Friendly clubroom and bar serves drinks and ices, sells bread and newspapers and has the usual games machines. Attractive, heated, covered swimming pool (16 x 8 m; 1/5-15/9) with open air children's pool and sun terrace. Playground. Table tennis, multi-court, tennis court and boules. Bicycle hire. Off site: Fishing, riding or golf within 1 km. Windsurfing, sailing, sand yachting, canoeing, swimming, climbing and shooting nearby. Cinema, disco and casino near.

At a glance

Welcome & Ambience	✓✓✓	Location	✓✓✓✓
Quality of Pitches	✓✓✓	Range of Facilities	✓✓✓✓

Directions

Site is on outskirts of Fort Mahon Plage, on D32 from Quend (which is on D940 Berck - Le Tréport road).

Charges 2004

Per pitch 95 sq.m. incl. electricity and 3 persons	€ 16,00 - € 25,00
pitch 120 sq.m, as above	€ 19,00 - € 28,00
extra person (over 1 yr)	€ 6,80
dog	€ 2,50

Reservations

Essential for July/Aug; made with deposit (€ 40 per week) and fee (€ 10). Tel: 03 22 23 40 30. E-mail: info@campingleroyon.com

Open

5 March - 1 November.

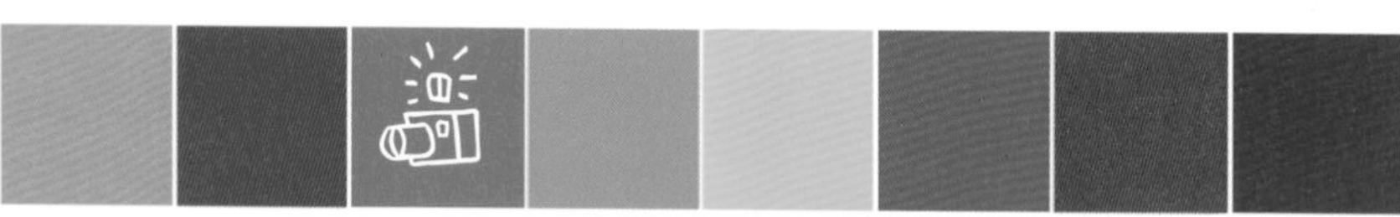

FR80090 Camping Caravaning Le Val d'Authie

20 route de Vercourt, 80120 Villers-sur-Authie (Northern France)

In a village location, this well organised site is fairly close to several beaches, but also has its own excellent pool complex, small restaurant and bar. The owner has carefully controlled the size of the site, leaving space for a leisure area. There are 170 pitches in total, but with many holiday homes and chalets, there are only 60 for touring units. These are on grass, some divided by small hedges, with electricity and 15 with full services. Ideas for excursions include the 15/16th century chapel and the Aviation Museum at Rue and the steam railway which runs from Le Crotoy to Cayeux-sur-Mer around the Baie de Somme.

Facilities

Good modern toilet facilities include some shower and washbasin units, washbasins in cubicles, and limited facilities for disabled people and babies. Facilities may be under pressure in high season and a reader reports poor cleaning at that time. Ice pack service. Shop for basics (not in October). Bar/restaurant serving good value meals (1/5-15/9; hours vary according to season). Swimming pool with small jacuzzi and paddling pool (1/5-15/9, with lifeguards in July/Aug). Good playground for small children, club room with TV, and weekend entertainment in season (discos may be noisy until late). Multi-court, beach volleyball, football, boules and tennis court (all free). Fitness trail and running track, mountain bike circuit. Barbecues are not permitted.

At a glance

Welcome & Ambience	✓✓✓✓	Location	✓✓✓✓
Quality of Pitches	✓✓✓✓	Range of Facilities	✓✓✓✓

Directions

Villers-sur-Authie is about 25 km. NNW of Abbeville. From A16 junction 24 take N1 to Vron, then left on D175 to Villers-sur-Authie. Or use D85 from Rue, or D485 from Nampont St Martin. Site is at southern end of village at junction of minor road (easy to miss).

Charges 2004

Per person	€ 6,00
child (under 7 yrs)	€ 3,00
pitch	€ 5,00
electricity (4-10A)	€ 4,00 - € 8,00

Camping Cheques accepted.

Reservations

Advisable for high season, peak weekends and B.Hs. Tel: 03 22 29 92 47. E-mail: camping@valdauthie.fr

Open

1 April - 31 October.

FR80070 Camping La Ferme des Aulnes

1 rue du Marais, Fresne-sur-Authie, 80120 Nampont-St Martin (Northern France)

This peaceful site has been developed on the grassy meadows of a small, 17th century farm on the edge of the village of Fresne and is lovingly cared for by its enthusiastic owner and his hard-working team. Restored outbuildings house reception and the site's facilities, arranged around a central, landscaped courtyard that now boasts a fine heated swimming pool. Of the 120 pitches, 55 are available for touring units, with most of the remainder occupied by or for sale to private owners for holiday mobile homes. All tourist pitches have electricity (6A) and are fairly level. Many are individual and divided by shrubs and young trees, others are on an open, slightly sloping, grassy area.

Facilities

Sanitary fittings are smart, modern and well maintained, including washbasins in cubicles with a large cubicle for disabled people. Facilities are uni-sex but there are four new individual cabins for ladies. Dishwashing and laundry sinks. Small shop with local produce and necessities (all season, as are all other facilities). Piano bar and restaurant. TV room. Swimming pool from 26 March (16 x 9 m; heated and with cover for cooler weather). Fitness room. Aquagym and Balneo therapy. Playground for small children. Beach volleyball, table tennis, boules and archery. Off site: Fishing is possible in river 50 m. from site. Golf 3 km. Riding 8 km.

Open

26 March - 1 November.

At a glance

Welcome & Ambience	✓✓✓✓✓	Location	✓✓✓✓✓
Quality of Pitches	✓✓✓✓	Range of Facilities	✓✓✓✓

Directions

At Nampont St Martin (on the N1 between Montreuil and Abbeville) turn west off the N1 on to the D485 (site is signed), towards Villers-sur-Authie. Site is on right after about 3 km in village of Fresne.

Charges 2004

Per adult	€ 7,00
child (under 7 yrs)	€ 4,00
pitch	€ 6,00
dog	€ 4,00
electricity (6A)	€ 5,00

Camping Cheques accepted.

Reservations

Contact site for details. Tel: 03 22 29 22 69.
E-mail: contact@fermedesaulnes.com

FR77030 Camping International de Jablines

Base de Loisirs, 77450 Jablines (Paris & Ile de France)

Redesigned in 1997, Jablines replaces an older site in an upmarket, modern style which, with the accompanying leisure facilities of the adjacent 'Espace Loisirs', provides an interesting, if a little impersonal alternative to other sites in the region. The whole complex close to the Marne has been developed around old gravel workings. Man-made lakes provide marvellous water activities – dinghy sailing, windsurfing, canoeing, fishing and supervised bathing, plus a large equestrian centre. In season the activities at the leisure complex are supplemented by a bar/restaurant and a range of very French style group activities. The 'Great Lake' as it is called, is said to have the largest beach on the Ile-de-France! The site itself provides 132 pitches, most of a good size with gravel hardstanding and grass, accessed by tarmac roads and clearly marked by fencing panels and newly planted shrubs. All have 10A electrical connections, 60 with water and waste connections also.

Facilities

Two identical toilet blocks, heated in cool weather, are solidly built and well equipped. They include some washbasins in cubicles, indoor dishwashing and laundry facilities with washing machine and dryer. Motorcaravan service (charged). Shop (all season). Play area. Bar/restaurant adjacent at leisure centre/lake complex along with a range of watersports including 'water cable ski', riding activities, tennis and minigolf. Whilst staying on the campsite, admission to the leisure complex is free. Internet point. Ticket sales for Disneyland, Asterix and Sea Life.

Open

25 March - 30 October.

At a glance

Welcome & Ambience	✓✓✓✓	Location	✓✓✓✓
Quality of Pitches	✓✓✓✓	Range of Facilities	✓✓✓✓

Directions

From A4 Paris - Rouen take A104 before Disneyland. Take exit 8 on D404 Meaux/Base de Loisirs Jablines. From the A1 going south, follow signs for Disneyland after Charles de Gaulle airport using the A104. Take exit 6A Clay-Souilly on N3 (Meaux). After 6 km. turn right on D404 and follow signs.

Charges 2005

Per unit incl. 2 persons, electricity	€ 19,00 - € 22,00
luxury pitch incl. water and waste	€ 22,00 - € 24,00
extra person	€ 3,00 - € 5,50

Camping Cheques accepted.

Reservations

Essential for July/Aug. and made with booking form from site and 30% deposit. Tel: 01 60 26 09 37. E-mail: welcome@camping-jablines.com

FR78040 Camping Municipal de l'Etang d'Or

Route du Château d'Eau, 78120 Rambouillet (Paris & Ile de France)

This is a pleasant site in a peaceful forest location, with good tarmac access roads, site lighting and 190 touring pitches of varying size and surfaces. Some of the individual pitches are divided by hedges, others are more open and sunny. All have electricity, 83 also have water and drainage, with a few hard-standings. Campers get a discount brochure for local sites or activities (e.g. the municipal swimming pool, animal park, bowling and billiards, bicycle hire), and a special permit for the fishing lake. There are many good cycle and footpaths in the area. It is possible to visit Paris by rail, the Mobilis 'transport package' ticket is available from the railway station. Rambouillet itself is an interesting town and Chartres and Versailles are within reach.

Facilities

Two heated sanitary buildings include British and Turkish style WCs, washbasins (some in cubicles), dishwashing and laundry sinks, plus basic facilities for baby changing and for disabled persons. Facilities could be a little stretched during the high season. Washing machine and dryer. One block is closed in winter. Motorcaravan service point (€1.29). Café/bar and small shop. Good playground. Off site: Large supermarket at southern end of the town.

Open

All year, excl. 19 Dec - 30 Jan.

At a glance

Welcome & Ambience	✓✓✓	Location	✓✓✓✓
Quality of Pitches	✓✓✓	Range of Facilities	✓✓✓✓

Directions

Rambouillet is 52 km. southwest of Paris, midway between Versailles and Chartres. Site is southeast of town: from N10 southbound take Rambouillet/Les Eveuses exit, northbound take Rambouillet centre exit, loop round and rejoin N10 southbound, taking next exit. Pass under N10, following signs for site.

Charges 2005

Per person	€ 3,90 - € 4,30
child (2-10 yrs)	€ 2,70 - € 3,00
pitch	€ 4,30 - € 4,90
dog	€ 1,50
electricity (6-10A)	€ 3,00 - € 3,80

Reservations

Contact site for details. Tel: 01 30 41 07 34. E-mail: rambouillet.tourisme@wanadoo.fr

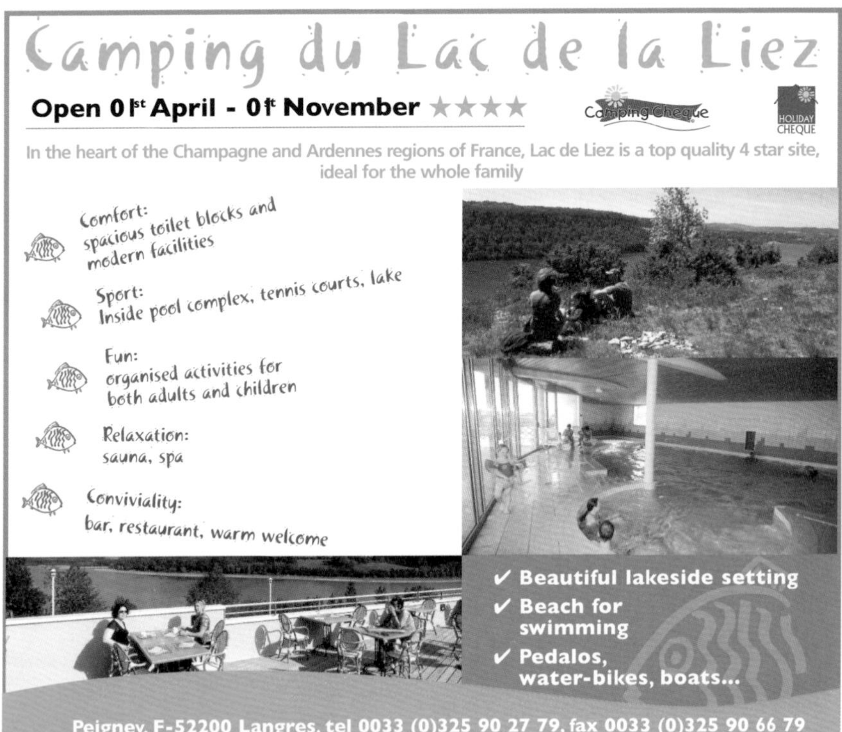

FR52030 Camping Lac de la Liez

Peigney, 52200 Langres (Eastern France)

Managed by the enthusiastic Baude family, this newly renovated lakeside site is near the city of Langres. With its old ramparts and ancient city centre, Langres was elected one of the 50 most historic cities in France. Situated only 10 minutes from the A5, Camping Lac de la Liez provides an ideal spot for an overnight stop en-route to the south of France. There is also a lot on offer for a longer stay, including the lake and an impressive indoor pool complex, with a sauna. The site provides 144 fully serviced, terraced pitches with panoramic views of the lake. The 200 hectare lake has a sandy beach for play and swimming, a play area and a small harbour where boats and pedaloes may be hired. Access to the lake from the campsite is down steps and across what is quite a fast road (in total 150 m).

Facilities

Two new toilet blocks have all facilities in cabins. Facilities for disabled people. Laundry facilities. Motorcaravan services. Shop, bar and restaurant (with takeaway food). Indoor pool complex with spa and sauna. Extensive games area and tennis court (free in low season). Off site: Lake with beach and boat hire. Bicycle hire and cycle tracks around the lake. Riding 5 km. Fishing 100 m. Golf 40 km.

Open

1 April - 1 November

At a glance

Welcome & Ambience	✓✓✓✓	Location	✓✓✓✓
Quality of Pitches	✓✓✓✓	Range of Facilities	✓✓✓✓

Directions

From Langres take the N19 towards Vesoul. After approximately 3 km. turn right, straight after the large river bridge, then follow site signs.

Charges 2005

Per person	€ 6,00
child (under 7 yrs)	€ 3,00 - € 3,00
pitch	€ 8,00
electricity	€ 4,00 - € 4,00
dog	€ 1,50

Camping Cheques accepted.
Reductions in low season.

Reservations

Contact site. Tel: 03 25 90 27 79.
E-mail: campingliez@free.fr

FR67030 Camping Caravaning du Ried

Route de Rhinau, 67860 Boofzheim (Eastern France)

The area between the main road from Strasbourg to Colmar and the river Rhine is usually bypassed by those who are exploring Alsace or passing through to Switzerland and Italy. However, if looking for a night stop or a different base in the region, Camping du Ried could well fit the bill. Situated on the edge of a small, picturesque village, it has 100 tourist pitches (with 5A electricity) amongst the 120 rental and 55 private static caravans. Most of these are under tall trees, on grass and separated by hedges. One might think that this is just another reasonable campsite until one sees the excellent pool complex just inside the site entrance which has an attractive outdoor pool for use in July and August and a heated indoor one open from May to September. There is also a lake and small beach on site. We found this a pleasant site with very friendly management who would like to welcome more British visitors although no English is spoken.

Facilities

The main, heated toilet block is quite a large building and was refurbished in 2002. It is well tiled and has all the usual facilities including those for disabled people. Washing machines and dryer. Additional small units by lake or reception. Bar/restaurant (weekends 1/4-30/6 & 1/9-30/9, daily 1/7-31/8). Splendid indoor and outdoor pools (bracelets must be worn). These also have toilets and showers. Motorcaravan Service Point. Playground. Boules. Minigolf. Canoeing. High season animation for children and daily programme including a variety of excursions, guided canoe trips and competitions. Library. Archery. Fitness trail around lake. Volleyball. Fishing. Off site: Large Super 'U' supermarket outside gates, also has an ATM, fuel station and car wash (open 08.00-20.00). Markets at Benfeld Mondays and Selestat Tuesdays. Cycle hire 1 km. Riding 4 km. Golf 18 km.

At a glance

Welcome & Ambience	✓✓✓✓	Location	✓✓✓
Quality of Pitches	✓✓✓✓	Range of Facilities	✓✓✓✓

Directions

Leave N83 Strasbourg - Colmar road at Benfeld and go east on D5 to Boofzheim. Site is 500 m. beyond village towards Rhinau.

Charges 2005

Per unit incl. 2 persons	€ 13,00 - € 17,50
extra person	€ 3,00 - € 5,50
hiker	€ 7,00 - € 9,00
dog	€ 2,50 - € 3,00
electricity	€ 5,00

Security barrier card deposit €30.
Discount for longer stays.

Reservations

Made with deposit and fee; contact site.
Tel: 03 88 74 68 27. E-mail: info@camping-ried.com

Open

1 April - 2 October.

FR88040 Camping Club du Lac de Bouzey

19 rue du Lac, 88390 Sanchey (Eastern France)

Camping-Club Lac de Bouzey is eight kilometres west of Épinal, overlooking the lake, at the beginning of the Vosges Massif. It is well placed for exploring the hills, valleys, lakes and waterfalls of the south of Alsace Lorraine. The word 'Club' has been added to the name to indicate the number of activities organised in high season. The 160 individual 100 sqm. back-to-back grass pitches are arranged on either side of tarmac roads with electricity (6 -10A). They are on a gentle slope, divided by trees or beech hedging, under a cover of tall, silver birch trees and some overlook the 130 ha. lake. Units can be close together when the site is busy. The lake has a number of sandy beaches. Many water sports may be enjoyed, from pedaloes to canoes, windsurfing and sailing. The large, imposing building at the entrance to the site houses a restaurant and bar with terraces overlooking the lake. Two bars by the lake would indicate that the lake-side is popular with the public in summer but the camping area is quiet, separated by a road and well back and above the main entrance. An 'all year' site, there is lots going on for teenagers. English is spoken. A 'Sites et Paysages' member.

Facilities

The central sanitary block, partly below ground level, includes a baby room and one for disabled people (although there is up and down hill walking on the site). In winter a small, heated section in the main building with toilet, washbasin and shower is used. Good laundry and dishwashing facilites. Motorcaravan service point. Well stocked shop. Bar, restaurant. Heated swimming pool (1/5-30/9) of an original shape and backed by two sunbathing terraces. Fishing, riding, volleyball, games room, archery and bicycle hire on site. Below ground, under the restaurant, is a sound-proof room for cinema shows and discos for those staying on site only. Staff escort young people back to their pitch at the end of the evening. High season programme of activities for all ages, including excursions, entertainment, sports and a mini-club.
Off site: Golf 8 km.

At a glance

Welcome & Ambience	✓✓✓✓	Location	✓✓✓✓
Quality of Pitches	✓✓✓	Range of Facilities	✓✓✓✓✓

Directions

Site is 8 km. west of Épinal on D460 and is signed from some parts of Épinal. Follow signs for Lac de Bouzey and Sanchey.

Charges 2005

Per unit incl. 2 adults	€ 15,00 - € 23,00
extra person	€ 5,00 - € 7,00
child (4-10 yrs)	free - € 5,00
electricity (6/10A)	€ 4,00 - € 5,00
dog	free - € 3,00

Reservations

Made with deposit (€ 12 per day booked) and fee (€ 25). Tel: 03 29 82 49 41.
E-mail: camping.lac.de.bouzey@wanadoo.fr

Open

All year.

FR17230 Camping de L'Océan

La Passe, La Couarde sur Mer, 17670 Ile de Ré (Vendée/Charente)

L'Océan lies close to the centre of the Ile de Ré, just 50 metres from a sandy beach. There are 338 pitches here with around 200 for touring units, the remainder occupied by mobile homes and chalets. The camping area is well shaded and pitches are of a reasonable size, most with electricity (10A) and 60 with water and drainage. Pride of place goes to the large heated swimming pool which is surrounded by an attractive sunbathing terrace. Bicycle hire is popular here as the island offers over 100 km. of interesting cycle routes. There is a pleasant bar/restaurant with a terrace overlooking the pool. In peak season a range of entertainment is organised including disco evenings. Future plans include a new toilet block, internet access in the bar and an indoor pool.

Facilities

The sanitary blocks are modern and well maintained with facilities for disabled visitors and a dog shower. Shop. Bar/restaurant and takeaway (all season). Swimming pool. Riding. Bicycle hire. Tennis court. Fishing pond adjacent. Basketball. Play area. Charcoal barbecues are not permitted. Off site: South facing beach 50 m. La Couarde (nearest restaurants, shops etc.) 2.5 km. Golf 5 km.

Open

25 March - 25 September.

At a glance

Welcome & Ambience	✓✓✓✓	Location	✓✓✓✓
Quality of Pitches	✓✓✓✓	Range of Facilities	✓✓✓✓

Directions

After crossing the toll bridge onto the island, join D735 which runs along the north side of the island until you pass La Couarde. The site is 2.5 km beyond the village (in the direction of Ars en Re).

Charges 2004

Per unit incl. 2 persons	€ 14,00 - € 35,00
extra person	€ 4,00 - € 8,80
electricity	€ 5,00
dog	€ 1,70 - € 4,20

Camping Cheques accepted.

Reservations

Contact site. Tel: 05 46 29 87 70.
E-mail: campingdelocean@wanadoo.fr

FR17010 Camping Bois Soleil

2 avenue de Suzac, 17110 St Georges-de-Didonne (Vendée/Charente)

Close to the sea and the resort of St Georges, Bois Soleil is a fairly large site in three separate parts, with 165 serviced pitches for touring units and a few for tents. All touring pitches are hedged, and have electricity, with water and a drain between every two. There are a few pitches with lockable gates for late night entry and exit. The main part, 'Les Pins', is mature and attractive with ornamental trees and shrubs providing shade. Opposite is 'La Mer' which has direct access to the beach. It has some areas with rather less shade and a raised central area for tents. The sandy beach here is a wide public one, sheltered from the Atlantic breakers although the sea goes out some way at low tide. The third part of the site, 'La Forêt', is for static holiday homes. The areas are well tended with the named pitches (not numbered) cleared and raked between clients and with an all-in charge including electricity and water. This lively site offers something for everyone, whether they like a beach-side spot or a traditional pitch, plenty of activities or the quiet life – it is best to book for the area you prefer. It can be full mid-June - late August.

Facilities

Each area is served by one large sanitary block, supplemented by smaller blocks providing toilets only. Another heated block is near reception. Well designed and appointed buildings, cleaned twice daily, they include washbasins in cubicles, facilities for disabled people (WC, basin and shower) and for babies. Launderette. Nursery for babies. Supermarket, bakery (July/Aug) and beach shop. Restaurant and bar by pool. Excellent takeaway (from April). Heated swimming pool. 'Parc des Jeux' with tennis, table tennis, bicycle hire, boules and children's playground. TV room and library. Comprehensive tourist information and entertainment office. Internet terminal. Charcoal barbecues are not permitted but gas ones can be hired by the evening. Pets are not accepted. Off site: Fishing and riding within 500 m. Golf 20 km.

At a glance

Welcome & Ambience	✓✓✓✓✓	Location	✓✓✓✓✓
Quality of Pitches	✓✓✓✓✓	Range of Facilities	✓✓✓✓✓

Directions

From Royan centre take coast road (D25) along the sea-front of St Georges-de-Didonne towards Meschers. Site is signed at roundabout at end of the main beach.

Charges 2004

Per unit incl. 2 persons,	
6A electricity	€ 16,00 - € 27,50
3 persons	€ 19,00 - € 27,50
tent incl. 2 persons	€ 13,00 - € 24,50
extra person	€ 3,50 - € 5,00
child (3-7 yrs)	€ 1,50 - € 3,50
electricity (10A)	€ 3,40 - € 5,00

Camping Cheques accepted.
Less 20% outside July/Aug.

Reservations

Made with 25% deposit and € 26 fee.
Tel: 05 46 05 05 94.
E-mail: camping.bois.soleil@wanadoo.fr

Open

3 April - 30 November.

FR85040 Castel Camping La Garangeoire

St Julien-des-Landes, 85150 La Mothe-Achard (Vendée/Charente)

La Garangeoire is one of a relatively small number of seriously good sites in the Vendée, situated some 15 km. inland near the village of St Julien des Landes. One of its more memorable qualities is the view of the château through the gates as you drive in. Imaginative use has been made of the old Noirmoutiers 'main road' which passes through the centre of the site and now forms a delightful, quaint thoroughfare, nicknamed the Champs Elysée. Providing a village like atmosphere, it is busy at most times with the facilities opening directly off it. The site is set in the 200 ha. of parkland surrounding the small château of La Garangeoire. The peaceful fields and woods, where campers may walk, include three lakes, one of which is used for fishing and boating (life jackets supplied from reception). With a spacious, relaxed atmosphere, the main camping areas are arranged on either side of the old road, edged with mature trees. The 300 pitches, each with a name not a number and individually hedged, are especially large (most 150-200 sq.m.) and are well spaced. Most have electricity (12A), some water and drainage also. The site is popular with tour operators (144 pitches).

TRAVEL SERVICE SITE

TO BOOK CALL 0870 405 4055 OR www.alanrogersdirect.com

Facilities

Ample sanitary facilities are of good standard, well situated for all areas. One excellent block has facilities for babies and disabled people. All have washbasins in cabins. Good laundry facilities. Motorcaravan service point. Good shop. Full restaurant, takeaway and a separate crêperie with bars and attractive courtyard terrace overlooking the swimming pool complex (from 1/5) with water slides, fountains and a children's pool. Large play field with play equipment for children's activities, whether organised or not. Games room. Two tennis courts. Bicycle hire. Table tennis, crazy golf, archery and volleyball. Riding in July/Aug. Fishing and boating. Off site: Beaches 15 km.

At a glance

Welcome & Ambience	✓✓✓✓✓	Location	✓✓✓✓
Quality of Pitches	✓✓✓✓	Range of Facilities	✓✓✓✓✓

Directions

Site is signed from St Julien; the entrance is to the east off the D21 road, 2.5 km north of St Julian-des-Landes.

Charges 2004

Per unit incl. 2 persons	€ 14,00 - € 27,00
with electricity	€ 17,00 - € 30,00
with services	€ 18,50 - € 33,50
extra person	€ 4,50 - € 6,00
child (under 10 yrs)	€ 2,50 - € 3,00
dog	€ 3,00

Camping Cheques accepted.

Reservations

Made for min. 7 days with deposit (€ 61) and fee (€ 22.87). Tel: 02 51 46 65 39.
E-mail: garangeoire@wanadoo.fr

Open

5 April - 24 September.

Bois Soleil

Camping ★★★★
Charente-Maritime

Surrounded by pine trees and a sandy beach on the Atlantic Coast, with one direct access to the beach, Bois Soleil proposes to you many attractions like tennis, tabletennis, children playgrounds and entertainment.
Shops, take-away and snack-bar with big TV screen.

Spring and Summer 2005

2, avenue de Suzac - 17110 ST GEORGES DE DIDONNE
Tel: 0033 546 05 05 94 - Fax: 0033 546 06 27 43
www.bois-soleil.com / e-mail: camping.bois.soleil@wanadoo.fr

FR17140 Castel Camping Sequoia Parc

La Josephtrie, 17320 St Just-Luzac (Vendée/Charente)

Approached by an impressive avenue of flowers, shrubs and trees, Séquoia Parc is a Castel site set in the grounds of La Josephtrie, a striking château with beautifully restored outbuildings and a spacious courtyard. The site itself is designed to a high specification with reception in a large, light and airy room retaining its original beams and leading to the courtyard area where you find the shop, bar and restaurant. The pitches are 140 sq.m. in size with 6A electricity connections and separated by young shrubs. The pool complex with water slides, a large paddling pool and sunbathing area is impressive. The site has some 400 mobile homes and chalets, of which 125 are used by tour operators. This is a popular site with a children's club and entertainment all season and reservation is necessary in high season.

TRAVEL SERVICE SITE

TO BOOK CALL 0870 405 4055 OR www.alanrogersdirect.com

Facilities

Three luxurious toilet blocks, maintained to a high standard, include units with washbasin and shower, a laundry, dishwashing sinks, facilities for disabled visitors and baby baths. Motorcaravan service point. Gas supplies. Shop. Restaurant/bar and takeaway. Impressive swimming pool complex with paddling pool. Tennis, volleyball, football field. Games and TV rooms. Bicycle hire. Pony trekking. Organised entertainment all season.

Open

15 May - 11 September, with all services.

At a glance

Welcome & Ambience	✓✓✓✓	Location	✓✓✓✓
Quality of Pitches	✓✓✓✓✓	Range of Facilities	✓✓✓✓✓

Directions

Site is 2.5 km. southeast of Marennes. From Rochefort take D733 south for 12 km. Turn west on D123 to Ile d'Oléron. Continue for 12 km. and turn southeast on D728 towards Saintes. Site signed (1 km. on the left).

Charges 2004

Per unit incl. 2 persons and electricity	€ 15,00 - € 35,00
extra person	€ 6,00 - € 8,00
child (3-7 yrs)	€ 3,00 - € 5,00

Camping Cheques accepted.

Reservations

Made with 25% deposit and € 30 booking fee. Tel: 05 46 85 55 55. E-mail: sequoia.parc@wanadoo.fr

FR85120 Haven Camping Le Bois Masson

149 rue des Sables, 85160 St Jean-de-Monts (Vendée/Charente)

Le Bois Masson is a large, lively site with modern buildings and facilities in the seaside resort of St Jean-de-Monts. As with other sites here, the long, sandy beach is a few minutes away by car, reached through a pine wood. This site offers 500 good sized pitches, all with electricity. Most are occupied by mobile homes. Pitches are of sandy grass, mostly separated by hedges, with medium sized trees providing some shade. There are some pitches with water and drainage and an area kept for those who prefer a quieter pitch. There is plenty of on-site entertainment over a long season. The pool complex is impressive and includes a large outdoor pool, a paddling pool, a separate slide and an indoor pool. A jacuzzi, sauna and fitness room are also provided together with many other sports. Very busy in high season, this is not a site for those seeking somewhere quiet, but there is plenty to do for those perhaps with older children.

Facilities

Four sanitary blocks of excellent design provide modern showers with mixer taps, washbasins in cabins and British style WCs. Facilities for disabled visitors and babies. Dishwashing room (with dishwashers). Laundry. Comprehensive amenities housed in modern buildings fronting on to the road include a good supermarket, a large, lively bar with entertainment room, overlooking the pools, a restaurant and a creperie. Many activities including tennis, volleyball, table tennis and bicycle hire. Gas barbecues only are permitted. Mobile homes and rooms to rent. Off site: Riding, golf, squash, watersports near.

At a glance

Welcome & Ambience	✓✓✓✓✓	Location	✓✓✓✓
Quality of Pitches	✓✓✓✓	Range of Facilities	✓✓✓✓✓

Directions

From the roundabout at the southeast end of the St Jean de Monts bypass road, turn into town following signs to 'Centre Ville' and site, which is on the right after 400 m.

Charges 2004

Per pitch (incl. 2 persons and electricity	€ 13,00 - € 34,00

Reservations

Contact site. Tel: 02 51 58 62 62. E-mail: boismasson@haven.fr

Open

19 March - 10 October.

FR85150 Camping La Yole

Chemin des Bosses, Orouet, 85160 St Jean-de-Monts (Vendée/Charente)

La Yole is an attractive, popular and well run site, two kilometres from a sandy beach. It offers 278 pitches (100 touring pitches), the majority under trees with ample shade and separated by bushes and the trees. All have electricity (10A), water and drainage and are of 100 sq.m. or more. The pool complex is surrounded by a paved sunbathing area and overlooked by a new bar and restaurant which have a large terrace. A pleasant walk through pine woods then by road leads to two sandy beaches. The security barrier is closed at night. Used by tour operators (50%). A 'Sites et Paysages member'. This a friendly, popular site with welcoming owners.

Facilities

Two toilet blocks of older design, one refurbished, include washbasins in cabins, units for disabled people and baby baths, all kept very clean. The third block in the newer part of site is very modern with baby room. Laundry with washing machine, dryer and iron. Well stocked shop. Takeaway. Bar (1/5-1/9) and restaurant (18/5-31/8). Swimming pool with water slide, paddling pool and an indoor heated pool with jacuzzi. Play area on sand, large field for ball games and a club room. Tennis. Table tennis, pool and video games. Organised entertainment in high season. Only gas barbecues are permitted. Off site: Fishing, golf and watersports 6 km. at St Jean.

At a glance

Welcome & Ambience	✓✓✓✓✓	Location	✓✓✓✓
Quality of Pitches	✓✓✓✓	Range of Facilities	✓✓✓✓✓

Directions

Signed off the D38, 6 km. south of St Jean de Monts in the village of Orouet.

Charges 2005

Per unit incl. 2 persons, electricity, water and drainage	€ 17,00 - € 28,70
tent incl. 2 persons, electricity and water	€ 15,00 - € 23,00
extra person	€ 3,65 - € 5,90
child (2-9 yrs)	€ 2,05 - € 4,30
baby (0-2 yrs)	free - € 3,25

Camping Cheques accepted.

Reservations

Advised, particularly for June, July and Aug. Tel: 02 51 58 67 17. E-mail: contact@la-yole.com

Open

2 April - 30 September.

FR85330 Camping Naturiste Cap Natur'

151 ave de la Faye, 85270 St Hilaire-de-Riez (Vendée/Charente)

Situated on the northern outskirts of the busy resort of St Hilaire-de-Riez, and only about 1 km. from the nearest beach (6 km. from the nearest official naturist beach) this family campsite for naturists is in an area of undulating sand dunes and pine trees. The 140 touring pitches nestle among the dunes and trees and offer a wide choice to suit most tastes. Despite the undulating terrain, some pitches are quite level and thus suitable for motorcaravans. The modern facilities are excellent and include both open air and indoor pools, and a jacuzzi. Around the pool is an ample paved sunbathing area, including a stepped 'solarium'. The indoor complex is a designated non-smoking area. There is an air of peace and quiet about this site which contrasts with the somewhat frenzied activity which pervades many of the resorts in this popular tourist area, with a friendly, warm welcome from the family that own it.

Facilities

Sanitary facilities are basic, but clean, consisting of one indoor (heated) and one outdoor (but roofed) block. Both blocks have open plan hot showers, British style WCs, washbasins, baby baths and children's toilets. Small shop (with takeaway pizza) and restaurant, good sized bar, with TV, pool tables and indoor table games. Indoor and outdoor swimming pools. Fitness classes in high season. Massage room. Play area on soft sand. Volleyball and archery. Torches useful. Bicycle hire. Not suitable for American motorhomes. Off site: Beach 2 km. Fishing 5 km. Naturist beach 6 km. Golf, riding and boat launching 10 km.

Open

9 April - 1 November.

At a glance

Welcome & Ambience	✓✓✓✓	Location	✓✓✓✓
Quality of Pitches	✓✓✓✓	Range of Facilities	✓✓✓✓

Directions

Site is on the north side of St Hilaire. From Le Pissot roundabout go south on the D38, follow signs for St Hilaire at first roundabout (first exit), then at second roundabout turn right signed 'Terre Fort'. At third Y-shaped junction right again signed 'Parée Prèneau'. Site is 2 km along this road on left.

Charges 2004

Per unit incl. 2 adults	€ 14,50 - € 26,50
child (under 13 yrs)	€ 1,60 - € 4,10
electricity (10A)	€ 4,20

Camping Cheques accepted.

Reservations

Advised in high season and for French holidays. Made with 25% deposit and booking fee (€ 27.44). Single male visitors are not accepted. Tel: 02 51 60 11 66. E-mail: info@cap-natur.com

FR85300 Camping La Grand' Métairie

8 rue de la Vineuse en Plaine, 85440 St Hilaire la Forêt (Vendée/Charente)

Just five kilometres from the super sandy beach at Jard sur Mer, La Grand' Métairie offers many of the amenities of its seaside counterparts, but with the advantage of being on the edge of a delightful, sleepy village, otherwise untouched by tourism. It is a busy well run site with a lively entertainment programme in high season. The site has 180 pitches (69 for touring), all with electricity, water and drain. As yet there is little shade but pitches are separated by small trees and bushes and are reasonable in size.

Facilities

Two modern toilet blocks are kept very clean and include washbasins mainly in cabins. Units for disabled people. Washing machines and dryers. Fridge hire. Basic provisions kept with village store just 100 m. Smart bar/restaurant (1/5-10/9). Attractive, kidney-shaped heated pool, indoor pool, jacuzzi and paddling pool. Tennis, minigolf (both free in low season). Internet access. Not suitable for American motorhomes. Off site: Riding and fishing within 5 km.

Open

1 April - 30 September.

At a glance

Welcome & Ambience	✓✓✓✓✓	Location	✓✓✓✓
Quality of Pitches	✓✓✓✓	Range of Facilities	✓✓✓✓

Directions

Site is in centre of St Hilaire la Forêt. From Les Sables d'Olonne take D949 (La Rochelle) towards Talmont St Hilaire and Luçon 7 km. after Talmont turn right on D70 to St Hilaire la Forêt. Site is on the left before village centre.

Charges 2004

Per unit incl. 2 persons and electricity (6A)	€ 16,00 - € 24,00
extra person	€ 4,00 - € 7,00

Reservations

Advised for high season with 25% deposit and fee (€ 25). Tel: 02 51 33 32 38. E-mail: grand-metairie@wanadoo.fr

TRAVEL SERVICE SITE

TO BOOK CALL 0870 405 4055 OR www.alanrogersdirect.com

FR85210 Camping Les Ecureuils

Route des Goffineaux, 85520 Jard-sur-Mer (Vendée/Charente)

Les Ecureuils is a wooded site in a quieter part of the southern Vendée. It is undoubtedly one of the prettiest sites on this stretch of coast, with an elegant reception area, attractive vegetation and large pitches separated by low hedges with plenty of shade. Of the 261 pitches, some 120 are for touring units, each with water and drainage, as well as easy access to 10A electricity. Jard is rated among the most pleasant and least hectic of Vendée towns. The harbour is home to some fishing boats and rather more pleasure craft, and has a public slipway for those bringing their own boats. This site is very popular with tour operators (126 pitches). And in case you are curious, yes there are squirrels on site, including red ones! An indoor pool and spa were added in 2002.

Facilities

Two toilet blocks, well equipped and kept very clean, include baby baths, and laundry rooms. Small shop. Takeaway service (pre-order). Snacks and ice-creams available from the friendly bar. Good sized L-shaped swimming pool and separate paddling pool. New indoor pool. Modern play area. Minigolf, table tennis and a pool table. Club for children (5-10 yrs) daily in July/Aug. Bicycle hire. Only gas barbecues are allowed. Dogs are not accepted. Off site: Nearest beach 400 m. Fishing 400 m. Many places to eat at nearby marina or in town which has good supermarket and weekly market.

Open

15 May - 15 September.

At a glance

Welcome & Ambience	✓✓✓✓	Location	✓✓✓✓✓
Quality of Pitches	✓✓✓✓	Range of Facilities	✓✓✓✓

Directions

Jard-sur-Mer is on the D21 road between Talmont St Hilaire and Longeville sur Mer. Site is well signed from the main road - caravanners will need to follow these signs to avoid tight bends and narrow roads.

Charges 2005

Per person	€ 6,50
child (0-4 yrs)	€ 2,00
child (5-9 yrs)	€ 4,50
per pitch with water and drainage	€ 11,50
with electricity (10A)	€ 15,50

Less 10% outside 30/6-1/9.

Reservations

Advised for July/Aug. Tel: 02 51 33 42 74.
E-mail: camping-ecureuils@wanadoo.fr

France

TRAVEL SERVICE SITE

TO BOOK CALL 0870 405 4055 OR www.alanrogersdirect.com

FR37030 Camping Le Moulin Fort

37150 Francueil-Chenonceaux (Loire Valley)

Camping Le Moulin Fort is a tranquil, riverside site that has been redeveloped by British owners, John and Sarah Scarratt. The 137 pitches are enhanced by a variety of trees and shrubs offering some shade and 80 pitches have electricity (6A). The attractive (unheated) swimming pool is accessed by a timber walkway over the mill race from the snack bar terrace adjacent to the restored mill building. The picturesque Chateau of Chenonceaux is little more than one kilometre along the Rive Cher and many of the Loire châteaux are within easy reach, particularly Amboise and its famous Leonardo de Vinci museum. Although not intrusive there is some noise from the railway line across the river and a few trains run at night. The site is more suitable for couples and families with young children.

Facilities

Two toilet blocks with all the usual amenities of a good standard, including washbasins in cubicles and baby baths. Shop, bar, restaurant and takeaway (all 15/5-30/9). Swimming pool (15/5-30/9). Minigolf. Games room and TV. Regular family entertainment including wine tasting, quiz evenings, activities for children and light-hearted games tournaments. Fishing. Bicycle hire. Off site: Riding 12 km. Golf 20 km.

Open

1 April - 31 October.

At a glance

Welcome & Ambience	✓✓✓✓✓	Location	✓✓✓✓✓
Quality of Pitches	✓✓✓✓✓	Range of Facilities	✓✓✓✓

Directions

Site is well signed from the N76 Tours - Vierzon road. From the D40 Tours - Chenonceaux road, go through the village and after 2 km. turn right on D80 to cross the river at Chisseaux. Site is on left just after the bridge.

Charges 2005

extra adult	€ 4,00 - € 5,00
child (4-112 yrs)	€ 2,00 - € 4,00
electricity (6A)	€ 4,00
dog	€ 2,00 - € 3,00

Reservations

Advised for high season and for large units at any time; contact site. Tel: 02 47 23 86 22. E-mail: lemoulinfort@wanadoo.fr

FR37010 Camping de la Mignardière

22 avenue des Aubépines, 37510 Ballan-Miré (Loire Valley)

Southwest of the city of Tours, this site is within easy reach of several of the Loire châteaux, notably Azay-le-Rideau. In addition, there are many varied sports amenities on the site or very close by. The site has 177 numbered pitches of which 139 are for touring units, all with electricity (6/10A) and 37 with drainage and water. The pitches are of a good size on rather uneven grass with limestone gravel paths (which are rather 'sticky' when wet). The site's facilities are supplemented by a small 'parc de loisirs' just across the road which provides a bar and refreshments, pony rides, minigolf, small cars, playground and other amusements. The barrier gates (coded access) are closed 22.30 - 07.30 hrs. Reservation is essential here for most of July/August.

Facilities

Two toilet blocks, one new near the site entrance, the other totally refurbished, include washbasins in private cabins, a unit for disabled people, baby bath and laundry facilities. Motorcaravan service point. Shop (15/5-15/9). Takeaway (1/7-31/8). Two large, heated swimming pools (15/5-15/9). Good tennis court. Table tennis. Bicycle hire. Off site: Attractive lake catering particularly for windsurfing 300 m. (boards can be hired or use your own) and family fitness run. Fishing 500 m. Riding 1 km. Golf 3 km. Tours centre 8 km.

Open

10 April - 25 September.

At a glance

Welcome & Ambience	✓✓✓✓✓	Location	✓✓✓✓
Quality of Pitches	✓✓✓✓	Range of Facilities	✓✓✓✓

Directions

From A10 autoroute take exit 24 and D751 towards Chinon. Turn right after 5 km. at Campanile Hotel following signs to site. From Tours take D751 towards Chinon.

Charges 2004

Per unit incl. 2 persons	€ 13,50 - € 19,00
with electricity, water and drainage	€ 19,00 - € 26,50
extra person	€ 4,00 - € 5,00
child (2-10 yrs)	€ 2,60 - € 3,00

Camping Cheques accepted.

Reservations

Made for any length with 30% deposit (min. € 40). Tel: 02 47 73 31 00. E-mail: info@mignardiere.com

FR37060 Camping L'Arada Parc

Rue de la Baratière, 37360 Sonzay (Loire Valley)

A good, well maintained site in a quiet location, Camping L'Arada Parc is a popular base from which to visit the numerous châteaux in this beautiful part of France. The 81 grass pitches all have electricity and 22 have water and drainage. The clearly marked pitches, some slightly sloping, are separated by maturing trees and shrubs that will, in time, provide some shade. An attractive, heated pool is on a pleasant terrace beside the restaurant and campers can enjoy their meal or a drink overlooking the pool. Entertainment, themed evenings and activities for children are organised in July/August. This is a new site with modern facilities which is developing well.

Facilities

Two modern toilet blocks provide unisex toilets, showers and washbasins in cubicles. Excellent baby room, Facilities for disabled visitors (wheelchair users may the gravel in front of the lower block difficult). Dishwashing and laundry sinks under cover at each block. Laundry with washing machine, dryer and ironing board. Shop, bar, restaurant and takeaway (27/3-31/10). Swimming pool (no Bermuda style shorts; 1/5-13/9). Play area, covered games area. Boules, volleyball, badminton and table tennis. TV room. Bicycle hire.
Off site: Tennis 200 m. Riding 7 km. Fishing 9 km. Golf 12 km.

At a glance

Welcome & Ambience	✓✓✓✓✓	Location	✓✓✓✓
Quality of Pitches	✓✓✓✓	Range of Facilities	✓✓✓✓✓

Directions

Sonzay is northwest of Tours. Take D959 Tours - Château-la-Vallière road, then D6 to Sonzay and follow camping signs. Site is signed from the D959.

Charges 2004

Per unit incl. 2 persons	€ 14,50
extra person	€ 4,50
child (2-7 yrs)	€ 3,00
electricity (10A)	€ 3,00

Camping Cheques accepted.

Reservations

Made with deposit (30%); contact site.
Tel: 02 47 24 72 69. E-mail: laradaparc@free.fr

Open

1 April - 1 November.

FR37090 Camping du Château de La Rolandière

37220 Trogues (Loire Valley)

This is charming little site set in the grounds of a small château which has the appearance of a Queen Anne style dolls house. There are 30 medium sized, flat pitches, some gently sloping front to rear, and all separated by neat hedges. All but four have 10A electricity and water taps nearby and the parkland trees give shade. The château and adjoining buildings contain rooms to let and a small swimming pool serves them and the campsite. An eighteen hole minigolf meanders through the parkland and there is an area set aside for ball games, swings and slides for younger children. Sabine Toulemonde and her husband offer a very warm welcome. Situated on the D760 between Ille Bouchard and St Maure-de-Touraine, the site is five kilometres west of the A10, convenient for an overnight break or for longer stays to explore the châteaux at Chinon, Loches or Azay-le-Rideau and the villages of Richelieu and Crissay-s-Manse.

Facilities

The refurbished French style toilet block provides showers, washbasins, dishwashing and laundry areas. Separate provision for disabled visitors. One washbasin cabin in both the male and female units. Washing machine and dryer available via reception. Bar with terrace and snacks. Small shop in reception. Swimming pool. Minigolf. Play area. Bicycle hire. Off site: Fishing 1 km. to River Vienne. Restaurant 5 km. adjacent to A10 junction. St Maure 8 km.

Open

15 April - 30 September.

At a glance

Welcome & Ambience	✓✓✓✓✓	Location	✓✓✓✓
Quality of Pitches	✓✓✓✓	Range of Facilities	✓✓✓✓

Directions

The site is 5 km. west from junction 25 on A10 at St Maure-de-Touraine on the D760 towards Chinon. The entrance is clearly signed.

Charges 2005

Per person	€ 5,00 - € 6,00
child	€ 2,50 - € 3,00
pitch	€ 7,00 - € 8,50
animal	€ 1,50 - € 2,00
electricity	€ 3,50

No credit cards.

Reservations

Contact site. Tel: 02 47 58 53 71.
E-mail: contact@larolandiere.com

FR41070 Camping Caravanning La Grande Tortue

3 route de Pontlevoy, 41120 Candé-sur-Beuvron (Loire Valley)

This is a pleasant, rustic site that has been tastefully developed in the surroundings of an old forest. It provides 169 touring pitches set amongst trees which provide shade as well as some sunshine. The majority of the pitches are more than 100 sq.m. and all have 6/10A electricity. The family owners continue to develop the site with a new multi-sports court already created and a covered swimming pool planned. During July and August, they organise a programme of trips including wine/cheese tastings, canoeing and horse riding excursions. Used by tour operators.

Facilities

Three sanitary blocks offer British style WCs, washbasins in cabins and push-button showers. Very basic chemical emptying point. Laundry with deep sinks, washing machine, dryer and ironing board. Shop selling provisions. Terraced bar and restaurant with reasonably priced food and drink (15/5-15/9). Swimming pool and two shallower pools for children (15/5-30/9). Trampolines, a ball crawl with slide and climbing wall, bouncy castle, table tennis. New multi-sport court. Off site: Walking and cycling. Bicycle hire 1 km. Fishing 500 m. Golf 7 km. Riding 8 km.

Open

9 April - 30 September.

At a glance

Welcome & Ambience	✓✓✓✓✓	Location	✓✓✓✓
Quality of Pitches	✓✓✓	Range of Facilities	✓✓✓✓

Directions

Site is just outside Candé-sur-Beuvron on the D651, midway between Amboise and Blois. From Amboise, turn right just before entering Candé, then immediately left into the campsite (well signed from the road).

Charges 2004

Per unit incl. 2 persons	€ 13,00 - € 21,00
incl. electricity	€ 17,00 - € 24,00
extra adult	€ 4,50 - € 5,90
child (under 9 yrs)	€ 3,20 - € 4,20
animal	€ 2,90

Camping Cheques accepted.

Reservations

Necessary in July and August. Tel: 02 54 44 15 20. E-mail: grandetortue@libertysurf.fr

FR49040 Camping de l'Etang

Route de St Mathurin, 49320 Brissac (Loire Valley)

Originally the farm of the Château de Brissac (yet only 24 km. from the lovely town of Angers), this rural campsite retains the tranquillity and ambience of by-gone days and added the necessary comforts expected by today's campers. The 150 level touring pitches have pleasant views across the countryside. Separated and numbered, some have shade and all have electricity with water and drainage nearby. A small bridge crosses the river Aubance which runs through the site and there are two lakes where fisherman can enjoy free fishing. The site has its own vineyard and the wine produced can be purchased on the campsite and is highly recommended. Tour operators use 18 pitches.

TRAVEL SERVICE SITE

TO BOOK CALL 0870 405 4055 OR www.alanrogersdirect.com

Facilities

Three well maintained toilet blocks provide all the usual facilities. Laundry room with washing machines and dryers. Excellent baby room. Disabled visitors are well catered for. Motorcaravan service point. The adapted farmhouse houses reception, small shop and takeaway (from 19/5). Across the courtyard is a bar/restaurant serving crêpes, salads, etc (evenings form 15/6, all day 1/7-31/8). Swimming pool (heated and covered) and paddling pool. Fishing. Play area. Bicycle hire. Variety of evening entertainment in high season. Off site: Adjacent Parc de Loisirs (free for campers) is a paradise for young children with many activities including boating, pedaloes, pony rides, miniature train, water slide, bouncy castle and swings. Golf and riding 10 km.

At a glance

Welcome & Ambience	✓✓✓✓✓	Location	✓✓✓✓
Quality of Pitches	✓✓✓✓	Range of Facilities	✓✓✓✓

Directions

Take D748 south from Angers. Follow signs to Brissac-Quincé but do not enter the town, proceed to site along D55 (well signed) in direction of St Mathurin.

Charges 2005

extra person	€ 4,50 - € 6,00
child (0-10 yrs)	€ 3,00 - € 3,50
electricity	€ 3,00
dog	€ 2,00

Reservations

Contact site. Tel: 02 41 91 70 61.
E-mail: info@campingetang.com

Open

14 May - 10 September.

FR49020 Camping de Chantepie

St Hilaire-St Florent, 49400 Saumur (Loire Valley)

The drive along the winding road bordered by apple orchards and vineyards is well rewarded on arriving at the colourful, floral entrance to Camping de Chantepie. A friendly greeting awaits at the attractive reception office set beside the tastefully restored farmhouse. Linked by gravel roads (which can be dusty), the 150 grass pitches are level and spacious, with some new larger ones for long units (state preference when booking). Most pitches have electricity (5/10A) and are separated by low hedges of flowers and trees which offer some shade. The panoramic views over the Loire from the pitches on the terraced perimeter of the meadow are stunning and from here a footpath leads to the river valley. Leisure activities for all ages are catered for in July/Aug. by the Chantepie Club, including wine tastings, excursions and canoeing. This is a good site for families.

Facilities

The toilet block is very clean and the provision of facilities is adequate with washbasins in cubicles, new showers (men and women separately) and facilities for disabled visitors. Well stocked shop. Bar, terraced café and takeaway (from 19/5). Covered and heated pool, outdoor pool and paddling pool protected from the wind by a stone wall. Play area. Terraced minigolf. Volleyball, TV, video games and table tennis. Pony rides. Bicycle and mountain bike hire.
Off site: Fishing 200 m. Golf 2 km. Riding 6 km.

Open

14 May - 10 September.

At a glance

Welcome & Ambience	✓✓✓✓✓	Location	✓✓✓✓
Quality of Pitches	✓✓✓	Range of Facilities	✓✓✓✓✓

Directions

From Saumur take D751 signed Gennes. Turn right at roundabout in St Hilaire-St Florent and continue until you reach Le Poitrinea and campsite sign, then turn left. Continue for about 3 km. and then turn right into road leading to site.

Charges 2005

Per unit incl. 2 persons	€ 15,00 - € 24,00
extra person	€ 4,50 - € 6,00
child (010 yrs)	€ 3,00 - € 3,50
electricity	€ 3,00
dog	€ 2,00

Reservations

Made with € 11 fee; contact site.
Tel: 02 41 67 95 34.

FR49010 Castel Camping L'Etang de la Brèche

Route Nationale 152, 5 Impasse de la Breche, 49730 Varennes-sur-Loire (Loire Valley)

The Saint Cast family has developed L'Etang de la Brèche with loving care and attention on a 25-hectare estate four kilometres northeast of Saumur on the edge of the Loire behind the dykes. It is a peaceful base from which to explore the famous châteaux, abbeys, wine cellars, mushroom caves and Troglodyte villages in this region. The site provides 201 large, level pitches with shade from mixed tall trees and bushes, facing central, less shaded grass areas used for recreation. There are electrical connections to all pitches (in some cases a long cable may be required due to the size of the pitches), with water and drainaway on 63 of them. The restaurant, also open to the public, blends well with the existing architecture and, together with the bar area and terrace, provides a social base and is probably one of the reasons why the site is popular with British visitors. The swimming complex includes three pools: one with a removable cover, one outdoor, and a lovely pool for toddlers. The site includes a small lake (used for fishing) and wooded area ensuring a quiet, relaxed and rural atmosphere and making L'Étang de la Brèche a comfortable holiday base for couples and families. Used by tour operators (85 pitches).

Facilities

Three toilet blocks, modernised to good standards, include facilities for babies with two units for people with disabilities. Washing up sinks and laundry. Shop and epicerie. Restaurant, pizzeria and takeaway. Three heated pools. Tennis, basketball, minigolf and a field for football. Bicycle hire. General room, games and TV rooms. Well organised, varied sporting and entertainment programme (10/7-25/8). Child minding is arranged in afternoons. Internet point. Torch useful. Off site: Riding 2 km. Golf 8 km.

Open

15 May - 15 September.

At a glance

Welcome & Ambience	✓✓✓✓✓	Location	✓✓✓✓
Quality of Pitches	✓✓✓✓	Range of Facilities	✓✓✓✓✓

Directions

Site is 100 m. north off the main N152, about 4 km. northeast of Saumur on the north bank of the Loire.

Charges 2004

Per unit incl. 2 persons	€ 16,50 - € 27,00
incl. 3 persons	€ 20,50 - € 33,00
extra person	€ 4,00 - € 6,00
child (under 10 yrs)	€ 2,50 - € 3,00
electricity (10A)	free - € 3,00
water and drainage	€ 2,50

7th night free in low season.

Reservations

Made for min. 7 nights in high season (3 days in low season) with deposit and fee. Tel: 02 41 51 22 92.
E-mail: mail@etang-breche.com

FR86040 Camping Le Futuriste

86130 St Georges-les-Baillargeaux (Loire Valley)

On raised ground with panoramic views over the strikingly modern buildings and night-time bright lights that comprise the popular attraction of Futuroscope, Le Futuriste is a neat, modern site, open all year. It is ideal for a short stay to visit the park which is only 1.5 km. away (tickets can be bought at the site) but it is equally good for longer stays to see the region. With a busy atmosphere, there are early departures and late arrivals. Reception is open 08.00-22.00 hrs. There are 112 individual, flat, grassy pitches divided by young trees and shrubs which are beginning to provide some shelter for this elevated and otherwise rather open site (possibly windy). There are 28 pitches without electricity for tents, 22 with 6A electricity and a further 62 with electricity, water, waste water and sewage connections. All are accessed via neat, level and firmly rolled gravel roads. Of course, the area has other attractions and details are available from the enthusiastic young couple who run the site. Note: it is best to see the first evening show at Futuroscope otherwise you will find youself locked out of the site - the gates are closed at 23.30 hrs.

Facilities

Excellent, very clean sanitary facilities are housed in two modern blocks which are insulated and can be heated in cool weather. The facilities in the newest block are unisex. and include some washbasins in cabins and facilities for disabled people. Dishwashing and laundry sinks. Washing machine and dryer. Small shop (1/5-30/9) provides essentials (order bread the night before). New bar/restaurant. Snack bar and takeaway. Two outdoor pools, one with a slide and paddling pool (1/5-30/9). Free fishing in lake on site. Youth groups are not accepted. Off site: Bicycle hire 500 m. Golf 5 km. Riding 10 km. Supermarkets near.

Open

All year.

At a glance

Welcome & Ambience	✓✓✓✓	Location	✓✓✓✓
Quality of Pitches	✓✓✓✓	Range of Facilities	✓✓✓✓

Directions

From either A10 autoroute or the N10, take Futuroscope exit. Site is located east of both roads, off the D20 to St Georges-Les-Baillargeaux. From all directions follow signs to St Georges. The site is on the hill; turn by the water tower and site is on the left.

Charges 2004

Per pitch incl. 1-3 persons	€ 12,75 - € 17,50
extra person	€ 1,65 - € 2,35
electricity	€ 2,35 - € 3,20
dog	€ 1,60

Camping Cheques accepted.

Reservations

Phone bookings accepted for min. 2 nights.
Tel: 05 49 52 47 52.
E-mail: camping-le-futuriste@wanadoo.fr

FR86090 Camping du Parc de Saint Cyr

86130 Saint Cyr (Loire Valley)

This well organised, five hectare campsite is part of a 300 hectare leisure park, based around a large lake with sailing and associated sports, and an area for swimming (supervised July/Aug). Land-based activities include tennis, two half-courts, table tennis, fly fishing, badminton, pétanque, beach volleyball, TV room, and a well equipped fitness suite, all of which are free of charge. In high season there are extra free activities including a kids club, beach club, archery and an entertainment programme. Also in high season, but charged for, are sailing school, aquatic toboggan, windsurfing, canoe, kayak, water bikes and stunt bikes. Campers can also use the 9 and 18 hole golf courses (with 20% discount for the 18 hole). If all this sounds a bit too exhausting, you could escape to the small, peaceful formal garden in the centre of the site. The campsite has around 179 tourist pitches and 11 mobile homes for rent. The marked and generally separated pitches are all fully serviced with electricity (10A), water and drain.

Facilities

The main toilet block is modern and is supplemented for peak season by a second, recently refitted unit, which should prove adequate for demand, although they do attract some use by day-trippers to the leisure facilities. They include washbasins in cubicles, dishwashing and laundry sinks, washing machines and dryers, and facilities for babies and disabled persons. Shop, restaurant and takeaway (April - Sept). Playground on the beach. Bicycle hire. Barrier locked 22.00-07.00 hrs (10 deposit for card).

Open

1 April - 30 September.

At a glance

Welcome & Ambience	✓✓✓✓	Location	✓✓✓✓
Quality of Pitches	✓✓✓	Range of Facilities	✓✓✓✓

Directions

Saint Cyr is approx. midway between Châtellerault and Poitiers. Site is signed to the east of the N10 at Beaumont along the D82 towards Bonneuil-Matours, and is part of the Parc de Loisirs de Saint Cyr.

Charges 2004

Per pitch incl. electricity, water and drainage	€ 6,00 - € 12,00
adult	€ 2,50 - € 5,00
child (1-7 yrs)	€ 1,50 - € 2,00
animal	free - € 1,50

Reservations

Advisable for high season, made with fee (€ 7.62). Tel: 05 49 62 57 22. E-mail: contact@parcdesaintcyr.com

FR21000 Camping Lac de Panthier

21320 Vandenesse-en-Auxois (Burgundy)

An attractively situated lakeside site in Bungundy countryside, Camping Lac de Panthier is divided into two distinct campsites. The first, smaller section houses the reception, shop, restaurant and other similar facilities. The second, larger area is 200 m. along the lakeside road and is where the site activities take place and the pool can be found. The 200 pitches (136 for touring units) all have electricity connections and are mostly on level grass, although in parts there are shallow terraces. The most obvious attraction here is the proximity to the lake with its many watersports facilities. The site's restaurant has panoramic views over the lake. Used by tour operators. A 'Sites et Paysages' member.

Facilities

Four unisex toilet blocks (two for each site) also provide for babies and disabled people. Shop, bar and restaurant (all from 15/5). Swimming pool, children's pool and water-slide (15/5-15/9). Indoor pool, sauna and fitness equipment. Fishing. Riding. Watersports. Off site: Boat excursions from Pouilly en Auxois (8 km). Dijon, Autun and Beaune are also within easy reach.

Open

24 April - 29 September.

At a glance

Welcome & Ambience	✓✓✓✓	Location	✓✓✓✓
Quality of Pitches	✓✓✓✓	Range of Facilities	✓✓✓✓

Directions

From the A6 join the A38 and immediately exit at junction 24. Take N81 towards Arnay Le Duc (back over the A6), then almost immediately turn left on D977 for 5 km. Fork left again for Vandenesse en Auxois. Continue through village on D977 for 2.5 km, turn left again and site is on left.

Charges 2004

Per adult	€ 3,70 - € 6,10
child (under 7 yrs)	€ 1,80 - € 3,00
pitch	€ 4,10 - € 6,80
electricity	€ 4,00
dog	€ 1,50

Camping Cheques accepted.

Reservations

Contact site. Tel: 03 80 49 21 94.
E-mail: info@lac-de-panthier.com

FR21040 Camping de l'Etang de Fouché

Rue du 8 Mai 1945, 21230 Arnay le Duc (Burgundy)

Useful as an overnight stop en-route to or from the Mediterranean or indeed for longer stays, this quite large but peaceful, lakeside site has good facilities and the added advantage of being open all year. It can be very busy during the school holidays, and is probably better visited outside the main season. There are 190 good sized pitches, on fairly level grass and all with 10A electricity (some with water). This part of Burgundy is popular and Arnay le Duc itself is an attractive little town with an interesting history and renowned for its gastronomy, with many hotels and restaurants. The pitches, many hedged, offer a choice of shade or more open aspect. In July/August there are regular activities for children and adults.

Facilities

At the time of the inspection, only two of the four sanitary blocks were open. They are reasonably modern and well maintained, including some British style WCs, washbasins in cabins, facilities for disabled visitors. Washing machines and dishwashing under cover. Shop (with bread), bar, restaurant, takeaway (all 15 May to 15 Sep). TV/games room. Boules. Table tennis. Playground. Off site: Site is within 800m of the town centre, which has tennis courts, shops etc. At the supervised lakeside beach next to the site - small play-ground, water slides, pedaloes, canoes, soft drinks.

Open

1 April - 15 October.

At a glance

Welcome & Ambience	✓✓✓✓	Location	✓✓✓✓
Quality of Pitches	✓✓✓✓✓	Range of Facilities	✓✓✓✓

Directions

Site is on east side of town (well signed), 15 km. from A6 autoroute (exit at péage de Pouilly en Auxois).

Charges 2004

Per unit incl. 2 persons	€ 8,50 - € 11,70
extra person	€ 2,50 - € 3,20
child (under 7 yrs)	€ 1,24 - € 1,60
electricity	€ 3,30
animal	€ 1,00

Reservations

Advised for Jul/Aug; contact site. Reservation fee €10, deposit €30. Tel: 03 80 90 02 23.
E-mail: info@campingfouche.com

FR58010 Camping des Bains

15 avenue Jean Mermoz, 58360 St Honoré-les-Bains (Burgundy)

You are assured of a warm welcome at this attractive family run site, which is well situated for exploring the Morvan area in the heart of Burgundy – an area of rolling countryside, woods, rivers and villages, ideal for walking or cycling. The spacious 120 level grassed pitches (all with electricity) are mostly separated by hedges with a variety of mature trees offering shade. Next to the site is the 'thermal spa' where there are opportunities to 'take the waters' for a three day session or a full cure of three weeks! An excellent restaurant is almost opposite the entrance. A 'Sites et Paysages' member.

Facilities

The two main sanitary units have mostly British style WCs, washbasins in separate cabins and ample hot showers. Laundry. Facilities for disabled people. Family bar (1/6-30/9) also provides food and a takeaway service (15/6-15/9). Small swimming pool (12 x 12 m) with a separate slide and new paddling pool (15/6-15/9). Excellent play area. Table tennis. Minigolf. Entertainment weekly for children in July/Aug. Off site: Bicycle hire or riding 500 m. Fishing 5 km. Canal-side cycle route from Vandenesse (6 km).

Open

1 May - 10 October.

At a glance

Welcome & Ambience	✓✓✓✓	Location	✓✓✓✓
Quality of Pitches	✓✓✓✓	Range of Facilities	✓✓✓✓

Directions

From Nevers, travel east on D978; turn right onto D985 towards St Honoré-les-Bains, from where site is signed 'Camping des Bains', on entering town. Care is needed at narrow site entrance.

Charges 2005

Per unit incl. 2 persons	€ 15,50
extra person	€ 4,50
child (2- 7 yrs)	€ 2,85
electricity (6A)	€ 3,20
dog	€ 1,50

Reservations

Write to site with deposit (€ 65) and fee (€ 12.20). Tel: 03 86 30 73 44.
E-mail: camping-les-bains@wanadoo.fr

FR71020 Le Village des Meuniers

71520 Dompierre-les-Ormes (Burgundy)

In a tranquil setting with panoramic views, the neat appearance of the reception building sets the tone for the rest of this attractive site. The main part has 113 terraced, grassy pitches, some with hardstanding, are all fairly level, each with electricity and ample water points. Of these, 75 also have waste water outlets. A second section, used only in high season contains 16 standard pitches. All pitches enjoy stunning views of the surrounding countryside - the Beaujolais, Maconnais, Charollais and the Clunysois. An extensive sunbathing area surrounds the attractively designed swimming pool complex. This is a superb site, tastefully landscaped, with a high standard of cleanliness in all areas. As the hedges and trees mature they will offer more shade. This is an area well worth visiting, with attractive scenery, interesting history, excellent wines and good food. Used by tour operators (12 pitches) and 15 chalets to rent.

Facilities

Sanitary facilities mainly in an unusual, purpose designed hexagonal block, with modern fittings. Smaller unit in the lower area of the site, plus further toilets in the main reception building. Motorcaravan service point in car park. Café (high season). Bar, shop and takeaway from 1/6. Swimming pool complex with three heated pools and toboggan run (from 1/6). Children's activities organised in high season. Football. Minigolf. Internet access.
Off site: Village 500 m. Fishing 1.5 km. Riding 10 km.

Open

15 May - 15 September.

At a glance

Welcome & Ambience	✓✓✓✓	Location	✓✓✓✓
Quality of Pitches	✓✓✓✓✓	Range of Facilities	✓✓✓✓

Directions

Town is 35 km. west of Macon. Follow N79/E62 (Charolles, Paray, Digoin) road and turn south onto D41 to Dompierre-les-Ormes (3 km). Site is clearly signed through village.

Charges 2005

Per person	€ 5,00 - € 7,00
child (2-12)	€ 3,00 - € 4,00
pitch	€ 6,00 - € 8,50
electricity	€ 3,00 - € 4,00
car	€ 1,00

Reservations

Advised for July/Aug. Tel: 03 85 50 36 60.
E-mail: levillagedesmeuniers@wanadoo.fr

FR71070 Castel Camping Château de l'Epervière

71240 Gigny-sur-Saône (Burgundy)

Peacefully situated on the edge of the little village of Gigny-sur-Saône, yet within easy distance of the A6 autoroute, this site nestles in a natural woodland area near the Saône river (subject to flooding in winter months). With 135 pitches, nearly all with 10A electricity, the site is in two fairly distinct areas. The original part has semi-hedged pitches on part-level ground with plenty of shade from mature trees, close to the château and fishing lake - you may need earplugs in the mornings because of the ducks! The centre of the second area has a more open aspect, with large hedged pitches and mature trees offering shade around the periphery and central open grass area. A partly fenced road across the lake connects the two areas of the site (care is needed with children). The managers, Gert-Jan and Francois, and their team enthusiastically organise a range of activities for visitors that includes wine tastings in the cellars of the château and a Kids' Club in July/Aug. Used by tour operators (60 pitches). A member of 'Les Castels' group.

Facilities

Two well equipped toilet blocks, one beside the château and a newer one on the lower section include washbasins in cabins, dishwashing and laundry areas under cover. Washing machine and dryer. Shop providing bread and basic provisions (1/5-30/9). Tastefully refurbished restaurant in the château with a distinctly French menu (1/4-30/9). Second restaurant with more basic menu and takeaway. A converted barn houses an attractive bar, large screen TV and games room. Unheated swimming pool (1/5-30/9), with many sunloungers, partly enclosed by old stone walls protecting it from the wind, plus a smaller indoor heated pool with jacuzzi, sauna and paddling pool. Well equipped play area. Outdoor paddling pool. Bicycle hire.
Off site: Riding 15 km. Golf 20 km.

At a glance

Welcome & Ambience	✓✓✓✓✓	Location	✓✓✓✓
Quality of Pitches	✓✓✓✓	Range of Facilities	✓✓✓✓✓

Directions

From N6 between Châlon-sur-Saône and Tournus, turn east on D18 (just north of Sennecey-le-Grand) and follow site signs for 6.5 km. From A6, exit Châlon-Sud from the north, or Tournus from the south.

Charges 2004

Per person	€ 5,40 - € 6,40
child (under 7 yrs)	€ 3,30 - € 4,30
pitch	€ 6,90 - € 9,60
dog	€ 2,20 - € 2,70
electricity	€ 3,30 - € 4,30

Camping Cheques accepted.

Reservations

Contact site. Tel: 03 85 94 16 90.
E-mail: domaine-de-leperviere@wanadoo.fr

Open

1 April - 30 September.

France

TRAVEL SERVICE SITE

TO BOOK CALL 0870 405 4055 OR www.alanrogersdirect.com

FR39040 Sunêlia La Pergola

39130 Marigny (Franche Comté)

Close to the Swiss border and overlooking the sparkling waters of Lac de Chalain, La Pergola is a neat, tidy and terraced site set amongst the rolling hills of the Jura. Awaiting discovery as it is not on the main tourist routes, La Pergola is very well appointed, with 350 pitches, mainly on gravel and separated by small bushes, and all with electricity, water and drainage. Arranged on numerous terraces, connected by steep steps, some have shade and the higher ones have good views over the lake. A tall fence protects the site from the public footpath that separates the site from the lakeside but there are frequent access gates. The entrance is very attractive and the work that Mme. Gicquaire puts into the preparation of the flower-beds is very evident. The bar/restaurant terrace is beautiful, featuring grape vines for welcome shade and a colourful array of spectacular flowers leading on to a landscaped waterfall area next to the three swimming pools and entertainment area. English is spoken. Used by tour operators (120 pitches).

Facilities

The latest sanitary block serving the lower pitches is well appointed with private cabins. Slightly older blocks serve the other terraces. Visitors with disabilities are advised to select a lower terrace where special facilities are provided. Washing machines and dryers. Bar. Restaurant. Pool complex, two pools heated. Good play area and children's club. Table tennis and volleyball. Windsurfing, pedaloes and small boats for hire. Organised programme in high season includes cycle tours, keep fit sessions and evening entertainment with disco twice weekly. Off site: Riding 3 km.

Open

30 April - 11 September.

At a glance

Welcome & Ambience	✓✓✓✓	Location	✓✓✓✓
Quality of Pitches	✓✓✓✓	Range of Facilities	✓✓✓✓✓

Directions

Site is 2.5 km. north of Doucier on Lake Chalain road D27.

Charges 2004

Per unit incl. 2 persons and electricity	€ 20,00 - € 35,00
extra person	€ 4,50 - € 5,50
child (2-6 yrs)	free - € 4,50
dog	€ 2,00

Camping Cheques accepted.
Various special offers available.

Reservations

Made with deposit (€ 122) and fee (€ 27).
Tel: 03 84 25 70 03. E-mail: contact@lapergola.com

FR73030 Camping Les Lanchettes

73210 Peisey-Nancroix (Savoie)

This site is in the beautiful Vanoise National Park and at 1,470 m. is one of the highest campsites in this guide. There is a steep climb to the site, not recommended for underpowered units, although the spectacular scenery is well worth the effort. A natural, terraced site, it has 90 good size, reasonably level and well drained, grassy/stony pitches, with 80 used for touring units, 70 having electricity (3-10A). Because it is very cold in winter and quite cold on some spring and autumn evenings (warm bedding necessary) there are no outside taps. In winter about 30 of the pitches at the bottom of the site are unused as they become part of a cross country ski run. For those who love mountains, wonderful scenery, flora and fauna and for those wanting a walking/biking summer holiday, from novice to expert, this is the site for you. In winter it is ideal for the serious skier being close to the famous resort of Les Arcs (via free bus service and cable car).

Facilities

Comprehensive facilities are all in the basement of the house, very cosy in winter. The large, open entrances are closed during cold weather and when the evenings are cold allowing the building to be heated. Motorcaravan service point. Restaurant with takeaway (July/Aug. and mid Dec-mid April). Playground. Club/TV room. Large tent/marquee used in bad weather for a meeting place and as a dormitory by those with small tents. In winter a small bus (free) runs to all the hotels, bars, ski tows etc. and calls at the campsite. A wide range of footpaths and mountain bike rides is available in the valley and mountains around. Some chair lifts carry bikes up to the walking/bike tracks high up in the mountains; the descent is breathtaking. The roads around are ideal for the serious road cyclist.
Off site: Accompanied walks (one free) in the National Park. Riding next to site. Village of Peisey-Nancroix with a few restaurants, bars and shops 3 km. Les Arcs winter sports centre 6 km. Outdoor swimming pool and bicycle hire 6 km. Golf and indoor pool 8 km.

At a glance

Welcome & Ambience	✓✓✓✓	Location	✓✓✓✓
Quality of Pitches	✓✓✓✓	Range of Facilities	✓✓✓

Directions

From Albertville take N90 towards Bourg-St-Maurice, through MoΩtiers and Aime and 9 km. further turn right on D87, signed Landry and Peisey-Nancroix. Follow road down and then up a reasonably wide, steep, winding hill (with hairpin bends) for 10 km. Pass through Peisey-Nancroix and Nancroix; site is on right about 1 km. beyond Nancroix.

Charges 2004

Per unit incl. 2 persons	€ 11,10 - € 12,80
extra person	€ 3,80 - € 4,30
child (2-7 yrs)	€ 2,30 - € 2,50
electricity (3-10A)	€ 2,90 - € 7,30
dog	€ 1,00 - € 1,20

Camping Cheques accepted.

Reservations

Made with 25% deposit and fee (€ 10).
Tel: 04 79 07 93 07. E-mail: lanchettes@free.fr

Open

15 December - 15 October.

FR74070 Camping Caravaning L'Escale

74450 Le Grand-Bornand (Haute-Savoie)

You are assured a good welcome from the Baur family at this beautifully maintained, picturesque site. Situated at the foot of the Aravis mountain range, beside the picture postcard ski resort of Le Grand-Bornand, L'Escale has wonderful views, is surrounded by fields of flowers in summer and is clearly popular all year round. The 149 fairly sunny pitches (142 for touring) are of average size, clearly marked with a part grass, part gravel surface and separated by trees and shrubs. All have electricity and 86 pitches are fully serviced. Rock pegs are essential. The village (200 m.) has all the facilities of a major resort with ongoing activity for summer or winter holidays. In summer a variety of well signed footpaths and cycle tracks provide forest or mountain excursions of all degrees of difficulty. In winter the area provides superb facilities for down-hill and cross-country skiing and apres-ski entertainment. La Maison du Patrimoine is a must to visit. A 'Sites et Paysages' member.

Facilities

The very good toilet blocks (heated when cold) have all the necessary facilities. Two chalet buildings provide further facilities. Large drying room with sinks, dryer and washing machines. Separate room for skis and boots. Superb new complex with interconnected indoor and outdoor pools and paddling pools (June-Aug). Bar/restaurant (July/Aug). Play area. Tennis and table tennis. Torches essential (no street lighting). Off site: The village (5 minutes walk) has shops, bars, restaurants, municipal pool complex, archery, para-gliding, hang-gliding, 150 km. of signed walks. Activities are organised for children and adults. Ice skating and ice hockey in winter. Bicycle hire 200 m. Riding and golf 3 km.

Open

All year excl. October and November.

At a glance

Welcome & Ambience	✓✓✓✓✓	Location	✓✓✓✓✓
Quality of Pitches	✓✓✓✓	Range of Facilities	✓✓✓✓✓

Directions

Probably the best access is via Annecy following the D16 and D909 roads towards La Clusaz. Shortly before La Clusaz, at St Jean-de-Sixt, turn left at roundabout on D4 signed Le Grand Bornand. Just before entering village turn right signed Vallée de Bouchet and camping. Site is just over 1 km. at a roundabout on right.

Charges 2005

Per unit incl. 1 or 2 persons	€ 15,50 - € 21,00
extra person	€ 4,30 - € 5,50
electricity (2-10A)	€ 3,30 - € 7,90
animal	€ 2,20 - € 2,30

Camping Cheques accepted.

Reservations

Made with deposit (€ 71) and fee (€ 10).
Tel: 04 50 02 20 69.
E-mail: contact@campinglescale.com

TO BOOK CALL 0870 405 4055 OR www.alanrogersdirect.com

TRAVEL SERVICE SITE

FR33080 Domaine de la Barbanne

Route de Montagne, 33330 St Emilion (Gironde)

La Barbanne is a pleasant, friendly, family-owned site in the heart of the Bordeaux wine region, only 2.5 km. from the famous town of St Emilion. With 160 pitches, the owners have transformed it into a carefully maintained, well equipped site. The original parts of the site bordering the lake have tarred roads, good shade and pleasant surroundings, whilst the newer area has younger trees, some shade and gravel access roads. The pitches are being re-numbered and are all large, level and grassy with dividing hedges and electricity connections. La Barbanne has an attractive entrance and reception area with ample space for parking or turning. The owners run a free minibus service three times a day to St Emilion and also organise excursions to local places of interest, including Bordeaux. A 'Sites et Paysages' member.

Facilities

Two toilet blocks, the original one fully refurbished, the other in the newer area being very modern. Most washbasins are in private cabins. Visitors with disabilities are well catered for. Motorcaravan service point. Small, well stocked shop. Bar with terrace, takeaway and restaurant (1/7-31/8). Two landscaped swimming pools, one heated with cork-screw water slide (15/4-20/9). Fully enclosed play area with seats for parents and an organised children's club (from 1/7). Tennis, boules, volleyball, table tennis and minigolf. The lake provides superb free fishing, pedaloes, canoes and lakeside walks. Bicycle hire. Off site: St Emilion and shops 2.5 km. Riding 8 km.

At a glance

Welcome & Ambience	✓✓✓✓✓	Location	✓✓✓✓✓
Quality of Pitches	✓✓✓✓	Range of Facilities	✓✓✓✓

Directions

At St Emilion take D122 for 2.5 km. Turn right just before Montagne and site is on left after 400 m. Caravans and motorhomes are forbidden through the village of St Emilion. They must approach the site by taking the D243 from Libourne or from Castillon on the D936 via D130/D243.

Charges 2004

Per person	€ 4,00 - € 6,50
child (under 7 yrs)	€ 2,50 - € 5,20
pitch incl. electricity	€ 14,00 - € 21,00
animal	free - € 2,00

Camping Cheques accepted.

Reservations

Made for min. 4 days. Tel: 05 57 24 75 80.
E-mail: barbanne@wanadoo.fr

Open

1 April - 20 September.

TO BOOK CALL 0870 405 4055 OR www.alanrogersdirect.com

TRAVEL SERVICE SITE

FR33110 Airotel Camping de la Côte d'Argent

33990 Hourtin-Plage (Gironde)

Spread over 20 hectares of undulating sand-based terrain and in the midst of a pine forest, this large site is well placed and well equipped for leisurely family holidays. It also makes an ideal base for walkers and cyclists, with over 100 km. of cycle lanes leading through the Medoc countryside. Hourtin-Plage is a pleasant invigorating resort on the Atlantic coast and a popular location for watersports enthusiasts, or those who prefer spending their days on the beach. More appealing though may be to stay on site, for Côte d'Argent's top attraction is its pool complex with wooden bridges connecting the pools and islands, on which there are sunbathing patios and play areas. A super new indoor heated pool is a recent addition. There are 750 touring pitches which are not clearly defined and in the trees, some on soft sand-based ground. The site is well organised and ideal for children. Entertainment takes place at the bar near the entrance (until 12.30). There are 48 hardstandings for motorcaravans outside the site, providing a cheap stop-over, but with no access to site facilities.

Facilities

Five very clean sanitary blocks of various ages include provision for disabled visitors. Plenty of laundry machines. Motorcaravan service points. Large supermarket, restaurant, takeaway and pizzeria bar. Four outdoor pools with waterslides and flumes. New indoor pool. Massage. Astronomy once a week. Two tennis courts. Pool tables. Four play areas. Mini-club and organised entertainment in season. Charcoal barbecues are not permitted. Fishing. Riding. Bicycle hire. Off site: Path to the beach 300 m. Golf 30 km.

Open

13 May - 18 September.

At a glance

Welcome & Ambience	✓✓✓✓	Location	✓✓✓✓
Quality of Pitches	✓✓✓	Range of Facilities	✓✓✓✓✓

Directions

Turn off D101 Hourtin-Soulac road 3 km. north of Hourtin. Then join D101E signed Hourtin-Plage. Site is 300 m. from the beach.

Charges 2004

Per unit incl. 2 persons	€ 19,00 - € 30,00
tent incl. 2 persons	€ 15,00 - € 25,00
extra person	€ 3,00 - € 5,00
child (2-10 yrs)	€ 2,00 - € 4,00
electricity (6A)	€ 5,00
dog	€ 2,00 - € 4,00

Camping Cheques accepted.

Reservations

Necessary for July/August. Tel: 05 56 09 10 25. E-mail: info@camping-cote-dargent.com

FR40060 Camping Eurosol

Route de la Plage, 40560 Vielle-St Girons (Landes)

The sandy beach 700 metres from Eurosol has supervised bathing in high season. The site also has its own swimming pool with paved sunbathing areas which are planted with palm trees giving quite a tropical feel. The site itself is on undulating ground amongst mature pine trees giving good shade and the pitches on the slopes are mainly only suitable for tents. The 417 pitches for touring units are numbered (although with nothing to separate them, there is little privacy) and 209 have electricity with 120 fully serviced (86 with mobile homes). A family site with entertainers who speak many languages, many games and tournaments are organised and a beach volleyball competition is held each evening in front of the bar.

Facilities

There are four main toilet blocks all refurbished to include washbasins in cabins. Two smaller blocks have facilities for babies and disabled people. Motorcaravan service point. Fridge rental. Well stocked shop (8/5-18/9). Bar (8/5-18/9), restaurant and takeaway (1/7-31/8). Raised deck area and a stage for live shows (mainly performed by the very versatile staff) arranged in July/Aug. and finishing by midnight. Outdoor swimming pool (8/5-18/9). Tennis. Multi-sport court for basketball, handball and football. Bicycle hire. Charcoal barbecues are not permitted. Off site: Riding school opposite. Fishing 700 m.

At a glance

Welcome & Ambience	✓✓✓✓	Location	✓✓✓✓
Quality of Pitches	✓✓✓	Range of Facilities	✓✓✓✓✓

Directions

Turn off D652 at St Girons on D42 towards St Girons-Plage. Site is on left before coming to beach (4.5 km).

Charges 2004

Per unit incl.1 or 2 persons	€ 10,00 - € 22,00
with electricity	€ 12,50 - € 26,50
with water and drainage	€ 12,50 - € 29,50
extra person (over 4 years)	€ 4,00
dog	€ 2,50

Reservations

Made for min. 1 week with deposit (€ 95) and fee (€ 25). Tel: 05 58 47 90 14. E-mail: contact@camping-eurosol.com

Open

8 May - 18 September.

Aquatic complex of 3500 m^2 :
water slides, jacuzzis, covered and heated swimming pool

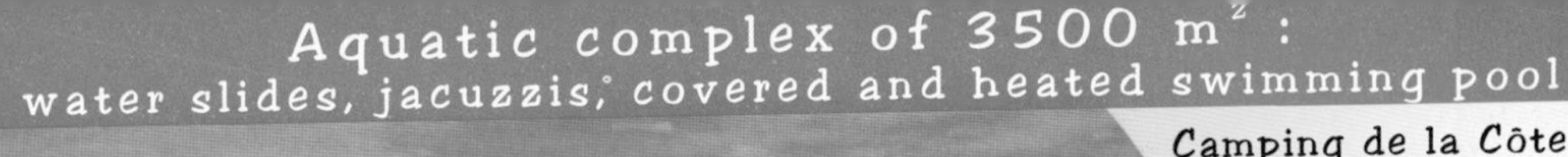

Camping de la Côte d'Argent occupies an area of 20 hectares situated in the heart of a pine forest, but only 300 m from a huge beach, and just 4 km away from one of the biggest natural lakes in the whole of the France. A characterful site protected from the wind by the forest and nearby sand dunes. The site enjoys an ideal climate in natural, pleasant, surroundings, perfect for a relaxing holiday.

Terre de Vacances

Airotel Camping Caravaning
de la Côte d'Argent ★★★

Club Airotel

Hourtin Plage
South Atlantic

Cottages and mobil-homes to rent

Special Offers
(except july and august)
14 = 11 and 7 = 6
camping or rental

✱ SHOPS ✱ SPORT ACTIVITIES ✱ TENNIS ✱ HORSE RIDING ✱ ARCHERY
✱ KIDS-CLUB ✱ GAMES ROOM ✱ SAILING (4KM) ✱ SURF (300M)

Airotel Camping Caravaning de la Côte d'Argent 33990 Hourtin Plage
Tél : + 33 5.56.09.10.25 Fax : +33 5.56.09.24.96
www.camping-cote-dargent.com www.cca33.com www.campingcoteouest.com

e brochure on demand -Alan Rogers 2005
me. . . . . First name. . . . .
dress. . . . .
wn. . . . . Country. . . . .

FR33130 Camping Caravaning Les Grands Pins

33680 Lacanau-Océan (Gironde)

This Atlantic coast holiday site with direct access to a fine sandy beach, is on undulating terrain amongst tall pine trees. A large site, it provides 570 pitches, with about 44 private and rental mobile homes, leaving around 525 pitches of varying sizes for touring units. The site is well served by tarmac access roads, and although not noticeably divided, one half of the site is a traffic free zone (except for arrival or departure day, caravans are placed on the pitch, with separate areas outside the zone for car parking). There is a good number of tent pitches, those in the centre of the site having some of the best views, and especially useful for tenters are safety deposit and fridge boxes which are available for rent. The large sandy beach is a 350 m. stroll from the gate at the back of the site.

Facilities

Five toilet blocks include washbasins in cubicles, dish-washing and laundry sinks, a dog and wetsuit washing area, baby room and facilities for disabled people (not all units are open in low season). Well equipped launderette. Motorcaravan services. Good sized supermarket, surf boutique. Bar, restaurant and snack bar with takeaway. Heated swimming pool (20 x 10 m, from 1/5 with lifeguard in July/Aug) with large paved sunbathing surround. Jacuzzi. Free fitness activities (aquagym, etc). Games room. Fitness suite. Tennis (charge in July/Aug). Two playgrounds. Bicycle hire. Organised activities for children (July/Aug). Entrance barrier with keypad access. Only gas barbecues permitted. Off site: Fishing, golf, riding and bicycle hire 5 km.

Open

1 May - 15 September

At a glance

Welcome & Ambience	✓✓✓✓	Location	✓✓✓✓✓
Quality of Pitches	✓✓✓	Range of Facilities	✓✓✓✓

Directions

From Bordeaux take N125/D6 west to Lacanau, continue on D6 to Lacanau Ocean. At second roundabout, take second exit: Plage Nord and follow signs to camps sites. Les Grand Pins is signed to the right at the far end of the road. If approaching from northern France you could use the ferry from Royan to Le Verdon.

Charges 2004

Pitch incl. 2 persons and electricity	€ 20,00 - € 34,00
extra person	€ 6,00 - € 9,00
child (2-12 yrs)	free - € 4,00
dog	€ 3,00 - € 4,00

Reservations

Essential for high season, made with deposit and fee. Discounts for early booking. Tel: 05 56 03 20 77. E-mail: reception@lesgrandspins.com

FR40140 Camping Caravaning Lou P'tit Poun

110 avenue du Quartier Neuf, 40390 St Martin de Seignanx (Landes)

The manicured grounds surrounding Lou P'tit Poun give it a well kept appearance, a theme carried out throughout this very pleasing site. It is only after arriving at the car park that you feel confident it is not a private estate. Beyond this point the site unfolds to reveal an abundance of thoughtfully positioned shrubs and trees. Behind a central sloping flower bed lies the open plan reception area. The avenues around the site are wide and the 168 pitches are spacious. All have electricity (6/10A), 30 are fully serviced and some are separated by low hedges. The jovial owners not only make their guests welcome, but extend their enthusiasm to organising weekly entertainment for young and old during high season. A 'Sites et Paysages' member.

Facilities

Two unisex sanitary blocks, maintained to a high standard and kept clean, include washbasins in cabins, a baby bath and provision for disabled people. Dishwashing sinks and laundry facilities with washing machine and dryer. Motorcaravan service point. Café, bread and ices (1/7-31/8). Swimming pool (1/6-15/9) Play area. Games room, TV. Half court tennis. Table tennis. Bicycle hire. Caravan storage. Off site: Bayonne 6 km. Fishing or riding 7 km. Golf 10 km. Sandy beaches of Basque coast ten minute drive.

Open

1 June - 15 September.

At a glance

Welcome & Ambience	✓✓✓✓✓	Location	✓✓✓✓
Quality of Pitches	✓✓✓✓✓	Range of Facilities	✓✓✓✓

Directions

Leave A63 at exit 6 and join N117 in the direction of Pau. Site is signed at Leclerc supermarket. Continue on N117 for 5.5 km. and site is then clearly signed on right.

Charges 2004

Per pitch incl. 1 or 2 persons	€ 10,00 - € 22,00
with 4A electricity	€ 12,00 - € 24,00
with water and drainage	€ 18,00 - € 28,00
extra person	€ 5,00 - € 6,00
child (under 7 yrs)	€ 2,00 - € 4,00
pet	€ 3,00 - € 4,00

Reservations

Made with deposit (25%) and fee (€ 20).
Tel: 05 59 56 55 79. E-mail: ptitpoun@club-internet.fr

FR40170 Haven Camping La Résreve

Gastés, 40160 Parentis-en-Born (Landes)

La Resérve, now run by Haven Europe, is a large site set in a pine wood. It has access to a large lake with a beach and small harbour and the Atlantic beaches are nearby (20 km). The lake shelves gradually so is good fun for for children and there are good facilities for windsurfing and sailing; powered boats for water ski-ing are also permitted here. The 700 numbered pitches (200 for touring) are of above average size (mostly 120 sq.m.) set on mainly flat ground and marked by stones in the ground. Most have electricity. A variety of entertainment, sports and activities are organised in the Haven Europe tradition, often in and around the super pool complex.

Facilities

Five toilet blocks, with en-suite facilities in one, include washbasins in cabins. Washing machines. When visited they were in some need of care and maintenance - this is being addressed. Well stocked supermarket. Restaurant and large bar with entertainment all season. Swimming pool complex with water slides, paddling pools, etc. (lifeguards on duty). Children's club. Two tennis courts (floodlit in the evening), minigolf, table tennis and volleyball. Boat hire, windsurfing courses and water ski-ing. TV room, general room and amusement machines. Fishing. Bicycle hire. Dogs are not accepted. Off site: Atlantic beaches 20 km.

At a glance

Welcome & Ambience	✓✓✓✓	Location	✓✓✓✓
Quality of Pitches	✓✓✓	Range of Facilities	✓✓✓✓✓

Directions

Turn west off D652 Gastes - Mimizan road on southern outskirts of Gastes by campsite sign, then 3 km. to site.

Charges 2004

Per pitch incl. 2 persons	€ 12,00 - € 34,00
with electricity	€ 14,00 - € 39,00
extra person	€ 3,00 - € 6,00

Reservations

Accepted at any time for min. 4 days; no booking fee. Contact site or Haven Europe in the UK on 0870 242 7777 for information or reservation.
Tel: 05 58 09 74 79. E-mail: lareserve@haven.fr

Open

23 April - 25 September.

FR40160 Camping Les Vignes

Route de la Plage du Cap de L'Homy, 40170 Lit-et-Mixe (Landes)

Les Vignes is a large holiday site close to the Atlantic coast with 450 pitches, of which 250 are occupied by a mix of mobile homes, bungalows and tents, most of which are for rent. The 157 tourist pitches are relatively level on a sandy base, all serviced with electricity (10A) and water, some with waste water drains. The site's amenities, including a supermarket, restaurant and bar, are located at the entrance to the site. The rather stylish pool complex includes a six lane water slide. A wide range of activities is provided and during July and August a great variety of entertainment options for adults and children, some of which take place in the new entertainment 'Big Top'.

Facilities

Four virtually identical sanitary units (not all open in low season) provide combined washbasin and shower cubicles, dishwashing and laundry sinks, washing machines and dryers, facilities for babies and disabled people. Large supermarket (15/6-10/9). Restaurant and bar (15/6-10/9). Takeaway (July/Aug). Swimming pool complex (1/6-15/9). Tennis. Table tennis. Golf driving range. Minigolf. Volleyball, basketball. Pétanque. Kids club and playground. Bicycle hire. Barrier closed 23.00-07.00 hrs. Off site: Golf course, canoeing, kayaking, surfing, riding. Many cycle tracks.

At a glance

Welcome & Ambience	✓✓✓✓	Location	✓✓✓✓
Quality of Pitches	✓✓✓	Range of Facilities	✓✓✓✓

Directions

Lit-et-Mixe is on the D652 20 km. south of Mimizan. Turn west on D88 1 km. south of town towards Cap de l'Homy for 1.5 km. where site entrance is on left.

Charges guide

Per pitch incl. 2 persons incl. electricity and water	€ 14,50 - € 33,00
extra person (over 5 yrs)	€ 4,00 - € 5,00
child (under 5 yrs)	€ 1,50 - € 3,00

Reservations

Advisable for high season, made with deposit and fee. Tel: 05 58 42 85 60. E-mail: contact@les-vignes.com

Open

1 June - 15 September.

FR40190 Camping Airotel Saint Martin

Avenue de l'Océan, 40660 Moliets-Plage (Landes)

A family site aimed mainly at couples and young families, Airotel St Martin is a welcome change to most of the sites in this area in that it has only a small number of mobile homes (77) compared to the number of touring pitches (583). First impressions are of a neat, tidy, well cared for site and the direct access to the beach is an added bonus. The pitches are mainly typically French in style with low hedges separating them plus some shade. There is also a 'free and easy' area under tall trees. Electric hook ups are 11-15A and a number of pitches also have water and drainage. Entertainment in high season is low key (with the emphasis on quiet nights) – daytime competitions and a 'mini-club' and the occasional evening entertainment, well away from the pitches and with no discos or karaoke.

Facilities

Six toilet blocks of a high standard and very well maintained, have washbasins in cabins, large showers, baby rooms and facilities for disabled visitors. Motorcaravan service point. Washing machines and dryers. Fridge rental. Very good supermarket and various bars, restaurants and takeaways are at the entrance, owned by the site (Easter - 30/10). Attractive indoor pool, jacuzzi and sauna (open all season, charged for in July/Aug). Large outdoor pool area with pools, jacuzzi and paddling pool (15/6-15/9). Multi sports pitch. Small play area. Internet access. Only electric barbecues are permitted. Off site: Tennis or golf 700 m. Riding 7 km. This is an excellent area for cycling.

At a glance

Welcome & Ambience	✓✓✓✓	Location	✓✓✓✓✓
Quality of Pitches	✓✓✓✓	Range of Facilities	✓✓✓✓

Directions

From the N10 take D142 to Lèon, then D652 to Moliets-et-Mar. Follow signs to Moliets-Plage, site is well signed.

Charges 2004

Per unit incl. 1 or 2 adults, 1 child	€ 16,50 - € 26,50
with electricity	€ 19,50 - € 30,00
with services	€ 22,50 - € 36,00
extra person	€ 3,00 - € 5,00

Prices are for reserved pitches.

Reservations

Contact site. Tel: 05 58 48 52 30.
E-mail: contact@camping-saint-martin.fr

Open

Easter - 2 November.

FR40180 Camping Le Vieux Port

Plage sud, 40660 Messanges (Landes)

The area to the north of Bayonne is heavily forested and several very large campsites are attractively located close to the superb Atlantic beaches. Le Vieux Port is probably the largest and certainly one of the most impressive of these. A well established destination appealing particularly to families with teenage children, this lively site has no fewer than 1,406 open pitches. They are of mixed size, most with electrical hook-ups (6/8A) and some with water and drainage. Sprawling beneath the pine trees, the camping area is well shaded and pitches are generally of a good size, attractively grouped around the toilet blocks. At least a third of the site is taken up with mobile homes and there are a large number of tour operators here (30%). The heated swimming pool complex is exceptional boasting no less than five outdoor pools and three large water slides. There is also a heated indoor pool. At the back of the site a path leads across the dunes to a superb beach. A little train also trundles to the beach on a fairly regular basis in high season (small fee). All in all, a lively site with a great deal to offer an active family.

Facilities

Nine well appointed toilet blocks are all of modern design and well maintained. Facilities for disabled people. Motorcaravan service point. Good shopping facilities, including a well stocked supermarket and various smaller shops. Several restaurants (including takeaway service) and bars (all open all season). Large swimming pool complex (no bermuda shorts). Three tennis courts, two football pitches, a multi-sport pitch, minigolf etc. Bicycle hire. Well run and popular riding centre. Large animation team organise a wide range of activities in high season including frequent discos and karaoke evenings. Only communal barbecues are allowed.

At a glance

Welcome & Ambience	✓✓✓	Location	✓✓✓✓✓
Quality of Pitches	✓✓✓✓	Range of Facilities	✓✓✓✓✓

Directions

Leave RN10 at Magescq exit heading for Soustons. Pass through Soustons following signs for Vieux-Boucau. Bypass this town and site is clearly signed to the left at second roundabout.

Charges 2005

Per unit incl. 2 persons	€ 12,00 - € 33,00
extra person	€ 3,50 - € 6,00
child (under 10 yrs)	€ 2,50 - € 4,00
electricity (6/8A)	€ 4,00 - € 6,50
animal	€ 2,00 - € 3,50

Reservations

Essential in high season. Tel: 05 58 48 22 00.
E-mail: contact@levieuxport.com

Open

1 April - 30 September.

France

TRAVEL SERVICE SITE

TO BOOK CALL 0870 405 4055 OR www.alanrogersdirect.com

FR40100 Camping du Domaine de la Rive

Route de Bordeaux, 40600 Biscarosse (Landes)

Set in pine woods, La Rive has a superb beach-side loaction on Lac de Sanguient. It provides mostly level, numbered and clearly defined pitches of 100 sq.m. all with electricity connections (6A). The swimming pool complex is wonderful, with various pools linked by water channels and bridges, the four-slide pool having a wide staircase to the top to speed up enjoyment. There is also a jacuzzi, paddling pool and two large, unusually shaped swimming pools, all surrounded by paved sunbathing areas and decorated with palm trees. An indoor pool is heated and open all season. The beach is excellent, shelving gently to provide safe bathing for all ages. There are windsurfers and small craft can be launched from the site's slipway. This is a friendly site with a good mix of nationalities.

Facilities

Five modern, very good quality toilet blocks have washbasins in cabins and mainly British style toilets. Visitors with disabilities well catered for in three blocks. Baby baths. We found the facilities very clean. Motorcaravan service point. Well stocked shop with gas (1/5-15/9). Bar serving snacks and takeaway. Games room adjoining. Restaurant with reasonably priced family meals (1/5-10/9). Swimming pool complex supervised July/Aug (outdoor pool 1/5-15/9). Play area. Two tennis courts. Bicycle hire. Hand-ball or basketball court, table tennis, boules, archery and football. Fishing. Water skiing. Watersports equipment may be hired and tournaments in various sports are arranged in June-Aug. Skateboard park, trampolines with safety harness and an enlarged and upgraded play area. Discos and karaoke evenings organised outside bar with stage and tiered seating. Mini-club for children twice daily. Charcoal barbecues not permitted on pitches (central area available). Caravan storage. Off site: Riding 5 km. Golf 10 km.

At a glance

Welcome & Ambience	✓✓✓✓	Location	✓✓✓✓
Quality of Pitches	✓✓✓	Range of Facilities	✓✓✓✓✓

Directions

Take D652 from Sanguinet to Biscarrosse and site is signed on the right in about 6 km.

Charges 2004

Per pitch incl. 2 persons	
and electricity	€ 20,00 - € 34,00
with water and drainage	€ 23,00 - € 37,00
extra person	€ 3,40 - € 5,90
child (3-10 yrs)	€ 2,30 - € 4,50
boat	€ 5,00 - € 6,00
dog	€ 2,10 - € 3,50

Camping Cheques accepted.

Reservations

Advised for July/Aug; write or fax site. (deposit € 100) Tel: 05 58 78 12 33.
E-mail: info@camping-de-la-rive.fr

Open

1 April - 30 September.

FR64090 Camping Airotel La Chêneraie

Chemin Cazenave, 64100 Bayonne (Pyrénées-Atlantiques)

La Chêneraie is only eight kilometres from the coast at Anglet with its long sandy beach and large car park, but with the calm and tranquillity of this site you would think you were much further away from all the hustle and bustle of the coast. The distant views of the Pyrénées from various points all add to the feeling of tranquility. There are 210 pitches arranged on neat grass, with most partially divided by trees and shrubs, so quite well shaded. Many have electricity, some with water and drainage. One area is very sloping but it has been terraced to give level pitches. Wooded walks lead to a small lake which can be used for inflatable boats or fishing (no swimming). A tour operator uses 20 pitches.

Facilities

Large, central toilet block with washbasins in cabins, with three smaller blocks around the site providing additional facilities. In high season these facilities may be under pressure and maintenance and cleaning could be variable. Dishwashing and laundry sinks. Washing machine and dryers, baby baths, and facilities for disabled people. Shop, restaurant with all day snacks and takeaway (all main season). Medium sized swimming pool open June - end August (longer if the weather is good). Playground. Tennis courts (free outside July/Aug). TV room. Table tennis. Off site: Bicycle hire 5 km. Riding 6 km. Golf 7 km.

Open

Easter - 30 September (full services 1/6-15/9).

At a glance

Welcome & Ambience	✓✓✓✓	Location	✓✓✓✓
Quality of Pitches	✓✓✓	Range of Facilities	✓✓✓

Directions

Site is 4 km. northeast of Bayonne just off main N117 road to Pau, signed at traffic lights. From new autoroute A63 take exit 6 marked 'Bayonne St Esprit'.

Charges 2004

Per person	€ 3,70 - € 4,40
child (under 10 yrs)	€ 2,15 - € 2,75
pitch	€ 9,45 - € 11,43
with water and electricity	€ 13,75 - € 18,00
tent pitch	€ 7,65 - € 8,85
dog	€ 2,30

Less 10-20% outside 1/6-1/9. No credit cards.

Reservations

Made for min. 1 week with deposit (€ 62) and fee (€ 15,24). Tel: 05 59 55 01 31.

FR64110 Camping du Col d'Ibardin

64122 Urrugne (Pyrénées-Atlantiques)

This family owned site at the foot of the Basque Pyrénées is highly recommended and deserves praise. It is well run with emphasis on personal attention, the smiling Madame, her staff and family ensuring that all are made welcome and is attractively set in the middle of an oak wood. Behind the forecourt, with its brightly coloured shrubs and modern reception area, various roadways lead to the 178 pitches. These are individual, spacious and enjoy the benefit of the shade (if preferred a more open aspect can be found). There are electricity hook-ups (4/10A) and adequate water points. From this site you can enjoy the mountain scenery, be on the beach at Socoa within minutes or cross the border into Spain approximately 14 km. down the road. Used by tour operators (20 pitches).

Facilities

Two toilet blocks, one rebuilt to a high specification, are kept very clean. WC for disabled people. Dishwashing facilities in separate open areas. Laundry unit with washing machine and dryer. Motorcaravan service point. Small shop selling basic food and gas, with orders taken for bread (1/7-31/8). Catering and takeaway in July/Aug. Bar and occasional evening entertainment which includes Flamenco dancing. Swimming pool and paddling pool. Children's playground and club with adult supervision. Tennis courts, boules, table tennis, video games. Bicycle hire. A multi-purpose sports area is planned. Not suitable for American motorhomes. Off site: Riding 2 km. Fishing 5 km. Large supermarket and shopping centre 5 km. Golf 7 km.

Open

1 April - 30 September.

At a glance

Welcome & Ambience	✓✓✓✓	Location	✓✓✓✓
Quality of Pitches	✓✓✓✓	Range of Facilities	✓✓✓✓

Directions

Leave A63 autoroute at St Jean-de-Luz sud, exit no. 2 and join the RN10 in the direction of Urrugne. Turn left at roundabout (signed Col d'Ibardin) on the D4 and site is on right after 5 km. Do not turn off to the Col itself, but carry on towards Ascain.

Charges 2004

Per unit incl. 2 persons	€ 12,00 - € 19,50
extra adult	€ 2,60 - € 4,50
child (2-7 yrs)	€ 1,55 - € 2,80
electricity (4/10A)	€ 2,75 - € 5,20
animal	€ 1,00 - € 1,60

Reservations

Are accepted - contact site. Tel: 05 59 54 31 21. E-mail: info@col-ibardin.com

FR64140 Sunêlia Bérrua

Rue Berrua, 64210 Bidart (Pyrénées-Atlantiques)

Berrua Village Camping, set only 1 km. from the sea, is an ideal location for visiting the beaches here in southwest France. A neat and tidy site, it has 270 level pitches (120 for touring units) set amongst trees. Most places have electricity (6A) and some are fully serviced. The attractive swimming pool has sunbeds around for sunbathing and a paddling pool. A new complex is planned for 2005. Some animation is organised in high season for both adults and children, for example guided walks, dances, sporting competitions, bingo and karaoke. A member of the Sunêlia group.

Facilities

Toilet facilities are good (unisex) consisting of two blocks with washbasins in cabins, baby rooms, facilities for disabled visitors, washing machines and dishwashing sinks (cold water only). Motorcaravan service point. Shop (July/Aug). Bar/restaurant and takeaway (15/4-15/9). Swimming pool. Games room. Play area (3-10 yrs only). Bicycle hire. Archery and boule. Off site: Fishing 1 km. Golf or riding 3 km. Beach 1 km.

Open

6 April - 5 October.

At a glance

Welcome & Ambience	✓✓✓✓	Location	✓✓✓✓
Quality of Pitches	✓✓✓✓	Range of Facilities	✓✓✓✓✓

Directions

From A63 exit 4, take N10 south towards Bidart. At roundabout after the 'Intermarche' supermarket, turn left. Bear right then take next right (site signed).

Charges 2004

Per unit incl. 2 persons	€ 14,50 - € 23,60
extra person	€ 2,95 - € 5,30
child (2-10 yrs)	€ 2,00 - € 3,15
electricity (6A)	€ 2,65 - € 4,00
animal	free - € 4,00

Camping Cheques accepted.

Reservations

Contact site. Tel: 05 59 54 96 66.
E-mail: contact@berrua.com

TRAVEL SERVICE SITE

TO BOOK CALL 0870 405 4055 OR www.alanrogersdirect.com

FR12150 Camping Marmotel

12130 St Geniez-d'Olt (Aveyron)

The road into Marmotel passes various industrial buildings and is a little off-putting – persevere, as they are soon left behind. The campsite itself is a mixture of old and new. The old part provides many pitches with lots of shade and separated by hedges. The new area is sunny until the trees grow. These pitches each have a private sanitary unit, with shower, WC, washbasin and dishwashing. New and very well designed, they are reasonably priced for such luxury. All the pitches have electricity (10A). A lovely restaurant has a wide terrace with views of the hills and overlooking the heated swimming and paddling pools. These have fountains, a toboggan and sun beds either on grass or the tiled surrounds. The Lot river runs alongside the site where you can fish or canoe.

Facilities

Good sanitary facilities include baby baths and facilities for disabled visitors. Shower cubicles are a little small. Washing machines. Bar/restaurant and takeaway (all season). Swimming pools. Small play area. Multi-sports area (tennis, volleyball, basketball). Entertainment for all ages in July/Aug. including a disco below the bar, cinema screen, karaoke, dances and a mini club for 4-12 yr olds. Bicycle hire. Fishing. Canoeing. Off site: Large supermarket 500 m. Riding 10 km. Bicycle tours and canoe trips on the Lot and rafting on the Tarn are organised.

Open

1 May - 10 September.

At a glance

Welcome & Ambience	✓✓✓✓	Location	✓✓✓✓
Quality of Pitches	✓✓✓	Range of Facilities	✓✓✓✓✓

Directions

Heading south on autoroute 75 (free) take exit 41 and follow signs for St Geniez d'Olt. Site is at western end of village. Site is signed onto D19 to Prades d'Aubrac, then 500 m. on left.

Charges 2005

Per unit incl. 1 or 2 persons, and 10A electricity	€ 17,00 - € 28,80
extra person	€ 2,90 - € 5,40
child under 4 yrs	€ 1,00 - € 3,10
animal	free - € 1,60

Camping Cheques accepted.
Less 30% outside July/Aug.

Reservations

Made with deposit (€ 100) and fee (€ 16).
Tel: 05 65 70 46 51. E-mail: info@marmotel.com

France

TRAVEL SERVICE SITE

TO BOOK CALL 0870 405 4055 OR www.alanrogersdirect.com

FR12020 Camping Caravaning Les Rivages

Avenue de l'Aigoual, Route de Nant, 12100 Millau (Aveyron)

Les Rivages is a large site on the outskirts of the town. It is well organised and well situated, being close to the high limestone Causses and the dramatic gorges of the Tarn and Dourbie, the latter of which runs past the back of the site. Smaller pitches, used for tents and small units, abut a pleasant riverside space suitable for sunbathing, fishing or picnics. Most of the 314 pitches are large, 100 sq.m. or more, and well shaded. A newer part of the site (on the right as you enter) has less shade but pitches are larger. All pitches have electricity (6A), and 100 have water and drainage. The site offers a very wide range of sporting activities close to 30 in all (see facilities). Millau is a bustling and pleasant town. Don't miss the night markets, but don't eat before you get there – there are thousands of things to taste, many of them grilled or spit roasted. The gates are shut 10 pm.- 8 am, with night-watchman.

Facilities

Four well kept modern toilet blocks have all necessary facilities. Special block for children with baby baths, small showers and toilets, as well as ironing facilities. Shop for most essentials (1/6-15/9). Terrace restaurant and bar overlooking a good-sized main swimming pool and children's pool (from 10/5). Play area. Much evening entertainment, largely for children, along with child-minding and a mini-club. Tennis (indoor and outdoor). Squash (can be viewed from the bar). Table tennis. Floodlit petanque. Many river activities, walking, bird watching and fishing. Off site: Rafting and canoeing arranged. Bicycle hire 1 km. Riding 10 km. Hypermarket in Millau.

At a glance

Welcome & Ambience	✓✓✓✓✓	Location	✓✓✓✓✓
Quality of Pitches	✓✓✓✓	Range of Facilities	✓✓✓✓

Directions

From Millau, take D991 road south towards Nant. Site is about 400 m. on the right.

Charges 2004

Per pitch incl. 2 persons and electricity	€ 15,50 - € 24,00
with water and drainage	€ 17,50 - € 26,00
extra person (over 3 yrs)	€ 3,00 - € 4,50
pet	free - € 3,00

Reservations

Advisable for July/Aug. with deposit (€ 61) and fee (€ 15,24). Tel: 05 65 61 01 07.
E-mail: campinglesrivages@wanadoo.fr

Open

1 May - 30 September.

FR12010 Castel Camping Le Val de Cantobre

12230 Nant-d'Aveyron (Aveyron)

This very pleasant terraced site has been imaginatively and tastefully developed by the Dupond family over a 25 year period. In particular, the magnificent carved features in the bar create a delightful ambience, complemented by a recently built terrace. True, the ground is hard in summer but reception staff supply robust nails if your awning pegs prove a problem. Most of the 200 pitches (all with electricity and water) are peaceful, generous in size and blessed with views of the valley. The pools have a new surround, bedecked by flowers and crowned by a large urn which dispenses water into the paddling pool. But it is the activity programme that is unique at Val de Cantobre, supervised by qualified instructors in July and August, some arranged by the owners and some at a fair distance from the site. Passive recreationists appreciate the scenery, especially Cantobre, a medieval village that clings to a cliff in view of the site. Nature lovers will be delighted to see the vultures wheeling in the Tarn gorge alongside more humble rural residents. Butterflies in profusion, orchids, huge edible snails, glow worms, families of beavers and the natterjack toad all live here. It is easy to see why - the place is magnificent. Although tour operators occupy around 40% of the pitches, the terrace design provides some peace and privacy, especially on the upper levels and a warm welcome awaits from the Dupond family.

Facilities

The impressive, fully equipped toilet block is beautifully appointed with a huge indoor dishwashing area. Laundry. Fridge hire. Shop, although small, offers a wide variety of provisions; including many regional specialities (comparing well with local shops and markets). Attractive bar, restaurant, pizzeria and takeaway facility (some steepish up and down walking from furthest pitches to some facilities). Three adjoining swimming pools. Minigolf. Table tennis. Play area. Around 15 types of activity including river rafting, white water canoeing, rock climbing or jumps from Millau's hill tops on twin seater steerable parachutes. All weather sports pitch. Torch useful. Off site: Fishing 4 km. Riding 15 km. Bicycle hire 25 km.

At a glance

Welcome & Ambience	✓✓✓✓✓	Location	✓✓✓✓✓
Quality of Pitches	✓✓✓✓	Range of Facilities	✓✓✓✓

Directions

Site is 4 km. north of Nant, on D991 road to Millau. From Millau direction take D991 signed Gorge du Dourbie.

Charges 2004

Per unit incl. 2 persons and 4A electricity	€ 19,00 - € 29,00
extra person (4 yrs and over)	€ 4,00 - € 7,00
dog	free - € 2,00

Camping Cheques accepted.

Reservations

Made for any length with 25% deposit, fee (€ 25) and optional cancellation insurance.
Tel: 05 65 58 43 00. E-mail: info@valdecantobre.com

Open

14 May - 11 September, with all facilities.

FR12080 Camping Club Les Genêts

Lac de Pareloup, 12410 Salles Curan (Aveyron)

This family run site is on the shores of Lac de Pareloup and offers both family holiday and watersports facilities. The 162 pitches include 102 grassy, mostly individual pitches for touring units. These are in two areas, one on each side of the entrance lane, and are divided by hedges, shrubs and trees. Most have electricity (6A) and many also have water and waste water drain. The site slopes gently down to the beach and lake with facilities for all watersports including waterskiing. A full animation and activities programme is organised in high season, and there is much to see and do in this very attractive corner of Aveyron. The site is not suitable for American style motorhomes. Used by tour operators (25 pitches). A 'Sites et Paysages' member.

Facilities

Two main sanitary units include washbasins in cubicles and a suite for disabled people. Refurbishment of the older unit is planned, whilst the other unit is new. Baby room. Dishwashing and laundry sinks. Laundry room. Very well stocked shop. Bar and restaurant. Snack bar serving pizzas and other snacks in main season. Swimming pool and spa pool (both from 1/6; unsupervised). Playground. Minigolf, volleyball and boules. Bicycle hire. Red Indian style tee-pees. Hire of pedaloes, windsurfers and kayaks. Fishing licences available.

Open

31 May - 11 September.

At a glance

Welcome & Ambience	✓✓✓✓	Location	✓✓✓✓✓
Quality of Pitches	✓✓✓✓	Range of Facilities	✓✓✓✓✓

Directions

From Salles-Curan take D577 for about 4 km. and turn right into a narrow lane immediately after a sharp right hand bend. Site is signed at junction.

Charges 2004

Per unit incl. 1 or 2 persons and 6A electricity	€ 11,00 - € 28,00
lakeside pitch	€ 11,00 - € 36,00
extra person	€ 4,00 - € 6,00
child (under 2 yrs)	free
pet	€ 3,00 - € 4,00

Refundable deposits for barrier card € 20 and for pool bracelet € 8 per person.

Reservations

Advised for July/Aug. and made with deposit (€ 155) and fee (€ 29). Tel: 05 65 46 35 34.
E-mail: contact@camping-les-genets.fr

FR12160 Camping Caravaning Les Peupliers

Route des Gorges du Tarn, 12640 Rivière-sur-Tarn (Aveyron)

Les Peupliers is a friendly, family site on the banks of the Tarn river. Most of the good-sized pitches have shade, and all have electricity, water and a waste water point. The river has a landing place for canoes and a small beach. In a lovely, sunny situation is the swimming pool with a paddling pool and sun beds, all protected by a beautifully clipped hedge and with a super view to the surrounding hills and the Chateau du Preylarde perched above the village. The site has its own canoes (to hire). Some English is spoken. A treat for us at dusk was to watch beavers playing on the river bank.

Facilities

Large, light and airy toilet facilities are a good provision with adjustable showers, washbasins in cubicles and mainly British style WCs. Good baby facilities with baths, showers and WCs. Facilities for disabled visitors. Washing machines. Shop (1/6-30/9). Bar with TV and internet point. Snack bar and takeaway (1/5-30/9). Swimming pool (from 1/5). Games and competitions organised in July/Aug. Fishing. Volleyball, football, badminton. Play area. Above reception is a balcony with fitness equipment. Play area. Weekly dances organised in July/Aug. Canoe hire. Off site: Village with shops and restaurant 300 m. Riding 0.5 km. Bicycle hire 2 km. Golf 25 km.

Open

1 April - 30 September.

At a glance

Welcome & Ambience	✓✓✓✓	Location	✓✓✓✓
Quality of Pitches	✓✓✓✓	Range of Facilities	✓✓✓✓

Directions

Heading south from Claremot Ferrand to Milau on the A75 autoroute, take exit 44 signed Aguessac and Gorges du Tarn. In Aguessac follow signs to Rivière-sur-Tarn (5 km. away) and site is clearly indicated.

Charges 2004

Per person	€ 5,00 - € 7,00
child (under 5 yrs)	€ 2,00 - € 3,00
pitch	€ 4,00 - € 6,00
electricity (6A)	€ 3,00
dog	€ 1,50

Camping Cheques accepted.

Reservations

Made with deposit (€125) and fee (€25).
Tel: 05 65 59 85 17.
E-mail: lespeupliers12640@wanadoo.fr

FR12070 Camping La Grange de Monteillac

12310 Sévérac-l'Église (Aveyron)

La Grange de Monteillac is a modern, well equipped site in the beautiful, well preserved small village of Sévérac L'Église. A spacious site, it provides 105 individual pitches, 70 for touring, on gently sloping grass, separated by flowering shrubs and young trees offering little shade. All pitches have access to electricity (6A, long leads may be required), water and waste water connections. They include 35 chalets, mobile homes and tents for rent in separate areas. The friendly owner and his welcoming staff will advise about the visits to a château evening with candlelight banquet, an angora farm, and a local pottery that are run weekly in main season. An evening stroll around this delightful village is a must.

Facilities

The toilet block central to the touring area is modern, spacious and clean, with all washbasins in cubicles. Facilities for babies and disabled people. Dishwashing and laundry sinks. Washing machine and dryer. Shop at reception (1/7-31/8). Poolside restaurant/snack-bar serving pizzas, grills etc. and takeaway in high season. Music or groups feature in the bar (July-Aug). Two swimming pools with toilets and changing rooms below (1/6-15/9). Large well equipped playground. Organised activities include children's club, bicycle hire and archery lessons. Off site: Shops in village 1.5 km. Fishing 2 km. Riding 9 km.

At a glance

Welcome & Ambience	✓✓✓	Location	✓✓✓✓
Quality of Pitches	✓✓✓	Range of Facilities	✓✓✓✓

Directions

Site is on the edge of Sévérac-l'Église village, just off N88 Rodez - Sévérac Le Château road. From A75 use exit 42.

Charges 2004

Per unit incl. 2 persons and electricity	€ 21,50
extra person	€ 3,80
child (under 7 yrs)	€ 2,50

Less 30% outside July/Aug.

Reservations

Contact site. Tel: 05 65 70 21 00.
E-mail: info@la-grange-de-monteillac.com

Open

1 May - 15 September.

FR16060 Camping Marco de Bignac

Lieudit 'Les Sablons', 16170 Bignac (Charente)

The small village of Bignac is set in peaceful countryside not too far from the N10 road, north of Angoulême. Since buying the campsite in 1994, the Marshall family have worked hard to improve this tranquil site which is arranged along one side of an attractive lake on a level, grassy meadow. The 89 pitches are marked at each corner by a tree so there is shade, and electricity (3/6A) is available. At the far end of the site is a hedged swimming pool and plenty of grassy space for ball games. The lake shores are home to ducks and the lake itself is used for fishing and small boats. The reception office is part of the owner's home and near to it is a bar, snack bar and restaurant with tables outside and views across the lake. This site is popular with British visitors and is a peaceful, relaxing location for couples or young families. There is no noisy entertainment and all the activities are free of charge.

Facilities

Two traditional style toilet blocks have functional facilities all in cabins opening from the outside. British style WCs. Washing machine. Bar and snack bar (1/6-31/8; closed Mon. until high season). Essentials kept in the bar and baker calls daily (high season). Swimming pool (15/6-31/8, unsupervised). Football field, badminton, tennis, table tennis, pedaloes, minigolf a boule pitch and fishing, all free. Library. Play area. Pets corner. Special evenings, outings and competitions organised in high season. A torch may be useful. Off site: Riding 5 km. Bicycle hire 10 km. Golf 25 km.

At a glance

Welcome & Ambience	✓✓✓✓	Location	✓✓✓✓✓
Quality of Pitches	✓✓✓✓	Range of Facilities	✓✓✓✓

Directions

From N10 south of Poitiers, 14 km. north of Angoulême, take D11 west to Vars and Basse. Where you turn right onto D117 to Bignac. Site is signed at several junctions and in village (Camping Bignac).

Charges 2005

Per pitch incl. 2 persons	€ 13,00 - € 19,00
extra person	€ 3,00 - € 5,00
electricity (3/6A)	€ 2,50 - € 4,00

Reservations

Made with deposit (€ 30). Tel: 05 45 21 78 41.
E-mail: camping.marcodebignac@wanadoo.fr

Open

15 May - 15 September.

FR24010 Castel Camping Château Le Verdoyer

Champs Romain, 24470 St Pardoux (Dordogne)

Le Verdoyer is a Dutch, family-owned site developed in the park of a restored château. We particularly like this site for its beautiful buildings and lovely surroundings. It is situated in this lesser known area of the Dordogne sometimes referred to as the Périgord Vert, with its green forests and small lakes. The 37 acre estate has two such lakes, one in front of the Château for fishing and one accessed by a foot-path, with sandy beach and safe swimming area. There are 150 marked, level, terraced pitches (some a little rocky). Mostly of a good size (100-150 sq.m), all have electricity (5/10A), with a choice of wooded area or open field, where hedges have been planted and have grown well; 120 are 'confort' pitches with more planned. There is a swimming pool complex and in high season activities are organised for children (5-13 yrs) but there is definitely no disco! The courtyard area between reception and the bar is home to evening activities, and provides a pleasant place to enjoy drinks and relax. The Château itself has rooms to let and its excellent lakeside restaurant is also open to the public. Used by a Dutch tour operator (15 pitches).

Facilities

Recently completely renewed, three very well appointed toilet blocks include washbasins in cabins, facilities for disabled people and baby baths. Serviced launderette. Motorcaravan service point. Fridge rental. Multi-purpose shop with gas. Bar (with snacks and takeaway) and restaurant, both open all season (and also open to the public). Good value bistro serving meals (July/Aug). Two pools (25 x 10 m. and 10 x 7 m; the smaller one can be covered in low season), slide (36 m. long) and paddling pool. Play areas. All-weather tennis court. Volleyball, basket-ball and badminton. Table tennis. Minigolf. Bicycle hire (tennis and bicycles free in low season). Small library.
Off site: Riding 3 km.

At a glance

Welcome & Ambience	✓✓✓✓✓	Location	✓✓✓✓✓
Quality of Pitches	✓✓✓✓	Range of Facilities	✓✓✓✓

Directions

Site is 2 km. from the Limoges (N21) - Chalus (D6bis-D85) - Nontron road, 20 km. south of Chalus and is well signed from the main road. Site is on the D96 about 4 km. north of village of Champs Romain.

Charges 2005

Per unit incl. 2 persons and electricity	€ 18,00 - € 29,00
extra adult	€ 5,00 - € 6,00
child (under 4 yrs)	free
dog	free - € 3,00

Camping Cheques accepted.
Between 9/7-20/8 stay 14 nights, pay for twelve.

Reservations

Write to site. Tel: 05 53 56 94 64.
E-mail: chateau@verdoyer.fr

Open

23 April - 15 October.

FR24070 Camping Lestaubière

Pont St Mamet, 24140 Douville (Dordogne)

Set just off the main N21 road near Pont St Mamet, mid-way between Bergerac and Perigueux, this quiet and charming site is well situated for exploring the western side of the Dordogne and the Bergerac vineyards. There are 90 pitches, mostly on fairly flat, shaded wooded ground at the top of the site, with some on more sloping open meadow with views across the valley. Pitches are marked and all have electrical connections although long leads may be necessary for some pitches. The swimming pool and small lake with diving platform and beach encourage longer stays. A pleasant, shaded patio terrace under vines and maples leads to a general room with a bar and a separate room for young people. There are many British and Dutch visitors, but no tour operators. Good English is spoken by the friendly Dutch owners.

Facilities

Two toilet blocks include some washbasins in private cabins in the larger block. Baby baths and large family shower room. Ample dishwashing and laundry sinks. No facilities for disabled visitors. Small shop. Bar. Library. Swimming pool (unsupervised) and paddling pool. Excellent adventure style play area. Volleyball, boules and fishing. Occasional organised activities. Off site: Tennis 500 m.

Open

1 May - 1 October.

At a glance

Welcome & Ambience	✓✓✓✓	Location	✓✓✓✓
Quality of Pitches	✓✓✓	Range of Facilities	✓✓✓

Directions

Site is 19 km. NE of Bergerac. From N21 Bergerac - Perigueux road take exit for Pont St Mamet. Site is 500 m. north of the village, on eastern side of road, and is well signed. After you turn off main road at this point the site entrance is on the left.

Charges guide

Per person	€ 4,60 - € 5,20
pitch	€ 5,10 - € 6,90
electricity (4/10A)	€ 2,70 - € 4,00

Reservations

Advised for July and August. No deposit and booking fee. Tel: 05 53 82 98 15. E-mail: lestaubiere@cs.com

FR24080 Camping Caravaning Le Moulin de David

Gaugeac, 24540 Monpazier (Dordogne)

Owned and run by a French family who continually seek to improve it, this pleasant and attractive site is one for those who enjoy peace, away from the hustle and bustle of the main Dordogne attractions, yet sufficiently close for them to be accessible. Set in a 14 hectare. wooded valley, it has 160 pitches split into two sections; 102 for tourers - 33 below the central reception complex in a shaded situation, the others above, partly terraced and with varying degrees of shade. All pitches have electricity. Spacing is good. The site has been planted with a pleasing variety of shrubs and trees, and combined with the small stream that runs through the centre they create a beautiful, tranquil setting. A delightful wooded walk via a long distance footpath to Château Biron, 2-3 km. distance. A 'Sites et Paysages' member.

TRAVEL SERVICE SITE

TO BOOK CALL 0870 405 4055 OR www.alanrogersdirect.com

Facilities

All three toilet blocks are good, including washbasins in cabins, facilities for disabled visitors and babies in each. Adequate dishwashing and laundry sinks. Laundry room. Good shop. Bar/restaurant with shaded patio and takeaway. Swimming pool and children's paddling pool, plus freshwater pool with waterslide. Play area. Boules, half-court tennis, table tennis, volleyball, basketball, trampolining and football area. Library. Bicycle hire. Events, games and canoe trips organised (1/7-31/8). Off site: Small supermarket and cash point in Monpazier 2.5 km.

Open

14 May - 10 September.

At a glance

Welcome & Ambience	✓✓✓✓	Location	✓✓✓✓
Quality of Pitches	✓✓✓✓✓	Range of Facilities	✓✓✓✓

Directions

From Monpazier take the D2 Villeréal road. Take third turning left (after about 2 km), signed to Moulin de David and 'Gaugeac mairie'. Site is about 500 m. along this road on the left.

Charges 2004

Per person (over 2 yrs)	€ 3,65 - € 6,40
normal pitch	€ 5,00 - € 9,30
large pitch incl. water and drainage	€ 8,00 - € 12,00
electricity (3/10A)	€ 3,35 - € 5,65

Camping Cheques accepted.

Reservations

Advisable for Jul/Aug, with deposit (€ 65 per week reserved) and fee (€ 19) for stays between 26/6 and 21/8). Tel: 05 53 22 65 25. E-mail: info@moulin-de-david.com

FR24090 Camping Soleil Plage

Vitrac, 24200 Sarlat (Dordogne)

This spacious site is in one of the most attractive sections of the Dordogne valley, right on the riverside. The site has a total of 199 pitches, divided into two sections, of which around 114 are available for touring units. The smaller section surrounds the main reception and other facilities, which are housed in a renovated farmhouse, whilst the larger section of the site is about 250 m. from the reception and pool areas, and offers river bathing from a sizeable pebble bank. All pitches are bounded by hedges and are of good size – in the larger section there are a few pitches for large families. Most pitches have some shade, all have electricity and a few have water and a drain. Various activities are organised in high season including walks and tournaments, with canoe hire from the site. Once a week there is a 'soirée' with a band and wine - worth catching! The site is popular, although in late August it begins to empty.

Facilities

Toilet facilities are in two modern unisex blocks. Washing machines. Motorcaravan service point. Pleasant bar with extensive and good value takeaway menu, refurbished restaurant serving excellent Périgourdine menus, and well stocked shop (all 12/5-15/9). Very impressive swimming pool complex includes main pool, paddling pool, spa pool and two water slides. Tennis court, devilish minigolf, table tennis, volleyball and football pitches. TV room. Playground. Fishing. Canoe and kayak hire. Currency exchange. Off site: Golf 1 km. Bicycle hire 2 km. Riding 5 km.

Open

1 May - 30 September.

At a glance

Welcome & Ambience	✓✓✓✓✓	Location	✓✓✓✓
Quality of Pitches	✓✓✓✓✓	Range of Facilities	✓✓✓✓

Directions

Site is 8 km. south of Sarlat. From D703 Vitrac - Carsac-Aillac road turn southeast at 'Rochebois' golf course (site signed). Follow road to the end, turn right at T-junction, and follow the road along and around to the left. Site is on left just after turning the corner.

Charges 2004

Per person	€ 4,00 - € 6,40
child (2-10 yrs)	€ 2,40 - € 3,70
pitch	€ 6,00 - € 10,60
with electricity (6A)	€ 8,50 - € 14,00
with full services	€ 11,50 - € 19,00

Reservations

Made for exact dates: min. 1 week with deposit (€ 65) and fee (€ 35); send for booking form. Tel: 05 53 28 33 33. E-mail: info@soleilplage.fr

FR24170 Camping Le Port de Limeuil

24480 Allés-sur-Dordogne (Dordogne)

At the confluence of Dordogne and Vézère rivers, opposite the picturesque village of Limieul, this delightful family site has a peaceful, relaxed ambience. There are 90 grassy, flat and numbered pitches, some very spacious and all with electricity connections (5A). The buildings are intraditional Périgourdine style and surrounded with flowers and shrubs – it is a very pretty site. The young French owners have been steadily developing the facilities. A sports area on a large open grassy space between the river bank and the main camping area adds to the feeling of space, and provides an additional recreation and picnic area (there are additional unmarked pitches along the bank here). This is an ideal location for visiting the west central part of the Dordogne département, and is recommended for long stays.

Facilities

Two clean, modern toilet blocks provide excellent facilities. Bar/restaurant with snacks and takeaway (all 20/5-5/9). Small shop. Swimming pool with jacuzzi, paddling pool and children's slide (1/5-30/9). Badminton, football, boules and volleyball. Mountain bike hire. Canoe hire - launched from the site's own pebble beach. Off site: The pretty medieval village of Limeuil 200 m. Riding 1 km. Golf 10 km.

Open

1 May - 30 September.

At a glance

Welcome & Ambience	✓✓✓✓✓	Location	✓✓✓✓
Quality of Pitches	✓✓✓✓	Range of Facilities	✓✓✓✓

Directions

Site is 7 km south of Le Bugue. From D51/D31E Le Buisson - Le Bugue road turn west onto D51 towards Limeuil. Just before the bridge into the village of Limeuil, turn left (site signed), across another bridge. Site is about 100 m. along this road on the right.

Charges 2004

Per pitch incl. 2 persons	€ 13,51 - € 19,30
extra person	€ 3,36 - € 4,80
electricity (5A)	€ 2,13 - € 3,05

Reservations

Advised for mid July - end August.
Tel: 05 53 63 29 76. E-mail: didierbonvallet@aol.com

FR24330 Camping de l'Etang Bleu

24340 Vieux-Mareuil (Dordogne)

Set halfway between the historic towns of Perigueux and Angoulême, this tranquil countryside site in a mature woodland setting has recently been acquired by enthusiastic British owners Mark and Jo Finch. The site has 169 pitches, with 108 available to touring units. The remainder are taken up by two small tour operators and site owned mobile homes and ready erected tents for rent. The pitches are of a good size, flat and grassy, with mature hedging and trees providing privacy and plenty of shade. All pitches have water and 90 have electricity (10/16A). At the bottom of the site is a fishing lake stocked with carp (no permit required), and various woodland walks start from the campsite grounds. The bright and cheerful 'bistro bar' provides good value food and drinks, and becomes a focal point for evening socialising on site. This site is ideal for couples or families with young children who are looking for a quiet and relaxing holiday away from the hustle and bustle of the busiest tourist areas, but still within reach of some of the area's major towns.

Facilities

Two modern, clean and well maintained toilet blocks provide mostly British style toilets, washbasins (some in cubicles), showers, facilities for babies and disabled people. Laundry. Dishwashing facilities. Small playground with paddling pool. Swimming pool (20m x 10m) with sun terrace and loungers. Pleasant bar and terrace with 'bistro' food (all season), Takeaway. Small shop (items not stocked can be ordered on request). Table tennis, boules. Canoe and bicycle hire. Various entertainments, sporting activities and excursions organised in high season. (Floodlit tennis court, minigolf and adventure type playground are planned for summer 2004). Off site: Restaurant - Auberge de L'Etang Bleu - adjacent to campsite, small supermarket, post office etc. in Mareuil (7 km).

Open

18 March - 18 October.

At a glance

Welcome & Ambience	✓✓✓✓	Location	✓✓✓✓
Quality of Pitches	✓✓✓✓	Range of Facilities	✓✓✓✓

Directions

From Angoulême take D939 south, from Perigueux take D939 north. From either direction after about 45 km. the village of Vieux Mareuil is signed on north side of the road. Turn here on D93, and follow narrow road through the village. Just after leaving village site is signed on right, just past Auberge de L'Etang Bleu. Follow signs down long gravel drive to site entrance. NOTE: American-style motorhomes and larger caravans may find it easier to access site by taking the D708 Mareuil - Nontron road, and turning south on the D93, avoiding the narrow access roads in Vieux Mareuil village.

Charges 2004

Per adult	€ 3,50 - € 5,00
child (2-7 yrs)	€ 2,00
pitch	€ 6,00 - € 7,00
with electricity	€ 7,50 - € 11,00
pet	€ 3,00

Less 30% in low seasons.

Reservations

Advisable for high season. Tel: 05 53 60 92 70. E-mail: marc@letangbleu.com

FR46050 Camping Le Rêve

46300 Le Vigan (Lot)

Le Rêve is a very peaceful site situated in the heart of rolling countryside where the Perigord runs into Quercy. Le Rêve continues to impress us with its tranquillity and the young Dutch owners are keen to develop the site in such a way that this will not be lost. The 56 touring pitches are all of good size, with access to electricity (6A), and divided by shrubs. A few of the pitches are situated at the edge of the forest, and provide plenty of shade. Plenty of large grassy areas give lots of space for children to play and make this site particularly suitable for young families.

Facilities

The modern toilet block includes a heated enclosed area for cooler weather. Washbasins in cabins, special cubicles for disabled people and a baby room. Washing machine and dryers. Small shop for basics (bread, milk etc.), pleasant bar, restaurant and takeaway (all open all season). Small, clean, solar heated swimming pool and large paddling pool with Off site: Riding 2 km. Fishing 5 km. Golf 20 km.

Open

9 April - 24 September.

At a glance

Welcome & Ambience	✓✓✓✓	Location	✓✓✓
Quality of Pitches	✓✓✓✓	Range of Facilities	✓✓✓✓

Directions

From N20 Souillac-Cahors road take D673 3 km. south of Payrac. After 2 km. site is signed down small lane on west side of the road. Turn here, and follow signs for another 2.5 km. to site.

Charges 2005

Per person	€ 2,50 - € 3,50
child (under 7 yrs)	€ 1,60 - € 2,50
pitch	€ 12,00 - € 17,00
electricity (6A)	€ 2,50

Less 20-30% outside July/Aug. No credit cards.

Reservations

Advised for high season and made for any length with deposit (€ 70) and fee (€ 5). Tel: 05 65 41 25 20. E-mail: info@campinglereve.com

FR46010 Castel Camping Le Domaine de la Paille Basse

46200 Souillac-sur-Dordogne (Lot)

Set in a rural location some eight kilometres from Souillac, this family owned, high quality site is easily accessible from the N20 and well placed to take advantage of excursions into the Dordogne. It is part of a large domaine of 80 hectares, which is available to campers for walks and recreation. The site is quite high up and there are excellent views over the surrounding countryside. The 250 pitches are in two main areas - one is level in cleared woodland with good shade, and the other on grass in open ground without shade. Numbered and marked, the pitches are a minimum 100 sq.m. and often considerably more. All have electricity (3/6A) with about 80 also equipped with water and drainage. A wide range of activities and entertainment are organised in season (animation was of a very high standard when we stayed). For good reason, the site can get very busy in high season and is popular with tour operators (25%), but there is more space available from mid August.

Facilities

Three main toilet blocks all have modern equipment and are kept very clean. Laundry facilities. Shop for essentials. Good restaurant, bar with terrace and takeaway. Crêperie. Good pool complex, with main swimming pool (25 x 10 m), a smaller one (10 x 6 m), paddling pool (unheated) and water slides. Sun terrace with loungers. Sound-proofed disco room (twice weekly in season). TV rooms (with satellite). Cinema room below the pool area. Archery, tennis (charged), football, volleyball and table tennis. Play area. Off site: Golf 4 km.

Open

15 May - 15 September.

At a glance

Welcome & Ambience	✓✓✓✓	Location	✓✓✓✓
Quality of Pitches	✓✓✓✓	Range of Facilities	✓✓✓✓

Directions

From Souillac take D15 road leading northwest towards Salignac-Eyvignes and after 6 km. turn right at camp sign and follow steep and narrow approach road for 2 km.

Charges 2004

Per person	€ 4,70 - € 5,80
child (under 7 yrs)	€ 3,10 - € 3,80
pitch	€ 7,20 - € 8,90
incl. water and drainage	€ 8,80 - € 10,90
dog	€ 3,80

Camping Cheques accepted.
Less 20% outside 15/6-1/9.

Reservations

Advised mid-July - mid-Aug. and made for min. 1 week with deposit and booking fee.
Tel: 05 65 37 85 48. E-mail: paille.basse@wanadoo.fr

TRAVEL SERVICE SITE

TO BOOK CALL 0870 405 4055 OR www.alanrogersdirect.com

FR47010 Camping Caravaning Moulin du Périé

47500 Sauveterre-la-Lemance (Lot et Garonne)

Set in a quiet area and surrounded by woodlands this peaceful little site is well away from much of the tourist bustle. Its 125 grass pitches, divided by mixed trees and bushes, are reasonably sized and extremely well kept, as indeed is the entire site. All pitches have electricity (6A) and most enjoy good shade, with a wide variety of trees and shrubs. The picturesque old mill buildings, adorned with flowers and creepers, now house the bar and restaurant where the food is to be recommended, as is the owner's extensive knowledge of wine that he is pleased to share with visitors. The attractive front courtyard is complemented by an equally pleasant terrace at the rear. Two small, clean swimming pools overlook a shallow, spring water lake, ideal for inflatable boats and paddling, and bordering the lake, a large grass field is popular for games. A quiet, friendly site with regular visitors - reservation is advised for July/Aug. A 'Sites et Paysages' member.

TRAVEL SERVICE SITE

TO BOOK CALL 0870 405 4055 OR www.alanrogersdirect.com

Facilities

Two clean, modern and well maintained toilet blocks include facilities for disabled visitors. Motorcaravan service point. Fridge, cot, barbecue and chemical toilet hire (book in advance). Shop for essentials (with gas). Bar/reception and restaurant (including takeaway). Two small swimming pools (no bermuda-style shorts). Football and volleyball. Boules, table tennis, outdoor chess. Playground and trampoline. Small, indoor play area. Bicycle hire. In season various activities are arranged; including canoeing, riding, wine tasting visits, sight seeing trips plus weekly barbecues and gastronomic meals. Winter caravan storage.
Off site: Fishing 1 km. Small supermarket in village and larger stores in Fumel.

Open

23 April - 20 September.

At a glance

Welcome & Ambience	✓✓✓✓	Location	✓✓✓
Quality of Pitches	✓✓✓✓	Range of Facilities	✓✓✓

Directions

From D710 Fumel - Périgueux road, turn southeast into village of Sauveterre-le-Lemance across the railway line. Continue straight through village and turn left (northeast) at far end on C201 minor road signed to campsite, Château Sauveterre and Loubejec. Continue straight along this road and site is 3 km. on the right.

Charges 2004

Per unit incl. 2 persons	€ 12,10 - € 20,50
with electricity	€ 15,70 - € 24,10
extra person	€ 3,90 - € 6,10
child (under 7 yrs)	€ 1,65 - € 3,25
animal	€ 2,00 - € 3,30

Camping Cheques accepted.

Reservations

Advised for July/Aug. and made with deposit (€ 140) and fee (€ 20). Tel: 05 53 40 67 26.
E-mail: moulinduperie@wanadoo.fr

FR23010 Castel Camping Le Château de Poinsouze

Route de la Châtre, BP 12, 23600 Boussac-Bourg (Creuse)

Le Château de Poinsouze is a recently developed site with 145 pitches arranged on the open, gently sloping, grassy park to one side of the Château's main drive - a beautiful plane tree avenue. It is a well designed, high quality site. The 112 touring pitches, some with lake frontage, all have electricity (6-25A), with water, waste water and sewage connections to many. The Château (not open to the public) lies across the lake from the site. Exceptionally well restored outbuildings on the opposite side of the drive house a new restaurant, other facilities and the pool area. The site has a friendly family atmosphere, there are organised activities in main season including dances, children's games and crafts, family triathlons, and there are marked walks around the park and woods. All facilities are open all season, though times may vary. This is a top class site with a formula which should ensure a stress-free, enjoyable family holiday. Boussac (2.5 km) has a market every Thursday morning. The massive 12/15th century fortress, Château de Boussac, is open daily all year.

Facilities

The high quality, double glazed sanitary unit is entered via a large utility area equipped with dishwashing and laundry sinks, foot-pedal operated taps, sinks accessible for wheelchair users, drinks machine and two smaller rooms with washing machines, dryer and ironing. Four spacious rooms are very well equipped including some washbasins in cubicles, baby baths, changing mats and child's WC, and two suites for disabled people. Good motorcaravan service point. Well stocked shop. Takeaway, Comfortable bar with games, TV and library room above. New restaurant. Well fenced swimming pool with slide, children's pool (children wear colour coded bracelets, deposit required). Fenced playground designed with safety in mind. Table tennis, petanque, pool table and table football games. Bicycle hire. Free fishing in the lake (if you put the fish back); boats and lifejackets can be hired. Football, volleyball, basketball, badminton and other games. Dogs are not accepted in high season (9/7-19/8).

At a glance

Welcome & Ambience	✓✓✓✓✓	Location	✓✓✓✓✓
Quality of Pitches	✓✓✓✓	Range of Facilities	✓✓✓✓

Directions

Site entrance is 2.5 km north of Boussac on D917 (towards La Châtre).

Charges 2005

Per pitch incl. 2 persons	€ 12,00 - € 19,00
with electricity (6A), water, waste water	€ 18,00 - € 26,00
with electricity (10A), water, waste water, sewage connection	€ 23,00 - € 28,00
extra adult	€ 3,00 - € 5,50
child (2-7 yrs)	€ 2,00 - € 4,50
electricity 10-25A	€ 2,50 - € 5,00

Camping Cheques accepted.

Reservations

Advisable during July/Aug; made with 30% deposit and € 15 fee. Tel: 05 55 65 02 21. E-mail: info.camping-de.poinsouze@wanadoo.fr

Open

13 May - 18 September.

France

TRAVEL SERVICE SITE

TO BOOK CALL 0870 405 4055 OR www.alanrogersdirect.com

FR48020 Camping de Capelan

48150 Meyrueis (Lozère)

The Lozère is one of France's least populated departements but offers some truly spectacular, rugged scenery, wonderful flora and fauna and many old towns and villages. The little town of Meyrueis, accessible from the campsite via a riverside walk, marks the start of the Gorges de la Jonte, with the better known Gorges du Tarn running a little to the north. Le Capelan is a friendly family site with English and Dutch spoken. It has 120 grassy pitches strung out alongside the river, most with some shade and all with electrical connections (6/10A). Around 40 pitches are used for mobile homes. The site has direct river access and trout fishing is popular. Although there are special facilities, the site is not ideal for disabled visitors. A 'Sites et Paysages' member.

Facilities

Two very good toilet blocks are of recent construction and well maintained. Facilities for disabled visitors (but see above). 3 bathrooms (bath, shower, basin and WC) for rent. Small shop (from 1/6). Spacious bar (from 1/6) with satellite TV, internet access, pool table. Takeaway (from 1/7). Swimming and paddling pools with sunbathing terrace (from 1/6), accessible only via 60 steps. Multi-sports terrain. Play area. Range of leisure activities including supervised rock climbing. Fishing. Communal barbecue area; only gas and electric barbecues permitted on site. Off site: Town centre with shops, restaurants, banks, etc. 1 km. Bicycle hire 1 km. Riding 3 km. Canoeing. The Cévennes national park with innumerable walking and cycling opportunites. Several excellent caves. Vulture visitor centre.

At a glance

Welcome & Ambience	✓✓✓✓	Location	✓✓✓✓
Quality of Pitches	✓✓✓	Range of Facilities	✓✓✓✓

Directions

Site is 1 km. west of Meyruels on the D996, the road to La Jonte. It is well signed from the centre of the town.

Charges 2004

Per pitch and 2 persons including electricity	€ 13,00 - € 18,00
extra person	€ 3,70
child (under 7 years)	€ 2,40

Camping Cheques accepted.

Reservations

Contact site. Tel: 04 66 45 60 50.
E-mail: camping.le.capelan@wanadoo.fr

Open

30 April - 19 September.

FR07140 Camping Les Lavandes

Le Village, 07170 Darbres (Ardèche)

Although slightly less sophisticated than some others in the region, this site should appeal to those seeking the real France for a pleasant family holiday. Situated to the northeast of Aubenas, in a quieter part of this region, Les Lavandes is surrounded by magnificent countryside, vineyards and orchards. A ride along the panoramic road to Mirabel is a must. The enthusiastic French owners, who speak good English, run a site that appeals to all nationalities. The 70 pitches (58 for touring) are arranged on low terraces separated by a variety of trees and shrubs that give welcome shade in summer. Visit at the end of May to see the campsite trees laden with luscious cherries. There is no problem with electricity, most pitches having 6A but a few have 10A. Water taps are not so abundant. Traditional buildings house the reception (full of tourist information including a touch screen), shop, restaurant, takeaway and cosy bar offering excellent views over the swimming pool to the village (just a stroll away) and hillside beyond. Organised activities include wine tasting, shows, musical evenings and children's games.

Facilities

The recently refurbished facilities are comprehensive and well maintained. Excellent room with facilities for disabled people and a baby room. Washing machine. Small shop (1/7-31/8). Cosy bar and terrace (1/6-31/8). Restaurant (1/7-31/8). Takeaway (14.4-31.8). Swimming pool and paddling pool surrounded by paved sunbathing area with larger grass area adjacent, all with super views. Two small play areas for younger children. Table tennis, table football and pool table. Electric barbecues are not permitted.
Off site: Fishing 1 km. Bicycle hire 3 km. Tennis 5 km. Canoeing, walking, cycling, riding and carting nearby. Caves, troglodyte villages, historical villages, interesting geological formations and museums. Wonderful area for birds (Golden Orioles and Bonellis eagle).

At a glance

Welcome & Ambience	✓✓✓✓	Location	✓✓✓✓
Quality of Pitches	✓✓✓✓	Range of Facilities	✓✓✓

Directions

You are advised to approach the site from the south. From Montélimar take the N102 towards Aubenas. After passing through Villeneuve, in Lavilledieu, turn right at traffic lights on D224 to Darbres (10 km). In the village of Darbres turn very sharp left by the post office (care needed) and follow signs to site.

Charges 2004

Per unit incl. 2 persons	€ 11,00 - € 16,00
extra person	€ 2,80 - € 3,50
child under 8 yrs	€ 1,00 - € 2,60
electricity	€ 3,50
dog	free - € 3,50

Reservations

Made with deposit (€ 85) and fee (€ 15).
Tel: 04 75 94 20 65. E-mail: sarl.leslavandes@online.fr

Open

Easter - 15 September.

FR07090 Castel Camping Le Domaine des Plantas

07360 Les Ollières-sur-Eyrieux (Ardèche)

A good quality site in a spectacular setting on the steep banks of the Eyrieux river, Domaine des Plantas offers an attractive alternative to those in the more popular southern parts of the Ardèche. The Eyrieux valley is less well known, but arguably just as attractive as those further south and a good deal less crowded, particularly in the main season. Perhaps the only drawback to this site is the narrow twisting three kilometre approach road which, although by no means frightening, may present something of a challenge to those with large outfits - however, the helpful owners have an ingenious convoy system designed to assist campers on departure. There is a sandy beach beside the quite fast-flowing, but fairly shallow, river (used for bathing) and a swimming pool and paddling pool with tiled surrounds for sunbathing. The old, original buildings house the reception, restaurant and bar. The terrace provides a stunning viewpoint. The 162 pitches (90 for touring) are steeply terraced and shaded. They have electricity connections (10A, long leads may be needed). Much up and down walking is required making this site unsuitable for those with walking difficulties.

Facilities

Two excellent toilet blocks (one can be heated) are very well equipped. There are some facilities which will certainly please the very young. Dishwashing and laundry sinks. Washing machine. Motorcaravan service point. Small shop (bread to order). Bar, restaurant and disco. Heated kidney shaped swimming pool and paddling pool. Adventure play area beside river. High season animation for children organised six days a week, and discos for 14-18 year olds held in cellar twice weekly (strictly no alcohol). Many activities and excursions are possible, arranged according to campers' motivations. Only gas and electric barbecues are allowed. Off site: Riding 15 km. Mountain biking, canoeing, canyoning, rifding and walking. A wonderful area for touring.

At a glance

Welcome & Ambience	✓✓✓✓	Location	✓✓✓✓
Quality of Pitches	✓✓✓✓	Range of Facilities	✓✓✓✓

Directions

From A7 take exit 15 (Valence Sud). Immediately after the péage turn right to Valence centre, then follow signs to Montélimar via the N7 for 7 km. Turn right towards Charmes sur Rhône, thence to Beauchastel. On leaving Beauchastel follow signs to Ollieres sur Eyrieux. In the village cross the river and follow campsite signs (3 km).

Charges 2004

Per unit incl. 2 persons and electricity	€ 18,00 - € 28,00
extra person over 4 yrs	€ 4,00 - € 7,00
animal	€ 2,00

Camping Cheques accepted.

Reservations

Made with deposit (€ 110) and fee (€ 20).
Tel: 04 75 66 21 53.
E-mail: plantas.ardeche@wanadoo.fr

Open

8 May - 18 September.

FR07020 Camping Caravaning L'Ardéchois

Le Chambon, Gluiras, 07190 St Sauveur-de-Montagut (Ardèche)

This attractive site is quite a way off the beaten track and the approach road is winding and narrow in places. However, it is worth the effort, to find in such a spectacular setting, a hillside site offering a wide range of amenities. There are 106 pitches (83 for touring) laid out on steep terraces, of varying sizes and many separated by trees and plants. Some are alongside the small, fast-flowing stream, while the rest (60%) are on higher, sloping ground nearer the restaurant/bar and pool. All 83 touring pitches have electricity (10A). The main site access roads are tarmac but are quite steep and larger units may find access to some terraces difficult. The amenities have been created by the careful conversion of old buildings which provide modern facilities in an attractive style (all from Easter). The friendly Dutch owners have developed an extensive excursion programme for exploring this attractive area on foot or by car. There are two entrances to the site so, on arrival, park outside on the road and go to reception on foot. A 'Sites et Paysages' member.

Facilities

Two good sanitary blocks provide washbasins in private cabins, baths and showers for babies and facilities for people with disabilities. Dishwashing and laundry rooms. Motorcaravan service point. Shop, bar/restaurant and takeaway (1/5-25/9). New restaurant planned. Swimming pool (heated in low season; no Bermuda style shorts; 1/5-25/9) with adjacent bar, snack bar and terrace, plus a paddling pool for children. TV room. Table tennis. Volleyball. Bicycle hire, archery and fishing. Comprehensive entertainment programme. Off site: Canyoning, climbing, river walking and canoeing trips organised.

Open

Easter - 31 October.

At a glance

Welcome & Ambience	✓✓✓✓	Location	✓✓✓
Quality of Pitches	✓✓✓✓	Range of Facilities	✓✓✓✓

Directions

From Valence take N86 south for 12 km. At La Voulte-sur-Rhône turn right onto D120 to St Sauveur de Montagut (site well signed), then take D102 towards Mézilhac for 8 km. to site.

Charges 2005

Per unit incl. 2 persons	€ 19,00 - € 25,50
extra person	€ 4,00 - € 5,50
child (0-3 yrs)	free
animal	€ 3,00 - € 4,00

Camping Cheques accepted.
Low season price for over 55s.

Reservations

Write with deposit (€ 69) and fee (€ 23); min. 10 days 6/7-24/8. Tel: 04 75 66 61 87.
E-mail: ardechois.camping@wanadoo.fr

FR07070 Camping Les Ranchisses

Route de Rocher, Chassiers, 07110 Largentière (Ardèche)

Combining farming, wine-making, running an Auberge and a friendly family campsite is no simple task, but the Chevalier family seem to manage it quite effortlessly. Well run and with the emphasis on personal attention, this is a highly recommended site. In a somewhat lesser known area of the Ardèche, the site has developed from an original 'camping à la ferme' into a very well equipped modern campsite. There are 165 good-sized, level, grassy pitches, 88 for tourists with electricity (10A) which include 42 multi-serviced pitches (electricity, water, waste water). The pitches are in two distinct areas - the original site which is well shaded, and the lower part which is more open with less shade, serviced by tarmac and gravel access roads. The site runs parallel to the road and there may be background traffic noise in some areas. There is a small lake (unfenced) connected to the river, providing opportunities for bathing, fishing or canoeing (free life jackets) with one part of the bathing area quite safe for youngsters. The site's own Auberge is set in the original 1824 building that once used to house silk worms. It serves meals and takeaway food at lunch-time and evenings (all season) either inside the cave-like restaurant or outside on the attractive, shaded terrace.

Facilities

Two modern, comprehensively equipped toilet buildings include washbasins in cubicles, dishwashing and laundry sinks and facilities for babies and disabled persons. It is an excellent provision, kept immaculate. Laundry in separate building. Motorcaravan service point. Small shop, takeaway and bar with terrace (all 10/4-19/9). Excellent pool complex with two large pools (both heated all season) and paddling pool. Adventure style playground. Organised amusements for children in high season. Tennis court. Minigolf. Table tennis. Boules. Canoeing. Off site: Canoe and kayaking arranged from the site each Monday and Wednesday (mid - June - end Aug). Medieval village of Largentière (1.5 km.) with Tuesday market and medieval festival in July. Take to the back roads to see the real Ardèche and don't miss the wonderful old villages of Balazuc and Labaume.

At a glance

Welcome & Ambience	✓✓✓✓	Location	✓✓✓✓
Quality of Pitches	✓✓✓✓	Range of Facilities	✓✓✓✓✓

Directions

Largentière is southwest of Aubenas and is best approached using the D104. After 16 km. just beyond Uzer at a roundabout turn northwest on the D5. After 5 km. at far end of Largentière, fork left downhill signed Valgorge. Site is on left in about 1.8 km.

Charges 2004

Per unit incl. 2 persons	€ 19,00 - € 25,00
serviced pitch	€ 25,50 - € 32,00
extra person	€ 4,50 - € 6,00
child (1-10 yrs)	€ 4,50 - € 6,00
electricity	€ 4,50

Camping Cheques accepted.

Reservations

Made with 30% deposit plus booking/insurance fee (€ 15). Tel: 04 75 88 31 97. E-mail: reception@lesranchisses.fr

Open

10 April - 19 September.

France

TRAVEL SERVICE SITE

TO BOOK CALL 0870 405 4055 OR www.alanrogersdirect.com

FR07120 Camping Nature Parc L'Ardéchois

Route touristique des Gorges, 07150 Vallon-Pont-d'Arc (Ardèche)

This very high quality, family run site is within walking distance of Vallon-Pont-d'Arc. It borders the River Ardèche and canoe trips are run, professionally, direct from the site. This site is ideal for families with younger children seeking an active holiday. The comprehensive facilities are of a very high standard, particularly the central toilet block. Of the 244 pitches, there are 197 for tourers, separated by trees and individual shrubs. All have electricity and 125 have full services. The focal point of the site is the bar and restaurant (good menus), with terrace and stage overlooking the attractive heated pool, large paddling pool and sunbathing terrace. There is a well thought out play area plus plenty of space for youngsters to play on the site and along the river. Activities are organised all season; these are family based – no discos. Patrols at night ensure a good night's sleep. Access to the site is easy and suitable for large outfits.

Facilities

Two well equipped toilet blocks, one superb with 'everything' working automatically. Facilities are of the highest standard, very clean and include good facilities for babies, those with disabilities, washing up and laundry. Four bathrooms to hire. Washing machines. Well stocked shop. Swimming pool and paddling pool (no Bermuda shorts). Football, volleyball, tennis and table tennis. Very good play area. Internet access. Organised activities, canoe trips. Only gas barbecues are permitted. Communal barbecue area. Off site: Canoeing, rafting, walking, riding, mountain biking, golf, rock climbing. Vallon-Pont-d'Arc 800 m.

At a glance

Welcome & Ambience	✓✓✓✓✓	Location	✓✓✓✓
Quality of Pitches	✓✓✓✓	Range of Facilities	✓✓✓✓✓

Directions

From Vallon-Pont-d'Arc (western end of the Ardèche Gorge) at a roundabout go east on the D290. Site entrance is shortly on the right.

Charges 2004

Per pitch incl. 2 persons	€ 23,00 - € 35,00
140 sq.m. pitch with water/drain	€ 29,00 - € 42,50
extra person	€ 5,20 - € 7,50
electricity	€ 4,20

Reservations

Made with deposit (€ 95) and fee (€ 35).
Tel: 04 75 88 06 63. E-mail: ardecamp@bigfoot.com

Open

Easter - 30 September.

FR07150 Camping Domaine de Gil

Route de Vals-les-Bains, Ucel, 07200 Aubenas (Ardèche)

This very attractive and well organised, smaller site in a less busy part of the Ardèche should appeal to couples and families with younger children. The 80, good sized, level pitches (43 touring) are surrounded by a variety of trees offering plenty of shade. All have 5A electricity. The focal point of the site is formed by the very attractive swimming pool, paddling pool and large sunbathing area, with the bar, restaurant and well appointed children's play areas all adjacent. A spacious sports area and shady picnic/play area are alongside the river Ardèche - an ideal spot to cool off on a hot day. You will receive a warm welcome from the enthusiastic and friendly, new Dutch owners (who speak excellent English).

Facilities

All the excellent facilities are in a single, cheerful, modern block adjacent to the pool. Most washbasins are in cabins. Plenty of dishwashing and laundry sinks plus a washing machine and iron. Motorcaravan service point. Small shop for basics. Bar/restaurant and takeaway (from June). Swimming pool and paddling pool, heated all season (proper trunks only). Two play areas. Volleyball, boules, minigolf, football, tennis court. Canoeing, boating and fishing in the river. Some activities in high season. In July/Aug. charcoal barbecues not permitted. Off site: Shops, etc. at Vals-les-Bain 1.5 km. Organised canoe trips and canyoning on the river Ardèche. Bicycle hire, riding 4 km.

At a glance

Welcome & Ambience	✓✓✓✓✓	Location	✓✓✓✓
Quality of Pitches	✓✓✓✓	Range of Facilities	✓✓✓✓

Directions

Site is just north of Aubenas at Ucel. From southeast on N102, just after a tunnel, turn right at roundabout (Privas) into Pont d'Ucel. At roundabout, take last exit (Ucel). Shortly turn left (narrow road, Ucel D18) and then right (Ucel D578B). Site is about 2 km on the left.

Charges 2004

Per unit incl. 2 persons	€ 13,00 - € 22,50
extra person	€ 3,20 - € 5,50
electricity	€ 3,60

Reservations

Made with deposit (€ 120) and fee (€ 15).
Tel: 04 75 94 63 63. E-mail: raf.garcia@wanadoo.fr

Open

15 April - 15 September.

FR26030 Sunêlia Le Grand Lierne

B.P. 8, 26120 Chabeuil (Drôme)

In addition to its obvious attraction as an overnight stop, fairly convenient for the A7 autoroute, this site provides a pleasant base to explore this little known area between the Ardèche and the Vercors mountains and the Côte du Rhône wine area. It has 161 marked, stony pitches, 76 for touring units, mainly separated by developing hedges or oak trees. Many have good shade, some are on flat ground and all have electricity (6/10A). A more open area exists for those who prefer less shade and a view of the mountains, but this area contains many mobile homes. English and Dutch are spoken. Used by tour operators (30%).

Facilities

Two sanitary blocks include washbasins in cabins, facilities for disabled people and a small WC for children. Washing machines (powder provided), dryers and lines by the blocks. Motorcaravan services. Shop/restaurant and terrace (20/5-31/8). Bar/takeaway (all season). Fridge rental. Excellent pool complex with three pools, one very small open all season and covered and heated in low season (other pools 15/5-31/8; no Bermuda shorts). Paddling pool and 50 m. water slide. Playgrounds. Mini-tennis, minigolf, table tennis, volleyball, archery and football field. Bicycle hire. Library. Extensive entertainment programme, including excursions (from end-May). Only gas and electric barbecues are permitted. Dogs and other pets are not accepted in high season (3/7-21/8). Caravan storage. Off site: Golf 3 km. Bicycle hire 4.5 km. Fishing 5 km. Riding 7 km. Canoe/kayak near. Vercors mountains. Chabeuil 5 km.

At a glance

Welcome & Ambience	✓✓✓	Location	✓✓✓
Quality of Pitches	✓✓✓	Range of Facilities	✓✓✓

Directions

Site signed in Chabeuil about 11 km. east of Valence (18 km. from autoroute). It is best to approach Chabeuil from the south side of Valence via the Valence ring road, thence onto the D68 to Chabeuil itself. Site is off the D125 to Charpey, 5 km. from Chabeuil, but well signed.

Charges 2004

Per unit incl. 2 adults	€ 16,00 - € 27,80
extra person	€ 6,60 - € 7,80
child (2-7 yrs)	€ 3,40 - € 5,60
electricity (6/10A)	€ 4,00 - € 5,50
animal	€ 4,00

Camping Cheques accepted.

Reservations

Accepted with 25% deposit and fee (€ 30).
Tel: 04 75 59 83 14. E-mail: contact@grandlierne.com

Open

23 April - 12 September, with all services.

FR84020 Domaine Naturiste de Bélézy

84410 Bédoin (Vaucluse)

At the foot of Mt Ventoux, Bélézy is an excellent naturist site with many amenities and activities and the ambience is essentially relaxed and comfortable. The site has two areas joined by a short pedestrian tunnel and the 238 marked and numbered pitches are set amongst many varieties of trees and shrubs. Electricity points (12A) are plentiful but you may need a long cable in places. The emphasis is on informality and concern for the environment and during high season cars are banned from the camping area to the supervised parking areas nearby. So far as naturism is concerned, the emphasis is on personal choice (and weather conditions!), the only stipulation being the requirement for complete nudity in the pools and pool area. The leisure park side of the site is an area of natural parkland with an orchard, fishpond and woodland, with a good range of sports facilities including tennis courts and swimming pools. The largest pool is for swimming and relaxation, the smaller pool (heated 25/3-30/9) is also used for watersports and aquarobics. Near the pool area is the smart restaurant, with terrace, and the mellow old Mas (Provencal farmhouse) that houses many of the activities and amenities. There is a hydrotherapy centre to tone up and revitalise with qualified diagnosis. Member 'France 4 Naturisme'.

Facilities

Sanitary blocks are a little different. The newer ones are of a standard type and excellent quality, with free hot showers in cubicles with separators, and washbasins in cabins. One block, refurbished in 2003, has heating in low season. Another has an attractive children's section. In the same area the adult block has hot showers in the open air, separated by natural stone dividers and washing up areas again mostly in the open. Shop (1/4-30/9). Restaurant provides excellent food, waiter service, and takeaway meals at affordable prices. Three swimming pools. Sauna. Two tennis courts. Boules and table tennis. Adventure play area. Activities include painting and pottery courses and language lessons (not in July/Aug). Archery. Music (bring your own instrument). Guided walks. Children's clubs in holiday periods. Library and information centre. Disco. Hydrotherapy centre (1/4-30/9) - treatments include steam baths, massage and seaweed packs, osteopathy, Chinese medicine (including acupuncture) and Bach therapies. Barbecues are prohibited but there is a central barbecue area. Dogs and pets are not accepted.

At a glance

Welcome & Ambience	✓✓✓✓	Location	✓✓✓✓
Quality of Pitches	✓✓✓✓	Range of Facilities	✓✓✓✓✓

Directions

From A7 autoroute or RN7 at Orange, take D950 southeast to Carpentras, then northeast via D974 to Bédoin. Site is signed in Bédoin, being about 1.5 km. northeast of the village

Charges 2005

Per unit incl. 1 adult	€ 13,00 - € 25,00
incl. 2 adults	€ 18,50 - € 31,50
incl. 3 adults	€ 24,50 - € 39,00
extra adult	€ 5,50 - € 10,50
child (3-8 yrs)	€ 4,00 - € 7,50
electricity (12A)	€ 4,20

Camping Cheques accepted.
Various offers and reductions outside high season.

Reservations

Write with deposit (25%) and fee (€ 30).
Tel: 04 90 65 60 18. E-mail: info@belezy.com

Open

21 March - 2 October.

FR04020 Castel Camping Le Camp du Verdon

Domaine du Verdon, 04120 Castellane (Alpes-de Haute-Provence)

Close to the 'Route des Alpes' and the Gorges du Verdon, this is a very popular holiday area, the gorge, canoeing and rafting being the main attractions, ideal for active families. Two heated swimming pools and numerous on-site activities during high season help to keep non-canoeists here. Du Verdon is a large level site, part meadow, part wooded, with 500 partly shaded, rather stony pitches (350 for tourists). Numbered and separated by bushes, they vary in size, have 6A electricity, and 120 also have water and waste water. They are mostly separate from the mobile homes (63) and pitches used by tour operators (110). Some overlook the unfenced river Verdon, so watch the children. One can walk to Castellane without using the main road. Dances and discos in July and August suit all age groups - the latest finishing time is around 11 pm. (after that time patrols make sure that the site is quiet). The site is popular and very busy in July and August.

Facilities

The toilet blocks have been refurbished with British style WCs and up-to-date equipment. One block has facilities for disabled visitors. Washing machines and irons. Motorcaravan service and car wash points. Popular restaurant with terrace and bar including room with log fire for cooler evenings. Large well stocked shop. Pizzeria/crêperie. Takeaway (open twice daily). Two heated swimming pools and new paddling pool with 'mushroom' style fountain (all open all season). Entertainers provide games and competitions for all (July and August). Playgrounds. Minigolf, table tennis, archery, basketball and volleyball. Organised walks. Bicycle hire. Riding. Small fishing lake. ATM. Off site: Castellane and the Verdon Gorge 1 km. Riding 2 km. Boat launching 4.5 km. Golf 20 km. River Verdon and many water sports.

At a glance

Welcome & Ambience	✓✓✓	Location	✓✓✓✓✓
Quality of Pitches	✓✓✓✓	Range of Facilities	✓✓✓✓

Directions

From Castellane take D952 westwards towards Gorges du Verdon and Moustiers. Site is 1 km. on left.

Charges 2004

Per unit with up to 4 persons	€ 15,00 - € 26,00
with 6A electricity	€ 19,00 - € 30,00
dog	€ 2,50

Camping Cheques accepted.

Reservations

Made for any length with deposit (€ 80 - € 110 depending on pitch) and fee (€ 20). Tel: 04 92 83 61 29. E-mail: contact@camp-du-verdon.com

Open

15 May - 15 September.

FR04100 Camping International

Route Napoleon, 04120 Castellane (Alpes-de Haute-Provence)

Camping International has very friendly, English speaking owners and is a reasonably priced, less commercialised site situated in some of the most dramatic scenery in France with good views. The 250 pitches, 130 good sized ones for touring, are clearly marked, separated by trees and small hedges, and all have electricity and water. The bar/restaurant overlooks the swimming pool with its sunbathing area set in a sunny location, and all have fantastic views. In high season English speaking young people entertain children (3-8 years) and teenagers. On some evenings the teenagers are taken to the woods for campfire 'sing-alongs' which can go on till the early hours without disturbing the rest of the site. There are guided walks into the surrounding hills in the nearby Gorges du Verdon – a very popular excursion, particularly in high season. The weather in the hills here is very pleasant without the excessive heat of the coast. Access is good for larger units.

Facilities

Several small toilet blocks are of an older design with small cubicles and, although they are quite basic, the showers are fully controllable (these blocks are due to be replaced soon). One newer block has modern facilities, including those for disabled visitors, but this is not open early and late in the season. Washing machines, dryer and irons and a baby room. Chemical disposal at motorcaravan service point. Fridge hire. Shop. Restaurant/takeaway. Swimming pool (all 1/5-30/9). Club/TV room. Children's animation and occasional evening entertainment in July/Aug. Children's play area. Volleyball, football and boules pitches. Internet access. Off site: Riding 800 m. Castellane (1.5 km) is a very attractive little town with a superb river, canyon and rapids, ideal for canoeing, rafting and canyoning etc. Good area for walking and biking. Boat launching 5 km.

At a glance

Welcome & Ambience	✓✓✓✓	Location	✓✓✓✓
Quality of Pitches	✓✓✓✓	Range of Facilities	✓✓✓✓

Directions

Site is 1 km. north of Castellane on the N85 Route Napoleon.

Charges 2004

Per unit incl. 2 persons	€ 12,00 - € 19,00
extra person	€ 3,00 - € 4,00
electricity (6A)	€ 3,00 - € 4,00
dog	€ 2,00

Camping Cheques accepted.

Reservations

Necessary for July/Aug. and made with deposit (€ 45), no booking fee. Tel: 04 92 83 66 67. E-mail: info@campinginternational.fr

Open

1 April - 30 September.

FR04080 Camping Caravaning L'Etoile des Neiges

04140 Montclar (Alpes-de Haute-Provence)

This attractive, family run site near the mountain village and ski resort of St Jean Montclar is open most of the year so is suitable for both summer and winter holidays. This beautiful alpine region offers all the usual alpine activities. Being at an altitude of 1,300 m. the nights can get quite cold even in summer. The 121 shady pitches, with 80 for touring, are laid out in terraces and separated by small shrubs and alpine trees. All pitches are close to electricity and water points. An attractive bar and restaurant overlooks the two swimming pools, with the shallow pool having a water slide ideal for children. The site has no shop as the local shops are only a few minutes walk away. Although situated in the southern high Alps, the site can be reached without climbing any stiff gradients. A 'Sites et Paysages' member.

Facilities

The central toilet block, heated in winter, includes washbasins in cabins. Separate room containing facilities for disabled visitors. Two washing machines. Motorcaravan service point. Bar/restaurant (mid June - Sept). Swimming pool (from 1 June). Tennis, table tennis and boules. Two play areas. Rafting and walking organised in July/Aug.
Off site: Shops in village a few minutes walk. Bicycle hire and riding in village. Fishing 1.5 km. Watersports and beach at Lac Serre Ponçon 7 km.

Open

1 January - 30 September and 22-31 December.

At a glance

Welcome & Ambience	✓✓✓✓✓	Location	✓✓✓✓
Quality of Pitches	✓✓✓✓	Range of Facilities	✓✓✓✓

Directions

Site is 35 km. south of Gap via the D900B. Beyond Serre Ponçon, turn right onto D900 signed Selonnet and St Jean Montclar. On entering St Jean Montclar turn left, go past chalets and shops and fork right to the campsite on the left. The roads (at 1,300 m.) are steep and can be snowy and icy in winter.

Charges 2005

Per unit incl. 2 persons	€ 12,50 - € 21,00
extra adult	€ 4,00 - € 5,00
electricity (6A)	€ 3,00 - € 4,00

Camping Cheques accepted.

Reservations

Advised for July/Aug. Deposit of 30% plus € 15 fee.
Tel: 04 92 35 01 29.
E-mail: contact@etoile-des-neiges.com

FR04010 Sunêlia Hippocampe

Route de Napoléon, 04290 Volonne (Alpes-de Haute-Provence)

Hippocampe is a friendly, 'all action' lakeside site situated in a beautiful area of France. The perfumes of thyme, lavender and wild herbs are everywhere and the higher hills of Haute Provence are not too far away. There are 447 level, numbered pitches (243 for touring units), medium to very large (130 sq.m) in size. All have electricity (10A) and 220 have water and drainage, most are separated by bushes and cherry trees. Some of the best pitches border the lake. The restaurant, bar, takeaway and shop have all been completely renewed (2004). This is a family run site with families in mind, with games, competitions, aerobics, entertainment and shows, plus a daily club for younger family members in July/August. A soundproof underground disco is set well away from the pitches and is very popular with teenage customers. Staff tour the site at night ensuring a good night's sleep. The site is, however, much quieter in low season and, with its good discounts, is the time for those who do not want or need entertaining. The Gorges du Verdon is a sight not to be missed and rafting, paragliding or canoe trips can be booked from the site's own tourist information office. Being on the lower slopes of the hills of Haute-Provence, the surrounding area is good for walking and mountain biking. This is a very good site for an active or restful holiday and is suitable for outfits of all sizes. Used by tour operators (20 pitches). English is spoken.

Facilities

Toilet blocks vary from old to modern, all with good facilities that include washbasins in cabins. They are very clean. Washing machines. Motorcaravan service point. Fridge rental. Bread available from reception (from 28/4), shop (26/6-3/9). Bar (1/5-12/9). Restaurant, pizzeria and barbecue chicken shop (all 15/5-12/9). Large, attractive pool complex (from 1/5-30/9) with two pools of differing sizes and depths, heated in early and late seasons. Tennis (free outside 3/7- 21/8). Fishing, canoeing, boules. Large selection of sports facilities to choose from, some with free instruction, including archery (high season). Charcoal barbecues are not permitted. Off site: Bicycle hire 2 km. Riding 6 km. Village of Volonne 600 m. Rafting, canoeing, canyoning, torrent walking, mountain biking, paragliding and hang gliding.

At a glance

Welcome & Ambience	✓✓✓✓✓	Location	✓✓✓✓
Quality of Pitches	✓✓✓✓✓	Range of Facilities	✓✓✓✓✓

Directions

Approaching from the north turn off N85 across river bridge to Volonne, then right to site. From the south right on D4, 1 km. before Château Arnoux.

Charges 2004

Per simple pitch incl. 2 persons	€ 12,00 - € 26,00
with electricity	€ 15,00 - € 31,00
with water/drainage 100 sq.m.	€ 15,00 - € 33,00
with water/drainage 140 sq.m.	€ 19,00 - € 38,00
extra person (over 4 yrs)	€ 2,50 - € 6,00

Camping Cheques accepted.

Reservations

Made with deposit (varies with size of pitch from € 50 - € 95) and booking fee (€ 25). Tel: 04 92 33 50 00. E-mail: camping@l-hippocampe.com

Open

1 April - 30 September.

France

TRAVEL SERVICE SITE

TO BOOK CALL 0870 405 4055 OR www.alanrogersdirect.com

FR32010 Le Camp de Florence

Route Astaffort, 32480 La Romieu (Gers)

Camp de Florence is an attractive site on the edge of an historic village in pleasantly undulating Gers countryside. It is run by the Mynsbergen family who are Dutch (although Susan is English) and they have sympathetically converted the old farmhouse buildings to provide facilities for the site. The 183 pitches (95 for tourers) are all over 100 sq.m. plus. Terraced where necessary, all have electricity, 10 with hard-standing and 25 fully serviced. They are arranged around a large field (full of sunflowers when we visited) with rural views, giving a feeling of spaciousness. The 13th century village of La Romieu is on the Santiago de Compostela pilgrim route and the collegiate church, visible from the site, is well worth a visit (the views are magnificent from the top of the tower), as is the local arboretum, the biggest collection of trees in the Midi-Pyrénées. The Pyrénées are a two hour drive, the Atlantic coast a similar distance. There are 20 tour operator pitches.

Facilities

Two unisex toilet blocks include some washbasins in cabins. Washing machine and dryer. Motorcaravan services. Water points are limited. Good upstairs, air-conditioned restaurant, open to the public as well as campers, serves a range of food, including local specialities and an à la carte menu (1/5-30/9, closed Weds, with a barbecue instead). Takeaway. Bread on site in season. Swimming pool area with jacuzzi, central island and protected children's pool (all open to the public in the afternoons). Adventure play area, games area and pets area. Games room, tennis, table tennis, volleyball and petanque. Bicycle hire. Video shows, discos, picnics, animation and musical evenings and excursions organised. Internet access.

Open

1 April - 10 October.

At a glance

Welcome & Ambience	✓✓✓✓✓	Location	✓✓✓✓
Quality of Pitches	✓✓✓✓	Range of Facilities	✓✓✓✓✓

Directions

Site is signed from D931 Agen - Condom road. Small units can turn left at Ligardes (signed) and follow D36 for 1 km. and take right turn for La Romieu (signed). Otherwise continue until outskirts of Condom and take D41 left to La Romieu and pass through village to site.

Charges 2004

Per unit incl. 2 persons and electricity	€ 13,50 - € 27,50
extra person	€ 3,50 - € 6,50
child (4-9 yrs)	€ 2,60 - € 4,50
water and drainage	free - € 3,00
dog (max 2)	€ 1,50 - € 2,00

Camping Cheques accepted.
Special prices for groups, rallies, etc.

Reservations

Write or phone for information (English spoken).
Tel: 05 62 28 15 58.
E-mail: info@campdeflorence.com

FR09020 Camping L'Arize

Lieu-dit Bourtol, 09240 La Bastide-de-Sérou (Ariège)

You will receive a warm welcome from Dominique and Brigitte at this friendly little family site and Brigitte speaks excellent English. The site sits in a delightful, tranquil valley among the foothills of the Pyrénées and is just east of the interesting village of La Bastide de Sérou beside the River Arize (good trout fishing). The river is fenced for the safety of children on the site, but may be accessed just outside the gate. Deer and wild boar are common in this area and may be sighted in quieter periods. The owners have built this site from ground level over the last few years and have put much love and care into its development. The 70 large pitches are neatly laid out on level grass within the spacious site. All have 3/6A electricity (French type sockets) and are separated into bays by hedges and young trees. Discounts have been negotiated for several of the local attractions (details are provided in the comprehensive pack provided on arrival - in your own language). This is a comfortable and relaxing base for touring this beautiful part of the Pyrénées with easy access to the medieval town of Foix and even Andorra for duty-free shopping.

Facilities

The central sanitary block (unheated) includes washbasins in cabins and good facilities for babies and disabled people. Laundry room with dryer. Dishwashing under cover. Chemical disposal (into a large holding tank - the organic sewage system is incompatible with chemicals). Small swimming pool with paved sunbathing area. Entertainment in high season, weekly barbecues and welcome drinks on Sundays. Fishing, riding and bicycle hire on site.
Off site: Golf 5 km. Several restaurants and shops are within a few minute's drive and the nearest restaurant, which is located at the national stud for the famous Merens horses just 200 m. away, will deliver takeaway meals to your pitch.

At a glance

Welcome & Ambience	✓✓✓✓✓	Location	✓✓✓✓✓
Quality of Pitches	✓✓✓✓	Range of Facilities	✓✓✓✓

Directions

Site is southeast of the village La Bastide-de-Sérou. Take the D15 towards Nescus and site is on right after approx. 1 km.

Charges 2005

Per pitch incl. 2 persons and electricity	€ 15,20 - € 22,60
extra adult	€ 4,00 - € 5,20
child (0-7 yrs)	€ 3,00 - € 3,60
dog	free - € 1,50

Discounts for longer stays in mid and low season.

Reservations

Made with 25% deposit and fee (€ 10).
Tel: 05 61 65 81 51. E-mail: camparize@aol.com

Open

28 March - 4 November.

FR65060 Castel Camping Pyrénées Natura

Route du Lac, 65400 Estaing (Haute-Pyrénées)

Pyrénées Natura, at an altitude of 1,000 metres, on the edge of the National Park. is the perfect site for lovers of nature. Eagles and vultures soar above the site and a small open air observatory with seats and binoculars is provided. The Ruysschaert family's aim is that you go home from a holiday here feeling at peace with the world, having hopefully learned something about the flora and fauna of the High Pyrénées. Groups are taken walking in the mountains to see the varied flora and fauna (there are even a few bears but they are seen very rarely). The 60 pitches, all with electricity, are in a large, level, open and sunny field. Around 75 varieties of trees and shrubs have been planted – not too many to spoil the view though, which can only be described as fantastic. The reception and bar are in a traditional style stone building with tiled floors and an open staircase. The small shop in the old water mill is quite unique. Stocking a variety of produce, including wine, it is left unmanned and open all day and you pay at reception - very trusting, but they have not been let down yet. The last weekend in May is when the local shepherds take their flocks up to the high pastures. Campers help by walking up with them and then helping to separate the different flocks. Returning to the site by bus, with a good old sing-song with the shepherds, the site provides food for everyone. That sounds like a trip worth making.

Facilities

First class toilet facilities with high quality fittings include a cubicle for children, full facilities for disabled visitors and, in the same large room, baby bath, shower and changing mat. Dishwashing and laundry sinks. Washing machine and airers (no lines allowed). Motorcaravan service point. Small shop. Small takeaway (15/5-15/9). Small bar (15/5-15/9) and lounge area. Lounge, library and TV (mainly used for videos of the National Park). Sauna and solarium. Auditorium. Play area for the very young. Table tennis, boule and giant chess. Weekly evening meal in May, June and Sept.
Off site: Village has two restaurants.

Open

1 May - 20 September.

At a glance

Welcome & Ambience	✓✓✓✓✓	Location	✓✓✓✓✓
Quality of Pitches	✓✓✓✓✓	Range of Facilities	✓✓✓✓

Directions

From Lourdes take N21 to Argelès-Gazost. At roundabout at Argelès, take D918 signed Aucun, turning left after 8 km. on D13 to Bun. After Bun cross the river and right on D103 to site (5.5 km). Some parts are narrow but with passing places.

Charges 2005

Per unit incl. 2 persons and electricity (3A)	€ 14,50 - € 22,00
extra person	€ 4,00
child (under 8 yrs)	€ 2,50

Less in low season.

Reservations

Made with deposit (€55). Tel: 05 62 97 45 44.
E-mail: info@camping-pyrenees-natura.com

FR65080 Camping Le Lavedan

Lau-Balagnas, 65400 Argelès-Gazost (Haute-Pyrénées)

Reasonably priced, Camping du Lavedan is an old established and very French site set in the Argelès Gazost valley south of the Lourdes. It is beside the road so there is some daytime road noise. The 105 touring pitches are set on grass with some shade. All have electricity, water and waste water point. The area is fine for walking, biking, rafting and of course in winter, skiing. There is a pool which can be covered in inclement weather and a twice weekly event is organised in July/Aug and weekly in June.

Facilities

The toilet block, though quite old with some Turkish style toilets and also bidets, has recently been refurbished. Showers are quite small, but some washbasins are in cabins. Baby shower and bath. Facilities for disabled visitors. Washing machines and dryer in separate small block which is heated in winter. Restaurant/takeaway (1/5-15/9). Bar (all year). No shop but bread delivery daily (1/5-15/9). Swimming pool (with cover), paddling pool and sunbeds. Good play area. Off site: Fishing or bicycle hire 1 km. Supermarket or rafting 2 km. Riding 5 km. Golf 15 km.

Open

All year.

At a glance

Welcome & Ambience	✓✓✓✓	Location	✓✓✓
Quality of Pitches	✓✓✓	Range of Facilities	✓✓✓✓

Directions

Site is on the right side of the N21 (Lourdes - Cauterets), south of Argelès and just past the village of Lau Balagnas, which is 15 km. south of Lourdes.

Charges 2004

Per unit incl. 2 persons	€ 13,00 - € 17,00
incl. 3 persons	€ 17,00 - € 20,00
extra person	€ 4,50 - € 5,50
child (under 7 yrs)	€ 3,50 - € 4,00
electricity (2-6A)	€ 2,00 - € 6,00
dog	€ 2,00

Camping Cheques accepted.

Reservations

Contact site. Tel: 05 62 97 18 84.
E-mail: contact@lavedan.com

FR65090 Camping Soleil du Pibeste

16 Avenue du Lavedan, 65400 Agos Vidalos (Haute-Pyrénées)

Soleil du Pibeste is a quiet rural site with well tended grass and flower beds. It has 23 mobile homes to rent and 67 pitches for tourers. All pitches have electricity (3-15A) and there is some shade. The Dusserm family welcomes all arrivals with a drink and are clearly determined to ensure you have a good stay. They are particularly keen on developing eco-toursim in the Pyrenees. At times some domestic matters could perhaps have a little more attention. It is a perfect site for the active as many activities are organised from the site - from gentle ones like painting and Chinese dancing to walking, rafting, parasailing, climbing, riding and of course in the winter skiing. There is no shop but the supermarket is only 5 km. and bread is delivered. The swimming pool is on a terrace above the pitches with sunbeds, a paddling pool and waterfall and the most magnificent view of the mountains. The same wonderful view can be enjoyed whilst doing the washing up. A new by-pass should eliminate most of the road noise.

Facilities

Two heated toilet blocks have washbasins in cabins and large showers. Cleaning can be variable. Baby room. Facilities for disabled visitors (key). Washing machine and dryer. Motorcaravan services. Bar serving snacks with piano and internet access. Room for cards or reading. Swimming and paddling pools. Small play area. Boule, archery, basketball and volleyball. Table tennis. Bicycle hire. Off site: Fishing 800 m. Golf 10 km. Rafting 2 km. Skiing 2 km.

Open

All year.

At a glance

Welcome & Ambience	✓✓✓✓✓	Location	✓✓✓✓
Quality of Pitches	✓✓✓	Range of Facilities	✓✓✓✓

Directions

Agos Vidalos is on the N21, 5 km. south of Lourdes. Leave express-way at second exit, signed Agos Vidalos and continue to site on the right in a short distance.

Charges 2004

Per unit incl. 2 persons and 3A electricity	€ 15,00 - € 19,00
extra person	€ 3,00 - € 4,00
6A electricity	€ 3,00

Reservations

Made with 25% deposit and €26 fee.
Tel: 05 62 97 53 23.
E-mail: info@campingpibeste.com

FR81060 Camping Les Clots

81190 Mirandol-Bourgnounac (Tarn)

Les Clots is a very rural, simple site in the heart of the countryside with 48 touring pitches and 15 used for chalets and caravans for rent. The 2.5 km. road from the nearest village of Mirandol is quite narrow but if you make sure that you arrive after 1 pm there should be no problem. Set around an old farmhouse, the outbuildings have been sympathetically converted into reception, the toilet facilities and a laundry room, all giving the site lots of character. The site has been carved out of a steep hillside giving variously sized terraces taking from 1 to 10 units. Nearly all pitches have electricity (6A). A few pitches, mainly for tents, are set well away the others giving lots of seclusion. Being amongst the trees there is some sunshine in places. A quiet site with no entertainment at all – the noisiest things we heard were the owls. A river borders the site but it is quite a long walk down the hillside to it.

Facilities

Toilet blocks are quite basic but have everything needed and are kept very clean. Baby bath. Facilities for disabled visitors. Washing machines. Bar (July/Aug). Shop with basic provisions incl. bread (July/Aug). Simple swimming and paddling pools (1/7-30/9). Table tennis. Minigolf. In July/Aug an evening meal is prepared (to order). Fishing. Leaflets for walks in the area. Site is not suitable for American style motorhomes. Off site: Riding 15 km.

Open

1 May - 1 October.

At a glance

Welcome & Ambience	✓✓✓✓	Location	✓✓✓✓
Quality of Pitches	✓✓✓✓	Range of Facilities	✓✓✓

Directions

Heading south on N88 from Rodez, take D911 at Baraqueville towards Villefranche. In 19 km. at Rieupeyrove take D905 south to La Salvetat, then on to Mirandol (approx. 22 km). On the outskirts of Mirandol, site is signed to the right.

Charges 2004

Per unit incl. 3 persons	€ 19,00
child (under 8 yrs)	€ 2,80
electricity (6A)	€ 2,70

Low season reductions.

Reservations

Contact site. Tel: 05 63 76 92 78.
E-mail: campclots@wanadoo.fr

FR11060 Yelloh! Village Domaine d'Arnauteille

11250 Montclar (Aude)

Enjoying some beautiful and varied views, this rather unusual site is ideally situated for exploring, by foot or car, the little known Aude Département, the area of the Cathars and for visiting the walled city of Carcassonne (10 minutes drive). However, access could be difficult for large, twin axle vans. The site itself is set in 115 hectares of farmland and is on hilly ground with the original pitches on gently sloping, lightly wooded land and newer ones of good size with water, drainage and electricity (5/10A), semi-terraced and partly hedged. The facilities are quite spread out with the swimming pool set in a hollow basin surrounded by green fields and some newly developed pitches. The reception building is vast; originally a farm building, with a newer top floor being converted to apartments. This is a developing site with enthusiastic owners. Some up and down walking between the pitches and facilities is unavoidable. A 'Sites et Paysages' member.

Facilities

The main, heated sanitary block is now a distinctive feature, rebuilt to a very high specification with a Roman theme. Three other smaller blocks (one rebuilt) are located at various points. They include washbasins in cabins, dishwashing under cover (hot water), laundry, facilities for disabled people and a baby bath. Motorcaravan service point and gas. Small shop (15/5-30/9 - the site is a little out of the way). Restaurant in converted stable block offers plat du jour, grills, takeaway (15/5-30/9). Swimming pool (25 x 10 m.) with children's pool. Games court. Boules. Play area. Table tennis and volleyball. Riding (1/7-31/8). Day trips organised. Off site: Fishing 3 km. Bicycle hire 8 km. Golf 10 km. Rafting and canoeing near, plus many walks with marked paths.

At a glance

Welcome & Ambience	✓✓✓✓✓	Location	✓✓✓✓
Quality of Pitches	✓✓✓✓	Range of Facilities	✓✓✓✓✓

Directions

Using D118 from Carcassonne, after bypassing the small village of Rouffiac d'Aude, there is a small section of dual carriageway. Before the end of this, turn right to Montclar up a rather narrow road (with passing places) for 2.5 km. Site is signed very sharp left and up hill before the village.

Charges 2005

Per pitch incl. 2 persons	€ 13,50 - € 25,00
with 6A electricity	€ 17,00 - € 29,00
electricity, water and drainage	€ 20,00 - € 33,00
extra person	€ 4,00 - € 6,80

Camping Cheques accepted.

Reservations

Made with deposit (25%) and fee (€ 23).
Tel: 04 68 26 84 53. E-mail: Arnauteille@mnet.fr

Open

1 April - 30 September.

FR11070 Camping Les Mimosas

Chaussée de Mandirac, 11100 Narbonne (Aude)

Being some six kilometres inland from the beaches of Narbonne and Gruissan, this site benefits from a somewhat less hectic situation than others in the popular seaside environs of Narbonne. The site itself is, however, quite lively with plenty to amuse and entertain the younger generation while, at the same time, offering facilities for the whole family. A purchase of a club card is required in July/Aug. to use the children's club, gym, sauna, tennis, minigolf, billiards etc. (€ 26 per family for your entire stay). A very large, purpose built entertainment centre is under construction. The 150 pitches are mainly of good size, most with electricity (6A), including a few 'grand confort', and they benefit from a reasonable amount of shade, mostly from 2 m. high hedges. This could be a very useful site offering many possibilities to meet a variety of needs, on-site entertainment (including an evening on Cathare history), and easy access to popular beaches, interesting towns such as Narbonne itself, Béziers or the 'Cité de Carcassonne', the Canal du Midi and Cathare castles.

Facilities

Four sanitary buildings, all refurbished to high standards, include washbasins in cabins, some British WCs, baby baths, laundry and dishwashing sinks, and washing machines. Shop (1/4-31/10). Bar. Small lounge, amusements. Auberge with takeaway (1/4-30/9). Heated pool complex including new, landscaped pool with slides and islands, the original pool and a children's pool (open 1/5-31/8 when weather is suitable). Adventure play area. Minigolf. Mountain bike hire. Off site: Riding near. Windsurfing/sailing school 300 m. Gruissan's beach 10 minutes by car. Lagoon for boating and fishing can be reached via footpath (about 200 m).

Open

24 March - 31 October.

At a glance

Welcome & Ambience	✓✓✓✓	Location	✓✓✓✓
Quality of Pitches	✓✓✓✓	Range of Facilities	✓✓✓✓✓

Directions

From A9 take exit 38 (Narbonne Sud) and go round roundabout to last exit taking you back over the autoroute (site signed from here). Follow signs to La Nautique and then Mandirac and site (total 6 km. from autoroute). Also signed from Narbonne centre.

Charges 2004

Per basic pitch incl. 1 or 2 persons	€ 12,70 - € 19,00
pitch with electricity	€ 15,50 - € 24,00
with electricity, water and waste water	€ 20,00 - € 28,00
extra person	€ 3,70 - € 5,10
child (2-7 yrs)	€ 2,15 - € 3,30
animal	€ 1,45 - € 2,40

Camping Cheques accepted.

Reservations

Made with deposit (€ 100) and fee (€ 22).
Tel: 04 68 49 03 72. E-mail: info@lesmimosas.com

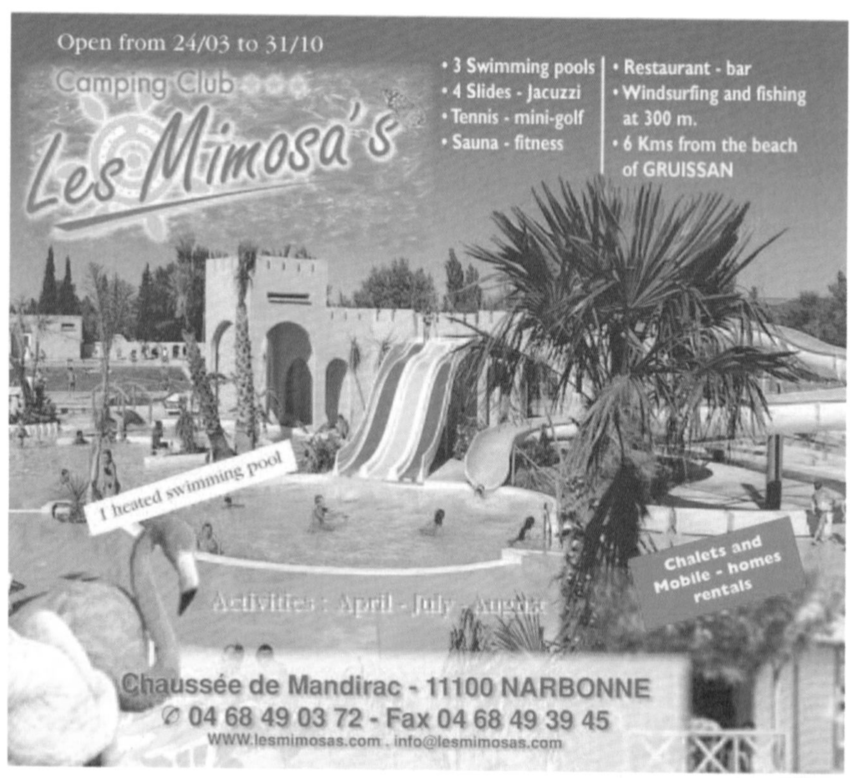

FR11080 Camping La Nautique

La Nautique, 11100 Narbonne (Aude)

This extremely spacious site is situated on the Etang de Bages, where flat water combined with strong winds make it one of the best windsurfing areas in France and is owned and run by a very welcoming Dutch family. The site is fenced off from the water for the protection of children and windsurfers can have a key for the gate (with deposit) that leads to launching points on the lake. La Nautique has 390 huge, level pitches (a small one is 130 sq.m), including a good number used for site owned mobile homes and chalets and 30 tour operator pitches. There are also six or seven overnight pitches with electricity in a separate area. The wide range of evergreens, flowering shrubs and trees on site give a pleasant feel and each pitch is separated by hedges making some quite private and providing shade. All have electricity (10A) and water. The difference between this and other sites is that each pitch has an individual toilet cabin. Various entertainment is organised for adults and children in July/Aug, plus a sports club for supervised surfing, sailing, rafting, walking and canoeing (some activities are charged for). The unspoilt surrounding countryside is excellent for walking or cycling and locally there is horse riding and fishing. English is spoken in reception by the very welcoming Schutjes family. This site caters for families with children including teenagers (in fact they say 8 months to 86 years!)

Facilities

Each individual cabin has a toilet, shower and washbasin (key deposit) and, as each pitch empties, the facilities are cleaned in readiness for the next. Special pitches for disabled people. Two fully equipped laundry areas. Shop at entrance. Bar/restaurant with splendid new terrace (evenings only May and Sept) plus large TV. Takeaway. All 1/5 - 15/9. Snack bar 1/7 - 31/8. Swimming pools (solar heated), slide and paddling pool with fountain and slide, and poolside bar (1/7-31/8). New play areas and active children's club. Tennis, table tennis, basketball, volleyball, football, minigolf and boules. Teenagers' disco in high season. Recreation area with TV for youngsters. Internet connection. Only electric barbecues are permitted.
Off site: Large sandy beaches at Gruissan (10 km) and Narbonne Plage (15 km). Narbonne 4 km. Walking and cycling. Canoeing, sailing and windsurfing on the Etang.

At a glance

Welcome & Ambience	✓✓✓✓✓	Location	✓✓✓✓
Quality of Pitches	✓✓✓✓	Range of Facilities	✓✓✓✓✓

Directions

From A9 take exit 38 (Narbonne Sud). Go round roundabout to last exit and follow signs for La Nautique and site, then further site signs to site on right in 3 km.

Charges 2004

Per unit incl. electricity, water and sanitary unit	€ 7,40 - € 17,50
person	€ 4,00 - € 5,20
child (1-7 yrs)	€ 2,00 - € 3,60
dog or cat	€ 1,35 - € 2,35

Reservations

Made with deposit (€ 130) and fee (€ 20).
Tel: 04 68 90 48 19.
E-mail: info@campinglanautique.com

Open

1 February - 25 November.

FR30190 Camping International des Gorges du Gardon

Chemin de la Barque Vieille, 30210 Vers-Pont-du-Gard (Gard)

Probably the main attraction in the Gardon area of France is the Pont du Gard, an amazing Roman aqueduct built around 50AD. There are, however, other attractions worthy of a visit, such as the medieval village of Castillon-du-Gard perched on a rocky peak with narrow cobbled streets, and Collias at the bottom of the gorge from where you can hire canoes. Camping International is within easy (walking or cycling) distance of these attractions. It provides 200 level, good-sized pitches with electricity (6-16A); some are open while others are shaded. There is direct access to the river where swimming is permitted, although in summer the water level may be a little low. Unsupervised heated pools provide an alternative. The owners, Joseph and Sylvie Gonzales speak a little English, and visitors will always receive a warm and friendly welcome from them. Tourist information is in the reception (open all day) and Sylvie will share her local knowledge if you need any additional help.

Facilities

Two toilet blocks provide unisex facilities: showers, washbasins (some in cabins), and toilets. Facilities for disabled visitors in building nearest reception. Baby room. Washing machine, dishwashing and laundry sinks. Bar and restaurant (table service and takeaway). Swimming and paddling pools (unsupervised). Play areas. Table tennis. Games room and TV. Organised family entertainment during July/Aug. Off site: Pont du Gard approx 4 km. Collias 5 km. Canoeing arranged from site. Good area for walking and cycling.

Open

15 March - 30 October.

At a glance

Welcome & Ambience	✓✓✓✓✓	Location	✓✓✓✓✓
Quality of Pitches	✓✓✓✓	Range of Facilities	✓✓✓✓

Directions

Exit A9 at Remoulins, then take D981 towards Uzès. Follow campsite signs from this road – about 2 miles from the town.

Charges 2004

Per unit incl. 2 persons	€ 12,00 - € 16,00
extra adult	€ 3,50 - € 6,00
child (under 7 yrs)	€ 2,50 - € 3,00
electricity	€ 3,00
dog	€ 2,00

Reservations

Advisable during July and August.
Tel: 04 66 22 81 81.
E-mail: camping.international@wanadoo.fr

FR30160 Camping Caravaning Le Boucanet

B.P. 206, 30240 Le Grau-du-Roi (Gard)

On the beach between Grande Motte and Le Grau-du-Roi, this is a sunny site with only a little shade. Many trees have been planted but as yet most are not tall enough to give much shade. As to be expected, the 458 pitches are sandy and level. The 343 for touring units are separated by small bushes, most with electricity (6A). Plenty of flowers decorate the site and the pleasant restaurant overlooks the large heated pool (open lunchtimes and evenings). An excellent shopping arcade provides groceries, fruit, newspapers, a butcher and cooked meats, rotisserie and pizzas. In July and August organised activities include games, competitions, gymnastics, water polo, jogging and volleyball for adults. There is access to the river for paddling and swimming and horse riding on the white horses of the Camargue is to be found within a few kilometres.

Facilities

The toilet blocks are convenient for the pitches providing washbasins in cubicles and some British style toilets in two blocks, the remainder Turkish style (about 70%). Some washbasins in cabins. Facilities for disabled people at two blocks. Baby rooms. Dishwashing and laundry sinks have warm water. Washing machines, dryers, irons and fridge hire. Motorcaravan service point. Range of shops. Restaurant. Bar with snacks. Large swimming pool and paddling pool. Play area on sand and miniclub in July/Aug. Table tennis, tennis. Bicycle hire. Dogs are not accepted. Off site: Riding 500 m. Bicycle hire 15 km. Golf 40 km. Shops, restaurants and bars within 3 km.

At a glance

Welcome & Ambience	✓✓✓	Location	✓✓✓✓
Quality of Pitches	✓✓✓	Range of Facilities	✓✓✓✓✓

Directions

Site is between La Grand Motte and Le Grau-du-Roi on the D255 coastal road, on the seaward side of the road.

Charges 2005

Per unit incl. 2 persons	€ 17,00 - € 31,00
with electricity	€ 20,50 - € 34,50
pitch on first row of beach, plus	€ 5,00 - € 6,00
extra adult	€ 6,00 - € 9,00
child (under 7 yrs)	€ 4,50 - € 7,50

Camping Cheques accepted.

Reservations

Necessary for July/Aug. and made with 25% deposit and booking fee (€ 25); by money order or credit card only. Tel: 04 66 51 41 48.
E-mail: contact@campingboucanet.fr

Open

16 April - 25 September.

France

TRAVEL SERVICE SITE

TO BOOK CALL 0870 405 4055 OR www.alanrogersdirect.com

FR34070 Yelloh! Village Le Sérignan Plage

Le Sérignan Plage, 34410 Sérignan (Hérault)

A large, friendly, family-orientated site with direct access to superb sandy beaches, including a naturist beach, Serignan Plage exudes a strongly individualistic style which we find very attractive. However, those who look for 'manicured' sites may be less impressed, as its situation on 'the littoral' and proximity to the beach makes it difficult to keep things neat and tidy. With some 450 mainly good sized, level touring pitches, including some (with little shade) actually alongside the beach, coupled with perhaps the most comprehensive range of amenities we've come across, the hugely enthusiastic owners, Jean-Guy and Katy Amat continually surprise us with new ideas and developments. New for 2004 was a superb 1,800 sq.m. 'Spa Water Fitness centre' with more new pools, a fitness centre and jacuzzi. The amenities are just too extensive to describe in detail, but they include a pool complex, with slides surrounded by large grassy sunbathing areas with sun loungers, and another indoor pool. Perhaps the most remarkable aspect is the cluster of attractive buildings which form the 'heart' of this site with courtyards housing attractive bars, a smart restaurant, shops, takeaway, a stage for entertainment, disco, etc. – all very attractive and with a very special ambience.

Facilities

Nine unisex toilet blocks. The older circular ones with a mixture of British and Turkish style WCs are nearest the sea and central 'village' area, seasonal units and mobile homes, etc. and thus take most of the wear and tear. The touring area, furthest from the sea has three modern blocks of individual design. Well planned with good facilities, these include large controllable hot showers with washbasin and WC en-suite, well equipped baby rooms, facilities for disabled people. Dishwashing and laundry facilities in all blocks and washing machines. At peak times maintenance can be a little variable. Well stocked supermarket, bakery, tabac, ATM and market stalls. Poissonnerie and boucherie (7/6-8/9). Central launderette. Hairdresser. Bars, restaurant and takeaway (all 7/4-10/9). Much animation for children and a range of evening entertainment. Secluded roof-top bar (9 pm - 1 am). - ask for a 'Cucaracha'! Soundproof disco. Heated indoor pool and outdoor pool complex (also heated) with lifeguards in the main season and an ID card system (April - Sept). Sporting activities organised. Bicycle hire. Off site: Riding 2 km. Golf 10 km. Bicycle hire. Sailing and windsurfing school on beach (lifeguard in high season).

At a glance

Welcome & Ambience	✓✓✓✓	Location	✓✓✓✓✓
Quality of Pitches	✓✓✓✓	Range of Facilities	✓✓✓✓✓

Directions

From A9 exit 35 (Béziers Est) follow signs for Sérignan on D64 (9 km). Don't go into Sérignan, but take sign for Sérignan Plage for 4 km. At small multi sign (blue) turn right on single carriageway. At T-junction turn left over small road bridge and after left hand bend, site is 100 m. after Sérignan Plage Nature.

Charges 2004

Per unit incl. 1 or 2 persons and 5A electricity	€ 15,00 - € 36,00
extra person	€ 6,00 - € 6,50
pet	€ 3,00

Camping Cheques accepted.
Low season offers.
Discounts in low season for children under 7 yrs.

Reservations

Made from 1 Feb. with deposit (25%) and fee (€ 30).
Tel: 04 67 32 35 33.
E-mail: info@leserignanplage.com

Open

10 April - 22 September.

FR34140 Haven Camping La Carabasse

Route de Farinette, 34450 Vias-sur-Mer (Hérault)

La Carabasse, a Haven Europe holiday park, is on the outskirts of Vias Plage, a popular place with lots of shops and restaurants. The site has everything you could need with two good pools, and its own bars and a restaurant. Very much orientated to British visitors. There are lots of activities for young families and teenagers. The bars and restaurant provide live music in the evenings and entertainment. There are 950 pitches in total, 400 for touring, with many mobile homes. The touring pitches are set amongst tall poplar and birch trees on level hard ground, all have electricity and partial shade. Some have private sanitary facilities. The wonderful Mediterranean beaches are close and La Carabasse has its own beach club. It is a lively busy site in high season, and Vias Plage itself can also be quite hectic. Haven Europe are continuing to develop and improve the site with a wide range of facilities for children and teenagers. Football coaching from U.F.A. qualified staff, for two hours a day, five days a week, can be booked from € 40 or you can learn snorkelling, life saving or body-boarding and become a 'wave rider'!

Facilities

Two of the toilet blocks are modern and fully equipped. With an older block used in high season. Some pitches have their own private sanitary cabin providing a WC and shower (extra charge). Bars, restaurant and swimming pools. Beach club for windsurfing and pedaloes. Wealth of daytime activities (some charged for) from golf lessons to aqua-aerobics and tennis tournaments. Children's clubs and multi-sports unit. Evening entertainment. Off site: Vias town with twice weekly market. Modern resort of Cap d'Adge nearby with Aqualand and golf course (18 holes).

At a glance

Welcome & Ambience	✓✓✓✓	Location	✓✓✓✓
Quality of Pitches	✓✓✓	Range of Facilities	✓✓✓✓✓

Directions

Site is south of Vias. From N112 (Agde - Beziers) road turn right for Vias-Plage (D137) and site (on the left).

Charges 2004

Per pitch incl. up to 6 persons and electricity	€ 11,00 - € 37,00
with private sanitary cabin	€ 12,00 - € 43,00

Reservations

Accepted at any time for min. 4 days; no booking fee.
Tel: 04 67 21 64 01.
E-mail: europe.website@bourne-leisure.co.uk

Open

16 April - 13 September.

Le Sérignan Plage

The magic of
the Mediterranean

Passerelles RC 87 B 302

Imagine – hot sunshine, blue sea, vineyards, olive and eucalyptus trees, alongside a sandy beach – what a setting for a campsite – not just any campsite either !

With three pool areas, one with four toboggans surrounded by sun bathing areas, an indoor pool for baby swimmers plus a magnificent landscaped, Romanesque spa-complex with half Olympic size pool and a superb range of hydro-massage baths to let you unwind and re-charge after the stresses of work.

And that's not all – two attractive restaurants, including the atmospheric "Villa" in its romantic Roman setting beside the spa, three bars, a mini-club and entertainment for all ages, all add up to a fantastic opportunity to enjoy a genuinely unique holiday experience.

Le Sérignan-Plage - F-34410 SERIGNAN
Tel: 00 33 467 32 35 33 - Fax: 00 33 467 32 26 36
info@leserignanplage.com - www.leserignanplage.com

yelloh! VILLAGE

FR30100 Camping Naturiste de la Sablière

Domaine de la Sablière, St Privat de Champclos, 30430 Barjac (Gard)

Spectacularly situated in the Cèze Gorges, this naturist site with a surprising 604 pitches tucked away within its wild terrain offers a wide variety of facilities, all within a really peaceful, wooded and dramatic setting. Pitches are grouped in areas - 'Mesange' (mainly for tents with cars parked 200 m. away) and 'Fauvette' at the bottom of the gorge alongside the river at some points close to the main access road, which is well surfaced but steep and winding. A newer area, 'Pinson', is near the top of the hill. The pitches themselves are mainly flat on terraces, attractively situated among a variety of trees and shrubs (some with low overhang). Many are of a good size and have electricity (6/10A). A pool complex (dynamited out of the hill and built in local style) provides a new children's pool area and two large pools, one of which can be covered by a sliding dome, sunbathing terraces, saunas and a bar. This is a family run and orientated site and the owner, Gaby Cespedes, provides a personal touch that is unusual in a large site. This no doubt contributes to the relaxed, informal atmosphere and first time naturists would find this a gentle introduction to naturism. You must expect some fairly steep walking between pitches and facilities, although there is a minibus shuttle service in high season. Member France 4 Naturisme.

Facilities

Six good unisex sanitary blocks (most refurbished 2003) have excellent free hot showers in typical open plan, naturist style, washbasins (cold water), baby baths and facilities for people with disabilities. Dishwashing and laundry sinks. Laundry. Supermarket. Open air, covered restaurant (all season) with good value waiter service meals and a takeaway. Swimming pool complex. Bar with TV room and disco. Small café/crêperie. Varied activities include walking, climbing, swimming, canoeing, fitness trail, fishing (permit required), archery, tennis, minigolf and volleyball, book binding, pottery, yoga etc. Entertainment for adults and children (mid June - end Aug). Mobile homes, caravans, chalet and tents to rent. Torch useful. Off site: Barjac with its Antiques Fair at Easter and mid-August. Alès, Chemin de Fer des Cevennes.

At a glance

Welcome & Ambience	✓✓✓✓	Location	✓✓✓✓
Quality of Pitches	✓✓✓	Range of Facilities	✓✓✓✓✓

Directions

From Barjac take D901 east for 3 km. Site is signed just before St Privat-de-Champclos and is approx. 3 km. on narrow roads following camp signs.

Charges 2004

Per pitch incl. 2 persons	€ 11,40 - € 28,40
extra person	€ 3,42 - € 6,34
child (under 8 yrs)	free - € 5,82
electricity	€ 3,55
dog	€ 1,00 - € 2,50

Camping Cheques accepted.

Reservations

Made with deposit (25%) and fee (€ 30)- contact site. Tel: 04 66 24 51 16. E-mail: sabliere@club-internet.fr

Open

27 March - 3 October.

FR34150 Yelloh! Village Nouvelle Floride

34340 Marseillan Plage (Hérault)

Marseillan Plage is a small, busy resort just east of Cap d'Adge and La Nouvelle Floride enjoys a super position immediately beside a long gently shelving sandy beach. It is a good quality site, very traditional in style and set under tall trees with neat hedges to separate the 520 pitches (370 for tourers). These are on sandy soil and all have water and electricity (6A). Some of the pitches in the newer area (across a small lane) and the hardstanding pitches near the beach have little shade as yet. There are a number of mobile homes but the site is mainly for tourers. Amenities and facilities are generally of excellent quality and include a strikingly attractive bar area overlooking the beach with a raised stage for entertainment. Alongside the play area is a multi-purpose ball court and fitness centre, also on sand with robust machines with the idea of keeping Mum and Dad fit whilst still keeping an eye on the children. Essentially a 'holiday site', there is an extensive programme of entertainment and activities catering for all ages, and a good heated pool complex. However, the main attraction for most will almost certainly be the direct access to a fine beach. The gates on the beach entrance are locked at 9 pm. for security. This is a well run, family run site aimed at families.

Facilities

The four toilet blocks are impressive, including two with a number of en-suite showers and washbasins, otherwise washbasins all in cabins. Baby rooms, excellent facilities for disabled visitors and even a dog shower. The showers and washing up areas are closed between 23.00-07.00 hrs. Motorcaravan service point. Bar and restaurant. Shop all season, plus a range of shops at Charlemagne across the road. Pool complex with slides, jacuzzi, paddling pools, etc (all season). Play area, fitness centre and multi-purpose ball court. Table tennis. Weekly films (DVD) and variety of organised games, competitions, dances and discos. Mini-club in school holidays. Bicycle hire. Off site: Riding and bicycle hire 500 m. Golf 5 km.

At a glance

Welcome & Ambience	✓✓✓✓	Location	✓✓✓✓✓
Quality of Pitches	✓✓✓✓	Range of Facilities	✓✓✓✓✓

Directions

From A9 autoroute exit 34, follow N312 to Agde then take N112 towards Sete. Watch for signs to Marseillan Plage from where site is well signed.

Charges 2005

Per unit incl. 1 or 2 persons, water and electricity	€ 15,00 - € 43,00
extra person (over 1 yr)	€ 5,00 - € 8,50
animal	€ 3,00 - € 3,50

Reservations

Contact site. Tel: 04 67 21 94 49. E-mail: info@nouvelle-floride.com

Open

19 March - 24 September.

FR66190 Sunêlia Les Tropiques

Bvd de la Méditerranée, 66440 Torreilles-Plage (Pyrénées-Orientales)

Les Tropiques makes a pleasant holiday venue, only 400 metres from a sandy beach and also boasting two pools. There are 450 pitches with 200 given over to mobile homes and chalets. Pleasant pine and palm trees with other Mediterranean vegetation give shade and provides an attractive environment. Activities are provided for all including a large range of sports, caberets and shows but an identity bracelet for entry to the site is obligatory in high season (small payment required).

Facilities

Modern, fully equipped sanitary facilities include provision for disabled visitors. Launderette. Bar, restaurant with takeaway meals and pizzeria (all 14/6–15/9). Shop. Two outdoor swimming pools (1/6–30/9) Tennis, table tennis, football, volleyball and pétanque. Archery (1/7-31/8). TV and billards room. Play area. Disco (every evening and club for 6-12 yr old children in July/Aug. New car-wash installed. Off site: Minigolf 300 m. Windsurf board hire and sea fishing 400 m. Riding 400 m. Bicycle hire 5 km. Golf 15 km.

Open

9 April - 7 October.

At a glance

Welcome & Ambience	✓✓✓✓	Location	✓✓✓✓
Quality of Pitches	✓✓✓✓	Range of Facilities	✓✓✓✓✓

Directions

From autroute A9 take exit for Perpignan Nord and follow D83 towards Le Barcarès for 9 km. Take D81 suth towards Canet for 3 km. before turning left at roundabout for Torreilles Plage. Site is the last but one on the left.

Charges 2005

Per unit incl. 2 persons with electricity	€ 17,00 - € 33,00
extra person	€ 3,60 - € 6,00
child (0-13 yrs)	€ 2,70 - € 4,50
animal	€ 4,00

Camping Cheques accepted.

Reservations

Contact site. Tel: 04 68 28 05 09.
E-mail: camping.tropiques@wanadoo.fr

TO BOOK CALL 0870 405 4055 OR www.alanrogersdirect.com

TRAVEL SERVICE SITE

FR06080 Camping Caravaning Les Cigales

505 ave. de la Mer, 06210 Mandelieu-la-Napoule (Alpes-Maritimes)

It is hard to imagine that such a quiet, peaceful site could be in the middle of such a busy town and so near to Cannes - we were delighted with it. The entrance (easily missed) with reception and parking has large electronic gates that ensure that the site is very secure. There are only 115 pitches (40 used for mobile homes) so this is really quite a small, personal site. There are three pitch sizes, from small ones for tents to pitches for larger units. All are level with much needed shade in summer, although the sun will get through in winter when it is needed, and all have electricity (6A), some also with water and waste water. The site is alongside the Canal de Siagne and for a fee, small boats can be launched at La Napoule, then moored outside the campsite's side gate. Les Cigales is open all year so it is useful for the Monte Carlo Rally, the Cannes Film Festival and the Mimosa Festival, all held out of the main season.

Facilities

Two well appointed unisex toilet blocks are kept very clean, one heated for the winter months. Washbasins in cabins and facilities for babies and disabled visitors. Dishwashing and laundry sinks. Washing machine. Motorcaravan service point. Restaurant at entrance also serves takeaways (April - 30 Sept). Swimming pool, quite new with large sunbathing area (March - Oct, heated mid-March - mid-Oct). Small play area. Table tennis. Fishing possible in the canal (but not many fish!). Off site: Beach 800 m. The town is an easy walk. Two golf courses within 1 km. Railway station 1 km. for trains to Cannes, Nice, Antibes and Monte Carlo. Centre commercial (supermarket and 40 shops) 2 km.

At a glance

Welcome & Ambience	✓✓✓✓✓	Location	✓✓✓✓✓
Quality of Pitches	✓✓✓✓✓	Range of Facilities	✓✓✓✓

Directions

From A8 take exit 40 and bear right. Remain in right hand lane and continue right signed Plages-Ports and Creche-Campings. New supermarket is on the right. Continue under motorway to T-junction. Turn left and site is 60 m. on left opposite Chinese restaurant.

Charges 2004

Per person	€ 5,00
child (under 5 yrs)	€ 2,50
pitch	€ 13,50 - € 27,00

Reservations

Made with deposit (€ 77). Tel: 04 93 49 23 53.
E-mail: campingcigales@wanadoo.fr

Open

All year.

TO BOOK CALL 0870 405 4055 OR www.alanrogersdirect.com

TRAVEL SERVICE SITE

FR06120 Camping Green Park

159, Vallon des Vaux, 06800 Cagnes-sur-Mer (Alpes-Maritimes)

Green Park has had a very extensive renewal programme over the past 18 months with many of the facilities having been rebuilt to a high standard of which the owning family are justifiably proud. Situated just over 4 km from the beaches at Cagnes-sur-Mer, Green Park is at the centre of the Cote d'Azur. There are two parts to Green Park, one newly constructed and very active site to keep every member of the family occupied for most of the day and evening, with club activites for children, teenagers and even adults, while on the other side of the apporach road there is a quieter and more traditional site, with limited facilities. Activities and facilities are interchangeable. There are 78 touring pitches mostly on the left or west side of the site, mainly on grass, all with electricity of which 24 are the 'Grand Comfort' style, plus 67 mobile homes and chalets. The site has two swimming pools (one on each side of the road which is not busy and goes 'nowhere' further up the valley). Green Park is situated in an area which benefits from a 'micro climate'. Hot during the day but pleasantly cooler at night.

Facilities

All the toilets are modern and mostly British, with facilities for children and disabled visitors (the disabled facilities are superb). Showers and washbasins are modern and kept very clean. Dishwashing and laundry sinks and three washing machines. Bar, restaurant and takeaway. Two swimming pools - one heated. Internet point. Games room. Green Park is secure - with an electronic barrier (€ 5 card deposit) and a gate keeper on duty all night. Off site: Golf 12 km. Riding 10 km.

Open

29 March - 17 October.

At a glance

Welcome & Ambience	✓✓✓✓✓	Location	✓✓✓✓
Quality of Pitches	✓✓✓✓	Range of Facilities	✓✓✓✓✓

Directions

Coming from Aix on the A8, take exit 47 onto the N7 towards Nice. Go straight on at traffic lights by the racecourse for 2 km. then turn left towards Val Fleuri on Av. du Val Fleuri. Go over roundabouts onto Chemin Vallon des Vaux to site on right in 2 km. From Nice on N98 coast road, turn right at Le Port du Cros de Cagnes and follow camping signs. It is important to avoid the town centre.

Charges 2004

Per unit incl. 2 persons	€ 12,00 - € 30,60
extra person	€ 3,50 - € 3,90
child (2-7 yrs)	free - € 2,80
electricity	€ 3,60 - € 4,80
dog	€ 2,00 - € 2,50

Camping Cheques accepted.

Reservations

Contact site. Tel: 04 93 07 09 96.
E-mail: info@greenpark.fr

FR06140 Ranch Camping

06110 Le Cannet (Alpes-Maritimes)

Recommended by our agent, we hope to include a full report on this wooded Riviera campsite in a future inspection programme. Le Ranch is just 2 km. from the beaches and the glistening resort of Cannes. The site offers 130 shady pitches of varying sizes, priced according to size, and an attractive range of amenities. Mobile homes for rent.

Facilities

Sanitary building. Swimming pool (covered in low season). Playground. Small shop. Table tennis. Games room.
Off site: Tennis 200 m. Regular bus service to Cannes, Cannes centre 2 km, nearest beach 2 km.

Open

1 April - 30 October.

Directions

Take the Le Cannet exit from the A8 autoroute, then follow signs to La Bocca on the D809 , to L'Aubarede, from where the site is clearly signposted.

Charges year

Per unit incl. 1 person	€ 10,00 - € 16,00
extra person	€ 5,00
child (5-10 yrs)	€ 2,00
electricity (6A)	€ 3,00

Reservations

Contact site; minimum 7 nights. Tel: 04 93 46 00 11.

FR06030 Camping Caravaning Domaine de la Bergerie

Route de la Sine, 06140 Vence (Alpes-Maritimes)

La Bergerie is a quiet, family owned site, situated in the hills about three kilometres from Vence and ten kilometres from the sea at Cagnes-sur-Mer. This extensive, lightly wooded site has been left very natural and is in a secluded position about 300 m. above sea level. Because of the trees most of the pitches are shaded and all are of a good size. It is a large site but because it is so extensive it does not give that impression. There are 450 pitches, 300 with electricity (2/5A) and 65 also with water and drainage. Because of the nature of this site, some pitches are a little distance from the toilet blocks. There are no organised activities and definitely no groups allowed.

Facilities

Both toilet blocks have been refurbished and include washbasins in cabins and excellent provision for disabled people (pitches near the block are reserved for disabled people). Very good shop, small bar/restaurant with takeaway (all 1/5-30/9). Large swimming pool, paddling pool and spacious sunbathing area (5/6-30/9). Playground. Bicycle hire. Table tennis, tennis courts and 10 shaded boules pitches with competitions in season. Barbecues are not permitted. Off site: Riding 6 km. Fishing 10 km. Golf 12 km. Hourly bus service (excl. Sundays) to Vence.

Open

25 March - 15 October.

At a glance

Welcome & Ambience	✓✓✓✓	Location	✓✓✓✓
Quality of Pitches	✓✓✓	Range of Facilities	✓✓✓✓

Directions

From A8 exit 47 take Cagnes-sur-Mer road towards Vence. Site is west of Vence; follow 'toutes directions' signs around the town to join the D2210 (Grasse). Follow this to roundabout (2 km), turn left and follow site signs for 1 km. Site is on right in light woodland.

Charges 2004

Per unit incl. 2 persons	€ 13,50 - € 19,00
with electricity (2A)	€ 17,23 - € 23,00
water, drainage, electricity (5A)	€ 22,00 - € 29,00
extra person	€ 4,60

Camping Cheques accepted.
Less 10-15% for longer stays.

Reservations

Necessary only in July/Aug. for the special pitches and made with 25% deposit and € 12.96 fee.
Tel: 04 93 58 09 36.

FR83020 Camping Caravaning Esterel

Avenue des Golf, 83700 St Raphaël (Var)

For caravans only, Esterel is a quality site east of St Raphaël, set among the hills at the back of Agay. Developed by the Laroche family over the last 27 years, the site has an attractive quiet situation with good views of the Esterel mountains. The site is 3.5 km. from the sandy beach at Agay where parking is perhaps a little easier than at most places on this coast. In addition to a section for permanent caravans, it has some 250 pitches for tourists, on which caravans of any type are taken but not tents. Pitches are on shallow terraces, attractively landscaped with good shade and a variety of flowering plants, giving a feeling of spaciousness. Each pitch has an electricity connection and tap, and 18 special ones have their own individual en-suite washroom adjoining. Some maxi pitches from 110 to 160 sq.m. are now available. A pleasant courtyard area contains the shop and bar, with a terrace overlooking the attractively landscaped (floodlit at night) pool complex, which has recently been extended. Wild boar come to the perimeter fence each evening to be fed by visitors. This is a very good site, well run and organised in a deservedly popular area. A member of 'Les Castels' group.

Facilities

Toilet facilities in three blocks have been refurbished and are excellent. They can be heated and include washbasins mostly in cabins. Individual toilet units on 18 pitches. Facilities for disabled people. Laundry room. Motorcaravan service point. Shop. Takeaway. Bar/restaurant. Five circular swimming pools (two heated), one large for adults, one smaller for children and three arranged as a waterfall (1/4-30/9). Disco. Archery, volleyball, minigolf, two tennis courts, pony rides, petanque and squash court. Playground. Bicycle hire. Events and entertainment are organised in season. Barbecues of any type are forbidden. A new nursery and restaurant have been built. Off site: Good golf courses very close. Trekking by foot, bicycle or by pony in the surrounding natural environment of L'Esterel forest park. Beach 3 km.

Open

19 March - 1 October.

At a glance

Welcome & Ambience	✓✓✓✓	Location	✓✓✓✓✓
Quality of Pitches	✓✓✓✓	Range of Facilities	✓✓✓✓✓

Directions

You can approach from St Raphaël via Valescure but easiest way is to turn off the coast road at Agay where there are good signs. From Fréjus exit from autoroute A8, follow signs for Valescure throughout, then for Agay, and site is on left. (Reader's comment: If in doubt, follow golf complex signs, or Leclerc). The road from Agay is the easiest to follow.

Charges 2004

Per unit incl. 2 persons,	
standard pitch	€ 22,00 - € 40,00
de-luxe pitch	€ 30,00 - € 52,00
extra person	€ 8,00
child (1-7 yrs)	€ 6,00
animal	€ 2,00

Reservations

Necessary for high season and made for min. 1 week with deposit (€ 80) and fee (€ 30). CD brochure available from site. Tel: 04 94 82 03 28.
E-mail: contact@esterel-caravaning.fr

FR83010 Camping Caravaning Les Pins Parasols

Route de Bagnols, 83600 Fréjus (Var)

Not everyone likes very big sites and Les Pins Parasols with its 189 pitches is of a size which is quite easy to walk around. It is family owned and run. Although on very slightly undulating ground, virtually all the pitches are levelled or terraced and separated by hedges or bushes with pine trees for shade. They are around 100 sq.m. and all have electricity. What is particularly interesting is that 48 of the pitches are equipped with their own fully enclosed, tiled sanitary unit, consisting of WC, washbasin, hot shower and dishwashing sink, all quite close together. These pitches naturally cost more but may well be of interest to those seeking extra comfort. The nearest beach is the once very long Fréjus-Plage (5.5 km) now reduced a little by the new marina, and adjoins St Raphaël. (See note on La Baume entry concerning traffic delays at the D4/N7 road junction.) Used by tour operators (10%).

Facilities

Besides the individual units there are three toilet blocks of good average quality providing washbasins in cabins and facilities for disabled people. One block can be heated when necessary. Small shop with reasonable stocks and restaurant with takeaway (both 1/5-20/9). General room with TV. Swimming pool (200 sq.m) with attractive rock backdrop and separate long slide with landing pool and small paddling pool (heated). Half-court tennis.
Off site: Bicycle hire or riding 2 km. Fishing 6 km. Golf 10 km. Bus from the gate into Fréjus 5 km. Beach 6 km.

Open

Easter - 30 September.

At a glance

Welcome & Ambience	✓✓✓✓	Location	✓✓✓✓
Quality of Pitches	✓✓✓✓	Range of Facilities	✓✓✓✓

Directions

From A8 take exit 38 for Fréjus Est. Turn right on leaving pay booths on a small road which leads across to D4, where right again and under 1 km. to site.

Charges 2004

Per normal pitch with electricity	
incl. 2 persons	€ 17,40 - € 24,90
pitch with sanitary unit	€ 22,00 - € 31,00
extra person	€ 4,40 - € 6,00
child (under 7 yrs)	€ 2,90 - € 3,65

Reservations

Necessary for July/Aug. only and made for min. 10 days for exact dates with deposit (€ 100) but no fee. Tel: 04 94 40 88 43.
E-mail: lespinsparasols@wanadoo.fr

uxury mobil homes for rent nd maxi pitches for touring aravans and camping cars !

range of high quality services !

Heated Swimming pools !

ON-STOP lively activities !

A Paradise for children !

Avenue des Golfs
530 Saint-Raphaël
FRANCE

FR83060 Camping Caravaning de la Baume

Route de Bagnols, 83618 Fréjus (Var)

La Baume is large, busy site that has been well developed with much investment. It is about 5.5 km. from the long sandy beach of Fréjus-Plage, but it has such a fine and varied selection of swimming pools on site that many people do not bother to make the trip. The pools with their palm trees are a feature of this site and are remarkable for their size and variety (water slides, etc.) – the very large 'feature' pool a highlight. The site has nearly 500 pitches of varying but quite adequate size with electricity, water and drainage, with another 200 larger ones with mains sewerage to take mobile homes. Separators are being installed to divide the pitches and shade is available over most of the terrain. Although tents are accepted, the site concentrates mainly on caravanning. It is likely to become full in season, but one section with unmarked pitches is not reserved, and there is plenty of space off-peak. La Baume's convenient location has its 'downside' as there is some traffic noise from the nearby autoroute - somewhat obtrusive at first but we soon failed to notice it. A popular site with tour operators. Adjoining La Baume is its sister site La Palmeraie, containing self-catering accommodation, its own landscaped pool and providing some entertainment to supplement that at La Baume.

Facilities

The seven toilet blocks should be a satisfactory supply. Two have been enlarged recently, the others refurbished to provide mainly British style toilets with a few Turkish; washbasins in cabins and sinks for clothes and dishes with hot water. Supermarket and several other shops. Bar with external terrace overlooking pools and TV. Restaurant and takeaway. Five swimming pools (heated all season). Fitness centre. Tennis courts. Archery (July/Aug). Oganised events - sports, competitions, etc. in daytime and some evening entertainment partly in English. Amphitheatre for shows. Discos daily in season. Off site: Bus to Fréjus passes the gate.

Open

26 March - 30 September, with full services

At a glance

Welcome & Ambience	✓✓✓	Location	✓✓✓✓
Quality of Pitches	✓✓✓✓	Range of Facilities	✓✓✓✓✓

Directions

Site is 3 km. up the D4 road, which leads north from N7 just west of Fréjus. From west on autoroute A8 take exit for Fréjus/St Raphaël (junction 37), turn towards them and after 4 km., turn left on D4. From east take exit for Fréjus/St Raphaël (junction 38); after exit turn right immediately on small road marked 'Musée' etc. which leads you to D4 where right again.

Charges 2005

Per unit incl. 2 persons, 6A electricity, water and drainage	€ 18,00 - € 37,00
extra person	€ 4,00 - € 8,00
child (under 7 yrs)	free - € 5,00
car	€ 3,50 - € 4,00

Min. stay for motorhomes 3 nights.
Large units should book.

Reservations

Essential for high season, and made for exact dates with substantial deposit and fee (€ 31.25), from 1 Jan. Tel: 04 94 15 88 88.
E-mail: reception@labaume-lapalmeraie.com

FR83240 Camping Caravaning Moulin des Iscles

83520 Roquebrune-sur-Argens (Var)

A haven of peace and tranquillity, Moulin des Iscles is hidden down 0.5 km. of private, unmade road - an unusual find in this often quite hectic part of Provence. Based around a former mill, it is a small, pretty site beside the river Argens with access to the river in places for fishing, canoeing and swimming, with a concrete bank and fenced where deemed necessary (some sought after pitches overlook the river). The 90 grassy, level pitches with electricity (6A) and water to all, radiate out from M. Dumarcet's attractive, centrally situated home which is where the restaurant and shop are situated. A nice mixture of deciduous trees provide natural shade and colour and the old mill house rests comfortably near the entrance which has a security barrier closed at night. This is a quiet site with little on site entertainment, but with a nice little restaurant. A good effort has been made to welcome handicapped visitors. It is a real campsite not a 'camping village'.

Facilities

The toilet block is fully equipped, including ramped access for disabled visitors. Some Turkish style toilets. Washbasins have cold water, some in cubicles. Baby bath and changing facilities en-suite. Covered laundry and dishwashing sinks. Small separate unisex provision for pitches near the entrance. Washing machine. Restaurant with home cooked dish-of-the-day on a weekly rotation. Surprisingly well stocked shop. Library - some English books. TV room incl. satellite, Pool table, table tennis. Play area, minigolf and boules all outside the barrier for more peace and quiet on site. Internet terminal. Canoeing possible. Off site: Riding and golf 6 km. Bicycle hire 2 km. (new bicycle way to St Aygulf). Beach 7 km.

At a glance

Welcome & Ambience	✓✓✓✓	Location	✓✓✓✓
Quality of Pitches	✓✓✓✓	Range of Facilities	✓✓✓

Directions

Follow as for site no. 8320, Les Pecheurs, but continue past it through the village of Roquebrune towards St Aygulf for 1 km. Site signed on left. Follow private unmade road for approx. 500 m. to site entrance in front of you.

Charges 2005

Per unit incl. 2 or 3 persons	€ 19,00
extra adult	€ 3,20
child (over 10 yrs)	€ 2,20
electricity	€ 2,70

Camping Cheques accepted.
Prices are lower out of high season.

Reservations

Contact site. Tel: 04 94 45 70 74.
E-mail: moulin.iscles@wanadoo.fr

Open

1 April - 30 September.

Heated sanitary blocks
Marked-out pitches
5 swimming pools
6 water-slides
5km from the beaches of
Frejus and St Raphael

Provencal chalets, mobile homes and apartments for 4 to 6 people for hire

Special rates in low season

Heated swimming pool

Route de Bagnols Rue des Combattants d'Afrique du Nord
83618 FREJUS Cedex
Tel: + 33 494 19 88 88 - Fax: + 33 494 19 83 50
www.labaume-lapalmeraie.com
E-mail : reception@labaume-lapalmeraie.com

FR83070 Caravaning L'Etoile d'Argens

83370 St Aygulf (Var)

First impressions of L'Etoile d'Argens are of space, cleanliness and calm. Reception staff are very friendly and English is spoken (open 24 hrs). This is a site run with families in mind and many of the activities are free, making for a good value holiday. There are 493 level grass pitches (265 for touring units) laid out in typical French style, separated by hedges. There are five sizes of pitch, ranging from 50 sq.m. (for small tents) to 250 sq.m. These are exceptionally large and two families could easily fit two caravans and cars or one family could have a very spacious plot with a garden like atmosphere. All pitches are fully serviced with fresh and waste water and 10A electricity, with mainly good shade although the site is not overpowered by trees which leads to a spacious feeling. The pool and bar area is attractively landscaped with old olive and palm trees on beautifully kept grass. Two heated pools (one for adults, one for children) have been added recently – both very much with families in mind, not teenagers as there are no big slides. The river runs along one side of the site and a free boat service (15/6-15/9) runs every 40 minutes to the beach. It is also possible to moor a boat or fish. This is a good family site for the summer but also good in low season for a quiet stay in a superb location with excellent pitches. Tour operators take 85 pitches and there are 175 mobile homes but for a large site it is unusually calm and peaceful even in July.

Facilities

Two new toilet blocks were added in 2000, whilst all but 4 of the 20 original small unisex blocks have been renovated. All are well kept and include some washbasins in cubicles. Dishwashing sinks and laundry with outside clothes line. Supermarket and gas supplies. Bar, restaurant, pizzeria, takeaway. Two adult pools (one heated), paddling pool, jacuzzi and solarium. Tennis (two of the four courts are floodlit) with coaching and minigolf (both free in low season), aerobics, archery (July/Aug), football and swimming lessons. Volleyball, basketball, table tennis and boule. Play area with rubber base. Children's entertainer in July/Aug. Activity programme includes games, dances for adults and escorted walking trips to the surrounding hills. within 3 km. Off site: Golf 2 km. Riding 3 km. Beach 3.5 km.

Open

Easter - 30 September, with all services.

At a glance

Welcome & Ambience	✓✓✓✓	Location	✓✓✓✓
Quality of Pitches	✓✓✓✓✓	Range of Facilities	✓✓✓✓✓

Directions

Leave A8 at exit 36 and take N7 to Le Muy and Fréjus. After about 8 km. at roundabout take D7 signed Roquebrune and St Aygulf. In 9.5 km. (after roundabout) turn left signed Fréjus. Watch for site sign and ignore width and height limit signs as site is 500 m. to right.

Charges 2004

Per tent pitch (100 sq.m.) with electricity and 2 persons	€ 20,00 - € 37,00
'comfort' pitch (100 sq.m.) incl. 3 persons, water and drainage	€ 27,00 - € 46,00
'luxury' pitch incl. 4 persons 180 sq.m	€ 39,00 - € 62,00
extra person	€ 5,50 - € 8,00
child (under 7 yrs)	€ 3,50 - € 6,00
car and dog	€ 4,00

Reservations

Made for any period with substantial deposit and fee. Tel: 04 94 81 01 41. E-mail: info@etoiledargens.com

FR83250 Sunêlia Douce Quiétude

3435 boulevard Jacques Baudino, 83700 St Raphaël (Var)

Douce Quiétude is only seven kilometres from the beaches at Saint Raphaël and Agay but is quietly situated at the foot of the Estérel massif. There are 400 pitches, but only 70 of these are for touring units (around half are used for mobile homes) set in pleasant pine woodland or shaded, green areas. The pitches are of a comfortable size, separated by bushes and trees with electricity (6A), water, drainage and telephone/TV points provided. This mature site offers a wide range of services and facilities complete with a pool complex. It can be busy in the main season yet is relaxed and spacious. Security is good with the wearing of identity bracelets mandatory throughout your stay.

Facilities

Fully equipped modern toilet blocks have changing facilities for babies and provision for disabled visitors. Launderette. Bar and restaurant with takeaway and pizzeria (1/6-3/9). Shop. Three outdoor swimming pools (two heated), water slide and jacuzzi. Play area. Children's club and activities for teenagers (all July/Aug). Sports area for volleyball, basketball and petanque. Games room (July/Aug). Tennis. Table tennis and billards. Minigolf. Archery. Fitness centre and sauna (July/Aug). Evening entertainment with shows, karaoke and discos. Mountain bike hire. Only gas barbecues are permitted. Off site: Golf and riding 5 km. Windsurf hire and sea fishing 7 km.

At a glance

Welcome & Ambience	✓✓✓✓	Location	✓✓✓✓
Quality of Pitches	✓✓✓✓	Range of Facilities	✓✓✓✓✓

Directions

Take exit 38 from A8 autoroute signed Fréjus/St Raphaël. Follow directions for Valescure then Agay on the D100, then site signs (takes you round the back of Frejus/St Raphaël). Site can also be reached from the N98 coast road turning north at Agay on D100; continue past Esterel Camping to pick up site signs.

Charges 2004

extra person	€ 6,00 - € 8,00
child (3-12 yrs)	€ 5,00 - € 6,00
animal	€ 2,00 - € 4,00

Camping Cheques accepted.

Reservations

Contact site. Tel: 04 94 44 30 00.
E-mail: info@douce-quietude.com

Open

3 April - 2 October.

L'Etoile d'Argens

2005

" 36 years experience with you "

ESE Communication - draguignan - tél : 04.94.67.06.00

www.etoiledargens.com

E-mail : info@etoiledargens.com

3370 St Aygulf - Tél. +33 4 94 81 01 41

FR83200 Camping Caravaning Les Pêcheurs

83520 Roquebrune-sur-Argens (Var)

Developed over three generations by the Simoncini family, this peaceful, friendly site is set in more than four hectares of mature, well shaded countryside at the foot of the Roquebrune Rock. It will appeal to families who appreciate natural surroundings together with many activities, cultural and sporting. Interspersed with a number of mobile homes, the 130 touring pitches are all of a good size with electricity (6/10A) and separated by trees or flowering bushes (there are 24 mobile homes and 75 pitches used by tour operators). The Provencal style buildings are delightful, especially the bar, restaurant and games room, with its terrace down to the river and the site's own canoe station (locked gate). Adjacent to the site, across the road, is a lake used exclusively for water skiing with a sandy beach, a restaurant and minigolf. Activities include climbing the 'Rock' with a guide. We became more and more intrigued with stories about the Rock, as unfolded by Sabine Simoncini. The Holy Hole, the Three Crosses and the Hermit all call for further exploration which Sabine is happy to arrange, likewise trips to Monte Carlo, Ventiniglia (Italy) and the Gorges du Verdon, etc. The medieval village of Roquebrune is within walking distance.

Facilities

Modern, well designed toilet facilities are in three blocks, one new and attractively designed in the local style, the other two refurbished. Overall, it is a good provision, open as required, with washbasins in cabins (warm water only), baby baths and facilities for disabled visitors. Dishwashing and laundry sinks (H&C). Washing machines. Sheltered swimming pool (heated in low season) with separate paddling pool (child-proof gates, lifeguard in high season; closed lunch times in July/Aug.) with ice cream bar. Shop. Bar, restaurant and games room (all open all season). New play field with nets and play equipment. Fishing. Canoeing (free) and water skiing. Animation arranged in main season for children and adults, visits to local wine caves and sessions at rafting and diving schools. Only gas or electric barbecues are permitted. Only one dog per pitch is accepted. Off site: Bicycle hire 1 km. Riding and golf 6 km (reduced fees).

At a glance

Welcome & Ambience	✓✓✓✓✓	Location	✓✓✓✓
Quality of Pitches	✓✓✓✓	Range of Facilities	✓✓✓✓✓

Directions

From A8 autoroute take Le Muy exit and follow N7 towards Frèjus for approx. 13 km. bypassing Le Muy. After crossing over the A8, turn right at roundabout towards Roquebrune sur Argens. Site is on left after 2 km. just before bridge over river (watch carefully for fairly narrow entrance).

Charges 2005

Per unit incl. 2 persons	€ 18,00 - € 31,00
extra person	€ 4,00 - € 6,00
child (under 7 yrs)	€ 3,00 - € 5,00
electricity (6/10A)	€ 4,00 - € 5,00
dog (max 1)	€ 3,00

Camping Cheques accepted.

Reservations

Made for touring pitches with deposit and fee. Tel: 04 94 45 71 25. E-mail: info@camping-les-pecheurs.com

Open

23 March - 30 September.

FR83220 Camping Caravaning Cros de Mouton

B.P. 116, 83240 Cavalaire-sur-Mer (Var)

Cros de Mouton is a reasonably priced campsite in a popular area. High in the hills on a steep hillside, 1.5 km. from Cavalaire and its popular beaches, the site is a calm oasis away from the hectic coast. There are stunning views of the bay but, unfortunately, due to the nature of the terrain, some of the site roads are very steep - the higher pitches with the best views are especially so. However, Olivier and Andre are happy to take your caravan up with their 4x4 Jeep if you are worried. There are 199 terraced pitches under cork trees which include 46 for mobile homes, 73 suitable only for tents with parking close by, and 80 for touring caravans. These are large and have electricity (10A), some also with water. The restaurant terrace and the pools share the wonderful view of Cavalaire and the bay. English is spoken by the welcoming and helpful owners.

Facilities

Two clean and well maintained toilet blocks have all the usual facilities including washbasins in cubicles. Washing machine at each and a fully fitted facility for disabled customers (although site is perhaps a little steep in places for wheelchairs). Bar/restaurant serving reasonably priced meals, plus takeaways. Swimming and paddling pools with lots of sunbeds on the terrace and small bar for snacks and cold drinks. Small play area and games room.
Off site: Beach 1.5 km. Bicycle hire 1.5 km. Riding 16 km. Golf 20 km.

Open

15 March - 1 November.

At a glance

Welcome & Ambience	✓✓✓✓✓	Location	✓✓✓✓
Quality of Pitches	✓✓✓✓	Range of Facilities	✓✓✓✓

Directions

Take the D559 to Cavalaire-su-Mer (not Cavalière 4 km. away). Site is about 1.5 km. north of the town, very well signed from the centre.

Charges 2004

Per person	€ 5,80 - € 7,10
child (under 7 yrs)	€ 4,00
pitch	€ 5,80 - € 7,10
electricity (10A)	€ 4,00
dog	free - € 2,00

Camping Cheques accepted.

Reservations

Made with deposit (€ 80) and fee (€ 20).
Tel: 04 94 64 10 87.
E-mail: campingcrosdemouton@wanadoo.fr

FR83170 Camping Domaine de la Bergerie

Vallée du Fournel, 83520 Roquebrune-sur-Argens (Var)

This excellent site near the Côte d'Azur will take you away from all the bustle of the Mediterranean to total relaxation amongst the cork, oak, pine and mimosa. The 60 hectare site is quite spread out over terrain that varies from natural, rocky, semi-landscaped areas for mobile homes to flat, grassy avenues of 200 separated pitches for touring caravans and tents. All pitches average over 80 sq.m. and have electricity, with those in one area also having water and drainage. The restaurant/bar, a converted farm building, is surrounded by shady patios, whilst inside it oozes character with high beams and archways leading to intimate corners. Activities are organised daily and, in the evening, shows, cabarets, discos, cinema, karaoke and dancing at the amphitheatre prove popular (possibly until midnight). A superb new pool complex supplements the orginal pool adding more outdoor pools with slides and a river feature, an indoor pool and a fitness centre with jacuzzi, sauna, massage and gym.

Facilities

Four toilet blocks are kept clean and include washbasins in cubicles, facilities for disabled people and babies, plus dishwashing and laundry areas with washing machines. Well stocked supermarket. Bar/restaurant. Takeaway. New pool complex (1/4-30/9) with indoor pool and fitness centre (body building, sauna, gym, etc). Five tennis courts and two half courts. Archery, roller skating and minigolf. Volleyball and mini football. Mini-farm for children. Fishing. Only gas barbecues are permitted. Off site: Riding or golf 4 km. Bicycle hire 7 km. Beach, St Aygulf or Ste Maxime 7 km. Water skiing and rock climbing nearby.

Open

Touring: 1 June - 15 September; mobile homes: 15 March - 15 October.

At a glance

Welcome & Ambience	✓✓✓✓✓	Location	✓✓✓✓✓
Quality of Pitches	✓✓✓✓	Range of Facilities	✓✓✓✓✓

Directions

Leave A8 at Le Muy exit on N7 towards Fréjus. Proceed for 9 km. then right onto D7 signed St Aygulf. Continue for 8 km. and then right at roundabout on D8; site is on the right.

Charges 2004

Per unit incl. 2 adults and electricity (5A)	€ 17,00 - € 28,00
3 persons and electricity, water and drainage	€ 24,50 - € 40,00
extra person	€ 3,00 - € 5,40
child (under 7 yrs)	€ 4,00 - € 6,80
electricity (10A)	€ 1,80 - € 2,70
dog	free - € 3,00

Reservations

Made with deposit (€ 200) and fee (€ 20). Touring: 1 June - 15 September; mobile homes: 15 March - 15 October. Tel: 04 98 11 45 45. E-mail: info@domainelabergerie.com

FR83230 Camping Domaine du Colombier

Route de Bagnols-en-Forêt, 83600 Fréjus (Var)

Domaine du Colombier is a busy site alongside a main road, so a few of the pitches will have some road noise. The majority however are down a hillside and pine trees help to deaden the noise. The pitches (326 for touring units out of 470) vary in size from smallish ones to quite large ones, of which 40 are fully serviced. The hillside is terraced, with all pitches level and with electricity. The pool area with palm trees, a tiled surround and free sunbeds is in a sunny location. There are also three slides and water polo nets for competitions. A disco is underground to deaden the noise. Like the cabarets and competitions all these facilities operate in high season. This is a family site and no groups are accepted. The only downside is that the swimming pool is at the bottom of the site, giving a long pull back up to the majority of pitches, although there is now a new snack bar beside the pool. Much new planting of attractive trees and shrubs has taken place after the fires of 2003.

Facilities

Well maintained and positioned toilet blocks are fully equipped, including baby rooms. Three blocks have en-suite units for people in wheelchairs. Two can be heated on cooler days. Well equipped laundry. Well stocked shop. Bar/restaurant with takeaway. Snack bar (from 1/6). Disco. Large heated swimming pool (30 x 20 m) and paddling pool (all season). Communal barbecue areas for July/Aug. Internet terminal. Two play areas of excellent quality on safety bases. Games room, mini-club room. Half court tennis, volleyball, basketball and boule. Tourist office with bookings to major attractions possible. Only gas or electric barbecues are permitted. Off site: Bus passes the gate.

At a glance

Welcome & Ambience	✓✓✓✓	Location	✓✓✓✓
Quality of Pitches	✓✓✓✓	Range of Facilities	✓✓✓✓✓

Directions

From A8 autoroute take 38 and follow D4 for Frejus. Site is on left, well signed.

Charges 2005

Per unit incl. 2 or 3 persons	€ 19,00 - € 43,00
extra person	€ 6,00 - € 7,50
child (under 10 yrs)	€ 4,00 - € 5,50

Camping Cheques accepted.
Special low season offers.

Reservations

Made with 25% deposit plus booking fee (€ 25).
Tel: 04 94 51 56 01.
E-mail: info@domaine-du-colombier.com

Open

19 March - 1 October.

FR83080 Au Paradis des Campeurs

La Gaillarde-Plage, 83380 Les Issambres (Var)

Having direct access to a sandy beach (via an underpass) and being so well maintained are just two of the reasons which make Au Paradis so popular. Family owned and run, it now has 180 pitches, all with 6A electricity and 132 with water tap and drainaway. The original pitches vary in size and shape but all are satisfactory and most have some shade. The newer pitches are all large but at present have little shade although trees and bushes have been planted and shade is developing. There is no entertainment which gives peaceful nights. The gates are surveyed by TV (especially the beach gate) and a security man patrols all day. The site has become popular and it is essential to book for June, July and August.

Facilities

Two toilet blocks, refurbished to an excellent standard with high quality fittings and well maintained, include the majority of washbasins in cabins. Facilities for children are very good with baby baths and a shower at suitable height. En-suite unit for disabled visitors. Dishwashing, laundry sinks, two washing machines and dryer. Motorcaravan service point. Shop and restaurant (with takeaway service) front onto main road and open all season. TV room. Two excellent play areas, catering for the under and over 5s, both with top quality safety bases. Boules. Car wash area. Off site: Bicycle hire 2.5 km. Riding 3 km. Golf 6 km.

At a glance

Welcome & Ambience	✓✓✓✓	Location	✓✓✓✓
Quality of Pitches	✓✓✓✓	Range of Facilities	✓✓✓✓

Directions

Site is signed from N98 coast road at La Gaillarde, 2 km. south of St Aygulf.

Charges 2005

Per unit incl. 2 persons	€ 12,60 - € 19,50
with water and drainage	€ 14,50 - € 23,50
extra person	€ 5,00
child (under 4 yrs)	€ 2,80
electricity (6A)	€ 3,40

Reservations

Advised for main season. Tel: 04 94 96 93 55.

Open

20 March - 15 October.

FR20040 Domaine Naturiste Riva Bella

B.P. 21, 20270 Alèria (Haute-Corse)

A relaxed, informal naturist site beside a glorious beach, Riva Bella is arguably camping and caravanning at its very best. Although offering a large number and variety of pitches, they are situated in such a huge area of varied and beautiful countryside and seaside that it is difficult to believe it could ever become overcrowded. The site is divided into several distinct areas - pitches and bungalows, alongside the sandy beach, in a wooded glade with ample shade, behind the beach, or beside the lake/lagoon which is a feature of this site. The ground is undulating, so getting an absolutely level pitch could be a problem in the main season. Although electric hook-ups are available in most parts, a long cable is probably a necessity. There is an interesting evening entertainment programme. A recent addition is a therapy centre with treatments and massages based on marine products. Noël Pasqual is fully proud of his site and the fairly unobtrusive rules are designed to ensure that everyone is able to relax, whilst preserving the natural beauty of the environment. There is, for example, a restriction on the movement of cars in certain areas (but ample free parking). Generally the ambience is relaxed and informal with nudity only obligatory on the beach itself. Member 'France 4 Naturisme'.

Facilities

Toilet facilities in several blocks have been completely refurbished. Whilst fairly typical in design for naturist sites, they are fitted and decorated to the highest standards facilities for disabled people and babies. Large well stocked shop (15/5-30/9). Fridge hire. Excellent restaurant (all season) with reasonable prices overlooks the lagoon. Snack bar beside the beach during the main season (1/6-30/9). Watersports including sailing school, fishing, sub-aqua etc. Therapy centre. Sauna. Volleyball, aerobics, table tennis, giant draughts and archery. Fishing. Mountain bike hire. Half-court tennis. Herd of llamas to watch. The police/fire service ban barbecues during the summer as a safety precaution Off site: Riding 5 km.

At a glance

Welcome & Ambience	✓✓✓✓✓	Location	✓✓✓✓✓
Quality of Pitches	✓✓✓✓	Range of Facilities	✓✓✓✓✓

Directions

Site is approx. 8 km. north of Aleria on N198 (Bastia) road. Watch for signs and unmade road to it and follow for 4 km

Charges 2004

Per unit incl. 2 persons	€ 17,00 - € 30,00
extra person	€ 4,00 - € 8,50
child (3-8 yrs)	€ 2,00 - € 5,00
electricity	€ 3,50
dog	€ 3,00 - € 3,00

Camping Cheques accepted.
Special offers and half-board arrangements available.

Reservations

Made with deposit and fee/cancellation insurance.
Tel: 04 95 38 81 10. E-mail: riva-bella@wanadoo.fr

Open

12 April - 11 October.

PAS-DE-CALAIS 62
NORD 59
NORTHERN FRANCE
SOMME 80
SEINE-MARITIME 76
AISNE 02
ARDENNES 08
OISE 60
MEUSE 55
MOSELLE 57
BAS-RHIN 67
MANCHE 50
CALVADOS 14
EURE 27
PARIS ILE DE FRANCE
MARNE 51
MEURTHE-ET-MOSELLE 54
NORMANDY
ORNE 61
EURE-ET-LOIR 28
AUBE 10
HAUTE-MARNE 52
VOSGES 88
FINISTERE 29
COTES-D'ARMOR 22
ILLE-ET-VILAINE 35
MAYENNE 53
HAUT-RHIN 68
BRITTANY
SARTHE 72
LOIRET 45
YONNE 89
HAUTE-SAONE 70
MORBIHAN 56
COTE-D'OR 21
TERRITOIRE-DE-BELFORT 90
LOIRE VALLEY
FRANCHE-COMTE
LOIRE-ATLANTIQUE 44
MAINE-ET-LOIRE 49
LOIR-ET-CHER 41
INDRE-ET-LOIRE 37
BURGUNDY
DOUBS 25
CHER 18
NIEVRE 58
JURA 39
INDRE 36
SAONE-ET-LOIRE 71
VENDEE 85
VIENNE 86
ALLIER 03
HAUTE-SAVOIE 74
AIN 01
VENDEE CHARENTE
DEUX-SEVRES 79
CREUSE 23
CHARENTE-MARITIME 17
HAUTE-VIENNE 87
PUY-DE-DOME 63
LOIRE 42
RHONE 69
SAVOY DAUPHINY ALPS
SAVOIE 73
CHARENTE 16
LIMOUSIN/AUVERGNE
ISERE 38
CORREZE 19
HAUTE-LOIRE 43
RHONE VALLEY
DORDOGNE 24
CANTAL 15
HAUTES-ALPES 05
DROME 26
ARDECHE 07
GIRONDE 33
PROVENCE
LOT 46
LOZERE 48
ALPES-DE-HAUTE-PROVENCE 04
LOT-ET-GARONNE 47
AVEYRON 12
ATLANTIC COAST
VAUCLUSE 84
GARD 30
ALPES-MARITIMES 06
TARN-ET-GARONNE 82
LANDES 40
MEDITERRANEAN
TARN 81
GERS 32
MIDI-PYRENEES
BOUCHES-DU-RHONE 13
HERAULT 34
VAR 83
HAUTE-GARONNE 31
PYRENEES-ATLANTIQUES 64
AUDE 11
HAUTES-PYRENEES 65
ARIEGE 09
PYRENEES-ORIENTALES 66

For administrative purposes France is actually divided into 23 official Regions covering the 95 départements (similar to our counties). However, theses do not always coincide with the needs of tourists (for example, the area we think of as the 'Dordogne' is split between two official regions. We have, therefore, opted to feature our campsites within unofficial 'tourist' regions.We use the departement numbers as the first two digits of our campsite numbers so, for example, any site in the Manche departement will start with the number 50.

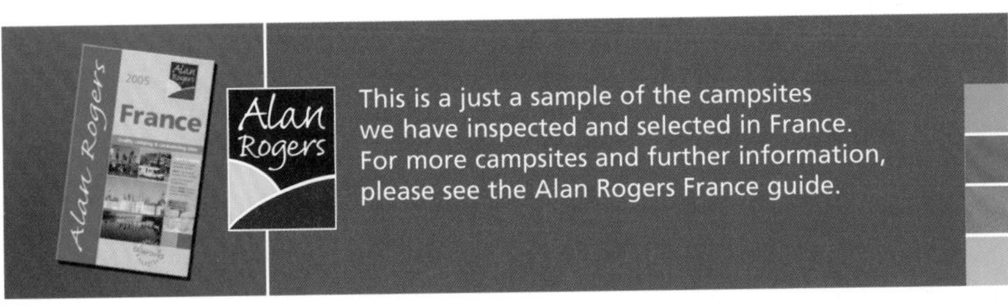

With its wealth of scenic and cultural interests, Germany is a land of contrasts. From the flat lands of the north to the mountains in the south, with forests in the east and west, regional characteristics are a strong feature of German life and present a rich variety of folklore and customs.

Each region in Germany differs greatly to the next. Home of Lederhosen, beer and sausages is Bavaria in the south, full of charming forest villages, beautiful lakes, and towering mountains dotted with castles. In the south west, Baden Württemberg is famous for its ancient Black Forest, with dense woodlands, medieval towns and scenic lakes, this region is a walkers paradise. Further west is the stunningly beautiful, Rhine Valley full of romantic castles, wine villages, woodland walks and river trails. Eastern Germany is studded with lakes and rivers, undulating lowlands that give way to mountains. The north has its lively ports such as Bremen and Hamburg and picturesque coastal towns, where watersports are a popular pastime in the North Sea. The capital city of Berlin, situated in the north east of the county, is an increasingly popular tourist destination, with its blend of old and modern architecture and huge variety of entertainment on offer.

Population

83.2 million

Capital

Berlin

Climate

Temperate climate. In general winters are a little colder and summers a little warmer than in the UK

Language

German

Currency

The Euro

Telephone

The country code is 00 49

Banks

Mon-Fri 08.30-12.30 and 14.00-16.00. Late opening on Thurs until 18.00

Shops

Mon-Fri 08.30/09.00 to 18.00/18.30

Public Holidays

New Year's Day; Good Fri; Easter Mon; Labour Day; Ascension; Whit Mon; Unification Day 3 Oct; Christmas, 25, 26 Dec. In some areas: Epiphany 6 Jan; Corpus Christi 22 Jun; Assumption 15 Aug; Reformation 31 Oct; All Saints 1 Nov

Motoring

An excellent network of (toll-free) motorways (Autobahns) exists in the 'West' and the traffic moves fast. Remember in the 'East' a lot of road building is going on amongst other works so allow plenty of time when travelling and be prepared for poor road surfaces

Tourist Office

German National Tourist Office
PO Box 2695
London W1A 3TN
Tel: 020 7317 0908
Fax: 020 7495 6129
Email: gntolon@d-z-t.com
Internet: www.germany-tourism.de

VISIT THE DELIGHTFUL SPA TOWN OF BADEN-BADEN IN SOUTHERN GERMANY AND PAMPER YOURSELF WITH A DIP IN ONE OF THE WORLD-FAMOUS THERMAL BATHS.

DE3003 Camping Wulfener Hals

23769 Wulfen auf Fehmarn (Schleswig-Holstein)

If you are travelling to Denmark or on to Sweden, taking the E47/A1 then B207 from Hamburg, and the ferry from Puttgarden to Rødbyhavn, this is a top class all year round site, either to rest overnight or as a base for a longer stay. Attractively situated by the sea, it is a large, mature site (34 hectares) and is well-maintained. It has over 800 individual pitches of up to 160 sq.m. (half for touring) in glades and some separated by bushes, with shade in the older parts, less in the newer areas nearer the sea. There are many hardstandings and 462 pitches have electricity, water and drainage. There is much to do for old and young alike with a small outdoor heated pool (unsupervised), but the sea is naturally popular as well. The site also has many sporting facilities including its own golf courses and schools for watersports.

Facilities

The four heated sanitary buildings have first class facilities including showers on payment (€ 0.50) and both open washbasins and private cabins (more of these for ladies). Facilities for disabled people, dishwashing and laundry, each available in most but not all the buildings. Motorcaravan services. Shop, bar and restaurants, (one waiter, one self-service and takeaway (all year). Swimming pool (May - Oct). Sauna. Solarium. Sailing and windsurfing school. Diving school. Golf courses (18 hole, par 72 and 9 hole, par 27). Roller skating. Riding. Fishing. Archery. Football area. Table tennis. Good play equipment for younger children. Bicycle hire. Only small dogs are accepted. Off site: Naturist beach 500 m. Village mini-market 2 km.

At a glance

Welcome & Ambience	✓✓✓✓	Location	✓✓✓✓✓
Quality of Pitches	✓✓✓✓	Range of Facilities	✓✓✓✓✓

Directions

From Hamburg take A1/E47 north to Puttgarden, cross the bridge onto the island of Fenmark and turn right twice to Avendorf and follow the signs for Wulfen and the site.

Charges guide

Per person	€ 3,40 - € 6,70
child (2-14 yrs)	€ 1,60 - € 4,60
pitch (plus surcharges over 110 or 130 sq.m.)	€ 6,70 - € 17,90
electricity (10A)	€ 2,30
dog	€ 1,00 - € 6,70

Many discounts available and special family prices.

Reservations

Probably not necessary for short stay.
Tel: 04371 86280. E-mail: camping@wulfenerhals.de

Open

All year.

DE3002 Ferienpark Schlei-Karschau

24407 Rabenkirchen-Faulück (Lower Saxony)

With an impressive landscaped entrance, a shop and restaurant to one side and reception to the other and a barrier which is closed in the evening, this is a good quality site. It is a rural area with attractive villages, plenty of water and woodland, near to the interesting old port of Bremerhaven with its 29 km. of quays and maritime and fishing museums. The heart of this site is a deep set, small fishing lake and beach. Lightly wooded, pitches are accessed by circular roadways on differing levels and terraced where necessary. Because of the design you don't realise that there are 380 pitches, nearly all with electricity (6A) and clearly defined by shrubs and trees (250 for touring units).

Facilities

Two heated toilet blocks, one adjoining reception and one nearer the lake (access to this is by steps from the varying levels). The provision is good and well kept, with one block recently renovated. Motorcaravan services. Shop, restaurant, bar and takeaway. Children's playground. Minigolf. Table tennis. Fishing. Beach volleyball. Bicycle hire. Large screen TV. Barbecue facility with roof. Off site: Zoo for small animals nearby, also a riding school with Icelandic horses which are small, quiet and very safe for children with a good value inclusive daily rate, including lunch. Watersports near. Swimming pool behind the hotel opposite the site is open and free to campers. Horse riding 2 km. Golf 5 km.

At a glance

Welcome & Ambience	✓✓✓✓	Location	✓✓✓✓
Quality of Pitches	✓✓✓✓	Range of Facilities	✓✓✓

Directions

Follow B 73 North from Hamburg and take exit for Wingst (Spiel and Sportpark) signed 'camping platz'. Then take first left.

Charges 2004

Per person	€ 4,00
child (3-14 yrs)	€ 3,00
pitch	€ 9,00
small tent with motorcycle	€ 3,00
dog	€ 2,00
electricity	€ 2,00

No credit cards.

Reservations

Contact site. Tel: 04642 920820. E-mail: info@ferienpark.de

Open

1 March - 31 October, with all facilities.

DE3005 Camping Schnelsen Nord

Wunderbrunnen 2, 22457 Hamburg (Hamburg)

Situated some 15 kilometres from the centre of Hamburg on the northern edge of the town, Schnelsen Nord is a suitable base either for visiting this famous German city, or as a night stop before catching the Harwich ferry or travelling to Denmark. A large number of trees and shrubs offer shade and privacy. There is some traffic noise because the autobahn runs alongside (despite efforts to screen it out) and also some aircraft noise. However, the proximity of the A7 (E45) does make it easy to find. The 145 pitches for short-term touring are of about 100 sq.m, on grass with access from gravel roads. All have 6A electricity, are numbered and marked out with small trees and hedges. Only basic food supplies are stocked in reception as the site is about ten minutes walk from the restaurants and shops in town. Apart from some road traffic 'hum', as previously mentioned, this is a quiet, well laid out site.

Facilities

A deposit is required for the key to the single sanitary block, a well constructed modern building with good quality facilities and heated in cool weather. Hot water is free for the washbasins (some in cabins) and dishwashing. Good facilities for disabled visitors, with special pitches close to the block. Washing machines and dryers. Motorcaravan service point (for site guests only). Shop (basics only). Table tennis. Playground. Off site: Swimming pool, tennis courts, golf and fishing nearby.

Open

1 April - 31 October.

At a glance

Welcome & Ambience	✓✓✓✓	Location	✓✓✓✓
Quality of Pitches	✓✓✓✓	Range of Facilities	✓✓✓

Directions

From A7 autobahn take Schnelsen Nord exit. Stay in outside lane as you will soon need to turn back left; follow signs for Ikea store and site signs.

Charges 2005

Per person	€ 5,00
child (3-13)	€ 3,50
tent	€ 7,20 - € 7,40
electricity (6A)	€ 2,50
caravan	€ 7,40
motorcaravan	€ 9,70 - € 11,20

Reservations

Said to be unnecessary. Tel: 040 5594225. E-mail: service@campingplatz-hamburg.de

DE3020 Campingplatz Freie Hansestadt Bremen

Am Stadtwaldsee 1, 28359 Bremen (Bremen)

Five kilometres from the city centre and in pleasant 'green belt' surroundings near the university, this is a useful small site. There is no need to take your vehicle into the city, as the site has excellent public transport connections. There is bus stop in front of the site. Despite the easy accessibility of the city, the site has a distinctly rural feel with quite an abundance of wildlife. It has 115 large pitches (75 for touring units) of at least 100 sq.m on flat grass and marked out by stones, all with 6A electricity and 12 with hardstanding for motorcaravans. What helps make this site so appealing is the pleasant reception accorded to guests and the helpful English speaking staff. Being a popular spot, it can become very busy and full here over a long season and on certain pitches some road noise may be experienced.

Facilities

An excellent, heated building includes some washbasins in cabins, provision for disabled visitors and a baby room. Washing machines and dryer. Motorcaravan services. Gas supplies. Cooking facilities. Good reasonably priced restaurant/bar (March-Oct). Takeaway (all year). Small shop (all year, but limited in low season - fresh bread to order). General room. Playground. Sports field. Bicycle hire. Barbecue area. Off site: 20 hectare lake suitable for swimming and boating 500 m. Bus stop at the entrance, tram service only minutes away. Good cycle rides and walks in the municipal woodland adjacent (avoid the male naturist area!)

At a glance

Welcome & Ambience	✓✓✓✓✓	Location	✓✓✓✓
Quality of Pitches	✓✓✓✓	Range of Facilities	✓✓✓✓

Directions

From A27 autobahn northeast of Bremen take exit 19 for 'Universitat' and follows signs for University and site.

Charges 2004

Per person	€ 4,10
child (under 16 yrs)	€ 2,50
caravan	€ 6,00
tent	€ 4,00 - € 6,00
car on pitch	€ 1,40
motorcaravan acc. to size	€ 8,50 - € 10,00

Reservations

Made for any length with deposit. Tel: 0421 212002. E-mail: campingplatz-bremen@t-online.de

Open

All year.

DE3010 Kur und Feriencamping Röders Park

Ebsmoor 8, 29614 Soltau (Lower Saxony)

Although near Soltau centre (1.5 km), Ebsmoor is a peaceful location, ideal for visits to the famous Luneburg Heath or as a stop on the route to Denmark. The site is run by the third generation of the Röders family who make their visitors most welcome and speak excellent English. The central feature of the wooded site is a small lake crossed by a wooden bridge. An abundance of trees and shrubs gives a secluded setting to an already well cared for appearance. Röders' Park only offers a tranquil stay - there is no entertainment. Many sports activities are available locally. The site has 100 pitches (75 touring), all with 6A electricity and 70 with water and drainage also. Most have hardstanding and there is reasonable privacy between pitches.

Facilities

Two modern, very clean sanitary blocks (one with under-floor heating) contain all necessary facilities with a laundry room and an excellent, separate unit (including shower) for wheelchair users. Motorcaravan services. Gas supplies. Simple shop. Restaurant (both Easter - Oct). Children's play area. Bicycle hire. Off site: Thermal swimming pool 1 km. Fishing and riding 1.5 km. Golf 3 km. 999 km. of cycle paths in the surrounding area.

Open

All year.

At a glance

Welcome & Ambience	✓✓✓✓✓	Location	✓✓✓✓✓
Quality of Pitches	✓✓✓	Range of Facilities	✓✓✓✓

Directions

From Soltau take B3 road north and turning to site is on left after 1.5 km. (opposite DCC camping sign) at yellow town boundary sign.

Charges 2005

Per person	€ 5,00
child (4-14 yrs)	€ 4,00
pitch	€ 11,00
dog	€ 2,00
electricity (6A)	€ 0,45

Reservations

Contact site. Tel: 05191 2141. E-mail: info@roeders-park.de

DE3025 Alfsee Ferien-und Erholungspark

Am Campingpark 10, 49597 Rieste (Lower Saxony)

There have continued to be major improvements to this already well-equipped site. There are now over 800 pitches (many long stay but with 400 for tourers) on flat grass, 120 with 16A electricity, with some shade for those in the original area. A new camping area provides 100 large, serviced pitches. Alfsee offers a really good base for enjoying the many watersports activities available here on the two lakes. The smaller one has a 780 m. water-ski 'tug' ski lift style (on payment) and there is also a separate swimming area here with a sandy beach (and beach volleyball). A little further along is a 600 m. go-kart track and a smaller track for youngsters. The Alfsee itself is a very large stretch of water with a sailing school, windsurfing, motor boats, row boats, canoes and pedaloes as well as fishing and a cafe/restaurant open daily. This site has plenty to offer for the active family and children of all ages.

Facilities

Three older, but still very good sanitary blocks serve the original area with two new first class, heated buildings with family bathrooms, baby rooms and laundry facilities. Washing machines and dryers. Cooking facilities. All is nicely decorated and well maintained. Motorcaravan services. Gas supplies. Shop, restaurants and takeaway (all year). New pub and internet point. Watersports. Football practice field. Children's playground and entertainment. Grass tennis courts. Trampoline. Minigolf. Go-kart track. General room with amusement machines. Fishing. Bicycle hire. Riding. Off site: Golf 8 km.

At a glance

Welcome & Ambience	✓✓✓✓✓	Location	✓✓✓✓✓
Quality of Pitches	✓✓✓✓✓	Range of Facilities	✓✓✓✓✓

Directions

From A1 autobahn north of Osnabrück take exit 67 for Neuenkirchen and follow signs for Rieste, Alfsee and site.

Charges 2004

Per unit incl. 2 persons	€ 7,60 - € 10,70
extra adult	€ 3,20 - € 5,20
child or student	€ 2,80 - € 3,40
dog	€ 1,70 - € 2,70
electricity (once only plus meter)	€ 1,40
overnight pitch (17.00 - 10.00 hrs)	€ 7,50 - € 9,50

Reservations

Made for any length without deposit.
Tel: 05464 92120. E-mail: info@alfsee.com

Open

All year.

DE3045 Knaus Camping Park Walkenried

Ellricher Straße 7, 37445 Walkenried (Lower Saxony)

The southern Harz area offers much for walkers and anglers and this site organises many outings ranging from free walks to coach trips to the highest mountain in the area at Brocken (1,142 m). It also has the benefit of an indoor pool, sauna and solarium. Outdoor activities available in the area include tennis, riding and watersports. There are 160 touring pitches here of 80-100 sq.m. and arranged in well shaded groups on mainly slightly sloping grass and gravel. Most are separated by bushes or trees and have 4A, 2 pin electrical connections. There are some smaller hardstandings for motorhomes and a separate area for visitors with dogs.

Facilities

The satisfactory tiled and heated sanitary facilities are in the main building by the entrance, with washbasins in cabins for ladies (some curtained for men) and a toilet for disabled visitors. Laundry and cooking facilities. Gas supplies. Motorcaravan services. Shop and restaurant (closed Tuesdays). Order bread at reception. Indoor swimming pool, free for campers (open 9-12 and 3-6,). Sauna and solarium. Large play area. Barbecue area with some seating here and by the small lake. Fishing in lake. Large screen TV. Beach volleyball. Bicycle hire. Off site: Golf 2 km.

Open

All year except November, with all facilities.

At a glance

Welcome & Ambience	✓✓✓✓✓	Location	✓✓✓✓
Quality of Pitches	✓✓✓✓	Range of Facilities	✓✓✓✓

Directions

Walkenried is signed from B4 Erfurt-Magdeburg road just north of Nordhausen and from B243 Seesen-Nordhausen road. The site is signed in the town.

Charges 2004

Per person	€ 6,00
child (3-14 yrs)	€ 3,00
pitch	€ 3,00 - € 8,00
dog	€ 2,00
electricity	€ 2,00
serviced pitch	€ 1,00

No credit cards.

Reservations

Contact the site. Tel: 05525 778.

Germany

DE3065 Camping am Bärenbache

Bärenbachweg 10, Hohegeiss, 38700 Braunlage (Lower Saxony)

Pleasantly situated and over 600 meters high in the Harz, Campingplatz Bärenbache is a quiet, attractive, well run family site having direct access to the forests that surround it. This terraced site on a south facing slope reaps the maximum benefit from the sun throughout the year and offers views of the surrounding hills in an area known for its fresh air. At the lower end of the site is a large, heated, outdoor swimming pool complex adjoined by a bar/restaurant. Of the 140 pitches 90 are reserved for tourists all having 10A electrical connections. The level pitches are separated by hedges and are of various sizes, some suitable for one, others for several units. The Harz is a region steeped in geological, mythical, industrial and cultural history and the reception has a good selection of tourist information. In addition, the site owners are only too happy to give tourist advice. Roses, rambling, narrow gauge railways, witches, mines, mineral collections and medieval towns such as Goslar, all have their place in this fascinating region.

Facilities

As can be expected in a site that also has a winter season, all facilities are housed internally in the modern, well maintained and heated toilet block. Showers are free. Baby room. Laundry room with washing machines, dryers and iron, drying room. Dishwashing sinks. Small kitchen with cooking rings. Playground. Table tennis. Volleyball. Large outdoor heated pool with two separate pools for children. Bar/restaurant (all year) beside the pool. Off site: Shopping in the village centre is only a few minutes walk from the campsite.

At a glance

Welcome & Ambience	✓✓✓✓✓	Location	✓✓✓✓✓
Quality of Pitches	✓✓✓✓	Range of Facilities	✓✓✓✓✓

Directions

The village of Hohegeiß is 10 km. southeast of Braunlage on the B4 road. Leaving Hohegeiß in the direction of Zorge. site is signed.

Charges 2004

Per person	€ 4,35
child (2-15 yrs)	€ 2,50
pitch	€ 4,70
electricity/ kwH	€ 0,45

Reservations

Contact site. Tel: 05583 1306.
E-mail: info@campingplatz-hohegeiss.de

Open

All year.

DE3030 Regenbogen-Camp Tecklenburg

Grafenstrasse 31, 49545 Tecklenburg-Leeden (North Rhine-Westphalia)

This is a well designed and attractive countryside site with lots of trees and hedges where modern buildings have been built in keeping with the traditional, half timbered style of the region. The site has an excellent indoor and outdoor swimming pool complex. There are 500 grass touring pitches arranged on large, open areas divided by tall hedges. Trees provide good shade and all pitches have electrical connections. Facilities on this site are really good, from the modern heated pool complex, to the large half timbered historical bar/restaurant with its thick wooden beams and adjoining beer garden. Access from the A30 autobahn is convenient, although this is offset by the fact that some noise from the autobahn is evident in the touring pitch area. The old town of Tecklenburg is well worth visiting, Convenient parking is the old town (Altstadt) car park, with a small supermarket adjoining. It is signposted and located just above the church and from there it is only a short walk to the town centre.

Facilities

Four modern, heated toilet blocks have free showers and provision for disabled visitors. Washing machines and dryer. Cooking facilities. Chemical disposal facilities and motorcaravan service point. Shop, bar and restaurant (Easter- end October and Christmas). Pool complex with indoor and outdoor pools and paddling pool. Play area. Minigolf. Table tennis. In-line skating. Volleyball.

Open

All year.

At a glance

Welcome & Ambience	✓✓✓✓✓	Location	✓✓
Quality of Pitches	✓✓✓✓	Range of Facilities	✓✓✓✓✓

Directions

Leave A30/E30 autobahn at exit 13 towards Tecklenburg. Between the autobahn exit and Tecklenburg, at a roundabout, the site is signed.

Charges 2004

Per person	€ 6,80
child (4-13 yrs)	€ 3,40
pitch	€ 10,00
electricity	€ 2,50

Prices are lower out of high season.

Reservations

Formal ones are complicated and require pre-payment. Suggest phoning or sending a card before arrival. Tel: 05405 1007.
E-mail: tecklenburg@regenbogen-camp.de

Germany

DE3180 Camping Sonnenwiese

Borlefzen 1, 32602 Vlotho (North Rhine-Westphalia)

Sonnenwiese is a first class, family run campsite where care has been taken to make everyone feel at home – there is even an insect hotel! The site is tastefully landscaped with lots of flowers, an ornamental pond crossed by a wooden bridge and large grass areas extending to the river. Situated between wooded hills to the north and bordering the river Weser to the south, this 500 pitch site offers 60 touring pitches, all with electricity and most also having water and drainage. In addition, there are special pitches with their own shower, toilet and washbasin unit. The site is particularly orientated towards families with children, having spacious play areas and in summer and at holiday weekends, entertainment programmes. Outside the bar/restaurant is a small railway where children can ride, while parents finish their meal or enjoy a drink. On the Weser there are fishing and water sports and the site has its own slipway. Bicycles can be hired at reception where tour maps are available.

Facilities

The toilet block is modern and maintained to the highest standard. Showers are token operated. Baby room. Laundry room with washing machines, dryer and ironing board. Cooking facilities. Supermarket. Restaurant. Snack bar. Sauna, solarium and fitness room. Club room. Large adventure play area. Volleyball and basketball. Table tennis. Grass bordered lake for swimming. Fishing. Bicycle hire.

Open

All year.

At a glance

Welcome & Ambience	✓✓✓✓✓	Location	✓✓✓✓
Quality of Pitches	✓✓✓✓✓	Range of Facilities	✓✓✓✓✓

Directions

Leave A2 at exit 31 or 33. Just north of bridge over the Weser is the turn for the site. After 3 km. on the right are two sites. Sonnenwiese is on the left.

Charges 2004

Per person	€ 4,60
child (5-14 yrs)	€ 1,80 - € 3,40
pitch	€ 7,00 - € 8,60
electricity	€ 1,50

No credit cards.

Reservations

Contact site. Tel: 05733 8217.
E-mail: info@sonnenwiese.com

DE3182 Ferienpark Teutoburger Wald

Fischteiche 4, 32683 Barntrup (North Rhine-Westphalia)

Our German agent has recommended this wooded site and we plan to conduct a full inspection in 2005. Ferienpark Teutoburgerwald can be found around 20 minutes drive south of Hamlin and offers a varied camping area, ranging from small tent pitches to a number of larger super pitches equipped with private sanitary facilities. A range of leisure amenities, administered by the town, are available on-site.

Facilities

Swimming pool. Tennis. Playground, children's club. Organised walking and mountain biking. Chalets for rent. Off site: Hamlin 20 km, Bad Pyrmont 12 km.

Open

20 March - 31 October.

Reservations

Advised for high season. Tel: 05263 2221.
E-mail: info@ferienparkteutoburgerwald.de

Directions

Barntrup is on the B66 which leads off the main Hameln - Detmold road (B1), about 10 km before reaching Detmold. Site is signed within the town.

Charges 2004

Per unit incl. 2 persons, electricity	€ 13,00 - € 18,00
'super' pitch plus	€ 10,00
extra adult	€ 4,00
child (2-15 yrs)	€ 2,00

DE3185 Campingplatz Münster

Laerer Werseufer 7, (Wolbecker Strasse), 48157 Münster (North Rhine-Westphalia)

This is a first class site on the outskirts of Münster. Of a total of 570 pitches, 120 are touring units, each with electricity, water, drainage and TV socket. The pitches are level, most with partial hardstanding and others are separated into groups by mature hedges and a number of trees provide shade. The university city of Münster with its many historical buildings and over 500 bars and restaurants, many offering local traditional dishes, is only 5 km. from the site. Next to the reception desk is a small shop and on the first floor of the building a comfortable bar/restaurant with terrace. Bicycles are available for hire and there are cycle tour maps for the area. For those who wish to avoid the stress of driving in busy foreign cities and the even worse problem of finding a parking place, public transport offers a good solution.

Facilities

The two toilet blocks are well designed, modern and maintained to the highest standards. Controllable showers are token operated. Two units for disabled guests. Baby room. Cooking facilities. Laundry room. Sauna and solarium. Hairdressing salon. Motorcaravan services. Shop. Bar/restaurant. Table tennis. Minigolf. Play area. Tennis court. Bicycle hire. Barrier deposit € 10. Off site: Bus stop.

Open

All year.

At a glance

Welcome & Ambience	✓✓✓✓✓	Location	✓✓✓✓
Quality of Pitches	✓✓✓✓✓	Range of Facilities	✓✓✓✓

Directions

Site is 5 km. southeast of the city centre. Leave A1 at exit 78 (Münster Süd) and take B51 towards Münster. After 2 km. stay on the B51 in the direction of Bielefeld/Warendorf. After 5 km. turn south (right) towards Wolbeck. WDR. Follow camping site signs.

Charges 2004

Per unit incl. 2 persons, electricity	€ 23,00 - € 42,00
extra adult	€ 4,00
child (4-12 yrs)	€ 2,50

Reservations

Contact site. Tel: 0251 311982.
E-mail: campingplatz-muenster@t-online.de

DE3202 Erholungszentrum Grav-Insel

Gravinsel 1, 46487 Wesel (North Rhine-Westphalia)

Grav-Insel claims to be the biggest family camping site in Germany, providing entertainment and activities to match, with over 2,000 permanent units as well as those for touring. It is a well maintained site, attractively situated on an island in the Rhine and is a good base for swimming (with a sandy beach by a quiet inlet), fishing and boating (with boat park). A long section for the touring units runs beside the water to the left of the entrance. The pitches are flat, grassy, mostly without shade and of about 100 sq.m. Some are marked by water points and there are electricity boxes with multiple outlets (10/16A). A brand new building behind the modern reception is enormous and houses excellent sanitary facilities including some for disabled visitors, a restaurant with wheelchair access, terraces for a snack bar and ices, play rooms (including a large area for wet weather play) and a supermarket. However, these amenities are a long walk from some of the touring pitches. This is a busy, well managed site where the peacocks add to the holiday atmosphere.

Facilities

Excellent, new sanitary facilities, augmented by older, very basic portakabin units in the touring area, have toilets with washbasins, some very large showers with triple sprays, baby room, launderette, dishwashing. Solarium. Supermarket (hours acc. to season). Restaurant (all year). Riding. Fishing. Swimming. Large play area on sand plus wet weather indoor area. Animation in high season. Boat park. Sailing. Off site: Warner Bros. Movie-World-Park 20 minutes drive.

At a glance

Welcome & Ambience	✓✓✓✓	Location	✓✓✓✓
Quality of Pitches	✓✓✓✓	Range of Facilities	✓✓✓✓

Directions

From the A3 Arnhem - Düsseldorf exit 6 take B58 towards Wesel, then right towards Rees. Turn left at sign for Flüren, through town and left to site after 1.5 km.

Charges guide

Per person	€ 3,00
child (under 14 yrs)	€ 1,50
pitch	€ 6,50
electricity	€ 3,00

Reservations

Not made. Tel: 0281 972830.
E-mail: grav-insel@t-online.de

Open

All year.

DE3210 Campingplatz Biggesee Sondern

Am Sonderner Kopf 3, 57462 Olpe-Sondern (North Rhine-Westphalia)

Biggesee-Sondern is a high quality leisure complex site, in an attractive setting on the shores of a large lake in the Südsauerland National Park, offering many leisure opportunities, as well as excellent camping facilities. It is therefore deservedly popular, and reservation is almost always advisable. Well managed, the same company also operates two other sites on the shores of the lake, where space may be available, which is useful as it is also popular for a short stay, being quite near the A45 and A4 roads. There are 300 flat or sloping numbered pitches of 100 sq.m, of which about 250 are available for tourists, either in rows or in circles, on terraces, with 6A electricity and water points grouped throughout. The leisure activities available are numerous. Watersports include diving, sailing and windsurfing, with lessons available. You may launch your own small boat, and also swim from the shore in a roped off area.

Facilities

Excellent sanitary facilities are in two areas, heated when necessary but bring your own paper. Many washbasins in cabins and special showers for children. Facilities for babies, laundry (keys from reception) and people with disabilities. Motorcaravan services. Car wash area. Cooking facilities. Roller-skating. Playroom and playground for smaller children. Skiing. Watersports. Walks around the lake. Football pitch. Table tennis. Fishing. Bicycle hire. Solarium and sauna. Entertainment and excursions. Off site: Tennis near. Riding 8 km. Golf 12 km. Restaurant and snacks 300 m (Easter - 31/10).

At a glance

Welcome & Ambience	✓✓✓✓	Location	✓✓✓✓✓
Quality of Pitches	✓✓✓✓	Range of Facilities	✓✓✓✓

Directions

From A45 (Siegen-Hagen) autobahn, take exit 18 to Olpe (N), and turn towards Attendorn. After 6 km. turn to Bigge-Stausee. Site is well signed.

Charges guide

Per person	€ 3,10 - € 3,90
child (3-15 yrs)	€ 1,80 - € 2,40
pitch incl. electricity	€ 10,50 - € 13,10
dog	€ 2,30 - € 2,40

No credit cards.

Reservations

Advised for much of the year, but phone site.
Tel: 02761 944111. E-mail: biggesee@t-online.de

Open

All year.

DE3280 Camping und Ferienpark Teichmann

An der B252, 34516 Vöhl-Herzhausen (Hesse)

Situated by a six hectare lake (the Edersee) with tree-covered hills all around, this well cared for site blends in attractively with its surroundings. Windsurfing, rowing boats, pedaloes (no motor-boats), swimming and fishing are possible, all in different areas, and the site is also suitable for a winter sports holiday (with ski runs near). There are many local walks and the opportunity exists for taking a pleasure boat trip and riding home by bicycle. The 460 pitches (half for touring units) are mainly on flat grass, all with 6A electricity and with some hardstandings. The many amenities include a mini-market and café. A good site for families, there are many activities (listed below) and a pitch can usually be found even for a one night stay. A very large open air model railway is a special attraction.

Facilities

Three good quality sanitary blocks can be heated and have some private cabins, with baby rooms in two with facilities for wheelchair users. Café and shop (both summer only). Restaurant by entrance open all day (Feb-Dec). Watersports. Boat and bicycle hire. Lake swimming. Football. Fishing. Minigolf. Beach volleyball (high season). Tennis. Table tennis. Playground. Large working model railway. Sauna and solarium. High season disco. Off site: Cable car (you can take bikes), Aquapark, toboggan run.

Open

All year.

At a glance

Welcome & Ambience	✓✓✓✓	Location	✓✓✓✓
Quality of Pitches	✓✓✓✓	Range of Facilities	✓✓✓✓

Directions

From A44 Oberhausen - Kassel autobahn, take exit for Korbach. Site is between Korbach and Frankenberg on the B252 road, 1 km. to the south of Herzhausen, about 45 km. from the A44.

Charges guide

Per unit with 2 persons, electricity, water and waste water	€ 9,50 - € 14,00
extra adult	€ 3,60 - € 5,70
child (3-16 yrs)	€ 2,60 - € 3,60
electricity (6A)	€ 2,10

Reservations

Made with deposit (€ 50) and fee (€ 5); write to site. Tel: 05635 245. E-mail: camping-teichmann@t-online.de

DE3205 Campingplatz der Stadt Köln

Weidenweg 35, 51105 Köln-Poll (North Rhine-Westphalia)

The ancient city of Cologne offers much for the visitor, with museums, art galleries, opera and open-air concerts, as well as the famous Cathedral. The wooded park is pleasantly situated along the river bank, with wide grass areas (the manager takes great pains to keep it well) on either side of narrow tarmac access roads with low metal barriers separating it from the public park and riverside walks. Of 140 unmarked, level or slightly undulating touring pitches, 50 have 10A electricity and there is shade for some from various mature trees. Tents have their own large area. Because of its position close to the autobahn bridge over the Rhine, there is road and river noise, but when we stayed the location and friendly atmosphere generated by the Eckhardt family more than made up for it.

Facilities

Small toilet block has fairly basic facilities, but is heated with free hot water (06.00-12.00, 17.00-23.00 hrs) in the washing troughs and by token in the showers. Large open-fronted room for cooking and eating (free hot water). Washing machine and dryer. Small shop (mid May-Sept). Microwave evening snacks (March-Oct). Fishing. Bicycle hire. Drinks machine. Off site: Bar/café by entrance. Trams and buses to city centre 1 km. across the bridge. Golf 3 km.

Open

25 April - 5 October.

At a glance

Welcome & Ambience	✓✓✓✓✓	Location	✓✓✓✓
Quality of Pitches	✓✓✓✓	Range of Facilities	✓✓✓

Directions

Leave autobahn A4 at exit no. 13 for Köln-Poll (just to west off intersection of A3 and A4). Turn left at first traffic lights and follow site signs through a sometimes fairly narrow one-way system to the riverside, back towards the motorway bridge.

Charges 2004

Per person	€ 4,50
child (4-12 yrs)	€ 2,00
pitch incl. car	€ 4,50 - € 6,00
electricity	€ 1,00

Reservations

Write to site. Tel: 0221 831966.
E-mail: campingkoeln@epost.de

DE3225 Naturpark Camping Suleika

Lorch bei Rüdesheim am Rhein, 65391 Rüdesheim am Rhein (Hesse)

On a steep hillside in the Rhine-Taunus Nature Park and approached by a narrow and steep system of lanes through the vineyards, this situation is not for the faint hearted. Having said that, it is a popular site for caravan rallies. Once you reach the site, it is steeply arranged in small terraces up the side of the wooded hill with a stream flowing through - the water supply is direct from springs. The surroundings are most attractive, with views over the vineyards to the river below. The Riesling Walk footpath passes above the site. Of the 100 pitches, 50 are available for tourists. These are mostly on the lower terraces, in numbered groups of up to four units. There is a special area for younger campers. All have electricity and there are water points around. Cars have to be parked away from the pitches near the entrance. A central block contains a very pleasant restaurant and small shop for basics (bread to order), with sanitary facilities alongside. With steep walks from most pitches to the facilities, this is probably not a site for visitors with disabilities; however, it is an attractive situation and reception staff are very friendly. This particular area is famous as it was briefly a 'Free State' (1919-23) and you will be able to taste and buy the site owner's wine and other items as souvenirs. There are many local attractions (as well as the Lorelei) shown on a large map, and the helpful owner speaks good English.

Facilities

The excellent toilet block is heated in cool weather and provides some washbasins in cabins for each sex and a nicely furnished baby washroom, with WC, shower and bath. Laundry service. Motorcaravan services. Gas supplies. Restaurant (closed Mon. and Thu.). Small shop (bread to order). Children's playground. Some entertainment in season. Off site: Bicycle hire. Fishing 300 m. Riding 4 km.

Open

15 March - 31 October.

At a glance

Welcome & Ambience	✓✓✓✓	Location	✓✓✓✓
Quality of Pitches	✓✓✓✓	Range of Facilities	✓✓✓

Directions

There is a direct entrance road from the B42 (for cars only), between Rudesheim and Lorch, with a height limitation of 2.25 m. under a railway bridge. Higher vehicles will find the site signed on the south side of Lorch. Site is reached via a one-way system of lanes – follow the signs.

Charges 2004

Per person	€ 4,50
child	€ 2,50
caravan or tent	€ 3,00 - € 4,50

No credit cards.

Reservations

Made with € 26 deposit, so only worthwhile for a longer stay. Tel: 06726 9464.

DE3265 Lahn Camping

Schleusenweg 16, 65549 Limburg an der Lahn (Hesse)

Pleasantly situated on the bank of the river Lahn (with direct access to it) between the autobahn and the town - both the autobahn viaduct and the cathedral are visible - this is a useful overnight stop for travellers along the Köln-Frankfurt stretch of the A3. You may, however, be tempted to stay longer as there are other attractions here, notably a very fine swimming pool complex nearby and the attractive old town of medieval buildings a gentle stroll away. The site is on level grass with 200 touring pitches (out of 250 altogether and 140 have 6A electricity - may need long cable)) on either side of gravel tracks at right angles from the main tarmac road, which runs the length of the site. There are some trees but it is mainly open. It is very popular with many nationalities and can become crowded at peak times, so arrive early. Some road and rail noise.

Facilities

The main sanitary block near reception is rather old but improvements have been made (showers need a token). A new, high quality heated block at the other end of the site is a welcome addition. Washing machines, dryers, cookers. Gas supplies. Motorcaravan services. Bar/restaurant (open evenings and Sundays) offers drinks, simple meals and takeaway. Small shop for basic supplies (not Sunday p.m.). Fishing (permit on payment). Play area. Bicycle and motorcycle hire. Off site: Swimming pool opposite. Riding 5 km. Golf 15 km. Supermarkets and good range of shops and restaurants in town. Pleasure cruises.

Open

18 April - 26 October.

At a glance

Welcome & Ambience	✓✓✓✓	Location	✓✓✓✓
Quality of Pitches	✓✓✓	Range of Facilities	✓✓✓

Directions

Leave A3 autobahn at Limburg-Nord exit and follow road into town and then signs for 'Camping-Swimming'.

Charges guide

Per person	€ 3,50
child (3-14 yrs)	€ 2,00
car	€ 1,60
motorcycle	€ 1,50
caravan	€ 3,50
motorcaravan	€ 5,10
2 person tent	€ 2,50

No credit cards.

Reservations

May be possible - phone site. Tel: 06431 22610. E-mail: lahncamping@limburg-net.de

DE3275 Camping Seepark

36275 Kirchheim (Hesse)

Kirchheim is just five kilometres from the A7 (50 km. south of Kassel) and also close to the Frankfurt to Dresden autobahns A5-A4 in eastern Hesse, which has the largest forested area in Germany. Pleasantly situated on the side of a valley, this is a large terraced park and is probably unique in offering a service for diabetics, with special food available and dialysis arranged in Bad Hersfeld hospital. There are 170 touring pitches (5 for people with disabilities) generally in their own areas (out of 370 altogether), varying in size from about 80 to 110 sq.m many marked with young trees in the corners. All have 16A electrical connections, just under half with water and drainage. They are mostly numbered in cul-de-sacs with access from tarmac roads leading up to an open area for larger vehicles and a tent field at the top. Thousands of bushes and trees have been planted over the years (but providing little shade for the pitches) and flowers are prominent around the service buildings. Opposite the entrance is a mainly sloping overnight area (including electricity and shower). This area of eastern Hesse has many areas of interest - Bad Hersfeld is an ancient town with an annual Festival of Drama and Opera from mid June to mid August, Fulda is an ecclesiastical centre and near it is Schloss Fasanerie, a good example of baroque architecture with a fine collection of porcelain and beautifully furnished.

Facilities

The original sanitary facilities are in the complex at the entrance with further very good facilities at the modern restaurant building higher up the site (high season and holidays). They have under-floor heating and private cabins. The tent area is currently served by a portable unit. Launderette. Drive over motorcaravan service point. Shop. Restaurant (breakfast available) open all year. Small free heated open air raised swimming pool (June-Aug; 1 m. deep; parents must supervise children which also applies to the lake swimming area at the left side of the site). Tennis. Table-tennis. Football. Volleyball. Minigolf. Diabetic service. Play areas. Tennis. Fishing. Volleyball. Football field. Water-skiing. Barbecue area. Off site: Close by on the lake there is water-skiing, boat hire, trampolining, adventure pool, roller skating rink, indoor tennis and fishing. Golf 3 km.

At a glance

Welcome & Ambience	✓✓✓✓	Location	✓✓✓✓
Quality of Pitches	✓✓✓✓	Range of Facilities	✓✓✓✓

Directions

From A7 Kassel - Fulda/Wurzburg take exit 87 for Kirchheim and follow signs to Seepark for 4.5 km. The park is on a minor road between the small villages of Rimboldshausen and Kemmerode, just west of the lake.

Charges guide

Per unit incl. up to 6 persons	€ 17,50
electricity	€ 2,00
water	€ 0,80

Reservations

Advisable Easter, Whitsun and June - September, although overnight should be possible if arriving early. Tel: 06628 1525. E-mail: info@campseepark.de

Open

All year.

DE3404 Odenwald Campingpark

Langenthalerstraße 80, 69434 Hirschhorn am Neckar (Hesse)

This site has recently been acquired by young owners who are working hard on improving it. Just north of the town, it is bisected by a tributary of the river Neckar, the Ulfenbach, which makes a popular and safe place for children to play. Besides the 180 well tended seasonal pitches, there are 150 marked and numbered level touring pitches with electricity (6/16A). About 40 have cable TV connections. There is a separate area for tents. Two of the four sanitary blocks are old, and do not provide hot water to the washbasins, but all are reasonably clean and well cared for. The heated outdoor pool is popular, and a picnic area, sauna and solarium are nearby.

Facilities

Four sanitary blocks, two heated. Showers (free). Washing machines and dryer. Baby room. Toilets for disabled visitors. Motorcaravan service point. Gas. Shop. Good restaurant, bar and takeaway. Swimming pool (20 x 9 m). TV room. Playground. Minigolf. Table tennis. Basketball. Bicycle hire. Off site: Fishing 1.2 km. Golf 13 km. Riding 15 km.

Open

Easter - 15 October.

At a glance

Welcome & Ambience	✓✓✓✓	Location	✓✓✓✓
Quality of Pitches	✓✓✓✓✓	Range of Facilities	✓✓✓✓

Directions

From Hirschhorn, take L3105 road north towards Wald-Michelbach. Site is on left after about 1.5 km.

Charges guide

Per person	€ 4,50
child (5-14 yrs)	€ 1,80 - € 3,10
pitch	€ 6,20
electricity	€ 1,00

No credit cards.

Reservations

Contact site. Tel: 06272 809.
E-mail: odenwald-camping-park@t-online.de

DE3258 Camping Sägmühle

67705 Trippstadt (Rhineland Palatinate)

Camping Sägmühle has been in the same family for over 50 years, during which time it has undergone several major developments which have turned it into a first class site. It is peacefully situated beside a lake, in a wooded valley in the heart of the Palatinate Nature Park, and there are many kilometers of walks to enjoy, as well as castles to explore. A first class restaurant offers you some of the fine local wines, and there is plenty for younger children to enjoy with fishing, swimming and boating in the lake (pedaloes for hire), a fort, minigolf and tennis. The 200 touring pitches (half the total) are at least 80 sq.m. or more on flat grass, each with electricity (4A or more) and TV connections, with plenty of water points around. There are three separate areas of pitches, one of which is close to the lake, and it is a pleasant change to find a site that keeps the lakeside pitches for tourers.

Facilities

Each area has its own sanitary facilities, those beside the lake and the back being first class, with those at the side being renovated. Private cabins, baby bathroom, facilities for disabled people, launderette. Motorcaravan services. Restaurant and takeaway (lunchtime and evening). Bread available from the accessory shop in high season. Solarium. Two tennis courts. Play areas. Table tennis, football area, basketball. Mountain bike hire. Boules, giant chess. Minigolf. Fishing in lake. Entertainment daily in high season. Off site: Shops 10 minutes walk in Trippstadt. Riding 4 km.

Open

1 January - 31 October, and 16 December - 31 December.

At a glance

Welcome & Ambience	✓✓✓✓	Location	✓✓✓✓
Quality of Pitches	✓✓✓✓	Range of Facilities	✓✓✓✓

Directions

At Kaiserslautern on A6, take exit 15 (Kaiserslautern West) onto B270 towards Pirmasens. Turn left after 8 km. towards Karlstal/Trippstadt and follow the campsite signs. From the A65 between Karlsruhe and Neustadt take exit 15 or 17 towards Annweiler on the B10. After Annweiler right on B48 to Rinnthal and on towards Kaiserslautern/Johanniskreuz. After 20 km left to Kaiserslautern/Trippstadt and the next left to Trippstadt. Follow site signs into the valley.

Charges 2005

Per person	€ 5,70 - € 6,90
child (under 14 yrs)	€ 2,20 - € 2,80
pitch incl. electricity (4A)	€ 4,50 - € 8,00

Reservations

Contact site. Tel: 06306 92190.
E-mail: info@saegmuehle.de

DE3212 Landal GreenParks Wirfttal

Wirftstraße, 54589 Stadtkyll (Rhineland Palatinate)

Peacefully set in a small valley in the heath and forest of the hills of the northern Eifel, near the Belgian border Wirfttal has 250 numbered pitches of which 150 are for tourers. They mostly back onto fences, hedges etc. on fairly flat ground of different levels (steel pegs are required for tents and awnings). The pitches are 80 sq.m or more, and all have electricity (6A) and TV aerial points with water points around. 17 individual pitches have their own water and waste water points. Also part of the site, but separate from the camping, is a large holiday bungalow complex. A short walk up the hill is an outdoor swimming pool complex with three pools, one heated, and minigolf. Additionally, at the site entrance, is a small indoor pool, and a sports centre with two outdoor tennis courts (floodlit), a super adventure playground, bowling and an indoor tennis and squash centre. Fishing (but not swimming) is allowed in the small lake.

Facilities

There is one main toilet block (the only one open out of main season), and two small units, all heated. All ladies' washbasins and one for men in the main block are in cabins. Shop. Restaurant and snacks (high season). Swimming pool complex (with discount for campers). Indoor pool (free) and sauna and solarium (on payment) Tennis (indoor and outdoor). Riding. Fishing (free). Bicycle hire. Sports centre adjacent with squash hall. Children's play equipment around site and main adventure playground. Winter sports. Bicycle and sledge hire. Animation in season in activity hut.

Open

All year.

At a glance

Welcome & Ambience	✓✓✓✓	Location	✓✓✓✓
Quality of Pitches	✓✓✓✓	Range of Facilities	✓✓✓✓✓

Directions

Site is 1.5 km. south of Stadtkyll on road towards Schüller.

Charges guide

Per unit incl. 2 persons and electricity	€ 26,00
extra person	€ 2,50
dog	€ 3,00
electricity (6A)	€ 2,30

Less in low season. Special 5, 8 or 10 day rates.

Reservations

Made (Fri.- Fri. only in high season) with 50% deposit. Office open 7 days/week. Tel: 06597 92920. E-mail: info@landal.de

DE3215 Camping Goldene Meile

Simrockweg 9 - 13, 53424 Remagen (Rhineland Palatinate)

This site is on the banks of the Rhine between Bonn and Koblenz, and adjacent to a large complex of open-air public swimming pools (campers pay the normal entrance). Although there is an emphasis on permanent caravans, there are about 300 pitches for tourists (out of 550), 50 with water and waste water connections (more extra large ones are being added) and 14 with waste water, and an area for tents. They are either in the central, more mature area or in a newer area where the numbered pitches of 80-100 sq. m. are arranged around an attractively landscaped small fishing lake. Just 5 are by the busy river, but it is more peaceful the further back you are. There are electricity connections in most areas (6A). They claim always to find space for odd nights, except perhaps at B.Hs. This site is in a popular area and, although busy in high season, appears to be well run.

Facilities

The main toilet block to one side of the site is a good quality building, heated and kept clean, with some washbasins in cabins, showers with token from machine and facilities for wheelchair users. Shower and wash rooms are locked at 10 pm. A smaller block serves the newer pitches near the lake (no showers). Dishwashing and laundry sinks, washing machine and dryer. Cooking facilities. Motorcaravan services. Gas supplies. Small shop with bread to order (1/4-30/10 and some weekends). Bar, restaurant and takeaway (1/4-30/10 and some weekends). Playgrounds. Entertainment for children in July/Aug. Beach volleyball. Basketball. Football. Bicycle hire. Main gate locked at 10 pm. (also 1-3 pm). Off site: Swimming pools adjacent (May-Sept).

Open

All year.

At a glance

Welcome & Ambience	✓✓✓✓✓	Location	✓✓✓✓✓
Quality of Pitches	✓✓✓✓	Range of Facilities	✓✓✓✓

Directions

Remagen is 23 km. south of Bonn on no. 9 road towards Koblenz. Site is on road running close to the Rhine from Remagen to Kripp and is signed from the N9 south of Remagen, which avoids the congested town (signs also for Allwetterbad). From A61 autobahn take Sinzig exit.

Charges 2005

Per person	€ 5,50
child (6-16 yrs)	€ 4,50
pitch	€ 7,50
with services	€ 9,00
tent	€ 3,50
electricity	€ 2,25

Eurocards accepted.

Reservations

Can be made for at least a few days. Tel: 02642 22222. E-mail: info@camping-goldene-meile.de

DE3242 Country Camping Schinderhannes

56291 Hausbay-Pfalzfeld (Rhineland Palatinate)

Country Camping could be a useful transit stop en-route to the Black Forest, Bavaria, Austria and Switzerland, as well as a family holiday. High in the Hunsruck (a large area with forests, ideal for walking and cycling), Schinderhannes himself was a legendary 'Robin Hood' character, whose activities were curtailed in Mainz, at the end of a rope. Lying about 30 km south of Koblenz, west of the Rhine and south of the Mosel, it is set in a 'bowl' of land which catches the sun all day long, with trees and parkland all around, making it a very peaceful and picturesque setting. There are 250 permanent caravans in a separate area from 90 overnight pitches on hardstanding, which are on two areas near reception. For those staying longer, the site becomes visually more attractive as you drive down into the area around the lake to a further 160 numbered pitches. These are of over 80 sq.m. on grass, some with hardstanding and all with European electrical connections (10A) and with water points around. You can position yourself for shade or sun. The lake is used for swimming and inflatable boats and for fishing. English is spoken by the helpful reception staff.

Facilities

The sanitary buildings, which can be heated, are of a high standard with one section, in the reception/shop building, for the overnight pitches and the remainder close to the longer stay places. Facilities for disabled people. Laundry. Bar. Pleasant large restaurant with takeaway, featuring an open fire, rest area with TV and a skittle alley downstairs. Shop (all amenities 1/3-31/10 and maybe Xmas). Tennis (on payment). Basketball. Fishing. Play area. Rallies welcome. Torches useful. Barrier closed 22.00-07.00 hrs. Off site: Bicycle hire 1 km. (cycle down to the Rhine and catch the train back).

At a glance

Welcome & Ambience	✓✓✓✓✓	Location	✓✓✓✓✓
Quality of Pitches	✓✓✓✓✓	Range of Facilities	✓✓✓✓

Directions

From A61 Koblenz - Ludwigshafen road, take exit 43 Pfalzfeld (30 km. south of Koblenz) and on to Hausbay where site is signed.

Charges 2005

Per person	€ 5,00
child	€ 3,00
pitch incl. electricity	€ 8,00
dog	€ 2,00

Reservations

For groups only, contact site. Tel: 06746 80280. E-mail: info@countrycamping.de

Open

All year.

DE3220 Camping Burg Lahneck

Ortsteil Oberlahnstein, 56112 Lahnstein (Rhineland Palatinate)

The location of this site is splendid, high up overlooking the Rhine valley and the town of Lahnstein - many of the pitches have their own super views. Adjacent is a good outdoor swimming pool with extensive grassy areas, and the mediaeval castle Burg Lahneck (the home of the camp proprietor, which may be visited) with its smart restaurant. It is in the best part of the Rhine valley, and close to Koblenz and the Mosel. A 'Kurzentrum', under 2 km. from the site, has a thermal pool from warm springs (reduced admission to campers) with sauna and solarium. The site, which consists partly of terraces and partly of open grassy areas, has a cared for look and all is very neat and clean. One can usually find a space here, though from early July to mid-August it can become full. There are 100 individual touring pitches (out of 107 altogether) marked but not separated and mostly level, all with electricity (16A). Campers are sited by the management. Reception staff at the site are friendly and charges reasonable. There are some tour operator pitches.

Facilities

The single central, heated toilet block is of a good standard, and well maintained and cleaned. There are some cabins for both sexes. Showers are on payment. Washing machine and dryer. Motorcaravan services. Gas supplies. Small shop. Small playground. Off site: Cafe/restaurant adjoining site serves drinks, snacks, ices, etc. with some hot evening food; meals also in Burg Lahneck restaurant. Town swimming pool (reduced charges for campers, 15/5-31/8). Tennis nearby. Riding 500 m. Fishing 3 km. Bicycle hire 2 km.

Open

Easter/1 April - 31 October.

At a glance

Welcome & Ambience	✓✓✓✓	Location	✓✓✓✓✓
Quality of Pitches	✓✓✓✓	Range of Facilities	✓✓✓

Directions

From B42 road bypassing the town, take Oberlahnstein exit and follow signs 'Kurcentrum' and Burg Lahneck.

Charges 2004

Per person	€ 5,50
children (3-14 yrs)	€ 3,00
caravan	€ 5,50
motorcaravan	€ 7,50 - € 8,50
electricity	€ 0,50
dog	€ 1,00

No credit cards.

Reservations

Made without deposit for exact dates. Tel: 02621 2765.

DE3222 Camping Gülser Moselbogen

Am Gülser Moselbogen 20, Güls, 56072 Koblenz (Rhineland Palatinate)

The provision of first class sanitary facilities here, combined with the location being very convenient for sightseeing along the rivers Mosel and Rhein and the easy access to Koblenz, the A48 and A61, make this an attractive proposition for a short or longer-term stay. The site is set quite high up from the river (safe from flooding) but with no direct access to it, and has a pleasant outlook to the forested valley slopes. A large proportion of the 16 acre site is taken up by privately owned bungalows, but the touring section of 66 large individual pitches, near the entrance, is self contained and accessed by gravel paths leading off the main tiled roads. The flat pitches have little shade yet, but all have connections for TV and 16A electricity and there are water points in each section. A new area of gravel hardstanding has been developed and RVs are accepted.

Facilities

Entry to the really excellent, heated sanitary building is by a coded card that also operates the hot water to the showers (free to the washbasins, many of which are in cabins). Unit for disabled visitors, baby room, dishwashing and cooking rings (charged). Laundry. Gas supplies. Motorcaravan services. Bread and milk may be ordered at reception. Children's play area. Bicycle hire. Off site: Fishing 200 m. A special area for swimming in the Mosel 200 m. Restaurant 500 m. Güls village 1.5 km. Riding 3 km.

Open

All year.

At a glance

Welcome & Ambience	✓✓✓✓✓	Location	✓✓✓✓✓
Quality of Pitches	✓✓✓✓	Range of Facilities	✓✓✓✓

Directions

Site is 1.5 km. west of village of Güls, and is accessed from the B416 that runs along the north bank of the Mosel from Koblenz (where it joins the B9) towards Cochem. From the A61 take exit 38 towards Koblenz-Metternich. After 2 km. turn right towards Winningen/Flughaven/Güls (white sign) and keep on main road for Güls till the B416, turn right towards Cochem and watch for site signs in 1.5 km.

Charges 2004

Per person	€ 5,00
child (3-14 yrs)	€ 2,50
pitch	€ 5,00 - € 8,00
electricity (plus 1.00 connection)	€ 1,50
dog	€ 2,00
chip card deposit	€ 5,00

Reservations

Not normally necessary. Tel: 0261 44474. E-mail: moselbogen@paffhausen.com

DE3232 Family Camping

Wiesenweg 25, 56820 Mesenich bei Cochem (Rhineland Palatinate)

Situated beside the River Mosel with views of forest and vineyard, this attractive family run site has the added advantage of being on a stretch of the river well away from the railway. The 75 touring pitches are among the vines, mainly level, individual ones with electric hook-ups (6/8A), separated by bushes and the older ones with shade. Thirteen pitches have their own water tap and there are 48 tents for rent on the site. The site roads are relatively narrow and are not ideal for larger units (definitely unsuitable for American RVs or twin axle caravans). On arrival you must stop in the lay-by provided on the approach road while booking in at reception (a short walk). A very popular site in July and August with many activities organised for youngsters, the site has small outdoor pool and a children's pool. There is direct access to the riverside path and good walks and cycling opportunities all around the site. Good English is spoken.

Facilities

Well equipped, heated toilet facilities provide good sized showers (on payment), washbasins mainly in cubicles or curtained. Good unisex babyroom. Laundry with washing machines and dryer. Shop, bar and restaurant (1/7-1/9). Swimming pools (1/6-15/9, weather dependant). Play area. Disco evenings and wine tours in July/Aug. River fishing. Dogs are not accepted in July/Aug. Off site: Bicycle hire 300 m. Golf or riding 10 km. Wine museum nearby. Cochem with its castle, and a large leisure centre is only 15 km.

Open

8 April - 3 October.

At a glance

Welcome & Ambience	✓✓✓✓	Location	✓✓✓✓✓
Quality of Pitches	✓✓✓✓	Range of Facilities	✓✓✓✓

Directions

Mesenich is about 15 km. southwest of Cochem, on the opposite side of the River Mosel. From the B49 at Senheim, cross the river and follow signs to Mesenich. Site is in the village on left (signed). Alternatively cross the river at Cochem and follow the L98 riverside road south to Mesenich. It can also be reached from the scenic B421 Kirchberg to Zell road, turning to Senheim 15 km. after Kirchberg (rather winding, steep road at the end).

Charges 2004

Per unit incl. 2 persons	€ 10,00 - € 20,50
extra person	€ 4,00 - € 4,50
child (2-12 yrs)	€ 3,00 - € 4,50
electricity	€ 2,20
dog (excl. July/Aug)	€ 2,50

No credit cards.

Reservations

Essential for July/Aug. Tel: 02673 4556.
E-mail: info@familycamping.de

DE3233 Campingplatz Holländischer Hof

56820 Senheim / Moselle (Rhineland Palatinate)

This campsite lies along a bend of the river Moselle, surrounded on three sides by hills, and on the other by the river. An arm of the river intrudes here and a harbour for small boats has been made. A road bridge passes over the very last pitches at one end of the site, but this did not seem to generate any noise nuisance. There are some seasonal pitches, but the site caters mostly for tourists. All 150 pitches have electricity points (6/10A). Many wine producing villages and towns are within easy reach, the largest and best known being Cochem (16 km. downstream). Boat trips are also a feature of the area. As well as the many events taking place in the villages, the site organises a good programme of daily activities. Dogs are not allowed on the site, but there are a dozen pitches outside the barrier for those who have dogs with them.

Facilities

Main sanitary block – washbasins with hot and cold water (some in cubicles), showers (by token), unit for disabled visitors. Laundry sinks, washing machines, dryer and irons. Other toilet facilities in a 'portacabin' unit. Motorcaravan service point. Good shop. Gas. Pleasant restaurant, snack bar, pizzeria and takeaway (with children's menu) and terrace. Playground. TV room. Arcade games, table football, table tennis. Sports field with volleyball. Fishing in river. Off site: Tennis 300 m. Bicycle hire 2 km. ATM point 2 km. Golf 4 km.

Open

Easter - 1 November.

At a glance

Welcome & Ambience	✓✓✓✓	Location	✓✓✓✓✓
Quality of Pitches	✓✓✓✓✓	Range of Facilities	✓✓✓✓

Directions

From Cochem (on the west bank) take B49 upstream (south). At Nehren, cross bridge towards Senheim. From the bridge the site is below on the left. If coming from upstream, take the B49 north from Alf.

Charges 2005

Per person	€ 3,85
child (3-10 yrs)	€ 2,80
pitch	€ 6,70
electricity per kw	€ 0,55

No credit cards.

Reservations

Made for 7 July - 31 Aug. only with fee (€ 16).
Tel: 02673 4660. E-mail: holl.hof@t-online.de

DE3245 Landal GreenParks Sonnenberg

54340 Leiwen (Rhineland Palatinate)

With attractive views over the Mosel as you climb the approach road, four kilometres from the wine village of Leiwen and the river, this pleasant site is on top of a hill. It has a splendid free leisure centre incorporating an indoor activity pool with child's paddling pool, whirlpool, cascade and slides. Also in this building are tenpin bowling, a sauna, solarium and fitness room, tennis and badminton, plus a snack bar. Combining a bungalow complex (separate) with camping, the site has 150 large, individual and numbered grassy pitches on terraces with electricity (6A) and TV connections. Excursions and entertainment are organised in season, with ranger guided walks, wine-tasting, daily cruises from Leiwen to Bernkastel and coach trips to the Rhine (both May-Oct). There are two good restaurants and shop, and the site is efficiently managed with a friendly and helpful English speaking reception staff.

Facilities

The single toilet block has under-floor heating, washbasins in cabins (all for women, a couple for men). It is stretched in busy times. Large laundry. Motorcaravan services. Shop. Restaurant, bistro, bar and snacks (one restaurant only in low season). Indoor multi-purpose leisure centre with activity pool, climbing wall, 10 pin bowling, tennis and badminton. Volleyball. Football pitch. Minigolf. Children's playground. Bicycle hire in high season. Disco, entertainment and excursions at busy times (not all every day). Deer park. Off site: Fishing 5 km. Riding or golf 12 km.

Open

21 February - 3 November.

At a glance

Welcome & Ambience	✓✓✓✓	Location	✓✓✓✓
Quality of Pitches	✓✓✓✓	Range of Facilities	✓✓✓✓✓

Directions

From Trier-Koblenz A48/A1 take new exit 128 for Bekond, Föhren, Hetzerath and Leiwen. Follow signs for Leiwen and in town follow signs for Ferienpark, Sonnenberg or Freibad on very winding road up hill 4 km. to site.

Charges guide

Per unit incl. 2 persons and electricity	€ 18,00 - € 31,00

Special 5, 8 or 10 day rates.

Reservations

Essential mid July - end August. Write with deposit (Fri. - Fri. only in high season). Tel: 06507 93690. E-mail: info@landal.de

DE3250 Landal GreenParks Warsberg

54439 Saarburg (Rhineland Palatinate)

On top of a steep hill in an attractive location, this site and the long winding approach road both offer pleasant views over the town and surrounding area. A chair lift with a terminal 800 metres from the site links it to the town - it is well worth a ride, as is the new 530 metre long 'Rodelbahn' toboggan (both with small fee). A large, well organised site, there are 500 numbered touring pitches of quite reasonable size on flat or slightly sloping ground, separated in small groups by trees and shrubs, with electrical connections (6A) available in most places. There are some tour operator pitches and a separate area of holiday bungalows to rent. There are plenty of games facilities here, a restaurant, large shop and a magnificent, brand new heated indoor swimming pool complex, close to a large area of play equipment on sand. This is a site with friendly, English speaking reception staff, which should appeal to all age groups. July and August are very busy.

Facilities

Three toilet blocks of very good quality provide washbasins (many in private cabins) and a unit for disabled visitors. Large launderette by reception. Motorcaravan services. Gas supplies. Shop. Restaurant and takeaway, games rooms adjacent. Swimming pools (15/5-15/9). Tennis. Minigolf. Bicycle hire. Football field. Large playground. Bowling. Outdoor chess and draughts. Entertainment in season for all ages. Reception opens 9 - 12 and 2 - 5.30 (Sunday 10-12 only). Off site: Riding and fishing 5 km.

Open

29 March - 4 November.

At a glance

Welcome & Ambience	✓✓✓✓	Location	✓✓✓✓
Quality of Pitches	✓✓✓✓	Range of Facilities	✓✓✓✓

Directions

From Trier on road 51 site is well signed in the northwest outskirts of Saarburg off the Trierstrasse (signs also for 'Ferienzentrum') and from all round town. Follow signs up hill for 3 km.

Charges guide

Per unit incl. 2 persons	€ 17,00 - € 22,00
with electricity (6A)	€ 19,00 - € 25,00
extra person	€ 2,50
dog	€ 3,00

Special 5, 8 or 10 day rates.

Reservations

Advisable and only made for July/Aug. Sat-Sat with 50% deposit. Tel: 06581 91460. E-mail: info@landal.de

Germany

DE3254 Camping Harfenmühle

55758 Asbacherhütte (Rhineland Palatinate)

Harfenmühle is situated in a wooded valley in the Hunsrück, an attractive area of Germany just below the Mosel. It is also unusual to find a site which has its own gourmet restaurant and wine cellar. It is essentially a friendly, relaxed partly terraced site, with 80 touring pitches, mostly individual and ranging in size up to 150 sq.m. with 16A electricity. With a separate meadow for tents, there are also 60 seasonal units and 26 chalets. There is plenty to keep youngsters happy and precious stones 'Edelsteinen' and minerals can be searched for here without payment.

Facilities

Satisfactory, heated sanitary facilities are in the main building, with some private cabins, curtained showers on payment, children's showers and bath. Launderette. Kiosk with fresh bread daily. Takeaway (1/5-31/10). Wine cellar/bar. Restaurant with local menu, plus regular gourmet days. Swimming lake. Water play area (max 30 cm). Table tennis. Ski hire. Aviary (meet Gustaf the 80 year old parrot). Off site: 1500 km. of marked walks through the Naturpark. Riding 3 km. and 4.5 km. Bicycle hire 5 km. Golf 10 km.

Open

All year.

At a glance

Welcome & Ambience	✓✓✓✓	Location	✓✓✓✓
Quality of Pitches	✓✓✓✓	Range of Facilities	✓✓✓✓

Directions

From the B41 Saarbrücken - Bad Kreuznach, exit north at Fischbach signed towards Herrstein and then on tthrough Morschied to Asbacherhütte, with site entrance on right.

Charges 2005

Per person	€ 4,00
child (2-15 yrs)	€ 2,50
pitch	€ 6,00 - € 7,50
electricity per kwh	€ 0,50

Reductions in low season for stays over 5 nights.

Reservations

Contact site. Tel: 06786 7076.
E-mail: camping-harfenmuehle@t-online.de

DE3415 Camping Adam

Campingstraße 1, 77815 Bühl (Baden-Württemberg)

This very convenient lakeside site is by the A5 Karlsruhe-Basle autobahn near Baden-Baden, very easily accessed from exit 52 Bühl (also from the French autoroute A35 just northeast of Strasbourg). It is also a useful base for the Black Forest. There is a lake that is divided into separate areas for bathing or boating and windsurfing, with a long slide - the public are admitted to this on payment and it attracts many people on fine weekends. All the touring pitches (180 from 490 total) have electricity connections (10A), many with waste water outlets too. Those for caravans are individual ones, with some special ones near the lake with water and drainage. Tents go along the lake surrounds and there are some places with hard paved centres to eliminate wet weather problems. At very busy times, units staying overnight only may be placed close together on a lakeside area of hardstanding. The shop and restaurant/bar remain open virtually all year (not Monday or Tuesday in low season), so this is a useful site to use out of season. In general the site has a well tended look and good English is spoken by the pleasant staff.

Facilities

Two heated sanitary buildings for tourers, one rebuilt to a high standard. Mostly private cabins in the new block, hot showers on payment, facilities for babies and disabled people. Washing machine and dryer. Gas. Motorcaravan services. Shop (1/4-31/10). Restaurant (1/3-30/10). Takeaway (1/5-31/8). Tennis. Playground. Bicycle hire. Fishing. Off site: Riding or golf 5 km.

Open

All year.

At a glance

Welcome & Ambience	✓✓✓✓	Location	✓✓✓✓
Quality of Pitches	✓✓✓✓	Range of Facilities	✓✓✓✓

Directions

Take A5/E35-52, exit 52 (Bühl), turn towards Lichtenau, go through Oberbruch and left to site. From French autoroute A35 take exits 52 or 56 onto D2 and D4 respectively then turn onto A5 as above.

Charges 2004

Per person	€ 4,50 - € 6,50
child (3-16 yrs)	€ 2,00 - € 3,50
pitch with services	€ 6,50 - € 8,00
electricity	€ 2,00

Reservations

Write to site. Tel: 07223 23194.
E-mail: webmaster@campingplatz-adam.de

DE3450 Ferien-Campingplatz Münstertal

Dietzelbachstr. 6, 79244 Münstertal (Baden-Württemberg)

Münstertal is an impressive site pleasantly situated in a valley on the western edge of the Black Forest. It has been one of the top graded sites in Germany for 20 years, and first time visitors will soon realise why when they see the standard of the facilities here. There are 300 individual pitches in two areas, either side of the entrance road on flat gravel, their size varying from 70-100 sq.m. All have electricity (16A) and 200 have waste water drains, many also with water, TV and radio connections. The large indoor swimming pool with sauna and solarium, and the outdoor pool, are both heated and free and there is a large, grass sunbathing area. The health and fitness centre provides a range of treatments, massages, etc. Children are very well catered for here with a play area and play equipment, tennis courts, minigolf, a games room with table tennis, table football and pool table and fishing. Riding is popular and the site has its own stables. The latest addition is an ice rink for skating and ice hockey in winter. There are 250 km. of walks, with some guided ones organised, and winter sports with cross-country skiing directly from the site (courses in winter - for children or adults and ski hire). The site becomes full in season and reservations, especially in July, are necessary.

Facilities

The three toilet blocks are of truly first class quality, with washbasins, all in cabins, showers with full glass dividers, baby bath, a unit for disabled visitors and individual bathrooms, some for hire, others for general use. Dishwashers in two blocks. Laundry with washing machines, spin and tumble dryers. Drying room. Motorcaravan services. Well stocked shop (all year). Restaurant, particularly good and well patronised (closed Nov.). Heated swimming pools, indoor all year 07.30-21.00, outdoor (with children's area) May-Oct. New health and fitness centre. Sauna and solarium. Games room. Bicycle hire. Tennis courses in summer Off site: Village amenities near. Golf 15 km. Freiburg and Basel easy driving distances for day trips.

At a glance

Welcome & Ambience	✓✓✓✓✓	Location	✓✓✓✓✓
Quality of Pitches	✓✓✓✓✓	Range of Facilities	✓✓✓✓✓

Directions

Münstertal is south of Freiburg. From A5 autobahn take exit 64, turn southeast via Bad Krozingen and Staufen and continue 5 km. to the start of Münstertal, where camp is signed from the main road on the left.

Charges guide

Per person	€ 6,20 - € 7,40
child (2-10 yrs)	€ 4,10 - € 4,65
pitch	€ 9,85 - € 11,80
dog	€ 2,60

No credit cards.

Reservations

Made without deposit. Tel: 07636 7080. E-mail: info@camping-muenstertal.de

Open

All year.

DE3440 Camping Kirchzarten

Dietenbacher Str. 17, 79199 Kirchzarten (Baden-Württemberg)

There are pleasant views of the Black Forest from this municipal site which is within easy reach by car of Titisee, Feldberg and Todtnau, and eight kilometres from the large town of Freiburg in Breisgau. It is divided into 500 numbered pitches with electricity, 370 of which are for tourists (some used by tour operators). Most pitches, which are side by side on level ground, are of quite reasonable size and marked out at the corners, though there is nothing to separate them and there are some hardstanding motorcaravan pitches. From about late June to mid-August it does become full. The fine swimming pool complex adjoining the site is free to campers and is a main attraction, with pools for diving, fun, swimming and children, surrounded by spacious grassy sunbathing areas and a children's play area on sand. It is only a short stroll from the site to the village centre, which has supermarkets, restaurants, etc.

Facilities

Splendid new sanitary building includes a large, central chidren's section, private cabins (some for hire). Laundry room. Cooking stoves, washing machines, dryers, irons, sewing machines (all on meter). Restaurant/bar. Shop (May - Sept). Swimming pool complex (15/5-15/9). Large playground. Table tennis. Minigolf. Organised recreation programme in high season. Dogs are not accepted in July/Aug. Off site: Tennis (covered court, can be booked). Adventure playground, fitness track, tennis and minigolf near. Riding 2 km. Golf 4 km.

Open

All year.

At a glance

Welcome & Ambience	✓✓✓✓✓	Location	✓✓✓✓✓
Quality of Pitches	✓✓✓✓✓	Range of Facilities	✓✓✓✓✓

Directions

From Freiburg take B31 road signed Donaueschingen to Kirchzarten where site is signed (it is south of the village).

Charges 2004

Per person	€ 5,00 - € 7,90
child (4-16 yrs)	€ 2,90 - € 4,20
third child or more	€ 1,85 - € 2,35
pitch	€ 5,30 - € 6,60
electricity	€ 1,10
unreserved pitch	€ 1,10 - € 15,40

Every 15th day free.

Reservations

Made for min. 1 week without deposit.
Tel: 07661 9040910.
E-mail: info@camping-kirchzarten.de

DE3406 Camping Kleinenzhof

75323 Bad Wildbad (Baden-Württemberg)

In the northern Black Forest, a very good area for walking and cross-country skiing, this site runs along the sloping bank of a stream. There are excellent facilities, which the owner is still working on improving. The land is terraced and accommodates around 200 seasonal pitches, and 100 touring pitches. All have 16A electricity and all but five have water and a drain. At the far end of the site is a hotel with indoor and outdoor pools which are free to campers. A full programme of activities is arranged, including walks, visits to the site's own distillery, films and barbecues at weekends.

Facilities

Four sanitary blocks, all heated, are clean and well maintained with many washbasins in cabins and free showers. Facilities for disabled visitors. Baby rooms, children's bathroom, 12 free family bathrooms and many for rent. Washing machines, dryers and drying room. Motorcaravan services. Gas supplies. Shop (closed 15/11-15/12). Bar and restaurant (at hotel). Indoor pool (all year), outdoor pool (May-Sept) and small paddling pool. Playground. TV and games room. Internet. Table tennis, table football, basketball, football. Bicycle hire. Off site: Fishing 3 km. Riding 8 km. Golf (18 hole) 25 km.

At a glance

Welcome & Ambience	✓✓✓✓✓	Location	✓✓✓✓
Quality of Pitches	✓✓✓✓✓	Range of Facilities	✓✓✓✓✓

Directions

From Pforzheim take B294 south through Birkenfeld and Neuenbürg to Calmbach (20 km.) From here continue on B294 to Kleinenzhof (another 3 km).

Charges 2005

Per person	€ 5,80
child (1-12 yrs)	€ 3,70
pitch	€ 7,50
electricity (plus € 0.55 per kw)	€ 1,00

Reservations

Made in high season with deposit (€ 50).
Tel: 07081 3435. E-mail: info@kleinenzhof.de

Open

All year.

DE3455 Gugel's Dreiländer Camping

Oberer Wald 3, 79395 Neuenburg (am Rhein) (Baden-Württemberg)

Neuenburg is ideally placed not only for enjoying and exploring the south of the Black Forest, but also for night stops when travelling from Frankfurt to Basel on the A5 autobahn. Set in natural heath and woodland, Gugel's is an attractive site which recently won a prestigious environmental award, where permanent caravans set away from the tourist area, with their well-tended gardens, enhance rather than detract from the natural beauty. There are 200 places for tourists either in small clearings in the tall trees which cover the site, in open areas or on a large hardstanding section used for single night stays. All have electricity (6A), and some are now individual pitches including one group of 30 with electricity, water, waste water and satellite TV connections. Opposite the entrance is a meadow where late arrivals and those who wish to depart before 7 am. may spend the night. A social room has been added with satellite TV where guests are welcomed with a glass of wine and a slide presentation of the attractions of the area. The Rhine is within walking distance. There may be some road noise near the entrance. The site may become very busy in high season and at Bank Holidays but you should always find room. In general there is a good atmosphere and it can be recommended for both short and long stays.

Facilities

Three good quality heated sanitary blocks include some washbasins in cabins, one baby room and one for disabled visitors. Washing machines and dryers. Motorcaravan services. Large shop (all year). Excellent restaurant, popular with both campers and non-residents (all year). Takeaway (weekends and daily in high season). Indoor pools (all year). Boules. Tennis courts with racquet and ball hire. Fishing. Minigolf. Table tennis. Chess. Barbecue. Bicycle hire. Community room with TV. Activity programme with organised walks, excursions, etc. and sports and competitions for children (high season). Large, play area and another with electric cars and motorcycles (on payment). Off site: Riding 1.5 km. Golf 5 km. Neuenburg, Breisach, Freiburg and Basel are just some of the interesting places to visit as well as the Black Forest.

At a glance

Welcome & Ambience	✓✓✓✓	Location	✓✓✓✓✓
Quality of Pitches	✓✓✓✓	Range of Facilities	✓✓✓✓✓

Directions

From autobahn A5 take Neuenburg exit, turn left and then almost immediately turn left at traffic lights, left at next junction and follow signs for 2 km. to site (called 'Neuenburg' on most signs).

Charges guide

Per person	€ 5,75
child (2-15 yrs)	€ 2,90
caravan or tent	€ 5,20
small tent	€ 3,50
car	€ 4,00
motorcaravan	€ 5,20 - € 8,40

Discount every 10th night, persons free.
No credit cards.

Reservations

Made for min 2 weeks in July/Aug. with deposit. Write specifying tent or caravan. Tel: 07631 7719. E-mail: info@camping-gugel.de

Open

All year.

DE3445 Camping Belchenblick

Münstertäler Straße 43, 79219 Staufen (Baden-Württemberg)

The quality site stands at the gateway, so to speak, to the Black Forest. Not very high up itself, it is just at the start of the long road climb which leads to the top of Belchen, one of the highest summits of the forest. It is well situated for excursions by car to the best areas of the forest, for example the Feldberg-Titisee-Höllental circuit, and many excellent walks are possible nearby. Staufen is a pleasant little place with character. The site has 210 pitches (180 for touring units) with many electrical connections (10-15A), and 50 pitches have TV, water and waste water connections. On site is a small heated indoor pool and adjacent is a municipal sports complex, including an open-air pool and tennis courts. Reservation is necessary from early June to late August at this popular site, which is not a cheap one. However, charges do include free hot water and the indoor pool. A little tractor will site your caravan if required.

Facilities

Three high quality sanitary blocks are heated and have free hot water, individual washbasins (6 in private cabins), plus 21 family cabins with WC, basin and shower (some on payment per night for exclusive use). Washing machine. Gas. Motorcaravan services. Shop (1/5-31/10). Bar (all year). Snacks and takeaway (1/5-31/10). Indoor and outdoor pools. Sauna and solarium. Tennis. Playground. Volleyball. Basketball. Skating. Hockey and football fields. Bicycle hire. Off site: Restaurant near. Fishing 500 m. Riding 2 km.

Open

All year.

At a glance

Welcome & Ambience	✓✓✓✓	Location	✓✓✓✓✓
Quality of Pitches	✓✓✓✓	Range of Facilities	✓✓✓✓✓

Directions

Take autobahn exit for Bad Krozingen, south of Freiburg, and continue to Staufen. Site is southeast of the town and signed, across an unmanned local railway crossing near the entrance.

Charges 2005

Per person	€ 6,00 - € 7,50
child (2-12 yrs)	€ 4,00
pitch	€ 8,00
dog	€ 2,50
electricity (p/kw per hour)	€ 0,60
water connection	€ 0,50

Reservations

Made without charge. Tel: 07633 7045.
E-mail: camping.belchenblick@t-online.de

DE3437 Camping Hochschwarzwald

79674 Todtnau-Muggenbrunn (Baden-Württemberg)

Hochschwarzwald is a small, peaceful, quality site in an attractive wooded valley high up in the Black Forest. This is an extremely popular area, with many summer visitors enjoying walking and cycling, but it is also ideal for winter stays, with skiing from the site. At the back of the park, as well as being able to walk in the woods, you can paddle in a flat area of the stream which tumbles town the hill and there is an attractive barbecue area with seating as well as table tennis. Of 85 marked pitches (some with shade), 50 are for tourers (all with 10A electrical connections) on level terraces of grass and gravel. There is an area at the entrance for overnight stays in high season.

Facilities

Two modern, heated sanitary buildings have good installations, with a few private cabins, a family room, a unit for the disabled, washing machine, dryer and spin dryer, plus dishwashing, inside or out. Small shop has essentials from 12.00 hrs. Restaurant/bar (closed Thursdays), both closed for 2 weeks in March and November. Off site: Walking and skiing directly from the site. Heated indoor pool, tennis court and ski school in Muggenbrunn. Todtnau waterfalls are 3km. Freiburg and Titisee are both 25 km.

At a glance

Welcome & Ambience	✓✓✓✓	Location	✓✓✓✓
Quality of Pitches	✓✓✓✓	Range of Facilities	✓✓✓✓

Directions

Site is about 1 km. beyond Muggenbrunn on the road from Todtnau towards Freiburg

Charges 2005

Per person	€ 4,30
child (2-12 yrs.)	€ 2,70
pitch	€ 4,00 - € 5,60
electricity per kwh	€ 0,50

Reservations

Contact site. Tel: 07671 1288.
E-mail: camping.hochschwarzwald@web.de

Open

All year.

DE3411 Campingplatz Heidehof

Blaubeurer Straße 50, 89150 Laichingen (Baden-Württemberg)

This site is at an altitude of 725 m. in the pleasant countryside of the Swabian Alb. Although there is an emphasis on permanent caravans, there are about 110 pitches for tourists. For overnight stays, these are in an area outside the barrier, and for longer stays pitches are inside the site. All have electricity connections (16A), and the overnight section also has an area for tents. A hotel/restaurant (open all year), although not actually in the campsite, is attached to it and immediately accessible from it. The city of Ulm and the recently opened Legoland are within easy reach. Being just off the autobahn makes it an ideal overnight stop on the way to or from Munich, southern Bavaria or Austria.

Facilities

Five good quality toilet blocks, all heated, clean and well maintained. Some washbasins are in cabins, and free showers. Four blocks have facilities for disabled visitors. Baby changing rooms. Dishwashing and laundry sinks. Washing machines, dryers and drying room. Motorcaravan service point. Gas supplies. Shop. Bar and restaurant (at hotel). Swimming pool (25 x 8 m.) and paddling pool. Playgrounds. Club for children at weekends in July/Aug. Table tennis, volleyball, football, minigolf. Bicycle hire. Main gate locked at 10 pm. (also 1.00 - 2.30 pm). Off site: Riding within 1 km. Fshing 6 km. Golf (9 hole) 10 km.

At a glance

Welcome & Ambience	✓✓✓✓✓	Location	✓✓✓✓
Quality of Pitches	✓✓✓✓	Range of Facilities	✓✓✓✓

Directions

From A5/E52 (Stuttgart -; Ulm) autobahn take exit 61. Follow L1230 south to Machtolsheim (about 3 km). Heidehof is about 2 km. further south on the L1220 (towards Blaubeuren).

Charges guide

Per person	€ 5,00
child (under 15 yrs)	€ 2,50
pitch	€ 4,00 - € 6,00
electricity	€ 1,50

Reservations

Made without charge. Tel: 07333 6408.
E-mail: heidehof.camping@t-online.de

Open

All year.

DE3420 Freizeitcenter Oberrhein

79244 Rheinmunster (Baden-Württemberg)

This large, well equipped holiday site provides much to do and is also a good base for visiting the Black Forest. To the left of reception are a touring area and a section of hardstanding for motorcaravans. The 250 touring pitches - out of 700 overall - all have electricity connections (mostly 16A, 3 pin, a few with 2 pin), and include 86 with water and drainage, but little shade. Two of the site's lakes are used for swimming (with roped-off areas for toddlers) and non-powered boating (the water was very clean when we visited), the third small one is for fishing. This site is well worth considering for a holiday, especially for families with young and early teenage children. Occasional live music is organised until late.

Facilities

Seven top quality, heated toilet buildings have free hot water and very smart fittings. Some have special rooms for children, babies and families. Excellent dog shower! Family washcabins to rent. Motorcaravan services. Gas supplies. Shop (1/4-31/10). Lakeside restaurant; snack bar (both 1/4-31/10). Modern play areas on sand. Small zoo. Tennis. Table tennis. Bicycle hire. Minigolf. Windsurf school. Swimming and boating lakes. Fishing (charged).
Off site: Supermarket 3 km. Riding 4 km. Golf 5 km.

Open

All year.

At a glance

Welcome & Ambience	✓✓✓	Location	✓✓✓✓
Quality of Pitches	✓✓✓✓	Range of Facilities	✓✓✓✓✓

Directions

Site is signed from Rheinmünster, 16 km. southwest of Rastatt on B36. From north on A5/E35-52 take exit 51 (Baden-Baden/Iffezheim) via Hügelsheim then south onto B36. From south take exit 52 (Bühl) and via Schwarzach and Rheinmünster or exit 52 to Rheinau then north on B36 to Stollhofen. Then follow signs from the roundabout.

Charges 2004

Per person	€ 5,00 - € 8,00
child (6-16 yrs)	€ 3,00 - € 6,00
child under 6 yrs	€ 2,50 - € 4,50
pitch with car	€ 5,00 - € 7,50
dog	€ 2,50 - € 4,50
electricity	€ 2,00

Reservations

Made for at least a week with deposit (€ 125) and fee (€ 10). Tel: 07227 2500.
E-mail: info@freizeitcenter-oberrhein.de

DE3427 Ferienparadies Schwarzwälder Hof

77960 Seelbach (Baden-Württemberg)

This recently refurbished site lies in a wooded valley, just south of the pleasant village of Seelbach in the Black Forest. The old buildings have been replaced by very attractive ones built in the old traditional style, but containing very modern facilities. There are 160 well drained touring pitches, either grass or hardstanding, all with electricity (10A), water supply and waste water outlet. There is also space for groups in tents. Just at the entrance is the family hotel with a restaurant. Besides a comprehensive general menu, there are also menus for children and older people with smaller appetites. A short walk from the site is a well-equipped municipal swimming pool and surrounding grass area. From 2004, entry to this will be free to campers. In July/August a good range of activities is organised for all ages, including a children's club. Fishing is possible in the stream which runs along the bottom of the site. The surrounding countryside is good for walking and cycling, and Europa Park is 30 km.

Facilities

Three sanitary blocks, all heated, clean and well maintained, include many washbasins in cabins and free showers. Facilities for wheelchair users. Family rooms (free). Baby changing room, superb children's bathroom, child size toilets and washbasins. Dishwashing and laundry sinks. Washing machines and dryers. Motorcaravan services. Gas supplies. Small shop. Restaurant, snacks and takeaway. TV and club room. Playground. Off site: Swimming 150 m. Bicycle hire 1 km. ATM in Seelbach (1 km.) Riding 3 km. Golf 5 km.

Open

All year.

At a glance

Welcome & Ambience	✓✓✓✓✓	Location	✓✓✓✓✓
Quality of Pitches	✓✓✓✓	Range of Facilities	✓✓✓✓

Directions

From A5/E35 autobahn, leave at exit 56 (Lahr). Follow road east through Lahr, until turn south to Seelbach. Go through Seelbach and the site is about 1 km. further on.

Charges guide

Per person	€ 5,50
child (0-13 yrs)	€ 3,50
pitch with services	€ 6,50 - € 8,00
tent pitch	€ 4,00 - € 5,50
dog	€ 2,00
electricity	€ 2,00

No credit cards.

Reservations

Made for any length with deposit (€ 25).
Tel: 078 23 27 77. E-mail: camping@seelbach.org

DE3428 Terrassen-Camping Oase

Mühlenweg 34, 77955 Ettenheim (Baden-Württemberg)

This pleasant well run site lies on wooded land on the western edge of the Black Forest, a very good region for walking and cycling. The level area near the entrance holds the main facilities and 200 touring pitches, all with 6A electricity. Pitches for tents are on grass and there is grass or hardstanding for caravans and motorcaravans. On sloping land further away are 75 terraced seasonal pitches. Just outside the entrance is the family hotel/restaurant, which also has a playground, all open to campers. A short walk from the site is a large swimming pool and an excellent surrounding leisure area. Europa Park is 10 km. away, and the city of Freiburg is 40 km. to the south. The site is only 5 km. from the A5/E35 autobahn, which makes it an ideal overnight stop on the way to Basel and Switzerland.

Facilities

Two sanitary blocks are heated, clean and well maintained. Many washbasins are in cabins. Showers are coin-operated. Facilities for wheelchair users. Baby changing room, children's bathroom. Dishwashing and laundry sinks. Motorcaravan services. Gas supplies. Shop. Restaurant and takeaway (at hotel). TV and club room. Off site: Swimming pool area 300 m. (supervised 50 m. pool and two paddling pools, snack bar, playground, three small football pitches, table tennis, volleyball, badminton, minigolf, boules, 30 sunbeds). Tennis, riding and bicycle hire within 1 km. Fishing 3 km. Golf 5 km.

Open

Week before Easter - 12 October.

At a glance

Welcome & Ambience	✓✓✓✓	Location	✓✓✓✓
Quality of Pitches	✓✓✓✓	Range of Facilities	✓✓✓

Directions

From A5/E35 autobahn, exit 57 (Ettenheim), follow L103 road southeast to Ettenheim (about 2.5 km). From here site is signed, and is a further 1 km. along the same road.

Charges guide

Per person	€ 3,50 - € 4,00
child (6-17 yrs)	€ 1,50 - € 3,00
pitch	€ 10,00 - € 15,50
car	€ 2,00
electricity	€ 1,80
dog	€ 2,00 - € 3,00

No credit cards.

Reservations

Contact site. Tel: 07822 445918.
E-mail: info@camping-oase.de

DE3432 Bonath Schwarzwald Camping Wolfach

Schiltacher Straße 80, 77709 Wolfach-Halbmeil (Baden-Württemberg)

This new site, which is still being developed, is set on the side of an valley in the Black Forest, set back from the road in a quiet position. If you would like to dine or wake up to beautiful views across an alpine valley and watch herds of wild deer graze in the meadows opposite, then this is the site for you. Terraced but with little shade as yet, the site has fairly level pitches, many with electricity (20A), water and drainage, and an area used for tents. In front of the main building is an area of hardstanding for overnight visitors, also with electricity. Herr Bonath advises on local attractions which include the waterfalls near Triberg which have been visited by, amongst others, Ernest Hemingway and Otto von Bismark.

Facilities

First class sanitary facilities include private cabins, large free showers including one multi-head, laundry, dishwashing, family bathrooms for hire and a kitchen, in the main building close to the entrance. It also houses reception with a small shop and the restaurant open daily all year. Off site: Wolfach 2 km. Golf 2 km. Outdoor pool 5 km.

Open

All year.

At a glance

Welcome & Ambience	✓✓✓✓✓	Location	✓✓✓✓✓
Quality of Pitches	✓✓✓✓	Range of Facilities	✓✓✓✓

Directions

From A5 Karlsruhe - Freiburg, take exit 55 Offenburg on B33/E531 to Haslach, then on 33/294 through Hausach. Soon after left on 294 to Wolfach. Go through tunnel and stay on 294 for about 3 km. to Halbmeil. Site is on the left at the end of the village

Charges guide

Per person	€ 5,90 - € 6,30
child (2-13 yrs)	€ 2,50 - € 3,20
pitch	€ 4,80 - € 5,30

Reservations

May be advisable for July/August. Tel: 07834 859309. E-mail: info@camping-online.de

DE3442 Terrassen Campingplatz Herbolzheim

Im Laue, 79336 Herbolzheim (Baden-Württemberg)

This well equipped campsite is in a quiet location on a wooded slope to the north of Freiburg. It is useful as a night stop when travelling between Frankfurt and Basel, and is just 10 km. from Europa Park, only a short way from the A5 autobahn. There are 70 caravan or motorcaravan pitches for tourists plus a few for motorcyclists, all with electricity (16A) on terraces lwith a little shade for some. This is good walking country and with only occasional entertainment, the site makes a very pleasant place in which to relax between daily activities, the many trees, shrubs and plants giving a pleasant, peaceful atmosphere.

Facilities

The main toilet facilities are modern, with new facilities for babies and disabled visitors. Motorcaravan services. Bar/restaurant (Easter - 1/10 daily). Shop for basics (order bread). Table tennis. Volleyball. Play area. Dogs are not accepted 15/7-15/8 Off site: Large open-air heated municipal pool complex adjacent (1/4-15/9). Bicycle hire 1 km. Restaurants and shops in village (3 km). Riding 5 km.

Open

Easter - 3 October.

At a glance

Welcome & Ambience	✓✓✓✓✓	Location	✓✓✓✓✓
Quality of Pitches	✓✓✓✓✓	Range of Facilities	✓✓✓✓

Directions

From A5 (Frankfurt - Basel) take exit 57, 58 or 59 and follow signs to Herbolzheim. Site is signed in south side of town near the swimming pool. Go through the pool car park, about 400 m. past pool entrance.

Charges 2005

Per person	€ 5,00
child (0-15 yrs)	€ 3,00
pitch	€ 6,00 - € 7,00
electricity	€ 2,00

Reservations

Contact site. Tel: 07643 1460. E-mail: s.hugoschmidt@t-online.de

DE3454 Kur- und Feriencamping Badenweiler

Weilertalstrasse 73, 79410 Badenweiler (Baden-Württemberg)

Badenweiler is a very pretty village on the edge of the southern Black Forest, easily accessed from the A5 or B3, but far enough from them to be peaceful. This campsite is on a hillside close to the village, with pleasant views, and is owned and run by the Wiesler family, with a little English spoken. Reception is part of a building which also houses a bar/café, opening hours as for reception, with takeaway snacks in the evenings in high season, basic supplies and a downstairs children's room. There are four terraces with 100 large, individual grass pitches, 93 for touring and all with electricity (16A).

Facilities

Top quality toilet blocks, one with toilets, the other with free showers and washbasins. Facilities for disabled visitors. Washing machines and dryers. Motorcaravan services. Gas. Shop for basics. Play area. Games room. Internet point. Off site: Outdoor, heated pool (free entry) 200 m. Restaurants 200 m. Shop 300 m. Golf 12 km.

Open

All year except 15 December - 15 January.

At a glance

Welcome & Ambience	✓✓✓✓	Location	✓✓✓✓✓
Quality of Pitches	✓✓✓✓✓	Range of Facilities	✓✓✓✓

Directions

From the A5 midway between Freiburg and Basel take exit 65 on B378 to Müllheim, then the L131 signed Badenweiler-Ost from where site is signed.

Charges 2004

Per person	€ 5,90
pitch	€ 8,00 - € 8,50
electricity (per kwh)	€ 0,40

No credit cards.

Reservations

Highly recommended all summer. Tel: 07632 1550. E-mail: camping.badenweiler@t-online.de

DE3452 Terrassen-Camping Alte Sägemühle

Badstrasse 57, 79295 Sulzburg (Baden-Württemberg)

This delightful site celebrates its 50th anniversary in 2005 and has constructed a large, traditional style water-wheel. By a peaceful road leading only to a natural swimming pool and an hotel, beyond the picturesque old town of Sulzburg with its narrow streets, this attractive location is perfect for those seeking peace and quiet. Set in a tree-covered valley with a stream running through the centre, the site has been kept as natural as possible. It is divided into terraced areas - tents have their own - and 42 of the 45 touring pitches (90% are 125 sq.m.) have electrical connections (16A) mainly German type, although long leads may be needed. The main building by the entrance houses reception, a small shop and the sanitary facilities. Run by the Geuss family (Frau Geuss speaks reasonable English) the site has won an award from the state for having been kept natural, for example, no tarmac roads, no minigolf, no playgrounds, etc. There are opportunities for walking straight from the site into the forest, and many walks and cycle rides are shown on maps available at reception. The tiny 500 year old Jewish Cemetery reached through the site has an interesting history.

Facilities

In the main building, facilities are of good quality with two private cabins, separate toilets, dishwashing, washing machine and dryer. Small shop for basics, beer and local wines (all year). Natural, unheated swimming pool adjacent (June-Aug) with discount to campers. Torch may be useful. A new motorhome service point has been installed.
Off site: Restaurants and other shops in Sulzburg (1.5 km). Bicycle hire in Sulzburg. Riding 5 km. Europa Park is less than an hour away.

Open

All year.

At a glance

Welcome & Ambience	✓✓✓✓✓	Location	✓✓✓✓✓
Quality of Pitches	✓✓✓✓✓	Range of Facilities	✓✓✓

Directions

Site is easily reached (25 minutes) from autobahn A5/E35. Take exit 64 for Bad Krozingen just south of Freiburg onto the B3 south to Heitersheim, then on through Sulzburg, or if coming from the south, exit 65 through Müllheim, Heitersheim and Sulzburg. Park is on the right edge of the road just before the main building.

Charges 2005

Per person	€ 5,50
child (1-15 yrs)	€ 3,00
pitch	€ 4,00 - € 6,50
electricity (plus meter)	€ 0,50
dog	€ 1,50

Reservations

Advised in high season. Tel: 07634 551181.

DE3436 Campingplatz Bankenhof

Bruderhalde 31, 79822 Titisee (Baden-Württemberg)

This peacefully located, fairly informal woodland site, with a friendly atmosphere, is situated just beyond the western end of Lake Titisee. The 190 pitches are on sparse grass and gravel, with some shade from a variety of trees, and 30 are occupied by seasonal units. The site is generally level, although there is a separate grassy area for tents which does have a slight slope. All pitches have electric hook-ups (16A), with gravel roads, and water taps for each area. Although there is some site lighting a torch might be useful for the darker areas under the trees. There is enough space for American RVs and other large units (welcomed, but booking is advised). Unusual features of the site are the glass walled technical area in the sanitary facilities, where the inquisitive can check the temperature of the water before taking their morning shower, and the totally separate sanitary unit with bright cheerful child-sized facilities for the under 10's. A popular bar and restaurant is open all year round (except November). Children also have an excellent fenced adventure playground. The lake and beach are only 300 m. via a direct path. A quick-stop facility just outside the site entrance, is available at reduced rates. An excellent site for exploring this part of the Black Forest and the Titisee area.

Facilities

Two sets of quality sanitary facilities plus three family bath/shower rooms for rent. Well equipped and heated, they include controllable hot showers and some washbasins in cubicles. A separate building houses facilities for disabled campers, and a unit for children (under 10 yrs). Kitchen facilities provide an electric hob and a dishwasher (on payment). Laundry. Motorcaravan service point. Shop. Restaurant (excl. Nov). Fitness room. TV and cinema room. Adventure play area. Youth Room. Bicycle, go-kart and buggy hire. Football field. Beach volleyball. Table tennis. Recycling centre for glass, paper, metal, batteries. Internet terminal. Off site: Fishing 0.5 km. Golf, riding and boat launching within 3 km. The Ski Museum at Hinterzarten 10 km. Railway Museum and steam trains at Blumberg or Germany's highest waterfall at Triberg both around 50 km.

At a glance

Welcome & Ambience	✓✓✓✓	Location	✓✓✓✓
Quality of Pitches	✓✓✓✓	Range of Facilities	✓✓✓✓

Directions

From Freiburg take road B31 east to Titisee, then from town centre follow camping signs for Jugendherberge and Bankenhof.

Charges guide

Per person	€ 4,10 - € 5,40
child (3-16 yrs)	€ 2,30 - € 2,60
pitch	€ 5,90 - € 7,40
electricity per kw.	€ 0,45
dog	€ 1,60

Reservations

Contact site. Tel: 07652 1351.
E-mail: info@bankenhof.de

Open

All year.

DE3465 Camping Wirthshof

Steibensteg 12, 88677 Markdorf (Baden-Württemberg)

Lying seven kilometres back from the Bodensee, twelve kilometres from Friedrichshafen, this friendly site with good facilities could well be of interest to Britons with young children. The 324 individual touring pitches have electrical connections (10A) and are of about 80 sq.m. on well tended flat grass, adjoining access roads. There are some larger pitches with water, waste water and electricity. No dogs are accepted in July/Aug. and there is a special section for campers with dogs at other times. On site is a pleasant heated outdoor pool (1/5-15/9) with a grassy lying-out area; it is free to campers but is also open to outsiders on payment so can be busy in season. Many activities are organised for children and adults over a long season.

Facilities

The three heated toilet blocks provide washbasins in cubicles, a unit for disabled people and a children's bathroom. Solar heated unit for dishwashing and laundry. Gas supplies. Motorcaravan services. Shop. Restaurant/bar with takeaway. Swimming pool (25 x 12.5 m; open 10/5-10/9). Sports field with goal posts. Two adventure playgrounds. Bicycle hire. Normal minigolf; also 'pit-pat', played at table height with billiard cues. Activity programme. Dogs not accepted July/Aug. Off site: Tennis near. Riding 8 km. Golf and fishing 10 km.

Open

15 March - 30 October.

At a glance

Welcome & Ambience	✓✓✓✓✓	Location	✓✓✓✓✓
Quality of Pitches	✓✓✓✓✓	Range of Facilities	✓✓✓✓✓

Directions

Site is on eastern edge of Markdorf, turn south off B33 Ravensburg road. The site is signed (but not named) from Markdorf.

Charges guide

Per person	€ 5,50
child (1-14 yrs)	€ 4,50
pitch incl. electricity	€ 10,50
serviced pitch incl. electricity	€ 13,00
dog (not allowed July/Aug)	€ 2,00

No credit cards.

Reservations

Made with deposit and fee. Tel: 07544 2325.
E-mail: info@wirthshof.de

DE3467 Isnycamping

Lohbauerstr. 59-69, 88316 Isny (Baden-Württemberg)

Isny is a delightful spot for families and for others looking for a peaceful stay in a very well-managed environment. The site has been developed to a high standard by the former owner of Donau-Lech (3630) and lies just south of the village, in a wood by a lake. Leading down from reception, with the lake to your left, you come to an open area of 45 individual 100 sq.m. hardstanding pitches (just beyond the toilet block), with a circular access road. A further area on a terrace above is under development. A café with light snacks during the week and meals at the weekends is open long hours in high season. It has a terrace that overlooks the lake, which is used for swimming (unsupervised) daily until early evening, and was pleasantly warm when we swam in it. A low metal rail marks the area for non-swimmers and there is a large grass sunbathing area. Latest developments include a large family play area and fly fishing for trout in Sept/October.

Facilities

The main sanitary unit (deposit required for the key) is first class, and is cleaned a minimum of 5 times a day. It has private cabins as well as vanity style washbasins, large controllable showers, with full curtain, token operated. Further facilities near the reception house showers, wc's, washbasins, and a good unit for disabled visitors. Dishwashing room. Laundry. Basic motorcaravan services. Café/bar. Reception keeps a few basic supplies. Bicycles to borrow. Off site: A pathway through the woods leads to a tennis club, a large recreation area, with children's play area, walks and communal Barbecue area. Restaurant and supermarket 1.5 km.

At a glance

Welcome & Ambience	✓✓✓✓	Location	✓✓✓✓
Quality of Pitches	✓✓✓✓	Range of Facilities	✓✓✓✓✓

Directions

From the B12 between Lindau and Kempten, turn south at sign in Isny and follow signs up into the woods.

Charges 2005

Per person	€ 6,40
child per year of age	€ 0,40
pitch	€ 9,00
electricity per kw	€ 0,50
dog	€ 1,00

Special rates for senior citizens (low season).

Reservations

Contact site. Tel: 07562 2389.

Open

All year except November and December.

DE3627 Azur Camping Ellwangen

Rotenbacher Strasse, 73479 Ellwangen (Baden-Württemberg)

In a quiet position on the edge of town, with the River Jagst along one side, this modern six hectare site, from which you can see the large hilltop castle, has a park-like appearance with mature trees giving some shade. The 95 large, flat, grassy pitches (8 hardstandings) are unmarked off tarmac access roads. Electricity is available for about half the pitches from central boxes (16A). All the facilities are in one area to the left of the site entrance in modern units, with reception, the small shop and a bar/restaurant.

Facilities

Heated sanitary facilities provide some private cabins. Dishwashing facilities, both inside and out, a small laundry, and room for babies and disabled visitors. Laundry facilities. Gas supplies. Motorcaravan services. Shop. Restaurant/bar. Some play equipment for children is on sand. Fishing is very popular. Off site: Cycle paths. Heated indoor municipal wave-pool 200 m. Numerous other local attractions.

Open

All year; 18 November - 28 February by reservation.

At a glance

Welcome & Ambience	✓✓✓✓	Location	✓✓✓✓
Quality of Pitches	✓✓✓✓	Range of Facilities	✓✓✓

Directions

From A7 Ulm - Würzburg autobahn take exit 113 and go into Ellwangen from where site is signed on road to Rotenbach village. It is next to the Hallenbad, with a fairly tight left turn into the entrance road.

Charges guide

Per person	€ 4,50 - € 6,00
child (2-12 yrs)	€ 3,50 - € 4,50
pitch	€ 5,50 - € 7,50
electricity	€ 2,10

No credit cards.

Reservations

Contact site. Tel: 07961 7921.
E-mail: info@azur-camping.de

DE3650 Camping Gitzenweiler Hof

Gitzenweiler 88, 88131 Lindau-Oberreitnau (Bavaria (S))

Gitzenweiler Hof has been developed into a really well-equipped, first-class site for a family holiday. In a country setting it has about 380 permanent caravans as well as about 450 places for touring units (it is advisable to book for July/Aug). In the tourist section many pitches are without markings with siting left to campers, the others in rows between access roads. There are 450 electricity connections (6/16A) and 56 pitches for motorcaravans with water, drainage and TV connections. A large open-air swimming pool has attractive surrounds with seats (free for campers). Lindau is an interesting town, especially by the harbour, and possible excursions include the whole of the Bodensee (Lake Constance), the German Alpine Road, the Austrian Vorarlberg and Switzerland. This is a pleasant, friendly, well-run site with a separate area just outside for overnight stops.

Facilities

The toilet blocks have been beautifully renovated and include some washbasins in cabins, a children's bathroom and baby bath, plus a dog shower. Washing machines, dryers and dishwasher. Motorcaravan services. Shop (limited hours in low season). Two restaurants with takeaway. Large swimming pool in summer (33 x 25 m). Volleyball. Basketball. Two playgrounds and play room with entertainment in summer. Organised activities for adults and children all year. Hens, rabbits, ducks and ponies for the children. Ground for football, etc. Free fishing in lake. Table tennis. Minigolf. Club room with arcade games and internet points. Library (including books in English). Doctor comes if needed; hospital near. American motorhomes accepted up to 10 tons.

At a glance

Welcome & Ambience	✓✓✓✓✓	Location	✓✓✓✓✓
Quality of Pitches	✓✓✓✓✓	Range of Facilities	✓✓✓✓✓

Directions

Site is signed from the B12 about 4 km. north of Lindau. Also from A96 exit 3 (Weißensberg), and from in and around Lindau.

Charges 2005

Per person	€ 6,50
child (3-9 yrs)	€ 2,00
child (10-15 yrs)	€ 4,50
pitch	€ 8,00 - € 14,00
tent pitch	€ 5,00 - € 8,00

Discounts for stays over 14 days and in low season.

Reservations

Made with deposit (€ 103). Tel: 08382 94940.
E-mail: info@gitzenweiler-hof.de

Open

All year.

DE3602 Camping Romantische Straße

97993 Creglingen-Münster (Baden-Württemberg)

The small village of Münster is on a scenic road just three kilometres from Creglingen (also the 100 km. long Tauber valley cycle route) and about 16 kilometres from the tourist town of Rothenburg which, although fascinating, is also extremely busy and commercialised. This site would, therefore, be much appreciated for its peaceful situation in a wooded valley just outside Münster, with 110 grass touring pitches (out of 150), many level, others with a small degree of slope. They are not hedged or fenced, to keep the natural appearance of the woodland. All the pitches have electricity (16A), some shade, and are situated either side of a stream (fenced off from a weir at the top of the site). Good English is spoken by the friendly owners, who also own the restaurant, and they have long term plans to further develop this attractive site, having already renovated the pool, sauna, solarium and changing rooms and made an open air chess and boules area in a peaceful spot higher up the site. Bird watchers will be interested that the White-throated Dipper is regularly seen here.

Facilities

The main sanitary facilities are of good quality, with free hot water for washbasins (two for each male/female in private cabins) and showers. A small unit further into the site is not of the same quality. Launderette. Motorcaravan services. Small shop for basic supplies. Gas supplies. Large, pleasant bar/restaurant at the entrance (1/4-31/10, closed Mondays). Barbecue and covered sitting area. Heated indoor swimming pool (bathing caps required) and sauna. Minigolf. Children's play area. Table tennis. Bicycle hire. Rooms to let. Off site: Large lakes for swimming 100 m. and fishing 1 km. Riding 3 km.

Open

15 March - 15 November.

At a glance

Welcome & Ambience	✓✓✓✓✓	Location	✓✓✓✓
Quality of Pitches	✓✓✓	Range of Facilities	✓✓✓✓

Directions

From the Romantische Strasse between Rothenburg and Bad Mergentheim, exit at Creglingen to Münster (3 km) and site is just beyond this village.

Charges 2004

Per person	€ 4,50 - € 5,50
child (3-14 yrs)	€ 3,50 - € 3,80
pitch	€ 6,00 - € 7,00
small tent pitch	€ 3,00 - € 3,50
dog	€ 1,00
electricity	€ 2,00

No credit cards.

Reservations

Advised for Whitsun, July/Aug. and made without deposit for British visitors Tel: 07933 20289.
E-mail: camping.hausotter@web.de

DE3630 Camping Donau-Lech

Campingweg 1, 86698 Eggelstetten (Bavaria (S))

The Haas family have developed this friendly site just off the 'Romantische Strasse' well and run it very much as a family site, providing a useful information sheet in English. The lake provides swimming and wildlife for children and adults to enjoy. Alongside it are 50 marked touring pitches with 16A electrical connections, on flat grass arranged in rows either side of a tarred access road. With an average of 120 sq.m. per unit, it is a comfortable site with an open feeling and developing shade. There are three separate pleasant, flat, grass areas near the entrance for people with tents (including youngsters, cyclists or motorcyclists) with unmarked pitches. Pitches for long stay visitors are located beyond the tourers. Very basic food supplies are kept with bread to order. Suitable not only as a night stop on the way south, the site is also not far from Augsburg or Munich (a Family Railticket costs about €21, valid for the return journey to Munich and the city's transport system) and the local area is very attractive.

Facilities

All amenities are housed in the main building at the entrance with reception. Sanitary facilities are downstairs with free showers now, warm water washbasins, (no cabins), dishwashing and laundry room, all of a satisfactory standard. Sauna. Washing machine and dryer. Motorcaravan services. Large bar area with terrace. Small shop for basics (1/4-31/10). General room. Youth room. Table tennis. Children's play area. Lake for swimming on site (own risk). Off site: Larger lake used for sailboarding 400 m. Golf course and driving range 1 km. Restaurants and other amenities a short drive.

Open

All year except November.

At a glance

Welcome & Ambience	✓✓✓✓	Location	✓✓✓✓
Quality of Pitches	✓✓✓✓	Range of Facilities	✓✓✓

Directions

Turn off main B2 road about 5 km. south of Donauwörth at signs for Asbach-Bäumenheim Nord towards Eggelstetten, then follow camp signs for over 1 km. to site.

Charges guide

Per person	€ 4,50
child (2-15 yrs)	€ 2,50
caravan	€ 5,00 - € 6,00
tent	€ 3,50 - € 5,00
car	€ 1,28
motorcaravan	€ 5,00 - € 6,00

Reservations

Not needed - said to be always space at present.
Tel: 09090 4046.
E-mail: info@donau-lech-camping.de

DE3672 Camping Elbsee

Am Elbsee 3, 87648 Aitrang (Bavaria (S))

This attractive site, with its associated hotel and restaurant about 400 m. away, lies on land sloping down to the lake. This is not an area well known to tourists, although the towns of Marktoberdorf (14 km), Kaufbeuren (16 km) and Kempten (21 km) merit a visit. With this in mind, the owners have set about providing good facilities and a developing program of activities. All the 120 touring pitches have access to electricity (16A) and 50 also have water and drainage. Some of the pitches restricted to tents slope slightly. In high season there are organised outings, musical performances on site or at the hotel, and children's activities. Next to the site is a supervised lake bathing area, operated by the municipality, with a kiosk selling drinks and snacks, and a playground. Entrance to this is at a reduced price for campers.

Facilities

Two clean, well appointed heated sanitary blocks include free showers, washbasins all in cabins, a children's bathroom and family bathrooms to rent. Facilities for disabled visitors. Motorcaravan service point. Shop (bread can be ordered for following day). Playground and activity rooms. TV, games and meeting rooms. Sports field. Activity programme (20/7-31/8). Off site: At hotel, restaurant, takeaway and bar. Boat hire. Fishing. Bicycle hire 2 km. Shop 2 km. Golf 12 km.

Open

15 December - 5 November.

At a glance

Welcome & Ambience	✓✓✓✓✓	Location	✓✓✓✓
Quality of Pitches	✓✓✓✓✓	Range of Facilities	✓✓✓✓

Directions

From centre of Marktoberdorf, take minor road northwest to Ruderatshofen and from there take minor road west towards Aitrang. Just south of Aitrang, site is signed to south of the road. The road to the site (2 km.) is winding and narrow, but two caravans can just about pass.

Charges guide

Per person	€ 3,60
child (4-14 yrs)	€ 2,60
pitch incl. car	€ 10,00 - € 13,00
electricity per kw.	€ 0,60

Reservations

Contact site. Tel: 08343 248.
E-mail: camping@elbsee.de

DE3642 Lech Camping

Seeweg 6, 86444 Mühlhausen bei Augsburg (Bavaria (S))

Situated just north of Ausgberg, this beautifully run site is a pleasure to stay on. Gabi Ryssel, the owner, works very hard to cater to every wish of her guests – from the moment you arrive and are given the key to a very clean toilet block and are given plenty of tourist information you are in very capable hands. The site has a comprehensive camping shop (only a few basic foodstuffs as there is a supermarket over the road) and an excellent restaurant overlooking a small lake. A paddling pool (part of the lake cordoned off) is provided for children with a safe little sandy area along with sunbeds to enjoy the view over the lake. The 40 level, grass and gravel pitches are not separated but you will be shown to an area with plenty of space between units and shade from pine trees. Electricity is available (10/16A). Although this is a rural site, there is easy access by bus to Ausberg, a beautiful German town.

Facilities

The new toilet block (cleaned many times daily) includes good showers. Baby room. Separate family bathroom for rent. Five star facilities for disabled visitors. Separate room with washing machine and laundry sinks, plus dishwashing sinks. Motorcaravan service point. Small shop. Restaurant. Small playground (partially fenced). Bicycle hire. Off site: Football field 300 m. Easy access to main E52 Stuttgart - Munich road. Bus service to city. Legoland 25 minute drive.

Open

Easter - 15 September.

At a glance

Welcome & Ambience	✓✓✓✓✓	Location	✓✓✓✓✓
Quality of Pitches	✓✓✓✓	Range of Facilities	✓✓✓✓✓

Directions

Site is northeast of Augsberg. Leave E52 /A8 Munich - Stuggart motorway at exit 73 and follow signs to Neuburg/Pottmes. After 3 km. (past airport) on U49 is Muhlhausen sign. Lech Camping is on right.

Charges 2004

Per person	€ 5,00
child (2-15 yrs)	€ 2,50
pitch	€ 7,00
electricity	€ 2,50
animal	€ 2,50

Reservations

Contact site. Tel: 08207/2200.
E-mail: lech-camping-gmbh@t-online.de

DE3635 Camping München-Obermenzing

Lochhausenerstraße 59, 81247 München (Bavaria (S))

On the northwest edge of Munich, this site makes a good stopover for those wishing to see the city or pass the night. The flat terrain is mostly covered by mature trees, giving shade to most pitches. Caravan owners are well off here as they have a special section of 130 individual drive-through pitches, mainly separated from each other by high hedges and opening off the hard site roads with easy access. These have 10A electricity connections and about 30 have water and waste water connections also. About 200 tents and motorcaravans are taken on quite large, level grass areas, with an overflow section so space is usually available. There is a shop and rest room with TV and a drinks machine (including beer). There is some road noise, but we spent another reasonably undisturbed night here, helped by the new earth bank, and it is a very convenient site.

Facilities

The single central sanitary block is large, having been extended, and it should now be adequate in size. Cleaning appears satisfactory and there is heating in the low season. It provides individual washbasins, many in curtained cubicles and most with free hot water. Hot showers require tokens (meter outside so make sure taps are turned off). Cooking facilities on payment. Washing machine and dryers. Gas supplies. Motorcaravan services. Shop (from May). Bar (from July). TV room. Charcoal barbecues not permitted. Off site: Baker and café nearby. Riding or golf 5 km. Bicycle hire 8 km. Public transport services are available to the city from very close by. By car the journey might take 20-30 minutes depending on the density of traffic.

At a glance

Welcome & Ambience	✓✓✓✓	Location	✓✓✓✓
Quality of Pitches	✓✓✓✓	Range of Facilities	✓✓✓

Directions

Site is in the northwest of the city. From Stuttgart, Nuremberg, Deggendorf or Salzburg, leave A99 at München - Lochhausen 'Kreiss-West'.

Charges 2004

Per person	€ 4,50
child (2-14 yrs)	€ 2,00
car	€ 6,00
tent	€ 3,85
caravan or motorcaravan	€ 6,00
electricity (plus slot meter)	€ 0,50

No credit cards.

Reservations

Not made. Tel: 089 8112235.
E-mail: campingplatz-obermenzing@t-online.de

Open

15 March - 31 October.

DE3640 Camping Municipal München-Thalkirchen

Zentralländstraße 49, 81379 München (Bavaria (S))

Now under new management, this well cared for municipal site is pleasantly and quietly situated on the southern side of Munich in parkland formed by the River Isar conservation area, four kilometres from the city centre (there are subway and bus links) and tall trees offer shade in parts. The large city of Munich has much to offer and the Thalkirchen site becomes quite crowded during the season, There are 550 pitches (150 for caravans, most with 10A electricity, water and waste water shared; 100 for motor-caravans, mostly with electricity and a small area of hardstanding) of various sizes (some quite small), marked by metal or wooden posts and rails. Like many city sites, groups are put in one area. and American motorhomes are accepted. The site is very busy (and probably noisy) during the Beer Festival (14 Sept - 5 Oct), but is well maintained and kept clean.

Facilities

There are five refurbished toilet blocks, two of which can be heated, with seatless toilets, washbasins with shelf, mirror and cold water. Hot water for showers and sinks is on payment. Facilities for disabled people. Shop (7 am - 8.30 pm). Snack bar with covered terrace (7 am - 10 pm), Drinks machine incl. Beer. General room with TV pool and games. Good small children's playground. Tourist information, souvenirs and other services. Treatment room. Washing machines and dryers. Maximum stay 14 days. Bikes for hire. Dormitory accommodation for groups (schools, scouts and guides etc.) Office hours 7 am - 11 pm. Off site: Restaurant 200 m. Pleasant walks may be taken in the adjacent park and the world famous Munich zoo is just 15 minutes walk along the river from the site.

At a glance

Welcome & Ambience	✓✓✓✓	Location	✓✓✓✓
Quality of Pitches	✓✓✓	Range of Facilities	✓✓✓✓

Directions

From autobahns follow 'Mittel' ring road to SSE of the city centre where site is signed; also follow signs for Thalkirchen or the Zoo and site is close. Well signed now from all over the City.

Charges guide

Per person	€ 4,40
child (2-14 yrs)	€ 1,30
pitch incl. car	€ 9,70

Credit cards only accepted for souvenirs.

Reservations

Not made except for groups - said to be room up to 4 pm. daily. Tel: 089 7231707.
E-mail: munichtouristoffice@compuserve.com

Open

15 March - end October.

DE3667 Camping Bannwaldsee

Münchner strasse 151, 87645 Schwangau (Bavaria (S))

This well run site is within easy reach of the pleasant town of Füssen and the famous castles of Neuschwanstein and Hohenschwangau, and the extravagantly baroque Wieskirch (Church in the meadow) is 32 km. away. Situated on the edge of the lake, it has a beach, and a jetty at which pedaloes and rowing boats can be hired. The site is level, with 500 touring pitches. Those for caravans and motorcaravans are on grass or hardstanding, of good size, marked out and numbered. All are close to electrical points (10A or 16A), and 140 of them have electricity, water supply and waste water outlet. There is a separate grassed area for tents. In July and August there is a marquee for films, dances, music and other organised activities, and a club for young children. During this period, a travel agent is on site for those who wish to book excursions.

Facilities

Three clean and well maintained sanitary blocks, with some washbasins in cabins. Showers are free, although there might not be enough to avoid congestion in high season. Facilities for disabled visitors. Baby room. Very good laundry facilities including drying rooms. Cooking rings (charged). Motorcaravan sevice point. Restaurant (with bar, pizzeria, snacks, takeaway) and well stocked shop, both open all year. Bicycle and pedal car hire. Games and TV room. Fishing at lake. Church service on Sundays in high season. Off site: Bus stop at entrance. In Schwangau (2 km.) - indoor and outdoor swimming pools, riding, minigolf. Golf 15 km.

At a glance

Welcome & Ambience	✓✓✓✓✓	Location	✓✓✓✓
Quality of Pitches	✓✓✓✓	Range of Facilities	✓✓✓✓

Directions

From Füssen, take B17 road northeast towards Schwangau, Schongau, Landsberg and Augsburg. Site is signed from Schwangau, and is to the left of the road, about 3 km. further on.

Charges guide

Per person	€ 6,00 - € 7,00
child (6-15 yrs)	€ 4,50 - € 5,00
pitch	€ 5,00 - € 6,00
electricity	€ 2,00
dog	€ 2,50 - € 3,00

Reservations

Advised for high season and made with deposit (€ 65) and fee (€ 15). Tel: 08362 93000. E-mail: info@camping-bannwaldsee.de

Open

All year.

DE3670 Camping Hopfensee

Fischerbichl 17, 87629 Füssen im Königswinkel (Bavaria (S))

Hopfensee is a high class site with excellent facilities, catering for discerning visitors, by a lake. It is well placed to explore the very attractive Bavarian Alpine region which, along with the architecture and historical interest of the Royal Castles at Hohenschwangau and the Baroque church at Wies, makes it a very popular holiday area. The 377 tourist pitches for caravans and motorhomes, most with shade, each have 16A electricity, water, drain and cable TV connections. They are marked, numbered and of a good size. At the centre of the site is a large building with an open village-like square in the middle, adorned with cascading flowers. It houses the exceptional sanitary facilities and, on the upper floors, a swimming pool, treatment and physiotherapy suites, fitness centre, cinema and children's play room. There is direct access to the lake for sailing, canoeing etc. and a place for parking boats. Charges are high, but include the pool, super sports building, cinema, etc. Tents are not accepted.

Facilities

The exceptionally good, heated sanitary facilities provide British style WCs, free hot water in washbasins (some in cabins), large showers and sinks, laundry and washing-up rooms, as well as baby and children's wash rooms. Some private units are for hire. Motorcaravan services. Restaurant with terrace faces across the lake towards the setting sun. Bar. Takeaway. Shop. Indoor pool and fitness centre. Supervised courses of remedial water treatments, massage, etc. Sauna, solarium and steam bath. Children's playground and kindergarten. Large games room with table tennis, pool, etc. Bicycle hire. Tennis. Table tennis. Fishing. Ski school in winter. No tents taken. Off site: Riding 1 km.

Open

17 December - 6 November.

At a glance

Welcome & Ambience	✓✓✓✓	Location	✓✓✓✓
Quality of Pitches	✓✓✓✓✓	Range of Facilities	✓✓✓✓✓

Directions

Site is 4 km. north of Füssen. Turn off B16 to Hopfen and site is on the left through a car park. If approaching from the west on B310, turn towards Füssen at T-junction with the B16 and immediately turn right again for the road to Hopfen.

Charges 2005

Per person	€ 7,80 - € 8,90
child (2-12 yrs)	€ 4,70 - € 5,55
12-18 yrs	€ 6,00 - € 8,40
pitch with cable TV, electricity	€ 11,50 - € 12,80
local tax (over 18)	€ 1,20 - € 1,60
rubbish tax	€ 0,25

No credit cards.

Reservations

Made without deposit; min. 14 days 16 June - 1 Sept (unless shorter time fits into charts). Tel: 08362 917710. E-mail: info@camping-hopfensee.com

Germany

DE3671 Camping Öschlesee

Moos 1, 87477 Sulzberg (Bavaria (S))

Less than one kilometre northwest of Sulzberg, this well run site lies in the foothills north of the Alps, a cross country skiing area in winter, with good walking and cycling at other times. There is no pool, but just across the road is a swimming and picnic area on the edge of the lake. Most of the 100 touring pitches are on level ground and all have access to electricity (10A). In the section containing some new pitches, the newly planted trees are not yet big enough to provide shade. The nearby town of Kempten (7 kilometres) is worth a visit, and annually hosts the 9-day Allgäu Festival in mid August. The all year resort of Oberstdorf is 35 kilometres and the site is far enough (42 kilometres) from Füssen to avoid the high season crowds, but still near enough for a day trip to there and the castles of Neuschwanstein and Hohenschwangau. Its proximity to the autobahn makes it a good overnight stop on the way to or from places such as Oberammergau, Garmisch-Partenkirchen, Berchtesgaden and Salzburg.

Facilities

Two modern heated sanitary blocks are clean and well maintained, with free showers, some washbasins in cabins, baby changing room and facilities for disabled visitors. Laundry room. Motorcaravan service point. Bar, snack bar, takeaway and small shop, which also serves as reception. Gas sales. TV room, arcade games. Playground. Table tennis. Automatic skittle alley. Bicycle hire. Off site: Riding and fishing 1 km. Golf 10 km.

Open

All year.

At a glance

Welcome & Ambience	✓✓✓	Location	✓✓✓✓✓
Quality of Pitches	✓✓✓✓	Range of Facilities	✓✓✓

Directions

From A7/E43 autobahn at exit 136, turn on A980 heading west towards Waltenhofen and Isny. After about 2.5 km. at the first exit (Durach), take minor road south. Site is signed from here (about 1 km.)

Charges guide

Per person	€ 4,10
child (2-14 yrs)	€ 3,10
pitch	€ 9,80
tent pitch	€ 6,80
electricity	€ 1,60
dog	€ 1,10

No credit cards.

Reservations

Contact site. Tel: 08376 93040.
E-mail: camping.oschlesee@t-online.de

DE3680 Alpen-Caravanpark Tennsee

82494 Krün / Obb (Bavaria (S))

Tennsee is an excellent site in truly beautiful surroundings high up (1,000 m.) in the Karwendel Alps with super mountain views, and close to many famous places of which Innsbruck (44 km) and Oberammergau (26 km) are two. Mountain walks are plentiful, with several lifts close by. It is an attractive site with good facilities including 120 serviced pitches with individual connections for electricity (up to 16A and two connections), gas, TV, radio, telephone, water and waste water. The other 80 pitches all have electricity and some of these are available for overnight guests at a reduced rate. Reception and restaurants, bar, cellar youth room and a well stocked shop are all housed in attractive buildings. Many activities and excursions are organised to local attractions by the Zick family, who run the site in a very friendly, helpful and efficient manner.

Facilities

The first class sanitary block has under-floor heating, washbasins in cabins and private units with WC, shower, basin and bidet for rent. Unit for disabled people with the latest in flushing and warm air drying. Baby bath, dog bathroom and a heated room for ski equipment (with lockers). Washing machines, free dryers and irons. Gas supplies. Motorcaravan services. Cooking facilities. Shop. Restaurants with takeaway (waiter, self service and takeaway). Bar. Youth room with table tennis, amusements. Solarium. Bicycle hire. Playground. Organised activities and excursions. Bus service to ski slopes in winter.
Off site: Fishing 400 m. Riding or golf 3 km.

Open

All year except 8 November - 15 December.

At a glance

Welcome & Ambience	✓✓✓✓✓	Location	✓✓✓✓✓
Quality of Pitches	✓✓✓✓	Range of Facilities	✓✓✓✓✓

Directions

Site is just off main Garmisch-Partenkirchen/Innsbruck road no. 2 between Klais and Krün, 15 km. from Garmisch watch for small sign 'Tennsee + Barmersee' and turn right there for site.

Charges 2005

Per person	€ 7,00 - € 7,50
1-3 children (3-15 yrs)	€ 3,50 - € 5,00
other children	€ 3,00 - € 3,50
pitch	€ 8,00 - € 12,00
dog	€ 3,00
local tax	€ 1,15

Senior citizens special rates (not winter).

Reservations

Advised for July - Sept and Xmas and made for exact dates (no fee). Tel: 08825 170.
E-mail: info@camping-tennsee.de

DE3685 Camping Allweglehen

83471 Berchtesgaden (Bavaria (S))

Berchtesgaden is a National Park with magnificent scenery, in an area of mountains, lakes, valleys, castles and churches. Hitler built his 'Eagles Nest' on top of the Kehlstein, which is visible from the site and open to the public (bus service, no cars). This all year site occupies a hillside position, with spectacular mountain views. The site access road is steep (14%), particularly at the entrance, but the proprietor will use his tractor to tow caravans if requested. There are 180 pitches (160 for touring), arranged on a series of gravel terraces, separated by hedges or fir trees and all with good views and electrical connections (16A). There is a separate area on a sloping meadow for tents. The pleasant restaurant, with terrace, offers Bavarian specialities at reasonable prices. This is a useful base for sightseeing or relaxing.

Facilities

Two adjacent older style, heated toilet blocks near the restaurant. Cleaning and maintanence can be variable. Washing machines and dryers. Motorcaravan services. Gas. Restaurant. Kiosk for essentials (all year). Play area. Small heated pool (small charge, 15/5-15/10). Solarium. Minigolf. Table tennis. Fishing. Excursions. Off site: Winter sports near. Walks. Riding 2 km. Bicycle hire 3 km. Golf 5 km.

Open

All year.

At a glance

Welcome & Ambience	✓✓✓	Location	✓✓✓✓
Quality of Pitches	✓✓✓✓	Range of Facilities	✓✓✓

Directions

Easiest access is via the Austrian autobahn A10 (vignette necessary), Salzburg Sud exit and follow the B305. Alternatively take the B305 from Ruhpolding (winding and with 4 m. height limit), or the B20 from Bad Reichenhall. Site is 4 km. NE of Berchtesgaden.

Charges 2004

Per person	€ 4,50
pitch	€ 8,70 - € 9,20
electricity (per kw)	€ 0,45

Reservations

Write to site (in German!). Tel: 08652 2396.
E-mail: Campingplatz.Allweglehen@t-online.de

DE3695 Dreiflüsse Camping

94113 Irring b. Passau (Bavaria (S))

Although the site overlooks the Danube, it is in fact some 9 km. from the confluence of the Danube, Inn and Ilz. Dreiflüsse Camping occupies a hillside position to the west of Passau with pitches, flat or with a little slope on several rows of terraces. The 180 places for touring units are not all numbered or marked, although 16A electricity boxes determine where units pitch. Trees and low banks separate the terraces which are of gravel with a thin covering of grass. The energetic and very jolly owner is most popular with his regular visitors and he gives the site a very friendly air. This is a useful en-route stop or for a stay to explore Passau, and is popular with cyclists. There may some road and rail noise (24 hrs).

Facilities

The sanitary facilities are acceptable, if a little old, with two private cabins for women, one for men. Laundry. Motorcaravan services. Gas supplies. Pleasant restaurant at entrance, where the reception, shop and sanitary buildings are also located. Shop all season. Small heated indoor pool (May - 15 Sept on payment). Play area. Table tennis. Bicycle hire. Off site: Riding 3 km. Bus service for Passau from outside site (a little erratic and finishes at 6 pm).

Open

1 April - 31 October.

At a glance

Welcome & Ambience	✓✓✓✓	Location	✓✓✓✓
Quality of Pitches	✓✓✓✓	Range of Facilities	✓✓✓✓

Directions

From autobahn A3, take exit 115 (Passau-Nord) from where site is signed. Follow signs from Passau on road to west of city and north bank of Danube towards Windorf and Irring.

Charges 2004

Per person	€ 4,50
child (4-12 yrs)	€ 3,50
pitch	€ 5,00 - € 9,00
electricity (plus kw charge)	€ 1,00

No credit cards.

Reservations

Write to site. Tel: 08546 633.
E-mail: dreifluessecamping@t-online.de

DE3697 Kur und Feriencamping Dreiquellenbad

Singham 40, 94086 Bad Griesbach (Bavaria (S))

This site is southwest of Passau and is an exceptional site in a quite rural area, with over 200 pitches, some 190 of which are used for touring units. All pitches have electricity and water and 50 are fully serviced with electricity, water, drainage, TV and phone points. English is spoken at reception which also houses a shop and good tourist information. A luxury leisure complex includes a sauna, Turkish bath and jacuzzi. An adjoining building provides various beauty and complementary health treatments.

Facilities

Excellent sanitary facilities include private cabins and free showers, facilities for disabled visitors. Two private bathrooms for rent. Laundry facilities. Motorcaravan services. Shop. Internet point. Off site: Golf 2 km.

Open

All year.

At a glance

Welcome & Ambience	✓✓✓✓✓	Location	✓✓✓✓✓
Quality of Pitches	✓✓✓✓	Range of Facilities	✓✓✓✓✓

Directions

Site is 15 km. from A3 exit 118. Follow signs for Pocking. In 2 km. turn right on B388. Site is in Singham. Turn right into Karpfhan then left to site.

Charges 2004

Per person	€ 4,90
pitch	€ 7,80 - € 8,80
electricity (plus meter)	€ 1,00

Reservations

Would be advisable for July/August.
Tel: 085 32 96 13 50.

DE3688 Panorama Camping Harras

Harrasser Strasse 135, 83209 Prien am Chiemsee (Bavaria (S))

Panorama Harras is a popular, friendly site on a small wooded peninsula by the Chiemsee, with good views to the mountains across the lake. Sailing and windsurfing are very popular here and you can swim from the shingle beach. It is also a useful base for exploring this attractive area, with boat trips to the 'Herrenchiemsee' island with its castle, cycle trips and mountains to walk in. Pitches vary between 60 and 100 sq.m. (some available by the lake) with a separate, all numbered section of gravel hardstanding for motorhomes, and an area for tents also on gravelly grass. Most have electricty (6A), and 80 numbered pitches are marked by trees, which give some shade, but with no hedges, it can look crowded if full.

Facilities

Good quality sanitary facilities include family shower rooms with washbasin and toilet (no paper). Showers need a token. Baby room, launderette, inside dishwashing and a good unit for disabled people. Well stocked shop. Restaurant with bar and takeaway (all open for the whole season). Bicycle hire. Off site: Boat trips on the lake. Golf and riding 5 km. Automobile museum 20 km.

Open

9 April - 10 October.

At a glance

Welcome & Ambience	✓✓✓✓	Location	✓✓✓✓
Quality of Pitches	✓✓✓	Range of Facilities	✓✓✓✓

Directions

The Chiemsee is north of the A8 (E52,E60) between Munich and Salzburg. Take exit 106 north towards Prien and turn towards Harras in approx. 2.5 km. Follow signs for another 2 km.

Charges 2005

Per person	€ 5,40
child (under 14 yrs)	€ 3,90
pitch	€ 4,90
with electricity	€ 7,40

Surcharge 15% for stays of less than 4 nights.

Reservations

Contact site. Tel: 08051 904613.
E-mail: info@camping-harras.de

DE3715 Knaus Camping-Park Viechtach

Waldfrieden 22, 94234 Viechtach (Bavaria (S))

Camping-Park Viechtach, although reached via a small industrial area, is a relaxing place at which to stay, well laid out in a woodland setting on the edge of the village. The various trees and shrubs give a garden effect and there is good shade in most parts. A tarmac road winds its way between the grass pitches (most terraced) which are separated by rocks and trees and marked by plaques. There are 250 pitches (130 for touring units), all with 6A electricity, and size varies from small for some motorcaravans to quite large for bigger units (100 sq.m.). Whether for a night stop or for a longer stay to visit the Bavarian Forest, this site is well worth considering. English is spoken by the friendly reception staff.

Facilities

Two heated sanitary blocks have been renovated recently. One is central to the touring pitches, the other at the top end of the site on the ground floor of a larger building, with a drying room. Facilities are similar with washbasins (some private cabins), sinks and showers. Bread to order. There is an attractive bar/restaurant with reasonable prices, a small shop for basic supplies and a camping equipment shop. A heated indoor swimming pool has a sauna and solarium. Children's playgrounds for all ages. Table tennis. Beach volleyball. Bicycle hire. Two Small games rooms. Large screen TV. Several rooms for wet weather. Washing machines, dryers and irons. Gas supplies. Off site: Outdoor pool and tennis nearby.

At a glance

Welcome & Ambience	✓✓✓✓	Location	✓✓✓✓
Quality of Pitches	✓✓✓✓	Range of Facilities	✓✓✓✓

Directions

Take Viechtach exit from B85 Weiden - Passau road, and follow campsite signs for some way.

Charges 2004

Per unit incl. 2 persons and electricity	€ 17,50
extra person	€ 6,00
child (3-14 yrs)	€ 3,00
tent and motorcycle	€ 3,00
dog	€ 2,00
electricity	€ 2,00

No credit cards.

Reservations

Write to site. Tel: 09942 1095.
E-mail: knauscamp.viechtach@freenet.de

Open

All year except November (with all services).

DE3735 Spessart-Camping Schönrain

Schönrainstraße 4 - 18, 97737 Gemünden-Hofstetten (Bavaria (N))

Situated a short distance from the town of Gemünden, with views of forested hills beside the river Main, this is a very friendly, family run site, with excellent facilities. There are just 200 pitches, half of which are for touring. They are at least 100 sq.m. with some up to 200, most have 10A electricity and 20 also have water. A new area has been developed for tents. The site has an outdoor pool open from Whitsun to end Sept (weather permitting). A pleasant small restaurant and bar and a shop are on site with the local full-bodied Franconian wine and schnaps for sale. Frau Endres welcomes British guests and speaks a little English. There are opportunities for walking and riding in the adjacent woods, excursions are organised in the main season and it is possible to hire a bicycle, ride to Würzburg and catch the pleasure boat back, or take a combined bus and cycle ride. Fishing and boating are both very popular in the locality.

Facilities

A super new sanitary building has card operated entry - the card is pre-paid and operates the showers, washing machines and dryers, coffee machine, dishwashing, gas cooker, baby bathroom, jacuzzi etc. Two private bathrooms (complete with wine and balcony!) for rent. Motorcaravan services. General room with sections for very young children, a pool table and arcade games and a TV. Upstairs is a library and internet café, fitness room and solarium. The building has heating and automatic lighting and is a splendid addition. Bar/restaurant (closed Tuesdays). Shop. Swimming pool. Playground. Outdoor chess. Table tennis. Bicycle hire. Excursions organised. Off site: Riding 200 m. Fishing 400 m. Canoeing, cycling and walking near.

Open

1 April - 30 September.

At a glance

Welcome & Ambience	✓✓✓✓✓	Location	✓✓✓✓
Quality of Pitches	✓✓✓✓	Range of Facilities	✓✓✓✓

Directions

From Frankfurt - Würzburg autobahn, take Weibersbrunn-Lohr exit and then B26 to Gemünden. Turn over Main river bridge to Hofstetten. From Kassel - Wurzburg autobahn, leave at Hammelburg and take B27 to Gemünden, and as above.

Charges 2004

Per pitch 100 sq.m.	€ 6,70
pitch 150 sq.m.	€ 9,70
hikers or cyclists and small tent	€ 4,20
person	€ 5,70
child (under 14 yrs)	€ 3,60
dog	€ 2,60

Swimming pool included. Less 10% for stays over 14 days in mid and low seasons.

Reservations

Write to site. Tel: 09351 8645.
E-mail: info@spessart-camping.de

DE3610 Knaus Campingpark Nürnberg

Hans Kalb Strasse 56, 90471 Nürnberg (Bavaria (N))

This is an ideal site for visiting the fascinating and historically important city of Nuremberg. Since acquiring this pleasantly situated site, the Knaus group have undertaken improvements and it now ranks as one of the best city sites anywhere. There are 150 shaded pitches on mainly flat grass among the tall trees, some marked out with 'ranch' style boards, others still attractively 'wild', some others with hard-standing. 118 have 10A electricity. There is sufficient space for them to be quite big and many have the advantage of being drive through. All the Knaus parks are well run and they welcome British tourers. There may be some noise if there is an event on at the Stadion, so it may be worthwhile checking.

Facilities

A brand new heated sanitary building offers first class facilities Washing machines and dryers, cooking facilities, unit for disabled visitors. Gas supplies. Motorcaravan services. Shop. Bar/bistro area with terrace and light meals served. Children's play area in woodland. Tennis court. Bicycle hire. Large screen TV. Off site: Swimming pool and football stadium 200 m. City centre 4 km. (a 20 minute walk following signs takes you to the underground station).

Open

All year.

At a glance

Welcome & Ambience	✓✓✓✓	Location	✓✓✓✓
Quality of Pitches	✓✓✓✓	Range of Facilities	✓✓✓✓

Directions

From autobahns, take Nürnberg-Fischbach exit from A9 München-Bayreuth east of Nürnberg. Proceed 3 km. on dual carriageway towards city then left at camp sign. From city follow 'Stadion-Messe' signs and site is well signed and along from the Stadion.

Charges 2004

Per person	€ 6,00
pitch	€ 9,50

No credit cards.

Reservations

Not made and said to be unnecessary.
Tel: 0911 9812717.
E-mail: knaus.camp.nbg@freenet.de

DE3632 Azur Camping Altmühltal

Am Festplatz 3, 85110 Kipfenberg (Bavaria (N))

In the beautiful Altmühltal river valley, this Azur site is in pretty woodland, with lots of shade for much of it. On flat grass with direct access to the river, one looks from the entrance across to the old Schloss on the hill. Outside the main entrance is a large, flat, grass/gravel field for 60 overnight tourers (with electricity). The main site has 277 pitches, of which 178 are for touring, plus two small areas for tents and one large one. Ranging in size up to 90 sq.m. most are in small groups marked by trees or bushes. This well-run site is a popular base for walking, cycling, fishing, canoeing and other watersports.

Facilities

The main sanitary facilities are good, with free hot water (no private cabins), baby room, unit for wheelchair users, plus dishwashing. Launderette. Kitchen with ovens and cooking rings. 'Portacabin' style at the other end of the site (toilets only in low season). Motorcaravan services. Shop. Snacks July-August. Play area. Fishing. Off site: Supermarket 100 m. Restaurants 300 m. Bicycle and canoe hire in town.

Open

All year.

At a glance

Welcome & Ambience	✓✓✓✓	Location	✓✓✓✓
Quality of Pitches	✓✓✓✓	Range of Facilities	✓✓✓✓

Directions

From A9/E45 (Munich - Nuremberg) exit 58 Eichstätt or 59 Denkendorf or and follow Kipfenberg signs.

Charges guide

Per person	€ 4,50 - € 6,00
child (2-12 yrs)	€ 3,50 - € 4,50
pitch	€ 5,50 - € 7,50
electricity	€ 2,10

Reservations

Probably not necessary for overnight. For longer stays in high season and school holidays contact site.
Tel: 08465 905167. E-mail: info@azur-camping.de

DE3710 Azur Ferienzentrum Zwiesel

Waldesruhweg 34, 94227 Zwiesel (Bavaria (N))

Bayerischerwald is a large site on the edge of town with views to the hills. Pleasantly situated nearly 2,000 feet up (it can be cool at night) on a slight slope, there are around 500 pitches, just under 400 for tourers, but there is not much shade. There are various areas, with motorhomes taken on a flat open, grassy section, whilst for caravans there are some flat and many sloping or undulating pitches, all with electricity, along the central road. The site is also open for winter camping, with ski-lifts quite near.

Facilities

Two tiled sanitary blocks have some private cabins. Facilities for disabled people. Baby room. Bread orders at reception. Pleasant restaurant/bar (closed Nov). Launderette. Open air chess. Table tennis. Off site: Large swimming pool complex next door (open June-Sept). For other dates or rainy days there is an indoor pool (all are free for campers).

Open

All year.

At a glance

Welcome & Ambience	✓✓✓✓	Location	✓✓✓✓
Quality of Pitches	✓✓✓✓	Range of Facilities	✓✓✓✓

Directions

Site is on north side of Zwiesel. From autobahn A3 Regensburg-Passau, take Deggendorf exit and then B11 to Zwiesel. Take Zwiesel Nord exit and follow Azur signs.

Charges 2004

Per person	€ 4,50 - € 6,50
pitch	€ 5,50 - € 7,50
electricity	€ 2,30

Reservations

Write to site. Tel: 09922 802 595.
E-mail: zwiesel@azur-camping.de

DE3720 Internationaler Campingplatz Naabtal

93188 Pielenhofen (Bavaria (S))

Regensburg is an ancient city on the Danube, near the Bavarian Forest which, although not as well known as the Black Forest, is a lovely area of natural beauty. Naabtal is a very pleasant, attractive riverside site in a beautiful tree-covered valley and makes an excellent night stop when travelling to or from Austria or Hungary or a base for exploring this interesting part of Germany. Sixty per cent of the site is taken up by static caravans used for weekends and holidays. The 130 large, flat or gently sloping pitches for tourists (all with 10A electricity, some individual) are mostly under willow and other types of trees by the riverside or in an open field. There is good shade in some parts and hills covered with trees rise all around - this is good walking and mountain biking country, with marked trails. Small boats can be launched on the placid river (where you may also swim at your own risk) and there are two good size tennis courts.

Facilities

A new sanitary building serves the tent area so thay have their own showers now, while two original, heated toilet blocks are part of larger buildings. Some washbasins are in cabins, showers are on payment. Washing machines, dryers and irons. New, first class unit for disabled people. Gas supplies. Motorcaravan services. Sauna and solarium. Bar/restaurant (1/4-31/10 plus Xmas/New Year). Small shop (Easter – end Sept.). Skittle alley and tarmac curling rink. Children's playground with imaginative fixed apparatus. Large meeting room with catering facilities, a stage and a youth room with table tennis and video games. Tennis. Football field. Volleyball. Bicycle hire. Fishing (permit required). Small boats on river. Reception will advise on local excursions, walks, cycle routes and sports.
Off site: Village shop 1.5 km. Golf 15 km.

At a glance

Welcome & Ambience	✓✓✓✓	Location	✓✓✓✓
Quality of Pitches	✓✓✓✓	Range of Facilities	✓✓✓✓

Directions

Take exit 97 Nittendorf from A3 Nürnberg - Regensburg, and follow road to Pielenhofen (Camping Naabtal is signed from exit). Cross river and turn right to site. Site is about 11 km. from autobahn exit. From A93 exit 39 onto B8 towards Nittendorf, then at Etterzhausen turn towards Pielenhofen.

Charges 2005

Per person	€ 5,05
child	€ 3,10
pitch	€ 5,80
dog	€ 2,00
electricity (plus meter)	€ 0,45

No credit cards.

Reservations

Needed in high season; contact site. Tel: 09409 373. E-mail: camping.pielenhofen@t-online.de

Open

All year.

DE3739 Camping Katzenkopf

Am See, 97334 Sommerach am Main (Bavaria (N))

This is an excellent family run site, on the banks of the Main to the east of Wurzburg. For peace and quiet this site is likely to be at the top of the list. There are 250 pitches with some 150 for touring units. All pitches have electricity (16A) and 6 provide electricity, water, and drainage. English is spoken at reception which also houses a shop and good tourist information. Wurzburg is an important commercial and cultural centre that was substantially destroyed by bombing and has risen again from the ashes. The town is the home of the excellent Franconian wine. The village of Sommerach, a few minutes walk from the site, is surrounded by vineyards which produce a special local vintage.

Facilities

Excellent, modern toilet blocks include private cabins, free showers and facilities for disabled people and children. Laundry and dishwashing facilities. Motorcaravan service point. Restaurant, bar and takeaway. Fishing. Boat launching. Sailing courses. Dogs accepted in part of the site only. Off site: Sailing. Shops and vineyards.

Open

1 April - 6 November.

At a glance

Welcome & Ambience	✓✓✓✓✓	Location	✓✓✓✓✓
Quality of Pitches	✓✓✓✓	Range of Facilities	✓✓✓✓

Directions

From the A3 take Kitzingen exit and turn towrads Schwarzach. After 4 km. turn right towards Sommerach. Just before the village turn left and site is well signed.

Charges 2004

Per person	€ 4,80 - € 5,00
child (0-14 yrs)	€ 2,70 - € 3,00
pitch	€ 5,00 - € 6,00
electricity	€ 2,00
dog	€ 1,80

Reservations

Advised for July/August. Tel: 09381 9215.

DE3750 Camping Schloss Issigau

Schloss Issigau, 95188 Issigau (Bavaria (N))

This is a handy, pleasant little family run site with very good facilities – less than 50 pitches and all for tourers. It is just over 5 km. from the A9 Berlin - Nuremberg in northeast Bavaria, on the edge of the pretty village with views across it and fields to woods. Entering a large grass courtyard there are several sections, part terraced and with some old trees giving a little shade in places. As you go through the site it opens up to a largish, sloping tent area. Around half the pitches are individual ranging up to 120 sq.m, all with 16A electricity. There is a delightful café/bar and restaurant in the interesting old 'Schloss' (circa 1398 - a large fortified house is how we might describe it) with a museum of old armour.

Facilities

Satisfactory heated sanitary facilities are in an old building with some modern fittings and some washbasins in cabins. Laundry facilities. Baby room. Café/bar and restaurant (open daily from 12.00 to 22.00). Table tennis and games room. Hotel accommodation. Off site: Small supermarket 300 m.

Open

15 March - 31 October and 18 December - 9 January.

At a glance

Welcome & Ambience	✓✓✓✓	Location	✓✓✓✓
Quality of Pitches	✓✓✓	Range of Facilities	✓✓✓✓

Directions

From A9 Berlin - Nuremberg, 45 km. north of Dreieck Bayreuth/Kulmbach take exit 31 Berg/Bad Steben to Issigau and follow signs in village - narrow in places.

Charges 2005

Per person	€ 4,50
child (4-14 yrs)	€ 2,50
pitch	€ 5,00 - € 6,00

No credit cards.

Reservations

Probably unnecessary. Tel: 09293 7173.
E-mail: info@schloss-issigau.de

DE3850 Camping Strandbad Aga

Reichenbacherstrasse 14, 07554 Gera-Aga (Thuringia)

Strandbad Aga is a useful night stop near the A4/A9 and within reach of Dresden, Leipzig and Meissen. It is situated in open countryside on the edge of a small lake, with 350 fenced pitches, mostly fairly level, without shade. The 200 touring pitches all have 16A electricity – for stays of more than a couple of days, over-nighters being placed on an open area. The lake is used for swimming, boating and fishing (popular with day visitors at weekends) and there is a small play area on one side (close to a deep part). Entertainment is organised in July and the enthusiastic owner is improving the facilities each year.

Facilities

The sanitary building is at one side, with some washbasins in cabins and hot showers on payment. Large (4 x 4 m.) room for wheelchair users. Washing machines and dryers. Motorcaravan services. Restaurant. High season kiosk for drinks, ice creams, etc. Play area. Small lake. Entertainment in high season. No English spoken. Off site: Shop in village (200 m). Riding. Tennis 1 km.

Open

1 April - 1 November.

At a glance

Welcome & Ambience	✓✓✓✓	Location	✓✓✓✓✓
Quality of Pitches	✓✓✓✓✓	Range of Facilities	✓✓✓

Directions

From A4/E40 Chemnitz - Erfurt autobahn take Gera exit (no. 58) then the B2 towards Zeitz, following Bad Köstritz signs at first then site signs.

Charges guide

Per person	€ 4,00
child (3-13 yrs)	€ 2,00
pitch incl. car	€ 6,00

No credit cards.

Reservations

Write to site. Tel: 036695 20209.
E-mail: info@campingplatz-strandbad-aga.de

DE3855 Camping Oberhof

Am Stausee (Bergstrasse 14), Oberhof, 99330 Frankenhain (Thuringia)

Oberhof has been purchased by the owners of DE3242 Schinderhannes and they have already begun upgrading the site. 150 pitches for tourers and electricity connections are available, of which 20 are on hardstanding with water. Situated just 2 km. from the German winter sports centre, with cross country skiing possible from the site, there are also 100 km. of waymarked walks, the Beerberg and Schneekopf mountains (978 m) nearby and many famous towns within a half hour drive (Erfurt, Weimar etc).

Facilities

New sanitary facilities should be ready. Takeaway. Lakeside beach, fishing, boat hire and diving school. Children's play area. Table tennis, volleyball. Bicycle hire.

Open

All year.

Reservations

Contact site. Tel: 036205 76518.
E-mail: info@oberhofcamping.de

At a glance

Welcome & Ambience	✓✓✓	Location	✓✓✓✓
Quality of Pitches	✓✓✓	Range of Facilities	✓✓✓✓

Directions

From A4 (Eisenach -Dresden) exit 42 (Gotha) on B247 south towards Oberhof. At 'Wegscheide' guesthouse (3 km. before Oberhof) turn left into parking area and take track on right for 1 km. downhill to site (fairly steep in places). From Erfurt on A71 take Ilmenau, Geschwanda exit on B88 (Ohrdruf/Gotha) to Frankenhain from where turn left on track towards Lütsche Talsperre and site.

Charges 2004

Per person	€ 5,00
pitch incl. electricity	€ 8,00

DE3833 Camping und Freizeitpark LuxOase

Arnsdorfer Straße 1, Kleinröhrsdorf, 01900 Dresden (Saxony)

This is a pleasantly situated new park about half an hour from the centre of Dresden, in a very peaceful location with good facilities. It is owned and run by a progressive young family. On open grassland with views across the lake (access to which is through a gate in the site fence) to the woods and low hills beyond, this is a sun-trap with little shade at present. There are 138 large touring pitches (plus 50 seasonal in a separate area), marked by bushes or posts on generally flat or slightly sloping grass. All have 10/16A electricity and 92 have water and waste water facilities. At the entrance is an area of hard-standing (with electricity) for late arrivals. The main entrance building houses the amenities and in front of the building is some very modern play equipment on bark. You may swim, fish or use inflatables in the lake. Entertainment is organised for children in high season. There are many interesting places to visit apart from Dresden and Meissen, with the fascinating National Park Sächsische Schweiz (Saxon Switzerland) on the border with the Czech Republic offering some spectacular scenery. Boat trips on the Danube can be taken from the tourist centres of Königstein and Bad Schandau and Saxony is also famous for its many old castles, for which an English language guide is available. Bus trips are organised to Prague.

Facilities

A brand new sanitary building provides modern, heated facilities with private cabins, a family room, baby changing room, units for disabled visitors and two units for hire. Rooms for cooking, laundry and dishwashing. Gas supplies. Motorcaravan services. Shop (am. all year, pm. in high season). Bar and restaurant with good value meals (Apr - Oct evenings and w/end lunchtimes). Bicycle hire. Lake swimming. Sports field with basketball and volleyball. Fishing. Children's play area. Sauna. Train, bus and theatre tickets from reception. Internet point. Minigolf. Off site: Riding next door. Public transport to Dresden 1 km. Golf 7.5 km. Nearby Dinosaur park, zoo and indoor karting etc.

Open

All year.

At a glance

Welcome & Ambience	✓✓✓✓✓	Location	✓✓✓✓✓
Quality of Pitches	✓✓✓✓	Range of Facilities	✓✓✓✓

Directions

From A4 (Dresden - Görlitz) take exit 85 towards Radeberg, soon following signs to site via Leppersdorf and Kleinröhrsdorf.

Charges 2004

Per person	€ 4,00 - € 4,50
child (2-14 yrs)	€ 2,20 - € 2,50
motorcaravan or caravan/car	€ 7,20 - € 8,00
tent	€ 6,50 - € 7,50
car or motorcycle	€ 1,70
electricity	€ 2,00

Various special offers in low season.

Reservations

Advisable for July/August. You must contact site if you intend to visit in winter (8 Nov. - 28 Feb). Tel: 035952 56666. E-mail: camping.luxoase@t-online.de

DE3847 Campingplatz Auensee

Gustav-Esche Strasse 5, 04159 Leipzig (Saxony)

It is unusual to find a first-class site in a city, but this large, neat and tidy site is one. It is far enough away from roads and the airport to be reasonably peaceful during the day and very quiet overnight and has 168 pitches of which about 150 are for short-term tourers. It is set in a mainly open area with tall trees and very attractive flower arrangements around, with some chalets and 'trekker' huts for rent in the adjoining woodland, home to the shoe-stealing foxes. The individual, numbered, flat grassy pitches are large (at least 100 sq.m.), all 16A electrical connections and five on hardstanding, arranged in several sections with a separate area for young people with tents. Three central points supply water and barbecue areas are provided. Children of all ages are well catered for with forts, an ultra-modern climbing frame all on sand, a super-swing and an enclosed court with tennis, football and basketball. A modern restaurant and snack bar (breakfast, lunch and supper), plus a small shop are open all year round. A popular site, it is best to arrive early.

Facilities

Five sanitary buildings (all in one area and mind your head if you are over 6 feet tall) have differing mixtures of very modern equipment and offer many washbasins in cabins and showers on payment (token). Well equipped rooms for babies and disabled visitors (key from reception). Dishwashing facilities (open air and inside). Kitchen and laundry rooms. All the buildings can be heated. Shop in restaurant and snack bar (all year). Entertainment rooms. Several play areas. Bicycle hire. Fishing close by. Barbecue with seating. Kitchen. Motorcaravan service point. Dog walk. English usually spoken. Off site: Public transport to the city centre goes every 10 minutes from just outside the site.

Open

All year.

At a glance

Welcome & Ambience	✓✓✓✓	Location	✓✓✓✓✓
Quality of Pitches	✓✓✓✓	Range of Facilities	✓✓✓✓

Directions

Signs to site are hard to find but should be signed 5 km. from Leipzig centre on the B6 to Halle. From the A9 Berlin - Nurnberg take exit 17 at Schkeuditz onto the B6 towards Leipzig. Turn right to Auensee at the Church just 3 km before the centre of the town. If you pass the railway station you are too far. Turn back and turn left at the Church.

Charges guide

Per person	€ 4,09
child (6-13 yrs)	€ 2,95
child (14-18 yrs)	€ 3,07
caravan	€ 6,14
tent	€ 5,11
small tent (under 4 sq.m.)	€ 3,07

Reservations

Contact site. Tel: 0341 4651 600.

DE3827 Camping Sanssouci-Gaisberg

An der Pirschheide, Templiner See 41, 14471 Potsdam (Brandenburg)

Sanssouci is an excellent base for visiting Potsdam and Berlin, about two kilometres from Sanssouci Park on the banks of the Templiner See in a quiet woodland setting. Looking very attractive, reflecting the effort which has been put into its development, with modern reception, shop, takeaway, restaurant and bar. There are 240 pitches in total with some 90 odd being seasonal pitches but all the 150 touring pitches now have 6/10amp electricity, many also with their own water and waste water connections. Tall trees mark out the tourist pitches, and access is good for larger units. There is a separate area for tents by the lake. Reception staff are helpful with English spoken and a comprehensive English language information pack has been prepared by the owners for local attractions. Free transport in the mornings and evenings is operated by the site to the nearby station. Tickets for public transport, boat trips and fishing can be bought at reception.

Facilities

Top class sanitary facilities are in an excellent, modern, heated block containing hot showers, washbasins in cabins and facilities for babies. Dishwashing on payment and laundry, plus a very good facility for wheelchair users. A separate smaller toilet building also. New building with bathroom to rent, kitchen, hairdressers and solarium. Gas supplies. Motorcaravan services. Restaurant/bar. Shop. Rowing boats, motorboats and pedaloes for hire. Fishing. Swimming in the lake. Play area in central woods. Bicycle hire. Internet café. Site closed to vehicles 13.00-15.00 hrs. Off site: The pool, sauna, solarium and skittle alley at the nearby Hotel Semiramis may (100 m.) be used by campers at a discount. Riding 3 km. Golf 10 km.

Open

1 April - 4 November.

At a glance

Welcome & Ambience	✓✓✓✓	Location	✓✓✓✓✓
Quality of Pitches	✓✓✓	Range of Facilities	✓✓✓✓

Directions

From A10 take Potsdam exit 7, follow B1 to within 4 km. of city centre then sign to right for camp just before the railway bridge. Or A10 exit 12 on the B2 into town and follow signs for Brandenburg/Werder. Site is southwest of Sanssouci Park on the banks of the Templiner See off Zeppelinstrasse 1.2 km. along a woodland drive.

Charges 2005

Per person	€ 8,60
child (2-15 yrs)	€ 1,00
pitch	€ 8,40
tent pitch	€ 1,20
dog	€ 4,00

Special low season offers. No credit cards.

Reservations

Not normally necessary. Tel: 03327 55680.
E-mail: info@recra.de

DE3842 Camping am Schlosspark

03222 Lubennau (Brandenburg)

Situated about halfway between Berlin and Dresden, this is an attractive proposition for a short visit as well as a night stop, in a delightful, woodland setting, about ten minutes walk from the centre of the much visited old town, on the banks of the Hauptspree. Taking 125 units (they may be rather close together at very busy times), all have electrical connections. They are mainly on flat grass but with a central hardstanding area for motorcaravans and a long area for tents at the end. You can paddle your own boat, go for a trip in a gondola, explore the Spreewald or just look round the interesting old town from this pleasant site. A public path passes between the site and the river; insect repellent is advisable. At public holidays and during the high season, the site can be very busy and facilities may be stretched.

Facilities

The refurbished, heated sanitary facilities are quite good with free hot water for the washbasins (some private cabins), but the showers require tokens from reception. A kitchen is provided as well as dishwashing and laundry. Small shop for basics at reception (all year). Small children's play area. Boat and bicycle hire. Fishing. Motorcaravan service point. Off site: Shops in the adjacent town, with a 'Tiergarten' café just 200 m. away and the Schlosspark hotel and restaurant through the woods. Riding 5 km.

Open

All year.

At a glance

Welcome & Ambience	✓✓✓✓✓	Location	✓✓✓✓✓
Quality of Pitches	✓✓✓✓	Range of Facilities	✓✓✓

Directions

From the A13 (Berlin - Dresden) take exit 9, turning right onto the B115 into Lübbenau then following site signs. At weekends the town is busy, requiring extra care and patience. We found it easier to enter Lübbenau from the southeast via the A15 Boblitz exit (no. 2).

Charges 2005

Per person	€ 4,50
child (4-14 yrs)	€ 2,00
caravan or motorcaravan	€ 7,00
tent	€ 4,00
dog	€ 2,00
electricity (plus meter)	€ 1,50

Reservations

Essential probably only for May Day and Whitsun weekends. Tel: 03542 3533.
E-mail: info@spreewaldcamping.de

DE3820 Camping Havelberge am Woblitzsee

17237 Groß Quassow (Mecklenburg-West Pomerania)

The Müritz National Park is a very large area of lakes and marshes, popular for birdwatching as well as watersports, and Havelberge is a large, well-equipped site to use as a base for enjoying the area. It is quite steep in places here with many terraces, most with shade, less in newer areas, with views over the lake. There are 250 pitches in total with 80 good sized, numbered touring pitches most with electrical connections (10A). Over 170 seasonal pitches with a number of attractive chalets and an equal number of mobile homes in a separate areas. In the high season this is a busy park with lots going on to entertain families of all ages, whilst in the low seasons this is a peaceful base for exploring an unspoilt area of nature.

Facilities

Three sanitary buildings provide very good facilities, with a few private cabins and showers on payment. Cooking rings and dishwashing. Laundry. Motorcaravan service point. Small shop and modern restaurant (May - Sept). The lake provides fishing, swimming from a small beach and non-powered boats can be launched - canoes, rowing boats, windsurfers and bikes can be hired. Play areas and animation in high season. Volleyball. Off site: Riding 3.5 km.

Open

All year.

At a glance

Welcome & Ambience	✓✓✓✓✓	Location	✓✓✓✓✓
Quality of Pitches	✓✓✓✓	Range of Facilities	✓✓✓✓

Directions

From A19 Rostock - Berlin road take exit 18 and follow B198 to Wesenberg and go left to Klein Quassow and follow site signs.

Charges 2004

Per person	€ 3,00 - € 5,60
child (2-14 yrs)	€ 1,20 - € 3,80
caravan and car	€ 5,00 - € 11,30
tent	€ 2,50 - € 6,20
motorcaravan	€ 3,40 - € 6,70
electricity	€ 2,00

Reservations

Contact site for high season and school holidays. Tel: 03981 24790. E-mail: info@haveltourist.de

Centrally located in Europe, Hungary comprises mountain ranges, hilly regions and flat plains, with the River Danube running through its length. The country also has over one thousand lakes, an abundance of thermal baths, Europe's largest cave system and several notable wine regions.

An increasingly popular destination, Budapest is divided into two parts by the Danube, the hilly side of Buda on the western bank and the flat plain of Pest on the eastern bank. A cruise along the river will enable you to appreciate this picturesque city with its grand buildings, romantic bridges, museums and art galleries. It also has plenty of spas to tempt you. North of the city, the Danube Bend is one of the grandest stretches of the river, along the banks of which you'll find historic towns and ruins. Further afield in the north-eastern hills, the caves at Aggtelek are another firm favourite.

One of the largest in Europe, Lake Balaton covers an area of nearly 600 square miles and is great for swimming, sailing, windsurfing and waterskiing. It has two distinct shores; the bustling south with its string of hotels, restaurants and beaches, and the north offering a quieter pace with beautiful scenery and sights.

Population

10.2 million

Capital

Budapest

Climate

There are four fairly distinct seasons – hot in summer, mild spring and autumn, very cold winter with snow

Language

The official language is Magyar, but German is widely spoken

Currency

Hungarian forints

Telephone

The country code is 00 36

Banks

Mon-Fri 09.00-14.00, Sat 09.00-12.00

Shops

Mon-Fri 10.00-18.00, Sat 10.00-14.00. Food shops open Mon-Fri 07.00-19.00, Sat 07.00-14.00

Public Holidays

New Year; 15 March; Easter Mon; Labour Day; Whitsun; Constitution Day 20 Aug; Republic Day 23 Oct; All Saints Day 1 Nov; Christmas 25, 26 Dec

Motoring

Main roads are very good, as is sign-posting. Dipped headlights are compulsory at all times but main beams should not be used in towns. Most of the roads are single carriage. Motorway stickers must be purchased for Hungary for the M1 from the Austrian border to Budapest; the M7 from Budapest to Lake Balaton and also on the M3 eastward. Separate toll is charged on the full length of the M5 (Budapest - Kiskunfelegyhaza). Give way to trams and buses at junctions and if pulling away from the kerb. Cross railways at walking pace. Carrying spare fuel in a can is not permitted.

Tourist Office

Hungarian National Tourist Office
46 Eaton Place, London SW1X 8AL
Tel: 020 7823 1032
Fax: 020 7823 1459
Email: htlondon@btinternet.com
Internet: www.hungarytourism.hu

TRY SAMPLING THE LOCAL WINE - HUNGARY HAS PLENTY TO OFFER INCLUDING THE CELEBRATED *BULL'S BLOOD.*

HU5080 Balatontourist Diana Camping

8241 Aszófô (Veszprem County)

Once a very large site of about twelve hectares, Diana was developed many years ago as a retreat for the 'party faithful'. Now just 8 hectares are used by Mr and Mrs Keller-Toth, who have leased it from the Balatontourist organisation and run it as a quiet, friendly site. There is a great feeling of space and naturally, much woodland around in which you may wander. There are 27 hedged pitches of 120 sq.m. (where two 60 sq.m. ones have been joined) on grass. Many have shade from trees including about 65 smaller individual ones. The remainder are amongst the trees which mark them out. There is no exact number of pitches, but about 150 units are taken, all with electrical connections (2 pin, 6 or 10A) on sloping ground. The fair-sized restaurant, open all season, has tables, benches and flowers in troughs outside. Animation is organised in high season with Hungarian musicians and animators, including occasional 'Diana days' with Hungarian folklore and goulash soup.

Facilities

Toilet facilities have beeen largely refurbished and are open 06.00-12.00 and 15.00-23.00 hrs. Very smart, new sections now provide large showers with private dressing for men and women and washbasins with hot water. Splendid, new children's washroom (key from reception), with 3 shower/baths, 2 designed for handicapped children. Washing machines, dryers and ironing (key from reception). Motorcaravan service point. Large kitchen with 3 cookers. Well stocked shop (open 08.00-17.00 low season or 22.00 high season). Restaurant (all season). Children's play area, with animation in high season. Volleyball. Tennis. Table tennis under cover. Club room with video nights for adults at weekends. Off site: Many walking opportunities. Lake fishing 3 km. Riding or bicycle 5 km.

At a glance

Welcome & Ambience	✓✓✓✓	Location	✓✓✓✓
Quality of Pitches	✓✓✓✓	Range of Facilities	✓✓✓✓

Directions

From road 71 on the north side of the lake, turn towards Azsófö just west of Balatonfüred, through the village and follow the signs for about 1 km. along access road (bumpy in places).

Charges 2005

Per person	HUF 700 - 990
child (6-14 yrs)	HUF 400 - 600
pitch incl. electricity	HUF 1500 - 2350

Special rates for disabled persons and low season long stays.

Reservations

Write to site. Tel: 87 445 013.
E-mail: dianacamping@freemail.hu

Open

7 May - 17 September.

HU5090 Balatontourist Camping Füred

8230 Balatonfüred (Veszprem County)

This is a large international holiday village rather than just a campsite, pleasantly decorated with flowers and shrubs, with a very wide range of facilities and sporting activities. All that one could want for a family holiday can be found on this site. Directly on the lake with 800 m. of access for boats and bathing, it has a large, grassy lying out area, a small beach area for children with various watersports organised. There is also a swimming pool on site with lifeguards. Mature trees cover about two-thirds of the site giving shade, with the remaining area being in the open. The 944 individual pitches (60-120 sq.m), all with electricity (4-10A), are on either side of hard access roads on which pitch numbers are painted. Many bungalows are also on the site. Along the main road that runs through the site, are shops and kiosks, with the main bar/restaurant and terrace overlooking the lake. Other bars and restaurants are around the site. A water ski drag lift is most spectacular with its four towers erected in the lake to pull skiers around the circuit. Coach trips and pleasure cruises are organised. The site is part of the Balatontourist organisation and, while public access is allowed for the amenities, security is good. Some tour operators - Danish and German.

Facilities

Six fully equipped toilet blocks around the site include hot water for dishwashing and laundry. Private cabins for rent. Laundry service. Gas supplies Numerous bars, restaurants, cafés, food bars and supermarket (all 15/4-15/10). Stalls and kiosks with wide range of goods, souvenirs, photo processing. Hairdresser. Excellent swimming pool with separate children's pool (20/6-25/9). Sauna. Fishing. Water ski lift. Windsurf school. Sailing. Pedaloes. Play area on sand. Bicycle, moped and jetski hire. Dodgem cars. Tennis. Minigolf. Video games. Internet point. Dogs are not accepted. Off site: Riding 5 km. Close by a street of fast food bars, about 10 in all, offering a variety of Hungarian and international dishes with attractive outdoor terraces under trees.

At a glance

Welcome & Ambience	✓✓✓✓	Location	✓✓✓✓✓
Quality of Pitches	✓✓✓	Range of Facilities	✓✓✓✓✓

Directions

Site is just south of Balatonfüred, on Balatonfüred - Tihany road and is well signed. Gates closed 1-3 pm. except Sat/Sun.

Charges 2005

Per person	€ 2,46 - € 5,33
child (2-14 yrs)	€ 2,05 - € 4,30
pitch incl. electricity (120 sq m)	€ 11,89 - € 20,08
100 sq.m.	€ 11,07 - € 18,36
70 sq m	€ 9,22 - € 14,14
60 sq m	€ 7,17 - € 11,68

Reservations

Write to site. Tel: 87 343 823.
E-mail: cfured@balatontourist.hu

Open

15 April - 15 October.

HU5070 Balatontourist Camping Kristof

8220 Balatonalmádi (Veszprem County)

This is a delightfully small site with just 33 marked pitches and many tall trees. Square in shape, the generously sized pitches are on either side of hard roads, on level grass. There is some shade and all pitches have electricity points (6A). It is situated between the main road and railway line and the lake. Although there is no direct access to the lake, a public lakeside area adjoins the site, and site fees include the entry price. This is a neat little site with a kiosk with terrace for breakfast and dinner (steaks, etc) drinks, bread, milk and ice cream. Balatonalmádi is at the northern end of the lake and well placed for excursions around the lake or to Budapest. Kristof is very suitable for anyone seeking a small, friendly site without the bustle of the larger camps. Good English is spoken.

Facilities

The excellent, fully equipped toilet facility is part of the reception building. Laundry room with washing machine (small charge), kitchen and sitting room with TV. Motorcaravan service point. Café (12/5-19/9). Playground and organized entertainment every day except Sunday. Tennis court. Basketball. Paddling pool. Off site: Fishing and beach 50 m. Bicycle hire and boat launching 500 m. Village shops and supermarket 500 m. Riding 5 km.

At a glance

Welcome & Ambience	✓✓✓✓✓	Location	✓✓✓✓✓
Quality of Pitches	✓✓✓✓	Range of Facilities	✓✓✓✓

Directions

Site is on road no. 71 at Balatonalmádi, between the railway line and the lake and is signed.

Charges 2005

Per pitch	HUF 2150,00 - 3510
adult	HUF 575 - 995
child (2-14 yrs)	HUF 450 - 820
dog	HUF 755 - 780

Reservations

Essential July - 20 Aug. Write for booking form. Tel: 88 584 201. E-mail: ckristof@balatontourist.hu

Open

12 May - 19 September.

HU5385 Balatontourist Camping Levendula

H-8243 Balatonakali (Veszprem County)

Levendula is the latest addition to the Balatontourist chain of sites on the north side of Lake Balaton. It has 127 level unmarked pitches, varying in size from 60 - 90 sq.m, and separated by low hedges. Almost all have views of the lake and all have electricity (4/10A). The site is attractively landscaped with shrubs and flowers and there is direct access to the lake. The north side of Lake Balaton has much to offer culturally. The Veszprém county has a rich history with baroque towns, castles, old churches and several items of interest such as the watermill and Protestant cemetery from the first decades of the 19th century with its heart shaped tombs. As part of the Balatontourist organisation, Levendula has similar amenities to the other sites, including a full entertainment program for children in high season, but without the noise of its larger brothers. The new toilet buildings are worth mentioning – they are among the best we've seen in Central Europe.

Facilities

Two new toilet blocks with all modern fittings, including one washbasin in cabin for men and women, en-suite facilities for disabled people and a heated baby room with bath and changing mat. Laundry with sinks, 2 washing machines, dryer and ironing board (iron from reception). Camper's kitchen with cooking rings on request. Fish cleaning area. Dog shower. Bar/restaurant with terrace. Shop. Playground with colourful equipment. Watersports. Table tennis. Beach volleyball. Games room with billiards. Animation programme 6 days a week, 3 times a day. Tours on Lake Balaton. Day trips to Budapest. Off site: Riding 1.5 km.

At a glance

Welcome & Ambience	✓✓✓✓	Location	✓✓✓✓
Quality of Pitches	✓✓✓✓	Range of Facilities	✓✓✓✓

Directions

Follow 71 road towards Keszthely and site is signed in Balatonakali.

Charges guide

Per person	€ 2,81 - € 4,39
child (2-14 yrs)	€ 2,23 - € 3,46
pitch incl. electricity	€ 7,01 - € 16,39
dog	free - € 3,46

Reservations

Call or e-mail site before mid-May. Tel: 87 544 011. E-mail: levendula@balatontourist.hu

Open

25 May - 15 September.

HU5370 Balatontourist Camping Napfeny

8253 Révfülöp (Veszprem County)

Camping Napfény is designed for families with children of all ages looking for an active holiday, and has a 200 m. frontage on Lake Balaton. There are steps to get into the lake and canoes, boats and pedaloes for hire. An extensive entertainment programme is designed for all ages and there are several bars and restaurants of various styles. There are souvenir shops and a supermarket. In fact, you need not leave the site at all during your holiday, although there are several excursions on offer, including to Budapest or to one of the many Hungarian spas, a trip over Lake Balaton or a traditional wine tour. The site's 450 pitches vary in size (60-110 sq.m). Located further from the water than the pitches at the Venus site, almost all have shade - very welcome during the hot Hungarian summers - and 4-10A electricity. This site is larger and therefore more crowded than the Venus site. As with most of the sites on Lake Balaton, a train line runs just outside the site boundary.

Facilities

Three sanitary blocks, two new and one partly refurbished, have toilets, washbasins (open style and in cabins) with hot and cold water, spacious showers (both pre-set and controllable), child size toilets and basins, and two bathrooms with bath, basin and toilet (hourly charge). Heated, unisex baby room with baby bath. Facilities for disabled people. Launderette with washing machines, a dryer, spin dryer and ironing board (irons for hire). Dishwashing and sinks under cover with free hot water. Dog shower. Motorcaravan services. Supermarket. Several bars and restaurants and souvenir shops Fenced sports field, Tennis court. Basketball and handball. Minigolf. Fishing. Bicycle hire. Canoe, rowing boats and pedalo hire. Extensive entertainment program for all ages. Off site: Riding 3 km.

At a glance

Welcome & Ambience	✓✓✓✓	Location	✓✓✓✓✓
Quality of Pitches	✓✓✓	Range of Facilities	✓✓✓✓✓

Directions

Follow the M71 from Veszprém southeast to Keszthely. Site is in Révfülöp on the left hand side of the road.

Charges 2005

Per person	HUF 750 - 1200
child (2-14 yrs)	HUF 570 - 900
pitch incl. electricity	HUF 1650 - 4600
dog	HUF 570 - 900

Reservations

Made from mid-May; contact site. Tel: 87 563 031. E-mail: cnapfeny@balatontourist.hu

Open

1 May - 30 September.

HU5380 Balatontourist Camping Venus

8252 Balatonszepezd (Veszprem County)

For those who want to be directly beside Lake Balaton, but would like a reasonably quiet location, Camping Venus site is probably the best spot. Apart from the rather noisy train that passes the site a few times an hour, this is a quiet site with views of the lake from almost all the pitches. From the front row of pitches you could almost dangle your feet from your caravan in the warm water of the lake. Varying in size from 70 to 90 sq.m, there are 150 flat pitches, all with at least 4/10A electricity and almost all with shade. Given the small size of the site, Mária Ekes, the manager, gets to know every guest in person and she will make you very welcome. This is a well managed site with modern, well kept sanitary blocks and 24 hour security at the gate. Lake Balaton with its water temperature of about 25 degrees Celsius in summer, is obviously the main attraction here, but you can also make several excursions, for example a trip to Budapest or a gipsy night in Riza.

Facilities

Two sanitary blocks, one new, provide toilets, washbasins (open style and in cabins) with hot and cold water, pre-set showers, facilities for disabled people and child size toilets and basins. Launderette with washing machine, sinks and ironing board (iron for hire at reception). Motorcaravan services. Shop for basics. Bar. Restaurant. Snack bar. Playground. Table tennis. Daily activity program with pottery, fairy tale reading, horse shows, tournaments in Sümeg, trips over the lake and to Budapest. Canoe, pedalo, rowing boats and bicycle hire. Dogs are not accepted.
Off site: Riding 3 km.

At a glance

Welcome & Ambience	✓✓✓✓✓	Location	✓✓✓✓✓
Quality of Pitches	✓✓✓	Range of Facilities	✓✓✓✓

Directions

Follow the M71 from Veszprém to the southeast towards Keszthely. Site is in Balatonszepezd on the left hand side of the road.

Charges 2005

Per person	HUF 705 - 1100
child (2-14 yrs)	HUF 540 - 870
pitch incl. electricity	HUF 1470 - 4160

Reservations

Made before mid-May; contact site. Tel: 87 568 061.
E-mail: cvenus@balatontourist.hu

Open

14 May - 10 September, with all services

HU5100 Ozon Camping

Erdei Malom köz 3, 9400 Sopron (Gyor-Moson-Sopron County)

Sopron, close to the border, was not over-run by the Turks or bombed in WW2, so 350 historic buildings and monuments remain intact, making it the second major tourist centre after Budapest. It also has a music festival from mid-June to mid-July and is close to the Löverek hills. This surprisingly pleasant campsite is just over 4 kilometres from the centre, with the modern, chalet style reception at the entrance from where the oval site opens out into a little green valley surrounded by trees. It is peaceful and comfortable with many trees within the site offering shade. Concrete access roads lead to 60 numbered grass pitches, all with electricity (6A), and 12 with water and waste water are in the lower level on the left, where siting is more difficult for caravans. They are mostly flat, some with a slight slope, separated by hedges and vary from 40 sq.m. for tents up to 80 sq.m. for larger units. One member of staff spoke English when we visited.

Facilities

Sanitary facilities in two heated buildings are identical except that one has a laundry (free) whilst the other, near the swimming pool, has a sauna. Curtained showers with communal changing, close to washbasins therefore could be a little cramped. Both blocks have free cookers, fridges and dishwashing. Gas supplies. Restaurant with good value meals (all season). Room with TV. Money exchange at reception. Small swimming pool and paddling pool (15/5-11/10). Off site: Shops 150 m. Bicycle hire 1 km. Tennis and fishing 2 km. Riding 3 km. Bus service to town centre.

At a glance

Welcome & Ambience	✓✓✓✓	Location	✓✓✓✓
Quality of Pitches	✓✓✓	Range of Facilities	✓✓✓✓

Directions

From A3 south of Wien, follow roads 16 (Kingenbach) and 84 to Sopron. Site is on road to Brennerberganya, well signed in Sopron.

Charges 2004

Per person	HUF 1100
child (under 10 yrs)	HUF 800
pitch	HUF 1500
dog	HUF 500

Reservations

May be advisable in high season and are made if you write in German. Tel: 99 523 370.
E-mail: ozoncamping@sopron.hu

Open

15 April - 15 October.

HU5110 Dömös Camping

Duna-Part, 2027 Dömös (Komarom-Esztergom County)

The area of the Danube Bend is a major tourist attraction and here at Dömös is a lovely modern, well maintained and presented, friendly, peaceful site with large pitches and easy access. The Danube is just over 50 m. away and quite fast flowing. There are views of the river and the hills on the other bank from some pitches. With Budapest just 45 kilometres, Esztergom (the ancient capital of Hungary) 15 kilometres and the small town of Visegrad, with its impressive cliff fortress close by, this could make an ideal base from which to explore the whole area. There are about 100 quite large pitches, of which 80 have 6A electricity, in sections on flat grass, numbered and divided by small plants and some with little shade. At the top of the site is an inviting open-air swimming pool with a grass lying out area and tiny children's pool with a large bar with pool tables alongside. Sightseeing tours to Budapest, Esztergom and Szentendre are arranged.

Facilities

The modern, long, brick built sanitary building is tiled with sliding doors and includes large showers with individual changing, and facilities for children and disabled visitors. Dishwashing and cooking area. Laundry with washing machines. Motorcaravan services. New restaurant (all season). Small café with terrace. Bar. Shop for basics (1/6-26/8). Swimming pool (20 x 10 m, all season). Small play area on grass. English is spoken. Off site: Fishing 50 m. Village facilities 300 m. Tennis, minigolf and football field adjacent. Riding 2 km. Bicycle hire 8 km. Mountain walking tours.

Open

1 May - 15 September.

At a glance

Welcome & Ambience	✓✓✓✓	Location	✓✓✓✓✓
Quality of Pitches	✓✓✓✓	Range of Facilities	✓✓✓✓

Directions

Site is between the village and the Danube, off road 11 Esztergom - Visegrad - Szentendre.

Charges 2005

Per person	HUF 830
child (2-14 yrs)	HUF 620
caravan	HUF 930
car	HUF 420
tent	HUF 830
motorcaravan	HUF 1300

No credit cards (cash only).

Reservations

Not normally made, but may for British visitors for period 15/7-15/8. Tel: 33 482 319. E-mail: domoscamping@klein.hu

HU5120 Gasthof Camping Pihenö

I-es föút, 9011 Györszentivan-Kertváros (Györ-Moson-Sopron County)

This privately owned site makes an excellent night stop when travelling to and from Hungary as it lies beside the main no. 1 road, near to the end of the motorway to the east of Györ. It is set amidst pine trees with pitches which are not numbered, but marked out by small shrubs, in a small clearing or between the trees. With space for about 40 touring units, all with electrical connections (6A), and a dozen simple, one roomed bungalows and four en-suite rooms. On one side of the site, fronting the road, is the reception, bar and pleasant restaurant with terrace (menu in English). The food is of excellent quality and very well priced (typical main course and coffee £3.50). The management offer a very reasonably priced package (if desired) which includes pitch and meals. A very friendly German speaking owner runs the site and restaurant with his wife and daughters who speak a little English.

Facilities

A single, small toilet block has just two showers for each sex (10 ft for one minute) and curtained, communal dressing space. Baby room. Room for washing clothes and dishes with small cooking facility. Washing machine. Bar. Restaurant with good menu and reasonable prices. Solar heated swimming pool and children's pool (10 x 5 m, open June -Sept). Order bread at reception the previous evening. Off site: Györ with shops and swimming pool.

Open

1 April - 30 October.

At a glance

Welcome & Ambience	✓✓✓✓	Location	✓✓✓✓
Quality of Pitches	✓✓✓✓	Range of Facilities	✓✓✓✓

Directions

Coming from Austria, continue through Györ following signs for Budapest. Continue on road no. 1 past start of motorway for 3 km. and site is on left. From Budapest, turn right onto road no. 10 at end of motorway, then as above.

Charges year

Per pitch	€ 2,26
electricity	€ 0,87
dog	€ 0,87

Less 10% for stays over 4 days, 20% after 8.

Reservations

Write to site. Tel: 96 523 008. E-mail: piheno@arrabonet.gyor.hu

HU5150 Fortuna Camping

Dózsa György út 164, 2045 Törökbálint (Pest County)

This superb and pretty site lies at the foot of a hill with views of the vineyards, but Budapest is only 25 minutes away by bus. The owner, Csaba Szücs, will provide visitors with a map and instructions on how to see the town in the best way. The site is surrounded by mature trees and Mr Szücs will proudly name all 150 varieties of bushes and shrubs which edge some of the pitches. The site has a small restaurant with very reasonable prices but it is only open from 18.00-20.00 (although when we visited the last order was taken at 21.00). A new, open air swimming pool with flume will help you to cool off in summer with an indoor pool for cooler weather. Concrete and gravel access roads lead to terraces where there are 170 individual pitches most bordered with hedges, all with electricity (16A, long leads may be needed), and 14 with water, on slightly sloping ground. A special field area provides for group bookings, and has separate facilities. Mr Szücs and his family will endeavour to make your stay a comfortable one. His daughter organises tours to Budapest or the surrounding countryside, and will also explain the mysteries of public transport in Budapest.

Facilities

Four fully equipped sanitary blocks (one with heating) with good facilities for disabled people. Washing up facilities, plus six cookers in sheltered area. Washing machine and dryer. Gas supplies. Motorcaravan services. Restaurant and bar (all year). Snack bar. Shop (1/6-20/8 or essentials from reception, order bread previous day). Outdoor swimming pool with slide (15/5-15/9). Indoor pool. Small play area. Excursions organised. English spoken. Off site: Close to bus terminal for city centre 1 km.

Open

All year.

At a glance

Welcome & Ambience	✓✓✓✓✓	Location	✓✓✓✓✓
Quality of Pitches	✓✓✓✓	Range of Facilities	✓✓✓✓

Directions

From M1 Györ - Budapest, exit for Törökbálint following signs for town and then site. Also accessible from M7 Budapest - Balaton road.

Charges guide

Per person	€ 5,00
child (4-14 yrs)	€ 4,00
pitch	€ 5,00
electricity	€ 2,00
dog	€ 2,00

No credit cards.

Reservations

Advised for high season - write to site. Tel: 23 335 364. E-mail: fortunacamping@axelero.hu

HU5180 Jumbo Camping

Budakalászi út 23-25, 2096 Üröm (Pest County)

Jumbo Camping is a modern, thoughfully developed site in the northern outskirts of Budapest. Situated on a hillside 15 km from Budapest centre, with attractive views of the Buda hills and with public transport to the city near, this is a pleasant and comfortable small site (despite the name) where you will receive a warm welcome. It is possible to park outside the short, steepish entrance which has a chain across. Reception, where you are given a comprehensive English language information sheet, doubles as a café/bar area. The concrete and gravel access roads lead shortly to 55 terraced pitches of varying size, a little on the small size for large units, and some with a fair degree of slope. Hardstanding for cars and caravan wheels, as well as large hardstandings for motorhomes. There is a steep incline to some pitches and use of the site's 4x4 may be required. All pitches have 6A electricity (may require long leads) and there are 8 caravan pitches with water and waste water. They are mostly divided by small hedges and the whole area is fenced.

Facilities

Sanitary facilities are excellent, with large showers (communal changing). Dishwashing undercover. Terrace with chairs and tables. Washing machine, iron and cooking facilities on payment. Motorcaravan services. Café where bread (orders taken), milk and butter available. Small, attractive swimming pool (10/6-10/9). Playground with covered area for wet weather. Barbecue area. English spoken and information sheet provided in English. Off site: Shop and restaurant 500 m. The 'Old Swabian Wine-Cellar' said to serve extremely good food. Bus to city 500 m. every 30 minutes. Riding 4 km and tennis can be arranged. Fishing 8 km.

Open

1 April - 31 October.

At a glance

Welcome & Ambience	✓✓✓✓	Location	✓✓✓✓✓
Quality of Pitches	✓✓✓✓	Range of Facilities	✓✓✓✓

Directions

Site is signed on roads to Budapest - nos. 11 from Szentendre and 10 from Komarom. If approaching from Budapest use 11 but note that the site sign appears very quickly after a sharp right hand bend (site signs and entry are clearer if using road 10). You can also approach via Györ on M1/E60 and Lake Balaton on M7/E71. The turn into the site is quite acute and uphill.

Charges 2004

Per pitch acc to size and season	HUF 1100 - 1600
adult	HUF 1100
child (3-14 yrs)	HUF 690
electricity	HUF 570

No credit cards (cash only).

Reservations

Write to site. Tel: 26 351 251.

HU5210 Diófaház Guest House

Ady Endre út 12, 3348 Szilvásvárad (Heves County)

Diófaház is an ideal base in northeast Hungary for exploring this wooded part of the country, to visit the stud farm of the famous Lippizaner horses (one of only five in the world) or to visit the town of Eger, world famous for its culture and red wine. The site is in private grounds on the edge of the village and provides a maximum of six pitches, all with electricity, which makes it quiet and peaceful. Gyöngyi Pap, the owner provides a warm welcome and if you're lucky you may arrive for weekly barbecue or the home made Hungarian goulash soup. There are plenty of opportunities for cycling or walking tours, or there is a lakeside beach within 6 km. In winter this is a skiing resort and there is a local spa. English is spoken.

Facilities

The single toilet block includes washbasins in cabins with hot and cold water, controllable showers and sinks with free hot water. Fresh rolls to order every day with home made jam but no shop. Discounts at two restaurants in the village if you show your campers card. Individual barbecues are not permitted (communal barbecue available). Off site: Riding 200 m. Bicycle hire 500 m. Fishing 6 km.

Open

All year.

At a glance

Welcome & Ambience	✓✓✓✓✓	Location	✓✓✓✓✓
Quality of Pitches	✓✓✓	Range of Facilities	✓✓✓

Directions

Take the no. 25 road from Eger north to Szilvásvárad. Site is signed when entering the village.

Charges 2004

Per unit incl. 2 persons	€ 8,00 - € 9,60
extra person	€ 2,80

Reservations

Contact site. Tel: 36 355 595.
E-mail: info@diofahaz.hu

HU5300 Kek-Duna Camping

Hösök Tere 23, 7020 Dunafoldvar (Tolna County)

Dunafoldvár is a most attractive town of 10,000 people and you are in the heart of it in just two or three minutes by foot from this site, easily reached via the wide towpath on the west bank of the Danube. For a town site, Kék-Duna is remarkably peaceful. Apart from the obvious attractions of the river, with a large island opposite and pleasant walks possible, the ancient town has a most interesting museum, the 'Burg', with a genuine dungeon and cells, Roman relics and with a panoramic view of the town and river from its top floor. There are in fact too many places of interest within easy reach to list here. This is a pleasant small site on the banks of the Danube, fenced all round and locked at night, with flat concrete access roads to 50 pitches. All have electricity (16A), the first half being open, the remainder well shaded.

Facilities

Modern, tiled sanitary building with nicely decorated ladies' section offers curtained showers with communal changing. The rest of the facilities are of above average standard. Dishwashing outside with cold water. Washing machine. Shop and café (from mid June), town shops close. Bicycle hire. Excursion information. English speaking receptionist Off site: Tennis 50 m. Thermal swimming pool 200 m (under the same ownership). Riding 5 km.

Open

All year.

At a glance

Welcome & Ambience	✓✓✓✓	Location	✓✓✓✓✓
Quality of Pitches	✓✓✓✓	Range of Facilities	✓✓✓

Directions

From no. 6 Budapest - Pecs road take exit at Dunafoldvár for Kecskemed road no. 52, and follow until slip road on right which leads on to the riverside towpath. Site is well signed.

Charges guide

Per adult	HUF 500
pensioner, student or child	HUF 250
caravan, car and electricity	HUF 1200
motorcaravan and electricity	HUF 1100
tent and car	HUF 550
electricity for tent	HUF 220

Reservations

Advisable for July/Aug. or arrive early.
Tel: 75 541 107.

HU5260 Jonathermál Motel-Camping

Kökút 26, 6120 Kiskunmajsa (Bacs-Kiskun County)

Situated three kilometres to the north of the town of Kiskunmajsa, a few kilometres west of road no. 5 (E75) from Budapest (140 km.) to Szeged (35 km.) this is one of the best Hungarian campsites. The camping area is large, reached by tarmac access roads with 250 unmarked pitches are in several areas around the motel and sanitary buildings. Some shade is available and more trees are growing. All the 120 large pitches have electricity (6A) and are set on flat grass where you place the pitch number allocated to you. Entrance to the pool complex is charged (weekly tickets available) which gives you a huge 100 x 70 m. open air pool with a beach along one side, the indoor pool, children's pool, thermal, sauna and cold dip and an open air thermal pool, plus various places to eat and drink. This professionally run site offers the chance of relaxation but is also well placed for visiting Szeged, Csongrad or Szolnok, as well as being close to the borders with Romania and the former Yugoslavia. A conference room is being added next to reception which will also function as a social room for campers and a new thermal bath is planned.

Facilities

A heated sanitary block provides first class facilities including washbasins in cabins and a unit for disabled visitors. Launderette. Gas supplies. Kiosk on site for bread and basics. etc. Smart bar and rest room. Restaurant by pool complex. Large swimming and thermal complex with other facilities (1/5-1/10). Massage (on payment). Children's playground including carved wooden animals. Volleyball, tennis and minigolf. Fishing lake (day permits). Bicycle hire. Riding. German spoken. Accommodation to rent.
Off site: Shop opposite entrance, 120 m. Restaurants near.

Open

All year.

At a glance

Welcome & Ambience	✓✓✓✓✓	Location	✓✓✓✓
Quality of Pitches	✓✓✓✓	Range of Facilities	✓✓✓✓

Directions

From no. 5 (E75) Budapest - Szeged road take Kiskunmajsa exit and site is well signed 3 km. north of the town.

Charges 2004

Per person	HUF 550 - 700
child (6-14 yrs)	HUF 200 - 300
caravan	HUF 260 - 340
motorcaravan	HUF 500 - 680
tent	HUF 200 - 300
car or motorcycle	HUF 200 - 300

Less 5-10% for longer stays. No credit cards.

Reservations

Possibly necessary mid-July - mid-Aug.
Tel: 77 481 855.
E-mail: jonathermal@mail.datanet.hu

HU5025 Zalatour Thermal Camping

Gyogyfurdo 6, 8749 Zalakaros (Zala County)

The Zalatour Thermál Camping in Zalakaros has 280 attractively laid out, level pitches, all with 10A electricity and varying in size from 30-100 sq.m. (the larger pitches need to be reserved). There are 250 for touring units on grass and gravel (firm tent pegs may be needed) and around 10 hardstandings for larger units and motorcaravans. Mature trees provide useful shade an access roads are gravel. Zalatour attracts many elderly people who spend their day at the thermal spa 200 metres down the road – the waters are good for rheumatism and other joint problems. This site is good for rest and relaxation in the shade with the added benefit of the healing waters of the spa. Lake Balaton is close, as is the Balaton cycle route (taking you all the way around the lake) and the Kis Balaton Nature Reserve.

Facilities

Modern and comfortable toilet facilities with British style toilets, open washbasins and controllable, hot showers (free). Facilities for disabled visitors. Full-service laundry including ironing. Campers' kitchen. Motorcaravan service point and car wash. Shop. Bar/restaurant. Massage, acupuncture and pedicure. Sauna. Hairdresser. Bicycle hire.
Off site: Fishing and beach 3 km. Golf 500 m. Riding 2 km.

Open

1 April - 30 September.

At a glance

Welcome & Ambience	✓✓✓✓	Location	✓✓✓
Quality of Pitches	✓✓✓	Range of Facilities	✓✓✓✓

Directions

On E71 travelling northeast from Nagykanisza, take exit for Zalakaros. Follow good site signs.

Charges 2004

Per person	HUF 1000
child (2-14 yrs)	HUF 500
pitch incl. electricity	HUF 750,00 - 1500
dog	HUF 300

Reservations

Necessary for larger pitches; contact site.
Tel: 93 34 01 05. E-mail: thermal@zalatour.hu

HU5315 Camping Forras

7394 Magyarhertelend (Baranya)

This well established site is close to the historic city of Pécs, in a part of Hungary with Mediterranean style climate. Camping Forras, or 'Bij Balázc' as it is called by some Dutch guests, is also close to the Mescék National Park, where there are many marked walking routes. The site has 120 pitches, all for tourers, off gravel and grass access roads. Of these, 80 are marked and have 6A electricity connections. The remaining pitches are used mainly for tents. The whole site looks well cared for with many different varieties of trees giving a pleasant atmosphere and providing useful shade in summer. Forras is opposite a pool – not a thermal spa according to the owner, although it is advertised as such! There is a restaurant here, with a small bar on the site for drinks. This is a good site for those seeking relaxation in beautiful, natural surroundings.

Facilities

The traditional toilet block provides acceptable facilities with British style toilets, open washbasins and controllable showers (free). Washing machine and spin dryer. Dishwashing. Bar with library. Basic playground. Minigolf. Torch useful. Off site: Fishing 3 km. City of Pécs is close.

Open

7 May - 30 September.

At a glance

Welcome & Ambience	✓✓✓	Location	✓✓✓✓
Quality of Pitches	✓✓✓✓	Range of Facilities	✓✓✓

Directions

From Pécs, take no. 66 road north towards Sásd. Turn left in Magyarszék towards Magyarhertelend and follow signs. Site is just outside village on the left.

Charges 2004

Per person	HUF 650
child (2-13 yrs)	HUF 350
pitch incl. car	HUF 500 - 800
electricity	HUF 400
dog	HUF 300

No credit cards.

Reservations

Contact site. Tel: 6 13 34 166 222.
E-mail: h.verwejj@tomaatnet.nl

HU5290 Kemping Nap a Szivemben

Petofi Sándor u. 38-D, 7081 Simontornya (Tolna County)

This small, immaculate looking site is under Dutch ownership and was newly opened in 2004. It only has 15 pitches on well kept, grassy lawns, all with 18/22A electricity. The toilet block is amongst the best we have seen in Central Europe. The site is on the main road but it did not appear to be too disturbing. The owner, Mrs Van Rijn, organises Hungarian breakfasts with visits to the Castle (where a Dutch noble family once lived) and wine tastings in their own vineyard. A cycle route has been set out in the local area. Nap a Szivemben is about 35 km. from Lake Balaton and close to the historic city of Pécs. There is a swimming pool in the town but according to Mrs Van Rijn, this is not clean – she suggests that you use site's own small pool (10 x 5 m). There is a small bar in one of two former garages with an interesting painting of a tow truck on the wall – the site owners also operate a towing service for stranded Dutch and German drivers.

Facilities

One immaculate, modern toilet block has British style toilets, open washbasins and controllable, free showers. Facilities for disabled visitors. Laundry service at the owner's house. Outdoor pool (10 x 5 m). Excursions and activities organised. Bar with Dutch satellite TV. Off site: Fishing and riding 2 km.

Open

Easter - 15 October.

At a glance

Welcome & Ambience	✓✓✓✓	Location	✓✓✓
Quality of Pitches	✓✓✓✓	Range of Facilities	✓✓✓

Directions

Site is on the main 61 road running through town. Take exit just before the petrol station on the right on leaving Simontornya.

Charges 2004

Per unit incl. 2 persons, electricity	€ 20,00
child	€ 3,00 - € 3,50

No credit cards.

Reservations

Contact site. Tel: 36 74 586 060.

Whether you want to explore historical cities, stroll around mediaeval hill towns, relax on sandy beaches or simply indulge in opera, good food and wine, Italy has it all. Roman ruins, Renaissance art and beautiful churches abound. For the more active, the Italian Alps are a haven for winter sports enthusiasts and also offer good hiking trails.

Italy only became a unified state in 1861, hence the regional nature of the country today. With 20 distinct regions each one has retained its own individualism which is evident in the cuisine and local dialects.

In the north, the vibrant city of Milan is great for shopping and home to the famous opera house, La Scala, as well as Leonardo's Last Supper fresco. It is also a good jumping-off point for the Alps; the Italian Lake District, incorporating Lake Garda, Lake Como and Lake Maggiore; the canals of Venice and the lovely town of Verona. Central Italy probably represents the most commonly perceived image of the country and Tuscany, with its classic rolling countryside and the historical towns of Florence, Siena, San Gimignano and Pisa, is one of the most visited areas. Further south is the historical capital of Rome and the city of Naples. Close to some of Italy's ancient sites such as Pompei, Naples is within easy distance of Sorrento and the Amalfi coast.

Population

57.8 million

Capital

Rome

Climate

The south enjoys extremely hot summers and mild, dry winters, whilst the mountainous regions of the north are cooler with heavy snowfalls in winter

Language

Italian. There are several dialect forms and some German is spoken near the Austrian border

Currency

The Euro

Telephone

The country code is 0039

Banks

Mon-Fri 08.30-13.00 and 15.00-16.00

Shops

Mon-Sat 08.30/09.00-13.00 and 15.30/16.00-19.30/20.00, with some variations in larger cities

Public Holidays

New Year; Easter Mon; Liberation Day 25 Apr; Labour Day; Assumption 15 Aug; All Saints 1 Nov; Immaculate Conception 8 Dec; Christmas 25, 26 Dec; plus some special local feast days

Motoring

The standard pink EU driving licence is recognised in Italy but holders of the older green UK type will need to change it for a photocard driving licence, or use an International Driving Permit. An Italian translation of a British driving licence is no longer accepted. Tolls are payable on the extensive Autostrada network. If travelling distances, save time by purchasing a `Viacard' from pay booths or service areas. An overhanging load, ie. bicycle rack, must be indicated by large red/white hatched warning square. Failure to do so will result in a fine

Tourist Office

Italian State Tourist Board
1 Princes Street
London W1B 2AY
Tel: 020 7408 1254
Fax: 020 7399 3567
Email: italy@italiantouristboard.co.uk
Internet: www.enit.it

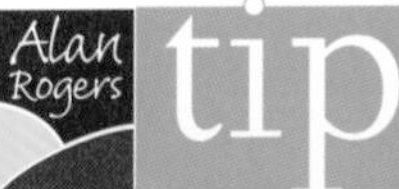

tip

THERE ARE PLENTY OF PERFORMING ARTS AND OPERA FESTIVALS TO ENJOY THROUGHOUT THE YEAR, ESPECIALLY IN SUMMER, INCLUDING THE FESTIVAL OF TWO WORLDS IN SPOLETO AND THE ARENA OPERA FESTIVAL IN VERONA.

IT6220 Camping Mombarone

Settimo Vittone Reg., 10010 Torre Daniele (Piedmont)

This is a small rustic all year site alongside the SS26 road. It would be a useful stop if entering Italy from the northwest through the Mont Blanc tunnel. It has 120 pitches, with space for about 40 touring units on the grassy space between the permanent units. The Peretto family take pride in looking after their guests and English is spoken. The site is thoughtfully laid out in a valley with attractive plants, shrubs and trees for shade and is surrounded by high mountains and wooded hills, with vines bedecking the eastern slopes. This is an ideal base for climbers as the mountains in this area are extremely popular. The many famous valleys including Valle di Champorcher and Valle di Gressony are within easy driving distance, as is the Parco Nazionale del Gran Paradiso. The site has a small wooden bar and a simple, inexpensive restaurant is 50 metres away. Shops and good restaurants are close by in the village of Quincinetto. There is a small framed and supported pool for children or they can paddle in the shallow river and catch tiddlers on the northern boundary. If you are here in October help the family pick their own grapes, make the wine (in the Nebbiolo style) and share the fun; The wine is sold at the bar - it is good!

Facilities

The sanitary facilities are adequate with both British and Turkish WCs and a washing machine. When you leave tell them how many showers taken and settle up accordingly! Bar. Toddlers' pool. Volleyball, table tennis, table football. Fishing. Off site: Riding 5 km. Shops and restaurants in the town.

Open

All year.

At a glance

Welcome & Ambience	✓✓✓✓✓	Location	✓✓✓
Quality of Pitches	✓✓✓	Range of Facilities	✓✓✓

Directions

From the A5 motorway take exit for Quiuinetto onto the SS26. On the SS26 Aosta – Turin road, the site is between the 45 and 46 km. markers between Pont St Martin and Sethimo Vittone.

Charges 2004

Per person	€ 4,00
child (under 10 yrs)	€ 3,00
pitch	€ 5,00 - € 5,50
electricity	€ 2,00

No credit cards.

Reservations

Write to site. Tel: 0125 757907.

IT6245 Camping Riviera

Via Casali Darbedo 2, 28822 Cannobio (Piedmont)

With scenic views across the water and surrounding mountains, this 22,000 sq.m. site is directly beside Lake Maggiore. Under the same active ownership as Valle Romantica, the whole site has a well cared for appearance and it is certainly one of the best lakeside sites in the area. Over 250 numbered pitches are on flat grass, either side of hard surfaced access roads and divided by trees and shrubs. There are 220 with 5A electricity (long cables may be needed). There is a small jetty and easy access to the lake for boats, swimming and other watersports. Sailing and windsurfing regattas are organised. The site could make a suitable base for exploring the area, although progress on the busy winding road may be slow!

Facilities

The five sanitary blocks, one new and two with facilities for disabled visitors, are of good quality. Washing machines. Fridge boxes for hire. Gas supplies. Motorcaravan services. Well stocked site shop. Pleasant bar/restaurant with covered terrace, providing waiter service and takeaway. Pizzeria. Swimming pool (1/5-15/9). Fishing (licence required). Boat slipway. Sailing and windsurfing schools. Off site: The town is only a short distance. Bicycle hire 500 m.

Open

27 March - 31 October.

At a glance

Welcome & Ambience	✓✓✓✓	Location	✓✓✓✓✓
Quality of Pitches	✓✓✓	Range of Facilities	✓✓✓

Directions

Site is about 4 km. from the Swiss border in the town of Cannobio which is on the SS34 Locarno – Verbania road. It is the last site before the bridge, at the lakeside (on the east).

Charges 2004

Per person	€ 5,50 - € 6,50
child (1-11 yrs)	€ 3,50 - € 4,50
pitch	€ 9,00 - € 12,00
dog	€ 4,00
electricity (4A)	€ 3,00

No credit cards.

Reservations

Made for min. 14 nights with deposit (€ 60) and fee (€ 40). Tel: 0323 71360.
E-mail: riviera@riviera-valleromantica.com

IT6246 Camping Village Isolino

Via per Feriolo 25, 28924 Verbania Fondotoce (Piedmont)

Lake Maggiore is one of the most attractive Italian lakes and Isolino Camping Village is one of the largest sites in the region. The long entrance road to the site – rolled gravel and fairly uneven – is rather off-putting but then the stunning location and attractive swimming pool with its lovely views across the lake to the fir-clad mountains beyond is breathtaking and worth finding. Most of the 710 tourist pitches have shade from a variety of trees and are of a good size in regular back-to-back rows. All have electrical connections (6A). There is a small sandy beach and a wide range of watersports (no jet-skis) can be enjoyed on the lake. The social life of the campsite is centred around the large bar which has a stage for musical entertainment, pool-side terrace and takeaway with a restaurant on the floor above sharing the magnificent views across the lake. The site is owned by the friendly Manoni family who also own Camping Continental Lido at nearby Lake Mergozzo and good English is spoken.

Facilities

Six well-built toilet blocks, most refurbished, have free hot water. Washing machines and dryers. Fridge boxes for hire. Motorcaravan service point. Large well stocked supermarket. Most attractive swimming pool with children's pool at one end and sunbathing area. Football pitch. Tennis courts. Fishing. Watersports. Bicycle hire and guided mountain bike tours. Beach volleyball and organised activities for children and adults and weekly disco in July/Aug. Raised barbecues are permitted. Off site: Golf 3 km. Riding 12 km. Site is well situated for visiting the many attractions of the region which include famous gardens on the islands in the lake and at the Villa Taranto, Verbania. The Swiss mountains and resort of Locarno are quite near.

At a glance

Welcome & Ambience	✓✓✓✓	Location	✓✓✓✓
Quality of Pitches	✓✓✓	Range of Facilities	✓✓✓✓

Directions

Leave A26 motorway at exit for Stresa/Baveno, turn left towards Fondotoce and follow signs to site on right.

Charges 2005

Per unit incl. 2 persons and electricity	€ 17,55 - € 34,05
extra person	€ 4,10 - € 6,75
child 3-5 yrs	€ -2,00 - € 5,50
child 6-11 yrs	€ 3,05 - € 5,50
dog	€ 3,05 - € 6,75

Credit cards accepted with 1.4% commission.

Reservations

Contact site. Tel: 0323 496080. E-mail: info@isolino.com

Open

18 March - 19 September.

IT6240 Camping Valle Romantica

Via Valle Cannobina, 28822 Cannobio (Piedmont)

The pretty little town of Cannobio is situated between Verbania and Locarno on the western shore of Lake Maggiore. It could make a base for exploring the Lake and its islands, although progress along the winding lakeside road, hemmed in by mountains, is slow. Serious mountain walkers are well catered for, and the Swiss resort of Locarno is not far. Steamers cross the Lake, but the only car ferry across is between Verbania and Locarno. In a scenic situation, this lovely site was established about 40 years ago by the present owner's father, who planted some 20,000 plants, trees and shrubs. These are all now well established and maintained to make a delightful garden setting. The site's swimming pool is in a sunny position and there is a pool in the river, where, except after heavy rain, children can play. The 188 numbered pitches for touring units are on flat grass among the trees, which provide good shade and serve to separate the pitches (but mean some narrow site roads). Electricity (4A) is available on most pitches, although long cables are necessary in some parts. Used by tour operators (30 pitches). The owner takes a keen and active personal interest in the site, and English is spoken.

Facilities

The three sanitary blocks provide good facilities with free showers of a reasonable size, with hooks, screen and a small dressing space, controlled by taps. Washing machines. Gas supplies. Motorcaravan services. Small, well stocked supermarket. Pleasant bar/restaurant with waiter service and takeaway. Pizzeria. Swimming pool (1/5-15/9). Fishing (licence required). Sailing and windsurfing schools. Fridge box hire. Off site: Bicycle hire 500 m. Boat launching 1.5 km.

Open

27 March - 30 September.

At a glance

Welcome & Ambience	✓✓✓✓	Location	✓✓✓✓
Quality of Pitches	✓✓✓✓	Range of Facilities	✓✓✓

Directions

The site is approx. 4 km. from the Swiss border in Cannobio which is on the SS34 Locarno - Verbania road. Follow site signs from SS34 turning west (away from lake) at the southern outskirts of Cannobio and travel 1.5 km. to site.

Charges 2004

Per person	€ 5,50 - € 6,50
child (1-12 yrs)	€ 3,50 - € 4,50
pitch	€ 9,00 - € 12,00
electricity (4A)	€ 3,00

No credit cards.

Reservations

Contact site. Tel: 0323 71249.
E-mail: valleromantica@riviera-valleromantica.com

IT6261 Camping Del Sole

Via per Rovato, 26, 25049 Iseo (Lombardy)

Camping Del Sole lies on the southern edge of Lake Iseo, just outside the pretty lakeside town of Iseo and near the delightful waterfront area where you can enjoy classic Italian architecture, stroll around the shops or enjoy a meal in one of the many restaurants. The campsite is alongside the beautiful lake where there is a boat launching facility. In total the site has 360 pitches, some taken up with chalets and mobile homes, and many with fine views of the surrounding mountains and the lake. The pitches are generally flat and of a reasonable size, most with electrical connections. The site has a wide range of excellent leisure amenities, notably a large swimming pool and smaller children's paddling pool. There is a pleasant bar and restaurant with a pizzeria near the pool and entertainment area and a second bar that serves snacks by the lake. A lively entertainment programme is provided and excursions around the lake are organised, notably to Lake Iseo's three islands where you can sit at a street café or enjoy a walk while enjoying the magnificent scenery. Excursions are also organised to the wine cellars of Franciacorta.

Facilities

Sanitary facilities are modern and well maintained, including special facilities for disabled visitors. Washing machines and dryers. Bar, restaurant, pizzeria and snack bar. Supermarket. Motorcaravan service point. Bicycle and pedal boat hire. Tennis. Volleyball. Entertainment in high season. Off site: Golf 5 km. Riding 6 km.

Open

22 April - 25 September.

At a glance

Welcome & Ambience	✓✓✓	Location	✓✓✓✓✓
Quality of Pitches	✓✓✓	Range of Facilities	✓✓✓✓

Directions

From the A4 Milan – Venice autostrada take Rovato exit. Head towards Lago d'Iseo for 12 km. and the site is well signed. If you miss site signs follow signs to Rovato from Iseo town centre (1 km)

Charges 2004

Per person	€ 4,30 - € 7,80
child	€ 3,80 - € 6,30
pitch incl. electricity	€ 8,30 - € 16,50
tent pitch	€ 6,30 - € 13,50

Reductions in low season.

Reservations

Contact site. Tel: 030 980288.
E-mail: info@campingdelsole.it

IT6250 Camping Au Lac de Como

Via Cesare Battisti 18, 22010 Sorico (Lombardy)

Au Lac du Como is situated in a most pleasant location at the head of Lake Como in the centre of the village of Sorico facing south down the water and surrounded by wooded mountains. There is direct access to the lake for swimming, boating and other watersports, with windsurfing appearing to be the most popular pastime. Static units predominate but the camping area is directly by the lake where there is said to be room for 74 touring units, with 3A electricity connections. However, as pitches are not marked out, pitching can be a little haphazard and the area may become crowded at times, particularly in high season when advanced booking is advised. Cars are parked just away from tents and caravans and there is further parking outside the entrance. The owner speaks good English and insists on respect for other residents so ball games, barbecues and loud music are not allowed. The site is well situated for exploring the area, with Switzerland nearby via the Splugen Pass. There are also marked paths and trails for walking and biking in the mountains with an interesting nature park close. Although it makes a good night stop when passing this way, many visitors find it interesting and stay longer. Most guests are German or Dutch but British find their way here and are welcome.

Facilities

There is one good sanitary block in the centre of the static part and two smaller basic ones, all with mainly British style WCs. Hot water in the larger block is on payment but free in the other two except for dishwashing and laundry. Washing machine and dryer. Motorcaravan services. Supermarket. Hotel bar and restaurant open all day, offering excellent buffet breakfast service and evening meals. Heated swimming pool (21 x 7 m). Sauna and solarium. Fishing. Range of watersports possible. Canoe, kayak and bicycle hire.

Open

All year.

At a glance

Welcome & Ambience	✓✓✓✓✓	Location	✓✓✓✓✓
Quality of Pitches	✓✓✓	Range of Facilities	✓✓✓

Directions

Easiest route is north on SS36 from Lecco to Nuovo Olonio and west on SS402 (signed Gravelona) to Sorico; site is then on the left in centre of village. Can be approached on SS340 from Como on lakeside road which is quite narrow in places but an interesting drive (not advised for larger units).

Charges guide

Per person	€ 6,50
child	€ 4,50
pitch	€ 11,00
dog	€ 6,00
extra car	€ 6,00 - € 0,00

Less 10-50% for over 1 night outside July/August.

Reservations

Advised for high season; write to site.
Tel: 034 484035. E-mail: infoaulac@aulacdecomo.com

IT6251 Camping La Riva

Via Poncione, 3, 22010 Sorico (Lombardy)

La Riva was opened in 2000 and lies at the northern end of Lake Como, close to the nature reserve of 'Pian di Spagna' and within walking distance of Sorico, a pretty town with a range of bars and restaurants. This is a small, quiet site which enjoys direct lake access and is well located for trekking in the surrounding mountains or for mountain biking. It is also ideally located for exploring the beautiful Lake Como area and even into Switzerland and St Moritz. Pitches are generally level and of a reasonable size (typically 80 sq.m). They are marked by trees and many have attractive views across the river to the mountains. Most have electrical connections. Close by, the campsite reception houses a small bar, which incorporates a snack bar and takeaway, and a small shop. A new heated outdoor pool was opened for the 2004 season.

Facilities

The centrally located sanitary building contains modern showers (tokens needed), toilets and washbasins and is kept very clean. Facilities for disabled people. Washing machine. New swimming pool (charged) and solarium. Bicycle hire. Fishing, water skiing. Canoe and dinghy hire. Off site: Guided walks. Cycling/walking track from site to Sorico. Riding. Golf. Local market.

Open

1 April - 3 November.

At a glance

Welcome & Ambience	✓✓✓✓	Location	✓✓✓✓✓
Quality of Pitches	✓✓✓✓	Range of Facilities	✓✓✓

Directions

Site is located on the River Mera as it joins Lake Como at Sorico. Approaching on S340 from Menaggio you pass site shortly before reaching Sorico.

Charges 2004

Per person	€ 6,00
child (0-7 yrs)	€ 4,50
pitch	€ 9,00
incl. electricity	€ 12,00
dog	€ 3,00

Discounts in low season.

Reservations

Contact site. Tel: 034 494571.
E-mail: info@campinglariva.com

IT6229 Camping Levico

Pleina 1, 38056 Levico Terme (Trentino - Alto Adige)

Our Italian agent has recommended this lakeside site and we plan to conduct a full inspection in 2005. Camping Levico is the only site with direct access to Lake Levico but also boasts an attractive swimming pool. The 270 pitches are grassy and of a good size, mostly with electrical connections. A range of watersports are available here, and the site organises a varied activity programme, including walking and cycling trips. Mobile homes and chalets for rent.

Facilities

Bar, restaurant and takeaway. Shop. Lakeside beach. Swimming pool and paddling pool, Playground. Children's club. Entertainment programme in high season.
Off site: Levico Terme 2 km. Trento 16 km. Riding, cycle and walking trails.

Open

1 April - 9 October.

Directions

Bardolino is located to the north of the S47 Trento - Bassano road. The site is to the south of the town, approaching from the S47.

Charges 2004

Per person	€ 5,00 - € 7,80
child (3 - 12 years)	€ 4,30 - € 5,50
pitch incl. electricity (6A)	€ 6,70 - € 15,90

Reservations

Advised for high season; contact site.
Tel: 0461 706491. E-mail: mail@campinglevico.com

IT6201 Camping Antholz

39030 Antholz (Trentino - Alto Adige)

Appearances can be deceptive and this is the case with Camping Antholz, an all year campsite in the heart of the Dolomites. At first sight the 130 pitches, numbered but only roughly marked out, make this a very ordinary looking campsite. Just inside the entrance is a pleasant looking building with reception and a smart restaurant. It is when one investigates the sanitary accommodation that one realises that this is no ordinary site, as the facilities are of an extremely high standard. High up in the Anterselva valley, the site has splendid views of near and distant peaks. There are few trees on the site but many provide a pleasant background. The pitches have electrical connections. This is good skiing country in winter (ski bus, ski school, ski lifts) and, with a new National Park near, provides good walking in summer.

Facilities

The toilet block with under-floor heating, in addition to the normal facilities, also provides a hair salon, cosmetics room and a baby room. Washing machine and dryer.
Motorcaravan services. Restaurant (all year). Shop for basics. Playground. TV room. Table tennis. Bicycle hire. Limited entertainment programme for children in high season.
Off site: Tennis near. Winter sports, summer walking.

Open

All year.

At a glance

Welcome & Ambience	✓✓✓	Location	✓✓✓✓
Quality of Pitches	✓✓✓	Range of Facilities	✓✓✓

Directions

From Bressanone exit on A22, go east on SS49 through Brunico and turn north (signed Antholz) for about 12 km. Pass Antholz village and site is on right.

Charges 2004

Per unit incl. 2 persons and electricity	€ 18,50 - € 23,50
extra person	€ 4,50 - € 6,00
child (3-13 yrs)	€ 2,00 - € 4,60
dog	€ 2,00 - € 3,00

Reservations

Write to site. Tel: 0474 492204.
E-mail: info@camping-antholz.com

IT6210 Camping Steiner

Kennedy Straße 32, 39055 Laives (Bolzano) (Trentino - Alto Adige)

Camping Steiner is very central for touring with the whole of the Dolomite region within easy reach, as well as Bolzano, Merano and other attractive places. It has its share of overnight trade but, with much on site activity, one could spend an enjoyable holiday here, especially now the S12 by which it stands has a motorway alternative. It is a fairly small site with part taken up by bungalows. The individual touring pitches, mostly with good shade and hardstanding, are in rows on either side of access roads. There are electricity connections. This friendly, family run site has a long tradition of providing a happy camping experience in the more traditional style – the owner remembers Alan Rogers who stayed here on many occasions. There is a family style restaurant and indoor and outdoor pools to provide exercise and relaxation.

Facilities

The two sanitary blocks, one new, can be heated in cool weather. Excellent small restaurant and takeaway service, with good choice. Cellar bar with taped music, dancing at times. Shop. Two free swimming pools on the site - an open air one, 20 x 10 m. (May-Sept. and heated in spring), and a 12 x 6 m. enclosed, heated pool (open all season, except July/Aug). Playground and paddling pool. Table tennis.
Off site: 18 hole golf course 30 minutes away.

Open

28 March - 7 November.

At a glance

Welcome & Ambience	✓✓✓✓	Location	✓✓✓✓
Quality of Pitches	✓✓✓	Range of Facilities	✓✓✓

Directions

Site is by the S12 in northern part of Leifers, 8 km. south of Bolzano. From motorway if approaching from north, take Bolzano-Süd exit and follow Trento signs for 7 km; from south take Ora exit and proceed for 14 km. towards Bolzano.

Charges 2004

Per person	€ 5,00 - € 6,50
child (0-9 yrs)	€ 3,00 - € 4,50
pitch incl. car and 6A electricity	€ 11,00 - € 13,00
dog	€ 5,00

Less in low season. Less 5-10% after 2 weeks stay.

Reservations

Made for min. one week with reasonable deposit. Tel: 0471 950105. E-mail: steiner@dnet.it

IT6230 Camping San Cristoforo

Via dei Pescatori, 38057 Pergine Valsugana (Trentino - Alto Adige)

This part of Italy is becoming better known by those wishing to spend time by a lake in splendid countryside, but away from the more crowded, better-known resorts. Lake Caldonazzo is one of the smaller lakes, but is excellent for watersports. There are several grassy garden areas dotted arond the lake not far from the campsite. Camping San Cristoforo is a relatively new site on the edge of the small town of the same name and is separated from the lake by a minor road, but with easy access. Owned by the friendly Oss family whose policy is to get to know their guests and build a family atmosphere. Excellent English is spoken. The site has 160 pitches on flat grass with tarmac access roads and separated by shady trees, the pitches are of a good size, numbered in front and with electricity. The lake is very close offering watersports and fishing. This quiet mountain site has a well cared for air.

Facilities

The modern sanitary block provides some washbasins in cabins. Facilities for disabled people. Washing machine and dryer. Small shop. Attractive bar/restaurant (all year) serving food and takeaway. Swimming pool (20 x 20 m.) with small padlling pool. Bicycle hire. Minigolf. Off site: Village shops close. Fishing and boating 200 m. Golf 2 km. Riding 5 km.

Open

29 May - 5 September.

At a glance

Welcome & Ambience	✓✓✓	Location	✓✓✓✓
Quality of Pitches	✓✓✓✓	Range of Facilities	✓✓✓✓

Directions

Site is southeast of Trento, just off the SS47 road, well signed from the village of San Cristoforo.

Charges 2004

Per person	€ 6,00 - € 8,00
child (2-11 yrs)	€ 4,00 - € 6,00
pitch	€ 10,00 - € 12,80
dog	€ 2,00 - € 3,00

No credit cards.

Reservations

Not accepted. Tel: 0461 512707.
E-mail: info@campingclub.it

IT6232 Camping Al Sole

38060 Molina di Ledro (Trentino - Alto Adige)

Lake Ledro is only 9 km. from Lake Garda, its sparkling waters and breathtaking scenery offering a low key alternative for those who enjoy a natural setting. The drive from Lake Garda is a real pleasure and prepares you for the treat ahead. This site has been owned by the same friendly family for over 40 years and their experience shows in the layout of the site with its mature trees and the array of facilities provided. Situated on the lake with its own pretty grass and sand beach, the facilities are constantly upgraded and include a new pool and a play area. There is a 10 km. walk around the lake with board-walks installed in the less accessible areas. It came as no surprise to hear that many people choose to return to Camping al Sole year after year. The local community welcomes tourists and offers free hiking programmes beginning with a Monday evening information night so that you can choose the most appropriate guided walks. This is a very nice, peaceful site for extended stays or sightseeing.

Facilities

The newly refurbished sanitary block has plenty of hot water and good facilities for disabled campers. Washing machines. Freezer. Small supermarket. Pleasant restaurant and pizzeria with outdoor terrace. Bar serving snacks and takeaway. Large screen TV. Swimming pool with sunbeds and shower. Play area. Table tennis. Lake for swimming, boating, wind-surfing, fishing and canoeing. Live music and dancing twice weekly in July/Aug. Torches needed in some areas. Bicycle hire. Off site: Pedaloe hire nearby. Hiking, mountain biking, climbing and canyoning. Riding 2 km. Golf 20 km.

At a glance

Welcome & Ambience	✓✓✓✓	Location	✓✓✓✓
Quality of Pitches	✓✓✓✓	Range of Facilities	✓✓✓✓

Directions

From autostrada A22 exit for Lake Garda North to Riba del Garda. In Riva follow sign for Ledro valley. Site is well signed as you approach Lago di Ledra.

Charges 2004

Per person	€ 5,50 - € 7,00
child (3-11yrs)	€ 4,00 - € 5,00
pitch incl. electricity	€ 7,00 - € 9,50
dog	€ 3,50 - € 4,50

Reservations

Advised for high season. Tel: 0464 508496. E-mail: info@campingalsole.it

Open

20 April - 30 September.

IT6237 Camping Al Porto

38069 Torbole (Trentino - Alto Adige)

This is a small unassuming site built on what was the owner's family farm 50 years ago (ask to see the wonderful photos of the family farming). It is peaceful, set back from the main road, close to the water. Lake access is about 80 m. along a road to the rear of the site near a tiny marina. There is a gently shelving beach ideal for launching windsurfers (the area is a mecca for windsurfing). Near the modern reception there is a small bar and terrace area where coffee and snacks are served. Although the services on site are limited it is in the heart of Torbole where there is a choice of places to eat. The grass pitches are level with trees providing shade. Hedges separate the two camping areas, one with numbered pitches with electricity for tourers. The other, less formal area for tents (no electricity) has a secure hut for windsurfing equipment to one side. A no-frills site which is good for stop-overs.

Facilities

The clean, modern toilet block has British and Turkish style WCs and hot water throughout. Facilities for disabled campers. Washing machines. Motorcaravan services. Bar with snacks incl. light breakfasts. Play area.
Off site: Swimming, windsurfing and sailing in the lake. Mountain biking, hiking, climbing, canoeing, canyoning and fishing nearby. Shops and cafés a short walk.

Open

1 April - 6 November.

At a glance

Welcome & Ambience	✓✓✓✓	Location	✓✓✓✓
Quality of Pitches	✓✓✓✓	Range of Facilities	✓✓✓

Directions

Site is on the northeast tip of Lake Garda. Take Roverto south exit for Lake Garda north, then A240 for Nago. From Nago to Torbole and leave Torbole in direction of Riva del Garda. Site is immediately on left before Torbole town exit bridge.

Charges 2004

Per person	€ 6,50 - € 8,50
pitch	€ 7,50 - € 8,50
incl. electricity	€ 8,30 - € 9,30

Discounts in low season. No credit cards.

Reservations

Not taken. Tel: 0464 505891.
E-mail: alporto@torbole.com

IT6280 Camping Villagio Weekend

Via Vallone della Selva 2, 25010 San Felice del Benaco (Lombardy)

Created among the olive groves and terraced vineyards of the Chateau Villa Louisa, which overlooks it, this modern well equipped site enjoys some superb views over the small bay which forms this part of Lake Garda. On reaching the site you will pass through a most impressive pair of gates. Although the site is 400 metres from the lake via a steep footpath, for many campers the views resulting from its situation on higher ground will be ample compensation for it not being an actual lakeside site. Being set in quiet countryside, it provides an unusually tranquil environment, although even here it can become very busy in the high season. The site has a supervised pool (25 x 12 m) and a paddling pool which make up for its not actually having frontage onto the lake, and some visitors, particularly families with children, will doubtless prefer this. There are 230 pitches, all with electricity, of which about 30% are taken by tour operators and statics. The touring pitches are in several different areas, and many enjoy superb views. Some pitches for larger units are set in the upper terraces on steep slopes and manoeuvring can be challenging, and low olive branches may cause problems for long or high units. The large, attractive restaurant has a thoughtfully laid out terrace and lawn from where there are more wonderful views.

Facilities

The three sanitary blocks, one below the restaurant/shop, are modern, well maintained and include hot water to showers, basins and dishwashing areas. Mainly British style WCs, a few washbasins in cabins and facilities for disabled people in one. Reports of congestion in the facilities at peak periods. Washing machines and dryer. Bar/restaurant (waiter service). Takeaway. Shop. Supervised swimming pool and paddling pool. Volleyball. Barbecues. Entertainment programme in season. All facilities are open througout the season. Two playgrounds. First aid room. English spoken.
Off site: Fishing 2 km. Golf 6 km. Riding 8 km. Windsurfing, water skiing and tennis near.

At a glance

Welcome & Ambience	✓✓✓✓	Location	✓✓✓✓✓
Quality of Pitches	✓✓✓✓	Range of Facilities	✓✓✓✓

Directions

Approach from Saló (easier when towing) and follow site signs. From Milano - Venezia autostrada take Desenzano exit towards Saló and Localita Cisano - S. Felice. Take care not to miss narrow right fork at Cisano when the road starts to descend.

Charges 2004

Per person	€ 5,00 - € 7,50
child (3-10 yrs)	€ 3,90 - € 5,70
pitch incl. electricity	€ 10,40 - € 15,00
dog	€ 3,90 - € 6,00

Reservations

Contact site. Tel: 0365 43712.
E-mail: info@weekend.it

Open

24 April - 26 September.

IT6254 Camping Lido

Via Peschiera 2, 37017 Pacengo (Veneto)

Camping Lido is one of the largest and best of the 120 campsites around Lake Garda and is situated in the southeast corner of the lake. There is quite a slope from the entrance down to the lake so many of the 700 grass touring pitches are on terraces which give lovely views across the lake. They are of varying size, separated by hedges and all have electrical connections. This is a most attractive site with tall, neatly trimmed trees standing like sentinels on either side of the broad avenue which runs from the entrance right down to the lake. A wide variety of trees provide shade on some pitches and flowers add to the overall appearance. Near the top of the site is a large, well designed pool and a fitness centre. The site has its own beach with a landing stage that marks off a large area for swimming on one side and on the other an area where boats can be moored. Every night in high season there is a free bus service for teenagers to a local disco returning at 2am. One could happily spend all the holiday here without leaving the site but with so many attractions nearby this would be a pity.

Facilities

Seven modern toilet blocks have the usual facilities including provision for disabled visitors and three family rooms with baths. Washing machines and dryer. Fridge rental. Restaurant, bars, pizzeria, takeaway and well stocked supermarket. Swimming and paddling pools. Fitness centre with gym, sauna and Turkish bath. Playground. Football field. Tennis. Bicycle hire. Watersports. Fishing (permit required). Volleyball. High season organised activities. Shingle beach with landing stage for boats. Dogs are not accepted in high season (6/7-15/8). Off site: Gardaland Theme Park.

At a glance

Welcome & Ambience	✓✓✓✓✓	Location	✓✓✓✓
Quality of Pitches	✓✓✓✓	Range of Facilities	✓✓✓✓

Directions

Leave A4 Milan - Venice motorway at exit for Peschiera. Head north on east side of lake on SS249. Site entrance on left after Gardaland Theme Park.

Charges guide

Per person	€ 4,10 - € 5,90
child (3-5 yrs)	free - € 3,60

Reservations

Contact site. Tel: 045 759 0030.
E-mail: info@campinglido.it

Open

1 April - 18 October.

IT6357 Campings Cisano & San Vito

Via Peschiera 48, 37010 Cisano di Bardolino (Veneto)

This is a combination of two sites and some of the 700 pitches have superb locations along the kilometre of shaded lakeside contained in Cisano. Some are on sloping ground and most are shaded but the San Vito pitches have no lake views. Both sites have a family orientation and considerable effort has been taken in the landscaping to provide maximum comfort even for the largest units. The support facilities are constantly upgraded, although visitors with disabilities should select their pitch carefully to ensure an area appropriate to all their needs (there are some slopes in Cisano). A pleasant family style restaurant (some road noise) also sells takeaway food and is accessed through a tunnel under the road. Excellent pools and play equipment, along with a children's club and animation in high season are all here. The friendly efficient staff speak English at both sites. San Vito is the smaller and more peaceful location with no lakeside pitches and shares many of the facilities of Cisano which is a short walk across the road. Each site has its own reception and Cisano's three pools with spa are great.

Facilities

Plentiful, good quality sanitary facilities are provided in both sites (9 blocks at Cisano and 2 at San Vito) including facilities for disabled visitors. Shop, bar, restaurant (open all season). TV in restaurant. Pleasant swimming pool. Play area. Fishing and sailing from site. Free windsurfing and canoeing. Boat launching and storage. No ball games allowed on beach. Dogs are not accepted (cats are). Motorcycles not allowed on site (parking provided). Off site: Indoor pool, bicycle hire and tennis 2 km. Riding 15 km. Golf 20 km.

Open

29 March - 6 October.

At a glance

Welcome & Ambience	✓✓✓✓✓	Location	✓✓✓✓✓
Quality of Pitches	✓✓✓	Range of Facilities	✓✓✓

Directions

Leave A4 autoroute at Pescheria exit and head north towards Garda on lakeside road. Pass Lazise and site is signed (small sign) on left halfway to Bardolina. Site is 12 km. beyond the Gardaland theme park.

Charges guide

Pitch	€ 8,00 - € 15,50
adult	€ 3,00 - € 8,00
child	free - € 4,00

Reservations

Accepted in high season only with deposit (Sat - Sat only). Tel: 045 622 9098.
E-mail: cisano@camping-cisano.it

The Lido campsite is on the Veronese shore of Lake Garda, between the well-known towns of Peschiera and Lazise. It is situated right beside the lake, which is known for its clear water. It offers modern efficient facilities, equipment for tents, caravans and bungalows. Our bungalows are brick houses with 4 beds and a terrace with veranda. Dishes, sheets and blankets are not supplied. Large swimming pool for adults and children. Marina for boats. We recommend low season for those seeking complete relaxation.

NEW: Fitness Centre.

IT6359 Camping Serenella

Loc. Mezzariva, 37011 Bardolino

A reader has recommended this lakeside site and we hope to include a full report in a future edition of this guide. Serenella is just outside the pretty resort of Bardolino on Lake Garda's eastern shores. Pitches are of a reasonable size and most have electrical connections. A range of watersports are available here, and the site organises a varied activity programme. Mobile homes and chalets for rent.

Facilities

Bar, restaurant/pizzeria and takeaway meals. Supermarket. Lakeside beach, swimming pool and paddling pool. Playground. Children's club. Entertainment programme in high season. Off site: Bardolino 1 km, Gardaland theme park, riding, cycle trails, Verona 35 km.

Open

12 March - 23 October.

Directions

Bardolino is on the S249 which runs along the eastern shores of Lake Garda. Site is signed from the resort.

Charges 2004

Per person	€ 3,50 - € 8,40
child (4-10 yrs)	€ 2,00 - € 4,00
pitch incl. electricity	€ 8,00 - € 15,50

Reservations

Advised for high season. Tel: 0457 211333.
E-mail: serenella@camping-serenella.it

IT6255 Camping La Quercia

37017 Lazise sul Garda (Veneto)

A spacious, popular site on a slight slope leading down to Lake Garda, La Quercia is decorated by palm trees and elegantly trimmed hedges. The security is very good, with passes used for most areas. Pitches are in regular double rows between access roads, all with electricity (6A). Most are shaded by mature trees, although those furthest from the lake are more open to the sun. Siting is not always easy but staff do help in high season. La Quercia, which can accommodate up to 1,000 units, has a fine sandy beach on the lake, with diving jetties and a roped-off section for launching boats or windsurfing (high season). Much of the activity centres around the newly renovated pool with its fantastic slides and the terrace bar, restaurant and pizzeria which overlook the entertainment stage. Another self-service restaurant serving traditional Italian food is located closer to the beach. The evening entertainment is very professional with the young team working hard to involve everyone – smaller children and some parents love it! The site is a short distance from the exquisite lakeside towns of Lazise and Peschiera, which have a wide choice of restaurants, and is a short drive from Verona, one of Italy's finest cultural centres where the open-air Opera in the Roman Amphitheatre is a unique experience. La Quercia has always been a popular site, even though its prices are a little higher, it does offer a great deal for your money, including a wide choice of organised activities and amenities, most free. Many of the courses require enrolment on a Sunday. The families we spoke to during our visit commented on how much they enjoyed La Quercia.

Facilities

The six toilet blocks are perfectly sufficient and are of a very high standard. Laundry. Supermarket. General shop. Bar, restaurant, self-service restaurant and pizzeria. Swimming pool, paddling pool and large, landscaped spa pool (small charge). Tennis court. Table tennis. Riding stables. Football. Aerobics and yoga. Facilities for boats on the lake. Scuba club. Playground with water play. Organised events (sports competitions, games, etc.) and free courses (e.g. swimming, surfboarding). Canoeing. Roller blading. Archery, climbing, judo, multi-gym. Volleyball. Minigolf. Evening entertainment or dancing. Baby sitting service. Internet. ATM. Free weekly excursion. Medical service. Off site: Supermarkets en-route to Verona. Gardaland and the enormous Caneva Aqua Park nearby.

At a glance

Welcome & Ambience	✓✓✓	Location	✓✓✓✓✓
Quality of Pitches	✓✓✓✓	Range of Facilities	✓✓✓✓✓

Directions

Site is on south side of Lazise. From north on Trento - Verona A22 autostrada take Affi exit then follow signs for Lazise and site. From south take Peschiera exit and site is 7 km. towards Garda and Lazise.

Charges 2004

Per person	€ 5,05 - € 9,40
child (4-7 yrs)	€ 3,00 - € 6,30
pitch	€ 9,95 - € 25,30
dog	€ 3,00 - € 6,40

Low season discount for pensioners.

Reservations

Are made Sat - Sat for certain pitches.
Tel: 045 6470577. E-mail: laquercia@laquercia.it

Open

10 days before Easter - 30 September.

IT6275 Fornella Camping

Via Fornella 1, 25010 San Felice del Benaco (Lombardy)

Fornella Camping is one of the few campsites on Lake Garda still surrounded by farmed olive trees and with a true country atmosphere. Parts of the site have lake views, others a back drop of mountains and attractive countryside. The 268 pitches are on flat grass, terraced where necessary and most have good shade, all with 6A electricity, 40 have water and waste as well. The owners speak excellent English and have family connections with the UK. This site has top class facilities for boat owners, having recently purchased the adjoining marina. There are two separate lake accesses for boats and windsurfers. The suberb new swimming pool complex includes a clover shaped swimming pool with a surface area of over 900 sq.m, a jacuzzi, water games and a paddling pool, all with lifeguard cover. There are 3,000 sq.m. of grassy pool gardens for sunbathing and a bar/café area. The owner describes animation here as 'soft' – lots of sport and activities with an emphasis on the environment and countryside, no loud speakers but live music in the evenings for campers. The well appointed bar and restaurant are located on the lakeside with a terrace offering splendid views over the lake.

Facilities

Three very clean, modern toilet blocks, well dispersed around the site, have mainly British type WCs and hot water in washbasins (some in cabins), showers and sinks. Facilities for disabled people. Washing machines, dryer and irons. Motorcaravan services. Bar/restaurant. Pizzeria and takeaway at certain times. Shop. Supervised swimming pool and paddling pool (15/5-15/9). Tennis. Table tennis. Volleyball. Two playgrounds and animation for children in season. Beach. Fishing. Small marina, boat launching and repairs. Off site: Bicycle hire 4 km. Golf 8 km. Riding 10 km.

Open

1 May - 23 September.

At a glance

Welcome & Ambience	✓✓✓✓	Location	✓✓✓✓✓
Quality of Pitches	✓✓✓✓	Range of Facilities	✓✓✓✓

Directions

From main SS572 Desenzano-Salo road on the west side of the lake, head for San Felice and follow signs.

Charges 2004

Per person	€ 4,60 - € 8,80
child (3-7 yrs)	€ 3,60 - € 6,80
pitch incl. electricity (6A)	€ 9,30 - € 16,50
boat	€ 4,50 - € 11,50
dog	free - € 5,90

Charges acc. to season and pitch location.
Various low season discounts.

Reservations

Made with deposit and fee; contact site.
Tel: 0365 62294. E-mail: fornella@fornella.it

TRAVEL SERVICE SITE

TO BOOK CALL 0870 405 4055 OR www.alanrogersdirect.com

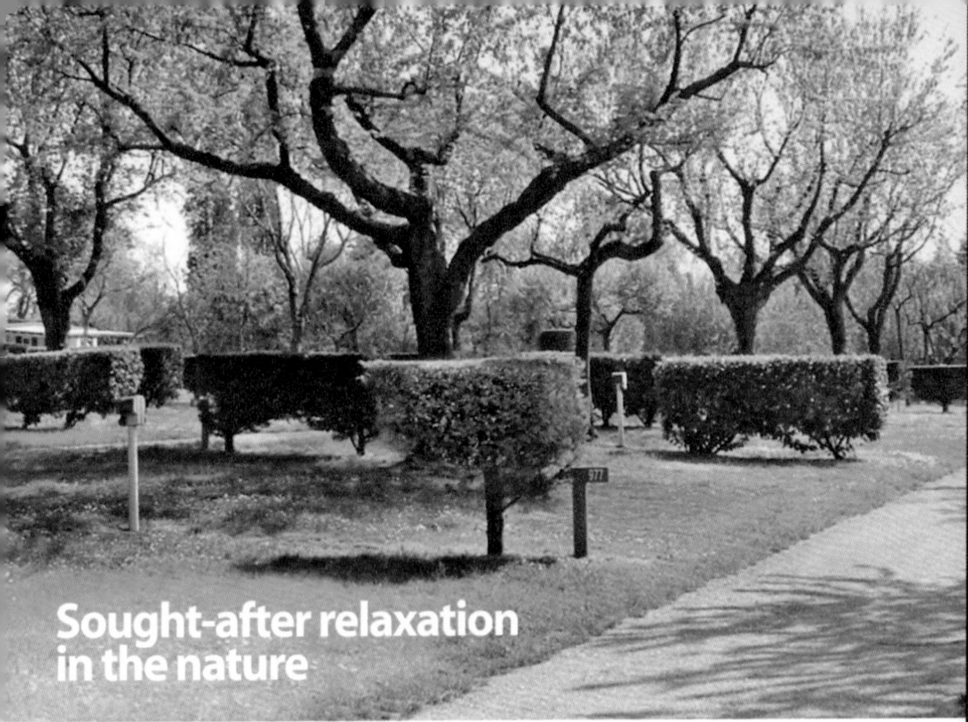

The Camping No. 1 of Lake Garda!

Enjoy a unique relax in the **Camping La Quercia,**
in a clean and safe environment with an exceptional comfort.
In the spirit of the true camping, we make people happy since 45 years.

If you wish a place where everything smiles on you,
discover our hospitality in the midst of Nature.

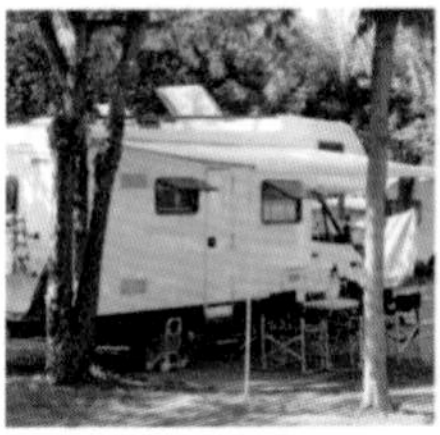

Shadow for everybody, in a place of extraordinary beauty.

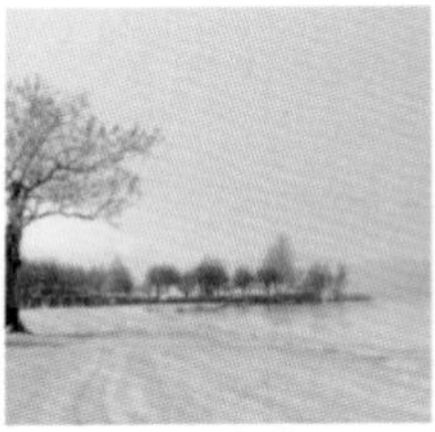

A very clean beach where one can play in all safety.

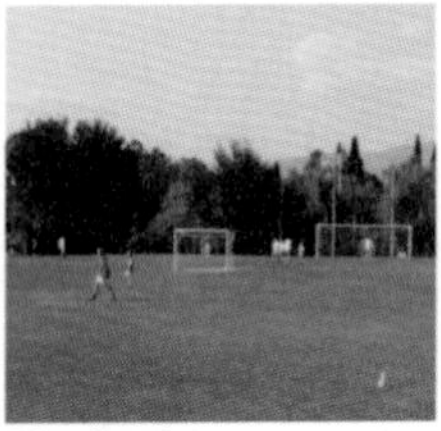

A lot of services for a vacation of true relax.

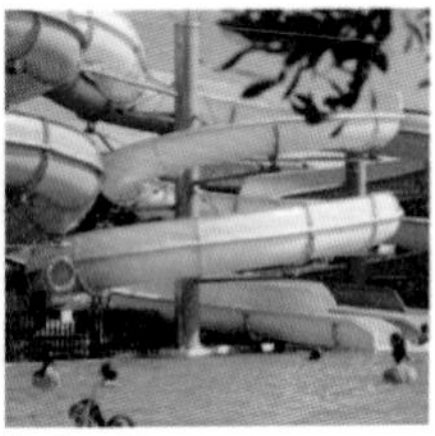

Try AquaFun, an exciting amusement.

Shady parking places – Warmed toilet services for both grownups and children – Warm water 24 hours out of 24 – Restaurant – Pizzeria – Cocktail Bar – Funny Bar on the beach – Swimming-pools and 'Maxicaravan'-slides with sight on the lake – Professional animateurs – Animation for both children and boys – Warmed underwater massage bath – Full-comfort bungalows for 4 and 5 people – The widest beach in the lake – Theatre – Supermarket – Butcher's shop – Pastry-shop and bakery – Typical products of the lake – Fresh fruits and vegetables all days – Tobacconist's shop – International news-stall – Rent-a-car service – Fax service Tennis – Canoes – Archery – Surfing – Judo – Football – Fitness hall – Fencing – Spinning – Horse-riding.

Reserve at once your relax vacation! Call now!

++39.045.6470577

• For Nation of origin at least 1.250 km away.

• For at least 14 nights stay.

• For stay of 3 nights:
from 19/03/05 to 13/05/05
from 29/05/05 to 25/06/05
from 04/09/05 to 02/10/05

For more information:
service@laquercia.it
www.laquercia.it/csa

CAMPING ★★★★ LA QUERCIA
...more than a camping!

LAZISE SUL GARDA
VERONA - **ITALY**

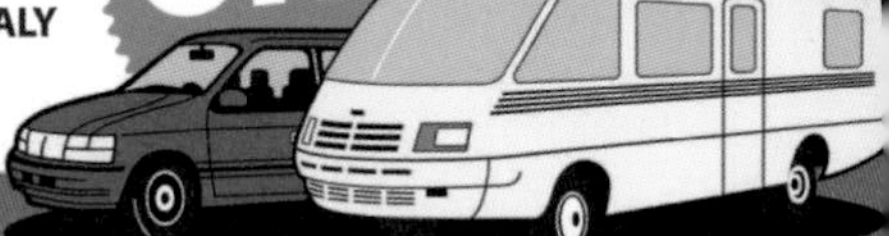

Information
www.**laquercia**.it
laquercia@laquercia.it

New! ***The only camp-site with V.S.C.***
Vehicle Safety Check *for cars and camper vans.*
Free check-up for: *Brakes, Suspension, Tyres, Lights, Windscreen wipers, Exhaust fumes.*
Immediate release of a safety certificate.

IT6263 Camping Bella Italia

Via Bella Italia 2, 37019 Peschiera del Garda (Veneto)

Peschiera is a picturesque village on the southern shore of Lake Garda and Camping Bella Italia is an attractive, large, well organised site, just one kilometre west from the centre of the village. In the grounds of a former farm, the site slopes gently down to the lake with access to the water for swimming and boating and to the lakeside public path which includes a series of fitness stations. Although about one third of the total area is taken by the site's own accommodation (apartments and bungalows) and tour operators, there are some 700 tourist pitches, most towards the lakeside and reasonably level on grass under trees. All have electricity (3A) are separated by shrubs and numbered on the campsite plan but not on the ground. They are grouped in regular rows on either side of hard access roads which are named after composers (east side) and artists (west side) of the wide central road which leads to the shops, pleasant restaurants and terrace and entrance to lakeside path. There are fine views across the lake from many parts. A feature of the site is the group of pools of varying shape and size with an entertainment area at the road end of the site. A range of supervised activities is organised. Regulations are in place to ensure a peaceful site particularly during the afternoon siesta and during the hours of darkness. English is spoken by the friendly management.

Facilities

The six toilet blocks are all new within the last few years and have British style toilets, free hot water in washbasins (some in cabins), showers and facilities for disabled visitors. Good provision for dishwashing and laundry. Washing machines. Motorcaravan services. Shops. Bars. Waiter service restaurant and terrace with splendid views across to the opposite shore and new restaurant in the old farm building. Swimming pools. Tennis. Football. Volleyball. Basketball. Playgrounds (small). Games and TV room. Watersports. Bicycle hire. Organised activities. Dogs are not accepted. Off site: Fishing 1 km. Numerous excursions possible and Gardaland, Italy's most popular theme park is about 2 km. east of Peschiera.

At a glance

Welcome & Ambience	✓✓✓	Location	✓✓✓✓✓
Quality of Pitches	✓✓✓	Range of Facilities	✓✓✓✓✓

Directions

From Peschiera exit on A4 (Milan - Venice) autostrada, turn left and drive through town to site 1 km. from centre, on the lakeside.

Charges 2004

Per person	€ 4,00 - € 9,00
child (3-5 yrs)	free - € 5,00
pitch	€ 9,00 - € 19,00

Four charging seasons.
No credit cards.

Reservations

Advised for high season; contact site.
Tel: 045 640 0688.
E-mail: bellaitalia@camping-bellaitalia.it

Open

Two weeks before Easter - mid October.

IT6265 Camping Ideal Molino

Via Gardiola 1, 25010 San Felice del Benaco (Lombardy)

Molino is a small, garden-like site with charm and character which may appeal to those who do not like the larger sites. A friendly family atmosphere is maintained at the site by the daughter of the original owners. Ingeborg is delightful and speaks perfect English. The family house, of which the charming restaurant is part, has a huge water wheel constantly turning which was used to crush the olives from the local area. This explains the name of the campsite and the old mill equipment can still be seen under the house, although it is now disconnected. The site is mainly on fairly level ground beside Lake Garda with a hill rising quite sharply behind. It is in two main parts divided by the site buildings, and pitches vary in character, some by the lake, some for tents on terraces, and many in rows with pergolas and flowering shrubs. All pitches are well shaded, have electricity, water and drainage, and can be reserved (in high season most advisable). The excellent restaurant has superb lake views and a huge lakeside barbecue operates twice weekly. Accompany these with the delicious local Lugana wines. A pleasant stony beach is at one end; elsewhere one steps straight down into shallow water. Boats can be launched and there is a floating pontoon for sunbathing and diving. The management does not like loud radios or any noise after 11 pm. A shallow stream runs along the western boundary and there is a pretty pond by reception.

Facilities

All three small sanitary blocks have been rebuilt to a very high standard, with automatic lighting and facilities for disabled visitors. British style WCs, individual washbasins with hot water and adjustable hot showers. Laundry (attended). Motorcaravan services. Shop. Restaurant/bar. Bicycle hire. Table tennis. Fishing. Water skiing. Free organised entertainment in season. Dogs are not accepted.

Open

16 March - 30 September.

At a glance

Welcome & Ambience	✓✓✓✓	Location	✓✓✓✓✓
Quality of Pitches	✓✓✓	Range of Facilities	✓✓✓

Directions

From Desenzano at southerly end of lake Garda follow S572 north towards Salô. Turn off towards lake, following signs for San Felice, then yellow signs bearing camp name. Watch for sudden stop sign on final descent to site! Site is about 4 km. outside Salô.

Charges 2004

Per person	€ 4,50 - € 7,70
child (2-10 yrs)	€ 3,90 - € 6,20
pitch incl. electricity	€ 9,60 - € 16,00

Discount for over-60s in low season.
No credit cards.

Reservations

Made for min 7 days from January with deposit.
Tel: 0365 62023. E-mail: info@campingmolino.it

The campsite Villaggio Bella Italia, surrounded by huge trees, is directly situated on a romantic beach of Garda Lake, only a few steps from the picturesque centre of the small town Peschiera del Garda. Here you can relax in a peaceful and green landscape or enjoy our professional entertainment program. **At Your disposal:** free windsurf courses, swimming lessons, aerobic courses, tennis lessons, cinema for kids, entertainment and plays, parties und funny evenings for everybody. **And much more.**

Via Bella Italia 2
I-37019 Peschiera del Garda (VR)
Tel. 0039/045640068 8
Fax 0039/0456401410
E-mail: bellaitalia@camping-bellaitalia.it
Http://www.camping-bellaitalia.it

GardaCamp
TO FAMILY, IN GARDALAKE

IT6256 Camping del Garda

Via Marzan 6, 37019 Peschiera del Garda (Veneto)

Although Camping del Garda is not directly on the lake (a cul-de-sac leading to a watersports centre runs between camp and water) it has access via a large gate to the beach and for launching boats. This is one of the largest campsites around Lake Garda and more a self contained holiday village. There are many trees, some providing shade on the 800 level grass tourist pitches which are back-to-back in 59 numbered rows. With access from hard roads and trees marking corners, all have electricity. Several days of heavy rain immediately before our visit prevented the mowing of some pitches but otherwise it was a neat, tidy site with flower beds adding to its attraction. It is within easy walking distance of the picturesque little town of Peschiera and the busy waterfront from where boat trips can be made. There are two large swimming pools (from 1/6) with lifeguards. A variety of sports is available, entertainment for children and adults are provided and there is provision for boat enthusiasts to launch boats.

Facilities

Eleven good quality toilet blocks have the usual facilities with free hot water in sinks, washbasins and showers. Facilities for disabled visitors in two blocks. Washing machines and dryers. Bars, restaurant and takeaway. Supermarket. Swimming pools. Tennis courts and tennis school. Minigolf. Watersports including windsurf school. Fishing. Playground. Full programme of organised activities in high season. Table tennis. Bowls. Dogs or motorcycles are not accepted. Off site: Gardaland, Zoo Safari, Verona, etc.

At a glance

Welcome & Ambience	✓✓✓✓	Location	✓✓✓✓
Quality of Pitches	✓✓✓✓	Range of Facilities	✓✓✓✓

Directions

Leave A4 (Milan - Venice) motorway at Peschiera exit, head towards town. Follow signs from roundabout.

Charges guide

Per person	€ 4,00 - € 7,00
child (under 5 yrs)	free - € 4,50
pitch incl. electricity (4A)	€ 9,00 - € 15,00

Reservations

Contact site. Tel: 045 755 0540.
E-mail: campingdelgarda@icmnet.net

Open

1 April - 30 September.

IT6284 Camping Belvedere

Via Cavalle, 5, 25080 Manerba del Garda (Lombardy)

Situated along a promontory reaching into Lake Garda, this campsite has been landscaped with terracing to give many of the 84 pitches a good vantage point to enjoy the wonderful views. There is plentiful access to the long pebbly beach for a relaxing swim and a dedicated area for boat launching. The delightful restaurant and bar with pretty flowers is under shady trees at the water's edge. The site has lots of grassy areas and alternated with attractive olive trees are others to give a cool canopy for campers. There are no facilities for disabled campers and young children would require supervision as the terracing is unguarded in places and there are steep slopes which may hinder the infirm. Italian villages with lots of atmosphere are close by as are the huge theme parks the area is known for. The landscaping and atmosphere are delightfully Mediterranean with charming Italian vistas. This is a good site from which to explore all the exciting sights the area has to offer.

Facilities

Five decent sanitary blocks are very much to the sites credit, however, with no facilities for disabled visitors. Shop selling basics. Restaurant, bar and takeaway. Play area. Full size tennis court. Music in bar. TV. Torches useful. Off site: Golf and bicycle hire 2 km. Riding 4 km. Fishing. Watersports. Theme parks. Bars and restaurant (limited menu).

Open

11 March - 9 October.

At a glance

Welcome & Ambience	✓✓✓	Location	✓✓✓✓✓
Quality of Pitches	✓✓✓✓✓	Range of Facilities	✓✓✓✓

Directions

From Desezano head north on road 572 towards Salo and take minor road to Manerba from where Belvedere is signed. Site is on road Cavadella along with two other campsites (San Biago and La Rocca).

Charges 2004

Per adult	€ 3,75 - € 6,00
child	€ 3,00 - € 4,80
pitch with electricity	€ 7,80 - € 12,00

Reservations

Accepted with a deposit. Tel: 03 65 55 11 75.
E-mail: info@camping-belvedere.it

IT6252 Camping San Francesco

Strada Vicinale, 25015 Rivoltella (Lombardy)

A large site is situated to the west of the Simione peninsula on the southeast shores of Lake Garda. The pitches are of average size, generally on flat gravel and sand and enjoy shade from mature trees. There are different standards of pitch from 'lakeside large' through 'superior' to 'standard' and all have 6A electricity. A wooded beach area of about 400 metres on the lake can be used for watersports and it has a jetty for boating. The sports centre, pools and entertainment area are all located across a busy road away from the pitches. These can be reached via a tunnel under the road located near the reception and car park area. Siesta is from 13.00 - 15.00 during which time reception is closed and there is no access to or from the campsite for campers' vehicles. On our visit we found there was a long queue to gain access after 15.00 (in low season). There may be some noise in the campsite from the adjoining holiday complex in high season however this should abate by 23.00.

Facilities

Sanitary facilities are in two large, modern, centrally located buildings. Very clean when seen, they offer every facility a camper could want with hot water at all points. Excellent facilities for disabled campers. Shop. Restaurant. Bar. Pizzeria and snacks. Takeaway. In a separate area across the road: swimming pools (15/4-20/9) and jacuzzi, sports centre, football stadium and tennis. Playground. Entertainment programme, organised activities and excursions. Big screen satellite TV. RC chapel in high season. Bicycle hire arranged. The busy reception will organise tours and ferry trips. Torches required in some areas. Off site: Riding 5 km. Golf 10 km.

At a glance

Welcome & Ambience	✓✓✓✓✓	Location	✓✓✓✓✓
Quality of Pitches	✓✓✓✓	Range of Facilities	✓✓✓✓✓

Directions

From autostrada A4, between Brescia and Verona, exit towards Sirmione and take S11 to Rivoltella. Site is well signed.

Charges 2004

Per person	€ 5,40 - € 8,80
child (under 6 yrs)	free - € 7,70
pitch incl. electricity	€ 11,30 - € 19,10
superior pitch	€ 13,30 - € 22,70

Reservations

Contact site. Tel: 0309 110245.
E-mail: info@campingsanfrancesco.it

Open

1 April - 30 September.

IT6010 Camping Village Capalonga

Via della Laguna 16, 30020 Bibione-Pineda (Veneto)

A quality site right beside the sea, Capalonga is a large site with 1,350 pitches of variable size (70-90 sq.m). Nearly all marked out, all have electrical connections, some have water and drainage, and there is good shade almost everywhere. The site is pleasantly laid out – roads run in arcs which avoids the square box effect. Some pitches where trees define the pitch area may be tricky for large units. The very wide, sandy beach is cleaned by the site and never becomes too crowded; a concrete path leads out towards the sea to avoid too much sand-walking. The seabed shelves extremely gently so is very safe for children and the water is much cleaner here than at most places along this coast. A large lagoon runs along the other side of the site where boating (motor or sail) can be practised and a landing stage and moorings are provided. There is also a swimming pool on site. Capalonga is an excellent site, with comprehensive facilities.

Facilities

The seven toilet blocks are well and frequently cleaned. Two newer blocks built side by side have facilities for disabled people and very fine children's rooms with basins and showers at the right height. British and some Turkish style toilets, some washbasins in private cabins and a whole wall of mirrors. Launderette. Motorcaravan services. Large supermarket. General shop for beach goods, cards, papers, etc. Self-service restaurant and separate bar. Swimming pool (25 x 12-5 m; 19/5-15/9). Boating. Fishing. Playground. Large playing field provides exercise stations, football pitch and a general area for ball games and there are play areas with equipment on the beach. Free animation programme with wide range of sport, fitness and entertainment. First-aid room. Dogs are not accepted.

At a glance

Welcome & Ambience	✓✓✓	Location	✓✓✓✓
Quality of Pitches	✓✓✓✓	Range of Facilities	✓✓✓✓

Directions

Bibione is about 80 km. east of Venice, well signed from afar on approach roads. 1 km. before Bibione turn right towards Bibione Pineda and follow camp signs.

Charges guide

Per person	€ 5,70 - € 9,80
child (1-4 yrs)	free - € 4,50
child (5-10 yrs)	free - € 6,50
pitch with electricity	€ 10,50 - € 19,00
pitch with water and drainage	€ 11,00 - € 20,00
boat	€ 6,50 - € 12,00

Reservations

Advised for July/Aug. and made Sat to Sat only, with large deposit and fee. Tel: 0431 438351. E-mail: capalonga@bibionemare.com

Open

1 May - 28 September.

IT6015 Camping Village Il Tridente

Via Baseleghe 12, 30020 Bibione-Pineda (Veneto)

This is an unusual site as only half the area is used for camping. Formerly a holiday centre for deprived children, it occupies a strip of woodland 200 m. wide and 400 m. long stretching from the main road to the sea. It is divided into two parts by the Residence, an apartment block of first class rooms with air conditioning and full cooking and bathroom facilities which are for hire. The 250 tourist pitches are located amongst tall pines in the area between the entrance and the Residence. Pitch size varies according to the positions of the trees, but they are of sufficient size and have electricity connections. The ground slopes gently from the main building to the beach of fine sand and this is used as the recreation area with two swimming pools - one 25 x 12.5 m. and a smaller children's pool - tennis courts, table tennis and sitting and play places. With thick woodland on both sides, Il Tridente is a quiet, restful site with excellent facilities.

Facilities

The three sanitary blocks, two in the main camping area and one near the sea, are of excellent quality. All have similar facilities with mixed British and Turkish style WCs in cabins with washbasins and facilities for disabled people. Washing machines and dryers. Motorcaravan services. The Residence includes an excellent restaurant, bar and well stocked supermarket. Swimming pools. Playground. Tennis. Table tennis. Mini-football. Volleyball. Animation programme includes activities for children in high season. Boats may be kept at the quay on the sister site, Capalonga (no. 6010), about 1 km. away. Dogs are not accepted.

At a glance

Welcome & Ambience	✓✓✓	Location	✓✓✓✓
Quality of Pitches	✓✓✓✓	Range of Facilities	✓✓✓✓✓

Directions

From A4 Venice - Trieste autostrada, take Latisana exit and follow signs to Bibione and then Bibione Pineda and camp signs.

Charges guide

Per person	€ 5,70 - € 9,00
child (1-4 yrs)	free - € 4,20
child (5-10 yrs)	free - € 6,30
pitch incl. electricity	€ 10,50 - € 18,00

Reservations

Contact site. Tel: 0431 439600. E-mail: tridente@bibionemare.com

Open

12 April - 28 September.

IT6020 Camping Union Lido Vacanze

Via Fausta 258, 30013 Cavallino (Veneto)

This well known site is extremely large but has first class organisation and it has been said that it sets the standard that others follow. It lies right by the sea with direct access to a long and broad sandy beach which fronts the camp. Shelving very gradually, the beach, which is well cleaned by the site, provides very safe bathing. The site is regularly laid out with parallel access roads under a covering of poplars, pine and other trees typical of this area providing good shade. These mark out the numbered pitches of adequate size (2,600 for touring units), all with electricity and 1,684 also with water and drainage. There are separate areas for caravans, tents and motorcaravans, plus one mixed part. The entrance provides a large off-road overnight parking area with electrical connections, toilets and showers for those arriving after 9 pm. An aqua-park includes a swimming pool, lagoon pool for children, heated whirlpool and a slow flowing 160 m. long 'river' for paddling or swimming. Covering 5,000 sq.m. this is supervised by lifeguards and is open mornings and afternoons. There is also a heated pool for hotel and apartment guests, available to others on payment. A selection of sports is offered in the annexe across the road and fitness programmes under qualified staff are available in season. The golf 'academy' with professional in attendance, has a driving range, pitching green, putting green and practise bunker, and a diving centre has a school and the possibilty of open water dives. There are regular entertainment and activity programmes for adults and children. Union Lido is above all an orderly and clean site and this is achieved partly by strict adherence to regulations suiting those who like comfortable camping undisturbed by others and good management.

Facilities

Fifteen well kept, fully equipped toilet blocks which open and close progressively during the season include hot water to all facilities, footbaths and deep sinks for washing dishes and clothes. Eleven blocks have facilities for disabled people. Launderette. Motorcaravan service points. Gas supplies. Comprehensive shopping area set around a pleasant piazza has wide range of shops including a large supermarket (all open till late). There are seven restaurants and several pleasant and lively bars. Aqua-park (from 15/5). Tennis. Riding. Table tennis. Minigolf. Skating rink. Bicycle hire. Archery. Two fitness tracks in 4 ha. natural park with play area and supervised play for children. Boat excursions. Recreational events for adults and children, day and evening. Golf academy. Diving centre and school. Windsurfing school in season. Church service in English in Jul/Aug. Exchange facilities and cash machine. Hairdessers for ladies and men. First aid centre, doctor's surgery with treatment room and ambulance. Dogs are not accepted. Off site: Boat launching 3.5 km.

At a glance

Welcome & Ambience	✓✓✓✓✓	Location	✓✓✓✓✓
Quality of Pitches	✓✓✓✓✓	Range of Facilities	✓✓✓✓✓

Directions

From Venice - Trieste autostrada leave at exit for airport or Quarto d'Altino and follow signs first for Jesolo and then Punta Sabbioni, and camp will be seen just after Cavallino on the left.

Charges 2005

Per person	€ 6,00 - € 9,00
child (under 3 yrs)	€ 3,50 - € 6,20
child (3-12 yrs)	€ 5,00 - € 7,80
pitch with electricity	€ 11,10 - € 20,30
pitch with water and drainage	€ 14,20 - € 23,40

Three different seasons: (i) high season 29/6-31/8; (ii) mid-season 18/5-29/6 and 31/8-14/9, and (iii) off-season, outside these dates.

Reservations

Made for the letting units only, but site provides 'priority cards' for previous visitors. Tel: 041 2575111. E-mail: info@unionlido.com

Open

1 May - 30 September, with all services.

IT6021 Camping Italy

Via Fausta 272, 30013 Cavallino (Veneto)

There are over 30 campsites on the Littorale del Cavallino between Lido di Jesolo and Punta Sabbioni and Camping Italy, under the same ownership as the better known Union Lido which it adjoins, is suggested for those who prefer a smaller site where less activities are available (although those at Union Lido may be used). The 180 tourist pitches are on either side of sand tracts from hard access roads under a cover of trees. Being on the small size (60-70 sq.m), they may be difficult for large units, particularly in high season when cars may have to be parked away from some pitches. All have electricity connections and some have water as well. There is direct access to a gently sloping sandy beach and a good, heated, pool. Strict regulations regarding undue noise make this a peaceful site and with lower charges than some, this a good site for families with young children where it is possible to book in advance.

Facilities

Two good quality, fully equipped sanitary blocks include facilities for disabled visitors. Washing machines. Shop. Restaurant. Bar beside beach. Heated swimming pool (17 x 7 m). Small playground, mini-club and children's disco. Weekly dance for adults. Barbecues are only permitted in a designated area. Dogs are not accepted. Off site: Sports centre 500 m. Golf or riding 500 m.

Open

20 April - 18 September.

At a glance

Welcome & Ambience	✓✓✓✓	Location	✓✓✓✓
Quality of Pitches	✓✓✓	Range of Facilities	✓✓✓✓✓

Directions

From Venice - Trieste A4 autostrada leave at exit for airport or Quarto d' Altino and follow signs for Jesolo and Punta Sabbioni. Site on left after Cavallino.

Charges 2005

Per person	€ 4,50 - € 7,10
child (under 6 yrs)	€ 3,00 - € 5,60
pitch with electricity	€ 7,60 - € 17,20
pitch with electricity and water	€ 8,10 - € 18,50

Three charging seasons.

Reservations

Contact site. Tel: 041 968 090. E-mail: info@campingitaly.it

1955
2005

UNION LIDO Vacanze

★★★★

30013 CAVALLINO - VENEZIA - ITALIA
Camping Park & Resort
Tel. Camping +39 041 25 75 111
Tel. Hotel +39 041 96 80 43
Telefax +39 041 53 70 355
info@unionlido.com - booking@unionlido.com
www.unionlido.it

CAMPING
PARK & RESORT

In 2005 Union Lido will be celebrating it's 50th Anniversary. All are welcome to join in the celebrations that will last all season. Union Lido is situated on the green Riviera of Cavallino, a tourist park between Venice and the Adriatic Sea.

Open from the 1st of May until the 30th of September.

Parco Turistico di Cavallino Treporti

The Leading Camping & Caravaning Parks of Europe

SINCERT UNITER CERTIFIED QUALITY MANAGEMENT SYSTEM ISO 9001

SINCERT UNITER CERTIFIED ENVIROMENTAL MANAGEMENT SYSTEM ISO 14001

MANIFESTO Turistico Ambientale VENETO

Make yourselves at home
Well equipped, level and spacey emplacements under the cover of pine trees and many other trees, for tents, caravans and campers. Very modern sanitary blocks, equipped for wheelchairs and a special corner for children too. Unbeatable offers on Bungalows and mobile homes, all with TV and many with air-conditioning.
Union Lido Park Hotel: is the only 4 Star Hotel in Cavallino, with it's own swimming pool, children's pool and whirlpool too.

Enjoy life the Italian way
The Gourmet Club of Union Lido - the 7 bars and 7 restaurants – offer a sensational range of delights, with traditional Italian and regional dishes, all of the highest quality.
Two Supermarkets with a large variety of products, numerous shops that satisfy every need from the latest bathing articles, daily newsagents to fresh fruit and vegetables from the local area.

Something for everyone!
Mini and Junior Club, Scout Camp (July and August), Football school for 6-15 year olds, day assistance and Crèche for the youngest and the Baby Disco.
Artistic activities, painting course, Top Model school, games and hobbies, diving centre, Golf academy, riding school, tennis, archery and a multi-sports ground.
Amphitheatre; concerts and musical entertainment.

Water is the element of life
Exclusive beach 1 kilometre long and 200 metres wide.
Water Park; 5,000 metres squared with a lagoon with slide, slow river, waterfall and whirl pools.

New for 2005
A second Water Park is in programme to celebrate the 50th Anniversary of Union Lido, it will be a very special attraction, especially with the white sand lagoon that is nearly 1000 metres squared!
There will also be a spacious and comforting Health Spa.
A European preview is in programme; of a new prototype of Mobile Home, built in line with bio-building principles.

Unlimited Free time
Experience the wonderful adventure of exploring the local lagoon area on your own bicycle, worth a visit no matter what the season. Choose from themany excursions around the Veneto Region or choose the charm of Venice itself.

The main birthday party will be on the 15th of May 2005.
Over 500 staff are looking forward to your visit.
The Anniversary Programme can be seen on our web-site: www.unionlido.it

Enter these co-ordinates into your Navigation System 45.28.03N 012.31.53 E and let yourselves be guided to the magical world of Union Lido!

IT6205 Camping International Dolomiti

Via Campo di Sotto, 32043 Cortina d'Ampezzo (Veneto)

Cortina is a large provincial town with many interesting shops and restaurants. A bus from outside the gate of the campsite will take you the three kilometres to the town centre. The strength of this site is its beautiful mountain scenery and quiet location in a grassy meadow beside a fast flowing river (no fences). The site is dedicated to tourers with 390 good sized pitches, most with electricity and about half with shade. There is a heated swimming pool on site, but otherwise it is a simple and uncomplicated site which makes a good centre for touring the Dolomites or for more active pursuits such as mountain walking. The site does not take reservations so arrive early in the day in the first three weeks of August to improve your chance of obtaining a pitch.

Facilities

The main toilet block is large and should be adequate. Some British style WCs but mainly Turkish. Washbasins have hot water sprinkler taps. A heated block provides facilities for disabled visitors. Washing machines and ironing boards. Gas supplies. Coffee bar and small shop (long hours). Swimming pool (1/7-31/8). Basic playground (hard base). Dogs are not accepted. Off site: Restaurant 600 m. Fishing 1 km. Golf 2 km. Bicycle hire and riding 3 km.

Open

1 June - 15 September.

At a glance

Welcome & Ambience	✓✓✓	Location	✓✓✓
Quality of Pitches	✓✓✓✓	Range of Facilities	✓✓✓

Directions

Camping International is approx. 2 km. off the S51 (Dobbiaco - Veneto), to the west at the southern outskirts of Cortina (site signed from S51 at turn off). The S48 travels west of Cortina to the A22 between Bolzano and Triste, however this road can be difficult to locate from Cortina (follow signs to Falzarego). This road (S48) has incredible alpine views as it travels over two mountain passes, however it is extremely slow between Cortina and Canazei due to the topography (chains required in winter).

Charges 2004

Per person	€ 4,50 - € 7,50
child (under 6 yrs)	€ 2,50 - € 4,00
pitch incl. electricity	€ 7,00 - € 9,00

Reservations

Not made; contact site for information only.
Tel: 0436 2485. E-mail: campeggiodolomiti@tin.it

IT6035 Camping Mediterraneo

Via delle Batterie 38 Ca, 30010 Cavallino-Treporti (Veneto)

This large site has been considerably improved in recent years and is near Punta Sabbioni from where boats go to Venice. Mediterraneo is directly on the Adriatic Sea with a 480 m. long beach of fine sand which shelves gently and also two large pools (one for adults, the other for children) and a whirlpool. Sporting, fitness and entertainment programmes are arranged and swimming in the sea is supervised at designated hours by lifeguards. The 750 touring pitches, of which 500 have electricity (from 4A), water and drainaway, are partly in boxes with artificial shade, some larger without shade, with others in unmarked zones under natural woodland equipped with electric hook ups where tents must go. Used by tour operators (145 pitches). This is an organised and efficient site.

Facilities

Eight modern sanitary blocks are of good quality with British type WCs and free hot water in washbasins, showers and sinks. Washing machines. Motorcaravan services.
Refrigerator hire. Commercial centre with supermarket and other shops with a restaurant, bars and a pizzeria near the pools. Swimming pool. Playground. Tennis court. Minigolf. Table tennis. Bicycle hire. Surf and swimming school. Regular monthly programme of sports, organised games, excursions etc; dancing or shows 3 times weekly in main season. Fitness programme. Dogs are not accepted.
Off site: Riding and golf 3 km.

Open

22 April - 25 September.

At a glance

Welcome & Ambience	✓✓✓✓	Location	✓✓✓✓
Quality of Pitches	✓✓✓	Range of Facilities	✓✓✓✓

Directions

Site is well signed from Jesolo-Punta Sabbioni road near its end after Ca' Ballarin and before Ca' Savio. Follow camp signs, not those for Treporti as this village is some way from the site.

Charges 2005

Per person	€ 3,90 - € 8,40
child (1-6 yrs) or senior (over 60 yrs)	€ 2,70 - € 6,60
pitch with electricity	€ 7,50 - € 19,10
pitch with 3 services	€ 8,30 - € 20,90
tent pitch with electricity	€ 6,00 - € 17,00

Four rates.

Reservations

Made with large deposit. Tel: 041 966721.
E-mail: mediterraneo@vacanze-natura.it

IT6030 Camping dei Fiori

Via Pisani 52, Ca'Vio, 30010 Ca' Vio Treporti (Veneto)

The Lido del Cavallino peninsula, stretching from the outskirts of Lido del Jesolo to Punta Sabbioni, has over 30 good sites directly on the Adriactic sea and convenient for visiting Venice and other interesting places in northeast Italy. Dei Fiori stands out amongst the other small camps in the area. As its name implies, it is aflame with colourful flowers and shrubs in summer and presents a neat and tidy appearance whilst providing a quiet atmosphere. The 420 pitches, with electricity, are either in woodland where space varies according to the trees which have been left in their natural state, or under artificial shade where regular shaped pitches are of reasonable size. Well built bungalows for rent enhance the site and are in no way intrusive, giving a village-like effect. About a quarter of the pitches are taken by static units, many for rent. Shops and a restaurant are in the centre next to the swimming pools. Nearby is the hydro-massage bath which is splendidly appointed and reputed to be the largest in Italy. The long beach is of fine sand and shelves gently into the sea. Regulations ensure the site is quiet between 11 pm - 7.30 am and during the afternoon siesta period. Venice is about 40 minutes away by bus and boat and excursions are arranged from the site. The site is well maintained by friendly, English speaking management.

Facilities

Three sanitary blocks are conveniently situated around the site and are of exceptional quality with British style WCs, well equipped baby rooms, good facilities for disabled people and washing machines and dryers. Motorcaravan services. Restaurant. Snack bar. Shops. Swimming pools and whirl pool. Fitness centre, hydro-massage bath and programmes (1/5-30/9) under the supervision of qualified staff (a charge is made during middle and high seasons but not in low season). Tennis. Table tennis. Minigolf. Basketball. Children's club and play area. Windsurfing. Organised activities, entertainment and excursions. Dogs are not accepted. Off site: Bicycle hire 2 km. Riding 4 km.

Open

22 April - 3 October.

At a glance

Welcome & Ambience	✓✓✓✓	Location	✓✓✓
Quality of Pitches	✓✓✓✓	Range of Facilities	✓✓✓✓

Directions

Leave A4 Venice - Trieste autostrada either by taking exit for airport or Quarto d'Altino and follow signs for Jesolo and then Punta Sabbioni and camp signs just after Ca'Ballarin.

Charges guide

Per person	€ 4,20 - € 8,50
child (1-4 yrs) or senior over 65 yrs	€ 3,20 - € 7,50
pitch with 3 services	€ 9,30 - € 19,80
pinewood pitch with electricity	€ 8,00 - € 18,40
tent pitch in pinewood with electricity	€ 6,60 - € 16,50

Min. stay 7 days in high season (4/7-29/8).

Reservations

Advised for high season (incl. Whitsun) and made for min. 7 days. Write for application form as early as possible. Tel: 041 966448.
E-mail: fiori@vacanze-natura.it

IT6032 Camping Cavallino

Via delle Batterie 164, 30013 Cavallino (Veneto)

This large, well ordered site is run by a friendly, experienced family who have other sites in this guide. It lies beside the sea with direct access to a superb beach of fine sand, which is very safe and enjoys the cover of lifeguards. The site is thoughtfully laid out with large numbers of unusually large pitches shaded by olives and pines. All pitches have electricity and there is a 10% tour operator presence. If you wish to visit Venice a bus service runs to the ferry at Punta Sabbioni, some 20 minutes distance. You then catch an interconnecting ferry which, after a charming journey of 40 minutes, drops you directly at Saint Marco Square after negotiating its way around the gondolas. A late return will mean a 2 km. walk at the end of a different bus service, but the night views of Venice from the sea are wonderful. Be sure to pay independently at the ferry rather than using the supposed cheap 'all-in' tickets which in fact are more expensive.

Facilities

Clean and modern toilet blocks are well spaced and provide a mixture of Turkish and British style WCs with facilities for disabled campers. Launderette. Motorcaravan services. Large shop providing most requirements. Swimming pools (May-Sept). Restaurant with large terrace offering rapid service and takeaway. The menu is varied and reasonably priced with some excellent shell-fish and pasta dishes. Pizzeria. Table tennis. Minigolf. Play area. Ambitious animation programme aimed mostly at younger guests. Dogs are not accepted.

Open

11 April - 11 October.

At a glance

Welcome & Ambience	✓✓✓	Location	✓✓✓✓
Quality of Pitches	✓✓✓	Range of Facilities	✓✓✓✓

Directions

From Venice - Trieste autostrada leave at exit for airport or Quarto and Altino. Follow signs, first for Jesolo and then Punta Sabbiono, and site signs will be seen just after Cavallino on the left.

Charges guide

Per person	€ 3,30 - € 7,30
child (1-6 yrs) or over 60's	€ 2,80 - € 5,90
pitch incl. electricity	€ 9,30 - € 18,50

Min. stay in high season I week.
No credit cards.

Reservations

Made for letting units only, but site provides priority cards for previous visitors. Tel: 041 966133.
E-mail: info@campingcavallino.com

IT6003 Centro Vacanze Pra' Delle Torri

P.O. Box 176, 30021 Caorle (Veneto)

Pra' delle Torri is another Italian Adriatic site which has just about everything! Pitches for camping, hotel, accommodation to rent, one of the largest and best equipped swimming pools in the country and a golf course where lessons for beginners are also available. Many of the 1,300 grass pitches (with electricity) have shade and they are arranged in zones – when you book in at reception you are taken by electric golf buggy to select your pitch. There are two good restaurants, bars and a range of shops arranged around an attractive square. The swimming pool complex is the crowning glory, but other amenities include a large grass area for ball games, a good playground, a babies' car track, and a whole range of sports, fitness and entertainment programmes, along with a medical centre, skincare and other therapies. The site has its own sandy beach and Porto Santa Margherita and Caorle are nearby. One could quite happily spend a whole holiday here without leaving the site but the attractions of Venice, Verona, etc. might well tempt one to explore the area.

Facilities

Sixteen excellent, high quality toilet blocks with the usual facilities including very attractive 'Junior Stations', units for disabled visitors, washing machines and dryers. Motorcaravan service point. Large supermarket and wide range of shops, restaurants, bars and takeaways. Tennis courts. Football field. Minigolf. Table tennis. Fishing. Watersports. Archery. Basketball and volleyball. Diving. Aqua gym, fitness programmes and keep fit track. Bowls. Mountain bike track. Wide range of organised sports and entertainment. Off site: Riding 3 km.

Open

3 April - 25 September.

At a glance

Welcome & Ambience	✓✓✓✓	Location	✓✓✓✓
Quality of Pitches	✓✓✓✓	Range of Facilities	✓✓✓✓✓

Directions

From A4 (Venice - Trieste) motorway leave at exit for Sto Stino di Livenze and follow signs to Caorle then Sta Margherita and signs to site.

Charges guide

Per person	€ 3,55 - € 7,95
child (1-5 yrs)	€ 2,45 - € 5,95
senior (over 60 yrs)	€ 2,60 - € 6,75
pitch incl. electricity	€ 6,80 - € 18,70
tent pitch	€ 4,75 - € 14,80

Min. stay 2 nights.

Reservations

Contact site. Tel: 0421 299063.
E-mail: torri@vacanze-natura.it

IT6022 Portofelice Camping Village

Viale Dei Fiori 15, 30020 Eraclea Mare (Veneto)

Portofelice is a typical Italian coastal site with a sandy beach and plenty of well organised activity. It is unusual in being separated from the sea by a protected pine wood with a gravel path between the two. It is of medium size for this part of Italy with 546 tourist pitches and 230 occupied by static caravans, bungalows and tour operators' accommodation. The pitches are arranged in rectangular blocks or zones in regular rows, separated by hedges from hard access roads and with either natural or artificial shade. Cars are parked in numbered places under shade at the side of the zones. All pitches have electricity and 224 also have water, drainage and TV sockets. The social life of the site is centred around the pool complex where the shops, pizzeria, bar, café and restaurant are also located. A wide range of entertainment and activities is organised.

Facilities

Two modern sanitary blocks have the usual facilities with slightly more Turkish style toilets than British. New toilet block for children (0-12 yrs). Facilities for disabled people. Shops. Pizzeria. Restaurant with good menu at reasonable prices and most tables on a covered terrace with waiter service. Swimming pools with an area specifically equipped for disabled guests, whirlpool massage and sunbathing. Playgrounds. Tennis, football, basket and volleyball, open spaces and a sandy beach. Bicycle hire. Organised activities for children. Activity and entertainment programmes, Off site: Riding 200 m. Golf 6 km.

At a glance

Welcome & Ambience	✓✓✓✓	Location	✓✓✓✓
Quality of Pitches	✓✓✓✓	Range of Facilities	✓✓✓✓

Directions

From A4 Venice - Trieste motorway take exit 'S Dona/Noventa' and go south through S Dona di Piave and Eraclea to Eraclea Mare where site is signed.

Charges 2004

Per person	€ 3,00 - € 8,40
senior (over 60 yrs)	€ 2,40 - € 6,80
child (1-5 yrs)	free - € 6,20
pitch depending on type	€ 6,70 - € 17,70

Reservations

Write to site. Tel: 0421 66411.
E-mail: info@portofelice.it

Open

8 May - 19 September.

IT6008 Camping Sabbiadoro

Via Sabbiadoro 8, 33054 Lignano Sabbiadoro (Friuli - Venézia Giúlia)

This is a large, quality site with a huge entrance and efficient reception. It has over 1,250 pitches and is ideal for families who like all their amenities to be close by. The local resort town is just 200 m. away and buzzes with activity in high season. The fine beach is 250 m. distant and safe for children. The pitches vary in size, are shaded by attractive trees and have electricity. The facilties are all in excellent condition and well thought out especially the pool complex. Everything here is very modern, safe and clean. You may wish to cover your car and unit to prevent sap covering it over time. A second site close by is opened for younger customers in high season – they use the main site facilities.

Facilities

Well equipped sanitary facilities include superb facilities for disabled visitors. Washing machines and dryers. Motorcaravan service point. Huge supermarket 12/4-29/9). Bazaar. Good restaurant and snack bar (31/5-29/9). Heated outdoor pool complex with separate fun pool area, slides and fountains (late May - Sept). Table tennis. Disco. TV Room. Internet. Play areas. Tennis. Fitness centre. Volleyball. Electronic games. Petrol station. Small boat launching. Range of entertainment in the main season. Dogs are not accepted in high season. Off site: Fine beach near particularly good for children. Windsurfing. Bicycle hire. Shops, restaurants and bars. Riding, sailing and golf 2 km.

At a glance

Welcome & Ambience	✓✓✓✓	Location	✓✓✓✓
Quality of Pitches	✓✓✓✓	Range of Facilities	✓✓✓✓

Directions

Leave A4 at Latisana exit, west of Trieste and head to Latisano. From Latisano follow Lignano road and then Sabbiadoro. Site is well signed approaching town.

Charges guide

Per adult	€ 3,90 - € 7,30
child (3-12 yrs)	€ 2,60 - € 4,20
pitch	€ 6,20 - € 11,40
pitch with electricity	€ 7,00 - € 12,20

Reservations

Made for min. 15 days with € 50 deposit.
Tel: 0431 71455. E-mail: campsab@lignano.it

Open

23 March - 29 September.

IT6042 Camping Alba d'Oro

Via Triestina s.s.14, km 10, Ca, 30030 Mestre (Veneto)

This well managed site is ideal for visiting Venice and the site's bus service takes you directly to the bus station on the west side of the city. There is always room here and on arrival you can select your own pitch. There is a separate area for backpackers and yet another for families. The 140 pitches, all with electricity, are of reasonable size and separated. The good sized pool is especially welcome after a hot day spent visiting Venice. The site has its own new marina (with crane) and if you wish to bring your own boat you can enjoy the pleasant 40 minute trip into Venice the easy way. The site is close to the airport and loud aircraft noise will be heard on some pitches especially to the east. However, as there is no night flying allowed it is worth staying here to be close to the city rather than driving to the sites in Cavallino and having the resultant long journey into Venice. The clientele staying here changes rapidly and is very cosmopolitan, with a very large backpacker element in new tents and mobile homes, but the site is not terribly noisy.

Facilities

The four modern sanitary blocks are kept very clean. One block has facilities for disabled campers. Sinks for washing dishes and clothes. Launderette. Motorcaravan services. Restaurant with a most pleasant terrace overlooking the pool and serving good food at reasonable prices, is very busy every night. Part of the same complex, is a lively bar with entertainment in season including pool parties and 'happy hours'. Pizzerias. Table tennis. Bicycle hire. Marina on site. Bus service 1 April - Oct. Shuttle bus to Verona for walking tour (Tuesday and Friday, 1.75 hrs).

At a glance

Welcome & Ambience	✓✓✓✓	Location	✓✓✓✓✓
Quality of Pitches	✓✓✓✓	Range of Facilities	✓✓✓✓

Directions

From Venice - Trieste autostrada leave at exit for airport and follow signs for Jesolo on the SS14. Site is on right at 10 km. marker.

Charges 2004

Per person	€ 7,00 - € 8,00
child (3-10 yrs)	€ 4,50 - € 5,50
caravan / motorhome	€ 13,00 - € 14,00
car & tent	€ 13,00 - € 14,00

Reservations

Contact site. Tel: 041 5415102.
E-mail: albadoro@tin.it

Open

1 January - 31 December.

IT6053 Camping Fusina

Via Moranzani, 79, 30030 Fusina (Veneto)

There are some sites that take one by surprise – this is one. This is old fashioned camping, but what fun, and we met English speaking people who have been coming here for 30 years. Choose from 500 well shaded, flat and grassy informal pitches or a position with views over the lagoon to the towers in Saint Mark's Square. With water on three sides there are welcoming cool breezes and fortunately many trees hide the industrial area close by. The site owns a large ferry car park and a 700-boat marina which accepts and launches all manner of craft. A deep water channel carries huge ships close by and the water views are never boring. Fusina offers a very easy and comfortable, 20 minute ferry connection to the cultural heart of Venice. Several site buildings, including some of the showers and toilets, were designed by the famous modern architect Scarpa. These are heritage listed and are visited by design students, although this listing makes development and improvement difficult. Those who don't wish to be disturbed by the lively bar can choose from the many waterside pitches on the far end of the site.

Facilities

Despite planning difficulties sanitary facilities are clean and appropriate, including well equipped new units for disabled campers. Many washing machines and dryers. Motorcaravan service point. Charming restaurant (no credit cards; English breakfast served). Shop (March - 31 Oct). Many of the staff are mature Australian/New Zealand people and English is used everywhere. Playground. Volleyball. Very lively bar entertainment. Boat hire. TV with satellite. Pizzeria and beer garden. Marina with cranes, moorings,and maintenance facilities. Air-conditioned London Cyber bus (really!). ATM. Torches useful. Off site: Excellent public transport and ferry connections to Venice. Boat trips along the Brenta Canal.

At a glance

Welcome & Ambience	✓✓✓✓	Location	✓✓✓✓✓
Quality of Pitches	✓✓✓✓	Range of Facilities	✓✓✓✓

Directions

From SSII Padua - Venice road follow site sign on road east of Mira, turning right as signed. Site is in Fusina at end of peninsula and is well signed (also indicated as 'Fusina parking').

Charges guide

Per unit	€ 14,00
person	€ 7,00
child (5-12yrs)	€ 4,00

Reservations

No need to book for motorcaravans or tents, otherwise contact site. Tel: 041 547 0055. E-mail: info@camping-fusina.com

Open

All year.

IT6050 Camping Della Serenissima

Via Padana 334/a, 30030 Oriago (Veneto)

This is a delightful little site of some 140 pitches (all with 16A electricity) where one could stay for a number of days whilst visiting Venice (12 km), Padova (24), Lake Garda (135) or the Dolomites. There is a good service by bus to Venice and the site is situated on the Riviera del Brenta, a section of a river with some very large old villas. Used mainly by Dutch and British visitors, with some Germans, it is calm and quiet. A long, narrow and flat site, numbered pitches are on each side of a central road. There is good shade in most parts with many trees. The management is very friendly and good English is spoken.

Facilities

The single sanitary block is just adequate with hot water in washbasins, showers and sinks. Mainly Turkish style WCs. Motorcaravan services. Gas supplies. Shop (all season). Bar. Restaurant and takeaway (1/6-31/10). Play area. Fishing. Bicycle hire. Reduced price bus ticket to Venice if staying for 3 days. No organised entertainment but local markets etc. all well publicised. Off site: Golf or riding 3 km.

Open

Easter - 10 November.

At a glance

Welcome & Ambience	✓✓✓✓✓	Location	✓✓✓✓
Quality of Pitches	✓✓✓✓	Range of Facilities	✓✓✓

Directions

From the east take road S11 at roundabout SSW of Mestre towards Padova and site is 2 km. From west, leave A4 at Dolo exit, follow signs to Dolo, continue on main road through village and left at T-junction. Continue on S11 for site about 6 km on left.

Charges 2004

Per person	€ 6,00 - € 7,00
child (3-10 yrs)	€ 4,00 - € 5,00
pitch and car	€ 10,00 - € 12,00

Reservations

Are made; contact site. Tel: 041 921850. E-mail: camping.serenissima@shineline.it

IT6283 Camping La Rocca

Via Cavalle 22, 25080 Manerba del Garda (Lombardy)

Set high on a peninsula, there are delightful views from this very friendly, family-orientated campsite. With 200 attractive touring pitches enjoying shade from the tree canopy which also protects the campers from the summer heat, this is a 'real' campsite (20 of the pitches have lake views). The director Livio is charming and very engaging with his pleasant, halting English. Located in the idyllic Gulf of Manerba on Lake Garda, near the La Rocca natural park, it has the choice of two pretty, pebble lakeside beaches which can be accessed from the site, and a very nice pool complex. Close to traditional Italian villages and modern theme parks there is something for everyone here. The site has a friendly family feel with all modern amenities without losing its distinctive Italian ambience. Nothing is too much trouble for the management.

Facilities

Two sanitary blocks with smart new units for disabled campers and baby changing areas which are kept in pristine condition at all times. Washing machines. Restaurant for basic meals with a pleasant terrace shared with the bar. Small shop for basics (town close). Swimming pools. Tennis courts. Play area. Volleyball. Table tennis. Bicycle loan. Fishing (with permit). Small boat launching. Music in the evenings. Mini-club in high season. Torches required on beach steps and tunnel. Off site: Bars and restaurants close. Theme parks. Fishing. Sailing. Golf 2 km. Riding 3 km.

Open

26 March - 2 October.

At a glance

Welcome & Ambience	✓✓✓✓	Location	✓✓✓✓✓
Quality of Pitches	✓✓✓✓	Range of Facilities	✓✓✓✓

Directions

From A4 autostrada take Desenzano exit and follow SS572 towards Salo. Take minor road to Manerbafrom where site is signed. It is on road Cavadella together with two other campsites.

Charges guide

Per adult	€ 3,80 - € 6,50
child	€ 3,00 - € 5,00
pitch	€ 7,00 - € 12,00

Reservations

Advised for July/Aug. (min. 1 week) with deposit. Tel: 0365 551 738. E-mail: info@laroccacamp.it

IT6054 Camping Oasi

Via A. Barbarigo 147, 30019 Sottomarina (Veneto)

Camping Oasi is a traditional, old style Italian family site, possibly suitable for an overnight stay. Many Italian families return here all summer so it would be a good place to practice your Italian language skills. There is an excellent marina just outside the campsite gates for launching boats. Pitches are small, flat and mostly shaded except closer to the beach area. A modest restaurant, shop and terrace are on the campsite and another small beach bar is at the fine grey sandy beach which is a long walk through the campsite and sports areas. The site has a good swimming pool with a small flume and a good sports area. There is a large characterless town nearby.

Facilities

Two older sanitary blocks each have one British style toilet but no facilities for disabled visitors. The numbers are low so facilities could get very busy. Good swimming pool and flume. Small play area. Sports area, beach volleyball, basketball, table tennis and boules.

Open

27 March - 30 September.

At a glance

Welcome & Ambience	✓✓✓	Location	✓✓✓
Quality of Pitches	✓✓✓	Range of Facilities	✓✓✓

Directions

Site is off the S309 near Chioggia. Follow signs to Sottomaria then campsite. Site signs can be a little unclear, but the turn off the busy road is at a set of lights. Continue 3 km. down narrow road to site.

Charges 2004

Per person	€ 4,50 - € 6,75
child (1-5 yrs)	€ 2,25 - € 3,50
pitch	€ 7,50 - € 15,50

Reservations

Contact site. Tel: 041 490801.
E-mail: info@campingoasi.com

IT6000 Camping Mare Pineta

Sistiana 60 D, Duino - Aurisina, 34019 Trieste (Friuli - Venézia Giúlia)

This site is 18 km. west of Trieste, and is on raised ground near the sea with views over the Sistiana Bay, Miramare Castle and the Gulf of Trieste. A pebbly beach, with a car park, lies just beyond the site, a drive of about a kilometre (a free bus service runs every 40 minutes from 9 am.-7 pm). Alternatively there is a large swimming pool (unheated) on site with a new terrace. The development of this site continues with modern reception buildings and improved sanitary facilities. Over 350 of the 500 individual pitches are available for touring units. They are on gravel hardstanding (awnings possible) in light woodland, all with electricity and with water nearby. Space is nearly always available (1-15 Aug. is the busiest). For arrivals outside office hours, a waiting area has water and toilet facilities. The Rilke footpath runs along the seaside border of the site. It is reported that a weekend disco on the beach below the campsite involves noisy vehicle departures at 3 am. The site is used by a tour operator.

Facilities

Six toilet blocks of varying quality, some recently modernised and extended, provide some washbasins in cabins and some for children (the hot water supply does not always cope with the demand) and WCs of both British and Turkish style. Facilities for disabled people. Sinks for laundry and dishwashing, most with hot water. Laundry with dryer and ironing. Motorcaravan service point. Shop (all season). Bars. Pizzeria with terrace. Disco. Swimming pool (1/6-15/9) with lessons. Playground. Facilities for football, volleyball and mini-basket. Tennis. Table tennis. Games room. Organised entertainment in season. Dogs or other animals are not accepted. Off site: Bicycle hire 500 m. Fishing 1 km. Riding 2 km. Golf 10 km.

At a glance

Welcome & Ambience	✓✓✓	Location	✓✓✓✓
Quality of Pitches	✓✓✓✓	Range of Facilities	✓✓✓✓

Directions

From west take Sistiana exit from A4 autostrada, turn right and site is 1 km. on right; from the east approach on the S14.

Charges guide

Per person	€ 3,90 - € 7,00
child (3-12 yrs)	€ 3,00 - € 5,50
pitch incl. electricity and water	€ 8,00 - € 16,00
pitch with view of the bay	€ 11,00 - € 20,00

Reservations

Made with 40% deposit and € 15.49 fee.
Tel: 040 299264. E-mail: info@marepineta.com

Open

12 April - 30 September.

IT6005 Villaggio Turistico Camping Europa

PO Box 129, 34073 Grado (Friuli - Venézia Giúlia)

This large flat site beside the sea can take almost 650 units. All the pitches are marked, nearly all with good shade, and there are electrical connections in all areas. The terrain is undulating and sandy in the areas nearer the sea, where cars have to be left in parking places and not by your pitch. There is direct access to the beach but the water is shallow up to 200 metres from the beach, with growing seaweed. However, a narrow wooden jetty is provided which one can walk along to deeper water. For those who prefer, there is a swimming pool near the sea and, on the site itself, a medium sized heated pool and smaller paddling pool. This is a good honest, improved site which is probably the best in the area.

Facilities

Six identical toilet blocks should make up a good supply, with free hot water in all facilities, half British style WCs and facilities for disabled people. Washing machines. Motorcaravan services. Large supermarket; small general shop (May - Sept). Large bar and restaurant/pizzeria, with takeaway (all season). Swimming pools (May - Sept; 10.00 - 19.00). Two tennis courts. Football pitch. Table tennis. Fishing. Bicycle hire. Playground. Dancing at times in season; some organised activities June/Aug. Dogs are accepted in a special section and in limited numbers. Off site: Golf 0.5 km. Riding 4 km.

Open

10 April - 26 September.

At a glance

Welcome & Ambience	✓✓✓	Location	✓✓✓
Quality of Pitches	✓✓✓	Range of Facilities	✓✓✓✓

Directions

Site is 4 km. east of Grado on road to Monfalcone. If road 35L is taken to Grado from west, continue through the town to Grado Pineta.

Charges 2004

Per person	€ 5,50 - € 8,00
child (3-12 yrs)	free - € 5,50
pitch incl. electricity acc. to season and location	€ 8,00 - € 16,00
dog	€ 2,50 - € 6,00

Less 10% for longer stays out of season.

Reservations

Advised for high season and made for min. 1 week from Sat. to Sat., with deposit in high season (50% of total). Tel: 0431 80877. E-mail: info@villageeuropa.com

IT6045 Camping Marina di Venezia

Via Montello 6, 30010 Punta Sabbioni (Veneto)

This is a very large site (2,300 pitches) with much the same atmosphere as many other large sites along this appealing stretch of coastline. Marina di Venezia, however, has the advantage of being within walking distance of the ferry to Venice. It will appeal particularly to those who enjoy an extensive range of entertainment and activities, and a lively atmosphere. The site's excellent sandy beach is one of the widest along this stretch of coast and has a pleasant beach bar. The main pool is Olympic sized and there is also a very large children's pool adjacent. Individual pitches are marked out on sandy ground, most separated by trees or hedges. They are of an average size for the region (around 80 sq.m). Most are equipped with electricity, and some have water and drainage.

Facilities

Ten modern toilet blocks are maintained to a high standard with good hot showers and a reasonable proportion of British-style toilets. Good provision for disabled visitors. Washing machines and dryers. Shopping facilities include a fish shop, sports shop and a shoe shop, to name but three! Several bars, restaurants and takeaway facilities. Swimming pools (no slides). Several play areas. Tennis, football, beach volleyball, windsurf and catamaran hire. Wide range of organised entertainment. Church on site.

At a glance

Welcome & Ambience	✓✓✓✓	Location	✓✓✓✓
Quality of Pitches	✓✓✓	Range of Facilities	✓✓✓✓

Directions

From A4 take Jesolo exit. After Jesolo continue towards Punta Sabbioni. Site is signed to the left towards the end of this road, close to Venice ferries.

Charges 2004

Per person	€ 3,95 - € 7,80
child or senior (under 5 and over 60)	€ 3,35 - € 6,35
pitch incl. services	€ 9,95 - € 19,00

Reservations

Essential for high season. Tel: 041 530 2511. E-mail: camping@marinadivenezia.it

Open

23 April - 30 September.

IT6401 Camping Villaggio dei Fiori

Via Tiro a Volo 3, 18038 San Remo (Ligúria)

Open all year round, this open and spacious site has high standards and is ideal for exploring the Italian Riviera or for just relaxing by the enjoyable, filtered sea water pools. If you prefer, there is a path to a secluded and pleasant beach overlooked by a large patio area. The beach surrounds are excellent for snorkelling and fishing. Unusually, most of the pitch areas at the site are totally paved and there are some extremely large pitches for large units (ask reception to open another gate for entry). There is ample shade from mature trees and shrubs, which are constantly watered and cared for in summer, and pleasant views over the sea from the western pitches. All pitches have electricity (only 3A) and there is an outside sink and cold water for every four. Some super pitches overlook the beach edge. The friendly management speak excellent English and will supply detailed tourist plans. Excursions are offered (extra cost) along the Italian Riviera dei Fiori and the French Côte d'Azur. Buses run from outside the site to Monte Carlo, Nice, Cannes, Eze and many other places of interest. This is a very good site for visiting all the attractions in the local area.

Facilities

Three clean and modern sanitary blocks have British and Turkish style WCs and hot water throughout with two private cabins in each. Facilities for disabled campers. Washing machines, dryer and irons. Motorcaravan services. Large restaurant with fine menu and extensive terrace with giant children's toys close by. Bar sells essential supplies. Pizzeria and takeaway (all year). Sea water swimming pools (one for children, and both with a small extra charge in high season) and sophisticated whirlpool spa (June-Sept). Tennis. Table tennis. Volleyball. Play area. Fishing. Animation for children and adults in high season. Excursions. Bicycle hire. Dogs or other animals are not accepted. Off site: Shop 150 m. Riding and golf 2 km.

At a glance

Welcome & Ambience	✓✓✓✓	Location	✓✓✓✓
Quality of Pitches	✓✓✓	Range of Facilities	✓✓✓✓

Directions

From main SS1 Ventimiglia - Imperia road, site is on right side of road just before town of San Remo. There is a sharp right turn if the site is approached from the west. From autostrada A10 take San Remo Ouest exit. Site is well signed.

Charges 2004

Per pitch incl. up to 4 persons	€ 24,00 - € 49,00
half pitch incl. 2 persons, no car	€ 17,00 - € 30,00
electricity	€ 2,00

Some charges due on arrival. Discounts for stays in excess of 7 days. Discount for readers 10% in low season.

Reservations

Contact site for details. Tel: 0184 660635. E-mail: info@villaggiodeifiori.it

Open

All year.

IT6403 Camping Baciccia

Via Torino 19, 17023 Ceriale (Ligúria)

This friendly, family run site is a popular holiday destination. There is always a family member by the gate to greet you, and Vincenzina and Giovanni, along with their children Laura and Mauro, work tirelessly so ensure that you enjoy your stay. Tall eucalyptus trees shade the 120 tightly packed pitches which encircle the central facilities block. The pitches are on flat ground and all have electricity. Baciccia was the nick-name of the present owner's grandfather who grew fruit trees and tomatoes on the site. The informal restaurant overlooks a large swimming pool and, as no frozen food is served, the menu is necessarily simple but is traditional Italian food cooked to perfection. There is a half size tennis court and boule as well as organised water polo and pool games. If you have forgotten anything by way of camping equipment just ask and the family will loan it to you. The beach is a short walk and the town has the usual seaside attractions but it is worth visiting the tiny traditional villages close by. This may suit campers who wish for a family atmosphere and none of the brashness of large seaside sites. Free shuttle service to Ceriale's beaches.

Facilities

Two clean and modern sanitary blocks near reception have British and Turkish style WCs and hot water throughout. Washing machines, dryer and irons. Motorcaravan services. Restaurant/bar. Shop. Pizzeria and takeaway. Two swimming pools (20/3-31/10). Tennis. Table tennis. 5-a-side football. Volleyball. Bowls. Play area. Wood-burning stove and barbecue. Internet point. Fishing. Diving. Animation for children and adults in high season. Excursions. Bicycle hire. Off site: Department store 150 m. Riding and golf 5 km.

Open

All year.

At a glance

Welcome & Ambience	✓✓✓✓	Location	✓✓✓✓
Quality of Pitches	✓✓✓	Range of Facilities	✓✓✓

Directions

From the A10 (E80) between Imperia and Savona, take Albenga exit. Turn left towards Ceriale and Savona, turning left after 3 km. at traffic lights and follow signs to site.

Charges 2005

Per unit incl. up to 3 persons (over 2 yrs)	€ 23,00 - € 44,00
extra person	€ 4,00 - € 8,00
half pitch incl. 2 persons, no car	€ 15,00 - € 29,00
dog	€ 2,00 - € 4,00

Discounts for stays in excess of 7 days.
Discount for readers 10% in low season.

Reservations

Contact site. Tel: 0182 990 743.
E-mail: info@campingbaciccia.it

IT6410 Camping Genova Est

Via Marconi-loc Cassa, 16031 Bogliasco (Ligúria)

This wooded site is set on very steep slopes close to the Genoa motorways coming from the north or west and, although it has very limited facilities, it is quite near the town. There is a regular free bus service to the beach in high season, or if you are extremely fit a set of steep stairs will take you there in 15 minutes. The Buteros who run and own the site both speak good English and are very enthusiastic and anxious to please. The approach from the main road twists and climbs steeply with a tight final turn at the site entrance. There are 54 touring pitches with electricity available. The small play area is set on a narrow terrace and children should be supervised. A pretty small bar and a little restaurant with a terrace give fine views over the sea. Torches are needed at night in several parts of the site. This is a site to be used for exploring Genoa and Riviera di Levante, rather than for extended stays.

Facilities

One of the two sanitary blocks provides free hot showers and en-suite cabins (WC, washbasin and shower). Washing machine. Motorcaravan services. Shop and bar/restaurant (both Easter - 30/9). Essential daily goods form restaurant. Towing vehicle available. Gas supplies. Site is not suitable for disabled people. Off site: Fishing 1.5 km.

Open

I5 March - 20 October.

At a glance

Welcome & Ambience	✓✓✓✓	Location	✓✓✓
Quality of Pitches	✓✓✓	Range of Facilities	✓✓

Directions

From autostrada A10 take Nervi exit and turn left (south) on the SS1 towards La Spezia. In Bogliasco look for a sharp left turn with a large sign for the site. Follow narrow winding road for 2 km. to site.

Charges guide

Per person	€ 5,00 - € 5,30
child (3-10 yrs)	€ 3,30 - € 3,60
caravan	€ 5,40 - € 5,70
small tent	€ 4,60

Less 5% for holders of the current Alan Rogers Guide.

Reservations

Contact site. Tel: 010 3472053.
E-mail: camping@dada.it

IT6414 Camping Arenella

Loc. Arenella, 19013 Deiva Marina (Ligúria)

Situated at the back of the town of Deiva Marina, Arenella is accessed from the A12 autostrada via a reasonable but twisting 5 km. stretch of road. The site is on a hillside amongst pines and there are some good views. There are around 70 pitches for permanent units with a further 50 pitches for tourists with electricity connections available. Cars must be parked in a separate area. The most interesting tourist option is a visit to Cinque Terre, five villages which can only be reached by rail, boat or cliff footpath. Their history is one of fishing but they now also specialise in wines. There are very pleasant walks and treks in the Ligurian woods nearby.

Facilities

Two centrally situated, and quite dated sanitary blocks have predominantly Turkish style WCs and free hot water in showers and washbasins. Small snack bar and shop (June – Sept). Free bus service to the beach.
Off site: Beach 1.5 km.

Open

All year excl November.

At a glance

Welcome & Ambience	✓✓✓	Location	✓✓✓
Quality of Pitches	✓✓	Range of Facilities	✓✓

Directions

Leave A12 autostrada at Deiva Marina exit and follow signs to Deiva Marina. Site is well signed and can be found to the right.

Charges 2004

Per person	€ 6,80 - € 8,00
child (under 6 yrs)	€ 3,40 - € 4,00
pitch and car	€ 6,80 - € 8,00
electricity	€ 2,00

Reservations

Advised in high season. Tel: 01 87 82 52 59.
E-mail: campingarenella@libero.it

IT6412 Villaggio Camping Valdeiva

Loc. Ronco, 19013 Deiva Marina (Ligúria)

A mature and peaceful site three kilometres from the sea between the famous Cinque Terre and Portofino, Valdeiva is open all year. It is situated in a valley amongst dense pines so views are restricted. On flat ground and separated, most of the 125 pitches are used for permanent Italian units. There are spaces for at most 14 touring units and on a terrace adjacent space for tents. With shade in most parts, the touring pitches are of varying size with electricity connections. Cars may be required to park in a separate area depending on the pitch. The site does have a small swimming pool, which is very welcome if you do not wish to take the free bus to the beach. The beach is pleasant and the surrounding village has several bars and restaurants. There are very pleasant walks and treks in the unspoilt woods of Liguria nearby or the most interesting tourist option is a visit to Cinque Terre, five villages, some of which can only be reached by rail, boat or by cliff footpath. Their history is one of fishing but now they also specialise in wines. Unusually some of the vineyards can only be reached by boat. We see this as a transit site rather than for extended stays.

Facilities

The toilet block nearest the touring pitches provides cramped facilities. There is a new block in the centre of the site. WCs are mainly Turkish, but there are some of British style. Washbasins have hot water and hot showers are free. Shop for basics only (15/6-15/9). Bar/restaurant with reasonable menu and pizzas cooked in a traditional wood fired oven (15/6-15/9). Small swimming pool. New play area. Table tennis. Electronic games. Excursions. Free bus to the beach. Torches required. Bicycle hire. Off site: Fishing and boat launching 3 km.

At a glance

Welcome & Ambience	✓✓✓	Location	✓✓✓✓
Quality of Pitches	✓✓✓	Range of Facilities	✓✓✓

Directions

Leave autostrada A12 at Deiva Marina exit and follow signs to Deiva Marina. Signs are clear at the first junction and site is on left approx. 3 km. down this road.

Charges guide

Per pitch incl. 2 persons	€ 14,98 - € 22,21
3 persons	€ 18,08 - € 29,95
4 persons	€ 21,17 - € 34,09

Reservations

Contact site. Tel: 0187 824174.
E-mail: camping@valdeiva.it

Open

All year.

IT6603 Camping Ecochiocciola

Via Testa 70, 41050 Maserno di Montese (Emília-Romagna)

Tucked away in the Apennines in a small village, this interesting little campsite is open all year and has many surprises. 'Ecochiocciola' (named for the camper after the snail wearing his house on his back) is being developed by the owner Ottavio Mazzanti as a place to enjoy the natural geographic, geological, botanical and zoological features of the area. Comforts such as the swimming pool are designed to enhance the experience. Ottavio speaks excellent English and there are mementos of his extensive travels in the reasonably priced restaurant, which serves Indian and German dishes as well as Italian. The 50 small touring pitches are on level or gently sloping ground with some terraces, many enjoying superb views. Ottavio has begun to develop many of his unique ideas into features which will entertain and interest his guests, including a guided tour through the adjacent 'didactic' park complete with illustrative boards, which analyse the environment. There is also an orchard with ancient fruits and a garden with kitchen and medicinal herbs. The region is only 60 km. from historic Bologna, the surrounding area is very pretty and there are many areas of interest nearby including the Ferrari gallery at Maranello. This is a peaceful site with a distinctly rustic feel for people who enjoy natural settings.

Facilities

Two mature but clean sanitary blocks have some British style WCs and coin-operated hot showers. Facilities for disabled campers. Washing machine. Motorcaravan services. Restaurant. Bar. Pizzeria. Games room, large multipurpose room for entertainment. Swimming pool with shallow area for children (14/6-31/8) with nearby barbecue and grill. Football, volleyball tennis and skating area. Bicycle hire. Torches necessary. Off site: Riding trails, guided tours and mountain biking. No shop on the site but the village is 300 m. Local bus stop in village. Riding 3 km.

At a glance

Welcome & Ambience	✓✓✓✓	Location	✓✓✓✓
Quality of Pitches	✓✓✓	Range of Facilities	✓✓✓

Directions

From tha A1 take Moderna South exit through Vignola, Montese, Sesta la Fanano, to Maserno di Montese. Site is 200 m. from the village, well signed.

Charges 2004

Per person	€ 4,00 - € 6,00
child (2-8 yrs)	€ 3,00 - € 5,00
pitch	€ 8,00 - € 12,00
electricity (6A)	free
dog	€ 1,50 - € 3,00

Reservations

Contact site. Tel: 059 980065.
E-mail: info@ecochiocciola.com

Open

8 March - 9 November and 20 December - 2 February.

IT6602 Camping Hotel Città di Bologna

Via Romita 12 - 4A, 40127 Bologna (Emília-Romagna)

This spacious site was established in 1993 on the edge of the Trade Fair Centre of this ancient and historic city and is very clean and modern. The reception is impressively efficient and friendly with excellent English spoken. Although near enough to the motorway to be aware of vague traffic hum, the site is surrounded by fields and trees giving a peaceful atmosphere. The intention was not only to make a campsite, but to provide high quality motel-type rooms for use by those visiting trade fairs. The 150 pitches are numbered and marked out by trees giving some shade. On level grass with hard-standings (open fretwork of concrete through which grass can grow) in two areas, there are electrical connections in all areas. You will always find space here as there is huge over capacity. Recent improvements include the closure of the poorly used caravan storage area allowing a potential increase to 300 pitches with associated facilities planned. This site is excellent for an overnight stop or for longer stays to explore the most attractive and unusual city of Bologna and Emilia-Romagna. Bologna is obviously not Venice or Verona but it has a beauty of its own, we think a visit is a must. There are 40 km. of porticos so you can even sight-see in the rain! In every corner there is something of historic interest. Talk to the manager Doctor Osti - he is an enthusiast.

Facilities

Modern sanitary blocks include excellent provision for disabled visitors (some British style WCs with free showers and alarms that ring in reception). Washing machines. Motorcaravan services. Smart bar with adjoining terrace where snacks are offered. Superb new heated and supervised swimming pool (free). Small play area. Table tennis. Football. Minigolf. Volleyball. Internet access. Medical room - doctor will call. Off site: Bicycle hire 5 km. Fishing 10 km. Bus service to city centre from site. Shops and restaurant 500 m.

At a glance

Welcome & Ambience	✓✓✓✓✓	Location	✓✓✓✓
Quality of Pitches	✓✓✓✓✓	Range of Facilities	✓✓✓

Directions

Site is well signed from 'Fiera' (fair) exit on the autostrada on the northeast of the city.

Charges 2004

Per person	€ 4,00 - € 7,00
child (5-9 yrs)	€ 3,00 - € 4,50
pitch incl. electricity	€ 8,00 - € 12,00

Reservations

Write to site. Tel: 051 325016.
E-mail: info@hotelcamping.com

Open

All year (except 10 days at Christmas).

IT6065 Camping Bungalow Park Tahiti

Viale Libia 133, 44020 Lido delle Nazioni (Emília-Romagna)

Tahiti is an excellent, extremely well run site, thoughtfully laid out less than a mile from the sea (a continuous small fun road-train link is provided). Flowers, shrubs, ponds and attractive wooded structures enhance its appearance and, unlike many campsites of this size, it is family owned and run. They have thought of everything here and the manager Stefano is a dynamo who seems to be everywhere, ensuring the impressive standards are maintained. The staff are smart and attentive. As well as the 25 x 12 m. swimming pool, there is a 'Atoll Beach' Caribbean style water-play fun area with palms, plus a jacuzzi, bar and terrace (small extra charge for 'wet' activities). A new 'Thermal Oasis' offers health and beauty treatments. The 469 pitches are of varying size, back to back from hard roads and defined by trees with shade in most areas. There are 30 pitches with a private unit containing a WC and washbasin. Electricity is available throughout and 100 pitches also have water and drainage. English is spoken by the friendly management, although the British have not yet really discovered this site, which is popular with other European campers. The site is very busy in season with much to-ing and fro-ing, but all is always under control – it is superb, especially for families with children. It is also keen on recycling and even has a facility for exhausted batteries.

Facilities

All sanitary blocks are of a very high standard, nicely decorated with plants and potted shrubs. They have a mix of British and Turkish style WCs and free hot water for washbasins, sinks and showers. The newest block has a baby room and make-up/hairdressing room. Large supermarket and kiosk. Two waiter service restaurants with extensive menus. Bar. Pizzeria, takeaway. Swimming pools. New fitness centre with beauty and fitness treatments. Several playgrounds and mini-club, bouncy castles and mini go-carts. Well equipped gym. Archery. Tennis. Floodlit sports area. Table tennis. Minigolf. Basketball. Volleyball. Football pitch. Bicycle hire. Electronic games. Free transport to the beach. Organised entertainment in outdoor theatre and excursions in high season. New 'disco-pub'. Daily medical service. ATM. Internet terminals. Torches needed in some areas. Dogs are not accepted. Off site: Fishing 300 m. Riding 500 m.

At a glance

Welcome & Ambience	✓✓✓✓	Location	✓✓✓✓
Quality of Pitches	✓✓✓✓✓	Range of Facilities	✓✓✓✓✓

Directions

Turn off SS309 35 km. north of Ravenna to Lido delle Nazioni (north of Lido di Pomposa) and follow camp signs.

Charges 2004

Per person	€ 4,50 - € 8,10
child (2-8 yrs)	free - € 6,10
pitch acc. to season and type and facilities	€ 8,20 - € 26,90
pitch with sanitary facility	€ 22,90 - € 35,90

Reservations

Made for min. 1 week (2 weeks in high season) with deposit. Tel: 0533 379500.
E-mail: info@campingtahiti.com

Open

3 April - 26 September.

IT6623 Centro Vacanze San Marino

Strada San Michele 50, Cailungo, 47893 Repubblica di San Marino

According to one guide book, the Republic of San Marino is 'an unashamed tourist trap which trades on its falsely preserved autonomy'. It has its own mint, produces its own postage stamps, issues its own car registration plates, has a small army and a unique E-mail address, but in all other respects, is part of Italy. However, tourists do seem to find it interesting, particularly those with patience to climb to the battlemented castles on the three highest ridges. Centro Turistico San Marino is 4 km. below this, standing at 400 m. above sea level and spreading gently down a hillside, with lovely views across to the Adriatic. This excellent, modern site has a variety of well cared for trees offering shade. The main grass pitches are roomy, on level terraces accessed from tarmac or gravel roads. Separated by hedges, all have water, waste and electricity connections, 10 with satellite TV connections. There are smaller pitches on lower terraces for tents. The irregularly shaped pool has an pretty flower bedecked island. There is a pleasant open feel to this site. There are mobile homes and bungalows to rent and the site is used by a tour operator (30 pitches). Make sure you visit the ancient city of San Marino at the top of the mountain. Despite scores of tourist shops it is very beautiful and there are some real bargains.

Facilities

Four high quality heated toilet blocks, kept very clean, are well located around the site with British and Turkish style WCs and hot water in washbasins, sinks and showers. Washing machines and dryers. Motorcaravan services. Gas supplies. Shop with limited supplies (all year, closed Tuesday in winter). Kitchen with fridge and gas cooker for campers and TV room (satellite). Attractive restaurant/pizzeria with good menu and pleasant terrace overlooking the pools (all year). Swimming pool (20/5-31/8) with jacuzzi and solarium. Several play areas. Games room with video games and internet point. Table tennis. Volleyball. Football. Archery. Boules. Tennis. Bicycle hire. Small amphitheatre for entertainment. Animation programme for children (high season). New central barbecue area. Bus service on market days and Sundays. Minibus and car hire at extremely competitive rates (local taxis are very expensive).

At a glance

Welcome & Ambience	✓✓✓✓✓	Location	✓✓✓✓✓
Quality of Pitches	✓✓✓✓	Range of Facilities	✓✓✓✓✓

Directions

Leave autostrada A14 at exit Rimini-Sud (or SS16 where signed), follow SS72 west to San Marino. Site is signed from about 15 km. This is the only campsite in the Republic.

Charges 2004

Per person	€ 5,50 - € 8,50
child (2-10 yrs)	€ 3,00 - € 6,00
caravan	€ 4,00 - € 11,00
car	€ 2,00 - € 4,00
motorcaravan	€ 6,00 - € 13,00
dog	€ 1,00 - € 5,00

Reservations

Write to site. Tel: 0549 903964.
E-mail: info@centrovacanzesanmarino.com

Open

All year.

IT6621 Villagio Camping delle Rose

Via Adriatica, 29, Gatteo a Mare (Emilia-Romagna)

Recommended by our agent, we hope to include a full report on this popular seaside campsite in a future inspection programme. Delle Rose is a large bustling site to the north of Rimini. A bus runs to the nearest beach. Pitches are mostly shaded, many with electricity. Mobile homes and chalets for rent.

Facilities

Swimming pool, children's pool, pool bar, sports field, restaurant / pizzeria, snack bar, supermarket, take-away meals, modern sanitary buildings, children's playground, table tennis, games room, TV room, children's club, entertainment programme in high season. Off site: Beach 1 km, Ravenna 35 km, San Marino 36 km, Rimini 16 km. Po Delta park 20 km, Atlantica water park 5 km.

Open

23 April - 25 September.

Directions

Take the Cesena exit from the A14 Bologna - Ancona motorway. Head east to join the SS16 and then south to Gatteo a Mare. The site is clearly signed.

Charges year

Per person	€ 4,20 - € 8,20
pitch	€ 9,00 - € 16,00

Reservations

Advised for high season; contact site.
Tel: 0547 86213. E-mail: info@villaggiorose.it

IT6600 Camping Barco Reale

Via Nardini 11 - 13, 51030 San Baronto (Tuscany)

Just forty minutes from Florence and an hour from Pisa, this site is beautifully situated high in the Tuscan hills close to the birthplace of Leornado da Vinci, and the fascinating town of Pistoia. Part of an old walled estate, there are impressive views of the surrounding countryside and pleasant walks available in the grounds. It is a quiet site of 15 hectares and 250 pitches with good shade from mature pines and oaks, Some pitches are huge with great views and others are very private. Most are for tourers, but some have difficult access (site provides tractor assistance). All have electricity and 50 have water and drainage. The site has an attractive bar, a smart restaurant with terraces (try the brilliant traditional dishes), and a leased shop (prices are a little high). The pools have really stunning views to the west (on a clear day you may see the island of Capraia) This is a most attractive and popular site, which will appeal to those who prefer a quiet site but with plenty to do for all age groups. In high season there is an information kiosk which supplies tourist information, makes bookings and help in general. Used by tour operators.

Facilities

Two modern sanitary blocks are well positioned and kept very clean. Good facilities for disabled people (dedicated pitches close by) and a pretty baby room. Laundry facilities. Motorcaravan services. Restaurant. Bar. Disco. Shop. Supervised swimming and paddling pools (caps required; 1/5-15/9). Ice cream shop (1/6-31/8). Play areas. Volleyball. Football. Chess. Bowls. Bicycle hire. Internet point. Tuscan cooking lessons.Entertainment and adventure park. Roman style amphitheatre for children's animation in high season. Excursions on foot and by bus (all season). No charcoal fires permitted. Off site: Village and shops 1 km. Disco and indoor pool 5 km. Fishing 8 km. Golf 15 km.

Open

1 April - 30 September.

At a glance

Welcome & Ambience	✓✓✓	Location	✓✓✓✓
Quality of Pitches	✓✓✓	Range of Facilities	✓✓✓✓

Directions

From Pistoia take Vinci - Empoli - Lamporecchio signs to San Baronto. From Empoli follow signs to Vinci and San Baronto. Final approach is around a sharp bend and up a steep slope. The drive from the autoroute is pretty but very winding and extremely time consuming!

Charges 2004

Per person	€ 6,70 - € 8,70
child (0-3 yrs)	€ 3,00 - € 4,00
child (3-12 yrs)	€ 4,00 - € 5,30
caravan	€ 6,20 - € 8,00
tent	€ 5,50 - € 7,00
car	€ 3,70 - € 4,80

Credit cards accepted for amounts over € 155.

Reservations

Write to site. Tel: 0573 88332.
E-mail: info@barcoreale.com

IT6624 Camping Villaggio Rubicone

Via Matrice Destra 1, 47039 Savignano (Emília-Romagna)

This is a sophisticated, professionally run site where the very friendly owners, Sandro and Paolo Grotti are keen to fulfil your every need. The reception area is most attractive, spacious and efficient, operating an effective security system and offering a booking service for local attractions including trips to Venice, Rimini and other places of interest. Rubicone covers over 30 acres of thoughtfully landscaped, level ground by the sea and has a large private beach where guests can enjoy the luxurious facilities, including free parasols. There is shade from poplar trees for some of the 600 touring pitches which vary in size (up to 90 sq.m). Arranged in back to back double rows, in some areas the central pitches are a little tight for manoeuvring larger units. All the pitches are kept very neat with hedges and all have electricity connections, 40 with water and drainage and 20 with private sanitary facilities. There are many bars around the site from beach bars to night club bars and the restaurant offers excellent food and efficient service at very reasonable prices. The animation programme is for both young and old and is staged in a circular terraced area near the main bar. The site has an amazing array of activities on offer (e.g. judo lessons) and many sporting opportunities including a smart modern double tennis court. Across the railway line (via an underpass) is a huge complex including excellent swimming pools for adults and children.

Facilities

In addition to the 20 private sanitary units, there are modern toilet blocks with hot water for the showers and washbasins (half in private cabins), mainly British style toilets, baby rooms and two excellent units for disabled visitors. Washing machines. Motorcaravan services. Bars. Restaurant, snack bar and excellent shop (from 10/5). Pizzeria (all season). Swimming pools (from 1/5; bathing caps mandatory). Play areas. Games room with internet access. Tennis. Solarium. Jacuzzi. Mini racing track. Water motorbikes. 'Powered' trampolines. Beach with lifeguard and showers. Fishing. Boat launching. Sailing and windsurfing schools. Gas supplies. Dogs are not accepted. Off site: Bicycle hire 500 m. Riding 2 km. Golf 15 km.

At a glance

Welcome & Ambience	✓✓✓✓	Location	✓✓✓✓
Quality of Pitches	✓✓✓✓	Range of Facilities	✓✓✓✓✓

Directions

Site is 15 km. northwest of Rimini. From Bologna exit the A14 at Rimini north and head for the S16 to Bellaria and San Mauro a Mare; site is well signed.

Charges 2004

Per person	€ 4,60 - € 8,50
child (2-8 yrs)	€ 3,50 - € 7,00
pitch (small, medium, large)	€ 9,80 - € 14,70
electricity	€ 2,10

No credit cards.

Reservations

Contact site. Tel: 0541 346377.
E-mail: info@campingrubicone.com

Open

1 May - 30 September.

IT6608 Camping Torre Pendente

Viale delle Cascine 86, 56122 Pisa (Tuscany)

Torre Pendente is a friendly site, well run by the Signorini family who speak good English and make everyone feel welcome. It is within walking distance of the famous leaning tower of Pisa (but via a dimly lit underpass). Obviously its position means it is busy throughout the main season. A medium sized site, it is on level, grassy ground with tarmac or gravel access roads and some shade. There are 220 touring pitches, 160 with electricity. All site facilities are near the entrance including a most pleasant swimming pool complex with pool bar and a large terrace. Here you can relax after hot days in the city and enjoy drinks and snacks or find more formal fare in the restaurant. This is a very busy site in high season with many nationalities discovering the delights of Pisa. It is ideal for exploring the fascinating leaning tower and other attractions.

Facilities

Three toilet blocks (two new) are clean and smart with British and Turkish style toilets with new facilities for disabled campers. Hot water at sinks. Washing machine. Motorcaravan services. Mini market. Restaurant, bar and takeaway. Swimming pool with pool bar, paddling pool and spa. Playground. Boules. Accomodation. Off site: Bicycle hire. Riding 3 km.

Open

1 April - 15 October.

At a glance

Welcome & Ambience	✓✓✓✓	Location	✓✓✓✓✓
Quality of Pitches	✓✓✓	Range of Facilities	✓✓✓✓

Directions

From autostrada A12, exit at Pisa Nord and follow signs for 5 km. to Pisa. Do not take first sign to town centre. Site is well signed at a later left turn into the town centre (Viale delle Cascine) and is then a short distance on the left hand side.

Charges 2005

Per adult	€ 8,00
child (3-10 yrs)	€ 3,50 - € 4,50
pitch	€ 10,00 - € 11,50
dog	€ 1,60

Reservations

Contact site. Tel: 050 561704.
E-mail: torrepen@campingtoscana.it

IT6611 Camping Il Poggetto

Via Il Poggetto 143, 50010 Troghi - Firenze (Tuscany)

This superb new site has a lot to offer. It benefits from a wonderful panorama of the Colli Fiorentini hills with acres of the Zecchi family vineyards to the east adding to its appeal and is just 15 km. from Florence. The charming and hard-working owners Marcello and Daniella have a wine producing background and you can purchase their fine wines at the site's shop. Their aim is to provide an enjoyable and peaceful atmosphere for families. All 90 pitches are of a good size and have electricity and there are a few in excess of 100 sq.m. for larger units. On arrival you are escorted to view available pitches then assisted in taking up that place. The restaurant offers some fine Tuscan fare along with pizzas and pastas. An attractive large terrace overlooks the two pools. A regular bus service runs directly from the site to the city (discounted tickets). English is spoken. There are plans to extend the site.

Facilities

Two spotless sanitary blocks with subtle piped music are a pleasure to use with a mix of British and Turkish style WCs, washbasins and showers. Three private sanitary units for hire. Five very well equipped units for disabled campers and pretty baby room. Laundry facilities. Motorcaravan services. Gas supplies. Shop. Bar. Restaurant. Takeaway. Volleyball. Swimming pools and jacuzzi (15/5-30/9). Games room. Table tennis. Bicycle and scooter hire. Playground and animation for children all season. Excursions twice weekly and organised trekking. Internet point. Off site: Tennis 100 m. Fishing and riding 2 km. Golf 12 km.

At a glance

Welcome & Ambience	✓✓✓✓✓	Location	✓✓✓✓
Quality of Pitches	✓✓✓✓✓	Range of Facilities	✓✓✓✓✓

Directions

Leave A1 at 'Incisa Valdarno' exit and turn left towards Incisa after 400 m. turn right on Sp1 road towards Firenze. Site is 5 km. at Troghi, well signed.

Charges 2005

Per person	€ 7,50
child (0-12 yrs)	€ 5,20
pitch	€ 13,00

Reservations

Contact site. Tel: 055 8307323.
E-mail: poggetto@tin.it

Open

19 March - 16 October.

IT6632 Camping Valle Gaia

Via Cecinese 87, 56040 Casale Marittimo (Tuscany)

Valle Gaia is a delightful family site with a friendly, laid back atmosphere, which is in marked contrast to some of the busy sites on the coast. Yet it is located just 9 km. from the sandy beaches at Cecina. This pretty site has two enticing pool complexes, both with children's pools and generous sunbathing terraces, and is just a short drive away from the mediaeval Manhattan of San Gimignano, Volterra and Siena. The 150 pitches are of a reasonable size (90 sq.m), well shaded by pine or cypress trees and surrounded by oleanders. Most have electrical connections. The bar and restaurant are both very popular, the latter located in a splendidly converted farmhouse and specialising in local cuisine.

Facilities

Three toilet blocks of modern construction are maintained to a high standard with mainly British style toilets. Some washbasins in cubicles. Washing machines and dryers. Shop. Tennis courts, 5-a-side pitch, table tennis and games room. Bicycle hire. Only gas barbecues are permitted. Off site: Shops at Casale Marittimo 3.5 km. Riding 4 km.

Open

3 April - 16 October.

At a glance

Welcome & Ambience	✓✓✓	Location	✓✓✓✓
Quality of Pitches	✓✓✓✓	Range of Facilities	✓✓✓✓

Directions

From A12 autostrada, take Rosignano Marittimo exit, following signs to Roma, joining the E80. Take Casale Marittimo exit and follow signs to the town. The site is clearly signed from here.

Charges 2004

Per pitch	€ 8,10 - € 13,40
adult	€ 4,30 - € 7,40
child (under 10 yrs)	€ 3,18 - € 5,43

Reservations

Essential for high season - made with deposit.
Tel: 0586 681 236. E-mail: info@vallegaia.it

IT6629 Camping Tripesce

Via Cavalleggeri 88, 57018 Vada (Tuscany)

Recommended by our agent, we plan to conduct a full inspection of this site in 2005. Tripesce is a popular Tuscan site with direct access to a sandy beach. The 240 pitches are well shaded and many are equipped with electrical connections. Tripesce runs a varied activity and entertainment programme, and even has its own diving school. Excursions are organised to nearby places of interest, notably Florence, Pisa and Lucca. Mobile homes and chalets for rent.

Facilities

Bar, restaurant and pizzeria. Takeaway. Supermarket. Playground and children's club. Bicycle hire, Riding. Tennis. Sports field. Entertainment programme in high season. Excursions. Direct beach access. Off site: Florence, Siena, San Gimignano, Lucca, Cecina 10 km (nearest town with a range of restaurants and shops).

Open

19 March - 22 October.

Directions

Leave the S1 (Livorno - Grossetto road) at the Vada exit (south of Rossignano Maritimo, and follow signs to Vada, from where the site is well indicated.

Charges year

Per person	€ 4,00 - € 7,00
pitch incl. 5A electricity	€ 9,00 - € 13,00

Reservations

Advised for high season; contact site.
Tel: 0586 788167. Email : info@campingtripesce.com

IT6636 Camping Le Capanne

Via Aurelia km 273, 57020 Bibbona (Tuscany)

Marina di Bibbona is a relatively little known resort situated a little to the south of Livorno and close to the better known resort of Cecina. The area retains much charm and a number of popular beaches are close at hand. The site's new owners have some ambitious development plans, many of which are already fulfilled. The site is very easily accessed from the main S1 Via Aurelia road (Livorno - Rome). There are 320 good sized pitches, most with electricity. They are nearly all well shaded by pine, olive and eucalyptus trees. A modern mobile home area has a sunnier, more open setting with around 75 pitches taken up with mobile homes or chalets belonging to the site or to tour operators.

Facilities

Toilet blocks are of a traditional design but kept clean, with plenty of hot water and toilets of mixed British and Turkish style. Dishwashing and laundry sinks. Washing machines. Mini-market and 'bazaar'. Bar and popular restaurant away from camping area near site entrance specialising in Tuscan cuisine. Large swimming pool and large play area. Bicycle hire. Entertainment programme in high season. Off site: Beach 2 km. with bus from the site in high season. Riding 2 km. Fishing 2.5 km.

At a glance

Welcome & Ambience	✓✓✓✓	Location	✓✓✓✓
Quality of Pitches	✓✓✓✓	Range of Facilities	✓✓✓✓

Directions

Take A12 autostrada (Livorno - Rosignano Marittimo) to its end and join the Via Aurelia (S1) heading south. Exit at Bibbona and follow signs to the campsite.

Charges 2004

Per person	€ 4,50 - € 8,30
pitch (incl. electricity)	€ 7,80 - € 13,60

No credit cards.

Reservations

Necessary for the high season. Tel: 0586 600 064. E-mail: info@campinglecapanne.it

Open

1 April - 30 September.

IT6641 Blucamp

57021 Campiglia Marittima (Tuscany)

Blucamp is a simple site in a tranquil setting near the pretty village of Campiglia Marittima. The famous islands of Elba and Capraia can be sighted whilst checking in at the reception block, and there are fabulous views over green hills and the sea from some of the upper pitches. The 100 small pitches (all with 3A electricity, 6 fully serviced) are terraced and on steep slopes; one area is for tents only and has the most amazing views. There is a tractor (free) to help you install your unit if required (this site is not really suitable for very large units). Cars are parked off the pitches in numbered bays. All pitches have young trees that provide some shade but others are more open. It is busy in high season, but is very quietly situated, 8 km. back from the sea, just 700 m. from the medieval village of Campiglia Marittima. As the site is set so high it catches any welcome cool breezes. The local area has a history of Etruscan metal mining, with the fascinating miner's castle of the Temperino Valley, or walk in the footsteps of the Etruscan civilisation in the grotto tombs of Populonia. There is a ferry to Elba and Corsica 19 km. away.

Facilities

Two satisfactory toilet blocks have British and Turkish style WCs, individual washbasins with cold water and free hot showers. Six private sanitary units for hire. Washing machine. Small friendly restaurant/bar. Attractive medium-sized swimming pool. Electronic games. Table tennis. Internet. Torches required in some areas. Off site: Riding 2 km. Fishing 8 km.

Open

17 May - 7 September.

At a glance

Welcome & Ambience	✓✓✓✓	Location	✓✓✓✓
Quality of Pitches	✓✓✓	Range of Facilities	✓✓✓

Directions

Take exit for S. Vincenzo Sud off the main S1 road Livono to Follonica. Follow signs for Campiglia Marittima then follow camping signs from the town. Site is about 1 km. from the town.

Charges 2004

Per person	€ 7,50
child (0-8 yrs)	€ 5,15
pitch	€ 9,60 - € 13,80

Less 30% outside July/Aug.

Reservations

Made with deposit; contact site. Tel: 0565 838553. E-mail: info@blucamp.it

IT6662 Camping Le Marze

Strada Provinciale 158, km 30,200, 58046 Marina di Grosseto (Tuscany)

This natural site is four kilometres north of Marina di Grosseto and has 180 generously sized pitches for touring units. Separated by hedges, all have electricity and most enjoy natural shade from mature pine trees. On sand and with easy access, there is a background noise of 'cicadas' (crickets) from the lofty pines and squirrels entertain high above. A private beach is across the main road. Bicycles are an asset and you could also enjoy a cycle ride to the town along a beach track. The beach is worth the walk as it is the strongest feature here, being soft sand which shelves slowly. There are secluded dunes, and a lifeguard. The beach bar is excellent and operates as a disco at night thus protecting the site from noise. The site layout is circular with the restaurant, bar and shop complex in the centre. Two identical swimming pools are unusual in that they are in supported structures above ground (1.3 m. deep) in order to not impact on the environment. Le Marze is well placed to visit local Etruscan villages, such as Ventulania and Roselle, or Pienza, a late Romanesque town created by Pope Pio II. There is a large tour operator presence but these are on the outer ring of the site and not intrusive.

Facilities

The four toilet blocks are of a high standard, two of them new, with British style WCs. Facilities for disabled campers in the new blocks along with baby facilities and private bathrooms. Motorcaravan service point. Market with amazing choice of goods and a bazaar alongside. Bar, restaurant, pizzeria and takeaway. Swimming pools. Aqua-aerobics and watersports. Two play areas. Ambitious entertainment programme in season, excursions and activities including gym with a personal trainer (extra charge). Barbecue areas. Evening entertainment. Bicycle hire. Torches required in some areas. Off site: Riding and boat launching 3 km. Golf 5 km.

At a glance

Welcome & Ambience	✓✓✓	Location	✓✓✓✓
Quality of Pitches	✓✓✓✓	Range of Facilities	✓✓✓✓

Directions

Camping Le Marze is on the road between Castiglione delle Pescaia and Marina di Grosseto, known as the SS322 or SP158 in places. Site is well signed on the west side of the road about 3 km. from Marina di Grosseto.

Charges 2004

Per person	€ 5,90 - € 9,90
child (2-12 yrs)	€ 3,50 - € 5,40
pitch	€ 8,10 - € 13,40

Reservations

Contact site. Tel: 0564 35501.
E-mail: lemarze@ecvacanze.it

Open

1 May - 3 October.

IT6665 Camping Le Soline

Via delle Soline, 51, 53010 Casciano di Murlo (Tuscany)

Le Soline is a country hillside site with wonderful views of the Tuscan hills from its steep slopes. Just 20 km. south of Siena and 800 m. from the village of Casciano, it has 80 neat pitches for large units and 60 tents on seven terraces with electricity. Many trees including olives provide shade for the pitches, most having views. There is a full entertainment programme in high season and some free guided tours of the area. The kind and attentive Broggini family spare no efforts in making your stay a pleasant memory. The restaurant has an excellent menu and the terraces look over the pool to the hills beyond.

Facilities

A good quality, heated toilet block on the third terrace has mixed British and Turkish style WCs, facilities for disabled campers and hot water in basins but showers are on payment. Motorcaravan services. Gas. Laundry. Restaurant. Pizzeria (all season). Shop (15/3-10/11). Swimming pools (Easter-15/10). Playground. Bicycle hire. Organised excursions (June-Aug). Barbecue area (not on pitches). Off site: Riding 600 m. Bicycle hire 1 km. Fishing 3 km.

At a glance

Welcome & Ambience	✓✓✓✓	Location	✓✓✓✓
Quality of Pitches	✓✓✓✓	Range of Facilities	✓✓✓✓

Directions

From Siena, turn off SS223 (Siena - Grosseto) left to Fontazzi (20 km.) and keep right for Casciano.

Charges 2004

Per person	€ 5,00 - € 7,00
pitch incl. electricity	€ 8,50 - € 9,50

Reservations

Contact site. Tel: 0577 817410.
E-mail: camping@lesoline.it

Open

All year.

IT6645 Parco Delle Piscine

Via del Bagno Santo 29, 53047 Sarteano (Tuscany)

On the spur of Monte Cetona, Sarteano is a spa, and this large smart site utilises that spa in its very open environs. The novel feature here is the three unique swimming pools fed by the natural thermo-mineral springs. These springs have been known since antiquity as 'del Bagno Santo' which flows at a constant temperature of about 24 degrees. Two of these pools (the largest is superb with water cascade and hydro-massage, and the other large shallow pool is just for children) are set in a huge park-like ground with many picnic tables. They are free to all those staying on the site. A third excellent pool is on the campsite itself and is opened in the main season for the exclusive use of campers. A very big building alongside the spa-pool houses a select restaurant on the first floor and a pizzeria on the second floor, the terrace gives fine views over the local area. There are 450 individual, flat pitches, all of good size and fully marked with high neat hedges giving really private pitches. Delle Piscine is really good as a sight-seeing base or as an overnight stop from the Florence - Rome motorway (it is 6 km. from the exit). Access to the attractive town is directly outside the site gate and it is worth exploring, especially the massive fortress with its drawbridge (straight out of a toy-box!) This spacious site is well run with an excellent infrastructure and there is a friendly welcome from the English speaking staff.

Facilities

Two heated toilet blocks are of high quality with mainly British style WCs and numerous sinks for laundry and dishwashing (with hot water). Motorcaravan services. Restaurant/pizzeria/bar. Takeaway. Coffee bar. Newspaper kiosk. Swimming pools (one all season). TV room, satellite TV room and mini-cinema with 100 seats and a very large screen. Tennis. Soccer field. Table tennis. Exchange facilities. Free guided cultural tours. Internet. Gas supplies. Dogs are not accepted. Off site: Bicycle hire 100 m. Riding 3 km.

Open

1 April - 30 September.

At a glance

Welcome & Ambience	✓✓✓✓	Location	✓✓✓✓
Quality of Pitches	✓✓✓✓✓	Range of Facilities	✓✓✓✓

Directions

From autostrada A1 take exit for Chiusi and Chianciano, from where Sarteano is well signed (6 km). In town of Sarteano follow camping signs to site (entrance sign reads Piscine di Sarteano).

Charges 2004

Per adult	€ 9,50 - € 12,00
child (3-10 yrs)	€ 5,50 - € 7,50
tent or caravan	€ 9,50 - € 12,00
car	€ 3,50 - € 6,00
motorcaravan	€ 13,00 - € 18,00
electricity	€ 3,50

Reservations

Write to site, or book by e-mail. Tel: 0578 26971. E-mail: info@bagnosanto.it

IT6660 Camping Maremma Sans Souci

58043 Castiglione della Pescaia (Tuscany)

This delightful seaside site is owned and run by the Perduca family and sits in natural woodland on the coast between Livorno and Rome. Only 3 km. from Castiglione della Pescaia, a lively holiday town with an old walled village and castle at the centre, it is on a small cliff overlooking a marina. Maremma Sans Souci has a welcoming and relaxing atmosphere. The minimum amount of undergrowth has been cleared to provide 400 individually marked and hedged, flat pitches for camping enthusiasts. This offers considerable privacy in individual settings. A positive feature of this site is that there are no seasonal pitches. Some pitches are small and cars may not remain with tents or caravans but must go to a numbered, shaded and secure car park near the entrance. There is a wide road for motorcaravans but other roads are mostly narrow and bordered by trees (this is a protected area, and they cannot fell the trees). Access to some parts is difficult so each pitch is earmarked either for caravans or for tents. There are electrical connections for all caravan pitches. An excellent sandy beach is less than 100 m. from one end of the site (400 m. from the other) and is used only by campers. The restaurant with several terraces is in the centre of the site and offers outstanding Italian food at extremely good prices along with a fine choice of wines. Maremma is a most friendly site right by the sea which should appeal to many people who like a relaxed style of camping in a comfortable woodland setting with a real personal touch.

Facilities

Five small, very clean, mature toilet blocks are well situated around the site. Free showers and hot water at the sinks, plus lots of little extras such as hair dryers and soap dispensers, etc. Three blocks have additional private cabins each with WC, basin and shower and there are separate facilities for disabled campers. Washing machines. Motorcaravan services. Laundry. Doctor's surgery and facilities for disabled visitors. Shop. Excellent restaurant (self service in season) serving a range of local fish and fresh pasta. Bar with pizzas and other snacks. Well stocked shop. Free freezer. Volleyball. Car wash. Sailing school. Torches required in some areas. Dogs are not accepted between 16/6-31/8. Off site: Excursions organised to Elba and Rome.

At a glance

Welcome & Ambience	✓✓✓✓	Location	✓✓✓✓
Quality of Pitches	✓✓✓✓	Range of Facilities	✓✓✓✓

Directions

Site is 2.5 km. northwest of Castiglione on road to Follonica.

Charges 2004

Per person	€ 6,00 - € 8,50
child (2- 6 yrs)	€ 4,00 - € 6,00
pitch and car	€ 7,00 - € 15,00

Reservations

Necessary for July/Aug. and will be made for min. 1 week with deposit (€ 2.58). Tel: 0564 933765. E-mail: info@maremmasanssouci.it

Open

1 April - 31 October.

IT6661 Toscana Village

Via Fornoli, 9, 56020 Montopoli (Tuscany)

Five years ago a forest stood here and was part of the attractive medieval Tuscan village of Montopoli. Toscana Village has been thoughtfully carved out of the mature pines and it is ideal for a sightseeing holiday in this central area. The 150 level pitches (some large) are on shaded terraces and are carefully maintained. Some pitches have full drainage facilities and water, most have electricity (3A). The amenities are centrally located at the top pf the hill in a pleasant modern building. The restaurant has a terrace where there are views of the forest. For a swim or sunbathe and to relax, the unusually shaped pool is in a separate area of the site and will be a welcome break after touring the sights in Pisa, Florence and Lucca. This site is being improved and enlarged each year, and it is a quality site tucked away from the hustle and bustle of the cities. English is spoken by the helpful reception staff.

Facilities

One modern central block has excellent facilities including British style toilets, hot water at all the stylish sinks, private cabins and two large en-suite cubicles which may be suitable for disabled campers. Washing machines and dryer. Motorcaravan service point. Shop. Gas. Restaurant with terrace (limited menu). Takeaway. Bread to order. Swimming pool (lifeguard 11.30-18.30 hrs; disclaimer signed if you use the pool out of these times; open May – Sept). Play area. 5-a-side football. Bicycle hire. Organised activities. Doctor's room. Torches useful. Off site: Walk to Montopoli village (1 km). Fishing 6 km. Golf and riding 7 km.

At a glance

Welcome & Ambience	✓✓✓✓✓	Location	✓✓✓✓
Quality of Pitches	✓✓✓✓	Range of Facilities	✓✓✓✓

Directions

From A12 (Genove – Florence) take Pisa Centro exit. Take the F1,P1,L1 and then the Montopoli exit. Opposite large cemetery just before the town is Via Masoria leading to Via Fornoli and site (well signed).

Charges 2004

Per person	€ 4,00 - € 6,30
child (2-10 yrs)	free - € 5,00
pitch	€ 7,50 - € 11,50
electricity	€ 2,00
water and drainage	€ 2,50

Reservations

Made with 20% deposit. Tel: 0571 449032. E-mail: info@toscanavillage.com

Open

Easter - 31 October.

IT6663 Camping Semifonte

Via Ugo Foscolo 4, 50021 Barberino (Tuscany)

Barberino lies in the heart of Tuscany between Florence and Siena, an area rich in history and known for that special Italian wine Chianti. Camping Semifonte is a small basic, terraced site with fine views over the surrounding hills. The 90 pitches (76 for caravans and motorcaravans, the remainder without electricity for tents) are on steep terraces, small and tight for manoeuvring. Each terrace has a tap and electricity connections. There is a very small shop selling basics. The small pools are separate and of the supported type, neither has security fencing and the paddling pool is alongside the play area, so children must be supervised at all times here. The prices are reasonable but the facilities are limited and you would be advised to arrive with full cupboards. The site is unsuitable for disabled visitors. A good restaurant is 500 m. from the site with another in the small village a short walk away.

Facilities

Two small sanitary blocks have a mixture of British and Turkish toilets, few showers and are under much pressure at peak periods. Motorcaravan service point. Small supported swimming pool for adults – no safety barrier. Children's supported pool with no safety fence – next to small play area. Off site: Regular bus route to/from Florence and Siena. Bicycle hire 0.5 km. Riding 1 km. Golf 15 km.

Open

1 April - 20 October.

At a glance

Welcome & Ambience	✓✓✓	Location	✓✓✓✓
Quality of Pitches	✓✓✓	Range of Facilities	✓✓

Directions

From Florence-Siena autostrada take Tavarmelle exit to Barberina Val Elsa. Take first left on entering village and site is 500 m.

Charges 2004

Per person	€ 6,00 - € 6,50
child (3-10 yrs)	€ 4,00 - € 4,50
pitch with electricity	€ 11,00 - € 13,00
tent	€ 7,50 - € 10,00

Reservations

Made with € 5.50 fee (non refundable).
Tel: 055 807 5454. E-mail: semifonte@semifonte.it

IT6633 Camping Free Time

Via dei Cipressi, 57020 Marina di Bibbona (Tuscany)

Free Time is a modern site just 700 metres from an attractive sandy beach and 500 metres from the little resort of Marina di Bibbona. Pitches are on level ground, most with electricity connections and reasonably shaded. There is a good, well-stocked supermarket and a bar/restaurant/pizzeria complex overlooking the pool. The main pool is large and there is a separate, smaller paddling pool.

Facilities

The toilet blocks are modern and well maintained with special facilities for disabled visitors. Some pitches have private sanitary facilities (extra charge). Motorcaravan service point. 5-a-side football pitch. Fishing lake. Play area. Lively 'animation' programme in peak season (including aqua gym in the pool and disco evenings). Dogs are not accepted in high season. Off site: Beach 700 m. Cecina 5 km.

Open

11 April - 5 October.

At a glance

Welcome & Ambience	✓✓✓✓	Location	✓✓✓✓
Quality of Pitches	✓✓✓✓✓	Range of Facilities	✓✓✓✓✓

Directions

From Livorno – Civitavecchia road ('superstrada') take La California exit and follow signs to Marina di Bibbona. Site is well signed.

Charges guide

Per pitch	€ 9,00 - € 13,00
person	€ 6,00 - € 10,00
child (1-9 yrs)	€ 4,00 - € 6,00
electricity 3A	€ 0,50

Reservations

Contact site. Tel: 0586 600934.
E-mail: freetime@camping.it

IT6671 Camping International Argentario

Localita Torre Saline, 58010 Albinia (Tuscany)

Argentario is really two separate campsites with a large holiday villa complex, all sharing the common facilities. The pools, animation area and bar area, like the villa complex are new and elegantly designed. The large irregularly shaped pool and smaller circular paddling pool are very inviting. Entertainment is organised daily by the team where there is something for everyone, young and old. The 404 pitches are smaller than usual, but mostly flat and on a surface of dark sand and pine needles, being shaded by tall pines. The area is quite dusty and many of the pitches are a very long way from the amenities. Motorcaravans are parked in a large separate open square. Some campers may find the long walks trying, especially as the older style facilities are tired and stressed during peak periods. A basic restaurant and pizzeria is remote from the touring section and has no views. The beach of dark sand has attractive views across to the mountains. We see this site more for short stays than extended holidays and as unsuitable for disabled campers.

Facilities

Three mature blocks have mostly Turkish style toilets, a few cramped showers with hot water and cold water at the sinks (showers are very busy at peak periods). There are facilities for disabled campers but we think this site would prove very difficult because of the sand surface and remoteness of some facilities. Washing machines. Motorcaravan service point. Shop. Restaurant, bar and takeaway. Swimming pools. Tennis. Boat hire. Minigolf. Volleyball. Basketball. Archery. Tennis. ATM. Cars are parked in a separate car park in high season. Torches very useful. Dogs are not accepted. Off site: Bar and restaurant on the beach. Boat launching and riding 1 km. Golf 20 km.

At a glance

Welcome & Ambience	✓✓✓✓	Location	✓✓✓
Quality of Pitches	✓✓✓	Range of Facilities	✓✓✓✓

Directions

Site is off the SS1 at the 150 km. mark, signed Porto S. Stefano. It is on the right, clearly marked but be careful to ignore the first 'combined' campsite sign and proceed another 300 m. to the main entrance with reception.

Charges guide

per pitch	€ 6,00 - € 10,00
adult	€ 6,00 - € 10,00
child (1 - 6 yrs)	€ 4,00 - € 5,00

Reservations

Made for the full month only in August (no deposit). Tel: 0564 870 302. E-mail: info@argentariocampingvillage.com

Open

Easter/1 April - 30 September.

IT6664 Camping Toscana Colliverdi

Via Marcialla 349, Loc. Marcialla, 50020 Certaldo (Tuscany)

New owners Chiaro and Guiseppe Bondi are developing this small country hillside site in Tuscany. A new small bar and tiny terrace offer welcoming cool drinks, excellent coffee and fresh bread in the mornings. Other supplies and good restaurants are available in the village of Marcialla 700 metres away. Toscana Colliverdi has space for 45 large units on deep terraces and two areas for tents. All the terrace pitches have electricity. One part of the access road is tarmac the other rough gravel - large units should use the tarmac for ease of access on the steep slopes. There are excellent panoramic views of the surrounding countryside (unfortunately in some areas marred by overhead wires and a pylon supporting them sitting at the bottom of the site). The site is well positioned to visit the many historic and cultural places of interest in the area, including the birthplace of Leornardo de Vinci which is very close by. A new pool set above ground is inviting after a hot day, maybe after exploring the nearby castle. We met Alan Rogers readers Wendy and Roger while visiting in June, who were delighted with the site which was covered with yellow and red wildflowers at the time. The site is dark at night and the centre steps are a challenge as some are of differing depths, thus a good torch is required. If you are content to be self-supporting and want expert assistance in exploring Tuscany along with the advantage of reasonable campsite fees, then this could be for you.

Facilities

A small, clean toilet block is on the second terrace with British style toilets, showers and washbasins, plus dishwashing and laundry sinks, all with hot water. No facilities for disabled campers. Washing machine. Small bar and terrace (basic supplies available). Good size above ground pool. Off site: Restaurant, shop, butcher, greengrocer, post office 1 km.

Open

1 April - 30 September.

At a glance

Welcome & Ambience	✓✓✓✓✓	Location	✓✓✓✓
Quality of Pitches	✓✓✓	Range of Facilities	✓✓

Directions

From A1 autostrada Florence - Siena, take Tavarnelle exit and head for Tavarnelle. At the village follow signs for Marcialla. Site entrance is on the left 700 m. after the village of Marcialla.

Charges 2004

Per person	€ 6,00 - € 6,50
child (1-9 yrs)	€ 4,00 - € 4,50
pitch incl. car	€ 7,50 - € 10,00
electricity	€ 1,50
dog	€ 1,50 - € 2,00

No credit cards.

Reservations

Write to site. Tel: 0571 669334. E-mail: toscolverdi@virgilio.it

IT6612 Camping Norcenni Girasole Club

Via Norcenni 7, 50063 Figline Valdarno (Tuscany)

The Norcenni Girasole Club is a brilliant, busy and well run resort style site in a picturesque, secluded situation with great views of Tuscan landscapes 19 km. south of Florence. Owned by the dynamic Cardini-Vannucchi family, care has been taken in its development and the buildings and infrastructure are most attractive and in sympathy with the surrounds. Absolutely everything is to hand and guests will only need to leave the site if they wish to explore the local attractions. There is an amazing choice of superb pools both in the lower area where there are new pools in the already fantastic complex (one for aerobics, a wading pool, a covered pool), and then at the top of the site where a lagoon with amazing acres of pools allows children to ride the large, exciting water flume free, play in the waterfall and feature pool or revert to other themed pools with slides. A modern health complex provides saunas, jacuzzi, steam bath, a fitness centre and massages (extra cost). Three attractive restaurants with terraces serve wonderful food, the Vecchio specialising in typical Tuscan fare (bookings advised). We also liked Lo Strettoio with its family atmosphere and the S. Andrea restaurant at the very top of the site which has fabulous views and offers more cosmopolitan food. There are 470 clean and roomy pitches for touring units, all with electricity (4A) and water, most shaded by well tended trees. The ground is hard and stony (tent pegs can be difficult). Although on a fairly steep hillside, pitches are on level terraces accessed from good roads. An extensive animation programme is published each week with music on three evenings and lots of activities for children. Courses in the Italian language, Tuscan cooking and wine tasting are provided. There are many English visitors and all information and most of the animation is in English.

Facilities

Sanitary facilities are very good with mixed British and Turkish style WCs. Hot water throughout. Five family bathrooms for rent (book in advance). Facilities for disabled visitors. Laundry facilities. Supermarket and gift shops. Wine shop. Bar and restaurants. Pizzeria. Gelateria. Tennis courts. Riding. Wonderful swimming pools, one covered and heated (supervised; hats required). Fitness centre (charged). Disco. Internet café. ATM. Off site: Excursions including evening tour of Florence with dinner in an historic palace. Daily bus to Florence and buses to the local railway station.

At a glance

Welcome & Ambience	✓✓✓✓	Location	✓✓✓✓
Quality of Pitches	✓✓✓✓	Range of Facilities	✓✓✓✓✓

Directions

From Florence take Al/E35 autostrada and Incisa exit. Turn south on route 69 towards Arezzo. In Figline turn right for Greve and watch for Girasole signs - site is 4 km up a twisting, climbing road.

Charges 2004

Per person	€ 6,70 - € 9,30
child (2-12 yrs)	€ 4,00 - € 5,50
pitch incl. car	€ 9,40 - € 13,30

Reservations

Made with deposit. Tel: 055 915141.
E-mail: girasole@ecvacanze.it

Open

30 March - 2 November.

IT6653 Camping Listro

Via Lungolago, 06061 Castiglione del Lago (Umbria)

This is a simple, pleasant, flat site with the best beach (private to the site) on Lake Trasimeno. As the lake is very shallow with some reeds (7 m. at its deepest), it has very gradually sloping beaches making it very safe for children to play and swim. This also results in very warm water, which is kept clean as fishing and tourism are the major industries hereabouts. Listro is a few hundred yards north of the historic town of Castiglione and the attractive town can be seen rising up the hillside from the site. It provides 110 pitches all with electricity with 70% of the pitches enjoying the shade of mature trees. Younger campers are in a separate area of the site, ensuring no noise and some of the motorcaravan pitches are right on the lakeside giving stunning views out of your windows. Facilities on the site are fairly limited with a small shop, bar and snack bar, and there is no organised entertainment. English is spoken and British guests are particularly welcome. If you enjoy peace and quiet in camping terms then this site is for you.

Facilities

Two screened sanitary facilities are very clean with British and Turkish style WCs. Facilities for disabled visitors. Washing machine. Motorcaravan services. Bar. Shop. Snack bar. Play area. Table tennis. Volleyball. Private beach.
Off site: The town is 800 m. and bars and restaurants are near, as are sporting facilities including a good swimming pool and tennis courts (discounts using the campsite card).

Open

1 April - 30 September.

At a glance

Welcome & Ambience	✓✓✓✓	Location	✓✓✓✓✓
Quality of Pitches	✓✓✓	Range of Facilities	✓✓✓✓

Directions

From A1/E35 Florence-Rome autostrada take Val di Chiana exit and join the Perugia (75 bis) superstrada. After 24 km. take Castiglione exit and follow town signs. Site is clearly signed just before the town.

Charges 2004

Per person (over 3 yrs)	€ 3,50 - € 4,20
pitch	€ 3,50 - € 4,20
car	€ 1,10 - € 1,60
motorcycle	€ 0,80 - € 1,05

Less 10% for stays over 8 days in low season.

Reservations

Contact site. Tel: 075 951193. E-mail: listro@listro.it

IT6667 Camping La Finoria

Via Monticello, 66, 58023 Gavorrano (Tuscany)

An unusual site set high in the mountains with incredible views, La Finoria is a rugged site with a focus on nature. Italian schoolchildren attend education programmes here. The three motorcaravan pitches are at the top of the site for those who enjoy a challenge, with a dozen caravan pitches on lower terraces accessed by a steep gravel track. Under huge chestnut trees there is a very pretty terraced area for tents. These have a private natural feel which some might say is what camping is all about. If you visit in November you can help collect the olives and make olive oil or a little earlier gather chestnuts for puree. Campers are invited to take part in the educational programmes. The restaurant reflects the owner's attention to detail – the food here is wonderful and after an exhausting day communing with nature, or exploring the area, there is a large pool for a refreshing swim before enjoying the night views.

Facilities

Two blocks provide British and Turkish style toilets, hot showers and cold water at washbasins and sinks. Facilities for disabled campers. Washing machines. Small shop (closed Jan/Feb). Good restaurant and bar (closed Jan/Feb). Swimming pool (May - Sept). Torches essential.
Off site: Riding 2 km. Tennis 3 km. Village 3 km. Bicycle hire 6 km. Golf 8 km. Beach and fishing 12 km.

Open

All year.

At a glance

Welcome & Ambience	✓✓✓✓	Location	✓✓✓✓✓
Quality of Pitches	✓✓✓	Range of Facilities	✓✓✓

Directions

From SS1 Follonica - Grosseto road take Gavorrano exit, then road to Finoria. This is a steady climb for some 10 minutes. As soon as you start to descend at a junction (the only one) look left downhill for a large white sign indicating the site off to the left.

Charges guide

Per person	€ 2,50 - € 8,50
pitch	€ 4,00 - € 10,00

Reservations

With only a few motorcaravan or caravan pitches it is best to phone ahead in high season.
Tel: 0566 844381. E-mail: info@campeggiolafinoria.it

IT6649 Camping Punta Navaccia

06069 Tuoro sul Trasimeno (Tuscany)

Situated on the north side of Lake Trasimeno and run by friendly and welcoming owners, this site is ideally located for exploring Umbria and its famous cities, such as Assisi and Perugia. Tuscany and its cities of Siena and Florence are also within easy reach and it is even possible to visit Rome for a day trip. The area surrounding the site also has a lot to offer, with an interesting historical past. It was here in 217BC that the historical battle of Tuoro del Trasimeno (battle of the Romans and Carthaginians) took place. However, the main attraction is of course the lake, ideal for swimming and a variety of water-sports. The site is large with over 70,000 sq.m. and 400 touring pitches (200 with 4A electricity) and all with shade. The campsite has a long (stony) beach with moorings. There are 60 mobile homes for rent.

Facilities

Sanitary block with British style WCs, showers and some private cabins. Washing machine and dryer. Motorcaravan service point. Heated swimming and paddling pools. Shop, restaurant and takeaway (April - November). Play area. Tennis. Basketball. Beach volleyball. Table tennis. Large covered amphitheatre. Disco. Cinema screen. Miniclub. Animation is organised in high season (in Italian, English, German and Dutch). Boat launching. Off site: Sandy beach 200 m. Windsurfing, sailing and canoeing 200 m.

At a glance

Welcome & Ambience	✓✓✓✓✓	Location	✓✓✓
Quality of Pitches	✓✓✓	Range of Facilities	✓✓✓✓

Directions

Going south from Florence (Firenze) to Rome on the A1, take Val di Chiana exit to Perugia near Bettolle. After 15 km. take exit for Tuoro; site is well signed.

Charges 2004

Per unit incl. 2 persons	€ 17,00 - € 24,00
extra person	€ 5,50 - € 8,00
child (2- 9 yrs)	€ 4,00 - € 6,00

Reservations

Contact site. Tel: 075 826357.
E-mail: navaccia@camping.it

Open

15 March - 31 October.

IT6652 Camping Villaggio Italgest

Via Martiri di Cefalonia, 06060 Sant Arcangelo Magione (Umbria)

Directly on the shore on the south side of Lake Trasimeno, which is almost midway between the Mediterranean and the Adriatic, Sant Arcangelo is ideally placed for exploring Umbria and Tuscany. The area around the lake is fairly flat but has views of the distant hills and can become very hot during summer. Villaggio Italgest is a pleasant site with 248 tourist pitches on level grass and, except for the area next to the lake, under a cover of tall trees. All pitches have electrical connections and cars are parked away from the pitches. The site offers a wide variety of activities, tours are organised daily and there is entertainment for children and adults in high season. The bar/disco remains open until 2 am. There is a good sized swimming pool area. This a most pleasant place to stay and English is spoken.

Facilities

The one large and two smaller sanitary block have mainly British style WCs and free hot water in the washbasins and showers. Facilities for disabled people. Motorcaravan services. Washing machines and dryers. Community room with stoves, fridges and freezers. Bar, restaurant, pizzeria and takeaway (all season). Mini-market. Swimming pool. Tennis. Football. Volleyball. Table tennis. Play area. Wide range of activities, entertainment and excursions. Marina for boats with crane. Entertainment (July/Aug). Excursions. TV (satellite) and games rooms. Disco. Films. Watersports, motor boat hire and lake swimming. Fishing. Mountain bike and scooter hire. Internet point.

At a glance

Welcome & Ambience	✓✓✓✓✓	Location	✓✓✓✓
Quality of Pitches	✓✓✓✓✓	Range of Facilities	✓✓✓✓

Directions

Site is on the southern shore of Lake Trasimeno. Take Magione exit from the Perugia spur from the Florence - Rome autostrada, proceed southwest round the lake to S. Arcangelo where the site is signed.

Charges 2005

Per person	€ 5,70 - € 8,00
child (3-9 yrs)	€ 4,00 - € 5,70
pitch	€ 6,00 - € 9,50
car	€ 1,80 - € 2,50

Reservations

During winter telephone 075/5847422 or write to site with 30% deposit. Tel: 075 848 238.
E-mail: camping@italgest.com

Open

24 March - 30 September.

IT6655 Camping Internazionale Assisi

S Giovanni in Campiglione 110, 06081 Assisi (Umbria)

Camping Internazionale is situated on the west side of Assisi and has high grade facilities which provide tourers with a good base to visit both Saint Francis' city and nearby Perugia and Lake Trasimeno. The excellent restaurant has a large terrace which can be completely enclosed serving reasonably priced meals, ranging from pizzas to local Umbrian dishes. Finish off with a drink in the enjoyable 'Stonehenge Bar' which stays open a little later. The city is lit up in the evenings to provide a beautiful backdrop from some areas in the site. The 175 pitches are large and clearly marked on flat grass, all with electricity. There is shade as it can be very hot in this part of Italy, and a welcome relief is the site's pleasant, large swimming pool. The site is pleasantly out of the city bustle and heat and offers a regular shuttle bus service. Assisi boasts one of the finest cathedrals in Christendom, among many other attractions, and a stay in this area should not be cut too short. The site organises many tours in the area for individuals and groups including artistic, religious, wine, food, archaeological and nature. In terms of value this is one of the cheapest sites we have seen in Northern Italy.

Facilities

The well appointed and clean toilet block has free hot showers, plenty of washbasins, mainly Turkish style WCs (only 4 British style in each block) and facilities for disabled people. Washing machine. Gas supplies. Motorcaravan services. Campers' kitchen tables and benches. Restaurant/pizzeria with self-service section (closed Wednesdays). Bar with snacks. Shop. Ice cream bar. Swimming pool, jacuzzi and circular paddling pool (bathing caps mandatory). Table tennis. Bicycle hire. Tennis. Volleyball. Roller skating area. Off site: Riding 2 km. Excursions to Assisi centre, Rome and Siena. Bus service to city three times daily from outside the site (one on Sundays except Easter).

Open

1 April - October.

At a glance

Welcome & Ambience	✓✓✓	Location	✓✓✓✓
Quality of Pitches	✓✓✓	Range of Facilities	✓✓✓✓

Directions

Site is on the south side of the SS147, which branches left off SS75 Perugia - Foligno road. Follow Assisi signs and, since there are several campsite signs in the town, look for un-named camping sign going off to the left (downhill) as you enter the city. Site is 4 km. from the city. At Violi a village just before Assisi there is a warning of a low bridge of 3.3 m. - in fact it is much higher at the centre of the curved bridge and even the highest units will pass through.

Charges 2004

Per person	€ 6,00 - € 7,00
child (3-10 yrs)	€ 4,00 - € 5,00
pitch incl. car	€ 8,00 - € 9,00
tent	€ 4,00 - € 5,00

Electricity included. Credit cards accepted min. € 50.

Reservations

Made for 1 week stays in high season, but not really necessary. Tel: 075 813710. E-mail: info@campingassisi.it

IT6656 Camping Il Collaccio

Azienda Agricola 11 Collaccio, 06047 Castelvecchio di Preci (Umbria)

Castlevecchio di Preci is tucked away in the tranquil depths of the Umbrian countryside. The natural beauty of the Monti Sibillini National Park is near (excursions are organised) and there are walking and cycling opportunities with many marked paths. Il Collaccio is owned and run by the Baldoni family who bought the farm over 30 years ago, rebuilt the derelict farmhouse in its original style and then decided to share it with holiday makers by developing a campsite and accommodation for rent. The farming aspect was kept, along with a unit producing salami (they run very popular salami making and Umbrian cookery courses over Easter and New Year - no preservatives!) and its products can be bought in the shop and sampled in the excellent restaurant. The camping area has been carved out of the hillside which forms a natural amphitheatre with splendid views. At first sight the narrow steep entrance seems daunting (the owner will assist) and the road which leads down to the somewhat steep camping terraces takes one to the exit. A pleasant restaurant and bar overlooks the upper pools and a bar is alongside the lower pools. The 93 large pitches are on level terraces with stunning views. Electricity (6A) is available - long leads useful. Thousands of trees, planted to replace those cut down by the previous owner, are maturing and provide some shade. With sparsely populated villages across the valley on the mountain slopes and embraced by stunning scenery, Il Collaccio and its surrounds are unusual and different.

Facilities

Three modern sanitary blocks are spaced through the site with British and Turkish style WCs, cold water in washbasins and hot, pre-mixed water in showers and sinks. Facilities for disabled visitors. Washing machine. Motorcaravan service point. Restaurant (all season). Shop (basics, 1/7-31/8). Two swimming pools both with paddling pools (15/5-30/9). Play area. Tennis. Volleyball. Table tennis. Boules. Entertainment (high season). Excursions. Off site: Cycling and walking. Canoeing and rafting 2 km. Fishing 10 km.

Open

1 April - 30 September.

At a glance

Welcome & Ambience	✓✓✓✓✓	Location	✓✓✓✓
Quality of Pitches	✓✓✓✓	Range of Facilities	✓✓✓✓

Directions

From SS77 Foligno-Civitonova Marche road turn south at Muccia for Visso from where Preci is signed. There is a direct route through a tunnel, if the site is approached north of Eggi which is 10 km. north of Spoleto. The tunnel exit is at Sant Anatolia di Narco SS209, where a left turn will take you to Preci.

Charges 2004

Per person	€ 5,50 - € 7,50
child (3-12 yrs)	€ 2,25 - € 4,00
pitch incl. electricity	€ 5,50 - € 9,00
car	€ 2,00 - € 3,50

Reservations

Write to site. Tel: 0743 939005. E-mail: info@ilcollaccio.com

IT6813 Camping Porticciolo

Via Porticciolo, 00062 Bracciano (Lázio)

This small family run site, useful for visiting Rome, has its own private beach on the southwest side of Lake Bracciano. Alessandro and his wife Alessandra, who have worked hard to build up this site since 1982, are charming and speak English. Alessandro is a Roman classical history expert and provides free documentary information on the local area and Rome. A pleasant feature is that the site is overlooked by the impressive castle in the village of Bracciano. There are 170 pitches (150 for tourers) split into two sections, some with lake views and 120 having electricity. Pitches are large and shaded by very green trees which are continuously watered in summer by a neat overhead watering system. The friendly bar has two large terraces, shared by the trattoria which opens for lunch and the pizzeria with its wood fired oven in the evenings. A small amount of entertainment is offered during the season and the lake is clean for swimming with powerboats banned (it is Rome's drinking water! Separate ancient pipes directly feed the two famous fountains in St Peter's Square). Small boats and windsurfers may be launched from the site. As an uncomplicated, lakeside site away from the heat and hassle of the city, it is ideal.

Facilities

Three somewhat rustic, but clean, sanitary units. Hot showers (by token), laundry facilities and washing machines. Motorcaravan services. Gas supplies. Shop (basics). Bar. Trattoria/pizzeria (15/5-5/9). Tennis. Five-a-side soccer. Play area. Table tennis. Volleyball. Bicycle hire. Fishing. Tourist information (from computer terminal by reception). Internet point. Torches required in some areas. Excursions 'Rome By Night' and nearby nature parks. Off site: Riding 2 km. Bus service from outside the gate runs to central Rome (about 1 hour - all day ticket known as a 'Birg' is very good value). Air conditioned train service from Bracciano (1.5 km) into the city – the site runs a connecting bus (09.00 daily).

Open

1 April - 30 September.

At a glance

Welcome & Ambience	✓✓✓✓	Location	✓✓✓✓
Quality of Pitches	✓✓✓✓	Range of Facilities	✓✓✓✓

Directions

From Rome ring road (GRA) northwest side take Cassia exit to Bracciano S493 (be careful not to confuse this exit with 'Cassia bis' which is further northeast). Follow signs to village of Bracciano on southwest shore of Lago di Bracciano. Two kilometres before village, just afer going under a bridge follow site signs and turn along the lake away from Anguillara. Site is 1 km. beside lake.

Charges 2004

Per person	€ 4,10 - € 5,50
child (3-10 yrs)	€ 3,30 - € 4,50
tent, caravan or motorcaravan	€ 4,10 - € 6,40
car	€ 1,60 - € 3,00
electricity	€ 1,80 - € 3,60
dog	€ 2,60 - € 3,50

Special low season offers.

Reservations

Write to site. Tel: 06 99803060.
E-mail: info@porticciolo.it

IT6812 Roma Flash Sporting

Via Settevene Palo km 19,800, 00062 Bracciano (Lázio)

This excellent family site is situated on the beautiful Lake Bracciano, the source of Rome's drinking water. Roma Flash Sporting is a friendly campsite which seems to improve each time we visit. The dynamic owners Elide and Edoardo speak excellent English and happily go out of their way to ensure guests enjoy their holiday. The simple restaurant has a large terrace and small indoor area both overlooking the lake where you can enjoy a basic menu and excellent pizza; a small shop shares this area. The lake area has very fine panoramic views and there are two beach areas to swim with grassy sunbathing areas. Boats and windsurfers can be launched (no power boats allowed). There is also a swimming pool and paddling pool on the site. Only 40 minutes from Rome there are regular buses to the local station. All guests are supplied with a campsite booklet full of useful information such as train timetables, a suggested itinerary for visiting Rome and places to eat in Rome etc. Mature trees provide cover for the 200 pitches, some which have good lake views. The ancient Etruscan ruins are fairly close by if you wish to visit something even older than Rome itself.

Facilities

One brand new large toilet block is very well appointed and we hear the second block will be replaced for 2005. All British style toilets, free hot water throughout and fully adjustable showers. Excellent dishwashing and laundry with washing machines. Facilities for disabled visitors. Washing machine. Gas supplies. Bar/pizzeria (all season). Small shop. Swimming pool and small paddling pool (caps compulsory). Table tennis. Beach handball. Play area. Watersports. Canoes-kayaks. Games room. Boule. Animation for children in high season. Excursions possible. Torches required in some areas. Dogs are accepted but not allowed in the restaurant or beach areas.

At a glance

Welcome & Ambience	✓✓✓✓	Location	✓✓✓✓
Quality of Pitches	✓✓✓✓	Range of Facilities	✓✓✓✓

Directions

From E35/E45 north of Rome, take Settebagni exit. Follow GRA orbital road west to Cassia exit. Follow sign for Lago Bracciano to town of Bracciano. Site is well signed from town.

Charges 2004

Per person	€ 5,00 - € 7,00
child (3-10 yrs)	€ 3,00 - € 5,50
pitch incl. car	€ 11,00 - € 14,00
small tent	€ 5,50 - € 6,50

Reservations

Contact site. Tel: 0699 805458.
E-mail: info@romaflash.it

Open

1 April - 30 September.

IT6809 Camping Tiber

Via Tiberina km 1,400, 00188 Roma (Lázio)

An excellent city site which is unusually peaceful, Camping Tiber is ideally located for visiting Rome with an easy train service (20 minutes to Rome) a free shuttle bus every 30 minutes and trams for later at night. The 350 tourist pitches are mostly shaded under very tall trees (with electricity) and many have very pleasant views over the river Tiber. This mighty river winds around two sides of the site boundary (safely fenced) providing a cooling effect for campers. There is a new section with little shade as yet and bungalows to rent are in another, separate area of the campsite. A small but pleasant outdoor pool with a bar awaits after a busy day in the city and the main bar, restaurant with terrace and takeaway are attractive and give good value. The site is extremely well run and especially good for campers with disabilities to visit the delights of Rome.

Facilities

Fully equipped sanitary facilities include modern British style toilets, hot water and good facilities for disabled campers. Washing machines and dryers. Drive-over motorcaravan service point. Market. Bar, restaurant, pizzeria and takeaway. Internet. Swimming pool (15/5-30/9). Free shuttle bus to underground. Night bus. Tourist information. Torches useful. Off site: Local bars, restaurants and shops. Golf or riding 20 km. River fishing.

Open

15 March - 31 October.

At a glance

Welcome & Ambience	✓✓✓✓	Location	✓✓✓✓✓
Quality of Pitches	✓✓✓✓	Range of Facilities	✓✓✓✓

Directions

From Florence, exit at Rome Nord Fiano on A1 and immediately turn south onto Via Tibernia and site is signed. From other directions on Rome ring road (known and signed as the GRA – like the M25 but less crowded) take exit 6 northbound on S3 Via Flaminia and the site is very well signed.

Charges guide

Per person	€ 8,50 - € 9,60
child (3-12 yrs)	€ 6,00 - € 7,00
pitch incl. car	€ 8,40 - € 10,70

Reservations

Advised and possible on-line, or by phone/fax.
Tel: 06 3361 0733. E-mail: info@campingtiber.com

IT6810 Camping Seven Hills

Via Cassia 1216, 00191 Roma (Lázio)

Close to Rome, this site provides a quieter, garden setting in some areas, but has a lively atmosphere in others. It is situated in a delightful valley, flanked by two of the seven hills of Rome and is just off the autostrada ring road to the north of the city (4 km. from the city centre. The site runs a bus shuttle service every 30 minutes to the local station and one return bus to Rome each day (09.00, returning at 18.00). Arranged in two sections, the top half, near the entrance, restaurant and shop consists of small, flat, grass terraces with two to four pitches on each, with smaller terraces for tents. Access to some pitches may be tricky. The flat section at the lower part of the site is reserved mainly for ready erected tents used by international tour operators who bring guests by coach. These tend to be younger people and the site, along with its often busy pool, has a distinctly youthful feel. Consequently there may be a little extra noise, so choose your pitch carefully. The site is a profusion of colour with flowering trees and shrubs and a good covering of trees provides shade. An unusual feature of the site is that numerous deer roam unhindered and peacocks strut around the terraces. The 80 pitches for tourers, with electricity (3A) to some are not marked, but the management supervise in busy periods. English is spoken and many notices are in English. All cash transactions on the site are made with a card from reception. This is an extremely busy and bustling site with up to 15 touring buses with their occupants on the site during high season, in addition to a very busy camping routine.

Facilities

Three soundly constructed sanitary blocks are well situated around the site, with open plan washbasins, and hot water in the average sized showers. Dishwashing under cover with cold water. Facilities for disabled campers. Washing machines. Well stocked shop. Bar/restaurant and terrace. Money exchange. Table tennis. Volleyball. Swimming pool at the bottom of the site with bar/snack bar (separate pool charge). Disco. Off site: Golf (good course) 4 km. Bus service to Rome. Excursions and cruises arranged. Internet. Torches required in some areas. Bungalows to rent.

Open

All year.

At a glance

Welcome & Ambience	✓✓✓	Location	✓✓✓✓
Quality of Pitches	✓✓✓	Range of Facilities	✓✓✓✓

Directions

Take exit 3 from the autostrada ring-road on to Via Cassia (signed SS2 Viterbo, NOT Via Cassia Bis) and look for camp signs. Turn right after 1 km (13 km. stone) and follow small road for about 1 km. to site.

Charges 2004

Per person (over 4 yrs)	€ 8,20 - € 8,90
tent	€ 5,00 - € 5,80
caravan	€ 6,50 - € 7,50
car	€ 4,00 - € 4,50
motorcaravan	€ 8,80 - € 9,80
motorcycle	€ 2,40 - € 2,90

No credit cards.

Reservations

Write to site. Tel: 0630 310826.
E-mail: seven_hills@camping.it

IT6780 Camping Roma

via Aurelia, 831, 00165 Roma (Lázio)

This is a new all year venture for the dynamic Cardini – Vannucchi groups who have two other city sites, Alba d'Oro (IT6042) in Venice and Michelangelo (IT6614) in Florence, as well as the amazing Norcenni Girasole resort style campsite in Tuscany (IT6612). This site has been chosen for its proximity to Rome and is to be developed as a comfortable city site. It has new swimming pools, restaurant, bar and small shop as well as internet points. The excellent local supermarket is across the busy road but can be accessed by a pedestrian bridge. The site has a large number of bungalows and many tents for hire. A regular shuttle bus service takes campers to the nearest station with direct access into Rome. We are eagerly awaiting developments at this site as all the facilities are being replaced (expected completion date 2006). Pitches are set high on the hill, they are mostly grass and established shade trees have recently been pruned but should have a good shade cover for the 2005 season. Power will be 6A for 2005.

Facilities

All the amenities are currently being upgraded, the old ones were still in use when we visited – they were clean but fairly basic. Excellent new restaurant and bar. Small shop. Swimming pools. Internet point. Shuttle bus to train station. Off site: Large supermarket across the road. Rome.

Open

All year.

At a glance

Welcome & Ambience	✓✓✓✓	Location	✓✓✓✓
Quality of Pitches	✓✓✓✓	Range of Facilities	✓✓✓✓

Directions

Site is within the circle of the GRA (Grande Raccordo Anulare), the motorway ring road encircling Rome. On western side of the GRA take exit no. 1 (Aurelia) towards San Pietro and 'Centro'. Site is on this road heading towards the city at km. 831 marker.

Charges 2004

Per person	€ 7,00 - € 8,00
child (3-10 yrs)	€ 4,50 - € 5,50
pitch	€ 13,00 - € 14,00

Reservations

Contact site. Tel: 06 662 3018.
E-mail: campingroma@ecvacanze.it

IT6814 Flaminio Village

Via Flaminia 821, 00191 Roma (Lázio)

We were impressed with Camping Flaminio – it is ideally situated for visiting 'the eternal city'. An attractive, quite large campsite with some shade, it is on ground which is sloping in parts. It is located about 400 metres up a lane leading off the main road, which results in its being surprisingly quiet. There is a regular bus/underground service into the centre of Rome from outside the site entrance, which operates until late evening. It is a site for those with culture in mind and the nearest antiquities, etc. are only 500 metres away. There is limited space for touring units, but the majority of these pitches are of average size, have electricity and are approached by 'environmentally approved' brick access roads. There are also some 80 well-equipped bungalows, quite attractively arranged in a village-style setting.

Facilities

The sanitary facilities are currently housed in somewhat ancient blocks, but a new block is planned. Bar-pizzeria and restaurant. Shop. Swimming pool and solarium (15/6-5/9 charged for in peak season). Fitness centre. Play area. Off site: Shops, supermarket, service station, bank and access to cycle route alongside river into the City. Buses and trains outside the gate.

Open

All year.

At a glance

Welcome & Ambience	✓✓✓✓	Location	✓✓✓✓✓
Quality of Pitches	✓✓✓	Range of Facilities	✓✓✓✓

Directions

From the ring road due north of the city take the Via Flaminia exit (6) south towards the city centre, and after 3 km. bear left to avoid tunnel. Site is 150 m. on the right after passing tunnel entrance.

Charges 2005

Per adult	€ 9,20 - € 10,30
child (under 12 yrs)	€ 6,40 - € 7,50
caravan and car	€ 11,30 - € 12,90
tent	€ 5,10 - € 6,60
motorcaravan	€ 10,10 - € 11,70

Reservations

Contact site. Tel: 06 333 2604.
E-mail: info@villageflaminio.com

IT6820 Camping Villaggio Baia Domizia

81030 Baia Domizia (Campania)

This large, beautifully maintained seaside site is about 70 kilometres northwest of Naples, and is within a pinewood, cleverly left in a natural state. It is the ideal place to recover from the rigours of touring or to relax and allow the professionals to organise tours for you to Rome, Pompei, Sorrento etc. Although it does not feel like it, there are 1,200 pitches in clearings, either of grass and sand, or on hardstanding, all with electricity. Finding a pitch may take time as there are so many good ones to choose from, but staff help in season. The entire site is attractive with shrubs, flowers and huge green areas. Most pitches are well shaded, but there are some in the sun for cooler periods. The site is very well organised with particular regulations (e.g. no dogs or loud noise), so the general atmosphere is relaxing and peaceful. Although the site is big, there is never very far to walk to the beach, and though it may be some 300 m. to the central shops and restaurant from the site boundaries, there is always a nearby toilet block. The central complex is superb with well designed buildings containing all your needs (the site is some distance from the town). Restaurants, bars and a gelaterie enjoy live entertainment and attractive water lily ponds surround the area. Near the entrance are two excellent pools, which are a pleasant alternative to the sea on windier days. The supervised beach is 1.5 km. of soft sand and a great attraction. A grassy field overlooking the sea is ideal for picnics and sunbathing. A range of sports and other amenities is provided. Charges are high, but this site is well above average and most suitable for families with children.

Facilities

Seven new toilet blocks have hot water in washbasins (many cabins) and showers. Excellent access and facilities for disabled people. Washing machines. Motorcaravan services. Gas supplies. Huge supermarket and general shop. Large bar and restaurants with pizzeria and takeaway. Ice cream parlour. Sports ground. TV. Playground. Tennis. Bicycle hire. Windsurfing hire and school. Disco. Church. Bureau de change. Doctor daily. Excursions to major attractions in the area. Torches required in some areas. Barrier closed 14.00 - 16.00. Dogs not accepted. Off site: Fishing or riding 3 km.

Open

1 May - 21 September.

At a glance

Welcome & Ambience	✓✓✓	Location	✓✓✓✓
Quality of Pitches	✓✓✓✓	Range of Facilities	✓✓✓✓

Directions

The turning to Baia Domizia leads off the Formia - Naples road 23 km. from Formia. From Rome - Naples autostrada, take Cassino exit to Formia. Site is to the north of Baia Domizia and well signed.

Charges 2004

Per person	€ 4,40 - € 10,20
child (1-3 yrs)	€ 3,30 - € 8,50
tent or caravan	€ 7,70 - € 15,10
car	€ 2,80 - € 5,70
motorcaravan	€ 10,20 - € 19,60

Electricity (5A) included.

Reservations

Not taken, but min. 1 week stay in high season (July/Aug). Tel: 0823 930164. E-mail: info@baiadomizia.it

IT6800 Camping Europe Garden

Via Belvedere 11, 64028 Silvi (Abruzzo)

This site is 13 km. northwest of Pescara, lying just back from the coast (2 km.) up a very steep hill with pleasant views over the sea. The 204 pitches, all with electricity, are mainly on good terraces – access may be difficult on some pitches. However, a tractor is available to help. Cars stand by units on over half of the pitches or in nearby parking spaces for the remainder, and most pitches are shaded. There is a good pool at the bottom of the site, with a small bar and an entertainment programme in season on a small stage and associated area within the pool boundary. The restaurant has olive trees penetrating the floor and ceilings of the eating area and good views but the terrace views are fabulous. The site has steep slopes and is not suitable for disabled or infirm campers.

Facilities

Two good toilet blocks are well cleaned and provide mixed British and Turkish style WCs. Washing machines. Restaurant. Bar. Tennis. Playground. Swimming pool (300 sq.m; swimming caps compulsory), small paddling pool and jacuzzi. Free bus service (18/5-7/9) to beach. Entertainment programme. Free weekly excursions (15/6-8/9). Dogs are not accepted.

Open

27 April - 20 September.

At a glance

Welcome & Ambience	✓✓✓✓	Location	✓✓✓✓
Quality of Pitches	✓✓✓✓	Range of Facilities	✓✓✓✓

Directions

Turn inland off S16 coast road at km. 433 stone for Silvi Alta and follow signs. From A14 take Pineto exit (from north) or Pescara Nord exit (from south).

Charges guide

Per person	€ 4,10 - € 5,10
child (0-3 yrs)	€ 3,60 - € 4,20
pitch incl. electricity	€ 11,10 - € 13,10

No credit cards. Low season discounts for long stays.

Reservations

Made with € 103 deposit for first 2 weeks of August (min 2 weeks), at other times without deposit. Tel: 085 930137. E-mail: info@europegarden.it

IT6819 Camping Villaggio Settebello

Via Flacca, km3600, 04022 Salto di Fondi (Lázio)

Recommended by one of our readers, Settebello is a popular seaside site half-way between Rome and Naples. We hope to conduct a full inspection in 2005. This large site has direct beach access and a good range of leisure amenities. The 480 pitches are well shaded and many offer electrical connections. A lively entertainment programme is organised in high season. The site is bisected by the SS213 Terracina - Gaeta road and is equipped with a subway accordingly. Mobile homes and chalets for rent.

Facilities

Bar and restaurant. Takeaway meals. Shop. Playground. Sports field. Tennis. Minigolf. Children's club. Entertainment programme in high season. Direct beach access.
Off site: Rome 110 km. Naples 110 km. Fondi 10 km. Riding. Watersports.

Open

1 March - 31 October.

Directions

The site is located on the SS213 between Terracina and Sperlonga and is clearly signed.

Charges 2004

Per person	€ 5,20 - € 9,30
child (3-12 yrs)	€ 4,40 - € 8,50
pitch incl. 6A electricity	€ 10,80 - € 22,10

Reservations

Contact site. Tel: 0771 599132
Email : settebello@settebellocamping.com

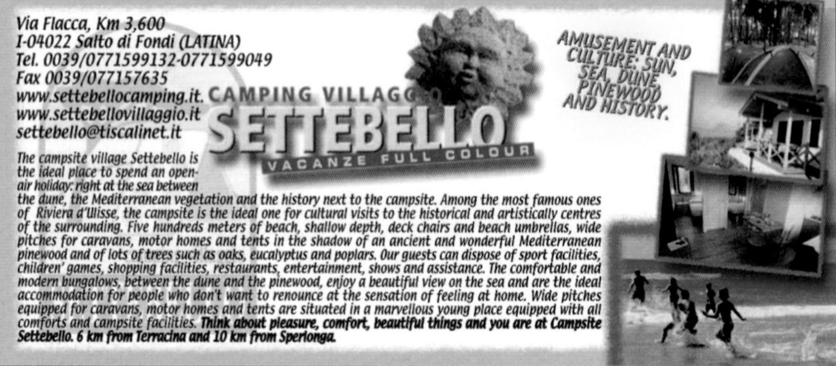

IT6830 Camping Zeus

Via Villa dei Misteri, 80045 Pompei (Campania)

The naming of this site is obvious once you discover it is just 50 metres from the entrance to the fantastic ruins at Pompei (closer than the car park). It is a reasonably priced, city type site perfect for visiting the famous Roman archaeological sites here. After experiencing Pompei, if you wish then to see Sorrento or Herculaneum (equally interesting and worth an extra days stay) the train station is just outside the gate and they are both just a 20 minute journey. This is by far the easiest way to get to these areas as the traffic here is impossible to describe (or navigate). The site's 80 pitches, all for tourers, are under mature trees which give shade. Pitching is informal with lines of trees dictating where units park. In high season it is a good idea to liaise with other units so that you can get out when you want to leave. It is worth noting that the ruins have limited disabled access so a telephone call is recommended. This site provides a safe central location and is of a high standard for the area, albeit with none of the holiday trimmings.

Facilities

The single sanitary block is clean and modernised, with British and Turkish type WCs. Showers have hot water with cold water in washbasins and dishwashing sinks. No facilities for disabled campers. Washing machines. Gas supplies. Bar/restaurant with good value daily menu at lunch times (evening in high season) with waiter service. Shop.
Off site: Pompei, Sorrento, Herculaneum, Amalfi coast.

Open

All year.

At a glance

Welcome & Ambience	✓✓✓✓	Location	✓✓✓✓
Quality of Pitches	✓✓✓	Range of Facilities	✓✓✓

Directions

Leave Napoli - Salerno autostrada at second Pompei exit (Pompei est and Scafati). After pay booth turn left at first intersection then continue 300 m. down this road to the end where turn left again (you are in the town so you need to adopt a forceful but defensive driving style and stay calm). Continue along this road around 500 m. towards the ruins of Pompei, turn up the hill to the ruins entrance gate and the campsite is 50 m. past this.

Charges 2004

Per adult	€ 5,00
child (under 8 yrs)	€ 3,00
pitch	€ 4,00 - € 6,00
car	€ 4,00

Reservations

Not taken. Tel: 081 8655320.
E-mail: campingzeus@libero.it

IT6834 Camping Santa Fortunata

Via Capo 39 AB, 80067 Sorrento (Campania)

The beautiful Amalfi coast and Isle of Capri are a mecca for tourists – if possible try to visit in May, June or September when the roads are less busy. Camping Santa Fortunata has been owned by the friendly De Angelis family for over 30 years. It is situated in the heart of the most popular areas to visit in the region including Sorrento, Capri, the Amalfi Coast, Pompei and Herculenium. There is a local bus stop at the gate for convenient access to the area or join the excursions which are arranged to the most popular attractions. A boat leaves the site daily for Capri where you can swim and enjoy the charming villages. Access to the site is easy which is unusual in this area. Pitches are of average size, although there are some spaces for larger units. They are on hard ground, most are shaded and some have stunning views over the bay. The toilet blocks are spread out throughout the quite large site. The good size pool is very popular, as is swimming from the rocky coastline at the lower end of the site (with access via a steep 250 m. incline). A large restaurant with terrace serves a simple menu of local dishes and delicious pizza which are also available for take away.

Facilities

Five older style refurbished sanitary blocks with adjustable hot showers. Hot water for dishwashing but not laundry sinks. Washing machine. Good restaurant/bar. Small well provisioned shop. Swimming pool. Volleyball. Excursions organised. Off site: Boat trips to Capri. Amalfi, Capri, Naples, Pompeii and Positano are all within easy reach.

Open

19 March - 16 October

At a glance

Welcome & Ambience	✓✓✓	Location	✓✓✓✓
Quality of Pitches	✓✓✓	Range of Facilities	✓✓✓

Directions

From the A3 between Naples and Salerno, follow signs to Pensisola Sorrentina exit at Castellammare di Stabia and on through Sorrento. Take SS145 towards Massa Lubrense, running along Via Capo. Site is about 1.5 km. past Sorrento. Sorrento itself can be extremely busy – the best time to travel this coastline is before 07.00 or between 13.00 and 15.00 during siesta when traffic conditions are greatly improved.

Charges 2004

Per person	€ 6,00 - € 9,00
child (4-10 yrs)	€ 4,00 - € 6,00
pitch	€ 9,00 - € 14,00
car	€ 4,00 - € 5,00

Reservations

Contact site. Tel: 081 807 3574. E-mail: info@santafortunata.com

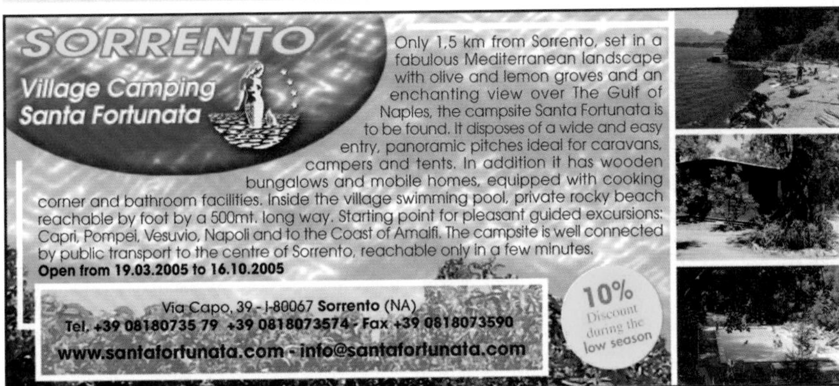

IT6842 Camping Sant' Antonio

Via Marina d'Equa 21, Seiano, 80069 Vico Equense (Campania)

A quiet place with very basic facilities, this little site is just across the road from Seiano marina and tiny beach (no views due to the high stone wall). There are only 150 pitches with shade offered by orange, lemon and walnut trees. Pitches are reasonably flat and have electricity on flat ground. In summer (mid-June - end Sept) there is a bus service to the Circumvesuviana railway. English is spoken by the Maresca family who run the site. Access to the site is challenging, down a long steep narrow road via a very sharp turn just after a tunnel and high overpass. The entrance is through a covered opening in a stone wall.

Facilities

The single sanitary block provides hot and cold showers, washbasins and British style WCs. Hot water is on payment. Small shop, bar and restaurant. Dogs are not accepted in August. Off site: Fishing and boat slipway 100 m.

Open

15 March - 30 October.

At a glance

Welcome & Ambience	✓✓✓	Location	✓✓✓✓
Quality of Pitches	✓✓✓✓	Range of Facilities	✓✓✓

Directions

Take route SS163 from Castellamare to Sorrento. Just 50 m. after tunnel by-pass around Vico Equense, watch for very hard right turn for Seiano beach and follow signs down the narrow road.

Charges 2004

Per person	€ 6,70 - € 7,75
child (3-8 yrs)	€ 4,70 - € 5,00
pitch	€ 7,80 - € 10,85

Reservations

Contact site. Tel: 081 802 8570.

Italy

IT6853 Camping Villagio Athena

Via Ponte di Ferro, 84063 Paestum (Campania)

This level site, which has direct access to the beach, has most facilities to hand. Much of the site is in woodland, but sun worshippers will have no problem here. The access is easy and the staff are friendly. There are 150 pitches, of which only 20 are used for static units and these are unobtrusive. There is no disco, although cabaret shows are staged in July/Aug. The management, the Prearo brothers, aim for a pleasant and happy environment.

Facilities

Toilet facilities in three blocks have mixed British and Turkish style WCs, washbasins and showers (cold water only) and hot showers on payment. Dishwashing and laundry sinks. Toilets for disabled people. Shop. Bar and restaurant (1/5-30/9). Riding. Watersports. Dogs and barbecues are not permitted. Off site: Tennis 1 km. Hourly bus service. Greek temples nearby.

Open

1 March - 30 October.

At a glance

Welcome & Ambience	✓✓✓✓	Location	✓✓✓✓
Quality of Pitches	✓✓✓✓	Range of Facilities	✓✓✓✓

Directions

Take SS18 through Paestum and, at southern end of town before the antiquities, turn right as signed and follow road straight down to sea. Site is well signed.

Charges guide

Per person	€ 4,65 - € 6,50
pitch incl. electricity	€ 8,50 - € 13,00

Reservations

Contact site. Tel: 0828 851105.
E-mail: vathena@tiscalinet.it

IT6845 Centro Turistico San Nicola

71010 Peschici (Puglia)

This is a really splendid site occupying a hill-side position, sloping down to a cove with a 500 metre beach of fine sand – a special feature is an attractive grotto at the eastern end. Surrounded by tree clad mountains, it is generally a quiet, well regulated site which is part of, but separate from, a tourist holiday complex in the same area. Hard access roads lead to spacious well constructed, grassy pitches, under shade from mature trees. Scores of pitches are on the beach fringes (no extra charge) and there is a separate area for campers with animals. There are 750 pitches of varying size, all with electricity. Cars may have to be parked away from the pitches in high season. There are no static caravans, but some bungalows are on site. With a neat, tidy appearance, many flowerbeds provide a garden atmosphere. The site is popular with German campers (tannoy announcements and most notices in German only) although English is spoken. It is fairly remote with some interesting hairpins in the last 14 km. of the 75 km. journey from the autostrada. However, we think it is well worth the drive if you enjoy high quality beach sites and wish to explore the Gargano National Park.

Facilities

Six modern toilet blocks, two in the beach part, the others around the site, are excellent with British and Turkish style toilets, hot water in the washbasins (some with toilets in private cabins), showers and dishwashing facilities. Washing machines and dryers. Supermarket, fruit shop and bazaar. Two beach bars (from 1/5; some evening noise until 22.30 hrs). Large bar/restaurant with terraces and separate pizzeria (all season). Electronic games. Tennis. Watersports. Playground. Organised activities and entertainment for young and old (July/Aug). Off site: Coach and boat excursions. Gargano National Park.

Open

1 April - 15 October.

At a glance

Welcome & Ambience	✓✓✓✓	Location	✓✓✓✓
Quality of Pitches	✓✓✓✓	Range of Facilities	✓✓✓✓✓

Directions

Leave autostrada A14 at exit for Poggio Imperiale, and proceed towards Peschici and Vieste. When signs for Peschici and Vieste diverge, follow Vieste signs keeping a sharp lookout for San Nicola and Camping Baia San Nicola signs. Then follow large pink campsite signs. It will take at least 1.5 hrs from the motorway.

Charges 2004

Per adult	€ 7,00 - € 11,00
child (1-8 yrs)	€ 4,00 - € 6,50
tent	€ 5,50 - € 8,50
caravan or trailer tent	€ 8,50 - € 13,50
car	€ 3,50 - € 6,00
motorcaravan	€ 10,00 - € 15,00

Reservations

Only made for site's own accommodation (min. 1 week). Tel: 0884 964024.
E-mail: sannicola@sannicola.it

IT6858 Camping Il Salice

Contrada Ricota Grande, 87060 Corigliano Cálabro (Calabria)

This is a site with attitude! Starting with the elegant, air-conditioned reception and welcoming coffees, there are attractive landscaped gardens, fountains and the most enormous pool in the shape of Calabria. There are many choices here – to visit the hairdresser, have a massage, enjoy the warm Ionian sea or have a relaxing drink by the pool. The large flat pitches are under tall pines and eucalyptus, many with views of the beach, some right alongside the sand. In the distance the mountains of Pollino National Park can be seen. Nearby are the famous sites of Archaic Sybaris, the capital of Magna Greece and many other attractions. It is a real treat to stay here and enjoy the facilities – we think it well worth the driving.

Facilities

One large heated and two small unheated toilet blocks provide high quality facilities including excellent units for disabled campers. Laundry. Restaurant, pizzeria, takeaway and bar. Shop. Hairdresser. Massage. Very large outdoor pool (fairly hefty family charge in high season € 36 - € 62). Solarium. Tennis courts. Bicycle hire. Electronic games room. Internet. Amphitheatre and entertainment. Pedaloes. Windsurfing. Off site: Fishing. Golf 20 km.

Open

All year.

At a glance

Welcome & Ambience	✓✓✓✓✓	Location	✓✓✓✓✓
Quality of Pitches	✓✓✓✓✓	Range of Facilities	✓✓✓✓✓

Directions

From A3 Salerno-Reggio Calabria autostrada take Sibari exit, followed by the SS106 road towards Crotone. At the km. 19 marker look for the campsite sign and turn for Centro Vacanze Il Salice towards the beach. Site is well signed through small 'estate'.

Charges 2004

Per person	€ 2,00 - € 10,00
child (3-6 yrs)	free - € 8,00
pitch	€ 3,00 - € 14,00
electricity (3-6A)	€ 2,00 - € 3,00

Reservations

Contact site. Tel: 09 83 85 11 69.
E-mail: info@salicevacanze.it

IT6865 Camping Riva di Ugento

Litoranea Gallipoli, S. Maria di Leuca, 73059 Ugento (Puglia)

There are some campsites where you can be comfortable, have all the amenities at hand and still feel you are connecting with nature. Under the pine and eucalyptus trees of the Bay of Taranto foreshore is Riva di Urgento. Its 950 pitches are nestled in and around the dunes and the foreshore area. They have space and trees around them and the sizes differ, as the environment dictates the shape of most. The sea is only a short walk from most pitches and some are at the water's edge. There are pools, although these are expensive in high season. We were sorry to leave the site which was by far the best we found in the area.

Facilities

Twenty toilet blocks are in two different styles, of which ten have complete amenities. Bar. Restaurant and takeaway. Swimming pool. Tennis. Watersports incl. windsurfing school. Cinema. TV in bar. Bicycle hire. Off site: Fishing.

Open

11 May - 30 September.

At a glance

Welcome & Ambience	✓✓✓✓	Location	✓✓✓✓✓
Quality of Pitches	✓✓✓✓✓	Range of Facilities	✓✓✓✓

Directions

From Bari take Brindisi road to Lecce, then SS101 to Gallipoli, followed by the SR274 towards S. Maria di Leuca, and exit at Ugento. Site is well signed and has a long bumpy approach road.

Charges 2004

Per pitch incl. 3 persons	€ 16,00 - € 35,00

Reservations

Contact site. Tel: 0648 72823.
E-mail: rivadiugento@rivadiugento.it

IT6875 Vascellero Villaggio Camping

87063 Cariati Marina (Calabria)

The superb, irregularly shaped pool with its bar and gelateria are the hub of Vascellero Village. Alongside is the air conditioned restaurant which is bedecked with tasteful artefacts. The pool area is a delightful place to while away the day and the beach is equally tempting. Here, through a secure gate, you will find a sophisticated beach bar serving food on terraces overlooking the sea. The camping area is just inside the gate and is modest, but there are 100 generous pitches of gravel and sand under artificial shade and giant poplars. Entertainment for children runs during the day, and evening entertainment is held for adults. Senora Franca aims to please her guests, whether it is for summer holidays or winter ski-ing.

Facilities

The single toilet block, kept clean at all times, provides mixed Turkish and British style toilets, six fully equipped cabins and facilities for disabled campers. Washing machines. Motorcaravan service point. Excellent restaurant. Pizzeria. Good swimming pool with pool bar. Two good play areas. Hairdresser. Tennis. Bicycle hire. Mini-club, entertainment and aerobics. Beach 250 m. Beach volleyball. Beach restaurant serving takeaway and casual food with stage and disco. Watersports. Excursion service. Dogs and other animals are not accepted in Aug.

At a glance

Welcome & Ambience	✓✓✓✓	Location	✓✓✓✓
Quality of Pitches	✓✓✓	Range of Facilities	✓✓✓✓

Directions

Take SS106 Taranto – Reggio road. At km. 299.2 marker in village of Carati turn towards beach at campsite signs. Site is well signed over the railway line.

Charges guide

Per person	€ 4,00 - € 10,00
child (2-5 yrs)	€ 3,00 - € 7,00
pitch incl. electricity	€ 5,50 - € 15,00

Reservations

Made with € 150 deposit. Tel: 0983 91127.
E-mail: villaggio@vascellero.it

Open

All year.

IT6885 Camping Costa Blu

Loc. Finocchiaro, 88050 Sellia Marina (Calabria)

This tiny campsite of just 50 clean flat pitches has remarkable features for its size plus an attractive Italian ambience. The generously sized pitches (with electricity) are shaded by pines and eucalyptus. The very attractive pool has a slide and separate paddling pool and close by there is a small, smart amphitheatre for children and adult entertainment, which again is unusual in a site this size. First class tennis and 'bocce' courts (artificial surfaces) are near the beach access. The clean beach is just 30 m. through a secure gate and it is excellent for relaxing and enjoying the tranquil atmosphere, to soak up the sun or swim in the cool Ionian sea. A small restaurant serves the menu of the day and the friendly owners and staff are very keen that you enjoy your stay, although little English is spoken. This is a great site if you think small is beautiful and is a cut above the other sites in this area and the prices in low season are very favourable.

Facilities

One block of sanitary facilities has mixed Turkish and British style toilets and unisex coin operated showers (20c). Washing machine. Motorcaravan service point. Small restaurant with dish of the day. Snack bar. Small shop. Very nice small pool complex with a slide. Paddling pool. Play area. Beach volleyball. Small amphitheatre. Animation and mini-club. Off site: Watersports. Fishing. Restaurants, bars and shops.

At a glance

Welcome & Ambience	✓✓✓✓	Location	✓✓✓✓
Quality of Pitches	✓✓✓✓	Range of Facilities	✓✓✓

Directions

Take SS106 Crotone - Reggio road. At km. 199.7 marker in village of Carati take turn towards the beach indicated by the campsite signs. Site is well signed over the railway line through a small estate. The entrance is a sharp turn off the village road.

Charges 2005

Contact site.

Reservations

Contact site. Tel: 044 960232.

Open

15 June - 3 September.

IT6890 Villaggio Camping Dolomiti sul Mare

SS 522 per Tropea km 16,5, 89817 Briatico (Calabria)

Set high above the gulf of Eufemia, 300 metres from the beach, Dolomiti is a large sprawling site where the focus is on bungalows. It is popular with Italians and the village area within the resort is growing fast resulting in a little chaos at times, especially at reception and the restaurant where it is advisable to book well ahead and then confirm on the day. The pitches are informally laid out in a large, somewhat dusty olive grove where the ground slopes to the sea (chocks useful). Campers share the pool, bar, restaurant and entertainment with the other residents, but the high standards of the main complex make a stay worthwhile. The view from the attractive traditional house which forms the restaurant, bar and terraces has stunning views to the sea. This is an excellent stop-over point when in the area and compares favourably with other local sites.

Facilities

One unit with mixed British and Turkish style toilets and hot showers provides adequate, clean facilities. Site is unsuitable for disabled campers (rough terrain). Washing machines and dryers. Motorcaravan service point. Shop. Bar and terrace with views. Self service restaurant and snack bar. Swimming pool plus spa and paddling pool. Aerobics. Play area. Bicycle hire. Amphitheatre with entertainment and mini-club. Dogs are accepted but contact site first. Torches useful. Off site: Riding and beach 500 m.

At a glance

Welcome & Ambience	✓✓✓	Location	✓✓✓✓
Quality of Pitches	✓✓✓	Range of Facilities	✓✓✓✓

Directions

Take E45 Cosenza – Reggio road and leave at Serre exit. Head for Vibo Valentia, then take the coast road and Briatico – the site is well signed.

Charges guide

Per person	€ 6,00 - € 12,00
pitch	€ 4,00 - € 17,00
dog	€ 3,00 - € 6,00

Reservations

Contact site. Tel: 0963 391355. E-mail: dolmar@tin.it

Open

All year.

IT6930 Camping Villaggio Marinello

Via del Sol, 17, 98060 Oliveri (Sicily)

Camping Village Marrinello is located alongside the sea with direct access to a lovely uncrowded beach with an informal marina at one end and a spit of sand and natural pool areas at the other. The 250 sandy pitches here are shaded by tall trees. We enjoyed a delicious traditional meal in the excellent terraced restaurant with its lovely sea views. Tours are arranged to major sightseeing destinations such as Mount Etna, Taormina and the nearby Eolian Islands. The Greco family have been here for over 30 years and work hard to ensure that their guests enjoy a pleasant stay. The nearby resort area town has lots of attractions for the tourist and the site is easily accessible from the ferry at Messina.

Facilities

Two sanitary blocks with free hot showers, one is to be refurbished and heated for the winter of 2004/5. Washing machines. Bazzar, market and supermarket. Bar with sea views. Restaurant and terraced eating area also with views. Electronic games. Piano bar in high season. Off site: Seaside resort style town of Oliveri.

Open

All year.

At a glance

Welcome & Ambience	✓✓✓✓	Location	✓✓✓✓
Quality of Pitches	✓✓✓	Range of Facilities	✓✓✓✓

Directions

From the A20 motorway take Falcone exit and follow signs to Oliveri. At the town turn north towards the beach (there should be a campsite sign), then turn west along the beach and continue about 1 km. to site.

Charges 2004

Per person	€ 4,50 - € 7,50
pitch with electricity	€ 11,80 - € 15,70
child (under 3 yrs)	free

Reservations

Contact site. Tel: 0941 313000.
E-mail: marinello@camping.it

IT6923 Camping Jonio

Via Villini a Mare, 2, Ognina 95126 Catania (Sicily)

This is a small, uncomplicated and tranquil city site with the advantage of being on top of the cliff at the waters edge. The level pitches are on gravel with shade from some tall trees and artificial bamboo screens. There are some clean high quality sanitary facilities (also some private facilities for hire), although these may be overcrowded in peak season. There is no pool but the views of the water compensate and there are delightful rock pools in the sea just a few steps from the campsite. A new attractive restaurant offers food in the summer high season. Camping Jonio is ideal for a short stay to unwind whilst basking on the rocky platforms and diving into the clear waters, or to take advantage of the many excursions to the local historical sites. Excellent winter rates are available for long stay visitors. Five languages including English are spoken and access to the site is good.

Facilities

Sanitary facilities are in one small block for men and another for women. Modern and clean, but low numbers of showers and hot water at timed periods will mean showers will frequently be under stress. Laundry. Motorcaravan service point. Shop. Bar and restaurant. Basic old style playground (parental supervision recommended). Animation in high season. Diving school. Access to rock pools and small gravel beach. Excusions arranged to local attractions including Mount Etna and Taormina. Dogs are not accepted in July/August. Off site: Large town of Catania, many local historical sites and Mount Etna.

At a glance

Welcome & Ambience	✓✓✓✓	Location	✓✓✓✓
Quality of Pitches	✓✓✓	Range of Facilities	✓✓✓

Directions

From A18 motorway take Catania exit and follow signs to the SS114 coast road in the direction of Ognina. Site is off the SS114 (signed) on the northeast outskirts of town.

Charges 2004

Per person	€ 5,00 - € 7,00
pitch	€ 5,00 - € 10,00
car	€ 3,00 - € 5,00
boat	€ 5,00 - € 7,00
electricity	€ 2,50

Reservations

Contact site. Tel: 095 491139.
E-mail: jonio@camping.it

Open

All year.

IT6925 Camping Il Peloritano

Ctra Tarantonio s. 113d., Rodia, 98161 Messina (Sicily)

Set in a 100 year old olive grove which provides shade for the fifty informally arranged pitches, Camping Il Peloritano is a quiet uncomplicated site with clean facilities. It is a 200 metre walk to the sandy beach and approximately two kilometres to the nearest village. The friendly owners Patrizia Mowdello and Carlo Oteri provide assistance to arrange excursions to the Eolian Islands, Taormina and Mount Etna and will do their best to make your stay a pleasant one.

Facilities

Hot showers (by token). Washing machine. Motorcaravan service point. Small shop. Meals can be ordered in from local restaurants. Excursions arranged. Off site: Sandy beach 200 m. Small seaside village 2 km.

Open

1 March - 30 October.

At a glance

Welcome & Ambience	✓✓✓	Location	✓✓✓
Quality of Pitches	✓✓✓	Range of Facilities	✓✓

Directions

From A20 motorway take Villafranca / Gesso exit onto the S113 away from Gesso. At eastern outskirts of Villafranca turn on S113 dir. (this road may not be well signed but is the only main road continuing east along the coast and not up into the hills). Continue through Orto Liuzzo and the turn to site is about 3 km. down this road.

Charges 2004

Per person	€ 4,80 - € 6,00
child (3-7 yrs)	€ 2,80
pitch	€ 4,80 - € 7,00
car	€ 1,80 - € 2,40
electricity	€ 2,30

Reservations

Write, phone, or email. Tel: 090 348496.
E-mail: peloritano@camping.it

IT6950 Camping La Foce

Via Ampurias, 1 c.s, 07039 Valledoria (Sardinia)

English speaking Stefano Lamparti is the enthusiastic owner of La Foce which is a large sprawling site in the Golfo del Asinara. A river flows through the site into the sea and Stefano has a motorised punt to ferry campers to a secluded area of the coast on the other side of the river where they can enjoy the golden sand dunes and have a refreshing swim away from other beachgoers. The 300 sandy pitches vary in size and are informally arranged under tall shady eucalyptus trees stretching along the length of the site, some close to the river. This unpretentious site has a family atmosphere and there appears to be something for everyone here in a distinctly old style way, communing with nature. A pleasant surprise was the Gulliver Centre in a remote are of the campsite. This is a place for children from all over Italy and other parts of Europe to learn about the challenges of nature.

Facilities

Four mature toilet blocks house good facilities with British and Turkish style toilets but no facilities for disabled campers. Hot water is available 24 hours. Washing machine. Motorcaravan service point. Supermarket. Restaurant and snack bar. Play areas. Tennis. Bocce. Excursion service. Beaches – some by free punt. Boat launching. Windsurfing. Canoeing. Sub-aqua diving. Off site: Fishing. Sailing 1.5 km. Riding 2 km.

Open

1 May - 30 September.

At a glance

Welcome & Ambience	✓✓✓✓	Location	✓✓✓✓
Quality of Pitches	✓✓✓✓	Range of Facilities	✓✓✓✓

Directions

From Sassari take coast road go east to Castelsardo and Valledoria. As you arrive at the village watch for campsite signs towards beach.

Charges 2005

Per person	€ 6,00 - € 14,00
child (3-8 yrs)	free - € 8,00
electricity (4/6A)	€ 1,50 - € 3,80
dog	€ 1,50 - € 3,00

Reservations

Made for min 7 days - with deposit.
Tel: 079 582 109. E-mail: info@foce.it

IT6955 Camping Baia Blu La Tortuga

Pineta di Vignola Mare, 07020 Aglientu (Sardinia)

In the northeast of Sardinia near the Costa Smeralda and well situated for the Corsica ferry, Baia Blu is a large, professionally run campsite. The beach with its golden sand, brilliant blue sea and pretty rocky outcrops is warm and inviting. The site's 550 touring pitches are of fine sand and shaded by tall pines with banks of colourful oleanders and wide boulevards providing good access for units. This is a busy bustling site with lots to do and attractive restaurants. It is under the same ownership as Marepineta (no. IT6000) and is very popular with Italian families who enjoy the wide range of amenities here.

Facilities

Four blocks provide an exceptionally good ratio of facilities to pitches including combined private shower/washbasin cabins (for rent), free hot showers and mixed British and Turkish toilets. Numerous footbaths, basins for children, sinks for dishes and laundry. Facilities for disabled people. Washing machines and dryers. Motorcaravan services. Supermarket. Gas. Bazaar. Bar. Restaurant, pizzeria, snack bar and takeaway (May-Sept). Supermarket. Playground. Tennis. Volleyball. Football. Table tennis. Games and TV rooms. Windsurfing and diving schools. Entertainment and sports activities organised in season. Excursions. Barbecue area (not permitted on pitches). First aid. Torches useful. Used by tour operators. Off site: Disco 50 m. Riding 5 km.

At a glance

Welcome & Ambience	✓✓✓✓	Location	✓✓✓✓
Quality of Pitches	✓✓✓✓	Range of Facilities	✓✓✓✓

Directions

Site is on the north coast between towns of Costa Paradiso and S. Teresa di Gallura (18 km.) at Pineta di Vignola Mare and is well signed.

Charges guide

Per person	€ 4,30 - € 9,80
junior (4-10 yrs) or senior (over 60 yrs)	€ 3,20 - € 7,50
pitch incl. electricity	€ 8,30 - € 21,20
tent pitch incl. electricity	€ 6,70 - € 13,00
dog	€ 1,00 - € 4,65

Reservations

Made with 30% deposit and € 15.50 fee. Tel: 079 602060. E-mail: info@baiablu.com

Open

12 April - 28 September.

IT6963 Camping Villaggio Isuledda

Cannigione di Arzachena, 07020 Sardegna (Sardinia)

Located in the centre of the Arzachena Gulf, Isuleda has access to three kilometres of beaches. These include a small bay with a marina, a more rugged long, open beach and a small bay with some attractive coves. This high quality resort style operation has something for everyone, with an amazing choice of restaurants, activities and entertainment. The staff are professional and vibrant, campers appeared relaxed and happy. The central area buzzes with activity, although it is possible to find a quiet area to relax. There is a balance of activities for all age groups and a large range of pitch choice. Most of the 650 good sized, gravel pitches are shaded by eucalyptus trees and flat; some are on the water's edge and others enjoy sea views (book early for high season). This site takes camping in Sardinia a step further and can be considered at the cutting edge for the area.

Facilities

Four modern and two older blocks provide the sanitary facilities with mainly British style toilets and good facilities for disabled campers (we recommend the smaller blocks). Showers are on payment (€ 0,50). Washing machines. Motorcaravan service point. Large supermarket. Tabac and paper shops. Restaurants (à la carte and self service), pizzeria and snack bar. Aerobics. Play areas. Doctor. Bicycle and motor scooter hire. Small boat launching. Windsurfing. Sailing. Sub Aqua diving school. Beach volleyball. Marina. Mini-club, animation and entertainment. Excursion service. Disco and beer bar – both isolated for noise management. Dogs and other animals are not accepted. Off site: Riding 2 km. Golf 20 km.

At a glance

Welcome & Ambience	✓✓✓✓✓	Location	✓✓✓✓✓
Quality of Pitches	✓✓✓✓✓	Range of Facilities	✓✓✓✓✓

Directions

Site is on the Costa Smeralda in the northeast of Sardinia. From SS125 Olbia – Cannigione road, south of Arzachena, take road north to Baia Sardinia. Site is well signed off this road in about 12 km. Be sure to travel up the west side of the inlet.

Charges guide

Per person	€ 5,00 - € 10,00
child (2-12 yrrs)	€ 3,00 - € 6,00
pitch	€ 4,50 - € 23,00
electricity	€ 3,00

Reservations

Contact site. Tel: 0789 86003. E-mail: informazioni@isuledda.it

Open

8 April - 17 October.

IT6996 Camping Mariposa

Via Lido 22, 07041 Alghero (Sardinia)

Mariposa is situated right by the sea with its own beach and the range of sports available here probably makes it best suited for active young visitors. Kite surfing, diving, windsurfing, sailing, surfing and paragliding courses are all available here on payment, whilst evening entertainment is provided free. Pitch size ranges from 50 to 90 sq.m. so they are also better suited for tents, although they do all have 6A electrical connections and caravans and motorcaravans are welcome. Cars must be parked away from the pitches. Alghero (1.5 km.) still has a strong 'Catalan' flavour from its 400 year occupation by the Spanish. There are many small coves and the Neptune caves are well worth a visit.

Facilities

The sanitary facilities are fairly basic, partly open plan, with cold washbasins and troughs, dishwashing and laundry sinks and an equal amount of warm (token needed) and cold showers. Washing machines and dryer. Motorcaravan service point. Shop, self service restaurant and bar (all open all season). Bicycle hire. Dogs are not accepted in August.

Open

1 April - 31 October.

At a glance

Welcome & Ambience	✓✓✓✓	Location	✓✓✓✓
Quality of Pitches	✓✓✓✓	Range of Facilities	✓✓✓✓

Directions

Alghero is on the northwest coast, about 35 km. southwest of Sassari. Mariposa is at the north of the town.

Charges guide

Per person	€ 7,50 - € 10,50
child (3-12 yrs)	€ 4,00 - € 8,50
tent	free - € 10,00
caravan	free - € 10,00
motorcaravan	€ 3,50 - € 11,00
electricity	€ 2,50

Reservations

Tel: 079 950 360. E-mail: info@lamariposa.it

IT6972 Camping L'Ultima Spiaggia

Localita Planargia, 08042 Bari Sardo (Sardinia)

A great name for this campsite – 'the ultimate beach' – and the beach really is extremely good, along with the bright colourful décor and amenities. Tastefully laid out with a rather tropical feel, this is a very pleasant place to spend time. The 350 pitches are terraced on sand, some enjoying sea views, and large stone barbecues are provided. The good entertainment programme can be enjoyed from the terrace of the friendly restaurant which offers a reasonably priced menu which includes the local seafood specialities. Access to the fine beach (with lifeguard – unusual in these parts) with its watersports is gained through a security gate. Sub-aqua diving is extremely good hereabouts. Much thought has been put into the décor of the campsite and the effect is very relaxing. We think you will enjoy this clean and pleasant site where some English is spoken.

Facilities

Two toilet units include mainly Turkish style toilets and good facilities for disabled campers. Washing machines. Motorcaravan service point. Small supermarket. Restaurant and snack bar. Play areas. Football. Beach volleyball. Windsurfing. Aerobics. Riding. Tennis. Minigolf. Canoeing. Bicycle hire. Mini-club. Entertainment. Excursion service. Torches useful. Off site: Restaurants, bars and shops. Fishing. Boat launching.

Open

20 April - 30 September.

At a glance

Welcome & Ambience	✓✓✓✓	Location	✓✓✓✓✓
Quality of Pitches	✓✓✓✓	Range of Facilities	✓✓✓✓✓

Directions

Site is on east coast of Sardinia and is well signed from SS125 in village of Bari Sardo. Note that the roads are very winding from the north – allow lots of time for transit.

Charges guide

Per person	€ 5,50 - € 12,00
child (1-6 yrs)	€ 3,50 - € 4,50
pitch	€ 5,50 - € 11,50
dog	€ 1,50 - € 3,50

Reservations

Made without charge. Tel: 0782 29363.
E-mail: info@campingultimaspiaggia.it

IT6975 Camping Villaggio Porto Pirastu

Capo Ferrato, 09043 Muravera (Sardinia)

This delightful site situated at Capo Ferrato has a wide range of facilities in a tranquil area alongside the beautiful Mar Tirreno with its warm turquoise water, rocky outcrops and long stretches of sandy beach. This is a resort style venture with a professional approach. The attractive traditional buildings lend atmosphere to the main square and the restaurant has a charming ambience with its arched ceilings. There are shaded terraces and sitting out areas where you can relax and enjoy the sea breezes whilst enjoying an aperitif or ice-cream. The large staff provides excellent activities for adults and children including water aerobics at the beach. Tennis lessons are available, a cinema and lively entertainment. The 260 shaded, reasonably sized pitches are attractively spaced on gravel and sand, some having views of the water. Porto Piratsu is a quality site with innovative management who aim to provide an enjoyable holiday.

Facilities

Two very pleasant blocks of sanitary facilities with mainly style British toilets, facilities for disabled campers and some children's washbasins. Washing machine. Motorcaravan service point. Shop. Restaurant and snack bar. Play areas. Mini-club and entertainment all day in high season. Cinema. Tennis. Excursion service. Beach volleyball. Water aerobics. Sub-aqua diving. Windsurfing school. Torches useful.
Off site: Sailing 1.5 km. Bicycle hire 4 km. Golf, riding 5 km.

Open

1 April - 30 September.

At a glance

Welcome & Ambience	✓✓✓✓	Location	✓✓✓✓✓
Quality of Pitches	✓✓✓✓	Range of Facilities	✓✓✓✓✓

Directions

Site is in southeast corner of Sardinia in the north of the Costa Rei. From coast road SS125 at S. Priamo travel south to Villagio Capo Ferrato. Site is well signed from here.

Charges guide

Per person	€ 4,00 - € 11,50
child (3-9 yrs)	€ 3,00 - € 7,90
pitch	€ 7,20 - € 12,50

Reservations

Made with 50% deposit. Tel: 070 991 437.
E-mail: info@portopirastu.net

IT6995 Camping Torre del Porticciolo

C.P.n. 83, Sede lagale via G. Ferret 17, 07041 Alghero (Sardinia)

Torre del Porticciolo is set high on a peninsula with fabulous views over the sea and old fortifications. It is a friendly, family owned site with striking traditional old buildings, attractive landscaping and large pools. The owner Marisa Carboni and her friendly staff speak a little English and are very helpful. A wonderfully decorated restaurant is close to the large bar and terrace. Nearby is the equally attractive pizzeria with its own terrace. It is in this area that the evening entertainment takes place. It is a 300 m. walk out of the site down a steep slope with stunning views to the attractive beach and warm waters. The 333 pitches are sandy and shaded and average 100 sq.m. in size. There are some with views, although most are tucked in under the pine trees.

Facilities

Four good toilet blocks have mainly Turkish style toilets plus facilities for disabled campers. Washing machines. Motorcaravan service point. Big supermarket. Excellent restaurant. Snack bar. Good pool complex with paddling pool. Aerobics. Fitness centre. Play areas. Bicycle hire. Mini-club. Animation. Excursion service. Beach 100 m. down steepish slope. Excellent diving. Off site: Fishing. Sailing. Riding 1 km.

Open

1 June - 10 October.

At a glance

Welcome & Ambience	✓✓✓✓✓	Location	✓✓✓✓✓
Quality of Pitches	✓✓✓✓	Range of Facilities	✓✓✓✓✓

Directions

Take SS291 Sassari - Alghero road east, then SS55 to Capo Caccia. Turn to Porticciolo town where site is well signed.

Charges guide

Per person	€ 7,00 - € 12,50
junior or senior (under 12 and over 60 yrs)	€ 6,00 - € 10,00
pitch	€ 2,00 - € 5,00
dog	€ 3,00 - € 5,00

Reservations

Made with 30% deposit by bank draft.
Tel: 079 919010. E-mail: info@torredelporticciolo.it

Alan Rogers

This is a just a sample of the campsites we have inspected and selected in Italy. For more campsites and further information, please see the Alan Rogers Italy guide.

LA LICCIA ★★★
S.Teresa di Gallura (SS)
✆ +39 0789 755190

ACAPULCO ★★★
Punta Palau - Palau (SS)
✆ +39 0789 709497

CAPO D'ORSO ★★★
Golfo delle Saline - Palau (SS)
✆ +39 0789 702007

ISOLA DEI GABBIANI ★★★
Porto Pollo - Palau (SS) - ✆ +39 0789 704024

BAIA SARACENO ★★★
Punta Nera - Palau (SS) - ✆ +39 0789 709403

ISULEDDA ★★★★
Cannigione - Arzachena (SS) - ✆ +39 0789 86003

CUGNANA PORTO ROTONDO ★★★
Loc. Cugnana - Olbia (SS) - ✆ +39 0789 33184

TAVOLARA ★★★
Porto S.Paolo (SS) - ✆ +39 0789 40166

S.TEODORO LA CINTA ★★★
San Teodoro (NU) - ✆ +39 0784 865777

PEDRA E CUPA ★★★
Budoni (NU) - ✆ +39 0784 844004

SELEMA ★★★
S.Lucia di Siniscola (NU) - ✆ +39 0784 819068

LE CERNIE ★★★
Lotzorai (NU) - ✆ +39 0782 669472

TELIS ★★★
Loc. Portofrailis - Arbatax (NU) - ✆ +39 0782 667140

SOS FLORES ★★★
Loc. S.Gemiliano - Tortolì (NU) - ✆ +39 0782 667485

ORRI ★★★
Loc.Orrì - Tortolì (NU) - ✆ +39 0782 624695

PORTO CORALLO ★★★
Villaputzu (CA) - ✆ +39 070 997017

LE DUNE ★★★
Loc. Piscina Rei - Muravera (CA) - ✆ +39 070 9919057

CAPO FERRATO ★★
Costa Rei - Muravera (CA) - ✆ +39 070 991012

SPIAGGIA DEL RISO ★★★
Loc. Campolongu - Villasimius (CA)
✆ +39 070 797150

FLUMENDOSA ★★
S. Margherita Pula (CA)
✆ +39 070 9208364

PINI E MARE ★★
Quartu S.Elena (CA) - ✆ +39 070 803103

All our camping in

www.faitasardegna.it **faitasardegna@foce.it**

The independent principality of Liechtenstein is the fourth smallest country in the world. Nestled between Switzerland and Austria, it has a total area of 157.sq.km. (61 sq.miles).

If you like clean mountain air and peaceful surroundings, then a visit to Liechtenstein would be worthwhile. The little town of Vaduz (the Capital) is where you will find most points of interest, including the World Famous art collection (Kunstmuseum), which holds paintings by Rembrandt and other world famous artists. Above the town of Vaduz is the restored twelth century castle, now owned by the prince of Liechtenstein (not open to the public). Take a walk up to the top of the hill, you can view Vaduz and the mountains stretched out below. Situated on a terrace above Vaduz is Triesenberg village, blessed with panoramic views over the Rhine Valley, a pretty village with vineyards and ancient chapels. Malbun is Liechtenstein's premier mountain resort, popular in both winter and summer, for either skiing or walking.

FL7580 Camping Mittagspitze

Sägastrasse 29, FL 9495 Triesen

Camping Mittagspitze is attractively and quietly situated for visiting the Principality. Probably the best site in the region, it is on a hillside and has all the scenic views that one could wish. Extensive broad, level terraces on the steep slope provide unmarked pitches (a reader tells us that spacing causes problems in high season) and electricity connections are available. There is little shade. Of the 240 spaces, 120 are used by seasonal caravans. Liechtenstein's capital, Vaduz, is 7 km, Austria is 20 km. and Switzerland 3 km.

Facilities

Two good quality sanitary blocks (the one near reception is new) provide all the usual facilities. Washing machine, dryer and ironing. Room where one can sit or eat with cooking facilities. Shop (1/6-31/8). Restaurant (all year). Small swimming pool (15/6-15/8), not heated but very popular in summer. Playground. Fishing. Off site: Tennis and indoor pool nearby. Riding and bicycle hire 5 km.

Open

All year.

At a glance

Welcome & Ambience	✓✓✓	Location	✓✓✓✓
Quality of Pitches	✓✓✓	Range of Facilities	✓✓✓

Directions

From A3 take Trübbach exit and follow road towards Balziers. Then head towards Vaduz and site is 2 km. south of Triesen on the right.

Charges 2005

Per person	€ 8,50
child (under 14 yrs)	€ 4,00
caravan or large tent	€ 8,00 - € 10,00
car	€ 4,00
small tent	€ 5,00
dog	€ 4,00
electricity	€ 5,00

Reservations

Not made. Tel: 3923677.
E-mail: info@campingtriesen.li

The Grand Duchy of Luxembourg is an independent sovereign state, lying between Belgium, France and Germany. Divided into two areas: the spectacular Ardennes region in the north and the rolling farmlands and woods in the south, bordered on the east by the wine growing area of the Moselle Valley.

From wherever you are in Luxembourg you are always within easy reach of the capital, Luxembourg-Ville, home to about one fifth of the population. The city was built upon a rocky outcrop, and has superb views of the Alzette and Petrusse Valleys. Those who love the great outdoors must make a visit to the Ardennes, with its hiking trails, footpaths and cycle routes that take you through beautiful winding valleys and across deep rivers, a very popular region for visitors. If wine tasting takes your fancy, then head for the Moselle Valley, particularly if you like sweet, fruity wines. From late spring to early autumn wine tasting tours take place in cellars and caves. The Mullerthal region, known as the 'Little Switzerland', lies on the banks of the river Sûre, which forms the border with Germany; the earth is mostly made up of soft sandstone, so through the ages many fascinating gorges, caves and formations have emerged.

Population

435,700

Capital

Luxembourg City

Climate

A temperate climate prevails, the summer often extending from May to late October

Language

Letzeburgesch is the national language, with French and German also being official languages

Currency

The Euro

Telephone

The country code is 00 352

Banks

Mon-Fri 08.30/09.00-12.00 and 13.30-16.30

Shops

Mon 14.00-18.30. Tues to Sat 08.30-12.00 and 14.00-18.30 (grocers and butchers at 15.00 on Sat)

Public Holidays

New Year; Carnival Day mid-Feb; Easter Mon; May Day; Ascension; Whit Mon; National Day 23 June; Assumption 15 Aug; All Saints; All Souls; Christmas 25, 26 Dec

Motoring

Many holidaymakers travel through Luxembourg to take advantage of the lower fuel prices, thus creating traffic congestion at petrol stations, especially in summer. A Blue Zone area exists in Luxembourg City and various parts of the country (discs from tourist offices) but parking meters are also used

Tourist Office

Luxembourg National Tourist Office
122 Regent Street, London W1B 5SA
Tel: 020 7434 2800
Fax: 020 7734 1205
Email: tourism@luxembourg.co.uk
Internet: www.luxembourg.co.uk

LUXEMBOURG IS THE IDEAL PLACE TO BUY BEAUTIFUL PORCELAIN AND CRYSTAL. VILLEROY & BOCH'S CRYSTAL FACTORIES IN SEPTFONTAINES ARE OPEN TO VISITORS.

LU7670 Camping des Ardennes

L-9809 Hosingen

A good value, small municipal site, Camping Ardennes is located on the edge of this attractive small town with an easy level walk to all amenities and parks and some floral arrangements to admire during the summer season. The 48 touring pitches are level, open and grassy. All have electricity (10A) and are arranged on either side of surfaced roads, with a few trees providing a little shade in places. Adjacent sports complex with tennis and football, etc. This site is useful as a stopover if travelling along the N7.

Facilities

The single well appointed, modern, clean sanitary block can be heated in winter. Washing machine, dryer and clothes lines. Café/bar (opening variable). Barbecue. Playground. Volleyball. Boule. Skis and winter sports equipment for hire. English spoken. Rooms for rent (B&B).

Open

All year.

At a glance

Welcome & Ambience	✓✓✓	Location	✓✓✓
Quality of Pitches	✓✓✓	Range of Facilities	✓✓✓

Directions

Site is off the main N7 road north of Diekirch and is signed from town centre, with the sports complex.

Charges guide

Per pitch	€ 4,50
adult	€ 4,50
child (3-12 yrs)	€ 2,25
electricity	€ 2,25
dog	€ 2,25

Reservations

Write to site (no deposit). Tel: 921 911.

LU7880 Camping Trois Frontières

Maison 1, L-9972 Lieler

On a clear day, it's possible to see Belgium, Germany and Luxembourg from the campsite swimming pool, hence its name: Les Trois Frontières. Martin and Esther Van Aalst own and manage the site themselves and all visitors receive a personal welcome and immediately become part of a large happy family. Most of the facilities are close to the entrance, leaving the camping area quiet, except for the children's play area. The restaurant/takeaway provides good quality food at reasonable prices, served either inside or on the pleasant terrace with flower borders and overlooking the pool. The pool, paddling pool and grass sunbathing area with recliners are screened by an ornamental balustrade. There is no shop, however, Martin and Esther sell basic provisions such as bread, milk and newspapers.

Facilities

Unisex facilities include excellent showers, washbasins in cabins, British-style WCs, suite for visitors with disabilities, plus baby bath and changing station. More WCs in second building (down some steps). Laundry. Play area. Boules pitch, table tennis, games room, table football, table tennis, darts. Bicycle hire. Off site: Shops 2.3 km. Golf and riding 12 km. Clervaux 12 km, walking and cycling.

Open

All year.

At a glance

Welcome & Ambience	✓✓✓✓✓	Location	✓✓✓✓
Quality of Pitches	✓✓✓✓	Range of Facilities	✓✓✓✓

Directions

Take N7 northward from Diekirch. Continue past Weiswampach, then turn right onto CR338 signed Lieler. Site is on right as you enter the village.

Charges guide

Per pitch incl. 2 persons	€ 15,15 - € 17,50
extra adult	€ 5,10 - € 5,60
child (under 12 yrs)	€ 2,60 - € 3,10
electricity (4A)	€ 2,25

Reduction during low season for visitors over 55 yrs.

Reservations

Contact site. Tel: 998 608.
E-mail: camp.3front@cmdnet.lu

LU7620 Europacamping Nommerlayen

L-7465 Nommern

This is a top quality site, in central Luxembourg, with fees to match, but it has everything! A large, central building housing most of the services and amenities opens onto a terrace around an excellent swimming pool complex with two main pools (one heated 1/5-15/9) and an imaginative watery playground. The 396 individual pitches (70-120 sq.m.) on grassy terraces, all have access to electricity (2/16A) and water taps. Interestingly enough the superb new sanitary block is called 'Badtemple' (its architecture suggesting this title as the entrance with colonnades supporting a canopy is reminiscent of a Greek temple).

Facilities

A large, high quality, modern sanitary unit provides some washbasins in cubicles, facilities for disabled people, and family and baby washrooms. Private bathrooms for hire, including whirlpool bath. Laundry. Motorcaravan service point. Supermarket. Restaurant. Snack bar. Bar (all 15/3-15/11). Heated swimming pools (1/5-15/9). Solarium. Fitness programmes. Bowling. Table tennis. Snooker. Billiards. Volleyball. Playground. Large screen TV. Entertainment in season. Bicycle hire. Off site: Riding 1 km. Fishing and golf 5 km.

At a glance

Welcome & Ambience	✓✓✓✓✓	Location	✓✓✓✓
Quality of Pitches	✓✓✓✓✓	Range of Facilities	✓✓✓✓✓

Directions

Site is 5 km. from Larochette, on the west side of Nommern village. Follow signs 'Europa' Frum/Larochette in the centre of village.

Charges 2004

Per unit incl. 2 persons and 2A electricity, acc. to pitch	€ 18,00 - € 35,00
extra adult	€ 4,25
electricity (16A) plus	€ 3,00

Reservations

Essential for high season only, with deposit. Tel: 878 078. E-mail: nommerlayen@vo.lu

Open

All year except 15 December - 15 January.

LU7640 Camping Auf Kengert

L-7633 Larochette / Medernach

A friendly welcome awaits you at this peacefully situated, family run site, two kilometres from Larochette, northeast of Luxembourg city, providing 180 individual pitches, all with electricity (4/16A). Some in a very shaded woodland setting, on a slight slope with fairly narrow access roads. There are also six hardened pitches for motorcaravans on a flat area of grass, complete with motorcaravan service facilities (space really only suitable for four motorhomes). Further pitches are in an adjacent and more open meadow area. There are also six site owned chalets and caravans. This site is popular in season, so early arrival is advisable, or you can reserve.

Facilities

The well maintained sanitary block in two parts includes a modern, heated unit with some washbasins in cubicles, and excellent, fully equipped cubicles for disabled visitors. The showers, facilities for babies, additional WCs and washbasins, plus laundry room are located below the central building whicn houses the shop, bar.and restaurant. Motorcaravan services. Gas supplies. Playground and indoor play room. Swimming pool (Easter - 30 Sept). Paddling pool. Open area for ball games. Fishing. Bicycle hire.
Off site: Golf, fishing and riding 8 km.

At a glance

Welcome & Ambience	✓✓✓✓	Location	✓✓✓✓
Quality of Pitches	✓✓✓	Range of Facilities	✓✓✓✓

Directions

From Larochette take the CR118/N8 (towards Mersch) and just outside town turn right on CR119 towards Schrondweiler, site is 2 km. on right.

Charges 2005

Per person	€ 11,00 - € 14,00
child (4-18 yrs)	€ 5,00 - € 7,00
electricity	€ 2,00
dog	€ 1,25

10% reduction for students, walkers and cyclists.

Reservations

Write to site. Tel: 837186. E-mail: info@kengert.lu

Open

1 March - 8 November.

LU7870 Camping de la Sûre

Route de Gilsdorf, L-9234 Diekirch

The municipal Camping de la Sûre is within walking distance of the centre of Diekirch, a town that is brimming with things to see and do. Located on the banks of the Sûre, this site offers 175 flat grass pitches, most with a 16A electricity connection. One large building close to the entrance houses the reception and sanitary facilities, all of which were in pristine condition at the time of our visit. A walk/cycle path runs alongside the campsite; maps are available in the Syndicat d'Initiative in the town centre. Diekirch, with a donkey as its mascot, is a happy town and well worth a visit. A concert is held in the square every evening during the high season, there are free guided walks twice monthly during July and August, as well as a weekly entertainment programme for youngsters. Visitors to the campsite receive an information bag in their own language. There is an ongoing programme of improvements.

Facilities

One large building houses several heated rooms with modern facilities including showers and communal washbasins. Baby room and suite for visitors with disabilities. Laundry. Dishwashing. Play area. Children's entertainment organised during July and August.
Off site: Diekirch has leisure facilities within walking distance of campsite. Large park with skateboarding and bicycle ramps adjacent. Cycle path along site boundary.

Open

1 April - 1 October.

At a glance

Welcome & Ambience	✓✓✓✓	Location	✓✓✓✓
Quality of Pitches	✓✓✓✓	Range of Facilities	✓✓✓

Directions

Follow campsite signs from centre of Diekirch.

Charges guide

Per person	€ 4,70
child	€ 2,23
pitch	€ 3,72
dog	€ 0,74
electricity	€ 1,98

Reservations

Advisable in July and August, contact site.
Tel: 80 9425. E-mail: tourisme@diekirch.lu

LU7850 Camping Fuussekaul

4 Fuussekaul, L-9156 Heiderscheid

Children who visit Fuusse Kaul (the name means fox hole) won't want to leave as there is so much for them to do. Apart from a fun pool, exciting play areas, and an entertainment programme, children and parents can bake their own pizzas in the open-air oven. Of the 289 pitches, 196 of varying sizes are for touring units, all with a 10A electricity connection. The touring area (separate from the chalets and seasonal pitches) is well endowed with modern facilities, although there is no provision for visitors with disabilities. An entertainment programme continues throughout the main holiday season and includes mini shows and theatre productions, and sports. On the opposite side of the road (pedestrian access via an under-road passage) is a service and parking area for six motorhomes. Each pitch has a hook-up, fresh water tap and waste water disposal point. There's also a drive-over service point for those not wishing to stay the night.

Facilities

Four excellent sanitary blocks provide showers (token costs € 0.50), washbasins (in cabins and communal) and children and baby rooms with small toilets, washbasins and showers. Laundry. Parking and service area for motorcaravans. Suite with sauna and sunbeds etc. New beauty salon. Well stocked shop, bar, restaurant and takeaway. Swimming pools, playgrounds, cross country skiing when snow permits. Bicycle hire. Children's club included in site fees. Oven for baking pizzas. Off site: Castles, museums and walks all within a reasonable distance. Bus stops outside site entrance. Riding 500 m. Fishing 3 km. Supermarket and shops in Ettelbruckk 7 km.

At a glance

Welcome & Ambience	✓✓✓✓	Location	✓✓✓✓
Quality of Pitches	✓✓✓✓	Range of Facilities	✓✓✓✓✓

Directions

Take N15 from Diekirch to Heiderscheid. Site is on left at top of hill just before reaching the village. Motorhome service area is signed on the right.

Charges guide

Per unit incl. 2 persons	€ 14,50 - € 24,50
extra person	€ 2,00
electricity	€ 2,00
dog	€ 2,00

Reservations

Necessary in July and August with fee (€ 20). Tel: 268 8881. E-mail: info@fuussekaul.lu

Open

All year.

LU7590 Camping Belle-Vue 2000

29 rue de Consdorf, L-6551 Berdorf

Belle Vue would be ideal for those wanting a winter stopover. Residential and seasonal pitches are at the top end of the site and those reserved for touring units at the bottom end with views of the surrounding hills (site is split 70% residential: 30% touring). Two modern sanitary blocks serve the touring pitches, both equipped with all services. A large play area (hedged) offers a variety of equipment for young children. The campsite reception is in the same buildiong as the shop, which closes daily from 12.00-13.00 and at noon on Sundays.

Facilities

Two modern sanitary blocks with good clean facilities: showers, communal washbasins, British-style WCs, suite for visitors with disabilities, dishwashing sinks, and laundry. Hedged playground for pre-teen children. TV/meeting room. Table tennis. Well-stocked shop. Off site: Local shops, hotels for drinks and meals, and municipal sports complex with indoor swimming pool, fitness centre, tennis courts, minigolf etc. are just a few minutes walk away.

At a glance

Welcome & Ambience	✓✓✓	Location	✓✓✓✓
Quality of Pitches	✓✓✓	Range of Facilities	✓✓✓

Directions

Berdorf is 6 km. west of Echternach, the site is signed from centre of village in the direction of Consdorf.

Charges guide

Per person	€ 4,00
child (3-14 yrs)	€ 2,00
pitch	€ 4,00
electricity	€ 2,00

Reservations

Contact site. Tel: 79 0635.

Open

All year.

LU7610 Camping Birkelt

1 rue de la Piscine, L-7601 Larochette

This is very much a family site, the price representing the range of facilities provided. It is well organised and well laid out, set in an elevated position in attractive undulating good walking countryside. A tarmac road runs around the site with 400 large grass pitches, some slightly sloping, many with a fair amount of shade, on either side of gravel access roads in straight rows or circles. All pitches have an electricity point (6A). As well as the all weather swimming pool complex just outside the site entrance (free for campers), there is also a fitness centre with solarium and sauna. Entertainment for children is arranged in high season. The site is very popular with tour operators (140 pitches).

Facilities

Three modern sanitary buildings well situated around the site include mostly open washbasins (6 cabins in one block). Dishwashers (on payment), baby baths, facilities for wheelchair users. Washing machines and dryers. Motorcaravan service point. Shop. Coffee bar. Restaurant with terrace. All weather swimming pool. Outdoor pool for toddlers. Fitness centre. Playgrounds. Table tennis. Roller blade skating, Minigolf. Tennis. Football ground. Riding. Balloon flights. Internet points. Bicycle hire. Off site: Golf and bicycle hire 5 km. Fishing and Kayaking 10 km.

Open

1 April - 31 October.

At a glance

Welcome & Ambience	✓✓✓✓✓	Location	✓✓✓✓
Quality of Pitches	✓✓✓✓✓	Range of Facilities	✓✓✓✓✓

Directions

From N7 From N7 Diekirch - Luxembourg city, turn onto N8 at Berschblach (just past Mersch) towards Larochette. Site is signed on the right about 1.5 km. from Larochette. Approach road is fairly steep and narrow.

Charges 2004

Per unit incl. 2 persons	€ 20,00 - € 29,00
extra person	€ 3,75
electricity	€ 2,50
dog	€ 2,50

Less 25% in low season.

Reservations

Write to site for reservation application form. Tel: 879 040. E-mail: vilux@pt.lu

LU7680 Camping Kohnenhof

Maison 1, L-9838 Obereisenbach

Nestling in a valley with the River Our running through it, Camping Kohnenhof offers an agreeable location for a relaxing family holiday. From the minute you stop at the reception you are assured of a warm and friendly welcome. Numerous paths cross through the wooded hillside so this could be a haven for walkers. The river is shallow and safe for children to play in (parental supervision essential). The restaurant is part of an old farmhouse and, with its open fire to keep it warm, offers a wonderful ambience to enjoy a meal. A large sports field and play area with a selection of equipment caters for younger campers. During the high season, an entertainment programme is organised for parents and children. Some campers may be quite a distance from the sanitary facilities, bar and restaurant which are grouped together near the site entrance. This site is not suitable for visitors with walking disabilities.

Facilities

Heated sanitary block with showers and washbasins in cabins. Motorcaravan service point. Laundry. Bar, restaurant, takeaway. Games and TV room. Baker calls daily. Sports field with play equipment. Boule court. Bicycle hire. Off site: Bus to Clervaux and Vianden stops (4 times daily) outside site entrance. Riding 5 km. Castle at Vianden 14 km. Monastery at Clervaux 14 km. Golf 15 km.

Open

1 April - 7 November.

At a glance

Welcome & Ambience	✓✓✓✓	Location	✓✓✓✓
Quality of Pitches	✓✓✓✓	Range of Facilities	✓✓✓✓

Directions

Take N7 north from Diekirch. At Hosingen, turn right onto the narrow and winding CR324 signed Eisenbach. Follow campsite signs from Eisenbach or Obereisenbach.

Charges 2004

Per person	€ 4,60
pitch	€ 9,60

Reservations

Advised in high season with € 10 deposit. Tel: 929 464. E-mail: kohnenho@pt.lu

LU7660 Camping Kockelscheuer

22 route de Bettembourg, L-1899 Kockelscheuer

Camping Kockelscheuer is four kilometres from the centre of Luxembourg city and quietly situated (although there can be some aircraft noise at times). On a slight slope, there are 161 individual pitches of good size, either on flat ground at the bottom or on wide flat terraces with easy access, all with 16A electricity. There is also a special area for tents. For children there is a large area with modern play equipment on safety tiles and next door to the site is a sports centre. Charges are very reasonable. There is a friendly welcome although little English is spoken.

Facilities

Two fully equipped, identical sanitary buildings, both very clean at time of visit. Washing machines. Motorcaravan services. Shop. (order bread the previous day). Snack bar. Restaurant in adjacent sports centre also with minigolf, tennis, squash, etc. Rest room. No entry or exit for vehicles (reception closed) from 12.00-14.00 hrs. Off site: Swimming pool 5 km.

Open

Easter - 31 October.

At a glance

Welcome & Ambience	✓✓✓✓✓	Location	✓✓✓✓
Quality of Pitches	✓✓✓✓✓	Range of Facilities	✓✓✓✓

Directions

Site is SSW of Luxembourg city on the N13 to Bettembourg. Road is also known as the 186. From the south, exit A4 at junction signed Kockelscheuer onto N4. In 2 km. turn right (signed Kockelscheuer and campsite) and continue to follow the signs.

Charges 2005

Per person	€ 3,75
child (3-14 yrs)	€ 2,00
pitch	€ 4,50
electricity (1 or 2 days)	€ 1,75

Reservations

Are made but site says you should find space if you arrive by 5 p.m Tel: 471 815.
E-mail: mail@camp-kockelscheuer.lu

LU7700 Camping Gaalgebierg

L-4001 Esch-sur-Alzette

Occupying an elevated position on the edge of town, near the French border, this pleasant good quality site is run by the local camping and caravan club. Although surrounded by hills and with a good variety of trees, not all pitches have shade. There are 150 pitches (100 for tourists) 100 sq.m., most on grass, marked out by trees, some on a slight slope. There is a gravel area set aside for one night stays, plus four all-weather pitches for motorhomes although these are used mostly in the winter. All pitches have 16A electricity and TV points. The site operates its own minibus for visits to Luxembourg city and other excursions (free to campers) and also provides the Luxembourg card. Camping Gaalgebierg is justifiably proud of its new water saving policies and rubbish recycling system, and is one of only eight sites to receive the 'EcoLabel' from Luxembourg's Ministry of Tourism.

Facilities

The modern, well equipped toilet blocks can be heated and include some washbasins in cubicles, hot showers on payment and excellent facilities for disabled people and babies. Dishwashing and laundry sinks. Laundry. These facilities have a key-card entry system. Motorhome service point. Gas available. Shop for basics. Small bar and take-away on demand. TV room. Excellent playground. Volleyball. Table tennis. Boules. Badminton. Room with keep fit equipment and indoor table tennis (free). Entertainment and activities programme in high season. Off site: Restaurant within walking distance. Swimming pool and tennis nearby.

At a glance

Welcome & Ambience	✓✓✓✓✓	Location	✓✓✓✓
Quality of Pitches	✓✓✓✓	Range of Facilities	✓✓✓✓

Directions

Site is well signed from centre of Esch, but a sharp look out is needed as there are two acute right-handers on the approach to the site.

Charges guide

Per person	€ 3,50
child (3-12 yrs)	€ 1,75
pitch	€ 5,00
electricity (16A)	€ 1,50

Less 10% for stays of 7 days excl. July/Aug.
No credit cards.

Reservations

Write to site. Tel: 541 069. E-mail: gaalcamp@pt.lu

Open

All year.

With vast areas of the Netherlands reclaimed from the sea, nearly half of the country lies at or below sea level. The result is a flat, fertile landscape, criss-crossed with rivers and canals. Famous for its windmills and bulb fields, it also boasts some of the most impressive coastal dunes in Europe.

Netherlands

There is more to the Netherlands than Amsterdam and the bulb fields. Granted, both are top attractions and no visitor should miss the city of Amsterdam with its delight of bridges, canals, museums and listed buildings or miss seeing the spring-time riot of colour that adorns the fields and gardens of South Holland. This is a country with a variety of holiday venues ranging from lively seaside resorts to picturesque villages, idyllic old fishing ports and areas where nature rules. Favourite places include the Province of Overijssel, especially the Vecht valley, an area of natural beauty which centres around the town of Ommen. Giethoorn, to the northwest of the province is justly dubbed the 'Venice of the North'. Another appealing spot is around Dordrecht, southeast of Rotterdam. Here the Alblasserwaard polder, a typically Dutch landscape offers time to discover the famed windmills of Kinderdijk, cheese farms and a stork village. The lure of the islands of the Zeeland Provice is difficult to resist. These islands are joined by amazing feats of engineering, particularly the Oosterschelde storm surge barrier. Island hopping introduces lovely old towns such as Middelburg, the provincial capital Zierikzee with its old harbour or the quaint old town of Veere.

Population

15.9 million

Capital

Amsterdam

Climate

Temperature with mild winters and warm summers

Language

Dutch. English is very widely spoken, so is German and to some extent French. In Friesland a Germanic language, Frisian is spoken

Currency

The Euro

Telephone

The country code is 00 31

Banks

Mon-Fri 09.00-16.00/1700

Shops

Mon-Fri 09.00/09.30-17.30/18.00. Sat to 16.00/17.00. Later closing hours in larger cities

Public Holidays

New Year; Good Fri; Easter Mon; Queen's Birthday 30 Apr; Liberation Day 5 May; Ascension; Whit Mon; Christmas 25, 26 Dec

Motoring

There is a comprehensive motorway system but, due to the high density of population, all main roads can become very busy, particularly in the morning and evening rush hours. There are many bridges which can cause congestion. There are no toll roads but there are a few toll bridges and tunnels notably the Zeeland Bridge, Europe's longest across the Oosterschelde

Tourist Office

Netherlands Board of Tourism
15-19 Kingsway, 7th Floor, Imperial House
London WC2B 6UN
Tel: 020 7539 7950
Fax: 020 7539 7953
Email: information@nbt.org.uk
Internet: www.holland.com/uk

tip

GIVEN THE FLAT TERRAIN CYCLING IS A GREAT WAY TO TOUR THE COUNTRY, WITH MOST PLACES LINKED BY DEDICATED CYCLE PATHS. YOU CAN HIRE BIKES FROM TRAIN STATIONS AND FROM RENTAL SERVICES IN LARGER TOWNS.

NL5500 Vakantiepark Pannenschuur

Zeedijk 19, 4504 PP Nieuwvliet (Zeeland)

This is one of several coastal sites on the narrow strip of the Netherlands between the Belgian frontier near Knokke and the Breskens ferry. Quickly reached from the ports of Ostend, Zeebrugge and Vlissingen, it is useful for overnight stops or for a few days to enjoy the seaside. A short walk across the quiet coast road and steps over the dike bring you to the open, sandy beach. Quite a large site, most of the 595 pitches are taken by permanent or seasonal holiday caravans but there are also 165 pitches for tourists mostly in their own areas. Mostly in bays of six or eight units surrounded by hedges, all have electricity (6A), water and drainage connections. Cars are not parked by units but in separate parking areas. A star attraction is the complex that provides a super indoor heated swimming pool with baby and children's sections, jacuzzi, sauna, Turkish bath and solarium. Overall, this is a very good site.

Facilities

Five sanitary blocks including two new, heated buildings, provide first class facilities including children's washrooms, baby rooms and some private cabins. Hot water is now free (using a charged key - deposit €11). Launderette. Motorcaravan services. Gas supplies. Supermarket (restricted hours in low seasons). Restaurant, snack bar and takeaway. Swimming pool, sauna and solarium. All these amenities are closed 14/1-31/1. Large games room with snooker, pool tables, amusement machines, soft drinks bar. Children's playground and play field. Bicycle hire. Organised activities in season. Off site: Fishing 500 m. Riding 2 km. Golf 5 km.

At a glance

Welcome & Ambience	✓✓✓✓	Location	✓✓✓✓
Quality of Pitches	✓✓✓✓	Range of Facilities	✓✓✓✓

Directions

At Nieuwvliet, on Breskens - Sluis minor road, 8 km. southwest of Breskens, turn towards the sea at sign for Nieuwvliet-Bad and follow signs to site

Charges 2004

Per person (over 2 yrs)	€ 4,50
pitch incl. electricity	€ 19,00 - € 31,00
dog (max. 2 per unit)	€ 4,00

Rates available for weekly stays.

Reservations

Advised (high season Sat.- Sat. only) and made with deposit and fee. Tel: 0117 37 23 00. E-mail: info@pannenschuur.nl

Open

All year (all amenities closed 14/1-31/1).

NL5580 Camping de Veerhoeve

Veerweg 48, 4471 NC Wolphaartsdijk (Zeeland)

This is a family run site near the shores of the Veerse Meer which is ideal for family holidays. It is located in a popular area for watersports and is well suited for sailing, windsurfing or fishing enthusiasts, with boat launching 1 km. away. As with most sites in this area there are many mature static and seasonal pitches. However, part of the friendly, relaxed site is reserved for touring units with 60 marked pitches on grassy ground, all with electrical connections. A member of the Holland Tulip Parcs group.

Facilities

Sanitary facilities in three blocks have been well modernised with full tiling. Hot showers are on payment. Laundry facilities including ironing. Motorcaravan services. Supermarket (all season). Restaurant and snack bar (July/Aug. otherwise at weekends). TV room. Tennis. Playground and play field. Games room with table tennis and table football. Bicycle hire. Fishing. Accommodation for groups. Max. 1 dog per pitch. Off site: Riding 2 km. Slipway for launching boats 2 km. Golf 7 km.

Open

3 April - 30 October.

At a glance

Welcome & Ambience	✓✓✓✓	Location	✓✓✓✓✓
Quality of Pitches	✓✓✓✓	Range of Facilities	✓✓✓✓

Directions

From N256 Goes-Zierikzee road take Wolphaartsdijk exit. Follow through village and signs to site.

Charges 2005

Per pitch incl. up to 4 persons	€ 20,00 - € 23,20
with electricity (6A), water and drainage	€ 21,50 - € 24,50
with TV connection	€ 22,50 - € 26,00
extra person	€ 4,00

Reservations

Write to site. Tel: 0113 58 11 55.
E-mail: deveerhoeve@zeelandnet.nl

NL6920 Camping 't Veerse Meer

Veerweg 71, 4471 NB Wolphaartsdijk (Zeeland)

This well cared for family run site is situated beside the Veerse Meer on the island of Noord Beveland in Zeeland. Not only is its location idyllic for watersports enthusiasts, it is also an excellent and picturesque setting for cyclists and walkers. Emphasis at this site is on a neat and tidy appearance, quality facilities and a friendly reception. The site spreads over both sides of the road, and the area to the right is being developed to include pitches with individual sanitary facilities, plus the already established fully serviced hardstanding pitches for motorcaravans. The original part of the site is where you will find reception, a bar and the main sanitary block. There are 40 generous touring pitches, many fully serviced and separated by hedging. Further seasonal and static places are kept apart. A feature of this campsite is a narrow canal crossed by a bridge.

Facilities

One main sanitary block has showers (token operated), open style wash areas, two washcabins, child size WC and a baby bath. Dishwashing sinks. Laundry area. Motorcaravan service point. Bar. Play area. Organised events for all age groups in high season. Bicycle hire. Fishing.

Open

1 April - 31 October.

At a glance

Welcome & Ambience	✓✓✓✓	Location	✓✓✓✓
Quality of Pitches	✓✓✓✓	Range of Facilities	✓✓✓✓

Directions

From N256 Goes-Zierikzee road take Wolphaartsdijk exit. Follow through village and signs to site.

Charges guide

Per unit incl. 1 or 2 persons	€ 13,50 - € 15,50
incl. 3 or 4 persons	€ 16,00 - € 18,00
hiker or cyclist pitch (2 persons)	€ 11,50 - € 13,50
dog	€ 2,00

Reservations

Advisable in high season; contact site.
Tel: 0113 581423. E-mail: info@campingversemeer.nl

NL5570 Camping de Molenhoek

Molenweg 69a, 4493 NC Kamperland (Zeeland)

This family run site makes a pleasant contrast to the livelier coastal sites in this popular holiday area. It is rurally situated three kilometres from the Veerse Meer which is very popular for all sorts of water-sports. Catering both for 300 permanent or seasonal holiday caravans and for 100 touring units, it is neat, tidy and relatively spacious. The marked touring pitches are divided into small groups with surrounding hedges and trees giving privacy and some shade, and electrical connections are available. A large outdoor swimming pool is Molenhoek's latest attraction. Entertainment is organised in season (dance evenings, bingo, etc.) as well as a disco for youngsters. Although the site is quietly situated, there are many excursion possibilities in the area including the towns of Middelburg, Veere and Goes and the Delta Expo exhibition.

Facilities

Sanitary facilities in one fully refurbished and one newer block, include some washbasins in cabins, dishwashing and laundry sinks. Toilet and shower facilities for disabled visitors and provision for babies. Motorcaravan services. Small shop. Simple bar/restaurant with terrace and TV room. Swimming pool (15/5-15/9). Playground. Bicycle hire. Off site: Tennis and watersports close. Riding 1 km. Fishing 2.5 km.

Open

1 April - 28 October.

At a glance

Welcome & Ambience	✓✓✓✓✓	Location	✓✓✓✓
Quality of Pitches	✓✓✓✓	Range of Facilities	✓✓✓✓

Directions

Site is west of the village of Kamperland on the 'island' of Noord Beveland. From the N256 Goes - Zierikzee road, exit west onto the N255 Kamperland road. Site is signed south of this road.

Charges guide

Per unit incl. 2 persons	€ 22,50 - € 33,00
extra person	€ 4,00 - € 5,00
dog	€ 5,00
electricity	€ 2,50

No credit cards.

Reservations

Are made - details from site. Tel: 0113 37 12 02. E-mail: molenhoek@zeelandnet.nl

NL6930 Camping Schoneveld

Schoneveld 1, 4511 HR Breskens (Zeeland)

This site is well situated within walking distance of Breskens and it has direct access to sand dunes. It has around 200 touring pitches and has many static vans, but these are kept apart. Touring outfits are placed behind reception and laid out in fields which are entered from long avenues that run through the site, there are also twelve car parking bays. One ultra modern and very clean toilet block serves this area of the site. The complex at the site entrance houses reception, a restaurant and a recreation room. Also near the entrance are the indoor swimming pool, tennis courts and a football field. The ferry link to Breskens from Vlissingen takes pedestrians and cyclists only, a tunnel is to open for motor vehicles. A member of the Tulip Parc group.

Facilities

One large sanitary block provides showers, wash cubicles, child size toilets and washbasins, baby room, en-suite unit for disabled visitors. Motorcaravan service point. Restaurant. Fun Food Plaza and takeaway (5/4-31/10). Bowling. Swimming pool. Table tennis. Tennis. Football field. Play area. Organised entertainment in July/Aug. Bicycle hire. Off site: Fishing 200 m. Boat launching 3 km. Golf or riding 10 km.

Open

All year.

At a glance

Welcome & Ambience	✓✓✓✓	Location	✓✓✓
Quality of Pitches	✓✓✓	Range of Facilities	✓✓✓

Directions

From Breskens port follow N58 south for approx. 1 km and turn right at camping sign. Site is 500 m.

Charges 2004

Per unit incl. 2 persons	€ 16,15 - € 29,15
incl. 3 persons	€ 20,50 - € 33,50
incl. 5 persons	€ 23,85 - € 36,85
tent pitch incl. 1 or 2 persons	€ 9,75 - € 15,75

Weekly tariff and various discunts available.

Reservations

Contact site. Tel: 0117 38 32 20. E-mail: schoneveld@zeelandnet.nl

NL6960 Recreatiepark De Klepperstee

Vrijheidsweg 1, 3253 ZG Ouddorp (Zuid-Holland)

De Klepperstee is a good quality, family site offering excellent recreation areas that are spread over the centre of the site, giving it an attractive open parkland appearance which is enhanced by many shrubs, trees and grass areas. The variety of children's play equipment ensures hours of non-stop fun and there is a special evening house for older children with a television, etc. The site itself is peacefully located in tranquil countryside amid renowned nature reserves and just outside the village of Ouddorp in Zuid Holland. The 338 spacious touring pitches are in named avenues, mostly separated by hedging and spread around the perimeter, together with the seasonal and static caravans.

Facilities

One main sanitary block and a number of WC/shower units around the touring area provide hot showers (on payment), washbasins, some in cabins (hot water only), baby bath and shower, child size toilets and a unit for disabled people. Dishwashing sinks (hot water on payment). Laundry. Motorcaravan services. Supermarket. Restaurant, bar and takeaway. Small paddling pool. Play areas. Football field, netball, basketball and tennis. Table tennis. TV, pool and electronic games. Entertainment in high season. Bicycle hire. No animals are accepted and no single sex groups.

Open

Easter - 31 October.

At a glance

Welcome & Ambience	✓✓✓✓✓	Location	✓✓✓✓
Quality of Pitches	✓✓✓✓	Range of Facilities	✓✓✓✓

Directions

From Rotterdam follow A15 west to Rozenburg exit 12 and join N57 south for 22 km. Turn right at end of dual carriageway signed Ouddorp. Continue on local road following signs for Strand. Site on left after approx.3 km.

Charges guide

Per unit incl. up to 4 persons	
and 6A electricity	€ 28,50
with 10A electricity	€ 31,00
tent pitch incl. 2 persons	€ 14,50
extra person	€ 2,50

Reservations

Contact site for booking form, or telephone. Tel: 0187 681511. E-mail: info@klepperstee.com

NL6970 Camping 't Weergors

Zuiddijk 2, 3221 LJ Hellevoetsluis (Zuid-Holland)

A rustic style site built around old farm buildings, t'Weergors has a comfortable mature feel. At the front of the site is a well presented farmhouse which houses reception and includes the main site services. Around the courtyard area is one of the two sanitary blocks which is unsophisticated, but clean and functional with tiled walls and floor. There are 100 touring pitches, plus seasonal and static places. Some touring pitches are exceptionally large, divided by hedging with a 'drive in, drive out' system (cars charged if kept on pitch). Each pitch has a cable TV connection. An appealing feature of this site is the lake which lies to the rear, offering a quiet corner where you might head for an evening stroll.

Facilities

Two sanitary blocks have showers (by token), washbasins, some in cabins, child size WCs and a baby bath. Dishwashing sinks (token) and laundry area with washing machine and dryer. Motorcaravan service point. Small shop (Easter - 1/9). Restaurant, bar (all year). Snack bar (Easter - 1/9). Tennis. Football field. Recreation room/TV. Play area. Paddling pool. Organised entertainment in high season. Fishing. Bicycle hire. Rally field.

Open

Easter - 31 October.

At a glance

Welcome & Ambience	✓✓✓✓	Location	✓✓✓
Quality of Pitches	✓✓✓✓	Range of Facilities	✓✓✓

Directions

From Rotterdam join A15 west to Rozenburg junction 12 and join N57 south for 11 km. Turn left on N497 signed Hellevoetsluis and follow camp signs for 4.5 km. to roundabout. Turn right at roundabout and site is 1.5 km. on right.

Charges 2005

Per person	€ 3,50
child 3-12 yrs	€ 1,50
tent or caravan	€ 6,00
car on pitch	€ 2,50
electricity	€ 2,20
dog	€ 1,40

Reservations

Contact site. Tel: 0181 312430. E-mail: weergors@publishnet.nl

NL5600 Recreatiecentrum Delftse Hout

Korftlaan 5, 2616 LJ Delft (Zuid-Holland)

Pleasantly situated in Delft's park and forest area on the eastern edge of the city, this well run, modern site is part of the Koningshof group. It has 200 tourist pitches quite formally arranged in groups of 4 to 6 and surrounded by attractive young trees and hedges. All have sufficient space and electricity (10A). Modern buildings near the entrance house the site amenities. A good sized first floor restaurant serves snacks or full meals and has an outdoor terrace overlooking the swimming pool and pitches. Walking and cycling tours are organised and there is a recreation programme in high season. A special package deal includes tickets to local 'royal' attractions and a visit to the Royal Delftware factory.

Facilities

Modern, heated toilet facilities include a spacious family room. Laundry. Motorcaravan services. Shop for basic food and camping items (1/4-1/11). Restaurant and bar (1/4-1/10). Small outdoor swimming pool (15/5-15/9). Adventure playground. Table tennis. Volleyball. Recreation room. Bicycle hire. Gas supplies Off site: Fishing 1 km. Riding or golf 5 km. Regular bus service to Delft centre.

Open

All year.

At a glance

Welcome & Ambience	✓✓✓✓	Location	✓✓✓✓
Quality of Pitches	✓✓✓✓	Range of Facilities	✓✓✓✓

Directions

Site is 1 km. east of Delft. From A13 motorway take Delft/Pijnacker (exit 9), turn towards Pijnacker and then right at first traffic lights, following camping signs through suburbs and park to site.

Charges 2005

Per unit incl. 2 persons	€ 19,50 - € 24,00
supplement for services	€ 6,00
extra person (3 yrs and older)	€ 2,00
electricity (10A)	€ 3,50
dog (1 per pitch)	€ 2,00

Low season discounts and for over 55s.

Reservations

Essential for high season. Tel: 0152 13 00 40.
E-mail: info@delftsehout.nl

NL5610 Camping De Oude Maas

Achterzeedijk 1A, 2991 SB Barendrecht (Zuid-Holland)

This site is easily accessed from the A15 southern Rotterdam ring road and is situated right by the river, so it is well worth considering if you are visiting the city or want a peaceful stop. The entrance is the least inspiring part here and you have to drive right up to the barrier in order to activate the intercom. Once through this, you pass a long strip of mixed seasonal and touring pitches. There is a pleasant touring area for 12 units with electricity, water and drain in a hedged group near to the reception and river. The third section for seasonal units and mobile homes is in a woodland setting, well back from the river.

Facilities

One modern toilet block and a small 'portacabin' type unit provide all necessary facilities including a unit for disabled visitors, a baby room and dishwashing. Launderette. Fishing. Off site: Swimming pool near. Bicycle hire 5 km. Riding 8 km. Golf 10 km.

Open

1 March - 15 October.

At a glance

Welcome & Ambience	✓✓✓	Location	✓✓✓
Quality of Pitches	✓✓✓	Range of Facilities	✓✓✓

Directions

Best approached from A29 Rotterdam/Bergen op Zoom motorway. Leave A29 at exit 20 (Barendrecht) and follow signs for Heerjansdam and site

Charges 2005

Per person	€ 3,55
child (under 12 yrs)	€ 1,90
caravan/tent and car	€ 7,10
electricity (10A)	€ 1,90

Reservations

May be advisable high season. Tel: 0180 677 24 45.
E-mail: info@deoudemoas.com

NL5640 Vakantiecentrum Kijkduinpark

Machiel Vrijenhoeklaan 450, 2555 NW Den Haag (Zuid-Holland)

This is now an ultra-modern, all year round centre and family park, with many huts and bungalows for rent and a large indoor swimming pool complex. The wooded touring area is immediately to the left of the entrance, with 450 pitches in shady glades of bark covered sand. There are simple pitches for tents, some pitches with electricity only and many with water, waste water and cable TV connections as well. In a paved central area stands a supermarket, snack bar and restaurant. The main attraction here is the Meeresstrand, 500 m. from the site entrance. This is a long, wide sandy beach with flags to denote suitability for swimming. It is popular with windsurfers.

Facilities

There are five modern sanitary blocks (key entry, €20 deposit). Launderette. Snack bar. Shop. Restaurant. Supermarket (all year). Indoor pool. Bicycle hire. Special golfing breaks. Entertainment and activities organised in summer Off site: Fishing 500 m. Riding 5 km,

Open

All year.

At a glance

Welcome & Ambience	✓✓✓✓	Location	✓✓✓✓
Quality of Pitches	✓✓✓✓	Range of Facilities	✓✓✓✓

Directions

Site is southwest of Den Haag on the coast. Kijkduin is well signed as an area from all round Den Haag.

Charges 2004

Per unit incl. 2 persons, electricity	€ 16,00 - € 35,00
extra person	€ 1,21
child (under 15 yrs)	€ 0,47

Discounts for young families and over 55s.

Reservations

Advisable for high season, write to site.
Tel: 0704 48 21 00. E-mail: info@kijkduinpark.nl

NL5630 Camping Koningshof

Elsgeesterweg 8, 2231 NW Rijnsburg (Zuid-Holland)

This popular site is run in a personal and friendly way. The 200 pitches for touring units are laid out in groups of four or twelve, divided by hedges and trees and all with electrical connections (10A). Cars are mostly parked in areas around the perimeter and 100 static caravans, confined to one section of the site, are entirely unobtrusive. Reception, a pleasant good quality restaurant, bar and a snack bar are grouped around a courtyard style entrance which is decorated with seasonal flowers. The site has a small outdoor, heated pool (13.5 x 7 m), with a separate paddling pool and imaginative children's play equipment. Recent additions are a recreation hall, an indoor swimming pool and a unique children's play pool with water streams, locks and play materials. The site has a number of regular British visitors from club connections who receive a friendly welcome, with English spoken. Used by tour operators (25 pitches). A very useful local information booklet (in English) is provided for visitors. A member of the Holland Tulip Parcs group.

Facilities

Three good toilet blocks, two with under-floor heating, include washbasins in cabins and provision for disabled visitors. Laundry room with washing machines and dryers. Motorcaravan services. Gas supplies. Shop (1/4-15/10). Bar (1/4-1/11). Restaurant (1/4-10/9). Snacks and takeaway (1/4-1/11). Small outdoor pool (unsupervised; 15/5-15/9). Indoor pool complex (15/3-15/11). Solarium. Adventure playground and sports area. Tennis courts. Fishing pond (free). Bicycle hire. Entertainment in high season. Room for shows. One dog per pitch accepted in a limited area of the site. Off site: Riding or golf 5 km. Sandy beach 5 km. Den Haag 15 km. and Amsterdam 30 km.

Open

All year.

At a glance

Welcome & Ambience	✓✓✓✓✓	Location	✓✓✓✓
Quality of Pitches	✓✓✓✓✓	Range of Facilities	✓✓✓✓✓

Directions

From N44/A44 Den Haag - Amsterdam motorway, take exit 7 for Oegstgeest and Rijnsburg. Turn towards Rijnsburg and follow camp signs

Charges 2005

Per pitch incl. 2 persons	€ 26,50
extra person (over 3 years)	€ 3,50
dog (see text)	€ 2,50
electricity (10A)	€ 3,50

Senior citizen discounts, group rates and special packages.

Reservations

Necessary for July/Aug and made for any length with deposit and fee (payable by credit card).
Tel: 0714 02 60 51.
E-mail: info@koningshofholland.nl

NL5620 Camping Duinrell

Duinrell 1, 2242 JP Wassenaar (Zuid-Holland)

A very large site, Duinrell's name means 'well in the dunes' and the water theme is continued in the adjoining amusement park and in the extensive indoor pool complex. Entry to the popular pleasure park is free for campers - indeed the camping areas surround and open out from the park. The 'Tiki' tropical pool complex has many attractions which include slides ranging from quite exciting to terrifying (according to your age!), whirlpools, saunas and many other features. There are also free outdoor pools and the centre has its own bar and café. Entry to the Tiki complex is at a reduced rate for campers. Duinrell is open all year and a ski school (langlauf and Alpine) with 12 artificial runs, is a winter attraction. The campsite itself is very large with 1,150 tourist places on several flat grassy areas and it can become very busy in high season. As part of a continuing improvement programme, 950 marked pitches have electricity, water and drainage connections and some have cable TV. Amenities shared with the park include restaurants, a pizzeria and pancake house, supermarket and a theatre. There are now 425 smartly furnished bungalows to rent.

Facilities

Six toilet blocks, including two very good new ones, serve the tourist areas and can be heated in cool weather. Laundry facilities. Amusement park and Tiki tropical pool complex as detailed above. Restaurant, cafés, pizzeria and takeaways (weekends only in winter). Supermarket. Entertainment and theatre with shows in high season. 'Rope Challenge' trail and 'Forrest Frisbee' trail. Bicycle hire. Bowling. Artificial ski slopes and ski school (winter). Diving experience package. All activities have extra charges.

Open

All year.

At a glance

Welcome & Ambience	✓✓✓✓	Location	✓✓✓✓
Quality of Pitches	✓✓✓✓	Range of Facilities	✓✓✓✓✓

Directions

Site is signed from N44/A44 Den Haag-Amsterdam road, but from the south the turning is about 5 km. after passing sign for start of Wassenaar town - then follow camp signs.

Charges 2005

Per person over 3 yrs	€ 9,15
senior (over 65 yrs)	€ 6,50
pitch	€ 8,25
with electricity	€ 8,50
with water	€ 10,00
dog	€ 5,50

Special package offers. Overnight stays between 17.00-10.00 hrs (amusement park closed) less 25%.

Reservations

Advised for high season, Easter and Whitsun (min. 1 week), 50% payment required 6 weeks in advance plus fee (€ 7.00). Tel: 0705 15 52 57.

NL5680 Camping Noordduinen

Campingweg 1, 2221 EW Katwijk (Zuid-Holland)

This is a large, well managed site surrounded by dunes and sheltered partly by trees and shrubbery, which also separate the various camping areas. The 200 touring pitches are marked and numbered but not divided. All have electricity (10A) and 45 are fully serviced with electricity, water, drainage and TV connection. There are also seasonal pitches and mobile homes for rent. The latter are placed mostly away from the touring areas and are unobtrusive. You are escorted to an allocated pitch and sited in a formal layout and cars are parked away from the pitches. Entertainment is organised in high season for various age groups. Bicycles can be hired nearby and worth a visit is Space Expo.

Facilities

The three sanitary blocks are modern and clean, with washbasins in cabins, a baby room and provision for people with disabilities. Hot water for showers and dishwashing is on payment. Laundry. Motorcaravan services. Supermarket with fresh bread daily. Restaurant/bar which doubles as a function room. Takeaway service. Games room. Play area. Only gas barbecues are permitted. No dogs accepted. Off site: Beach and Katwijk within walking distance.

At a glance

Welcome & Ambience	✓✓✓	Location	✓✓✓
Quality of Pitches	✓✓✓	Range of Facilities	✓✓✓

Directions

Leave A44 at exit 8 (Leiden/Katwijk) to join N206 to Katwijk. Take Katwijk Noord exit; follow signs to site.

Charges guide

Per pitch	€ 21,50 - € 29,50
serviced pitch	€ 26,50 - € 32,50
electricity (10A)	€ 3,00

Reservations

Contact site. Tel: 0714 02 52 95. E-mail: info@noordduinen.nl

Open

31 March - 28 October.

NL5660 Camping Het Amsterdamse Bos

Kleine Noorddijk 1, 1187 NZ Amstelveen (Noord-Holland)

Het Amsterdamse Bos is a very large park to the southwest of Amsterdam, one corner of which has been specially laid out as the city's municipal site. Close to Schiphol Airport (we noticed little noise), it is about 12 kilometres from central Amsterdam. A high season bus service runs from the site during the day to the city (a local service at other times is 300 m). The site is well laid out alongside a canal, with unmarked pitches on separate flat lawns mostly backing onto pleasant hedges and trees, with several areas of hard-standing. It takes 400 tourist units, with 100 electrical connections (10A). An additional area is available for tents and groups.

Facilities

Two older style sanitary blocks rather let the site down, appearing somewhat small and well used. A third block is new. Hot water is on payment to the washbasins but pre-set hot showers are free. Laundry facilities. Motorcaravan services. Gas supplies. Small shop. Cafe/bar and snack bar. Fishing, boating, pancake restaurant in the park. Off site: Riding and bicycle hire 5 km.

Open

1 April - 15 October.

At a glance

Welcome & Ambience	✓✓✓✓	Location	✓✓✓✓
Quality of Pitches	✓✓✓✓	Range of Facilities	✓✓✓✓

Directions

Amsterdamse Bos and site are west of Amstelveen. From the A9 motorway take exit 6 and follow N231 to site (2nd traffic light).

Charges 2004

Per person	€ 5,00
child (4-12 yrs)	€ 2,50
pitch	€ 6,00 - € 6,50
electricity (10A)	€ 3,00
dog	€ 1,50

Group reductions.

Reservations

A limited number only will be made for 'serious enquirers'. Tel: 0206 41 68 68. E-mail: camping@dab.amsterdam.nl

NL5670 Gaasper Camping Amsterdam

Loosdrechtdreef 7, 1108 AZ Amsterdam (Noord-Holland)

Amsterdam is probably the most popular destination for visits in the Netherlands, and Gaasper Camping is on the southeast side, a short walk from a Metro station with a direct 20 minute service to the centre. On the edge of a large park with nature areas and a lake, the site is well kept and neatly laid out on flat grass with attractive trees and shrubs. There are 350 touring pitches in two main areas - one more open and grassy, mainly kept for tents, the other more formal with numbered pitches mainly divided by shallow ditches or good hedges. Areas of hardstanding are available and all caravan pitches have electrical connections (10A). There are 20 tent pitches with 10A connections. Some 60 seasonal and permanent units have their own area. In high season the site becomes very crowded and it is necessary to arrive during the day to find space (in July/Aug. check-ins start at 11.00 hrs). Although this is a typical, busy city site, it is better than many and there is a friendly welcome, with good English spoken.

Facilities

Three modern, clean toilet blocks (one unisex) for the tourist sections are an adequate provision. Some washbasins in cabins. Hot water for showers and some washing-up sinks on payment. Washing machine and dryer. Motorcaravan services. Gas. Supermarket (1/4-15/10). Café/bar plus takeaway (1/4-15/10). Play area. Off site: Riding 200 m. Fishing 1 km. Golf 4 km. Shopping centre nearby.

Open

15 March - 1 November.

At a glance

Welcome & Ambience	✓✓✓✓	Location	✓✓✓✓✓
Quality of Pitches	✓✓✓✓✓	Range of Facilities	✓✓✓

Directions

Take exit for Gaasperplas/Weesp (S113) from the section of A9 motorway which is on the east side of the A2. Do not take the Gaasperdam exit (S112) which comes first if approaching from the west.

Charges 2004

Per person	€ 4,50
pitch incl. car	€ 9,25 - € 10,00

No credit cards.

Reservations

Made only in writing for caravans or motorcaravans for min. stay of 7 nights (state whether single/double axle and with/without awning). Tel: 020 6967326.

NL5700 Molengroet Recreatieverblijven

Molengroet 1, 1723 PX Noord-Scharwoude (Noord-Holland)

Molengroet is a modern, pleasant site, close to a lake for watersports and 40 kilometres from Amsterdam. It is a useful stop on the way to the Afsluitdijk across the top of the Ijsselmeer or as an enjoyable stop for watersport enthusiasts. The 260 touring pitches are grouped according to services provided, ranging from simple pitches with no services, to those with electricity (4/10A), TV, water and waste water. The bar and restaurant are open all season and there is a snack bar in high season - order snacks from the restaurant. The nearby lake with surf school is an attractive proposition, particularly for those with teenagers. A site bus can take you to the local pool or the beach. Friendly multi-lingual staff provide local information. A member of the Holland Tulip Parcs group.

Facilities

The best sanitary facilities, in a modern, heated building, are near the serviced pitches. Supplemented by two other blocks, all necessary facilities are provided. Motorcaravan services. Gas. Shop (1/4-1/9), bread and milk from reception at other times. Restaurant/bar (1/4-1/9). Fishing. Bicycle hire. Surfboards and small boats for hire. Entertainment in high season and at weekends Off site: Watersports close. Tennis, squash, sauna, and swimming nearby. Riding or golf 5 km.

Open

19 March - 1 November.

At a glance

Welcome & Ambience	✓✓✓✓✓	Location	✓✓✓✓✓
Quality of Pitches	✓✓✓✓	Range of Facilities	✓✓✓✓

Directions

From Haarlem on A9 to Alkmaar take N245 towards Schagen. Site is southwest of Noord Sharwoude, signed to west on road to Geestermerambacht

Charges 2005

Per unit incl. 2 persons	€ 11,50 - € 18,50
with electricity (4/6A)	€ 17,50 - € 24,50
with private sanitary facility	€ 27,00 - € 34,00
extra person (over 2 yrs)	€ 3,50 - € 4,50

Reductions in low season and for longer stays.

Reservations

Made with 50% deposit on booking, balance 3 weeks before arrival. Tel: 0226 39 34 44. E-mail: info@molengroet.nl

NL5710 Camping It Soal

Sudersêleane 27, 8711 GX Workum (Friesland)

This is an attractive, child friendly site with 800 metres of beach, situated directly beside the Ijsselmeer with a canal on one side. It is ideal for those who enjoy water sports as there are many activities on the lake, including windsurfing, sailing, swimming and fishing, or you can launch your own boat. The site has 650 pitches here, of which 400 are good sized, individual, flat and grassy for tourers, with electrical connections. In separate areas, the other pitches are taken by seasonal guests and about 50 static units. Dogs are only allowed in one area and cars must be left in a car park. From the restaurant there are beautiful views over the Ijsselmeer. It Soal is close to Workum, a picturesque old village and one of the 11 cities of the famous 'Elfstedentocht' ice skating race. You can enjoy shopping or visiting the old buildings here including the Jopie Huisman Museum (a famous local painter).

Facilities

Modern sanitary facilities include toilets, washbasins (open and in private cabins) and free, controllable showers. Facilities for disabled visitors. Baby room with bath. Laundry with washing machines and dryers. Shop, restaurant and takeaway (1/4-1/10). Several small play areas. Table tennis. Tennis courts. Video games room. Skate track. Volleyball. Bicycle hire. Fishing. Boat launching. Beach. Surfboards and sailing boats for hire. Entertainment programme.
Off site: Golf 15 km. Riding 10 km. The surrounding areas are ideal for cycling, walking, skating and fishing.

At a glance

Welcome & Ambience	✓✓✓✓	Location	✓✓✓✓✓
Quality of Pitches	✓✓✓✓	Range of Facilities	✓✓✓✓

Directions

From Groningen on the A7 (via Drachten, Joure and Sneek), exit just before Bolsward on N359 towards Workum, then exit Workum and follow signs.

Charges 2004

Per unit incl. 1 or 2 adults with electricity (4/6A)	€ 19,50 - € 24,00
extra person	€ 3,50
dog	€ 3,50

Reservations

Contact site. Tel: 0515 541443. E-mail: info@itsoal.nl

Open

1 April - 31 october

NL6870 Kennemer Duincamping de Lakens

Zeeweg 60, 2051 EC Bloemendaal aan Zee (Noord-Holland)

De Lakens is part of the Kennemer Duincampings group and is beautifully located in the dunes at Bloemendaal aan Zee. De Lakens has 940 reasonably large, flat pitches with a hardstanding of shells. There are 410 for tourers (235 with 10A electricity) and the sunny pitches are separated by low hedging. This site is a true oasis of peace in a part of the Netherlands usually bustling with activity. From this site it is possible to walk straight through the dunes to the North Sea. Although there is no pool, a lake on the site can be used for swimming or, of course, there is the sea. A separate area is provided for groups and youngsters to maintain the quiet atmosphere.

Facilities

The six toilet blocks for tourers (two brand new) include controllable showers, washbasins (open style and in cabins), facilities for disabled people and a baby room. Launderette. Two motorcaravan service points. Bar/restaurant and snack bar. Supermarket. Adventure type playgrounds. Bicycle hire. Basketball, table football, table tennis and boules. Entertainment program in high season for all ages. Boat slipway. Fishing. Dogs are not accepted. Off site: Beach and riding 1 km. Golf 10 km.

At a glance

Welcome & Ambience	✓✓✓✓	Location	✓✓✓✓✓
Quality of Pitches	✓✓✓✓	Range of Facilities	✓✓✓✓✓

Directions

From Amsterdam go west to Haarlem and follow the N200 from Haarlem towards Bloemendaal aan Zee. Site is on the N200, on the right hand side.

Charges guide

Per pitch	€ 19,45 - € 23,85
with electricty	€ 22,35 - € 26,75

Reservations

Made with deposit and fee. Tel: 075 6472393.
E-mail: delakens@kennemerduincampings.nl

Open

1 April - 1 November.

NL5720 Camping Jachthaven Uitdam

Zeedijk 2, 1154 PP Uitdam (Noord-Holland)

Situated beside the Markermeer which is used extensively for watersports, this large site has its own private yachting marina (300 yachts and boats). It has 200 seasonal and permanent pitches, many used by watersports enthusiasts, but also offers 260 marked tourist pitches (120 with 6A electricity) on open, grassy ground overlooking the water and 14 mobile homes to rent. There is a special area for campers with bicycles. Very much dominated by the marina, this site will appeal to watersports enthusiasts, with opportunities for sailing, windsurfing and swimming, but it is also on a pretty stretch of coast, 15 kilometres northeast of Amsterdam.

Facilities

Two rather basic toilet blocks in fairly open buildings have hot showers on payment. A third block is of excellent quality. Motorcaravan services. Gas supplies. Shop (1/4-1/10). Bar/restaurant (weekends and high season). TV room. Tennis. Children's playground. Bicycle hire. Fishing. Yacht marina (with fuel) and slipway. Watersports facilities. Entertainment in high season.

Open

1 March - 1 November.

At a glance

Welcome & Ambience	✓✓✓✓	Location	✓✓✓✓✓
Quality of Pitches	✓✓✓✓	Range of Facilities	✓✓✓✓

Directions

From A10, take N247 towards Volendam then Monnickendam exit south in direction of Marken, then Uitdam.

Charges guide

Per unit incl. 2 persons	€ 20,50
extra person (over 3 yrs)	€ 4,50
tent	€ 17,00
tent without car	€ 13,50
dog	€ 3,50
boat on trailer	€ 6,50

Less 20% outside 1/5-7/9.

Reservations

Contact site. Tel: 0204 03 14 33.
E-mail: info@campinguitdam.nl

NL6820 Camping Westerkogge

Kerkebuurt 202, 1647 MH Berkhout (Noord-Holland)

Camping Westerkogge is near the A7 motorway and Hoorn, and close to the Ijsselmeer. The 300 pitches (100 for touring units) are on grassy fields, surrounded by high trees and bushes that provide shade; 80 pitches have 6A electricity and 28 of these also have water and drainage. From this site you can cycle through the lovely West Friesland countryside, sail on the Ijsselmeer or visit the attractive old town of Hoorn. It is also a good base for visiting Amsterdam or the harbour of Den Helder. After that you could tour through the polder by boat or hire a canoe. Fishing is even easier because it's possible on site. Besides all the activities in the area, the site itself has a lot to offer: Take a dive in the covered swimming pool, join in at the shows or bingo and for children there's organised activities including a weekly disco. This is a site for the whole family.

Facilities

Three toilet blocks include washbasins (open style and in cabins), child size washbasins and unisex showers. Facilities for disabled visitors. Laundry. Covered sinks with free hot water. Motorcaravan services. Shop (in reception). Café with bar and snacks. Covered pool (10 x 5 m) with separate paddling pool (also open to the public). Playground. Sports court. Tennis court. Bicycle hire. Go-kart and canoe hire. Boat trips through the polder. Off site: Riding 10 km. Golf 15 km. Beach 30 km.

At a glance

Welcome & Ambience	✓✓✓✓	Location	✓✓✓✓
Quality of Pitches	✓✓✓✓	Range of Facilities	✓✓✓✓

Directions

Follow the A7 from Amsterdam north towards Hoorn and take exit Berkhout/Hoorn. Follow signs for Berkhout and site.

Charges 2004

Per unit incl. 2 persons and 4A electricity	€ 18,15 - € 20,30
extra person	€ 2,90 - € 3,15
pet	€ 2,05 - € 2,30

Reservations

Contact site. Tel: 0229 55 12 08. E-mail: info@camping-westerkogge.nl

Open

1 April - 30 October.

NL5760 Camping de Kuilart

Kuilart 1, 8723 CG Koudum (Friesland)

De Kuilart is a well run, modern site by Friesland's largest lake and with its own marina and private boating facilities it attracts many watersports enthusiasts. The marina provides windsurfing and sailing lessons and boat hire, and there are special rates at the site for groups and sailing clubs. However, the site has an excellent indoor swimming pool as well as an area for lake swimming and on land there are sports facilities and woods for cycling and walking. It may also therefore appeal for a relaxing break in a pleasant area not much visited by British campers. The 560 pitches at De Kuilart are set in groups of 10 to 16 on areas of grass surrounded by well established hedges. There are 225 for touring units, 200 with electricity, water, waste water and TV connections. The restaurant provides good views of the lake and woodland. A member of the Holland Tulip Parcs group.

Facilities

Four modern, heated sanitary blocks well spaced around the site are of above average quality, although showers are on payment and most washbasins (half in private cabins) have only cold water. Launderette. Motorcaravan services. Gas. Restaurant/bar (23/3-4/11). Supermarket (20/4-2/9). Indoor pool (23/3-4/11). Sauna and solarium. Lake swimming. Sports field. Playground. Tennis. Bicycle hire. Fishing. Recreation team (high season). Marina (600 berth) with windsurfing, boat hire and boat shop. Dogs accepted in certain areas (if booked). Off site: Riding or golf 4 km.

Open

All year.

At a glance

Welcome & Ambience	✓✓✓✓	Location	✓✓✓✓✓
Quality of Pitches	✓✓✓✓	Range of Facilities	✓✓✓✓✓

Directions

Site is southeast of Koudum, on the Fluessen lake. Follow the camping sign off the N359 Bolsward - Lemmer road

Charges guide

Per unit incl. 2 persons	€ 15,00 - € 19,00
pitch with electricity, water and drainage	€ 16,50 - € 20,50
extra person (over 1 yr)	€ 4,00

Special weekend rates at B.Hs.

Reservations

Advised as site is very popular; made from Sat. - Sat. only in peak season. Tel: 0514 52 22 21. E-mail: info@kuilart.nl

NL6040 Recreatiecentrum Bergumermeer

Solcamastraat 30, 9262 ND Suameer (Friesland)

This site is located right beside Lake Bergum, so is ideal for lovers of watersports, with sailing, surfing, water skiing and canoeing possible, as well as swimming from two sandy beaches. There is also a large, heated indoor swimming pool and a solarium. There are 90 good sized, flat, touring pitches for both caravans and tents, some having an attractive view over the Margriet-channel and the countryside, others with views over the lake. In high season there are organised activites and entertainment. It is well worth spending an afternoon on the terrace of the restaurant which has been built to resemble the bridge of a ship. With a great view over the lake, you can watch the sailing boats pass by.

Facilities

Three sanitary buildings offer private cabins, children's toilets, baby bath and good facilities for disabled people. Laundrette. Freezer. Shop. Bar/restaurant (all season). Heated indoor pool. Solarium. Play area. Children's farm. Tennis courts. Minigolf. Fishing. Sailing dinghies, motorboats and canoes for hire. Entertainment. Club space with disco. Bicycle hire. Off site: Riding 5 km. Golf 19 km.

Open

27 March - 16 October.

At a glance

Welcome & Ambience	✓✓✓✓	Location	✓✓✓✓✓
Quality of Pitches	✓✓✓✓	Range of Facilities	✓✓✓✓

Directions

From Amsterdam via A7/E22 through Leeuwarden towards Drachten, or east from Amsterdam via A6, onto A7 at sign for Leeuwarden/Groningen, then onto N31 at sign for De Haven/Drachten and in either case onto N356 towards Bergum following site signs.

Charges guide

Per pitch incl. 2 persons	€ 21,00
incl. 10A electricity	€ 23,25
extra person	€ 3,50

Reservations

Contact site. Tel: 0511 46 13 85. E-mail: info@bergumermeer.nl

Netherlands

NL6080 Camping de Zeehoeve

Westerzeedijk 45, 8862 PK Harlingen (Friesland)

Superbly located, directly behind the sea dyke of the Waddensea and just a kilometre from the harbour of Harlingen, De Zeehoeve is an attractive and spacious site. It has 300 pitches (125 for tourers), all with electricity and 20 with water, drainage and electricity. This splendid location allows one the opportunity to watch the sun slowly setting from the sea dyke. You can also stroll through Harlingen or take the ferry to Vlieland or Terschelling. It is possible to moor your own boat at Harlingen, to hire a boat or book an organised sailing or sea fishing trip. Camping De Zeehoeve is ideal for rest and relaxation, for watersports or visit the attractions of Harlingen and Friesland. After a day of activity, one can wine and dine in the site restaurant or one of the many pubs in Harlingen.

Facilities

Three sanitary blocks include open style washbasins with cold water only, washbasins in cabins with hot and cold water, controllable showers (on payment), family showers and a baby bath. Facilities for disabled people. Cooking hob. Launderette. Sinks with free hot water. Motorcaravan services. Bar/restaurant (1/7-31/8). Playground. Volleyball. Bicycle hire. Pedaloes and canoes for hire. Fishing. Extensive entertainment programme in July/Aug. Off site: Beach 200 m. Riding 10 km.

Open

1 April - 15 October.

At a glance

Welcome & Ambience	✓✓✓✓✓	Location	✓✓✓✓✓
Quality of Pitches	✓✓✓✓	Range of Facilities	✓✓✓✓

Directions

From Leeuwarden take A31 southwest to Harlingen, then follow site signs.

Charges guide

Per person	€ 3,50
child (4-11 yrs)	€ 3,00
caravan or tent	€ 3,50
car or m/cycle	€ 2,00
motorcaravan	€ 5,50
electricity	€ 2,00

Reservations

Contact site. Tel: 0517 41 34 65.
E-mail: info@zeehoeve.nl

NL5770 Camping Stadspark

Campinglaan 6, 9727 KH Groningen (Groningen)

The Stadspark is a large park to the southwest of the city, well signed and with easy access. The campsite is within the park with many trees and surrounded by water. It has 200 pitches with 150 for touring units, of which 75 have 6A electricity and 30 are fully serviced. The separate tent area is supervised directly by the manager. Buses for the city leave from right outside and timetables and maps are provided by Mrs Van der Veer, the helpful, English speaking manager. Groningen is a very lively city with lots to do.

Facilities

Two sanitary blocks, one totally refurbished, provide hot water for showers and dishwashing is now free. Motorcaravan service point. Shop (15/3-15/10). Café, bar and takeaway (1/4-15/9). Bicycle hire. Fishing. Canoeing. Off site: Riding and golf 10 km.

Open

15 March - 15 October.

At a glance

Welcome & Ambience	✓✓✓✓	Location	✓✓✓✓✓
Quality of Pitches	✓✓✓✓	Range of Facilities	✓✓✓✓

Directions

From Assen on A28 turn left on the A7. Turn on N370 and follow site signs (Stadspark, quite close).

Charges 2005

Per unit incl. 2 adults	€ 15,00
extra adult	€ 2,30
child (2-12 yrs)	€ 1,50
electricity	€ 2,00

No credit cards.

Reservations

Contact site. Tel: 0505 25 1624.
E-mail: info@campingstadspark.nl

NL6120 Camping 't Strandheem

Parkweg 2, 9865 VP Opende (Groningen)

Camping Strandheem has some quite large, numbered pitches (110 sq.m.) some with hardstanding and suitable for motorcaravans. Of the 330 pitches, 180 are used for tourers, all electricity and partly separated by low hedges, although there is not much shade. 40 of the pitches also have water points and cable TV connections. Camping Strandheem provides a base for some interesting excursions, including visits to the fishing harbour of Lauwersoog or the little village of Eenrum where you can learn how to make mustard in Abraham's Mosterdmakerij, design wax candles in a candle factory and visit a wooden shoe factory. The site itself also has a lot to offer. For youngsters there is an entertainment program in high season with water games in the lake next to the site, real life theatre, games and craft work, or for adults there are card nights or films twice a week. De Bruinewoud family will give you a warm welcome.

Facilities

Two modern toilet buildings have washbasins (open style and in cabins), controllable showers, child size toilets and basins, a good baby room and fully equipped bathroom. Facilities for disabled people. Launderette. Motorcaravan service. Shop. Café with bar and snack bar. Covered swimming pool (5 x 5 m) with separate paddling pool and slide. Playgrounds. Minigolf. Fishing. Bicycle hire. Volleyball. Basketball. Boules. Lake with beach (€ 1 p/p per day). Extensive recreation program in July and August. Film and card nights. Off site: Lake with beach 100 m. Riding 6 km. Golf 15 km.

At a glance

Welcome & Ambience	✓✓✓✓✓	Location	✓✓✓✓
Quality of Pitches	✓✓✓✓	Range of Facilities	✓✓✓✓

Directions

Follow A7 west from Groningen towards Heerenveen and take exit 31. Follow camp signs from there.

Charges guide

Per unit incl. 2 persons	€ 18,50
extra person	€ 3,00
private sanitary facility	€ 8,50
electricity (4/10A)	€ 1,80 - € 2,50
dog	€ 2,50

Reservations

Made with 50% deposit. Tel: 0594 65 95 55. E-mail: info@strandheem.nl

Open

1 April - 1 October.

NL6090 Camping Lauwersoog

Strandweg 5, 9976 VS Lauwersoog (Groningen)

The focus at Camping Lauwersoog is very much on the sea and watersports. One can have sailing lessons or hire canoes, sailing boats or fishing boats and it is a short stroll from the site to the beach. The site is also close to the harbour of Lauwersoog where you can take the ferry to Schiermonnikoog and let the wind blow away the cobwebs on the large beaches of this beautiful, almost car free island (only residents may take cars onto the island). The site's restaurant specialises in seafood and even the entertainment programs for all ages have a water theme. The youngsters go treasure hunting on the beach or try to find Lavica the Zeemeerhix (mermaid), whilst adults may walk and cycle through the Lauwersmeergebied or join sailing trips organised from the site. Camping Lauwersoog has 450 numbered pitches with 225 for tourers. Electricity (4/6A) is available at 200 pitches and 80 have water, drainage, electricity and cable connections. The pitches are on level, grassy fields (some beside the beach), partly separated by hedges and some with shade from trees.

Facilities

The two toilet blocks for tourers provide washbasins (open style and in cabins), pre-set showers and child size toilets. Facilities for disabled people. Laundry. Ice pack service. Covered sinks with free hot water. Motorcaravan service. Shop (daily 9.00 - 18.00 in July/Aug) with delivery service. Seafood restaurant. Snack bar on the beach. Playground. Sailing school. Canoes, sailing boats and fishing boats for hire. Bicycle and go-kart hire. Volleyball. Boules. Extensive entertainment program for all ages in high season. Torch useful. Off site: Riding 5 km.

At a glance

Welcome & Ambience	✓✓✓✓	Location	✓✓✓✓✓
Quality of Pitches	✓✓✓✓	Range of Facilities	✓✓✓✓

Directions

Follow N361 from Groningen north to Lauwersoog and then follow site signs.

Charges 2004

Per unit incl. 2 persons, 6A electrcity	€ 23,50
serviced pitch (125 sq.m)	€ 26,50
extra person	€ 4,00
dog	€ 4,00

Reservations

Made with 50 deposit. Tel: 0519 34 91 33. E-mail: info@lauwersoog.nl

Open

All year.

NL6140 Camping de Valkenhof

Beilerstraat 13a, 9431 GA Westerbork (Drenthe)

De Valkenhof is a spacious family site with 180 pitches, partly in the woods and partly on open fields without hedges to separate them. With 160 pitches for touring units, there are 143 with 4A electricity. With 500 km. of cycle paths, De Valkenhof and its surroundings are ideal for enjoying the woods and moors of Drenthe. The site is also close to the former concentration camp of Westerbork, which is well worth a visit, the museum village of Orvelte, the Noorderdierenpark Zoo in Emmen, the Verkeerspark in Assen and troll country in Exloo. De Valkenhof does not allow cars on the campsite itself and this, together with the large pitches, provides for a really quiet holiday. Other than a recreation room for youngsters, a pool and sanitary buildings, the site has few amenities but you'll find all you need in the village. The large outdoor pool (over 1,000 sq.m), with its giant slide and recreational activities will certainly appeal to children.

Facilities

Two modern toilet blocks have washbasins (open style and in cabins, only one block with hot water at the basins), pre-set showers, toilets, showers and basins for children and a baby room. Laundry. Sinks under cover. Some snacks from reception. Swimming pool with slide and paddling pool. Extensive entertainment program in high season for children. Boules. Library. Games room. Only gas barbecues are permitted. Off site: Bicycle hire 2 km.

Open

1 April - 1 October.

At a glance

Welcome & Ambience	✓✓✓✓	Location	✓✓✓✓
Quality of Pitches	✓✓✓✓	Range of Facilities	✓✓✓

Directions

Travelling north from Zwolle on the A28, take exit Beilen/Westerbork. Follow N31 eastwards and take exit for Westerbork. From there follow site signs.

Charges guide

Per unit incl . 2 persons	€ 16,25
extra person	€ 3,00

No credit cards.

Reservations

Made with 50% deposit. Tel: 0593 337546. E-mail: info@camping-de-valkenhof.nl

NL5790 Rekreatiepark 't Kuierpadtien

Oranjekanaal NZ 10, 7853 TA Wezuperbrug (Drenthe)

Professionally run, this all year round site is suitable as a night stop, or for longer if you wish to participate in all the activities offered in July and August (on payment). These encompass canoeing, windsurfing, water shutes and the dry-ski slope, which is also open during the winter so that the locals can practise before going en-masse to Austria. There are three opportunities for swimming with an indoor pool supplemented by a heated outdoor pool (June-Aug) and the lake itself. The site itself is in a woodland setting on the edge of the village. The 320 flat and grassy pitches for touring units (650 in total) are of reasonable size. All have electricity and 10 are fully serviced. A member of the Holland Tulip Parcs group.

Facilities

Eight quite acceptable sanitary blocks, including a new one, with hot showers (17.30 - 10.00 in July/Aug). Motorcaravan services Supermarket (1/4-15/9) but bread all year. Restaurant and bar (all year). Indoor pool. Outdoor pool (1/4-1/9). Sauna, solarium and whirlpool. Tennis. Dry ski slope. Play areas. Boules, volleyball and basketball.

Open

All year.

At a glance

Welcome & Ambience	✓✓✓✓✓	Location	✓✓✓✓
Quality of Pitches	✓✓✓✓	Range of Facilities	✓✓✓✓✓

Directions

From N34 Groningen-Emmen road exit near Emmen onto N31 towards Beilen. Turn right into Schoonord where left to Wezuperbrug. Site is at beginning of village on the right.

Charges guide

Per person (over 1 yr)	€ 4,10
pitch	€ 8,50 - € 16,75
car	€ 2,75
dog (max. 1)	€ 2,75

No credit cards.

Reservations

Advised for July/Aug. and made with deposit. Tel: 0591 38 14 15. E-mail: info@kuierpad.nl

NL6160 Camping Ruinen

Oude Benderseweg 11, 7963 PX Ruinen (Drenthe)

Camping Ruinen (formerly Recreatiecentrum Engeland) is a large, spacious site with 450 pitches in the woods of Drenthe. All 205 touring pitches have electricity (4/10A) and include 40 serviced pitches with water, drainage, cable TV and electricity connections. The numbered pitches are over 100 sq.m. in size and are on large, grassy fields. They are separated by hedges and in the shade of trees. At this comfortable site you can relax by cycling or walking through the woods or over the moors, or join organised trips in groups on a regular basis. There is no need to worry about the children - they will have great fun with Engel and Bengel, who arrange daily adventures, crafts or water games. The site does not have its own pool but the municipal pool is around the corner (passes from reception). Local attractions for children include Speelstad Oranje, a very large play-town, Ponypark Slagharen, a large theme park, or Verkeerspark Assen where they can learn to drive (on the right hand side of the road, of course). Adult activities include a 'whisper tour' by boat through the 'De Weerlibben' national park or a visit to the 'water-town' of Giethoorn.

Facilities

Four well-spaced toilet blocks provide washbasins (open style and in cabins), child-size toilets, bathrooms, child-size baths and a baby room. Facilities for disabled visitors. Laundry. Motorcaravan services. Shop. Restaurant with children's menu. Pancake restaurant. Play areas between the pitches. Giant chess. Boules. Tennis courts. Minigolf. Bicycle hire. Full entertainment programme in high season. Dog are allowed on certain pitches only. Off site: Riding 500 m. Fishing 3 km. Golf 18 km.

Open

1 April - 1 October.

At a glance

Welcome & Ambience	✓✓✓✓	Location	✓✓✓✓
Quality of Pitches	✓✓✓	Range of Facilities	✓✓✓✓

Directions

From Zwolle follow A28 north and take Ruinen exit. Follow site signs from there.

Charges guide

Per unit incl. 2 persons	€ 15,60 - € 20,25
extra person	€ 3,30
serviced pitch, plus	€ 5,00
dog	€ 3,25

No credit cards.

Reservations

Made with € 5.75 booking fee; contact site.
Tel: 0522 47 17 70. E-mail: engeland@etrade.nl

NL5980 Camping De Roos

Beerzerweg 10, 7736 PJ Beerze-Ommen (Overijssel)

De Roos is a family run site in a area of outstanding natural beauty, truly a nature lover's campsite, cosseted in an atmosphere of tranquillity. It is situated in Overijssel's Vecht Valley, a unique region set in a river dune landscape on the River Vecht. The river and its tributary wend their way unhurriedly around and through this spacious campsite. It is a natural setting that the owners of De Roos have carefully preserved. Conserving the environment is paramount here and the 285 pitches and necessary amenities have been blended into the landscape with great care. Pitches, many with electricity hook-up, are naturally sited, some behind blackthorn thickets, in the shadow of an old oak, or in a clearing scattered with wild flowers. De Roos is a car-free campsite during peak periods – vehicles must be parked at the car park (except arrival and departure). Swimming, fishing and boating are possible in the Vecht and there is a children's pool and beach area, also landing stages with steps. The enthusiastic owners have compiled walking and cycling routes (in English) to follow the ever-changing countryside of the Vecht Valley.

Facilities

Four well maintained sanitary blocks are kept fresh and clean. The two larger blocks are heated and include baby bath/shower and wash cabins. Dishwashing sinks. Launderette. Motorcaravan services. Health food shop and tea room (1/5-1/9). River swimming. Fishing. Bicycle hire. Volleyball. Basketball. Boules. Table tennis. Several small playgrounds and field for kite flying. Gas supplies. Dogs are not accepted (and cats must be kept on a lead!). Torch useful. Off site: Riding 6 km. Golf 10 km.

Open

9 April - 2 October.

At a glance

Welcome & Ambience	✓✓✓✓	Location	✓✓✓✓✓
Quality of Pitches	✓✓✓✓	Range of Facilities	✓✓✓✓

Directions

Leave A28 at Ommen exit 21 and join N340 for 19 km. to Ommen. Turn right at traffic lights over bridge and immediately left on local road towards Beerze. Site on left after 7 km. just after Beerze village sign.

Charges 2005

Per person over 3 yrs	€ 2,60 - € 3,20
pitch	€ 12,50 - € 14,50
electricity	€ 2,10

Discounts in low season and special packages.

Reservations

Contact site; reservations made with € 6.81 fee.
Tel: 0523 25 12 34. E-mail: info@campingderoos.nl

NL6480 Camping De Molenhof

Kleysenweg 7, 7667 RS Reutum/Weerselo (Overijssel)

De Molenhof is a pleasant family site where you can enjoy the real Twent hospitality. It has 450 well laid out pitches of which 420 are for touring units, all with water, drainage, electricity (10A) and cable connections. The remaining 30 pitches are currently occupied by mobile homes, but these are to be replaced with touring pitches in the next two years. This is a real family site and children under the age of 12 years will particularly enjoy themselves in the covered, adventure playground, the two swimming pools (one outdoor, one covered) with a large slide on the outside and with the entertainment team that provides a full daily programme in high season. The highlight for youngsters will probably be the new sanitary block which has a special 'fairy tale' style children's area. Taking a shower here will be a real treat. Older guests are not forgotten – you can explore the rich Twent surroundings by bike or go shopping in Almelo, Hengelo, Enschede or even in Germany, since you are close to the border.

Facilities

Four toilet blocks, one in 'fairy tale style' for children, provide washbasins (open style and in cabins), adult and child size toilets and basins, controllable showers, bathrooms and a baby room. Laundrette. Motorcaravan service. Well stocked shop. Bar/restaurant. Pancake restaurant. Swimming pools. Playgrounds (1 covered). Sports court. Tennis court. Fishing. Bicycle and go-kart hire. Boules. Extensive entertainment program in high season. Off site: Beach and riding 6 km. Golf 8 km.

At a glance

Welcome & Ambience	✓✓✓✓✓	Location	✓✓✓✓
Quality of Pitches	✓✓✓✓	Range of Facilities	✓✓✓✓✓

Directions

Follow A1 from Amsterdam east to Hengelo and take exit 31, Hengelo Noord. Go through Deurningen to Weerselo and from there the N343 towards Tubbergen and site signs.

Charges 2004

Per fully serviced pitch incl. 2 persons	€ 29,00
extra person	€ 5,00

Reservations

Made with 50% deposit. Tel: 0541 661201. E-mail: info@demolenhof.nl

Open

19 March - 2 October.

NL5780 Holiday Park de Zanding

Vijverlaan 1, 6731 CK Otterlo (Gelderland)

De Zanding is a family run, highly rated site that offers almost every recreational facility, either on site or nearby, that active families or couples might seek. Immediately after the entrance, a lake is to the left where you can swim, fish, sunbathe or try a canoe. There are many sporting options and organised high season programmes for all ages. Minutes away is the Hoge Veluwe National Park for a great day out either cycling, walking or visiting the Kröller-Müller Museum. There are 463 touring pitches spread around the site (all with electricity), some individual and separated, others in more open spaces shaded by trees. Some serviced pitches are in small groups between long stay units and there is another area for tents. Seasonal units take a further 508 pitches. A member of the Holland Tulip Parcs group.

Facilities

First class sanitary facilities are housed in five modern blocks that are clean, well maintained and well equipped. Good provision for babies and people with disabilities. Laundry. Kitchen. Motorcaravan services. Gas supplies. Supermarket. Restaurant/bar (15/5-15/9). Lake swimming. Fishing. Tennis. Minigolf. Boules. Volleyball. Five children's play areas. Bicycle hire. Organised activities. Dogs are not accepted.

Open

24 March - 30 October.

At a glance

Welcome & Ambience	✓✓✓✓✓	Location	✓✓✓✓✓
Quality of Pitches	✓✓✓✓✓	Range of Facilities	✓✓✓✓✓

Directions

Leave A12 Utrecht - Arnhem motorway at Oosterbeek at exit 25 and join N310 to Otterlo. Then follow signs to site, watching carefully for entrance.

Charges 2005

Per unit incl. 2 persons and 4A electricity	€ 17,20 - € 27,55
tent pitch incl. 2 persons	€ 12,00
extra person	€ 3,00
10A electricity	€ 1,35

Reservations

Not necessary. Tel: 0318 596111. E-mail: zanding@zanding.nl

Netherlands

NL5810 Recreatiepark de Luttenberg

Heuvelweg 9, 8105 SZ Luttenberg (Overijssel)

This woodland site is near the Sallandse Heuvelrug nature reserve and is well placed for relaxing walking and cycling tours. It is a large park with 120 seasonal pitches around the perimeter and 220 touring pitches (all with 4A electricity) in a central area off tarmac access roads. The large, individual pitches are numbered and separated, in rows divided by hedges and trees, with easy access. A separate cluster is for dog owners and some areas are car free. There is a large bar and eating area with terrace and a small, separate restaurant The new 25 m. swimming pool and a small one for children, with the on-site activities and an animal enclosure, provide plenty to keep younger visitors happy. A member of the Holland Tulip Parcs group.

Facilities

New heated sanitary block with controllable showers gives a satisfactory overall provision together with two other blocks. All are heated and each provides hot showers on payment. Outside, under cover dishwashing points. Motorcaravan services. Gas supplies. Small shop for essentials including bread. Bar and restaurant (low season: Tues. and Fri-Sun). Barbecue with seating. Swimming pool (15/5-15/9). Tennis. Table tennis. Football. Volleyball. Boules. Bicycle hire. Minigolf. Off site: Fishing 1.5 km. Riding 6 km.

Open

31 March - 1 October.

At a glance

Welcome & Ambience	✓✓✓✓	Location	✓✓✓✓
Quality of Pitches	✓✓✓✓	Range of Facilities	✓✓✓✓

Directions

From N35 Zwolle - Almelo turn on N348 Ommen road east of Raalte, then turn to Luttenberg and follow signs. From A1 (Amsterdam - Hengelo) take exit 23 at Deventer on N348, then as above.

Charges 2005

Per unit incl. 2 persons and electricity	€ 24,00
4 persons	€ 31,00
hikers and cyclists (2 persons)	€ 14,00
extra person (over 1 yr)	€ 3,50
dog	€ 3,50

Less 15% outside 15/7-1/9. No credit cards.

Reservations

Made with fee; contact site. Tel: 0572 30 14 05.
E-mail: info@luttenberg.nl

NL5960 Camping De Wielerbaan

Zoomweg 7-9, 6705 DM Wageningen-Hoog (Gelderland)

This family run park has an interesting history and a natural setting at a point where the Veluwe, the valley of Gelderland and the picturesque area of Betuwe meet. Translated 'Wielerbaan' means 'cycle race-track' which still stands in the heart of this site. The owners have utilised this area to accommodate recreation facilities which include an indoor pool. Touring pitches in a meadow setting are serviced with water, electricity and drainage. Planned cycles routes are available at reception, or maps to choose your own way. It is possible to go by boat to Arnhem and worth visiting is the Burgers Zoo, the Zoo of Ouwehand or seeking out the nearby parks (discounted entrance cards are available from the site).

Facilities

Four toilet blocks of a reasonable standard provide wash cabins, showers and a baby room. Launderette. Gas supplies. Shop. Small restaurant. Snacks and takeaway. Library. Swimming pool. Minigolf. Boules. Ten small play areas and organised entertainment in high season. Off site: Golf 500 m. Fishing 5 km. Boat launching.

Open

All year.

At a glance

Welcome & Ambience	✓✓✓✓	Location	✓✓✓✓
Quality of Pitches	✓✓✓✓	Range of Facilities	✓✓✓✓

Directions

Leave A12 at exit 24 towards Wageningen and continue for 4.5 km. to second roundabout, where site is clearly signed. Follow signs to site, 1.5 km. from the town.

Charges guide

Per unit incl. 2 persons and electricity	€ 15,80 - € 23,95
extra person	€ 1,80
dog (max. 2)	€ 2,80

Less 10% for over 55s at certain times.

Reservations

Advisable in high season. Tel: 0317 41 39 64.
E-mail: info@wielerbaan.nl

NL6290 Camping Eiland van Maurik

Rijnbandijk 20, 4021 GH Maurik (Gelderland)

Camping Eiland van Mourik is beside a lake at the Nederrijn, in the centre of an extensive nature and recreation area. These surroundings are ideal for all sorts of activities - swimming, windsurfing, water-skiing or para-sailing, relaxing on the beach or fishing. There is even an animal farm for the children. In the event of bad weather, the site has a gym including volleyball, badminton and table tennis and a covered 'play palace' – Avontura, where in high season games and activities are organised for children. The site has 365 numbered, flat pitches. All the 155 for touring units have 10A electricity and cable TV connections and 64 also have water and drainage. There is direct access from the site onto the beach. You could enjoy the pancakes in the 'Oudhollandse' restaurant - also enjoy the views over the water if you do! This is a site for families.

Facilities

The three toilet blocks for tourers include washbasins (open style and in cabins), controllable showers and a baby room. Launderette with ironing board and iron. Dishwashing sinks. Shop. Bar/restaurant (1/4-1/10). Play areas (1 indoors). Play field. Tennis. Minigolf. Table tennis. Bicycle hire. Riding (part of the entertainment programme). Tennis. Volleyball. Water skiing. Para-sailing. Animal farm. Entertainment program in high season. Gate key deposit € 50.
Off site: Shop, restaurant and bar nearby. Golf 9 km.

Open

1 April - 1 October.

At a glance

Welcome & Ambience	✓✓✓✓✓	Location	✓✓✓✓✓
Quality of Pitches	✓✓✓✓	Range of Facilities	✓✓✓✓✓

Directions

From Rhenen take the N320 road towards Mourik and signs for 'Eiland van Mourik'.

Charges 2004

Per unit incl. 2 persons and electricity	€ 17,00 - € 22,00
extra person (under 2 yrs free)	€ 3,00
dog	€ 3,50
boat per night (not on pitches)	€ 6,50
hikers and cyclists (2 persons)	€ 13,50

Reservations

Made with 50% deposit, balance due on arrival. Tel: 0344 691502. E-mail: info@eilandvanmaurik.nl

NL5850 Camping de Hooge Veluwe

Koningsweg 14, 6816 TC Arnhem (Gelderland)

Its situation at the entrance to the Hoge Veluwe National Park with its moors, forests, sand drifts, walking routes and cycle paths, makes this a highly desirable holiday base. The site itself is well managed and laid out in an orderly fashion, with 260 touring pitches, including 85 fully serviced places of 300 sq.m. All have electricity (4/6A), are numbered and laid out in small fields which are divided by hedging. Some are traffic free which means cars must be left in a nearby car park. Mobile homes are discreetly placed mostly in the centre of the site, but the many trees and shrubbery make them unobtrusive, in fact, many have enviable garden areas. The adjacent National Park incorporates the Kroller Muller Museum and the Museonder Underground Museum. The Burgers Zoo and Safari Park and Burgers Park are also near, all of which make interesting visits. There is some road noise.

Facilities

Five excellent, heated sanitary blocks with all facilities, are easily identified by colourful logos. Launderette. Motorcaravan services. Gas supplies. Supermarket. Restaurant. Takeaway. All facilities open all season. TV room. Heated outdoor and indoor pools, and a paddling pool. Several small play areas. Recreation hall. Dedicated playground with football pitch, tennis, cycle track, basket-ball, minigolf, etc. Bicycle hire. Organised activities.
Off site: Riding 50 m. Golf 6 km. Beach 12 km.

Open

26 March - 30 October.

At a glance

Welcome & Ambience	✓✓✓✓✓	Location	✓✓✓✓✓
Quality of Pitches	✓✓✓✓✓	Range of Facilities	✓✓✓✓✓

Directions

Leave A12 motorway at exit 25 (Oosterbeck) and follow signs for Hooge Veluwe. Site is on right in approx. 6 km. From the A50, take exit 21 to Schaarsbergen and follow signs.

Charges guide

Per unit incl. 2 persons and electricity	€ 15,00 - € 25,00
extra person	€ 3,00
dog	€ 3,25

Reservations

Necessary in high season. Tel: 0264 43 22 72. E-mail: info@dehoogeveluwe.nl

NL5870 Camping de Vergarde

Erichemseweg 84, 4117 GL Erichem (Gelderland)

Situated north of 's Hertogenbosch and west of Nijmegen and Arnhem, De Vergarde has two sections on either side of a lake. Static holiday caravans are on the left, with 207 touring pitches in named sections on the right (about one third seasonal). With good access, pitches are numbered on flat grass and include 30 with electricity (6A) and TV connections. There are trees all round the perimeter (but no shade on the pitches) and the site has a spacious, open feeling with the lake adding to its attractiveness. The shop opens daily and the restaurant/bar in high season plus weekends in low season. Lots of ducks and geese gather around the lake, which can be used for fishing (but not swimming). A member of the Holland Tulip Parcs group.

Facilities

Excellent sanitary facilities are in three blocks, including family showers and baby bathrooms. Most, but not all, hot water is on payment. Washing machines. Motorcaravan services. Heated swimming pools (1/5-1/9). Shop (1/5-1/10). Restaurant (1/5-1/10). Play area and large indoor games room for wet days. Pony riding. Pets corner. Minigolf. Bicycle hire. Games room. Two tennis courts. Fishing.

Open

1 March - 30 October.

At a glance

Welcome & Ambience	✓✓✓✓	Location	✓✓✓✓
Quality of Pitches	✓✓✓✓	Range of Facilities	✓✓✓✓

Directions

From A15 Dordrecht - Nijmegen road exit at Tiel West (also MacDonald's) and follow signs to Erichem.

Charges 2004

Per unit incl. 2 persons	€ 18,00
with electricity, water and drainage	€ 20,00
with satellite TV	€ 23,00
extra person (over 2 yrs)	€ 3,00
dog (max 1)	€ 3,00

Special weekly rates. Low season less 20%.

Reservations

Contact site. Tel: 0344 57 20 17.
E-mail: info@devergarde.nl

NL5950 Rekreatiecentrum Heumens Bos

Vosseneindseweg 46, 6582 BR Heumen (Gelderland)

The area around Nijmegen, the oldest city in the Netherlands, has large forests for walking or cycling, nature reserves and old towns to explore, as well as being quite close to Arnhem. Mr Van Velzen and his sons took over this site in 2002 and are planning new buildings. The site covers 16 ha. and is open over a long season for touring families (no groups of youngsters allowed) and all year for bungalows. It offers 165 level, grass touring pitches for touring units, all with electricity and cable TV connections. Numbered but not separated, in glades of 10 and one large field, all have easy access with cars parked away from the caravans. One small section for motorcaravans has some hardstandings. An open air swimming pool with a small children's pool is maintained at 28 degrees by a system of heat transfer from the air.

Facilities

The main, high quality sanitary building, plus another new block, are modern and heated, providing showers on payment, rooms for families and disabled people and hot water to private cabins and other washbasins. Another smaller building has acceptable facilities. Smart launderette. Motorcaravan services. Gas supplies. Shop. Bar, restaurant and snack bar (all season). Heated swimming pool (from 1/5). Bicycle hire. All weather tennis courts. Boules. Table tennis. For children a separate glade area with play equipment on sand and grass, Activity and excursion programme (high season). Large wet weather room. Off site: Riding 300 m. Fishing 2 km. Golf 10 km.

At a glance

Welcome & Ambience	✓✓✓✓	Location	✓✓✓✓
Quality of Pitches	✓✓✓	Range of Facilities	✓✓✓✓

Directions

From A73 (Nijmegen - Venlo) take exit 3 (4 km. south of Nijmegen) and follow site signs.

Charges 2005

Per pitch incl. 2 persons	€ 15,25 - € 27,00
electricity	€ 2,20
dog (max 1)	€ 4,00

Special low season weekends (incl. restaurant meal) and special deal for over 55 yr olds.

Reservations

Made without charge and essential for public holidays and July/Aug. Tel: 0243 58 14 81.
E-mail: info@heumensbos.nl

Open

1 April - 1 November.

NL6310 Camping Arnhem

Kemperbergerweg 771, 6816 RW Arnhem (Gelderland)

Camping Arnhem is a wooded site in the Veluwe region of the Netherlands, close to the 'Hooge Veluwe' National Park. The 484 pitches are partly in the sun and partly in the shade of tall trees and there are 260 for touring units (10 for tour operators), some with hardstanding. This is a perfect base for visiting the National Park, the Kroller Muller museum or the outdoor museum. You could also go riding or play golf close to the site or experience the silence high up in the air in a glider from the Terlet airport. There is also plenty to do on the site including tennis, table tennis, boules or minigolf. Children will be entertained by the professional entertainment team - if you don't look out, the clowns may take you for a healthy dive in the adventure pond.

Facilities

Modern sanitary blocks provide free hot showers, facilities for disabled visitors and a baby room. Fully equipped launderette with ironing facilities. Motorcaravan services. Supermarket. Café. Bar. Tennis. Volleyball. Basketball. Minigolf. Table tennis. Sports field. Boules. Open air theatre. Several playgrounds. Adventure pond. Swimming pool and paddling pool. Entertainment programme in high season. Bicycle hire. Off site: Arnhem for shopping. Burgers Zoo. Kroller Moiler museum. Airborn museum. Riding and golf. Gliding. Balloon trips and boat trips.

At a glance

Welcome & Ambience	✓✓✓✓	Location	✓✓✓✓✓
Quality of Pitches	✓✓✓✓	Range of Facilities	✓✓✓✓

Directions

From the A50 take exit 21 for Schaarsbergen. Go to Schaarsbergen and follow the camp signs.

Charges 2004

Per unit incl. 2 adults, 2 children and 4A electricity € 20,85 - € 29,10

Reservations

Contact site. Tel: 026 443 1600.
E-mail: arnhem@holiday.nl

Open

1 April - 26 October.

NL5900 Beekse Bergen Safari Campsite

Beekse Bergen 1, 5081 NJ Hilvarenbeek (Noord-Brabant)

Beekse Bergen is a large impressive leisure park set around a very large, attractive lake near Tilberg. The park offers a range of amusements which should keep the most demanding of families happy! These include not only water based activities such as windsurfing, canoeing, jetski, rowing and fishing, but also a small amusement park, a cinema, tennis courts, minigolf and many more. The lake is bordered by sandy beaches, children's playgrounds, open-air swimming areas and water slides. Transport around and across the lake is provided by a little train or a sightseeing boat (in high season). These and most of the amenities are free to campers. Part of the resort is the Beekse Bergen Safari Park with reduced entry for campers, where you can see the many wild animals from either your own car, a safari bus or two safari boats, the Stanley and the Livingstone. On the far side of the lake, as well as the bungalows and tents, there are two distinct campsites - one on flat meadows surrounded by hedges and trees near the lake, the other in a more secluded wooded area reached by a tunnel under the nearby main road. The 600 numbered pitches are about 100 sq.m, and all have electrical connections. The Safari Campsite has a 'typical safari environment' and a viewpoint over the Safari Park (with free, unlimited entry for campers staying here. Open 24 April - 2 Sept). There is an independent central complex with catering, playground and launderette, plus an entertainment team. This is an area with many other recreational activities, including the award winning Efteling amusement park.

Facilities

Sanitary facilities are quite adequate in terms of numbers, cleanliness and facilities including some washbasins in private cabins. Launderettes. Restaurants, cafés and takeaway (weekends only in low seasons). Supermarket. Children's playgrounds and indoor pool. Beaches and lake swimming. Watersports including rowing boats (free) and canoe hire. Amusements. Tennis. Minigolf. Fishing. Recreation programme. Bicycle hire. Riding. Twin axle caravans not accepted. Off site: Golf 5 km.

Open

28 March - 26 October.

At a glance

Welcome & Ambience	✓✓✓✓✓	Location	✓✓✓✓
Quality of Pitches	✓✓✓✓	Range of Facilities	✓✓✓✓

Directions

From A58/E312 Tilburg - Eindhoven motorway, take exit to Hilvarenbeek on the N269 road. Park and campsite are signed Beekse Bergen.

Charges guide

Per person (from 2 yrs)	€ 3,75
standard pitch incl. electricity	€ 11,00 - € 18,90
serviced pitch	€ 14,45 - € 22,35

Discounts for weekly stays, camping packages available.

Reservations

Necessary for high season and B.Hs.
Tel: 013 5491100. E-mail: beeksebergen@libema.nl

NL5540 Camping De Katjeskelder

Katjeskelder 1, 4904 SG Oosterhout (Noord-Brabant)

This site is to be found in a wooded setting in a delightful area of Noord Brabant. This is idyllic cycling and walking countryside and many well known attractions such as the Efteling theme park and the Biesbosch nature park lie within a short drive. It is a well established, family run site offering extensive facilities with a new and impressive ultra-modern reception area. Around the 25 hectare site are mobile homes and bungalows but there are 200 touring pitches, all with electricity and water (between two pitches), plus 13 fully serviced pitches with hardstanding for motorcaravans. Cars are prohibited alongside the pitches, but may be parked nearby. The site has a 'cat' theme, hence the cat names including that of the restaurant, the 'Gelaarsde Kat' (Puss in Boots) which is situated in the 'Tropikat' complex. This tropical indoor water playground with slide is free for campers and the site also has an outdoor swimming pool and children's pool, both supervised. A member of the Holland Tulip Parcs group.

Facilities

Three modern, heated sanitary blocks provide facilities including a family shower/wash room, baby room and provision for disabled people. Laundry. Motorcaravan services. Supermarket. Restaurant, bar, snack bar, pizzeria ('pizzacat') and takeaway (the 'Hapjeskat') Indoor tropical pool. Outdoor swimming pools (15/5-31/8). Play field. Tennis. Bicycle hire. Minigolf. Several play areas for small children, plus a large adventure playground and organised entertainment for children all season. Off site: Oosterheide nature park and Dorst forest.

At a glance

Welcome & Ambience	✓✓✓✓	Location	✓✓✓✓✓
Quality of Pitches	✓✓✓✓	Range of Facilities	✓✓✓✓✓

Directions

From A27 Breda/Gorinchem motorway take exit 17 Oosterhout Zuid and follow signs for 7 km to site

Charges guide

Per unit incl. 2 persons, electricity, water and TV connections	€ 19,00 - € 33,00
3-4 persons	€ 23,50 - € 33,50
dog	€ 5,00

Reservations

Necessary in high season. Tel: 0162 453 539. E-mail: kkinfo@katjeskelder.nl

Open

All year.

NL6790 Camping de Kienehoef

Zwembadweg 35 - 37, 5491 TE Sint-Oedenrode (Noord-Brabant)

Camping de Kienehoef is at Sint Oedenrode in Noord Brabant, which boasts many historical sights, including two castles. The site is well cared for and attractively laid out with reception to the right of the entrance and the site facilities to the left. Behind this area is a heated swimming pool. The generous pitches are mostly laid out in bays and placed between trees and shrubs to the right of a long avenue leading through the site. A few are to the left, alongside bungalows which are discreetly placed in the trees. In what is known as the red area, cars must be parked away from the pitches.

Facilities

Two modern, clean and well maintained toilet blocks include pre-set showers and some shower/wash cubicles, also family and baby rooms. Separate dishwashing and laundry area with iron and board. Shop, restaurant/bar and snacks (all 1/5-15/9). Heated swimming pool (1/5-15/9). Lake fishing. Bicycle hire. Sports field, tennis court, volleyball. Dogs and other pets are not accepted. Off site: Golf 1 km. Riding 15 km.

Open

28 March - 28 October.

At a glance

Welcome & Ambience	✓✓✓	Location	✓✓✓
Quality of Pitches	✓✓✓✓	Range of Facilities	✓✓✓✓

Directions

Leave A2 'sHertogenbosh - Eindhoven motorway at exit 27 and follow signs to Sint Oedenrode. Site is well signed from village.

Charges guide

Per unit incl. 2 persons and electricity	€ 22,00 - € 26,00
extra person	€ 3,50 - € 27,60
hiker tent pitch	€ 7,00 - € 8,00

Reservations

Contact site. Tel: 0413 47 28 77. E-mail: info@kienehoef.nl

NL5910 Vakantiecentrum de Hertenwei

Wellenseind 7-9, 5094 EG Lage Mierde (Noord-Brabant)

Set in the southwest corner of the country quite close to the Belgian border, this relaxed site covers a large area. In addition to 100 quite substantial bungalows with their own gardens (some residential, 30 to let and 32 mobile homes), the site has some 350 touring pitches. These are in four different areas on oblong meadows surrounded by hedges and trees, with the numbered pitches around the edges. There is a choice of pitch size (100 or 150 sq.m.) and all have 6A electrical connections, water and drainage, and even a cable TV connection as well. The most pleasant area is probably the small one near the entrance and main buildings – these are a long walk from some of the furthest pitches. Indoor and outdoor pool and recreation programme in season with films, dances or disco, sports, bingo, etc.

Facilities

Four toilet blocks are of slightly differing types, all of quite good quality and well spaced around the site. Virtually all washbasins in private cabins and the blocks can be heated in cool weather. Units for disabled people, hair washing cabins and baby baths. Launderette. Gas supplies. Motorcaravan services. Supermarket (Easter - end Oct). Bar by indoor pool (12 x 6 m. open all year,admission charged). Three outdoor pools, the largest 25 x 10 m. (15/5-29/8). Restaurant, cafeteria with snack bar (all year). Disco. Two tennis courts. Children's playgrounds and play meadows. Sauna, solarium and jacuzzi. Bicycle hire.
Off site: Supermarket 2 km. Bus service to Tilburg or Eindhoven with stop at entrance. Fishing and riding 4 km.

At a glance

Welcome & Ambience	✓✓✓✓	Location	✓✓✓✓
Quality of Pitches	✓✓✓✓	Range of Facilities	✓✓✓✓

Directions

Site is by N269 Tilburg - Reusel road, 2 km. north of Lage Mierde and 16 km. south of Tilburg

Charges 2005

Per unit incl. 2 persons and electricity	€ 29,50 - € 32,75
extra person	€ 4,00

Less 25-40% in low seasons.

Reservations

Made for min. 1 week, in summer Sat to Sat. only, with deposit. Tel: 0135 09 12 95.

Open

All year.

NL6560 Camping De Maasvallei

Dorperheideweg 34, 5944 NK Arcen (Limburg)

Set in the pretty countryside around Noord-Limburg and close to the German border this fairly large site has 463 pitches. There are also static caravans, a number of which are to rent. It is well situated for boating on the Maas, or if preferring to relax on site there is a lake and beach. Being a mature site it is surrounded by trees and some pitches benefit from shade. The main facilities such as the restaurant, bar, takeaway, shop, games room and swimming pool are a short walk from reception, with the lake towards the rear of the site. This is mainly a campsite geared for families, or it would appeal to those seeking a break where walking and cycling are the main attractions of the area. Arcen is a pretty village and draws many visitors.

Facilities

Two clean and heated sanitary blocks provide showers, washcabins, baby baths and a family room, Dishwashing and laundry sinks, washing machines and dryers. Motorcaravan service point. Restaurant and bar. Shop. Swimming pool. Table tennis, basketball, volleyball. Bicycle hire. Organised activities in July/August. Dogs are accepted, but only one per family and in a special area.

Open

All year.

At a glance

Welcome & Ambience	✓✓✓✓	Location	✓✓✓
Quality of Pitches	✓✓✓	Range of Facilities	✓✓✓✓

Directions

Leave A77 Boxmeer - Goch motorway at exit 2 to join N271 south in the direction of Venlo. Follow N271 for 27 km. and turn left at traffic lights on dual-carriageway on local road (signed Lingsfort). Continue on local road for 1.8 km. and turn left. Site is on right after 1.6 km.

Charges 2004

Per unit incl. 2 persons	€ 17,00 - € 22,50

Reservations

Contact site. Tel: 077 4731564.
E-mail: info@demaasvallei.nl

NL5890 Kampeercentrum Klein Canada

Dorpstraat 1, 5851 AG Afferden (Limburg)

Following the war, the family who own this site wanted to emigrate to Canada - they didn't go, but instead created this attractive site with the maple leaf theme decorating buildings, pool and play equipment. Pleasant, farm style buildings adorned with flowers house the main amenities near the entrance and the site has a sheltered atmosphere with many ornamental trees. There are three touring areas, one on an island surrounded by an attractive, landscaped moat used for fishing, the other on flat ground on the other side of the entrance. They provide 195 large, numbered pitches, all with electricity (6-10A), water, drainage and TV connections. The newest area will offer 80 pitches each with its own sanitary unit and car park space. Some 200 permanent and seasonal pitches form other areas to the back of the site. There is a small indoor pool, sauna and solarium and an outdoor pool (with large slide) and children's pool with a grassy sunbathing area. Cars are parked in separate areas. This is a good quality site with a lot to offer for a comfortable stay in charming surroundings. A member of the Holland Tulip Parcs group.

Facilities

Mixed toilet facilities include some with washbasins in cubicles, and family facilities in a fully tiled and heated room. Some pitches have individual units. Motorcaravan services. Gas supplies. Supermarket, Bar, restaurant, snack bar and takeaway (all 1/4-31/10). Outdoor pool (May - Sept). Indoor pool (all year). Sauna and solarium. Pool table. Table top minigolf. Tennis. Fishing. Children's playground. Animals enclosure. Bicycle hire. Off site: Riding 5 km.

Open

All year.

At a glance

Welcome & Ambience	✓✓✓✓✓	Location	✓✓✓✓
Quality of Pitches	✓✓✓✓	Range of Facilities	✓✓✓✓

Directions

Afferden is on the N271 between Nijmegen and Venlo, just south of the A77/E31 motorway into Germany. Site is on the N271 and is signed.

Charges 2005

Per unit incl. 6A electricity, water & TV	€ 11,60 - € 17,00
'super comfort' pitch plus	€ 5,75
person	€ 3,60
child (1-12 yrs)	€ 2,80
dog	€ 2,50

Reservations

Made with € 10 deposit. Tel: 0485 531223. E-mail: info@kleincanada.nl

NL5970 Camping De Paal

Paaldreef 14, 5571 TN Bergeyk (Noord-Brabant)

A first class campsite, De Paal is especially suitable for families with young children. Situated in 42 hectares of woodland, there are 530 touring pitches, ranging in size up to 150 sq.m. (plus 70 seasonal pitches). The pitches are numbered and separated by trees, with cars either parked on the pitch or in a dedicated parking area. All have 6A electricity, TV, water, drainage and a bin. With child safety in mind, there is a play area on each group of pitches, in addition to the large open sand-based adventure play area and large barn for wet weather. In high season an animation team provides further entertainment. The high quality indoor heated pool consists of play pools for babies and children, with a deeper one for parents. The heated outdoor and toddlers pools are also shallow. Maps can be purchased in reception showing the many walking and cycling opportunities in this attractive area. Whilst catering foremost for families with young children, outside the high season there are many regular adult visitors to this friendly site, very capably run by the Martens family and staff.

Facilities

High quality sanitary facilities are ultra modern, including washcabins, family rooms and baby baths, all with lots of space. Facilities for disabled visitors. Launderette. Motorcaravan services. Underground supermarket. Restaurant (high season), bar and snack bar (all season). Indoor pool (all season, supervised in high season). Outdoor pool (May - Sept). Bicycle hire. Tennis. Play areas. Theatre. Bicycle storage room. Off site: Within short walk of the entrance is a tennis complex with 6 indoor courts (Sept-May) with 10 outdoor all weather courts (all equipment available for hire) and pleasant lounge bar. Horse riding and covered wagons for hire 500 m.

At a glance

Welcome & Ambience	✓✓✓✓✓	Location	✓✓✓✓
Quality of Pitches	✓✓✓✓	Range of Facilities	✓✓✓✓

Directions

From E34 Antwerpen-Eindhoven road take exit 32 (Eersel) and follow signs for Bergeyk and site (2 km. from town).

Charges guide

Per pitch incl. 2 persons and services	€ 21,00 - € 31,00
extra person (over 1 yr)	€ 4,00 - € 5,00
cyclist	€ 8,00
dog	€ 4,00

Discounts outside 5/7-16/8 daily 30%, over 7 days 35%, (over 55's 45% for more than 7 days).

Reservations

Essential for July/Aug. and made for min. 1 week Sat to Sat. Tel: 0497 57 19 77. E-mail: info@depaal.nl

Open

Easter/1 April - 31 October.

NL6510 Rekreatiecentrum de Schatberg

Midden Peelweg 5, 5975 MZ Sevenum (Limburg)

In a woodland setting of 86 hectares, this family run campsite is more reminiscent of a holiday village, with a superb range of activities, making it an ideal venue for families. It is well situated for visits to Germany and Belgium, also easily accessible from the port of Zeebrugge. The surrounding countryside offers the opportunity to commune with nature, either by cycling or walking. For the more 'stay on site' visitor the location is excellent with several lakes for fishing, windsurfing and swimming, plus an extensive range of activities and a heated outdoor swimming pool. The 600 touring pitches, with electricity (6/10A), water and drainage, average 100 sq.m. in size and are on rough grass terrain mostly with shade, but not separated. A range of rented and private accommodation is unobtrusively placed in separate areas and includes some very smart, brick-built bungalows for rent. A feature at De Schatberg is the attractive restaurant/bar area and the reception and indoor pool, manned by friendly staff. After a fire this area has been rebuilt to a modern design and is very user-friendly. Look out for the wallabies and the deer!

Facilities

Three modern, fully equipped toilet blocks, supplemented by two small wooden toilet units to save night time walks, receive heavy use in high season. There are showers, washbasins (some in cabins), family shower rooms, baby baths and en-suite units for disabled visitors. Dishwashing and laundry sinks. Washing machines and dryers. Motorcaravan service point. Supermarket. Restaurant, bar and takeaway. Indoor and outdoor swimming pools. Football. Tennis. Minigolf. Trampoline. Play areas. Fishing. Watersports. Bicycle hire. Bowling, casino, underground disco, entertainment for children and adults in high season. Dogs are only accepted in certain areas. Off site: Golf 4 km.

At a glance

Welcome & Ambience	✓✓✓✓✓	Location	✓✓✓✓
Quality of Pitches	✓✓✓	Range of Facilities	✓✓✓✓

Directions

Leave A67 Eindhoven/Venlo motorway at Helden exit 38 and follow signs for 1 km. to site.

Charges 2005

Per unit incl. up to 4 persons	€ 17,50 - € 30,70
extra person over 3 yrs	€ 4,50

Reservations

Contact site. Tel: 0774 67 77 77.
E-mail: info@schatberg.nl

Open

All year.

NL6710 Kampeerterrein De Achterste Hoef

Troprijt 10, 5531 NA Bladel (Noord-Brabant)

This quite large campsite is to be found off the N284 at Bladel in Noord Bradant. It is an ideal location for cycling, walking and is close to the Belgian border. A family oriented site, it offers good quality facilities which are well maintained and kept very clean. On entering the site you find all the main service buildings alongside reception. There are about 320 touring pitches, all fully serviced and 28 with their own sanitation and sited near the lake. There are also seasonal and static caravan places, but these are kept apart and mostly in one area. The touring pitches are 100 - 150 sq.m. in size with many amongst the trees, but some are in open meadows and some divided by young shrubs. To the rear of the site is the lake and beach area, with a dedicated section for swimming.

Facilities

Four sanitary blocks have showers, washbasins, both open and in cabins, a bathroom and a baby bath. Dishwashing sinks, laundry room, washing machine and dryer. Motorcaravan service point. Supermarket. Restaurant/bar and snack bar. Disco. Recreation room. Pitch and putt. Football. Tennis. Heated swimming pool. Minigolf. Bicycle hire. Watersports. Play areas. Animal corner. Organised activities in July/Aug. Off site: Fishing 3 km. Riding 15 km. Golf 20 km.

At a glance

Welcome & Ambience	✓✓✓✓✓	Location	✓✓✓✓
Quality of Pitches	✓✓✓✓	Range of Facilities	✓✓✓✓

Directions

Travelling east or west on the N284 Eindhoven - Reusel Road turn south at second traffic lights in Bladel and follow camping signs to site.

Charges 2004

Per unit incl. 1 person	€ 15.25 - € 23.35
incl. 2 persons	€ 17.85 - € 29.75
extra person over 2 yrs	€ 4.40
dog (max 1)	€ 4.40
local tax	€ 0.72

Camping Cheques accepted.

Reservations

Contact site. Tel: 0497 381579.
Email: info@achterstehoef.nl

Open

Easter - 31 October.

NL6530 Terrassencamping Gulperberg Panorama

Berghem 1, 6271 NP Gulpen (Limburg)

Gulperberg Panorama is just 3 km. from the attractive village of Gulpen. Visitors are assured of a warm welcom and if arriving (or leaving) on a Saturday are welcomed (or bade farewell) by the 'Aartje Twinkle'. Pitches are large and flat on terraces overlooking the village on one side and open countryside on the other. Many have full services. English is spoken in reception, although all information is written in Dutch - don't hesitate to ask if you require a translation. This is good walking country and maps are available for a small charge from the reception. Gulperberg Panorama is a haven for children with a weekly entertainment programme. The site is not suitable for visitors with disabilities.

Facilities

Four modern sanitary blocks have excellent facilities (showers require a token). Family shower room and baby room. Laundry. Shop (27/4-31/8). Bar. Takeaway. New restaurant and takeaway planned for 2004. Swimming pool (29/4-15/9). Three play areas. Volleyball, basketball, table tennis. Giant 'air-cushion'. TV and games room. Extensive entertainment programme for children plus family entertainment. Off site: Golf and bicycle hire 3 km. Fishing 4 km. Riding 5 km.

Open

10 April - 28 October.

At a glance

Welcome & Ambience	✓✓✓✓	Location	✓✓✓✓✓
Quality of Pitches	✓✓✓✓	Range of Facilities	✓✓✓✓

Directions

Gulpen is east of Maastricht. Take N278 Maastricht - Aachen. Site is signed just as you enter Gulpen (look for them on the right). Turn right and follow camping signs for approx. 3 km.

Charges 2004

Per unit incl. 2 persons	€ 12,50 - € 16,50
with electricity (6A)	€ 14,30 - € 18,75
with services	€ 17,90 - € 22,40
extra person (over 2 yrs)	€ 2,10 - € 3,00
pet (max 2)	€ 1,90 - € 2,50

Reductions for the over-55s.

Reservations

Advised in July and August. Tel: 0434 50 23 30.
E-mail: info@gulperberg.nl

NL6520 Camping BreeBronne

Lange Heide 9, 5993 PB Maasbree (Limburg)

Said to be one of the top campsites in the Netherlands, BreeBronne is set in a forest region beside a large lake. There are 370 pitches, of which 220 are for touring units. They are at least 80 sq.m. in size and all have electricity (10A), water, waste water and cable TV connections. Touring pitches are separated from the static units. The lake provides a sandy beach with water slide and opportunities for swimming, sailing and windsurfing. Alternatively, you can swim in the heated open-air pool (May-Aug) or the 'sub-tropical' heated indoor pool with its special children's area (April-Oct), nicely decorated with trees and a water slide.

Facilities

The sanitary facilities are top class with a special section for children, decorated in fairy tale style, and excellent provision for disabled visitors and seniors. Launderette. Dog shower. Solarium. Private bathrooms for hire. 'De Bronn' restaurant with regional specialities. Bar. Takeaway. Shop. Play area. Play room. Internet. Tennis. Animation. Off site: The local area has a rich history, with pretty villages and museums.

Open

All year.

At a glance

Welcome & Ambience	✓✓✓✓✓	Location	✓✓✓✓✓
Quality of Pitches	✓✓✓✓	Range of Facilities	✓✓✓✓✓

Directions

Breebronne lies between the towns of Sevenum and Maasbree. From autobahn A67 towards Venlo take exit 38 and fork right. After 3 km. take turn for Maasbree, then left (marked Maasbree) and continue to a roundabout. Take third exit and from here BreeBronne is signed. Go through town and fork right after 2 km. to site on the left.

Charges 2005

Per unit incl 4 persons	€ 26,00 - € 42,00
extra person	€ 4,50
dog	€ 5,00
private bathroom	€ 11,00

Reservations

Contact site. Tel: 077 465 23 60.
E-mail: info@breebronne.nl

A land full of contrasts, from magnificent snow capped mountains, dramatic fjords, vast plateaux with wild untamed tracts, to huge lakes and rich green countryside. With nearly one quarter of the land above the Arctic Circle it is not surprising that Norway has the lowest population density in Europe.

Norway is made up of five regions. In the heart of the eastern region and the oldest of the Scandinavian capitals, Oslo is situated among green hills and vast forest areas, rich in Viking folklore and traditions. If your main reason for visiting Norway is to see the fjords then head to the west. They are magnificent, with waterfalls and mountains that plunge straight down into the fjords. Trondheim, the third largest city, is in the heart of central Norway, steeped in history with a mixture of old wooden houses and modern architecture. Southern Norway sees the most sun, a popular holiday destination for the Norwegians, with a coastline ideal for swimming, sailing, scuba diving and fishing. The north is the 'Land of the Midnight Sun', where the sun never sets in summer and in winter it fails to rise. Fishing, scuba diving and whale safaris are popular. The scenery is diverse with forested valleys, stark mountains and lush valleys, and there are also coastal cities to explore, including Tromsø, which boasts the world's most northerly brewery.

Population

4.4 million

Capital

Oslo

Climate

Weather can be unpredictable, although less extreme on the west coast. Some regions have 24 daylight in summer but none in winter

Language

Norwegian, but English is widely spoken

Currency

Norwegian Krone

Telephone

The country code is 00 47

Banks

Mon-Fri 09.00-15.00. Every large village and town in Norway has a bank, although rural branches may have restricted opening hours

Shops

Mon-Fri 09.00-16.00/17.00, Thu 09.00-18.00/20.00 and Sat 09.00-13.00 /15.00

Public Holidays

New Year's Day; Holy Thursday; Good Friday; Easter Monday; May Day; Constituition Day 17 May; Ascension; Whit Monday; Christmas 25, 26 Dec

Motoring

Roads are generally uncrowded around Oslo and Bergen but be prepared for tunnels and hairpin bends. Certain roads are forbidden to caravans or best avoided (advisory leaflet from the Norwegian Tourist Office). Vehicles must have sufficient road grip and in the winter it may be necessary to use winter tyres with or without studs or chains. Vehicles entering Bergen on week-days must pay a toll and other tolls are also levied on certain roads

Tourist Office

Norwegian Tourist Board
Charles House, 5 Lower Regent Street
London SW1Y 4LR
Tel: 09063 022 033
Fax: 020 7839 6014
Email: infouk@ntr.no
Internet: www.visitnorway.com

THE LARGEST MAINLAND GLACIER IN EUROPE IS AT JOSTEDALSBREEN, NEAR STRYN. DAILY GLACIER WALKS ARE ORGANISED IN SUMMER BY EXPERIENCED GUIDES. CONTACT THE GLACIER CENTRE AT JOSTEDALSBREEN FOR DETAILS.

NO2340 Mo Camping

Steinsdalsvegen 117, 5601 Norheimsund (Hordaland)

This attractive site appears to be alongside a small lake but is actually at the head of an arm of Hardanger fjord, one of the 'Big Three' of Norway's spectacular fjords. Only 74km from the ferry at Bergen, Mo makes an ideal first stop on entering Norway or the last night as the ferry can be reached in a comfortable 1.5 hours. It also makes a pleasant base to explore this part of the country. Within walking distance of the site, accessed along a footpath at the side of the road, the spectacular Steinsdals Falls draw half a million visitors annually to view the falls from behind! This little site is part of a small working farm run by the Mo family. It has 35 unmarked touring places, with 25 electrical connections possible, on a curve of flat grass with areas of hardstanding for poor weather. The camping is divided from the working part of the farm by a line of charming, traditional, wooden farm buildings which include the family home, owners own personal mini museum, (ask to be shown), the reception and toilet facilities. Although offering only the basics, this site is looked after and well situated with many good walks in the area, free fishing on site and a two-seater canoe for hire. Two rooms and an apartment for rent. Good mobile phone reception.

Facilities

Heated sanitary facilities (in a converted barn) include for each sex a shower (10Nkr - 5 mins) and two washbasins. British style toilets. A little restricted, all sanitary facilities are hard-pressed when the site is full. One room provides a laundry sink, washing machine and dryer plus 2 sinks for dishwashing. Hot water on payment. Motorcaravan services. Off site: Shop and filling station 200 m. Town 1 km. Bicycle hire 5 km. Riding 7 km.

At a glance

Welcome & Ambience	✓✓✓✓	Location	✓✓✓✓
Quality of Pitches	✓✓✓	Range of Facilities	✓✓✓

Directions

Site is well signed on road 7 1 km west of Norheimsund.

Charges 2004

Per unit incl. 2 adults and electricity NOK 120

No credit cards.

Reservations

Not necessary. Tel: 56 55 17 27.

Open

1 June - 31 August only.

NO2320 Odda Camping

Borsta, 5750 Odda (Hordaland)

Bordered by the Folgefonna glacier to the west and the Hardangervidda plateau to the east and south, Odda is an industrial town with electro-chemical enterprises based on zinc mining and hydro-electric power. At the turn of the century Odda was one of the most popular destinations for the European upper classes - the magnificent and dramatic scenery is still there, together with the added interest of the industrial impact which is well recorded at the industrial museum at Tyssedal. This municipal site has been attractively developed on the town's southern outskirts, just over a kilometre from the centre on the shores of the Sandvin lake (good salmon and trout fishing) and on the minor road leading up the Buar Valley to the Buar glacier, Vidfoss Falls and Folgefonna ice-cap. It is possible to walk to the ice face but in the later stages this is quite hard-going! The site is spread over 2.5 acres of flat, mature woodland, which is divided into small clearings by massive boulders deposited long ago by the departing glacier. Access is by well tended tarmac roads which wind their way among the trees and boulders. There are 50 tourist pitches including many with electricity. The site fills up in the evenings and can be crowded with facilities stretched from the end of June to early August.

Facilities

A single timber building at the entrance houses the reception office (often unattended) and the simple, but clean sanitary facilities which provide, for each sex, 2 WCs, one hot shower (on payment) and 3 open washbasins. Small kitchen with dishwashing. Washing machine and dryer in the ladies washroom. Off site: Town facilities close.

Open

1 June - 31 August.

At a glance

Welcome & Ambience	✓✓✓	Location	✓✓✓✓
Quality of Pitches	✓✓✓	Range of Facilities	✓✓✓

Directions

Site is on the southern outskirts of Odda, signed off road to Buar, with a well marked access.

Charges guide

Per unit NOK 75 - 90

electricity NOK 20

Reservations

Write to site. Tel: 53 64 34 10.

NO2325 Sundal Camping

P.O. Box 5476, 5476 Mauranger (Hordaland)

This is an excellent gateway site for fjordland, from either Stavanger or Bergen. Maurangerfjord is a steep-sided arm leading off the eastern shore of the middle reaches of the Hardangerfjord. The village of Mauranger commands magnificent views across the waters. Cutting through the village is a turbulent stream, popular with those in search of trout. Its waters are ice-cold, for they descend from the nearby Folgefonn ice-cap and its renowned glacier, an hour's brisk walk from the village. Sundal Camping is divided into two sections: a wooded waterfront site, between the local road and the fjord, which combines camping with a small marina; and an open meadow site uphill of the local road. Sundal is not only ideally situated for Folgefonn; it is also the nearest good site to the charming small town of Rosendal, famous for the stately home of the celebrated Rosenkrantz family.

Facilities

Well equipped toilet blocks provide most facilities. Stream and lake fishing. Canoe and rowing boat hire. Small shop. Pleasant small hotel adjacent with attractive restaurant/bar.

Open

Contact site.

At a glance

Welcome & Ambience	✓✓✓	Location	✓✓✓✓
Quality of Pitches	✓✓✓	Range of Facilities	✓✓✓✓

Directions

Route 48 crosses Hardangerfjord by ferry from Gjermundshavn to Lofallstrand from where a clearly marked local road runs northeast for 16 km. along the fjord waterfront to Mauranger.

Charges guide

Per pitch incl. 2 persons	NOK 80 - 120

Reservations

Contact site. Tel: 53 48 41 86.

NO2315 Ringoy Camping

5782 Ringoy (Hordaland)

Although the village of Ringoy is quiet and peaceful, it occupies a pivotal position, lying not only midway between two principal ferry ports of Upper Hardangerfjord (Kinsarvik and Brimnes), but also by the junction of two key roads (routes 7 and 13). There are several sites at the popular nearby resort town of Kinsarvik, but none compares for situation or atmosphere with the small, simple Ringoy site. This site is basically a steeply sloping field running down from the road to the tree-lined fjord, with flat areas for camping along the top and the bottom of the field. The owners, the Raunsgard family are particularly proud of the site's remarkable shore-side barbecue facilities. On arrival you find a place as there is no reception - someone will call between 8 and 9 pm.

Facilities

The toilet block is small and simple (with metered showers), but well designed, constructed and maintained. It is possibly inadequate during peak holiday weeks in July. Rowing boat (free). Off site: Village mini-market and garage within a minute's walk.

At a glance

Welcome & Ambience	✓✓✓	Location	✓✓✓
Quality of Pitches	✓✓✓	Range of Facilities	✓✓✓

Directions

Site is on route 13, between Kinsarvik and Brimnes.

Charges guide

Per unit	NOK 80
electricity (10A)	NOK 15

Reservations

Write to site. Tel: 53 66 39 17.

Open

All year.

NO2330 Eikhamrane Camping

5776 Nå (Hordaland)

Sorfjord, well known for its fruit growing, has long been on a popular route for travellers across Norway via Utne (where Norway's oldest hotel is a tourist attraction in its own right) and a short ferry crossing across Hardangerfjord. Travellers are also attracted by the Folgefonn ice cap, the most accessible of the great glaciers, which lies at the head of Sorfjord. About halfway along the western shore of Sorfjord is Eikhamrane Camping. Arranged on a well landscaped and partly terraced field which slopes alongside the road to a pebbly lakeside beach, it was formerly part of an orchard which still extends on both sides of the site and uphill across the road. There is room for 50 units (about 20 caravans or motorcaravans and 30 tents) on unmarked, well kept grass with 20 electrical hook ups (10A).

Facilities

Two small timber toilet blocks, one for toilets with external access, the other for washbasins (open) and showers (on payment). Both are simple but very well kept. Small kitchen with dishwashing facilities (hot water on payment). Some supplies kept at reception office in the old farmhouse, home of the owner (bread and milk to order). Watersports (sailing, canoeing and rowing), and fishing in lake. Off site: Digranes nature reserve (birdwatching) nearby.

At a glance

Welcome & Ambience	✓✓✓	Location	✓✓✓
Quality of Pitches	✓✓✓	Range of Facilities	✓✓✓✓

Directions

Site is on road 550 just outside the village of Nå, on the western shore of Sorfjord, 32 km. south of Utne and 16 km. north of Odda.

Charges guide

Per person	NOK 10
pitch incl. electricity	NOK 85

No credit cards.

Reservations

Write to site. Tel: 53 66 22 48.

Open

1 June - 31 August only.

NO2350 Espelandsdalen Camping

5736 Granvin (Hordaland)

If one follows Hardangerfjord on the map and considers the mighty glacier which once scooped away the land along its path, it is easy to imagine that it started life in Espelandsdalen. Here is the textbook upper glacial valley. Espelandsdalen runs from Granvin to Ulvik, both of which lie at the heads of their respective arms of Hardangerfjord. A minor road (route 572) links the two small towns with sharp climbs at either end (tricky for caravans). The valley bed here is occupied by a series of connected lakes, popular with canoeists. For generations farmers have struggled to make a living out of the narrow strip of land between water and rock. One of these farmers has converted a narrow, sloping field bisected by the road (572) into a modest lake-side camp site taking about 40 units. The grassy meadow pitches below the road run right down to the lake-shore, and the whole site occupies just over an acre. There are a few electrical hook ups (8-10A). Campers come here for the fishing, walking or skiing, or just to marvel at the views of the valley and its towering mountain sides.

Facilities

A basic sanitary block consists of a washing trough with hot water, a shower on payment and WCs. Some basic foodstuffs are kept in the office. Swimming, fishing and boating in lake. Boat hire. Off site: Ski track 2 km.

Open

1 May - 31 August.

At a glance

Welcome & Ambience	✓✓✓	Location	✓✓✓✓
Quality of Pitches	✓✓✓	Range of Facilities	✓✓✓

Directions

The northern loop of the 572 road follows Espelandsdalen and the campsite is on this road, about 6 km. from its junction with route 13 at Granvin (steep gradients - see above)

Charges guide

Per person	NOK 10
child (4-12 yrs)	NOK 5
pitch	NOK 60
electricity	NOK 20

No credit cards.

Reservations

Contact site. Tel: 56 52 51 67.
E-mail: post@espelandsdalencamping.no

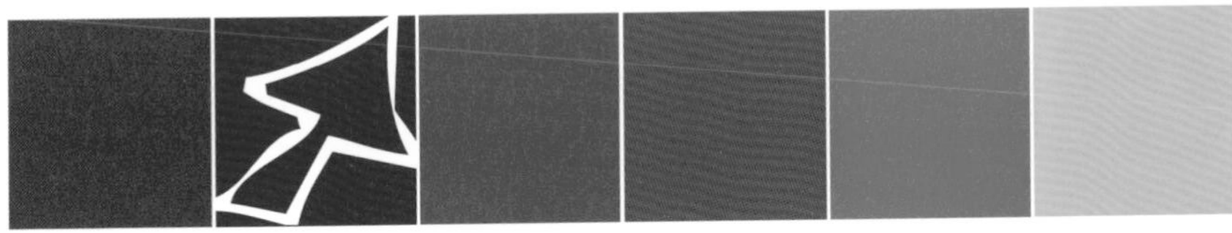

NO2370 Botnen Camping

5950 Brekke (Sogn og Fjordane)

For those setting forth north on route 1 from Bergen there are suprisingly few attractive sites until one reaches the southern shore of mighty Sognefjord. At Brekke is a well known tourist landmark, the remarkable Breekstranda Fjord Hotel, a traditional turf-roofed complex which tourist coaches are unable to resist. A mile or two beyond the hotel, also on the shore of the fjord, is the family run Botnen Camping. An isolated, simple (2-star) site which slopes steeply, it is well maintained. It has its own jetty and harbour, with rowing boats and canoes for hire, and commands a splendid view across the fjord to distant mountains.

Facilities

Children's play area. Swimming, fishing and boating in fjord. Boats and canoes for hire.

Open

May - 1 September.

At a glance

Welcome & Ambience	✓✓✓	Location	✓✓✓
Quality of Pitches	✓✓✓	Range of Facilities	✓✓✓✓

Directions

Site is 2 km off the coast road running west from Brekke.

Charges guide

Per person	NOK 10
child	NOK 5
caravan	NOK 40
tent	NOK 30
electricity	NOK 15

Reservations

Contact site. Tel: 57 78 54 71.

NO2360 Ulvik Fjord Camping

5730 Ulvik (Hordaland)

Ulvik was discovered by tourists 150 years ago when the first liners started operating to the head of Hardangerfjord, and to this day, a regular stream of cruise liners work their way into the very heartland of Norway. A century and a half of visitors has meant that Ulvik is now a well-established tourist destination, describing itself as 'the pearl of Hardanger'. This pretty little site is 500 m. from the centre of the town. It occupies what must once have been a small orchard running down to the lake beside a small stream. There is room for about 30 units on undulating ground which slopes towards the fjord, with some flat areas and a few electrical connections and some site owned cabins.

Facilities

There are no facilities other than a small wooden building which houses reception and the well kept sanitary facilities. For each sex there are 2 open washbasins, WCs and 2 modern showers on payment. Small kitchen with cooker and sink. Boat slipway, fishing and swimming in fjord. Off site: Hotel opposite, shops and restaurants in town.

Open

20 May - 31 August.

At a glance

Welcome & Ambience	✓✓✓	Location	✓✓✓
Quality of Pitches	✓✓✓	Range of Facilities	✓✓✓

Directions

Ulvik is reached by road no. 572; the site is on the southern side of the town. There is a ferry from road no. 7 at Brimnes. Cars and caravans can now connect with road 7 via a tunnel.

Charges guide

Per person	NOK 15
child (4-12 yrs)	NOK 10
pitch incl. car	NOK 650 - 65
hiker or cyclist and tent	NOK 35
electricity	NOK 20

Reservations

Write to site. Tel: 05 52 65 77.

NO2380 Tveit Camping

6894 Vangsnes (Sogn og Fjordane)

Located in the district of Vik on the south shore of Sognefjord, four kilometres from the small port of Vangsnes, Tveit Camping is part of a small working farm and it is a charming neat site. Reception and a kiosk open most of the day in high season, with a phone to summon assistance at any time. Four terraces provide 40 pitches with 30 electricity connections (10A) and there are also site owned cabins. On the campsite you will find a restored Iron Age burial mound dating from 350-550AD, whilst the statue of 'Fritjov the Intrepid' towers over the landscape at Vangsnes. Visit the Kristianhus Boat and Engine Museum or see traditional Gamalost cheese making in Vik. It is also possible for families do do easy hikes on the glacier at Nigardsbreen but not at Fjaerland where it is more challenging.

Facilities

Modern, heated sanitary facilities provide showers on payment, a unit for disabled visitors, kitchens with facilities for dishwashing and cooking, and a laundry with washing machine, dryer and iron (hot water on payment). Motorcaravan services. Kiosk (15/6-15/8). TV rooms. Children's playground. Harbour for small boats, slipway and boat/canoe hire. Fishing. Bicycle hire. Off site: Shop, café and pub by ferry terminal in Vangsnes 4 km. Riding 15 km.

At a glance

Welcome & Ambience	✓✓✓	Location	✓✓✓✓
Quality of Pitches	✓✓✓	Range of Facilities	✓✓✓

Directions

Site is by Rv 13 between Vik and Vangsnes, 4 km. south of Vangsnes.

Charges 2004

Per person (over 5 yrs)	NOK 10
pitch	NOK 90
electricity	NOK 20

No credit cards.

Reservations

Contact site. Tel: 57 69 66 00. E-mail: tveit@online.no

Open

10 May - 10 October.

NO2390 Kjornes Camping

6856 Sogndal (Sogn og Fjordane)

A simple farm site in a prime fjordside location, ideal for those on a budget. Occupying a long open meadow which slopes down to the tree lined waterside, this site is ideal for those who enjoy peace and quiet, lovely scenery or a spot of fishing. Access is via a narrow lane with passing places, which drops down towards the fjord 3 km. from Sogndal. The site takes 100 touring units, but with only 36 electrical connections (16A). A scenic route (Rv 55) runs along the entire north shore of Sognefjord and the Sogndalfjord to Sogndal and then continues across the Jotunheimen mountain plateau towards Lom.

Facilities

The sanitary unit is basic but clean, providing mostly open washbasins, and 2 showers per sex (on payment). Small kitchen with dishwashing sink, double hot-plate and fridge. 'Al fresco' laundry with small roof covering the sink, washing machine and dryer.

Open

1 June - end August.

At a glance

Welcome & Ambience	✓✓✓	Location	✓✓✓
Quality of Pitches	✓✓✓	Range of Facilities	✓✓✓

Directions

Site is off the Rv 5, 3 km. east of Sogndal, 8 km. west of Kaupanger.

Charges guide

Per person	NOK 15
pitch	NOK 45
small tent	NOK 30
electricity	NOK 20

Reservations

Write to site. Tel: 57 67 45 80.
E-mail: camping@kjornes.no

NO2385 PlusCamp Sandvik

Sandvik Sor, 6868 Gaupne (Sogn og Fjordane)

Sandvik is a compact, small site on the edge of the town of Gaupne close to the Nigardsbreen Glacier. It provides 60 touring pitches, 32 with electrical connections (8/16A), arranged on fairly level grassy terrain either side of a gravel access road. A large supermarket, post office, banks, etc. are all within a level 500 m. stroll. A café in the reception building is open in summer for drinks and meals and the small shop sells groceries, ices, soft drinks, sweets, etc. This is a useful site for those using the spectacular Rv 55 high mountain road from Lom to Sogndal or for visiting the Nigardsbreen Glacier and Jostedalsbreen area of Norway.

Facilities

The single, fully equipped, central sanitary unit includes washbasins with dividers and two hot showers per sex (on payment). Multi-purpose unit for families or disabled people. Small campers' kitchen has dishwashing, hot-plates, oven and fridge (all free of charge) together with tables, chairs and TV. Separate laundry. Shop and small restaurant (1/6-31/8). Playground. Boat hire. Fishing.

At a glance

Welcome & Ambience	✓✓✓	Location	✓✓✓
Quality of Pitches	✓✓✓	Range of Facilities	✓✓✓

Directions

Signed just off Rv 55 Lom-Sogndal road on eastern outskirts of Gaupne.

Charges guide

Per pitch incl. up to 4 persons	NOK 120
electricity	NOK 25

Reservations

Write to site. Tel: 57 68 11 53.
E-mail: sandvik@pluscamp.no

Open

All year.

NO2436 Byrkjelo Camping

6826 Byrkjelo (Sogn og Fjordane)

This neatly laid out and well equipped small site offers 50 large marked and numbered touring pitches, 40 with electrical connections (10A) and 15 with gravel hardstandings. It is a good value site in a village location with neatly mown grass, attractive trees and shrubs with a warm welcome from the young and enthusiastic owners. Fishing is possible in the river adjacent to the site. Reception and a small kiosk selling ices, sweets and soft drinks, are housed in an attractive cabin and there is a bell to summon the owners should they not be on site when you arrive. A garage, mini-market and cafe are just 100 m.

Facilities

The good heated sanitary unit includes 5 shower rooms each with washbasin, on payment. A multi-purpose unit serves the needs of families with babies and disabled visitors, incorporating a WC, basin and shower with handrails, etc. Campers' kitchen with dishwashing sinks, hot-plates and dining area (all free). Separate laundry with sink, washing machine, dryer and airing rack. Motorcaravan services. Kiosk. TV room. Minigolf. Small children's playground. Fishing. Off site: Riding 4 km. Golf 15 km. Ideal base for Nordfjord and Jostedalsbreen.

At a glance

Welcome & Ambience	✓✓✓✓	Location	✓✓✓✓
Quality of Pitches	✓✓✓✓	Range of Facilities	✓✓✓

Directions

Site is beside the Rv 1 in the village of Byrkjelo, 19 km. east of Sandane.

Charges 2005

Per person	NOK 10
pitch	NOK 85
electricity	NOK 30

No credit cards.

Reservations

Advisable in peak season. Tel: 57 86 74 30.
E-mail: byrkjelocamping@sensewave.com

Open

20 May - 1 September.

NO2400 PlusCamp Jolstraholmen

postboks 11, 6847 Vassenden (Sogn og Fjordane)

This well presented, family run site is situated on the E39 between Sognelfjord and Nordfjord. It is actually located between the road and the fast-flowing Jolstra River (renowned for its trout fishing), 1.5 km. from the lakeside village of Vassenden, behind the Statoil filling station, restaurant and supermarket complex which is also owned and run by the site owner and his family. The 80 pitches (some marked) are on grass or gravel, all with electricity (10A). A river tributary runs through the site and forms an island on which some additional tent pitches are located, and there are also 19 cabins. Guided walking tours are organised, and a recently created riverside and woodland walk follows a 1.5 km. circular route from the site and has fishing platforms and picnic tables along the way.

Facilities

The main heated sanitary facilities, fully equipped in rooms below the complex, include showers on payment) plus one family bathroom per sex. Small unit located on the island. Two small kitchens (cooking facilities free of charge). Laundry. Supermarket. Restaurant. Garage. Covered barbecue area. Playground. Volleyball. Water slide (open summer, weather permitting). Rafting. Fishing. Guided walks. Boat hire. Off site: Minigolf. 50 m. Ski-slopes 1 km.

At a glance

Welcome & Ambience	✓✓✓✓	Location	✓✓✓✓
Quality of Pitches	✓✓✓	Range of Facilities	✓✓✓✓

Directions

Site is beside the E39 road, 1.5 km. west of Vassenden, 18 km. east of Forde.

Charges 2004

Per unit incl. 1-4 persons	NOK 120 - 155
electricity	NOK 30

Reservations

Write to site. Tel: 57728907.
E-mail: jolstraholmen@pluscamp.no

Open

All year.

NO2428 Andenes Camping

Storgata 53, 8483 Andenes (Nordland)

Many campsites in Norway have simple and basic facilities wih little evidence of security. Often, one arrives, finds a pitch and you pay later when reception opens. Andenes Camping is a classic example but included in this guide for very special reasons. This extremely popular exposed site at sea level with picturesque mountain backdrop, is only three kilometres from the base of 'Whalesafari'. This company is deemed the world's largest, most successful Arctic whale watching operation for the general public. The site is also an exceptional location for the midnight sun. Lying on the west coast of Andøy between the quiet main road (82) and white sandy beaches, an area of uneven ground provides space for an unspecified number of touring units and you park where you like. The ground is mainly of grass with some hardstanding. Twenty units only can access 16A electricity connections and if you want electricity you are highly advised to arrive by mid-afternoon.

Facilities

The reception building houses clean separate sex sanitary facilities providing for each 2 toilets, 2 showers (10Nkr for 5 mins). with curtain to keep clothes dry and 3 washbasins. In each one toilet is suitable for disabled people and includes a hand basin. Small kitchen with one sink also includes a 4 ring cooker with oven and two additional hot plates (free). Motorcaravan service point. Picnic tables about site and swings for children. Off site: Well stocked supermarket 250 m. On approach to town a garage, caravan dealer and another supermarket. From the nearby village of Bleik (8 km), trips for deep sea fishing and visits to Bleiksøya one of Norway's most famous bird cliffs to include 800 pairs of puffins and 60 kittiwakes.

At a glance

Welcome & Ambience	✓✓✓	Location	✓✓✓✓
Quality of Pitches	✓✓✓	Range of Facilities	✓✓✓

Directions

Travelling north on road 82, site is on left 3 km. before Andenes.

Charges 2004

Per unit	NOK 120
incl. electricity	NOK 130
tent	NOK 90

Reservations

Not required. Tel: 76 14 12 22.
E-mail: erna.strom@norlandia.no

Open

1 June - 30 September.

NO2432 Harstad Camping

Nesseveien 55, 9411 Harstad (Troms)

For those visiting or exiting Lofoten and Vesterålen, this well established, popular site close to Harstad, provides an excellent stopping point on Hinnøya, the largest island in Norway. In a delightful setting with fine views, the campsite has space for 120 units as it slopes down to Vågsfjorden. Pitches are not marked but by the waters edge a flat area porvides most of the 33 electricity hook-ups (16A). This part of the site is sought after and we advise a mid-afternoon arrival for the possibility of a level pitch and/or electricity connection. A small island very close to the site plays host to a colony of arctic tern. The clean sanitary block has two coin operated showers for each sex and one may have to wait if the site is busy. Catches of fish from the shore are not prolific, although hiring one of the site's boats (rowing or motor) will soon transport you to nearby areas where you are likely to catch good sized cod. The site also has 16 cabins for rent.

Facilities

Good facilities include British style WCs, washbasins and showers (Nkr 10 for 4 mins). Room for disabled visitors. Laundry room with sinks (hot water Nkr 5), washing machine and dryer. Kitchen with hot plates (free), tables and chairs. Chemical disposal point. Reception (manned 0800-2300 high season) has a small selection of soft drinks, ices, sweets, crisps, some tinned foods and postcards (no bread or milk). Off site: One of northern Norway's largest shopping centres, including a supermarket and garage at 2 km.

At a glance

Welcome & Ambience	✓✓✓✓	Location	✓✓✓✓
Quality of Pitches	✓✓✓	Range of Facilities	✓✓✓✓

Directions

Travelling north on road 83, site is on right 3 km. before Harstad. After turning right, turn immediate left and site is 1 km. along firm unmade road (site signed from either direction).

Charges 2004

Per unit	NOK 140
incl. electricity	NOK 165

Reservations

Not made. Tel: 77 07 36 62.
E-mail: postmaster@harstad-camping.no

Open

All year.

NO2480 Bjorkedal Camping

Bjorkedal, 6120 Folkestad (Møre og Romsdal)

On the Rv 1 north of the Nordfjord is a lovely bowl shaped valley famous throughout Norway for traditional boat building. Bjorkedal Camping is situated on a grassy open plateau about 300 m. off the main road and overlooking the farmland and mountains around the lake. There is space for 25 tents or vans with 10 electricity connections and 5 log cabins. For a thousand years boats have been hand built in this valley by the Bjorkedal family. Site owner, Jakob Bjorkedal, will be pleased to show you the old water powered saw mill that he has reconstructed, and there are usually some examples of his boat building craft in the magnificent workshop with a most spectacular cathedral-style timber roof. There is an extensive network of footpaths both in the valley and leading up into the surrounding circle of mountains where you can see the old cabins of the herdsmen, one dating back to the 17th century.

Facilities

A small, modern and spotlessly clean sanitary unit includes washbasins with dividers and curtains, one shower per sex (on payment), plus a WC and washbasin unit with ramped access for disabled people. Kitchen with dishwashing sink and full cooker (free). Laundry with sinks and washing machine. TV lounge. Small game hunting. Freshwater fishing. Off site: Site is convenient base from which to explore Geiranger, Runde, West Cape or Strynefjellet.

At a glance

Welcome & Ambience	✓✓✓✓	Location	✓✓✓✓
Quality of Pitches	✓✓✓	Range of Facilities	✓✓✓

Directions

Signed off the Rv 1, midway along the western side of Bjorkedal lake and 21 km. north of Nordfjordeid.

Charges guide

Per person	NOK 10
pitch	NOK 40
electricity (16A)	NOK 15

Reservations

Write to site. Tel: 70 05 20 43.

Open

All year.

NO2460 Prinsen Strandcamping

Gåseid, 6015 Ålesund (Møre og Romsdal)

Prinsen is a lively, fjordside site, five kilometres from the attractive small town of Alesund. It is a more attractive option than the more crowded sites closer to town, even so, this is mainly a transit and short-stay site. Divided by trees and shrubs, and sloping gently to a small sandy beach with views down Borgundfjord, the site has 125 grassy pitches, 27 cabins and 7 rooms, 110 electricity connections (16A) and 75 cable TV hook-ups. Reception shares space with the small shop. Alesund has lovely Art Nouveau architecture and Sunnmøre Folk Museum has a boat collection and medieval and Viking artefacts.

Facilities

The main heated sanitary unit in the reception building is fully equipped with mostly open washbasins, showers on payment and a sauna for each sex. Small kitchen with cooking facilities. Laundry. Motorcaravan service point. Shop (1/6-1/9). TV room. Barbecue areas. Playground. Slipway and boat hire. Fishing. Bicycle hire.
Off site: Restaurant 800 m.

At a glance

Welcome & Ambience	✓✓✓✓	Location	✓✓✓✓
Quality of Pitches	✓✓✓✓	Range of Facilities	✓✓✓

Directions

Turn off E136 at roundabout signed to Hatlane and site. Follow signs to site.

Charges guide

Per unit incl. up to 6 persons	NOK 150
electricity	NOK 20

Reservations

Write to site. Tel: 70 15 52 04.

Open

All year.

NO2490 Skjerneset Camping

Ekkilsoya, 6553 Bremsnes (Møre og Romsdal)

The tiny island of Ekkilsøya lies off the larger island of Averoy and is reached via a side road and bridge (no toll) from the main Rv 64 just south of Bremsnes. Although the fishing industry here is not what it used to be it is still the dominant activity and Skjerneset Camping has been developed by the Otterlei family to give visitors an insight into this industry and its history. Most of the old 'Klippfisk' warehouse is now a fascinating 'fisherimuseum' and aquarium, with the remainder housing the sanitary facilities. There is space for 20 units on gravel hardstandings around a rocky bluff and along the harbour's rocky frontage and all have electricity (16A). A small grassy area for 10 tents is under pine trees in a hollow on the top of the bluff. Note: this is a working harbour with deep unfenced water very close to the pitches.

Facilities

Unisex sanitary facilities are heated, but basic, and perhaps a little quirky in their layout but include washbasins in cubicles. Kitchen. Small laundry. All were free when we visited. Kiosk for basic packet foods, crisps, ices, sweets, postcards etc. TV. Motor or rowing boat hire. Organised sea-fishing or sightseeing trips, and for non-anglers who want a fish supper, fresh fish are always available on site.

At a glance

Welcome & Ambience	✓✓✓	Location	✓✓✓
Quality of Pitches	✓✓✓	Range of Facilities	✓✓✓✓

Directions

Site is on the little island of Ekkilsøya which is reached via a side road running west from the main Rv 64 road, 1.5 km. south of Bremsnes.

Charges guide

Per unit incl. electricity	NOK 110

Reservations

Write to site. Tel: 71 51 18 94.

Open

All year.

NO2450 Bjolstad Camping

6445 Malmefjorden (Møre og Romsdal)

This is delightful small, rural site, which slopes down to Malmefjorden, a sheltered arm of Fraenfjorden. Bjolstad has space for just 45 touring units on grassy, fairly level, terraces either side of the tarmac central access road. A delight for children is a large, old masted boat which provides hours of fun playing at pirates or Vikings, plus the more conventional swings and a trampoline. At the foot of the site is a waterside barbecue area, a shallow, sandy, paddling area for children and a jetty. Both rowing and motorboats (with lifejackets) can be hired, one can swim or fish in the fjord. This site is an ideal base for visiting Molde International Jazz Festival (annually mid-July), or the famous Varden viewpoint with its magnificent views over this 'Town of Roses', the fjord and 222 mountain peaks, both only 15 minutes drive from the site. Further afield, the small town of Bud is famous for its WW2 German coastal fortress, or one can drive the fantastic and scenic Atlantic Highway (now free) as it threads its way across the many islands and bridges to the west of Kristiansund.

Facilities

The basic, clean, heated sanitary unit includes two showers per sex (token on payment), plus washbasins with dividers, one in cubicle (for ladies). Small campers' kitchen with two dishwashing sinks and hot-plate. Laundry service at reception. Playground. Boat hire. Fjord fishing and swimming. Dogs are not accepted. Off site: Riding 9 km. Golf 12 km.

Open

1 June - 30 Sept (may before on request).

At a glance

Welcome & Ambience	✓✓✓✓	Location	✓✓✓✓
Quality of Pitches	✓✓✓	Range of Facilities	✓✓✓✓

Directions

Turn off Rv 64 on northern edge of Malmefjorden village towards village of Lindset (lane is oil bound gravel). Site is 1 km.

Charges 2005

per person	NOK 10
child	NOK 5
caravan or tent	NOK 100
motorcaravan	NOK 80
electricity	NOK 20

Reservations

Write to site. Tel: 71 26 56 56.
E-mail: post@bjolstad.no

NO2505 Magalaupe Camping

Rute 5, 7340 Oppdal (Sør Trøndelag)

This is a rural, good value, riverside site in a sheltered position with easy access from the E6. Fairly simple facilities are offered but there are a host of unusual activities in the surrounding area, including caving, canyoning, rafting, gold panning, mineral hunting, and musk oxen, reindeer and elk safaris. In winter the more adventurous can also go snow-mobiling or skiing in the high Dovrefjell National Park. The 75 unmarked and grassy touring pitches (36 with 10/16A electricity) are in natural surroundings amongst birch trees and rocks on several different levels and served by gravel access roads. There are also 8 attractive and fully equipped site owned cabins. As the site rarely fills up, the simple facilities should be adequate at most times.

Facilities

Small, but very clean, heated sanitary unit fully equipped but the showers are on payment. Extra WC/washbasin units in reception building.Small kitchen with dishwashing facilities, hot-plate and freezer, plus a combined washing/drying machine. Kiosk for ices, soft drinks, etc. Bar (mid June - Aug). TV lounge. Fishing. Bicycle hire. Off site: Supermarkets and other services in Oppdal (11 km). Riding or golf 12 km.

At a glance

Welcome & Ambience	✓✓✓✓	Location	✓✓✓✓✓
Quality of Pitches	✓✓✓	Range of Facilities	✓✓✓

Directions

Site is signed to western side of the E6, 11 km. south of Oppdal.

Charges 2005

Per unit incl. 4 persons	NOK 90
tent and car	NOK 90
electricity	NOK 10

No credit cards.

Reservations

Write to site. Tel: 72 42 46 84.
E-mail: camp@magalaupe.no

Open

All year.

Norway

NO2510 Håneset Camping

Osloveien, 7460 Roros (Sør Trøndelag)

At first sight Håneset Camping it is neither promising, lying between the main road and the railway, nor is the gritty sloping ground of the site very imaginatively landscaped - for grass, when it grows up here, is rather coarse and lumpy. However, as we soon discovered, it is the best equipped campsite in the town, and ideal to cope with the often cold, wet weather of this bleak high plateau. The 50 unmarked touring pitches all have access to electricity (10/16A), and most facilities are housed in the main complex building. People flock from all over Europe to visit this remarkably well preserved mining town. For over 300 years it was one of Europe's leading copper mines, and during all that time it never suffered serious fire. As a result it occupies a special place on UNESCO's world heritage list for its unique concentration of historic wooden houses.

Facilities

Heated sanitary facilities provide three separate rooms for each sex, fully equipped with showers on payment. Washing machine and two clothes washing sinks. Kitchen. Shop and cafeteria (mid June-August) and huge sitting/TV room and two well equipped kitchens which the owners, the Moen family, share fully with their guests, plus rooms for rent. Playground. Off site: Town 20 minutes walk.

At a glance

Welcome & Ambience	✓✓✓✓	Location	✓✓✓
Quality of Pitches	✓✓✓	Range of Facilities	✓✓✓

Directions

Site is on the Rv 30 leading south from Roros to Os, 3 km. from Roros.

Charges guide

Per pitch incl. electricity NOK 130 - 155

No credit cards.

Reservations

Write to site. Tel: 72 41 06 00.

Open

All year.

NO2500 Tråsåvika Camping

Orkanger, 7354 Viggja (Sør Trøndelag)

On a headland jutting into the Trondheimfjord some 40 km. from Trondheim, Trasavika commands an attractive position. For many this compensates for the extra distance into town. The 65 pitches (some slightly sloping) are on an open grassy field at the top of the site, or on a series of terraces below, which run down to the small sandy beach, easily accessed via a well designed gravel service road. There are 48 electricity connections (10A). To one side, on a wooded bluff at the top of the site, are 14 cabins (open all year), many in traditional style with grass rooves. The smart reception complex also houses a small shop, licensed café with lounge area and a terrace overlooking the panorama. In September 2005 the E39 opens which will virtually remove the occasional road noise. Nobody travelling so far would dream of not visiting the unusually interesting and attractive city of Trondheim, for long Norway's capital.

Facilities

The neat, fully equipped, sanitary unit includes two controllable hot showers per sex (on payment). Hot water on payment in kitchen and laundry which have a hot-plate, dish and clothes washing sinks, washing machine and dryer. Shop. Café (20/6-30/8). TV/sitting room. Play area. Jetty and boat hire. Free fjord fishing with catches of good sized cod from the shore.

At a glance

Welcome & Ambience	✓✓✓✓	Location	✓✓✓✓
Quality of Pitches	✓✓✓	Range of Facilities	✓✓✓✓

Directions

Site is west of Viggja with access from the E39 between Orkanger and Buvik, 21 km. from the E6 and 40 km. west of Trondheim.

Charges 2004

Per pitch NOK 140

electricity NOK 30 - 110

Reservations

Contact site. Tel: 72 86 78 22.
E-mail: jowiggen@start.no

Open

1 May - 10 September.

NO2495 Vegset Camping

7760 Snasa (Nord-Trøndelag)

This small, basic but pleasant site is seven kilometres south of Snåsa, directly beside the E6 road on the banks of Lake Snåsavatn. It consists of ten site owned chalets, a number of static units and a small area for about 20 touring units on slightly sloping ground. There are electricity connections available. Snåsa is a centre for the South Lapp people who have their own boarding school, museum and information centre there. The Bergasen Nature Reservation is close to the village and is famous for its rare flora, especially orchids. The Gressamoen National Park is also near.

Facilities

The satisfactory toilet block provides showers (Nkr. 10), plus a shower with toilet suitable for disabled people. Kitchen. Kiosk selling emergency groceries doubles as a TV room (end June - mid Aug). Swimming, boat hire and fishing (licence from site).

At a glance

Welcome & Ambience	✓✓✓✓	Location	✓✓✓
Quality of Pitches	✓✓✓	Range of Facilities	✓✓✓

Directions

Site is just off the E6 road, 7 km. south of Snåsa.

Charges 2005

Per pitch incl. electricity NOK 140

Reservations

Contact site. Tel: 74 15 29 50.
E-mail: mveg@online.no

Open

Easter - 10 October.

NO2485 Krokstrand Camping

Krokstrand, 8630 Storforshei (Nordland)

This site is a popular resting place on the long trek to Nordkapp and it is only 18 km. from the Arctic Circle with its Visitor Centre. There are 45 unmarked pitches set amongst birch trees with electrical connections (16A) for 28 units. In late spring and early summer the river alongside, headed by rapids is impressive with the possibility of mountains close by still being snow-capped. The small reception kiosk is open 16.00 - 22.00 hrs in high season, otherwise campers are invited to find a pitch and pay later. For those interested in WW2 history there is the neatly tended grave of a Russian soldier by the site gate.

Facilities

Well maintained, spotlessly clean, small sanitary unit includes two showers per sex (on payment). Laundry with washing machine and dryer. Small kitchen with double hot-plate and dishwashing sink. Motorcaravan services. Brightly painted children's playground with trampoline, well maintained. Minigolf. Fishing. Off site: Hotel with café/restaurant just outside site entrance (same ownership as the site) with good meals, snacks and very basic provisions. Souvenir shop.

At a glance

Welcome & Ambience	✓✓✓✓	Location	✓✓✓✓
Quality of Pitches	✓✓✓✓	Range of Facilities	✓✓✓✓

Directions

Entrance is off E6 at Krokstrand village opposite hotel, 18 km. south of the Arctic Circle.

Charges 2004

Per person	NOK 10
pitch	NOK 80
electricity	NOK 30

No credit cards.

Reservations

Write to site. Tel: 75 16 60 02.

Open

1 June - 20 September.

NO2475 Saltstraumen Camping

Bok 85, 8056 Saltstraumen (Nordland)

On a coastal route, this extremely popular site, in a very scenic location with a magnificent backdrop, is close to the largest Maelstrom in the world. It is an easy short walk to this outstanding phenomenon where in the course of six hours between 33,800 and 82,700 billion gallons of water are pressed through a narrow strait at a rate of about 20 knots. The effect is greatest at new or full moons. The fjord close by (walking distance) is reknowned for the prolific numbers of coalfish and cod caught from the shore. Most on site 'have a go' to catch their evening meal. As well as 20 cabins, the site has 60 plain touring pitches mostly on level, gravel hardstandings in rows, each with electricity. The site is 33 km. from Bodø and 50 km. from Fauske. You are advised to arrive by late afternoon.

Facilities

Basic but heated sanitary facilities are clean and fully equipped. Separate shower areas for men and women have dividers, shower curtains and communal changing (free). Kitchen with two full cookers, fish cleaning area and fish freezer. (free). Laundry. Motorcaravan service point. TV room. Playground. Minigolf. Fishing. Off site: Mini supermarket outside entrance. Hotel and cafeteria nearby.

Open

All year.

At a glance

Welcome & Ambience	✓✓✓✓	Location	✓✓✓✓✓
Quality of Pitches	✓✓✓	Range of Facilities	✓✓✓✓

Directions

Travelling from the south: Before Rognan take Rv 812 signed Saltstraumen (good, scenic road with an easy maximum 8% gradient). At junction with Rv 17 turn right and site is on left after second bridge. From the north: from Rv 80 (Fauske -Bodø) turn south on Rv 17, site is 12 km. at Saltstraumen.

Charges 2004

Per unit incl. 2 persons	NOK 90 - 120
electricity	NOK 30

Reservations

Not accepted. Tel: 75 58 75 60. E-mail: saltstraumen@pluscamp.no

NO2465 Lyngvær Lofoten Bobilcamping

Postboks 30, 8310 Kabelvag (Nordland)

Some camping sites on Lofoten are very basic with extremely limited facilities but Lyngvaer is in complete contrast. This established site is very popular, with many customers returning. In the centre of Lofoten alongside a tidal fjord with mountains all around, the setting and location is quite idyllic. Large terraces provide fine views for most of the 200 pitches, mainly grass, some with hardstanding, with electricity for 110 (10/16A). Fresh water, waste water and chemical disposal is free for guests. Boat hire is available and the site has its own waters for salmon and trout fishing. The owners bake their own bread to order, with all other foodstuffs available in the attractive town of Henningsvaer (10 km).

Facilities

Toilet facilities are spotlessly clean and good with showers in small cubicles (Nkr 10 for 6 mins). Extra unisex showers and toilets are beside reception. Communal kitchen with cooking, dishwashing and fish freezer (free). Large sitting area with satellite TV. Play areas. Boat hire. Fishing.

Open

1 May - 30 September.

At a glance

Welcome & Ambience	✓✓✓✓	Location	✓✓✓✓✓
Quality of Pitches	✓✓✓✓	Range of Facilities	✓✓✓✓

Directions

From ferry (Skutvik - Svolvaer) turn southwest on E10 signed Lofoten. Site is on left in 18 km.

Charges 2005

Per unit incl. 1 person	NOK 100
electricity	NOK 20

Eighth night free.

Reservations

Not necessary. Tel: 76 07 87 81. E-mail: relorent@c2i.net

NO2455 Ballangen Camping

8540 Ballangen (Nordland)

Ballangen is a pleasant, lively site conveniently located on the edge of a fjord with a small rocky beach, with direct access off the main E6 road. The 150 marked pitches are mostly on sandy grass, with electricity (10/16A) available to 120. There are a few hardstandings, also 50 cabins for rent. A TV room has tourist information, a coffee and games machines and there is a small outdoor pool and waterslide with free fjord fishing, and boat hire. An interesting excursion is to the nearby Martinstollen mine where visitors are guided through the dimly lit Olav Shaft 500 m. into the mountain. Narvik with its wartime connections and museums is 40 km.

Facilities

Toilet facilities in a new building with modern fittings include some washbasins in cubicles. Facilities for disabled visitors, sauna and solarium. Kitchen with dishwashing sinks, full cooker, hot-plates and covered seating area. Laundry. Motorcaravan services. Well stocked shop. Café and takeaway (main season). TV/games room. Swimming pool and waterslide (charged). Tennis. Minigolf. Fishing. Golf. Boat and bicycle hire. Off site: Riding 2 km. Ballangen 4 km, has supermarket and other services.

At a glance

Welcome & Ambience	✓✓✓✓	Location	✓✓✓✓
Quality of Pitches	✓✓✓	Range of Facilities	✓✓✓✓

Directions

Access is off the E6, 4 km. north of Ballangen, 40 km. south of Narvik.

Charges 2005

Per unit incl. 4 persons	NOK 150
electricity	NOK 30

Reservations

Contact site. Tel: 76 92 76 90.
E-mail: ballcamp@c2i.net

Open

All year.

NO2445 Slettnes Fjordcamp

9047 Oteren (Troms)

Slettnes is a useful stopover southeast of Tromso beside the E6 road. Beside a narrow fjord and surrounded by snowy capped mountains, this is a large site mainly for permanent caravans but with room for 20 touring units. A very well kept site, there are neat flower beds outside reception.

Facilities

Sanitary facilities consist of two toilets each for male and female with washbasins with mirror, etc. There are three showers each, communal but with no charge and good hot water. A kitchen houses a sink unit, full size cooker and microwave.

At a glance

Welcome & Ambience	✓✓✓	Location	✓✓✓
Quality of Pitches	✓✓✓	Range of Facilities	✓✓✓

Directions

Site is beside the E6 road near Oteren.

Charges guide

Per unit	NOK 100

Reservations

Contact site. Tel: 77 71 45 08.

Open

Contact site.

NO2425 Kirkeporten Camping

9763 Skarsvag (Finnmark)

This is the most northerly campsite in the world (71° 06' 50") and considering the climate and the wild unspoilt location it has to be one of the best sites in Scandinavia, and also rivals the best in Europe. An added bonus is that the reindeer often come right into the campsite to graze. The 30 pitches, 22 with electricity (16A), are on grass or gravel hardstanding in natural 'tundra' terrain beside a small lake, together with 10 rental cabins and 5 rooms. Sea fishing and photographic trips by boat can be arranged and buses run 4 times a day to Honningsvåg or the Nordkapp Centre. We suggest you follow the marked footpath over the hillside behind the campsite, from where you can photograph Nordkapp at midnight if the weather is favourable. We also advise you pack warm clothing, bedding and maybe propane for this location. Note: Although overnighting at Nordkapp Centre is permitted, it is on the very exposed gravel car-park with no electric hook-ups or showers.

Facilities

Excellent modern fully sanitary installations in two under-floor heated buildings, linked by a covered timber walkway. They include a sauna, two family bathrooms, baby room, and excellent unit for disabled visitors. Laundry with washing machine and dryer. Kitchen, with hot-plates, sinks and a dining area. All have quality fittings, excellent tiling and beautiful woodwork - the owner is a carpenter by profession. Good motorcaravan service point. Reception/cafeteria at the entrance open daily (15/6-15/8).

At a glance

Welcome & Ambience	✓✓✓✓	Location	✓✓✓✓
Quality of Pitches	✓✓✓✓	Range of Facilities	✓✓✓

Directions

On the island of Magerøya, from Honningsvåg take the E69 for 20 km. then fork right signed Skarsvåg. Site is on left after 3 km. just as you approach Skarsvåg.

Charges guide

Per person	NOK 20
pitch	NOK 110
electricity	NOK 30

Reservations

Not usually necessary. Tel: 78 47 52 33.

Open

20 May - 1 September.

NO2435 Solvang Camping

Transfarelv, 9500 Alta (Finnmark)

This is an old-style, restful little site with a welcoming atmosphere. It is set well back from the main road, so there is no road noise. The site overlooks the tidal marshes of the Altafjord, which are home to a wide variety of bird-life, providing ornithologists with a grandstand view during the long summer evenings bathed by the Midnight Sun. The 30 pitches are on undulating grass amongst pine trees and shrubs, and are not marked, although there are 12 electric hook-ups (16A). The site is run by a church mission consequently only limited funds are available for repairs and refurbishment. However, all facilities are clean and in good order (out of season, the site provides holidays for needy children and carers).

Facilities

Basic, heated sanitary facilities in a fairly old building, include mostly open washbasins. Kitchen with two full cookers. Small laundry with washing machine and spin dryer. In its own little kiosk outside is the modern stainless steel chemical disposal point and outside a waste water drain which, with a little ingenuity, is possible to use for draining a motorcaravan tank. TV lounge. Playground.

At a glance

Welcome & Ambience	✓✓✓	Location	✓✓✓✓
Quality of Pitches	✓✓✓	Range of Facilities	✓✓✓

Directions

Site is signed off the E6, 10 km. north of Alta.

Charges guide

Per unit	NOK 90
electricity	NOK 30

No credit cards.

Reservations

Write to site. Tel: 78 43 04 77.

Open

1 June - 10 August.

NO2415 Kautokeino Fritidssenter & Camping

Suonpatjavri, 9520 Kautokeino (Finnmark)

This is a newly developed, friendly, lakeside site, eight kilometres south of Kautokeino. The 30 pitches are not marked but are generally on a firm sandy base amongst low growing birch trees, with 20 electric hook-ups (10A) available. There are also cabins and motel rooms for rent. Although the grass is trying to grow, the ground is frozen from September until May so it takes many years to establish. During the season when there are enough guests, the owner arranges an evening campfire around two Sami tents, with 'lectures' about the Sami people. There are good walks in the area to some special Sami sites. Shops and other services are in Kautokeino and the site is 35 km. north of the Finnish Border.

Facilities

The modern sanitary building is heated and well maintained, with 2 British style WCs, 2 open washbasins and 2 showers (on payment) per sex. Small kitchen with full cooker, dishwashing sinks and refrigerator. Laundry with washing machine, dryer and ironing facilities. Separate bathroom for disabled people, also containing baby facilities. Football. Volleyball. Site rents canoes, boats and pedalos and free fishing available in lake.

At a glance

Welcome & Ambience	✓✓✓✓	Location	✓✓✓✓
Quality of Pitches	✓✓✓	Range of Facilities	✓✓✓✓

Directions

Site is 8 km. south of Kautokeino on the Rv 93 (do not confuse with a site of similar name in the town).

Charges guide

Per person	NOK 10
pitch	NOK 65 - 75
electricity	NOK 25

Reservations

Write to site. Tel: 78 48 57 33.

Open

1 June - 30 September.

NO2515 Gjelten Bru Camping

2560 Alvdal (Hedmark)

Located just a few kilometres west of Alvdal, this peaceful little site, with its traditional turf roof buildings, makes an excellent base from which to explore the area. The 50 touring pitches are on level neatly trimmed grass, served by gravel access roads and with electricity available to 37. Some pitches are in the open and others under tall pine trees spread along the river bank. Across the bridge on the other side of the river and main road, the site owners also operate the local, extremely well stocked mini-market and post office. The UNESCO World Heritage town of Roros is 75 km. to the northeast of this charming little site, and the Dovrefjell National Park is also within comfortable driving distance.

Facilities

Heated toilet facilities are housed in two buildings. One unit has been refurbished, the other is of newer construction. There is a mix of conventional washbasins and stainless steel washing troughs, and hot showers on payment. Separate unit with WC, basin, shower and handrails for disabled campers. Two small kitchens, one at each block, provide dishwashing facilities, hot-plates and an oven all free of charge. Fishing. Off site: Supermarket and post office nearby. Bicycle hire 5 km.

At a glance

Welcome & Ambience	✓✓✓	Location	✓✓✓
Quality of Pitches	✓✓✓✓	Range of Facilities	✓✓✓

Directions

On the Rv 29 at Gjelten 3.5 km. west of Alvdal. Turn over the river bridge opposite village store and post office, and site is immediately on right.

Charges 2004

Per unit	NOK 120
electricity	NOK 20

No credit cards.

Reservations

Write to site. Tel: 62 48 74 44.

Open

All year.

NO2545 Rustberg Hytteulerie & Camping

2636 Oyer (Oppland)

Conveniently located beside the E6, 23 km. from the centre of Lillehammer, this attractive terraced site provides a comfortable base for exploring the area. Like all sites along this route it does suffer from road and train noise at times, but the site's facilities and nearby attractions more than compensate for this. There are 90 pitches with 60 for touring units, most reasonably level and with some gravel hard-standings for motorcaravans. There are 50 electrical connections. A small open air, heated swimming pool with water-slide is open 1/6-31/8 (weather permitting). Lillehammer has a pleasant pedestrian precinct, the '94 Olympic Ski jump and Mailhaugen outdoor museum. We recommend a visit to the latter and pay parking for the day, it is cheaper. At Oyer and Hunderfossen (5 km) you will find a road museum, fairytale park and the more adventurous can ride the Olympic bobsleigh track.

Facilities

Heated, fully equipped sanitary facilities include washbasins in cubicles, showers on payment and free saunas. Two good family bathrooms. Unit for disabled people. Campers' kitchen and dining room with dishwashing, microwave oven and double hob (all free). Laundry. Motorcaravan services. Solarium (on payment). Kiosk stocking basic foods. Free swimming pool and water-slide. Billiard golf. Playground. Off site: Forest walks directly from site. Fishing in the nearby river, day licence from reception. Golf 7 km.

At a glance

Welcome & Ambience	✓✓✓✓	Location	✓✓✓
Quality of Pitches	✓✓✓✓	Range of Facilities	✓✓✓✓

Directions

Site is well signed from the E6, 20 km. north of Lillehammer (North) exit.

Charges 2004

Per unit	NOK 155
electricity (10A)	NOK 20

Reservations

Write to site. Tel: 61 27 58 50.
E-mail: rustberg@online.no

Open

All year.

NO2550 Strandefjord Camping

2920 Leira (Oppland)

Fagernes lies on the north shore of an impressive glacial lake - Strandefjorden, and just four kilometres to the southeast at Leira, on a corner of this lake, is Strandefjord Camping. This undulating, woodland site behind a light industrial estate, has 70 touring pitches, but can take up to 250 units in scattered clearings amongst the trees and beside the lake. Many pitches are only suitable for tents and only 75 have electricity (10A). Also 30 seasonal units, 31 cabins and rooms on site. Saunas (which are equipped with TV!) are to be found under the main site complex which also houses reception, a licensed restaurant and conference room. Fishing and swimming in the lake are possible.

Facilities

The main heated, but rather basic, sanitary unit could be hard pressed in high season. It includes some washbasins in cubicles, but only 2 showers per sex (on payment). Separate rooms house a small kitchen with dishwashing and cooking facilities (free) and a laundry. Extra showers and WC's with saunas. Restaurant (June-Aug). CPlay areas. Lake swimming. Fitness track. Tennis. Beach volleyball. Minigolf. Boat hire. Off site: Village mini-market 2 minute walk.

At a glance

Welcome & Ambience	✓✓✓	Location	✓✓✓✓
Quality of Pitches	✓✓✓	Range of Facilities	✓✓✓✓

Directions

Turn off E16 Oslo road onto the Rv 51, at Leira village 4 km. east of Fagernes. Site entrance is within 50m.

Charges guide

Per caravan or motorcaravan	NOK 120
tent and car	NOK 100
electricity	NOK 25

Reservations

Write to site. Tel: 61 36 23 65.

Open

All year.

NO2590 Sandviken Camping

3650 Tinn Austbygd (Telemark)

Sandviken is a remote, lakeside site, in scenic location, suitable for exploring Hardangervidda. With its own shingle beach, at the head of Tinnsjo Lake, it provides 150 grassy, mostly level, pitches. In addition to 50 seasonal units and 12 cabins, there are 100 numbered tourist pitches with electricity (5A), plus an area for tents, under trees along the waterfront. A 1 km. stroll takes you to the tiny village of Tinn Austbygde which has a mini-market, bakery, café, bank, garage and post office.

Facilities

Tidy heated sanitary facilities includes some washbasins in cubicles, showers on payment, sauna, solarium and a dual-purpose disabled/family bathroom. Kitchen and laundry rooms (hot water on payment). Motorcaravan services. Kiosk (1/6-15/9). Playground. TV and games room. Minigolf. Fishing and watersports. Boat hire.

Open

All year.

At a glance

Welcome & Ambience	✓✓✓	Location	✓✓✓
Quality of Pitches	✓✓✓	Range of Facilities	✓✓✓✓

Directions

Easiest access is via the Rv 37 from Gransherad along the western side of the lake.

Charges guide

Per person	NOK 15
pitch	NOK 70 - 95
electricity	NOK 25

'Quickstop' (8 pm-9 am) 70 - 85. No credit cards.

Reservations

Write to site. Tel: 35 09 81 73.
E-mail: kontact@sandviken-camping.no

NO2570 Fossheim Hytte & Camping

3550 Gol (Buskerud)

Centred on the country town of Gol is one of Norway's favourite camping areas, Hallingdal. This small touring site lies just 4 km. west of the town, on the Hallingdal river bank, shaded by tall birch trees. From reception downstream there are mini rapids. Despite being just below the main road and with a railway in the trees on the opposite side of the river, surprisingly little noise penetrates this idyllic setting. There are 50 grassy touring pitches, with electricity (10/16A) for 40. Most overlook the river. In addition there are 10 cabins and 4 rooms for rent. Trout fishing with a specially constructed wooden walkway and platform for anglers with disabilities. In Gol, which is a small ski centre in the winter, you will find a replica of the towns Stave Church (1250) and worth visiting. Services are held in the church each week.

Facilities

A modern heated toilet unit includes some washbasins in cubicles, separate unit for disabled people and a sauna for each sex. Small kitchen and laundry rooms. Cooking (free of charge). Shop with basic provisions and bread to order (1/6-31/8). Large TV lounge overlooking the river. Motorcaravan services. Play area. Canoe hire, fishing licence from site. Bicycle hire in Gol. Off site: Riding 4 km. Golf 18 km.

At a glance

Welcome & Ambience	✓✓✓✓	Location	✓✓✓✓
Quality of Pitches	✓✓✓✓	Range of Facilities	✓✓✓✓

Directions

Site is 4 km. west of Gol on route Rv 7 to Geilo.

Charges 2004

Per unit incl. 2 persons	NOK 120 - 170
electricity	NOK 30

Reservations

Not necessary. Tel: 32 02 95 80.
E-mail: foshytte@online.no

Open

All year.

NO2615 Olberg Camping

Olberg, 1860 Trogstad (Østfold)

Olberg is a delightful small farm site, close to lake Øyeren and within 70 kilometres of Oslo. There are 35 large, level pitches and electricity connections (16A) are available for 28 units located on neatly tended grassy meadow with newly planted trees and shrubs. The reception building also houses a small gallery with paintings, glasswork and other crafts. In high season fresh bread is available (not Sunday). A short drive down the adjacent lane takes you to the beach on Lake Øyeren, and there are many woodland walks in the surrounding area. The old church and museum at Trøgstad, and Båstad church are worth visiting. Please bear in mind that this is a working farm. Forest and elk 'safaris' are arranged.

Facilities

Excellent, heated sanitary facilities in a purpose built unit created in the end of a magnificent large, modern barn are fully equipped and include a ramp for wheelchair access and one bathroom for families or disabled visitors. Dishwashing under cover with hot and cold water. Washing machine and ironing board. Small kitchenette with full size cooker and food preparation area. Kiosk. Snacks available. Craft gallery. Playground. Bicycle hire. Off site: Tennis nearby. Riding 2 km. Fishing 3 km. Golf 18 km.

At a glance

Welcome & Ambience	✓✓✓✓	Location	✓✓✓✓
Quality of Pitches	✓✓✓✓	Range of Facilities	✓✓✓

Directions

Site is signed on Rv 22, 20 km. north of Mysen on southern edge of Båstad village.

Charges 2004

Per unit incl. 2 adults	NOK 125
tent incl. 2 persons	NOK 125
electricity	NOK 30

Reservations

Write to site. Tel: 69 82 86 10.
E-mail: post@olberg.no

Open

1 April - 1 October, other times by arrangement.

NO2612 Holt Camping

4900 Tvedestrand (Aust-Agder)

Tvedestrand is an attractive small resort with a pretty harbour, which is very popular with the Norwegians for their own holidays. Holt Camping is quite pleasantly situated beside the main E18 road, some three kilometres from the town - there is a little noise from the road during the day but we were not disturbed when staying overnight. The campsite is part level, part sloping grassland and about half of the pitches have 16A electrical connections with a number of cabins. This site could be very useful en-route to Oslo from the ferry at Kristiansand or for a break in a part of Norway frequented more by the Norwegians themselves than by visitors from abroad.

Facilities

The single small sanitary block has excellent, well maintained facilities including hot showers on payment (1 per sex), washbasins (H&C) and provision for dishwashing and laundry (washing machine and dryer). Serving both the touring pitches and the cabins, the facilities may well be under pressure during busy times. Shop/café immediately outside site entrance. Children's play area.

At a glance

Welcome & Ambience	✓✓✓	Location	✓✓✓
Quality of Pitches	✓✓✓	Range of Facilities	✓✓✓

Directions

Site is beside the main E18 coast road (which actually bypasses the town), about 1 km. south of the turn off to the town itself.

Charges guide

Per unit incl. 2 persons and electricity	NOK 100
without electricity	NOK 80

Reservations

Contact site. Tel: 37 16 02 65.

Open

1 June - 31 August.

NO2600 Rysstad Feriesenter

4748 Rysstad (Aust-Agder)

Setesdal is on the upper reaches of the Otra river which runs north from the southern port of Kristiansand and right up to the southern slopes of Hardangervidda. It offers a wide range of scenery, often spectacular where the valley cuts through high, steep sided mountains. It is an area famous for its colourful mining history (silver) and for its vibrant art (especially music) and folklore. Thanks to a major hydro-electric project, a spectacular mountain road now links Setesdal with Sirdal to the west, bringing Setesdal within easy and pleasant driving range of Stavanger. At the junction of this road and Setesdal is the small village of Rysstad, named after the family who have developed camping in this area. Trygve Rysstad now runs the Rysstad Feriesenter, founded by his father in the '50s. The site occupies a wide tract of woodland between the road and the river towards which it shelves gently, affording a splendid view of the valley and the towering mountains opposite. The site is in effect divided into two sections; one is divided by trees and hedges into numbered pitches, some occupied by chalets, the other is an adjacent open field and 20 electricial connections are available.

Facilities

Good modern sanitary facilities under the reception block have showers on payment, washbasins in cubicles, dishwashing sinks and a cooker. Laundry facilities with washing machine. Children's play area and amusement hut. Sports field. Fishing, swimming and boating (boats for hire). Fitness track. Bicycle hire. TV room. Centre includes café, shop, bank, garage and restaurant. Attractive area on the river's edge for barbecues and entertainment with an arena type setting. Off site: Village within walking distance.

Open

1 May - 1 October.

At a glance

Welcome & Ambience	✓✓✓✓	Location	✓✓✓✓
Quality of Pitches	✓✓✓	Range of Facilities	✓✓✓✓

Directions

Site is about 1 km. south of junction between route 9 (from Kristiansand) and the extended route 45 (from Stravanger).

Charges guide

Per person	NOK 20
child	NOK 10
caravan or tent	NOK 130
hiker	NOK 60
electricity	NOK 25

Reservations

Write to site. Tel: 37 93 61 30.
E-mail: post@rysstadferie.no

NO2610 Neset Camping

4741 Byglandsfjord (Aust-Agder)

On a semi-promontory on the shores of the 40 kilometres long Byglandsfjord, Neset is a good centre for activities or as a stop en route north from the ferry port of Kristiansand (from England or Denmark). Byglandsfjord offers good fishing (mainly trout) and the area has marked trails for cycling, riding or walking in an area famous for its minerals. Neset is situated on well kept grassy meadows by the lake shore with the water on three sides and the road on the fourth and provides 200 unmarked pitches with electricity and cable TV available. The main building houses reception, a small shop and a restaurant with fine views over the water. This is a well run, friendly site where one could spend an active few days.

Facilities

Three modern sanitary blocks which can be heated, two with comfortable hot showers on payment, washing up facilities (metered hot water) and a kitchen. Restaurant and takeawy (1/7-15/8). Shop. Campers' kitchen. Children's playground. Lake swimming, boating and fishing. Barbecue area. Bicycle, canoe and pedalo hire. Climbing, rafting and canoeing courses arranged (including trips to see beavers and elk). Cross-country ski-ing possible in the area in winter.

At a glance

Welcome & Ambience	✓✓✓	Location	✓✓✓✓
Quality of Pitches	✓✓✓	Range of Facilities	✓✓✓✓✓

Directions

Site is on route 9, 2.5 km. north of the town of Byglandsfjord on the eastern shores of the lake.

Charges 2005

Per unit	NOK 150
tent and motorcycle	NOK 120
adult	NOK 10
child (5-12 yrs)	NOK 5
electricity	NOK 30
cable TV	NOK 25

Reservations

Write to site (also for details of courses).
Tel: 37 93 42 55. E-mail: post@neset.com

Open

All year.

Poland

Situated in the heart of Europe, Poland is a country rich in culture and heritage. Having transformed itself after years of invasions and interference from its neighbours, it has now become an ideal place for those looking for something a little different.

The northern part of Poland is varied, well-forested and gently undulating, with the coastline providing miles of sandy beaches, bays, cliffs and dunes. The flat central plain is the main agricultural area and heading south the terrain rises, with the mountainous regions being dominated by two big ranges, the Sudetens in the west and the Carpathians in the south. Here you'll find plenty of caves to explore. Poland also has over 9,000 lakes; the majority located in the north east in the Pomeranian and Masurian Lake districts. These lakes offer many opportunities for water sports enthusiasts, anglers, nature lovers and bird watchers.

Completely ravaged by the Second World War, Warsaw has been rebuilt and developed into a thriving capital, with plenty of churches, palaces, galleries and museums to visit. Unlike the capital, Kraków still retains its original character and wealth of architecture, having come through the war unscathed to become one of the world's twelve most significant historic sites as listed by UNESCO.

Population

38.6 million

Capital

Warsaw

Climate

Temperate climate, with warm and sunny summers, cold winters with large snowfalls. Hottest and sunniest days are in June and July but these months also seem to have more rainfall than at any other time of year - be prepared!

Language

Polish

Currency

The Zloty

Telephone

The country code is 00 48

Shops

Mon-Fri 6.00/7.00 - 18.00/19.00. Sat: 7.00 -13.00. Supermakets usually stay open until 21.00/22.00

Public Holidays

New Year; Easter Mon; Labour Day; Constitution Day; Corpus Christi; Assumtion, All Saints; Independence Day; Christmas 25, 26 Dec

Motoring

International Driving Permit is required. Between October and March it is compulsory to have head-lights switched on at all times while driving. Be aware that some of the roads and motorway surfaces are badly rutted - drive with caution. Motorcyclists must keep their lights on all year round.

Tourist Office

Poland National Tourist Office
Remo House, 310-312 Regent St,
London W1B 3AX
Tel: 020 7580 8811
Fax: 020 7580 8866
E-mail: info@visitpoland.org.
Internet: www.visitpoland.org

POLAND HAS STRONG THEATRICAL AND MUSICAL TRADITIONS AND A RICH FOLKLORE HISTORY. SMALL LOCAL FEASTS, FAIRS AND CONTESTS OCCUR THROUGHOUT THE COUNTRY, PARTICULARLY IN THE SUMMER.

PL3050 Camping Tramp Nr. 33

ul. Kujawska 14, 87-100 Torun (Kujawsko-Pomorskie)

Torun, a Gothic jewel built originally by the Teutonic Knights and now listed by UNESCO as a world heritage site, like so many Polish towns has a long, interesting and troubled history. Famous as the birth place of Copernicus, it is today a prosperous university city on the wide River Wisla. The old walled town is worth a visit in its own right, and with a major part of it pedestrianised, walking over the Wisla bridge from the campsite is a perfect way to enjoy your visit. Inevitably the town has a planetarium which has two shows a day in English. Camping Tramp has a pleasant appearance and lies in a basin below the level of the roads which run on both sides of the site. A variety of trees cover part of the site where pitches (with electric hook-ups) mingle with holiday bungalows. The other, larger field is an open meadow, where half the pitches have electricity. The 100 pitches, reached from hard access roads, are neither marked nor numbered but the position of electric boxes define where to go. Some pitches are separated by low hedging. The main E75 runs along one side of the campsite just before a busy junction and river bridge resulting in continuous traffic noise. Whilst we would not recommend this as a 'holiday' base, it makes a good night stop when travelling between Germany and the Baltic coast or to visit Torun.

Facilities

One refurbished and fully tiled, traditional style toilet block with toilets, hot showers and washbasins. Clean and smelling fresh when visited but without dressing space. Dishwashing sinks. Facilities for disabled visitors (with ramped access). Welcoming bar/restaurant (good value) with basic food supplies.Basketball. Playing field. Fishing. Off site: Town with restaurants and shops 2 km. Golf 10 km. Riding 5 km.

Open

1 May - 30 October.

At a glance

Welcome & Ambience	✓✓✓✓	Location	✓✓✓✓
Quality of Pitches	✓✓✓✓	Range of Facilities	✓✓✓

Directions

From the south approaching the town you have a choice – fork left for a restricted height route (max 3.2 m.) or straight on. If you fork left go under the railway bridge and turn right immediately to site 300 m. on the left. If straight on, turn back towards the main bridge and site access is on the right before the river crossing. From the north go over the Wisla bridge and turn left before the railway to site in 300 m. on the left.

Charges 2004

Per person	PLN 7,00
child (under 10 rrs)	PLN 4,00
pitch	PLN 15,00 - 30,00
electricity (10A)	PLN 9,00

Reservations

Write to site (in English). Tel: 056 6547187.

PL3090 Kemping Nr. 19 Kamienny Potok

Ul. Zamkowa Góra 25, 81-713 Sopot (Pomorskie)

Sopot is a popular seaside resort on the Gulf of Gdansk with a sandy beach, promenade and pier against a background of wooded hills. There are many attractions nearby including 'Opera-in-the-Woods' with 5,000 seats, an annual pop concert and other centres of historic interest. From the pier a ferry service departs for Gdansk, Gdynia or to Hel on the Baltic Sea sea peninsula and it is possible to travel from Gdansk to Finland. Kamienny Potok is set back from the beach and, by Polish standards, is a large site with 400 tourist pitches, some back to back on either side of concrete access roads, others in open meadows. Places are numbered but not marked out, of grass on sand and 150 pitches have electricity (6-20A). With well mown grass, the site was neat and tidy. There are many tall trees around the site, although not much shade in camping areas. It is an easy 25 minute train ride from the site to Gdansk and the station is only 500 m. walk. Dutch clubs rally here and the whole campsite has a pleasant quiet atmosphere, although there is some road noise near the entrance.

Facilities

Three toilet blocks (one old, two refurbished to high standards) with toilets, open style washbasins, hot showers and sinks for dishwashing. Facilities for disabled visitors. Motorcaravan service point. Washing machine. Open air bar with food service. Playgrounds. Fishing. Volleyball. Basketball. TV room. Billiard club with electronic dart boards. Off site: New swimming pool complex with giant slide 200 m. Beaches 500 m. Riding 1 km. Bicycle hire 1.5 km. Boat launching/hiring 2 km. Shell garage with basic food supplies. Ferry service to Gdansk, Gdynia and Hel 1 km.

Open

1 May - 15 September.

At a glance

Welcome & Ambience	✓✓✓✓✓	Location	✓✓✓✓✓
Quality of Pitches	✓✓✓✓	Range of Facilities	✓✓✓

Directions

Site is 2 km. north of Sopot on main road behind Shell garage.

Charges guide

Per person	PLN 12,00
child (4-15 yrs)	PLN 7,00
caravan	PLN 10,00
tent	PLN 5,00 - 7,00
car	PLN 9,00
motorcaravan	PLN 16,00 - 22,00

Reservations

Write to site in German. Tel: 058 550 0445.

PL3170 Camping-Pension Galindia Mazurski Eden

Bartlewo 1, 12-210 Iznota (Warminsko-Mazurskie)

Mazurski Eden is in the centre of the beautiful Mazurian Lake District surrounded by the interesting flora and fauna of the Piska forest. It is a quite amazing place approached by a 6 kilometre sand road, easily negotiable by caravans, with the entrance flanked by tall pine posts of carved figures. Wood carvings abound with statues by the water's edge, on buildings and inside the hotel. The camping area with room for 100 units, is grass on sand under tall trees which serve to determine the pitches, with electrical connection boxes topped with lamps for night illumination. A wealth of activities includes organised photographic safaris, canoeing and hiking trips, cycle excursions, visits to the Kadzidlowo nature reserve with wolves, bisons, beavers and other wildlife. Sailing and other watersports are arranged and even fishing under the ice in winter. Parties, picnics and barbecues are organised with dancing and folk bands. Various national days are noted, with open air workshops for painters and sculptors and church festivals are celebrated in a family atmosphere. The manager has a great interest in the social history of the ancient people of this area and this is reflected in the entertainment offered to group conferences being held in the hotel, to which campers are also invited.

Facilities

Excellent, newly tiled sanitary block (caveman style) with toilets, basins and showers. Dishwashing sinks with free hot water. Laundry service in the hotel. Motorcaravan service point. Kayaks, canoes, sailing boats and pedaloes for hire. Beach. Boat mooring. 'Cave men' festivities. Bar in cave under the pension with billiards. Open air bar near the lake. 'Cave men style' restaurant. Lounge with TV with English and German channels. Cave men style events organised with 'Chief Galindia'. Off site: Skiing and sailing.

Open

All year.

At a glance

Welcome & Ambience	✓✓✓✓✓	Location	✓✓✓✓✓
Quality of Pitches	✓✓✓	Range of Facilities	✓✓✓✓

Directions

Take 609 road from Mikolajki to Ukta and turn off towards Iznota on to sand road. Pass through Nowy Most to Iznota and follow camp signs.

Charges guide

Per person	PLN 18,00
pitch	PLN 13,00 - 26,00
electricity	PLN 20,00

Reservations

Write to site in English. Tel: 087 423 1416.
E-mail: galindia@galindia.com.pl

PL3280 Korona Camping Nr. 241

Gaj 51, 32-031 Gaj (Slaskie)

This site, with direct access from the main road, is 10 km. from Krakow. It is down a slope, some 100 metres back from the road, so is not noisy and it has lovely views over the villlage. The site is terraced, but caravans and motorcaravans tend to use a flat area near the toilet block. Tent pitches are slightly sloping. It is a family run site that takes about 100 units, all with 6A electricity, and pitches are separated by young trees. To the back of the site is a large pond for fishing (well fenced) and a large, covered barbecue place. Mrs Trepizynska has fresh bread roles available each morning and cooks a delicious stroganoff soup. Mr Trepizynska keeps four sheep, wandering over the site, to cut the grass – they are shy but give the site a rural feel. There are buses from the main road into Krakow, but each evening Mr Trepizynska will ask if anyone wishes to make the trip and if he finds ten people, will take them in his own minibus for a small charge. Similarly he will take people to the Wieliczka salt mines (16 km). Auschwitz is 64 km. and impressing enough to spend a day.

Facilities

One modern toilet block (could be under pressure in high season) with hot showers, washbasins and toilets, all clean and well maintained. Baby bath in both sections. Dishwashing under cover. Bar with open air terrace and some basics. Fishing pond. Playing field. Volleyball. Playground. Trip to Kraków and the Wieliczka salt mines. Off site: Kraków 10 km. Riding 3 km. Tennis 2 km. Bar/restaurant 500 m. Beach 20 km.

Open

May - September.

At a glance

Welcome & Ambience	✓✓✓✓✓	Location	✓✓✓✓✓
Quality of Pitches	✓✓✓✓	Range of Facilities	✓✓✓

Directions

Site is 10 km. south of Kraków off the E77 Kraków - Zakopane road. Take care because access to the site is directly off the motorway and is particularly difficult when coming from Zakopane because one has to cross the motorway.

Charges guide

Per person	PLN 10,00
child (5-10 yrs)	PLN 5,00
pitch incl. car	PLN 14,00 - 20,00
tent pitch	PLN 6,00 - 18,00
electricity	PLN 8,00
dog	PLN 5,00

Reservations

Contact site. Tel: 012 270 1318.

PL3100 Camping Przy Plazy Nr. 67

ul . Bitwy pod Plowcami 73, 81-731 Sopot (Pomorskie)

Sopot is Poland's most popular seaside resort and one of the large sandy beaches is only 25 m. from this site, with the town only a short walk away. The town was first established as a sea bathing centre in 1824 and its heyday came in the interwar years when it attracted the richest people in Europe. The pier and the main street contain many bars, restaurants and cafes and is a pleasant place to enjoy a beer and the sea air. In the wooded hills behind the town is the Opera Lesna built in 1909 and the venue for the annual International Song Festival held at the end of August. The impressive Grand hotel, built in 1924/7, in Sopot overlooks the beach and the Gulf of Gdansk and is a good place to go for a coffee. This is a large site with 180 unmarked pitches of which 160 have electricity.

Facilities

Each sanitary block has toilets and showers and is clean although a little worn. Motorcaravan draindown available. Small covered campers' kitchen with sinks. Small shop. Off site: Sopot and the beach plus numerous shops, bars and restaurants.

Open

15 June - 31 August.

At a glance

Welcome & Ambience	✓✓✓✓	Location	✓✓✓✓
Quality of Pitches	✓✓✓✓	Range of Facilities	✓✓✓

Directions

Sopot is between Gdansk and Gydnia on Poland's Baltic coast. To find this site you need to be on the coastal road between Sopot and Gdansk. The site is next to the new Novotel at the southern end of the town. It is well signed from the town.

Charges 2004

Per adult	PLN 11,00
child (7-16 yrs)	PLN 8,90
pitch incl. car	PLN 19,00 - 21,00
electricity	PLN 9,00

Reservations

Not necessary. Tel: 0585 516523.

PL3160 Camping Echo

11-511 Rydzewo (Warminsko-Mazurskie)

This is a very good, small family campsite run by Barbara Nowakowska. With only space for about 40 pitches, all with electricity, it would be a good choice for a short or medium term stop while you explore and enjoy the Masurian Lakes. It is on the banks of Lake Neogocin which is popular with water-sports enthusiasts and swimmers alike. The Masurian Lakes area is a very popular holiday spot but despite this the countryside remains unspoiled with many rare plants and birds thriving here. The lakes are interlinked by rivers and canals and are suitable for canoeing and yatching trips. The district is also a paradise for ramblers and those who delight in discovering secret spots. To the east the woods conceal overgrown bunkers built by the Germans in World War 2. The site is itself is just the place to rest and recuperate and enjoy the peace and quiet.

Facilities

The small sanitary block has toilets and hot showers which are immaculate. Washing machine. Chemical disposal point. Small restaurant and bar. Boat launching possible. Off site: Mazurian Lakes and not far away the Wolfslair, Hitler's bunker.

Open

1 May - 30 September.

At a glance

Welcome & Ambience	✓✓✓✓✓	Location	✓✓✓✓✓
Quality of Pitches	✓✓✓✓✓	Range of Facilities	✓✓✓✓

Directions

Rydzewo is south of Gizycko and the site is easy to find just on the northern outskirts of the village. It is on the banks of Lake Neogocin.

Charges 2004

Per person	PLN 10,00
child	PLN 7,00
pitch incl. car	PLN 20,00 - 23,00
electricity	PLN 9,00
dog	PLN 5,00

Reservations

Not needed. Tel: 087 421 1186.

PL3300 Camping Polana Sosny Nr. 38

Os. Na Polenie Sosny, 34-441 Niedzica (Malopolskie)

The small village of Niedzica is south of the Pieniny mountain range in the Dunajec valley and about 40 km. northeast of Zakopane. This excellent little campsite is right alongside the Dunajec dam and the river, at the eastern end of the Czorsztynskie lake. With 35 touring pitches, all with electricity, it is a good short or long stay. Adjacent is the Dwor restaurant which is open from 10.00 to 22.00 all the year. The raft ride on the river that flows through the limestone mountain gorges is one of the best-known tourist attractions in Poland. At first the rafts move with deceptive calm, but as they approach the gorge behind the cloister ruins the water becomes rougher as the river twists and winds. This lasts for about 8 km. after which the water once again flows more slowly. The exhilarating ride ends in Szczawnica, a well-known health resort. The start of this ride is just 3 km. from the campsite and a bus will bring you back. In addition the Slovakian border is just 2 km. away.

Facilities

The new small sanitary block near reception has toilets and showers and two good sets of facilities for disabled visitors. Chemical toilet disposal. Small campers' kitchen with sinks and electric rings. Off site: Niedzica and the Czorsztynskie Lake. Slovakian border 2 km.

Open

All year.

At a glance

Welcome & Ambience	✓✓✓✓	Location	✓✓✓✓
Quality of Pitches	✓✓✓✓	Range of Facilities	✓✓✓✓

Directions

From Nowy Targ head east on the 969. In village of Debno turn right towards Niedzica. The Czorsztynskie lake is on the left and Czorsztyn Castle is ahead. After the castle approach Niedzica and the dam. Just before the Dunajec dam bridge turn right and site is immediately on the left.

Charges 2004

Per person	PLN 4,00 - 6,00
pitch	PLN 20,00 - 30,00

Reservations

Not necessary. Tel: 0182629403.
E-mail: dworek@pro.onet.pl

PL3320 Auschwitz Centre

Ul. M. Kolbego 1, 32-602 Oswiecim (Malopolskie)

Oswiecim is a name that many foreigners will not have heard, but any mention of the German equivalent, Auschwitz, evokes fear in almost everyone. Founded in 1992 this centre gives the outward appearance of being a first class hotel. Its aim is to create a venue for meetings, exchanges, education, reflection and prayer for all those who visit Auschwitz and are moved by what happened here. To further this aim campers are welcome to use the landscaped gardens with tents, motorcaravans or caravans and use the centre's facilities. Electricity has been provided (6A) with 14 pitches either on the grass or on the large parking area. The state museum in Oswiecim – Auschwitz/Birkenau, now a UNESCO World Heritage site, is only a few minutes walk away, and is open almost every day of the year. No visitor can leave unmoved. Guided tours are available in English, alternatively you could buy the English guide book and walk around on your own, entrance is free.

Facilities

Showers and toilets are provided and are new, clean and well maintained. The restaurant in the centre is available for campers use. Off site: Owiecim and the museums of Auschwitz and Birkenau.

Open

All year.

At a glance

Welcome & Ambience	✓✓✓✓	Location	✓✓✓✓
Quality of Pitches	✓✓✓✓	Range of Facilities	✓✓✓✓

Directions

The centre is 600 m. from the Auschwitz museum in the road to the south running parallel to road that serves the museum. It is on the 950/933 road and is situated between a roundabout and a large electricity substation. It appears to be a first class hotel from the outside and has facilities to match.

Charges 2004

Per person	€ 5,00 - € 6,00

Reservations

Unlikely to be needed. Tel: 033 843 1000.
E-mail: biuro@center-dialogu.oswiecim.pl

Portugal is a relatively small country occupying the southwest corner of the Iberian peninsula, bordered by Spain in the north and east, with the Atlantic coast in the south and west. In spite of its size, the country offers a tremendous variety in both its way of life and traditions.

Most visitors looking for a beach type holiday head for the busy Algarve, with its long stretches of sheltered sandy beaches, and warm, clear Atlantic waters, great for bathing and watersports. With its monuments and fertile rolling hills, central Portugal adjoins the beautiful Tagus river that winds its way through the capital city of Lisbon, on its way to the Altantic Ocean. Lisbon city itself has deep rooted cultural traditions, coming alive at night with buzzing cafes, restaurants and discos. Moving southeast of Lisbon the land becomes rather impoverished, consisting of stretches of vast undulating plains, dominated by cork plantations. Consequently most people head for the walled town of Evora, an area steeped in two thousand years of history. The Portuguese consider the Minho area in the north to be the most beautiful part of their country, with its wooded mountains and wild coastline, a rural and conservative region with picturesque towns.

Population

10 million

Capital

Lisbon

Climate

The country enjoys a maritime climate with hot summers and mild winters with comparatively low rainfall in the south, heavy rain in the north

Language

Portuguese

Currency

The Euro

Telephone

The country code is 00 351

Banks

Mon-Fri 08.30-11.45 and 13.00-14.45. Some large city banks operate a currency exchange 18.30-23.00

Shops

Mon-Fri 0900-1300 and 1500-1900. Sat 0900-1300

Public Holidays

New Year; Carnival (Shrove Tues); Good Fri; Liberty Day 25 Apr; Labour Day; Corpus Christi; National Day 10 June; Saints Days; Assumption 15 Aug; Republic Day 5 Oct; All Saints 1 Nov; Immaculate Conception 8 Dec; Christmas 24-26 Dec

Motoring

The standard of roads is very variable, even some of the main roads can be very uneven. Watch Portuguese drivers, as they tend to overtake when they feel like it. Tolls are levied on certain motorways (auto-estradas) out of Lisbon, and upon southbound traffic at the Lisbon end of the giant 25th Abril bridge over the Tagus. Parked vehicles must face the same direction as moving traffic.

Tourist Office

ICEP Portuguese Trade & Tourism Office
2nd Floor 22/25a Sackville Street
London W1S 3LY
Tel: 09063 640 610 (60 p per minute)
Fax: 020 7494 1868
E-mail: iceplondt@aol.com
Internet: www.portugalinsite.com

tip

THE FESTA DE SÃO JOÃO (JUNE) SEES PEOPLE DANCING THROUGH THE STREETS, AMICABLY HITTING EACH OTHER OVER THE HEAD WITH LEEKS, AND THE FEIRA DE SÃO MARTINHO (NOV) HAS RIDING CONTESTS AND BULLFIGHTS.

PO8230 Camping Olhao

Pinheiros de Marim, 8700 Olhao (Faro)

This site, taking around 1,000 units and open all year, has mature trees to provide reasonable shade. The pitches are marked, numbered and in rows divided by shrubs with electricity and water to all parts. Permanent and long stay units take 20% of the pitches and the tourist pitches fill up quickly in high season, so arrive early. Amenities include very pleasant pools and tennis courts, a reasonable bar and restaurant, all very popular with the local Portuguese, and a café/bar with TV and games room. There is some noise nuisance from an adjacent railway. The large, sandy beaches in this area are on islands reached by ferry and are, as a result, relatively quiet (some reserved for naturists). This site can get busy in peak periods. A large, low season British contingent was enjoying the low prices when we visited.

Facilities

Eleven sanitary blocks are adequate, clean when seen, and are specifically sited to be a maximum of 50 m. from any pitch. One block has facilities for disabled visitors. Laundry. Supermarket. Kiosk. Restaurant/bar (all year). Café and general room with TV. Playgrounds. Swimming pools (April - Sept) and tennis courts (fees for both). Volleyball. Bicycle hire. Internet. Off site: Bus service 50 m to the nearest ferry at Olhao. Riding 1 km. Fishing 2 km. Golf 20 km.

Open

All year, as are all facilities.

At a glance

Welcome & Ambience	✓✓✓✓	Location	✓✓✓✓✓
Quality of Pitches	✓✓✓	Range of Facilities	✓✓✓✓

Directions

Just over 1 km. east of Olhao, on EN125, take turn to Pinheiros de Marim. Site is 300 m. on left. Look for white triangular entry arch as the site name is different on the outside wall - a foible of the owner.

Charges 2004

Per person	€ 1,95 - € 3,60
child (5-12 yrs)	€ 1,10 - € 2,00
car	€ 1,50 - € 3,00
tent	€ 1,50 - € 4,00
caravan	€ 2,45 - € 7,00
motorcaravan	€ 2,50 - € 7,20

Less for longer winter stays.

Reservations

Contact site. Tel: 289 70 03 00.
E-mail: parque.campismo@sbsi.pt

PO8202 Parque de Campismo Turiscampo

Estrada Nacional, 125, Espiche, 8600 Lagos (Faro)

This site has been taken over by the previous owners of Camping L'Amfora in Spain and has been recommended by our Spanish agent. With their experience and expertise, the new owners are fully refurbishing the site and are adding new toilet blocks, a large swimming pool, new bungalows and much more. It will be open all year round and should prove to be one of the best campsites in Portugal. There are 300 pitches, all with electricity and water and trees provide some shade. The sea is 2 km. and the city of Lagos 4 km. with all the attractions of the Algarve within easy reach.

Facilities

Two toilet blocks are supplemented by a further block in high season. Washing machines. Shop. Restaurant/bar. Swimming pool. Bicycle hire. Internet point. Entertainment in high season on the bar terrace. Bungalows to rent.
Off site: Praia da Luz village 1 km.

Open

1 January - 31 December.

Directions

From Lagos on road N125 towards Sagres, site is 3 km.

Charges 2005

Per person	€ 2,75 - € 4,80
child	€ 1,50 - € 2,50
pitch	€ 2,25 - € 6,00
car	€ 2,25 - € 3,50
electricity	€ 2,50 - € 3,00
dog	€ 1,00 - € 1,50

Reservations

Contact site. Tel: 351 282 789 265.
E-mail: info@turiscampo.com

PO8200 Orbitur Camping Valverde

Estrada da Praia da Luz, Valverde, 8600 Lagos (Faro)

A little over one kilometre from the village of Praia da Luz and its beach and about 7 km. from Lagos, this large, well run site is certainly worth considering for your stay in the Algarve. It has 600 numbered pitches, of varying size, which are enclosed by hedges. All are on flat ground or broad terraces with good shade in most parts from established trees and shrubs. The site has a swimming pool with a long curling slide and a paddling pool (under 10s free, adults charged). This is an excellent site with well maintained facilities and good security. It attracts a good number of long-term winter visitors. The site, which is one of the better Orbitur sites, is extremely well managed by Sra. Pinto, who is helpful and friendly.

Facilities

Six large, clean, toilet blocks have some washbasins and sinks with cold water only, and hot showers. Units for disabled people. Laundry. Motorcaravan services. Supermarket, shops, restaurant and bar complex with both self-service and waiter service in season (all April - Oct). Takeaway. Coffee shop. Swimming pool with slide and paddling pool (June - Sept). Playground. Tennis court. Disco. Pub. General room with TV. Excursions. Medical post. Off site: Fishing and bicycle hire 3 km. Golf 10 km. The road to the beach is quite narrow with fast traffic.

Open

All year.

At a glance

Welcome & Ambience	✓✓✓✓✓	Location	✓✓✓✓
Quality of Pitches	✓✓✓✓	Range of Facilities	✓✓✓✓

Directions

Fork left on N125 road 3 km. west of Lagos to Praia da Luz and site is under 1 km.

Charges 2004

Per person	€ 2,60 - € 5,00
child (5-10 yrs)	€ 1,30 - € 2,50
tent	€ 2,20 - € 6,70
caravan	€ 3,10 - € 7,70
car	€ 2,20 - € 4,50
motorcaravan	€ 3,80 - € 8,40

Off season discounts (up to 70%).

Reservations

Contact Orbitur - Central de Reservas, Rua Diogo do Couto, 1149–042 Lisboa. Tel: 21/811 70 00 or 811 70 70. Email: info@orbitur.pt

PO8210 Parque de Campismo Albufeira

EN 125 Ferreiras-Albufeira, 8200-555 Albufeira (Faro)

The spacious entrance to this site will accommodate the largest of units (watch for severe speed bumps at the barrier). One of the better sites on the Algarve, it has pitches are on fairly flat ground with some terracing, trees and shrubs giving reasonable shade in most parts. There are some marked and numbered pitches of 50-80 sq.m. Winter stays are encouraged with many facilities remaining open including a heated pool. An attractively designed complex of traditional Portuguese style buildings on the hill forms the central area of the site, has pleasant views and is surrounded by a variety of flowers, shrubs and well watered lawns, complete with a fountain. The waiter and self-service restaurants, a pizzeria, bars and a sound proofed disco, have views across the three pools.

Facilities

The toilet blocks include hot showers. Washing machines. Waiter and self-service restaurants, and pizzeria. Bars. Sound proof disco. Swimming pools. Playground. ATM. Car hire. Off site: Site bus service to Albufeira (2 km).

Open

All year.

At a glance

Welcome & Ambience	✓✓✓✓✓	Location	✓✓✓✓
Quality of Pitches	✓✓✓✓	Range of Facilities	✓✓✓✓✓

Directions

From N125 coast road or N264 (from Lisbon) at new junctions follow signs to Albufeira. Site is approx. 1 km. from junctions, on left.

Charges 2004

Per person	€ 4,85
child (410 yrs)	€ 2,60
car	€ 4,60
tent or caravan acc. to size	€ 4,60 - € 6,30
motorcaravan	€ 7,70 - € 11,40

Reservations

Made without de posit or fee; contact site. Tel: 289 587629. Email: campingalbufeira@mail.telepac.pt

PO8220 Orbitur Camping Quarteira

Estrada da Fonte Santa, 8125 Quarteira (Faro)

This is a large, busy attractive site on undulating ground with some terracing, taking 795 units. On the outskirts of the popular Algarve resort of Quarteira, it is 600 m. from a sandy beach which stretches for a kilometre to the town centre. Many of the unmarked pitches have shade from tall trees and there are a few small pitches of 50 sq.m. with electricity and water for reservation. There are 680 electrical connections. Like other sites along this coast, long winter stays are encouraged. The pools here are excellent (extra charge). The large restaurant and supermarket have separate entrances for local trade.

Facilities

Five sanitary blocks provide British and Turkish style toilets, individual washbasins with cold water, hot showers plus facilities for disabled visitors. Washing machines. Motorcaravan services. Gas supplies. Supermarket, self-service restaurant (Feb - Nov). Takeaway (from late May). Swimming pools (June - Sept). General room with bar and TV. Tennis. Kiosk. Open air disco. Medical room. Off site: Fishing 1 km. Bicycle hire 1 km. Golf 4 km.

Open

All year.

At a glance

Welcome & Ambience	✓✓✓✓✓	Location	✓✓✓✓✓
Quality of Pitches	✓✓✓✓	Range of Facilities	✓✓✓✓

Directions

Turn off N125 south towards Quarteira in Almancil (8 km. west of Faro). Site is 5 km. from the junction

Charges 2004

Per person	€ 2,60 - € 5,00
tent	€ 2,20 - € 6,70
caravan	€ 3,10 - € 7,70
car	€ 2,20 - € 4,50
motorcaravan	€ 3,80 - € 8,40

Off season discounts (up to 70%).

Reservations

Contact Orbitur - Central de Reservas, Rua Diogo do Couto, 1149–042 Lisboa. Tel: 21/811 70 00 or 811 70 70. Email: info@orbitur.pt

PO8410 Parque de Campismo de Armacao de Pera

8365 Armacao de Pera (Faro)

A modern site with a wide attractive entrance and a large external parking area, the 1,200 pitches are in zones on level grassy sand. They are marked by trees that provide some shade, and are easily accessed from tarmac and gravel roads. Electricity is available for most of the pitches. The facilities are good. The restaurant, self service café and bar, and supermarket should cater for most needs, and you can relax around the pools. The disco near the entrance is soundproofed which should ensure a peaceful nights.

Facilities

Three modern sanitary blocks provide British and Turkish style WCs, some with bidets, washbasins, showers with hot water on payment, and facilities for disabled campers. A reader reports that maintenance can be variable. Laundry. Supermarket. Restaurant (1/5-30/9). Self service café. Three bars (1/5-30/9). Kiosk. Games and TV rooms. Tennis. Play area. Swimming and paddling pools (May - Sept). ATM. Off site: Fishing, bicycle hire and watersports nearby.

Open

All year.

At a glance

Welcome & Ambience	✓✓✓✓✓	Location	✓✓✓✓
Quality of Pitches	✓✓✓✓	Range of Facilities	✓✓✓✓✓

Directions

Site is west of Albufeira. Turn off N125/ IC4 road in Alcantarilha, taking the EN269-1 towards the coast. Site is on left side before Armacao de Pêra. There are other sites with similar names in the area, so be sure to find the right one.

Charges 2004

Per person	€ 2,50 - € 5,50
tent or caravan	€ 2,00 - € 6,00
car	€ 1,50 - € 3,50
motorcaravan	€ 2,50 - € 6,00

Min. stay 3 nights 1 June - 31 Aug.

Reservations

Write to site. Tel: 282 31 22 96.

PO8430 Orbitur Camping Sagres

Cerro das Moitas, 8650 Sagres (Faro)

Camping de Sagres is a pleasant site at the western tip of the Algarve, not very far from the lighthouse in the relatively unspoilt southwest corner of Portugal. With 960 pitches for tents and 120 for tourers, the pitches are sandy and located amongst pine trees giving good shade. There are some hardstandings for motorhomes and electrical connections throughout. The fairly bland restaurant, bar and café/grill provide a range of reasonably priced meals. The beaches and the town of Sagres (the departure point of the Portuguese navigators) with its fort, are a short drive.

Facilities

Three spacious toilet blocks are showing some signs of wear but provide hot and cold showers, washbasins with cold water. Washing machines. Motorcaravan services. Supermarket (1/4-1/11). Restaurant/bar and café/grill (all 1/4-30/9). TV room. Bicycle hire. Barbecue area. Playground. Fishing. Off site: Beach 2 km. Golf 12 km.

Open

All year.

At a glance

Welcome & Ambience	✓✓✓✓	Location	✓✓✓✓
Quality of Pitches	✓✓✓✓✓	Range of Facilities	✓✓✓✓

Directions

Turn off road N268 east to EN268, after about 2 km. after turn to Sagres, site (as a camping site only – no name) is signed off to right.

Charges 2004

Per person	€ 2,40 - € 4,30
pitch incl. car	€ 4,20 - € 9,90

Off season discounts (up to 70%).

Reservations

Contact Orbitur - Central de Reservas. Tel: 21/811 70 00 or 811 70 70. Email: info@orbitur.pt

PO8440 Parque de Campismo Quintos dos Carriços

Praia da Salema, Vila do Bispo, 8650-196 Budens (Faro)

This is an attractive and peaceful, valley site with a dedicated naturist area. A traditional tiled Portugese style entrance leads you down a steep incline into this excellent and well maintained site which has a village atmosphere. With continuing improvements, the site has been developed over the years by the Dutch owner. It is spread over two valleys (which are real sun-traps), with the 300 partially terraced pitches marked and divided by trees and shrubs (oleanders and roses). A small stream (dry when seen) meanders through the site. The most remote part, 250 m. from the main site, is dedicated to naturists. Although the site is lit, torches may be required in more remote areas. A very popular site for summer and winter sun-worshippers, within easy driving distance of resorts. The many fine beaches in the region provide ample opportunities for diving, swimming and fishing.

Facilities

Four modern, spacious sanitary blocks, well tiled with quality fittings, are spotlessly clean and include washbasins with cold water and hot showers on payment (€ 0.60). Dishwashing, laundry sinks and washing machine. Excellent facility for disabled people. Gas supplies. Well stocked mini-market (all year). Restaurant (daily 1/3-15/10). Bar (daily in season, once a week only 15/10-1/3). TV room. Internet. Library. Games room. Bicycle, scooter, moped and m/cycle hire. Off site: Nearby tennis, squash and excellent walks. Fishing, golf and beach 1 km. Riding 8 km. Bus service operates from the site.

At a glance

Welcome & Ambience	✓✓✓✓✓	Location	✓✓✓✓
Quality of Pitches	✓✓✓✓	Range of Facilities	✓✓✓✓

Directions

Turn off RN125 (Lagos-Sagres) road at junction to Salema (17 km. from Lagos); site is signed.

Charges 2005

Per person	€ 4,20
child	€ 2,10
tent	€ 4,20 - € 5,40
caravan	€ 5,90
car	€ 4,20
motorcycle	€ 3,00

Discounts for long winter stays.

Reservations

Contact site. Tel: 282 69 52 01.
E-mail: quintacarrico@oninet.pt

Open

All year.

PO8350 Camping Markádia

Barragem de Odivelas, Apartado 17, 7920-999 Alvito (Beja)

A tranquil, lakeside site in an unspoilt setting, this will appeal most to those nature lovers who want to 'get away from it all' and to those who enjoy country pursuits such as walking, fishing or riding. The lake is in fact a 1,000 hectare reservoir, and more than 120 species of birds can be found in the area. The open countryside and lake provide excellent views and a very pleasant environment, albeit somewhat remote. The stellar views in the very low ambient lighting are wonderful at night. The site is lit but a torch is required. There are 130 casual unmarked pitches on undulating grass and sand with ample electricity connections (16A). The friendly Dutch owner has carefully planned the site so each pitch has its own oak tree to provide shade. The bar/restaurant with a terrace is open daily in season but weekends only during the winter. One can swim in the reservoir and rowing boats, pedaloes and windsurfers are available for hire. You may bring your own boat, although power boats are not allowed on environmental grounds.

Facilities

Four modern, clean and well equipped toilet blocks are built in traditional Portuguese style with hot water throughout. Dishwashing and laundry sinks are open air. Washing machines and ironing boards. Motorcaravan services. Bar and restaurant (1/4-30/9). Shop (all year, bread to order). Lounge. Playground. Fishing. Boat hire. Tennis. Riding. Medical post. Car wash. Dogs are not accepted in July/August. Facilities and amenities may be reduced outside the main season.

Open

All year.

At a glance

Welcome & Ambience	✓✓✓✓✓	Location	✓✓✓✓✓
Quality of Pitches	✓✓✓✓✓	Range of Facilities	✓✓✓✓✓

Directions

From A2 between Setabul and the Algarve take exit 10 on IP8 signed Ferreira and Beja. Take road to Torrao and 13 km. later at 1 km. north of Odivelas, turn right towards Barragem and site is 3 km. after crossing head of reservoir following small signs (one small section of poor road).

Charges 2005

Per person	€ 4,40
child (5-10 yrs)	€ 2,00
tent or caravan	€ 4,40
car or motorcycle	€ 4,40
motorcaravan	€ 8,80
electricity	€ 2,20

Discounts of 10-20% outside June - Aug, and for longer stays. No credit cards.

Reservations

Contact site for details. Tel: 284 76 31 41.

PO8170 Parque de Campismo Sao Miguel

Sao Miguel, Odeceixe, 7630-592 Odemira (Beja)

Nestled in green hills near two pretty white villages, four kilometres from the beautiful Praia Odeceixe (beach) is the attractive camping park Sao Miguel. The main building (with its traditional Portuguese architecture) is built around two sides of a large grassy square. It houses reception, restaurant, bars and supermarket. There are 'Lisbon Arcade' style verandas to sit under and enjoy a drink, coffee or meal while enjoying the view across the square to the pool, tennis courts and camping which is hidden under a canopy of trees. Unusually the site works on a maximum number of 700 campers, you find your own place (there are no defined pitches) under the tall trees, there are ample electrical points, the land slopes away gently. The wooden chalet style accomodation is in a separate area, but some mobile homes share the two traditional older style but clean sanitary blocks. An outdoor cinema operates in summer showing films for children and adults. The self serve restaurant and bars are excellent, there is a pizzeria by the pool with its own terrace (summer only) and for those who want to self cater the supermarket has a bakery, as well as wide range of goods including fresh fruit and vegetables.

Facilities

Two older style sanitary buildings with British style WCs and free hot showers. Washing machines, dishwashing and laundry sinks are at the end of the block under cover. Toilets and basins for disabled campers but no shower. Shop (Jun -Sep). Restaurant/bar (March - Oct) Bar, snacks and pizzeria (June - Sept). Children's playground. Tennis courts (extra charge). Swimming pool (extra charge). No animals are accepted. Torches useful. Off site: Village has a range of shops bars and restaurants. Historic village of Odemira 2 km. Fishing/sailing 4 km. Riding 20 km. Camping is situated inside the Nature Park of Alentejo.

Open

Easter - September.

At a glance

Welcome & Ambience	✓✓✓✓✓	Location	✓✓✓✓
Quality of Pitches	✓✓✓✓	Range of Facilities	✓✓✓✓✓

Directions

Between Odemira and Lagos on the N120 just before the village of Odeceixe on the main road well signed.

Charges guide

Per person	€ 2,60 - € 4,00
child (5-10 yrs)	€ 1,40 - € 2,25
tent	€ 2,60 - € 6,00
caravan	€ 4,00 - € 5,50
car	€ 2,60 - € 3,50
motorcaravan	€ 5,00 - € 8,00

Plus 7% VAT.

Reservations

Write to site. Tel: 282 947145.
E-mail: camping.sao.miguel@mail.telepac.pt

Open

Easter - September.

PO8150 Orbitur Camping Costa da Caparica

Ava. Alfonso de Albuquerque, Quinta de Ste Antonio, 2825 Costa da Caparica (Setubal)

This is very much a site for 600 permanent caravans but it has relatively easy access to Lisbon (just under 20 kilometres) via the motorway, by bus or even by bus and ferry if you wish. It is situated near a small resort, favoured by the Portuguese themselves, which has all the usual amenities plus a good sandy beach (200 m. from the site) and promenade walks. There is a small area for touring units which includes some larger pitches for motorcaravans. We see this very much as a site to visit Lisbon rather than for prolonged stays. Activities and shows are organised in season in an outdoor disco/entertainment area.

Facilities

The three toilet blocks have mostly British style toilets, washbasins with cold water and some hot showers - they come under pressure when the site is full. Facilities for disabled visitors. Washing machine. Motorcaravan services. Supermarket. Large bar/restaurant (Feb-Nov). Playground. Doctor calls daily in season. Gas supplies. Off site: Fishing 1 km. Riding 4 km. Golf 5 km.

Open

All year.

At a glance

Welcome & Ambience	✓✓✓✓	Location	✓✓✓✓
Quality of Pitches	✓✓✓	Range of Facilities	✓✓✓✓

Directions

Cross the Tagus bridge (toll) on A2 motorway going south from Lisbon, immediately take the turning for Caparica and Trafaria. At 7 km. marker on IC20 turn right (no sign) - the site is at the second roundabout.

Charges 2004

Per person	€ 2,40 - € 4,50
child (5-10 yrs)	€ 1, 20 - € 2,45
tent	€ 2,20 - € 6,50
caravan	€ 3,10 - € 6,50
car	€ 2,20 - € 4,40
motorcaravan	€ 3,80 - € 7,80

Off season discounts (up to 70%).

Reservations

Contact Orbitur - Central de Reservas,
Rua Diogo do Couto, 1149–042 Lisboa.
Tel: 21/811 70 00 or 811 70 70.
Email: info@orbitur.pt

PO8130 Orbitur Camping Guincho

E.N. 247, Lugar da Areia - Guincho, 2750-053 Cascais (Lisbon)

Although this is a popular site for permanent Portuguese occupants with 1,295 pitches, it is nevertheless quite attractively laid out among low pine trees and with the A5 autostrada connection to Lisbon (30 km), it provides a useful alternative to sites nearer the city. Located behind sand dunes and a wide, sandy but somewhat windswept beach, the site offers a wide range of facilities. These include a fairly plain bar/restaurant, supermarket (all year), general lounge with pool tables, electronic games, TV room and a good laundry. There is a choice of pitches (small - mainly about 50 sq.m.) mostly with electricity, although siting amongst the trees may be tricky, particularly when the site is full. This is viewed as an alternative for visiting Lisbon, not a holiday site.

Facilities

Three sanitary blocks, one refurbished, are in the older style but are clean and tidy. Washbasins with cold water but hot showers. Dishwashing sinks have cold water. Three washing machines, two dryers. Facilities for disabled visitors. Motorcaravan services. Gas supplies. Supermarket. Restaurant, bar and terrace (all year). General room with TV. Tennis. Playground. Entertainment in summer. Medical post. Car wash. Off site: Excursions. Riding 500 m. Beach 800 m. Fishing 1 km. Golf 3 km.

Open

All year.

At a glance

Welcome & Ambience	✓✓✓✓	Location	✓✓✓✓
Quality of Pitches	✓✓✓✓	Range of Facilities	✓✓✓✓

Directions

Approach from either direction on N247. Turn inland 6.5 km. west of Cascais at camp sign. Travelling direct from Lisbon, the site is well signed as you leave the A5 autopista.

Charges guide

Per unit icl. 2 persons, electricity, water	€ 15,20 - € 28,30
extra adult	€ 2,40 - € 4,40
child (5-10 yrs)	€ 1,20 - € 2,20

Off season discounts (up to 70%).

Reservations

Contact Orbitur - Central de Reservas, Rua Diogo do Couto, 1149–042 Lisboa. Tel: 21/811 70 00 or 811 70 70. Email: info@orbitur.pt

PO8450 Parque de Campismo Colina do Sol

2465 Sao Martinho do Porto (Leiria)

This is a well appointed site with its own pool and near to the beach. Only 1 km. from the small town of S. Martinho do Porto, it has around 350 pitches marked by fruit and ornamental trees on grassy terraces. Electricity (6 or 10A) is available to all, although some may need long leads. The attractive entrance with its beds of bright flowers, is wide enough for even the largest of outfits, and the surfaced roads are very pleasant for manoeuvring. There is a warm welcome and good English is spoken. A well stocked supermarket and a restaurant, cafeteria, and a bar with a delightful paved terrace beside the large clean pools. The beach is at the rear of the site, with access via a gate which is locked at night. This is a convenient base for exploring the Costa de Prata.

Facilities

Two large, clean and modern toilet blocks provide British style WCs (some with bidets), washbasins - some with hot water. Dishwashing and laundry sinks. Motorcaravan services. Supermarket, restaurant/café with bar.
Off site: Shop, restaurant and bar within 200 m.

Open

All year except 15 December - 15 January.

At a glance

Welcome & Ambience	✓✓✓✓	Location	✓✓✓✓
Quality of Pitches	✓✓✓✓	Range of Facilities	✓✓✓✓

Directions

Turn from EN 242 (Caldas-Nazaré) road northeast of San Martinho do Porto. Site is clearly signed.

Charges guide

Per person	€ 2,87
child (4-10 yrs)	€ 1,37
pitch incl. car	€ 4,84 - € 5,94

Less 25-50% in low seasons.

Reservations

Contact site. Tel: 262 98 97 64.
E-mail: geral@colinadosol.com

PO8480 Orbitur Camping Foz do Arelho

EN360 - km 3, Foz do Arelho, 2500 Caldas da Rainha (Leiria)

This is a large and roomy ex-municipal site, 2 km. from the beach. It has a new central complex with a most impressive pool. The large two storey, brick-faced building contains all the site's leisure facilities but has no ramped access and there are no sanitary facilities anywhere on site for disabled campers. The building is somewhat sterile and the furniture is bland but there are pleasant views over the pool from the restaurant and terrace. Pitches are generally sandy with some hardstandings, vary in size and are unmarked on two levels with wide tarmac roads. There is a little shade and some permanent Portuguese units occupied in high season and weekends at other times. All touring pitches have electricity.

Facilities

Four identical modern sanitary buildings (solar heating) with seatless British and Turkish style WCs and free showers. Washing machine in one. No facilities for disabled campers. No chemical disposal point. Supermarket. Children's club. Games room. Table tennis. Small new amphitheatre. Electronic games. Bar/snacks and restaurant. (April - Sept). Playground. Torches useful. Off site: Bus 500 m. Seaside town with shops, bars and restaurants 2 km. Fishing 2 km. Watersports 3 km. Riding 15 km. Golf 35 km.

At a glance

Welcome & Ambience	✓✓✓✓	Location	✓✓✓✓
Quality of Pitches	✓✓✓	Range of Facilities	✓✓✓✓

Directions

Site is north of Lisbon west of Caldos. From A8 Take N360 to Foz de Arelho. Site is well signed.

Charges 2004

Per person	€ 2,10 - € 4,00
pitch incl. car	€ 5,50 - € 6,50

Reservations

Contact Orbitur - Central de Reservas.
Tel: 21/811 70 00 or 811 70 70.
Email: info@orbitur.pt

Open

All year.

PO8110 Orbitur Camping Valado

E.N. 8-5 Alcobaca - Valado, 2450 Nazaré (Leiria)

This popular site is close to the traditional fishing port of Nazaré which has now become something of a holiday resort. The large sandy beach in the town (about 2 km. steeply downhill from the site) is sheltered by headlands and provides good swimming. The campsite is on undulating ground under tall pine trees, has 503 pitches and, although some smallish individual pitches with electricity and water can be reserved, the bulk of the site is not marked out and units could be close together especially during July/August. The functional restaurant, bar and supermarket are contained in one white-walled block.

Facilities

The three toilet blocks have British and Turkish style WCs, washbasins (some cold water) and 17 hot showers, all very clean when inspected. Laundry. Motorcaravan services. Gas. Supermarket. Bar, snack bar and restaurant with terrace (Feb - Nov). TV/general room. Playground. Tennis. Medical post. Car wash. Off site: Bus service 20 m. Fishing and bicycle hire 2 km.

Open

1 February - 30 November.

At a glance

Welcome & Ambience	✓✓✓✓	Location	✓✓✓✓
Quality of Pitches	✓✓✓✓	Range of Facilities	✓✓✓✓

Directions

Site is on the Nazaré - Alcobaca N8-5 road, 2 km. east of Nazaré.

Charges guide

Per unit incl. 2 persons, electricity, water	€ 12,30 - € 22,20
child (5-10 yrs)	€ 0,95 - € 1,70

Off season discounts (up to 70%).

Reservations

Contact Orbitur - Central de Reservas,
Rua Diogo do Couto, 1149–042 Lisboa.
Tel: 21/811 70 00 or 811 70 70.
Email: info@orbitur.pt

PO8460 Camping Caravaning Vale Paraiso

E.N. 242, 2450-138 Nazaré (Leiria)

A pleasant, well managed site, Vale Paraiso is by the main N242 road in eight hectares of undulating pine woods. It provides over 600 shady pitches, many on sandy ground only suitable for tents. For other units there are around 250 individual pitches of varying size on harder ground with electricity. A range of sporting and leisure activities includes a good outdoor pool with sunbathing areas, a new pool and a play area for children, plus a small adventure playground. There is a bar, takeaway and a slightly bland restaurant/bar. Several long beaches of white sand are within 2-15 kilometres allowing windsurfing, sailing, surfing or body-boarding. Animation for children and evening entertainment is organised in season. Nazaré is an old fishing village with narrow streets, a harbour and marina, with a lift to Sitio. There is much of historical interest in the area although the mild Atlantic climate is also conducive to just relaxing. The owners are keen to welcome British visitors and English is spoken.

Facilities

Toilet facilities are good, with hot water for washbasins, showers, laundry and dishwashing sinks. Facilities for disabled people. Baby baths to borrow. Washing machine and dryers. Motorcaravan services. Shop. Restaurant (March - Sept). Café/bar with TV (all year). Takeaway. Tabac. Supermarket (March - Sept). Swimming pool and paddling pool (March - Sept; free for children under 11 yrs). Petanque. Volleyball. Basketball. Football. Badminton. Leisure games. Amusement hall. Bicycle hire. Safety deposit. Gas supplies. E-mail and fax facilities (read free, send for a fee). Bus service from gate. Apartments to rent.
Off site: Fishing 1.5 km. Riding 5 km.

At a glance

Welcome & Ambience	✓✓✓✓	Location	✓✓✓✓
Quality of Pitches	✓✓✓✓✓	Range of Facilities	✓✓✓✓✓

Directions

Site is 2 km. north of Nazaré on the EN242 Marinha Grande road.

Charges 2005

Per person	€ 3,00 - € 4,00
child (3-10 yrs)	€ 1,50 - € 2,00
caravan	€ 3,60 - € 4,40
motorcaravan	€ 4,50 - € 5,50
tent	€ 2,60 - € 5,00
car	€ 2,80 - € 3,40

Reservations

Contact site. Tel: 262 56 18 00.
E-mail: info@valeparaiso.com

Open

1 January - 18 December & 27-31 December.

PO8100 Orbitur Camping Sao Pedro de Moel

Rua Volta do Sete, 2430 Sao Pedro de Moel (Leiria)

This quiet and very attractive site is situated under tall pines, on the edge of the rather select small resort of Sao Pedro de Moel. The attractive, sandy beach is about 500 m. walk downhill from the site (you can take the car, although parking may be difficult in the town) and is sheltered from the wind by low cliffs. The shady site can be crowded in July/Aug, and the 525 pitches are in blocks and unmarked (cars may be parked separately) with 404 electrical connections. A few pitches are used for permanent units. Although there are areas of soft sand, there should be no problem in finding a firm place. The large restaurant and bar are modern as is the superb swimming pool, paddling pool and flume (there is a lifeguard).

Facilities

Four clean toilet blocks have mainly British style toilets (some with bidets), some washbasins with hot water. Hot showers are mostly in one block. Laundry. Motorcaravan services. Gas supplies. Supermarket. Large restaurant and bar with terrace (April-Sept). Swimming pools (June-Sept). TV and games room. Playground. Table tennis. Tennis. Medical post. Car wash. Off site: Bus service 100 m. Beach 500 m. Fishing 1 km.

Open

All year.

At a glance

Welcome & Ambience	✓✓✓✓✓	Location	✓✓✓✓✓
Quality of Pitches	✓✓✓✓✓	Range of Facilities	✓✓✓✓✓

Directions

Site is 9 km. west of Marinha Grande, on the right as you enter Sao Pedro de Moel.

Charges guide

Per unit ncl. 2 persons, electricity, water	€ 13,70 - € 24,90
extra adult	€ 2,10 - € 4,00
child (5-10 yrs)	€ 1,05 - € 2,00

Off season discounts (up to 70%).

Reservations

Contact Orbitur - Central de Reservas, Rua Diogo do Couto, 1149–042 Lisboa. Tel: 21/811 70 00 or 811 70 70. Email: info@orbitur.pt

PO8400 Campismo O Tamanco

Casas Brancas II, 3100-231 Louriçal (Leiria)

O Tamanco is a peaceful countryside site, with a homely almost farm-stead atmosphere, you will have chickens and ducks wandering around and there is a Burro here. The young Dutch owners, Irene and Hans, are sure to give you a warm welcome at this delightful little site. The swimming pool is very pleasant as is the small bar and a restaurant (with vegetarian menu options). Courses in printing and sculpture are arranged at certain times of the year. There may also be entertainment for the children during the day. The site is very popular with the Dutch, mature couples and winter campers. The 100 good sized pitches are separated by cordons of all manner of fruit trees, ornamental trees and flowering shrubs, on level grassy ground. There is electricity (6/16A) to 72 pitches and 5 pitches are suitable for large motorhomes. The site is lit and there is nearly always space available. One can fish or swim in a nearby lake and the resort beaches are a short drive. There may be some road noise on pitches at the front of the site.

Facilities

The single toilet block provides very clean and generously sized facilities including washbasins in cabins, with easy access for disabled visitors. As facilities are limited they may be busy in peak periods. Dishwashing and laundry sinks outside, under cover. Hot water throughout. Washing machine. Bar/restaurant. New roofed patio with fireplace. TV room/lounge. Swimming pool. Off site: Lake 2 km. Beach 11 km. Market in nearby Lourical every Sunday.

Open

1 February - 31 October.

At a glance

Welcome & Ambience	✓✓✓✓✓	Location	✓✓✓✓✓
Quality of Pitches	✓✓✓✓✓	Range of Facilities	✓✓✓✓

Directions

From N109/IC1 (Leira-Figuera de Foz) road, 25 km. south of Figuera in Matos de Carriço, turn on to N342 road (signed Louri≤al 6 km). Site is directly off the behind high hedges 1.5 km. on left.

Charges 2004

Per person	€ 3,15
child (up to 5 yrs)	€ 1,70
tent	€ 2,35 - € 3,05
caravan	€ 3,40
car	€ 2,35
motorcaravan	€ 5,65

Winter discounts up to 40%. No credit cards.

Reservations

Contact site. Tel: 236 95 25 51.
E-mail: campismo.o.tamanco@mail.telepac.pt

PO8050 Orbitur Camping São Jacinto

E.N. 327, km 20, São Jacinto, 3800 Aveiro (Aveiro)

This small site is in the São Jacinto nature reserve, on a peninsula between the Atlantic and the Barrinha, with views to the mountains beyond. The area is a weekend resort for locals and can be crowded in high season - it may therefore be difficult to find space in July/Aug, particularly for larger units. Swimming and fishing are both possible in the adjacent Ria, or the sea, 20 minutes walk from a guarded back gate. There is a private jetty for boats and the manager will organise hire of the decorative 'Moliceiros' boats used in days gone by to harvest seaweed for the land. This is not a large site, taking 169 units on unmarked pitches, but in most places trees provide natural limits and shade. A deep bore-hole supplies the site with drinking water.

Facilities

Two toilet blocks, very clean when inspected, contain the usual facilities. Dishwashing and laundry sinks. Washing machine and ironing board in a separate part of the toilet block. Motorcaravan services. Shop. Restaurant/bar (all May - Sept). Playground. Table tennis. Tourist information.
Off site: Bus service 20 m. Fishing 200 m. Bicycle hire 10 km.

Open

February - November.

At a glance

Welcome & Ambience	✓✓✓✓✓	Location	✓✓✓✓✓
Quality of Pitches	✓✓✓✓	Range of Facilities	✓✓✓✓

Directions

Turn off N109 at Estarreja to N109-5 to cross bridge over Ria da Gosta Nova and on to Torreira and São Jacinto. Or from Porto go south N1/09 turn for Ovar on the N327 which leads to São Jacinto.

Charges 2004

Per person	€ 2,00 - € 3,50
child (5-10 yrs)	€ 1,00 - € 1,75
caravan	€ 2,20 - € 5,70
tent	€ 1,65 - € 4,90
car	€ 1,80 - € 3,40
motorcaravan	€ 2,40 - € 6,10

Off season discounts (up to 70%).

Reservations

Contact Orbitur - Central de Reservas,
Rua Diogo do Couto, 1149–042 Lisboa.
Tel: 21/811 70 00 or 811 70 70.
Email: info@orbitur.pt

PO8030 Orbitur Camping Rio Alto

E.N. 13 - km 13 - Rio Alto-Est, 4490 Póvoa de Varzim (Porto)

This site makes an excellent base for visiting Porto (by car) which is some 35 kilometres south of Estela. It has around 700 pitches on sandy terrain and is next to what is virtually a private beach (access via a novel double tunnel under the dunes). The beach shelves steeply at some tidal stages. The 18 hole golf course is adjacent and huge nets along one side of the site protect campers from any stray balls. There are some hardstandings for caravans and motorcaravans and electrical connections to most pitches. The area for tents is furthest from the beach and windswept, stunted pines give some shade. There are special arrangements for car parking away from camping areas in peak season. There is a quality restaurant, snack bar and a large swimming pool plus a paddling pool across the road from reception. The beach tunnel is open 09.00-19.00 and the beach has a lifeguard 15/6–15/9.

Facilities

Four well equipped toilet blocks have hot water. Dishwashing and laundry sinks under cover. Washing machines and ironing facilities. Facilities for disabled campers. Gas supplies. Restaurant, bar and snack bar (1 Jan - 30 Nov), mini-market (15 May - 15 Sept). Swimming pool (1 June - 30 Sept). Tennis. Playground. Games room. Surfing. TV. Medical post. Car wash. Evening entertainment twice weekly in season. Off site: Fishing 800 m. Golf 1 km. Bicycle hire 13 km. Riding 19 km.

Open

All year.

At a glance

Welcome & Ambience	✓✓✓✓✓	Location	✓✓✓✓✓
Quality of Pitches	✓✓✓✓	Range of Facilities	✓✓✓✓✓

Directions

Site is reached via a cobbled road leading directly off the EN13 coast road towards the sea (just north of Estela), 12 km. north of Póvoa de Varzim. Travel 2.6 km. along narrow cobbled road and look right for an Orbitur sign (well back from the road). Take this for 0.8 km. to site (speed bumps). Go through intensive greenhouse farming for the last 2 km. but keep going it is worth it!

Charges 2004

Per person	€ 2,40 - € 4,50
child (5-10 yrs)	€ 1,20 - € 2,25
tent	€ 2,20 - € 6,50
caravan	€ 3,10 - € 7,40
motorcaravan	€ 3,80 - € 7,80
car	€ 2,20 - € 4,40

Off season discounts (up to 70%).

Reservations

Contact Orbitur - Central de Reservas, Rua Diogo do Couto, 1149–042 Lisboa. Tel: 21/811 70 00 or 811 70 70. Email: info@orbitur.pt

PO8370 Parque de Campismo de Cerdeira

4840 Campo do Gerês (Braga)

Placed in the National Park of Peneda Gerês, amidst spectacular mountain scenery, this excellent site offers modern facilities in a truly natural area. The well fenced, professional and peaceful site has some 600 good sized unmarked, mostly level, grassy pitches in a shady woodland setting. Electricity (5/10A) is available for most pitches, though some long leads may be required. A very large timber complex, tastefully designed with the use of materials, granite and wood provides a superb restaurant with a comprehensive menu. There are unlimited opportunities in the area for fishing, riding, canoeing, mountain biking and climbing, so take advantage of this quality mountain hospitality.

Facilities

Three very clean sanitary blocks provide mixed style WCs, controllable showers and hot water. Laundry. Gas. Mini-market. Restaurant/bar (15/4- 30/9). Playground. Bicycle hire. TV room. Medical post. Good tennis courts. Mini Golf. Car wash. Barbecue area. Torches useful. Dogs not accepted in July/August. Off site: Fishing and riding 800 m.

Open

All year.

At a glance

Welcome & Ambience	✓✓✓✓✓	Location	✓✓✓✓✓
Quality of Pitches	✓✓✓✓✓	Range of Facilities	✓✓✓✓✓

Directions

From north, N103 (Braga-Chaves road), turn left at N205 (7.5 km north of Braga). Follow N205 to Caldelas Terras de Bouro and Covide where site is clearly marked to 'Campo do Geres'.

Charges 2004

Per person	€ 3,15 - € 4,20
child (5-11 yrs)	€ 1,90 - € 2,65
pitch	€ 4,20 - € 8,95

Reservations

Contact site. Tel: 253 35 1005. E-mail: parque.cerdeira@portugalmail.pt

Slovakia

Slovakia is a small scale country in the heart of Europe, consisting of a narrow strip of land between the spectacular Tatra Mountains and the river Danube. Picturesque, with historic castles, evergreen forests, rugged mountains, cave formations, and deep lakes and valleys.

Slovakia has a lot to offer the visitor with an abundance of year round natural beauty. Its terrain varies impressively; the Carpathian Arc Mountains take up nearly half the country and include the Tatra Mountains, with their rugged peaks, deciduous forests and lakes. Southern and eastern Slovakia is mainly a lowland region and home to many thermal springs, with several open to the public for bathing. Over the years many Hungarians have moved to this area and there is a strong Hungarian influence.

Slovakia has over four thousand registered caves, twelve are open to the public and vary from drop stone to glacial; each one claims to have healing benefits for respiratory disorders. The capital, Bratislava is situated on the river Danube and directly below the Carpathian Mountains. Although it may not be as glamorous as Prague, it contains many fascinating buildings from nearly every age and is a lively cheerful city.

Population

5.4 million

Capital

Bratislava

Climate

Cold winters and mild summers. Hot summers and some rain in the eastern lowlands

Language

Slovak

Currency

The Koruna

Telephone

The country code is 00 421

Banks

Mon-Fri 08.00-13.00 and 14.00-17.00

Shops

Mon-Fri 09.00-12.00 and 14.00-18.00. Some remain open at midday. Sat 09.00-midday

Public Holidays

New Year; Easter Mon; May Day; Liberation Day 8 May; Saints Day 5 July; Festival Day 6 July; 28 Oct; Christmas 24- 26 Dec

Motoring

A full UK driving licence is acceptable.The major route runs from Bratislava via Trencin, Banska, Bystrica, Zilina and Poprad to Presov. A windscreen sticker which is valid for a year must be purchased at the border crossing for use on certain motorways. Vehicles must be parked on the right.

Tourist Office

Czech & Slovak Tourist Centre
16 Frognal Parade
Finchley Road
London NW3 5HG
Tel: 020 7794 3263
Fax: 020 7794 3265
E-mail: info@czechtravel.co.uk

WHY NOT TAKE A TRIP UP THE SPECTACULAR HIGH TATRAS, THE VIEWS FROM ABOVE THE TREE LINE ARE BREATHTAKING.

SK4920 Autocamping Trencin

Na Ostrove, P.O. Box 10, 911 01 Trencin (Trencin)

Trencin is an interesting town with a long history and dominated by the partly restored castle which towers high above. The small site with room for 30 touring units (all with electricity) stands on an island about 1 km. from the town centre opposite a large sports complex. Pitches occupy a grass area surrounded by bungalows, with the castle high on one side and woods and hills on the other. There is some road and rail noise. This is a neat, tidy and friendly site with English spoken during our visit.

Facilities

Toilet block is old but tiled and clean with hot water in the washbasins (in cabins with curtains) and showers (doors and curtains) under cover but not enclosed. Cookers, fridge, tables and chairs. Little shade. Bar in high season. Boating and fishing in river. Off site: Restaurants 200 m. Shops 300 m. Tennis, indoor and outdoor pools within 400 m.

Open

15 May - 15 September.

At a glance

Welcome & Ambience	✓✓✓✓	Location	✓✓✓
Quality of Pitches	✓✓✓	Range of Facilities	✓✓✓

Directions

Site is signed in places in town, otherwise head for town sports centre.

Charges guide

Per person	SKK 120
child (6-12 yrs)	SKK 70
caravan	SKK 80
tent	SKK 40 - 70
car	SKK 70

Reservations

Write to site. Tel: 032 743 4013. E-mail: autocamping.tn@mail.pvt.sk

SK4900 Autocamping Trusalová

038 53 Turany (Zilina)

Autocamping Trusalová is situated right on the southern edge of the Malá Fatra National Park, north-east of the historic town of Martin which has much to offer to tourists. The town is perhaps best known for the engineering works which produced most of the tanks for the Warsaw Pact countries before the recent revolution and change to a more democratic regime. Paths from the site lead into the Park making it an ideal base for walkers and serious hikers who wish to enjoy this lovely region. The site is in two halves, one on the left of the entrance and the other behind reception on a slight slope. Surrounded by trees with a stream rushing along one side, pitches are grass from a hard road with room for about 150 units and there are some bungalows for rent. Information on the area is available from reception. We received a most friendly welcome at this quiet and pleasant site from the German speaking staff.

Facilities

Each half has its own old, but clean and acceptable, toilet provision including hot water in basins, sinks and showers. Motorcaravan service point. Each section has a covered barbecue area. Volleyball. Table tennis. TV lounge. Playground. Outdoor chess . Bicycle hire. Off site: Bar just outside site. Restaurants 500 m. or 1 km. Shops 3 km.

Open

1 June - 15 September.

At a glance

Welcome & Ambience	✓✓✓✓✓	Location	✓✓✓✓
Quality of Pitches	✓✓✓✓	Range of Facilities	✓✓✓✓

Directions

Turn north at Motorest Fatra on the road 18/E50 near village of Turany to site.

Charges guide

Per person	SKK 95
child (6-15 yrs)	SKK 45
pitch	SKK 75 - 120
car	SKK 70

No credit cards.

Reservations

Write to site in German. Tel: 043 4292 636.

SK4910 Autocamping Turiec

Kolonia huiezda 92, 036 08 Martin (Zilina)

Turiec is situated in northeast Slovakia, 1.5 kilometres from the small village of Vrutky, four kilometres north of Martin, at the foot of the Lucanska Mala Fatra mountains and with castles nearby. Holiday activities include hiking in summer, skiing in winter. There is room for about 30 units on slightly sloping grass inside a circular tarmac road with shade from tall trees. Electrical connections are available for all places. A wooden chalet by the side of the camping area has a TV rest room and a small games room. You will receive a friendly welcome.

Facilities

One acceptable sanitary block to the side of the camping area, but in winter the facilities in the bungalow at the entrance are used. Cooking facilities. Snack bar in summer. Badminton. Volleyball. Swimming pool 1.5 km. Rest room with TV. Small games room. Covered barbecue. Off site: Shop outside entrance.

Open

All year.

At a glance

Welcome & Ambience	✓✓✓✓	Location	✓✓✓✓
Quality of Pitches	✓✓✓	Range of Facilities	✓✓✓

Directions

Site is signed from E18 road (Zilina - Martin) in the village of Vrutky, 3 km. north of Martin. Follow signs to Martinské Hole.

Charges 2004

Pitch incl. 2 persons and electricity	€ 11,00

Reservations

Contact site. Tel: 043 428 4215. E-mail: recepcia@autocampingturiec.sk

SK4925 Camping Lodenica

Sinava 1, 921 01 Piestany (Trnava)

This site is 1.5 kilometres from the most important spa in the Slovak Republic and lies in a quiet forest setting on the shores of the Sinava lake, close to the town Piestany. The site is only four kilometres from the main motorway between Bratislava and Trencin and therefore useful as a night stop when travelling between Poland and Hungary or the Czech Republic. Lodenica is divided into three main camping areas with 250 pitches (150 with electricity), the first right behind the entrance and a large, circular field with pitching close to the electricity boxes. Pitches on the second field to the back are separated by low hedges and the third field is in the 'Arena' and surrounded by a wooden fence, rather like a fortress. Among the pitches are mature trees which provide shade. The lake offers numerous possibilities for watersports and in the town of Piestany are swimming pools, tennis courts, a fitness centre and some historic monuments. Right at the entrance of the site stands a welcoming and good value restaurant. Disappointing at this site are the toilet blocks, which are old and need refurbishing.

Facilities

One traditional toilet block with toilets, open style washbasins (cold water only) and hot showers. Laundry with 5 sinks. Campers' kitchen with gas hob and oven. Good value bar/restaurant. Playing field. Rowing boats, canoes and surfboards for hire at the lake. Waterskiing. Bicycle hire. Off site: Fishing and beach 200 m. Piestany town with shops, hot food, bars, indoor and outdoor pools 1.5 km. Riding 5 km.

Open

1 May - 30 September.

At a glance

Welcome & Ambience	✓✓✓✓	Location	✓✓✓✓✓
Quality of Pitches	✓✓✓✓	Range of Facilities	✓✓✓✓

Directions

Take motorway form Bratislava towards Trencin and exit at Piestany. Go through village and pick up campsite signs.

Charges guide

Per person	SKK 40
caravan	SKK 40 - 80
car	SKK 80
motorcaravan	SKK 120
electricity	SKK 60

Reservations

Said to be unnecessary. Tel: 033 76 26 093.

SK4950 Autocamping Zlaté Piesky

Senecka cesta c2, 821 07 Bratislava (Bratislava)

Bratislava undoubtedly has charm, being on the Danube and having a number of interesting buildings and churches in its centre. However, industry around the city, particularly en-route to the camp from the south, presents an ugly picture and gives no hints of the hidden charms. Zlate piesky (golden sands) is part of a large, lakeside sports complex which is also used during the day in summer by local residents. The site is on the edge of town with 200 touring pitches, 120 with electrical connections, on level grass under tall trees. Twenty well equipped and many more simple bungalows hire are spread around the site. Attractive lakeside recreation area also has pedaloes for hire and fitness area in the park. For a night stop or a short stay, if you are looking for a quieter site with fewer facilities, Intercamp may suit.

Facilities

Four toilet blocks, two for campers and two for day visitors, are of marginal quality and may be hard pressed. Two restaurants, one with waiter service, the other self service. Many small snack bars. Shops. Lake for swimming and watersports with large beach area. Table tennis. Minigolf. Children's play areas. Room with billiards and electronic games. Disco.

Open

1 May - 15 October.

At a glance

Welcome & Ambience	✓✓✓	Location	✓✓✓✓✓
Quality of Pitches	✓✓	Range of Facilities	✓✓✓✓

Directions

Follow signs on road no. 61 for Zillina and airport and pick up signs for camp. Zlaté piesky is on the left on entering the sports area, Intercamp is on the right

Charges guide

Per person	SKK 60 - 70
child (4-15 yrs)	SKK 30 - 40
caravan	SKK 80 - 90
motorcaravan	SKK 90 - 140
tent	SKK 30 - 60
electricity	SKK 80

No credit cards.

Reservations

Write to site. Tel: 0744 257 373.
E-mail: kempi@netax.sk

What Slovenia lacks in size it makes up for in exceptional beauty. Situated between Italy, Austria, Hungary and Croatia, it has a diverse landscape with stunning Alps, rivers, forests and the warm Adriatic coast.

With its snow capped Julian Alps and the picturesque Triglav National park that include the beautiful lakes of Bled and Bohinj, and the peaceful Soca River, it is no wonder that the northwest region of Slovenia is so popular. Stretching from the Alps down to the Adriatic coast is the picturesque Karst region, with pretty olive groves and thousands of spectacular underground caves, including the Postojna and Skocjan caves. Although small, the Adriatic coast has several bustling beach towns such as the Italianised Koper resort and the historic port of Piran, with many opportunities for watersports and sunbathing. The capital Ljubljana is centrally located, with Renaissance, Baroque and Art Nouveau architecture, you will find most points of interest are along the Ljubljana river. Heading eastwards the landscape becomes gently rolling hills, and is largely given over to vines (home of Lutomer Riesling). Savinja with its spectacular Alps is the main area for producing wine.

Population

1.9 million

Capital

Ljubljana

Climate

Warm summers, cold winters with snow in the Alps.

Language

Slovene, with German often spoken in the north and Italian in the west.

Currency

Slovene Tolar

Telephone

The country code is 386

Banks

Mon-Fri 8.30-16.30 with a lunch break 12.30-14.00, plus Saturday mornings 8.30-11.30.

Shops

Shops usually open by 8am sometimes 7am. Closing times vary widely.

Public Holidays

New Year 1, 2 Jan; Preseren Day 8 Feb; Easter Monday; Resistance Day 27 Apr; Labour Day 1-2 May; National Day 25 Jun; Assumption; Reformation Day 31 Oct; All Saint's Day; Christmas Day; Independence Day 26 Dec

Motoring

Small but expanding network of motorways radiating from Ljubljana (there may be tolls). Secondary roads often poorly maintained. Tertiary roads are often gravel (known locally as 'white roads' and shown thus on road maps). Road markings and signs are generally good.

Tourist Office

Slovenian Tourist Office
New Barn Farm, Tadlow,
Royston SG8 0EP
Tel: 0870 225 5305
Fax: 01767 631 166
E-mail: info@slovenian-tourism.co.uk
Internet: www.slovenia-tourism.co.uk

THE WORLD FAMOUS POSTOJNA CAVES ARE WELL WORTH A VISIT. GUIDED TOURS BY SPECIAL CAVE TRAINS TAKE YOU THROUGH EXTENSIVE AND MARVELLOUS ROCK FORMATIONS.

SV4210 Camping Sobec

Sobceva cesta 25, 4248 Lesce

Sobec is situated in a valley between the Julian Alps and the Karavanke Mountains, in a pine grove between the Sava Dolinka river and a small lake. It is only three kilometres from Bled and 20 kilometres from the Karavanke Tunnel. There are 450 unmarked pitches on level, grassy fields off tarmac access roads (390 for touring units, all with 16A electricity). Shade is provided by mature pine trees and younger trees separate some pitches. Camping Sobec is surrounded by water - the Sava river borders it on three sides and on the fourth is a small, artificial lake with grassy fields for sunbathing. Some pitches have views over the lake, which has an enclosed area providing safe swimming for children. This site is a good base for an active holiday, since both the Sava Dolinka and the Sava Bohinjka rivers are suitable for canoeing, kayaking, rafting and fishing), whilst the nearby mountains offer challenges for mountain climbing, paragliding and canyoning.

Facilities

Three traditional style toilet blocks (two refurbished, one old) with mainly British style toilets, washbasins in cabins and controllable hot showers. Child-size toilets and basins. Well equiped, attractive baby room. Facilities for disabled visitors. Laundry with sinks, washing machines and dryer. Dishwashing under cover. Motorcaravan service point. Supermarket. Bar/restaurant with stage for live performaces. Playgrounds on grass and stone. Rafting, canyoning and kayaking organised. Mini-club. Tours to Bled and the Narodni National Park organised. Off site: Golf and riding 2 km.

At a glance

Welcome & Ambience	✓✓✓✓✓	Location	✓✓✓✓✓
Quality of Pitches	✓✓✓✓	Range of Facilities	✓✓✓✓

Directions

Site is off the main road from Lesce to Bled and well signed just outside Lesce.

Charges guide

Per person	€ 8,06 - € 9,50
child (7-14 yrs)	€ 6,00 - € 7,02
dog	€ 2,50

Reservations

Write to site in English. Tel: 04 5353 700. E-mail: sobec@siol.net

Open

Easter - 30 September.

SV4235 Kamp Klin

Lepena 1, 5232 Soca

Kamp Klin is next to the confluence of the Soca and Lepenca rivers and is surrounded by mountains. The park is close to the Triglavski National Park and from here it is only a short drive to the highest point of Slovenia, the Triglavski mountain and its beautiful viewpoint with marked walking routes. Being next to two rivers, the site is also a suitable base for fishing, kayaking and rafting. Kamp Klin is privately owned and there is a 'pension' next door, all run by the Zorc family, who serve the local dishes with compe (potatoes), cottage cheese, grilled trout and local salami in the restaurant. The campsite has only 50 pitches, all for tourers and with electricity, on one large, grassy field, connected by a circular, gravel access road. The site is attractively landscaped with flowers and young trees, but this also means there is not much shade. Some pitches are right on the bank of the river (unfenced) and there are beautiful views of the river and the mountains. Like so many Slovenian sites in this area, this is a good holiday base for the active camper.

Facilities

One modern toilet block and a 'portacabin' style unit with toilets and controllable showers. Laundry with sinks. Dishwashing (inside). Bar/restaurant. Play field. Beach volley-ball. Fishing (permit € 60/day). Torch useful. Off site: Riding 500 m. Bicycle hire 10 km.

Open

All year.

At a glance

Welcome & Ambience	✓✓✓✓	Location	✓✓✓✓✓
Quality of Pitches	✓✓✓✓	Range of Facilities	✓✓✓

Directions

Site is on the main Kranjska Gora - Bovec road and is well signed in Soca. Access is via a sharp turn from the main road and over a small bridge that may be difficult for larger units.

Charges guide

Per person	€ 5,50 - € 7,20
child (7-12 yrs)	€ 2,80 - € 3,60
electricity	€ 2,40

Reservations

Write to site in English. Tel: 05 3889 356. E-mail: kampklin@volja.net

SV4360 Camp Smlednik

Dragocajna 14a, 1216 Smlednik

Camp Smlednik is relatively close to the capital, Ljublijana, yet within striking distance of Lake Bled, the Karawanke mountains and Julian Alps. It provides a good touring base, set above the river Sava, and also provides a small, separate enclosure for those who enjoy naturism. Situated beside the peaceful tiny village of Dragocajni, in attractive countryside, the site provides 190 places for tourers each with electricity (6/10A). Although terraced, it is probably better described as large plateau with tall pines and deciduous trees providing some shade. Amongst the many species of birds you have every chance of seeing the Golden Oriole. Near reception and the security barrier is a bar that provides limited food at weekends. Boasting a dartboard, it radiates an atmosphere typical of a British pub and is used by local villagers in the evenings accentuating that feeling. From a grass sunbathing area there is stepped access to the river for swimming. Good size fish can be caught by the angler (licence required). The Sava is excellent for canoeing or kayaking. The naturist area measuring only some 30 x l00 m. accommodates 15 units in a delightful setting adjacent to the river (INF card not required).

Facilities

Three fully equipped sanitary blocks are of varying standards, but it is an adequate and clean provision. In the main camping area a fairly new, solar powered two storey block has free hot showers, the lower half for use within the naturist area. Normally heated showers in the old block are on payment. Dishwashing and laundry sinks. Washing machine. Toilet for disabled visitors (level access). Supermarket at entrance. Bar (all year), limited food at weekends. Two good quality clay tennis courts (charged). Table tennis, basketball and area to kick a ball. Swings for children. River swimming and fishing.

At a glance

Welcome & Ambience	✓✓✓✓	Location	✓✓✓✓✓
Quality of Pitches	✓✓✓✓	Range of Facilities	✓✓✓

Directions

Travelling on road no.1, both Smlednik and the site are well signed. From E61 motorway, Smlednik and site are again well signed at the Vodiice exit.

Charges 2004

Per person	SIT 1300
child (7-14 yrs)	SIT 650
electricity (6-10A)	SIT 700

Reservations

Only necessary for naturist section. Tel: 01362 7002.

Open

1 May - 15 October.

SV4150 Kamp Kamne

Franc Voga, Dovje 9, 4281 Mojstrana

For visitors proceeding down the A1 towards the prime attractions of the twin lakes of Bled and Bohinj, a delightfully informal little site is to be found just outside the village of Mojstrana. Owner Frank Voga opened the site as recently as 1989, on a small terraced orchard. He has steadily developed the facilities, adding a small pool, then a tennis court. The little reception doubles as a bar where locals wander up for a beer and a chat while enjoying the view across the valley of the Julian Alps. The site is popular with walkers as three valleys lead west into the mountains from Mojstrana, including the trail to the ascent of Triglav, at nearly 3,000 metres, the highest point of the Julian Alps.

Facilities

Basic facilities only (classified as third class) but of high quality and well maintained. Reception/bar. Small swimming pool. Tennis court. Frank's English is rather basic, but his daughter Anna is fluent. Off site: Walking trails.

Open

All year.

At a glance

Welcome & Ambience	✓✓✓✓	Location	✓✓✓✓
Quality of Pitches	✓✓✓	Range of Facilities	✓✓✓

Directions

Site is well marked on north side of the A1, just to west of exit for Mojstrana.

Charges guide

Per person	€ 3,50 - € 4,50
child (7-14 yrs)	€ 3,00 - € 3,50
electricity	€ 1,50

Reservations

Contact site: Address: Dovje 9, 64281 Mojstrana. Tel: 064/891 105. Tel: 04 589 1105. E-mail: kamp.kamne@g-kabel.si

SV4310 Camping Adria

Jadranska Cesta 25, 6280 Ankaran

Camping Adria is on the south side of the Milje/Muggia peninsula, right on the shore of the Adriatic Sea and is surrounded by cypress, laurel, olive and fruit trees. It has a concrete promenade with access to the sea, complemented by an Olympic size pool filled with sea water. The site has 500 pitches (250 for tourers), all with 10A electricity, set up on one side of the site close to sea. The remainder of the site is used for holiday bungalows. Pitching is off tarmac access roads, running down to sea and most pitches are between 80 and 90 sq.m. There are six fully serviced pitches for motorcaravans with electricity, water and waste water. Pitches at the beach have beautiful views of the Adriatic and the historic ports of Koper and Izola. This part of the Slovenian Riviera is suitable for a beach holiday and also has much to offer architecturally and culturally. You can visit the Adria hotel (once the Benedictine monastery of Saint Nicholas) and the site organises boat trips to the historic fishing ports of Piran and Portoroz.

Facilities

Five modern toilet blocks with British and Turkish style toilets, open style washbasins (cold water only) and pre-set showers (on payment). Facilities for disabled visitors. Laundry room with sinks. Fridge box hire. Dishwashing (inside). Supermarket. Beach shop. Newspaper kiosk. Bar/restaurant with terrace. Swimming pool (40 x 15 m.) with large slide. Playground on gravel. Playing field. Tennis. Minigolf. Fishing. Basketball. Table tennis. Jetty for mooring boats. Boat launching. Canoe hire. Disco and bowling club. Off site: Historic towns of Koper, Izola, Piran and Portoroz are close.

At a glance

Welcome & Ambience	✓✓✓✓	Location	✓✓✓✓✓
Quality of Pitches	✓✓✓✓	Range of Facilities	✓✓✓✓

Directions

From Koper drive north to Ankaran. Site is immediately on the left after entering Ankaran.

Charges guide

Per person	€ 6,60 - € 8,26
child (under 10 yrs)	€ 2,70 - € 3,30
electricity	€ 2,50
dog	€ 2,10

Reservations

Write to site in English. Tel: 05 6637 350.
E-mail: adria.tp@siol.net

Open

1 May - 30 September.

SV4405 Camping Menina

Varpolje 105, 3332 Recica ob Savinji

The Menina site is in the heart of the 35 kilometres long Upper Savinja Valley, surrounded by 2,500 m. high mountains and unspoilt nature. This site has existed here for 40 years and used to be very popular during socialist times, but was closed at the beginning of the war in 1992. It reopened three years ago and the new, energetic and enthusiastic owner, Jurij Kolenc tells many interesting storys about all that has happened to his country. Menina has 200 pitches, all for touring units, on grassy fields under mature trees and with access from gravel roads. All have 4-10A electricity. The Savinja river runs along one side of the site, but if its water is too cold for swimming, the site also has a lake which can be used for swimming as well. This site is a perfect base for walking or mountain biking in the mountains (a wealth of maps and routes is available from reception). Rafting, canyoning and kayaking, or visits to a fitness studio, sauna or massage salon are organised.

Facilities

The traditional style toilet block has modern fittings with toilets, open plan basins and controllable hot showers. Dishwashing under cover. Bar/restaurant with open air terrace (evenings only) and open air kitchen. Playing field. Fishing. Mountain bike hire. Volleyball. Basketball. Giant chess. Russian bowling. Excursions (52). Live music and gatherings around the camp fire. Off site: Fishing 2 km. Recica and other villages with much culture and folklore are close.

Open

1 April - 15 November.

At a glance

Welcome & Ambience	✓✓✓✓✓	Location	✓✓✓✓✓
Quality of Pitches	✓✓✓	Range of Facilities	✓✓✓

Directions

From Ljubljana take A1 towards Celje. Exit at Trnava and turn north towards Mozirje. Follow signs Recica ob Savinj from there. Continue through Recica to Nizka and follow site signs.

Charges 2005

Per adult	€ 5,00 - € 6,50
child (5-15 yrs)	€ 3,50 - € 4,50
electricity	€ 2,00 - € 2,20
dog	€ 2,00 - € 2,20

Reservations

Possible, but probably not necessary.
Tel: 03 5835 027. E-mail: info@campingmenina.com

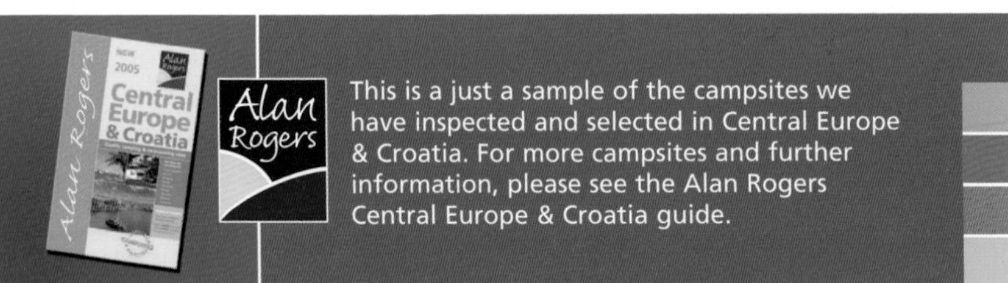

SV4250 Camping Danica Bohinj

Triglavska 60, 4265 Bohinjska Bistrica

For those wanting to visit the famous Bohinj valley, which stretches like a fjord right into the heart of the Julian Alps, there is a choice of two or three campsites. Our choice is the spacious Danica Bohinj site which lies in the valley 3 km. downstream of the lake. Danica occupies a rural site that stretches from the main road leading into Bohinj from Bled to the bank of the newly formed Sava river. It is basically flat meadow, broken up by lines of natural woodland. That this is essentially a site for real campers rather than budget holiday makers is evident from the predominance of tents and touring vans. There are 150 pitches, 135 for touring units, and all with 6A electricity.

Facilities

Two adequate toilet blocks with toilets, open plan washbasins and hot showers. Facilities for disabled visitors. Laundry. Volleyball. Football. Tennis. Small shop. Café. Fishing. Bicycle hire. Organised excursions in the Triglavski National Park. Off site: Riding 5 km.

Open

May - September.

At a glance

Welcome & Ambience	✓✓✓✓	Location	✓✓✓✓
Quality of Pitches	✓✓✓✓	Range of Facilities	✓✓✓✓

Directions

Driving from Bled to Bohinj, the well signed site lies just behind the village of Bohinjska Bistrica on the right-hand (north) side of the road.

Charges 2005

Per person	€ 5,10 - € 7,30
electricity	€ 2,00

Less 10% for stays over 7 days.

Reservations

Contact site. Tel: 04 572 1055.
E-mail: tdbohinj@bohinj.si

SV4330 Camping Pivka Jama

Veliki Otok 50, 6230 Postojna

Postojna is renowned for its extraordinary limestone caves which form one of Slovenia's prime tourist attractions. Pivka Jama is a most convenient site for the visitor, being mid-way between Ljubljana and Piran and only about an hour's pleasant drive from either. The site is deep in what appears to be primeval forest, cleverly cleared to take advantage of the broken limestone forest bedrock. The 300 pitches are not clustered together but nicely segregated under trees and in small clearings, all connected by a neat network of paths and slip-roads. Some level, gravel hardstandings are provided. The facilities are both excellent and extensive and run with obvious pride by enthusiastic staff. It even has its own local caves (the Pivka Jarma) which can spare its visitors the commercialisation of Postojna.

Facilities

Two toilet blocks with very good facilities. Washing machines. Motorcaravan service point. Campers' kitchen with hobs. Supermarket. Swimming pool and paddling pool. Volleyball. Basketball. Tennis. Table tennis. Bicycle hire. Daytrips to Postojna Caves and other excursions organised. Off site: Fishing 5 km. Riding or skiing 10 km.

Open

All year, excl. January.

At a glance

Welcome & Ambience	✓✓✓✓	Location	✓✓✓✓✓
Quality of Pitches	✓✓✓✓	Range of Facilities	✓✓✓

Directions

Site is 5 km. from Postojna. Take the road leading west from Postojna (just off the A10 trunk road) towards the Postojna Cave. Site is well signed.

Charges guide

Per person	€ 9,00
child (7-14 yrs)	€ 7,00
electricity	€ 4,00

Reservations

Contact site Tel: 05 720 39 93.
E-mail: avtokamp.pivka.jama@siol.net

SV4400 Camp Dolina Prebold

Vozlic Tomaz Dolenja vas 147, 3312 Prebold

Prebold is a quiet village about 15 km. west of the large historic town of Celje. It is only a few kilometres from the remarkable Roman necropolis at Sempeter. Dolina is little more than the garden of the house, taking 50 touring units, 15 with electricity. It belongs to Tomaz and Manja Vozlic who look after the site and its guests with loving care. It has been in existence for 40 years and is one of the first private enterprises in the former Yugoslavia. To the south of Prebold lies some of Slovenia's best walking country and to the north lies the upper Savinja valley. It is an easy drive up the Savinja to its spectacular source in the Logar Valley; beyond its semi-circle of 2,000 metre peaks lies Austria.

Facilities

The small, heated toilet block would certainly qualify for Slovenia's 'best loo' award. Washing machine and dryer. Reception with bar in the old stable. Small swimming pool (heated, 1/5-30/9). Sauna. Bicycle hire. Excursions are organised. Off site: Good supermarket and restaurant 200 m. Tennis and indoor pool within 1 km. Fishing 1.5 km.

Open

All year.

At a glance

Welcome & Ambience	✓✓✓✓✓	Location	✓✓✓✓
Quality of Pitches	✓✓✓✓	Range of Facilities	✓✓✓✓

Directions

Site is well signed in a small side street on the northern edge of Prebold. Best reached via a signed exit on the Ljubljana - Celje motorway.

Charges 2005

Per person	SIT 1500
electricity (6A)	SIT 800
dog	SIT 500

No credit cards.

Reservations

Contact site. Tel: 041 79 05 90.
E-mail: dolina@email.si

One of the largest countries in Europe with glorious beaches, a fantastic sunshine record, vibrant towns and laid back sleepy villages, plusa diversity of landscape, culture and artistic traditions, Spain has all the ingredients for a great holiday.

Spain has a huge choice of beach resorts to choose from. With charming villages and attractive resorts, the Costa Brava boasts spectacular scenery with towering cliffs and sheltered coves. There are plenty of lively resorts, including Lloret, Tossa and Calella, plus several quieter ones. Further along the east coast, the Costa del Azahar stretches from Vinaros to Almanzora, with the great port of Valencia in the middle. Orange groves abound. The central section of the coastline, the Costa Blanca, has 170 miles or so of silvery-white beaches. Benidorm is the most popular resort. The Costa del Sol lies in the south, home to more beaches and brilliant sunshine, whilst in the north the Costa Verde is largely unspoiled, with clean water, sandy beaches and rocky coves against a backdrop of mountains.

Beaches and sunshine aside, Spain also has plenty of great cities and towns to explore, including Barcelona, Valencia, Seville, Madrid, Toledo and Bilbao, all offering an array of sights, galleries and museums.

Population

39.5 million

Capital

Madrid

Climate

Spain has a very varied climate. The north is temperate with most of the rainfall; dry and very hot in the centre; subtropical along the Mediterranean

Language

Castilian Spanish is spoken by most people with Catalan (northeast), Basque (north) and Galician (northwest) used in their respective areas

Currency

The Euro

Telephone

The country code is 00 34

Banks

Mon-Fri 09.00-14.00. Sat 09.00-13.00

Shops

Mon-Sat 09.00-13.00/14.00 and 15.00/16.00-19.30/20.00. Many close later

Public Holidays

New Year; Epiphany; Saint's Day 19 Mar; Maundy Thurs; Good Fri; Easter Mon; Labour Day; Saint's Day 25 July; Assumption 15 Aug; National Day 12 Oct; All Saints Day 1 Nov; Constitution Day 6 Dec; Immaculate Conception 8 Dec; Christmas Day

Motoring

The surface of the main roads is on the whole good, although secondary roads in some rural areas can be rough and winding and have slow, horse drawn traffic. Tolls are payable on certain roads and for the Cadi Tunnel, Vallvidrera Tunnel (Barcelona) and the Tunnel de Garraf on the A16

Tourist Office

Spanish National Tourist Office,
22/23 Manchester Square, London W1U 3PX
Tel: 020 7486 8077
Fax: 020 7486 8034
Email: info.londres@tourspain.es
Internet: http://www.tourspain.es

THERE IS MORE TO SPANISH CUSINE THAN PAELLA. HEAD TO YOUR LOCAL TAPAS BAR TO SAMPLE THE DELICIOUS REGIONAL SPECIALITIES ON OFFER.

ES8020 Camping Internacional de Amberes

Playa de la Rubina, 17487 Empúria-brava (Girona)

Situated in the 'Venice of Spain', Empuria Brava is interlaced with inland waterways and canals, where many residents and holiday-makers moor their boats directly outside their homes on the canal banks. Internacional Amberes is a large friendly site 50 m. from the wide, sandy beach, which is bordered on the east and west by the waterway canals (no access into them from the beach, only by car on the main road). The site can arrange temporary moorings for boats at Empuria Brava on request. The sea breeze here appears regularly during the afternoon so watersports are very good and hire facilities are available. Amberes is a surprisingly pretty and hospitable site where people seem to make friends easily and get to know other campers and the staff. The site has 798 touring pitches, most enjoying some shade from strategically placed trees. All have electricity and water connections. The restaurant and bar are close to the site entrance and the cuisine is so popular that locals use it too. Unusually the swimming pool is on an elevated terrace, raised out of view of most onlookers with sunbathing areas and a small children's pool adjoining. A shallow river runs through the site and the children can amuse themselves catching the colourful crawfish that abound here. A 'secret garden' style minigolf course is special to this site.

Facilities

Toilet facilities are in five fully equipped and recently renovated blocks. Washing machines. Motorcaravan services. Supermarket. Restaurant/bar. Disco bar and restaurant. Takeaway. Pizzeria. Watersports - windsurfing school. Boat moorings. Organised sports activities, children's programmes and entertainment. Swimming pool. Playgrounds. Football. Table tennis. Tennis. Volleyball. Apartments. Off site: Bicycle hire, riding and fishing 500 m. Golf 12 km.

Open

1 April - 15 October.

At a glance

Welcome & Ambience	✓✓✓✓	Location	✓✓✓✓✓
Quality of Pitches	✓✓✓✓	Range of Facilities	✓✓✓✓

Directions

Empuria Brava is reached by the C260 Figueres - Roses road. Site is signed from main roundabout leading into Empuria Brava but it is easier to continue to second roundabout, turn towards Empuria Brava and follow road for some distance. Watch for site entrance on left on one of the many bends.

Charges 2005

Per person over 3 yrs	€ 3,00
pitch incl. electricity (55 sq.m.)	€ 7,80 - € 20,00
pitch 70 sq.m.	€ 10,00 - € 23,20
pitch 85 sq.m.	€ 11,80 - € 25,10
pitch 100 sq.m.	€ 13,00 - € 28,00

Less 20% for pensioners for stays of 15 days or over in low seasons.

Reservations

Contact site for booking form. Tel: 972 450 507. E-mail: info@inter-amberes.com

ES8040 Camping Las Dunas

Ctra Sant Marti d'Empuries - Sant Pere, 17470 Sant Pere Pescador (Girona)

Las Dunas is an extremely large, impressive and well organised site with many on site activities and an ambitious programme of improvements. It has direct access to a superb sandy beach that stretches along the site for nearly one kilometre with a windsurfing school and beach bar. There is also a much used swimming pool with large double children's pools. Las Dunas is very large, with 1,500 individual hedged pitches of around 100 sq.m. laid out on flat ground in long, regular parallel rows. Electrical connections are provided on all pitches and shade is available in some parts of the site. Much effort has gone into planting palms and new trees here and the results are very attractive (find the 600 year old olive tree - it is easier than you think). Pitches are usually available, even in the main season. The large restaurant and bar have spacious terraces overlooking the pools and you can enjoy a very pleasant more secluded cavern styled pub. A magnificent disco club is close by in a soundproof building (although people returning from this during the night can be a problem for pitches in the central area of the site). With free quality entertainment of all types in season and positive security arrangements, this is a great site for families with teenagers. Everything is provided on site so you don't need to leave it during your stay.

Facilities

Five excellent large toilet blocks (with cleaners 07.00-21,00) have British style toilets, controllable hot showers and washbasins in cabins. One block has underfloor heating and automatic doors for cooler weather. Excellent facilities for youngsters, babies and disabled people. Laundry facilities. Motorcaravan services. Extensive supermarket with bakery, good butcher and other shops. Large bar with terrace. Large restaurant. Takeaway. Ice-cream parlour. Beach bar in main season. Disco club. Swimming pool (30 x 14 m) with children's pool. Playgrounds. Tennis. Minigolf. Football and rugby pitches. Basketball. Boule. Volleyball. Sailing and windsurfing school and other watersports. Organised programme of events - sports, children's games, evening shows, partly in English (15/6-31/8). Exchange facilities .ATM. Safety deposit. Torches required in some areas.

At a glance

Welcome & Ambience	✓✓✓✓	Location	✓✓✓✓✓
Quality of Pitches	✓✓✓✓	Range of Facilities	✓✓✓✓✓

Directions

From A7 take exit 5 towards L'Escala (G1623) and turn north 2 km. before reaching L'Escala at sign to Sant Marti d'Ampurias. Site well signed on this road.

Charges 2004

Per person	€ 3,00
child (2-10 yrs)	€ 2,50
standard pitch incl. electricity	€ 13,00 - € 38,00
water and drainage	€ 1,00 - € 3,00
dog (one section only)	€ 3,00 - € 4,00

All plus 7% VAT.

Reservations

Made for numbered pitches with deposit and fee. Address for information: Apdo. de Correus 23, 17130 La Escala (Girona). Tel: 972 521 717. E-mail: info@campinglasdunas.com

Open

9 May - 25 September.

Spain

ES8030 Camping Nautic Almata

Ctra Sant Pere Pescador, km 11.6, 17486 Castelló d'Empuries (Girona)

Situated in the Bay of Roses, south of Empuria Brava and beside the Parc Natural dels Aiguamolls de l'Empordá, this is a site of particular interest for nature lovers (especially bird watchers). Beautifully laid out, it is arranged around the river and waterways, so will suit those who like to camp close to water or and those who enjoy watersports and boating. It is worth visiting because of its unusual aspects and the feeling of being on the canals, as well as being a high quality beach-side site. As you drive through the natural park to the site watch for the warning signs for frogs on the road and enjoy the wild flamingos alongside the road. It is a large site with 1,109 well kept, large, numbered pitches, all with electricity and on flat, sandy ground. There are some pitches right on the beach. The name no doubt derives from the fact that boats can be tied up at the small marina within the site and a slipway also gives access to a river and thence to the sea. Throughout the season there is a varied entertainment programme for children and adults. The facilities on this site are impressive. Some tour operators use the site.

Facilities

Sanitary blocks all of a high standard, attractively decorated. include some en-suite showers with basins, taps to draw hot water for dishwashing, laundry sinks and baby baths. Good facilities for disabled visitors and ramps where necessary. Washing machines. Gas supplies. Excellent supermarket. Restaurant and bar (recently refurbished), rotisserie and pizzeria near pool. Two separate bars by beach where discos held in main season. Water-ski and windsurfing schools. 300 sq. m. swimming pool. Tennis, squash, volleyball, fronton all free. Minigolf. Games room with pool and table tennis. Extensive riding tuition with own stables and stud. Children's play park (near river). Car, motorcycle and bicycle hire. Hairdresser. Torches are useful near beach. Off site: National Park and wetlands around site. Canal trips 18 km. Aquatic Park 20 km. Adventure sports 40 km. Excursions to Barcelona, Monserrat, Andorra and Dahli's museum.

At a glance

Welcome & Ambience	✓✓✓✓✓	Location	✓✓✓✓✓
Quality of Pitches	✓✓✓✓✓	Range of Facilities	✓✓✓✓✓

Directions

Site is signed at 26 km. marker on C252 between Castello d'Empuries and Vildemat, then 7 km. to site. Alternatively, on San Pescador - Castello d'Empuries road head north and site is signed on right.

Charges 2005

Per pitch	€ 18,00 - € 36,00
person (over 3 yrs)	€ 1,65 - € 3,30
dog	€ 3,85 - € 4,90
boat or jetski	€ 6,30 - € 8,50

All plus 7% VAT. No credit cards.

Reservations

Write to site. Tel: 972 454 477. E-mail: info@almata.com

Open

14 May - 18 September, including all facilities.

ES8060 Camping La Ballena Alegre 2

17470 Sant Pere Pescador (Girona)

La Ballena Alegre 2 is partly in a lightly wooded setting, partly open, and with some 1,800 m. of frontage directly onto an excellent beach of soft golden sand (which is cleaned daily). They claim that none of the 1,629 pitches is more than 100 m. from the beach. The site has won Spanish tourist board awards and is keen on ecological fitness. The grass pitches are individually numbered and of decent size (over 200 are 100 sq.m.). Electricity (5A) is available in all parts and there are 70 fully serviced pitches. Restaurant and bar areas are beside the pleasant terraced pool complex (four pools including a children's pool). For those who wish to drink and snack late there is a pub open until 03.00 hrs. The soundproof disco has a covered approach and is firmly managed - a discount card doubles for easy identification of customers. A little train ferries people along the length of the site. Activities include a well managed watersports centre, with sub-aqua, windsurfing and kite surfing, where equipment can be hired and lessons taken. A comprehensive open air fitness centre is near the beach and there is a full entertainment programme all season. An area across the road provides extra parking and sports activities. A great site for families.

Facilities

All seven toilet blocks have been refurbished to a very high standard and are well maintained. These feature large pivoting doors for showers, wash cabins, etc, special low facilities for children, baby baths and facilities for disabled campers. Launderette. Motorcaravan services. Gas supplies. Supermarket. Chemist. Bar and self-service restaurant. Full restaurant (evenings all season). Takeaway. 'Croissanterie'. Pizzeria and beach bar in high season. Swimming pool complex (all season). Three tennis courts. Table tennis. Watersports centre. Fitness centre. Bicycle hire. Playgrounds. Sound proofed disco. Dancing twice weekly and organised activities, sports, entertainment, etc. all season but it is generally a quiet site. Safe deposit. Cash point. Resident doctor and site ambulance. Car wash. Internet point. Torches useful in beach areas. Off site: Go-karting nearby with bus service. Fishing 300 m. Riding 2 km.

At a glance

Welcome & Ambience	✓✓✓✓	Location	✓✓✓✓✓
Quality of Pitches	✓✓✓✓	Range of Facilities	✓✓✓✓✓

Directions

From A7 Figueres - Girona autopista take exit 5 to L'Escala GI 623 for 18.5 km. At roundabout take sign to Sant Marti d'Empúries and follow camp signs. Access has now been entirely asphalted.

Charges 2004

Per person	€ 3,30
child (3-9 yrs)	€ 2,50
pitch incl. electricity	€ 14,90 - € 35,00
serviced pitch plus	€ 6,00 - € 11,00
dog (one section only)	€ 2,10 - € 4,00

All plus 7% VAT. Discount of 10% on pitch charge for pensioners all season. No credit cards.

Reservations

Made with deposit (€ 200), min. 10 days 10/7-10/8. Winter address: Ave. Roma 12, 08015 Barcelona. Tel: 902 510 520. E-mail: infb2@ballena-alegre.com

Open

15 May - 27 September.

3 km of beach in "Els Aiguamolls de l'Empordà" nature reserve
Nautic Almata
Camping Caravaning
Private jetty with direct access to the sea
50% DISCOUNT LOW SEASON
15% DISCOUNT MEDIUM SEASON
lmata
Camping Nautic Almata
E-17486 Castelló d'Empúries (Girona) Spain
Tel.(34)972 454477-Fax (34) 972 454686
E-Mail: info@almata.com
Internet: http://www.almata.com
1st CLASS
F La Jonquera Figueres Castelló d'Empúries Sant Pere Pescador

ES8050 Camping Aquarius

Ctra de la Platja s/n, 17470 Sant Pere Pescador (Girona)

A smart and efficient family site, Aquarius has direct access to a quiet sandy beach that slopes gently and provides good bathing (the sea is shallow for quite a long way out). The site is ideal for those who really like sun and sea, with a quiet situation. One third of the site has good shade with a park-like atmosphere with the great variety of plants here being carefully labelled (Mr Rupp the owner is an enthusiast). An extension with less shade provided an opportunity to enlarge the pitches and they are now all at least 70-100 sq.m. which is good for Spain. There are 447 numbered pitches, all with electrical connections (6A). Only five pitches are not for touring. The owner has an architectural background and a wealth of knowledge on the whole Catalan area and culture. He has written a booklet of suggested tours (from reception). The whole family is justifiably proud of their most attractive site and they continually make improvements. The fountain at the entrance, the fishponds and the water features in the restaurant are soothing and pleasing. A small stage close to the restaurant is used for live entertainment in season. The spotless beach bar complex with shaded terraces and minigolf has marvellous views over the Bay of Roses. The 'Surf Center' with rentals, school and shop is ideal for enthusiasts and beginners alike.

Facilities

Attractively tiled, fully equipped, large toilet blocks provide some cabins for each sex. Excellent facilities for disabled people, plus baths for children and hot water for sinks. A superb new block has under-floor heating and features family cabins with showers and basins. Laundry facilities. Gas supplies. Car wash. Motorcaravan services. Full size refrigerators. Supermarket with butcher. Pleasant restaurant and bar with terrace. Takeaway. Children's play centre (with qualified attendant), playground near the beach and games hall. TV room with giant screen and ample comfortable seating. 'Surf Center'. Table tennis. Volleyball. Minigolf. Bicycle hire. Football field. Boules. Barbecue and dance once weekly when numbers justify. Security boxes. Exchange facilities. ATM. Electronic games. Dogs are accepted in one section. (Note: no pool). Off site: Fishing and boat launching 3 km. Riding 6 km. Golf 15 km.

At a glance

Welcome & Ambience	✓✓✓✓	Location	✓✓✓✓✓
Quality of Pitches	✓✓✓	Range of Facilities	✓✓✓

Directions

From A7 motorway take exit 3 (Figueres/Roses) and take N11 south to join C260 towards Roses. At roundabout near Castello d'Empuries take road to and through Sant Pere Pescador. Site signed to left shortly after bridge south of town.

Charges 2005

Per person	€ 2,75 - € 3,30
child (2-12 yrs)	free - € 2,40
pitch acc. to season and facilities	€ 6,80 - € 33,35
electricity	€ 2,50

All plus 7% VAT. No credit cards.

Reservations

Made for any length with £50 deposit and £15 fee. (you are strongly advised to book early for any pitch near the beach). Tel: 972 520 003. E-mail: camping@aquarius.es

Open

All year except 11 January - 14 March.

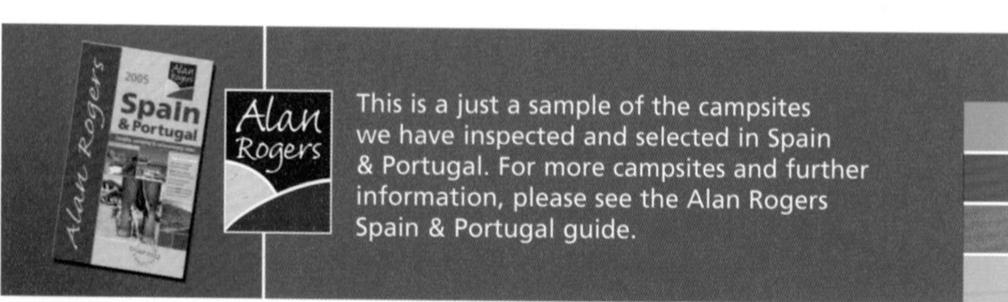

This is a just a sample of the campsites we have inspected and selected in Spain & Portugal. For more campsites and further information, please see the Alan Rogers Spain & Portugal guide.

ES8012 Camping Mas Nou

Ctra Figueres - Roses, km 38, 17486 Castelló d'Empúries (Girona)

Some two kilometres from the sea on the Costa Brava, this is a surprisingly tranquil site. Split into two parts, one contains pitches and sanitary blocks and the other houses the impressive leisure complex. There are 450 neat, level and marked pitches on grass and sand, a minimum of 70 sq.m. but most 80-100 sq.m, and 300 with electrical connections (6/10A). The leisure complex is 80 metres from the main site across a very quiet road and features a huge L-shaped swimming pool with a paddling area. A formal restaurant has ajoining bar, pleasant terrace crêperie and rotisseria under palms. Another barbecue-rotisseria in another part of the site offers takeaway meals (in season). The site owns the large souvenir shop on the entrance road. There are many traditional bargains here and it is worth having a good look around as the prices are extremely good. Lots of time and money goes into the cleanliness of this site and it is good very for families. Ask about the origin of the site coat of arms. The Bay of Roses and the Medes islands have a natural beauty and a visit to Dali's house or the museum (the house is fascinating) will prove he was not just a surrealist painter.

Facilities

Three excellent, fully equipped sanitary blocks include baby baths, good facilities for disabled visitors. These are amongst the best we have seen. Dishwashing and laundry sinks. Washing machines. Supermarket and other shops close by. Bar/restaurant. Takeaway. Swimming pool with life guard (from 1/6). Tennis. Minigolf. Basketball. Volleyball. Football. Mini club in dedicated building(July/Aug). Table tennis. Children's playground. Electronic games.
Off site: Riding 1.5 km. Fishing or bicycle hire 2 km. Beach 2.5 km. National Park. Aquatic Park. Romanica tour of famous local churches.

Open

12 April - 28 September.

At a glance

Welcome & Ambience	✓✓✓✓✓	Location	✓✓✓✓✓
Quality of Pitches	✓✓✓✓✓	Range of Facilities	✓✓✓✓✓

Directions

From A7 use exit 3. Mas Nou is 2 km. east of Castelló d'Empúries, on the Roses road, some 10 km. from Figueres.

Charges 2005

Per person	€ 3,75 - € 5,95
child (4-11 yrs)	€ 3,15 - € 4,20
caravan or tent	€ 3,75 - € 5,95
car or motorcycle	€ 3,75 - € 5,95
motorcaravan	€ 7,50 - € 11,90
electricity	€ 2,75 - € 3,20

All plus 7% VAT.

Reservations

Write to site. Tel: 972 454 175.
E-mail: info@campingmasnou.com

Spain

ES8074 Camping Paradis

Avenida de Montgó 260, 17130 L'Escala (Girona)

If you prefer a quieter site out of the very busy resort of L'Escala then this site is an excellent option. This large, friendly, family run site has a dynamic owner Marti, who is a most pleasant man with excellent English and very keen to help. The site is divided by the beach access road and has its own private access to the very safe and unspoilt beach. The site has 646 pitches, all with electricity (10A), some on sloping ground although the pitches themselves tend to be flat. Established pine trees provide shade for most places with more coverage on the western side of the site. Non-stop maintenance ensures that all facilities at this site are of a high standard. There are three swimming pools, the largest with an idyllic and most unusual setting on the top of a cliff overlooking the Bay of Roses. The site operates its own well equipped sub-aqua diving school and campers can experience a free diving experience in the pool or more adventurous coastal diving where appropriate. A CCTV security system monitors the pools and general security from a purpose built centre.

Facilities

Modern, fully equipped sanitary blocks are kept very clean. Washing machines and dryers. Shop (1/4-30/9). Extensive modern complex of restaurants, bars and takeaways (1/4-30/9). Takeaway(1/4-15/9). Swimming pools (1/5-20/10). Pool bar. Play areas. Fishing. Basketball, volleyball and badminton. Kayak hire. Sub aqua school. Organised activities for children in high season. ATM machine. Private access to beach. Off site: Cala Montgo beach 100 m. with a charming bay of soft sand offering all manner of watersports, pretty restaurants and a disco in season. Road train service to town centre from outside site. Riding 2 km. Golf 10 km.

At a glance

Welcome & Ambience	✓✓✓✓✓	Location	✓✓✓✓✓
Quality of Pitches	✓✓✓✓✓	Range of Facilities	✓✓✓✓✓

Directions

Leave autopista A7 at exit 5 heading for Viladimat, then L'Escala. Site is well signed from town centre.

Charges 2005

Per person	€ 2,70 - € 4,58
child (3-9 yrs)	€ 1,92 - € 3,22
pitch	€ 10,40 - € 21,58
electricity	€ 3,27

Plus 7% VAT. No credit cards.

Reservations

Advisable in high season. Tel: 972 770 200. E-mail: info@campingparadis.com

Open

19 March - 14 October.

ES8035 Camping L'Amfora

Avenida Josep Tarradellas 2, 17470 Sant Pere Pescador (Girona)

This is a large, friendly family site with a Greek theme, which is manifested mainly in the restaurant and pool areas. The site is clean and well kept and the owner is keen to operate in an environmentally friendly way. There are 850 pitches (730 for touring), all with 10A electrical connections and most with a water tap, on level grass with small trees and shrubs. Of these, 64 pitches are large (180 sq.m.) and made for two units per pitch, each with an individual sanitary facility (toilet, shower and washbasin). Some 200 more recently developed pitches have limited shade as yet. An inviting terraced bar and self-service restaurant overlook three large swimming pools (one for children) and a new one with two water slides. Ambitious evening entertainment (pub, disco, shows) and children's animation are organised in season and a choice of watersports activities is available on the beach.

Facilities

In addition to the individual units, the two main sanitary blocks (one heated) offer free hot water, washbasins in cabins, hairdryers and baby rooms. There is extra provision near the pool area. Access is good for disabled visitors. Laundry facilities. Supermarket. Terraced bar, self service and waiter service restaurants, takeaway and pizza service. Restaurant and bar on the beach with limited menu (high season). Disco-bar for the young. Swimming pools (1/5-30/9). Table tennis. Tennis courts. Bicycle hire. Minigolf. Football. Volleyball. Playground. Entertainment and organised activities for children. Evening shows. Windsurfing school. Sailing. Fishing. Doctor daily in season. Exchange facilities. Internet point. Car wash. Torches required in beach areas. Off site: Boat laumching 1 km. Riding 6 km. Golf 15 km.

Open

19 March - 30 September.

At a glance

Welcome & Ambience	✓✓✓✓	Location	✓✓✓✓✓
Quality of Pitches	✓✓✓✓	Range of Facilities	✓✓✓✓✓

Directions

From A7 motorway take exit 3 (Figueres/Roses) on N-11 towards Girona/Barcelona. Exit on C260 for Figueres/Roses towards Roses and, at roundabout near Castello d'Empuries turn right to Sant Pere Pescador. Site is signed through town.

Charges 2005

Per person	€ 3,32 - € 4,28
child (2-9 yrs)	free - € 3,42
pitch (100 sq.m.)	€ 13,05 - € 33,12
with individual sanitary facilities	€ 19,00 - € 48,00
dog	€ 1,30 - € 3,60

Electricity (10A) included. Plus 7% VAT. Discounts for pensioners for longer stays. No credit cards.

Reservations

Made with deposit (€ 61) and fee (€ 15.03); write to site. Tel: 972 520 540. E-mail: info@campingamfora.com

ES8120 Kim's Camping

Font d'en Xeco 1, 17211 Llafranc (Girona)

This attractive, terraced site is arranged on the wooded slopes of a narrow valley leading to the sea and there are many trees including huge eucalyptus. A steep lower area rises to a very pleasant plateau where all the amenities are located. There are 350 grassy and partly shaded pitches, all with electric hook-ups (6A). Many of the larger pitches are on the plateau from which great views can be enjoyed, whilst those on the terraces are connected by winding drives, narrow in places. The site has an excellent swimming pool (with lifeguard) and children's pool, a bar, and a pleasant restaurant with 'al fresco' eating. There are high standards of cleanliness and efficiency. The site is under 1 km. from the resort of Llafranc. This is a pleasant place for holidays where you can enjoy the bustling atmosphere of the village and beach, while staying in a quieter environment. Entertainment is provided in high season and visits to local sub-aqua schools for all levels of diving can be arranged. There is an outstanding view along the coastline from Cap Sebastian close by. English is spoken by the very friendly management and staff.

Facilities

Sanitary provision is adequate and includes a small brand new block and toilet facilities for disabled visitors. Laundry facilities. Motorcaravan services. Gas. Good shop. Bar. Bakery. Cafe/restaurant (15/6-20/9). TV room. Swimming pools. Excursions arranged. Play areas and kid's club. Torches required. Off site: Fishing, Glass bottomed boat in Llafranc. Bicycle hire 500 m. Riding 4 km. Golf 9 km.

Open

Easter - 30 September.

At a glance

Welcome & Ambience	✓✓✓✓	Location	✓✓✓✓
Quality of Pitches	✓✓✓	Range of Facilities	✓✓✓✓

Directions

Llafranc is southeast of Palafrugell. Turn off the Palafrugell - Tamariu road at turn (GIV 6542) signed 'Llafranc'. Site is on right 1 km. further on.

Charges 2004

Per person	€ 2,50 - € 6,00
child (3-10 yrs)	free - € 3,00
pitch incl. electricity	€ 12,00 - € 25,00

Plus 7% VAT. Discounts for long stays and for senior citizens.

Reservations

Made with deposit (€ 90). Tel: 972 301 156. E-mail: info@campingkims.com

ES8080 Camping El Delfin Verde

Ctra de Torroella de Montgri, 17257 Torroella de Montgri (Girona)

A large, popular and high quality site in a quiet location, El Delfin Verde has its own long beach along its frontage. A feature of the site is an attractive large pool in the shape of a dolphin with a total area of 1,800 sq.m. An elevated area with a large bar and full restaurant with wonderful views over the huge pool. This is a large site with nearly 6,000 visitors at peak times, well managed with friendly staff. Level grass pitches nearer the beach are marked and many are separated by small fences and new hedges. All have electricity and there is shade in some of the older parts. El Delfin Verde is a large and cheerful holiday site with many good facilities, sports and a free family entertainment programme in season.

Facilities

Six excellent large toilet blocks plus a seventh smaller block have fully controllable showers using desalinated water and some washbasins in cabins. Laundry facilities. Motorcaravan services. Supermarket and other shops. Swimming pools. Two restaurants, grills and pizzerias. Three bars. Large sports area. Dancing and floor shows weekly in season. Disco. Excursions. General room with TV. Video room. Games room. Bicycle hire. Minigolf. Playground. Trampolines. Badminton. Fishing. Hairdresser. Car repairs. Gas. Dogs not accepted in high season (11/7-14/8).
Off site: Golf 4 km (20% discount). Riding 4 km.

At a glance

Welcome & Ambience	✓✓✓	Location	✓✓✓✓
Quality of Pitches	✓✓✓	Range of Facilities	✓✓✓✓✓

Directions

Site has a long approach road leading off the C31 (Torroella de Montgri-Palafrugell) east of Girona.

Charges 2005

Per person	€ 3,50
child (2-9 yrs)	€ 3,00
pitch incl. electricity	€ 13,00 - € 38,00

Plus 7% VAT. Discounts on low season long stays.

Reservations

Write (all year) with deposit (€ 91) to Apdo. 43, 17257 Torroella de Montgri. Tel: 972 758 454. E-mail: info@eldelfinverde.com

Open

19 March - 16 October, incl. all amenities.

ES8072 Camping Les Medes

Paratge Camp De L'Arbre, 17258 L'Estartit (Girona)

Les Medes is different from some of the 'all singing, all dancing' sites so popular along this coast and the friendly family of Pla-Coll are rightly proud of their award winning site. Set back from busy L'Estartit itself, it is only 800 metres to the nearest beach and a little train runs from near the site (June - Sept) to the town. With just 172 pitches, the site is small enough for the owners to know their visitors and, being campers themselves, they have been careful in planning their top class facilities. The level, grassy pitches range in size from 60-80 sq.m. depending on your unit. All have electricity and the larger ones (around half) also have water and drainage. All are clearly marked in rows, but with no separation other than by the deciduous trees which provide summer shade. A cheery children's pool with fountains is behind the unusually shaped pool ringed by palms. This is part of an attractively landscaped feature with a false island, producing a relaxing atmosphere in front of the old Catalan farmhouse buildings. The open air dance floor has music twice weekly (in season). A classy indoor pool (heated) with sauna and solarium and good access for disabled campers is a great option out of high season. The Medes islands are very pretty and worth exploring or a bad weather day could be used to visit Salvador Dali's amazing house.

Facilities

Two modern, spacious sanitary blocks, can be heated and are extremely well maintained, providing washbasins in private cabins, top class facilities for disabled people and baby baths. Washing machines and dryer. Dishwashing and laundry sinks. Motorcaravan services. Bar with TV and snacks (all year). Restaurant (1/4-31/10). Shop (all year, but only basics in winter). Outdoor swimming pool and paddling pool (15/6-15/9) with drinks stall. Indoor pool with sauna, solarium (15/9-15/6). Masseur. Play area. Indoor children's area. TV room. Internet terminals. Excursions organised in July/Aug. Diving activities arranged. Giant chess. Table tennis. Volleyball. Boules. Quality information folder on arrival. Bicycle hire. Tours arranged. Dogs accepted in parts of two low season periods - check with the site. Environmentally friendly. Torches are useful. Off site: Riding 400 m. Fishing 800 m. Nearest beach 800 m. Medes Natural Reserve 1.5 km. Estartit 2 km. Golf 8 km.

At a glance

Welcome & Ambience	✓✓✓✓✓	Location	✓✓✓✓✓
Quality of Pitches	✓✓✓✓✓	Range of Facilities	✓✓✓✓✓

Directions

Site is signed from the main Torroella de Montgri - L'Estartit road GE641. Turn right after Camping Castel Montgri, at Joc's hamburger/pizzeria and follow signs.

Charges 2005

Per person	€ 6,00
child (0-10 yrs)	€ 4,30
pitch	€ 13,50
electricity	€ 3,50

All plus 7% VAT. Discounts outside high season and special offers for low season longer stays. No credit cards.

Reservations

Advised for July/Aug. Write to site with € 31 deposit. Tel: 972 751 805. E-mail: info@campingslesmedes.com

Open

All year except November.

ES8090 Camping Cypsela

Ctra de Pals - Platja de Pals, 17256 Platja de Pals (Girona)

This impressive, de-luxe site with lush vegetation and trees has many striking features, one of which is the sumptuous complex of sport facilities and amenities near the entrance. This provides a fine large swimming pool, a good children's pool and playgrounds, two excellent squash courts, a tennis court, fitness room, and other entertainment rooms. There is a playroom with mini-club for children and organised entertainment (including video screen), an amusements room with pool tables, football tables, video games, and a luxurious air conditioned lounge. The 'Les Moreres' is a pleasant al fresco restaurant offering a varied menu plus good wines (it can become very busy). Another indoor restaurant offers a similar excellent service. You have the choice of a smart bar or the air conditioned cocktail bar. The mainpart of the camping area is pinewood, with 661 clearly marked touring pitches on sandy gravel, all with electricity and some with full facilities. The 202 'Elite' pitches of 120 sq.m. are impressive. If you wish to travel to the beach there is a regular free bus service from the site. Cypsela is a busy, well administered site, only 2 km. from the sea, which we can thoroughly recommend, especially for families. It is very efficiently run, with good quality fixtures and fittings, all kept clean and maintained to a high standard. The gates are closed at night. Several tour operators use the site (299 pitches).

Facilities

Four stylish sanitary 'houses' are of excellent quality with comprehensive cleaning schedules. Using solar heating, three have washbasins in cabins and three have amazing children's rooms. Facilites for disabled people are superb. Serviced launderette. Ironing. Supermarket and other shops. Restaurant, cafeteria and takeaway. Bar. Hairdresser. Swimming pools. Tennis. Squash. Table tennis. Football field. Minigolf. Fitness room. Air conditioned social/TV room. Barbecue and party area. Children's club. Comprehensive animation programme. Organised sports and games activities. Games room. Air conditioned telephone parlour. Business and internet centre. Doctor always on site; well equipped treatment room. Car wash. Gas supplies. ATM. Dogs are not accepted. Off site: Bicycle hire 150 m. Golf 1 km. Fishing 2 km.

At a glance

Welcome & Ambience	✓✓✓✓✓	Location	✓✓✓✓
Quality of Pitches	✓✓✓✓	Range of Facilities	✓✓✓✓✓

Directions

Cypsela is on the EN6502 road to Platja de Pals, leaving the C31 (Figueres - Palamos) road at roundavout near Pals.

Charges 2004

Per person	€ 5,30
child (2-10 yrs)	€ 4,25
pitch acc. to season and services	€ 16,47 - € 47,69

Reservations

Contact site. Tel: 972 667 696.
E-mail: info@cypsela.com

Open

15 May - 26 September.

ES8103 Camping El Maset

Playa de Sa Riera, 17255 Begur (Girona)

A delightful little gem of a site in lovely surroundings, El Maset has 116 pitches, of which just 20 are for caravans or motorcaravans (the site reports there are some larger pitches for 2005), the remainder suitable only for tents. The owner of some 40 years, Senor Juan Perez is delightful, as is his secretary Josaphine, and longer stay customers may be presented with a memento of their visit. The site entrance is steep and access to the caravan pitches can be quite tricky. However, a new road has been cut out of the hillside and the owner's son will tow your caravan to your pitch. All these pitches have electricity, water and drainage with some shade. Access to the tent pitches, which are more shaded on attractive rock-walled terraces on the hillside, seems quite straightforward, with parking for cars not too far away - of necessity the pitches are fairly small. All steep terraced pitches are safely fenced for children. For a small site the amenities are quite extensive, including an unusual elliptical shaped swimming pool. A bar and very homely restaurant offering excellent food, with a terrace giving very pleasant views over the pool and towards the other side of the valley. This small site provides the standard of service normally associated with the very best of the larger sites. It is situated in the tiny resort of Sa Riera with access to the beach (300 m), in a beautiful protected bay with traditional fishing boats taking up one end of the sand. Begur, with its beautiful, small, quite unspoilt bay and beach, is 10 minutes by car.

Facilities

Sanitary facilities are superb with marble tops, hair and hand dryers and soap. In three small blocks and very clean, they include baby facilities. Washing machines and dryers. Unit for disabled campers. Bar/restaurant, takeaway (all season). Shop (from May). Swimming pool (all season). Solarium. Play area. Football and basketball. Excellent games room. Internet point. Dogs not accepted. Off site: Fishing 300 m. Golf and bicycle hire 1 km. Riding 8 km.

Open

2 April - 25 September.

At a glance

Welcome & Ambience	✓✓✓✓	Location	✓✓✓✓
Quality of Pitches	✓✓✓	Range of Facilities	✓✓✓

Directions

From C31 (Figueres - Palamos) south of Pals, north of Palafrugell, take GI653 to Begur. Site is 2 km. north of town; follow signs for Playa de Sa Riera and site.

Charges 2005

Per person	€ 4,30 - € 6,00
child (1-10 yrs)	€ 3,00 - € 4,30
caravan	€ 5,40 - € 7,60
tent	€ 3,30 - € 7,00
car	€ 4,00 - € 5,30

Plus 7% VAT. Discount in low season for 7 day stay.

Reservations

Write to site. Tel: 972 623 023.
E-mail: info@campingelmaset.com

ES8102 Camping Mas Patoxas

Ctra Palafrugell-Pals, km 339, 17256 Pals (Girona)

This is a mature and well laid out site for those who prefer to be apart from, but within easy travelling distance of the beaches (5 km.) and town (1 km). It has a very easy access and is set on a slight slope with wide avenues on level terraces providing 400 grassy pitches of a minimum 72 sq.m. All have electricity (5A) and water, many have drainage as well. There are some very pleasant views and shade from a variety of mature trees. An air-conditioned restaurant/bar provides both waiter service meals and take-away food to order (weekends only mid Sept - April) and entertainment takes place on a stage below the terraces during the high season. Both bar and restaurant terraces give views over the pools and distant hills. The restaurant menu is varied and very reasonable. We were impressed with the children's mini-club activity when we visited. There is a large, supervised irregularly shaped swimming pool with triple flume, a separate children's pool and a generous sunbathing area of the poolside and surrounding grass. Used by tour operators (40).

Facilities

Three modern sanitary blocks provide controllable hot showers, some washbasins with hot water, baby bath and three children's cabins with washbasin and shower. No specific facilities for disabled people, although access throughout the site looks to be relatively easy. Dishwashing facilities under cover (H&C). Laundry facilities. Restaurant/bar (1/4-30/9). Pizzeria. Takeaway. Well stocked shop (1/4-30/9). Swimming pool (15/6-30/9). Tennis. Table tennis. Volleyball. Football field. Entertainment in high season. Fridges for rent. Gas supplies. Torches useful in some areas. Off site: Bus service from site gate. Bicycle hire or riding 2 km. Fishing or golf 4 km.

At a glance

Welcome & Ambience	✓✓✓✓	Location	✓✓✓✓
Quality of Pitches	✓✓✓✓	Range of Facilities	✓✓✓✓

Directions

Site is east of Girona and approx. 1.5 km. south of Pals at km. 339 on the C31 Figueres-Palamos road, just north of Palafugel.

Charges 2004

Per person	€ 3,60 - € 5,00
child (1-10 yrs)	€ 2,50 - € 3,00
caravan pitch	€ 17,00 - € 24,00
tent pitch with car	€ 14,00 - € 21,00
dog	€ 2,10

Plus 7% VAT. Special low season offers.

Reservations

Write to site. Tel: 972 636 928.
E-mail: info@campingmaspatoxas.com

Open

All year, except 19 December - 13 January.

ES8104 Camping Begur

Ctra D'Esclanya, km 2, 17255 Begur (Girona)

The new owners here have made a massive investment in making the site a pleasant place to spend some time. Begur has some good supporting facilities including a pleasant swimming pool and paddling pool at its centre. The bar and snack bar are part of this new pool complex and it has been well designed with terraces and sunbathing area. The touring areas are protected from the sun by mature trees and the 317 pitches are informally arranged on sloping sandy ground (chocks useful). Most pitches have electrical connections (10A), water and drainage. A few mobile homes and apartments are scattered around the slopes. Environmental activities are encouraged including visits to the revolutionary water cleansing plant deep in the woods. There are many sporting facilities including a well equipped weight training room (free). A huge supermarket is just outside the gate, used by locals and the new restaurant here is now open. The bays of the Costa Brava are just 1.5 km. away.

Facilities

Two modern toilet blocks are fully equipped and include really large showers. Excellent facilites for disabled campers. Baby bath. Washing machines and dryers. Motorcaravan services. Bar and snacks. Restaurant and supermarket just outside gate. Swimming pools (all season). Table tennis. Boules. Weight training room. Play area. Volleyball. Football. Some animation in high season. Area for children with playground and entertainment and games in high season. Little farm with ponies, goat and chickens. Internet access. Off site: Village and beaches 1.5 km. Fishing 3 km. Golf 10 km. Riding 15 km.

At a glance

Welcome & Ambience	✓✓✓✓	Location	✓✓✓✓
Quality of Pitches	✓✓✓✓	Range of Facilities	✓✓✓✓✓

Directions

From Girona take road east to La Bisbal and Palafrugell then Begur. Turn south towards Fornells, the site is well signed 3 km. south of Begur.

Charges 2005

Per adult	€ 2,80 - € 4,90
child (3-10 yrs)	€ 1,30 - € 2,60
pitch with electricity	€ 7,60 - € 16,60
animal	€ 2,40 - € 3,80

Reservations

Possible with € 100 deposit. Tel: 972 623 201. E-mail: info@campingbegur.com

Open

29 April - 25 September.

ES8130 Camping Internacional de Calonge

Ctra S Feliu/Guixols - Palamos, 17251 Calonge (Girona)

This spacious, well laid out site has access to the fine beach by a footbridge over the coast road, or you can take the little road train as the site is on very sloping ground. Calonge is a family site with two good sized pools on different levels, a paddling pool plus large sunbathing areas. These are overlooked by the restaurant terrace which has great views over the mountains. The site's 800 pitches are on terraces and all have electricity (5A) with 167 available for winter use. A large proportion are suitable for touring units (the remainder for tents) being set on attractively landscaped terraces. Access to some pitches may be a little difficult. There is good shade from the tall pine trees and some views of the sea through the foliage. A nature area within the site is used for walks or picnics. A separate area within the site is set aside for visitors with dogs (including a dog shower!)

Facilities

Generous sanitary provision in new or renovated blocks include some washbasins in cabins. One block is heated for winter use. Laundry facilities. Motorcaravan services. Gas supplies. Shop (19/3-31/10). Bar/restaurant (19/3-23/10). Patio bar (pizza and takeaway). Swimming pools with lifeguard (19/3-30/9). Playground. Electronic games. Rather noisy disco two nights a week (but not late). Bicycle hire. Table tennis. Tennis. Volleyball. Hairdresser. ATM. Internet. Torches necessary in some areas. Off site: Fishing 300 m. Golf 3 km. Riding 10 km. Supermarket 500 m.

Open

All year.

At a glance

Welcome & Ambience	✓✓✓✓✓	Location	✓✓✓✓✓
Quality of Pitches	✓✓✓✓✓	Range of Facilities	✓✓✓✓✓

Directions

Site is on the inland side of the coast road between Palamos and Platja d'Aro, take C31 south to the 661 at Calonge. At Calonge follow signs to the C253 towards Platja d'Aro and on to site (well signed).

Charges 2005

Per person	€ 3,40 - € 6,25
child (2-10 yrs)	€ 1,75 - € 3,45
pitch incl. electricity	€ 11,75 - € 22,00
motorcaravan incl. electricity	€ 11,10 - € 18,50

All plus 7% VAT. Discounts for longer stays Oct - end May. No credit cards.

Reservations

Write with deposit (€ 37). UK contact: Mr J Worthington (0161) 799 9562. Tel: 972 651 233. E-mail: info@intercalonge.com

ES8232 Camping Bella Terra

Platja de S'Abanell, 17300 Blanes (Girona)

Camping Bella Terra is a very Spanish site, set in a shady pine grove facing a white sandy beach on the Mediterranean coast. There are 870 pitches with 590 for touring units, the rest taken by bungalows to rent (80) and by Spanish 'residents' (200). All pitches have 5/6A electricity and 24 are fully serviced. The site is in two sections, each with its own reception, on either side of a road which leads only to another campsite. The older part, with direct access to the beach, always fills up first and has the small supermarket with its own bakery, and the bar in front of which the activities and the evening entertainment take place. Main reception is on the right of the road as you approach, as are the restaurant with its own bar and the swimming pool. This site has a real Spanish feel.

Facilities

The older sanitary blocks are quite adequate and fully equipped with provision for disabled visitors and laundry. The block on the newer side is much more modern and spacious, and an unusual feature is the suite of half-size showers, toilets and washbasins for young campers on both male and female sides. Shop, restaurant, bar and takeaway and outdoor swimming pool (all May - Sept). Playground. Fishing. Off site: Bicycle hire 500 m. Golf and riding 5 km.

At a glance

Welcome & Ambience	✓✓✓✓	Location	✓✓✓✓
Quality of Pitches	✓✓✓	Range of Facilities	✓✓✓✓

Directions

Site is south of Blanes. Follow signs from the town centre and site is just after Camping Blanes.

Charges 2004

Per person	€ 4,15 - € 4,50
child (3-10 yrs)	€ 3,40 - € 3,70
pitch	€ 12,80 - € 24,15

Reservations

Contact site. Tel: 972 348017.
E-mail: cbellaterra@cbellaterra.com

Open

5 April - 30 September.

ES8160 Camping Cala Gogo

Ctra S Feliu-Palamos, km 46.5, 17251 Calonge (Girona)

Cala Gogo is a large traditional campsite with a pleasant situation on a wooded hillside with mature trees giving shade to most pitches. A small cove of considerable natural beauty has a coarse sand beach and there is access to a further two small beaches along the sand. If you prefer fresh water there are two pools on the site (one heated in low season). The site facilities are contained in terraced buildings which have a supermarket, shops, small restaurant and a bar all with an adjoining terrace enjoying views over the pools down to the sea. A second floodlit bar, pleasant restaurant and a takeaway are on the beach and open in high season. The 619 shaded touring pitches varying in size are in terraced rows, some with artificial shade, all have 10A electricity and 250 have water and drainage. There may be road noise in eastern parts of the site. Some pitches are right by the beach, the remainder are up to 800 metres uphill, but the 'Gua gua' (South American Spanish for bus) tractor train, operating all season, takes people between the centre of the site and the beach adding to the general sense of fun. The management aim to make the site attractive to families. It is an active, bustling place, with over 2,500 campers when full. A huge aqua-park close by offers amazing waterslides, waves and all manner of water enjoyment and there is a bus from the site. Used by tour operators (60 pitches), 170 mobile homes and chalets to rent.

Facilities

Seven toilet blocks are of a high standard and are continuously cleaned. Some washbasins are in private cabins. Laundry. Motorcaravan services. Gas supplies. Supermarket. General shop. Restaurants and bars. Swimming pools (25 x 12 m.) and paddling pool (lifeguards). Playground. Crèche and babysitting service for smaller children (extra charge). Sports centre with tennis, volleyball, basketball, etc, plus a mini-club. Programme of animation including sports, TV and video programmes daily, tournaments, entertainment. Bicycle hire. Limited table tennis. Kayaks (free). Fishing. Bureau de change. Medical service; nurse daily, doctor alternate days. Good 24 hr security service including video surveillance. Sponsored bus to local disco. Dogs are not accepted from mid June - end August. Off site: Bicycle hire and golf 4 km. Riding 10 km. Huge Aqua Park nearby with bus from site.

At a glance

Welcome & Ambience	✓✓✓✓	Location	✓✓✓✓
Quality of Pitches	✓✓✓✓	Range of Facilities	✓✓✓✓

Directions

Site is on inland side of coast road between Palomos and Platja d'Aro on the C253 at km 46.5 (4 km. south of Palomos). Avoid town centre by using C31 (Girona - Palomos) road, leaving at km 320, dropping down to Sant Antoni de Calonge, and turning right on C253.

Charges 2005

Per person	€ 3,25 - € 6,00
child (3-12 yrs)	€ 1,00 - € 2,70
caravan or trailer tent	€ 12,10 - € 24,50
motorcaravan	€ 10,55 - € 23,60
tent	€ 10,10 - € 19,50
dog	€ 2,00

Electricity (5A) included. All plus 7% VAT. Low season discounts. No credit cards.

Reservations

Made for min. 1 week with deposit (€ 150). Tel: 972 651 564. E-mail: calagogo@calagogo.es

Open

29 April - 25 September.

ES8170 Camping Valldaro

Aptdo 57, Avda. Castell d'Aro, 17250 Platja d'Aro (Girona)

Valldaro is 600 metres back from the sea at Platja de Aro, a small, bright resort with a long, wide beach and plenty of amusements. It is particularly pleasant out of peak weeks and is popular with the British. Like a number of other large Spanish sites, Valldaro has been extended and many pitches have been made larger, bringing them up to 80 or 100 sq.m. There are now 1,200 pitches with 660 available for tourers. The site is flat, with pitches in rows divided up by access roads. You will probably find space here even at the height of the season. The newer section has its own vehicle entrance (the nearest point to the beach) and can be reached via a footbridge; it is brought into use at peak times. It has some shade and its own toilet block, as well as a medium-sized swimming pool of irregular shape with grassy sunbathing area and adjacent bar/snack bar and take-away. The original pool (36 x 18 m.) is adjacent to the good Spanish-style restaurant which also offers takeaway fare. There are 400 permanent Spanish pitches and 150 mobile-homes and chalets to rent, but these are in separate areas and do not impinge on the touring pitches.

Facilities

Sanitary facilities are of a good standard and are well maintained. Children's size toilets. Washbasins (no cabins) and adjustable showers (temperature perhaps a bit variable). Two supermarkets and general shops. Restaurant. Large bar. Swimming pools. Tennis. Table tennis, minigolf with snack bar. Playgrounds. Sports ground with football and basketball. Organised entertainment in season. Hairdresser. Air conditioned telephone/internet parlour. Gas supplies. Keen interest in environmental issues with many recycling bins. Off site: Fishing, bicycle hire and golf 1 km. Riding 4 km.

At a glance

Welcome & Ambience	✓✓✓✓✓	Location	✓✓✓✓
Quality of Pitches	✓✓✓✓	Range of Facilities	✓✓✓✓✓

Directions

Site is off the C31 Girona-Palamós road; follow signs for Platja de Aro.and site is signed off roundabout.

Charges 2005

Per person	€ 3,25 - € 5,20
child (2-10 yrs)	€ 2,20 - € 3,05
pitch incl. electricity	€ 15,00 - € 25,00
dog	€ 2,30

All plus 7% VAT. Discounts in low seasons.

Reservations

Made only in the sense of guaranteeing admission without deposit. Tel: 972 817 515. E-mail: info@valldaro.com

Open

18 March - 2 October.

ES8100 Camping Inter-Pals

Avenida Mediterrania, 17256 Platja de Pals (Girona)

Sister site to no. ES8170 and set on sloping ground, with tall pine trees providing shade and about 500 metres from the beach, this site has 625 terraced pitches (including 280 for touring units and 250 for tents), on terraces and levelled plots, mostly with shade. Some of the terraced pitches have views of the sea through the trees. The main entrance and its drive resembles a pretty village street as the bungalows are set on both sides of the street, lined with traditional lampposts. Continuing the village theme is a row of shops where you will find most camper's needs. The site is close to Platja de Pals which is a long sandy unspoilt stretch of beach, a discreet area, part of which is now an official naturist beach. The formal restaurant with good value menu and choice of takeaway overlooks the pools. The pretty town of Pals is close by along with a good golf course. The site will assist with touring plans of the area.

Facilities

Three well maintained toilet blocks include individual washbasins, dishwashing and laundry sinks and facilities for disabled campers. Washing machines and dryers. Gas supplies. Fridge/TV rental. Medical centre. Excursions. ATM. Diving and watersport arranged. Shops. Restaurant/bar with Pizzeria/croissenterie with dancing and entertainment area. Cafe/bar by entrance. Swimming pool. Basketball, volleyball and badminton courts. Tennis. Children's playground and organised activities and entertainment in high season. Electronic games. Pool tables. Some breeds of dog are excluded - check with site. Torch useful. Off site: Fishing 200 m. Bicycle hire 500 m. Golf 1 km. Riding 10 km.

Open

19 March - 2 October.

At a glance

Welcome & Ambience	✓✓✓✓✓	Location	✓✓✓✓
Quality of Pitches	✓✓✓✓✓	Range of Facilities	✓✓✓✓✓

Directions

Site is on the road leading off the Torroella de Montgri-Bagur road north of Pals and going to Playa de Pals (Pals beach).

Charges 2004

Per person	€ 3,50 - € 4,95
child (3-10 yrs)	€ 2,50 - € 2,90
pitch	€ 15,50 - € 26,90
small tent and car	€ 13,50 - € 18,60
dog	€ 2,60

Plus 7% VAT. Discounts for long stays in low season. No credit cards.

Reservations

Made in the sense of guarantee to admit only, without deposit. Tel: 972 636 179. E-mail: interpals@interpals.com

TRAVEL SERVICE SITE
TO BOOK CALL 0870 405 4055 OR www.alanrogersdirect.com

ES8240 Camping Botánic Bona Vista Kim

Ctra N-II, km 665, 08370 Calella de la Costa (Barcelona)

While Calella itself may conjure up visions of mass tourism, this site is set on a steep hillside some three kilometres out of the town. Apart from perhaps some noise from the nearby coast road and railway, it is a quite delightful setting with an abundance of flowers, shrubs and roses (1,700 in total, all planted by the knowledgeable owner Kim, who has won several top Catalonian prizes for his roses). The site design successfully marries the beautiful botanic surrounds with the attractive views of the bay. Of the 160 pitches, all with electricity, 130 are available for tourers, they are 60-80 sq.m. or more and are situated on flat terraces on the slopes, with some shade. On arrival, park at the restaurant and choose a pitch – Kim is most helpful with siting your van. The access road is steep, with many of the pitches enjoying lovely views. The bar/restaurant is close to reception at the bottom of the site and is unusual in the attractive choice of Spanish décor and in having a circular, central open-hearth fire/cooker. There are two roof top terraces, the first terrace has service from the restaurant and bar and above that (for over 16 year olds), is the computer controlled sauna, jacuzzi with pool sized filter, a well equipped gymnasium and a sunbathing area, all enjoying views over the sea. There are quite good beaches just across the road and railway, accessible via a tunnel and crossing (including a naturist beach). The site has recently won environmental awards.

Facilities

The standard of design in the three sanitary blocks is quite outstanding for a small site (indeed for any site). Some washbasins in cabins in the newest block. Baby room. Dishwashing under cover. Washing machines. Motorcaravan services. Bar/restaurant, takeaway and shop (1/4-1/10). Large children's playground. Recreation park. Satellite TV. Internet point. Games room. Barbecue and picnic area. No cycling allowed on site. Off site: Fishing 100 m. Bicycle hire 1 km. Riding and golf 3 km. Watersports near.

Open

All year.

At a glance

Welcome & Ambience	✓✓✓✓	Location	✓✓✓✓
Quality of Pitches	✓✓✓✓	Range of Facilities	✓✓✓

Directions

From N11 coast road site is signed travelling south of Calella (at km. 665), and is on right hand side of road - care is needed as road is busy and sign is almost on top of turning (entrance shared with Camping Roca Grossa). Entrance is very steep. From Barcelona, after passing through Sant Pol de Mar, go into outside lane shortly after 'Camping 800 m.' sign and keep signalling left. Site entrance is just before the two lanes merge. (From C32 toll motorway, leave at exit 22 for Calella to join N11 south, then as above).

Charges 2005

Per person	€ 5,15
child (3-10 yrs)	€ 4,40
pitch	€ 10,30

All plus 7% VAT. No credit cards.

Reservations

Write to site. Tel: 93 769 24 88.
E-mail: info@botanic-bonavista.net

ES9140 Camping Repos del Pedraforca

Ctra B400, km 13.5, 08699 Saldés (Barcelona)

Looking up through the trees in this steeply terraced campsite in the area of the Cadi-Moixero Natural Parc, you see the majestic Pedraforca mountain. A favourite for Catalan climbers and walkers, its amazing rugged peak in the shape of a massive stone fork gives it its name. The long scenic drive through the mountains to reach the site is breathtakingly beautiful. The natural beauty of the area, pretty villages, wild flowers, wonderful walks, and interesting local attractions including sea salt mountain and historic coal mines are what attract people to this area. The campsite owner, Alicio Font, is a charming hostess who speaks English. She has created excellent summer and winter facilities including an indoor heated pool, sauna, jacuzzi and gym complex, a large outdoor pool, rooftop relaxation area, upstairs social room, excellent restaurant and popular bar, plus some log cabins to rent. This is generally a very environmentally conscious campsite. Access to the site is via a steep, curving road which could challenge some units. Pitches vary in size and accessibility, although there are excellent pitches for larger units.

Facilities

Two clean, modern sanitary blocks are fully equipped (but at peakperiods there may be queues). Facilities for disabled campers. Separate family room with baby baths, showers, etc. Washing machines and dryer. Restaurant/bar and small supermarket for basic items (both w/ends all year, then 15/5-30/9). Heated indoor pool, gym and spa. Outdoor pool (15/5-30/9). Play areas. Animation for children and adults in high season. Games and social rooms. Rooftop relaxation area. Table tennis. Torches required. Off site: Motorcaravan service point close but not within site. Mountain biking.

Open

All year.

At a glance

Welcome & Ambience	✓✓✓✓	Location	✓✓✓✓✓
Quality of Pitches	✓✓✓	Range of Facilities	✓✓✓✓✓

Directions

Site is approx. 90 minutes from Barcelona. Access to the site is gained from the C-16 Burga road. 2 km. south of Guardiola de Bergueda. Turn west to Saldes and site is well signed (13.5 km. to site from C-16).

Charges 2005

Per person	€ 4,85
child (1-10 yrs)	€ 3,90
pitch	€ 12,20
electricity (3-5A)	€ 3,50 - € 4,40
dog	€ 1,80

Discounts for stays of more than 3 nights and other offers for long stays (excluding high season).

Reservations

Contact site for details. Tel: 938 258 044.
E-mail: pedra@campingpedraforca.com

ES8200 Camping Cala Llevadó

Ctra de Tossa a Lloret, km. 3, 17320 Tossa de Mar (Girona)

For splendour of position Cala Llevadó can compare with almost any in this book. A beautifully situated cliff-side site, it has fine views of the sea and coast below. It is shaped something like half a bowl with steep slopes. There are terraced, flat areas for caravans and tents on the upper levels of the two slopes, with a great many individual pitches for tents scattered around the site. Some of these pitches (without electricity) have fantastic settings and views. There is usually car parking close to these pitches, although in some areas cars may be required to park separately. Electrical connections cover all caravan sectors and one tent area. High up in the site with a superb aspect, is the attractive restaurant/bar with a large terrace overlooking a play area and the pleasant pool. One beach is for all manner of watersports within a buoyed area and there is a sub-aqua diving school. Some other pleasant little coves can also be reached by climbing down on foot (with care!). The steepness of the site would make access difficult for disabled people or those with limited mobility. Cala Llevadó is luxurious and has much character and the atmosphere is informal and very friendly. Only 204 of the 575 touring pitches are accessible for caravans, so reservation in high season is essential. There are a few tour operator pitches (45). It is peacefully situated but only five minutes away from the busy resort of Tossa – take a look at the town where the castle is beautifully lit by night. The owner has recently added a botanic garden on the site with many of the plants, flowers and trees of the region, an explanation of its history and including a historic windmill.

Facilities

Four very well equipped toilet blocks are well spaced around the site, built in an attractive style and immaculately maintained, with some washbasins in cabins, well equipped showers, and baby baths. Washing machines and dryer. Laundry service. Motorcaravan services. Gas supplies. Fridge hire. Large, well stocked supermarket. New restaurant/bar with terrace (5/5-28/9). Swimming pool (20 x 10 m.) and semi-circular children's pool. Three play areas. New garden. Entertainment for children (4-12 yrs). Sailing, water ski and windsurfing school. Fishing. Scuba diving. Excursions. Torches are definitely needed in some areas. Off site: Bicycle hire 3 km. The site is alongside a larger complex where all manner of sophisticated sports and adventure activities are available. Campers can also use the other pools here

At a glance

Welcome & Ambience	✓✓✓✓✓	Location	✓✓✓✓✓
Quality of Pitches	✓✓✓	Range of Facilities	✓✓✓✓✓

Directions

Cala Llevadó is signed off the G1682 Lloret - Tossa road at km 18.9, about 3 km. from Tossa.

Charges 2005

Per person	€ 4,85 - € 7,60
child (4-12 yrs)	€ 3,00 - € 4,15
car or motorcycle	€ 4,85 - € 7,60
tent	€ 4,85 - € 7,60
caravan	€ 5,60 - € 8,10

Plus 7% VAT.

Reservations

Accepted with deposit and fee. Tel: 972 340 314. E-mail: info@calallevado.com

Open

1 May - 30 September, including all amenities.

ES8390 Camping Vilanova Park

Ctra de l'Arboc, km 2.5, 08800 Vilanova i la Geltru (Barcelona)

Sitting on the terrace of the bustling but comfortable restaurant at Vilanova Park, it is difficult to believe that back in 1908 this was an old Catalan farm and then, quite lacking in trees, it was known as 'Rock Farm'. If you find this hard to believe look at the old photos in the restaurant. Since then imaginative planting has resulted in there being literally thousands of trees and gloriously colourful shrubs making a most attractive large site, with an impressive range of high quality amenities and facilities open all year. These now include a second pool higher up in the site with marvellous views across the town to the sea. By 2005 this area will have a second, more intimate restaurant for that romantic dinner. The original pool has water jets and a coloured floodlit fountain playing at night time, which complement the dancing and entertainment taking place on the stage in the coutyard overlooking the pool. An unusual attraction is a Nature Park and mini-zoo with deer and bird-life, which has very pleasant picnic areas and views. At present there are 865 pitches with many occupied by bungalows and chalets carefully designed to fit into the environment There are 248 pitches for touring units in separate areas with 133 having a water supply. Marked and of 70-100 sq.m, all have 6A electricity and some larger pitches (100 sq.m.) also have water and drainage. The terrain, hard surfaced and mostly on very gently sloping ground, has many trees and considerable shade. Plans include an indoor pool, sauna and gym which will be appreciated by winter visitors. There is a transfer service from Barcelona and Reus airports.

Facilities

All toilet blocks are of excellent quality, can be heated and have washbasins (over half in cabins) with free hot water, and others of standard type with cold water. Serviced laundry. Motorcaravan services. Supermarket (Easter - 30/9). Souvenir shop. Restaurants. Bar with simple meals (both all year). Swimming pools (Easter - 15/10). Play areas. Sports field for football, basketball and volleyball. Games room. Tennis. Bicycle hire. Tennis. ATM and exchange facilities. Off site: Fishing 4 km. Golf 5 km. Barcelona is easily accessible - hourly buses in the main season or train from Vilanova i la Geltru. Vilanova town and beach 4 km.

Open

All year.

At a glance

Welcome & Ambience	✓✓✓✓	Location	✓✓✓✓
Quality of Pitches	✓✓✓✓✓	Range of Facilities	✓✓✓✓✓

Directions

Site is 4 km. northwest of Vilanova i la Geltru towards L'Arboc (BV2115). From Barcelona on A16/1C32 take exit 26 towards El Vendrall (C31), then take L'Arboc exit (km. 153) and narrow road uphill to site on right. From Tarragona use exit 16 signed L'Arboc but go right under autopista for 2 km. to site on left.

Charges 2004

Per person	€ 4,15 - € 6,70
child (4-12 yrs)	€ 2,50 - € 4,20
pitch incl. electricity	€ 12,30 - € 17,60
with water	€ 14,90 - € 20,00
dog	€ 2,24 - € 4,50

All plus 7% VAT. Long stay discounts.

Reservations

Made with deposit; contact site. Tel: 93 893 34 02. E-mail: info@vilanovapark.es

ES8502 Camping Caravaning Montblanc Park

Ctra Prenafeta, km 1,8, 43400 Montblanc (Tarragona)

Taking current trends into account, Montblanc Park may be described as a campsite of the future. Purpose designed, there are 213 terraced pitches for touring units and about 60 for wooden chalets, with more being developed, on the upper terraces. Visitors have first class facilities, including a very high quality restaurant serving typically Spanish dishes along with dishes to suit any palate and a terrace area for those who would choose a less formal atmosphere. Both the restaurant and terrace enjoy views of the exceptionally large, lagoon-style pool and further across the valley, over the autoroute towards the town of Montblanc and the Prades mountains of the Sera del Prades. The pitches are on terraces so take advantage of the mountain views and gentle cooling afternoon breezes. They vary in size, with hedging but little shade yet, and are sloping (chocks useful). There is much emphasis on activities for children and an animation team keep children amused during the day in July and August so parents can have a break. There is organised sport and live entertainment on Saturday night. This is a very professional operation, ideal for a relaxing holiday or exploring the many attractions of the local area. Medieval Montblanc itself is worth exploring and nearby Poblet with its monastery.

Facilities

Two purpose built toilet blocks feature en-suite facilities including superb facilities for disabled campers and a well equipped baby room. Washing machines and dryers. Supermarket. Restaurant. Snack bar. Swimming pool and large paddling pool. Play areas. Football. Boules. Basketball. Table tennis. Electronic games. Bicycle hire. Entertainment for children (wwekends and main holiday season). Tents for hire. Off site: Riding 4 km. Beach or golf 35 km. Mountain activities: climbing, caving, canyoning and orienteering. Paint ball. Quad biking and trips by 4x4.

Open

All year.

At a glance

Welcome & Ambience	✓✓✓✓	Location	✓✓✓✓
Quality of Pitches	✓✓✓✓	Range of Facilities	✓✓✓✓✓

Directions

Site is 3 minutes off the autopista. From A2 (Barcelona - Lleida) take exit 9 and follow N240 (Reus - Tarragona), then road to Prenafeta and site stands out on the left. It is 1.8 km. out of Montblanc and signed in the town.

Charges 2004

Per person	€ 3,00 - € 5,00
child (0-10 yrs)	free
pitch incl. electricity	€ 12,00 - € 18,00
water	€ 2,00
dog	€ 1,00 - € 2,00

Reservations

Contact site. Tel: 977 862544.
E-mail: info@montblancpark.com

ES8480 Camping & Bungalow Park Sanguli

Prolongacion Calle, Apdo de Correos 123, 43840 Salou (Tarragona)

Sanguli is a superb site boasting excellent pools and ambitious entertainment. Owned, developed and managed by a local Spanish family, it provides for all the family with everything open when the site is open. It lies little more than 100 metres from the good sandy beach, across the coast road and a small railway level crossing (some train noise at times). Sister site to ES8481, although large, Sanguli manages to maintain a quality family atmosphere due to the efforts of the very keen and efficient staff. There are three very attractive pool areas, one (heated) near the entrance with a grassy sunbathing area partly shaded and a second deep one with water slides that forms part of the excellent sports complex (with fitness centre, tennis courts, minigolf and football practice area). The third pool is the central part of the amphitheatre area at the top of the site which includes an impressive Roman style building with huge portals, containing a bar and restaurant with terraces. An amphitheatre seats 2,000 campers and treats them to very professional free nightly entertainment (1/5-30/9). All the pools have adjacent amenity areas and bars. Located near the centre of Salou, the site can offer the attractions of a busy resort while still being private and it is only 3 km. from Port Aventura. The owners are striving to achieve the 'Garden of Eden' that is their dream. There are 1,220 pitches of varying size (75-90 sq.m) and all have electricity with about 160 used by tour operators and 140 with bungalows. A wonderful selection of trees, palms and shrubs provides natural shade. A real effort is made to cater for young people with a 'Hop Club' (entertainment for 13-17 year olds), along with an internet room. This is a large, professional site providing something for all the family, but still able to provide peace and quiet for those looking for it.

Facilities

The quality sanitary facilities are constantly improved and are always exceptional, including many individual cabins with en-suite facilities. A new block also has excellent facilities for babies. All are kept very clean. Launderette with service. Motorcaravan services. Bars and restaurant with takeaway. Swimming pools. Jacuzzi. Fitness centre. Sport complex with tennis, football practice ground, Sports area and fitness room (charged). Playgrounds including adventure play area. Mini club, teenagers club. Internet room. Upmarket minigolf. First-aid room. Gas supplies. Off site: Fishing and bicycle hire 100 m. Riding 3 km. Golf 6 km. Resort entertainment.

Open

11 March - 1 November.

At a glance

Welcome & Ambience	✓✓✓✓✓	Location	✓✓✓✓✓
Quality of Pitches	✓✓✓✓✓	Range of Facilities	✓✓✓✓✓

Directions

On west side of Salou about 1 km. from centre, site is well signed from the coast road to Cambrils and from the other town approaches.

Charges 2005

Per person	€ 5,00
child (4-12 yrs)	€ 3,00
pitch incl. electricity	€ 12,00 - € 35,00
incl. water	€ 14,00 - € 37,00

All plus 7% VAT. Less 25-45% outside high season for longer stays. Special long stay offers for senior citizens.

Reservations

Advised for July/Aug. and made up to 1 March with sizeable booking fee. Tel: 977 381 641.
E-mail: mail@sanguli.es

ES8420 Camping Stel

Ctra N340, km 1182, 43883 Roda de Bará (Tarragona)

Camping Stel is situated between the pre-Littoral mountains and the sea. The rectangular site is between the N340 road and the excellent beach, with the railway running close to the bottom of the site. Beach access is gained through a gate and under the railway - there is rail noise on the lower pitches. The main facilities are grouped around the pools which are very pleasant with a large flume to an extension of the main pool (heated all season), an octagonal paddling pool and pleasant grass area carefully set out with palms. The central complex containing all the services is impressive with a large bar, terrace and snack area overlooking the pools. A small restaurant is behind the bar. The pitches are generally in rows with hedges around the rows but at the lower end of the site the layout is less formal. Many pitches have individual sinks. There is a separate area where no radio or TV is allowed ensuring peace and quiet. Just outside the gate is the famous Roman Arc de Bara which sits astride the original road.

Facilities

Four clean, fully equipped, sanitary blocks. One totally refurbished (2002) with facilities for children, excellent facilities for disabled campers and four high standard private cabins. Baby baths in the ladies' sections of blocks. Laundry. Motorcaravan services. Supermarket and tourist shop. Bar/restaurant and snack bar. Swimming pools.(4/4-28/9) Outdoor sports area. Gym. Animation for children and some adult entertainment in high season. Electronic games. Internet bar. Hairdresser. ATM. Overnight area for late arrivals. Dogs are not accepted. Torch useful. Off site: Golf, riding and bicycle hire 4 km. Travel to the area's many attractions is simple by the nearby autopista.

At a glance

Welcome & Ambience	✓✓✓✓	Location	✓✓✓✓✓
Quality of Pitches	✓✓✓✓✓	Range of Facilities	✓✓✓✓✓

Directions

Site is at 1182 km. marker on the N340 near Arc de Bara, between Tarragona and Vilanova.

Charges 2004

Per adult	€ 6,10
child (3-10 yrs)	€ 4,70
pitch incl. electricity	€ 18,90 - € 19,60
with water and drainage	€ 22,70 - € 23,50

All plus 7% VAT.

Reservations

Advisable in July/August. Tel: 977 802 002.
E-mail: rodadebara@stel.es

Open

9 April - 28 September.

PARC DE VACANCES
Sangulí Salou
CAMPING & BUNGALOW PARK
Prolongació carrer E, s/n
Apartat de Correus 123
43840 SALOU • Costa Daurada
Tarragona • España
tel. +34 977 38 16 41
fax +34 977 38 46 16
Better is Impossible...
mail@sanguli.es • www.sanguli.es
Salou • Costa Daurada • Catalunya • España

ES8481 Camping Cambrils Park

Apartado de Correos 123, 43850 Salou (Tarragona)

This is a superb site for a camping holiday providing for all family members, whatever their age. A drive lined with palm trees and flowers leads from a large, very smart round reception building at this impressive modern site. Sister site to ES8480, it is set 500 metres back from the excellent beach in a generally quiet setting with outstanding facilities. The 684 slightly sloping, grassy pitches of around 90 sq.m. are numbered and separated by trees. All have 10A electricity, 55 have water and waste water connections, some having more shade than others. The marvellous central lagoon pool complex with three pools and water slides is the main focus of the site with a raised wooden 'poop deck' sunbathing area with palm surrounds that doubles as an entertainment stage at night. There is a huge bar/terrace area for watching the magnificent floodlit spectacles, along with an excellent restaurant in the old farmhouse with an adjacent takeaway. By day there is a small bar at a lower level in the pool where you can enjoy a cool drink from submerged stools, plus a dryer version on the far side of the bar or just relax on the spacious grass sunbathing areas. There are a number of tour operator pitches and attractive thatched chalets. A fabulous jungle theme children's pool is nearer the entrance - they love it, especially the elephants! An extra pool for adults has been added here, along with a snack bar.

Facilities

Four excellent sanitary buildings provide some washbasins in cabins, superb units for disabled visitors and immaculate, decorated baby sections. Dishwashing and laundry sinks. Huge serviced laundry. Motorcaravan services. Car wash. Restaurant. Takeaway. Huge supermarket, souvenir shop and 'panaderia' (fresh-baked bread and croissants). Swimming pools with lifeguards. Minigolf. Tennis Football. Multi-games court. Basketball. Volleyball. Petanque. Animation and entertainment all season. Mini-club. Internet café. Doctor on site daily all season. ATM. Gas supplies. Dogs are not accepted. Off site: Beach 500 m. Fishing, bicycle hire 400 m. Riding 3 km. Port Aventura theme park 4 km. Golf 7 km.

Open

18 March - 9 October.

At a glance

Welcome & Ambience	✓✓✓✓	Location	✓✓✓✓
Quality of Pitches	✓✓✓✓✓	Range of Facilities	✓✓✓✓✓

Directions

Site is about 1.5 km west of Salou. From the A7 take exit 35 and at roundabout take signs for Cambrils. Follow new dual-carriageway around the back of Salou and site is signed at last roundabout towards Cambrils (you can see the bungalos from the dual-carriageway).

Charges 2005

Per person	€ 5,00
child (4-12 yrs)	free - € 3,00
pitch incl. electricity	€ 12,00 - € 35,00
incl. water and waste water	€ 14,00 - € 37,00

All plus 7% VAT. Special offers, plus low season discounts for pensioners.

Reservations

Contact site. Tel: 977 351 031.
E-mail: mail@cambrilspark.es

'My Sweet Camping'

This was the name of a unique photographic exhibition held at Cambrils Park and Camping Sanguli during the July and August 2004. In all, 90 poster-sized photographs were displayed around the two sites, all of which had been taken by the world renowned Portuguese photographer Aldo Soares. The images are all of holidaymakers who had spent their 2003 holidays at Cambrils and Sanguli, and each succeeded superbly in capturing the essence of each family's holiday experience.'

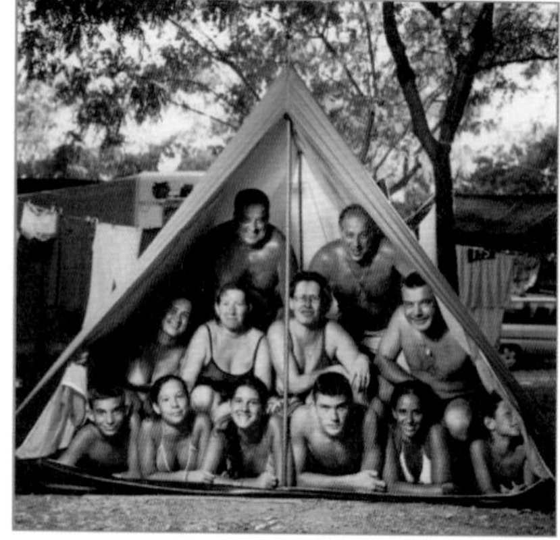

Spain

ES8392 Camping El Garrofer

Ctra C31 km 39, 08870 Sitges (Barcelona)

This large, pine covered site, alongside fields of vines, is 800 m. from the beach, close to the pleasant town of Sitges. It has over 500 pitches of which 380 with 6A electricity are for tourers, including 28 with water used for large motorcaravans. Everything is kept clean and the pitches are tidy and shaded, all with electricity. Dino is the young, dynamic, English speaking manager who has a vast programme of improvements which will make this a most attractive site. The permanent pitches are grouped in a completely separate area and the amenity buildings are along the site perimeter next to the road which absorbs most of the road noise. A varied menu is offered in the cosy restaurant with a small terrace. Everything is cooked to perfection and complemented with the wines of the Penedes DO made hereabouts (the restaurant has a local reputation and is used by non campers - the menu of the day is great value). A traditional bar is alongside and from here you can see the pretty mosaic clad play area (the 'Gaudi touch' which is also evident elsewhere). An ambitious animation programme is conducted for children in summer. Late evening Salsa classes were offered for adults when we visited. A small swimming pool with sunbathing areas is welcome on the hot summer days or you can walk to the very pleasant beach (ten minutes from a gate at the back of the site). The town of Sitges is an attractive resort with seaside entertainments and is well worth exploring. Open most of the year the site offers all manner of adventure activities (extra charge) which may be organized through reception and there are many things to see here - we especially recommend a visit to Monserrat.

Facilities

Two of the three sanitary blocks have been refurbished and provide roomy showers and special bright facilities for children. Separate baby room with bath. Good facilities for disabled campers. Laundry. Bar/restaurant. Shop (reception in low season). Swimming pool. Golf packages. Practice golf. Tennis. Play areas. Bicycle hire. Boules. Car wash. Bus link from outside site to Barcelona airport and city.
Off site: Golf, riding and fishing 0.5 km.

Open

17 January - 17 December.

At a glance

Welcome & Ambience	✓✓✓✓	Location	✓✓✓✓
Quality of Pitches	✓✓✓✓	Range of Facilities	✓✓✓✓✓

Directions

Sitges is 30 km. southwest of Barcelona. From A16/C32 exit 26 go towards Vilanova/St Pere Ribes. From Tarragona, go under autopista and back to roundabout on the other side to pick up site sign (towards Sitges). Take C246 to km. 39; site entrance is not too easy to see beside old large tree.

Charges 2004

Per person	€ 2,50 - € 4,40
child (1-9 yrs)	€ 1,70 - € 3,40
pitch incl. electricity	€ 13,40 - € 17,30

Plus 7% VAT.

Reservations

Contact site. Tel: 938 941 780.
E-mail: info@garroferpark.com

ES8410 Camping Playa Bara

Ctra N340, km 1183, 43883 Roda de Bará (Tarragona)

This is a most impressive, family owned site near the beach, which has been carefully designed and developed. On entry you find yourself in a beautifully sculptured, tree-lined drive with an accompanying aroma of pine and woodlands and the sound of waterfalls close by. Considering its size, with over 850 pitches, it is still a very green and relaxing site with an immense range of activities. It is well situated with a 50 metre walk to a long sandy beach via a tunnel under the railway (some noise) to a new promenade with palms and a quality beach bar and restaurant. Much care with planning and in the use of natural stone, palms shrubs and flowering plants gives a pleasing tropical appearance to all aspects of the site. The owners have excelled themselves in the design of the impressive terraced Roman-style pool complex, which is the central feature of the site. This complex is really amazing. Sunbathe on the pretty terraces or sip a drink whilst seated at the stools submerged in one of the pools or enjoy the panorama over the sea from the rooftop spa or the upper Roman galley bar surrounded by stylish friezes. A very well equipped gym with a dedicated instructor and a massage service. An attractive amphitheatre seats 2,000 and is used to stage ambitious entertainment in season. Pitches vary in size, the older ones terraced and well shaded with pine trees, the newer ones more open, with a variety of trees and bushes forming separators between them. Arrive early to find space in peak weeks.

Facilities

Excellent, fully equipped toilet blocks are of different sizes and types. Private cabins in some blocks, children's baths, basins and toilets and superb facilities for disabled visitors. Good private sanitary facilities for hire. Washing machines and dryers. Motorcaravan services. Supermarket. Butcher, bakery, papers, fruit, tabac and souvenir shops. Full restaurant and larger bar with simpler meals and takeaway, other bars, pleasant bar/restaurant on beach. Swimming pools. Jacuzzi/hydro-massage. Fronton and tennis (floodlit). Roller skating. Football. Junior club. Sports area. Doctor (24 hrs high season). Windsurfing school. Volleyball. Basketball. Gym. Petanque. Minigolf on a giant map of Europe. Fishing. Entertainment centre: amphitheatre with stage and dance floor. Animation in several languages. Large games room; video room, films. satellite TV, cocktail bar/disco room open 11 to 4 am. (weekends only in low season). ATM. Deposit boxes. Hairdresser. Internet points. Flights/excursions/tours booked. Off site: Bicycle hire 2 km. Riding 3 km. Golf 4 km.

At a glance

Welcome & Ambience	✓✓✓✓✓	Location	✓✓✓✓✓
Quality of Pitches	✓✓✓✓✓	Range of Facilities	✓✓✓✓✓

Directions

From the A7 take exit 31. Site entrance is at the 1183 km. marker on the N340 just opposite the Arco de Bara monument from which it takes its name.

Charges 2004

Per person	€ 3,11 - € 8,90
child (1-9 yrs)	€ 2,17 - € 6,20
large tent or caravan	€ 8,90
small tent	€ 6,20
car	€ 8,90
motorcycle	€ 6,20

All plus 7% VAT. Low season reductions for pensioners and all sports charges reduced by 90%.

Reservations

Contact site for details. Tel: 977 802 701.
E-mail: info@barapark.es

Open

11 March - 25 September, with all amenities.

ES8479 Camping Playa Cambrils – Don Camilo

Ctra Cambrils - Salou km 1.5, 43850 Cambrils (Tarragona)

Almost completely canopied by trees which provide welcome shade on hot days, the site is 300 m. from the beach across a busy road. It is mature and has had some recent renovations (2003). The small (60 sq.m.) pitches are on flat ground, divided by hedges, there are many permanent pitches and half the site is given up to chalet style accomodation. Large units are placed in a dedicated area where the trees are higher. The pool complex includes a functional glassed restaurant and bar with a distinct Spanish flavour reflected in the menu and tapas available all day. The pool is long and narrow with separate children's pool and a large paved area for soaking up the sun. Entertainment for chldren is organised by a good animation team. A big building at one end of the site consists of the supermarket, an attended electronic games room and a large play room. As this is a popular site with Spanish families it is a good place to practice your language.

Facilities

One modern sanitary building, and one large plus one small refurbished block offer reasonable facilities with British style WCs and free showers in separate buildings. Washing machines, dishwashing (some hot some cold) and laundry sinks (cold only) are at the end of the block under cover. Facilities for disabled campers near the swimming pool. Supermaket hop (Apr -Sep). Bar/snacks and separate restaurant (April-Sept). Playground. Animation in high season. Mini club. Huge electronic games room with attendant. Torches useful. Off site: Resort town has a range of shops, bars and restaurants. Bicycle hire 500 m. Fishing and golf 1 km. Riding 1.5 km.

At a glance

Welcome & Ambience	✓✓✓✓	Location	✓✓✓✓
Quality of Pitches	✓✓✓	Range of Facilities	✓✓✓

Directions

Leave A7 autopista at exit 37 and head for Cambrils and then to the beach. Turn left along beach road. Site is 1 km. east of Cambrils Playa and is well signed as you leave Cambrils marina.

Charges 2004

Per person	€ 1,50 - € 4,00
child (1-10 yrs)	free - € 3,00
pitch	€ 10,00 - € 23,00

Reservations

Write to site. Tel: 977 361 490.
E-mail: camping@playacambrils.com

Open

15 March - 12 October.

ES8530 Playa Montroig Camping Resort

Aptdo 3, N340 km 1136, 43300 Montroig (Tarragona)

What a superb site! Playa Montroig is about 30 kilometres beyond Tarragona set in its own tropical gardens with direct access to a very long soft sand beach. Bathing, windsurfing, surfboarding two diving rafts and many beach sports are available. The main part of the site lies between the sea, road and railway (as at other sites on this stretch of coast, there is some train noise) and there is a huge underpass. The site is divided into spacious, marked pitches with excellent shade provided by a variety of lush vegetation including very impressive palms set in wide avenues. There are 1,950 pitches, all with electricity and 330 with water and drainage. Some 48 pitches are directly alongside the beach – they are somewhat expensive and extremely popular. The site has many outstanding features. There is an excellent pool complex near the entrance with two pools (one heated for children). A quality restaurant serves traditional Catalunian fare (seats 150) and overlooks an entertainment area where you may watch genuine Flamenco dancing and buffet food is served (catering for 1,000). A large terrace bar dispenses drinks or if you yearn for louder music there is a disco and smaller bar. If you prefer international food there is yet another eating option in a very smart restaurant (seats 500). Above this is the 'Pai-pai' Caribbean cocktail bar where softer music is provided in an intimate atmosphere. Activities for children are very ambitious – there is even a ceramics kiln (multi-lingual carers). 'La Carpa', a spectacular open air theatre, is an ideal setting for daily keep fit sessions and the professional entertainment provided. If you are 5-11 years old you can explore the 'Tam-Tam Eco Park', a 20,000 sq.m. forest zone where experts teach the natural life of the area. You can even camp out for a night (supervised) to study wildlife (a once weekly activity). Adults are also allowed in to barbecues and other evening fun. This is an excellent site and there is insufficient space here to describe all the available activities. We recommend it for families with children of all ages and there is much emphasis on providing activities outside the high season.

Facilities

Fifteen sanitary buildings, some small, but of very good quality with toilets and washbasins, others really excellent, air conditioned larger buildings housing large showers, washbasins (many in private cabins) and separate WCs. Facilities for disabled campers and for babies. A 24 hour cleaning service operates. Water points around site (water said to be very pure from the site's own wells). Several launderettes. Motorcaravan services. Good shopping centre with supermarket, greengrocer, butcher, fishmonger, tobacconist and souvenir shops. Restaurants and bars. The 'Eurocentre', with 250 person capacity and equipped for entertainment and activities, large screen videos, films, shows and meetings (air conditioned). Fitness suite. Eco-park (see above). TV lounges (3) incl. satellite. Beach bar. Playground. Free kindergarten with multi-lingual staff. Skate-boarding. Jogging track. Sports area for volleyball, football and basketball. Tennis. Minigolf. Table tennis. Organised activities for children and adults including pottery and gardening classes. Windsurfing and water skiing courses. Surfboards and pedaloes for hire. Boat mooring. Hairdressers. Bicycle hire. Bureau de change. Safety deposit boxes. Telephone service. Internet café. Gas supplies. Dogs are not accepted. TVs are not allowed outside your vehicle. Off site: Riding and golf 3 km.

At a glance

Welcome & Ambience	✓✓✓✓	Location	✓✓✓✓✓
Quality of Pitches	✓✓✓✓✓	Range of Facilities	✓✓✓✓✓

Directions

Site entrance is off main N340 nearly 30 km. southwest from Tarragona. From motorway take Cambrils exit and turn west on N340 at 1136 km marker.

Charges 2004

Per unit incl 2 persons and electricity	€ 15,00 - € 56,00
premium pitch	€ 22,00 - € 80,00
extra person	€ 5,00
child (1-9 yrs)	free - € 4,00

All plus 7% VAT. Discounts for longer stays and for pensioners.

Reservations

Are possible and made with refundable booking fee (€ 30). Contact Dept. de Reservas, Apdo 3. at site address. Tel: 977 810 637. E-mail: info@playamontroig.com

Open

1 March - 31 October.

ES8470 Camping La Siesta

Calle Ctra Norte 37, 43840 Salou (Tarragona)

The palm bedecked entrance of La Siesta is only 250 metres from the pleasant sandy beach and close to the life of the resort of Salou. The town is popular with British and Spanish holidaymakers and has just about all that a highly developed Spanish resort can offer. For those who do not want to share the busy beach, there is a large, free swimming pool which is elevated above pitch level. La Siesta is divided into 470 individual pitches which are large enough and have electricity (10A), with smaller ones for tents. Many pitches are provided with artificial shade and within some pitches there is one box for the tent or caravan, and a shared one for the car. There is considerable shade from the trees and shrubs that are part of the site's environment. In high season, the siting of units is carried out by the management, who are friendly and helpful. Young campers are located separately to the rear of the site. The restaurant, which overlooks the good-sized pool, has a comprehensive menu and wine list, competing well with the town restaurants. A bar is alongside with TV and a large terrace, part of which is given over to entertainment in high season. A suprisingly large supermarket caters for most needs in season.

Facilities

Three bright and clean sanitary blocks provide very reasonable facilities. Motorcaravan services. Supermarket. Various vending machines. Self-service restaurant and bar with cooked dishes to take away. Dancing some evenings till 11 pm. Swimming pool (300 sq.m; open all season). Playground. Medical service daily in season. ATM point. Torches may be required. Off site: Huge numbers of shops, restaurants and bars near. Port Aventura is close. Bicycle hire 200 m. Fishing 500 m. Riding amd golf 6 km.

Open

14 March - 3 November.

At a glance

Welcome & Ambience	✓✓✓✓	Location	✓✓✓✓
Quality of Pitches	✓✓✓✓	Range of Facilities	✓✓✓✓✓

Directions

Leave A7 at exit 35 for Salou. Site is signed off the Tarragona/Salou road and from the one way system in the town of Salou. The site is in the town so keep a sharp eye for the small signs.

Charges 2004

Per person	€ 3,70 - € 6,80
child (4-9 yrs)	€ 3,00 - € 3,80
pitch and car	€ 7,40 - € 13,60
electricity	€ 2,50 - € 2,95

All plus 7% VAT. No credit cards.

Reservations

Advised 1 July - 20 Aug. and made in sense of guaranteeing a shady place, with electricity if required. Deposit required. Tel: 977 380 852. E-mail: info@camping-lasiesta.com

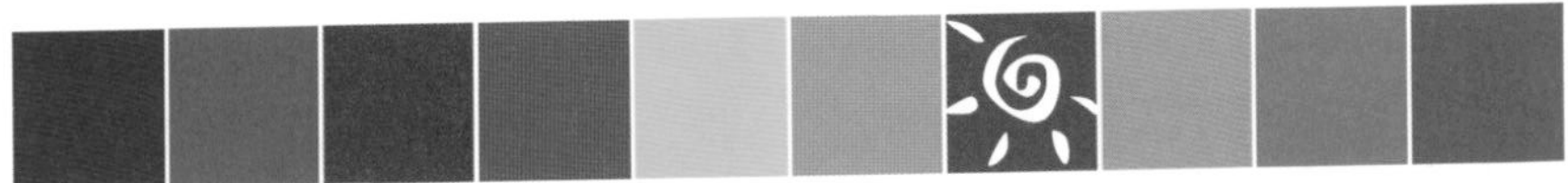

ES8482 Camping La Pineda de Salou

Ctra Costa Tarragona - Salou km 5, 43481 La Pineda (Tarragona)

La Pineda is just outside Salou towards Tarragona and this site is just 300 metres from the Aquapark and 2.5 kilometres from Port Aventura, to which there is an hourly bus service from outside the site entrance. There is some noise from this road. The site has a fair-sized swimming pool adjoining a smaller, heated one, open from mid June, behind large hedges close to the entrance. A large terrace has sun loungers, and various entertainment aimed at young people is provided in season. The 366 flat pitches are mostly shaded and of about 70 sq.m. All have 5A electricity. The beach is about 400 metres The simple restaurant/bar is shaded and has a large cactus garden to the rear. This is a plain, friendly and convenient site, with reasonable rates, probably best used for visiting Tarragona and Port Aventura, or exploring the local area, rather than for extended stays. Note: the site is reasonably close to a large industrial centre.

Facilities

Sanitary facilities are mature but clean with baby bath, dishwashing and laundry sinks. Facilities for disabled visitors. Two washing machines in each block. The second building is opened in high season only. Gas supplies. Shop (1/7-31/8). Restaurant and snacks (1/7-31/8). Swimming pools (1/7-31/8). Bar (all season). Five-a-side soccer pitch. Small TV room. Bicycle hire. Games room with videos and drink and snack machines. Playground (3-12 yrs). Entertainment (1/7-30/8). Torches may be required. Off site: Fishing 500 m. Golf 12 km.

Open

All year.

At a glance

Welcome & Ambience	✓✓✓	Location	✓✓✓
Quality of Pitches	✓✓✓	Range of Facilities	✓✓✓✓

Directions

From A7 just southwest of Tarragona take exit 35 and follow signs to La Pineda and Port Aventura then campsite signs appear.

Charges 2004

Per person	€ 3,70 - € 5,40
child (1-10 yrs)	€ 2,50 - € 4,00
pitch incl. car	€ 8,80 - € 17,50
electricity	€ 3,30
dog	€ 1,60 - € 0,27

All plus 7% VAT.

Reservations

Made for high season (min. 7 nights). Tel: 977 37 30 80. E-mail: info@campinglapineda.com

Spain

ES8537 Camping Naturista El Templo del Sol

43890 Hospitalet del Infante (Tarragona)

El Templo del Sol is a large, luxurious terraced naturist site with a distinctly Arabesque style and superb buildings in Moorish style. The owner has designed the magnificent main turreted building at the entrance with fountains and elaborate Moorish arches. Three large, tiered pools are wonderful with water cascading from one to the other and are part of a supporting complex containing a huge luxurious Jacuzzi with cracking views over the sea, a large bar with snacks, a games area, plus a sunbathing area on the roof. Also included is a 'Solar Park' where visitors may learn how solar energy is used and applied. The main building contains an impressive reception area and has an elegant restaurant and an elegant mosaic central, open area with a fountain. The site has 435 pitches, mainly rather small (60/70 sq.m), but 85 fully serviced. Pitches are on terraces giving rewarding views over the sea and ready access to the sandy beach. There is some shade. Site lighting is provided from pleasing serpent shaped light assemblies. The site is under French management and English is spoken. There is some daytime rail noise especially in the lower areas of the site where the larger pitches are located.

Facilities

The sanitary blocks are amongst the best you will find in Spain providing everything you could require and extensive services for disabled campers. Washing machines. Well stocked supermarket. Health shop. Souvenir shop. Bars. Restaurant and snack bar (1/4-10/10).Swimming pools (20/3-15/10). Jacuzzi. Cinema. Games area. Volley ball. Boule. Separate children's pool and play area. Miniclub. Doctor available. Library. Safety deposit boxes. Professional entertainment includes genuine Flamenco dancing. Hairdresser. Bicycle hire. ATM. Animals are not accepted. No jet skis. Off site: Fishing 100 m. Golf 2 km. Bicycle hire and boat launching 3 km. Riding 7 km. Theme parks.

At a glance

Welcome & Ambience	✓✓✓✓✓	Location	✓✓✓✓✓
Quality of Pitches	✓✓✓✓✓	Range of Facilities	✓✓✓✓✓

Directions

From N340 south of Tarragona, exit at km. 1123 in the direction of L'Hopitalet and follow signs.

Charges 2004

Per person	€ 3,00 - € 6,50
child (under 10 yrs)	€ 1,80 - € 5,00
pitch incl. electricity	€ 11,00 - € 21,00

Plus 7% VAT. Discounts for longer stays.

Reservations

Min. stay July/Aug. 5 nights, otherwise 3 nights. Naturist licence required. Contact site for details. Tel: 977 823 434. E-mail: info@eltemplodelsol.com

Open

20 March - 20 October.

ES8540 Yelloh! Village La Torre del Sol

Ctra N340, km 1136, 43300 Montroig (Tarragona)

A pleasant banana tree-lined approach road gives way to avenues of palms as you arrive at Torre del Sol, a member of the French Airotel chain and of the 'Yelloh' group of sites. Sister site to Templo del Sol (ES8537N), Torre del Sol is a very large site occuping a good position with direct access to the clean, soft sand beach, complete with a beach bar. Strong features here are 800 m of clean beach-front and entertainment is provided all season. There is a separate area where the 'Happy Camp' team will take your children to camp overnight in the Indian reservation, plus they can amuse them two days a week with other activities. The cinema doubles as a theatre to stage shows all season. A complex of three pools, thoughtfully laid out with grass sunbathing areas and palms has a lifeguard. There is good shade on a high proportion of the 1,500 individual, numbered pitches. All have electricity and are mostly of about 70-80 sq.m. There is usually space for odd nights but for good places between 10/7-16/8 it is best to reserve (only taken for a stay of five nights or more). Part of the site is between the railway and the sea so there is train noise. We were impressed with the provision of season-long entertainment and to give parents a break whilst children were in the safe hands of the animation team.

Facilities

Four very well maintained, fully equipped, toilet blocks include units for disabled people and babies, and some tiled units at three blocks with cabins with washbasins and hot showers. Washing machines. Gas supplies. Fridge hire. Large supermarket, bakery, and souvenir shops at entrance, open to public. Full restaurant with soft-toy playpen area. Takeaway. Bar with large terrace where entertainment held daily all season. Beach bar. Coffee bar and ice cream bar. Pizzeria. Open roof cinema with seating for 520; TV lounges (satellite); separate room for films or videos shown on TV. Well-soundproofed disco. Swimming pools (two heated). Solarium. Sauna. Tennis. Table tennis. Squash. Volleyball. Language school (Spanish). Minigolf. Multi purpose hardcourt. Sub aqua diving. Bicycle hire. Fishing. Windsurfing school; sailboards and pedaloes for hire. Playground and crèche. Library. Hairdressers. Car repair and car wash. No animals permitted. No jet skis. Off site: Theme parks. Beach fishing. Riding 3 km. Golf 4 km.

At a glance

Welcome & Ambience	✓✓✓✓✓	Location	✓✓✓✓✓
Quality of Pitches	✓✓✓✓✓	Range of Facilities	✓✓✓✓✓

Directions

Entrance is off main N340 road by 1136 km. marker, about 30 km. from Tarragona towards Valencia. From motorway take Cambrils exit and turn west on N340.

Charges 2005

Per pitch incl. 2 adults and electricity	€ 19,50 - € 55,00
extra person	€ 3,20 - € 8,50
child (0-10 yrs)	free - € 6,75

All plus 7% VAT. Discounts in low season for longer stays.

Reservations

Made with booking fee (€ 20); contact site first. Tel: 977 810 486. E-mail: info@latorredelsol.com

Open

15 March - 20 October.

ES8560 Camping Playa Tropicana

Playa Tropicana, 12579 Alcossebre (Castelló)

Playa Tropicana is the living dream of the owners Vera and Charlie. It has been given a tropical theme with scores of 'Romanesque' white statues around the site including in the sanitary blocks. It has a delightful position away from the main hub of tourism, alongside a good sandy beach which shelves gently into the clean waters. There is a shingle beach for fishing nearby and a pretty promenade in front of the site, with statues. It is in a quiet position and it is a drive rather than a walk to the centre of the village resort. The site has 300 marked pitches separated by lines of flowering bushes under mature trees. The pitches vary in size (50-100 sq.m), most are shaded and there are electricity connections throughout (some need long leads). There are 50 places for motorcaravans with water and drainage and there is a scale of charges for the different pitches. The site has several large water features by the high quality restaurant (some are very cheeky!), aviaries and small monkeys. Visit the restaurant and enjoy the pictures of the owners with famous people.

Facilities

Two sanitary blocks delightfully decorated, fully equipped and of excellent standard, include 16 washbasins in private cabins. Baby baths, some units with WC, basin and shower, and facilities for disabled people. Washing machine. Motorcaravan services. Gas supplies. Large supermarket (all season). Superb restaurant, a little expensive. (Easter - late Sept). Drinks served on terrace. Swimming pool (18 x 11 m.) and children's pool. Playground. Volleyball. Table tennis. Bicycle hire. Fishing. Torches necessary in some areas. No TVs allowed in July/Aug. Dogs are not accepted (but cats are). Off site: Fishing and watersports on the beach. Riding and boat launching 3 km. Golf 25 km.

Open

1 January - 31 December.

At a glance

Welcome & Ambience	✓✓✓✓✓	Location	✓✓✓✓✓
Quality of Pitches	✓✓✓✓✓	Range of Facilities	✓✓✓✓✓

Directions

Alcoceber (or Alcossebre) is between Peniscola and Oropesa. Turn off N340 at 1018 km. marker towards Alcossebre on CV142. Just before entering town proceed through the traffic lights to main road at next junction, turn right and follow coast road to site in 2.5 km.

Charges 2005

Per person	€ 3,00 - € 6,00
child (1-10 yrs)	€ 2,00 - € 5,00
pitch	€ 10,00 - € 43,00

Electricity and VAT included.
Discounts up to 45% out of season.

Reservations

Made for min. 10 days with deposit (25%).
Tel: 964 412 463. E-mail: info@playatropicana.com

ES8580 Bonterra Park

Avenida de Barcelona 47, 12560 Benicasim (Castelló)

If you are looking for a town site which is not too crowded and has good facilities, this one may be for you, as there are few quality sites in the local area and this is open all year. It is a 300 metre walk to a good, shady beach – and parking is not too difficult. Good beach for scuba diving or snorkelling - hire facilities are available at Benicasim. The site has 375 pitches (70-90 sq.m), all with electricity and a variety of bungalows on site. Bonterra has a clean and neat appearance with reddish soil, palms, grass and a number of trees which give good shade. There is a little road and rail noise. This is a well run, Mediterranean style site useful for visiting local attractions such as the Carmelite monastery at Desierto de las Palmas, six kilometres distant or the historic town of Castellon.

Facilities

Four attractive, well maintained sanitary blocks sensibly laid out, providing some private cabins, washbasins with hot water, others with cold. Showers have solar heating and include baby showers. Facilities for disabled campers. Laundry and motorcaravan services. Restaurant/bar. Shop (all year). Swimming pool, covered pool and children's pool. Playground (some concrete bases). Tennis. Multi-sport court. Table tennis. Disco. Bicycle hire. Off site: Town facilities. Fishing 500 m. Riding 3 km. Boat launching 5 km. Golf 10 km.

Open

All year.

At a glance

Welcome & Ambience	✓✓✓✓✓	Location	✓✓✓✓✓
Quality of Pitches	✓✓✓✓	Range of Facilities	✓✓✓✓

Directions

Site is east of Benicasim village, with entrance off the old main N340 road running a little back from the coast. Coming from the north, turn left at sign 'Benicasim por la costa'. On the A7 from the north use exit 45, from the south exit 46.

Charges 2005

Per adult	€ 3,10 - € 4,10
child (3-9 yrs)	€ 2,60 - € 3,60
pitch acc. to type and season	€ 9,10 - € 24,90
electricity	€ 3,10 - € 5,15

All plus 7% VAT. Less in low season and special long stay rates excl. July/Aug.

Reservations

Made if you write at least a month in advance.
Tel: 964 300 007. E-mail: info@campingbonterra.com

ES8570 Camping Torre La Sal 2

Cami L'Atall, 12595 Ribera de Cabanes (Castelló)

Torre La Sal 2 is a large site split in two by a fairly busy road, with a reception on each side. There are two pool complexes (one can be covered and heated) which are both on the west side, whilst the beach (shingle and sand) is on the east. Both sides have a restaurant (expensive) - the beach restaurant has two air conditioned wooden buildings and a terrace, but no views of the sea. Sports activities are on the western side, as is a children's park and a large disco. The pools and the park are locked for certain periods during the day. The 240 flat pitches vary in size, some very large with their own sinks, and most have either shade from trees or very high artificial shading rigged on frames. All have 10A electricity and are on sand, a few being close to the sea, but none with views. There is a plethora of bungalows, mobile homes, chalets and permanent pitches around the two areas. Many activities are organised in high season and the various amenities are scattered around the two locations - be sure to consult the lists and use your map to find your way around them all.

Facilities

Toilet facilities are of a good standard in both sections, four to the west and two to the east, with facilities for disabled campers in both. Baby rooms. Hot water to some sinks. British style toilets. Washing machines. Motorcaravan services. Shop, bars and restaurants (all year). Swimming pools and paddling pools - one heated and covered. Large play area. Games room. Disco. Football. Tennis. Volleyball. Basketball. Petanque. Fronton. Car wash. Security boxes. Medical room. Torches are required. Off site: Village has a range of shops bars and restaurants. Riding 10 km. Golf 20 km.

At a glance

Welcome & Ambience	✓✓✓	Location	✓✓✓✓
Quality of Pitches	✓✓✓✓	Range of Facilities	✓✓✓✓

Directions

From A7/E15 take exit 45 for Oropesa onto the N340. Move north to 1,000 km. marker and take road to the coast and town of Camil'atall. Site is well signed from here.

Charges 2004

Person	€ 5,10
child (1-9 yrs)	€ 4,60
pitch	€ 7,80
electricity	€ 4,60

Reservations

Write to site. Tel: 964 319 744.
E-mail: camping@torrelasal2.com

Open

All year.

ES8675 Camping Vall de Laguar

C/Sant Antonio 24, La Vall de Laguar, 03791 Campell (Alacant)

Near the pretty mountain-top village of Campell, this new campsite is perched high on the side of a mountain with breathtaking views of hilltop villages, the surrounding hills and distant sea. The pitches, pool, terrace and restaurant all share the views. Enrique and Consuello and their children Nico and Neus efficiently run this charming country site. Consuello cooks the most wonderful food and Nico is a font of information about the local area. A good time to be here is at the end of October when campers join in the festivities in the local village after the 'walk with history' when over a thousand people dine on paella. There are fascinating historic features in the area like the old (now disused) leper colony just a few hundred metres away and the ancient Moorish walk with over 6,500 carved rock steps (from a distance it looks like the Great Wall of China)! The 68 average size gravel pitches are on terraces and all have electricity and water. Trees and hedges have been planted but are yet to reach their potential. This is a great site to get away from the coastal hustle, bustle and high rise of the beaches. The restaurant has a pretty terrace and the pool is served by a small pool bar. There is a tight steep turn at the entrance although there is room to manoeuvre. This is a new site showing great promise for the future.

Facilities

Two new sanitary blocks have excellent clean facilities including some for disabled campers. Washing machines and dryers. Shop. Restaurant. Bar and pool bar. Swimming pool. Small entertainment programme in high season. Barbecue area with sinks. Torches useful. Off site: Attractive town close by. Donkey excursions 1 km. Golf and beach 18 km.

Open

All year.

At a glance

Welcome & Ambience	✓✓✓✓	Location	✓✓✓✓
Quality of Pitches	✓✓✓✓	Range of Facilities	✓✓✓

Directions

Site is about 20 km. west of Xabia/Javea. From A7/E15 take exit 62 and head to Beniarbeig on minor road. From there go to Sanet, Benidoleig and finally Vall de Laguar. Site is well signed from the town and sits above it. There are some winding and narrow sections on the way.

Charges guide

Per unit	€ 8,42 - € 12,02
person	€ 3,61 - € 3,61
child (over 3 yrs)	€ 3,00
electricity	€ 2,00

Minimun charge Easter week and July - August € 19.23

Reservations

Contact site. Tel: 699 773 509.
E-mail: info@campinglaguar.com

CAMPING TORRE LA SAL '2

CIUDAD DEPORTIVA

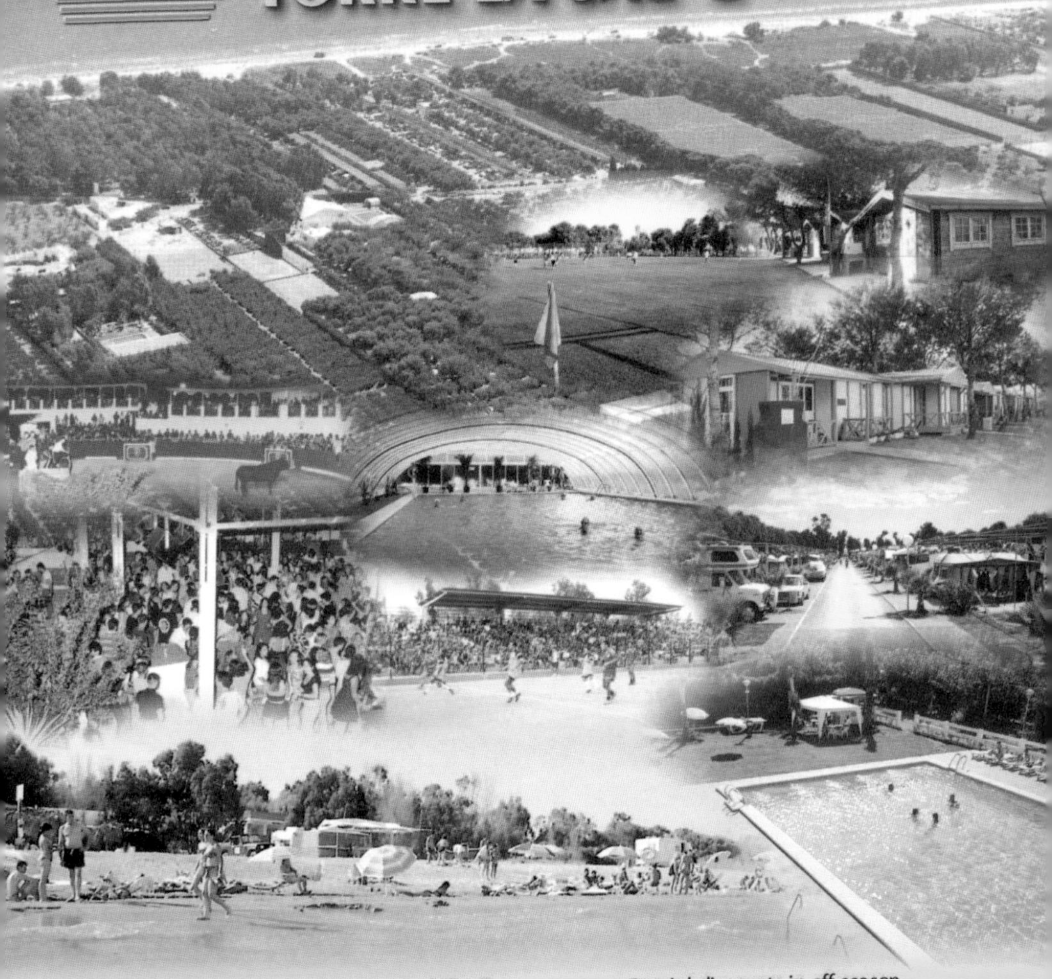

Situated in a paradisiacal spot, at the very beach, at 1 km from the natural region of Prat de Cabanes, at 2 km from the balneotherapy centre Marina d'Or and at 3 km from Oropesa de Mar con an ideal climate throughout the year. A nicely landscaped family camp site with 450 sites and 78 bungalows (46 'Nordicos' with heating and 32 'Gitotel de Luxe' with airco). The mulberry trees give lots of shade in summer and sun in winter. Our site is divided in sites of 80 to 140 sqm, separated by hedges. 282 of those sites have running water. 5 ablution blocks with free hot water and heated in winter. 4 swimming pools (2 of them covered and heated in winter). Tennis courts, squash, multi sport grounds with artificial grass, laundry, hair dresser's, 2 autom. washing machines, sauna, masseur serv. and Jacuzzi in winter, gymnastic for elderly people, social room, 2 children's playgrounds (the large one with monitor and animation in season), table tennis, supermarket, 2 restaurant-bars (one at beach and one next to the pools), various parkings, landscaped open air disco throughout the year and spectacular bullfight arena with young bulls (no violence). Organised animation (aerobic, monitors for sport and dancing...). Next to the site 'Ciudad Deportiva' only for campers with 2 football grounds with natural grass (105 x 64m and 80 x 50m). Caravan parking.

- Special discounts in off season
- Reservations possible
- Special fees for old age pensioners

from 1.30 till 30.6

Management: Fernando Fenollosa

CAMI L'ATALL, S/N.
E-12595 RIBERA DE CABANES
(CASTELLON)
TEL (34) 964319744 - 964319567
FAX (34) 964319744
A-7 exit 44 (12 km South)
or exit 45 (3 km North).
N-340 km 1000
camping@torrelasal2.com
www.torrelasal2.com

ideal also for sunny winter holidays on the beach.

Open all year

ES8536 Camping Caravanning Ametlla Village Platja

Apdo. Correus 240, Paraje Santes Creus, 43860 Ametlla de Mar (Tarragona)

This site within a protected area is new (2000), has been well thought out and is startling in the quality of service provided, the finish and the materials used in construction. The 373 pitches are on a terraced hillside above colourful coves with shingle beaches and two small associated lagoons (with a protected fish species). The site is environmentally correct, local planning regulations are extremely tight including the types of trees that may planted. The many bungalows here have been tastefully incorporated. There are great views, particularly from the friendly restaurant (which has a very good chef). Animation is organised for children in high season and there is a well equipped fitness room (free). There are good quality pools (with lifeguard) and a sub-aqua diving school operates on the site in high season and beginners may try a dive. This is a most attractive small site in an idyllic situation near the picturesque fishing village of L'Ametlla de Mar, famous for its fish restaurants, and within the Ebro Delta nature reserve. It is about 20 minutes from Europe's second largest theme park, Port Aventura, but as there is no regular bus service your own transport is required (the owners arrange free buses to the local disco each Wednesday). No transit traffic is allowed within the site in high season. Used by tour operators (30 pitches). This is a very good site for families or for just relaxing. There is some train noise.

Facilities

Three really good toilet blocks provide free hot water throughout, British style WCs, washbasins and some private cabins with WC and washbasin, plus others with WC, basin and shower. The showers are very clean, roomy and have hot water. Motorcaravan services. Gas supplies. Supermarket (1/4-30/9; small shop incl. bread at other times). Good restaurant with snack menu and bar. TV room (1/4-15/10). Swimming pool. Sub aqua diving. Kayaking. Fishing. Children's club and play area. Fitness room. Bicycle hire. Football. Basketball. Volleyball. Entertainment July/Aug. Barbecue area. Bicycle hire. Fishing. English is spoken. Off site: Boat launching 3 km. Golf 15 km. Riding 20 km. Theme parks.

Open

All year.

At a glance

Welcome & Ambience	✓✓✓✓	Location	✓✓✓✓
Quality of Pitches	✓✓✓✓	Range of Facilities	✓✓✓✓

Directions

From A7/E15 (Barcelona - Valencia) take exit 39 for L'Ametlla de Mar. Follow numerous large white signs on reaching village and site is 2.5 km. south of the village.

Charges guide

Per person	€ 2,06 - € 5,00
child (under 10 yrs)	€ 1,69 - € 4,10
tent or caravan	€ 2,18 - € 5,30
car	€ 2,18 - € 5,30
motorcaravan	€ 3,86 - € 9,40
electricity	€ 3,00 - € 3,50

All plus 7% VAT. Less for longer stays, especially in low season.

Reservations

Contact site. Tel: 977 267 784.
E-mail: info@campingametlla.com

ES8625 Kiko Park Rural

46317 Villargordo del Cabriel (Valencia)

Approaching Kiko Park Rural, you will see a small hilltop village appearing in a landscape of mountains, vines and a jewel-like lake. Kiko was a small village and farm and the village now forms the campsite and accomodation. Amenities are contained within the architectually authentic buildings, some old and some new. The restaurant serves delicious food that would compete favourably in any Spanish setting. Kiko Rural is run by four cousins from a family with 30 years of camping experience - a passionate and enthusiastic team with a vision of excellence. The 103 pitches (with 6A electricity) all have stunning views. Hundreds of trees planted in 2003 are yet to provide shade due to their size, although this will soon remedy itself. Generous hedge plantings have been made which already afford some privacy. There are swimming pools for adults and children, again with superb views. Kiko Rural is an ideal site for those folk, young and old, who enjoy adventurous activites, communing with nature, or relaxing with an occasional sightseeing excursion. A sister site to Kiko Park in Oliva Valencia (ES8615) Kiko Rural is like no other campsite. Old and new have combined to create an environment that is, within its catergory, outstanding.

Facilities

Three new sanitary blocks are very well equipped, including hot water throughout, preset showers and excellent facilities for disabled people.. Gas supplies. Motorcaravan services. Excellent restaurant. Well stocked shop with reasonable prices. Pleasant bar with TV. Swimming pool and paddling pool. Very good playground. Bicycle hire. Many adventurous activities can be undertaken here, including white water rafting, gorging, orienteering, trekking, bungee and riding. Special programmes organised on application. Large families and groups catered for. Animation for children and adults in high season.
Off site: All the arranged activities. Fishing, boating, canoening and windsurfing on the lake. Boat launching. Village 3 km. with usual facilites. Tours to 'bodegas'. Tours to Valencia.

At a glance

Welcome & Ambience	✓✓✓✓✓	Location	✓✓✓✓✓
Quality of Pitches	✓✓✓✓	Range of Facilities	✓✓✓✓

Directions

From autopista A7/E15 on Valencia ring road (near the airport) take N111 to the west. Villagordo del Cabriel is about 18 km. towards Motilla. Take the village exit and follow the signs which lead through the village and over a hill -; spot the village on a hill just 2 km. away. That village is the campsite!

Charges guide

Per pitch	€ 5,00 - € 10,00
person	€ 3,60
child up to 10 yrs	€ 2,80

Reservations

Contact site. Tel: 962 139 082.
E-mail: kikoparkrural@kikopark.com

Open

All year.

ES8615 Kiko Park

46780 Oliva (Valencia)

Kiko Park is a smart site nestled behind protective sand dunes, alongside a 'blue flag' beach. There are sets of attractively tiled steps over the dunes or a long boardwalk near the beach bar (good for prams and wheelchairs) to take you to the fine white sandy beach and the sea. There is an award-winning restaurant with architecture that reminds one of a ship near the tropical style beach-bar, both overlooking the marina, beautiful beach and sea. The 200 large pitches all have electricity and the aim is to progressively upgrade all these to serviced 'super' pitches. There are plenty of flowers, hedging and trees adding shade, privacy and colour. This is an excellent site for watersport enthusiasts, as it is beside a marina for boat launching. A variety of entertainment is provided all year. The children's club area has a mini zoo, with healthy looking animals (the 'burro' is popular, as are rabbits and the strange Chinese duck that dances rather than walks). Spanish lessons are held along with dance class and aerobics during the winter. The site is run by the second generation of a family involved in camping for 30 years and their experience shows. They are supported by a friendly, efficient team who speak many languages. The narrow roads leading to the site can be a little challenging for very large units but it is worth the effort.

Facilities

Four modern sanitary blocks are very clean and fully tiled with free hot water, large showers, washbasins (a few in cabins), British style WCs and excellent facilities for disabled visitors (who will find a large part of this site flat and convenient). Laundry facilities. Motorcaravan services. Gas supplies. Restaurant. Bar with TV. Beach-side bar and restaurant (all year). Supermarket (all year, excl. Sundays). Playground. Watersports facilities. Diving school in high season (from mid-June). Mini club. Entertainment for children from mid-June. Petanque. Bicycle hire. Beach volleyball. Exchange facilities. Off site: The yacht club also offers its facilities of swimming pool, bar, restaurant and TV room to campers at Kiko. The footpath to the marina leads into the town - about a 10 minute walk. Indoor pool 1 km. Golf 5 km. Riding 7 km.

At a glance

Welcome & Ambience	✓✓✓✓✓	Location	✓✓✓✓✓
Quality of Pitches	✓✓✓✓	Range of Facilities	✓✓✓✓

Directions

From A7 north of Benidorm take exit 61 to the town and then the beach; site is at the northwest end.

Charges 2005

child (under 10 yrs)	€ 2,20 - € 4,80
pitch acc. to services and season	€ 10,90 - € 29,00
dog	€ 0,60 - € 2,20
electricity (per kw)	€ 0,30

Reservations

Write to site. Tel: 962 850905.
E-mail: kikopark@kikopark.com

Open

All year.

ES8535 Camping-Pension Cala d'Oques

43890 Hospitalet del Infante (Tarragona)

This peaceful and delightful site has been developed with care and dedication by Elisa Roller over 30 years or so and she now runs it with the help of her daughter Kim. Part of its appeal lies in its situation beside the sea with a wide beach of sand and pebbles, its amazing mountain backdrop and the views across the bay to the town and part by the atmosphere created by Elisa, and staff - friendly, relaxed and comfortable. The restaurant with its homely touches has a super menu and a reputation extending well outside the site (the excellent cook has been there for many years) and the family type entertainment is in total contrast to that provided at the larger, brasher sites of the Costa Daurada. There are 255 pitches, mostly level and laid out beside the beach, with more behind on wide, informal terracing. Odd pine and olive trees are an attractive feature and provide some shade. Electricity is available although long leads may needed in places. Gates provide access to the pleasant beach with useful cold showers to wash the sand away. Torches are needed at night. For those interested, there is a naturist beach of fine sand around the little headland just south of the site. This is a pretty place to stay and Elisa gives a pleasant personal service but do not expect 'Costa' type entertainment. Ask how the nearby village of Hospitalet del Infante got its name - it's a royal riddle! The village itself is well worth exploring and if you are here in June watch for the fabulous fireworks of the celebration of St John. It is interesting to note that Cala d'Oques (Goose Bay) was where migrant geese landed on return from wintering in South Africa, hence the geese on the site logo and the guard goose watching the entrance.

Facilities

The main toilet facilities are in the front part of the building housing the restaurant, reception and the family home on the first level. Clean and neat, there is hot water to showers (hot water by token but free to campers - a device to guard against unauthorized visitors from the beach). New heated unit with toilets and washbasins for winter use. Additional small bock with toilets and washbasins at the far end of the site. Motorcaravan service point. Restaurant/bar and shop (1/4-30/9). Play area. Kim's kids club. Five-a-side soccer. Fishing. Internet point. Gas supplies. Torches required in some areas Off site: Village facilities, incl. shop and restaurant 1.5 km. Bicycle hire or riding 2 km.

Open

All year.

At a glance

Welcome & Ambience	✓✓✓✓✓	Location	✓✓✓✓✓
Quality of Pitches	✓✓✓✓	Range of Facilities	✓✓✓✓

Directions

Hospitalet del Infante is south of Tarragona, accessed from the A7 (exit 38) or from the N340. From the north take first exit to Hospitalet del Infante at the 1128 km. marker. Follow signs in the village, site is 2 km. south, by the sea.

Charges 2004

Per person	€ 4,85 - € 7,20
child (0-10 yrs)	free
pitch incl. car	€ 6,95 - € 15,00
electricity	€ 3,35
dog	€ 2,50 - € 2,85

Discounts for seniors and for longer stays.
No credit cards.

Reservations

Contact site. Tel: 977 823 254.
E-mail: eroller@nil.fut.es

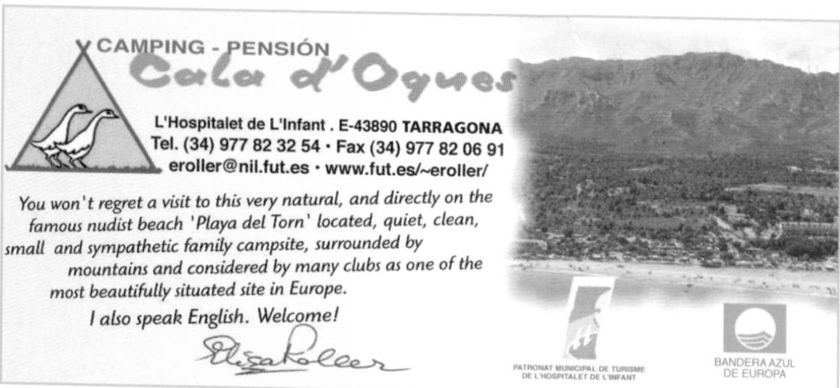

ES8620 Camping L'Alqueria

46730 Gandia (Valencia)

Recommended by our agent, we plan to conduct a full inspection of this site in 2005. Alqueria is a popular site to the south of Valencia and 1 km from a sandy beach. The 242 pitches are well shaded and most are equipped with electrical connections. This is a lively site in peak season with a varied activity and entertainment programme. Chalets are available for rent.

Facilities

Swimming pool, covered pool, bar, restaurant, takeaway meals, shop, sports field, children's playground, entertainment programme in high season, children's club. Off site: Nearest beach 1 km, golf 8 km, shops, restaurant etc. within 1 km.

Open

All year.

Directions

Leave the A7 at junction 60, joining the N332 (Valencia - Alicante road). At Gandia follow signs to Grao de Gandia. From here the site is well signed.

Charges year

Per person	€ 4,00 - € 7,00
child	€ 2,60 - € 3,60
pitch	€ 3,46 - € 4,27
electricity	€ 3.04

Reservations

Advised for high season; contact site.
Tel: 96 284 04 70. E-mail: info@campinggandia.com

ES8685 Camping Caravaning El Raco

Avda. Doctor Severo Ochoa, s/n, 03500 Benidorm (Alacant)

This purpose built site (opened in '96) with excellent facilities and very competitive prices provides about 1,000 pitches (180 for touring units). There is wide access from the Rincon de Loix road. The site is quietly situated 1.5 km. from the town, Levante beach and promenade. The road has both footpaths and a cycle track. There are wide tarmac roads and pitches of 80 sq.m. or more, separated by low, clipped cypress hedging and some trees which provide some shade. Free satellite TV connections are provided to each pitch and there are 94 with all services with (10A) electricity available. The whole site is on a slight downward slope away from the entrance and affords excellent views of the rugged mountains in the hinterland, although this open aspect could be a disadvantage in windy weather. The good value restaurant, bar and elegant outdoor and indoor pools are all at the entrance, some distance from the touring pitches. There are large numbers of permanent pitches and many seasonal pitches are occupied by wintering campers (lots of British) and the site has a mature, cheerful atmosphere.

Facilities

Four large toilet blocks are well equipped. Facilities for disabled people. Dishwashing sinks. Laundry facilities. Gas supplies. Motorcaravan services. Restaurant. Bar. Well stocked shop with reasonable prices. Busy bar with TV also open to public and good value restaurant. Outdoor swimming pool, no slides or diving board (1/4-31/10). Indoor heated pool (1/11-31/3). Playground. ATM. Off site: Beach 1 km. Bicycle hire 2 km. Golf 6 km. Theme parks.

Open

All year.

At a glance

Welcome & Ambience	✓✓✓✓	Location	✓✓✓✓
Quality of Pitches	✓✓✓✓	Range of Facilities	✓✓✓✓✓

Directions

From autopista take Benidorm (Levante) exit 65 and at second set of traffic lights turn left on N332 (main route to Altea and Valencia). After 1.5 km. turn right at lights (signed Levante Playa), then straight on at next lights for 300 m. to site on right. From north on N332 follow signs for Playa Levante (or Benidorm Palace). At traffic lights turn left (Playa Levante), straight on at next lights to site on right in 300 m.

Charges 2004

Per person	€ 4,80 - € 5,00
child (1-9 yrs)	€ 3,50 - € 3,70
pitch incl. car	€ 11,00 - € 13,60

Discounts for longer stays.
VAT included. No credit cards.

Reservations

Not accepted. Tel: 96 586 8552.
E-mail: campingraco@inicia.es

ES8743 Complejo Ecoturistico Marjal

Ctra N-332, km 73.4, 03140 Guardamar del Segura (Alacant)

MarJal is located beside the estuary of the Segura river, alongside the pine and eucalyptus forests of the Dunas de Guardamar natural park. It is a new site with a huge lagoon-style pool and a superb sports complex. Reception is housed within a delicately coloured building complete with a towering Mirador, topped by a weather-vane depicting the 'Garza Real' (heron) bird which frequents the local area and forms part of the site logo. There are 212 pitches on this award winning site, all with water, electricity, drainage and satellite TV points, the ground covered with crushed marble, making the pitches clean and pleasant. There is some shade and the site has an open feel with lots of room for manoeuvring. The large leased restaurant overlooks the pools and the river that leads to the sea in the near distance. This situation is shared with the taperia (high season) and bar with large terraces fringed by trees, palms and pomegranates. The impressive pool/lagoon complex (1,100 sq.m) has a water cascade, an island bar plus bridge, one part sectioned as a pool for children and a jacuzzi. The extensive sports area is also impressive with qualified instructors who will customise your fitness programme whilst consulting the doctor. No effort has been spared here, the quality heated indoor pool, light-exercise room, sauna, solarium, beauty salon, fully equipped gym and changing rooms, including facilities for disabled visitors, are of the highest quality. Aerobics and physiotherapy are also on offer. All activities are discounted for campers. A programme of entertainment is provided for adults and children in season by a professional animation team. The fine sandy beach can be reached through the forest (800 m).

Facilities

Three excellent heated toilet blocks have free hot water, elegant separators between sinks, spacious showers and some cabins. Each block has high quality facilities for babies and disabled campers, modern laundry rooms with washing machines, dryers, ironing boards and dishwashing rooms. Car wash. Well stocked supermarket. Restaurants. Bar. Large outdoor pool complex (1/6-31/10). Heated indoor pool (low season). Fitness suite and gym. Jacuzzi. Sauna. Solarium. Aerobics and aquarobics for the more mature camper. Play room for children. Minigolf. Floodlit tennis and soccer pitch. Volleyball. Bicycle hire. Games room. TV room. ATM. Business centre. Internet access.
Off site: Beach 800 m. Riding or golf 4 km.

At a glance

Welcome & Ambience	✓✓✓✓✓	Location	✓✓✓✓
Quality of Pitches	✓✓✓✓✓	Range of Facilities	✓✓✓✓✓

Directions

On N332 40 km. south of Alicante, site is on the sea side between 73 and 74 km. markers.

Charges 2004

Per person	€ 4,00 - € 6,00
child	€ 2,50 - € 4,00
pitch	€ 16,00 - € 28,00
dog	€ 2,00 - € 3,00
electricity (per kw, monitored by computer)	€ 0,25

All plus 7% VAT.

Reservations

Contact site. Tel: 966 725 022.
E-mail: camping@marjal.com

Open

All year.

ES8687 Camping Cap Blanch

Playa de Cap Blanch 25, 03590 Altea (Alacant)

This well run site, in a coastal location, is open all year and very popular for winter stays. It is alongside the beach road and has direct access to the pebble beach and is within a few hundred yards of all Albir's shops and restaurants. Campers can join in a host of activities organised by the site, from physical ones such as tennis and walking to gentler ones such as painting or lessons in Spanish in the pleasant classroom. The site tends to be full in winter and is very popular with several nationalities, especially the Dutch. For winter stays, it would pay to get there before Christmas as January and February are the peak months. Although it is on the coast, the site is well sheltered and something of a sun-trap, the 250 pitches on flat, hard gravel are of a good size and well maintained with 5A electricity. There is much to see in the Levant (this area takes its name from the Spanish word 'lavantarse' which means get up - as in sun!) and a visit to the mountains is recommended to sample traditional foods and the wonderful Jumilla and Yecla wines.

Facilities

The refurbished sanitary block can be heated and provides good facilities including some washbasins in cabins, baby facilities, a new shower room for children and a room for disabled visitors (both these accessed by key). Motorcaravan services. Gas supplies. Laundry. Bar and restaurant. Takeaway. Playground. Tennis. Boules. Fitness centre. Organised entertainment and courses. ATM.
Off site: Restaurants, shops and commercial centre close. Golf 0.5 km. Bicycle hire 1 km. Riding 5 km.

Open

All year.

At a glance

Welcome & Ambience	✓✓✓✓✓	Location	✓✓✓✓✓
Quality of Pitches	✓✓✓	Range of Facilities	✓✓✓✓

Directions

Site is on Albir - Altea coast road and can be reached from either end. From N332, north or south, watch for sign Playa del Albir and proceed through Albir until you reach the coast road. Site is on north side of Albir, well signed.

Charges 2004

Per person	€ 5,50
child (3-12 yrs)	€ 4,50
pitch incl. car	€ 8,50 - € 12,00
electricity	€ 5,50

VAT included. Less 10-35% for low season stays 7-30 days, special rates for long stays.

Reservations

Contact site. Tel: 965 845 946.
E-mail: capblanch@ctv.es

ES8742 Camping Internacional La Marina

Ctra N332 km 76, 03194 La Marina (Alacant)

Efficiently run by a friendly Belgian family, La Marina has 370 pitches of seven different types and size of pitch ranging from about 50 sq.m. for tents to 100 sq.m. with electricity (10A), TV, water and drainage. Artificial shade is provided and the pitches are extremely well maintained on level, well drained ground with a special area allocated for tents in a small orchard. The Lagoon swimming pool complex is absolutely fabulous and has something for everyone (with lifeguards). The quality restaurant and bustling terraces overlook the Lagoon making for a most relaxing meal. A fine fitness centre and covered, heated pool (14 x 7 m) are close by. A pedestrian gate is at the rear of the site to give access to the long sandy beach through the coastal pine forest that is a feature of the area. You can be assured of quality at La Marina and we recommend it very highly whatever type of holiday camper you may be.

Facilities

The elegant sanitary blocks offer the very best of modern facilities. Heated in winter, they include private cabins and facilities for disabled visitors. These facilities are amongst the best we have seen on the Mediterranean coast. Laundry facilities incl. irons. Modern motorcaravan services. Gas supplies. Supermarket. Bar/restaurant serving traditional Spanish dishes (all year). Swimming pools (1/4-15/10). Indoor pool. Fitness centre with massage. Sauna. Extensive activity and entertainment programme. New sports area. Tennis. Table tennis. Huge playground. Hairdresser. Good security. Off site: Fishing 800 m. Boat launching 5 km. Golf 7 km. Bicycle hire 8 km. Riding 15 km. Hourly bus service from outside the gate if you wish to explore Alicante or Murcia. Theme parks.

Open

All year.

At a glance

Welcome & Ambience	✓✓✓✓✓	Location	✓✓✓✓✓
Quality of Pitches	✓✓✓✓✓	Range of Facilities	✓✓✓✓✓

Directions

Site is 2 km. west of La Marina. Leave N332 Guardamara de Segura - Santa Pola road at the 75 km. marker if travelling north, or the 78 km. marker if travelling south. Site is well signed.

Charges 2005

Per person	€ 5,00 - € 7,20
child (under 10 yrs)	€ 3,50 - € 4,80
pitch acc. to type and season	€ 16,00 - € 37,20
electricity	€ 2,40 - € 3,00
dog	€ 1,00 - € 2,00

Plus 7% VAT. Seven grades of pitch. Less in low season, plus good discounts for longer stays 16/9-14/6, excluding Easter.

Reservations

Made with deposit (€ 50), min. 5 days Easter and Aug. Tel: 965 419 200. E-mail: info@campinglamarina.com

ES8689 Camping Playa del Torres

Partida Torres Norte 11, Apdo. Correus 243, 03570 Villajoyosa (Alacant)

Jacinto and Mercedes have a pretty beachside site with the lower part set under eucalyptus trees. Reception is placed in one of the site's tasteful wooden buildings close to the beach (excellent English is spoken). The 85 lower pitches, some large, are on flat ground with shade. 10 good pitches are right alongside the beach fence (book early). All have electricity (16A), some are fully serviced and there are ample water fountains around the site along with efficient, modern lighting. The upper levels of the site have chalets and mobile homes. A modest sized pool with a sunbathing area is set in the centre part of the site between the building housing the bar, cafeteria and shop and the separate clean sanitary block (a short walk from the beachside pitches). Boats can be launched from the sand and shingle beach, sub-aqua diving and other watersports can be organised. Benidorm with its beaches is close, along with many tourist activities including the Fuentes del Algar waterfall and the huge exiting new 'Terra Mittica' theme park. If you prefer small sites away from the 'high rise' and bustle of Benidorm which is of high quality this could be for you.

Facilities

The sanitary building is of a high specification, as are the fittings within, including excellent showers. Laundry. Bar. Cafeteria. Shop. Swimming pool. Children's play area. Petanque. Fishing. Barbecues. Freezer. Fridge hire. Reception will assist with all tourist activities. Off site: Riding 100 m. Golf 18 km. Serious or recreational walking and climbing is possible about 20 minutes away from the site. Benidorm is very close.

Open

All year.

At a glance

Welcome & Ambience	✓✓✓✓✓	Location	✓✓✓✓✓
Quality of Pitches	✓✓✓✓✓	Range of Facilities	✓✓✓

Directions

From Villajoyosa on N332, 1 km. after town, 300 m. past traffic lights, sign on right, follow road 800 m. to site. From Benidorm after 3 km. site on left, but left turn prohibited. Proceed 400 m. to traffic lights, circle onto other carriageway, then as above. From autoroute leave at Benidorm or Villajoyosa on N332, then as above. Do not confuse with two older sites (Hercules and Sartorium), adjacent beach sites.

Charges guide

Per person	€ 3,44 - € 3,82
child (4-13 yrs)	€ 2,57 - € 2,85
pitch	€ 3,22 - € 7,15
caravan	€ 3,57 - € 3,97
tent	€ 3,44 - € 3,82
car	€ 3,44 - € 3,83

Plus 7% VAT. Less 5-50% for low season stays of 7 days or more.

Reservations

Contact site. Tel: 966 810 031. E-mail: capto@ctv.es

Do as the sun does, spend your holidays at...
Welcome
RECOMENDED BY THE BEST EUROPEAN GUIDES
VACANCE-PARK
Camping Internacional
La Marina
CARAVANING - BUNGALOW PARK
1ª CATEGORIA
www.campinglamarina.com
Located at the Elche coastline,in the middle of nature, close to a beautiful beach of fine sand, distinguished with the ECC blue flag for optimal water quality. We offer luxurious installations: 3.000 m² thematic swimming complex, heated swimming-pool, fitness center, very high quality sanitary, entertainment to the highest level for children, young and adults. All free of charge for our clients. Prices in accordance with season and duration of the stays. Open all year.
FITNESS CENTER
and New Sport Complex
The Leading Camping & Caravaning Parks of Europe
CERTIFIED IQNet
AENOR
ER
Empresa Registrada
ER-1694/2001
CERTIFIED IN ISO 9001
CALIDAD TURISTICA
CV
COMUNITAT VALENCIANA
Costa Blanca
www.costablanca.org
Information and reservations
Ctra. N-332a Km.76 - E-03194 LA MARINA (Alicante) SPAIN
Telf.: (34) 96 541 92 00 - Fax: (34) 96 541 91 10
info@campinglamarina.com

ES8682 Camping Villamar

Carre Del Albir, 03503 Benidorm (Alacant)

A new all year site with all the amenities a camper could desire, Villamar is a superb site, operating to high standards and rules. The central Lake style pools and amenities complex with its extensive grassed areas, dotted with palms, is cleverly designed and very smart. Sit on the terraces looking over the tropical scenery as you enjoy an English breakfast or dinner later in the day, and you will find it difficult to remember the teeming town of Benidorm is close by. The 650 pitches are occupied by a myriad of foreign guests and we are told the owners hoped to create a small camping area. The pitches are very big, flat, with some shade from young trees. The entertainment programme and indeed the whole site is aimed at a mature population though there are few things for children to do (at present there is no children's play area, although one is planned for the future). The sports area has many courts for boules and other sedate activities such as darts, centred in the restaurant area. The restaurant is attractively decorated and has lounges and terraces for relaxation along with internet terminals and electronic games. All round this is a great site. There are no tour operator pitches.

Facilities

The four new sanitary blocks include open style washbasins (some partitioned), free controllable hot showers, baby areas and units for disabled campers. Dishwashing and separate laundry sinks outside each block. Well stocked shop with reasonable prices. Restaurant. Snack bar. Motorcaravan services. Car wash. Two outdoor swimming pools (one heated for the winter guests), one indoor pool (lifeguards in high season). Small play area. TV room, games room and leisure area. Boules. ATM. Internet point. Entertainment in the restaurant area. Dogs are not accepted. Off site: Resort town and beach close with usual attractions. Golf, riding, bicycle hire and boat launching 2 km. Excursions.

At a glance

Welcome & Ambience	✓✓✓✓✓	Location	✓✓✓✓
Quality of Pitches	✓✓✓✓✓	Range of Facilities	✓✓✓✓

Directions

Site is northeast of Benidorm at Platja de L'abril. From the A7, A19 or N11 take the exit for Benidorm (Platja de L'Abril). Once at the end of the exit road from the autoroute look for the very obvious camping signs.

Charges guide

Per person	€ 4,50 - € 6,90
child ((1-3 yrs)	€ 3,50 - € 4,30
pitch	€ 9,20 - € 16,00
electricity	€ 3,50

Reservations

Contact site. Tel: 96 681 1255.
E-mail: camping@campingvillamar.com

Open

All year.

ES8754 Camping Jávea

Ctra Cabo de la Nao, km 1, 03730 Jávea (Alacant)

The 200 metre access road to this site is a little unkempt as it passes some factories, but all changes on the final approach with palms, orange and pine trees, the latter playing host to a colony of parakeets. English is spoken at reception. The boxed hedges and palms surrounding this area with a backdrop of hills dotted with villas presents an attractive setting. Three hectares provides space for 246 numbered pitches with 146 for touring units. Flat, level and rectangular in shape, the pitches vary in size 60-80 sq.m. (not advised for caravans or motorhomes with an overall length exceeding 7 m). All have a granite chip surface and 8A electricity. Being a typical Spanish site, the pitches are not separated so units may be close to each other. Some pitches have artificial shade, although for most the pruned eucalyptus and pepper trees will suffice. The area has a large number of British residents so a degree of English is spoken by many shopkeepers and many restaurants provide multi language menus. Besides being popular for a summer holiday, Camping Javea is now open all year and could be of interest to those that wish to 'winter' in an excellent climate. Discounts can make an extended stay extremely viable.

Facilities

Two very clean, fully equipped, sanitary blocks include two children's toilets plus a baby bath, dishwashing and laundry sinks. Two washing machines. Fridge hire. Small bar and restaurant where in high season you purchase bread and milk. Large swimming pool and paddling pool with lifeguard and sunbathing lawns. Play area. Table tennis. Boules. Five-a-side football. Basketball. Electronic barriers (deposit for swipe card). Caravan storage. Off site: Sandy beach 3 km. Old and New Javea within easy walking distance with supermarkets and shops catering for all needs.

Open

All year.

At a glance

Welcome & Ambience	✓✓✓	Location	✓✓✓
Quality of Pitches	✓✓✓	Range of Facilities	✓✓✓

Directions

Exit N332 for Javea on A134, continue in direction of Port (road number changes to CV 734). On reaching roundabout and Lidl supermarket turn right signed Arenal Platges and Cabo de la Nao (also camping sign). Straight on at next roundabout to camping sign and slip road in 100 m. If you miss slip road go back from next roundabout.

Charges 2004

Per adult	€ 3,82 - € 4,50
child	€ 3,61 - € 4,25
pitch	€ 9,86 - € 15,45
electricity	€ 3,00
dog	€ 1,50 - € 2,00

Reservations

Necessary for high season. Tel: 965 791 070.
E-mail: info@campingjavea.com

ES8753 Caravaning La Manga

Autovia Cartagena-La Manga exit 15, 30370 La Manga del Mar Menor (Murcia)

The site is a very large well equipped, 'holiday style' site with its own beach and pool. With a good number of typical Spanish long stay units, the length of the site is impressive (1 kilometre) and a bicycle is very helpful for getting about. La Manga is a 22 km. narrow strip of land, bordered by the sea on one side and by the Mar Menor on the other. There are sandy beaches on both sides and considerable development in terms of hotels, apartments, restaurants, night clubs, etc. in between – a little reminiscent of Miami Beach! You cannot drive all round this narrow strip of land as there is a gap in the centre, however, the very end of the southern part is great for 'getting away from it all' (take a picnic for the beach and be sure to go over the little bridge for privacy). The campsite is situated on the approach to 'the strip' and enjoys the benefit of its own semi-private beach alongside the Mar Menor, with a sailing, canoeing and windsurfing school and the site's excellent restaurant (traditional Spanish Tapas and food) and bar right beside the beach. The beach is dotted with tall palm trees and the sea is very shallow and warm, so it is ideal for families with small children or choose between the outdoor or indoor pools. There are some 1,000 touring pitches of two sizes (84 or 110 sq.m), regularly laid out in rows on slightly sloping gravel. They are smart, separated and shaded by high hedges, all have electricity and water. This site's excellent facilities are ideally suited for holidays in the winter when the weather is pleasantly warm.

Facilities

Seven clean toilet blocks of standard design include washbasins with hot water in five blocks. Laundry. Gas supplies. Large well stocked supermarket. Restaurant. Bar. Snack bar. Swimming pool complex (April - Sept). Indoor pool, gym, sauna and jacuzzi. Open air cinema (April - Sept). Tennis. Petanque. Minigolf. Basketball. Volleyball. Football area. Play area. Watersports school. Off site: Golf 2 km. Bicycle hire or riding 5 km.

Open

All year.

At a glance

Welcome & Ambience	✓✓✓✓✓	Location	✓✓✓✓✓
Quality of Pitches	✓✓✓✓✓	Range of Facilities	✓✓✓✓✓

Directions

From MU312 dual-carriageway take exit 15 towards Cabo de Palos, signed Playa Honda (site signed also). Cross road bridge and double back. Site entrance is beside dual-carriageway with many flags flying.

Charges 2004

Per pitch incl. 2 persons	€ 17,00 - € 26,75
3 persons	€ 19,00 - € 29,75
4 persons	€ 21,50 - € 33,00

Electricity (10A) included. All plus 7% VAT. Discounts in low season.

Reservations

Contact site. Tel: 968 563 014.
E-mail: lamanga@caravaning.es

ES8755 Camping Caravanning Moraira

Camino Paellero 50, 03724 Moraira-Teulada (Alacant)

This small hillside site with some views over the town and marina is quietly situated in an urban area amongst old pine trees and just 400 metres from a sheltered bay. Terracing provides shaded pitches of varying size (access to some of the upper pitches may be difficult for larger units). A few pitches have water and waste water facilities and a few have sea and marina views. There are electricity connections (6/10A). A large, painted water tower stands at the top of the site. An attractive irregular shaped swimming pool with paved sunbathing terrace is below the small bar/restaurant with terrace. The pool has observation windows where you can watch the swimmers, and is used for sub-aqua instruction. The site runs a professional diving school for all levels (the diving here is good and the water warm, even in winter). A sandy beach is 1.5 km. There are plans to extend the reception building to provide a range of new facilities.

Facilities

The high quality toilet block, with polished granite floors and marble fittings, is built to a unique and ultra-modern design with extra large free hot showers. Washing machine and dryer in separate room. Motorcaravan services. Bar/restaurant and shop (1/7-30/9). Small swimming pool (all year). Sub-aqua with site boat and instruction. Tennis. Electronic games. Comprehensive security system. Torches may be required. Off site: Shops, bars and restaurants within walking distance. Beach 1.5 km. Fishing 400 m. Bicycle hire 1 km. Golf 8 km.

Open

All year.

At a glance

Welcome & Ambience	✓✓✓	Location	✓✓✓
Quality of Pitches	✓✓✓	Range of Facilities	✓✓✓

Directions

Site is best approached from Teulada. From A7 take exit 63 onto N332. In 3.5 km. turn right signed Teulada and Moraira. In Teulada fork right to Moraira. At junction at town entrance turn right signed Calpe and in 1 km. turn right into road to site on bend immediately after Res. Don Julio. Do not take the first right as the signs seem to indicate otherwise you will go round a loop.

Charges 2004

Per person	€ 4,50
child (4-9 yrs)	€ 3,50
pitch incl. car	€ 10,00 - € 12,00
electricity	€ 3,00

All plus 7% VAT. Less 15-60% in low seasons.

Reservations

Write to site for details. Tel: 965 745 249.
E-mail: campingmoraira@campingmoraira.com

ES8745 Camping La Fuente

Camino de La Bocamina, 30626 Banos de Fortuna (Murcia)

Located in an area known for its thermal waters since Roman and Moorish times and with just 62 pitches, La Fuente is a gem. The main attraction here is the huge pool complex where the water is constant at 22 degrees for 365 days of the year. Fed from thermal springs this is really good for old bones! Importantly there is a long gentle ramp into the pool for the not so agile. The site is in two sections, one where pitches are in standard rows and the other where they are in circles around blocks. The flat pitches have 10A electricity, some with shade, and all have their own modern mini-sanitary block.

Facilities

All pitches have their own high quality facilities including a unit for disabled campers. Washing machines and dryers. High quality restaurant. Pool (small charge). Snack bar by pool. Supermarket. Bicycle hire. Communal barbecues.

Open

All year.

At a glance

Welcome & Ambience	✓✓✓✓	Location	✓✓✓✓✓
Quality of Pitches	✓✓✓✓✓	Range of Facilities	✓✓✓

Directions

From A7/E15 (Alicante - Murcia) take C3223 to Fortuna then signs to Banos de Fortuna, then site.

Charges 2004

Per person	€ 2,25
pitch (with private sanitary facilities)	€ 9,50
electricity (per kw/h on meter)	€ 0,19

Reservations

Contact site. Tel: 968 685125.
E-mail: campingfuente@terra.es

ES8748 Camping Los Madriles

Ctra de la Azohia, km 4.5, 30868 Isla Plana (Murcia)

An extraordinary site with super facilities, Los Madriles is run by a hard working team, with constant improvments being made. Twenty kilometres west of Cartegena, the approach to the site and the surrounding area is fairly unremarkable, but the site is not. It provides huge rectangular and lagoon style pools with water sprays and jacuzzis which are fed by thermal waters used by the ancient Romans. Unbelievably the pools are emptied every night after they close at 10 pm. and are refilled by morning with fresh water, thus doing away for the need for chlorination. A fairly steep access road leads to the 311 flat, good to large size terraced pitches. Some have shade from large trees, with others in the newer area having less shade but panoramic views of the sea and behind to the mountains (ideal for winter visits). Private cabins are available. Simple snacks and prepackaged meals are served in the bar and attractive area near the pools. The campsite is immaculately clean and has excellent sports facilities. The guests we spoke to were really enjoying their stay. Local excursions can be made to the Campillo de Adrentro now a picnic spot, but once a military base. There are lots of walks in the region, and the ancient Roman city of Cartegena with its Roman ampitheatre, ancient bullring and port (once admired by Napoleon) is well worth a visit.

Facilities

Five sanitary blocks provide excellent facilities, including facilities for disabled campers. Washing machines and dryers. Motorcaravan services. Car wash. Restaurant/snack bar. Bar. Shop. Swimming pools with jacuzzi. Five-a-side football. Boules. Basketball. Table tennis. Play areas. Electronic games. Bicycle hire. ATM. Dogs and other animals are not accepted. Torches useful. Off site: Town close by. Fishing. Beach and boat launching 600 m. Riding 6 km. Golf 20 km. Excursions.

At a glance

Welcome & Ambience	✓✓✓✓	Location	✓✓✓✓
Quality of Pitches	✓✓✓✓	Range of Facilities	✓✓✓✓✓

Directions

From A7/E15 take km. 627 exit to Mazarron (southeast of Murcia) and go east on coast road towards Cartegena. Site is well signed before entering town of La Azohia.

Charges 2004

Per person	€ 4,00 - € 5,00
child (1-7)	€ 3,50 - € 4,50
pitch	€ 12,00 - € 15,00

Reservations

Contact site. Tel: 968 152 151.

Open

All year.

ES9285 Camping Las Lomas

Ctra de Sierra Nevada, 18160 Güejar-Sierra (Granada)

This site is high in the Güéjar Sierra and looks down on the Patano de Canales reservoir. After a wonderful drive to Güéjar-Sierra, you are rewarded with a site boasting excellent facilities. It is set on a slope but the pitches have been levelled to a great degree and are quite private, with high separating hedges and with many mature trees giving good shade (some pitches are fully serviced, with sinks and most have electricity). Development will mean that for 2005 there will be 120 pitches in all. The large bar/restaurant complex has a patio with wonderful views over the lake and an impressive huge central fire that is lit in winter. The pools also share this view and have a grassed area for sunbathing that runs down to the fence looking over the long drop to the lake below (safe fencing). A new feature is luxury rooms for rent, including one with a superb spa which is for hire by the hour. Any infirm visitors will need a car to get around as the inclines are extreme.

Facilities

Pretty blue tiled sanitary blocks (heated in winter) provide clean facilities. First class facilities for disabled campers and well equipped baby room (key at reception). Spa for hire. Motorcaravan services. Supermarket. Restaurant/bar. Swimming pool. Play area. Table tennis. Minigolf. Basketball. Many other activities available including parascending. Barbecue. Internet connection in reception. Torches useful. Off site: Buses run from outside site to village and Granada (15 km). Tours of the Alhambra organised with guides supplied if required. Useful site for winter skiing.

Open

All year.

At a glance

Welcome & Ambience	✓✓✓	Location	✓✓✓✓
Quality of Pitches	✓✓✓✓	Range of Facilities	✓✓✓✓

Directions

Using A323 (Jaén - Motril) take exit 135 at Granada to Sierra Nevada which brings you to the A395. At 4 km. marker take exit 5B for Sierra Nevada. Pass 7 km. marker and turn immediately right towards Cenes de la Vega and Güéjar-Sierra and right again after 200 m. onto GR420, then left to Güéjar-Sierra. Site is signed – drive uphill past the dam and enjoy the views to the site. Its easier than it sounds!

Charges 2004

Per person	€ 3,50
child	€ 2,40
pitch	€ 9,00

VAT included. No credit cards.

Reservations

Contact site. Tel: 958 484 742.
E-mail: laslomas@campings.net

ES9270 Camping Suspiro del Moro

Ctra Bailén-Motril, km 145., Puerto Suspiro del Moro, 18630 Granada (Granada)

Suspiro Del Moro is 11 km. south of Granada just off the Motril road or, alternatively, can be approached on the scenic mountain road from Almunecar. Based high in the Sierra Nevada mountain range, the area offers spectacular views from just outside the site, with trees and fences inhibiting the views inside. The site is small and rectangular with a cool and peaceful atmosphere and noise from the road is reduced by a high wall. Family run, it is well kept with gravel paths leading to the flat, grass pitches which benefit from the shade of the mature trees. The site is part of a business which includes a very attractive large swimming pool and there is a direct access from the site. Above this is a huge restaurant and bar.

Facilities

Clean and tidy, small toilet blocks are situated around the camping area with British style WCs and free hot showers. Laundry facilities. Small basic shop. Small restaurant/bar (high season). Small play area on gravel. Off site: Swimming pool and restaurant adjacent. Sierra Nevada and Granada.

Open

All year.

At a glance

Welcome & Ambience	✓✓	Location	✓✓✓
Quality of Pitches	✓✓✓	Range of Facilities	✓✓✓

Directions

Leave E902/A44 (Granada-Motril) at exit 144 from the south or 139 from the north and follow camping signs. At roundabout go towards Suspiro but then tun left (signed after turn). Site is 600 m. on right.

Charges 2004

Per person	€ 3,61
pitch incl. electricity	€ 10,31

Less 20% in low season.

Reservations

Contact site. Tel: 958 555 411.
E-mail: suspirodelmoro@eresmas.com

ES8783 Camping Naturista Almanat

Carril de la Torre Alta s/n, 29749 Almayate (Málaga)

With direct access to a 1 km. long grey sand and shingle naturist beach, this established all year naturist site, set on agricultural land with mountain backdrop, is proving a favourite with many British seeking winter sun. English is spoken at the modern reception. The site also has a night guard. The entire 2-hectare site is flat with a fine shingle surface on dirt. Many trees planted when the site opened in 1998 have now matured, providing much needed shade in the summer months. The 160 touring pitches with 16A electricity, vary in size and shape with the majority demanding physical manoeuvring of a touring caravan. Some pitches are long and narrow which could prevent the erection of an awning and you may feel quite close to your neighbour. The facilities on site are to a very high standard.

Facilities

The large, unisex toilet is fully equipped, regularly cleaned and all under cover. Good facilities for disabled campers near reception (approach surface may cause minor difficulty for wheelchairs). Between the site and beach are a grass area ideal for sunbathing. Bar/restaurant with terrace overlooking the sea provides good food at acceptable prices. Small shop for basic provisions. Large unheated swimming pool. Play area. TV in bar. Sauna and fully equipped gym. Basketball, paddle tennis. Cinema (56 seats) showing VHS tapes or DVD. Weather permitting, one is expected to be nude which is obligatory in the pool area and bar during the day. Off site: Torre del Mar is 2 km. Regular bus service (1 km). Fishing, riding nearby.

Open

All year.

At a glance

Welcome & Ambience	✓✓✓✓	Location	✓✓✓✓
Quality of Pitches	✓✓✓✓✓	Range of Facilities	✓✓✓✓✓

Directions

Approaching this site from the east (Torre del Mar) it is necessary to make a left turn to access the 600 m. single-track tarmac lane leading to the site. It is currently illegal to make that left turn and you will be fined if caught. We suggest exit the N340 at junction 265 signed Cajiz Iznate and Costa 340a. Take Costa direction and at coast turn left on 340a toward Torre del Mar. Site well signed in 4 km.

Charges 2004

Per person	€ 3,90
child (2-10 yrs)	€ 3,10
pitch	€ 7,80 - € 8,30
electricity (16A)	€ 2,30

All plus 7% VAT. No credit cards.

Reservations

Contact site. Tel: 952 556 462.
E-mail: almanat@arrakis.es

ES8782 Camping Caravaning Laguna Playa

Prolongacion Paseo Maritimo, 29740 Torre del Mar (Málaga)

Camping Laguna Playa is a pleasant and peaceful site run by a father and son team (the son speaks excellent English) and they give a personal service, alongside one of the Costa del Sol beaches. Trips are organised to the famous Alhambra Mosque in Granada on a weekly basis and the site is well placed for visits to Malaga and Nerja. The pitches are flat, of average size and with good artificial shade supplementing that provided by the many established trees on site. All pitches have electricity (5/10A). The busy restaurant with a terrace offers good value for money and many locals use it. The site has a distinctly Spanish flavour in August but in low season you will find lots of European 'snow birds' enjoying the warmth here. Animation is organised for children in high season and you could visit the new cinema near reception. Various competitions including petanque are organised in summer. Good off peak discounts are available.

Facilities

Two well equipped, modern, sanitary blocks, both recently refurbished, include baby baths and good facilities for disabled campers. Laundry facilities. Supermarket. Bar and busy restaurant also used by locals (all open all year). Swimming pools (open high season). Play area. Drinks machine. Children's entertainment. Off site: Beach promenade 200 m. Bicycle hire 500 m. Regular bus service 700 m. outside site. Golf 1.5 km. Riding 2 km.

Open

All year.

At a glance

Welcome & Ambience	✓✓✓✓	Location	✓✓✓✓
Quality of Pitches	✓✓✓	Range of Facilities	✓✓✓✓

Directions

Site is on the sea front west of the town of Torre del Mar, off the main N340 Malaga - Nerja road. Follow signs and take care not to enter the first camp site you meet on the beach as this is inferior and will be demolished in new development in the near future.

Charges 2004

Per person	€ 4,10
child	€ 3,20
tent	€ 4,10
caravan	€ 4,60
car	€ 4,10
motorcaravan	€ 8,70

Reservations

Write to site. Tel: 952 540 631.
E-mail: info@lagunaplaya.com

ES8802 Camping Cabopino

Ctra N340, km 194.7, 29600 Marbella (Málaga)

This large mature site is alongside the main N340 Costa del Sol coast road, 12 km. east of Marbella and 14 km. from Fuengirola. The Costa del Sol is also known as the Costa del Golf and fittingly there is a major golf course alongside the site. Just 600 metres from the beaches and dunes, a short walk over the road and down the hill brings you to a restaurant on the beach and an unofficial naturist area. A small yachting harbour with a range of restaurants and shops is a similar distance. The site is set amongst tall pine trees which provide shade for the sandy pitches (there are some huge areas for large units). The upper areas of the site are filled with permanent pitches and bungalows. The 400 touring pitches, a mix of leval and sloping, all have electrical connections (10A) and there is a separate area on the western side for groups of younger guests. At the other side of the site you will find a fenced swimming pool with a grass sunbathing area. Close to the entrance is an Italian restaurant serving good food and with a terrace that enjoys shade and is very pleasant.

Facilities

Four mature but clean sanitary blocks provide hot water throughout (may be under pressure at peak times). Washing machines. Bar/restaurant. Shop. Swimming pool (all season). Play area. Excursions can be booked. Torches necessary in the more remote parts of the site. Off site: Fishing, bicycle hire and riding within 1 km. Golf 7 km.

Open

All year.

At a glance

Welcome & Ambience	✓✓✓✓	Location	✓✓✓✓
Quality of Pitches	✓✓✓✓	Range of Facilities	✓✓✓✓

Directions

Site is 7 km. from Marbella. Approaching Marbella from the east, leave the N340 at the 194 km. marker (signed Cabopino). Site is off the roundabout at the top of the slip road.

Charges 2004

Per unit incl. 2 persons and electricity	15,55 - 26,15
extra person	€ 3,15 - € 5,25
child	€ 2,10 - € 4,25
dog	€ 2,25

Plus 7% VAT. Discounts outside high season and for over 7 days.

Reservations

Contact site. Tel: 952 834 373.
E-mail: info@campingcabopino.com

ES8850 Camping Paloma

Ctra Cadiz - Malaga, km 70, 11380 Tarifa (Cádiz)

A spacious, neat and tidy, family orientated site popular with Spanish families and young people of all nations in high season. Paloma is well established and the many tall palms around the site remind one of how close Africa and the romance of Tangier is. Paloma is 700 m. from a fabulous beach with white sands and enormous dunes, great for beachcombing, fishing and old fashioned seaside games. The area is famous for its ideal kite and windsurfing conditions. The site has 353 pitches on mostly flat ground, although the westerly pitches are sloping. They are of average size with some places for extra large units, some are separated by hedges and most are shaded by mature trees; around 200 pitches have electrical connections (10A). A large, smart restaurant serves excellent Spanish fare and the bar with large courtyard buzzes with activity, tapas and snacks are served here. There is a small swimming pool with a paved and grassed sunbathing area and an attractive thatched, stone bar.

Facilities

There are two sanitary blocks, one of a good size, although it is a long walk from the southern end of the site. The other block is smaller and open plan, serving the sloping areas of the site. The sanitary blocks have been refurbished to a high standard. WC's are British style with some Turkish, washbasins have cold water. Facilities for disabled visitors are in the smaller block with access from sloping ground, also a babies room. All very clean when seen. Washing machine. Gas supplies. Shop. Busy bar and good restaurant. Swimming pool with adjacent bar (high season only). Playground. TV in bar. Excursions (June-Sept).
Off site: Nearest beach 700m. Bicycle/scooter/quads hire 5 km. Riding 10 km. Tarifa 12 km. with lots of night life and bars. Golf 25 km.

At a glance

Welcome & Ambience	✓✓✓✓	Location	✓✓✓✓
Quality of Pitches	✓✓✓✓	Range of Facilities	✓✓✓✓

Directions

Site is signed off N340 Cadiz road at Punta Paloma, about 10 km. northwest of Tarifa, just west of km. 74 marker. Watch carefully for the site sign - no advance notice. Be sure to use the slip road to turn left if coming from Tarifa. Follow the signs down a sandy road for 300 m. and site is on the right.

Charges guide

Per person	€ 4,81
child	€ 3,91
car	€ 3,01
motorcycle	€ 2,70
tent	€ 3,31
caravan	€ 3,31

Reservations

Made for one part of site, for any length and without deposit. Tel: 956 684 203.

Open

All year.

ES8809 Camping El Sur

Ctra Ronda - Algeciras, km 1,5, Apartado de Correos 127, 29400 Ronda (Málaga)

The generous manoeuvring area and delightfully decorated entrance to this site are a promise of something different which is fulfilled in all respects. The very friendly family who run the site have worked hard for many years combining innovative thinking with excellent service. The 114 terraced pitches have electricity (5A) and water, and are partially shaded by olive and almond trees. Most have relaxing views of the surrounding mountains but at an elevation of 850 m. the upper pitches (the very top 45 pitches are for tents only) allow a clear view of the fascinating town of Ronda. The various leisure facilities are very clean, well maintained and the personal touches of the owners are obvious which make using them more enjoyable. This is one of the best small sites we have seen in Andalucia with prices that are extremely competitive. Enjoy the breathtaking 130 metre deep El Tajo gorge (where prisoners were thrown during the civil war) from the lovely 18th century bridge which joins the old and new parts of town. Look out also for the much-feared soldiers in tasselled red Fez headgear and green tunics. These are Franco's old crack unit; the infamous Spanish Africa Legion who are billeted here.

Facilities

The immaculate sanitary block is fully equipped (toilet paper purchased from reception). Laundry facilities in little separate blocks. Gas supplies. Bar and very large, high quality restaurant serving excellent food at reasonable prices (closed 71 15/1). Kidney shaped pool most welcome in summer as the temperatures soar (1/6-30/9). Children's playground and adventure play area. Separate camping area for groups. Minigolf. Dogs on leads with site permission. Barbeques on pitch with site permission. Off road bicycle hire. Internet terminal. Off site: The famous town of Ronda with all its attractions. The coast is approximately one hour drive. National parks to the north.

Open

All year.

At a glance

Welcome & Ambience	✓✓✓✓✓	Location	✓✓✓✓✓
Quality of Pitches	✓✓✓✓✓	Range of Facilities	✓✓✓✓✓

Directions

Site is well signed from the town centre (do not stray off the signed route as there are some very narrow roads) and it is off the Algeciras road, 1.5 km. south of Ronda.

Charges 2005

Per person	€ 4,00
child (under 10 yrs)	€ 3,80
tent	€ 4,00 - € 8,00
car or motorcycle	€ 4,00
motorcaravan	€ 8,00 - € 12,00
electricity (5-10A)	€ 3,50 - € 5,00

Plus 7% VAT. Less 40% in low season.
No credit cards.

Reservations

Advised for July/Aug. Tel: 952 875 939.
E-mail: info@campingelsur.com

ES8860 Camping Fuente del Gallo

Apto. 48, 11149 Conil de la Frontera (Cádiz)

Fuente del Gallo extends a warm welcome to British visitors, particularly as one half of the ownership is Irish. The attractive pool, restaurant and bar complex with its large, shaded terace, are very welcoming in the height of summer. The site is well maintained with 221 pitches for touring units. Although the actual pitch areas are generally a good size, the majority are long and narrow. This could, in some cases, prevent the erection of an awning and your neighbour may feel close. In low season it is generally accepted to make additional use of an adjoining pitch. Each pitch has 10A electricity and a number of trees create shade to some pitches. Good beaches are relatively near at 300 m. with access gained by steps through new houses with palm-lined roads. Helpful, friendly staff will assist in booking discounted trips to nearby attractions or even further afield to Africa. Cadiz, probably the oldest town in Spain, is worth a visit and in particular the old part with its narrow streets (many pedestrianised).

Facilities

Two modernised and very clean sanitary blocks include excellent services for babies and disabled visitors and hot water at all facilities. Laundry room with two washing machines. Motorcaravan services. Gas supplies. Well-stocked shop. Attractive bar and restaurant (breakfast served). TV and games rooms. Swimming pool (all season, lifeguard in high season when there is a small charge) with large grass area for sunbathing and children's pool. Play area. Excursions. Torches useful. Safety deposit boxes. Off site: Watersports on beach. Fishing 300 m. Riding 1 km. Bicycle and motor scooter hire 2 km. Golf 5 km.

At a glance

Welcome & Ambience	✓✓✓✓	Location	✓✓✓✓
Quality of Pitches	✓✓✓✓	Range of Facilities	✓✓✓✓

Directions

From Cadiz-Algeciras road (N340) at km. 23.00, follow signs to Conil de la Frontera town centre, then shortly right to Fuente del Gallo and 'playas'.

Charges 2005

Per person	€ 4,50
pitch	€ 7,50 - € 8,00
electricity	€ 4,00

All plus 7% VAT. Less for low season longer stays.

Reservations

Contact site. Tel: 956 440 137.
E-mail: camping@campingfuentedelgallo.com

Open

Easter - 3 September.

ES8873 Camping La Aldea

El Rocio, 21750 Almonte (Huelva)

This impressive site lies just on the edge of the Parque Nacional de Donana, southwest of Sevilla on the outskirts of El Rocio. The town hosts a fiesta at the end of May with over one million people attending the local shrine. They travel for days in processions to attend. If you want to stay this weekend book well in advance! The well planned, modern site is well set out and the 246 pitches have natural shade from trees or artificial shade and 10A electricity. There are 52 serviced pitches with water and sewerage. There are also pitches for tents and bungalows for rent. The facilities are new, large and very clean. A beautiful restaurant provides lovely local food. The staff are welcoming and helpful with plenty of tourist information to hand. Expeditions on horseback or by 4x4 vehicle can be arranged in the national park.

Facilities

Two sanitary blocks provide excellent facilities including provision for disabled visitors. Motorcaravan service point. Swimming pool (May - Oct). Restaurant and bar in separate new complex. Shop. Internet connection. Playground. Football/basketball court. Off site: Bus stop 5 minutes walk. Huelva and Sevilla are about an hour's drive. Beach 15 km.

Open

All year.

At a glance

Welcome & Ambience	✓✓✓✓✓	Location	✓✓✓✓
Quality of Pitches	✓✓✓✓✓	Range of Facilities	✓✓✓✓✓

Directions

From main Huelva – Sevilla road E1/A49 take exit 48 and go south through Almonte to outskirts of El Rocio. Site is on left just past 25 km. marker (go to the roundabout and back up to turn in.

Charges 2004

Per person	€ 3,75 - € 4,20
pitch incl. car	€ 4,20 - € 8,20
electricity	€ 3,75

Less 10-15% for low season stays over 3 days.

Reservations

Contact site. Tel: 95944 2677.
E-mail: info@campinglaaldea.com

ES9081 Camping Villsom

Ctra Sevilla-Cadiz, km 554.8, 41700 Sevilla (Sevilla)

This city site was one of the first to open in Spain and it is still owned by the same pleasant family. The administrative building consists of a peaceful and attractive bar with patio and satellite TV (where breakfast is served) and there is a pleasant, small reception area. There are no static caravans here, although there is an area for groups. It is a good site for visiting Seville with a frequent bus service to the centre (20 minutes, bus stop close by). Camping Villsom has around 180 pitches which are level and shaded. A huge variety of trees and palms are to be seen around the site and in summer the bright colours of the flowers are very pleasing. The site has a most inviting, palm surrounded pool which is quite secluded. A new hotel (in Spanish style) of nine rooms has been added for 2005 and new facilities for disabled visitors are planned. It is important to book if you intend to visit this site in peak weeks. It is not suitable for large motorhomes and there are few places for large caravans, but book.

Facilities

Sanitary facilities require modernisation in some areas. Some washbasins have cold water only. Laundry facilities. Small shop selling basic provisions. Bar with satellite TV (open July/Aug). Swimming pool (June-Sept). Putting. Table tennis. Drinks machine. Off site: Most town facilities including restaurant, supermarket, cinema and theatre.

Open

All year.

At a glance

Welcome & Ambience	✓✓✓	Location	✓✓✓
Quality of Pitches	✓✓✓	Range of Facilities	✓✓✓

Directions

On main Seville ñ Cadiz NIV road travelling from Seville take exit at km. 553 signed Dos Hermanos – Isla Menor. Go under concrete road bridge and turn immediately right (Isla Mentor) ad site is 80 m. on right. From Cadiz take same signed exit and at roundabout take fourth exit to go over main road and then down a slip road to go under bridege, then as above.Make sure you take the correct exit otherwise it is a lonfg drive along the main road before you can turn back.

Charges 2004

Per person	€ 3,60
child	€ 3,20
pitch incl. car	€ 5,00 - € 7,65
electricity	€ 2,40

All plus 7% VAT.

Reservations

Write to site. Tel: 954 720 828.
E-mail: camping.sevilla@turinet.es

ES9080 Camping Municipal El Brillante

Avenida del Brillante 50, 14012 Córdoba (Córdoba)

For a municipal site this is impressive. Cordoba is one of the hottest places in Europe - the 'frying pan' of Spain - and the superb pool here is more than welcome. This large site is on the north side of the river with a canal running through the centre (well fenced) and pleasant terraced gardens where you can sunbathe. If you really want to stay in the city, then this site is a good choice. It has 120 neat pitches of gravel and sand attractively spaced alongside the canal. The upper pitches are now covered by artificial and natural shade but the lower, newer area has little. Here there are 32 fully serviced pitches and an area for a few large motorhomes. The site becomes very crowded in high season. The entrance is narrow and may be congested so care must be exercised - there is a lay-by just outside and it is easier to walk in initially. The bar/restaurant is close to reception and there is a pleasant terrace bar/restaurant which overlooks the pool gardens in high season. Cordoba is a fascinating town and the Mosque/Cathedral is one of the great buildings of Europe and it is worth allowing two days here to investigate the area. Buses go from outside the site to town.

Facilities

The toilet blocks have been renovated and an impressive newer block has facilities for babies and disabled people. Motorcaravan services. Gas supplies. Bar and restaurant (1/4-30/9). Shop (all year). Swimming pool (15/6-15/9). Play area. Off site: Bus service to city centre from outside site. Commercial centre 300 m. (left out of site, right at traffic lights).

Open

All year.

At a glance

Welcome & Ambience	✓✓✓✓	Location	✓✓✓✓✓
Quality of Pitches	✓✓✓✓	Range of Facilities	✓✓✓✓

Directions

Site is on the north side of the river. From the NIV/E25 road from Madrid, take exit at km. 403 (the middle of three exits for Cordoba) and follow signs for Mosque/Cathedral into city centre. Pass it (on right) and turn right onto the main avenue. Continue and take right fork where the road splits, and follow signs for campsite and/or green signs for district of El Brillante. Site is on right up slight hill on this avenue.

Charges 2004

Per unit incl. 2 persons	€ 17,40
tent incl. 2 persons and car	€ 16,40
tent without car	€ 12,30
child (1-10 yrs)	€ 2,80
electricity	€ 2,80

No credit cards.

Reservations

Not made. It is essential to arrive early in high season. Tel: 957 403 836. E-mail: elbrillante@campings.net

ES9089 Camping Despeñaperros

Ctra Infanta Elena, 23213 Santa Elena (Jaén)

This site is on the edge of Santa Elena in a natural park with shade from mature pine trees. This is a good place to stay en-route from Madrid to the Costa del Sol or to just explore the surrounding countryside. Just to the north there are some stunning views of the narrow mountain gorge of Despeñaperros, definitely worth a visit. The site is run in a very friendly manner where nothing is too much trouble. The 116 pitches are fully serviced including a satellite TV/internet link. There is an excellent bar and a classy restaurant. A large swimming pool surrounded by grass overlook the beautiful mountains.

Facilities

Two traditional, central sanitary blocks have Turkish style WCs and well equipped showers. One washing machine (launderette in the town). Shop. Excellent bar (all year) and charming restaurant (12/3-20/10). Swimming pools (15/6-15/9). Tennis. First aid room. Caravan storage. Night security. Off site: Walking, riding and mountain sports.

Open

All year.

At a glance

Welcome & Ambience	✓✓✓✓✓	Location	✓✓✓✓✓
Quality of Pitches	✓✓✓✓	Range of Facilities	✓✓✓✓

Directions

Site is signed from the N1V between Bailén and Madrid. Take exit 259 and drive through the main street of Santa Elena to site on edge of town (there is another entrance for tall vehicles – ask at reception).

Charges 2004

Per person	€ 3,18
pitch incl. electricity	€ 8,50 - € 8,87

All plus 7% VAT.

Reservations

Contact site. Tel: 953 664 192.
E-mail: campingdesp@navegalia.com

ES9027 Camping Parque Natural de Monfrague

Ctra Plasencia-Trujillo km 10, 10680 Malpartida de Plasencia (Cáceres)

Situated on the edge of the Monfrague National Park, this well managed site owned by the Barrado family, has fine views to the Sierra de Mirabel and delightful surrounding countryside. It would prove difficult to find a more suitable location for those that savour peace, quiet, study of yesteryear, flora and fauna. Created as a National Park in 1979, Monfrague is now recognised as one of the best locations in Europe for anyone with any degree of interest in birdwatching. During our visit we saw Griffon, Black and Egyptian Vultures, Black and Red Kites, Bee-eater, White and the more rare Black Storks to name but a few. Nearby Plasencia has a medieval aqueduct, fine cathedral and the town's original twin ring of walls containing 68 towers. To the south, the classic historical towns of Merida, Caceres and Trujillo. Many of the 128 good-sized pitches are grassed on slightly sloping terraced ground. Scattered trees offer a degree of shade, there are numerous water points and electricity is rated at 10A. Used by locals, the air-conditioned restaurant provides good quality food at acceptable prices. A meal on the veranda as the sunsets will install fond memories of a rewarding holiday. The stork's nest perched precariously on a 15-metre pole near to the site entrance provided only a landmark when we visited as none had taken up residence. On rare occasions a goods train travels along the nearby railway line.

Facilities

Large modern toilet blocks, fully equipped, are very clean. Facilities for disabled campers and baby baths. Laundry. Supermarket/shop. Restaurant, bar and coffee shop. TV room with recreational facilities and fire for cooler times. Swimming pools (June - Sept). Play area. Tennis. Basketball. Bicycle hire. Riding. Animation for children in season. Barbecue areas. Off site: Large supermarket at Plasencia.

Open

All year.

At a glance

Welcome & Ambience	✓✓✓✓	Location	✓✓✓✓✓
Quality of Pitches	✓✓✓✓✓	Range of Facilities	✓✓✓✓

Directions

On the N630 - from the north take EX-208 (C524, Plasencia - Trujillo); site on left in 6 km. From south turn right just south of Plasencia on EX-108 (C511, Malpartida de Plasencia), then right on EX-208 to site.

Charges guide

Per person	€ 3,20
pitch	€ 4,50 - € 5,270
electricity	€ 2,50

VAT included.

Reservations

Write to site. Tel: 927 459 233.

ES9087 Camping Mérida

Ctra NV Madrid-Port, km 336.6, 06800 Mérida (Badajoz)

Mérida was the tenth city of the Roman Empire and the 60-arched Roman bridge, the amphitheatre and the National museum of Roman art are just some of the attractions that can be enjoyed here. Camping Mérida is situated alongside the main N-V road to Madrid, the restaurant, café and pool complex separating the camping site area from the road where there is considerable noise. The site has 80 good sized pitches, most with some shade and on sloping ground, with ample electricity connections (long leads may be needed). No English is spoken, but try out your Spanish. Camping Mérida is ideally located to serve both as a base to tour the local area or as an overnight stop en route when travelling.

Facilities

The central sanitary facility includes hot and cold showers, British style WCs, dishwashing sinks (H&C) and laundry sinks (cold only) under cover. Gas. Small shop for essentials. Busy restaurant/cafeteria and bar, also open to the public. Swimming pool with lifeguard (May-Sept). Bicycle hire. Play area (unfenced and near road). Caravan storage. Torches useful. Off site: Town 5 km.

Open

All year.

At a glance

Welcome & Ambience	✓✓✓	Location	✓✓✓
Quality of Pitches	✓✓✓	Range of Facilities	✓✓✓

Directions

Site is alongside NV road (Madrid-Lisbon), 5 km. east of Mérida, at km. 336.6. From east take exit 334 and follow camping signs (doubling back). Site is actuallty on the 630 road that runs alongside the motorway.

Charges 2004

Per person	€ 3,80
pitch incl. car	€ 5,10 - € 7,60
electricity	€ 3,00

All plus VAT.

Reservations

Write to site. Tel: 924 303 453. E-mail: proexcam@jet.es

ES9028 Camping Las Villueracas

Ctra Villanueva, 10140 Guadalupe (Cáceres)

This rural site nestles in an attractive valley northwest of Guadalupe. The pools and restaurant are of a very high standard (the locals eat there). The 70 pitches are level and of a reasonable size; some are marked, although the logic of the numbering is difficult to follow in places and large units may experience difficulty in getting into the more central pitches. There is limited shade from young trees and a more shaded area in a 'spinney'. A river runs alongside the site and we are told that the ground can be muddy in very wet periods. The site is co-located with hostel accommodation. An ideal location for visiting the Monastery and attractive town of Guadalupe in the Sierra de Guadalupe.

Facilities

The single toilet block is in the older style but very clean, one area for women and one for men, providing British type WCs, washbasins and free hot showers (although hot watercould be overwhelmed in busy periods). No facilities for disabled campers as yet. Restaurant. Bar. Swimming pools. Shop. Tennis. Small playground. Barbecue area. Safe deposit. Medical post. Car wash. No English spoken.

Open

All year.

At a glance

Welcome & Ambience	✓✓✓	Location	✓✓✓
Quality of Pitches	✓✓✓	Range of Facilities	✓✓✓

Directions

From NV/E90 (Madrid - Mérida) exit at Navelmoral de la Mata. Follow south to Guadalupe on CC713 (83 km). Site is 2 km. from Guadalupe, near the Monastery. From further southwest take exit 102 off E90/NV (northeast of Merida) to Guadalupe. Near 72 km. marker turn left to site, 100 m. on right.

Charges 2004

Per person	€ 3,00
pitch incl. electricity	€ 4,60 - € 5,00

No credit cards.

Reservations

Write to site. Tel: 927 367 139.

ES9094 Camping La Aguzadera

Ctra N-IV, km 197.5, 13300 Valdepeñas (Ciudad Real)

This is a small, unassuming site which will be useful to travellers, especially if you wish to enjoy some excellent Spanish fare in the restaurant. There are few other campsites open all year in this area. With pleasant views of the mountains, the site is part of a huge sports complex where there is lots of activity, although the site is quite separate with lots of room to manoeuvre. The 66 pitches are of average size and are on sloping sand with a few trees providing a little shade. There is some road noise as the site is just off the N4. It is primarily a transit site but useful if you are following the Valdepenas wine route.

Facilities

The central sanitary block is average, unheated, but clean. Washbasins have cold water only. Restaurant and bar. Essentials from bar. Swimming pool (high season only). Play area. Tennis. Large sports complex alongside (charges apply). Dogs are not accepted. Torches required.

Open

1 June - 30 September.

At a glance

Welcome & Ambience	✓✓✓	Location	✓✓✓
Quality of Pitches	✓✓✓	Range of Facilities	✓✓✓✓

Directions

Site is directly off N4 (Madrid-Cadiz) at 197 km. marker, Valdepenas exit. Look for 'Angel of Peace' statue – site is directly opposite and is well signed.

Charges guide

Per person	€ 3,55
child	€ 2,57
pitch	€ 5,88 - € 7,66

Reservations

Contact site. Tel: 926 310 769. E-mail: la-aguzadera@manchanet.es

ES9090 Camping El Greco

Ctra CM-4000 km 0,7, Puebla de Montalban, 45004 Toledo (Toledo)

Toledo was the home of the Grecian painter and the site that bears his name boasts a beautiful view of the ancient city from the restaurant, bar and superb pool. The friendly, family owners make you welcome and are proud of their site which is the only one in Toledo (it can get crowded). There is an attractive, tree-lined approach and ivy clad pergolas run down each side of the swimming pool. A large shaded terrace offers shelter from the sun which can be very hot here. The 150 pitches are of 80 sq.m. with electrical connections and shade from strategically planted trees. Most have hedges that separate and give privacy, with others in herring bone layouts that make for interesting parking in some areas. Access to some pitches may be tricky for caravans (narrow and at an angle) and some site roads are narrow. The river Tagus streches alongside the site but fishing in it is a better bet than swimming. This site makes a relaxing base to return to after a hard day visiting the amazing sights of the old city of Toledo or for something different visit the Warner Brothers Theme Park.

Facilities

Two sanitary blocks, both modernised include facilities for disabled campers and everything is modern and kept clean. Laundry. Motorcaravan services. Swimming pool (15/6-15/9; with charge). Restaurant/bar (1/4-30/9) with good menu and fair prices. Shop in reception. Volleyball. Playgrounds. Barbecues. Ice cube machine. Off site: Fishing in river. Golf 10 km. Riding 15 km. An hourly air-conditioned bus service runs from the gates to the city centre, touring the outside of the walls first. Warner Brothers movie theme park 40 mins. Madrid 1 hour drive.

Open

All year.

At a glance

Welcome & Ambience	✓✓✓✓✓	Location	✓✓✓✓✓
Quality of Pitches	✓✓✓✓✓	Range of Facilities	✓✓✓✓✓

Directions

Site is on C4000 road on the edge of the town, signed towards Puebla de Montelban; site signs also in city centre. From Madrid on N401, turn off right towards Toledo city centre but turn right again at the roundabout at the gates to the old city. Site is signed from the next right turn.

Charges guide

Per person	€ 4,40
child (3-10 yrs)	€ 3,70
caravan or tent	€ 4,24
car	€ 4,24
motorcycle	€ 3,50
motorcaravan	€ 8,49

Plus 7% VAT.

Reservations

Not made. Tel: 925 220 090.
E-mail: elgreco@retemail.es

ES9091 Camping Municipal Soto del Castillo

Soto del Rebollo s/n, 28300 Aranjuez (Madrid)

Aranjuez, supposedly Spain's version of Versailles, is worthy of a visit with its beautiful palaces, leafy squares, avenues and gardens. It is 47 km. south of Madrid and 46 km. from Toledo, and is therefore a useful and popular site, excellent for enjoying the unusual attractions or for an en-route stop. You can visit the huge, but slightly decaying Royal Palace or the Casa del Labrador (translates as farmer's cottage) which is a small neo-classical palace in unusual and differing styles. It has superb gardens commissioned by Charles II. Two little tourist road trains run from the site to the palaces daily. This unusally well equipped municipal site is alongside to the River Tajo in a park-like situation with mature trees. The 225 touring pitches, all with electricity (10A), are set on flat grass, unmarked amid tall trees. Siting is informal but pitches are of moderate size. Canoes may be hired from behind the supermarket and there is a lockable moat gate to allow access to the river. There is good security backed up with CCTV around the river perimeter.

Facilities

The largest of three modern and good quality sanitary blocks is heated in winter and well equipped with some washbasins in cabins. Two smaller blocks of more open design have been refurbished. Washing up facilities have only cold water. Laundry facilities. Gas supplies. Small shop (15/6-15/9). Bar/restaurant (all year) with attractive riverside patio (also open to the public). Takeaway. TV room. Swimming and paddling pools (15/6-15/9). Play area. Volleyball. Bicycle hire. Boat launching and Canoe hire. Drinks machines. Torch useful. Off site: Within easy walking distance of palace, gardens and museums. Riding 5 km. Golf 20 km.

Open

All year.

At a glance

Welcome & Ambience	✓✓✓✓✓	Location	✓✓✓✓✓
Quality of Pitches	✓✓✓✓	Range of Facilities	✓✓✓✓✓

Directions

Using the A305 from Madrid to Aranjuez look for the 8 km. marker on the outskirts of town. Then follow campsite signs - these lead you back onto the A305 (going north now) and the site is signed off right at 300 m. on the first left bend. Follow signs down the narrow road for 400 m. If coming from the south ensure that you have the A305 to Madrid - there are other roads signed to Madrid. If in doubt ask as it is very confusing if the A305 road is missed.

Charges guide

Per person	€ 3,00 - € 3,91
child (3-10 yrs)	€ 2,55 - € 3,15
caravan	€ 3,45 - € 4,36
tent	€ 2,70 - € 4,21
car	€ 2,55 - € 3,30
motorcaravan	€ 3,76 - € 4,81

Plus 7% VAT. Discounts for groups or long stays.

Reservations

Write to site. Tel: 918 911 395.

ES9200 Caravanning El Escorial

Apdo. Correos 8, Ctra M600, km 3500, 28280 El Escorial (Madrid)

There is a shortage of good sites in the central regions of Spain, but this is one (albeit rather expensive). It is well situated for sightseeing visits especially to the magnificent El Escorial monastery which is a short drive. Also, the enormous civil war monument of the Valle de los Caidos is very close plus Madrid and Segovia are both about 50 km. El Escorial is very large, there are 1,358 individual pitches with artificial shade (ensure you get a pitch without a low tree canopy if you have a 3 m. high motorcaravan. Of these, 750 are occupied by permanent units but are totally separate from the touring and tent areas – weekends can be lively and noisy on the site and in the bar. There are another 250 pseudo 'wild' spaces for tourists on open fields, with good shade from mature trees (long cables may be necessary for electricity). The general amenities are good and include three swimming pools (unheated), plus a paddling pool in a central area with a bar/restaurant with terrace and plenty of sitting out areas.

Facilities

Three large refurbished toilet blocks, plus two smart, small blocks for the 'wild' camping area, are all fully equipped with some washbasins in private cabins. Baby baths and facilities for disabled campers. The blocks can be heated in cool weather. Large supermarket (1/3-31/10) and souvenir shop. Restaurant/bar and snack bar (1/3-31/10). Disco-bar. Swimming pools. Three tennis courts. Two football pitches. Basketball. Fronton. Volleyball. Two well equipped playgrounds on sand. ATM. Off site: Town 3 km. Riding or golf 7 km.

Open

All year.

At a glance

Welcome & Ambience	✓✓✓✓✓	Location	✓✓✓✓
Quality of Pitches	✓✓✓✓✓	Range of Facilities	✓✓✓✓✓

Directions

From the south go through the town of El Escorial, follow the M600 - Guadarrama road - the site is between the 2 and 3 km. markers north of town on the right. If approaching from the north use the A6 autopista take exit 47 and the M600 towards El Escorial town. Site is on the left.

Charges 2005

Per person	€ 5,10
child (3-10 yrs)	€ 4,95
caravan, tent or car	€ 5,10
motorcaravan	€ 8,75
electricity	€ 3,50

VAT included. No credit cards.

Reservations

May be made in writing to guarantee admission. Tel: 918 902 412. E-mail: info@campingelescorial.com

ES9210 Camping Pico de la Miel

Ctra NI Madrid - France, km 58, 28751 La Cabrera (Madrid)

Pico de la Miel is a very large site, 70 kilometres north of Madrid. It is well signed and easy to find, two or three kilometres southwest off the main N1 road, with an amazing mountain backdrop. Mainly a long-stay site for Madrid hence there are a huge number of very well established, fairly old statics. There is a small separate area with its own toilet block for touring units. The 60 pitches are on rather poor, sandy grass, some with artificial shade. Others, not so level, are under sparse pine trees and there are yet more pitches for tents (the ground could be hard for pegs). Electricity connections are available. Tall hedges abound and trees make it resemble a giant maze, no internal signs are provided and the long walk to the pool can be a challenge. The noise level from the many Spanish customers is high and you will have a chance to practice your Spanish!

Facilities

Dated but clean tiled toilet block, with some washbasins in cabins and free hot water to laundry and washing up sinks. It can be heated and an en-suite unit with ramp is provided for disabled visitors. Motorcaravan services. Gas supplies. Shop. Restaurant/ Bar (all year). Excellent swimming pool complex, supervised (15/6-15/9). Tennis. Playground.
Off site: Bicycle hire and riding 200 m. Fishing 8 km.

Open

All year.

At a glance

Welcome & Ambience	✓✓✓✓	Location	✓✓✓✓
Quality of Pitches	✓✓✓✓	Range of Facilities	✓✓✓✓✓

Directions

Site is well signed from the N1. Going south use exit 60, going north exit 59 or 60, and follow site signs.

Charges 2004

Per person	€ 5,00
child (2-9 yrs)	€ 4,50
caravan or tent	€ 4,90
car	€ 4,70
motorcaravan	€ 7,85
electricity	€ 3,65

All plus 7% VAT. Less 10-25% for longer stays.

Reservations

Contact site. Tel: 918 688 082.
E-mail: pico-miel@picodelamiel.com

ES9019 Camping La Pesquera

Ctra de Caceres - Arrabal, 37500 Ciudad Rodrigo (Salamanca)

This modest site has just 54 pitches and is located near the Rio Agueda looking up to the magnificent fortress ramparts of Ciudad Rodrigo. A frontier city in its heyday, it has much of historic interest including the first Parador to be located in an historic building. Entry to the site is through a municipal park with a large play area. Whilst the site is small it can take even the largest units, the centrally located facilities have been refurbished to a high standard, the pitches are flat and grassy and the roads are well maintained gravel. The pitches are shaded by trees. There is a touch of old Spain directly alongside the site, an old farmhouse with its trailing grape vine and ancient well.

Facilities

Attractive new ochre/stone sanitary building with British WCs and free hot showers. Washing machine. Facilities for disabled campers. Basics sold from bar in high season. Bar/snacks (April - Sept). Playground outside gates. Torches useful. Off site: River fishing 1 km. Riding 5 km.

Open

25 April - 30 September.

At a glance

Welcome & Ambience	✓✓✓✓✓	Location	✓✓✓✓✓
Quality of Pitches	✓✓✓✓✓	Range of Facilities	✓✓✓

Directions

Site is southwest of Salamancar close to Ciudad Rodrigo. From the E80 N260, any direction, take the 526 to Coria. Site is alongside river directly off the road and well signed.

Charges guide

Per person	€ 2,80
child (up to 12 yrs)	€ 2,50
pitch	€ 2,50 - € 5,60

Reservations

Contact site. Tel: 923 481 348.

ES9025 Camping Regio

Ctra de Madrid, km 4, 37900 Santa Marta de Tormes (Salamanca)

Salamanca is one of Europe's oldest university cities, and this beautiful old sandstone city has to be visited. Find the famous frog which is hidden in the fabulous University facade and discover what unusual Spanish fortune will be granted you! This is also a useful staging post en-route to the south of Spain or central Portugal. The site is 7 km. outside the city on the old road to Madrid. It is behind the Hôtel Regio and campers can take advantage of the hotel facilities which include a quality restaurant, a cheaper cafeteria (discounts for campers), an excellent pool (small charge). The site itself has a small bar and restaurant. The pitches (with a large area for tents) are clearly marked on slightly sloping ground, with some shade in parts. There are plentiful electricity points (10A).

Facilities

Very large fully equipped sanitary block has very good facilities for disabled campers. Washing machines in a dedicated room - all very clean. Gas supplies. Excellent motorcaravan services. Restaurant, cafe and swimming pool at adjoining hotel. Bar. Supermarket (1/4-30/9). Play area. Tennis. Basketball. English is spoken. Off site: Bus to town. Fishing 2 km. Bicycle hire 4 km. Town centre and golf 7 km.

At a glance

Welcome & Ambience	✓✓✓	Location	✓✓✓✓
Quality of Pitches	✓✓✓✓✓	Range of Facilities	✓✓✓✓✓

Directions

Take main N501 route from Salamanca to Avila, then to St Marta de Tormes 7 km east of the city. Hôtel Regio is on the old road into St Marta on the left.

Charges 2005

Per person	€ 2,70 - € 3,20
pitch incl. car	€ 5,40 - € 6,40

Reservations

Write to site. Tel: 923 138 888.
E-mail: recepcion@campingregio.com

Open

All year.

ES9021 Camping Municipal Fuentes Blancas

Ctra Cartuja - M'flore, km 3,5, 09000 Burgos (Burgos)

Fuentes Blancas is a comfortable municipal site within easy reach of the Santander ferries. There are around 350 marked pitches of 70 sq.m. on flat ground, 112 with electricity (6A) and there is good shade in parts. A small shop caters for most needs, the typically Spanish bar serves snacks and in the evening a restaurant is open. The site has a fair amount of transit trade and reservations are not possible for August, so arrive early. Burgos is an attractive city, ideally placed for overnight stop en route to the south of Spain. The old part of the city is quite beautiful and there are pleasant walks along the river banks.

Facilities

Clean, modern, fully equipped sanitary facilities in five blocks, but not all open outside July/Aug. Facilities for babies. Washing machine. Motorcaravan services. Small shop (all season). Bar/snack bar (all season). Swimming pool (15/5-15/9). Playground. Table tennis. Basketball. Football. English is spoken. Off site: Fishing 150 m. Bicycle hire 2 km.

Open

1 April - 30 September.

At a glance

Welcome & Ambience	✓✓✓✓✓	Location	✓✓✓✓✓
Quality of Pitches	✓✓✓✓✓	Range of Facilities	✓✓✓✓

Directions

From the north (Santander) follow signs for E5/N1 (E80/N620) Valladolid - Madrid on main through road. Immediately after crossing river turn left at 'Fuente Blancas Parc' signs leading to yellow camp signs and follow river east in direction of Cartuja de Miraflores for 3 km. Site is well signed on left.

Charges guide

Per person	€ 3,50
pitch incl. caravan and electricity	€ 10,75

Reservations

Not made. Tel: 947 486 016.

ES9022 Camping El Folgoso

49361 Vigo de Sanabria (Zamora)

A pleasant drive through the Sanabria National Park takes you to this unspoilt site alongside a beautiful lake. It is a large site with most pitches given over to tents, as the terrain is rugged and strewn with large rocks, whilst being sheltered by fine dense oaks. The pitches are informal and tents are placed anywhere on terraces or the lower levels. Pitches for caravans and motorcaravans are in more formal lines at the far end of the site with electricity. Buildings are primarily of wood and stone and designed in sympathy with the surroundings. The nearby lake shores are public areas but there are picnic facilities. There are super walks all around and much to see in the area, from many spectacular canyons to Saint Martin's Monastery.

Facilities

Three sanitary blocks, two refurbished and one new unit close to the restaurant, provide pre-set showers on payment, facilities for disabled campers and a variety of washing facilities but all with cold water. Bar with snacks (all year). Restaurants (April - Oct.). Torches essential.
Off site: Supermarket (April - Oct.) just outside site.

Open

All year.

At a glance

Welcome & Ambience	✓✓✓	Location	✓✓✓✓
Quality of Pitches	✓✓✓	Range of Facilities	✓✓✓

Directions

From N525 Orense/Ourense - Benavente autovia or the parallel A525, take any exit for Puebla de Sanabria and follow signs for Sanabria National Park. This will place you on the ZA 104 heading north. Pass through villages of El Puente, Cubelo and Galende to 11 km. marker and site is signed to the right.

Charges guide

Per person	€ 3,46
pitch	€ 5,26 - € 7,67

Reservations

Not necessary. Tel: 980 626774.

ES9023 Camping Camino de Santiago

Casco Urbano, 09110 Castrojeriz (Burgos)

This tranquil and uncomplicated site lies to the west of Burgos on the outskirts of Castrojeriz, an unspoilt small Spanish rural town. In a superb location, almost in the shadow of the ruined castle high on the adjacent hillside, it will appeal to those who like peace and a true touring campsite without all the modern trimmings, and at a reasonable cost. Out of main season the bar/restaurant are closed but ask to be directed to the 'Taberna' restaurant in town for a real treat of old Spanish cuisine in classical surroundings. The 50 marked pitches are level, grassy and divided by hedges, with electricity (5A), water and drainage available to all. Mature trees provide shade and there is a pretty orchard in one corner of the site. English is spoken here.

Facilities

Adequate sanitary facilities with showers (three hot per sex), British and Turkish style WCs, and washbasins with cold water only. Dishwashing sinks with hot tap. These facilities are in older style, but are well maintained and clean. Washing machine. Small shop s (1/6-31/8). Bar. Coffee shop (1/6-31/8). Games room. Tennis. Play area. Bicycle hire.

Open

1 March - 30 November.

At a glance

Welcome & Ambience	✓✓✓✓✓	Location	✓✓✓✓✓
Quality of Pitches	✓✓✓✓	Range of Facilities	✓✓✓

Directions

From N120 (Osorno-Burgos) road, turn on BU404 for Villasandino and Castrojeriz. Turn left at crossroads on southwest side of town and then left at site sign.

Charges 2005

Per person	€ 3,75
tent or caravan	€ 3,50 - € 4,00
car	€ 3,00

All plus 7% VAT.

Reservations

Write or fax site for details. Tel: 947 377 255.
E-mail: campingcastro@eresmas.com

ES9250 Camping Costajan

Ctra NI/E5, km 162, 09400 Aranda de Duero (Burgos)

This site is well placed as an en-route stop for the ferries, being 80 km. south of Burgos. This is the capital of the Ribera del Duero wine region that produces many fine wines of Spain competing with the great Riojas. The welcome is warm and friendly here. With 225 unmarked pitches, all with electricity, there are around 100 for all types of tourer. Large units may find access to the variably sized pitches a bit tricky among dense olive and pine trees and on the slightly undulating sandy ground but trees provide good shade. In high season there is a good sized pool to relax in. There are many fascinating things to see in the area but we particularly recommend a visit to the suspended buildings at Gumiel de Izan.

Facilities

Good, heated, modern sanitary facilities. Facilites for disabled people. Washing machine. Gas supplies. Shop with essentials (all year). Cafe with snacks and bar. Large swimming pool open to public (all 15/5-15/9). Tennis. Football. Minigolf. Riding 2 km. Fishing 3 km.

Open

All year.

At a glance

Welcome & Ambience	✓✓✓✓	Location	✓✓✓
Quality of Pitches	✓✓✓✓	Range of Facilities	✓✓✓✓

Directions

From N1/E5 take exit to North signed Aranda de Duero at 164.5 km, follow N1 towards town and the campsite is at the 162 km mark.

Charges guide

Per person	€ 3,50 - € 3,65
pitch	€ 3,50 - € 7,35

Reservations

Said to be unnecessary. Tel: 947 502 070.
E-mail: costajan@circulopyme.com

ES9029 Camping El Astral

Camino de Pollos 8, 47100 Tordesillas (Valladolid)

The site is in a prime position alongside the wide River Duero (safely fenced). It is homely and run by a charming man, Eduardo Gutierrez, who has excellent English and is ably assisted by brother Gustavo and sister Lola. The site is generally flat with 154 pitches separated by hedges. They vary in size from 60 - 80 sq.m. with mature trees providing shade. We recommend a walk across the bridge to investigate the fascinating town of Tordesillas which is steeped in Spanish history. Also don't miss the Real Monasterio de Santa Clara known as the Alhambra of Castille - it is amazing. This is a friendly site ideal for exploring the area as you move through Spain. There is an electricity pylon tucked in the corner of the site but this does not detract from the pleasant ambience here and the quality stay offered.

Facilities

One attractive sanitary block including two cabins with WC, bidet and washbasin. Quality facilities provided for disabled campers, including ramps throughout site. Baby room in ladies' area. Washing machines. Motorcaravan services. Supermarket. Bar. Very good restaurant fequented by locals. Swimming and paddling pools (15/6-15/9; lifeguard at all times). Playground. Tennis. Minigolf. Local bus service. Animation daily in high season. Torches are useful.

Open

1 April - 30 September.

At a glance

Welcome & Ambience	✓✓✓✓✓	Location	✓✓✓✓✓
Quality of Pitches	✓✓✓✓✓	Range of Facilities	✓✓✓✓✓

Directions

Tordesillas is 28 km. southwest of Valladolid. From all directions, leave the main road towards Tordesillas and follow signs to site or 'Parador'.

Charges 2005

Per person	€ 3,85 - € 5,20
child (0-12 yrs)	€ 3,00 - € 4,25
pitch incl. car	€ 6,50 - € 9,60

Plus 7% VAT. Discounts in low season and for longer stays.

Reservations

Not necessary. Tel: 983 770 953.
E-mail: info@campingelastral.com

ES9024 Camping As Cancelas

Rue do 25 de Xulio 35, 15704 Santiago (A Coruña)

The beautiful city of Santiago has been the destination for European Christian pilgrims for centuries and they now follow ancient routes to this unique city, the whole of which is a national monument. There are many pilgrims' routes, including one commencing from Fowey in Cornwall. The As Cancelas campsite is excellent for sharing the experiences of these pilgrims in the city and around the magnificent cathedral. It has 156 marked pitches (30-70 sq.m), arranged in terraces and divided by trees and shrubs. On a hillside overlooking the city, the views are very pleasant, but the site has a steep approach road and access to most of the pitches can be a challenge for large units. Electrical hook-ups (5A) are available. There are many legendary festivals and processions here, the main one on 25 July, especially in holy years (when the Saint's birthday falls on a Sunday). Examine for yourself the credibility of the fascinating story of the arrival of the bones of St James at Compostela (Compostela translates as 'field of stars').

Facilities

Two very modern, luxurious toilet blocks are fully equipped, with ramped access for disabled campers. The quality and cleanliness of the fittings and tiling is outstanding. Dishwashing and laundry facilities. Small mini market (open July/Aug.). Restaurant. Bar/ TV. (open all year). Well kept, unsupervised swimming pool and children's pool. Small playground. Off site: Regular bus service runs into the city from the bottom of the hill outside site. Huge commercial centre five minutes level walk away.

Open

All year.

At a glance

Welcome & Ambience	✓✓✓✓✓	Location	✓✓✓✓✓
Quality of Pitches	✓✓✓✓	Range of Facilities	✓✓✓✓✓

Directions

From the east on N634 Lugo road site is signed at junction with N550 road (on dual-carriageway filter right following signs right for La Coruña N550 and also site). Turn at sports stadium. Site is 800 m. on left.

Charges 2005

Per person	€ 3,90 - € 4,80
child (up to 12 yrs)	€ 2,50 - € 3,90
car, tent or caravan	€ 3,90 - € 5,00
motorcaravan	€ 7,80 - € 10,00
electricity	€ 3,20

All plus VAT.

Reservations

Write to site. Tel: 981 580 476.
E-mail: info@campingascancelas.com

ES8942 Camping Los Manzanos

Ctra Sta Cruz - Meiras, km 0,7, 15179 Santa Cruz (A Coruña)

This large site is to the east of the historic port of La Coruña, not far from some ria (lagoon) beaches. The site has a steep sloping access and is divided by a stream into two main sections, linked by a wooden bridge. Some huge interesting stone sculptures create focal points and conversation pieces. The lower section is on a gentle slope. Pitches for larger units are marked and numbered, all with 10A electricity and there is a fairly large, unmarked field for tents. The site impressed us as being very clean, even when full, which it tends to be in high season. Señor Sanjurjo speaks good English and visitors are assured of a friendly welcome. Some aircraft noise should be expected (but only six aircraft per day – none at night).

Facilities

Two good toilet blocks provide modern facilities including free hot showers. Swimming pool - clean, with a lifeguard, free to campers, and open all season if you are tough enough! Small shop with fresh produce daily. High quality restaurant/bar (Easter - Sept). Playground. Barbecue area. Medical post. Excellent bungalows for hire. Off site: Beach 800 m. Bicycle hire 2 km. Golf and riding 8 km.

Open

Easter - 15 September.

At a glance

Welcome & Ambience	✓✓✓✓✓	Location	✓✓✓✓
Quality of Pitches	✓✓✓✓✓	Range of Facilities	✓✓✓✓

Directions

From A9/E1 going south, take exit 7 for 'O Burgo'. The site is on the Santa Cruz – Meiras road, north of Oleiras and is well signed from there.

Charges guide

Per person	€ 4,40
child	€ 3,40
pitch	€ 4,40 - € 8,80

All plus 7% VAT.

Reservations

Write to site. Tel: 981 614 825.
E-mail: info@camping-losmanzanos.com

ES8940 Camping Los Cantiles

Ctra N634, km 502,7, 33700 Luarca (Asturias)

Luarca is a picturesque little place with a pretty inner harbour and two sandy beaches, and Los Cantiles is two kilometres to the east of town on a cliff top that juts out into the sea, giving excellent views from some pitches and the sound of the waves to soothe you to sleep. The owners speak excellent English and Hubert, who is Dutch, and Cornelia, who is German, are charming and eager that you enjoy your stay here. The site is well maintained and is a pleasant place to stop along this under-developed coastline. The 230 pitches, 83 with electricity (6A) are mostly on level grass, divided by huge hedges of hydrangeas and bushes. Some pitches have gravel surfaces. There is a separate area for late arrivals in high season. You can take the car to the Laurca beaches and the small town is within walking distance downhill (the return is steep!). This is a pleasant site as a base for exploring the area or as a transit site if moving to or from Portugal.

Facilities

Two modern, fully equipped sanitary blocks (one in low season) are kept very clean, as is the whole site. Mainly British style toilets. The block used in winter is heated. Large solar heating system for hot water. Facilities for disabled people and babies. Water is recycled for flushing purposes - the owners have a 'green' attitude. Laundry. Freezer service. Gas supplies. Small shop (all year). Bar with hot snacks (15/6-1/10). Day room for backpackers with tables, chairs and cooking facilities (less gas). Lounge/reading room. Bicycle hire. Torches are required. English is spoken. Off site: Indoor swimming pool, sauna and fitness centre 300 m. Fishing 70 m. Riding 6 km.

Open

All year.

At a glance

Welcome & Ambience	✓✓✓✓✓	Location	✓✓✓✓✓
Quality of Pitches	✓✓✓✓✓	Range of Facilities	✓✓✓✓

Directions

Turn off main N632 at 154 km. marker onto N634. At the km 502.7 point east of Laurca, site is well signed through an estate.

Charges 2004

Per person	€ 3,70
child (4-10 yrs)	€ 3,25
tent	€ 3,60 - € 3,80
caravan	€ 4,30
motorcaravan	€ 7,00
car	€ 2,80

Plus 7% VAT. No credit cards.

Reservations

Advised for mid July - end Aug and made by post with deposit (€ 15). Tel: 985 640 938.
E-mail: cantiles@conectia.net

ES8960 Camping La Paz

Ctra N-634 Irun - Coruña, km 2, 33597 Vidiago-Llanes (Asturias)

On arrival here you may well be reminded of the fortress towns of old Spain. The reception building is opposite a solid rock face and many hundred feet below the site and the climb to the site is quite daunting but staff will place your caravan for you, although motorcaravan drivers will have an exciting drive to the top. Once there it is all worth it as the views are absolutely outstanding. The site is arranged on numerous terraces with lower areas in a valley floor. The way down to the beach is very steep but the views, both to the Picos de Europa and to seaward are most impressive. There are 434 pitches with electricity of between 30-70 sq.m, but many are only suitable for tents with no electricity. Because of the steep access, units may be positioned on upper terraces by site staff using Range Rovers. An area back from the beach is more suitable for very large units. There is a cliff-top restaurant and bar with commanding views over the ocean and beach. It is best to book in high season since the site is deservedly popular and one of the best managed along this coast. With the extreme slopes, we think it would appeal most to visitors who are not infirm. Children will require supervision on the steep slopes.

Facilities

Four first class sanitary blocks, with some interesting and unusual design features (such as being cut into solid rock), are modern, well equipped and spotlessly clean. They include hot showers with electronic controls and a baby bath. Full laundry and dishwashing facilities. Spring water is available from a number of taps throughout the site. Motorcaravan services. Mini-market. restaurant and bar. Lounge. Watersports. Table tennis. Games room. Fishing. Superb Beaches. Torches essential. English spoken. Off site: Well placed for excursions to the eastern end of the Picos de Europa.

Open

1 June - 20 September.

At a glance

Welcome & Ambience	✓✓✓✓✓	Location	✓✓✓✓
Quality of Pitches	✓✓✓✓✓	Range of Facilities	✓✓✓✓✓

Directions

From Santander take N634 towards Llanes. Site is signed from the main road at km.292, before you arrive in Vidiago.

Charges guide

Per adult	€ 3,58
child	€ 3,34
tent	€ 3,40
caravan	€ 4,78
car	€ 3,58
motorcycle	€ 2,98

All plus 7% VAT.

Reservations

Advised for peak weeks. Tel: 985 411 012. E-mail: delfin@campinglapaz.com

ES8961 Camping El Helguero

Ctra Santillana-Comillas, 39527 Ruiloba (Cantabria)

This site, surrounded by tall trees and impressive towering rock formations, caters for around 240 units on slightly sloping ground. There are many marked pitches on different levels, all with access to electricity (6A), but with only a little shade in parts. There are also attractive tent and small camper sections set close in to the rocks. The reasonably sized swimming pool and children's pool has an access lift for disabled campers. This is a good site for disabled visitors, in a peaceful location, and is excellent value out of main season. One can generally find space here even in high season, but arrive early. The site is used by tour operators and there are some site owned chalets. There is a large Spanish presence at weekends, especially in high season and if you do not wish to share the boisterous culture, choose one of the many pitches away from the restaurant area.

Facilities

Three well placed toilet blocks, although old, are clean and cared for, and include facilities for disabled visitors and children. Dishwashing, laundry sinks and washing machines. Motorcaravan services. Well-stocked supermarket (July/Aug. 9 am - 1 pm). bar snacks, separate more formal restaurant. Swimming pool with (limited opening with lifeguard on duty, caps compulsory - sold on site). Playground. Animation in high season. Games machines. Activities for children and entertainment for adults. Bicycle hire. ATM. Torches required. Off site: Restaurants in village. Fishing or riding 3 km. Santillana del Mar 12 km. Beaches near.

At a glance

Welcome & Ambience	✓✓✓✓	Location	✓✓✓✓
Quality of Pitches	✓✓✓✓✓	Range of Facilities	✓✓✓✓✓

Directions

From the C6316 road from Santillana del Mar to Comillas, turn left at Sierra. Site is signed as Camping Ruiloba (we don't know why) and is 200 m. on the left.

Charges 2005

Per person	€ 3,30 - € 3,90
child (4-10 yrs)	€ 2,80 - € 3,40
caravan or tent plus car	€ 6,60 - € 7,80
motorcaravan	€ 6,60 - € 7,80
electricity	€ 3,00

Reservations

Write to site. Tel: 942 722 124. E-mail: elhelguero@ctv.es

Open

1 April - 30 September.

ES9000 Camping Playa Joyel

Playa de Ris, 39180 Noja (Cantabria)

This very attractive holiday and touring site is some 40 kilometres from Santander and 70 kilometres from Bilbao. It is a high quality, comprehensively equipped busy site, by a superb beach; providing 1,000 well shaded, marked and numbered pitches, including 80 large pitches of 100 sq.m. Electricity is available (3A with blue Euro-sockets). The swimming pool complex with lifeguard is free to campers and the superb beaches are cleaned daily 15/6-20/9. One of the beach exits leads to the main beach, or if you turn left out of the other you will find a safe, placid estuary with water at rising tide. An unusual feature is the natural park within the site boundary which has a great selection of animals to see. It overlooks a protected area of marsh where European birds spend the winter. There are security patrols at night. This good value, well managed site has a lot to offer for family holidays with much going on in high season when it gets very busy. Used by tour operators (150 pitches).

Facilities

Six excellent, spacious and fully equipped toilet blocks (voted amongst the cleanest in Europe) include baby baths and dishwashing facilities. Large laundry. Motorcaravan services. Gas supplies. Freezer service. Supermarket (all season). General shop. Kiosk. Restaurant (14/4–29/9). Bar, café takeaway and snacks (14/4–28/9). Swimming pools, bathing caps compulsory (15/5-15/9). Entertainment organised with a soundproof pub/disco (July-Aug). Games hall. Gym park. Recreation area and sports field. Tennis. Children's playground. Riding.Fishing. Natural animal park. Barbecue area. Hairdresser (July/Aug). Pharmacy. ATM and money exchange. Torches necessary in some areas. Medical centre. Dogs are not accepted. Off site: Bicycle hire 500 m. Within 1 km – large complex with multiple facilities including golf and indoor pool (fee). Golf 20 km.

At a glance

Welcome & Ambience	✓✓✓✓✓	Location	✓✓✓✓✓
Quality of Pitches	✓✓✓✓✓	Range of Facilities	✓✓✓✓✓

Directions

From A8 (E70) toll-free motorway at Beranga (km.185) take the N634 then, almost immediately, take the S403 for Noja. Follow signs to site.

Charges 2005

Per person	€ 3,70 - € 5,50
child (under 10 yrs)	€ 2,50 - € 4,10
pitch	€ 10,70 - € 16,40
electricity	€ 2,50 - € 2,70

All plus 7% VAT. No credit cards.

Reservations

Made for 1 week or more. Early arrival or reservation is essential in high season. Tel: 942 630 081. E-mail: playajoyel@telefonica.net

Open

Easter - 30 September.

TRAVEL SERVICE SITE

TO BOOK CALL 0870 405 4055 OR www.alanrogersdirect.com

ES8971 Camping Caravaning Playa de Oyambre

San Vicente de la Barquera, Finca Peña Guerra, 39547 San Vicente de la Barquera (Cantabria)

This exceptionally well managed site is ideally positioned to use as a base to visit the spectacular Picos de Europa or one of the many sandy beaches along this northern coast. The site is in lovely countryside (good walking and cycling country), with some views of the fabulous Picos mountains, and near the Cacarbeno National Park. The owner's son Pablo and his wife Maria are assisted by Francis in providing a personal service and both men speak excellent English. The 200 marked pitches are mostly of a good size (average 80 sq.m. with the largest ones often taken by tightly packed seasonal units). They are arranged on wide terraces with little shade and with electricity (10A) in most places. All pitches are flat and most have water and drainage. The site is well lit and a guard patrols at night (high season). The site gets busy with a fairly large Spanish community in season and there can be the usual happy noise of them enjoying themselves at weekends.

Facilities

Good sanitary facilities are in one, well kept block, with cleaners on duty all day and evening. Showers are spacious but have a frustrating mixture of push-button hot and ordinary cold controls. Facilities for babies and disabled visitors. Dishwashing (H&C) and laundry sinks (cold only). Washing machines (tokens from reception). Motorcaravan services. Well stocked supermarket open until 10 pm. with deliveries of fresh fish three days a week (15/6-15/9). Restaurant features fresh local dishes. Bar/TV lounge. Games area with machines. Swimming pools with lifeguard (1/6-15/9). Playground. Basketball. Football. Off site: Fishing and superb beaches 1 km. Riding 5 km. San Vicente de la Barquera 5 km.

Open

Easter/1 April - 30 September.

At a glance

Welcome & Ambience	✓✓✓✓✓	Location	✓✓✓✓
Quality of Pitches	✓✓✓✓✓	Range of Facilities	✓✓✓✓✓

Directions

Site is signed at the junction to Comillas, at km. 265 on the E70, 5 km. east of San Vicente de la Barquera. The entrance is quite steep (take care with caravans). Exercise caution as there is another 'Camping Playa de Oyambre' within 500 m. (on the beach) which is not recommended.

Charges guide

Per person	€ 3,45
child	€ 2,95
pitch	€ 6,95
electricity	€ 2,50

All plus VAT.

Reservations

Advised, particularly if you have a large unit. Write to site. Tel: 942 711 461.
E-mail: camping@oyambre.com

ES8985 Camping Valderredible

Ctra Polientes - Ruerrero, S/n, Valderredible, 39220 Polientes (Cantabria)

This is a pleasant site owned by the Gutierrez brothers who designed and constructed this site using their past campsite experience. Jose and Jesus are very keen to welcome you to their establishment. If you approach the site from the east you will enjoy the vista of limestone valleys and pass a large ornate waterfall which is worth exploring. All facilities on site are modern and kept spotlessly clean. There are 100 flat pitches with 80 for tourers and 20 for tents. Most have electricity and trees have been planted, although there is little shade at the moment. The pools enjoy river and mountain views, as does the patio to the bar/restaurant. The bustling bar, with TV, is pleasantly decorated with local artefacts and offers a range of tapas in season. There are some lovely walks in this unspoilt area (ask for guidance). The site is about 80 km. south of Santander and is good as a stopover or for longer stays if you wish for a peaceful break. On the first Sat and Sun of August there is a Fiesta here with all night celebrations so the site is full and extremely noisy.

Facilities

The good central sanitary block is fully equipped and comfortable. Washing-up sinks outside but covered. Two washing machines (free) and a dryer. No facilities for disabled campers. Small well stocked shop. Bar selling tapas and more formal restaurant, good service and reasonably priced. Swimming pool and children's pool (caps required; June - Sept). Play area (supervision required). Volleyball. Bar billiards. Table football. Torch useful. Off site: Canoeing and fishing in river Ebro 200 m. (March - June). Riding and bicycle hire 15 km. Buses run to local village which has a few bars and some restaurants.

Open

1 April - 4 November.

At a glance

Welcome & Ambience	✓✓✓✓	Location	✓✓✓✓✓
Quality of Pitches	✓✓✓✓	Range of Facilities	✓✓✓✓

Directions

Exit from A623 Burgos - Santander road around the village of Quintanilla Escalada onto minor road to Polientes. The site is clearly signed along the 21 km. of road and is just past the village of Ruijas. It is a spectacular drive in from the main road.

Charges 2005

Per person	€ 3,30 - € 3,50
child (3-10 yrs)	€ 3,00 - € 3,10
tent	€ 3,40 - € 3,60
caravan	€ 3,40 - € 3,60
car	€ 3,40 - € 3,60
motorcaravan	€ 5,50 - € 5,80

Plus 7% VAT.

Reservations

Necessary in August. Tel: 942 776 138.
E-mail: valderrecamp@mundivia.es

ES9045 Camping Angosto

Ctra Villanane-Angosto no. 2, 01425 Villanañe (Araba)

This is a smart eco-friendly site with excellent facilities surrounded by wooded hills near the Valderejo National Park. Opened in 2002, the facilities are improving every year remaining smart and clean. A keen young team run things here, and there is an emphasis on adventure sports. The site is occasionally busy with parties of local youngsters enjoying the various activities organised by the management (it can be noisy when this happens). With ample manoeuvring space, the 71 pitches are flat and of average size, 25 having electricity. There is a large area for tents. Young trees have been planted around the site and are beginning to provide shade. An attractive pool has been built with a sliding roof for inclement weather. Attractive walks start just outside the site perimeter and we spotted deer several times, and the area has one of the largest colonies of vultures in Northern Spain. As the site is one hour from Bilbao we see it as a most pleasant stopover or a chance to sample the rustic simplicity of the area and enjoy the facilities and a tranquil setting.

Facilities

Central, fully equipped sanitary block of attractive design with facilities for disabled campers. Dishwashing sinks outside, under cover. Washing machine. Good shop also used by the local villagers. Stylish bar. Attractive and terraced restaurant. Small fenced children's play area close to entrance and grass toddler play area. Mountain bike hire. Fishing. Adventure sports incl. parascending organised. Table football. Table tennis. TV. Fishing. Ice machine. Drinks machine. Torches necessary in some areas. Off site: Bus service from pretty local village 1 km. Heated municipal pool 1.4 km.

Open

April - September (plus weekends September - March

At a glance

Welcome & Ambience	✓✓✓✓✓	Location	✓✓✓✓✓
Quality of Pitches	✓✓✓✓✓	Range of Facilities	✓✓✓✓✓

Directions

Nearest town is Miranda de Ebro. From Bilbao and the Longrono autoroute, exit at village of Pobes and take road to Salinas and Espejo (N625). Site is clearly signed. If towing a caravan continue to Miranda de Ebro proceed towards Burgos for one exit (no 4) and take the N1 to the N625 then north to Villanane.

Charges guide

Per person	€ 3,16
child	€ 2,70
tent	€ 2,85
caravan	€ 3,16
car	€ 2,85
motorcaravan	€ 4,81

All plus 7% VAT.

Reservations

Contact site. Tel: 945 353 271.
E-mail: info@camping-angosto.com

ES9043 Camping Caravanning Errota el Molino

31150 Mendigorria (Navarra)

This is an extremely large, sprawling site set by an attractive weir near the town of Mendigorria, alongside the river Arga. Regardless of the mini-windmill (molino) at the entrance, it really takes its name from an old disused water-mill close by (try to find it when you have a moment spare). Reception is housed in the lower part of a large prefabricated building along with the bar/restaurant which has a cool shaded terrace, there is a large separate more formal dining room and a supermarket and other support facilities. The chirpy owner Anna Beriain will give you a warm welcome. The upper floor is dormitory accommodation for backpackers. The site is split into separate permanent and touring sections. The touring area is a new development which is divided into sections. There are good-sized flat pitches with electricity and water for tourers, however there is no electricity in the tent area. Many trees have been planted around the site but there is little shade as yet. There is a small tour operator presence and backpackers and campers abound during the festival of San Fermin (bull running) in July, made famous in Pamplona (28 km.) by Ernest Hemingway. Tours of the local bodegas (groups of ten) to sample the fantastic Navarra wines can be organised by reception.

Facilities

The single, fully equipped, toilet block is very clean and well maintained, with cold water to washbasins. Services could become busy during San Fermin but then access is allowed to the sanitary facilities on the permanent side. Dishwashing (cold only) and laundry sinks (H&C). Facilities for disabled campers. Washing machine. Large restaurant, pleasant bar. Supermarket (Easter - Sept). Superb new swimming pools for adults and children. Football. Table tennis. Volleyball. Golf. Bicycle hire. Riding. Weekly animation programme (July/Aug) and many sporting activities. Pleasant river walk. Sophisticated dock and boat launching facility, pedaloes and canoes for hire and an ambitious water sport competition programme in season with a safety boat present at all times. Torches useful. Off site: Bus for town 1 km. Tours to Pamplona.

At a glance

Welcome & Ambience	✓✓✓✓✓	Location	✓✓✓✓✓
Quality of Pitches	✓✓✓✓✓	Range of Facilities	✓✓✓✓✓

Directions

From N111 Pamplona - Logroño road take exit to Puente la Reina. Take N6030 towards Mendigorria and after approx 6 km. take Larraga turn by the wide river Arga, where site is signed.

Charges guide

Per person	€ 3,60
child	€ 2,95
pitch incl. car and electricity	€ 10,50

Plus 7% VAT. Discounts outside high season.

Reservations

Made with 25% deposit. Advisable during San Fermin. Tel: 948 340 604.
E-mail: info@campingelmolino.com

Open

All year.

ES9060 Camping Peña Montañesa

Ctra Ainsa-Francia, km 2, 22360 Labuerda (Huesca)

A large, riverside site situated quite high up in the Pyrenees, near the Ordesa National Park, Pena Montanesa is easily accessible from Ainsa or from France via the Bielsa Tunnel (steep sections on the French side), and is ideally situated for exploring the beautiful Pyrenées. The site is essentially divided into three sections opening progressively throughout the season and all have shade. The 288 pitches on fairly level grass are of approximately 75 sq.m. and 10A electricity is available on virtually all. This is quite a large site which has grown very quickly and as such, it may at times be a little hard pressed, though it is very well run. Grouped near the entrance are the facilities that make the site so attractive. Apart from a fair sized outdoor pool and children's pool (lifeguard 1/3-1/10), there is a glass covered indoor pool (heated in winter) with jacuzzi and sauna (open all year) and an attractive bar/restaurant (with open fire) and terrace with the supermarket and takeaway opposite. The complete town of Ainsa is listed as a national monument of Spain and should be explored while you are here, along with the national park. There is an entertainment programme for children (21/6-15/9 and Easter weekend) and twice weekly for adults (July/Aug).

Facilities

A newer toilet block, heated when necessary, has free hot showers but cold water to open plan washbasins, facilities for disabled visitors and a small baby bathroom. An older block in the original area has similar provision. Washing machine and dryer. Bar. Restaurant. Takeaway. Supermarket. Outdoor swimming pool and children's pool (March - Oct). Pool complex (all year). Children's playground. Boules. Table tennis. Bicycle hire. Riding. Rafting. Only gas barbecues are permitted. Torches required in some areas. Off site: Fishing 100m. Skiing in season. Canoeing near.

At a glance

Welcome & Ambience	✓✓✓✓✓	Location	✓✓✓✓✓
Quality of Pitches	✓✓✓✓	Range of Facilities	✓✓✓✓✓

Directions

Site is 2 km. from Ainsa, on the road from Ainsa to France.

Charges guide

Per person	€ 4,40 - € 5,50
child (1-9 yrs)	€ 3,44 - € 4,30
pitch	€ 12,00 - € 15,00
dog	€ 2,64 - € 3,30
electricity	€ 4,30

All plus 7% VAT.

Reservations

Are made for camping with € 100 deposit by visa or giro. Tel: 974 500 032.
E-mail: info@penamontanesa.com

Open

All year.

ES9070 Centro de Vacaciones Pirineos

Ctra N240, km 300, 22791 Santa Cilia de Jaca (Huesca)

This pretty site which is open most of the year, is directly on the pilgrimage route to Santiago. As well as the campsite, with chalets to hire, there is a small hotel. It has a mild climate, being near the River Aragon, not too high and convenient for touring the Pyrenees. The trees provide good shade. There is an attractive irregular shaped swimming pool and children's pool. The restaurant with a varied menu and a good value menu of the day has a large comfortable terrace and a patio for drinks and snacks. There is an open fronted room for barbecuing and all equipment is provided. A major feature here is the huge recreational area with all manner of sports and amusements. It is a friendly site which is useful for transit stops and off-season camping on the large, mostly level wooded area which can accommodate 250 units (no marked pitches), with electric points throughout. There is some road noise along the south side of the site.

Facilities

One heated sanitary block is open all year, providing a quite satisfactory supply, including dishwashing and laundry sinks with hot water. A second, more modern block is open April - September only. Launderette. Restaurant. Bar. Supermarket (15/6-15/9, otherwise essentials kept in bar). Swimming pools (15/6-15/9). Two tennis courts. Table tennis. Playground. Playroom with electronic games. Petanque. Bicycle hire. Gas supplies. 5-side-soccer. Torches required in some areas. Off site: Fishing and bathing in river 200 m.

Open

All year excl. 3 November - 3 December.

At a glance

Welcome & Ambience	✓✓✓	Location	✓✓✓✓
Quality of Pitches	✓✓✓	Range of Facilities	✓✓✓✓

Directions

Site is 15 km. west of Jaca on N240 at km 300 (65 km. northwest of Huesca).

Charges guide

Per person	€ 4,80
child (2-9 yrs)	€ 4,45
caravan or tent	€ 4,80
car	€ 4,50
motorcaravan	€ 8,50
electricity (6A)	€ 3,90

All plus 7% VAT.

Reservations

Made with deposit (€ 60). Tel: 974 377 351.
E-mail: pirineos@pirinet.com

ES9125 Camping Lago Barasona

Ctra N - 123a, km 25, 22435 La Puebla de Castro (Huesca)

This site, alongside its associated 10 room hotel, is beautifully positioned in terraces by the shores of the Lago de Barasona (a large reservoir), with views of hills and the distant Pyrenees. There are two excellent restaurants here one being in the hotel the other with a pretty terrace with wonderful views. The menu and cooking is outstanding, specialising in the regional cuisine. The very friendly, English speaking owner is keen to please and has applied very high standards throughout the site. The grassy, fairly level pitches are generally around 100 sq.m. with 35 high quality pitches of 110 sq m for larger units. All have electricity (6/10A), many are well shaded and some have great views of the lake and/or hills. Waterskiing and other watersports are available in July and August. You may swim and fish in the lake which has a shallow area extending for around 20 m. If you prefer, the site has a round outdoor pool plus the pleasant standard pool in the hotel (these open from as early as April when the weather is often quite warm). The disco is well away from the site by the lakeside. The local administration has put together some excellent tourist and walking route information (in English) and the owner has matched this with his own quality brochure. The recently discovered Roman town of Labitolosa currently under excavation is just 1.5 kilometres away. This is a most pleasant and peaceful site in a lovely area and will suit families who wish for quality and choice in their camping. The views really are beautiful.

Facilities

Two toilet blocks in modern buildings have high standards and hot water throughout including cabins (3 for ladies, 1 for men). Bar/snack bar and two excellent restaurants (all season). Shop (15/5-15/9). Swimming pools (15/5-15/9). Tennis. Table tennis. Mountain bike hire. Canoe, windsurfing motor boat and pedalo hire. Mini-club. Lake swimming, fishing, canoeing, etc. Facilities for volleyball, football and a new children's play area were under construction. Walking (maps provided). Money exchange. Mini-disco. Off site: Riding 4 km.

Open

1 April - 30 September.

At a glance

Welcome & Ambience	✓✓✓✓	Location	✓✓✓✓✓
Quality of Pitches	✓✓✓✓	Range of Facilities	✓✓✓

Directions

Site is on the west bank of the lake, close to km. 25 on the N123A, 4.5 km. south of Graus (approx. 80 km. north of Lleida/Lerida).

Charges 2005

Per person	€ 3,70 - € 4,85
child (2-10 yrs)	€ 2,70 - € 3,70
car	€ 3,70 - € 5,20
caravan or tent	€ 3,70 - € 5,20
motorcaravan	€ 5,80 - € 8,30
electricity	€ 3,70

Plus 7% VAT .

Reservations

Made with 25-50% deposit, but probably not needed outside mid-July - mid-August. Contact site for details. Tel: 974 545 148. E-mail: info@lagobarasona.com

ES9095 Camping Ciudad de Albarracin

Junto al Polideportibo, 44100 Albarracin (Teruel)

Albarracin, in southern Aragon is set in the 'Reserva Nacional de los Montes Universales' and is a much frequented, fascinating town with a Moorish castle. The old city walls towering above date from its days when it attempted to become a separate country within Spain. This neat and clean family site is set on three levels on a hillside behind the town, with a walk of 1 km. to the centre. It is very modern and has high quality facilities including a superb building for barbecuing (all materials provided). There are 140 pitches (70 for touring units), all with electricity and separated by trees. Some require cars to be parked separately. The homely bar/restaurant, with a terrace and TV, is open all season and has a limited but very pleasant menu. The site is good value, is well run and is a good bet for exploring the area or just enjoying the peace and quiet in this area of natural beauty.

Facilities

The two spotless, modern sanitary buildings provide British style WCs, quite large showers and hot water throughout. Baby bath in the ladies' and a smart area for dishwashing and laundry with washing machines. Bar/restaurant (all season). Essentials from bar. Special room for barbecues with fire and wood provided. Play area. Fronton. 5-a-side soccer. Torches required in some areas. Off site: Municipal swimming pool 100 m. (high season). Town shops, bars and restaurants 500 m.

At a glance

Welcome & Ambience	✓✓✓	Location	✓✓✓✓✓
Quality of Pitches	✓✓✓	Range of Facilities	✓✓✓

Directions

From Teruel north on the N330 for about 8 km. then west onto A1512 for 30 km. Well signed in town.

Charges 2004

Per person	€ 2,70
child (under 14)	€ 2,00
pitch incl. car	€ 5,00 - € 5,45
electricity	€ 2,00

Plus 7% VAT.

Reservations

Contact site. Tel: 978 710 197.

Open

1 April - 31 October.

ES9105 Camping Lago Park

Ctra Alhama de Aragon-Nuevalos, 50210 Nuevalos (Zaragoza)

Lago Park is situated in an attractive area which receives many visitors for the Monasterio de Piedra just 3 km. distant and it enjoys pleasant views of the surrounding mountains. The site has a rather steep access and slopes so is probably unsuitable for disabled campers. It is just outside the attractive ancient village, between lake and mountains, and suitable as a base for exploring this really attractive area. Set on a steep hillside, the 300 pitches (250 for tourers) are on terraces. Only the lower rows of terraces are suitable for large caravans (access in some areas may be difficult). Facilities on site include a large pool (unheated and chilly with its mountain water). The restaurant is disappointing, but there are many good restaurants in town. The site is suitable for transit stops or if you wish to visit the monasterio as it is the only one hereabouts and appears to make the most of that fact. It is not recommended for long stays.

Facilities

The single sanitary block has Turkish and British style WCs. and controllable hot showers (no dividers). Restaurant/bar (June-Sept). Shop (all season). Swimming pool (late June-Sept). Play area. Gas. Off site: Fishing 300 m. Riding 2 km.

Open

1 April - 30 September.

At a glance

Welcome & Ambience	✓✓✓	Location	✓✓✓✓
Quality of Pitches	✓✓✓	Range of Facilities	✓✓✓

Directions

From Zaragoza (120 km.) take fast A2/N11/E90 road and turn on C202 beyond Calatayud to Nuévalos (25 km). From Madrid exit A2 at Alhama de Aragón (13 km). Follow signs for Monasterio de Piedra.

Charges 2004

Per person	€ 4,60
pitch incl. car	€ 8,90 - € 9,50
electricity (10A)	€ 3,90

Reservations

Contact site. Tel: 976 849 038.

ES8000 Camping Son Bou

Ctra de San Jaime km 3.5, Apdo. de Correus 85, Alayor, 07730 Menorca

The beautiful island of Menorca cries out to be explored. It is peaceful and tranquil, with characteristic dry stone walls, its low white buildings with terracotta tiled roof, its beautiful coastline and pretty villages with their cycle of fiestas. Camping Son Bou was only opened in July 1996 and has been purpose built in local style providing a large irregular shaped pool with marvellous view across to Monte Toro and overlooked by a pine shaded, terraced bar and restaurant. The 216 large pitches are arranged in circles radiating out from the main facilities and clearly edged with stones. Natural pine tree shade covers most but the outer ring. Electricity (6A) is available on nearly all pitches. The ground is hard and devoid of grass except where sprinklers operate. The site gets very busy with Spanish people from the mainland in high season. Earlier in the year it is quieter and greener. If you do not fancy the ferry crossings the site has some neat chalets and ready erected tents. The site will arrange ferries from Barcelona or Valencia (discounts).

Facilities

Well designed toilet block of good quality, open plan in places. Some washbasins in cabins. Baby baths. Facilities for disabled visitors. Washing up and laundry sinks all have cold water as do the washbasins. Serviced wash available. Shop (from 1/5). Bar. Restaurant. Outdoor pool (from 1/5). Tennis. Petanque. Football. Basketball. Volleyball. Play area. Bicycle hire. English spoken. Open air cinema most evenings. Occasional barbecue. Activity programme.
Off site: Riding 3 km. Village and beach 750 m.

At a glance

Welcome & Ambience	✓✓✓✓✓	Location	✓✓✓✓✓
Quality of Pitches	✓✓✓✓	Range of Facilities	✓✓✓✓

Directions

From Mahon (Mao) follow main road to Ciutadella. Go past town of Alaior (bypassed), for a further km. approx. Watch for restaurant on left and sign for San Jaime/Son Bou. Turn left on this road (surface not so good). Continue for 3.5 km.and site on right.

Charges 2005

Per person	€ 5,25 - € 6,40
pitch incl. car	€ 9,35 - € 11,35

All plus 7% VAT.

Reservations

Contact site. Tel: 971 372 605.
E-mail: info@campingsonbou.com

Open

22 March - 31 October.

With giant lakes and waterways, rich forests, majestic mountains and glaciers, and vast, wide open countryside, Sweden is almost twice the size of the UK but with a fraction of the population.

The beautiful southwest region, otherwise known as the 'Swedish Lake and Glass country', is easily accessible by ferry or overland from Norway. The area is dominated by two great lakes, Vänern and Vättern, Europe's second and third largest lakes. There are also many fine beaches with picturesque harbours and historic ports such as Gothenburg, Helsingborg and Malmö, which is now linked by a bridge to Copenhagen. Stockholm, the capital, is a delightful place built on fourteen small islands on the eastern coast. It is an attractive, vibrant city, with magnificent architecture, fine museums and historic squares. Moving northwards into central and northern Sweden, you'll discover beautiful forests and around 96,000 lakes, which are perfect for ice skating (in winter!) and you may even well see moose and reindeer. Today Sweden enjoys one of the highest standards of living in the world and a quality of life to go with it.

Population

8.8 million

Capital

Stockholm

Climate

Sweden enjoys a temperate climate thanks to the Gulf Stream. There is generally less rain and more sunshine in the summer than in Britain

Language

Swedish. English is fairly widely spoken

Currency

The Krona

Telephone

The country code is 00 46

Banks

Mon-Fri 09.30-15.00. Some city banks stay open til 17.30/18.00

Shops

Mon-Fri 09.00-18.00. Sat 09.00-13.00/16.00. Some department stores remain open until 20.00/22.00

Public Holidays

New Year; Epiphany; Good Fri; Easter Mon; Labour Day; Ascension; Whit Sun/Mon; Mid-summer Festival; All Saints; Christmas Dec 24-26

Motoring

Roads are much quieter than in the UK. Secondary roads may be gravel surfaced but are still good. Dipped headlights are obligatory. Away from large towns, petrol stations rarely open 24 hours. Buy diesel during working hours, it is rarely available at self service pumps.

Tourist Office

Swedish Travel and Tourism Council
Swedish House, 5 Upper Montagu Street
London W1H 2AG
Tel: 020 7870 5600
Fax: 020 7724 5872
Email: info@swetourism.org.uk
Internet: www.visit-sweden.com

tip

MOST SWEDISH CAMPSITES REQUIRE YOU TO SHOW A 'CAMPING CARD SCANDINAVIA'. THIS COSTS SKR. 90 AND CAN BE BOUGHT AT THE FIRST SITE YOU VISIT OR IN ADVANCE. VARIOUS SPECIAL OFFERS ARE ASSOCIATED WITH IT.

SW2705 Lisebergs Camping Karralund

Olbersgatan 1, S-416 55 Goteborg (Västra Götalands Län)

Well positioned for visiting the city, this busy, well maintained site has 200 marked pitches, 150 with electricity (10A) and cable TV, 42 hardstandings, and several areas for tents. Pitches do vary in size, some are fairly compact and there are no dividing hedges, consequently units can be rather close together. Additionally there are cabins for rent, a budget hotel and a youth hostel. All this makes for a very busy site in the main season, which in this case means June, July and August. An advance telephone call to check for space is advisable. A breakfast buffet is served in low season and there is a restaurant 300 m. from the site entrance. Reception has a range of tourist information, can provide advice on travel in the city, the Liseberg Amusement Park, and sells the Göteborg Card. The nearby Delsjö Camping (also a Lisebergs campsite) is only open in July.

Facilities

Two heated sanitary buildings, the larger one fairly new, and a smaller, older one with limited facilities, are well maintained and cleaned. They provide all the usual facilities, with controllable hot showers, a good suite for small children, dishwashing sinks and a laundry, kitchens with cooking facilities, and a complete unit for disabled visitors. Motorcaravan services. Shop. Restaurant and takeaway. Children's playground. TV room.

Open

All year (full services 10/5-25/8).

At a glance

Welcome & Ambience	✓✓✓✓	Location	✓✓✓✓
Quality of Pitches	✓✓✓	Range of Facilities	✓✓✓

Directions

Site is about 2.5 km. east of city centre. Follow signs to Kärralund and campsite symbol from E20, E6 or Rv 40.

Charges 2005

Per unit	SEK 155 - 300
electricity	SEK 45
tent & car	SEK 95 - 245

Only pitches with electricity available in high season.

Reservations

Advised from mid-June to end of August.
Tel: 031 840 200. E-mail: boende.lgab@liseberg.se

SW2706 Lisebergs Camping Askim Strand

Marholmsvagen, S-436 45 Askim (Västra Götalands Län)

Within easy reach of city, this is a very pleasantly located site, close to a long gently sloping beach which is very popular for bathing. As a result the area behind the campsite is populated by many holiday homes and cabins. A very open site with very little shade, it has 276 mostly level, grassy pitches all with 10A electricity, plus two areas for tents. Many pitches are fairly compact, although there are some larger ones. The keycard entry system operates the entrance barrier and access to the buildings and there is a night security guard (June-Aug). Reception has a range of tourist information, and can provide details of reductions on bus and taxi fares to the city, also selling the Göteborg Card.

Facilities

Two heated sanitary buildings, the larger one fairly new, the smaller recently refitted. Both are maintained to a high standard and provide all the usual facilities, including a good suite for small children, dishwashing sinks, laundry, kitchens with cooking facilities, and a unit for disabled visitors. Hot water is free. Motorcaravan services. Small shop (24/6-8/8, 08.00-21.00). Snack bar (July). Children's playground. TV room.

Open

10 May - 25 August (full services 20/6-11/8).

At a glance

Welcome & Ambience	✓✓✓✓	Location	✓✓✓✓
Quality of Pitches	✓✓✓	Range of Facilities	✓✓✓

Directions

About 10 km. south of Göteborg, take exit signed Mölndal S and ports (Hamnar). Take the Rv 159 towards Frolunda, and watch for a slip-road to the right, signed to Askim and follow signs to campsite.

Charges guide

Per unit	SEK 150 -190
electricity	SEK 40

Only pitches with electricity available for high season.

Reservations

Advised June-Aug. Tel: 031 286 261.
E-mail: boende.lgab@liseberg.se

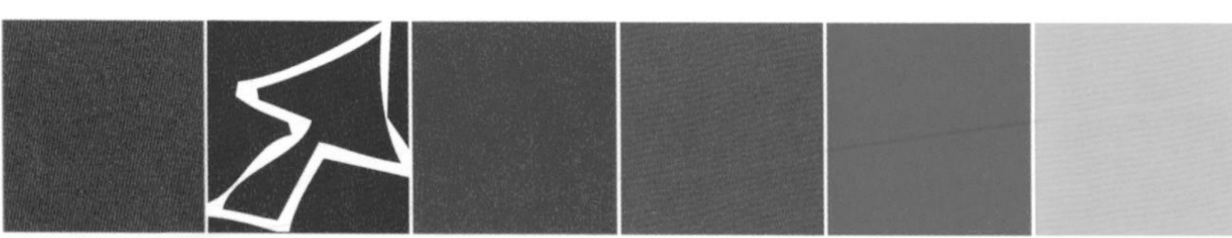

SW2650 Skånes Djurparks Camping

Jularp, S-243 93 Höör (Skåne Län)

This site is probably one of the most unusual we feature. It is next to the Skånes Djurpark - a zoo park with Scandinavian species - and has on site a reconstructed Stone Age Village. The site is located in a sheltered valley and has some 90 large, level grassy pitches for caravans and motorhomes all with 10A electricity, a few with waste water drain, and a separate area for tents. The most unusual feature of the site is the sanitary block – it is underground! The fully air-conditioned building houses a superb and ample complement of facilities. The site also has a number of underground, caveman style, 8 bed (dormitory type) holiday units which can be rented by families or private groups (when not in use by schools on educational trips to the Stone Age Village). They open onto a circular courtyard with a barbecue and camp fire area and have access to the kitchens and dining room in the sanitary block. There are good walks through the nature park and around the lakes, where one can see deer, birds and other wildlife. Well placed for the new Copenhagen - Malmo bridge or the ferries, this is also a site for discerning campers who want something distinctly different.

Facilities

The underground block includes roomy showers, two fully equipped kitchens, laundry and separate drying room and an enormous dining/TV room. Facilities for disabled people and baby changing. Cooking facilities. Laundry. Mini-shop (April - Oct). Café (June - Aug). Small heated family swimming pool (June - Aug). Children's playground. Stone Age Village. Off site: Restaurant just outside the camp entrance. Fishing 1.8 km. Bicycle hire 3 km. Riding and golf 8 km.

At a glance

Welcome & Ambience	✓✓✓✓	Location	✓✓✓✓
Quality of Pitches	✓✓✓✓	Range of Facilities	✓✓✓✓

Directions

Turn off no. 23 road 2 km. north of Höör (at roundabout) and follow signs for Skånes Djurpark. Campsite entrance is off the Djurpark car park.

Charges 2004

Per unit	SEK 140
electricity	SEK 30 - 40

Reservations

Advised for high season (July/Aug). Tel: 0413 553270. E-mail: info@grottbyn.se

Open

All year (full services 15/6-10/8).

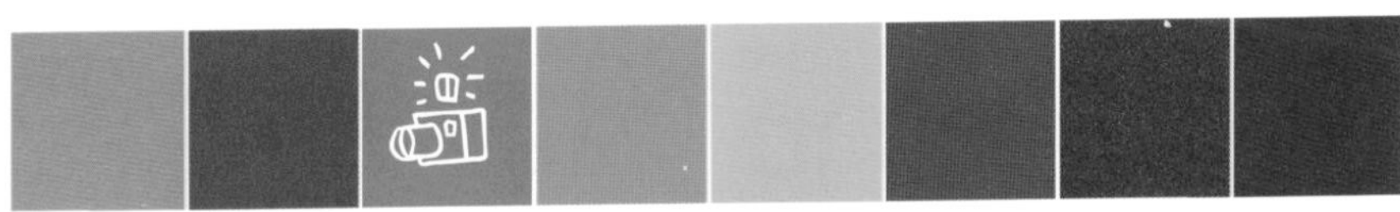

SW2640 Krono Camping Båstad-Torekov

S-260 93 Torekov (Skåne Län)

Part of the Kronocamping chain, this campsite is 500 metres from the fishing village of Torekov, 14 kilometres west of the home of the Swedish tennis WCT Open at Båstad on the stretch of coastline between Malmö and Göteborg. Useful en route from the most southerly ports, it is a very good site and worthy of a longer stay for relaxation. It has 510 large pitches (390 for touring units), all numbered and marked, mainly in attractive natural woodland (mostly pine and birch), with some on more open ground close to the shore. Of these, 400 have electricity (10A) and cable TV, 77 also having water and drainage. The modern reception complex is professionally run and is also home for a good shop, a snack bar, restaurant, and pizzeria. The spacious site covers quite a large area and there is a cycle track along the shore to the beach with bathing. Games for children are organised in high season and there is an outdoor stage for musical entertainment and dancing (also in high season). This well run site is a pleasant place to stay.

Facilities

Three very good sanitary blocks with free hot water and facilities in for babies and disabled visitors (in each block). Laundry. Cooking facilities and dishwashing. Motorcaravan service point. Restaurant, pizzeria and snack bar with takeaway (7/6-15/8). Bar. Shop and kiosk. Minigolf. Sports fields. Children's play areas. Bicycle hire. TV room. Beach. Fishing Off site: Tennis close. Golf 1 km. Riding 3 km. Games, music and entertainment in high season.

At a glance

Welcome & Ambience	✓✓✓✓	Location	✓✓✓✓
Quality of Pitches	✓✓✓✓	Range of Facilities	✓✓✓✓

Directions

From E6 Malmö - Göteborg road take Torekov/Båstad exit and follow signs for 20 km. towards Torekov. Site is signed 1 km. before village on right.

Charges 2004

Per unit	SEK 140 - 205
incl electricity/TV connection	SEK 185 - 250

Reservations

Advised in high season, contact site for details. Tel: 0431 364 525. E-mail: torekov@kronocamping.se

Open

8 April - 19 September.

SW2655 Tingsryds Municipal Camping

Mårdslyckesand, S-362 91 Tingsryd (Kronobergs Län)

A pleasant, well managed municipal site by Lake Tiken, Tingsryds Camping is well placed for Sweden's Glass District. The 129 large pitches are arranged in rows divided by trees and shrubs, with some along the edge of a lakeside path (public have access). All have electricity (10A) and there is shade in parts. The facilities are housed in buildings near the site entrance, with the reception building having the restaurant, cafe, bar and a small shop. Adjacent to the site is a small beach, grassy lying out area, playground and lake swimming area and three tennis courts. Hire of canoes, fishing and minigolf are available on site (public access also). Two large supermarkets, a heated indoor 'Waterworld', bowling alley, and further shops and restaurants are in the town (one kilometre), which can be reached via a level footpath/cycle track directly from the site. The town hosts a Folk Festival and market in July each year. This site is an ideal place from which to explore the factories and shops of the 'Kingdom of Crystal'.

Facilities

Heated sanitary installations are in two well maintained buildings, one including showers, mostly with curtains (on payment, communal undressing), the other a campers' kitchen with hobs and dining area, plus dishwashing sinks with further sinks outside under cover (hot water from separate tap). Facilities for disabled people and family room. Laundry with free ironing. Motorcaravan services. Shop (1/5-15/9). Restaurant, cafe, bar (1/5-15/9). Tennis. Minigolf. Playground. Boules. Lake swimming. Beach volleyball. Canoe hire. Fishing. Off site: Bicycle hire 1 km. Golf 15 km.

At a glance

Welcome & Ambience	✓✓✓✓	Location	✓✓✓✓
Quality of Pitches	✓✓✓✓	Range of Facilities	✓✓✓✓

Directions

Site is 1 km. from Tingsryd off road no. 120, well signed around the town.

Charges guide

Per unit	SEK 125 - 165
electricity	SEK 25

Reservations

Advised for high season. Write to site. Tel: 0477 10554.

Open

5 April - 20 October (full service 24/5-19/8).

SW2680 Krono Camping Saxnäs

S-386 95 Färjestaden (Kalmar Län)

Well placed for touring Sweden's Riviera and the fascinating and beautiful island of Öland, this family-run site, part of the Krono group, has 420 marked and numbered touring pitches. Arranged in rows on open, well kept grassland dotted with a few trees, all have electricity (10A), 320 have TV connections and 112 also have water. An unmarked area without electricity can accommodate around 60 tents. The site has about 130 long stay units and cabins for rent. Reception is efficient and friendly with good English spoken. In high season children's games are organised and dances are held twice weekly, with other activities on other evenings. The sandy beach slopes very gently and is safe for children. Nearby attractions include the seven kilometres long Öland road bridge and the 400 old windmills on the island (in the 19th century there were 20).

Facilities

Three heated sanitary blocks provide a good supply of roomy private showers, washbasins, some washbasin/WC suites and WCs. Facilities for babies and disabled visitors. Well equipped laundry room. Good kitchen with cookers, microwaves and dishwasher (free), and dishwashing sinks. Hot water is free throughout. Gas supplies. Motorcaravan services. Shop (1/5-30/8). Pizzeria, licensed restaurant and café (all 1/5-30/8). Bar (1/7-31/7). Playgrounds. Bouncing castle. Boules. Beach with volleyball. Fishing. Bicycle hire. Minigolf. Family entertainment and activities. Football. Off site: Golf 0.5 km. Riding 2 km. Kalmar and its castle, museums and old town on the mainland, Eketorp prehistoric fortified village, Öland Djurpark. The Danish Royal family's summer residence, Solliden, is well worth a visit.

At a glance

Welcome & Ambience	✓✓✓✓	Location	✓✓✓✓
Quality of Pitches	✓✓✓	Range of Facilities	✓✓✓✓✓

Directions

Cross Öland road bridge from Kalmar on road no. 137. Take exit for Öland Djurpark/Saxnäs, then follow campsite signs. Site is just north of the end of the bridge.

Charges guide

Per pitch	SEK 100 - 185
electricity/TV connection	SEK 40

Weekend and weekly rates available.

Reservations

Essential for high season (mid June - mid Aug). Tel: 0485 35700. E-mail: saxnas@kronocamping-oland.se

Open

17 April - 11 September.

SW2675 Västervik SweCamp Lysingsbadet

Lysingsvägen, S-593 53 Västervik (Kalmar Län)

One of the largest sites in Scandinavia, Lysingsbadet has unrivalled views of the 'Pearl of the East Coast' - Västervik and its fjords and islands. There are around 10 large, mostly marked and numbered pitches, spread over a vast area of rocky promontory and set on different plateau, terraces, in valleys and woodland, or beside the water. It is a very attractive site, and one which never really looks or feels crowded even when busy. There are 83 full service pitches with TV, water and electrical connections, 163 with TV and electricity and 540 with electricity only, the remainder for tents. Reception is smart, efficient and friendly with good English spoken. An hourly bus service to Västervik runs from the site entrance from May-September. On site facilities include a full golf course, minigolf, heated outdoor pool complex with water slide and poolside café, sauna and solarium, children's playgrounds, boat hire, tennis, basketball, volleyball and fishing. A licensed restaurant is supplemented by a café/takeaway and a range of on site shops. For children, Astrid Lindgren's World theme park at Vimmerby is an easy day trip away and for adults the delights of the old town of Västervik and its shopping.

Facilities

Ten modern sanitary blocks of various ages and designs house a comprehensive mix of showers, basins and WCs. All have good quality fittings and are kept very clean. Several campers' kitchens with dishwashing sinks, cookers and hoods, also 4 laundry rooms. Free hot water throughout and all facilities free of charge. Campers are issued with key cards which operate the entrance barriers and gain access to sanitary blocks, pool complex and other facilities. Motorcaravan services. Supermarket and shops (15/5-31/8). Restaurant and café/takeaway (1/6-15/8). Swimming pool complex (15/6-31/8). Golf. Minigolf. Tennis. Basketball. Volleyball. Bicycle and boat hire. Fishing. Entertainment and dances in high season. Children's playgrounds. Quick Stop service.Hairdresser. Bus service.

At a glance

Welcome & Ambience	✓✓✓✓	Location	✓✓✓✓✓
Quality of Pitches	✓✓✓✓	Range of Facilities	✓✓✓✓✓

Directions

Turn off E22 for Västervik and keep straight on at all junctions until first campsite sign. Follow signs to site.

Charges guide

Per unit	SEK 120 - 190
electricity	SEK 35

Reservations

Advisable for peak season (July/Aug). Write to site for details. Tel: 0490 88920. E-mail: lysingsbadet@vastervik.se

Open

All year.

SW2800 Glyttinge Camping

Berggårdsvägen, S-582 49 Linköping (Östergötlands Län)

Only five minutes by car from the Ikea Shopping Mall and adjacent to a good swimming pool complex, Glyttinge is a most attractive site with a mix of terrain - some flat, some sloping and some woodland. A top quality site with enthusiastic and friendly management, it is maintained to a very high standard and flowers, trees and shrubs everywhere give it a cosy garden like atmosphere. There are 239 good size, mostly level pitches of which 125 have electricity (10A) and 28 are fully serviced. Children are well catered for - the manager has laid out a wonderful, fenced and very safe children's play area and, in addition, parents can rent (minimal charge) tricycles, pedal cars, scooters and carts. There is also a wet weather playroom. Adjacent to the site, the heated outdoor pool complex has three pools (charged). Attractions nearby include the old town of Gamla Linköping, Aviation Museum, Land Museum and the Ikea Shopping Mall. Also ask at reception about canal tours.

Facilities

The main, central toilet block (supplemented by additional smaller facilities at reception) is modern, well constructed and exceptionally well equipped and maintained. It has showers in cubicles, washbasin and WC suites, hand dryers, and soothing music! Separate facilities for disabled visitors. Baby rooms. Laundry. Solarium. Superb kitchen and dining/TV room, fully equipped. Motorcaravan services. Shop and takeaway (15/6-15/8). Minigolf. Football. Bicycle hire. Children's playground. Off site: Swimming pool complex adjacent (15/5-25/8). Riding and golf 3 km. Fishing 5 km.

At a glance

Welcome & Ambience	✓✓✓✓	Location	✓✓✓✓
Quality of Pitches	✓✓✓✓	Range of Facilities	✓✓✓✓

Directions

Exit E4 Helsingborg - Stockholm road north of Linköping at signs for Ikea and site. Turn right at traffic lights and camp sign and follow signs to site.

Charges 2005

Per unit	SEK 140 - 165
electricity	SEK 35

Low season discounts for pensioners.

Reservations

Advised for July/Aug. Write to site for details. Tel: 013 174 928. E-mail: glyttinge@swipnet.se

Open

27 April - 1 October.

SW2670 Grannastrandens Familjecamp

Box 14, S-563 21 Granna (Jönköpings Län)

This large, lakeside site with modern facilities and busy continental feel, is set below the old city of Gränna. Flat fields separate Gränna from the shore, one of which is occupied by the 25 acres of Grännastrandens where there are 500 numbered pitches, including a tent area and some seasonal pitches. The site is flat, spacious and very regularly laid out on open ground with only a row of poplars by the lake to provide shelter, so a windbreak may prove useful against any onshore breeze. About 260 pitches have electricity (6/10A). Part of the lake is walled off to form an attractive swimming area with sandy beaches, slides and islands. Obviously the great attraction here is the lake. It offers beaches, bathing, fishing, sailing and superb coastal walks. Outstanding, however, is the 30 minute ferry crossing from the tiny harbour next to the site to Visingsö, the beautiful island reputedly inhabited for over 60 years. It is this excursion, complete with its gentle tour by horse drawn 'remmalag' which alone warrants Grännastrandens as your base. Gränna is also the centre of hot air ballooning and on 11 July each year there are ascents from Sweden's only 'balloon airport'.

Facilities

The large, sanitary block in the centre of the site has modern, well kept facilities including British style WCs, some with external access, washbasins, and free hot showers, some in private cubicles. Dishwashing and laundry sinks. Laundry facilities. Provision for disabled people. A further small, older block is by reception. Cooking facilities. Motorcaravan services. Shop. TV room. Children's playground. Lake swimming area. Boating and fishing. Off site: Café outside site (1/5-31/8) or town restaurants close.

At a glance

Welcome & Ambience	✓✓✓✓	Location	✓✓✓✓
Quality of Pitches	✓✓✓	Range of Facilities	✓✓✓✓

Directions

Take Gränna exit from E4 road (no camping sign) 40 km. north of Jönköping. Site is signed in the centre of the town, towards the harbour and ferry.

Charges guide

Per unit	SEK 150
electricity and satellite TV connection	SEK 30

Reservations

Write to site for details. Tel: 0390 10706.

Open

1 May - 30 September.

SW2665 Jönköping Swecamp Villa Björkhagen

Friggagatan 31, S-554 54 Jonkoping (Jönköpings Län)

Overlooking Lake Vättern, Villa Björkhagen is a good site, useful as a break in the journey across Sweden or visiting the city during a tour of the Lakes. It is on raised ground overlooking the lake, with some shelter in parts. There are 300 pitches on well kept grass which, on one side, slopes away from reception. Some pitches on the other side of reception are flat and there are 200 electrical (10A), 100 cable TV and 40 water connections available. Jönköping is one of Sweden's oldest trading centres with a Charter dating back to 1284 and several outstanding attractions. These must include the museums of the 'safety match', ceramics and weaponry and, particularly, the superb troll artistry of John Bauer.

Facilities

Heated sanitary facilities include hot showers on payment (some in private cubicles) and a sauna, plus provision for disabled visitors and babies. Laundry. Dishwashing facilities. Motorcaravan services. Gas supplies. Well stocked mini-market. Restaurant (May - Sept). Playground. TV room. Bicycle hire. Minigolf. Off site: Swimming pool complex 500 m. Fishing 500 m. Riding 7 km.

At a glance

Welcome & Ambience	✓✓✓✓	Location	✓✓✓✓
Quality of Pitches	✓✓✓	Range of Facilities	✓✓✓

Directions

Site is well signed from the E4 road on eastern side of Jönköping. Watch carefully for exit on this fast road.

Charges 2004

Per unit incl. all persons	SEK 170 - 220
electricity/TV connection	SEK 30

Prices may be increased if there is a local exhibition.

Reservations

Advised for July - write to site for details.
Tel: 036 122863. E-mail: villabjorkhagen@swipnet.se

Open

All year (full services 1 May - 30 September).

SW2720 Tidaholm-Hökensås Camping

Daretorp, S-522 91 Tidaholm (Västra Götalands Län)

Hökensås is located just west of Lake Vättern and south of Tidaholm, in a beautiful national park of wild, unspoiled scenery. The park is based on a 100 kilometres ridge, a glacier area with many impressive boulders and ice age debris but now thickly forested with majestic pines and silver birches, with a small, brilliant lake at every corner. This pleasant campsite is part of a holiday complex that includes wooden cabins for rent. It is relaxed and informal, with over 200 pitches either under trees or on a more open area at the far end, divided into rows by wooden rails. These are numbered and electricity (10A) is available on 130. Tents can go on the large grassy open areas by reception. The forests and lakes provide wonderful opportunities for walking, cycling (gravel tracks and marked walks) angling, swimming and when the snow falls, winter sports.

Facilities

The original sanitary block near reception is supplemented by one in the wooded area. Hot showers with communal changing area and some curtained cubicles are free. Separate saunas for each sex and facilities for the disabled and babies. Campers' kitchen at each block with cooking, dishwashing and laundry facilities (irons on loan from reception). Small, but well stocked shop with a comprehensive angling section. Café with takeaway. Children's playground. Tennis. Minigolf. Sauna. Lake swimming. Fishing.

At a glance

Welcome & Ambience	✓✓✓✓	Location	✓✓✓✓
Quality of Pitches	✓✓✓✓	Range of Facilities	✓✓✓✓

Directions

Approach site from no. 195 western lake coast road. at Brandstorp, about 40 km. north of Jönköping, turn west at petrol station and camp sign signed Hökensås. Site is about 9 km. up this road.

Charges 2005

Per unit	SEK 110
electricity	SEK 35 - 45

Prices are higher for Midsummer celebrations.

Reservations

Write to site for details. Tel: 0502 230 53. E-mail: info@hokensas-semesterby.com

Open

All year (full services 20/6-11/8).

SW2700 Boras Camping

PO Box 44022, S-500 04 Borås (Västra Götalands Län)

Borås Camping is in a park setting two kilometres north of the city centre. This pleasant municipal site is within easy walking distance of a swimming pool complex, Djurpark and shopping centre, and is convenient for ferries to and from Gothenburg. A tidy, well managed site, it provides 500 large, numbered, level pitches, carefully arranged in rows on well kept grass with good tarmac perimeter roads. Electricity (10A) is provided to 300 pitches and there is some shade in parts. Many activities are available both on the site and nearby, many free to campers; the excellent outdoor heated pool complex, Alidebergsbadet, is only 400 m. Canoes and pedaloes are available on the small canal running through the site. The shopping precinct at Knalleland is only 500 m, the Zoo (Djurpark) is 400 m. The site can issue the 'Boråscard' which gives free and discounted access to city car parks, transport, museums and attractions during your stay.

Facilities

Six good, modern sanitary blocks are clean and heated. Facilities for babies and disabled people, in various combinations (the largest block new in '99). Good campers' kitchens have hobs, extractor hoods, and dishwashing sinks (free of charge). Laundry facilities. Motorcaravan service point. Shop. Cafeteria and takeaway (full services 6/6-9/8). Several children's playgrounds. Minigolf. Bicycle hire.
Off site: Swimming, tennis, frisbee, badminton, football, croquet, table tennis, jogging tracks, basketball all nearby.

At a glance

Welcome & Ambience	✓✓✓	Location	✓✓✓✓
Quality of Pitches	✓✓✓✓	Range of Facilities	✓✓✓

Directions

Exit road no. 40 from Gothenburg for Borås Centrum and follow signs to Djurpark and road no. 42 to Trollhätten through the town. Turn left to site.

Charges year

Per unit	SEK 110 - 145
electricity	SEK 25

Reservations

One should always find room here. Tel: 033 353 280.

Open

All year.

SW2710 Lidköping SweCamp Kronocamping

Läckögatan, S-531 54 Lidköping (Västra Götalands Län)

This high quality, attractive site provides about 430 pitches on flat, well kept grass. It is surrounded by some mature trees, with the lake shore as one boundary and a number of tall pines have been left to provide shade and shelter. There are 274 pitches with electricity (10A) and TV connections and 91 with water and drainage also, together with 60 cabins for rent. A tour operator takes a few pitches and the site takes a fair number of seasonal units. There is a a small shop (a shopping centre is very close) and a coffee bar with conservatory seating area in the reception complex. Very good playgrounds are provided for children, together with a play field, TV room (cartoon videos shown) and an amusement and games room. The lake is available for watersports, boating and fishing with bathing from the sandy beach or there is a swimming pool complex (free for campers) adjacent to the site.

Facilities

Excellent, modern sanitary facilities are in two identical blocks with under-floor heating, attractive decor and lighting (and music). Hot water is free. Baby room and facilities for disabled people. Good kitchens with cookers and microwaves. Motorcaravan services. Small shop. Coffee bar with snacks. Minigolf. Volleyball. Solarium. Playgrounds. TV room. Games and amusements room. Bicycle hire. Play field. Lake swimming, fishing and watersports.
Off site: Swimming pool adjacent.

At a glance

Welcome & Ambience	✓✓✓	Location	✓✓✓✓
Quality of Pitches	✓✓✓✓	Range of Facilities	✓✓✓✓

Directions

From Lidköping town junctions follow signs towards Läckö then pick up camping signs turning right at second roundabout. Continue to site on left.

Charges 2004

Per unit	SEK 150 - 195
with electricity/TV connection	SEK 170 - 230

Reservations

Write to site for details. Tel: 0510 26804.
E-mail: info@kronocamping.com

Open

All year (full services 8/6-15/8).

SW2740 Laxsjons Camping och Friluftsgard

S-660 10 Dals Långed (Västra Götalands Län)

In the beautiful Dalsland region, Laxsjöns is an all year round site, catering for winter sports enthusiasts as well as summer tourists and groups. On the shores of the lake, the site is in two main areas – one flat, near the entrance, with hardstandings and the other on attractive, sloping, grassy areas adjoining. There are 300 pitches, all with electricity (10A), plus more for tents. The site has a good swimming pool with paddling pool. A restaurant is at the top of the site with a good range of dishes in high season. In addition, there is a lake for swimming, fishing and canoeing (boats available). The site is located in the centre of Dalsland, west of Lake Vänern, in an area of deep forests, endless lakes and river valleys, and is one of the loveliest and most interesting regions in this always peaceful and scenic country.

Facilities

The main toilet block has hot showers on payment (communal changing), open washbasins, WCs and a hairdressing cubicle. With a further small block at the top of the site, the provision should be adequate. Facilities for disabled visitors. Laundry with drying rooms for bad weather. Cooking rooms for tenters. Restaurant (high season). Shop. Tennis. Minigolf. Sauna. Playground. Swimming pool. Lake for swimming, Fishing and boating.

At a glance

Welcome & Ambience	✓✓✓	Location	✓✓✓✓
Quality of Pitches	✓✓✓✓	Range of Facilities	✓✓✓✓

Directions

From Åmål take road no. 164 to Bengtfors, then the 172 towards Dals Långed. Site is signed about 5 km. south of the town 1 km. down a good road.

Charges guide

Per unit incl. electricity	SEK 140 - 160

Reservations

Advisable in peak season. Tel: 0531 30010.
E-mail: info@laxsjonsfriluftsgard.com

Open

1 April - 30 September (full services 22/6-15/8).

SW2730 Ekuddens Camping

Strandbadet, S-542 00 Mariestad (Västra Götalands Län)

Ekuddens occupies a long stretch of the eastern shore of Lake Vänern to the northwest of the town, in a mixed woodland setting, and next door to the municipal complex of heated outdoor pools. The lake, of course, is used for swimming or boating and there are bicycles and canoes for hire. The spacious site can take 350 units (230 electrical hook-ups). Most pitches are under the trees but some at the far end of the site are on more open ground with good views over the lake. The site becomes busy in high season.

Facilities

Sanitary facilities are in three low wooden cabins, all clean and well maintained. Free hot showers, some with curtains and communal changing, some in private cubicles. Facilities for disabled visitors. Kitchens. Shop. Licensed bar. Takeaway (high season). Canoes and bicycles for hire. Playground. Minigolf. TV room. Entertainment in high season.
Off site: Swimming pools adjacent. Golf 2 km.

At a glance

Welcome & Ambience	✓✓✓✓	Location	✓✓✓✓
Quality of Pitches	✓✓✓✓	Range of Facilities	✓✓✓✓

Directions

Site is 2.5 km. northwest of the town, well signed at junctions on the ring road. From E20 motorway take exit for Mariestad S. and follow signs for Marieholm.

Charges guide

Per unit incl. electricity	SEK 130 - 160

Reservations

Essential in high season. Tel: 0501 10637.
E-mail: a.appelgren@mariestad.mail.telia.com

Open

1 May - 30 September (full services 15/6-15/8).

SW2750 Årjäng SweCamp Resort Sommarvik

Sommarvik, S-672 91 Årjäng (Värmlands Län)

This is a good site in beautiful surroundings with some of the 300 pitches overlooking the clear waters of the Västra Silen lake in peaceful countryside. The numbered pitches are arranged in terraces on a hillside interspersed with pines and birches, with half set aside for static units and 20 for tents. The remaining touring pitches all have 10A electricity hook-ups and 20 also include water and drainage. The site also has 60 chalets for rent. A large restaurant offers a full range of meals, soft drinks, beers, wines and takeaway meals. Close to reception, a heated swimming pool with a paddling pool, terraces and sun loungers has fine views down the lake. The pool and most activities on site attract daily charges. The lake with its sandy beach is popular and safe for children. There are plenty of activities available including canoeing, rowing boats, windsurfing, fishing, football, an attractive water featured minigolf, sauna, quizzes, guided walks and sightseeing trips. It is possible to ride trolleys around the area on disused railway tracks, go gold panning or slip into nearby Norway and visit Oslo. This site makes an ideal base to explore this scenic region in summer or winter when skiing is an additional attraction.

Facilities

Five sanitary units of varying sizes provide shower cubicles (hot showers on payment), washbasins, toilets, family bathrooms, facilities for disabled persons and baby changing. All are clean and acceptable but may be stretched in high season. Campers kitchens with cookers and sinks. Laundry facilities. Motorcaravan services. All activities and amenities are open 1/6-31/8. Small shop 1/5-30/9. Restaurant and takeaway. Good play areas. Bicycle hire. Internet access. 'Quick stop' pitches for overnight stays. Youth hostel and conference centre also on site. Off site: Indoor pool complex 3 km. Riding 5 km. Golf 9 km.

At a glance

Welcome & Ambience	✓✓✓✓	Location	✓✓✓✓
Quality of Pitches	✓✓✓	Range of Facilities	✓✓✓✓

Directions

Site is well signed on road 172.3km south of its junction with the E18 close to Årjäng.

Charges 2004

Per pitch	SEK 130
with electricity and water	SEK 160 - 240

Reservations

Advised for peak seasons (summer and winter). Tel: 0573 12060. E-mail: swecamp@sommarvik.se

Open

All year.

SW2760 Frykenbaden Camping

Frykenbaden PL 1405, S-655 00 Kil (County)

Frykenbaden Camping is in a quiet wooded area on the southern shore of Lake Fryken, taking 250 units on grassy meadows surrounded by trees. One area nearer the lake is gently sloping, the other is flat with numbered pitches arranged in rows, all with electricity (6/120A), and many with satellite TV and phone connections. Reception, a good shop and takeaway are located in a traditional Swedish house surrounded by lawns sloping down to the shore, with minigolf, a play barn and playground, with pet area also close by. Tables and benches are near the lake, where swimming and canoeing are possible. A good value restaurant is at the adjacent golf club which can be reached by a pleasant walk. Fryken is a long, narrow lake, said to be one of the deepest in Sweden, and it is a centre for angling. Frykenbadens Camping is a quiet, relaxing place to stay, away from the busier and more famous lakes. There are other activities in the area (golf, riding, ski-ing in winter) and Kil is not too far from the Norwegian border.

Facilities

The main sanitary block is of good quality and heated in cool weather with showers on payment, open washbasins, a laundry room and room for families or disabled people. With a further small block with equally good facilities, the overall supply is better than average for Swedish sites. Well equipped camper's kitchen with ovens, hobs and sinks. Small shop. Snack bar and takeaway. Minigolf. Children's play barn and playground. Lake swimming. Canoes and bicycles for hire. Off site: Golf 500 m. Go-karts, riding, jogging track 3 km.

At a glance

Welcome & Ambience	✓✓✓✓	Location	✓✓✓✓
Quality of Pitches	✓✓✓✓	Range of Facilities	✓✓✓✓

Directions

Site is signed from the no. 61 Karlstad - Arvika road, then 4 km. towards lake following signs.

Charges guide

Per unit	SEK 100 - 120
electricity	SEK 35
TV connection	SEK 15

Reservations

Write to site. Tel: 0554 40940. E-mail: frykenbaden@telia.com

Open

All year (full services 17/6-13/8).

SW2820 Skantzö Bad u. Camping

Box 506, S-737 27 Hallstahammar (Västmanlands Län)

A very comfortable and pleasant municipal site just off the main E18 motorway from Oslo to Stockholm, this has 180 large marked and numbered pitches, 165 of these with electricity (10A). The terrain is flat and grassy, there is good shade in parts and the site is well fenced and locked at night. There are 22 new alpine style cabins for rent with window boxes of colourful flowers. Reception is very friendly. Amenities include a very large, fenced, outdoor, heated swimming pool and waterslide (free), children's playground, tennis and minigolf (charged) and a games area complex. Direct access to the towpath of the Stromsholms Kanal and nearby is the Kanal Museum. The site provides hire and transportation of canoes for longer canal tours. There are good walks and cycle trails all around the area, and excellent tourist information is available.

Facilities

One sanitary block, located in the reception area, is maintained and equipped to a high standard, including free hot showers (in cubicles with washbasin), facilities for disabled people and baby changing. A new unit to the same high standards has been added at the far end of the site and both are heated. Good campers' kitchen, good laundry with drying room and lines, washing machine and dryer. Motorcaravan services. Barbecue grill area. Cafeteria and shop (18/5-19/8). Swimming pool and waterslide (19/5-19/8). Minigolf. Tennis. Children's playground. Bicycle hire. Fishing. Canoe hire. Off site: Golf 9 km.

At a glance

Welcome & Ambience	✓✓✓✓	Location	✓✓✓✓
Quality of Pitches	✓✓✓✓	Range of Facilities	✓✓✓✓

Directions

Turn off E18 at Hallstahammar and follow road no. 252 to west of town centre and signs to campsite.

Charges 2005

Per unit	SEK 125 - 150
electricity	SEK 35

Reservations

Write to site for details. Tel: 0220 24305.
E-mail: turism@hallstahammar.se

Open

1 May - 30 September.

SW2840 Flottsbro Stugor & Camping

PO Box 1073, S-141 22 Huddinge (Stockholms Län)

Flottsbro is a neat, small site with good quality facilities and very good security, located some 18 kilometres south of Stockholm. There are 100 large numbered pitches for caravans and motorhomes and a separate unmarked area for tents. Pitches are arranged on level terraces, 65 with electricity (10A), but the site itself is sloping and the reception and restaurant are at the bottom with all the ski facilities and further good sanitary facilities with a sauna. The reception area is remote from the entrance but a very good security system is in place, campers have keys to the barrier and toilet blocks, there is a night guard and an entry phone/camera surveillance system on the entrance for good measure. Once you have negotiated the entry phone you will find a friendly and more personal service at reception. Do not be tempted to walk to reception from the gate, it is a long way down and a steep climb back. Other facilities on site include the ski slope and lift, restaurant which serves a selection of simple meals and snacks, beer, tea, coffee and soft drinks. The site has a small lakeside beach and grassy lying out area with a playground and plenty of room for ball games. The area is also good for walking, cycling and cross-country skiing.

Facilities

In addition to the facilities at reception, two other small sanitary units are on the camping area. Modern facilities include free showers, a suite for disabled people, baby facilities and a family bathroom. Excellent campers' kitchen with electric cookers and sinks with hot water, all free. Washing machine, dryer (charged for) and sink. Sauna. Restaurant. Minigolf. Volleyball. Frisbee. Jogging track. Canoe hire. Children's playground. Off site: Large supermarket and the local rail station are 10 minutes by car from the site.

At a glance

Welcome & Ambience	✓✓✓✓	Location	✓✓✓✓
Quality of Pitches	✓✓✓✓	Range of Facilities	✓✓✓✓

Directions

Turn off the E4 at Vårby/Huddinge and turn left on road no.259. After 2 km. turn right and follow signs to Flottsbro.

Charges 2005

Per pitch	SEK 110 - 175
electricity	SEK 35

Reservations

Advisable for both summer and winter peak times. Write to site for details Tel: 08 535 327 00.
E-mail: info@flottsbro.com

Open

All year (full services 1 June - 31 August).

SW2842 Bredängs Camping

Stora Sällskapets väg 51, S-127 31 Skärholmen (Stockholms Län)

Bredängs is a busy city site, with easy access to Stockhom city centre. Large and fairly level, with very little shade, there are 500 pitches, including 115 with hardstanding and 180 with electricity (10A), and a separate area for tents. Reception is open from 07.00-23.00 in the main season (17/5-29/8), reduced hours in low season, and English is spoken. They can provide the Stockholm card, or a three-day public transport card. Stockholm has many events and activities all year round, you can take a circular tour on a free sightseeing bus, various boat and bus tours, or view the city from the Kaknäs Tower (155 m). The nearest Metro station is five minute walk, trains run about every ten minutes between 05.00 and 02.00, and the journey takes about twenty minutes. The local shopping centre is five minutes away and a two minute walk through the woods brings you to a very attractive lake and beach.

Facilities

Four heated sanitary units of a high standard provide British style WCs, controllable hot showers, with some washbasins in cubicles. One has a baby room, a unit for disabled people and a first aid room. Cooking and dishwashing facilities are in three units around the site. Laundry with washing machines and dryers, and separate saunas (18.00-21.00). Motorcaravan services and car wash. Well stocked shop (1/5-30/9). Small café serving fast food (1/5-9/9). Sauna. Children's playground. Bicycle hire. Off site: Fishing 0.5 km.

At a glance

Welcome & Ambience	✓✓✓	Location	✓✓✓✓
Quality of Pitches	✓✓✓	Range of Facilities	✓✓✓

Directions

Site is about 10 km. southwest of city centre. Turn off E3/4 at Bredängs signpost and follow clearly marked site signs.

Charges 2005

Per person	SEK 90 - 100
pitch	SEK 185 - 205
electricity	SEK 35

Discounts for pensioners in low season.

Reservations

Advised for main season. Tel: 08 977 071. E-mail: bredangcamping@telia.com

Open

18 April - 23 October.

SW2835 Orsa SweCamp

Box 133, S-794 22 Orsa (Dalarnas Län)

This quiet, budget priced site, adjacent to the Grönklitt Bear Park, is primarily designed for winter, with a ski slope adjacent. The site is a rather large and featureless gravel hardstanding, providing room for more than 50 units, with electricity (10A) available to all, but particularly good for larger motorcaravans. In summer, this quietly located site rarely has more than a dozen occupants, yet it is half the price of the crowded, often noisy sites in Orsa town 14 kilometres away. Reception is located in the holiday centre with its rental cabins, inn, tourist information and other services, about one kilometre below the camping area, and one should book in here and obtain a key for the sanitary unit before proceeding to the site. The Grönklitt Bear Park, with bears, wolves, and lynx is within a short scramble up the hillside from the site and there are magnificent views over this scenic lakeland area.

Facilities

The excellent, very modern, small sanitary unit is heated. It has one unisex WC with external access and, inside for each sex, there is one WC and washbasin cubicle, and two hot showers with curtains and communal changing area. Suite for disabled visitors. Drying room. Wel equipped kitchen with two hobs and two dishwashing sinks. All showers, hairdryers, hot water, drying and kitchen facilities are free of charge. Swimming pool (heated) and children's pool. Entertainment and activities for children. Jogging tracks. Minigolf. Off site: Nearest town 1 km.

At a glance

Welcome & Ambience	✓✓✓	Location	✓✓✓
Quality of Pitches	✓✓✓	Range of Facilities	✓✓✓

Directions

From Orsa town centre follow the signs to Grönklitt and 'Björn Park'. Site is 14 km.

Charges 2005

Per unit incl. all persons	SEK 105 - 170
electricity	SEK 40

Families only for Midsummer.

Reservations

Not necessary. Tel: 0250 46200. E-mail: fritid@orsa-gronklitt.se

Open

All year (full services 22/6-7/8).

SW2836 Mora Parkens Camping

Hantverkargatan 30, S-792 25 Mora (Dalarnas Län)

Mora, at the northern end of Lake Silijan is surrounded by small localities all steeped in history and culture. On the island of Sollerön, south of Mora, is evidence of a large Viking burial ground. Traditional handicrafts are still alive in the region. Travel to Nusnäs, an old village with documents going back to the Middle Ages and see the production of the brightly coloured wooden horse. Every household should have two for luck. Winding country roads lead you through rich farmland to the pretty half timbered houses in Bergkarlås/Vattnås. Mora is lively, friendly and attractive. The campsite which would be good for family holidays is only 10 minutes walk from the town. The camping area is large, grassy, open and flat. It is bordered by clumps of trees and a stream. The staff are pleasant and helpful. English is spoken.

Facilities

Toilet facilities are fully equipped. Camper's kitchen. Laundry. Shop. Restaurant/bar. Sauna. Boat and bicycle hire. Fishing. Cabins to rent. Full services mid June - mid August.

Open

All year.

At a glance

Welcome & Ambience	✓✓✓✓	Location	✓✓✓✓
Quality of Pitches	✓✓✓	Range of Facilities	✓✓✓

Directions

Follow signs to centre of town. Campsite is clearly signed from the town centre and is next to Zorngården and Zorunuse Et (the Zorn museum).

Charges guide

Per unit incl. electricity SEK 160 - 180

Reservations

Contact site. Tel: 0250 27600.
E-mail: moraparken@mora.se

SW2845 Svegs Camping

Kyrkogrand 1, S-842 32 Sveg (Jämtlands Län)

On the 'Inlandsvagen' route through Sweden, the town centre is only a short walk from this neat, friendly municipal site. Supermarkets, a café and tourist information office are adjacent. The 160 pitches are in rows, on level grass, divided into bays by tall hedges, and with electricity available to 70. The site has boats, canoes, cycles and rickshaws for hire, and the river frontage has a barbecue area with covered seating and fishing platforms. Alongside the river with its fountain, and running through the site is a pleasant well lit riverside walk. Places to visit include the town with its lovely church, some interesting old churches in the surrounding villages, and 16th Century Remsgården, 14 km. to the west.

Facilities

In the older style, sanitary facilities are functional rather than luxurious, providing stainless steel washing troughs, controllable hot showers with communal changing areas, and a unit for disabled visitors. Although a little short on numbers, facilities will probably suffice at most times as the site is rarely full. Kitchen and dining room with TV. Washing machine and dryers, and an ironing board (iron on loan from reception). Play area. TV room. Minigolf. Canoe, boat, rickshaw and bicycle hire. Fishing.

At a glance

Welcome & Ambience	✓✓✓	Location	✓✓✓✓
Quality of Pitches	✓✓✓✓	Range of Facilities	✓✓✓✓

Directions

Site is off road 45 behind the tourist information office in Sveg.

Charges 2004

Per unit	SEK 110 - 160
tent	SEK 60 - 70
electricity (10/16A)	SEK 30 - 40

Reservations

Contact site. Tel: 0680 10775.

Open

All year.

SW2850 Ostersunds Camping

Krondikesvagen 95, S-831 46 Ostersund (Jämtlands Län)

Östersund lies on Lake Storsjön, which is Sweden's Loch Ness, with 200 sightings of the monster dating back to 1635, and more recently captured on video in 1996. Also worthy of a visit is the island of Frösön where settlements can be traced back to pre-historic times. This large site has 300 pitches, electricity (10A) and TV socket available on 120, all served by tarmac roads. There are also 41 tarmac hardstandings available, and over 200 cottages, cabins and rooms for rent. Adjacent to the site are the municipal swimming pool complex with cafeteria (indoor and outdoor pools), a Scandic hotel with restaurant, minigolf, and a Statoil filling station. A large supermarket and bank are just 500 metres from the site, and Ostersund town centre is 3 km.

Facilities

Toilet facilities are in three units, two including controllable hot showers (on payment) with communal changing areas, suites for disabled people and baby changing. The third has four family bathrooms each containing WC, basin and shower. Two kitchens and excellent dining rooms. Washing machines, dryers and free drying cabinet. Very good motorhome service point. Playground.

At a glance

Welcome & Ambience	✓✓✓	Location	✓✓✓✓
Quality of Pitches	✓✓✓	Range of Facilities	✓✓✓

Directions

Site is to the south of the town off road 605 towards Torvalla, turn by Statoil station and site entrance is immediately on right. (well signed around the town).

Charges year

Per unit (incl. electricity/TV) SEK 90 - 150

Reservations

Contact site. Tel: 063 144 615.
E-mail: ostersundscamping@ostersund.se

Open

All year.

SW2853 Snibbens Camping & Stugby

S-870 16 Ramvik (Västernorrlands Län)

Probably you will stop here for one night as you travel the E4 coast road and stay a week. It is a truly beautiful location in the area of 'The High Coast' listed as a World Heritage Site. During high season Snibbens is a busy, popular site but remains quiet and peaceful. Besides 30 bungalows for rent there are 50 touring places set amongst delightful scenery on the shores of Lake Mörtsjön. The welcoming owners take you to your adequately sized grass pitch set amongst spacious birch trees interspersed with glacier smooth boulders. All the facilities are to the highest of standards, spotlessly clean, with entry to the toilets and showers (stretched in high season) by use of a swipe card presented to you on arrival. To one end of the site there is a beach where the waters are suitable for swimming. A little further on, is the site's restaurant where you can dine on the terrace overlooking the lake as the sun sets.

Facilities

Excellent, spotlessly clean facilities include free controllable showers and partitioned washbasins. Both men's and ladies toilets have baby changing. Two kitchens. Laundry room. Basic provisions at reception and bread to order. Rowing boats and pedalos for hire. Minigolf. Free fishing for site guests. Off site: Small supermarket 800 m.

Open

30 April - 15 September.

At a glance

Welcome & Ambience	✓✓✓✓✓	Location	✓✓✓✓✓
Quality of Pitches	✓✓✓✓	Range of Facilities	✓✓✓✓✓

Directions

Travelling north on the E4 and immediately prior to Höga Kusten bridge (one of the largest in Europe) take E90 signed Kramfors. Site is directly off E90 on left in 3 km, well signed.

Charges 2004

Per unit	SEK 140
incl. electricity	SEK 155

Reservations

Not made but they will hold a pitch until 17.00 if you phone on the morning of the day you intend to arrive. Tel: 061 240 505.

SW2855 Flogsta Camping

S-872 80 Kramfors (Västernorrlands Län)

Kramfors lies just to the west of the E4, and travellers may well pass by over the new Höga Kusten bridge (one of the largest in Europe), and miss this friendly little municipal site. This area of Ådalen and the High Coast, reaches as far as Örnsköldsvik. The attractive garden-like campsite has around 50 pitches, 21 with electrical connections (10A), which are arranged on level grassy terraces, separated by shrubs and trees into bays of 2-4 units. All overlook the heated outdoor public swimming pool complex (free entry for campers) and attractive minigolf course. The non-electric pitches are on an open terrace nearer reception. The town centre is a 20 minute walk through a housing estate, where a covered and elevated walkway crosses the main road and railway to the pedestrian shopping precinct.

Facilities

Acceptable sanitary facilities comprise nine bathrooms, each with British style WC, basin with hand dryer, shower (on payment 2Skr-2mins). Laundry with washing machine and dryer. More WCs and showers are in the reception building with a free sauna. A separate building houses a kitchen and TV/dining room (all free). The reception building has a small shop and snack-bar (staffed 08.00-22.00 hrs from 9/6-18/8 - outside these dates a warden calls daily). Playground.

At a glance

Welcome & Ambience	✓✓✓✓	Location	✓✓✓✓
Quality of Pitches	✓✓✓	Range of Facilities	✓✓✓

Directions

Signed from road 90 in the centre (not centrum) of Kramfors, the site lies to the west in a rural location beyond a housing estate and by the Flogsta Bad.

Charges 2004

Per unit	SEK 115
electricity	SEK 25

Reservations

Contact site. Tel: 0612 10005.
E-mail: flogsta@kramfors.se

Open

May - end September.

SW2857 Strömsund Swecamp

S-833 24 Strömsund (Jämtlands Län)

A quiet waterside town on the north – south route 45 known as the Inlandsväen, Stromsund is a good place to begin a journey on the Wilderness Way. This is route 342 which heads northwest towards the mountains at Gäddede and the Norwegian border. There is a wonderful feeling of space and freedom in Stromsund. Beside the main bridge is an excellent open air museum with a collection of buildings dating back several centurys, in the forests there are well marked trails. Walk here alone at midnight on Midsummer's Eve in an intense blue light - nothing moves as the path ahead leads deeper into the dense forest – it is a memorable experience. The campsite is set on a gentle grassy slope backed by forest. Another part of the site, across the road, overlooks the lake. The staff are friendly, happy and helpful.

Facilities

Excellent facilities include a shower block with underfloor heating. Laundry. Campers' kitchen. Bicycle and boat hire.

Open

All year.

At a glance

Welcome & Ambience	✓✓✓✓✓	Location	✓✓✓✓
Quality of Pitches	✓✓✓✓	Range of Facilities	✓✓✓

Directions

Site is 700 m. south of Stomsund on route 45.

Charges guide

Per unit incl. electricity	SEK 115 - 170

Full services mid June - mid August.

Reservations

Contact site. Tel: 0670 16410.
E-mail: stromsund.turism@stromsund.se

SW2860 Umeå Camping

S-901 84 Umeå (Västerbotens Län)

An ideal stop-over for those travelling the E4 coastal route, or a good base from which to explore, this popular municipal campsite is 6 km. from the centre of this university city. It is almost adjacent to the Nydalsjön lake, which is ideal for fishing and windsurfing. There are 320 grassy pitches arranged in bays of 10-20 units, divided by shrubs and small trees, all with electricity and some fully serviced. In the centre is a delightful mini garden. Outside the site adjacent to the lake, but with direct access, are football pitches, a small open-air swimming pool with slide, minigolf, mini-car driving school, a mini-farm and there are cycle and footpaths around the area. Umeå is also a port for ferries to Vasa in Finland (4 hrs).

Facilities

The large, heated, central sanitary unit is modern and well equipped including some controllable hot showers with communal changing areas, and a sauna for each sex. These facilities are stretched in high season. Well equipped kitchen with large dining room adjacent and TV. Laundry. Shop and snackbar (approx 25 May-20 August). Internet access in purpose building close to reception. Walk on chess, volley-ball, playgrounds. Bicycle hire. Rowing boat hire that can be used for fishing in the stocked lake (licence can be bought on site). Off site: Riding 15 km. Golf 18 km.

At a glance

Welcome & Ambience	✓✓✓✓	Location	✓✓✓✓
Quality of Pitches	✓✓✓✓	Range of Facilities	✓✓✓✓

Directions

A camping sign on the E4 at a set of traffic lights 5km north of the town directs you to the site. Direction also indicates Holmsund and Vassa.

Charges 2004

Per unit	SEK 160 - 175
unit with electricity	SEK 170 - 205
serviced pitch	SEK 205 - 230

Reservations

Contact site. Tel: 090 702 600.
E-mail: umea.camping@umea.se

Open

All year (full services approx. 11/6-12/8).

SW2865 Camp Gielas

Järnvägsgatan 111, S-933 22 Arvidsjaur (Norrbottens Län)

A modern site with excellent sporting facilities on the outskirts of the town, Gielas is well shielded on all sides by trees, providing a very peaceful atmosphere. The 150 pitches, 80 with electricity (16A) and satellite TV connections, are level on sparse grass and accessed by tarmac roadways. The sauna and showers, sporting, gym and internet facilities at the sports hall are free to campers. Also on site is a snack-bar. The lake on the site is suitable for boating, bathing and fishing and other amenities include tennis courts, minigolf, canoe and boat hire and playgrounds,

Facilities

Two modern, heated sanitary units provide controllable hot showers (on payment) and a unit for disabled visitors. Well equipped kitchens (free). Washing machine and dryer. The unit by the tent area also has facilities for disabled people. Snack bar. Minigolf. Playgrounds. Sauna. Sporting facilities. Boat and canoe hire. Lake swimming. Fishing. Winter golf course on snow on site. Off site: Golf 200 m. Riding 500 m. Bicycle hire 2 km. Bowling centre 500 m.

At a glance

Welcome & Ambience	✓✓✓✓	Location	✓✓✓✓
Quality of Pitches	✓✓✓✓	Range of Facilities	✓✓✓✓

Directions

Site is well signed from road 95 in the town.

Charges 2005

Per unit	SEK 140
electricity	SEK 25

Reservations

Contact site. Tel: 0960 55600.
E-mail: gielas@arvidsjaur.se

Open

All year.

SW2870 Jokkmokks Camping Center

Box 75, S-962 22 Jokkmokk (Norrbottens Län)

This attractive municipal site is just eight kilometres from the Arctic Circle. Large and well organised, the site is bordered on one side by the river and with woodland on the other, just three kilometres from the town centre. It has 170 level, grassy pitches, with an area for tents, plus 59 cabins and 26 rooms for rent. The site has a heated open-air pool complex open in summer. There are opportunities for snow-mobiling, cross-country skiing in spring, or ice fishing in winter. Nearby attractions include the first hydro-electric power station at Porjus, built 1910-15, with free tours (15/6-15/8), Vuollerim (40 km.) reconstructed 60 year old settlement, with excavations of the best preserved ice-age village, or try visiting for the famous Jokkmokk Winter Market (February) or the Autumn Market (end of August).

Facilities

Heated sanitary buildings provide mostly open washbasins and controllable showers, a few are in cubicles with divider. A unit by reception has a baby bathroom, a fully equipped suite for disabled visitors, games room, plus a very well appointed kitchen and launderette. Shop, restaurant and bar (in summer). Takeaway (high season). Swimming pools. Sauna. Bicycle hire. Playground. Minigolf. Football field. Fishing (licences sold). Off site: Riding 2 km.

At a glance

Welcome & Ambience	✓✓✓✓	Location	✓✓✓✓
Quality of Pitches	✓✓✓✓	Range of Facilities	✓✓✓✓

Directions

Site is 3 km. from centre of Jokkmokk on road 97.

Charges guide

Per unit incl. electricity	SEK 150

Reservations

Contact site. Tel: 0971 12370.
E-mail: campingcenter@jokkmokk.com

Open

All year.

A small, wealthy country, best known for its outstanding mountainous scenery, fine cheeses, delicious chocolates, Swiss bank accounts and enviable lifestyles. Centrally situated in Europe it shares its borders with four countries: France, Austria, Germany and Italy, each one having its own cultural influence on Switzerland.

The landscape of Switzerland boasts mountains, valleys, falls and glaciers. The Bernese Oberland is probably the most visited area, with picturesque villages, lakes and awe inspiring peaks, including the towering Eiger, Mönch and Jungfrau. The highest Alps are those of Valais in the southwest where the small busy resort of Zermatt gives access to the Matterhorn. The south east of Switzerland has densely forested mountain slopes and the wealthy and glamorous resort of St Moritz. Zurich in the north is a German speaking city with a wealth of sightseeing, particularly in the old town area with its 16th and 17th century houses. Geneva, Montreux and Lausanne on the northern shores of Lake Geneva make up the bulk of French Switzerland, with vineyards that border the lakes and medieval towns. The southernmost canton, Ticino, is home to the Italian speaking Swiss, with the Mediterranean style lakeside resorts of Lugano and Locarno.

Population

7.1 million

Capital

Bern

Climate

Mild and refreshing in the northern plateau. South of the Alps it is warmer, influenced by the Mediterranean. The Valais is noted for its dryness

Language

German in central and eastern areas, French in the west and Italian in the south. Raeto-Romansch is spoken in the southeast. English is spoken by many

Currency

Swiss franc

Telephone

The country code is 00 41

Banks

Mon-Fri 08.30-16.30. Some close for lunch

Shops

Mon-Fri 08.00- 12.00 and 14.00- 18.00. Sat 08.00-16.00. Often closed Monday mornings

Public Holidays

New Year; Good Fri; Easter Mon; Ascension; Whit Mon; Christmas 25 Dec; Other holidays are observed in individual Cantons

Motoring

The road network is comprehensive and well planned. An annual road tax is levied on all cars using Swiss motorways and the 'Vignette' windscreen sticker must be purchased at the border (credit cards not accepted), or in advance from the Swiss National Tourist Office, plus a separate one for a towed caravan or trailer

Tourist Office

Switzerland Tourism
Swiss Centre, 10 Wardour Street
London W1D 6QF
Tel: 020 7292 1550
Fax: 020 7292 1599
Email: info.uk@switzerland.com
Internet: www.myswitzerland.com

tip

ENJOY THE VIEW FROM EUROPE'S HIGHEST ALTITUDE RAILWAY STATION. THE SWISS JUNGFRAU RAILWAY IS A SCENIC TRACK THAT WINDS ITS WAY TO THE GLACIER SOME 12,000 FT HIGH.

CH9420 Camping Manor Farm 1

Manor Farm AG, CH-3800 Interlaken-Thunersee (Bern)

Manor Farm has been popular with British visitors for many years, as this is one of the traditional touring areas of Switzerland. The site lies outside the town on the northern side of the Thuner See, with most of the site between road and lake but with one part on the far side of the road. Interlaken is rather a tourist town but the area is rich in scenery, with innumerable mountain excursions and walks available. The lakes and Jungfrau railway are near at hand. The flat terrain is divided entirely into 570 individual, numbered pitches which vary considerably both in size (60-100 sq.m.) and price with 10A electricity available and shade in some places. There are 110 equipped with electricity, water, drainage and 55 also have cable TV connections. Reservations are made although you should find space except perhaps in late July/early August, but the best places may then be taken. Around 30% of the pitches are taken by permanent or letting units and there is a tour operator presence. Manor Farm is efficiently and quite formally run, with good English spoken.

Facilities

Six separate toilet blocks are practical, heated and soundly constructed. Fully equipped, they even include free hot water for baths. Twenty private units are for rent. Washing machine, dryer, ironing. Motorcaravan services. Gas supplies. Shop (1/4-15/10). Site-owned restaurant adjoining (1/3-30/11). Snack bar with takeaway on site (1/6-31/8). TV room. Football field. Playground and paddling pool. Minigolf. Bicycle hire. Table tennis. Sailing and windsurfing school. Swimming possible in the lake at two points and boats can be brought if a permit obtained. Boat hire. Fishing. Daily activity and entertainment programme in high season. Excursions. Tourist information. Off site: Golf 500 m.(handicap card). Riding 3 km. Area is good for cycling and walking.

Open

All year.

At a glance

Welcome & Ambience	✓✓✓✓	Location	✓✓✓✓✓
Quality of Pitches	✓✓✓✓	Range of Facilities	✓✓✓✓

Directions

Site is about 3 km. west of Interlaken along the road running north of the Thuner See towards Thun. Follow signs for 'Camp 1'. From the motor road bypassing Interlaken (A8) take exit marked 'Gunten, Beatenberg', which is a spur road bringing you out close to site.

Charges 2004

Per person	CHF 5,00 - 10,00
child 6-15 yrs	CHF 2,35 - 4,70
child under 6 yrs	free
pitch	CHF 7,80 - 38,00
electricity (0.5, 4 or 6A)	CHF 0,80 - 5,00
boat	CHF 3,00 - 8,00

Various discounts for longer stays.

Reservations

Taken for high season (min. 3 days) with booking fee (CHF 30). Tel: 033 822 22 64.
E-mail: manorfarm@swisscamps.ch

CH9440 Camping Jungfraublick

Gsteigstrasse 80, Matten, CH-3800 Interlaken (Bern)

The Berner Oberland is one of the most scenic and well known areas of Switzerland with Interlaken probably the best known summer resort. This second site is offered here as a contrast from the larger one on the opposite side of town. Situated in the village of Matten and within walking distance of the town centre (about one kilometre), Jungfraublick is a delightful, medium sized site with splendid views up the Lauterbrunnen valley to the Jungfrau mountain. The pink glow reflected from the sunset is a sight to behold when weather conditions allow. The motorway which bypasses the town runs in a deep cutting along one side of the site so traffic noise is screened out and an earth bank has been constructed alongside the access road reducing noise from here. The 100 touring pitches 60-75 sq.m. with electricity connections (2-6A) are in regular rows on level, well cut grass. A number of fruit trees adorn but do not offer much shade. The 35 static caravans are to one side of the tourist area and do not intrude. This is a very pleasant, quiet, tidy site with a friendly, English speaking owner who is pleased to advise on the attractions of the region.

Facilities

Fully equipped sanitary facilities are divided between two buildings near the entrance. Showers are on payment, as is hot water for dishwashing. Washing machines and dryers. Motorcaravan services. Shop for basic food requirements (from 1/6). Small swimming pool (12 x 8 m.) open mid-June - end-Aug. according to the weather. Heated rest room with TV and electronic games. Barbecues must be off the ground. Off site: Wilderswill train station is only 10 minutes walk. Bicycle hire 700 m. Restaurants and shops about 1 km. in the town. Golf, riding and fishing 4 km.

At a glance

Welcome & Ambience	✓✓✓✓	Location	✓✓✓
Quality of Pitches	✓✓✓✓	Range of Facilities	✓✓✓

Directions

Take the Lauterbrunnen exit from the N8 motorway bypass, turn towards Interlaken and site is on the left hand side.

Charges 2005

Per person	CHF 5,80 - 6,80
child (4-16 yrs)	CHF 3,80 - 4,20
pitch acc. to size and season	CHF 8,00 - 30,00
electricity (2-6A)	CHF 1,10 - 3,20

Reservations

Write to site with deposit (CHF. 30) and fee (10).
Tel: 033 822 44 14. E-mail: info@jungfraublick.ch

Open

1 May - 20 September.

CH9430 Camping Lazy Rancho 4

Lehnweg 6, CH-3800 Interlaken (Bern)

This super site is in a quiet location with fantastic views of the dramatic mountains of Eiger, Monch and Jungfrau. Neat, orderly and well maintained, the site is situated in a wide valley just one kilometre from Lake Thun and four kilometres from Interlaken. The English speaking owners lovingly care for the site and will endeavour to make you feel very welcome, offering advice on day trips out, and how to get the best bargains which can be had on the railway. The 155 pitches, of which 90 are for touring uints, are on well tended level grass (some with hardstanding), connected by tarmac roads. Each pitch has 10A electricity and there are 23 'super' pitches. This is a quiet friendly site, popular with British visitors.

Facilities

Two good sanitary blocks (one new, the other of an older design) are both heated with free hot showers, good facilities for disabled customers and a baby room. Laundry with washing machines, dryers and irons. Camper's kitchen with microwave, cooker, fridge and utensils. Motorcaravan service point. Well stocked shop. TV and games room. Play area on rubber base. Small swimming pool. Off site: Many cycle trails and way-marked footpaths. Riding 500 m. Golf 1 km. Bicycle hire 1 km. Lake Thun for fishing 1.5 km. Boat launching 1.5 km. Interlaken with good shops, bars and restaurants, and large leisure centre 4 km.

Open

15 April - 15 October.

At a glance

Welcome & Ambience	✓✓✓✓	Location	✓✓✓✓✓
Quality of Pitches	✓✓✓✓	Range of Facilities	✓✓✓✓

Directions

Site is on north side of Lake Thun. From road 8 (Thun – Interlaken) on south side of lake take exit signed Gunten, Beatenberg and campings. Follow towards lake at roundabout then follow signs for campings. Lazy Rancho is Camp 4. The last 0.5 km. is a little narrow but no problem and with good visibility.

Charges 2004

Per adult	CHF 6,00 - 7,50
child (6-15 yrs)	CHF 3,50 - 4,50
pitch	CHF 10,00 - 28,00
electricity (10A)	CHF 4,00
dog	CHF 3,00
local tax	CHF 1,60

Payment accepted in euros.

Reservations

Contact site. Tel: 033 822 87 16. E-mail: info@lazyrancho.ch

CH9460 Camping Jungfrau

CH-3822 Lauterbrunnen (Bern)

This friendly site has a very imposing situation in a steep valley with a fine view of the Jungfrau at the end. You can laze here amid real mountain scenery, though it does lose the sun a little early. There are naturally many more active things to do - mountain walks or climbing, trips up the Jungfrau railway or one of the mountain lifts or excursions by car. The site itself is quite extensive and is grassy with hard surfaced access roads. It is a popular site and, although you should usually find space, in season do not arrive too late. All 391 pitches (250 for touring) have shade in parts, electrical connections (10-15A) and 50 have water and drainage also. About 30% of the pitches are taken by seasonal caravans. The site is used by two tour operators and by groups of youngsters from many different countries - pitches at the top of the site may be quieter. The von Allmen family own and run the site and provide a warm welcome (English is spoken).

Facilities

Three fully equipped sanitary blocks can be heated in winter and include a good, new modern one at the far end of the site. The other two have been renewed and modernised. Facilities for disabled visitors, baby baths and footbaths. Washing machine, spin dryer and ironing. Motorcaravan services. Supermarket (all year). Self-service restaurant with takeaway (May - end Oct). Good general room with wooden tables and chairs, TV, jukebox, drink vending machines, amusements, with second one elsewhere. Well equipped and maintained children's playgrounds and covered play area. Excursions and some entertainment in high season. Mountain bike hire. Internet point. ATM. Off site: Free bus to ski station (in winter only).

Open

All year.

At a glance

Welcome & Ambience	✓✓✓✓	Location	✓✓✓✓✓
Quality of Pitches	✓✓✓✓	Range of Facilities	✓✓✓✓

Directions

Go through Lauterbrunnen and fork right at far end before road bends left, 100 m. before church. The final approach is not very wide.

Charges 2005

Per person	CHF 7,90 - 8,90
child (6-15 yrs)	CHF 3,90 - 4,40
pitch	CHF 14,00 - 20,00
car	CHF 3,50
dog	CHF 3,00
electricity (+ meter)	CHF 2,50

Discounts for camping carnet and for stays over 3 nights outside high season.

Reservations

Made for any period with deposit; write for details. Tel: 033 856 20 10. E-mail: info@camping-jungfrau.ch

CH9360 Camping Grassi

CH-3714 Frutigen (Bern)

This is a small site with about half the pitches occupied by static caravans, used by their owners for weekends and holidays. The 70 or so places available for tourists are not marked out but it is said that the site is not allowed to become overcrowded. Most places are on level grass with two small terraces at the end of the site. There is little shade but the site is set in a river valley with trees on the hills which enclose the area. It would make a useful overnight stop en-route for Kandersteg and the railway station where cars can join the train for transportation through the Lotschberg Tunnel to the Rhône Valley and Simplon Pass, or for a longer stay to explore the Bernese Oberland. Electricity is available for all pitches but long leads may be required in parts. There is a kiosk for basic supplies, but shops and restaurants are only a 10 minute walk away in the village.

Facilities

The well constructed, heated sanitary block is of good quality. Washing machine and dryer. Gas supplies. Motorcaravan services. Rest room with TV. Kiosk (1/6-31/8). Children's play area and play house. Mountain bike hire and tours. Fishing. Bicycle hire. Off site: Riding 2 km. Outdoor and indoor pools, tennis and minigolf in Frutigen. Skiing and walking.

Open

All year.

At a glance

Welcome & Ambience	✓✓✓✓	Location	✓✓✓✓
Quality of Pitches	✓✓✓	Range of Facilities	✓✓✓

Directions

Take Kandersteg road from Spiez and leave at Frutigen Dorf exit from where site is signed.

Charges 2005

Per person	CHF 6,40
child (1-16 yrs)	CHF 1,50 - 3,20
pitch	CHF 8,00 - 14,00
dog	CHF 1,50
local tax	CHF 0,40 - 0,80

No credit cards.

Reservations

Write to site. Tel: 033 671 11 49.
E-mail: campinggrassi@bluewin.ch

CH9495 Camping Balmweid

Balmweidstrasse 22, CH-3860 Meiringen (Bern)

This good, family run site is peaceful, just south of the village of Meiringen on the route to the Grimsel Pass. With a backdrop of steep cliffs it has good views of the adjacent mountains and forest-covered slopes. It provides 180 pitches of which 60 are for tourers, all with 10A electricity. A single main building houses all the facilities which are excellent and very well maintained. Close by you will find the Aare Gorge, with its mile long walkway, the glacier and gorge of Rosenlaul and the Reichenbach falls (where Sherlock Holmes fell to his death) and much much more. Whilst this is a good site on which to base a longer stay, it is also useful as an overnight stop en-route to the Grimsel Pass or for a rest having faced the challenges that the Pass has to offer.

Facilities

The excellent heated sanitary block in the reception building has WCs, showers and washbasins. Facilities for disabled visitors. Dishwashing area. Washing machines and dryer. Chemical disposal point. Motorcaravan service point. Restaurant and shop. TV Room. Playground.

Open

All year.

At a glance

Welcome & Ambience	✓✓✓✓	Location	✓✓✓✓
Quality of Pitches	✓✓✓	Range of Facilities	✓✓✓✓

Directions

From Meiringen the site is well signed to the south. At roundabout turn left and then left again in about 200 m. From Bern and Interlaken just go straight on at the roundabout signposted 'Grimsel'.

Charges 2005

Per person	CHF 7,00 - 8,00
child 6-16 yrs	CHF 3,50 - 4,00
tent	CHF 6,00 - 15,00
caravan	CHF 12,00 - 15,00
motorcaravan	CHF 12,00 - 18,00

Reservations

Advised for July and August Tel: 033 971 51 15.
E-mail: Info@camping-meiringen.ch

CH9480 Camping Gletscherdorf

CH-3818 Grindelwald (Bern)

Set in a flat river valley on the edge of Grindelwald, one of Switzerland's well known winter and summer resorts, Gletscherdorf enjoys wonderful mountain views, particularly of the nearby north face of the Eiger. The site has 120 pitches, 60 for touring units. Most are marked and have electricity connections (10A), with a few others in an overflow field. There is a good community room with tables and chairs. This is, above all, a very quiet, friendly site for those who wish to enjoy the peaceful mountain air, walking, climbing and exploring with a mountain climbing school in Grindelwald.

Facilities

Excellent small, heated, fully equipped, sanitary block. Washing machines and dryer. Motorcaravan services. Gas supplies. Small shop for basic food items. Torches useful. Dogs are not accepted. Off site: Bicycle hire or golf 1 km. Indoor pool 1 km. Town shops and restaurants within walking distance.

Open

1 May - 20 October.

At a glance

Welcome & Ambience	✓✓✓✓	Location	✓✓✓✓✓
Quality of Pitches	✓✓✓	Range of Facilities	✓✓✓

Directions

To reach site, go into town and turn right at camp signs after town centre; approach road is quite narrow and steep down hill but there is an easier departure road.

Charges 2004

Per person	CHF 6,90
child (6-15 yrs)	CHF 3,00
pitch	CHF 6,00 - 17,00
electricity	CHF 3,50 - 4,00
local tax (over 12 yrs)	CHF 2,30

Reservations

Essential for July/Aug. - contact site.
Tel: 033 853 14 29. E-mail: info@gletscherdorf.ch

CH9530 Camping International Giswil Sarnersee

Campingstrasse, CH-6074 Giswil (Unterwalden)

The peaceful Camping International Sarnersee has direct access to the Sarnersee lake with a sandy beach. It is in a quiet rural area, screened by trees and hedges, yet with excellent views of the surrounding peaks. It provides 165 pitches of which 100 are for tourers, all with 10Ap electricity supply. The seasonal pitches are spread throughout the site. The touring pitches are grass or gravel, level and some have lake views. The town is a short walk away.

Facilities

The main sanitary block just behind reception has WCs, hot showers on payment (half franc coin) and washbasins. Dishwashing area. Washing machines and dryer. Chemical disposal point. Motorcaravan service point. Small shop for basics. Restaurant and bar which will be rebuilt for 2005. TV room. Playground. Fishing Off site: Lucerne.

Open

1 May - 15 October.

At a glance

Welcome & Ambience	✓✓✓✓	Location	✓✓✓✓
Quality of Pitches	✓✓✓	Range of Facilities	✓✓✓

Directions

From Giswil head towards Grosstheil where the site is signposted. The single lane access road is quite long and you go past some farm buildings before the site becomes visible.

Charges 2005

Per person	CHF 5,75 - 8,00
child 2-6 yrs	CHF 1,60 - 2,00
child 6-16 yrs	CHF 3,20 - 4,00
pitch	CHF 14,40 - 18,00
electricity	CHF 2,50
local tax	CHF 0,80

Reservations

Advised for July and August Tel: 041 675 23 55.
E-mail: giswil@camping-international.ch

CH9510 Camping Aaregg

Seestrasse 26, CH-3855 Brienz am See (Bern)

Brienz in the Bernese Oberland is a delightful little town on the lake of the same name and the centre of the Swiss wood carving industry. Nearby at Ballenberg is the fascinating Freilichtmuseum, a very large open-air park of old Swiss houses which have been brought from all over Switzerland and re-erected in groups. Traditional Swiss crafts are demonstrated in some of these. Camping Aaregg is an excellent site situated on the southern shores of the lake with splendid views across the water to the mountains. There are 60 static caravans occupying their own area and 240 tourist pitches, all with electricity. Of these, 16 are large with hardstanding, water and drainage and many of these have good views of the lake. Pitches fronting the lake have a surcharge. The trees and flowers around the site make it an attractive and peaceful environment. It would make a good base from which to explore the many attractions of this scenic region, although it could also be useful as a night stop between Interlaken and Luzern.

Facilities

Well built, fully equipped, sanitary blocks refurbished to a high standard include some washbasins in cabins and showers on payment. Laundry facilities. Motorcaravan services. Pleasant restaurant with terrace and takeaway in season. Play area. English is spoken.

Open

1 April - 31 October.

At a glance

Welcome & Ambience	✓✓✓✓✓	Location	✓✓✓✓✓
Quality of Pitches	✓✓✓✓	Range of Facilities	✓✓✓✓

Directions

Site is on road B6 on the east of Brienz with entrance road between BP and Esso filling stations, well signed. From Interlaken-Luzern motorway, take Brienz exit and turn towards Brienz, site then on the left.

Charges 2005

Per person	CHF 6,00 - 9,00
child (6-16 yrs)	CHF 3,00 - 4,50
pitch	CHF 10,00 - 18,00
electricity (10A)	CHF 2,70 - 4,00

Low season less 20%.

Reservations

Made with deposit (CHF. 100); min. 14 days in July/Aug. Tel: 033 951 18 43. E-mail: mail@aaregg.ch

CH9110 TCS-Camping Seeland

CH-6204 Sempach-Stadt (Luzern)

Lucerne is a very popular city in the centre of Switzerland and Camping Seeland makes a peaceful base from which to visit the town and explore the surrounding countryside or, being a short way from the main N2 Basel - Chiasso motorway, is a convenient night stop if passing through. This neat, tidy site has 200 grass pitches for tourists, all with electricity, a few with gravel hardstanding on either side of hard roads under trees with further places on the perimeter in the open. A small river runs through the site with a connecting covered bridge. Bern, Zurich and Interlaken are less than an hour's drive away. The friendly, English speaking wardens will be pleased to advise on local attractions.

Facilities

Three good quality sanitary blocks have the usual facilities including excellent facilities for disabled visitors and a baby room. Washing machine and dryer. Motorcaravan service point. Excellent self-service bar/restaurant with pleasant terrace overlooking the play area, lake and surrounding tree covered hills. Shop. Table tennis. Fishing. Lakeside beach with lawn for sunbathing. Off site: Shops and restaurants a short distance away in the interesting and ancient village which has tennis courts, boats to rent and bicycle hire, minigolf and golf club.

At a glance

Welcome & Ambience	✓✓✓✓✓	Location	✓✓✓✓✓
Quality of Pitches	✓✓✓✓✓	Range of Facilities	✓✓✓✓✓

Directions

From the N2 take exit for Sempach and follow signs for Sempach and site.

Charges 2004

Per person	CHF 5,60 - 7,60
child	CHF 2,80 - 3,80
pitch	CHF 16,00 - 20,00
electricity (6A)	CHF 4,00

Reservations

Write with CHF 100 (CHF 20 fee). Tel: 041 460 14 66. E-mail: camping.sempach@tcs.ch

Open

27 March - 6 October.

CH9570 Camping Eienwäldli

Wasserfallstraße 108, CH-6390 Engelberg (Unterwalden)

This super site has facilities which must make it one of the best in Switzerland. It is situated in a beautiful location 3,500 feet above sea level, surrounded by mountains on the edge of the delightful village of Engelberg. Being about 35 kilometres from Luzern by road and with a rail link, it makes a quiet, peaceful base from which to explore the Vierwaldstattersee region, walk in the mountains or just enjoy the scenery. The indoor pool has recently been most imaginatively rebuilt as a Felsenbad spa bath with adventure pool, steam and relaxing grottoes, Kneipp's cure, children's pool with water slides, solarium, Finnish sauna and eucalyptus steam bath (charged for). Half of the site is taken up by static caravans which are grouped together at one side. The camping area is in two parts - nearest the entrance there are 57 hardstandings for caravans and motorcaravans, all with electricity(metered) and beyond this is a flat meadow for about 70 tents. The reception building houses the pool complex, shop, a café/bar and rooms and apartments to rent. There is also a restaurant opposite the entrance. The area is famous as a winter sports region and summer tourist resort.

Facilities

The excellent toilet block, heated in cool weather, has free hot water in washbasins (in cabins) and sinks and on payment in the showers. Washing machines and dryers. Shop. Café/bar. Small lounge. Indoor pool complex. Ski facilities. Playground. Torches useful. Off site: Golf driving range and 9-hole course near. Fishing and bicycle hire 1 km. Riding 2 km.

Open

All year.

At a glance

Welcome & Ambience	✓✓✓✓✓	Location	✓✓✓✓✓
Quality of Pitches	✓✓✓✓✓	Range of Facilities	✓✓✓✓✓

Directions

From N2 Gotthard motorway, leave at exit 'Stans-Sud' and follow signs to Engelberg. Turn right at T-junction on edge of town and follow signs to 'Wasserfall' and site.

Charges 2005

Per person	CHF 8,00
child (6-15 yrs)	CHF 4,00
caravan	CHF 12,00
tent	CHF 8,50 - 12,00
car	CHF 2,00
motorcaravan	CHF 14,00

Credit cards accepted (surcharge).

Reservations

Necessary for summer and winter high seasons. Made with CHF 50 deposit. Tel: 041 6371949. E-mail: info@eienwaeldli.ch

CH9130 Camping Vitznau

CH-6354 Vitznau (Luzern)

Camping Vitznau is situated in the small village of the same name, above and overlooking Lake Luzern, with splendid views across the water to the mountains on the other side. It is a small, neat and tidy site very close to the delightful village on the narrow, winding, lakeside road. The 120 pitches for caravans or motorhomes (max length 7 m.) have 15A electricity available to most. They are on level, grassy terraces with hard wheel tracks for motorcaravans and separated by tarmac roads, and although of sufficient rather than large size, with single rows on each terrace, all places have unobstructed views. However, larger units might have difficulty manoeuvring onto the pitches. There are separate places for tents. Trees provide shade in parts and this delightful site makes an excellent base for exploring around the lake, the town of Luzern and the nearby mountains.

Facilities

The single, well constructed sanitary block provides free hot showers (water heated by solar panels). Sinks for laundry and dishwashing are under cover with metered hot water. Washing machines and dryers. Gas supplies. Motorcaravan services. Well stocked shop (1/4-31/10). General room for wet weather. Games room and a well stocked shop. Small swimming pool and children's splash pool (15/5-15/9). Off site: Village restaurants about five minutes walk. Fishing or bicycle hire within 1 km. Watersports near. Golf 15 km.

At a glance

Welcome & Ambience	✓✓✓✓	Location	✓✓✓✓
Quality of Pitches	✓✓✓✓	Range of Facilities	✓✓✓✓

Directions

Site is signed from the centre of Vitznau.

Charges 2005

Per person	CHF 8,00 - 9,50
child (4-13 yrs)	CHF 4,00
pitch acc. to size and season	CHF 14,00 - 30,00
dog	CHF 3,00
electricity	CHF 4,00

Reservations

Write with deposit (CHF 20). Tel: 041 397 12 80. E-mail: camping-vitznau@bluewin.ch

Open

All year except November.

CH9015 Camping Tariche

Tariche, St Ursanne, CH-2883 Montmelon (Jura)

This lovely site is some six kilometres off the main road along a steep wooded valley, through which flows the Doub on its brief excursion through Switzerland from France. If you're looking for peace and tranquillity then this is a distinct possibility for a short or long stay. A very small friendly site, owned and managed by Vincent Gigandet, there are just 15 touring pitches. It is ideal for walking, fishing or for the more active, the possibility of kayaking along the Doub (the river is not suitable for swimming). Medieval St Ursanne, said to be the most beautiful village in the canton, is some 7 km. away. There you will find 16th century town gates and bridge and a 12th century church surrounded by ancient houses. Not too far distant is Delemont, the Jura's capital. A local artist, Michel Marchand, runs introductory lessons in watercolour painting.

Facilities

The modern, heated toilet block is of a high standard with free showers. Washing machine and dryer. Motorcaravan services. Good kitchen facilities include oven, hob and fridge. Restaurant with shaded terrace overlooking the play area so that adults can enjoy a drink and keep watch whilst enjoying the river views. Fishing. Off site: St Ursanne 7 km.

Open

1 March - 31 October.

At a glance

Welcome & Ambience	✓✓✓✓	Location	✓✓✓✓
Quality of Pitches	✓✓✓	Range of Facilities	✓✓✓

Directions

From the A16 take exit for St Ursanne (at the end of the tunnel). Turn left towards town and at roundabout turn left and go past first campsite. After 5.6 km. site is on the left next to the restaurant.

Charges 2004

Per person	CHF 8,20
child	CHF 4,00
pitch	CHF 8,00 - 15,00
electricity	CHF 3,00

Reservations

Worthwhile given it is a small site. Tel: 032 433 4619. E-mail: info@tariche.ch

CH9040 Camping des Pêches

Route du Port, CH-2525 Le Landeron (Neuchâtel)

This recently constructed, touring campsite is on the side of Lake Biel and river Thienne, and close to the old town of Le Landeron. The site is divided into two sections - on one side of the road is a well presented and neatly organised static caravan area, and on the other is the modern campsite for tourists. At the entrance an inviting reception building greets the visitor, also housing community room, small café and first-aid. The 200 pitches are all on level grass, numbered but not separated, a few with shade, all with electricity (10A) and many conveniently placed water points. All the facilities are exceptionally well maintained and in pristine condition during our visit throughout a busy holiday weekend.

Facilities

The spacious, modern sanitary block contains all the usual facilities including a food preparation area with six cooking rings, a large freezer and refrigerator. Payment for showers is by card. Baby room. Washing machines, dryers and irons. Motorcaravan service point. Children's playground. Bicycle hire. TV and general room. Treatment room. Card barrier. Off site: Fishing 300 m. Swimming pool 500 m (16/5-1/9; charged). Golf and riding 7 km.

Open

1 April - 15 October.

At a glance

Welcome & Ambience	✓✓✓✓	Location	✓✓✓✓
Quality of Pitches	✓✓✓✓	Range of Facilities	✓✓✓✓

Directions

Le Landeron is signed from the Neuchâtel - Biel motorway and site is well signed from the town.

Charges 2005

Per adult	CHF 8,00
child (6-16 yrs)	CHF 4,00
tent	CHF 7,50 - 9,50
caravan	CHF 10,50
motorcaravan	CHF 15,00
electricity	CHF 3,50

Reservations

Contact site. Tel: 032 751 29 00.
E-mail: info@camping-lelanderon.ch

CH9090 Camping Avenches Port-Plage

Camping-Port-Plage, CH-1580 Avenches (Vaud)

This is a large site by Swiss standards, located in a quiet, open situation directly on Lake Murten with its own marina and excellent access to the water. The site is well cared for, with 200 out of the 700 pitches available for tourists. These are of reasonable size (80 sq.m.) with shade in parts from tall trees and electrical connections on most (6A). At the centre of the site is a large building which houses a general shop, butcher, baker and the main sanitary facilities. A separate restaurant is nearer the lake shore. With its location directly on the shores of the lake, there are many leisure opportunities including watersports, fishing and sandy beaches for swimming or relaxing.

Facilities

Three toilet blocks, one new, are of excellent quality with British style WCs. Motorcaravan services. Restaurant. Shop, butcher and baker. First aid room. Children's playground. Special events are organised for adults and children in July/Aug. Watersports, boating and lake swimming. Pedaloes.

Open

1 April - 30 September.

At a glance

Welcome & Ambience	✓✓✓✓	Location	✓✓✓✓✓
Quality of Pitches	✓✓✓✓	Range of Facilities	✓✓✓✓✓

Directions

Site is signed near Avenches on the Bern - Lausanne road no.1 (not the motorway). Signed Neuchatel and Salavaux

Charges guide

Per person	CHF 8,30
child (4-16 yrs)	CHF 5,20
caravan	CHF 11,40
tent acc. to size	CHF 7,25 - 11,40
motorcaravan	CHF 15,50 - 20,70
electricity	CHF 4,00

Reservations

Write to site with CHF. 20 fee. Tel: 026 675 17 50.
E-mail: camping@avenches.ch

CH9240 Camping Le Petit Bois

CH-1110 Morges (Vaud)

This excellent TCS campsite is on the edge of Morges, a wine-growing centre with a 13th century castle, on Lake Geneva about eight kilometres west of Lausanne. Le Petit Bois is next to the municipal sports field complex with views across the lake to the mountains beyond. A good variety of flowers, shrubs and trees adorn the site and the neat, tidy lawns make a most pleasant environment. The site has 170 grass pitches for tourists, all with 6A electricity and laid out in a regular pattern from wide hard access roads on which cars stand. There are eight larger pitches for motorcaravans with electricity, water and drainage. Two tent like structures have electronic games in one with the other being used for entertainment. A fence separates the site from the lake with gates for access to the water. As well as being good for a long stay to explore this scenic and interesting region, it also makes a night stop when passing this way. The friendly managers speak good English, and will advise on local attractions.

Facilities

Two well built, fully equipped, modern toilet blocks include hot water in half the washbasins and sinks and on payment in the showers. Separate block with excellent baby room and cosmetics room. Facilities for disabled visitors. Washing machines, dryers and irons. Motorcaravan services. First class restaurant (with service) and takeaway. Well stocked shop. Playground. Boules. Bicycle and scooter hire. Small general room. Internet point. Some entertainment in high season. Picnic area. Off site: Next to the site is the very good heated town swimming pool and open space for ball games. Small harbour adjoining site has some moorings for campers' boats. Town centre within walking distance. Tennis.

At a glance

Welcome & Ambience	✓✓✓✓	Location	✓✓✓✓
Quality of Pitches	✓✓✓✓	Range of Facilities	✓✓✓✓

Directions

On Rue de Lac (B1) coming from Lausanne, leave Lausanne - Geneva motorway at exit 'Morges-ouest', from Geneva exit 'Morges'. Turn towards town and signs for site.

Charges 2004

Per person	CHF 5,80 - 7,20
caravan	CHF 18,00 - 22,00
pitch	CHF 10,00 - 25,00

Reservations

Made for min. 1 week with deposit (CHF. 80) and fee (20). Tel: 021 801 12 70.
E-mail: camping.morges@tcs.ch

Open

2 April - 24 October.

CH9000 Camping Waldhort

Heideweg 16, CH-4153 Reinach bei Basel (Basel-Land)

This is a satisfactory site for night halts or for visits to Basel. Although there are almost twice as many static caravan pitches as spaces for tourists, this is a quiet site on the edge of a residential district, within easy reach of the city. The site is flat, with 210 level pitches on grass with access from the tarmac road which circles round inside the site. Trees are now maturing to give some shade. All pitches have electricity (10A). Owned and run by the Camping and Caravanning Club of Basel, it is neat, tidy and orderly and there is usually space available. An extra, separate camping area has been added behind the tennis club which has pleasant pitches and good sanitary facilities.

Facilities

The good quality, fully equipped, central sanitary block includes facilities for babies and disabled people. Washing machine and dryer. Kitchen with gas rings. Fridge for ice packs. Motorcaravan services. Small shop with terrace for drinks. Playground with two small pools. Table tennis. Swimming pool and tennis next to site. Off site: Reinach is within walking distance for tram service into Basel.

Open

1 March - 29 October.

At a glance

Welcome & Ambience	✓✓✓✓	Location	✓✓✓✓
Quality of Pitches	✓✓✓	Range of Facilities	✓✓✓✓

Directions

Take Basel - Delémont motorway spur, exit at 'Reinach-Nord' and follow camp signs.

Charges 2005

Per person	CHF 8,00
child (6-16 yrs)	CHF 4,50
tent	CHF 11,00
caravan or motorcaravan	CHF 18,00

Electricity included.

Reservations

Made for main season; advance payment asked for single nights, otherwise no deposit.
Tel: 061 711 64 29. E-mail: camp.waldhort@gmx.ch

CH9150 Camping Seebucht

Seestrasse 559, CH-8038 Zürich-Wollishofen (Zürich)

Being a smallish site only 4.5 km. from the centre of the important town of Zürich and in a pleasant situation with well kept lawns, Seebucht has more demands on space than it can meet. With 300 touring pitches (all with 6/10A electricity), it may well pack units rather closely in season but there is much transit trade, so there are usually plenty of vacancies each day if you are early (reservations not made). Caravans go on flat hardstandings (cars cannot always stand by them); tents, for which space may be easier to find, go on lawns. The grassy strip alongside the lake is kept free for recreational use. Trains pass by the site regularly through the day and up until midnight; there is also some road noise.

Facilities

The single sanitary block has British style toilets, with some Turkish style for men, individual washbasins (cubicles for women) with cold water and hot water on payment for the showers. Motorcaravan services. Shop. Café for meals or drinks. Bar (1/6-31/8). Swimming is possible into fairly deep water. Fishing. Jetty where small boats can be launched. Off site: Bicycle hire 1 km. Golf 2 km.

Open

1 May - 30 September.

At a glance

Welcome & Ambience	✓✓✓	Location	✓✓✓✓
Quality of Pitches	✓✓✓	Range of Facilities	✓✓✓

Directions

Site is on southern side of the town and western side of the lake, at Wollishofen; well signed from most parts of town and at motorway exit. Situated on lakeside road no. 3 (southwards) signed Chur.

Charges 2004

Per person	CHF 8,00
child (4-16 yrs)	CHF 5,00
large tent or caravan	CHF 14,00
motorcaravan	CHF 16,00
car	CHF 5,00

Reservations

Not made. Tel: 01 482 16 12.
E-mail: ueli.g@bluewin.ch

CH9160 TCS Camping Rheinwiesen

CH-8246 Langwiesen (Schaffhausen)

Rheinwiesen is a friendly site in a very pleasant setting on the banks of the Rhine, with some tall trees, amongst which are some attractive willows. It is level and grassy, the first half quite open and the rest of the touring area wooded, with numbered pitches (mostly small – up to 70 sq.m.), many under tall trees. There are many day visitors in summer as the site is ideally placed for swimming, canoeing and diving in the Rhine. Dogs are not accepted at any time. Whilst here, you would not want to miss the impressive waterfalls at Schaffhausen, 150 m. wide and 25 m. high.

Facilities

For tourers, there is an old but clean building which might be under pressure at the busiest times. Washing machine and dryer. Two very deep, large waste collectors. Bar/snack bar with covered terrace for burgers etc. open daily. Bread to order, some essentials kept. Pool room. Two shallow open air paddling pools, with play area close by. Table tennis, table football. Off site: Shop 500m.

Open

27 April - 29 September.

At a glance

Welcome & Ambience	✓✓✓✓✓	Location	✓✓✓✓
Quality of Pitches	✓✓✓✓	Range of Facilities	✓✓✓

Directions

From Schaffhausen head east towards Stein am Rhein/Kreuzlingen for approx. 2.5km. to Langwiesen where the site is signed. If coming from the east, it is a tight turn into the site.

Charges guide

Per person	CHF 4,40 - 6,40
child (6-16yrs)	CHF 2,20 - 3,20
pitch	CHF 12,00 - 17,00
electricity	CHF 3,00

Reservations

Contact site. Tel: 052 659 3300.
E-mail: camping.schaffhausen@tcs.ch

CH9850 TCS-Camping Neue Ganda

CH-7302 Landquart (Graubünden)

Situated close to the Klosters, Davos road and the nearby town of Landquart, this valley campsite provides a comfortable night-stop near the A13 motorway. The 80 tourist pitches are not marked or separated but are all on level grass off a central tarmac road through the long, narrow wooded site. All pitches have 6/10A electricity. The many static caravans are mostly hidden from view situated in small alcoves. A modern, timber cladded building at the entrance houses all the necessary facilities - reception, community room and sanitary facilities. The restaurant/shop adjacent is open all the year.

Facilities

The toilet block is extremely well appointed and can be heated. Facilities for disabled visitors. Baby room. Washing machine and dryer. Drying room. Motorcaravan services. Restaurant. Shop. Internet access. Off site: Tennis, riding and canoeing nearby.

Open

6 April - 23 October and 19 December - 20 March

At a glance

Welcome & Ambience	✓✓✓✓	Location	✓✓✓✓
Quality of Pitches	✓✓✓	Range of Facilities	✓✓✓

Directions

From A13 take Landquart exit and follow road to Davos. After crossing large bridge, go down slip-road before petrol station where site is signed on right. At bottom turn left under road and right towards site.

Charges 2004

Per person	CHF 5,00 - 6,20
pitch	CHF 15,00 - 17,00
electricity	CHF 4,00

Reservations

Contact site. Tel: 081 322 39 55.
E-mail: camping.landquart@tcs.ch

CH9180 Camping Buchhorn

CH-9320 Arbon (Thurgau)

This small but clean and pleasant site is directly beside Lake Bodensee in the town's parkland. There is access for boats from the site, but powered craft must be under a certain h.p. (take advice on this from the management). There are splendid views across this large inland sea and interesting boats ply up and down between Constance and Lindau and Bregenz. The town swimming lido in the lake, with a restaurant, is quite close. The site is well shaded but few of the touring pitches are by the water's edge. An overflow field used for tents is next door. There are many static caravans but said to be room for 100 tourists. Pitches are on a mixture of gravel and grass, on flat areas on either side of access roads, most with 6A electricity. Cars may have to parked elsewhere. A railway runs directly along one side but one gets used to the noise from small and infrequent trains. A single set of buildings provide all the site's amenities. This is a beautiful area and the site is well placed for touring around Lake Bodensee.

Facilities

Toilet facilities are clean and modern, and should just about suffice in high season. Washing machine, dryer and drying area. Fridge. Shop (basic supplies, drinks and snacks - all season). General room. Playground. Gates closed 12-14.00 hrs daily. Dogs are not accepted. Off site: Tennis 150 m. Town swimming lido 400 m. Watersports and steamer trips are available on the lake, walks and marked cycle tracks around it. Nature reserve nearby.

Open

4 April - 3 October.

At a glance

Welcome & Ambience	✓✓✓	Location	✓✓✓✓
Quality of Pitches	✓✓✓	Range of Facilities	✓✓✓

Directions

On Arbon-Konstanz road 13. From the A1 take the Arbon West exit and head towards the town. Straight on at the lights and turn left just after the town sign. Turn left again and head towards the warehouses. Turn right and the site is straight ahead.

Charges 2004

Per person	CHF 6,75
child (6-16 yrs)	CHF 3,10
large tent, caravan or motorcaravan	CHF 11,40
small tent	CHF 5,70
car	CHF 3,10

Reservations

Advised for July/Aug; write to site.
Tel: 071 446 65 45. E-mail: info@camping-arbon.ch

CH9855 Camping Cavresc

CH-7746 Le Prese (Graubünden)

Le Prese is on the Tirano to St Moritz road, south of the Bernina Pass. Camping Cavresc is on grassy meadows in the Valposchiano valley and, with its southern climate, peaceful ambience and beautiful views, is a very good, newly built site with ultramodern sanitary facilities. There are 30 flat, level pitches, all with 10A electricity and water, plus a large area for tents. There is no shade. Le Prese is close to Italy and the Poschiavo Lake. When they say that the trains run through the town, they mean it, because through the length of this small town the main railway line runs along the main road and traffic is forced to the side each time a Red Glacier express arrives. If the campsite reception is unmanned, walk back into town, as the Sertori family who own the site also run the small well-stocked supermarket.

Facilities

The excellent toilet block is very well maintained. Showers on payment. Facilities for disabled visitors. Washing machine and dryer. Motorcaravan services. Restaurant/bar. Small shop. Swimming pool (high season). Off site: Le Prese 250 m. Windsurfing and sailing and of course skiing.

Open

All year.

At a glance

Welcome & Ambience	✓✓✓✓	Location	✓✓✓✓✓
Quality of Pitches	✓✓✓	Range of Facilities	✓✓✓✓

Directions

Coming from Italy on road no. 29, the site is towards the end of the town. Turn right towards Pagnoncini/Cantone and site is on right in about 100 m. Go over a humpback bridge at the entrance.

Charges 2004

Per person	CHF 9,00 - 12,00
child (6-16 yrs)	CHF 4,00 - 6,00
pitch	CHF 4,00 - 15,00
electricity	CHF 4,00

Reservations

Advised for high season. Tel: 081 844 07 97.
E-mail: camping.cavresc@bleuwin.ch

Switzerland

CH9820 Camping Pradafenz

Pradafenz 106, CH-7075 Churwalden (Graubünden)

In the heart of the village of Churwalden on the Chur - St Moritz road, Pradafenz makes a convenient night stop and being amidst the mountains, is also an excellent base for walking and exploring this scenic area. There are 38 ski lifts serving the district with one starting from the site entrance both for winter skiing and summer walking. Being at 1,200 m. above sea level and surrounded by pine-clad mountains, the views are breathtaking and the air fresh and clean. The absence of entertainment on site makes this a quiet, peaceful place although a variety of entertainment is offered in the region. At first sight, this appears to be a site for static holiday caravans but three large rectangular terraces at the front take 50 touring units. This area has a hardstanding of concrete frets with grass growing through and 'super-pitch' facilities of electricity (10A), drainage, gas and TV sockets. A flat meadow is also available for tents or as an over-flow for caravans. Although the gravel road which leads to the tourers' terrace is not very steep, the very friendly German speaking owner will tow caravans there with his tractor if required. Access is inadequate for twin axle caravans and very large motorcaravans.

Facilities

The main sanitary block is half underground, well appointed and heated. It includes some washbasins in cabins. Baby room and another with hair dryers. Another good, heated small block has been added in the tourist section. Washing machines, dryers and separate drying room. Boot drying room with freezer for ice packs. Motorcaravan services. Gas supplies. Small restaurant serving good, simple meals and selling basic provisions. General room. Walking. Skiing. Bicycle hire. Fishing. Torches useful. Off site: Restaurants and shops 300 m. in village. Municipal outdoor pool 500 m. Riding 3.5 km. Golf 5 km.

At a glance

Welcome & Ambience	✓✓✓✓	Location	✓✓✓✓✓
Quality of Pitches	✓✓✓✓	Range of Facilities	✓✓✓✓

Directions

From Chur take road towards Lenzerheide. It is initially a fairly long, steep climb with one tight hairpin. In centre of Churwalden turn right in front of the tourist office towards the site.

Charges 2004

Per person	CHF 7,00
child (2-16 yrs)	CHF 4,50 - 5,50
pitch	CHF 5,00 - 15,00
electricity	CHF 2,00
dog	CHF 3,00

Reservations

Advisable for winter; write to site.
Tel: 081 382 19 21. E-mail: camping@pradafenz.ch

Open

29 May - 30 October and 15 Dec - 15 April.

CH9830 Camping Sur En

CH-7554 Sur En / Sent (Graubünden)

Sur-En is at the eastern end of the Engadine valley, about ten kilometres from the Italian and Austrian borders. The area is, perhaps, better known as a skiing region, but has summer attractions as well. At nearby Scuol there is an ice-rink and thermal baths, plus a wide range of activities including mountain biking, white water rafting and excursion possibilities. As you approach on road 27 and spot the site way below under the shadow of a steeply rising, wooded mountain, the drop down may appear daunting. However, as you drive it becomes reasonable, although the site owner will provide assistance for nervous towers. A level site, it is in an open valley with little shade. They say there is room for 120 touring units on the meadows where pitches are neither marked nor numbered; there are electricity connections for all (6A). The friendly, English speaking owner seems to have created a very pleasant atmosphere and although the site might be used for a night stay during transit, it could well attract for a longer period.

Facilities

The modern, heated sanitary block is good with some extra facilities in the main building when required. Washing machine and dryer. Motorcaravan services. Shop and good restaurant (15/12-15/4 and 1/5-31/10) with covered terrace overlooking the play area. Takeaway (high season). Swimming pool (1/6-15/10). Bicycle hire. Fishing. Entertainment for adults and children is arranged in July/Aug. A symposium for sculptors is held during the second week in July. Excursions arranged in high season. Bus service to Scuol for train to St Moritz.
Off site: Golf 8 km.

Open

All year.

At a glance

Welcome & Ambience	✓✓✓✓	Location	✓✓✓✓
Quality of Pitches	✓✓✓	Range of Facilities	✓✓✓✓

Directions

From Zernez on road 27 go straight over at new roundabout at Scuol, then down hill. Ignore campsite at bottom and keep driving east. Note Sent village high above and a small lake in the valley below. Next you see the site also in the valley just before entering hamlet of Crusch. After 250 m. turn right signed Sur-En. The road is a steady, winding descent, Cross covered timber bridge (3.8 m.) and enter site.

Charges 2004

Per person	CHF 5,00 - 5,80
child (6-16 yrs)	CHF 2,50 - 2,90
pitch	CHF 11,10 - 15,00
electricity	CHF 2,80
dog	CHF 2,50

Reservations

Not made. Tel: 081 866 35 44.
E-mail: wb@bluewin.ch

CH9860 Camping Plauns

Morteratsch, CH-7504 Pontresina (Graubünden)

This is a mountain site in splendid scenery near St Moritz. Pontrasina is at the mouth of the Bernina Pass road (B29) which runs from Celerina in the Swiss Engadine to Titana in Italy. Camping Plauns, some four kilometres southeast of Pontresina, is situated in the floor of the valley between fir-clad mountains at 1,850 m. above sea level. A river runs through this long, narrow site with lovely views on each side with a small lake at one end. There are about 250 pitches for tourists in summer, all with electricity, some in small clearings amongst tall trees and some in a larger open space. In winter the number is reduced to 40. They are neither numbered nor marked and size depends on the natural space between the trees. Being in a mountain valley, the grass is thin over a stony base with tarmac roads running through. A new reception building houses a larger shop, TV room, enormous drying room and an intenet access point. This is a quiet site in a peaceful location and could make a useful night stop when travelling through or a base for exploring the region which is good walking country.

Facilities

Three fully equipped toilet blocks, one old and two new, modern and excellent, and can be heated in cool weather. Some washbasins in private cabins and showers on payment. Facilities for disabled visitors. Washing machines, dryers and drying room. Well stocked shop. Grill-snack bar for drinks or simple meals. TV room. Internet access. Bicycle hire. Playground. Torch useful. Off site: Restaurant 1 km. Entertainment programme offered, winter and summer, at nearby Pontresina.

At a glance

Welcome & Ambience	✓✓✓✓	Location	✓✓✓✓
Quality of Pitches	✓✓✓	Range of Facilities	✓✓✓

Directions

Site is on B29, the road to Tirano and Bernina Pass, about 4 km. southeast of Pontresina - well signed.

Charges 2004

Per person	CHF 8,50
child (6-15 yrs)	CHF 4,00 - 5,50
pitch	CHF 11,00 - 15,00
electricity	CHF 3,00 - 4,00
dog	CHF 3,00

Reservations

Made with CHF. 20 deposit. Tel: 081 842 62 85. E-mail: a.brueli@bluewin.ch

Open

1 June - 15 October and 15 December - 15 April.

CH9865 TCS-Camping Fontanivas

CH-7180 Disentis (Graubünden)

Many come to Switzerland to bury or hide their gold but if you go to Disentis/Müster you have the chance of finding some! The Medelser Rhine near Disentis is known to be the richest place in gold in the country. Since the 1980s when serious prospecting began there has been a gold rush in Disentis. Try your luck! That apart, this is an ideal holiday spot for both sports fans and nature lovers. Nestled in the Surselva valley with superb views the campsite with its own lake is also appealing. Surrounded by tall pine trees, the site is owned by the Touring Club of Switzerland, the Swiss version of the AA, and provides flat, level pitches, all with 6A electricity. There are plenty of opportunities for walks, nature trails and cycle rides, whilst the more adventurous can enjoy themselves canyoning, rafting, hang-gliding or mountain biking.

Facilities

The excellent sanitary block is well maintained with free showers for all and a hairdryer for the ladies. Facilities for disabled visitors. Baby room. Washing machine and dryer. Motorcaravan services. Shop. Restaurant/bar. Caravans and tent bungalows to rent. Off site: Disentis 700 m. Indoor pool. Fishing.

Open

End April - end September.

At a glance

Welcome & Ambience	✓✓✓✓	Location	✓✓✓✓
Quality of Pitches	✓✓✓	Range of Facilities	✓✓✓

Directions

From Andermatt take the Oberalppass to Disentis. Go through the town and at T-junction turn left towards Lukmanier. Go down the hill (past droopy power cables) and turn left into site.

Charges 2004

Per person	CHF 4,80 - 6,00
child (6-15 yrs)	CHF 2,40 - 3,00
pitch	CHF 5,00 - 16,00
electricity	CHF 4,00
dog	CHF 2,00 - 3,00

Reservations

Advised for high season. Tel: 081 947 44 22. E-mail: camping.disentis@tcs.ch

CH9520 Camping du Botza

CH-1963 Vétroz (Valais)

Situated in the Rhone Valley at a height of 450 m and not far from the autoroute, this is a pleasant site with views of the surrounding mountains. It is set in a peaceful wooded location, even though it is close to an industrial zone. There are 128 individual touring pitches, ranging in size (50-10 sq.m.) all with 16A electricity, many with some shade and 25 with water and drainage. Considerable investment has taken place recently in making the site environmentally friendly with solar power used to heat the pool and a large recycling facility. A pizzeria with a terrace overlooking the heated outdoor pool, serves a variety of dishes, whilst close to the entrance is the site's own restaurant, with live music and dancing on Friday, Saturday and Sunday evenings. English is spoken. The gates are locked at night.

Facilities

Some private cabins in the heated sanitary block. Washing machines and dryers. Shop. Pizzeria. Swimming pool open mid May to early September. Playground. Table tennis. Volleyball. Tennis court. Off site: Many walks alongside small streams nearby. Good cycle track. The historic town of Sion is 8 km. Riding 2 km. Golf 10 km.

Open

All year.

At a glance

Welcome & Ambience	✓✓✓✓	Location	✓✓✓
Quality of Pitches	✓✓✓	Range of Facilities	✓✓✓

Directions

From the A9/E62 between Sion and Martigny, take Conthey/Vetroz and go south towards Aproz. Turn right and follow signs through the Botza industrial estate to site.

Charges 2004

Per person	CHF 4,70 - 7,80
child (6-16 yrs)	CHF 2,30 - 3,90
pitch	CHF 10,50 - 12,50
electricity	CHF 3,30 - 4,40
dog	CHF 3,50

Reservations

Advised in high season. Tel: 027 346 1940. E-mail: info@botza.ch

CH9640 Camping de la Sarvaz

Route de Fully, CH-1913 Saillon (Valais)

The Rhone valley in Valais with its terraced vineyards provides a beautiful setting for this site. Family owned and run, Camping de la Sarvaz provides excellent facilities and would be a good base for relaxing or for the more energetic walking, cycling, climbing or skiing. The site adjoins a restaurant/bar. It has 22 level touring pitches all with electricity, 19 of which have water and drainage. Lovely mountain views surround the site and there are 14 chalets to rent. A new inflatable pool has been provided which is available from May to September. English is spoken.

Facilities

Modern, heated sanitary facilities are of very high standards, very well maintained. Free showers. Additional toilets on the first floor. Facilities for disabled people. Baby room. Washing machine and dryer. Motorcaravan services. Shop. Restaurant/bar. Volleyball. Good play area. Off site: Saillon 2 km. with Thermal centre and spa facilities.

Open

All year except 16 November - 15 December.

At a glance

Welcome & Ambience	✓✓✓✓	Location	✓✓✓✓
Quality of Pitches	✓✓✓✓	Range of Facilities	✓✓✓✓

Directions

From the A9 take exit 23 for Saxon/Saillon. Follow signs to Saillon then turn right towards the site, which is about 1 km. along the road.

Charges 2004

Per person	CHF 7,60
child (6-16 yrs)	CHF 3,80
pitch	CHF 16,00
electricity	CHF 3,30 - 4,40
dog	CHF 3,50

Reservations

Advised for high season. Tel: 027 744 13 89. E-mail: info@la-sarvaz.ch

CH9600 Camping Rive-Bleue

Bouveret Plage, CH-1897 Bouveret (Valais)

At the eastern end of Lac Léman, the main feature of this site is the very pleasant lakeside lido only a short walk of 300 m. from the site and with free entry for campers. It has an 'Aquaparc' pool with a water toboggan and plenty of grassy sunbathing areas, a bathing area in lake, boating facilities with storage for sailboards, canoes, inflatables etc, sailing school, pedaloes for hire. Also here and, like the lido, under same ownership as the campsite, is a quality hotel which at the rear has a café for food and drinks with access from the lido. The site itself has 200 marked pitches on well kept flat grass, half in the centre with 6A electricity, the other half round the perimeter.

Facilities

Two decent toilet blocks have washbasins with cold water in the old block, hot in the new, and pre-set free hot showers. Shop, restaurant by beach (both all season). Bicycle hire. Fishing. Covered area for cooking with electric rings and barbecue. Drying room. Motorcaravan services (Euro-relais; CHF. 12).

Open

1 April - 30 September.

At a glance

Welcome & Ambience	✓✓✓✓	Location	✓✓✓✓
Quality of Pitches	✓✓✓	Range of Facilities	✓✓✓

Directions

Approach site on Martigny-Evian road no. 21 and turn to Bouveret-Plage south of Le Bouveret.

Charges 2004

Per person	CHF 7,60 - 9,30
child (6-16 yrs)	CHF 5,30 - 6,30
car	CHF 1,90
tent	CHF 6,50 - 10,30
caravan	CHF 8,30 - 11,40
motorcaravan	CHF 10,10 - 13,20

Reservations

Are advised and made for any length with CHF. 20 non-refundable reservation fee. Tel: 024 481 21 61. E-mail: info@camping-rive-bleue.ch

CH9660 Camping Des Glaciers

CH-1944 La Fouly (Valais)

At 1,600 m. above sea level Des Glaciers is set amidst magnificent mountain scenery in a very quiet, peaceful location in the beautiful Ferret Valley. Being just off the main Martigny - Grand St Bernard route, it could make a night stop when travelling along this road but as this would entail a 13 km. detour along a minor road, it is more convenient for a longer stay. Those seeking the fresh mountain air or an opportunity for mountain walking would be well suited here. The site offers two types of pitches, about half in an open, undulating meadow with campers choosing where to go and the rest being level, individual plots of varying size in small clearings either between bushes and shrubs or under tall pines. A small stream runs through the site. Of the 170 places, 150 have 25A electricity so a small heater can be used if evenings become chilly. The charming lady owner, fluent in six languages, is always ready not only to welcome you to this peaceful haven but also to give information on the locality.

Facilities

Three sanitary units, all of exceptional quality and heated when necessary. The smallest is under reception, there is another in the centre of the open area and a block in the centre of the site. Hot water is all free. Washing machines and dryers. Gas supplies. Motorcaravan services. Small shop. Recreation room with TV. Playground. Torches may be useful. Off site: Shop and restaurant 500 m. Bicycle hire 500 m. Riding 8 km.

Open

20 May - 30 September.

At a glance

Welcome & Ambience	✓✓✓✓	Location	✓✓✓✓✓
Quality of Pitches	✓✓✓✓	Range of Facilities	✓✓✓✓

Directions

Leave Martigny-Gd St Bernard road (no. 21) at Orsieres and follow signs to La Fouly. Site is signed on right at end of La Fouly village.

Charges 2005

Per person	CHF 6,50
child (2-12 yrs)	CHF 3,50
pitch	CHF 10,00 - 16,00
electricity	CHF 3,50

Less 10% in May.

Reservations

Made without deposit; write to site. Tel: 027 783 17 35. E-mail: camping.glaciers@st-bernard.ch

CH9670 Camping de Molignon

CH-1984 Les Haudères (Valais)

The uphill drive from Sion in the Rhône Valley is enhanced by the Pyramids of Euseigne, through which the road passes via a short tunnel. These unusual structures, cut out by erosion from masses of morainic debris, have been saved from destruction by their unstable rocky crowns. De Molignon, surrounded by mountains, is a quiet, peaceful place 1,450 m above sea level; although there may be some road noise, the rushing stream and the sound of cow bells are likely to be the only disturbing factor in summer. The 100 pitches for tourists (75 with 10A electricity) are on well tended, level terraces leading down to the river. Although this is essentially a place for mountain walking (guided tours available), climbing and relaxing, there is a geological museum in Les Haudères, which has links with a British University, cheese making and interesting flora and fauna. Good English is spoken by the owner's son who is now running the site, who will be pleased to give information on all that is available from the campsite.

Facilities

Two fully equipped sanitary blocks, heated in cool weather, now include free hot showers. Baby room. Washing machines and dryer. Kitchen for hikers. Motorcaravan services. Gas supplies. Small shop for basic supplies (1/7-10/9). Restaurant good menu at reasonable prices (all year). Heated swimming pool with cover for cool weather (6 x 12 m). Sitting room for games and reading. Playground. Guided walks, climbing, geological museum, winter skiing. Fishing. Off site: Tennis and hang-gliding near. Bicycle hire 3 km. Riding 15 km. Skiing and langlauf in winter.

At a glance

Welcome & Ambience	✓✓✓✓	Location	✓✓✓✓
Quality of Pitches	✓✓✓	Range of Facilities	✓✓✓✓

Directions

Follow signs southwards from Sion for the Val d'Herens through Evolène to Les Haudères where site is signed on the right (3 km).

Charges guide

Per person	CHF 6,00
child (4-16 yrs)	CHF 2,90
pitch	CHF 8,00 - 16,00
dog	CHF 3,00
electricity	CHF 3,00

Less 10% in low season.

Reservations

Contact site. Tel: 027 283 12 40.
E-mail: molignon@swisscamps.ch

Open

All year.

CH9690 Camping Swiss-Plage

CH-3960 Sierre-Salgesch (Valais)

This is a good site and is well run by its English speaking owner and, although about half is occupied by static caravans, there are still 250 pitches for visiting tourists. The site is also slightly unusual in that much of the terrain has been deliberately left in its natural state. The wooded section gives good shade and tree formations and access roads determine where units go. There is a central open meadow and some quiet spots are a little further from the amenities. Most pitches, although unmarked, have 10A electric points available. One part of the site may be reserved but some space is usually available. The centre of the site has a natural lake which is kept dredged and clean and is suitable for small boats (not wind-surfers) and for swimming – the site say the water is tested weekly. It is possible to stroll along the banks of the Rhône and good walks are nearby.

Facilities

The central main block (heated in winter) and another block have recently been refurbished to a high standard, and with the third, less good block should be sufficient. Free hot water in washbasins in the main block, cold in some of the others, and hot showers on payment. Washing machine and dryer. Motorcaravan services. Shop. Terraced bar/ restaurant and snack bar with grills and pizzas. Takeaway. Lake. Paddling pool. Playground. Table tennis. Fishing (on payment). Volleyball. Badminton. Some entertainment in high season.

Open

7 April - 1 November.

At a glance

Welcome & Ambience	✓✓✓✓	Location	✓✓✓
Quality of Pitches	✓✓✓	Range of Facilities	✓✓✓

Directions

From either direction on road no. 9 or more recent bypasses, follow signs for Salgesch which should bring you past site entrance 3 km. northeast of Sierre. Care is required to spot the first sign in Sierre at a multi-road junction; site is well signed from here.

Charges 2005

Per person	CHF 6,80
child (4-16 yrs)	CHF 3,40
pitch	CHF 16,00
electricity	CHF 2,50
dog	CHF 3,00

Less 10% in low season. No credit cards.

Reservations

Necessary and made for any length with deposit.
Tel: 027 455 66 08. E-mail: info@swissplage.ch

CH9740 Camping Attermenzen

CH-3928 Randa (Valais)

'Location, Location, Location': this campsite has it! Randa, a picturesque Valais village, at 1,409 m. is a beautiful location for a campsite and an essential stopping place for those wishing to visit Zermatt only 10 km. away. The site is open all year excluding January, depending on the weather. For the summer season, reception is open from mid-June to mid-September – outside that time call at the restaurant (which is closed on Tuesdays). Unmarked pitches are on an uneven field with some areas that are fairly level and 6A electricity is within easy reach. This site is a paradise for walking, mountaineering, climbing and mountain biking (literally). Surrounded by famous 4,000 m. peaks, such as the Dom and Weisshorn, the site has good modern facilities and a restaurant and bar next door.

Facilities

The sanitary block is of a good standard and well maintained with free showers. Washing machine. Restaurant/bar. Off site: Zermatt 10 km.

Open

1 May - 31 October (summer season).

At a glance

Welcome & Ambience	✓✓✓	Location	✓✓✓✓✓
Quality of Pitches	✓✓✓	Range of Facilities	✓✓✓

Directions

From A9 at Visp turn right at roundabout towards Zermatt. Go through 3.3 km. long tunnel and follow road towards Zermatt. Go through Stalden then right at roundabout (Zermatt). Site is 1 km. after Randa.

Charges 2004

Per person	CHF 6,00
pitch incl. electricity	CHF 9,00 - 13,00

Reservations

Not taken for summer (reception only open 15/6-20/9. Contact site for details of winter camping. Tel: 027 967 13 79. E-mail: rest.camping@rhone.ch

CH9770 Camping Santa Monica

CH-3942 Raron (Valais)

We offer several different styles of campsite in the Rhône Valley including this pleasant, well tended site, that is open all year. The Simplon Pass is the only main route from Switzerland to Italy which avoids motorways. It is also an easy pass for caravans which is only closed occasionally in winter and, even then, is still possible by using the Brig-Iselle train ferry through the mountain. About half of this site is occupied by static caravans and chalets, but these are to one side leaving two flat, open meadows, so do not intrude on the tourist area. The 200 level pitches (100 for touring units) all have electricity (16A) and are roughly defined by saplings. Being right beside the main road 9 (some road noise), one does not have to deviate to find a night stop but it would also make a good base for exploring the area. Two cable ways start near the site entrance for winter skiers and summer mountain walkers.

Facilities

The single, heated toilet block is towards the entrance, has free hot water in washbasins and sinks and on payment in the showers. Facilities for disabled visitors. Motorcaravan services (Euro-Relais). Gas supplies. Bar, restaurant and shop (1/5-31/10). Small pool (1/6-30/9). Playground. Table tennis. Bicycle hire. Ski room. Off site: Restaurants and shops near. Tennis courts next door to site. Riding 10 km.

At a glance

Welcome & Ambience	✓✓✓✓	Location	✓✓✓
Quality of Pitches	✓✓✓✓	Range of Facilities	✓✓✓✓

Directions

On south side of road 9 between Visp and Susten.

Charges 2004

Per person	CHF 5,00 - 6,00
pitch incl. electricity	CHF 10,00 - 17,00

Reservations

Write to site. Tel: 027 934 24 24. E-mail: santamonica@rhone.ch

Open

All year.

CH9780 Camping Rhone

CH-3945 Gampel (Valais)

The Rhone valley provides a beautiful setting for this site. Family owned and run, it provides very good facilities and flat level pitches, all with 6A electricity. This is an excellent base for resting and relaxing or, for the more energetic, walking, cycling, climbing or skiing. About mid-way between Sion and Brig, it would be a good stop for those travelling and sightseeing. Sion has a dramatic backdrop, sheltered by the twin battlement hills of Valére and Tourbillon. The capital of Valais has kept much of its attractive medieval architecture. Brig on the other hand is the junction of a large number of road and rail routes and perhaps most importantly the Swiss end of the Simplon Pass.

Facilities

The good toilet block is well maintained with free showers. Facilities for disabled visitors. Baby room. Washing machine and dryer. Motorcaravan services. Restaurant/bar. Swimming pool. Play area. Off site: Gampel 1 km.

Open

April - mid October.

At a glance

Welcome & Ambience	✓✓✓✓	Location	✓✓✓✓
Quality of Pitches	✓✓✓✓	Range of Facilities	✓✓✓

Directions

From A9 turn right at roundabout (next to railway station) towards Gampel Steg. Go over Rhone Bridge and at base of the bridge turn left towards the site.

Charges 2004

Per person	CHF 6,80
pitch incl. electricity	CHF 10,20 - 11,70

Reservations

Advised for high season. Tel: 027 932 2041. E-mail: camping.rhone@swissonline.ch

CH9790 Camping Augenstern

Postfach 16, CH-3998 Reckingen (Valais)

The village of Reckingen is about half way between Brig and the Furka/Grimsel passes, although you can still get the train with car and caravan, or motorcaravan from Oberwald to Andermatt to avoid the steep climbs and descents of the Furka Pass. However, in doing so you will miss some unforgettable scenery and an experience never to be forgotten (we are assured that the nightmares diminish after a while). This family run site, at 1,326 m. provides 100 flat, level pitches for touring units, all with 10A electricity and not much shade. It provides an excellent base for walking, climbing or cycling. And perhaps, for the more adventurous, some rafting on the Rhone in the summer or skiing in the winter.

Facilities

The toilet block is good and is well maintained. Showers on payment. Motorcaravan services. Restaurant/bar. Shop in high season. Off site: Swimming pool complex 200 m. Reckingen 500 m.

Open

15 May - 15 October and 15 December - 31 March.

At a glance

Welcome & Ambience	✓✓✓✓	Location	✓✓✓✓
Quality of Pitches	✓✓✓	Range of Facilities	✓✓✓

Directions

From no. 19 road turn south in centre of Reckingen next to the church. Go down the hill, along one-way street and over the railway (carefully!) and a wooden bridge. Go over next bridge and turn right.

Charges 2004

Per person	CHF 6,50
pitch incl. electricity	CHF 12,50

Reservations

Advised for high season. Tel: 027 973 13 95.
E-mail: augenstern1@bluewin.ch

CH9890 Camping Campofelice

CH-6598 Tenero (Ticino)

The largest site in Switzerland and, now that three of the toilet blocks have been rebuilt and the other three renewed, Campofelice must rank among the best. It is bordered on the front by Lake Maggiore and on one side by the Verzasca estuary, where the site has its own harbour. The beach by the lake is sandy, long and wider than the usual lakeside ones. It shelves gently so that bathing is safe for children. Campofelice is divided into rows, with 1,030 individual pitches of average size on flat grass on either side of hard access roads. Mostly well shaded, all pitches have electricity connections (10A) and some also have water, drainage and TV connections. Pitches near the lake cost more (these are not available for motorcaravans) and a special area is reserved for small tents. Sporting facilities are good and there are cycle paths in the area, including into Locarno. English is spoken at this good, if rather expensive site.

Facilities

The six heated toilet blocks are of excellent quality. Washing machines and dryers. Motorcaravan services. Gas supplies. Supermarket. Restaurant. Tennis. Minigolf. Bicycle hire. Playground. Doctor calls. Dogs are not accepted Off site: Facilities nearby for watersports.

Open

18 March - 22 October.

At a glance

Welcome & Ambience	✓✓✓	Location	✓✓✓✓
Quality of Pitches	✓✓✓	Range of Facilities	✓✓✓✓

Directions

Site is very well signed on Bellinzona side of lakeside road no. 13 from Locarno.

Charges 2005

Per unit incl. 2 persons	CHF 38,00 - 84,00
extra person	CHF 8,00 - 12,00

Electricity included.

Reservations

Not made but there is usually space.
Tel: 091 745 1417. E-mail: camping@campofelice.ch

CH9970 TCS-Camping Parco al Sole

CH-6866 Meride (Ticino)

Meride is a small village in the extreme south of Switzerland with the Italian border close on three sides. A little remote, Parco al Sole is on a slight slope 1 km. before the village, with a steep mountain face on one side and views of others in the distance. A river runs across the top of the site and along one side and the reception office is accessed over a small wooden bridge. Apart from a little traffic noise from the road running past, it is a peaceful place. The road from the motorway is narrow in places and although this does not cause problems, Parco al Sole is better for a few days stay to explore the area rather than as a single night stop. There is space for 64 small units, with electricity connections (10A).

Facilities

A good quality sanitary block with the usual facilities is halfway up the site. 'Grotto Cafe' with log fire during cool weather where drinks and simple meals are offered and limited basic food supplies can be obtained. Heated swimming pool (12 x 6 m). Playground. Table tennis.

Open

1 May - 26 September.

At a glance

Welcome & Ambience	✓✓✓	Location	✓✓✓
Quality of Pitches	✓✓✓	Range of Facilities	✓✓✓

Directions

From N2 take Mendrisio exit (near Chiasso). Head to Rancate then Basazio, Arzo and Meride. Site is signed and is 6 km. The road to the site is narrow and the bridge in the last few yards has an awkward angle.

Charges 2004

Per person	CHF 5,80 - 7,40
pitch incl. electricity	CHF 16,00 - 24,00

Reservations

Write to site. Tel: 091 646 43 30.
E-mail: camping.meride@tcs.ch

OPEN ALL YEAR

The following sites are understood to accept caravanners and campers all year round, although the list also includes some sites that are open for at least ten months. These are marked with a star (*) – please refer to the site's individual entry for details.

Andorra
AN7143 Xixerella*
AN7145 Valira

Austria
AU0010 Nenzing*
AU0035 Alpin Seefeld
AU0155 Prutz*
AU0150 Riffler*
AU0040 Zugspitze
AU0220 Krismer
AU0060 Natterer See*
AU0170 Kranebitten
AU0070 Hofer
AU0100 Toni Brantlhof
AU0065 Seehof
AU0102 Stadlerhof
AU0140 Wilder Kaiser
AU0110 Tirol Camp
AU0180 Woferlgut
AU0160 Zell am See
AU0262 Oberwötzlhof
AU0306 Wien West*
AU0502 Im Thermenland
AU0440 Schluga
AU0480 Burgstaller

Baltic States - Lithuania
LI2030 Slenyje

Belgium
BE0560 De Lombarde
BE0580 Memling
BE0590 De Gavers
BE0620 Roosendael
BE0655 Lilse Bergen
BE0660 Baalse Hei*
BE0740 Eau Rouge
BE0780 Wilhelm Tell
BE0735 Petite Suisse
BE0670 La Clusure
BE0725 Val de L`Aisne
BE0530 Waux-Hall
BE0710 Vallée de Rabais

Czech Republic
CZ4640 Areal Jadran
CZ4590 Lisci Farma
CZ4880 Roznov
CZ4770 Dlouhá Louka
CZ4815 Triocamp

Denmark
DK2140 Jesperhus
DK2015 Ådalens
DK2020 Mogeltonder
DK2150 Solyst
DK2044 Hampen Sø
DK2032 Augustenhof
DK2046 Trelde Næs

Finland
FI2970 Nallikari
FI2850 Rastila

France
FR02030 Croix du Vieux Pont
FR78040 Etang d`Or*
FR88040 Lac de Bouzey
FR86040 Le Futuriste
FR73030 Les Lanchettes*
FR74070 Escale*
FR65090 Soleil du Pibeste
FR65080 Le Lavedan
FR06080 Les Cigales

Germany
DE3003 Wulfener Hals
DE3002 Schlei-Karschau
DE3010 Röders Park
DE3020 Bremen
DE3045 Walkenried*
DE3025 Alfsee
DE3030 Tecklenburg
DE3065 am Bärenbache
DE3180 Sonnenwiese
DE3185 Münster
DE3202 Grav-Insel
DE3210 Biggesee
DE3280 Teichmann
DE3275 Seepark
DE3258 Sägmühle*
DE3212 Wirfttal
DE3215 Goldene Meile
DE3242 Schinderhannes
DE3222 Moselbogen
DE3254 Harfenmühle
DE3415 Adam
DE3450 Münstertal
DE3406 Kleinenzhof
DE3440 Kirchzarten
DE3455 Gugel`s
DE3437 Hochschwarzwald
DE3445 Belchenblick
DE3420 Oberrhein
DE3411 Heidehof
DE3427 Schwarzwälder Hof
DE3432 Bonath
DE3454 Badenweiler*
DE3436 Bankenhof
DE3452 Alte Sägemühle
DE3467 Isnycamping*
DE3627 Ellwangen*
DE3650 Gitzenweiler
DE3630 Donau-Lech*
DE3672 Elbsee*
DE3667 Bannwaldsee
DE3670 Hopfensee*
DE3680 Tennsee*
DE3671 Öschlesee
DE3685 Allweglehen
DE3697 Dreiqueller
DE3715 Viechtach*
DE3710 Zwiesel
DE3610 Nürnberg
DE3632 Altmühltal
DE3720 Naabtal
DE3855 Oberhof
DE3833 LuxOase*
DE3847 Auensee
DE3842 Schlosspark
DE3820 Havelberge

Hungary
HU5150 Fortuna
HU5210 Diófaház
HU5300 Kek-Duna
HU5260 Jonathermál

Italy
IT6220 Mombarone
IT6250 Lac de Como
IT6201 Antholz
IT6042 Alba d`Oro
IT6053 Fusina
IT6401 Dei Fiori
IT6403 Baciccia
IT6414 Arenella*
IT6412 Valdeiva
IT6602 Bologna*
IT6623 San Marino
IT6665 Le Soline
IT6667 La Finoria
IT6810 Seven Hills
IT6780 Roma
IT6814 Flaminio
IT6830 Zeus
IT6875 Vascellero

IT6858 Il Salice
IT6890 Dolomiti sul Mare
IT6923 Jonio
IT6930 Marinello

Liechtenstein

FL7580 Mittagspitze

Luxembourg

LU7620 Nommerlayen*
LU7880 Trois Frontières
LU7670 Ardennes
LU7850 Fuussekaul
LU7590 Belle-Vue
LU7700 Gaalgebierg

Netherlands

NL5500 Pannenschuur*
NL6930 Schoneveld
NL5640 Kijkduinpark
NL5600 Delftse Hout
NL5630 Koningshof
NL5620 Duinrell
NL5760 Kuilart
NL6090 Lauwersoog
NL5790 Kuierpadtien
NL5960 Wielerbaan
NL5540 Katjeskelder
NL6560 Maasvallei
NL5910 Hertenwei
NL5890 Klein Canada
NL6510 Schatberg
NL6520 BreeBronne

Norway

NO2315 Ringoy
NO2400 Jolstraholmen
NO2385 Sandvik
NO2432 Harstad
NO2480 Bjorkedal
NO2460 Prinsen
NO2490 Skjerneset
NO2505 Magalaupe
NO2510 Håneset
NO2475 Saltstraumen
NO2455 Ballangen
NO2515 Gjelten Bru
NO2545 Rustberg
NO2590 Sandviken
NO2550 Strandefjord
NO2570 Fossheim
NO2615 Olberg*
NO2610 Neset

Poland

PL3170 Galindia Mazurski Eden
PL3300 Polana Sosny
PL3320 Auschwitz Centre

Portugal

PO8202 Espiche
PO8230 Olhao
PO8200 Valverde
PO8210 Albufeira
PO8220 Quarteira
PO8410 Armacao-Pera
PO8430 Sagres
PO8350 Markádia
PO8440 Quintos
PO8150 Caparica
PO8130 Guincho
PO8110 Valado*
PO8480 Foz do Arelho
PO8450 Colina-Sol*
PO8100 S Pedro-Moel
PO8460 Vale Paraiso*
PO8050 Sao Jacinto*
PO8370 Cerdeira
PO8030 Rio Alto

Slovakia

SK4910 Turiec

Slovenia

SV4235 Klin
SV4150 Kamne
SV4400 Dolina Prebold
SV4330 Pivka Jama*

Spain

ES8072 Les Medes*
ES8102 Mas Patoxas*
ES8130 Calonge
ES9140 Pedraforca
ES8240 Bona Vista Kim
ES8390 Vilanova Park
ES8502 Montblanc Park
ES8392 El Garrofer*
ES8560 Playa Tropicana
ES8580 Bonterra
ES8675 Vall de Laguar
ES8570 Torre La Sal 2
ES8536 Ametlla
ES8615 Kiko
ES8625 Kiko Rural
ES8535 Cala d'Oques
ES8685 El Raco
ES8743 Marjal
ES8687 Cap Blanch
ES8689 Playa del Torres
ES8742 La Marina
ES8754 Javea
ES8682 Villamar
ES8753 La Manga
ES8755 Moraira
ES8745 La Fuente
ES8748 Los Madriles
ES9285 Las Lomas
ES8783 Almanat
ES9270 Suspiro-Moro
ES8782 Laguna Playa
ES8802 Cabopino
ES8809 El Sur
ES8850 Paloma
ES8873 La Aldea
ES9081 Villsom
ES9080 El Brillante
ES9027 Monfrague
ES9089 Despenaperros
ES9028 Villueracas
ES9087 Merida
ES9091 Soto-Castillo
ES9090 El Greco
ES9200 El Escorial
ES9210 Pico-Miel
ES9025 Regio
ES9250 Costajan
ES9022 El Folgoso
ES9024 As Cancelas
ES8940 Los Cantiles
ES9043 Errota el Molino
ES9060 Peña Montañesa
ES9070 Pirineos*

Sweden

SW2705 Karralund
SW2650 Skånes
SW2675 Västervik Swe
SW2665 Rosenlund
SW2700 Boras
SW2720 Hökensås
SW2710 Lidköping
SW2760 Frykenbaden
SW2750 Sommarvik
SW2840 Flottsbro
SW2835 Orsa
SW2850 Ostersunds
SW2845 Svegs
SW2836 Mora Parkens
SW2857 Strömsund
SW2870 Jokkmokks
SW2860 Umeå
SW2865 Gielas

Switzerland

CH9420 Manor Farm
CH9460 Jungfrau
CH9495 Balmweid
CH9360 Grassi
CH9570 Eienwäldli
CH9130 Vitznau*
CH9855 Cavresc
CH9830 Sur En
CH9640 de la Sarvaz*
CH9520 Du Botza
CH9670 Molignon
CH9770 Santa Monica

DOGS

For the benefit of those who want to take their dogs with them or for people who do not like dogs at the sites they visit, we list here those sites that have indicated to us that they do not accept dogs. If you are, however, planning to take your dog we do advise you to check first – there may be limits on numbers, breeds, etc. or times of the year when they are excluded.

Never – **these sites do not accept dogs at any time:**

Austria

AU0306	Wien West

Baltic States - Lithuania

LI2010	Apple Island
LI2060	Viktorija

Belgium

BE0520	De Blekker
BE0735	Petite Suisse
BE0725	Val de L`Aisne

Croatia

CR6731	Valalta
CR6736	Valdaliso

Czech Republic

CZ4750	Bila Hora
CZ4690	Slunce

France

FR29140	Kerlann
FR17010	Bois Soleil
FR85210	Les Ecureuils
FR40170	La Réserve
FR84020	Bélézy
FR30160	Le Boucanet
FR34140	La Carabasse
FR06140	Ranch

Germany

DE3005	Schnelsen Nord
DE3182	Teutoburger Wald
DE3233	Holländischer Hof

Hungary

HU5090	Füred
HU5380	Venus

Italy

IT6229	Lévico
IT6357	Cisano & San Vito
IT6359	Serenella
IT6263	Bella Italia
IT6265	Ideal Molino
IT6256	Del Garda
IT6010	Capalonga
IT6015	Il Tridente
IT6020	Union Lido
IT6021	Italy
IT6035	Mediterraneo
IT6030	Dei Fiori
IT6003	Pra' Delle Torri
IT6032	Cavallino
IT6022	Portofelice
IT6000	Mare Pineta
IT6401	Dei Fiori
IT6414	Arenella
IT6065	Tahiti
IT6621	Delle Rose
IT6624	Rubicone
IT6629	Tripesce
IT6645	Delle Piscine
IT6671	Argentario
IT6780	Roma
IT6820	Baia Domizia
IT6819	Settebello
IT6853	Athena
IT6930	Marinello
IT6963	Isuledda

Netherlands

NL6960	Klepperstee
NL5680	Noordduinen
NL6790	Kienehoef
NL5970	De Paal

Norway

NO2320	Odda
NO2315	Ringoy
NO2325	Sundal
NO2330	Eikhamrane
NO2360	Ulvik Fjord
NO2490	Skjerneset
NO2445	Slettnes
NO2435	Solvang
NO2550	Strandefjord
NO2612	Holt
NO2600	Rysstad

Portugal

PO8170	São Miguel

Spain

ES8090	Cypsela
ES8103	El Maset
ES8420	Stel (Roda)
ES8481	Cambrils
ES8530	Playa Montroig
ES8537	Templo del Sol
ES8540	Torre del Sol
ES8560	Playa Tropicana
ES8620	L`AlqueriaL
ES8682	Villamar
ES8748	Los Madriles
ES9000	Playa Joyel

Switzerland

CH9480	Gletscherdorf
CH9160	Rheinwiesen
CH9180	Buchhorn
CH9890	Campofelice

Maybe – accepted but with certain restrictions:

Austria

AU0060	Natterer See	not 11/7-21/8
AU0400	Arneitz	not 11/7-21/8

Belgium

BE0670	La Clusure	max 1 in July/Aug

France

FR23010	Château de Poinsouze	not 11/7-21/8
FR26030	Grand Lierne	not 3/7 - 21/8

Germany

DE3232	Family Club	not 11/7-21/8
DE3440	Kirchzarten	not 11/7-21/8
DE3442	Herbolzheim	not 15/7-15/8
DE3465	Wirthshof	not 11/7-21/8

Italy

IT6210	Steiner	not 11/7-21/8
IT6254	Lido	not 6/7-15/8
IT6008	Sabbiaddoro	not 29/7- 15/8
IT6665	Le Soline	no cats
IT6660	Maremma	not 16/6-31/8
IT6633	Free Time	not 11/7-21/8
IT6842	Sant' Antonio	not 1/8-31/8
IT6845	San Nicola	not high season
IT6875	Vascellero	not 1/8-31/8
IT6996	Mariposa	not 1/8-31/8

Portugal

PO8350	Markádia	not 11/7-21/8
PO8370	Cerdeira	not 11/7-21/8

Spain

ES8080	Delfin Verde	not 12/7-15/8
ES8072	Les Medes	not 11/7-21/8
ES8160	Cala Gogo	not 1/7 - 26/8
ES8580	Bonterra	not 11/7-21/8

We have had very favourable feedback from readers concerning our choice of naturist sites, which we first introduced in our 1992 editions. Over the last few years we have gradually added a few more.

Apart from the need to have a 'Naturist Licence' (see below), there is no need to be a practising naturist before visiting these sites. In fact, as far as British visitors are concerned, many are what might be described as 'holiday naturists' as distinct from the practice of naturism at other times. The emphasis in all the sites featured in this guide at least, is on naturism as 'life in harmony with nature', and respect for oneself and others and for the environment, rather than simply on nudity. In fact nudity is really only obligatory in the area of the swimming pools.

There are a number of rules, which amount to sensible and considerate guidelines designed to ensure that no-one invades someone elses privacy, creates any nuisance, or damages the environment. Whether as a result of these rules, the naturist philosophy generally, or the attitude of site owners and campers alike, we have been very impressed by all the naturist sites we have selected. Without exception they had a friendly and welcoming ambience, were all extremely clean and tidy, and, in most cases, provided much larger than average pitches, with a wide range of activities both sporting and cultural.

The purpose of our including a number of naturist sites in our guide is to provide an introduction to naturist camping in Europe for British holidaymakers; we were actually surprised by the number of British campers we met on naturist sites, many of whom had 'stumbled across naturism almost by accident'. A Naturist Licence can be obtained in advance from either the British Naturist Association or on arrival at any recognised naturist site (a passport-sized photograph is required).

If you are planning to take your caravan, tent, trailer tent or motorcaravan to the continent you will need to be familiar with the rules, regulations and customs that pertain to driving abroad.

A recent survey looked at why many Britons would not entertain a holiday abroad and why many foreigners would not contemplate coming here. According to the findings, the biggest single put-off was driving on the 'wrong' side of the road. However, statistics clearly show that you are less at risk of being involved in accidents – and that includes minor shunts – when driving in another country. The theory is that motorists of that country recognise that the nationality plate on your vehicle means that you might be slightly hesitant and give you that extra few inches which makes the difference between a minor ding and a trouble free journey. Of course it could also be that when driving in another country we take things a bit easier, so we are less at risk of being involved in an accident.

With European harmonisation eliminating most of the differences between driving in your home country and another, there has never been a better time to consider driving abroad. Where there are differences, they are in the detail.

For example all European countries require you to carry your driving documents whenever you are behind the wheel; there's no three day's grace to get to your local police station. Amongst the documents you are required to carry is your vehicle registration document, the V5 (what used to be called the log book). If yours is a hire or company vehicle you may have difficulties getting your hands on the V5. However the police will accept a photocopy of the V5 provided it is accompanied by a brief letter – signed by the vehicle owner – saying you have their permission to take the vehicle abroad.

European harmonisation also means that most common road signs are the same in all countries. Where mainland Europe differs from the UK is in the use of direction signs. If you are following signs through a town and arrive at a junction without signage – don't panic. The logic is that if all major routes are straight on, you don't need another sign to tell you the obvious.

As to language difficulties, you will find that most continental road signs are similar in style to those in the UK, although what is written on them will be in the language of the country concerned (for example Barcelona is spelt Barcelone in French), so it's worthwhile mugging up some of the more important and/or more usual ones. See articles on individual countries – the main signs have been translated for you.

When it comes to traffic regulations around school entrances, the Europeans are also ahead of us. In mainland Europe the law, or common practice, is that you should not pass a parked school bus unless it is absolutely safe to do so. If you can pass, you must keep your speed to a walking pace. It is the same when you drive past a school when the children are outside. The law, or best practice, says you should reduce your speed to a crawl.

We would never dream of suggesting that you would ever break the speed limit, but if you are tempted it is worth remembering that European police seem to have as many speed cameras as British police. The difference between speeding in the UK and mainland Europe is in the way fines can be levied. If you are caught in a manned speed trap you may be expected to pay an on-the-spot fine, so it's no good arguing that you haven't got enough money to pay the fine. Most manned speed traps will take cash, traveller's cheques, debit and credit cards.

Checklist

Before you set off for a holiday abroad it's worth making yourself a checklist of things to do, and what to pack – we've been travelling abroad several times a year for more than thirty years and we still don't rely on our memory for this, so it's best to consult a checklist; here's the one we use:

- ☐ Passports
- ☐ Tickets
- ☐ Motor Insurance Certificate, including Green Card or Continental Cover clause
- ☐ V5 Registration Document and/or (if not your own vehicle) the owners authority
- ☐ Breakdown Insurance Certificate
- ☐ Driving Licence (The new PHOTO style licence is now MANDATORY in most European countries)
- ☐ Form E1-11 (to extend NHS Insurance to European destinations)
- ☐ Foreign Currency (EUROS, and Swiss Francs if appropriate) and/or Travellers Cheques
- ☐ Credit Card(s)
- ☐ Campsite Guide(s) and Tourist Guide(s)
- ☐ Maps/Road Atlas
- ☐ GB Stickers on car and caravan/trailer
- ☐ Beam deflectors to ensure that your headlights dip towards the right hand side
- ☐ Red Warning Triangle
- ☐ Spare vehicle/caravan driving light bulbs
- ☐ Torch
- ☐ First-Aid Kit, including mosquito repellent
- ☐ Fire extinguisher
- ☐ Basic tool kit (e.g screwdriver, pliers, etc)
- ☐ Continental mains connector/adaptor, and a long cable – for continental sites
- ☐ Polarity tester
- ☐ Spare fuses for car and caravan
- ☐ Spare fan/alternator belt

Finally bear in mind it's well worth having your car and caravan serviced before you go, and do check that your outfit is properly 'trimmed' before you set off.

Be sensible at all times and do not leave valuables in your vehicle or leave anything visible which could tempt a petty thief. Take care if waved down by anyone; in the past tactics like this have been used to get you to leave your car so an accomplice can have a field day rummaging through your belongings.

In theory European law means that a vehicle insured for use in the UK is still insured in any other European country. But some insurers know that doesn't really mean what you think it means. Somewhere in the fine print on page 37 of your policy you could find that if you take your vehicle abroad your insurance coverage is reduced to third party only. So two weeks before you venture abroad contact your vehicle insurer and find out if you need additional coverage.

Most vehicle breakdown insurance schemes claim to offer pan-European cover. But again it is worth asking just how good that cover is. If you car expires beside the road in a cloud of steam you don't want to have to try explaining the problem to a telephone receptionist who is fluent in every language – except yours.

The travel insurers Alan Rogers work with (see advert on page 523) operate language-specific call centres. If anything goes wrong you'll speak to somebody totally fluent in your language. What all insurers will insist on is that your vehicle must be in good condition before you set off on holiday. A full service a few weeks before your departure date will take care of that.

There is probably no subject which causes campers, caravanners and motor-caravanners venturing abroad more worries than insurance, so notwithstanding the notes above, if you're in any doubt about insurance it may be worthwhile you giving the subject some further thought, and the following will hopefully help to clarify things:

The problem with insurance is that there is often an 'overlap', so that sometimes one aspect is apparently covered on two insurance policies. To avoid confusion let's cut through the hype and take a clear look at the different types of insurance.

If you are planning on camping, caravanning or motorcaravanning abroad, this is what you will need.

Road traffic insurance

As previously stated, your ordinary car or motorcaravan road insurance will cover you anywhere in the EU. *However* many policies only provide minimum cover. So if you have an accident your insurance may only cover the cost of damage to the other person's property.

To maintain the same level of cover abroad as you enjoy at home you need to tell your vehicle insurer. Some will automatically cover you abroad with no extra cost and no extra paperwork. Some will say you need a Green Card (which is neither green or on card) but won't charge for it. Some will charge extra for the green card. Ideally you should contact your vehicle insurer 3-4 weeks before you set off, and confirm your conversation with them in writing.

A good insurance company will provide a European recognised accident report form. On this you mark details of damage to yours and the other party's property and draw a little diagram showing where the vehicles were in relation to each other. You give a copy of your form to the other motorist; he gives you a copy of his. It prevents all the shouting which often accompanies accidents in this country.

Holiday insurance

This is a multi-part insurance. One part covers your vehicles. If they breakdown or are involved in an accident they can be repaired or returned to this country. The best will even arrange to bring your vehicle home if the driver is unable to proceed.

Many new vehicles come with a free breakdown and recovery insurance which extends into Europe. Some professional motoring journalists have reported that the actual service this provides can be patchy and may not cover the recovery of a caravan or trailer. Our advice is to buy the motoring section of your holiday insurance.

The second section of holiday insurance covers people. It will include the cost of doctor, ambulance and hospital treatment if needed. If needed the better companies will even pay for English language speaking doctors and nurses and will bring a sick or injured holidaymaker home by air ambulance.

The third part of a good holiday insurance policy covers things. If someone breaks in to your motorhome and steals your passports and money, one phone call to the insurance company will have everything sorted out. If you manage to drive over your camera, it's covered.

An important part of the insurance that is often ignored is the cancellation section. Few things are as heartbreaking as having to cancel a holiday because a member of the family falls ill. Cancellation insurance can't take away the disappointment, but it makes sure you don't suffer financially as well.

There are a number of good insurance policies available including those provided for their members by the two major clubs and those offered by the leading camping holiday agents already mentioned in this guide.

Which ever insurance you choose we would advise not picking any of the policies sold by the High Street travel trade. Whilst they may be good, they don't cover the specific needs of campers, caravanners and motorcaravanners. And ideally you should arrange your holiday insurance at least four weeks before you set off.

Form E111

By arrangement between the British Government and rest of the European Community Governments, British holiday-makers can enjoy similar health care as that Government offers its own citizens. The form which shows you are entitled to take advantage of this arrangement is called E111.

E111 doesn't replace holiday insurance, but is in addition to. The form is available from all main UK Post Offices. Fill out one for every adult member of your family (children under 16 should be marked as dependents on your form). Get it stamped by the counter staff and take it on holiday with you.

Form E111 is valid indefinitely (unless you change your address).

And that is all you need to know about insurance. You know what they say about insurance, don't you? You'll only need it if you haven't got it.

3 FREE ISSUES!

THE UK'S FAVOURITE MOTORHOME MAGAZINES...

The UK's best selling motorhome magazine for 38 years, MMM is considered to be the only place to look for the latest news from the motorcaravanning world.

The UK's leading magazine for motorhome buyers, Which Motorcaravan has more hot news of new models and in-depth vehicle tests than any rival publication.

Reply now and you will get the next **3 issues of MMM for just £1 each** or the next **3 issues of Which Motorcaravan FREE!**

Then, if you like what you see - do nothing! Your subscription will continue at the LOW RATE of just £8 every 3 months for MMM, or £5 every 3 months for Which Motorcaravan, giving you a saving of up to 44% off the shop price!

100%
RISK FREE OFFER
If you feel that the magazine is not for you simply write to us within 10 days of receiving your third issue and you won't pay a penny more! Additionally, you may cancel your subscription at any time and we will refund in full the cost of all unmailed copies.

Call our Hotline today on **01778 391180**
(Please have your bank details ready & quote ref: ALANROGERS05)

Offer is open to UK residents and is a Direct Debit offer only. Your subscription will start with the next available issue. Please note, only one trial offer per magazine will be processed per household during a 12 month period.

HOLIDAY CHEQUE
£17.50 per night!

HOLIDAY
CHEQUE

Alan Rogers

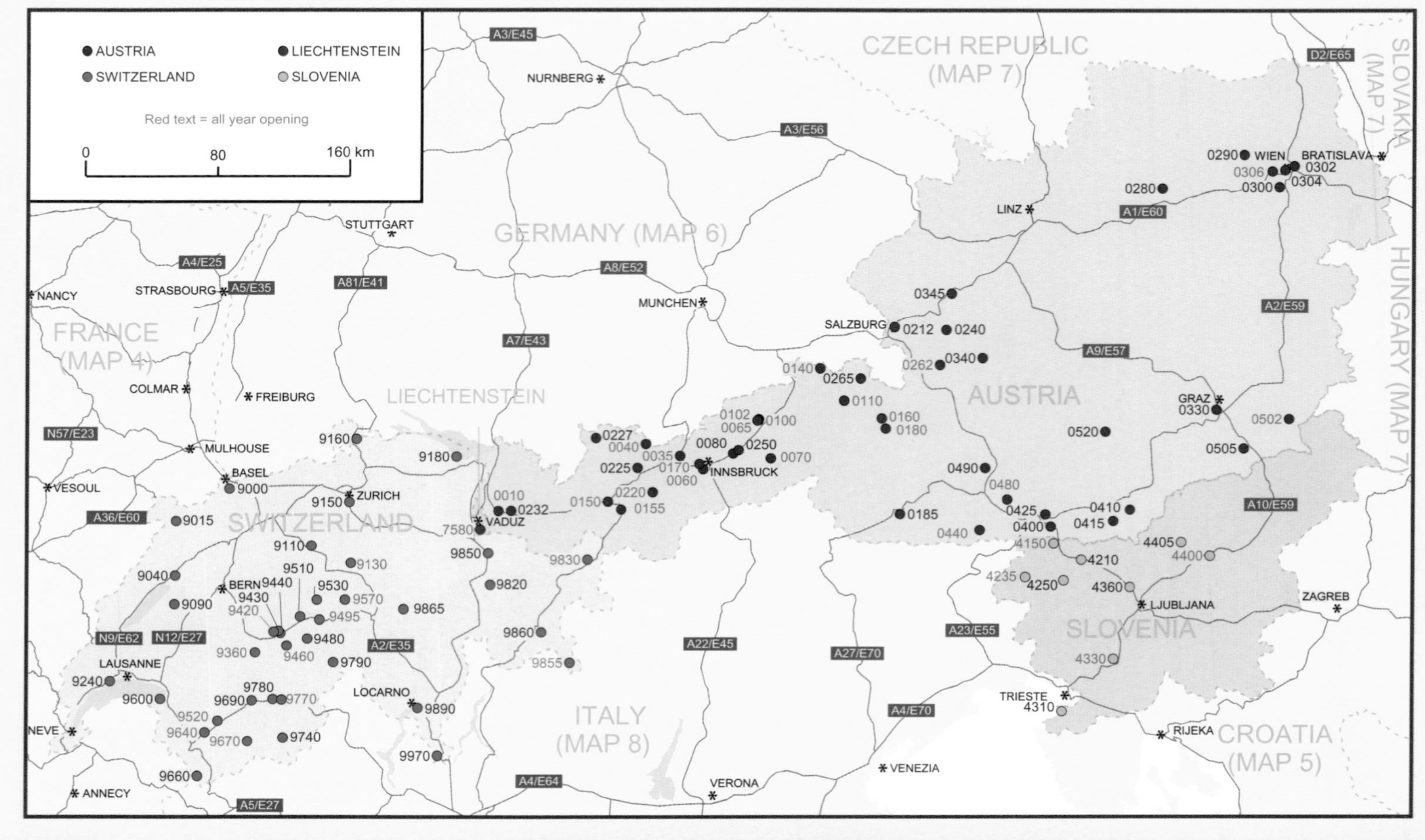

AUSTRIA
LIECHTENSTEIN
SWITZERLAND
SLOVENIA
Red text = all year opening
0
80
160 km
CZECH REPUBLIC (MAP 7)
SLOVAKIA (MAP 7)
HUNGARY (MAP 7)
GERMANY (MAP 6)
FRANCE (MAP 4)
ITALY (MAP 8)
CROATIA (MAP 5)
AUSTRIA
SWITZERLAND
LIECHTENSTEIN
SLOVENIA
NURNBERG
STUTTGART
MUNCHEN
NANCY
STRASBOURG
COLMAR
FREIBURG
MULHOUSE
BASEL
VESOUL
ZURICH
VADUZ
BERN
LAUSANNE
NEVE
ANNECY
LOCARNO
INNSBRUCK
SALZBURG
LINZ
WIEN
BRATISLAVA
GRAZ
LJUBLJANA
ZAGREB
TRIESTE
RIJEKA
VENEZIA
VERONA
A3/E45
A3/E56
D2/E65
A1/E60
A2/E59
A9/E57
A10/E59
A8/E52
A7/E43
A81/E41
A4/E25
A5/E35
N57/E23
A36/E60
N9/E62
N12/E27
A2/E35
A22/E45
A27/E70
A23/E55
A4/E70
A4/E64
A5/E27
0290
0306
0302
0304
0300
0280
0345
0212
0240
0262
0340
0140
0265
0110
0160
0180
0102
0065
0100
0080
0250
0070
0227
0040
0035
0225
0170
0060
0220
0150
0155
0010
0232
7580
0520
0330
0502
0505
0490
0480
0425
0400
0410
0415
0185
0440
4150
4405
4400
4210
4235
4250
4360
4330
4310
9160
9180
9000
9150
9015
9110
9130
9850
9830
9820
9040
9090
9440
9510
9530
9430
9420
9570
9495
9865
9480
9360
9460
9790
9860
9855
9240
9600
9780
9690
9770
9520
9640
9670
9740
9890
9970
9660

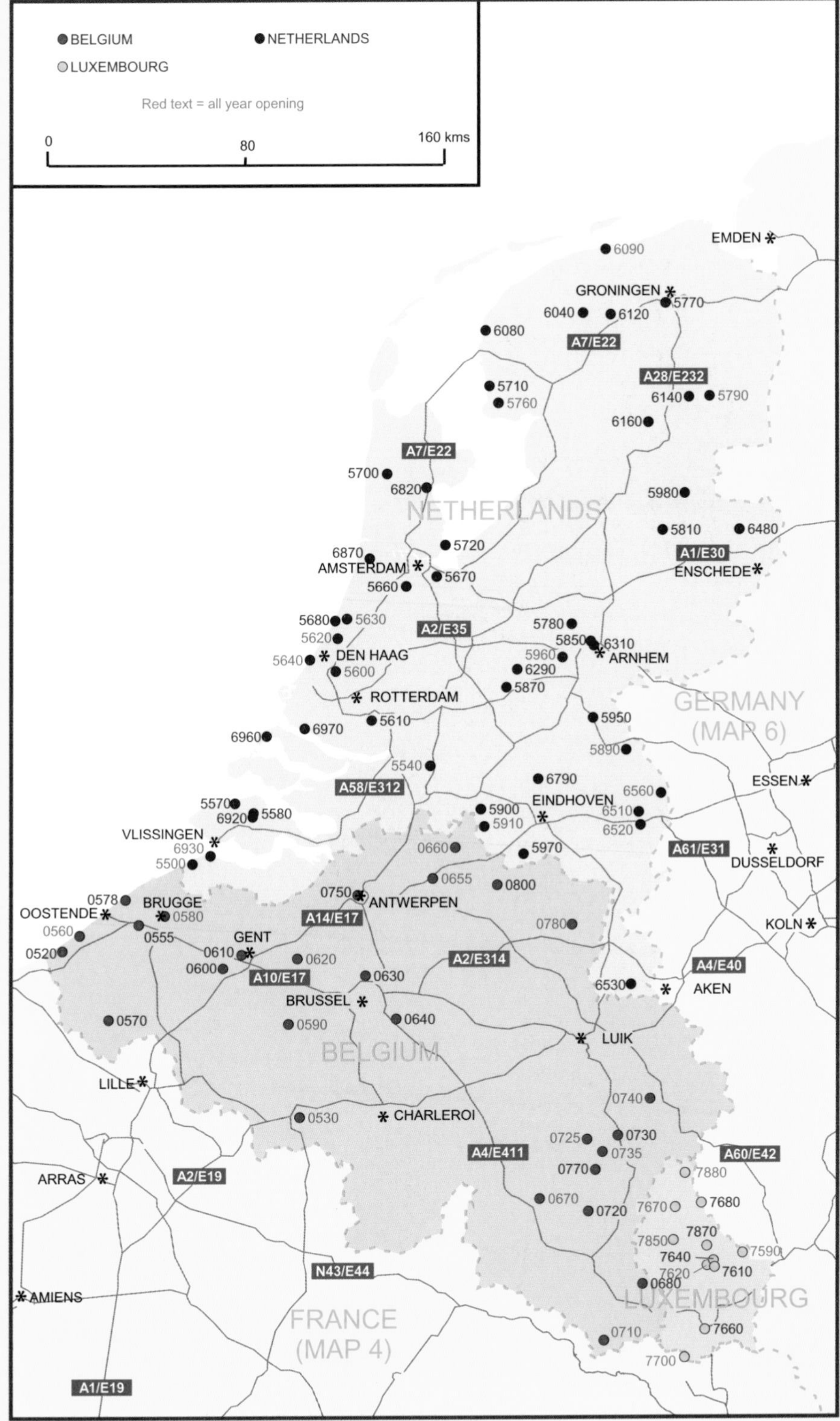
BELGIUM
NETHERLANDS
LUXEMBOURG
Red text = all year opening
0
80
160 kms
EMDEN
6090
GRONINGEN
6040
6120
5770
6080
A7/E22
A28/E232
5710
5760
6140
5790
6160
A7/E22
5700
6820
NETHERLANDS
5980
5810
6480
5720
A1/E30
6870
AMSTERDAM
5670
ENSCHEDE
5660
5680
5630
5620
A2/E35
5780
5850
6310
ARNHEM
5640
DEN HAAG
5600
5960
6290
5870
ROTTERDAM
5610
6970
6960
5950
GERMANY
(MAP 6)
5890
5540
A58/E312
6790
5570
6920
5580
5900
EINDHOVEN
6560
5910
6510
6520
VLISSINGEN
6930
5500
0660
5970
A61/E31
DUSSELDORF
ESSEN
0655
0800
0578
BRUGGE
0750
ANTWERPEN
OOSTENDE
0580
A14/E17
0560
0555
0780
KOLN
0520
GENT
0610
0620
0600
A10/E17
0630
A2/E314
A4/E40
6530
AKEN
BRUSSEL
0570
0590
0640
BELGIUM
LUIK
LILLE
0740
0530
CHARLEROI
0725
0730
0735
A4/E411
A60/E42
ARRAS
A2/E19
0770
7880
0670
0720
7670
7680
7850
7870
7590
7640
7620
7610
N43/E44
0680
AMIENS
LUXEMBOURG
FRANCE
(MAP 4)
7660
0710
7700
A1/E19

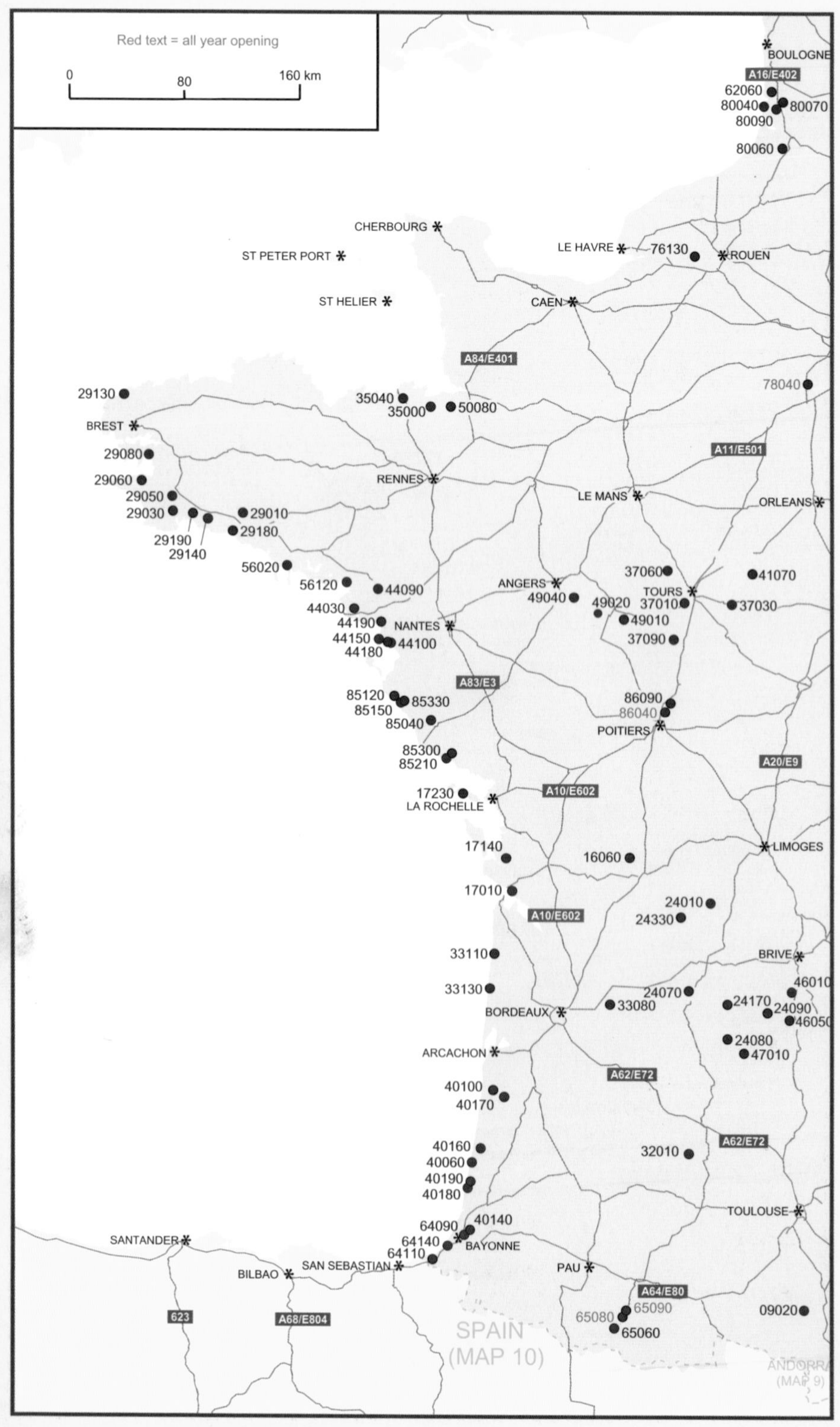
Red text = all year opening
0
80
160 km
BOULOGNE
A16/E402
62060
80040
80070
80090
80060
CHERBOURG
ST PETER PORT
LE HAVRE
76130
ROUEN
ST HELIER
CAEN
A84/E401
29130
35040
35000
50080
78040
BREST
29080
A11/E501
29060
RENNES
29050
LE MANS
ORLEANS
29030
29010
29190
29180
29140
56020
37060
41070
56120
44090
ANGERS
TOURS
44030
49040
49020
37010
37030
44190
NANTES
49010
44150
44100
37090
44180
A83/E3
85120
85330
86090
85150
86040
85040
POITIERS
85300
A20/E9
85210
17230
A10/E602
LA ROCHELLE
17140
16060
LIMOGES
17010
24010
A10/E602
24330
33110
BRIVE
46010
33130
24070
24170
33080
24090
BORDEAUX
46050
24080
47010
ARCACHON
A62/E72
40100
40170
40160
32010
A62/E72
40060
40190
40180
TOULOUSE
64090
40140
SANTANDER
64140
BAYONNE
64110
SAN SEBASTIAN
PAU
BILBAO
A64/E80
623
A68/E804
65080
65090
09020
65060
SPAIN
(MAP 10)
ANDORRA
(MAP 9)

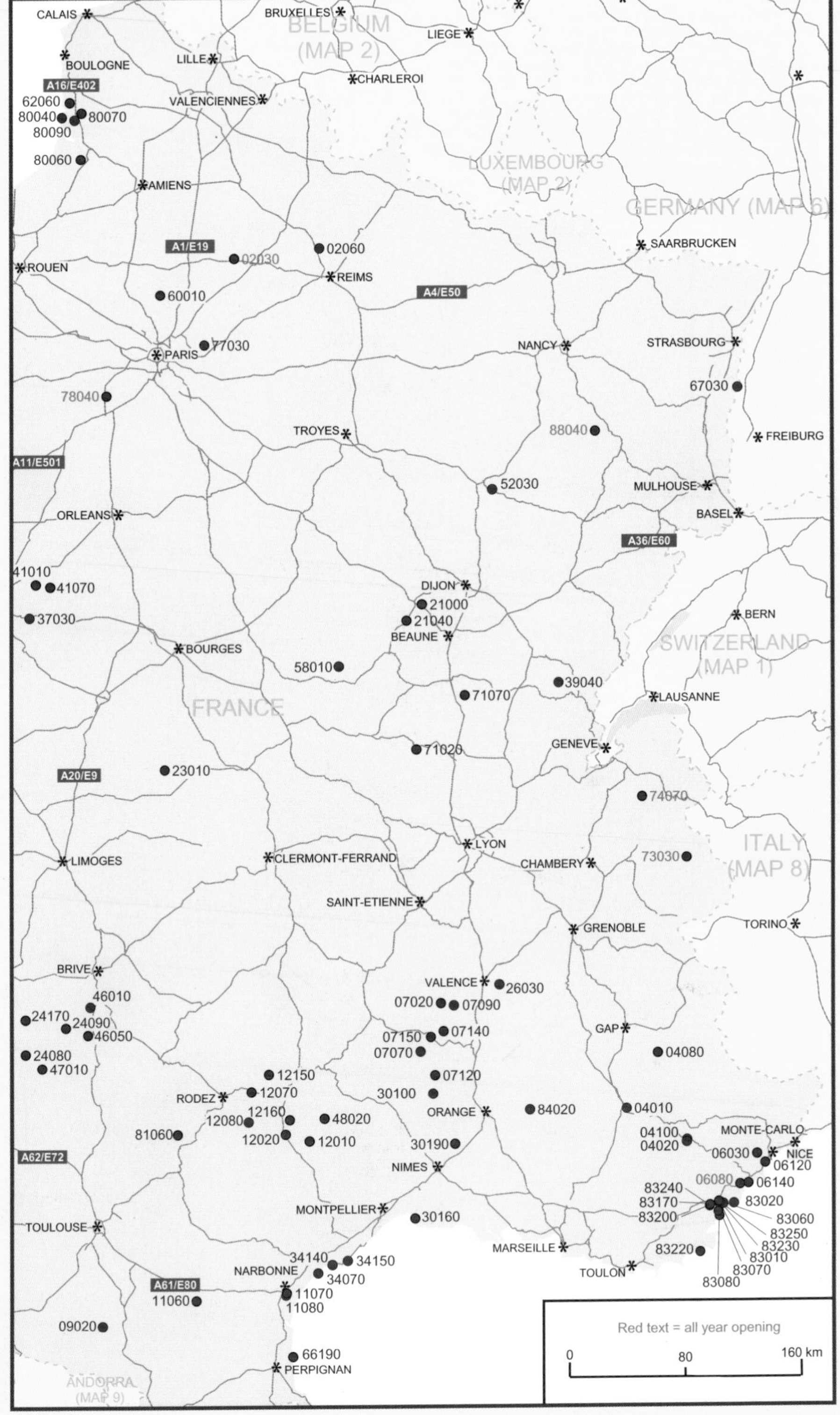
CALAIS
BRUXELLES
BELGIUM (MAP 2)
LIEGE
BOULOGNE
LILLE
CHARLEROI
A16/E402
62060
80040
80070
80090
VALENCIENNES
80060
LUXEMBOURG (MAP 2)
AMIENS
GERMANY (MAP 6)
SAARBRUCKEN
A1/E19
02030
02060
ROUEN
REIMS
A4/E50
60010
NANCY
STRASBOURG
77030
PARIS
67030
78040
TROYES
88040
FREIBURG
A11/E501
52030
MULHOUSE
BASEL
ORLEANS
A36/E60
41010
41070
DIJON
21000
21040
37030
BEAUNE
BERN
BOURGES
SWITZERLAND (MAP 1)
58010
39040
71070
LAUSANNE
FRANCE
71020
GENEVE
23010
A20/E9
74070
LYON
ITALY (MAP 8)
LIMOGES
CLERMONT-FERRAND
CHAMBERY
73030
SAINT-ETIENNE
GRENOBLE
TORINO
BRIVE
VALENCE
26030
46010
07020
07090
24170
24090
46050
07150
07140
GAP
07070
24080
04080
47010
12150
07120
RODEZ
12070
30100
12160
12080
48020
ORANGE
84020
04010
81060
12020
12010
30190
04100
04020
MONTE-CARLO
06030
NICE
06120
A62/E72
NIMES
06080
06140
83240
83170
83020
83200
83060
MONTPELLIER
30160
83250
TOULOUSE
83230
83010
MARSEILLE
83220
83070
34140
34150
TOULON
83080
NARBONNE
34070
A61/E80
11070
11060
11080
Red text = all year opening
0
80
160 km
09020
66190
PERPIGNAN
ANDORRA (MAP 9)

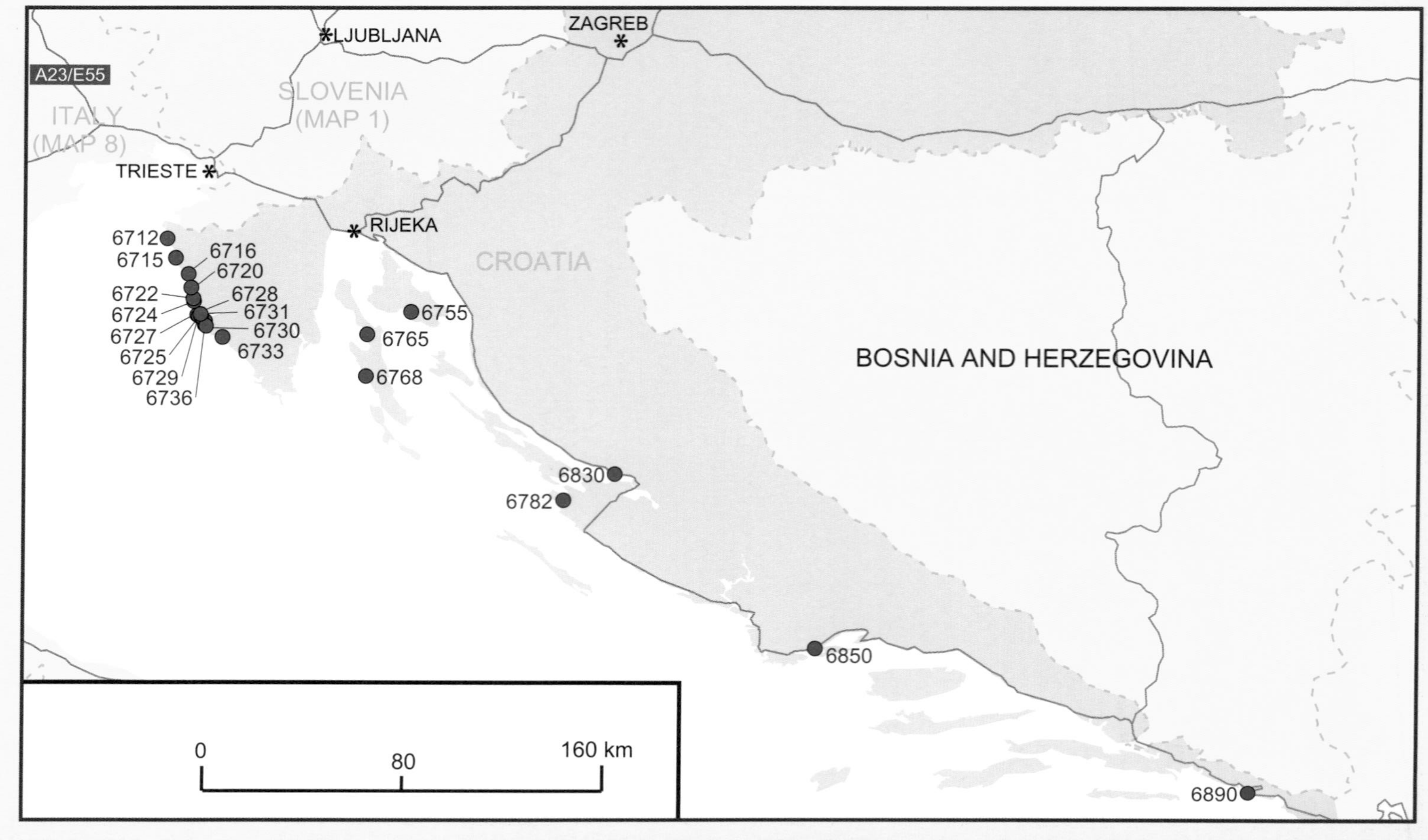
ZAGREB
LJUBLJANA
A23/E55
SLOVENIA
(MAP 1)
ITALY
(MAP 8)
TRIESTE
RIJEKA
CROATIA
BOSNIA AND HERZEGOVINA
6712
6715
6716
6720
6722
6728
6724
6731
6727
6730
6725
6733
6729
6736
6755
6765
6768
6830
6782
6850
6890
0
80
160 km

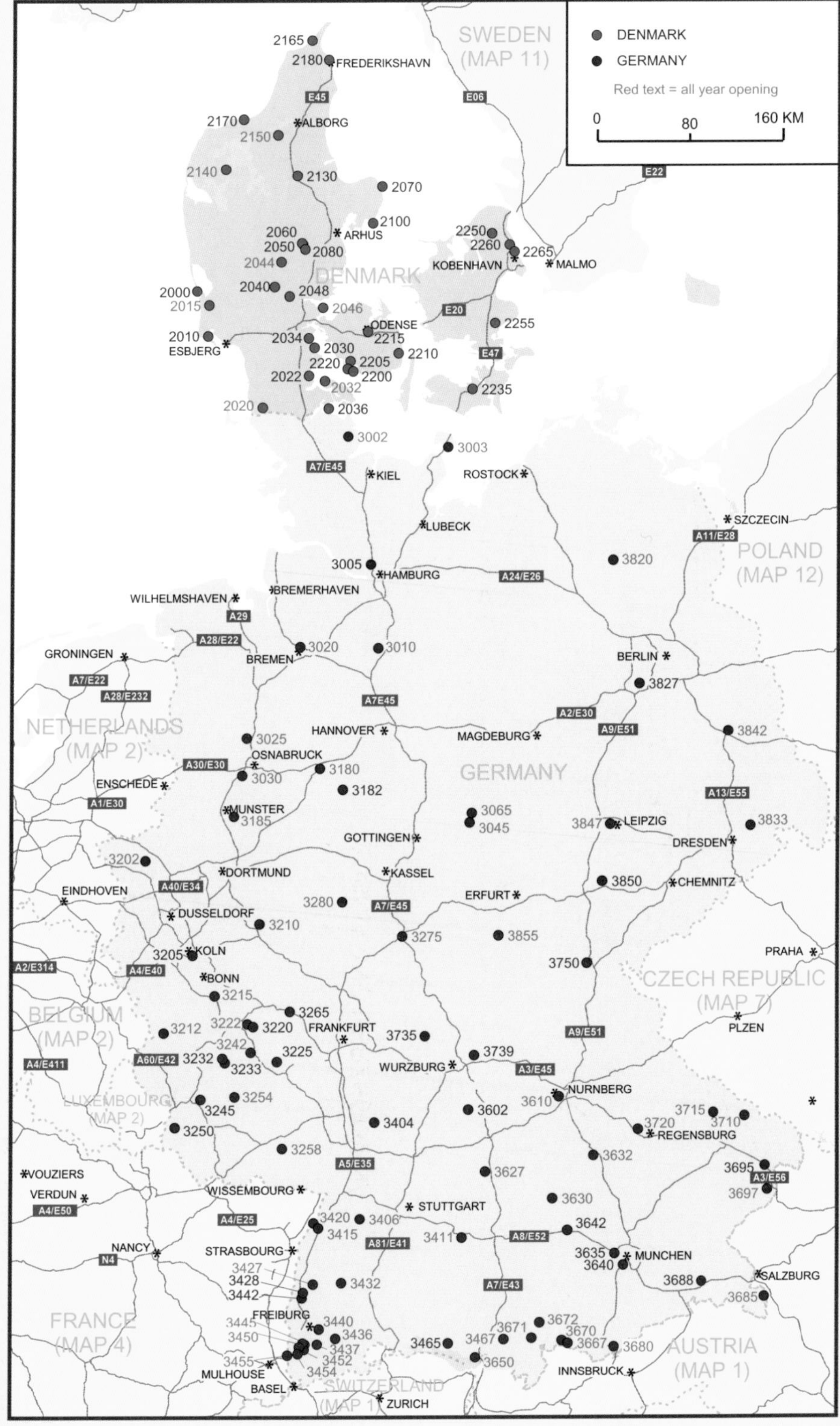
DENMARK
GERMANY
Red text = all year opening
0
80
160 KM
SWEDEN (MAP 11)
POLAND (MAP 12)
NETHERLANDS (MAP 2)
BELGIUM (MAP 2)
LUXEMBOURG (MAP 2)
FRANCE (MAP 4)
SWITZERLAND (MAP 1)
AUSTRIA (MAP 1)
CZECH REPUBLIC (MAP 7)
DENMARK
GERMANY
FREDERIKSHAVN
ALBORG
ARHUS
KOBENHAVN
MALMO
ODENSE
ESBJERG
KIEL
ROSTOCK
LUBECK
SZCZECIN
HAMBURG
BREMERHAVEN
WILHELMSHAVEN
GRONINGEN
BREMEN
BERLIN
HANNOVER
MAGDEBURG
OSNABRUCK
ENSCHEDE
MUNSTER
GOTTINGEN
LEIPZIG
DRESDEN
DORTMUND
KASSEL
EINDHOVEN
ERFURT
CHEMNITZ
DUSSELDORF
KOLN
BONN
PRAHA
PLZEN
FRANKFURT
WURZBURG
NURNBERG
REGENSBURG
VOUZIERS
VERDUN
WISSEMBOURG
STUTTGART
NANCY
STRASBOURG
MUNCHEN
SALZBURG
FREIBURG
MULHOUSE
BASEL
ZURICH
INNSBRUCK
E45
E06
E22
E20
E47
A7/E45
A11/E28
A24/E26
A29
A28/E22
A7/E22
A28/E232
A7E45
A2/E30
A9/E51
A30/E30
A1/E30
A13/E55
A40/E34
A7/E45
A2/E314
A4/E40
A4/E411
A60/E42
A9/E51
A3/E45
A5/E35
A3/E56
A4/E50
A4/E25
A81/E41
A8/E52
N4
A7/E43
2165
2180
2170
2150
2140
2130
2070
2100
2060
2050
2080
2044
2250
2260
2265
2040
2048
2000
2015
2046
2255
2010
2034
2215
2030
2210
2220
2205
2022
2200
2032
2235
2020
2036
3002
3003
3820
3005
3020
3010
3827
3025
3842
3030
3180
3182
3065
3045
3847
3833
3185
3202
3850
3280
3210
3275
3855
3205
3750
3215
3265
3222
3220
3212
3735
3242
3225
3739
3232
3233
3254
3245
3610
3602
3715
3710
3250
3404
3720
3258
3632
3695
3627
3697
3630
3420
3406
3415
3642
3411
3635
3640
3427
3428
3442
3432
3688
3685
3445
3450
3440
3436
3437
3672
3670
3671
3465
3467
3667
3680
3455
3452
3454
3650

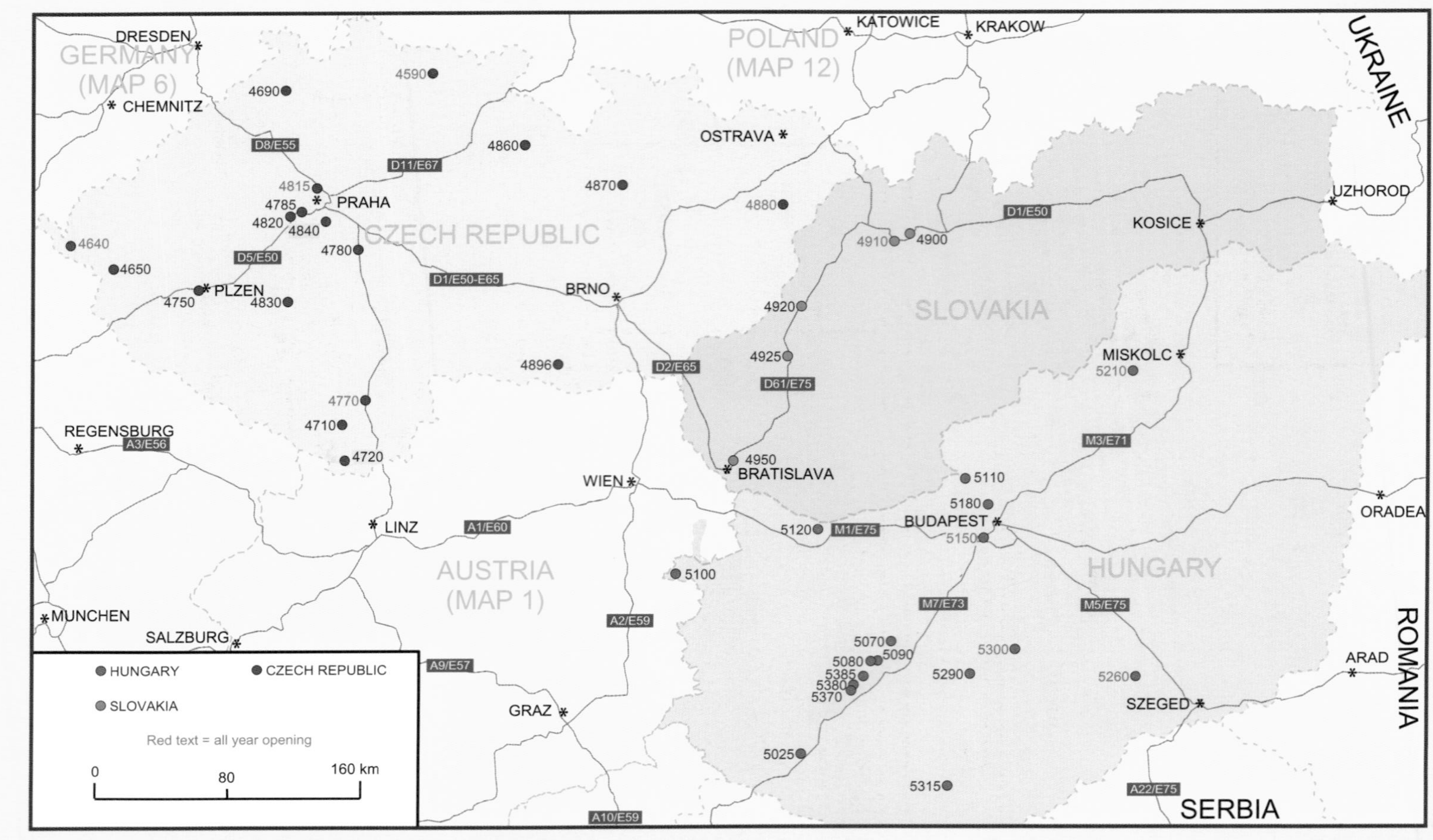

DRESDEN
GERMANY (MAP 6)
CHEMNITZ
KATOWICE
KRAKOW
POLAND (MAP 12)
UKRAINE
4690
4590
D8/E55
D11/E67
4860
OSTRAVA
4815
PRAHA
4785
4820
4840
4780
CZECH REPUBLIC
4870
4880
4910
4900
D1/E50
KOSICE
UZHOROD
4640
4650
D5/E50
PLZEN
4750
4830
D1/E50-E65
BRNO
4920
SLOVAKIA
4925
4896
D2/E65
D61/E75
MISKOLC
5210
4770
4710
4720
REGENSBURG
A3/E56
4950
BRATISLAVA
M3/E71
5110
WIEN
5180
ORADEA
LINZ
A1/E60
5120
M1/E75
BUDAPEST
5150
AUSTRIA (MAP 1)
5100
HUNGARY
MUNCHEN
SALZBURG
A2/E59
M7/E73
M5/E75
5070
5080
5090
5300
5385
5380
5370
5290
5260
A9/E57
ARAD
ROMANIA
GRAZ
SZEGED
5025
5315
A22/E75
SERBIA
A10/E59
HUNGARY
CZECH REPUBLIC
SLOVAKIA
Red text = all year opening
0
80
160 km

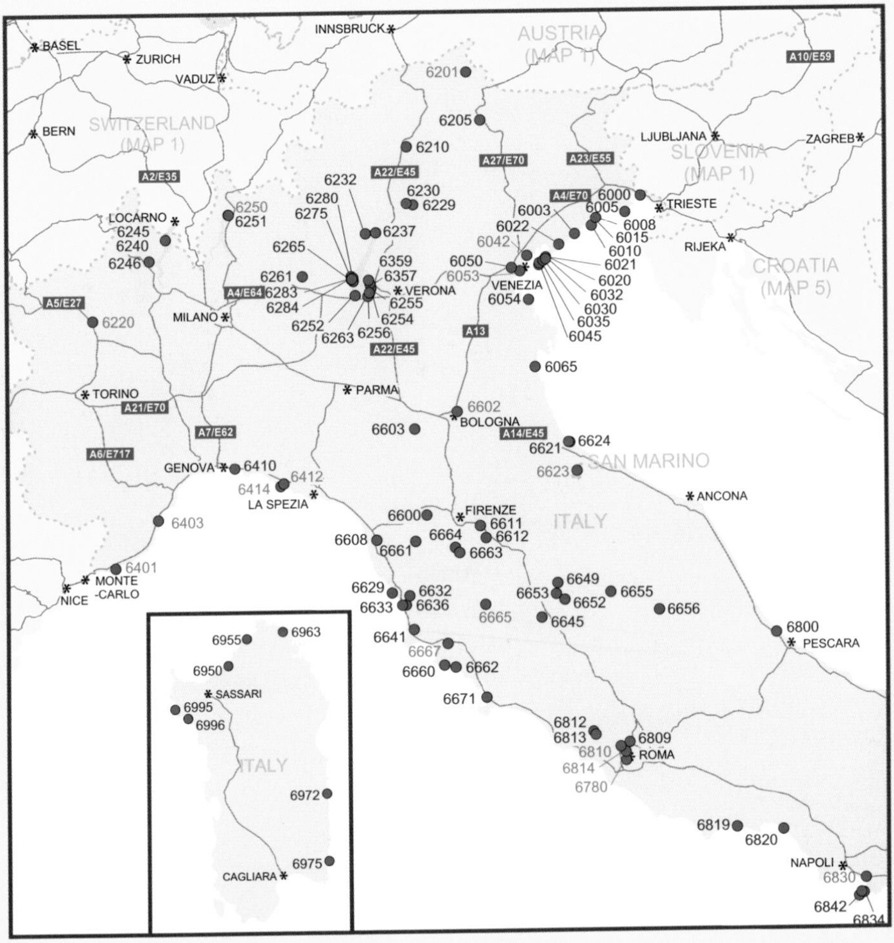

BASEL
ZURICH
INNSBRUCK
AUSTRIA (MAP 1)
A10/E59
VADUZ
6201
SWITZERLAND (MAP 1)
BERN
6205
6210
LJUBLJANA
ZAGREB
SLOVENIA (MAP 1)
A2/E35
A22/E45
A27/E70
A23/E55
6232
6280
6275
6230
6229
A4/E70
6000
6003
TRIESTE
LOCARNO
6250
6251
6005
6008
6245
6240
6237
6022
6015
6042
6010
RIJEKA
6265
6246
6359
6050
6021
CROATIA (MAP 5)
6261
6357
6053
6020
A4/E64
6283
VERONA
VENEZIA
A5/E27
6284
6255
6054
6032
6030
6254
6035
MILANO
6220
6252
6045
6263
6256
A13
A22/E45
6065
PARMA
TORINO
6602
A21/E70
BOLOGNA
6603
A7/E62
A14/E45
6624
6621
A6/E717
SAN MARINO
GENOVA
6410
6623
6412
6414
LA SPEZIA
ANCONA
FIRENZE
6600
6403
6611
ITALY
6612
6608
6664
6661
6663
6401
MONTE-CARLO
NICE
6649
6629
6632
6655
6653
6652
6633
6636
6656
6665
6645
6955
6963
6641
6800
PESCARA
6667
6950
6662
6660
SASSARI
6671
6995
6996
6812
6809
6813
6810
ROMA
ITALY
6814
6780
6972
6819
6820
NAPOLI
6975
CAGLIARA
6830
6842
6834

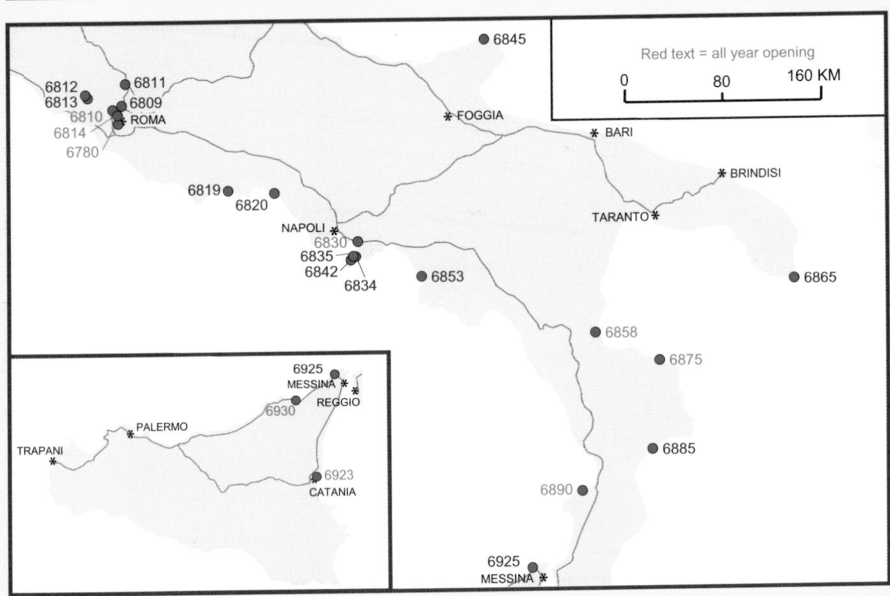

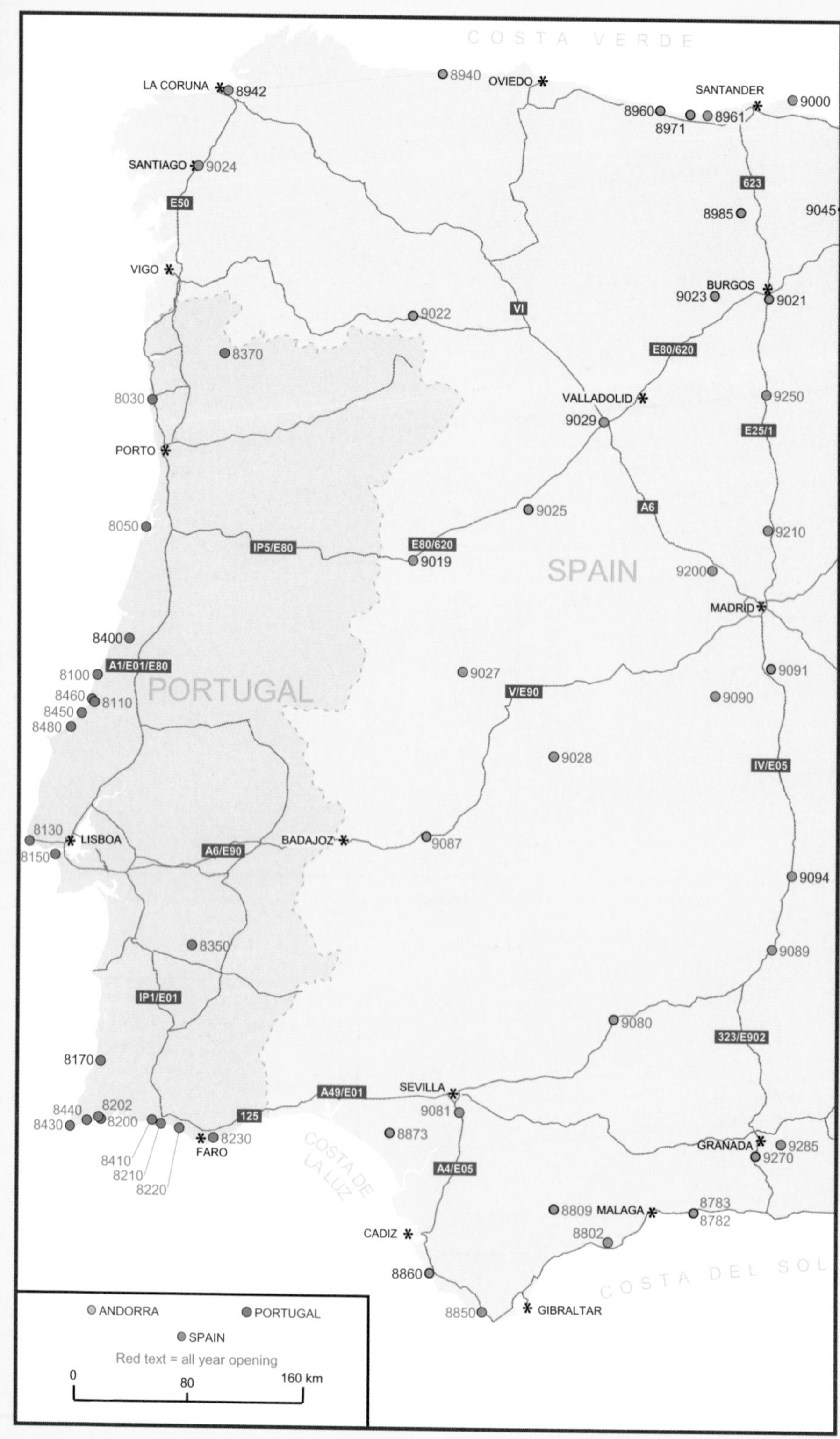
COSTA VERDE
LA CORUNA
8942
8940
OVIEDO
SANTANDER
8960
8971
8961
9000
SANTIAGO
9024
E50
623
8985
9045
VIGO
BURGOS
9023
9021
9022
VI
8370
E80/620
8030
VALLADOLID
9029
9250
PORTO
E25/1
9025
A6
8050
9210
IP5/E80
E80/620
9019
SPAIN
9200
MADRID
8400
A1/E01/E80
8100
9027
9091
8460
8110
V/E90
PORTUGAL
9090
8450
8480
9028
IV/E05
8130
LISBOA
A6/E90
BADAJOZ
9087
8150
9094
8350
9089
IP1/E01
9080
323/E902
8170
SEVILLA
A49/E01
8440
8202
9081
8430
8200
125
8873
8230
FARO
GRANADA
9285
9270
8410
8210
8220
COSTA DE LA LUZ
A4/E05
8809
MALAGA
8783
8782
CADIZ
8802
8860
COSTA DEL SOL
8850
GIBRALTAR
ANDORRA
PORTUGAL
SPAIN
Red text = all year opening
0
80
160 km

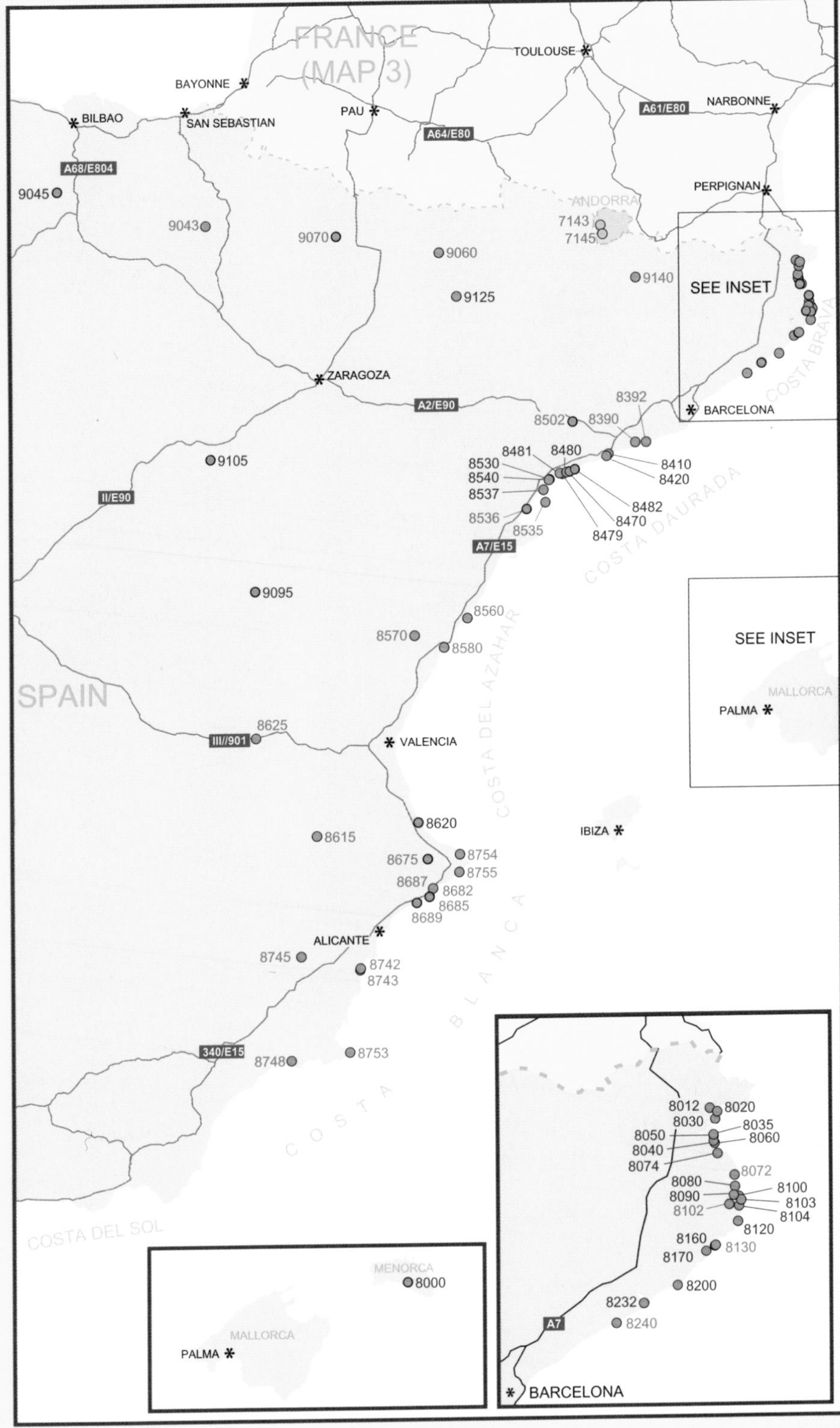
FRANCE (MAP 3)
TOULOUSE
BAYONNE
NARBONNE
A61/E80
PAU
BILBAO
SAN SEBASTIAN
A64/E80
A68/E804
PERPIGNAN
9045
ANDORRA
7143
7145
9043
9070
9060
9140
SEE INSET
9125
COSTA BRAVA
ZARAGOZA
A2/E90
8392
BARCELONA
8502
8390
8481
8480
8410
8420
8530
8540
8537
8536
8535
8482
8470
8479
9105
II/E90
A7/E15
COSTA DAURADA
9095
8560
8570
8580
SEE INSET
MALLORCA
PALMA
SPAIN
COSTA DEL AZAHAR
8625
III//901
VALENCIA
8620
8615
IBIZA
8675
8754
8755
8687
8682
8685
8689
ALICANTE
8745
8742
8743
340/E15
8748
8753
COSTA BLANCA
COSTA DEL SOL
MENORCA
8000
MALLORCA
PALMA
8012
8020
8030
8035
8050
8060
8040
8074
8072
8080
8100
8090
8103
8102
8104
8120
8160
8130
8170
8200
8232
A7
8240
BARCELONA

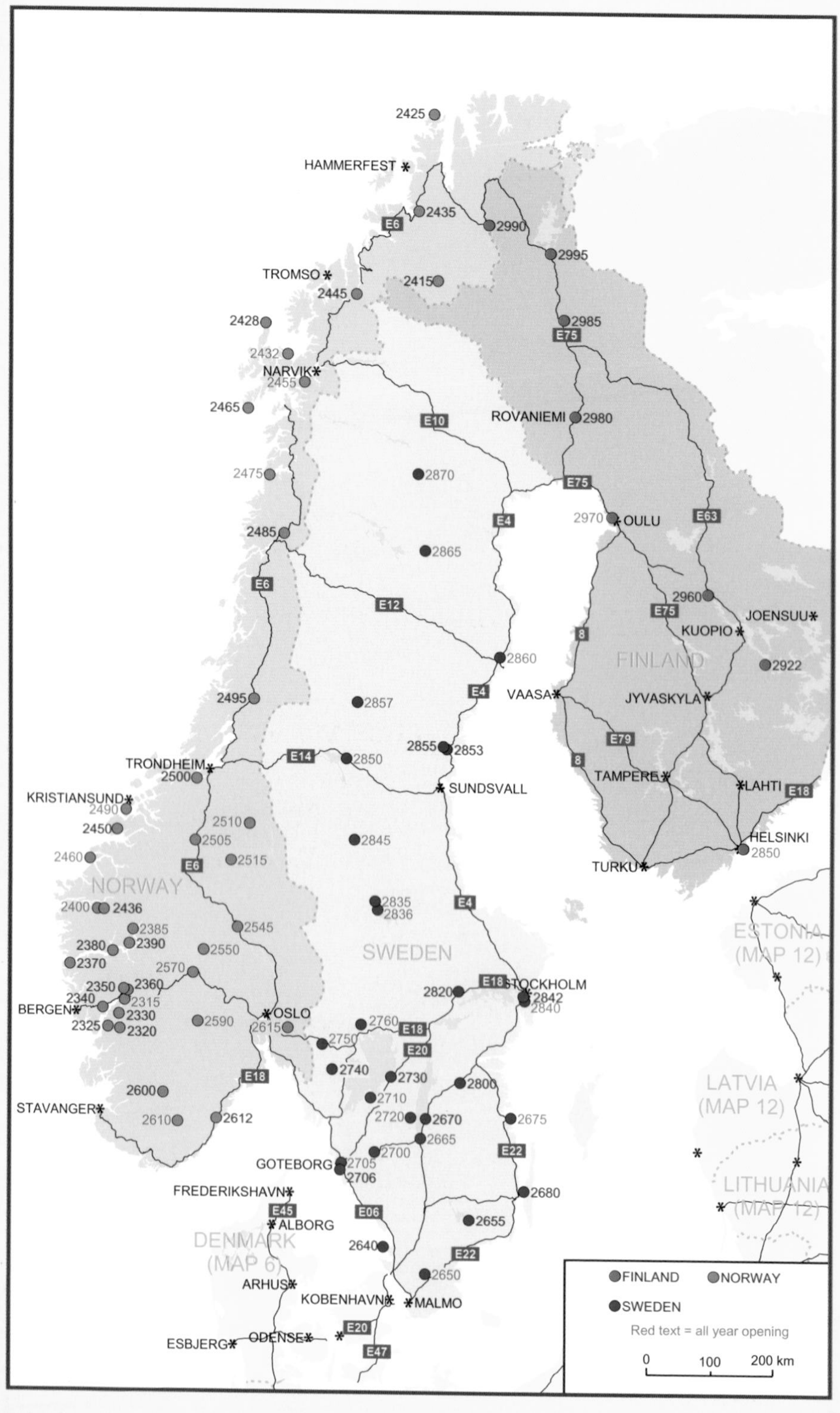
2425
HAMMERFEST
E6
2435
2990
2995
TROMSO
2445
2415
2428
2985
E75
2432
NARVIK
2455
2465
E10
ROVANIEMI
2980
2475
2870
E75
E4
2970
OULU
E63
2485
2865
E6
E12
2960
E75
JOENSUU
8
KUOPIO
2860
FINLAND
2922
2495
2857
E4
VAASA
JYVASKYLA
E79
2855
2853
TRONDHEIM
E14
2850
8
TAMPERE
LAHTI
E18
2500
SUNDSVALL
KRISTIANSUND
2490
2510
2450
2505
2845
HELSINKI
2850
2460
2515
TURKU
E6
NORWAY
E4
2400
2436
2835
2836
ESTONIA
(MAP 12)
2385
2545
2380
2390
2550
SWEDEN
2370
2570
E18
STOCKHOLM
2350
2360
2820
2842
2340
2315
2840
BERGEN
2330
OSLO
2325
2320
2590
2615
2760
E18
2750
E20
2740
2730
E18
2800
LATVIA
(MAP 12)
2600
2710
STAVANGER
2720
2670
2675
2610
2612
2665
E22
2700
GOTEBORG
2705
2706
LITHUANIA
(MAP 12)
FREDERIKSHAVN
2680
E45
E06
ALBORG
2655
DENMARK
(MAP 6)
2640
E22
2650
ARHUS
KOBENHAVN
MALMO
E20
ESBJERG
ODENSE
E47
FINLAND
NORWAY
SWEDEN
Red text = all year opening
0
100
200 km

ESTONIA
LATVIA
LITHUANIA
POLAND
Red text = all year opening
0
80
160 KM
HELSINKI
NARVA
0050
FINLAND (MAP 11)
0040
RUSSIA
TALLINN
0030
ESTONIA
TARFU
PARNU
E18
TOCKHOLM
VALMIERA
1020
SWEDEN (MAP 11)
LATVIA
REZEKNE
RIGA
1040
1060
DAUGAVPILS
E22
LIEPAJA
SIAULIAI
PANEVEZYS
2010
LITHUANIA
KLAIPEDA
VILNIUS
KAUNAS
2030
2060
RUSSIA
KALININGRAD
BELARUS
GDYNIA
3100
3090
3160
GDANSK
3170
BIALYSTOK
N1/E25
N51/E77
N8
BREST
TORUN
N10
BYDGOSZCZ
3050
UKRAINE
SZCZECIN
N10
N2/E30
A11/E28
WARSZAWA
POLAND
N17
POZNAN
LUBLIN
LODZ
RADOM
N24
GERMANY (MAP 6)
N8/E67
KIELCE
N5/E261
N14
N7/E77
WROCLAW
RZESZOW
A4/E40
KATOWICE
KRAKOW
3280
DRESDEN
3320
A13/E55
CZECH REPUBLIC (MAP 7)
OSTRAVA
3300
HRADEC KRALOVE
SLOVAKIA (MAP 7)

Germany

Hungary

TOWN AND VILLAGE INDEX continued

ACKNOWLEDGEMENTS

We would like to thank the following national and regional Tourist Boards for supplying photographs for use in this guide:

Andorra Tourist Office

Toerisme Vlaanderen

Croatian National Tourist Board

Danish Tourism Board

Bayern Tourismus

Hungarian Tourist Board

Italian Tourist Board

Lietchtenstein Tourist Board

Luxemburg Tourist Office
Bourscheid Castle © Konrad Scheel
Vianden Castle overlooking the Old Town © Marc Theis
Market town of Esch-sur-Sure © Marc Theis

Netherlands Tourist Board

Norwegian Tourist Board
North Cape Midnight Sun © Trym Ivar Bergsmo
Geirangerfjord © Per Eide
Sorlandet Lyngor © Niels Jorgensen

Portuguese National Tourism Office

Slovakia Travel

Turespana
L'Atmella de Mar © F. Ontanon
Broto © Oscar Masats

Costa Brava Girona Tourist Board

Sweden Travel & Travel Tourism Council

Switzerland Tourism

INSPECTED CAMPSITES & SELECTED

Tell Us About the Alan Rogers Guides!

We're keen to constantly improve our service to you and the key to this is information. If we don't know what makes our readers 'tick' then it's difficult to offer you more of what you want.

WIN A COMPLETE SET OF ALAN ROGERS GUIDES

Return this completed questionnaire and you could win a complete set of 2006 Alan Rogers Guides. Why not complete an on-line version of this? Go to www.alanrogers.com/feedback

About the Alan Rogers Guides

1 **For how many years have you used the Alan Rogers Guides?**

Never　1-2 yrs　3-6 yrs　7-10 yrs　Over 10 yrs

2 **How frequently do you refer to it?**

Never　Each year　Every 2 yrs　Every 3 yrs

3 **How frequently do you buy a new copy?**

Never　Each year　Every 2 yrs　Every 3 yrs

4 **If you lend it to friends, how many others might refer to it?**

1　2　3　4　Over 4

5 **Please rate the Alan Rogers Guides on a scale of 1–10 where 10 is excellent and 1 is extremely poor**

1　2　3　4　5　6　7　8　9　10

6 **Do you have any comments about the Alan Rogers Guides?**

7 **What do you consider to be the best thing about the guides?**

Independent reviews　Honest descriptions　Accurate information　Range of sites　Depth of information

Other

8 **What do you consider to be the worst thing about the guides?**

9 **How many sites featured in the guides have you visited in the past?** *(best estimate)*

10 **Can you comment on any other campsite guides?**

Title　Your opinion

About Your Holidays

11 **a) Do you own any of the following?**

Caravan　Motorhome　Trailer Tent　Tent

Other *(please specify)*

b) How many times a year do you use it?

1　2-3　4-6　7-10　More than 10

12 **When on holiday, do you participate in any of the following?**

Fishing　Golf　Cycling　Sailing/Boating　Walking　Bird Watching

Other *(please specify)*

13 **How many years have you been camping / caravanning?**

3 yrs or less　4 – 7 yrs　8 – 12 yrs　13 – 15 yrs　16 – 20 yrs　Over 20 yrs

WIN A COMPLETE SET OF ALAN ROGERS GUIDES

WIN A COMPLETE SET OF ALAN ROGERS GUIDES

About You

Mr/Mrs/Ms, etc. Initial Surname

Address

Post code

e-mail address @ Telephone

14 **Your age** 30 and under 31-50 51-65 Over 65

15 **Do you have children – if so, how old is the youngest?**
6 and under 7-12 Over 12

16 **Do you work (full or part time)?** Yes No

17 **Are you retired?** Yes No

About Your Leisure Time

18 **Are you a member of any caravan/motorhome clubs?**
The Caravan Club The Camping & Caravanning Club The Motor Caravanners Club

Other *(please specify)*

19 **Are you a member of the following?**
National Trust English Heritage RSPB CSMA Ramblers

20 **Which (if any) camping/caravanning magazines do you read regularly?**
MMM Practical Motorhome Practical Caravan Caravan Life Which Motorcaravan Motor-caravan Caravan

21 **Which other magazines do you read regularly?**

22 **Which newspapers do you read regularly?**
Express Mail Telegraph Times Guardian Observer Sun

Other (please specify)

23 **Do you enjoy any particular hobbies?** *(please specify)*

24 **Do you have regular access to the internet?** Yes No

If yes, which camping/caravanning websites do you visit regularly?

And Finally

25 **Do you have any useful camping/caravanning tips?**

26 **If you could change one thing about camping/caravanning holidays what would it be?**

We may wish to publish your comments, please tick this box if you would prefer us not to.

Might you be interested in becoming an Alan Rogers site inspector?
If so, please tick the box and we will send you further information

*Camping Cheque and Alan Rogers may use this data to send you information and Special Offers.
Please tick here if you do not wish to receive such information*

Thank you very much for your time and trouble in completing this questionnaire
Please return to: Alan Rogers Travel Service, FREEPOST NAT17734, Cranbrook, TN17 1BR